CONSUMER BEHAVIOR:
Concepts and Applications

McGRAW-HILL SERIES IN MARKETING

CONSUMER BEHAVIOR: Concepts and Applications

DAVID L. LOUDON
Northeast Louisiana University

ALBERT J. DELLA BITTA
University of Rhode Island

THIRD EDITION

McGRAW-HILL BOOK COMPANY

New York | St. Louis | San Francisco
Auckland | Bogotá | Caracas
Colorado Springs | Hamburg | Lisbon
London | Madrid | Mexico | Milan
Montreal | New Delhi | Oklahoma City
Panama | Paris | San Juan | São Paulo
Singapore | Sydney | Tokyo | Toronto

CONSUMER BEHAVIOR
Concepts and Applications

234567890 H A L H A L 89321098

ISBN 0-07-038764-8

This book was set in Times Roman by the College Composition Unit
in cooperation with Better Graphics, Inc.
The editor was Michael J. S. Asher;
the designer was Nicholas Krenitsky;
the production supervisor was Salvador Gonzales.
Drawings were done by FineLine Illustrations.
Arcata Graphics/Halliday was printer and binder.

Acknowledgments for Opening Example Photos
Rick Turgeon: Chapters 2, 5, 11, 12, 14, 15, 16, 19, 20, 22. Other chapters:

1   Photo courtesy of Stop & Shop Companies, Inc.
3   Photo courtesy of Wendy's International, Inc.
4   Photo courtesy of Merry Maids, Inc.
6   Photo by Andrew D. Bernstein. Courtesy of Los Angeles Clippers
7   Photo copyright © 1987 The Coca-Cola Company. All rights reserved. Coke and Coca-Cola
      are registered trademarks of the Coca-Cola Company.
8   Photo courtesy of Cunard Sea Goddess.
9   Photo courtesy of UndercoverWear, Inc.
10 Photo courtesy of Club Med, Inc.
13 Photo of Tim Davis Photography.
17 Photo courtesy of MasterCard International, Inc.
18 Photo courtesy of Healthcheck Corporation.
21 Photo courtesy of Ford Motor Company.

LIBRARY OF CONGRESS
Library of Congress Cataloging-in-Publication Data

Loudon, David L.
    Consumer behavior : concepts and applications / David L. Loudon,
Albert J. Della Bitta.—3rd ed.
      p. cm.—(McGraw-Hill series in marketing)
    Includes bibliographical references and index.
    ISBN 0-07-038764-8
    1. Consumers.   2. Consumers—Case studies.   I. Della Bitta,
Albert J.   II. Title.   III. Series.
HF5415.3.L68 1988
658.8'34—dc19
87-27979
    CIP

ABOUT
THE AUTHORS

David L. Loudon (Ph.D., Louisiana State University, 1971) is Professor of Marketing and head of the Department of Management and Marketing at Northeast Louisiana University. He has taught courses in consumer behavior, international marketing, marketing research, product management, and marketing management and has participated in executive development programs.

Dr. Loudon has conducted research in the United States, Europe, and Latin America on such topics as consumer behavior, international marketing, and marketing management. His findings have been published in a number of journals and in the proceedings of numerous professional conferences. In addition, he has authored several business cases which have been widely reprinted.

Dr. Loudon has served as a marketing consultant to a variety of organizations, and is president of a computer software firm. He enjoys boating, photography, and traveling.

Albert Della Bitta (Ph.D., University of Massachusetts, 1971) is Professor of Marketing and director of the Research Center in Business and Economics at the University of Rhode Island. His classroom teaching includes graduate and undergraduate courses in consumer behavior, marketing research, marketing management, pricing, and statistics. He has also presented executive development seminars in consumer behavior and marketing to national and international audiences.

Dr. Della Bitta has conducted research on a variety of consumer behavior issues. His articles have been published in various journals, including *Journal of Marketing Research, Decision Sciences, Journal of Business Research, Journal of Retailing, Journalism Quarterly, Journal of Macromarketing,* and *Journal of the Academy of Marketing Science.* His research papers have been presented at numerous national and regional conferences. Dr. Della Bitta has served as a reviewer for five leading academic journals and several professional conferences. He has also consulted for a variety of profit and not-for-profit organizations.

Professor Della Bitta enjoys fishing, photography, traveling with his family, and working in community youth programs. He also is an avid soccer fan.

CONTENTS

x

PART 2

UNDERSTANDING CONSUMERS AND MARKET SEGMENTS

PART 3

ENVIRONMENTAL INFLUENCES ON CONSUMER BEHAVIOR

PART 5
CONSUMER DECISION PROCESSES

PREFACE

This book is written for the beginning student of consumer behavior, whether he or she is at the undergraduate or the graduate level, with the purpose of blending both concepts and applications from the field of consumer behavior.

No special assumptions have been made regarding student preparation for this text. Although many will have had previous exposure to some of the behavioral concepts discussed, all can benefit from a review of these topics and an examination of them from a managerial perspective. Thus, the concepts presented here are regarded as extremely valuable for the career-oriented student in general and indispensable for the marketing major.

Considerable effort has been made to present the material clearly and in a style that is readable, interesting, and motivating to students. Unnecessary jargon has been avoided, and behavioral concepts have been defined in simple language. In addition to topical examples, a large number of graphics and other visuals help to clarify and reinforce text material. Each chapter begins with learning objectives, has a brief orienting example, and concludes with a managerial summary to reinforce major points.

As our title indicates, the book not only presents theoretical concepts of consumer behavior but also stresses the application of this conceptual material to marketing strategies and decision making in the private, public, and nonprofit sectors. At the conceptual level, it seeks to present an integrated framework around which the major areas of consumer-behavior knowledge can be discussed. The book is thoroughly documented and provides ample opportunity for the reader to pursue a particular area of interest in greater detail. The explosion of consumer research, however, has made it impossible to cite every study relevant to a specific topic; in any case, such detail tends to confuse the introductory student through information overload and often contradictory findings. Therefore, we have emphasized what is known about consumers, rather then dwell on the present uncertainty and its implications for future research. Nevertheless, controversial areas still exist and will continue to exist for quite some time, and the student is made aware of this fact.

For too long, consumer behavior texts have been crammed with theories and research findings while giving little attention to their pragmatic application in the marketplace. Our teaching experience has been that students, especially at the introductory level, are highly interested in discussions of potential and *actual* applications of these concepts. In addition to its motivating benefit, such an approach also allows students to gain a much greater appreciation of the conceptual material. Rather than just paying token attention to this, the third edition of the text continues to thoroughly incorporate marketing realism in several ways. First, throughout each chapter frequent reference is made to actual or potential applications of the concepts being discussed. Second, questions and projects at the end of each chapter offer opportunities for experiential learning. Here, research may be conducted, decisions made, or other creative activities undertaken,

students closer to the real world of marketing. Third, cases at the end of each part offer opportunities for more extensive discussion and for decision making through application of text material.

The third edition of this book offers important modifications. It has been updated to reflect the wealth of new evidence on consumer behavior that has been generated since publication of the last edition. This has been accomplished by rewriting sections, adding new material, and streamlining the discussion in places. In addition, a large number of recent examples and applications are incorporated to keep the book current. Further, many new cases have been added to allow students meaningful analysis and applications of concepts.

The third edition comprises six major sections:

Part 1, Studying Consumer Behavior, introduces the reader to the discipline of consumer behavior by defining and describing its scope and importance, discussing the marketing function, and providing numerous examples of consumer-behavior relevance in managerial decision making. Several conceptions of consumer behavior are briefly presented along with the authors' simplified framework. These serve as a foundation for studying and understanding the subject of consumer behavior.

Part 2, Understanding Consumers and Market Segments, begins with a brief treatment of some aspects of consumer research. This helps to prepare students for the discussion of specific studies, and it stresses the importance of consumer research as a prerequisite to many marketing decisions. Consumer behavior is of increasing interest to students who are not marketing majors, and some of them may be unfamiliar with important characteristics of the consumer market and the concept and methods of market segmentation. Consequently, consumer characteristics are discussed with a view toward selecting target markets and developing marketing programs.

Part 3, Environmental Influences on Consumer Behavior, examines the sociocultural influences on consumers and presents them in hierarchical order ranging from the broadest to the most immediate. The roles of culture, subculture, social class, social groups, family, and interpersonal influences are examined.

Part 4, Individual Determinants of Consumer Behavior, deals with the consumer's internal variables. These influence the ways in which the consumer proceeds through a decision process relating to products and services. Covered in successive chapters are the topics of motivation and involvement, information processing, learning and memory, personality and self-concept, attitudes, and attitude change.

Part 5, Consumer Decision Processes, discusses the way in which consumers make purchase decisions based on their environmental influences and individual determinants. Consumers' decision processes are described in a four-stage model consisting of problem recognition, information search and evaluation, purchasing processes, and post-purchase behavior.

Part 6, Additional Dimensions, is new to this edition. It presents the subject of consumerism, dealing with the consumer's position in society and some of the problems faced in the marketplace. In addition, ethical and social responsibilities of business, government, and consumers themselves are addressed and related to marketing responsiveness.

Instructors desiring alternative orders in material coverage will find the book very flexible. For example, if students have had an introductory course in marketing and marketing research, Chapters 3 to 5 may be minimized or eliminated. Those who prefer to discuss individual determinants of consumer behavior prior to environmental variables can simply reverse Parts 3 and 4. Finally, instructors facing time constraints will find the book quite flexible in regard to topics that can be covered over varying course lengths.

We are indebted to a number of people who helped us during the revision of this text. Robert E. Stevens, Northeast Louisiana University, wrote Chapter 22, which has been added to this edition. Dean Van McGraw, Northeast Louisiana University, and Dean Robert Clagett, University of Rhode Island, were supportive and offered administrative assistance. Our reviewers, who offered helpful suggestions that led to an improved manuscript, included: C. L. Abercrombie, Memphis State University; Dean Allmon, University of West Florida; Louis M. Capella, Mississippi State University; Richard Feinberg, Purdue University; and Peter L. Gillett, University of Central Florida.

Our editors at McGraw-Hill—Sam Costanzo, Michael Asher, and Laura Warner—provided outstanding support and assistance with this revision. Gloria Honeycutt, Marie Garofano, and Doris Russo were very helpful in typing the manuscript. In addition, Peter Hux aided at numerous stages of manuscript preparation. Finally, and most importantly, our families deserve special thanks for their patience, understanding, and encouragement. This work, like earlier editions, is dedicated to them.

David L. Loudon
Albert J. Della Bitta

CONSUMER BEHAVIOR:
Concepts and Applications

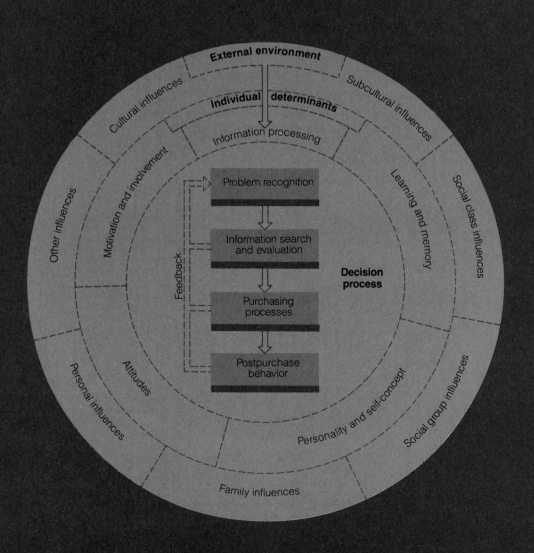

STUDYING CONSUMER BEHAVIOR

PART

1

INTRODUCTION

LEARNING OBJECTIVES

After studying this chapter, you should understand . . .

■ What is meant by the terms "ultimate consumer," "industrial buyer," and "customer"

■ What is implied by the term "consumer behavior"

■ How a study of the field of consumer behavior can be useful to you

■ How an understanding of consumer behavior is useful to marketing managers, administrators of nonprofit and social organizations, and those involved in consumer-protection or educational activities

Jim, a professor of journalism, was feeling quite down one Saturday about midway through the fall semester. The days were getting shorter and Jim dreaded the thought of winter. While reading the local paper, he noticed that the new shopping mall was opening that Saturday. The mall was not very large: it featured a department store, ten smaller stores, and a new Super Stop & Shop, a supermarket occupying 55,000 square feet of retail space.

In an effort to cheer up, Jim decided to take his kids and "check the place out." He didn't intend to buy anything—just to look around. They first went to the department store, which did not impress Jim much at all. The selection of merchandise in most departments was small. However, when they reached the toy section, his 8-year-old son spotted Marble Madness, a video game for the Commodore 64 computer, and "started in" on Jim until he finally agreed to buy it. They also "discussed" the purchase of Up Periscope, but Jim said that the next piece of software would have to wait until Christmas.

Jim's 14-year-old son, Craig, ran into (literally) a soccer ball display. While reassembling the display, Craig began to fondle a shiny gold Brine ball that had been the focus of his dreams for some time. Craig had heard from his friends that this ball incorporated the "exclusive wind-channeling design" that enabled you to kick very straight when you wanted to. It also came with a one-year warranty. Jim strongly resisted this $36 purchase, but he and Craig finally agreed to split the cost.

While walking further along the mall, they spotted a record shop and spent some time browsing around. Jim found a $28, five-record album of classic big band sounds that he had seen advertised on TV some time ago. Since his wife and he really enjoyed this type of music, Jim decided to surprise her with the purchase. Craig's request for Cyndy Lauper's new album, Jim rejected on the basis of "good taste." Craig didn't

1

respond well to that dig, but he soon forgot his anger when they reached the Super Stop & Shop store.

In addition to its regular supermarket offerings, this new store housed large seafood, bakery, deli, and produce departments and new, nontraditional areas such as appliance, automotive, furniture, and book departments. The kids were pleased with this concept, which was new to the area, but Jim experienced trouble with it—he felt strange having non-food-related departments in a store where he did grocery shopping. Also, the place seemed so large, requiring a lot of walking.

While looking through the book department, Jim noticed a title featuring the original story of Max Headroom—the computer-generated video character that had appeared in Coke commercials and had starred on its own talk show. Jim thought that the Headroom phenomenon would be relevant to his class on mass communications, and the book contained some ''neat stuff'' on how Max acquired his name. Thinking that this would be a good source of information to liven up some lectures, Jim decided to pay the $10.95 for the book. For the same reason, he also grabbed another about the McDonald's Corporation.

While being drawn by the aroma of freshly baked bread, the three passed a kiosk containing a computer with a touch-sensitive screen. This really impressed them all. It allowed one to touch in the name of a product, and the computer then drew a path to the product on a map of the store. In another function, the computer listed brands on sale and it also printed discount coupons for selected items. Jim thought this was great because it saved the inconvenience of having to clip and save coupons at home. The three of them had a ball with the machine for some time—it was almost like playing Pacman. When leaving, Jim grabbed a coupon for antifreeze and saved 30 cents on a gallon of Prestone.

Their last stop was at the bakery, where aromas had been luring all three for some time. They picked up two loaves of French bread, still warm, and Jim added in four chocolate croissants for the kids.

At the checkout counter they spotted the video department, which had an extensive selection of VCR tapes. Jim added the $20 membership fee onto his bill and then rented *Short Circuit* for the kids. He didn't have enough cash, but an automatic teller machine in the store enabled him to make a withdrawal from their savings account.

When the three arrived home, Jim was in much better spirits. The kids were also quite happy with their new purchases. When his wife asked about their trip, Jim mentioned some of the purchases and described his impressions of the stores. She didn't seem enthusiastic about shopping at such a large food store—it seemed like too much walking for the weekly trip to the market. However, she did agree to return the VCR tape and check it out for herself.

The example above illustrates the fascinating subject matter this book deals with—the behavior of consumers. Many who have seriously studied consumers find their behavior to be intricate, difficult to influence, and often mystifying. This consumer complexity is probably what motivates so many to learn more about the topic.

Chapter 1 serves as an introduction to this intriguing area of study. A useful way to begin is to examine several more actual situations involving various aspects of the nature and scope of consumer behavior.

HOSPITALS Rx? In many U.S. locations, hospitals have experienced a growing number of empty beds. Several factors are contributing to this situation, including implementation of new medical practices, more competition from health-care clinics and other hospitals, and the increasing resistance of many medical insurers, including Medicare, to pay for extended hospital stays. The impact is severe—in the period from 1985 to 1990, about 20 percent of the nation's hospitals are expected to fold, while others will drastically alter their operations.

Such prospects send shivers through the spines of hospital administrators. As a consequence, many have turned to the area of advertising to maintain or enhance their customer base. Ad spending by hospitals leaped from less than $50 million in 1983 to about $500 million in 1986. Some of these efforts focus on informing consumers about various wellness and health-care issues. Others are targeted at reducing the fear associated with a hospital stay and at building consumers' trust in the hospital and its staff.

While these actions appear appropriate, other actions seem less well-directed and, in some cases, very questionable. The problem is that often promotional methods developed for selling soap and other consumer products have been applied directly to hospital marketing without having been evaluated for their appropriateness to the situation. For example, free Cabbage Patch dolls and discount coupons have been offered to lure customers in. At one hospital a new method of disintegrating kidney stones has been advertised with the slogan, "Who Ya Gonna Call . . . Stonebusters!" More serious cases involving false and misleading promotional claims have prompted the American Hospital Association to reprimand some of its members. The questionable practices led one observer to remark, "What's next—two-for-the-price-of-one specials on major surgery?"[1]

LITTLE BIG STORE Along with other celebrities, Paul Newman shops there. In fact, this is the place Newman chose to introduce his own brand of spaghetti sauce. It's fairly small—only 30,000 square feet of retail space—but in another sense it's very large. In fact, it is claimed to be the world's largest dairy store. Its name is Stew Leonard's Dairy Market. Located in Norwalk, Connecticut, this highly successful store is operated according to several core marketing/consumer-oriented principles, including a focus on selling only a relatively small number of competitively priced, high-volume products and a belief that (1) shopping should be an interesting and pleasant experience, (2) store personnel should be well trained and eager to help customers, and (3) businesses should continually experiment with new ways to increase consumer satisfaction. Leonard's has shown that a solid knowledge of consumer behavior is required for successful implementation of these principles.

The result is discount merchandising with a very special flair. For example, the parking lot houses a petting zoo with hundreds of animals, and inside, customers can watch the operation of a large, glass-enclosed dairy plant. An average of only one out of every twenty-five job applicants is hired to serve customers, and these recruits are then trained quite extensively. Their motivation must also be high because they frequently must dress up as animals or cartoon characters for the enjoyment of customers.

Suggestion boxes are available for customer use and often result in operational changes. Also, a wide variety of new items and ideas are introduced regularly.

Store sales at Leonard's suggest strongly that management has a sound understanding of the pulse of area consumers. Annually, over 5 million people shop at Leonard's one store and purchase staggering amounts of food—20 tons of poultry per week, 100 tons of cottage cheese and 10 million quarts of ice cream per year, and over 20 times the number of croissants sold by any other in-store bakery in the country.[2]

These diverse examples involve the success of, and problems with, the offerings by for-profit and not-for-profit organizations and have implications for the implementation of public policy. They also involve the decision making of individuals and the impact of group behavior. One theme common to all the situations, however, is that they involve the behavior of consumers. Thus, whether we are aware of it or not, consumer behavior is occurring all around us. This might not always be very apparent, because many aspects of consumer behavior are actually quite hard to detect.

The study of consumers usually proves to be highly interesting to students. It is an exciting field, but for two reasons it is also one that requires serious study. First, the behavior of consumers can be quite subtle in nature, making it difficult to understand fully. Second, because consumer behavior is so prevalent, it significantly affects our lives through either our own actions or those of other consumers. Therefore, it has a great deal of practical relevance to our daily living.

To better appreciate the nature and scope of consumer behavior, the remaining sections of this chapter focus on two very basic questions:

1 What is the nature of consumer behavior?

2 Why should we study consumer behavior?

This material will provide a basis that we can build upon in subsequent chapters.

DEFINING CONSUMER BEHAVIOR

Before continuing, it is appropriate to offer a definition in order to clarify the focus of our study. Consumer behavior may be defined as:

. . . the decision process and physical activity individuals engage in when evaluating, acquiring, using, or disposing of goods and services.

Several aspects of this statement need emphasis and elaboration so that their meanings can be more fully appreciated.

CUSTOMERS AND CONSUMERS

The term "customer" is typically used to refer to someone who purchases from a particular store or company. Thus, a person who shops at A&P or who uses Texaco gasoline is viewed as a customer of these firms. The term "consumer" more generally refers to anyone engaging in any of the activities used in our definition of consumer behavior. Therefore, a customer is defined in terms of a specific firm while a consumer is not.

The traditional viewpoint has been to define consumers strictly in terms of *economic* goods and services. This position holds that consumers are potential *purchasers* of products and services offered for sale. This view has been broadened over time so that at least some scholars now do not consider a monetary exchange essential to the definition of consumers. This change implies that potential adopters of free services or even philosophies or ideas can also be encompassed by the definition. Consequently, organizations such as the Red Cross, United Way, or Foster Parents Plan, as well as religious and political groups, can view their various publics as "consumers." The rationale for this position is that many of the activities that people engage in regarding free services, ideas, or philosophies are quite similar to those they engage in regarding commercial products and services. Later sections of this and other chapters will expand on this idea.

THE ULTIMATE CONSUMER

Our primary attention will be directed toward *ultimate consumers,* those individuals who purchase for the purpose of individual or household consumption. Some have argued that studying ultimate consumers also reveals much about industrial or intermediate buyers and others involved in purchasing for business firms and institutions.[3] While not denying this, we must recognize that much industrial purchasing behavior is unique because it often involves different buying motives and the influence of a large variety of people.[4] For the sake of simplicity we will focus only on ultimate consumer behavior and will not become involved in drawing comparisons with industrial purchasing situations.

THE INDIVIDUAL BUYER

The most commonly thought of consumer situation is that of an individual making a purchase with little or no influence from others. However, in some cases a number of people can be jointly involved in a purchase decision. For example, planning a vacation or deciding on a new car can involve an entire family. In other cases the purchaser may just be acquiring a product for someone else who has asked for a certain item. These situations suggest that people can take on different roles in what we have defined as consumer behavior. Table 1-1 presents one way to classify these roles.

Some purchase situations involve at least one person in each of these roles,

TABLE 1-1

Some Consumer Behavior Roles

Role	Description
Initiator	The individual who determines that some need or want is not being met and authorizes a purchase to rectify the situation
Influencer	A person who by some intentional or unintentional word or action influences the purchase decision, the actual purchase, and/or use of the product or service
Buyer	The individual who actually makes the purchase transaction
User	The person most directly involved in the consumption or use of the purchase

Source: Gerald Zaltman and Philip C. Burger, *Marketing Research: Fundamentals and Dynamics*, p. 142. Adapted with permission of the authors.

while in other circumstances a single individual can take on several roles at the same time. For example, in one situation a wife (initiator and influencer) may ask her husband (buyer) to pick up a box of Total cereal on his shopping trip because their child (user) said she wanted it. At another time the husband could act as the initiator, buyer, and user by purchasing a health spa membership for himself.

Any study of consumer behavior would be incomplete if it treated only one consumer role. However, an emphasis on one role, while still devoting adequate treatment to the others, can simplify our study in many cases. When it becomes useful to consider only one role we will tend to choose the *buyer*—the individual who actually makes the purchase. This approach is useful because even when told what to purchase, the buyer often makes decisions regarding purchase timing, store choice, package size, and other factors. Therefore, focusing on the buyer, while allowing for the influence of others on the purchase decision, still gives considerable flexibility while concentrating on one consumer role.

THE DECISION PROCESS

The way in which our definition characterizes "behavior" also deserves special attention. That is, consumer behavior is seen to involve a *mental decision process* as well as *physical activity*. The actual act of purchase is just one stage in a series of mental and physical activities that occur during a period of time. Some of these activities precede the actual buying, while others follow it. However, since all are capable of influencing the adoption of products or services, they will be considered as part of the behavior in which we are interested.

An example will illustrate the benefits of this viewpoint. Suppose a photographer who regularly purchases one brand of film suddenly switches to a competing brand even though there has been no change in either the films or their prices. What has caused this shift in loyalty? Just noting that the individual's purchase behavior has changed does little to help our understanding of the situation. Perhaps the competing film received a strong recommendation by a friend, or possibly the photographer switched because he believed the competing brand best captured the colors of some subject matter of interest. On the other hand, his decision may have been caused either by general dissatisfaction with results from his regular film or from recent exposure to an advertisement for the competing brand.

This example suggests the complexity of decision processes and demonstrates the limitations of viewing consumer behavior as just the act of purchasing. Therefore, to understand consumers adequately we should stress that, in addition to just physical activities, their purchasing behavior involves a mental decision process that takes place over time.

A SUBSET OF HUMAN BEHAVIOR

Viewing consumer behavior in such a broad context suggests it is actually a subset of human behavior. That is, factors affecting individuals in their daily lives also influence their purchase activities. Internal influences, such as learning and motives, as well as external factors, such as social expectations and constraints, affect us in our role as consumers as well as in our other capacities. In fact, it is often difficult to draw a distinct line between consumer-related behavior and other aspects of human behavior. For example, next-door neighbors might find lawn problems a convenient topic for striking up a conversation. However, this can quickly lead to a serious discussion of the merits of Scott fertilizers, Lawn Bird Sprinklers, and Sears riding mowers.

The fact that consumer behavior is a subset of human behavior is to our advantage. The several disciplines collectively referred to as the *behavioral sciences* have studied human behavior for some time, and we can draw upon their contributions for understanding consumer behavior. This borrowing has been quite extensive and includes theories used in explaining behavior as well as methods useful in investigating it. In fact, this borrowing is so extensive that consumer behavior is often said to be *multidisciplinary* in nature. The behavior science disciplines that have most contributed to our understanding of consumers are:

1 *Psychology*. Study of the behavior and mental processes of individuals

2 *Sociology*. Study of the collective behavior of people in groups

3 *Social psychology*. Study of how individuals influence and are influenced by groups

4 *Economics*. Study of people's production, exchange, and consumption of goods and services

5 *Anthropology*. Study of people in relation to their culture

It has been argued that the multidisciplinary approach to consumer behavior has been based on inadequate means of borrowing from the behavioral sciences.⁵ This charge is based on a contention that when people act as consumers, certain aspects of their behavior are unique and distinct from other categories of human behavior. These unique aspects, it is argued, have not been adequately recognized by theories and concepts of behavior developed in other disciplines. Therefore, wholesale adoption of such concepts will not provide an adequate understanding of consumers.

This point is well taken. However, it does not mean that those interested in the behavior of consumers should never again borrow from the behavioral sciences. A better approach would involve critical examination of the theories and concepts available from other disciplines that might be useful for understanding consumers. The degree to which they would need modification for the purpose of understanding consumers could then be determined. In this way, the study of consumer behavior would have its own unique aspects, and those studying it would also be in a position to benefit from discoveries about human behavior in other disciplines.

WHY STUDY CONSUMER BEHAVIOR?

Understanding the reasons for studying a discipline enables one to better appreciate the contributions of that discipline; therefore, this section presents a justification for the time and effort that the reader will expend in learning about consumers.

SIGNIFICANCE IN DAILY LIVES

In a general sense, the most important reason for studying consumer behavior is the significant role it plays in our lives. Much of our time is spent directly in the marketplace, shopping or engaging in other activities. A large amount of additional time is spent thinking about products and services, talking to friends about them, and seeing or hearing advertisements about them. In addition, the goods we purchase and the manner in which we use them significantly influence how we live our daily lives. These general concerns alone are enough to justify our study. However, many seek to understand the behavior of consumers for what are thought to be more immediate and tangible reasons.

APPLICATION TO DECISION MAKING

Consumers are often studied because certain decisions are significantly affected by their behavior or expected actions. For this reason, consumer behavior is said to be an *applied discipline*. Such applications can exist at two different levels of analysis. The *macro* perspective applies knowledge of consumers to aggregate-level problems faced by large groups or by society as a whole. The *micro* perspective seeks application of this knowledge to problems faced by the individual firm or organization.

Macro Perspective   On the macro, or aggregate, level we know that consumers collectively influence economic and social conditions within an entire society. In market systems based on individual choice, consumers strongly influence what will be produced, for whom it will be produced, and what resources will be used to produce it. Consequently, the collective behavior of consumers has a significant influence on the quality and level of our standard of living.[6] For example, consider the overall impact of American consumers' strong desire for private automobile transportation. Vast amounts of resources have been used to produce cars, highway systems, and petroleum products used in their operation. It has also strongly influenced where many of us live (for example, suburbs) and how we run our daily lives (for example, what we eat, where we shop, and how we are entertained). Furthermore, this collective desire not only has led to the development of a strong transportation network but also has significantly contributed to our pollution problems and energy needs.

As this illustrates, understanding consumer behavior from a macro perspective can provide insight into aggregate economic and social trends and can perhaps even predict such trends. In addition, this understanding may suggest ways to increase the efficiency of the market system and improve the well-being of people in society.

Micro Perspective   The micro perspective involves understanding consumers for the purpose of helping a firm or organization accomplish its objectives. Advertising managers, product designers, and many others in profit-oriented businesses are interested in understanding consumers in order to be more effective at their tasks. In addition, managers of various nonprofit organizations have benefited from the same knowledge. For example, the United Way, the American Red Cross, and the American Cancer Society have been effective in applying an understanding of consumer behavior concepts to their activities.

APPLYING CONSUMER BEHAVIOR KNOWLEDGE

The following selections have been made from a variety of practical applications in the field of consumer behavior. Some involve a macro perspective while others illustrate a micro viewpoint. Together they underscore the importance of understanding consumers for solving a variety of contemporary problems.

CONSUMER BEHAVIOR AND MARKETING MANAGEMENT

Effective business managers realize the importance of marketing to the success of their firm. *Marketing* may be defined as:

. . . the process of planning and executing the conception, pricing, promotion, and distribution of ideas, goods, and services to create exchanges that satisfy individual and organizational objectives.[7]

Notice that the definition encompasses services and ideas as well as products.

A sound understanding of consumer behavior is essential to the long-run success of any marketing program. In fact, it is seen as a cornerstone of the *marketing concept,* an important orientation or philosophy of many marketing managers. The essence of the marketing concept is captured in three interrelated orientations:

Consumers' wants and needs. This focus is on identifying and satisfying the wants and needs of consumers. The intention of the firm is not seen as merely providing goods and services. Instead, want and need satisfaction is viewed as the purpose, and providing products and services is the means to achieve that end.

Company objectives. Consumers' wants and needs are numerous. Therefore, a firm that concentrates on satisfying a small proportion of all desires will most effectively utilize its resources. Company objectives and any of its special advantages are used as criteria to select the specific wants and needs to be addressed.

An integrated strategy. An integrated effort is most effective in achieving a firm's objective through consumer satisfaction. For maximum impact this requires that marketing efforts be closely coordinated and compatible with each other and with other activities of the firm.

Several limitations of the marketing concept have been noted, especially in regard to the degree to which attempting to satisfy consumers' wants and needs can generate negative consequences for society.[8] For example, convenience packaging has contributed to a solid waste disposal problem for society and the propellant formerly used in many aerosol sprays has been linked to depletion of the ozone layer of our atmosphere. Adjustments to the marketing concept which incorporate societal objectives have been suggested to alleviate such shortcomings.[9] However, the basic need to understand consumers is still fundamental to these revised schemes.

Several major activities can be undertaken by an organization that is market-

ing-oriented. These include market-opportunity analysis, target-market selection, and marketing-mix determination, which includes decisions on the proper combination of marketing variables to offer consumers. Each of these is briefly discussed below with examples to illustrate the relevance of consumer behavior to their accomplishment.

Market-Opportunity Analysis   This activity involves examining trends and conditions in the marketplace to identify consumers' needs and wants that are not being fully satisfied. The analysis begins with a study of general market trends, such as consumers' lifestyles and income levels, which may suggest unsatisfied wants and needs. More specific examination involves assessing any unique abilities the company might have in satisfying identified consumer desires.

A variety of recent trends have resulted in many new product offerings for consumer satisfaction. For example, companies attuned to the fitness interests of Americans have been quick to offer such new products as exercise bicycles, weight training books, and clothing. In the health care field, companies sensing consumers' unmet medical needs have offered coin-operated blood pressure testing machines at shopping centers and other convenient locations. Also, low-priced minor-surgery centers without meals or overnight accommodations are now available. In addition, a recently introduced device allows consumers to self-administer precisely calibrated medicine doses at home, thus eliminating the need for travel to the hospital.

Target-Market Selection   The process of reviewing market opportunities often results in identifying distinct groupings of consumers who have unique wants and needs. This can result in a decision to approach each market segment with a unique marketing offering. Consider the soft drink market. Here, major segments of ultimate consumers are distinguished by the type of purchase situation: (1) the food store segment, (2) the "cold bottle" or vending machine segment, and (3) the fountain market, which includes fast-food outlets. Unique packaging arrangements (container type and size), point of purchase promotions, and other variations are made for each segment.

In other cases, the marketer may decide to concentrate company efforts on serving only one or a few of the identified target markets. An excellent example of this occurred in the bath soap market. By segmenting consumers according to their lifestyle patterns and personalities, the Colgate-Palmolive company was able to identify a unique group of consumers in need of a certain type of deodorant soap. Development of Irish Spring for this target group led to the capturing of 15 percent of the deodorant soap market within three years of introduction.[10]

Marketing-Mix Determination   This stage involves developing and implementing a strategy for delivering an effective combination of want-satisfying features to consumers within target markets. A series of decisions are made on four major ingredients frequently referred to as the marketing mix-variables: product, price, place, and promotion. The following characterizes each area and provides a small sampling of how knowledge of consumer behavior is relevant for decision making.

PRODUCT   The nature of the physical product and service features are of concern here. Among decisions that are influenced by consumer behavior are:

What size, shape, and features should the product have?

How should it be packaged?

How many different models should be included in the product line?

What types of warranties and service programs should be provided?

What types of accessories and associated products should be offered?

CONVERSE VS. REEBOK   A good illustration of the problems and alternatives regarding product design is presented in the basketball shoe market. In 1917 Converse introduced a canvas basketball shoe and reigned as undisputed champion of this market until 1985 when it was finally out-sold by Nike. However, with the introduction then of a newer shoe by Converse, their sales again rose significantly.

The Converse philosophy had always been to emphasize quality, durability, and function while catering to the serious basketball athlete. Their designs emanate from "biomechanics laboratories," resulting in shoes with features such as high-tech arch pads, heel-comfort modules, and torsional stability. When Converse changed to what has become known as the modern "high top," the company considerably altered their shoe's design and construction to achieve better support and enhanced durability. Other manufacturers followed suit.

Enter Reebok, hot off their fantastic success in the aerobic shoe market. This company's achievements were based on the philosophy that a product's appearance and comfort are vitally important to its success in the marketplace. This was evidenced when they featured new designs of soft but not very durable garment leather to produce their very fashionable aerobic shoes, which were purchased by millions for casual wear.

Reebok's decision to enter the basketball shoe market was driven by some convincing consumer research results: Their highest degree of brand recognition was among the 15- to 24-year-olds, the group that also accounts for approximately 80 percent of all basketball shoe sales. To enter this market of buyers who traditionally purchased durable, functional shoes, the company designed three new models featuring enhanced performance and durability, but, consistent with Reebok philosophy, all having plenty of style.

Meanwhile, the fact that in 1984 sales of the Converse All Star really took off revealed to that company that a great percentage of the market purchases basketball shoes not to play basketball in but to use for casual wear. To take advantage of this fact and to combat style-oriented competition from Reebok, the company introduced the Converse Weapon in 1985—multicolored high tops constructed with garment leather."

GAINES   The situation faced by Gaines is considerably different. It illustrates that even when product users are not human, their reaction to a product can be the focus of considerable company interest. Gaines produces food for many of the nation's 43 million dogs that most owners treat as family members. Because of this, the bottom line is that if the product isn't devoured by Bowser with apparent relish, it probably

won't be purchased again. Since $3 billion of sales are at stake, it is not surprising that Gaines and its competitors spend millions of dollars yearly to maintain dog-food testing laboratories. Here, dogs' reactions to various ingredients (beans, cheese, and so on), food shapes (chunks versus bits), and moisture content are tested under controlled feeding conditions. Side-by-side taste tests comparing Gaines's products with different brands are also made with many dogs. Various measures of "dog satisfaction" are used, including the amount of each brand eaten, the extent of tail wagging and eye pupil dilation, and heartbeat rates. Results of these tests and nutrition information assist in making decisions on dog-food ingredients and new product ideas.[12]

PRICE   Marketers must make decisions regarding both a price to charge for the company's products or services and any modification to those prices. These decisions will determine the amount of revenues the firm will generate. A few of the factors involving consumer behavior are:

How price-aware are consumers in the relevant product category?

How sensitive are consumers to price differences between brands?

How large a price reduction is needed to encourage purchases during new product introductions and sales promotions?

What size discount should be given to those who pay with cash?

PRICE AWARENESS   Consumers' price awareness for certain product categories can be surprising. A recent study by *Progressive Grocer* magazine serves to illustrate. The focus was on price awareness of grocery items—goods for which many claim consumers have high price awareness and sensitivity. Results showed that only 22 percent of those interviewed immediately after their grocery store shopping could accurately identify (plus or minus 5 percent) prices of common grocery products. This was true even though they were asked about frequently purchased items. Also, the range of some estimates was staggering. For example, $4.86 separated the low and high estimate for a 6-ounce jar of Maxwell House instant coffee. Those shoppers who rated themselves as "very price aware" were only slightly better than others in their estimating ability.[13]

PRODUCT PRICES   However, for many products consumers show high concern for prices. As the watch market demonstrates, this certainly is not always directed at saving money. Amazingly, in times of uncertain economic conditions and inflation, Americans have joined many well-heeled Europeans in their interest in expensive watches. In fact, many retailers have noticed that the more a watch costs, the better it seems to sell. This market is not composed of people seeking a highly accurate timepiece, because such instruments can be obtained for a mere $500 or less. Instead, the "expensive" market is comprised of those who want to tell the world something about themselves— and their financial situation. Models to satisfy such buyers are priced from $1500 and some are in the $5000 to $8000 range. Top models frequently retail at approximately $15,000, while a special custom order has been known to sell for $4.3 million! For those who believe this expensive watch market is small, it should be noted that one New York dealer sold nearly 50,000 gold Swiss watches in one year alone.[14]

PLACE   This variable involves consideration of where and how to offer products and services for sale. It also is concerned with the mechanisms to transfer goods and their ownership to consumers. Decisions influenced by consumer behavior include:

What type of retail outlets should sell the firm's offering?

Where should they be located, and how many should there be?

What arrangements are needed to distribute products to retailers?

To what extent is it necessary for the company to own or maintain tight control over activities of firms in the channel of distribution?

What image and clientele should the retailer seek to cultivate?

RETAIL OUTLETS   Large retailers such as Sears, J. C. Penney, and K mart are located in most of the largest metropolitan centers. Growth requires these corporations to expand with ever-increasing markets. The question then becomes, Where are markets likely to develop and what type of outlets will best serve them? Many people in the industry are being persuaded by an impressive change in U.S. consumer demographics—a move back to smaller cities and towns. The result is that between 1979 and 1990 the ten largest metropolitan areas are projected to have an inflation-adjusted sales growth of only 37 percent, while the ten smallest metropolitan areas are expected to post 54 percent gains. This has led to development of what retailers are calling K30's and K40's. These 30,000 to 40,000 square-foot stores are designed for malls being developed in the smaller markets that were previously ignored because of low consumer density per square mile. They are frequently no more than one-half the size of large city stores and are built to emphasize merchandise that retailers believe will be the most profitable offerings for consumers in smaller markets. Consequently, the stores stress clothing, hardware, appliances, and automotive services but rarely include full furniture, carpet, or candy departments. Consumer reaction has been quite favorable and the major retailers have also been impressed with sales.[15]

ATMOSPHERICS   Although the location of retail outlets may be critical, it certainly does not guarantee sales. Thus, retailers are continuously searching for the proper product mix and service offerings to satisfy consumers. Sophisticated devices are also used by many to provide an atmosphere that is most pleasing to shoppers. Store background music is employed in this way. The type of songs and their programming are selected on the basis of consumer reactions. For example, the music on some systems increases in rhythm and beat until a climax is reached. This is followed by a period of silence after which the music begins to build again. Studies suggest that such programming gives consumers periodic psychological lifts. Benefits to the retailer are said to include a reduction in consumer complaints and a higher sales volume. In another vein, some psychologists have argued that consumers' sense of space can affect their purchase behavior. Higher-density conditions are said to generate a fairlike atmosphere which consumers perceive in a positive manner. The resulting potential for sales has led some to predict a new trend in ''high density'' store design. Methods designed to appeal to consumers do not stop there. For example, store colors are often used in ways that research has suggested will foster specific reactions. Artificial odors such as pizza and

chocolate chips are also available in aerosol cans, as are special timed-release devices to add to the food retailer's ''atmospherics.''[16]

PROMOTION   Of concern here are the goals and methods for communicating aspects of the firm and its offerings to target consumers. Consumer-related decisions include:

What methods of promotion are best for each specific situation?

What are the most effective means for gaining consumers' attention?

What methods best convey the intended message?

How often should a given advertisement be repeated?

NEW-IMAGE BUILDING   It is dark and wrinkled, and it certainly has little chance of winning any beauty contest. Also, most people associate it with ''regularity'' problems of elderly people. In fact, the prune is a fruit that is predominantly eaten by people over the age of 45 while others tend to ignore its existence. Both of these circumstances contributed to an unsatisfactory condition as far as California prune growers were concerned.

Previous advertisements directed at mothers and children positioned prunes as a healthy snack alternative to junk food. However, these efforts were not successful in building sales. What was needed was a means to draw attention to prunes, especially among younger consumers, and to develop a new image for the product as a tasty and healthful food. Therefore, the California Prune Board's promotional goals were set, and a search was activated to find the proper vehicle to accomplish these ends.

The result was a new promotional campaign employing a sweepstakes offer in an advertisement that stressed the healthy, nutritious, and tasty benefits of prunes. Prunes are a rich source of potassium, natural fiber, and vitamin A. In addition, cooking with prunes has been historically popular among the great chefs of France. That was the link—a stress on the double benefits of prunes: a healthful food that can also be associated with sophisticated gourmet dining. This seemed to be a natural for the new image.

The audience selected as the target was composed of younger, college-educated women of upper-middle income with children at home. Media chosen for advertisements fit the bill for reaching those who were interested in fine dining: *Bon Appetit, Gourmet,* and *Good Housekeeping* magazines were on the list. A modest number of geographical areas were selected as the focus for this new approach.

The attention-getting sweepstakes prizes were also tied into the theme. One prize was a twelve-day, all-expenses-paid eating tour of famous gourmet dining places in France. Another was a trip to a famous French cooking school located in Napa Valley, California.

Was it successful? Expectations were that 100,000 people would enter the sweepstakes. In fact, over 300,000 entries were received, and more than 50 percent of those who entered had purchased prunes. This news was treated with great enthusiasm by the promoters.[17]

COMPARATIVE ADVERTISING   Another area that often presents marketers with a dilemma is whether to use comparative advertising. This method of promotion is

designed to compare the company's brand directly against a competitor. The practice has been encouraged by the U.S. Federal Trade Commission under the belief that the technique is an effective way to present product information on which consumers can base their purchase decisions. It also is said to encourage competition between brands, which can lead to lower prices and product improvements. The problem is that evidence is not clear on how consumers react to comparative ads. There certainly seem to be successful aspects to numerous comparative campaigns—Vivitar, a photographic equipment manufacturer, ran an ad naming Kodak products and dramatically boosted their sales; public awareness of Avis and Datril increased significantly when they compared themselves to Hertz and Tylenol, respectively; and Pepsi claims to have increased its market share from its taste-test advertising campaign using Coke as the other brand. However, when responding to surveys about the issue, consumers frequently indicate a dislike of comparative ads because they find them lacking in reliability and usefulness. Studies have also found that such advertisements can confuse consumers and foster negative attitudes toward the promoted brand. As a result, consumers may respond by feeling they should disregard the advertisements and use their own judgment for purchase decisions. Perhaps the worst situation is when the competing brand responds in a hostile manner to a comparative ad, as Coke did to the ''Pepsi Challenge'' taste tests. The fighting that may occur (and did in this situation), can be perceived as childish or immature. This can quickly lead consumers to conclude that both companies lack credibility, and brand images may suffer accordingly.[18]

These examples indicate the relevance of consumer behavior to marketing-management decision making. However, it is also useful to consider other areas where knowledge of consumers has significant practical application.

CONSUMER BEHAVIOR AND NONPROFIT AND SOCIAL MARKETING

Can crime prevention, charitable contributions, or the concept of family planning be sold to people in much the same way that some business firms sell soap? A number of writers have suggested that various social and nonprofit organizations can be viewed as having services or ideas which they are attempting to market to target groups of ''consumers'' or constituents.[19] Such organizations include governmental agencies, religious orders, universities, and charitable institutions. Often these groups must also appeal to the public for support in addition to attempting to satisfy some want or need in society. Clearly, a sound understanding of consumer decision processes can assist their efforts.[20]

Consider, for example, the benefits such knowledge would have to administrators of the American Cancer Society. Two major tasks of this organization are (1) to solicit public contributions for support of cancer research and (2) to encourage regular physical examinations for early detection of the disease. Regarding the first task, fundamental information, such as the characteristics of potential contributors, what motivates their generosity, and how these motives can be most effectively appealed to are highly useful. Similarly, a sound basis for encouraging regular physical examinations would include specific knowledge of reasons why the exams are avoided—the expense, the time involved, the fear of learning about an illness, or some other reason.

Many other examples demonstrate the fundamental role a consumer orienta-

tion plays in nonprofit and social-marketing endeavors. The following serve as additional illustrations.

POLITICAL POSITION   Many political groups now base much of their platform on surveys and other methods devised to measure and influence the voting public. The presidential campaigns of Ronald Reagan serve as excellent examples. It is estimated that in 1980 Reagan's campaign spent $1.4 million on a survey program to determine the public's attitude on various issues, their perception of the candidates, and other information useful for designing campaign strategies. In 1984 Reagan's reelection budget for such surveying was estimated at $2 million. Early in October of 1984, 250 interviews were conducted every night to measure the attitudes and perceptions of Americans. By November of 1984 this number rose to 1000 nationally distributed interviews per night. These surveys enabled campaign strategists to determine what various groups of voters considered as important issues facing the nation and where they thought the candidates stood on these issues. In addition, selected audience reactions to debates and other candidate presentations were recorded second-by-second through the use of direct-response devices held by audience members. Hundreds of small-group interviewing sessions were conducted across the nation to identify themes useful for Reagan's positioning and to develop concise slogans such as "Leadership That's Working" for television advertisements. Reagan's leadership and speech-making styles were also constructed to appeal to certain voter characteristics identified in this research.[21]

RED CROSS   Traditionally the Red Cross has run a passive "good neighbor" theme to foster public awareness and favorable attitudes toward the organization. This approach was thought to gain high public acceptance and encourage financial contributions. However, an opinion survey requested by the organization cast doubt on these hopes. Results indicated that the public had low awareness and significant misperceptions about Red Cross activities. Few associated it with blood collection work, hospital volunteer activities, and water safety programs even though it was quite active in these areas. Although most respondents were aware of its disaster assistance, few felt any personal identification with this work. These findings led to further in-depth testing and subsequent development of specific topics designed to inform the public of the scope of Red Cross activities. The topics were bound together by the common theme of "Keep Red Cross Ready," to encourage volunteers and financial contributions more directly. Movie and TV personalities who possessed unique characteristics were carefully selected to present the points to obtain the greatest degree of message impact.[22]

Many other examples of consumer-oriented social marketing could be mentioned. However, not all of these efforts have met with significant success. For example, not long ago congressional hearings revealed that advertising valued at over $11 million was donated by media to encourage contributions for Radio Free Europe. Unfortunately, the effort was reported to have generated only $100,000 in revenues for the organization![23] This underscores the need for a sound understanding of consumers' decision processes as the basis for more effective social and nonprofit marketing.

In recent years the relevance of consumer-behavior principles to governmental decision making has become quite evident. Two major areas of activity have been affected: (1) government policies that provide services to the public or result in decisions that influence consumer behavior and (2) the design of legislation to protect consumers or to assist them in evaluating products and services.

Government Services   It is increasingly evident that government provision of public services can benefit significantly from an understanding of the consumers or users of these services. Numerous analysts have noted that our frequently failing mass-transportation systems will not be viable alternatives to private automobile travel until government planners fully understand how to appeal to the wants and needs of the public. In other cases, state and municipal planners must make a variety of decisions, including where to locate highways, what areas to consider for future commercial growth, and the type of public services (such as health care and libraries) to offer. The effectiveness of these decisions will be influenced by the extent to which they are based on an adequate understanding of consumers. This requires knowledge of people's attitudes, beliefs, perceptions, and habits as well as their tendencies to behave under a variety of circumstances.

PRODUCING NEW CURRENCY   In 1976, the U.S. government introduced a new two-dollar bill even though there were indications it would meet with some consumer resistance. One reason for developing this bill was to compensate for the dollar, which had declined in value due to inflation. However, the market proved more than resistant; it was nearly hostile. Retailers found no space for the two-dollar bills in cash register drawers. Consumers tended to confuse them with twenties and did not like the extra work of keeping track of one more paper denomination. Also, it appears that many people thought the twos would bring bad luck just as they do for dice throwers. Because of this unexpected consumer resistance the deuce failed. Disappointment but not defeatism seemed to characterize Treasury Department attitudes, because in 1979 it introduced the new Susan B. Anthony dollar coin. Apparently, the logic was that if the dollar is here to stay it should be in long-lasting coin form as opposed to nondurable bills. Remembering that in the early 1970s the Eisenhower dollar coin failed because its large size made it heavy, the Treasury Department made the Anthony coin only slightly larger than a quarter. To help distinguish it from the quarter, the Anthony had an eleven-sided design. However, design and considerable promotional efforts were not enough to guarantee success. Consumers rejected the coin in resounding fashion because to them it looked and felt like a quarter. Batting zero for three, reports were that government decisions makers were saying, ''Now, if we changed the coin's color to bronze and. . . .''[24]

LOCATING PARKS   City planners in Philadelphia decided to build a new recreational park for use by residents living in an impoverished area of the municipality. A central site was selected so that the park would be accessible to the greatest number of neighborhood children. A half-block expanse of swings, monkey bars, and play areas was then developed. Unfortunately, the park went basically unused. Apparently, the

city's administrators had unknowingly decided to build the park on an invisible dividing line separating the territories of two rival neighborhood gangs. Even though the area was centrally located, the fact that people perceived it as a "no man's land" virtually guaranteed that the park facilities would go unused.[25]

Consumer Protection Activities   Many agencies at all levels of government are involved with regulating business practices for the purpose of protecting consumers' welfare. Some government programs are also designed to influence certain consumer actions directly (such as the use of auto seatbelts) and discourage others (speeding, drug abuse, etc.). In addition, over thirty federal agencies, including the Department of Commerce, the Food and Drug Administration (FDA), and the Federal Trade Commission (FTC), have increased their efforts to provide consumers with information believed useful for making purchase decisions. The following serves to illustrate the nature of some of the issues government decision makers confront in their consumer protection efforts:

REGULATING ADVERTISEMENTS   Government agencies have developed many regulations to protect consumers from potentially misleading and deceptive advertisements. At the federal level, primary responsibility for this activity has been assigned to the FTC. Before the 1980s, the commission embarked on taking a more active regulatory role. In addition to declaring certain advertisements deceptive, it has now been able to require some firms to withdraw their offending promotions. In other cases, firms have also been ordered to sponsor communications designed to correct inappropriate impressions consumers may have formed from exposure to earlier advertisements. In all of these cases the FTC has focused on advertising copy—the words the firms use to make their claims. More recently, however, the commission has shown some interest in regulating the nonverbal (picture) content of advertisements. The justification given for this interest is that advertisers can use pictures to convey a considerable amount of meaning to consumers. Therefore, to regulate only verbal portions of ads is only attacking a part of the deception problem. An ad for Belair cigarettes serves as an example. The verbal part telling readers that Belair takes you "all the way to fresh" was evaluated as quite uninformative by a FTC deputy director, but he questioned the meaning consumers might derive from the full-page color picture of a couple frolicking in the ocean. The interpretation might be that Belair cigarettes make people healthy and happy. If such a message were conveyed in verbal form, it would likely draw an FTC deception investigation.

   Response from the advertising community has not been positive to such an argument. Many are concerned that the FTC staff is seeking to regulate legitimate attempts at advertising persuasion rather than deceptive practices. Others charge that hardly anything is known about how advertising pictures influence consumers. Therefore, any FTC judgments are bound to be quite arbitrary. FTC staffers tend to agree on this point, but they also have argued that it is possible to develop methods and standards for judging how such pictures influence consumers. In addition, they believe that a considerable amount of relevant information is presently available from consumer research studies that industry has already conducted for the purpose of developing effective advertising strategies. Industry spokespeople disagree and are quite concerned that an inadequate understanding of how consumers process pictorial stimuli could lead the FTC to develop inappropriate regulations.[26]

Unfortunately, it appears that the effect of many consumer protection efforts has been considerably less than expected, and in some cases the efforts may actually have had negative consequences for consumers. Often this occurs because officials have based their decisions on inadequate understanding of consumers and how they process information.[27]

CONSUMER BEHAVIOR AND DEMARKETING

U.S. history has long been characterized by intensive efforts of private enterprise to stimulate the public to greater levels of consumption. Various government policies have supported such efforts because of their favorable effect on economic development. Recently, however, it has become increasingly clear that we are entering an era of scarcity in terms of some natural resources such as oil, natural gas, and even water. These scarcities have led to promotions stressing conservation rather than consumption. The efforts of electric power companies to encourage reduction of electrical use serves as one illustration. In other circumstances, consumers have been encouraged to decrease or stop their use of particular goods believed to have harmful effects. Programs designed to reduce drug abuse, gambling, and similar types of consumption are examples. These actions have been undertaken by government agencies, nonprofit organizations, and other private groups.

The term "demarketing" refers to all such efforts to encourage consumers to reduce their consumption of a particular product or service. The following examples illustrate two demarketing programs:

ANTISMOKING CAMPAIGNS   The U.S. government has expended considerable effort to discourage cigarette smoking. Government activities have been supported with other programs mounted by nongovernment agencies such as the American Cancer Society and the Heart Association.

Communications to existing and potential smokers have involved using famous athletes to speak against smoking cigarettes, showing how the habit is socially offensive, and making very liberal uses of fear appeals. Fear campaigns have focused on how smokers increase their risks of developing heart disease, lung cancer, and other health problems. Celebrities who have been heavy smokers and have also been suffering from lung cancer have actually been used in some advertisements. The potential impact of smoking risks on family and loved ones has also served as an appeal in many communications.

Considerable funds have been spent on these programs. For example, in 1967 alone just one agency, the Department of Health, Education, and Welfare, spent $2.1 million in its antismoking campaign. Despite all of these efforts, cigarette smoking is still widespread.

ANTIDRUG EFFORTS   Swedish health authorities recently concluded that hashish smoking in Stockholm and other parts of that country had reached epidemic proportions. Concerns about new research evidence suggesting negative medical effects from the drug, and a belief that hash smoking led to using more serious narcotics, prompted Stockholm officials to act. It was decided that the best way to encourage people to reduce or discontinue their use of hash was to really "shake them up." This led to a series of posters and billboards dispersed throughout the city, graphically

showing potential negative consequences from using the drug. In one poster entitled "One Man's Bread," two men are shown counting money over a dead teenager lying next to a syringe. In another, a former teenage hashish-smoking soccer star is shown lying face down on an operating table. The caption reads: "Mickie: He first smoked hash five years ago. Here he lies today, dead at age 25 of an overdose of heroin." Meanwhile, in England the government is attempting a somewhat different strategy. The recent contention there is that young people rebel against authoritarian antidrug messages and that they would not associate themselves with addiction and death themes. Therefore, the new approach focuses on physical consequences of drug addiction, such as skin problems, glazed eyes, and limp hair. In one magazine ad, a girl with ugly skin blotches and a horrible complexion appears above the message "Skin Care by Heroin."[28]

Some demarketing efforts have met with considerable success while many others have made hardly any impact in changing long-established consumption patterns. An analysis of the successes and failures of various efforts strongly suggests that demarketing programs must be based on a sound understanding of consumers' motives, attitudes, and historically established consumption behavior.

CONSUMER BEHAVIOR AND CONSUMER EDUCATION

Consumers also stand to benefit directly from orderly investigations of their behavior. This can occur on an individual basis or as part of more formal educational programs. As we study what has been discovered about the behavior of others, we can gain insight into our own interactions with the marketplace. For example, when we learn that a large proportion of the billions spent annually on grocery products is used for impulse purchases, and not spent according to preplanned shopping lists, we may be more willing to plan our purchases in an effort to save money. In general, as we discover the many variables that can influence consumers' purchases, we have the opportunity to better understand how they affect our own behavior.

What is learned about consumer behavior can also directly benefit consumers in a more formal sense. The knowledge can serve as data for educational programs designed to improve their decision making regarding products and services. Such courses are now available at the high school and college level and are becoming increasingly popular. To be most effective, these educational programs should be based on a clear understanding of the important variables influencing consumers.

MANAGERIAL REFLECTIONS

For our product or service situation . . .

1   Who is likely to take on the roles described in Table 1-1? Do different purchase situations change this answer?

2   What are my target market's wants and needs?

3   Are there target markets which are sufficiently viable for our marketing effort?

4 What are the more critical decisions regarding the product?

5 How price-aware are consumers?

6 Are we selling in the proper retail outlets?

7 Are the promotional methods and advertising claims having an adverse effect on consumers?

8 Should any demarketing activities be considered?

9 What areas are in need of consumer education programs?

DISCUSSION TOPICS

1 A marketer in the cosmetics industry once remarked: "In the factory, we make cosmetics; in the drugstore we sell hope." How does this relate to the marketing concept and the need for marketers to understand consumer behavior?

2 Review the activities undertaken by marketing-oriented firms and show the relevance of consumer behavior to each activity.

3 What would you recommend to government officials interested in introducing a new type of currency (coin or bill) to the market?

4 Every consumer is unique, and any study that concentrates on the "average" consumer is meaningless. Comment on this statement.

5 In terms of understanding consumers, what are the advantages and disadvantages of viewing behavior as both a decision process and a physical activity as opposed to just a physical activity?

6 In what ways is the study of consumer behavior useful to consumer-advocate groups concerned with designing laws to assist and protect consumers?

7 Choose an actual nonprofit organization and suggest areas where knowledge of its "consumers" might improve the services it provides.

8 Refer to the Regulating Advertisements example on page 22. What aspects of consumers' behavior do you think need to be studied in order to resolve the issue raised by the FTC?

PROJECTS

1 Interview a business person. Ask this person to offer a definition of consumer behavior. Also, ask how he or she believes that greater knowledge of consumer behavior could help in job performance. To what degree do the responses reflect the philosophy of the marketing concept?

2 Choose an example of consumer protection legislation or of a regulation designed to protect consumers (for example, unit-pricing requirements, advertising codes, or information-disclosure requirements). Indicate where knowledge of consumers would be appropriate to possible revision of that legislation or regulation.

3 Find an example of a recent product, service, or program failure in such literature as *Business Week, The Wall Street Journal, Fortune, Forbes,* or other marketing publications. Suggest how knowledge of consumer behavior, or the lack of it, could have contributed to the success or failure of the effort.

NOTES

[1] Based on Fran Brock, "Advertising May Be Rx for What Ails Hospitals," *Adweek,* **35**:26–27, January 1985; and Stephen Koepp, "Hospitals Learn the Hard Sell," *Time,* January 12, 1987, p. 56.

[2] Based on Lisa McGurrin, "Hillbilly Music in the Frozen Peas at Stew Leonard's," *New England Business,* February 17, 1986, pp. 38–41.

[3] John A. Howard and Jagdish N. Sheth, *The Theory of Buyer Behavior,* Wiley, New York, 1969.

[4] Jagdish N. Sheth, "A Model of Industrial Buyer Behavior," *Journal of Marketing,* **37**:50–56, October 1973.

[5] See Jagdish N. Sheth, "The Surpluses and Shortages in Consumer Behavior Theory and Research," *Journal of The Academy of Marketing Science,* **7**:414–427, Fall 1979.

[6] W. T. Tucker, *Foundations for a Theory of Consumer Behavior,* Holt, New York, 1967, pp. 1–2.

[7] "AMA Board Approves New Marketing Definition," *Marketing News,* March 1, 1985, p. 1.

[8] Martin L. Bell and C. William Emery, "The Faltering Marketing Concept," *Journal of Marketing,* **35**:37–42, October 1971; and Lawrence P. Feldman, "Societal Adaptation: A New Challenge for Marketing," *Journal of Marketing,* **35**:54–60, July 1971.

[9] See James T. Rothe and Lissa Benson, "Intelligent Consumption: An Attractive Alternative to the Marketing Concept," *MSU Business Topics,* **22**:29–34, Winter 1974; George Fisk, "Criteria for a Theory of Responsible Consumption," *Journal of Marketing,* **37**:24–31, April 1973; and Philip Kotler, *Marketing Management: Analysis, Planning, and Control,* 3d ed., Prentice-Hall, Englewood Cliffs, N. J., 1976, pp. 16–18.

[10] "How Colgate's Brand Manager Applied Psychos to Market and Media for Irish Spring," *Media Decisions,* December 1976, pp. 70–71, 104–106.

[11] Based on Jane Simon, "Tip-off: Reebok vs. Converse," *New England Business,* June 16, 1986, pp. 28–33.

[12] Paul Gigot, "Pet Project: Pursuit of Tastier Dog Food Hounds the Beagles," *The Wall Street Journal,* June 16, 1981, pp. 1, 19.

[13] Jo-Ann Zbytniewski, "Shoppers Cry 'Remember the Price'—But Do They Practice What They Screech?" *Progressive Grocer,* **59**:119–122, November 1980.

[14] Lawrence Minard, "The More It Costs the Better It Sells," *Forbes,* December 22, 1980, pp. 59–62.

[15] Based on Steven Weiner, "With Many Cities Full of Stores, Chains Open Outlets in Small Towns," *The Wall Street Journal,* May 28, 1981, pp. 1, 19.

[16] See Bernard Wysocki, "Sight, Smell, Sound: They're All Arms in Retailers' Arsenal," *The Wall Street Journal,* April 17, 1979, pp. 1, 35, upon which this discussion is based.

[17] Betsy Gilbert, "Sweepstakes Gives Prunes a Face Lift," *Advertising Age,* August 15, 1985, pp. 36–37.

[18] See Nancy Giges, "Comparative Ads: Better Than . . . ?" *Advertising Age,* September 22, 1980, pp. 59+; Linda L. Golden, "Consumer Reactions to Explicit Brand Comparisons in Advertisements," *Journal of Marketing Research,* **16**:517–32, November 1979; William Wilkie and Paul Farris, "Comparison Advertising: Problems and Potential," *Journal of Marketing,* **39**:7–15, October 1975; Stephen Goodwin and Michael Etgar, "Experimental Investigation of Comparative Advertising: An Impact of Message Appeal, Information Load and Utility of Product Class," *Journal of Marketing Research,* **17**:187–202, May 1980; and William R. Swinyard, "The Interaction Between Comparative Advertising and Copy Claim Variation," *Journal of Marketing Research,* **18**:175–186, May 1981.

[19] Philip Kotler and Gerald Zaltman, "Social Marketing: An Approach to Planned Social Change," *Journal of Marketing,* **35**:3–12, July 1971; and F. Kelly Shuptrine and Frank A. Osmanski, "Marketing's Changing Role: Expanding or Contracting?" *Journal of Marketing,* **39**:58–66, April 1975.

[20] See Karen F. A. Fox and Philip Kotler, "The Marketing of Social Causes: The First Ten Years," *Journal of Marketing,* **44**:24–33, Fall 1980 for a recent evaluation of social-marketing programs.

[21] See Jack J. Honomichl, "The Marketing of a Candidate," *Advertising Age,* December 15, 1980, pp. 64–68; Gay Jervey, "Research Acts As Reagan's Eyes, Ears," *Advertising Age,* November 5, 1984,

pp. 1, 91; and Edwin Diamond and Stephen Bates, "The Media Campaign in '84: The Ads," *Public Opinion,* December/January 1985, pp. 55–57, 64.

[22] Based on "Red Cross Drive Result of Research," *Advertising Age,* January 15, 1979, p. 36.

[23] Leo Bogart, "The Marketing of Public Goods," *Conference Board Record,* November 1975, pp. 20–25.

[24] See "The Lady Vanishes," *Time,* August 11, 1980, p. 53; and "Numismatic Ms.," *Time,* July 9, 1979, p. 54.

[25] See "Mental Maps," *Time,* March 15, 1976, p. 71.

[26] See "Bell Attacks Measuring Nonverbal Signals in Ads," *Advertising Age,* November 27, 1978, p. 94; and "FTC is Seeking a Way to Decide If Pictures in Advertising Convey False Impressions," *The Wall Street Journal,* August 11, 1978, p. 8.

[27] See George S. Day, "Assessing the Effects of Information Disclosure Requirements," *Journal of Marketing,* **40**:42–52, April 1976; Jacob Jacoby, Donald Speller, and Carol Kohn Berning, "Brand Choice Behavior as a Function of Information Load: Replication and Extension," *Journal of Consumer Research,* **1**:33–42, June 1974; and Jagdish N. Sheth and Nicholas J. Mammana, "Recent Failures in Consumer Protection," *California Management Review,* **16**:64–72, Spring 1974.

[28] Mark Goldsmith, "Swedes Smoke Out Hashish Users," *Advertising Age,* February 23, 1981, p. 62; and "U.K. Launches Anti-Drug Ads," *Advertising Age,* July 22, 1985, p. 34.

A FOUNDATION FOR STUDYING CONSUMER BEHAVIOR

After studying this chapter, you should understand . . .

- The complex and largely unobservable nature of consumer behavior

- How theories and models are useful in attempting to understand consumers

- How useful contributions from related areas have been in our efforts to understand consumers

- Some of the physical and mental activities that consumers engage in before, during, and after purchasing products or services

For some time on an on-and-off basis, Craig had been considering the purchase of a stereo set for his family room. Craig was never much of a music buff, but recently he found himself enjoying "soft rock" on his car radio. That's when he began to think that it would be nice to continue listening to this music when relaxing at home. In fact, he even began to envision himself acquiring a few favorite records or tapes for home listening. Craig thought that if tapes or records were of interest to him, then a stereo system, as opposed to a radio, was the way to go. Also, since he wouldn't be caught dead with one of those "boom boxes," he felt that the best path would be a modestly priced component stereo system.

Craig felt like a fish out of water regarding stereo systems. He never was "into" stereo in college, where some of his friends seemed to have acquired their knowledge. Consequently, he really couldn't decide what his needs were and which products and brands would represent an intelligent buy for him. However, one weekend when he got together with his friend Joan, he decided to seek her advice. He asked her because she was a serious music listener and he trusted her opinions. Also, he had heard her $4000 system on several occasions, and the sound had blasted his socks off.

Joan told Craig that the way he planned to use a music system had a lot to do with what he needed. He described his casual musical interests, and when she asked him further about expected future interests, he answered the best he could. Joan decided that he would be best served by a modestly priced component system which included speakers, a receiver, and a cassette tape deck. When Craig mentioned that he still didn't know how to go about selecting between various models and brands, Joan offered to go with him to a stereo store, but she made sure that he agreed to make the purchase decision rather than asking her to choose for him.

2

When they got to the stereo shop, Joan spent about fifteen minutes showing Craig brands in the price range that she recommended. After dazzling him with her vast technical knowledge and with buzzwords like "power of 15 watts per channel, RMS at 8 ohms with less than 1 percent total harmonic distortion between 20 and 20,000 hertz," Craig was quite relieved when she finally recommended a Pioneer receiver and tape deck. However, when it came time to select speakers for the system, Joan said that this choice was "too personal," and Craig would have to select for himself.

At that point, Joan went to look at a digital disk player, and Craig stood there in complete confusion about speaker selection. A salesperson approached, asked if she could help, and Craig indicated that he was interested in a set of speakers to complete his system. He confessed he knew very little about stereos and asked her for a recommendation. Her response was that Craig should "let his ears" pick those speakers which were most suitable to him, and he should not be influenced by recommendations of others.

After over a half hour of listening, and a lot of questions to the salesperson, Craig had narrowed his selection down to two similarly priced speakers—Ohm-e and Genesis—and was obviously having great difficulty in choosing between them. Each had what he believed were desirable features that the other seemed to lack. Because of his confusion, he kept indicating to the salesperson that more information about the brands themselves was not enough. What he really needed was help in making a decision based on this information. The salesperson then interjected: "Look, only one has a really low bass response—that's the Ohm-e. Only one has a walnut cabinet—that's the Ohm-e, and only one allows you to adjust the frequency response—Ohm-e."

After a moment's deliberation Craig responded: "OK, then I guess I'll take the Ohm-e." Within four days Craig returned. He bought six blank cassette tapes and, without deliberating about any other brand, a second set of Ohm-e speakers for another room in his apartment.

The study of any subject is made easier by examining it in an organized fashion. This chapter will lay the foundation for such an approach to the topic of consumer behavior. Our first task is to better understand what consumer behavior actually entails. This will lead to a discussion of basic approaches to its study. Attention then will turn to the usefulness of models in describing and understanding consumers. After this review, the chapter ends by offering a simplified framework that is helpful for integrating the variety of information that will be presented in the text.

STUDYING CONSUMER BEHAVIOR

As suggested in Chapter 1, it is useful to view consumer behavior as part of human behavior because we can then study it by borrowing approaches that have been developed in the behavioral sciences. One such borrowed approach views consumer behavior as entailing a decision process involving considerable mental activity.[1] It treats the three classes of variables discussed below as being essential to understanding behavior.

CLASSES OF VARIABLES

Consumers are continuously confronting and reacting to a great variety of specific situations. Seeing an advertisement, learning of a new product, or experiencing dissatisfaction when using a good or service are examples of such situations. Three classes of variables are involved in understanding consumer behavior in any of these specific situations: stimulus variables, response variables, and intervening variables.

Stimulus variables, such as advertisements, other people, and products, exist in the individual's external environment and are also produced internally. For example, our stomachs produce certain stimuli when we desire food. The role of stimulus variables is to serve as inputs to consumers' behavior.

Response variables are the resulting activities of individuals who are initiated by stimulus variables to do something. These include observable actions such as gesturing, purchasing certain products, and changing the pitch of our voice slightly when we become excited. However, response variables can also include an increase in knowledge about a product, a change in attitudes toward it, or a reduction in an intention to purchase it. The distinction between these two groups of response variables is that some are *overt,* or easily observable, while others, such as an attitude, are *internal* to the individual and cannot be seen.

The third category of variables involved in specific situations consumers confront is referred to as *intervening variables* because they actually intervene between stimuli and responses. This suggests that at least some stimuli do not directly affect responses but their effects are modified by the influence of intervening variables. These variables are internal to the individual and can include motives, attitudes toward things and events, and perceptions of the world. Figure 2-1 graphically depicts the central role of intervening variables and how they can modify the influence of stimulus variables.

Intervening variables play a very important role in our study of consumer behavior. Because they exist, we cannot expect a given stimulus to produce the same response among all consumers. Even for the same individual, intervening variables can change during a period of time and have different influences. Consider, for example, how a consumer's reaction toward "old junk" found in her attic might change upon learning that the items are antiques of great value.

It should also be noted that the exact situation involved and the goals of any specific consumer study will strongly influence whether a given variable should be classified as a stimulus, response, or intervening variable. For example, attitudes may be thought of as response variables when the goal of some advertisement is to change consumers' attitudes about a particular brand. Alternatively, consumers'

FIGURE 2-1
A diagram of the relationship between stimulus, intervening, and response variables.

existing attitudes toward the same brand can be viewed as intervening variables when a retailer runs a one-day, 50-percent-off sale of the brand to reduce her inventory of it. Here, the response desired is probably purchase behavior, but attitudes toward the brand may intervene to influence consumers' purchase reactions toward the sale.

UNOBSERVABLE VARIABLES

It is important to realize that intervening variables and many response variables cannot be directly observed. This requires developing methods to determine whether such unobservable variables actually exist and what their characteristics are. One approach to the problem involves devising instruments which will measure or be related to the variables of interest. For example, methods have been developed to assess consumers' motives, personalities, attitudes, and purchase intentions. These measures, discussed in more detail in later chapters, involve consumers' own verbal assessments of their internal states (for example, attitudes), paper and pencil tests, and technically sophisticated electronic devices that record changes in eye pupil diameters and voice characteristics, as well as other potentially useful indicators of consumer reactions.

Another way to study unobservable variables can best be illustrated by the *black-box* concept first originated in electrical engineering.[2] Basically, as shown in Figure 2-2, we imagine a black box hiding some variable or process from our observation. We can view the stimulus inputs to the box and certain response outputs from it, but we can't see the intervening variables which connect these inputs and outputs.

Careful observation of inputs and visible responses enables a judgment to be made regarding the contents of the box. This process is termed an *inference*. For example, in high school chemistry we inferred the existence and nature of invisible oxygen by employing the black-box concept and observing its effect on

FIGURE 2-2
A diagram of the black-box approach to inferences about intervening variables.

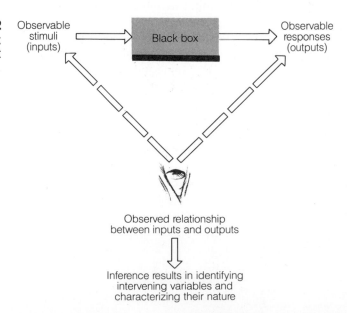

Observable stimuli (inputs)

Black box

Observable responses (outputs)

Observed relationship between inputs and outputs

Inference results in identifying intervening variables and characterizing their nature

combustion and life. As another illustration, assume that we show a friend a magazine advertisement using a scantily clad model to attract readers' attention. Upon seeing it, our friend frowns and says, "Disgusting." We might infer that this person has a negative attitude toward sexual exploitation in advertising.

These situations demonstrate that the names used to characterize unobservable variables are actually constructed (invented) by researchers. For this reason, such names are often referred to as *hypothetical constructs*. The constructs are called hypothetical because they are not observable and we cannot directly prove their existence. Instead, special measuring devices and the process of inference allows us to speculate about the characteristics of such variables and their role in influencing consumers.

PROBLEMS IN STUDYING CONSUMER BEHAVIOR

As our discussion suggests, studying consumer behavior is not necessarily an easy undertaking. A number of factors too lengthy to review here contribute to this difficulty. However, it is useful to treat briefly several of the more important constraints.

DIFFICULTY OF THE INFERENCE PROCESS

Unfortunately, even experts frequently disagree about the exact nature of intervening variables. This occurs because the variables are unobservable, they may have different aspects, and they can change over time. Thus, if we observe the effect of a variable at two different points in time, and the variable is changing over time, we could easily reach two different conclusions regarding its characteristics. The same would hold true if we happened to observe two different aspects of the same variable.

An important implication of this inference problem is that we must be prepared to face some uncertainty regarding the nature of variables that affect consumer behavior. We will even find different definitions and contradictory research conclusions about the nature of a given variable. Since such ambiguity is to be expected when dealing with complex unobservable behavior, it should be tolerated as we search for ways to minimize it.

SUBJECTIVITY OF BEHAVIOR

The past experiences of individuals influence how they view the world. Because the experiences of people differ, any given situation will be interpreted somewhat differently by each individual. Therefore, we must realize that consumers act on their subjective perceptions of the world, which are often considerably different from our own.

There often is a strong tendency to overlook this subjective aspect of behavior. Consequently, many unsuccessful marketing strategies are based on what managers *assume* are consumer motives, attitudes, and preferences, rather than on what we actually know about these variables. Researchers and consumer-protection advocates have also been misled by such faulty assumptions. We must be constantly on guard against falling into a similar trap ourselves.

LARGE NUMBER OF INPUT VARIABLES

The variety of input variables that can potentially influence consumer behavior is astounding. These may be categorized into internal and external dimensions.[3] One internal group comprises the individual's *physiological* requirements, which are only minimally influenced by his or her environment. Basic needs and drives such as the need for nourishment, water, and sleep belong to this category.

In addition to their physiological needs, individuals are also strongly influenced by their internal *psychological structure*. This includes processes such as attitude formation, information processing, and learning, as well as the individual's subjective knowledge, values, and beliefs that are formed from present and past experiences and influence future behavior. Collectively, the psychological structure is often said to contain *individual determinants* of behavior.

The external environment is also capable of influencing the individual's psychological condition and therefore his or her behavior. As with internal variables, the external environment consists of present, past, and future components. Aspects of the present environment are physical, economic, and social factors. Examples of physical variables include distance to stores, weather, and availability of transportation. Economic variables include the individual's wealth, the cost of various products, and the economic climate. Among others, social variables comprise the individual's social class and group influences. Many of these variables can be viewed as *situational determinants* of consumers' behavior.

Aspects of the past environment also have an influence. For example, consumers learn a great deal from past experiences. Interestingly, some of this learning becomes so strong that it is incorporated into habits without consumers even being aware of its effect.

Finally, expectations about the future can affect consumers' present behavior. To illustrate, expectations regarding future income, health, and job security can influence consumers' willingness to purchase capital goods (automobiles and washing machines, for example).[4]

The above paragraphs merely sample the types of specific variables relevant to studying consumer behavior. Many of these variables can go undetected because their influence is so subtle, and this can result in simple but incorrect explanations for complex behavior. Of course, the casual observer of consumers is in more danger of doing this than one who studies consumers in an organized fashion. We therefore must be constantly vigilant for additional variables influencing the behavior of consumers.

INTERACTION OF VARIABLES WITH EACH OTHER

Not only do numerous variables affect consumers, but they also frequently interact to magnify, cancel, or redirect each other's influence. For example, it seems that some advertisements may fail to persuade consumers to purchase the product because the announcer is not perceived as a believable source for the information.[5] In such cases, unfavorable perception of the announcer cancels out the positive effects of the message.

In addition, situations confronted by consumers can interact with other variables to modify their influence.[6] One study found that buyers of tableware were influenced by different sources of information depending on whether the tableware was being purchased as a gift or for personal use.[7] Such findings demonstrate the importance of being alert to the interactive effect of variables and their influence on the behavior of consumers.

While the four problems reviewed above in no way exhaust the list of constraints on studying consumer behavior, they do provide sufficient perspective for the reader. We now direct attention to models developed to facilitate our study.

MODELING BEHAVIOR

As just mentioned, studying consumer behavior can be quite complex, especially because of the many variables involved and their tendency to interact. Models of consumer behavior have been developed in an effort to overcome these difficulties.

DEFINITION OF A MODEL

A *model* can be defined as a simplified representation of reality. It simplifies by incorporating only those aspects of reality that interest the model builder. Other aspects that are not of interest only add to the complexity of the situation and can be ignored. Thus an architect's model of a building may not show furniture arrangements if that is not important to the building's design. Similarly, in modeling consumers we should feel free to exclude any aspects that are not relevant to their behavior. Since we have defined consumer behavior as involving a decision process, models that focus on this process will be of considerable interest to us.

TYPES OF MODELS

Any given property or process can be modeled in a variety of ways. We could model something by verbally describing it, by representing it with diagrams or mathematical symbols, or by characterizing it with some physical process such as electrical current. The most common consumer-behavior models are verbal.

Consumer-behavior models can also be classified in terms of scope. Some are designed to represent a very specific aspect of behavior, such as consumers' repetitive purchasing of the same brand over a period of time. Others are much more comprehensive because they attempt to include a great variety of consumer behaviors. These comprehensive models are less detailed in nature so that they can represent many diverse situations.

USES OF MODELS

Models are devised for a variety of reasons, but the two purposes for developing most consumer models are (1) to assist in constructing a theory that guides research on consumer behavior and (2) to facilitate learning what is presently known about consumer behavior. In both cases the model serves to structure systematic and logical thinking about consumers.[8] This entails (1) identifying the relevant variables, (2) indicating their characteristics, and (3) specifying their interrelationships, that is, how they influence each other.

Developing Theory A *theory* is an interrelated set of concepts, definitions, and propositions that presents a systematic view of some phenomenon.[9] It presents a

logical viewpoint that is useful in understanding some process or activity. More specifically, a theory has four major functions: description, prediction, explanation, and control. The *descriptive* function involves characterizing the nature of something such as the steps consumers go through while deciding on a purchase. In its *predictive* role a theory is used to foretell future events, as when learning theory is used to predict what brand names will be easier for consumers to remember. Theory can be used for *explanation* in order to learn the underlying *causes* of some event or activity. This would occur when we want to understand *why* a consumer regularly purchases the same brand of soup. Is it because of habit or loyalty to the brand? Although it is possible to predict events without understanding their causes, knowing why something happens greatly enhances our ability to predict its occurrence. *Control* is the ability to influence or regulate future events. This has been extremely difficult in the behavioral sciences due to the many variables involved and our lack of knowledge about them. Therefore, although marketers and others can sometimes influence consumers, we will find ample evidence that strict control of consumer behavior is far from present capabilities.

A useful relationship exists between models and theories because models can assist theory development by clearly delineating the relevant variables and their influence on each other. In this way models can present a unified view of what is known about consumer behavior and help identify what remains to be explored. This allows researchers to advance knowledge by selecting the most important aspects of consumer behavior for analysis and testing.

Facilitating Learning Our primary motivation for using models here is to serve as a learning aid. In this role, models provide a structure helpful for organizing knowledge about consumer behavior into a logical pattern that is easier to comprehend. They also remind us of the interrelationships between relevant variables. Therefore, as we concentrate on one particular variable, reference to the model will remind us to consider how it interacts with other variables to influence behavior.

MODELS OF CONSUMER BEHAVIOR

Comprehensive verbal models have been employed most often in the study of consumer behavior. A variety of such models exist, each taking a somewhat different view of consumers. Those chosen for presentation here are well known and represent a broad perspective. The first two represent traditional approaches to the study of consumers, while a more contemporary viewpoint is presented next.

TRADITIONAL MODELS OF CONSUMERS

The earliest comprehensive consumer models were actually devised by economists seeking to understand economic systems. Economics involves the study of how scarce resources are allocated among unlimited wants and needs.[10] Its two major disciplines—*macroeconomics* and *microeconomics*—have each developed alternative views of consumers. Partially because they have undergone some modernization, these models still influence contemporary views of consumers.

Microeconomic Model The classical microeconomic approach, developed early in the nineteenth century, focused on the pattern of goods and prices in the entire economy. It involved making a series of assumptions about the nature of the "average" consumer and then developing a theory useful in explaining the workings of an economy made up of many such people. Focus was placed on the consumer's *act of purchase,* which, of course, is only a portion of what we have defined as consumer behavior. Thus, microeconomists concentrated on explaining *what* consumers would purchase and in *what quantities* these purchases would be made. The tastes and preferences leading to these purchases were assumed to be known already. Therefore, microeconomists chose to ignore *why* consumers develop various needs and preferences and *how* consumers rank these needs and preferences.

The resulting theory was based on a number of assumptions about consumers. Primary among these were the following:

1 Consumers' wants and needs are, in total, *unlimited* and therefore cannot be fully satisfied.

2 Given a limited budget, consumers' goals are to allocate available purchasing dollars in a way that *maximizes* satisfaction of their wants and needs.

3 Consumers *independently* develop their own preferences, without the influence of others, and these preferences are consistent over time.

4 Consumers have *perfect knowledge* of the utility of an item; that is, they know exactly how much satisfaction the product can give them.

5 As additional units of a given product or service are acquired, the *marginal* (additional) satisfaction or utility provided by the *next* unit will be less than the marginal satisfaction or utility provided by previously purchased units. This is referred to as the *law of diminishing marginal utility.*

6 Consumers use the *price* of a good as the sole measure of the sacrifice involved in obtaining it. Price plays no other role in the purchase decision.

7 Consumers are *perfectly rational* in that, given their subjective preferences, they will always act in a deliberate manner to maximize their satisfaction.

Given these assumptions, economists argued that perfectly rational consumers will always purchase the good that provides them with the highest ratio of additional benefit to cost. For any given good this benefit/cost ratio can be expressed as a ratio of its marginal utility to price (MU/P). Therefore, it can be shown that the consumer would seek to achieve a situation where the following expression holds for any number (*n*) of goods:

$$\frac{MU_1}{P_1} = \frac{MU_2}{P_2} = \frac{MU_3}{P_3} = \cdots = \frac{MU_n}{P_n}$$

If any one product's ratio is greater than the others, the consumer can achieve greater satisfaction per dollar from it and will immediately purchase more of it. Provided there is an adequate budget, the consumer will continue purchasing until

the product's declining marginal utility reduces its MU/P ratio to a position equal to all other ratios. Additional purchasing *of that good* will then stop.

Although the microeconomic model has had an important influence on our understanding of consumers, it provides a severely limited explanation of consumer behavior, with a major deficiency being its highly unrealistic assumptions. For example, consumers frequently strive for acceptable and not maximum levels of satisfaction.[11] In addition, consumers lack perfect knowledge regarding products, and they often influence each other's preferences.[12] Also, they appear to use many variables in addition to price to assess a product's cost and may frequently use price as a measure of product quality as well as cost.[13] Finally, consumers simply do not appear to be perfectly rational in all their purchase decisions. These unrealistic assumptions may not have hindered the usefulness of this model in explaining the behavior of an entire economic system, but they certainly are not useful in understanding how actual consumers behave in specific purchase situations of concern to marketers and others.

An additional shortcoming of the microeconomic scheme occurs as a result of its focus on the specific act of purchase. We have argued that much consumer behavior occurs before and after this act. Considerable decision making and search for information can precede it, and purchase evaluation as well as additional purchases can follow it. Since the model does not address these activities, we cannot accept it as a comprehensive representation of consumer behavior.

Even with its limitations, the microeconomic model has been useful. It provides a perspective from which to better appreciate contemporary models of consumer behavior. In addition, we should now be more sensitive to the critical way in which the usefulness of a consumer model depends on its assumptions, and we should be ready to evaluate other models in terms of their dependence on stated or implied assumptions. Finally, because economists have modernized certain aspects of the microeconomic model, it continues to have an important influence on contemporary thinking regarding consumer behavior.

Macroeconomic Viewpoints   Macroeconomics focuses on aggregate flows in the economy—the monetary value of goods and resources, where they are directed, and how they change over time.[14] From such a focus, the macroeconomist draws conclusions about the behavior of consumers who influence these flows. Although the discipline has not generated a fully unified model of consumers, it does offer a number of insights into their behavior.

One interest centers on how consumers divide their income between consumption and savings. This deals with two economic facts of life: higher-income families spend a smaller proportion of their disposable income than do lower-income families, but as economic progress raises all income levels over time these proportions do not seem to change. That is, lower-income groups do not significantly change the proportion of income devoted to spending as economic progress results in an increase in their income. The *relative-income hypothesis* explains this apparent contradiction by arguing that peoples' consumption standards are mainly influenced by their peers and social groups rather than their absolute income levels.[15] Therefore, the *proportion* of a family's income devoted to consumption is expected to change only when an income change places the family in a different social setting. This will not happen when all income levels are rising at the same time.

Another macroeconomic proposition, the *permanent-income hypothesis,* explains why specific individuals are slow to change their consumption patterns even when their incomes do suddenly change. It proposes that consumers do not use *actual* income in any period to determine the amount of their consumption expenditures, but instead are influenced by their estimate of some *average,* long-term amount that can be consumed without reducing their accumulated wealth.[16] Sudden increases or decreases in income are viewed by the consumer as temporary and therefore are expected to have little influence on consumption activity.

A variety of other variables have been suggested by macroeconomists as influencing consumption patterns. Included are consumers' previous income experiences, accumulated liquid assets, and variations in taxes or credits. Although useful, these suggestions represent rather traditional approaches to studying consumers, stressing economic variables while tending to ignore the influence of psychological factors.

BEHAVIORAL ECONOMICS

Traditional economics focused on the *results* of economic behavior (supply, quantity demanded, prices, and the like) rather than the actual behavior of consumers themselves. As mentioned earlier, this occurred because economists' main focus of interest was on understanding how goods, services, and scarce resources are allocated among competing uses in the economy. Behavioral influences on consumers were viewed as complicating factors which could be assumed to cancel each other out when the interest was only in aggregate demand and supply of an entire economic system.

George Katona found such an approach lacking and argued that an appreciation of how psychological variables influence consumers could lead to a deeper understanding of the behavior of economic agents.[17] Katona's viewpoint, now known as *behavioral economics,* was fostered by important changes which occurred in our economy, especially after World War II. Rising income levels had given a large number of consumers significant discretionary income—spending power available after necessities had been purchased. In short, our economy had changed from one characterized as "much for a few" to one described as "more for many."[18] Presently, approximately 67 percent of the U.S. households have discretionary income levels high enough to be described as "affluent."[19]

What made discretionary income so interesting to Katona and others is that it has become a very important component of our economic system since a healthy portion of it is devoted to the purchase of durable goods such as stereos, washing machines, and VCRs. Because the cost of these items is usually high, consumers will tend to purchase them when they perceive the general economic climate and their personal situation as being favorable. Therefore, this important influence on our economy is somewhat volatile and is affected by consumers' perceptions and economic expectations.

A very simplified representation of Katona's viewpoint appears in Figure 2-3. As in traditional economic models, actual economic conditions are shown as

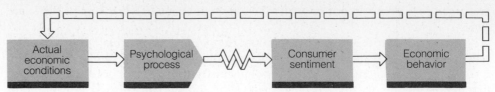

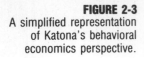

FIGURE 2-3
A simplified representation
of Katona's behavioral
economics perspective.

influencing consumers. These economic conditions include the rates of interest, inflation, and unemployment, the level of the GNP, as well as more personal economic situations such as the household's current status regarding taxes, income, and debt. However, as the diagram shows with a modulating arrow, rather than directly influencing the consumer, these actual economic conditions are modified by psychological factors which include consumers' motivations, knowledge, perceptions, and attitudes.

The diagram shows that consumer sentiment results from psychological processes modifying the effect of actual economic conditions on the consumer. *Consumer sentiment* may be thought of as the consumer's level of confidence about current economic conditions he faces, and his expectations about the status of economic conditions in the future. This consumer sentiment, in turn, is a deciding factor in the amount of discretionary spending that the consumer will engage in at any given point in time. For example, even when current economic conditions are quite acceptable, if the consumer expects that an economic downturn with possibilities of unemployment will occur in the near future, her purchase of a new car might be postponed until she is confident of her ability to handle future monthly payments. Katona argued that when many people in the economy share a similar view, a large number of consumers will hold back on discretionary spending and this is likely to lead to an economic downturn.

In order to test his arguments, in the early 1950s Katona turned to what was then a new and promising research method—sample surveys of large numbers of consumers.[20] The surveys asked a series of questions to assess consumers' level of economic confidence and expectations. Examples of these questions are:

> Now, looking ahead—do you think that a year from now you (and your family living there) will be better off financially, or worse off, or just about the same as now?

> Looking ahead, which would you say is more likely—that in the country as a whole we'll have continuous good times during the next five years or so, or that we will have periods of widespread unemployment or depression or what?[21]

Five key questions, such as the above, are combined into the *Index of Consumer Sentiment* (ICS), which is published on a regular basis.

Was Katona justified in proposing that psychological variables are needed to better understand the spending behavior of consumers and their effect on the economy? Has the ICS been a good predictor of changes in our economy? The left portion of Figure 2-4 shows a graph of the ICS from 1954 through the late 1970s. Also shown on the graph are times which have been officially identified by the

U.S. government as recessionary periods. The graph rather clearly shows that the ICS has declined prior to recessionary periods and, therefore, seems to be a predictor of their occurrence. The right-hand portion of Figure 2-4 shows a time-series graph of the ICS plotted against actual new car sales occurring three months later during the period from 1966 to 1982. Here, again, we see that car purchases clearly follow trends in the ICS. In fact, when the ICS was used as an explanatory variable in a regression analysis of new car sales, predictive power doubled when compared to using only income as an explanatory variable.[22] It appears quite reasonable for us to conclude that behavioral economics can contribute considerably to our understanding of aggregate behavior in a given economic system.

A SIMPLIFIED DECISION-PROCESS FRAMEWORK

As the study of consumers evolved into a distinct discipline apart from economic theory, newer, more psychologically oriented viewpoints were offered to describe and explain consumer behavior. These more contemporary views of consumers are in sharp contrast to early models because they concentrate on what traditional economists chose to ignore—the decision process and other mental activities consumers engage in regarding specific products, brands, and services.

A second and related distinguishing characteristic of these contemporary models is their extensive borrowing from material developed in the behavioral sciences. These newer models extend the behavioral orientation of Katona further, incorporating many variables which were originally identified in the fields of psychology, sociology, and related disciplines. Explanations of how these variables influence consumer behavior have also been borrowed from the behavioral sciences.

A third unique aspect of recent consumer-modeling efforts is their format, which generally portrays consumers' decision processes and actions in flowchart fashion as well as verbally. This provides a concrete structure which graphically portrays the sequence of activities involved in purchase decisions.

A large number of contemporary consumer models have been developed,

FIGURE 2-4
Association of the Index of Consumer Sentiment (ICS) with measures of aggregate economic activity.
Source: Richard T. Curtin, "Indicators of Consumer Behavior: The University of Michigan Surveys of Consumers," *Public Opinion Quarterly,* **46**:342, 347, 1982. Copyright © 1982 by The Trustees of Columbia University. Used with permission.

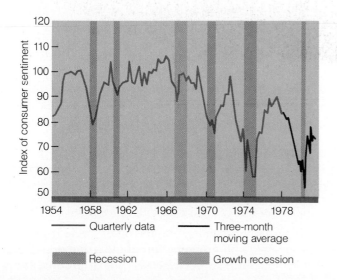

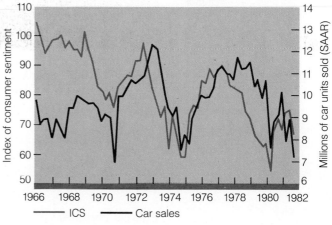

varying considerably in terms of their sophistication, precision, and scope.[23] Many insights can be derived from such models of consumers. These include:

1 Consumer behavior can best be viewed as an ongoing process in which the act of purchase represents only one stage.

2 Other aspects of behavior involve cognitive activity, which includes a decision process, and overt physical actions. All of these aspects of behavior can occur before, during, or after the act of purchase.

3 The decision process can be quite extensive and time-consuming or very automatic and short in duration.

4 The level of consumer involvement in the purchase decision is one variable influencing the amount of energy devoted to the decision process and to other activities.

5 Many variables, both internal and external to consumers, can influence consumer behavior. Many of these variables also interact with each other to form new or modified influences.

6 Because many of the variables influencing consumers are unobservable, the process of inference has been used to determine their existence and nature.

7 Because the study of consumers is still young, we should expect to find few concrete laws that explain their behavior. Instead, considerable diversity of opinion exists regarding many consumer behavior aspects.

A strength of most contemporary models is the intricate view they give of consumers. However, for those embarking on an initial study of the topic, these perspectives may lead to information overload. That is, their detailed views may be too complex for such an early stage of study. A strategy for handling this problem is to concentrate on the major aspects of behavior and show, on a more general level, how such variables may interact to affect consumers.

We have adopted such a simplified approach to guide our discussion, and a diagram of the result is presented in Figure 2-5. The framework represents an organized schematic of the major variables or processes that have been identified as the most important general influences on consumer behavior. It also represents an outline for Parts Three through Five of this text. As the reader's study progresses, the framework may be outgrown because of its simplicity. When this occurs, the detail provided by a more comprehensive model (such as the Engel-Blackwell-Miniard model cited in note 23) may serve as a useful outline for further analysis.

Reference to Figure 2-5 reveals that it is made up of three major sections: (1) external variables influencing behavior, (2) individual determinants of behavior, and (3) the consumer's decision process. These major sections are treated in Parts Three through Five, respectively, of the text.

External Variables The external environment depicted in the outer circle is made up of six specific influences and one catch-all grouping for all other factors. The six specific influences are culture, subcultures, social class, social groups, the family, and personal influences. The opened partitions denote the influence of these variables on individual determinants and on each other. These environmental influences are discussed in Part Three of the text.

The concept of culture has been characterized as "that complex whole that includes knowledge, belief, art, morals, law, custom, and any other capabilities and habits acquired by man as a member of society."[24] As such, it provides a basis for many of our values, beliefs, and actions as consumers. For example, the emphasis people in our society place on time and punctuality is unique and forms the basis for positive consumer reactions to such market offerings as fast-food franchises, express checkout lanes at supermarkets, and quartz watches. This topic and its influence on consumers is discussed in Chapter 6.

Subcultures are treated in Chapter 7. Here the emphasis is on segments of a given culture that have values, customs, traditions, and other ways of behaving that are unique and that distinguish them from others sharing the same cultural heritage. These aspects of uniqueness can have significant implications for the understanding of consumers and the development of successful marketing strat-

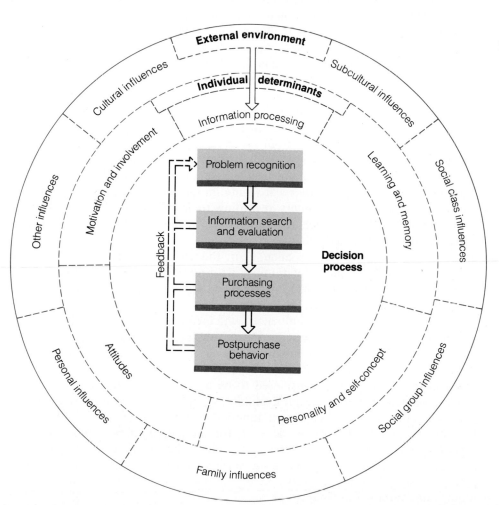

FIGURE 2-5
A simplified decision-process framework for studying consumer behavior.

egies. Subcultures distinguished on the basis of age and ethnic dimensions receive particular attention.

The term "social stratification" refers to the process by which people in a society rank one another into different social positions. The result is a hierarchy often referred to as a set of social classes. People within a given social class tend to share common beliefs, values, and methods of behaving. They also tend to associate more closely with one another than with people from different social classes. The values, wants, and interactions that develop in these distinct group-ings tend to have significant influences on consumers. They affect such basic factors as membership in a group, choice of neighborhoods, appreciation of certain styles, and choice of places to shop. Social class and its influence is discussed in Chapter 8.

A social group can be viewed as a collection of people who have a sense of relatedness resulting from some form of interaction with one another. These groups can have many functions. One that is particularly important from a consumer behavior perspective is the influence that group members can have on the individual. That is, the group can serve to persuade and guide the individual's values and behavior. The common interest that college students show in the latest fashions and in music serves as an illustration. Another interesting aspect of social groups is their role in providing consumers with various forms of information which can influence subsequent behavior. These topics are treated in Chapter 9.

The family is a special form of social group that is distinguished, at least in part, by numerous and strong face-to-face interactions among its members. The influence of different family members on purchase decisions is one area of interest in the field of consumer behavior. In some cases, decisions are made by one individual with little influence from other family members. In other cases, the interaction is so strong it is said to actually yield a joint decision rather than just an influence of one member on another. Of course, the nature and degree of influence in these decision-making patterns are quite important to marketers attempting to inform and persuade consumers regarding their offerings. Another aspect of family influence on consumer behavior is the way in which the stage of a family's life cycle (newly married, childhood years, and so on) influences the need for products and services. In a similar vein, the changing patterns of family and household structures, including families with working wives and those made up solely of singles, have significant implications for consumer behavior. These and related topics are considered in Chapter 10.

The process of personal influence, which can be described as the effects on an individual resulting from communications with others, has long been of interest to marketers. Interest in this subject is strong because personal influence has an important effect on the amount and type of information that consumers obtain about products. It is also considered to be a significant force acting on a con-sumer's values, attitudes, brand evaluations, and interest in a product. In fact, personal influence is an important function of opinion leaders. These opinion leaders are people that others look to for advice, opinions, and suggestions regarding purchase decisions. Personal influence also strongly affects the process of diffusion by which new product and service innovations spread in the market-place. Personal influence, diffusion of innovations, and other closely related topics are examined in Chapter 11.

The last category of environmental influences in Figure 2-5 is labeled "other influences." This general category encompasses influences on consumers that are not specifically treated in chapters dealing with the topics just reviewed. An example might be the effects of media that are not incorporated into one of the other categories. Many of these influences, including physical surroundings, the interpersonal setting, national events, and the consumer's available cash, have been summarized by the term "situational variables." The influence of these situational variables is treated at a number of points in later chapters.

Individual Determinants Major individual determinants of consumer behavior are portrayed in the inner ring of Figure 2-5. These variables influence how the consumer proceeds through a decision process regarding products and services. The decision process itself is shown in the center of the figure. An arrow leading from the external environment into individual determinants demonstrates that environmental stimuli do not directly influence consumers. Instead, the stimuli are modified by internal influences such as learning, attitudes, and motives. The opened circle between the decision process and these variables denotes the great influence they have on the decision process. The opened partitions between the individual determinants themselves represent the influence they have on each other.

Figure 2-5 shows the five major groups of individual determinants to be discussed further in Part Four of the text: motivation and involvement, information processing, learning and memory, personality and self-concept, and attitudes. Motives are internal factors that energize behavior and provide guidance to direct the activated behavior. Involvement describes the personal relevance or importance that the consumer perceives in a given purchase situation. High involvement will lead to a motivated state. Various types of involvement and motive situations, factors that influence them, and their influence on the behavior of consumers are subjects treated in Chapter 12.

The term "information processing" refers to the activities that consumers engage in when acquiring, integrating, and evaluating information. These activities involve actively seeking information or passively receiving it, attending to only certain parts of the information, integrating that which has been attended with information from other sources, and evaluating the information for the purpose of making decisions. Such activities are varied and occur at all stages of the decision process. They also strongly involve some individual factors including motivation, learning, and attitudes. Chapter 13 on information processing introduces these issues and also discusses several marketing strategy areas in which an understanding of the process can be of considerable benefit to the marketer. However, because of their importance, treatment of these issues is not reserved to just one chapter or section of this text. Several chapters in Part Four elaborate further on the subject. Additional discussion is also contained in Part Five where the critical role that information processing plays in the consumer's decision process is examined.

The important role of learning and memory is discussed in Chapter 14. What consumers learn, how they learn, and what factors govern the retention of learned material in memory are all issues of considerable importance for understanding consumers. Not only do consumers acquire and remember product names and

characteristics, but they also learn standards for judging products, places to shop, problem-solving abilities, behavior patterns, and tastes. Such learned material stored in memory significantly influences how consumers react to each situation that they confront.

Personality and self-concept are forces providing the consumer with a central theme. That is, they provide a structure for the individual so that a consistent pattern of behavior can be developed. In Chapter 15, several major personality theories are examined for their usefulness in understanding consumers. The chapter then discusses the importance of self-concept in understanding consumer behavior. How the self-concept develops, its role in influencing purchase decisions, and the practical relevance of the subject to the marketer are reviewed.

The topics of attitude and attitude change are examined in Chapters 16 and 17, respectively. Attitudes guide our basic orientation toward objects, people, and events. As such, attitudes strongly influence how consumers will act and react to products and services, and how they will respond to communications marketers develop to convince them to purchase their products. After reviewing the nature and function of attitudes, attention in Chapter 16 is turned to how attitudes are formed and how they are related to purchase behavior. Chapter 17 then discusses attitude change strategies, marketing communications, and how various aspects of a message, its source, and characteristics of the consumer himself can have a significant effect in modifying the consumer's attitudes.

The Decision Process   The inner portion of Figure 2-5 details the consumer decision process regarding products and services. The major steps in this process are shown as problem recognition, information search and evaluation, purchasing processes, and postpurchase behavior.[25]

The process may be viewed as starting when the consumer engages in problem recognition. *Problem recognition* occurs when the consumer is activated by awareness of a difference between her actual state of affairs and her concept of the ideal situation. This can occur through internal activation of a motive such as hunger, by confronting some external stimulus such as an advertisement, or by being affected by additional variables such as social or situational influences. In either case, however, action occurs only when the consumer perceives a sufficiently large discrepancy between the actual and ideal states.

Given that the consumer is aroused to action, the next stage is to undertake an information search. This usually starts with *internal search*—a quick and largely unconscious review of memory for stored information and experiences regarding the problem. This information is in the form of beliefs and attitudes which have influenced the consumer's preferences toward brands. Often such a review results in recognizing a strong brand preference, and a routine purchase occurs. However, if an internal search does not provide sufficient information about products, or how to evaluate them, the consumer continues with a more involved *external search* for information. This results in exposure to numerous informational inputs called *stimuli,* which can arise from a variety of sources including advertisements, printed product reviews, and comments from friends.

Any informational stimuli are subjected to *information processing* activities, which the consumer uses to derive meaning from stimuli. This process involves allocating attention to available stimuli, deriving meaning from these stimuli, and

holding this meaning in what is termed "short-term memory" where it can be retained briefly to allow further processing.

The alternative-evaluation phase involves comparing the information gained in the search process for alternative products and brands to the product-judging criteria or standards the consumer has developed. When such a comparison leads to favorable evaluations, the consumer is likely to develop a purchase intention toward that alternative receiving the most favorable evaluation.

As Figure 2-5 shows, a purchasing process usually follows strong purchase intentions. This involves a series of selections including the type of retail outlet as well as the specific brand or service to use. The consumer's purchase then leads to various outcomes. One such outcome is satisfaction as a result of direct experience in using the brand. Satisfaction will affect the consumer's beliefs about the brand. Other outcomes are dissatisfaction and postsale doubt. These can generate a heightened desire for additional information and influence subsequent problem recognition. In both cases, postpurchase experiences result in feedback to the problem recognition stage.

The above review provides a very general synopsis of most of the text. However, two topics of special interest have not been mentioned in this review. The first topic is the activity of consumer research and how some specific research approaches and techniques are employed to discover more about consumers. The second topic focuses on the concept of market segmentation, its potential benefits and costs to the marketer, and how some alternatives can be useful in understanding and selecting appropriate target markets from the aggregate consumer market. We will examine these two subjects before discussing environmental influences on consumers.

MANAGERIAL REFLECTIONS

For our product or service situation . . .

1   What are the various consumer response variables that are of interest?

2   What type of situational influences may affect the consumer?

3   What models or theories have we informally used when thinking about consumers?

4   How does consumer sentiment appear to influence consumers' reactions to our offerings?

5   What consumer motivations and problem-recognition situations may serve as sources for new product or service ideas?

6   Are there any typical consumer information search patterns we expect or assume for our products and services?

7   What evaluative criteria do consumers appear to have for our products or services and how are they developed?

8   What postpurchase processes are important?

9   Can we develop a general model of consumer behavior?

DISCUSSION TOPICS

1 What is a model? How can our study of consumer behavior benefit from using models?

2 Characterize the process of inference and indicate its importance to understanding consumer behavior.

3 A hard-nosed marketing manager was heard to remark: "All of this talk about consumers' decision process still just boils down to the same old fact—it's what the consumer buys, and how much of it, that's really important to the practicing marketer." What is your response?

4 Discuss the microeconomic model, indicating its contributions and limitations for the marketer, in terms of understanding consumer behavior.

5 What major contributions do contemporary models of consumer behavior make compared to traditional models?

6 How might producers of stereo equipment use Katona's model to understand better the consumers of their products? How might producers of chewing gum do the same?

7 Relate one of your experiences where postpurchase outcomes significantly influenced your future purchase behavior.

PROJECTS

1 Interview a business person and ask which variables are thought to be important influences on consumer behavior. Compare the responses to the variables reviewed in the chapter.

2 Design your own flowchart/verbal model of consumer behavior. Feel free to borrow useful aspects of models presented in the chapter, but also offer your original contributions.

3 Observe a consumer engaged in a shopping activity. Attempt to infer the variables involved in the situation and the nature of their influence. Be prepared to describe (a) the behavior you observed and (b) the inferences you drew from these actions.

NOTES

[1] For a review of other approaches see Robert L. Karen, *An Introduction to Behavior Theory and Its Applications,* Harper & Row, New York, 1974, pp. 8–18.
[2] Van Court Hare, Jr., *Systems Analysis: A Diagnostic Approach,* Harcourt, Brace & World, New York, 1967, p. 30.
[3] Suggested by Kurt Lewin as presented in Calvin S. Hall and Gardner Lindzey, *Theories of Personality,* Wiley, New York, 1957, pp. 206–223.
[4] George Katona, *The Powerful Consumer,* McGraw-Hill, New York, 1960.
[5] See F. Aronson and B. Golden, "The Effect of Relevant and Irrelevant Aspects of Communicator Credibility on Opinion Change." *Journal of Personality,* **30**:135–146, for some factors affecting credibility.

[6] See Russell W. Belk, "Situational Variables and Consumer Behavior," *Journal of Consumer Research,* **2**:157–164, December 1975.

[7] K. Gronhaug, "Buying Situation and Buyer's Information Behavior," *European Marketing Research Review,* **7**:33–48, September 1972.

[8] Rom J. Markin, Jr., *Consumer Behavior: A Cognitive Orientation,* Macmillan, New York, 1974, p. 79.

[9] Fred N. Kerlinger, *Behavioral Research: A Conceptual Approach,* Holt, New York, 1979, p. 64.

[10] Michael J. Brennan, *Theory of Economic Statics,* Prentice-Hall, Englewood Cliffs, N.J., 1965, p. 4.

[11] See James G. March and Herbert A. Simon, *Organizations,* Wiley, New York, 1958 for evidence of this in executive behavior.

[12] Thomas S. Robertson, *Innovative Behavior and Communication,* Holt, New York, 1971.

[13] Kent B. Monroe and Susan M. Petroshius, "Buyers' Perceptions of Price: An Update of the Evidence," in Harold H. Kassarjian and Thomas S. Robertson (eds.), *Perspectives in Consumer Behavior,* 3d ed., Scott Foresman, Glenview, Ill., 1981, pp. 43–55; and Werner W. Pommerehne, Friedrich Schneider, and Peter Zweifel, "Economic Theory of Choice and the Preference Reversal Phenomenon: A Reexamination," *The American Economic Review,* **72**:569–574, June 1982.

[14] Richard H. Leftwich, *The Price System and Resource Allocation,* 3d ed., Holt, New York, 1966, p. 8.

[15] J. S. Duesenberry, *Income, Saving, and the Theory of Consumer Behavior,* Harvard University Press, Cambridge, Mass., 1949.

[16] Milton Friedman, *A Theory of the Consumption Function,* Princeton University Press, Princeton, N.J., 1957; and J. William Levedahl, "The Impact of Permanent and Transitory Income on Household Automobile Expenditures," *Journal of Consumer Research,* **7**:55–66, June 1980.

[17] George Katona, "The Relationship Between Psychology and Economics," in S. Koch (ed.), *Psychology: A Study of a Science,* McGraw-Hill, New York, 1963.

[18] George Katona, *Essays on Behavioral Economics,* University of Michigan, Ann Arbor, 1980, p. 6.

[19] Victor J. Cook, "A New Role for Psychological Economics in Consumer Research," in Thomas C. Kinnear (ed.), *Advances in Consumer Research,* vol. 11, Association for Consumer Research, Provo, Utah, 1984, pp. 709–713.

[20] Until 1976, personal interviews were primarily used. However, since 1976 telephone surveys using random digit dialing (RDD) methods have been employed to collect the required information.

[21] Richard T. Curtin, "Indicators of Consumer Behavior: The University of Michigan Surveys of Consumers," *Public Opinion Quarterly,* **46**:351–352, 1982.

[22] Ibid., p. 349.

[23] For a review of a number of consumer behavior models heavily based on behavioral science contributions see Francesco M. Nicosia and Yoram Wind, *Behavioral Models for Market Analysis: Foundations for Marketing Action,* Dryden, Hindsdale, Ill., 1977; Gerald Zaltman and Melanie Wallendorf, *Consumer Behavior: Basic Findings and Management Implications,* Wiley, New York, 1979, pp. 515–542; Charles D. Schewe, "Selected Social Psychological Models for Analyzing Buyers," *Journal of Marketing,* **37**:31–39, July 1973; Philip Kotler, "Behavioral Models for Analyzing Buyers," *Journal of Marketing,* **29**:37–45, October 1965; John A. Howard and Jagdish N. Sheth, *The Theory of Buyer Behavior,* Wiley, New York, 1969; and James F. Engel, Roger D. Blackwell, and Paul W. Miniard, *Consumer Behavior,* 5th ed., CBS College Publishing, Hinsdale, Ill., 1986, pp. 22–40.

[24] Edward B. Tylor, *Primitive Culture,* Murray, London, 1891, p. 1.

[25] These steps are based on a more detailed series of activities proposed in Engel, Blackwell, and Miniard, *Consumer Behavior.*

CASES FOR PART ONE

CASE 1-1
PIER 1*

When Pier 1, Inc., opened its first retail store in 1962, it was perfectly positioned to serve an onslaught of baby boomers who were looking for inexpensive, exotic furnishings for dormitory rooms and first apartments. The stores featured India-print bedspreads (often used to cover unsightly walls), glass-bead curtains, bamboo fans, wicker chairs, and incense. Pier 1 stores often were managed by long-haired men and women who mirrored the hippies who shopped there. But now that baby boomers are older, the 205 Pier 1 stores have changed their merchandising strategy to fit a more mature audience.

The company's effort to understand its aging customers began with a series of focus-group interviews, followed by a survey of a random sample of 8750 regular customers. Now Pier 1 asks a 1500-member advisory board to answer four questionnaires a year. The company selected the people for its advisory board based on the demographic make-up of all Pier 1 customers. When the company introduces a new product or designs advertising, it is based on the demographics and psychographics of its customers, as revealed by the initial demographic survey and the advisory board surveys.

The surveys show, for example, that nearly 57 percent of Pier 1 customers graduated from college and another 30 percent attended some college, business, or technical school. Pier 1 stores now place informational cards near their products and at check-out lines to help customers learn more about the merchandise. Recent titles of the informational cards include "The Language of Fans," "Cleaning and Painting Rattan Furniture," "Planning a Most Unusual Party," and "How to Use Your Kamado Cooker." Other cards feature Greek recipes and the history of French glassware.

Pier 1 buyers are now looking for unusual imports to add to their merchandise mix, along with familiar items from the Far East. The customers, 85 percent of whom are women, have responded well to the opportunity to learn about merchandise as they browse. Today, Pier 1's best markets have a high concentration of young urban professionals, and the company has opened more stores in Minneapolis, Boston, Washington, and Fort Lauderdale.

*Doris Walsh, "Pier 1 Keeps Up," *American Demographics,* May 1986, pp. 16–17. Reprinted with permission.

Questions

1 How has Pier 1 used research information about consumer behavior to develop its marketing strategy?
2 What other information about consumers' behavior would be useful to Pier 1? How might such information be obtained?

CASE 1-2
THE AMERICAN RED CROSS*

When a company wants advertising or public relations results, it carefully studies its public and proceeds to target its message to the audience most likely to respond. So, too, does the Red Cross. The Red Cross has been growing increasingly sophisticated about its audiences. It is discovering more about those who are the primary users of Red Cross services, who gives blood and who provides financial support.

One of the most sophisticated models for awareness of audience specialization is the St. Paul Area Chapter, where the chapter is putting the concept to work by aiming a variety of publications at different groups. Understanding audiences is important because there are so many different jobs to do in the Red Cross. It is not like the Boy Scouts, which has a single purpose and mission.

Despite their diversity, most large chapters probably attempt to reach all their constituents with a single newsletter. But St. Paul Area Chapter uses a different approach. It has seven different publications aimed at seven different audiences, both internal and external, including chapter volunteers, blood region leaders, community leaders, and groups even as specialized as aspheresis donors. In the Central Ohio Blood Services region, the Red Cross has already changed its donor message to reflect what they've learned about today's self-aware population. They now talk a lot more about the benefits of donating blood, which include a sense of well-being, getting a mini-physical, and having a one-hour break from work. For the employer, it offers a chance to increase company morale because employees feel good about management that lets them give blood on the job.

The Red Cross is actively promoting in-depth audience analysis at the corporate level. At national headquarters, the focal point of the new audience awareness is in the audience communication division, which has analyzed the results of formal surveys, telephone polls, focus groups, and earlier research to develop a clearer image of the audiences that senior management has identified as critical to the Red Cross: blood donors, the military, business and industry, internal staff and volunteers at both the national and field level, and other segments of the public.

*Adapted from Jan Cook, "Red Cross Sensitizing Itself to Audiences," *Red Cross News,* **1**:7, June 1986. Courtesy of The American National Red Cross.

The Red Cross has concluded a large national survey that will support both communication development activities and efforts to improve and market core Red Cross services. This study is important for Red Crossers working on marketing and communication at all levels. It will create better profiles of current and potential financial contributors, blood donors, course takers, and volunteers, and it will help refine and target Red Cross messages.

One outcome of the new audience research is a five-year blood donor communication plan now undergoing final review. Because research shows that it is more cost-effective to convince current donors to donate blood more frequently than it is to recruit first-time donors, the plan advocates advertising and other communications that stress how frequently one can donate blood and emphasize the constant need for blood. Statistics also reveal that women represent a growing portion of the donor pool, so more messages than in the past will be targeted to women.

Blood regions are helping to fine-tune the plan. It was the suggestion of several regions that the plan give greater emphasis to strategies for involving chief executive officers of business and industry because of their impact on employee participation as donors.

When completed, the plan will be developed to reach the business and industry audience, which the Red Cross has targeted as its primary market for revenue-generating products. Currently, this audience makes up about 5 percent of all Red Cross contributions, fills volunteer leadership positions, and buys Red Cross courses. About 25 percent of all blood donations are collected in the workplace. A recent Red Cross survey of 1000 corporate decision makers revealed their high regard for the organization but their unfamiliarity with such organization services as organ and tissue banking and medical research. Development of a strategy that stresses coordination of all Red Cross programs working with business could provide a clearer picture of the Red Cross to the business audience. Acquiring in-depth information about such audiences and appropriately targeting Red Cross materials to them presumably will lead to a more reliable, better informed, responsive, and larger base of volunteers, donors, and supporters.

Question

How can a knowledge of consumer behavior benefit the American Red Cross?

CASE 1-3
MARKETING UNIVERSITIES*

Luckily, Hofstra administrators saw the handwriting on the wall. "We knew that if we didn't do something fast, we'd be out of business," says former board chairman George Dempster, a Long Island businessman, who along with Emil Cianciulli, a business partner and fellow Hofstra trustee, is credited with initiating the school's comeback. Together with the new president, James Shuart, they designed marketing plans aimed at repositioning Hofstra University within the nation's educational hierarchy and boosting its appeal to potential students. First, they developed sound fiscal management by balancing the budget and increasing the fund-raising efforts needed to enhance academic standards and physical facilities. Then, they began to identify and deal with other problems, such as the university's regional image. By the 1984–1985 academic year, Hofstra had record enrollment, and its endowment had grown from $5 million to over $17 million.

While not all of the nation's 3100 colleges and universities have had to engineer such dramatic turnarounds, the majority now realize that they can no longer sit back and wait for students to knock down their doors. In today's competitive environment, the institutions are paying attention—as well as committing large budgets—to the kind of strategic marketing and resource management techniques long used by corporate America. The result has been a resurgence in traditional recruitment practices—such as summer camps for high school students and college counselor visits to target high schools—and the genesis of new methods, such as creative financing programs and merit scholarships.

But the most pervasive tool in this increasingly sophisticated and costly business has become direct mail. Glossy, full-color brochures are sent annually to thousands of prospective students, promoting, among other things, unique campus atmospheres, enhanced academic programs, and renovated physical facilities.

At Emory University in Atlanta, the pursuit of the best and the brightest students during the past decade is reflected by the growth of its admissions office—from a staff of one with a $184,000 annual budget to a staff of twenty-five backed by a $1.1 million annual budget. Some of this money funds the 60,000 direct mail brochures sent out to students to fill a class of approximately 960.

*Adapted from Abby Livingston, "Embraceable U's," World, July–August 1985, pp. 11–13. Copyright © 1985, Peat, Marwick. Used with permission.

"You just don't have a strong student body without recruiting," says Bruce Moe, vice president of admissions and financial aid at St. Olaf College in Northfield, Minnesota. "And our brochures—like those of other schools—have become an important marketing tool. They're designed to get attention and a response."

The crux of the school's marketing plan is getting students' attention early. That's why St. Olaf, named in 1874 after the patron saint of Norway and associated with the American Lutheran Church, mailed out 100,000 brochures to high school juniors in 1983 to attract a freshman class of 830 for the 1984–1985 academic year. The approach worked: When 2035 applications (20 percent more than the previous year) arrived, St. Olaf was able to choose students who would best fit in amidst its low-keyed spiritual and high-powered academic atmosphere—especially its mathematics, chemistry, and music departments.

Colleges are scrambling these days to attract not only new students but also those who will stay four years and graduate. Toward that end, many institutions have sought to "position" themselves—that is, promote their own distinctive image and strengths. That's why Brandeis University in Waltham, Massachusetts—using a multifaceted promotional approach of direct mail, volunteer alumni organizations, phone-a-thons, and a strengthened public affairs department—positions itself as a university for the "serious" student. "Students are looking for a place that can launch them off into successful careers," explains David Gould, dean of admissions. "And a liberal-arts environment such as ours provides a broad foundation for future endeavors."

The school's selling point is that it offers students the facilities of a major research university along with the intimate atmosphere of a small college. (Indeed, the student/faculty ratio is about 10 to 1, and two-thirds of the classes have no more than twenty-five students.) And when it's time to graduate, the new Hiatt Career Development Center offers seniors up-to-date career counseling services and puts them in touch with well-connected alumni.

One element, however, that can probably make or break any school's recruitment effort is its financial aid options. Today, students—and their parents—are looking for ways to finance the college of their choice. "This is one of our greatest concerns, in light of federal cutbacks in student aid," says Brandeis president Evelyn Handler. As a result, in the two short years she's been at the helm, the school has prepared for a $200 million capital campaign that will include endowment funds for undergraduate scholarships and graduate fellowships.

St. Olaf has come up with some unique ways to deal with the financial dilemma. Realizing that students often mail in applications only if financial aid is available, administrators recently installed a computer near the admissions office so that visitors can obtain on-the-spot financial needs estimates. "In days past, students inquired about financial aid after they applied," says Harlan Foss, a St. Olaf veteran of thirty-nine years who served as president from 1980 through the 1984–1985 academic year. "But today, financial aid information can be the crucial element of a successful recruitment effort. After all, we're dealing with a major purchase."

Emory, too, has attracted an economically diverse student body—now that it has the resources to do so. In 1979, the institution received the largest single gift in the history of American philanthropy: more than $100 million donated by former Coca-Cola chairman Robert W. Woodruff. With one of the largest endowments in the nation, Emory has increased its scholarship fund from less than $1 million to nearly $6 million and has established the Woodruff scholarships, which are awarded on the basis of merit to as many as twelve freshmen each year.

Emory's new funding has also greatly increased its ability to keep enrolled students happy—by improving the quality of campus life. Says president James T. Laney, "A student's best education occurs with his or her own peers in settings of leisure and intellectual curiosity. So we want to have a lot of laboratories and libraries, but we also want to have a lot of the arts. And for that matter, a lot of sports."

At Hofstra capital improvements have also proved a useful marketing tool. Foreseeing the likelihood of attracting a more geographically dispersed student body, the school recently constructed seventeen new dormitories. Other new facilities include a sports complex with an olympic-size indoor swimming pool, an entertainment center and theater, and a new television institute. In addition, the library, recently expanded to house a million-volume collection and a new cultural center and art gallery on its top two floors, has strengthened the school's appeal.

The marketing process, however, does involve a certain amount of risk—especially in light of declining enrollments, higher costs, and reductions in federal aid. And as if these problems were not enough, administrators must grapple with the changing dreams and expectations of youth—who are the ultimate decision makers when it comes to attending a particular educational institution. That's why some experts voice concern over the possible adverse effects that marketing could have on higher education. Says Emory's Laney, "I have mixed feelings. While it's good for us in higher education to have sharp priorities and goals, I really do rue the competitive market. I think it confuses students. . . . Not every person should be pursued like a major league basketball player."

Given the current competitive climate, however, most administrators agree that marketing is here to stay. At the very least, more and more colleges are being forced to reexamine their goals, seek out new markets, and even redesign their programs and courses. Says Hofstra's Cianciulli, "We in higher education do need an accurate image of who we are. But we must build our infrastructures before we merchandise ourselves. How did Hofstra do that successfully? We had the flexibility to sustain growth. By that I mean we recognized problems in our marketplace early—and we reacted quickly by creating plans with clearly defined objec-

CASES FOR PART ONE

53

tives and goals—and most of all, by gaining a consensus among ourselves and never veering from our course."

Questions

1 What role does knowledge of consumer behavior play in determining marketing programs for universities?

2 What variables and information sources may influence students' decision processes?

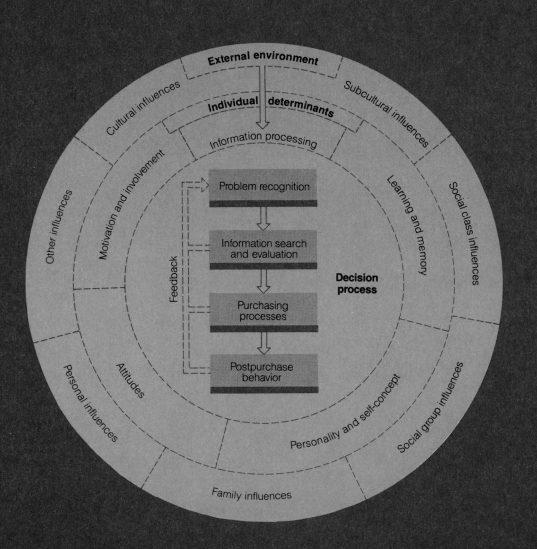

UNDERSTANDING CONSUMERS AND MARKET SEGMENTS

PART

2

RESEARCHING CONSUMER BEHAVIOR

LEARNING OBJECTIVES

After studying this chapter, you should understand . . .

■ The nature and significance of consumer research

■ The role of different consumer-research strategies

■ The different methods of gathering consumer information and the appropriateness of each

■ How researchers measure consumer characteristics

Wendy's—number 3 in the burger business—recently spent $1 million on consumer research to develop a better hamburger. After nine months of taste tests with 5200 people in six cities, The Big Classic was introduced with a different bun, a different box, and a different name from Wendy's previous burgers. The company tested 9 different buns, 40 special sauces, 3 types of lettuce, 2 sizes of tomato slices, 4 different boxes in 10 colors, and 500 names (including The Hunk, The Chief, The X.L., The Hot 'n Juicy, and The Max). Perhaps the biggest news the research uncovered was that the order of condiments makes a great difference to consumers. In other words, The Big Classic will taste different right side up or upside down depending on the way the burger's toppings hit your taste buds!'

3

THE NATURE AND SIGNIFICANCE OF CONSUMER RESEARCH

The following chapters will present a significant amount of evidence about consumers that has been generated by research investigations. Thus, it is useful first to gain an appreciation of the nature of consumer research, its applicability to marketing decision making, and some of the problems and limitations confronting the researcher. It is impossible to convey the breadth and depth of this subject in a single chapter. Consequently, no attempt is made to train the reader in research methods but merely to give exposure to a sample of important consumer-research concepts.

Consumer research may be defined as the systematic gathering, recording, and analyzing of information about consumers. Such studies are very important to our economy, and particularly to certain companies, as these examples indicate:

Companies interested in making their products sell better are compiling all sorts of facts about the personal lives of their customers:

Jockey International, Inc., knows how many undershorts we own.

Coca-Cola knows how many ice cubes we put in a glass (3.2) and how many of its commercials we see each year (69).

Procter & Gamble knows whether we fold or crumple our toilet paper.

Kimberly-Clark knows that we blow our nose an average of 256 times a year.

Paint makers know our first color choice for the outside of our houses is a shade of white, followed by pecan.

Bankers know we write an average of twenty-four checks a month.[2]

Marriott, like most of its hotel competitors did little consumer research, until recently. For example, room decor was chosen according to the personal taste of Marriott's decorators, with approval from the company president. But when in the early 1980s the company made a foray into consumer research, it was found that these decor decisions weren't popular with guests. Thus, Marriott's trademark reds and loud patterns were scrapped in favor of subtle shades of rust and beige. And when the corporation tested a new prototype midpriced hotel chain, hundreds of prospective customers were led through test rooms and questioned. They were very uncomfortable with a room 1 foot narrower in width but had little concern about trimming room length by 18 inches.[3]

One of the most successful consumer goods companies in the world is Procter & Gamble, which produces over eighty brands in the laundry-and-cleaning, personal-care, food, and other product categories. Procter & Gamble owes its success to maintaining close contact with consumers, tuning in to what consumers want, and making products that satisfy those wants. Because the company does business more frequently with consumers than does any other U.S. corporation—about 17 million transactions a day—it needs answers to questions about its customers.[4]

To gather useful information, Procter & Gamble puts a toll-free phone number on their packages or labels so that consumers can call in immediately with their thoughts

about the products (more than 500,000 have so far). In addition, Procter & Gamble each year phones or visits approximately 1.5 million people in connection with approximately 1000 research projects. These people are questioned extensively on their likes and dislikes concerning the company's products, including names, packaging, and other facets. Much continuing "basic" research concerns how people go about washing clothes, preparing meals, doing the dishes, and performing other household chores. Many specialized studies are also conducted on consumers' perceptions of products, reactions to advertisements, and responses in other areas. All of this information is processed and routed to every major segment of the company, where it is assessed for implications for Procter & Gamble's sales, advertising, manufacturing, and research-and-development operations.[5]

Even though batteries of tests and surveys may be conducted to discern what products buyers want, what brand name to choose, and how packages should be designed, new products may still flop. Sometimes researchers do not collaborate closely enough with managers such that the researchers may fail to ask the right questions, may present their results in a vague form that is not immediately actionable, or the research evidence gathered may be ignored by managers.[6]

Thus, no matter how good an idea may seem to be, failure to do sufficient research of the correct type and then to follow the recommendations of well-done research are quite likely to result in problems.

Of course, not every product that fails does so because of a lack of research. Unfortunately, research is simply not foolproof. Because of this fact, some companies have launched new products with little or no formal research. Minnetonka, Inc., for example, brought "Softsoap" (Figure 3-1) to the market with no research on the product's package design or color, name, or advertisements. The company credits intuition rather than formalized market research for the fact that the product captured 7 percent of the U.S. soap market in less than a year after its introduction.[7]

Nevertheless, the starting point for developing successful marketing strategy is a proper understanding of the consumer. Whether the marketer's "theory" of how the consumer will respond to a particular marketing mix is based on informal research or on a more formalized understanding, the essential ingredient for success is knowledge of the consumer. Chapter 3 will thus present an overview of research approaches by which the marketer may gain greater insights into consumer behavior.

In addition to such research conducted by many firms in the private sector, consumer research is also conducted by government agencies to solve public-policy issues, and by university researchers seeking to build better consumer-behavior theories. As mentioned in Chapter 1, the researcher may investigate any of several roles played by the consumer, such as user, buyer, initiator, or influencer. Therefore, the unit of analysis must be clearly specified when conducting consumer research.

CONSUMER RESEARCH STRATEGIES

Many strategies are available in the process of researching consumers. For example, studies may differ according to the goal of the research, the type of data

Softsoap™ or bar "soup"?
Now you have a choice at the sink.

It's ironic that the place where you use soap the most is the *one* place where it's always performed the worst.

At the sink.

What with the mess, the glop— there just had to be something better.

And now there is. SOFTSOAP brand liquid soap.

One touch of the pump and out it flows. In neat, metered amounts.

There's no mess, no drip, no soupy puddle at the side of your sink. Plus, there are over 300 wash-ups in each dispenser (the equivalent of 5-8 personal-size soap bars).

Softsoap™
Liquid soap

Soap without the "soupy" mess.

©1979
SOFTSOAP and design is a registered trademark of MINNETONKA, Inc
Minnetonka, Minnesota 55343 USA

FIGURE 3-1
Advertisement for Softsoap.
Courtesy of Minnetonka, Inc.

used, and the time frame of the investigation. Each of these approaches will be discussed in this section.

GOALS OF CONSUMER RESEARCH

Two major strategies of consumer research, classified according to their goals, are exploratory and conclusive studies.

Exploratory Research   Exploratory research is used to identify variables influencing consumers and discover how consumers may tend to react to these factors. This research occurs in situations when there is not enough known about consumers to draw conclusions about what variables are influencing their behavior. Two significant methods used in exploratory research are consumer suggestions and focus groups.

CONSUMER SUGGESTIONS   In the business world, many influences and problems encountered by consumers are discovered through the spontaneous suggestions of consumers themselves. For example, Procter & Gamble receives approximately 4000 ideas for new products each year, but for legal reasons it politely turns almost all of them down.[8] In addition, many retailers conduct an informal type of research similar to the familiar "suggestion box." Printed cards soliciting consumer feedback are placed for easy access, such as on tables in a restaurant or on sales counters in a retail store. Customers with complaints or compliments are able to express themselves instantly.

FOCUS GROUPS   Another popular technique for exploratory research is the focus-group interview. Focus groups generally bring together in a casual setting eight to ten people with similar backgrounds to apply the principles of group dynamics and free association to a marketing problem. A moderator guides the discussion but allows consumers to interact with each other. The sessions, which last about two hours, are usually videotaped. In addition, the group may be observed by other researchers or client representatives through a one-way mirror.

This type of qualitative research gives the marketer a chance to "experience" a "flesh-and-blood" consumer. That is, the marketer can better understand the framework in which the product is being used by learning about all of the satisfactions, dissatisfactions, rewards, and frustrations experienced by the consumer when buying and using the product.[9]

Focus groups can be helpful in specific ways to:

- Generate hypotheses about consumers and market situations.

- Suggest fresh and revitalized ideas.

- Check an advertisement, package, or product concept to determine if anything about it is confusing, misleading, or negative.

- Understand consumers' language and motivations.

- Understand consumers' lifestyles and personalities.

- Explore a new area as a prelude to a quantitative study.

- Do a postmortem on a failed product.[10]

It is important to appreciate that the primary objective of exploratory research such as focus-group interviewing is hypothesis formulation, that is, forming a conjectural statement about the relationship between two or more variables.

Conclusive Research   Conclusive research builds upon exploratory research. Specifically, the major goals of conclusive research are to describe fully consumers' behavior and to offer explanations for its causes. In addition, the prediction of consumers' behavior and methods of influencing it can be suggested by conclusive research. For example, a fast-food ethnic restaurant chain used focus groups to uncover all variables that appeared to be important in location decisions. Each variable was then tested in a quantitative study, resulting in a computer-based decision model incorporating the important variables.[11]

TYPE OF DATA USED

Two basic sources of data can be used in consumer research: primary and secondary data. *Primary data* are those the researcher gathers firsthand for the problem being investigated. However, there is a vast amount of information about consumers which is already compiled and readily accessible to the researcher who knows how to find and use it. Such data that have been collected for a purpose other than the research project at hand are termed *secondary data*. Before gathering primary data, the researcher should search through secondary sources to determine if any are applicable to the problem at hand. Because the types of secondary data are too numerous to describe here, an interested reader should refer to other sources for further information.[12] Our focus in this chapter will be on primary data and the methods used to gather them.

RESEARCH TIME FRAME

Generally speaking, in consumer research studies, primary data can be collected either at one time or over a period of time. We refer to these research designs as cross-sectional and longitudinal, respectively. These two approaches have different purposes.

Cross-sectional Research   Sometimes the researcher is interested in assessing the nature of some aspect of consumer behavior at one particular time instead of studying how it changes over time. As its name implies, the cross-sectional design is used to study such a situation by examining a cross section of behavior at any given time. For example, such a study may seek to determine the values and attitudes various consumers have about a particular product at one particular moment.

Longitudinal Research   Interest can also focus on how some aspect of consumer behavior occurs or changes over time. Marketers know, for example, that overall sales in product categories as well as brand shares can undergo striking weekly variations. To illustrate, supermarket reports in Chicago during a twelve-week period showed that a dishwashing detergent's share of market varied from a high of 60.6 percent to a low of 5.8 percent, while a paper towel's share ranged from 47.4 percent to 4.7 percent. Thus, what appears to be a stable national market for consumer-bought packaged goods can be actually highly volatile, paralleling the constant movement by consumers in buying plans and intentions and their switching of individual purchase preferences among brands.[13]

These situations are best studied by using a longitudinal design, which involves data gathering and analysis over a period of time. One popular type of longitudinal study is the continuous *consumer panel*. Consumers who are deemed representative of a particular group are chosen for inclusion in the panel, where the number of panel members may range from only a few people to several thousand households.

A continuous consumer panel provides the researcher with a fixed sample that can be repeatedly studied. By asking the same questions of panel members over a period of time, changes in their behavior, as well as reasons for these changes, can be determined. Panel members generally maintain a continuous record or diary of their consumption activities, such as shopping, purchase, use, and product/brand decisions, as well as demographic and attitudinal characteristics. For example, Kraft used diary purchase information about its Velveeta brand cheese loaf in determining whether to introduce Velveeta slices. The information provided data on how often the product was purchased, in what quantity, where it was bought, and by whom.[14]

METHODS OF GATHERING CONSUMER INFORMATION

In both cross-sectional and longitudinal designs, there are two general ways of collecting consumer behavior data: observation and communication. These two basic approaches can be further divided, however, into three information-gathering methods: observation, experiments, and surveys.

OBSERVATION

One way to study consumers is to observe their overt behavior. In some cases this alternative may be better than asking consumers how they act, because frequently discrepancies exist between how consumers say they behave and what they actually do. For example:

■ Soap makers have never been sure what to do about the color pink. Whenever they put different-colored bars of soap in front of us, we always point to the pink one as our favorite. But observation of store sales reveals that pink soaps are rarely among the best sellers.[15]

■ An anthropologist and his coworkers at the University of Arizona have for over the last decade been sorting through people's trash to observe what they consume. Recently, they found that eight of ten people said they drank no beer at home during the past week, but when sorting through garbage, researchers found that 50 percent threw away seven or more empty beer cans weekly.[16]

Another benefit of the observation method frequently is that it can be accomplished subtly, so that the consumers do not realize that they are subjects and thus change their behavior. Therefore, this method may be quite successful in obtaining certain types of behavioral information.

There are several illustrations of the observation technique being used in consumer research. Mechanical means of observation are sometimes used by researchers. For example, the A. C. Nielsen Company gathers television viewership data from a selected group of families by means of an electromechanical device that automatically records the times and channels of television viewing. This results in the famous Nielsen Television Ratings, which are issued every two weeks. Also, so-called people meters are being tested by various companies as a refinement to the traditional measurement approach. In these cases, household members enter code numbers into a keyboard when they begin and end their television viewing, thus providing a better indicator of who is watching what shows and commercials.[17] Some researchers believe that by the year 2001 even more accurate information will be obtained by means of tiny sensors—devices carried or worn—to monitor, store, and transmit data, not only about who the wearers are but even their physiological state as they respond to commercial messages on TV.[18]

In another application of the observation method, a technique has been developed using license-plate surveys to help retailers discover where their customers live.[19] Jewel Co. of Chicago conducted a study such as this for one of its supermarkets and found out exactly who shopped at that store, how far they traveled to get there, and in what sort of neighborhood they lived.[20]

Another form of mechanical observation is the use of cameras to observe eye movement and pupil dilation. Eye-movement tracking is able to document what actually attracts consumer attention. Also, by observing eye pupil dilation which accompanies the viewing of emotionally charged or interesting visual stimuli, the marketer is able to determine the interest-arousing potential of products, packages, and advertisements.[21] For example, a detailed diagnostic eye-tracking study of an advertiser's promotional letter and brochure showed that consumers focused only on certain locations of the brochure pages, exhibited erratic viewing patterns, and frequently failed to read key material. The letter and brochure were revised so that consumers increased their reading of the key copy and obtained greater involvement in the messages.[22]

Unobtrusive cameras have also been useful in understanding consumer behavior. For example, the question of where people set their home heating thermostats was researched for a group of electric utilities because their fuel-use projections, based partly on surveys of customers, were falling short of reality. TV cameras were put in the room where the thermostat was kept in 150 homes. Although people might have said they kept the thermostat at 68 degrees, it turned out that they fiddled with them all day long.[23]

Cameras are also used to observe shoppers' behavior in a store. This information can be very useful in many ways, such as in planning or improving a store's layout. For example, the shopping patterns of a supermarket's customers may be observed and recorded. The data can then be used to determine which aisles are most heavily traveled, where "traffic jams" occur, and whether more people pick up meat and dairy items first or last. Because subjects are unaware of being observed, hidden cameras have the potential advantage of being more accurate than personal observation methods. It should be noted, however, that critics of this method believe it is unethical to film shoppers without their permission.

A final observation technique that holds great promise for certain marketers is the use of automatic scanning devices in grocery stores. Scanning is a new measurement technique and a way of gathering data. When a product bearing a universal product code (UPC) containing information related to the brand is passed over an automated scanner at the checkout counter, the scanner translates the UPC. This information is transmitted to the store's computer file where the item's price is found and flashed back to the register. Price is printed on the customer receipt and the transaction is stored in the computer file. Although there are some problems with scanning (for example, not all grocery products are UPC encoded), there is, nevertheless, tremendous potential for this technique as a means of obtaining accurate data.[24] By the end of 1988, over 16,000 U.S. supermarkets will have such scanners in operation. This total will include almost all large outlets, and such scanner-equipped stores can be expected to account for 60 percent of the total food-store business by the end of the 1980s.[25]

The output from scanning systems creates the opportunity to expand the marketer's knowledge of the sales effects of advertising, sales promotions, and other marketing stimuli. However, the most important feature to many marketers is that such systems have the ability to segregate the purchases of an individual consumer electronically. Whereas traditional diary panels have relied on what the consumer said she did, an electronic diary panel offers the opportunity to record what the consumer actually did. Thus, the consumer no longer needs to memorize information about brand, price, coupon usage, and so on, because it is all done electronically.

For stores with such diary capability, panel members can be recruited, asked to fill out a demographic questionnaire, and given a card for each member of the household. Each panel member would shop normally, but present the panel identification card at the beginning of the checkout process. The checker can then record the card number and each individual transaction for the customer so it can be isolated and stored in the computer for future analysis. Such UPC scanner information can efficiently and economically provide answers to many marketing questions.[26] As scanner stores increase in number, marketers will gain a rich data base to help track and understand purchase behavior.

When scanner technology is used in conjunction with advanced cable television systems, the two offer additional research possibilities.[27] Scanner panel members in a city might be used to evaluate advertising effectiveness. If 2500 panel-member homes in one city were linked to cable television, half might receive the same commercials being shown to the general public and half could receive a set of test commercials. Purchase response at the store level would then show up via electronic scanning to indicate a measure of that test advertisement's effectiveness. Another system has been developed that enables companies to direct advertisements into homes that are not wired for cable television, so that companies can now test within a representative sample of an entire market.[28]

EXPERIMENTS

In experimental investigations the researcher selects consumers, stores, and so on (known as test units) and seeks to measure the effect of specific situations or conditions (known as experimental treatments) on a particular dependent variable such as consumers' attitudes or purchase behavior. In this process, an attempt is made to control or hold constant the effects of other so-called extraneous variables so that they will not influence the results. For example, if we wanted to determine whether the size of a magazine advertisement affects readers' attention, then the size of the ad might be varied, while such extraneous variables as the message or appeal used, and the color of the ads were held constant so that they would not influence the results and confuse the issue.

Consumer researchers may conduct experiments in the "field" (that is, the actual setting of the marketplace), or they may test hypotheses under "laboratory" conditions (which include any environment simulating real or actual conditions).

Field Experiments These provide a natural setting for research in order to overcome the problems of artificiality sometimes found in the laboratory. However, gaining realism from the marketplace environment can come at the cost of losing some control over the experimental situation.

Test marketing is one business equivalent of the scientist's field experiment.

In the market test, different marketing variables (such as prices and advertisements) are tried in several market areas to determine which receives the most favorable consumer response. New-product introductions may be tested for approximately six months to two years or more, during which the product is promoted and treated as if it were on the market in a full-scale way.[29]

In the case of test marketing, experimenters are faced with problems of control much different from those in the laboratory. For instance, competitors who are aware of a market test can interfere with the research by increasing their advertising, offering coupons, cutting prices, or making other strategy changes. These changes reduce the experimenter's control over the test and can hide the true effect of the variable or variables under study.

Unfortunately, the expense of many field experiments can be prohibitive, and the length of time involved also makes this type of research inappropriate for some studies. The fact that the field experiment is conducted in the marketplace, however, can enhance the credibility of the results.[30]

Laboratory Experiments   These are useful because they typically allow greater control over extraneous variables than is possible in the real world. Also the investigator may be better able to manipulate experimental treatments in the controlled environment of the laboratory. However, a potential problem with such experiments is that they can sometimes become too artificial, thereby insufficiently representing the real world. An example of a laboratory experiment could be to discover consumer taste preferences regarding Pepsi, Coke, and Royal Crown Cola. The laboratory situation allows control over extraneous variables such as temperature of the samples, types of containers, prices, and brand names. Thus, rather than using the products' bottles or cans, drinks could be presented to subjects in glasses of the same size and color with no brand name or price information on them.

Simulated test marketing (STM) is another example of laboratory experimentation, and one that has had much success. STM's are typically conducted in shopping malls or supermarkets, where a few hundred passersby are asked to step into a specially prepared room. There they view a television commercial or storyboard depicting the finished commercial and fill out questionnaires about what they saw. They are then given an opportunity to buy the product in a laboratory store or are given samples of the product to take home and use. They are followed up with phone interviews to measure their reactions and repeat-purchase intention. These responses are fed into a computer model and can provide reasonably accurate projections of share and repeat purchases of a product.[31]

SURVEYS

In the survey method of gathering data, consumers are not only aware of the fact that they are being studied, but they actively participate. Some companies, such as Kroger Co., are heavy users of surveys. Kroger holds more than 250,000 consumer interviews a year to define consumer wants more precisely.[32] There are three survey data-collection techniques: personal interviews, telephone surveys, and mail surveys. The usefulness of surveys is illustrated in the following example:

American Airlines seeks a competitive edge by relying on consumer research. They've been surveying their passengers for forty years, but deregulation has made it even more important for American to know its customers, their travel habits, and what they need. American's Continuous In-Flight Tracking Survey is taken on 1 percent of the airline's 1300 daily routes, so that every flight is surveyed about once every 100 days. Passengers are asked to rate services, detail their travel plans and the purpose of their trip, and give their age, occupation, income, sex, marital status, educational background, and zip code if they live in the United States. This information gives American a picture of its present customers. Daily telephone interviews of the public, surveys of other airlines' passengers, and the opinions of an advisory panel of over 200 frequent flyers reveal the habits of the larger market. American also takes as many as forty special surveys a year on specific topics.[33]

Personal Interviews   Direct face-to-face interaction between the interviewer and the respondent is perhaps the personal interview's greatest advantage over other types of surveys. A large amount of information can be obtained with a relatively high degree of accuracy by this approach. Flexibility is a further advantage, since questions can be modified to suit the situation or clarification can be provided if necessary. A major disadvantage of this approach, however, is its high cost. Personal interviews often occur in shopping malls because of the relative ease of obtaining a representative group of respondents. These are known as *mall intercept* interviews.

Telephone Surveys   The telephone survey can be a useful alternative to the personal interview because it provides for interviewer-respondent interaction and is quicker and less expensive to conduct than are personal interviews. Today, access to Wide Area Telephone Service (WATS) makes it easy for researchers to sample a vast geographic area for a comparatively low price. Telephone surveys work well when the objective is to measure certain behavior at the time of the interview or immediately prior to the interview, such as radio listening or television viewing. It is also easier to reach subjects by telephone, and many people who would not consent to a personal interview are willing to participate over the phone. These surveys generally achieve higher response rates than do mail surveys or personal interviews.

   Telephone surveys have some basic limitations, however. First, the amount of information that can be obtained is limited because of difficulty in keeping respondents on the phone and interested for any extended period. Second, the type of information obtainable is limited. For example, measuring the intensity of consumers' feelings is difficult, and questions containing numerous response options are cumbersome.

Mail Surveys   Although sometimes underestimated by market researchers, this approach has been successfully used by many companies. For example, *The Reader's Digest* spends $300,000 a year on mail research.[34] Mail-questionnaire surveys have long been used by researchers because of their low potential cost per respondent, their ability to reach widely dispersed consumers, and their ability to obtain large amounts of data and allow more sophisticated questioning techniques, such as measuring scales.

In this approach consumers receive a questionnaire in the mail, complete it at their leisure, and return it, usually in a postpaid envelope. Since respondents are seldom asked to identify themselves, a mail survey can reduce their reluctance to reveal sensitive information. Of course, there are also disadvantages to this type of survey. Mail interviews can result in a small number of responses, with many questionnaires ending up in wastebaskets. Another problem concerns the long time it may take for respondents to return the questionnaire. Follow-up letters to remind consumers of their delay can increase response rates but also boost costs. Also, since there is no interviewer-respondent interaction, questions must be worded carefully to avoid ambiguity and the questionnaire should be carefully pretested to detect any deficiencies.

No matter which survey method is used, the researcher must be concerned about *nonresponse error*—error introduced when those who are not reached or refuse to cooperate are different in important ways from those who do respond. For this reason researchers try to increase participation by such means as pre-notifying the individual that a questionnaire is on its way, offering inducements to participate (such as enclosing a dollar bill with the questionnaire), and making callbacks for not-at-homes.

MEASURING CONSUMER CHARACTERISTICS

Consumer research may also be classified according to whether demographic, activity, or cognitive information is sought. The following discussion will focus primarily on cognitive research approaches.

DEMOGRAPHIC MEASURES

Demographic research is concerned with gathering vital statistics about consumers—such characteristics as their age, income, sex, occupation, location, race, marital status, and education. Notice that since these characteristics are easily quantifiable, they enable the marketer to describe accurately and specifically and to understand certain consumer characteristics. For example, consider the use of demographic information in profiling consumers for the following situation:

The motorcycle industry keeps track of current owners of its product to determine how the market may be changing. Trade association data show that the market is approximately 94 percent male, with 60 percent of the men between 18 and 34 years of age, and a median age of 28 and rising. Approximately 45 percent of owners have had some college, 58 percent are married, and 77 percent have previously owned another bike. Information such as this may be very useful in aiming advertisements at potential buyers.[35]

Much of the demographic data on consumer markets is a product of federal, state, and local government sources. One of the best sources of demographic data is the U.S. Census Bureau. Population statistics and other official information are easily obtained and can be useful, even vital, for small businesses that cannot afford expensive marketing research. Whether it involves site location, choice of product lines, design of distribution systems, type of advertising, and so on, census information will normally play a part in the business decision.[36] Chapter 4 will describe in some detail the demographic characteristics of the U.S. consumer market; thus, little treatment of the topic is necessary at this point. However, it should be mentioned here that firms generally desire to obtain a demographic portrait of their customers. Such a profile may be constructed through research.

For those companies large enough to purchase outside research assistance, many research services offer the marketer detailed demographics either by census tracts (that is, statistical subdivisions within metropolitan areas containing an average 4000 population) or postal zip codes (more than 38,000 in the United States).[37]

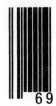

CONSUMER ACTIVITY MEASURES

Often the researcher seeks to understand various aspects of consumers' activities. For example, questions such as the following may be of interest: When do consumers buy this item? Which stores do they choose? How do they shop in these stores? How often do they shop or buy? How "loyal" are consumers to certain brands? Which information sources do they utilize in making a decision on which brand to purchase?

Clearly, many of the above questions have cognitive components to them, but at times interest may focus only on the observable aspects of such situations. To illustrate, brand loyalty has a cognitive dimension to it from the perspective of how psychologically committed the consumer is to the brand. Often, however, concern is directed toward the observable aspects of loyalty, such as measuring how regularly the consumer buys the brand (for example, eight out of ten times).

Many aspects of consumers' activities will be discussed in the last section of the text, in which purchasing processes are examined in detail. Therefore, we now turn our attention to cognitive measures in consumer research.

COGNITIVE MEASURES

Consumer researchers who desire to know more about their market than just demographic characteristics or activity patterns may attempt to collect cognitive information, that is, information about consumers' knowledge, attitudes, motivations, perceptions and information processing. Merely observing consumers cannot fully explain why they behave as they do, and questioning often does not provide reliable answers because of consumers' inability or reluctance to reveal true feelings to an interviewer. Thus, researchers attempt to utilize other techniques to explore intervening variables potentially useful in explaining consumer behavior.

This section describes associative and projective techniques that are used in consumer research to help explain the *why* of consumer behavior. Also, the depth interview is discussed because of its primary use in uncovering motives. Finally, attitudinal research approaches incorporating rating scales are presented. Research by Zales indicates the value of cognitive measures.

Zales jewelry store chain conducted an intensive three-year research analysis to understand its position in the jewelry market and to develop a new marketing strategy. A study of consumer attitudes confirmed Zales' position in the marketplace as a jeweler for middle America. However, the research also revealed that customers have little loyalty to Zales or to any other jeweler, partly as a result of the long purchase cycle.

Motivational studies found loyalty to relate in one way or another to reliability, selection, and sales personnel. In addition, a high level of anxiety was found to be attached to the jewelry shopping experience. In order to capitalize on its position, Zales developed new advertising to increase consumers' loyalty, and it also developed a guarantee program (Figure 3-2) to address the anxiety and reliability factors.[38]

Motivation Research During the 1950s companies became increasingly concerned with *why* consumers bought one product or brand instead of another. With the growth in income levels, particularly discretionary income, and as products became more alike, it grew even more important that marketers determine the attitudes, motives, values, perceptions, and images that might govern consumers' product/brand selections. To provide such answers a group of investigators termed "motivation researchers" came to the forefront of marketing studies using "qualitative" rather than "quantitative" research approaches.[39]

A set of projective techniques that had originally been developed by clinical psychologists was adapted and began to be used in consumer research along with various notions from the field of psychoanalysis. These techniques and notions became known by the general term of *motivation research,* or in its abbreviated form simply *MR.* It must be emphasized that these techniques are not used exclusively for studying consumers' motivations, nor do they include all the tools available for such study. Actually, motivation research shares many techniques with other areas of consumer research that are seeking to understand consumers. Several of these projective techniques are briefly characterized below.

FIGURE 3-2
Advertisement for Zales.
Courtesy of Zale Corporation.

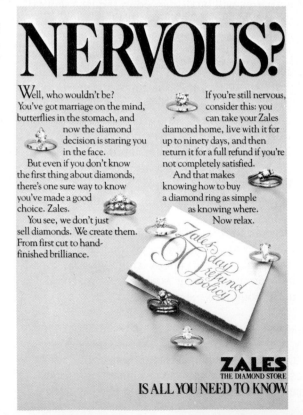

WORD-ASSOCIATION TESTS Word association is a relatively old and simple technique used by researchers. Respondents are read a list of words, one at a time, and asked to answer quickly with the first thing that comes into their minds after hearing each one. By answering rapidly, respondents presumably indicate what they associate most closely with the word offered, and they thereby reveal their true inner feelings. Word-association tests can be used in numerous other ways in consumer research such as to generate brand names, check their meaning, determine the effectiveness of advertising, and compare brand or company images.

The *sentence-completion* test is an adaptation of the word-association test in which the interviewer begins a sentence and the respondent finishes it. In conducting a study for a radio station, the interviewer might use the following statements:

1 WHJY plays music that appeals to . . .

2 The commercials on WHJY are . . .

3 A person who listens to WHJY is . . .

Frequently consumers respond to sentence-completion tests without realizing it, such as in contests that say, "Complete the following sentence in ten words or less."

A variation of word association that does not use direct questioning can be used to gain a better understanding of how consumers perceive product benefits. For example, in studies of soaps, respondents predictably say that a good soap makes them feel "clean and fresh" after a shower. But they have difficulty explaining what this cliché means to them, leaving copywriters with few ideas for new ways to appeal to them. One researcher tried a new approach, having consumers enlarge the context by separating the concept from the product. They forgot about soap and considered, instead, what the concept fresh and clean meant to them. In this free association they were encouraged to describe times they felt this way, to describe their mental pictures, to talk about their moods and feelings attached to it, to describe the music and colors that were brought to mind, and also to fantasize. Researchers learned that the idea of escape from ordinary life—getting away from cramped and rushed conditions in the city to being free, relaxed, unhindered, and surrounded by nature in the country—was a main theme. Although wholesomeness was prevalent, a connotation of sensuality also emerged. These results provided a fresh perspective for new creative approaches.[40]

The *story-completion* test is yet another expanded word-association test in which the respondent is told part of a story and is instructed to complete it in his or her own words, as in the following example:

Mrs. Jones reads in the newspaper that Land O' Lakes butter is on sale at the local supermarket. She decides to take advantage of the sale and goes to the supermarket to buy it. When she gets there, the manager informs her that there is no Land O' Lakes butter left.
How would Mrs. Jones react? Why?

The story technique can be useful in uncovering the images consumers have about stores and products, and this information can be applied in advertising and promotional themes.

PROJECTIVE TESTS   Projective tests call for the respondent to decide what another person would do in a certain situation. People may be reluctant to admit certain weaknesses or desires, but when they are asked to describe a neighbor or another person, they usually respond without hesitation. Thus projective techniques are based on the assumption that respondents express their own attitudes or motives as they infer the attitudes or motives of someone else.

A classic motivation research study regarding consumer attitudes toward instant coffee and based on this theory was conducted in 1950 by Mason Haire.[41] Direct-question interviews revealed a dislike of instant coffee because of the taste, but this was believed to be a stereotyped response rather than the true reason. In an effort to discover other reasons for this negative attitude, an indirect approach was used. Respondents were shown one of two identical grocery shopping lists, varying only in the brand and type of coffee. One list contained ''Nescafé Instant Coffee'' and the other, ''Maxwell House Coffee (drip ground).'' They were then asked to characterize the woman who purchased the groceries. Descriptions indicated that compared to the drip-ground buyer, the instant-coffee purchaser was thought to be lazy, a spendthrift, not a good wife, and one who failed to plan household purchases and schedules well. Although these findings are probably not true today, they were initially useful in better understanding consumer motivations. They indicated that respondents were not really dissatisfied with the taste of instant coffee, but rather the idea of using it was unacceptable. Respondents were projecting their own feelings about instant coffee into the descriptions of the woman who purchased it.

Another form of projective test makes use of pictures as stimuli. One example is the *Thematic Apperception Test (TAT),* in which respondents are shown ambiguous pictures concerning the product or topic under study and asked to describe what is happening in the picture. Because the pictures are so vague, it is believed that the respondents will actually reveal their own personalities, motivations, and inner feelings about the situation.

A modern form of the TAT looks like a comic strip with two characters discussing the topic under study. One character has a statement printed in the ''balloon'' above him, but above the other character is an empty balloon. Respondents are asked to fill in the balloon as they think the character would reply. Once again, respondents are answering for someone else but are expressing their own ideas. Figure 3–3 illustrates the cartoon technique.

DEPTH INTERVIEWS   As are the focus-group interviews, depth interviews are unstructured and informal. General questions are usually asked, followed by more specific questions that probe for needs, desires, motives, and emotions of the consumer. Also, the questioning is sometimes indirect, such as, ''Why do you think your friends smoke Marlboros?'' as opposed to the direct question, ''Why do you prefer Marlboro cigarettes?'' Again, this method attempts to circumvent inhibitions the respondent may have about revealing inner feelings. By carefully following cues given by the respondent, an interviewer can ask a series of questions that probe for underlying motivations.

While focus-group research can be a valuable tool for certain types of problems, such as those involved with new products, a useful alternative for many situations is the individual in-depth interview. This technique assumes that one person representing a specific market segment shares similar ideas and experiences with other members of the segment. If so, the hypotheses generated from one in-depth interview will not differ from those arising from a focus-group discussion with eight to ten people. Because the cost of recruiting respondents and obtaining facilities for focus-group research is so substantial, the in-depth interview is finding increased use. It also overcomes the problem of group-influence bias in focus groups.[42]

The key factor with depth interviewing (as well as focus-group interviewing) is the interviewer's skill, which calls for imagination and thoroughness in probing consumer leads while not influencing the respondent's answers. Because of their very nature, interview results are interpreted subjectively rather than quantitatively. Thus, there is a great possibility for bias. An additional source of error from depth and focus-group interviews may arise with the use of small samples, which may not be representative of the entire population.

Attitude-Measurement Scales Significant strides have been made in the area of measuring consumers' attitudes. This has resulted in the development of various self-reporting attitude-rating scales. The scales are termed self-reporting because consumers express their own evaluation of their attitudes by responding to the scale in the way they think most appropriate.

The many scales available differ mainly in their structure and in the degree to which they actually measure attitudes. This section presents two of the more widely used scales in consumer research—the Likert scale and the semantic differential.

FIGURE 3-3
The cartoon projective technique.

LIKERT (SUMMATED) SCALES Use of this approach involves compiling a list of statements relevant to the attitudes under investigation with agreement-disagreement response scales ranging, for example, from "strongly agree" to "strongly disagree." Consumers indicate which response most nearly expresses their attitude about the statement. The following is an example of an individual's response to a Likert scale:

	Strongly agree 5	Agree 4	Undecided 3	Disagree 2	Strongly disagree 1
Sears is generally a progressive store.		X			
Sears' stores are generally well stocked.	X				
Sears' merchandise is generally low-priced.		X			

Often the responses are added based on the numerical value assigned to them. This consumer's score of 13 indicates a very favorable attitude toward Sears. A lower total score, such as 6, would be interpreted as unfavorable.

SEMANTIC DIFFERENTIAL The semantic differential consists of pairs of bipolar adjectives or antonym phrases as ends of a continuum with response options spaced in between. This technique can be used in marketing to rate the psychological meaning of concepts, products, companies, or people.[43]

Typically, a seven-position scale is utilized between the adjectives with the middle value being neutral. A consumer is asked to mark the position that most closely corresponds to his or her attitude toward the subject being studied. Responses can be tabulated and profiled, a procedure which dramatically illustrates consumer attitudes.

Below is a sample set of semantic differential scales (with only a few adjectives shown) which might be used to have consumers express their attitudes toward three brands of bread. A profile of consumers' responses is also drawn in. Notice that consumers have a favorable attitude toward Brand A while Brand B is viewed somewhat neutrally, and attitudes toward C are quite negative. Such a finding would be of value to Brand C and could help guide the company in making strategy decisions to overcome this unfavorable image.

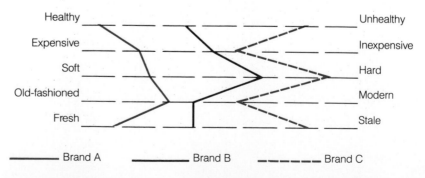

As in all of the approaches that have been discussed, the decision to use a specific method or scaling technique must depend on the type of information being sought by the researcher as well as the way in which the data are to be applied.[44]

MANAGERIAL REFLECTIONS

For our product or service situation . . .

1 What research studies have been conducted regarding our consumers?

2 How do these fit in with our present research information needs?

3 What do we need to know about our consumers, and which consumer behavior role is of interest to us?

4 Are the data we need available from secondary sources, or will we need to gather primary data?

5 What secondary data exist pertaining to our consumers?

6 Will cross-sectional or longitudinal data-gathering activities be necessary?

7 How will the information be gathered—by observation, survey, or experiment?

8 If by observation, what means will be used?

9 If by experimentation, will laboratory or field approaches be most relevant?

10 If by survey, will the information best be obtained by telephone, mail, or in person?

11 What is the demographic profile of our customers?

12 How may our buyers be categorized according to activity dimensions?

13 How may our buyers be described cognitively? What are the best ways to gather this information?

DISCUSSION TOPICS

1 Define consumer research.

2 Discuss the significance of consumer research to marketers, consumers, and the economy.

3 Discuss the role of focus-group interviewing. Find an example in the literature of its actual use by a company and briefly describe it to the class. Was the technique used properly?

4 Under what conditions should the marketer rely on secondary data? What potential limitations are there in their use?

5 Distinguish between cross-sectional and longitudinal research and illustrate each with an example.

6 Design and conduct a consumer panel for selected purchases among class members.

7 Recommend a design for the following types of consumer research on a subject of your choice: (*a*) observation, (*b*) survey, and (*c*) experiment.

8 With the objective of determining consumer attitudes toward instant coffee, design and conduct a cognitive research study using the following techniques: (*a*) word association, (*b*) projective tests, and (*c*) semantic differential. What differences are found in the results using these approaches?

PROJECTS

1 Conduct an in-class focus-group interview, using students in the class as subjects. Select one student to be moderator. Suggested topics include (*a*) ways to improve the campus bookstore, (*b*) opinions and attitudes towards a new product (bring in an advertisement), and (*c*) potential for opening a new restaurant near campus. The session should be videotaped if possible. Discuss how a researcher might use this information.

2 Administer the cartoon projective technique (Figure 3-3) to three friends not in the class. Compare results and list recommendations.

NOTES

[1] "Wendy's Introduces 'Classic' Burger," *News-Star-World,* September 19, 1986, p. 58.

[2] John Koten, "You Aren't Paranoid if You Feel Someone Eyes You Constantly," *The Wall Street Journal,* March 29, 1985, pp. 1, 12.

[3] Steve Swartz, "How Marriott Changes Hotel Design to Tap Midpriced Market," *The Wall Street Journal,* September 18, 1985, pp. 1, 16.

[4] Kent Larsson, "Retail Management Will Shift Focus from Merchandising to Marketing," *Marketing News,* May 30, 1980, p. 5.

[5] John A. Prestbo, "Good Listener," *The Wall Street Journal,* April 29, 1980, pp. 1, 35.

[6] Alan Andreasen, "Backward Market Research," *Harvard Business Review,* **63**:176, May–June 1985.

[7] "Minnetonka Credits 'Thinking,' Not Research, for Success of Softsoap," *Marketing News,* December 26, 1980, pp. 1, 6.

[8] Prestbo, "Good Listener," p. 35.

[9] Myril D. Axelrod, "Marketers Get an Eyeful When Focus Groups Expose Products, Ideas, Images, Ad Copy, etc. to Consumers," *Marketing News,* February 28, 1975, p. 6.

[10] Roger E. Bengston, "Despite Controversy, Focus Groups are Used to Examine a Wide Range of Marketing Questions," *Marketing News,* September 19, 1980, p. 25; and Yolanda Brugaletta, "Gives Guidelines to Set Up, Use, and Analyze Focus Groups," *Marketing News,* October 24, 1975, p. 1.

[11] Joe L. Welch, "Focus Groups for Restaurant Research," *The Cornell Hotel and Restaurant Administration Quarterly,* August 1985, p. 81.

[12] See Harper W. Boyd, Jr., Ralph Westfall, and Stanley F. Stasch, *Marketing Research: Text and Cases,* 5th ed., Irwin, Homewood, Ill., 1981; and Gilbert A. Churchill, Jr., *Marketing Research: Methodological Foundations,* 2d ed., The Dryden Press, Hinsdale, Ill., 1979, for a partial list of guides to secondary data.

[13] "Dramatic Market Volatility Will Be Revealed When Supermarket Sales Data Are Reported Nightly," *Marketing News,* January 18, 1985, p. 7.

[14] Anna Sobczynski, "Reading the Consumer's Mind," *Advertising Age,* May 3, 1984, p. M-17.

[15] Koten, "You Aren't Paranoid," p. 22.

[16] "Secrets of a Garbage Bin," *Better Homes and Gardens,* May 1986, p. 18.

[17] Brad Edmondson, "Attack of the People Meters," *American Demographics,* December 1985, p. 20.

[18] Brad Edmondson, "The Ultimate Measure," *American Demographics,* December 1985, p. 21.

¹⁹ Larry D. Crabtree and James A. Paris, "Survey Car License Plates to Define Retail Trade Area," *Marketing News*, January 4, 1985, p. 12.

²⁰ David J. Blum, "Census is Eagerly Awaited by Marketers," *The Wall Street Journal*, March 26, 1980, p. 48.

²¹ Herbert E. Krugman, "Some Applications of Pupil Measurement," *Journal of Marketing Research*, **1**:15, November 1964.

²² Neil Jesuele, "Combined Eye Tracking, Verbal Questioning Technique Now Helps Canadian Advertisers," *Marketing News*, April 18, 1980, p. 22.

²³ Frederick C. Klein, "Researcher Probes Consumers Using Anthropological Skills," *The Wall Street Journal*, July 7, 1983, p. 21

²⁴ See, for example, Jack J. Honomichl, "Turning a Dream Into a Reality," *Advertising Age*, February 9, 1981, pp. S-4–S-9; Carol Poston, "Dear Diary Panel . . ." *Advertising Age*, February 9, 1981, pp. S-10–S-11; Cecelia Lentini, "Research Scans Altered States," *Advertising Age*, April 13, 1981, pp. S-11–S-12; and Polly Summar, "Service Scans the Market," *Advertising Age*, April 27, 1981, pp. S-48–S-49.

²⁵ Fitzhugh L. Corr, "Scanners in Marketing Research: Paradise (Almost)," *Marketing News*, January 4, 1985, pp. 1, 15; and "1986 Nielsen Review of Retail Grocery Store Trends," *Progressive Grocer*, September 1986, p. 19.

²⁶ "Merchandising Ploys Effective? Scanners Know," *Marketing News*, January 4, 1985, p. 17; Michael Friedman, "Packing More Power into POS," *Chain Store Age Executive* (Retail Technology Section), January 1985, p. 3; Barbara Buell, "Big Brother Gets a Job in Market Research," *Business Week*, April 8, 1985, pp. 96–97; and "Test Prices, Evaluate Promotions Using Models, Supermarket Scanner Data, and Bump Analysis," *Marketing News*, March 1, 1985, pp. 16, 20.

²⁷ Joseph Poindexter, "Shaping the Consumer," *Psychology Today*, May 1983, pp. 64–68.

²⁸ Doris L. Walsh, "Rating the Test Markets," *American Demographics*, May 1985, pp. 38–43.

²⁹ See, for example, Jennifer Alter, "Test Marketing: No Shelving the Future," *Advertising Age*, February 9, 1981, pp. S-1, S-26; Carol Galginaitis, "What's Beneath a Test Market?" *Advertising Age*, February 9, 1981, pp. S-2–S-28; Mary McCabe English, "Marketers: Better Than a Coin Flip," *Advertising Age*, February 9, 1981, pp. S-14–S-16; Dylan Landis, "Durable Goods, Good for a Test?" *Advertising Age*, February 9, 1981, pp. S-18–S-20; and "Testing, Testing, Testing . . ." *Marketing & Media Decisions*, January 1981, pp. 60–61, 112.

³⁰ For a more complete presentation of the experimental approach see Keith Cox and Ben M. Enis, *Experimentation for Marketing Decisions*, International Textbook, Scranton, Pa., 1969; and M. Venkatesan and Robert J. Holloway, *An Introduction to Marketing Experimentation*, Free Press, New York, 1971.

³¹ Kevin Higgins, "Simulated Test Marketing Winning Acceptance," *Marketing News*, March 1, 1985, pp. 18–19; and Aimee L. Stern, "Test Marketing Enters a New Era," *Dun's Business Month*, October 1985, pp. 86–87.

³² "Marketing: The New Priority," *Business Week*, November 21, 1983, p. 96.

³³ Brad Edmondson, "Airline Research the American Way," *American Demographics*, November 1985, p. 18.

³⁴ Edward W. Whitley, "The Case for Postal Research," *Journal of the Market Research Society*, **27**:5–13, January 1985.

³⁵ "Open Throttle," *Marketing & Media Decisions*, December 1979, p. 102.

³⁶ Martha F. Riche, "The Business Guide to the Galaxy of Demographic Products and Services," *American Demographics*, June 1985, pp. 22–25, 28; and Sanford L. Jacobs, "Using Official Data Often Helps Avoid Mistakes, Find Customers," *The Wall Street Journal*, January 5, 1981, p. 15.

³⁷ "Census Update & ZIProfile Offer Detailed Demographics," *Marketing News*, November 30, 1979, p. 5; and Craig Reiss, "Marketers Target in on Geo-demographics," *Marketing & Media Decisions*, July 1981, pp. 46–47, 193–194.

³⁸ Tom Bayer, "Zale Sparkles in Strategy Shift," *Advertising Age*, October 5, 1981, pp. 4, 120.

³⁹ "Qualitative Research—A Summary of the Concepts Involved," *Journal of the Market Research Society*, **21**:107–124, April 1979.

⁴⁰ Judith Langer, "'Story Time' Is Alternative Research Technique," *Marketing News*, September 13, 1985, p. 24.

⁴¹ Mason Haire, "Projective Techniques in Marketing Research," *Journal of Marketing*, **14**:649–656, April 1950.

[42] Jack H. Grossman, "Individual In-Depth Interviews Are an Economical Alternative to Focus Groups," *Marketing News,* October 3, 1980, p. 4; and Hal Sokolow, "In-Depth Interviews Increasing in Importance," *Marketing News,* September 13, 1985, p. 26.

[43] William A. Mindak, "Fitting the Semantic Differential to the Marketing Problem," *Journal of Marketing,* **25**:28–33, April 1961.

[44] For a more complete presentation of cognitive research techniques see G. David Hughes, *Attitude Measurement for Marketing Strategies,* Scott, Foresman, Glenview, Ill., 1971.

MARKET SEGMENTATION: BASIC APPROACHES

LEARNING OBJECTIVES

After studying this chapter, you should understand . . .

■ The various ways markets may be viewed and the alternative strategies that result from such approaches

■ The concept of market segmentation, its attendant benefits and costs, criteria for using it, and steps in performing it

■ What is meant by the term "market"

■ Demographic, geographic, and socioeconomic characteristics of the American market and how specific facets may be used as bases for segmentation

■ The limitations of demographics in explaining and predicting consumer behavior

Merry Maids, Inc., is "cleaning up" from the trends that are reshaping American households—increases in working women, singles, and elderly people. The company was started in 1980, and now cleans over 40,000 homes each month. Calling itself "the McDonald's of home cleaning," Merry Maids has grown to hundreds of franchises and thousands of employees. Its growth is closely tied to demographic shifts, such as the fact that half of all mothers with children under age 3 are either working or looking for work. This helps the company recruit both employees and customers. Its main market is working women aged 35 to 54, in middle- to upper-middle-income neighborhoods, who realize fairly quickly that their time is worth more than the $50 to $60 charged each week to keep their house clean. To find new markets, Merry Maids uses data on home values for neighborhoods, even down to the number of bathrooms in a certain home. Metropolitan areas are divided into territories which are rated from A to D, with A being the most affluent. The franchises typically serve A or B neighborhoods but are located in nearby C or D neighborhoods to recruit employees.[1]

4

One of the most profound realizations to strike any marketer is that there is a great diversity among consumers. A closer inspection of the total market, however, shows that smaller groups of consumers have more homogeneity than the group as a whole in certain characteristics, especially their consumer behavior.

Chapter 4 introduces the concept of identifying and selectively marketing to such homogeneous groups of consumers. The major alternatives in selecting market targets are discussed, stressing the value of market segmentation. Some of the most important bases for segmenting markets are also discussed. In Chapter 5, the topic of segmentation is continued with an examination of additional methods by which markets may be selected. The associated concept of product positioning is also discussed there and is related to market segmentation.

VIEWS OF THE MARKET AND ALTERNATIVE MARKETING STRATEGIES

Marketers may approach target markets in their aggregate and heterogeneous form or as smaller, more homogeneous segments. The following section will discuss these two alternatives.

MARKET AGGREGATION

A market-aggregation strategy means, in effect, that little if any subdivision of the market is applied. With this approach, a firm would produce a single product and offer it to all consumers with a single marketing program. Although the marketer recognizes that not everyone will buy his product, he expects to attract a sufficient number for profitable operations. This approach has also been described as *undifferentiated marketing* or *product differentiation*.

In the past, a number of firms have used market-aggregation strategies, including soft-drink companies, cigarette manufacturers, gasoline marketers, many packaged food producers, and home appliance manufacturers. For example, Coca-Cola was for many years presented to consumers as a one-flavor soft drink available only in the familiar 6-ounce glass bottle and with the unchanging promotion theme "The Pause That Refreshes." Similarly, in the 1950s all major brands of American cigarettes were 87 millimeters long; without filters; made of nearly identical blends of Kentucky burley tobacco without special flavor additives; packed in soft, paper packets of twenty; and designed to appeal to masculine tastes.

The reasoning behind market aggregation is that although consumers may differ, they are sufficiently alike to approach as a homogeneous grouping for the product under consideration. Market aggregation, therefore, presents a standard product that differs little if any from competition, makes heavy use of mass promotion, and attempts to distinguish the product as being superior.[2] By so doing it seeks to have demand conform to what manufacturers are willing to supply.

The major advantage of pursuing such a strategy is lower costs of doing business. For example, efficiencies are gained from longer production runs with a single product. There may also be greater media discounts from a large-scale, undifferentiated advertising program.

There are dangers in this strategy, however. The marketer is exposed to competitive attacks by other firms pursuing a strategy of serving unfulfilled consumer needs. Consequently, by attempting to satisfy many consumers *reasonably* well, the company becomes vulnerable to other firms seeking to satisfy particular segments of the market *very* well. It is difficult for a product or brand to be all things to all people. During the last two decades particularly, companies have discovered that the demographic and lifestyle changes of the marketplace have dealt a severe blow to mass marketing and brand loyalty. Our population's once shared, homogeneous buying tastes have splintered into many—forming different consumer groups, each with special needs and interests.[3]

MARKET SEGMENTATION

In firms employing a strategy of segmentation, the market is viewed as being made up of smaller segments, each more homogeneous than the total in important characteristics. For example, the soft drink and cigarette markets of today are quite different from their earlier situations. The Coca-Cola Company now offers a variety of soft-drink flavors, calories, and containers. Similarly, today's cigarette market features nonfilters, high-filtration filters, menthol flavors, 100-mm cigarettes, feminine designs, upscale brands, generics, colored papers, and crushproof boxes, in addition to the traditional products. Thus, market segmentation is the process of partitioning the heterogeneous market into segments. The goal is to facilitate development of unique marketing programs which will be most effective for these specific segments.[4]

There are ranges of market segmentation alternatives. A firm might pursue *concentrated* marketing, which means that it would seek to serve only one of several market segments. Examples of brands that have at some point pursued this strategy are Volkswagen, Sony, Timex, and Gerber. On the other hand, a company may pursue market *atomization,* whereby each consumer is treated uniquely. Examples of firms that have adopted this approach abound in the specialty industrial goods field. In addition, those who custom-make cars, homes, and furniture are applying market atomization to consumer goods.

Most companies employing market segmentation, however, select several market segments to appeal to with different products, using different promotional efforts and prices, and perhaps selling through different distribution outlets. Many companies fit this description, such as General Motors with its various car divisions. Similarly, Procter & Gamble produces not only Ivory Snow but also Tide, Dash, Duz, Dreft and other detergents to meet different consumers' needs (at least as they are perceived by purchasers of these brands).

Benefits and Costs of Market Segmentation   Clearly, market segmentation conforms supply to what consumers demand. In addition, because the segments contain fewer and more similar consumers, the marketer is able to obtain more detailed knowledge about their characteristics. As one author suggests, potential benefits of this approach lie in its ability to aid the marketing manager to:

- Quickly detect trends in a rapidly changing market
- Design products that truly meet the demands of the market
- Determine the most effective advertising appeals

■ Direct the appropriate amounts of promotion in the right media to segments offering the greatest profit potential

■ Schedule promotional efforts during time periods when responsiveness is likely to be highest [5]

Although market segmentation produces benefits for the firm, it also boosts costs. Typically, manufacturing costs are higher because of shorter production runs. For example, the auto makers offer such a wide lineup of vehicles to meet every purse and purpose that in the last two decades it has added well over $1000 in overhead to the cost of the average car. Counting the different combinations of engines, transmissions, and optional accessories, a recent Ford model comes in more than 69,000 varieties![6] In addition, research costs are higher because of the need to investigate more segments, promotion costs are higher when quantity media discounts are lost, and overlapping market coverage may result in some "cannibalization" as one product steals sales from another in the same company's line. This occurred at General Foods when Maxim freeze-dried instant coffee was introduced. The brand name was selected to trade on the reputation of Maxwell House instant coffee, and as a result, stole millions of dollars in sales from the older product.[7] Ideally, a company would like to achieve what General Foods did when it introduced Cool Whip. Sales were taken away from competing aerosol toppings (which General Foods did not produce) rather than from its other brand of dessert topping, Dream Whip. Thus, market segmentation can result in greater sales for a company, but at higher costs. Of course, the goal is to increase revenue more than costs, thus raising profits.[8]

Market Criteria for Effective Segmentation　A decision to use a market segmentation strategy should rest on consideration of four important criteria that affect its profitability. In order for segmentation to be viable, the market must be (1) identifiable and measurable, (2) accessible, (3) substantial, and (4) responsive.

IDENTIFIABLE AND MEASURABLE　Segments must be identifiable so that the marketer can determine which consumers belong to a segment and which do not. However, there may be a problem with the segment's measurability (that is, the amount of information available on specific buyer characteristics) because numerous variables are difficult, if not impossible, to measure at the present time. For example, if it is discovered that consumers who perspire profusely favor a particular brand, what can the marketer do with this information? Probably very little, since the size of this particular segment will be difficult to estimate through measurement. Consequently, such a variable does not appear to represent an effective means of segmenting the market.

ACCESSIBLE　This criterion refers to the ease of effectively and economically reaching chosen segments with marketing efforts. Some desired segments may be inaccessible because of legal reasons; for example, liquor manufacturers are unable to market directly to young teenagers. It is more likely, however, that segments may be inaccessible because the marketer is unable to reach them at a reasonable cost and with minimum waste via existing promotional media and retail outlets.

SUBSTANTIAL   This criterion refers to the degree to which a chosen segment is large enough to support profitably a separate marketing program. As was cited previously, a strategy of market segmentation is costly. Thus, one must carefully consider not only the number of customers available in a segment but also the amount of their purchasing power. For some product categories the incidence and/or frequency of usage are so low that the entire market can support only one or two brands. Because a brand in this situation must appeal to all segments, segmenting a portion of the market may not be profitable. Another situation related to the substantiality criterion is when heavy users make up such a large proportion of the sales volume that they are the only relevant target. If only a very few consumers account for most of the sales volume, marketing efforts may have to be directed at this group. If this is so, additional segmentation may be meaningless unless the heavy-user group itself is of sufficient size or volume potential to permit a segmented approach.[9]

RESPONSIVE   There is little to justify the development of a separate and unique marketing program for a target segment unless it responds uniquely to these efforts. Therefore, the problem is to define market segments meaningfully so that they favorably respond to marketing programs designed specifically for them.[10] It is possible for the marketer, using readily available data, to measure differences among market segments in terms of their responsiveness to the marketing decision variables, and these measurements may successfully be used in developing marketing strategy.[11]

Market segmentation is not useful, however, when a brand is the dominant one in the market and is already appealing to the many segments. Targeting the product to only one or two segments of this market is not likely to benefit sales much, since these groups are already responding to the marketer's strategy.[12]

If the four criteria above are fulfilled, segmentation will be an attractive marketing strategy. The question remains, however: By which variables or bases may the market be segmented? Before exploring these bases in detail, we will first describe the process of performing market-segmentation studies.

Performing Market Segmentation   This section reviews the steps involved in a typical market-segmentation study in order to illustrate a successful approach that may often be taken.[13] The eight steps involved in the process are as follows:

1   *Define the problem or determine the usage to be made of the research.*
Market segmentation can be used to answer a wide range of questions about the response of market segments to the firm's marketing strategies (such as price or product changes, new product offerings, and advertising themes), as well as the selection of target market segments for the firm's offerings. Thus, the marketer doing concept testing studies, for instance, may want to know how interested and disinterested respondents for a new product concept differ by demographic, socioeconomic, or attitudinal characteristics. The marketer may also want to

know whether the market for new product concepts can be segmented in terms of some benefit sought by the respondents (such as low price) and what the concept evaluations, attitudes, product usage, demographics, and other background characteristics of these benefit-seeking groups may be.

2 *Select a segmentation basis.*

Segmentation studies are usually conducted by marketing practitioners using one of two general alternatives for choosing a segmentation basis: *a priori* and *clustering* methods. For purposes of illustration, the a priori approach will be described here. The clustering method will also be addressed briefly at the end of this section.

The a priori segmentation approach occurs when management decides *in advance* what basis to use for segmentation. If, for example, concern is with the likely impact of a price increase, consumer income or price sensitivity measures may be chosen as the segmentation basis. When conducting such a market segmentation approach, therefore, the marketer must begin by selecting some basis for it.

A number of bases for segmentation have been suggested as appropriate in certain situations. Generally, segmentation bases used by marketers can be categorized as falling into one of two major groupings: general consumer characteristics and situation-specific consumer characteristics. General consumer characteristics to be discussed later in this chapter include demographic, geographic, socioeconomic, and lifestyle characteristics. Situation-specific consumer characteristics to be examined include product usage, purchase patterns, and benefits sought in a product. Each of these approaches offers advantages as well as disadvantages, depending on the situation faced by the marketer. The relevant considerations for making a selection in the segmentation process are management's specific needs and the state of knowledge about each variable's relevance as a market-segmentation basis.

During selection of a segmentation basis, the criterion of differential responsiveness is a significant concept. It means that different demand elasticities exist for the marketing offerings of product, price, promotion, and distribution. Thus, the marketer is attempting to determine whether different elasticities exist among different groups and what factors cause or, at least, are associated with the differences among the groups. If these factors can be identified, they may then be used as bases to divide the market into segments. Notice that some bases may be the real *cause* of different demand elasticities, while others may not explain but simply be *correlates* of the elasticities. For example, demographic characteristics (age, income, and so on) of consumers who use a product such as a video recorder may be a useful basis for segmentation because these characteristics may correlate with differences in product purchase or usage patterns. However, this basis may not actually serve as an explanation for the differences in purchase or usage patterns. Other factors such as consumers' personalities or lifestyles, which may not be known to the marketer, can be the true cause of the different demand elasticities existing in the marketplace.

Of course, it is usually desirable to discover a basis which not only serves to distinguish market segments, but also causes the formation of such differing groups. However, since this goal is usually difficult to attain, the marketer often must settle for a basis that distinguishes segments but does not explain the existence of these groupings. In either case, the segmentation basis selected should be one that is appropriate to the decision-making needs of management. Although a segmentation basis may theoretically be the best one, if management cannot grasp it easily, it is not likely to be correctly used. Thus, there may be many possible and useful segmentation bases, but those that are easier to measure and understand, and those that suit the marketer's purpose and ability are the ones that will be chosen.

3 *Choose a set of descriptors that defines, characterizes, or relates to the segmentation basis.*

These descriptors of segments can include virtually any variable (sex, social class, and so on). To illustrate, the degree to which a person may respond to price deals may be linked to such demographic descriptors as age, income, and location. In fact, the enormous number of possible variables from which to select makes it a complex decision process for the marketer. There may be the problem of an often questionable link between the selected basis for segmentation and the segment descriptors. For example, segments with varying elasticities for marketing variables may not be identifiable in terms of standard demographics or other segment descriptors. Conversely, segments defined in terms of demographics may be identifiable, but they may not have varying elasticities for marketing variables. Thus, the marketer may not find a clear link between segment descriptors and a chosen basis for segmentation which could limit strategy implementation. Another problem involves management's ability to use information about those segment descriptors that discriminate between the segments as an input to the design of the firm's marketing strategy. The descriptors must be actionable so that management can relate findings to such decision variables. For example, it would be useful to find that not only do segments differ in age, but media habits also vary by age; thus, each segment can be reached with marketing messages through their own unique media.

4 *Select a sample of consumers that is representative of the larger population of interest.*

Here, the idea is to research and identify segments on a low-cost basis. Instead of gathering data from the entire population, a less-costly sample of consumers is selected. It is then determined if segments are identifiable within this sample. If this is the case, the next step is to project sample results to the relevant population in order to segment the entire market.

5 *Collect data on segment descriptors from the sample of consumers.*

When obtaining these data, the marketer may rely on primary data-collection efforts or on available secondary sources (for example, the Market Research Corporation of America offers clients a variety of measures on a national panel of consumers.)

6 *Form segments based on chosen consumer descriptors.*

Here the marketer must define and use a dividing line to determine to which segment each sample consumer will be assigned.[14] For example, if the marketer were segmenting consumers into heavy-use and light-use soft-drink users, the

decision might be to classify heavy users as those who purchase more than four liters of soft drinks per week.

7 *Establish profiles of segments.*

Once respondents have been classified into segments, profiles of these segments can be established on the basis of their key discriminating characteristics. For example, a segment of TV viewers who may be frequent watchers of TV movies may be profiled as having the following characteristics: have lower income and education; have traditional, conservative values; are compulsive TV viewers; take pride in a clean home; are unwilling to take risks; are concerned with security; are content with being homebodies; and are price consciousness. Several analytical techniques exist for accomplishing this process; however, discussion of their use is beyond the scope of this text.[15]

8 *Translate the results into marketing strategy.*

This is the most difficult aspect of any segmentation project. During this stage the marketer uses findings about the segments' estimated sizes and profiles to select target market groups and design appropriate marketing mixes for the chosen segments. Thus, the key to a successful segmentation study is the ability to interpret results and use them as guidelines for the design, execution, and evaluation of an appropriate marketing strategy. The selection of target segments is a complex "art" in which the marketer considers such factors as the segments' expected responses to marketing variables, their reachability, the nature of competitive activity within each segment, and the company's resources and ability to implement a segmented strategy. Information from the segment profile should help generate diverse ideas and creative strategies for appealing to chosen segments.

The a priori approach has been the traditional method of selecting a basis for segmentation. However, it has the serious potential limitation that the marketer may not have sufficient information in advance to select the best segmentation basis. Unless one is fortunate enough to begin the process by correctly identifying the most useful basis for segmentation, a less-than-optimum segmentation of the market is likely to occur. The *clustering* method presents an alternative which addresses this potential limitation of the a priori method. This approach, rather than selecting a basis for segmentation in advance, first attempts to see how a sample group of consumers may form their own groupings based on a variety of descriptor variables, such as needs, attitudes, benefits sought, and lifestyle characteristics. This procedure typically starts by measuring consumers on a wide variety of descriptors. Then, usually with computer-based grouping methods, the researcher attempts to find how consumers may cluster together on the basis of these measures. Such an approach is said to allow consumers to form "natural" groupings, instead of forming only those preestablished by the researcher when the a priori method is used. If such natural groupings are identified, the next step will be to determine what descriptor or set of descriptors may be associated with, or explain, these groupings. This information will then be used to form the basis or bases for segmentation. Although there are newer, hybrid segmentation methods that have been tried by some researchers, the two types just discussed are the most widely practiced approaches.[16]

The eight-step procedure outlined here is not to suggest, however, that segmentation studies should simply be done mechanically, following specific steps by rote. Too often, dissatisfaction occurs because marketers assume that clearcut and insightful segments will simply magically pop out of the mass of statistical output generated.[17]

The following guidelines may help lead to a successful study instead of one that is a waste of time and money:

■ Set clearly defined objectives and consider focusing on the development of communications strategies rather than on new products.

■ Organize carefully. This usually involves a project team with people from the creative, research, and account management functions.

■ Do substantial groundwork, including a review of past advertising and research and of significant market facts and trends.

■ Develop sensitive and reliable attitude measures.

■ Thoroughly examine alternative modes of segmentation.

■ Plan for follow-up activities such as testing ad copy in the target market and tracking studies to gain feedback on the marketing actions taken as a result of the segmentation research.[18]

The remainder of this chapter as well as Chapter 5 will now examine a number of popular segmentation bases in more detail. It should be noted again, however, that no one basis will be appropriate for all marketing decisions; in fact, a combination of approaches may lead to much better information for decision making.

DEMOGRAPHIC CHARACTERISTICS AND MARKET SEGMENTATION

It is essential for us to review the general characteristics of the American consumer market and of some of its major segments. Only with a clear understanding of major consumer characteristics can we begin to appreciate the implications of environmental and individual determinants of their behavior. Hence, the remainder of this chapter will be devoted to isolating the most significant demographic, geographic, and socioeconomic characteristics and trends of American consumers and discussing their relevance for developing segmentation strategies. Chapter 5 will expand on these approaches by incorporating more advanced segmentation concepts.

It is often said that a market consists of people with purchasing power and the willingness to buy. That is:

Market = people × purchasing power × willingness to buy

Consequently, if we examine these three elements of the consumer market, we will obtain useful insights for segmentation decisions. We will begin by studying

the first prerequisite in our definition of a market—people. The U.S. consumer market may be segmented along a number of demographic dimensions. This section discusses the major demographic characteristics with which the reader should be familiar.

U.S. POPULATION GROWTH

It is helpful first to examine the overall size of the population in the United States even though it does not represent a "segment" of interest to most firms. In 1986 the population stood at over 240 million. Tracing the history of our population growth since World War II, we find that two major distortions have occurred: the "baby boom" and the "baby bust." The baby boom, which began in 1946 and lasted until the early 1960s, generated approximately 4 million births annually. The number of children born to the average woman of childbearing age (age 15 to 44) has varied from 2.1 during the great depression, to 3.8 during the baby boom, to 1.8 at present. This latter statistic gives rise to the characterization of the current period as the baby bust. For our population to level off and reach zero population growth (ZPG), however, the birth rate will have to remain at a rate of 2.1 or less for several decades.[19] One forecast for U.S. population shows an increase until 2035 to 291 million, followed by a decline to approximately our present level of 241 million by the year 2150.[20]

The main reasons pointed to for the decline in the U.S. birthrate include the following:[21]

1 Modernization of our society such that it has become secular, industrialized, educated, and urban, and has shifted from a high birth-and-death rate to a low birth-and-death rate

2 Contraception and the growing availability of abortion

3 The women's liberation movement, which has challenged the traditional roles of motherhood and homemaking among women

4 The growing environmental concern that a large population will use up too much of the world's limited natural resources

5 Economic causes, such as inflation and the high cost of having and supporting children.[22]

Although low fertility seems here to stay according to most demographers, marketers can expect to see a new baby boom even with current fertility rates. This will be due to the increased number of annual births from the large pool of baby-boom women who have deferred childbearing. For example, 1985 marked the highest number of births (3.75 million) in any year during the previous two decades. The difference between the next potential baby boom and the one following World War II, though, will be that more women will be involved but each will average fewer children.[23]

THE CHANGING AGE MIX OF THE POPULATION

The mix of ages in the U.S. population can be an important factor to consider. The population age mix of the 1980 to 1990 decade will include more babies, fewer teenagers and young adults, and many more middle-aged and elderly adults than during the 1970s. Evidence of the changing age mix is that the median age in the United States has increased from 27.9 in 1970 to 30 in 1980, and it will rise to an expected 32.8 in 1990.[24] Table 4-1 summarizes trends in age groups to 1990.

Each decade may be characterized according to a "core market thrust"— that market which reflects the largest proportional growth. During the 1950 to 1960 period, the core market focus was babies and young children; in the 1960s, it was teenagers and young adults; during the 1970s, it was young marrieds; during the 1980s, it has been early middle-agers; and during the 1990s, the core market will be middle-agers.[25]

Demographers use the term "cohort" to mean the aggregate of persons born in any given year or specified period. Cohort factors, therefore, are the values and attitudes that a population group carries with it throughout life.[26] It will become clear in later chapters (especially Chapters 6 and 7) that values and attitudes differ among age groups within the population. For example, when General Mills asked adults and teens in the same families what expenditures they thought of as luxuries, they found that youngsters were far less likely than their parents to cite a new car each year or hired household help and were far more likely to classify having meat at most meals as a luxury.

Although cohort factors are difficult to predict, the following are observable trends compared with earlier decades.[27] First, there are more working wives. In spite of the fact that the increase amounts to only a percentage point or two, the growth is extremely meaningful because it has occurred largely among women who have small children. Hence, some suggest there will be demands for more company-sponsored day care and more paid maternity leave. Overall the proportion of women in the labor force jumped from 36.5 percent in 1960 to 54.1 percent in 1985 and is still rising. Among married women only 28 percent of wives between ages 25 and 34 were in the labor force in 1960, but 65 percent were in 1985. At present, in 60 percent of the families where the husband works, the wife or another family member also holds down a job.[28]

TABLE 4-1

Age Group Changes, 1970–1990

Age	Percentage of total population		
	1970	1980	1990 (projected)
0– 5	10.2	8.6	9.2
6–12	14.0	10.6	10.3
13–17	9.8	8.7	6.6
18–24	12.1	13.3	10.4
25–34	12.3	16.3	17.0
35–44	11.3	11.6	15.1
45–54	11.4	10.2	10.5
55–64	9.1	9.5	8.6
65 +	9.8	11.2	12.3

Source: U.S. Bureau of the Census.

Second there will continue to be few children per family. However, since a very large number of women are entering prime childbearing years, total births may jump to 4 million or more annually, in spite of a low overall birthrate.[29] Also, a large share of these births will be of first children—an estimated 40 percent births in 1985 versus only 25 percent in 1960. This is significant since it has been estimated that an additional $700 is spent by parents "tooling up" for the first child. In fact, a leading consulting firm estimates that during the first three years, first-born children account for over $2000 in retail sales. Thus, this expected baby boom could account for an incremental $1 billion in retail sales by 1990.[30] Parents' changing spending patterns are also causing a significant growth in the children's market. For instance, today's parents have more money to spend on kids because they have waited about two years later than their parents did to have children. The further along they are in their careers, the more money there is to spend. When parents decide their child must have something, cost may not matter.[31]

A third cohort factor is the growth in households (which are composed of those related and unrelated individuals who occupy a housing unit). Although the total population is an important factor, for many companies it is not nearly so critical as the number of total households. One of the reasons for the rapid growth in households is the high rate of divorce. The divorce rate for all marriages is currently 5 percent, and census experts estimate that approximately half of all children born in 1980 will spend a meaningful part of their childhood with only one parent.[32] At current rates, 60 percent of American women now in their 30s will go through at least one divorce. Among the 70 percent who remarry, 52 percent will go through a second divorce. Among women aged 25 to 29, 50 percent are projected to eventually divorce, while for women aged 45 to 49 the rate is 45 percent and for women 55 to 59 it is 28 percent.[33]

A more important reason for the large growth in households, however, is the increasing tendency for young singles to establish their own accommodations apart from their parents. There is also a growing segment of older adults who live apart from their children. Thus, the dramatic rise in number of households is occurring largely among single adults.

MARKETING IMPLICATIONS OF POPULATION CHANGES

There are a number of important marketing changes that have been wrought by shifts in the U.S. population. The baby bust, for instance, has caused some significant marketing reorientations among companies. For example, in the entertainment field Walt Disney World's Experimental Prototype Community of Tomorrow (EPCOT)—a facility designed to display technology from around the world—was developed by Disney in order to tap a new market. The company, which had long been dependent upon young children (a declining market) and families for its theme parks and movies, broadened its appeal to adults. In addition to its attempt to gain a larger share of the millions of tourists who visit Florida each year, Disney is now making more sophisticated movies in order to penetrate the older teenager and adult markets.[34]

The food and beverage industries have also been strongly affected by these new patterns. Companies that previously catered only to babies found during the baby bust that it pays to diversify. Thus, Gerber Products Co., the nation's largest producer of baby foods, has also gone into life insurance, printing, and pre-packaged meals for single diners. However, with the advent of a new baby boom, the company is optimistic.[35] Nevertheless, Gerber is also trying to expand its market by convincing teenagers to think of its baby food as dessert.[36]

The lifeblood of the soft-drink industry has been the 13 to 24 age group who, on the average, each consumes more than 820 cans per year. By the mid-1980s, the decline in this most lucrative age group is expected to reduce soft-drink companies' sales by more than 3 *billion* cans annually. Consequently, companies such as Coca-Cola have (1) carefully shifted their advertising and launched numerous new cola products to appeal to their aging market, (2) pushed expansion in foreign markets, and (3) diversified into other products such as wine, orange juice, coffee, and tea.[37]

Even the financial industry's products have changed because of demographic patterns. For example, Merrill Lynch started the Fund For Tomorrow, which purchases stocks and other securities said to be well-positioned to benefit from demographic changes affecting future consumer markets—such trends as the aging of baby boomers, growth in two-income households, and the rising number of high-income households.[38]

The changing age mix also brings about changes in consumer expenditures.[39] Reports by the Bureau of Labor Statistics show that a family headed by someone between 35 and 44 years of age has an income near that of one headed by someone 45 to 54. However, the younger family spends 16 percent less on personal care services, 21 percent less on over-the-counter drugs, but 10 percent more on meat. Similarly, compared to the under-25 age group, 25- to 34-year-olds spend 50 percent more on such household items as major appliances, furniture, curtains, rugs, and housewares.

The increase in the number of working wives means that companies will make greater attempts to attract these busier, more monied women. In addition, the growth of a new and large segment of mature mothers, women in their 30s and 40s who deferred parenthood until they felt financially and emotionally prepared, or who reversed previously ambivalent feelings about children, will have importance for marketers who may have to create new products, new positionings, or new ad campaigns to appeal to them. For example, H. J. Heinz Co. has introduced a line of premium-priced instant baby foods to appeal to mothers over age 30. Heinz aimed at this target group because they are quality conscious, have more money to spend, and want the best for their babies.[40]

The combination of two working parents and fewer children may also create a large potential market for selling what are now considered luxury goods. Assuming that inflation does not reach high levels for long periods and reduce the family's purchasing power, the demand is expected to be great for the services of airlines and hotels and for automobiles and leisure goods. Presently one-third of the nation's 87 million households are married couples in which both spouses work. But they account for 49 percent of the houses purchased and for the large share shown of the total spent for the following items: 60 percent on microwave ovens, 53 percent on dishwashers, 52 percent on power tools, 45 percent on china and dinnerware, 45 percent on clothes, 48 percent on VCRs, 49 percent on general sports equipment including bicycles, 52 percent on camping equipment, 52 per-

cent on hunting and fishing equipment, 46 percent on stereos, and 47 percent on records and tapes bought from clubs.[41]

The advent of smaller families will also affect the housing market, perhaps resulting in smaller units, more multiple-housing units, and locations closer to centers of population. Such a trend has obvious implications for furniture and appliance manufacturers. For example, Black & Decker has put its new-product emphasis on compact appliances designed for smaller living quarters. Similarly, General Electric Co. downsized its microwave oven and then modeled it to hang beneath kitchen cabinets, thus freeing valuable counter space.

Market planners across the United States anticipate that the customer of the future will be much more self-confident, discriminating, and independent. This will have important implications for products to be offered this market as well as for the nature of retail establishments to be patronized.

GEOGRAPHIC CHARACTERISTICS AND MARKET SEGMENTATION

The American consumer market may also be grouped along geographic dimensions, which is one of the oldest forms of segmentation. It has long been evident that regional differences sometimes result in differences in buyer preferences or variations in product usage; for example, products primarily geared to warm-weather climates, such as swimming pools and air conditioners, have marketing programs built partially on a geographic-segmentation strategy. Other examples of geographic segmentation include gasolines that are "localized" for driving conditions in the area of their sale; magazines that publish regional editions, allowing advertisers to tailor their messages and to pinpoint more accurately their audiences; and station wagons, which are primarily a suburban phenomenon and thus sold mainly by dealers in such areas. The technique can also be applied in nonprofit marketing situations. One of the most important roles for geographic segmentation in the nonprofit sector is in connection with charitable organizations which must solicit contributions, particularly those using house-to-house canvassing and direct mail. The American Lung Association, the Epilepsy Foundation, Easter Seals, and the American Heart Association are examples of organizations in which geographic segmentation of the market permits a division of the market according to who the high-dollar contributors are and where they are located. Such a segmentation approach can lead to an improved allocation of programs and to publicity and fund-raising efforts being directed toward the most productive target segments.[42]

This section discusses major geographic characteristics potentially useful in segmenting markets.

REGIONAL DISTRIBUTION OF THE U.S. POPULATION

Population is not distributed evenly across the United States but instead is concentrated in certain states and regions, with the states east of the Mississippi River accounting for the great bulk of our population.

Although current population data are important, one should not lose sight of the fact that population shifts are occurring that could dramatically alter the present picture. Between 1970 and 1980 certain areas of the United States gained population rapidly, while others gained slowly, and still others lost population. One of the most important shifts in population evident is the generally southwestward movement toward the *Sunbelt*, the lower arc of warm states. During 1980–1985 this group of states in the south and west accounted for more than 90 percent of the nation's population increase, and is expected to account for 82 percent between 1985 and 1995.[43]

The growing popularity of the Sunbelt is a result of many people's searching for a better quality of life. Escape from the colder weather and higher expenses in northern cities are two of the key motivations driving industry and individuals alike to relocate in this region. By the year 2030, the population of the south, for example, should overtake that of the northeast and midwest combined.[44] Figure 4-1 presents regional shifts expected during the period 1985 to 1995 among the four areas of the United States.

It is important to understand regional trends in population, since this understanding may be helpful in segmentation and marketing strategy decisions. For example, it has been demonstrated that personality differences exist among geographic regions of the United States, and these may be associated with differences in the demand for many products.[45] Even the design and character of some products varies across the different regions of the country. An obvious example is the differing architecture of housing across the country.[46] Many such differences result from climate, religion, social customs, and other factors. Consequently, gathering demographic data by region can lead to a useful understanding of sales patterns.

Using computers and laser scanners, companies are finding out how buying habits change from store to store around the country. Thus, marketers are increasingly learning that there are important regional differences in the United

FIGURE 4-1
Regional differences in U.S. population, employment, and income.
Source: "Regional Growth," *American Demographics,* November 1985, p. 58.

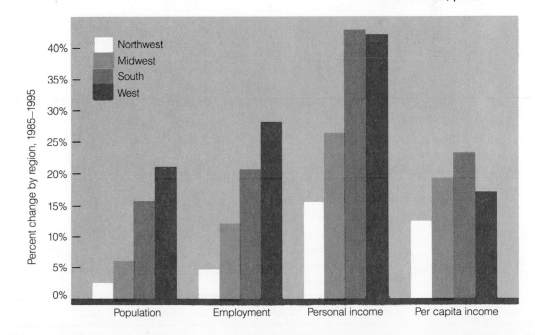

States and that for many products a shotgun approach of a single national advertising campaign is less effective than more precisely targeted regional strategies.

National brands are spending less, proportionately, on national media and more on regional television, radio, and newspapers. This new marketing approach emphasizes local color, appeals to regional tastes, problems, and styles, uses local celebrities for testimonials, ties in with local events, and sometimes offers a regionalized product. For example, S. C. Johnson & Son, maker of Raid bug killers, was concerned that its market share had plateaued. It began to study the regional bug market to understand better when and where different bugs would be crawling, flying, biting, and stinging. The company developed a regional promotion program that led to market share increases in sixteen of eighteen regions and of 5 percent in the U.S. insecticide market.[47]

Other studies have found large variations in consumer behavior among the different geographical regions.[48] For example, Table 4-2 presents selected data on regional differences in consumption, product ownership, and media usage. In addition, Table 4-3 illustrates other differences among consumers in four census regions and for the United States overall.

TABLE 4-2

Regional Differences
in Consumption,
Product Ownership,
and Media Usage

Product	Total U.S.	New England	East south central	West north central	Pacific
Percentage reporting use once a week or more					
Multiple vitamins	42	38	35	45	48
Chewing gum	37	35	46	39	34
Antiperspirant	75	66	74	76	71
Mouthwash	46	46	56	41	41
Perfume or cologne	77	50	79	79	82
Yogurt	12	17	8	9	16
Percentage owning					
35 mm camera over $150	24	30	17	22	29
Personal or home computer	10	17	10	10	9
Automatic dishwasher	51	42	49	50	62
Digital watch	55	45	60	55	56
Citizens band radio	36	33	42	36	33
Videotape recorder for TV	10	13	12	11	12
Percentage exposed					
Magazines:					
Newsweek	37	40	33	37	42
People	46	52	43	49	48
TV Guide	50	63	54	45	50
Playboy	27	27	26	29	30
Reader's Digest	66	54	66	71	69
True Story	10	11	14	10	9

Source: DDB Needham Worldwide, Inc., *Life Style Survey*, 1983.

Perhaps the most provocative view of the differences between regions has been offered by Joel Garreau in his book *The Nine Nations of North America*.[49] Garreau's thesis is that we should forget the artificial political boundaries between countries, regions, states, and provinces in North America and concern ourselves, instead, with cultural boundaries. His anthropological research incorporates demographic characteristics, interviews, and personal observations to yield differences in cultural value patterns between the various areas. Table 4-4 presents a summary of some of the significant features of each "nation."

Although one research study claims a relationship between the "nations" concept and values,[50] another study of these nine geographical areas found that the consumer values did not support this theory. In contrast, the values were more closely related to those of the Bureau of Census regions, thus implying that Garreau's segmentation of North America is not optimal.[51] Another researcher attempted to map the regions empirically using demographic, marketing, and political variables, which led to a picture of some similarities with Garreau's view but also showed consistent differences.[52] Thus, more research is needed.

How can a marketing manager use such a concept of regional variation in values held by consumers? First, it should be recognized that consumers may purchase various products and services based in part on the value fulfillment obtained from their ownership or use of them. Thus, some may buy a personal computer because they value a sense of accomplishment and like a challenge. Second, understanding that values of various regions may differ and knowing which values tend to predominate in a given region may give a clue to development of successful marketing strategies. For example, an advertising campaign for a brand of personal computer stressing how its features help to accomplish the individual's goals may be most effective in the east, less effective in the south, and still less effective in the west south central. Similarly, an appeal to security (such as, how a brand of personal computer can be used to control a home security system) may be more successful in certain parts of the south than in the west.[53]

TABLE 4-3

Regional Consumer
Activity Profile

	Percentage engaging in activity in past year				
Item	Total U.S.	New England	East south central	West north central	Pacific
Visited an art gallery or museum	41	38	33	43	50
Went bowling	31	33	21	34	32
Rode a bicycle	55	54	61	61	50
Went to an exercise class	24	30	20	25	26
Went to a pop or rock concert	15	18	16	19	12
Went to a classical concert	18	34	13	18	20
Went to a club meeting	53	49	48	59	55
Attended church	77	76	81	86	66
Cooked outdoors	82	81	81	79	84
Went to the movies	73	74	64	75	74

Source: DDB Needham Worldwide, Inc., *Life Style Survey*, 1983.

TABLE 4-4
Capsule Summaries of the Nine Nations

The Foundry

Capital: Detroit

Description: The industrialized northeast that is losing population, jobs, and investment to the other "nations" is marked by gritty "urban prison camps," decaying infrastructures, heavy trade unionism, obsolete technologies, and racial friction. "The whole point of living in the Foundry is work," Joel Garreau observes. "No one ever lived in Buffalo for its climate or Gary for its scenic vistas. Work is so central to the Foundry experience, that when people are thrown out of it they literally go crazy."

Outlook: This is the only "nation" on decline, due to soft demand for autos, steel, rubber, and its other major products. It no longer represents "America" in a business or social sense, even though it is home to 90 million people. However, it will bounce back in a different form, probably in the early 21st century, according to Garreau. The Foundry's major asset is water, which gives it a competitive edge over most of the other "nations."

MexAmerica

Capital: Los Angeles

Description: The southwest "nation" of North America has as its capital the second largest Mexican city in the world. Its language, culture, economics, food, politics, and lifestyle are under heavy Hispanic influence. "There are great numbers of Hispanics in the southwest who can't be told by Anglos to 'go back where you come from.' They *are* where they came from," Garreau said. Houston, which is starting to resemble Los Angeles, is the world's new energy capital, bordering MexAmerica on the east. Phoenix is now the 11th largest city in the U.S. MexAmerica is a watershed of the future, but its No. 1 problem is water, most of which is "imported."

Outlook: Is is rapidly becoming the most influential of all the nations. If a circle were drawn around Southern California, it would be the 14th wealthiest country in the world. A strong entrepreneurial spirit and "umlimited growth" perspective attract hard-working Anglos and Hispanics. But "northern" influences are creeping in. The southwestern "sombrero, siesta"; the Los Angeles "hot tub, laid-back, flakiness"; and the Houston "all (oil) well, cowboy hat" stereotypes are no longer accurate.

The Islands

Capital: Miami

Description: This "nation' consists of southern Florida, which looks south for its future, and the Caribbean, which sees Miami as its capital. The major industries are (1) the $55 billion illegal drug trade, (2) trade with the "Latin American Rim," and (3) non-Anglo tourism. The Latin American influence is strong and pervasive. The *Miami Herald* circulates editions in Central America. JC Penney stores in Miami stock fur coats in the summer—for tourists south of the equator who arrive during their own winter.

Outlook: The "weirdest and hardest to track civilization in North America," Garreau calls The Islands. Miami has become a world-class capital with a Caribbean influence, "although southern Florida doesn't want to admit it," he adds. The main point is that southern Florida has very little in common with the rest of the state, let alone Dixie.

Dixie

Capital: Atlanta

Description: Dixie is that "forever-underdeveloped North American nation across which the social and economic machine of the late 20th century has most dramatically swept," Garreau notes. Dixie is an emotion, an idea, a way of life in small towns and cities, calling oneself a "Southerner," the Confederate flag, and waving to strangers. It is knowing where and who you are.

Outlook: No longer predominantly backward, rural, poor, and racist, Dixie is undergoing the most rapid social and economic change on the continent. However, Dixie's growth is all "catch up," since most of its "impressive" growth statistics (per-capita income, for example) are still below the national average. Southern cities tend to annex surrounding towns with industries, thus creating "artificial" population growth. Yet, the people are among the most optimistic about the future. "Dixie isn't the 'sunbelt,'" Garreau warns. "There is no such place as the sunbelt."

New England

Capital: Boston

Description: With virtually no energy or raw materials, little agriculture, few basic industries, high taxes, and expensive home fuel and auto gas, New England is the poorest of the nine "nations" (poverty is actually chic). The oldest and most civilized Anglo "nation" on the continent has people who are environmentally aware, tolerant, intelligent, political, fair, but somewhat elitist, Garreau notes. They feel "we're all in this together."

Outlook: New England was the first "nation" to enter economic decline and post-industrial society. It is rebounding thanks to an influx of high-tech industries, the proprietors and employees of which like New England's charm and quality of life. New England is once again a land of pioneers, only this time they're resurrecting a fully depreciated "nation."

Empty Quarter

Capital: Denver

Description: The Intermountain West boasts wide-open spaces, energy (oil, gas, tar sands, oil shale), and minerals (gold, silver, copper, zinc, iron, magnesium, uranium, and hundreds of others). While it is the largest "nation" in terms of land area, it has the smallest population, which makes it politically weak-voiced. With its pristine environment, it is the true "west." There's plenty of fresh air, but the land is high and dry, and largely government-owned. It's not uncommon for residents to drive 200 miles to see a movie.

Outlook: The future of the Empty Quarter will largely be determined by outsiders: environmentalists who want to preserve its beauty, and the "rape-and-run boys," who want its energy, Garreau said. The people still believe in the "frontier ethic," but this "nation" will undergo radical change over the next 20 years. It's estimated that development of the Overthrust Belt alone could result in one million jobs and eight million additional population.

Breadbasket

Capital: Kansas City

Description: The Breadbasket is marked by agriculture and agriculture-related industries and economies. If there is a mainstream America, this is it—conservative, hard-working, religious residents."People in the Breadbasket are the ratifiers of social change," Garreau explains. "Ideas still must *play* in Peoria before they become accepted. When the people in Kansas started opposing the Vietnam War, you knew the war would soon be over.

Outlook: This nation works best. It is stable and at peace with itself by virtue of its enviable, prosperous, renewable economy. The Great Plains also have acquired great political power because of the strategic world importance of food. But farmers are being hurt financially by their own productivity: they are 3% of the population yet feed North Americans and millions of others around the world.

Quebec

Capital: Quebec City

Description: The French-speaking area of Canada, steeped in history, tradition, ethnic pride, and a homogeneous culture. It is blessed with plentiful hydroelectric power, prosperous transportation industries, a diversified economy, and a perspective conducive to the acceptance of high technology.

Outlook: Because they've had to struggle to maintain their identity since the first French settlers arrived, the Quebecois feel they've withstood the test of time. "They feel they're not only different from the rest of Canada, but different from the rest of the world," Garreau notes. Fiercely independent, the Quebecois make a habit of saying they want to be "maitres chez nous," or "masters of our own house." While Quebec may never separate from the rest of Canada, the important point is that the people feel they can, and would succeed on their own.

Ecotopia

Capital: San Francisco

Description: The only part of the west blessed with adequate water and renewable resources (and volcanoes). The home of "Silicon Valley," computer chips, aluminum, timber, hydroelectic power, fisheries, bioengineering, environmentalism, outdoor nature lovers, energy conservation, and recycling. "Quality of life" is a religion in the great Pacific Northwest, which considers the rest of North America "screwed up." Strongly antinuclear, with a penchant for seriously discussing "appropriate technology," and holistic medicine, Ecotopians have as their motto: "Leave. Me. Alone."

Outlook: Ecotopia's economy is interest-rate-based, so it won't explode with opportunity until interest rates fall, Garreau said. Still, the residents will only want clean, high-tech industries, and will cling to the "small-is-beautiful" ideology. Ecotopia is best positioned to exploit the growing Pacific Rim nations. Unlike the eastern part of the U.S. and Canada, which is European-oriented, Ecotopia looks to Asia for its future.

Note: The information and opinions in the capsule summaries are taken from *The Nine Nations of North America* and interviews with Joel Garreau.
Source: Adapted from Bernie Whalen, "The Nine Nations of North America," *Marketing News,* January 21, 1983, sec. 1, p. 18. Used with permission of American Marketing Association.

METROPOLITAN POPULATION IN THE UNITED STATES

Approximately three-fourths of the total population of the United States live in metropolitan areas, with the ten largest population centers accounting for approximately 25 percent of the total U.S. population. However, population has generally moved toward exurbia—out of the central cities and even beyond the larger metropolitan statistical area. Such trends have important implications for many firms. For example, Church's restaurant chain for many years opened its fried chicken outlets only in inner cities, primarily across the Sunbelt. According to one of its founders, the chain's philosophy involved locating stores where there was a crying need for such an operation and where real estate was cheaper, since money was needed to build and equip the stores. While other regional and national entrepreneurs adapted to the changing environment by opening in the suburbs, Church's maintained its approach so that most of its stores are still located in the inner cities.[54]

Although traditional U.S. population migration patterns have followed that of people moving from the country to the city, then to the suburbs, and finally to the exurbs, there are some countertrends. For example, approximately half of those people leaving rural areas are going to the suburbs rather than to the cities, and some of those leaving the suburbs are going back to central cities.[55] Many U.S. cities have benefited from this "gentrification" movement in which young professionals are reclaiming deteriorating neighborhoods convenient to downtown.

How do suburban consumers differ from those in the cities? According to Fabian Linden of the National Industrial Conference Board, the family that moves to the suburbs tends to be younger, to have more children, to have a higher level of educational accomplishments, and to be generally more affluent than the one that remains in the city. The typical city family, by contrast, tends to be older, less well-educated, and less fortunate financially.[56] Thus, there are substantial differences in the demographic characteristics and hence in the consumer-behavior patterns of the suburban versus urban consumers. The marketer needs to be aware of such differences because they may affect the strategy for a product or brand being used.[57]

With population migrating to the suburbs and spilling over the relevant political boundaries (such as towns and cities), old descriptions of market areas based on such political entities have become obsolete. Consequently, the federal government now uses the concept of a metropolitan statistical area (MSA) as a geographic unit for measuring market data. An MSA is regarded as a large population nucleus that includes adjacent areas which have a high degree of economic and social integration with that population nucleus. These MSAs are classified into four levels (A, B, C, and D), based on total population size. More than 350 metropolitan areas have been identified by the U.S. government. In addition, areas designated as primary metropolitan statistical areas (PMSAs) are urbanized county clusters linked together economically and socially within MSAs of 1 million or more population. Areas designated consolidated metropolitan statistical areas (CMSAs) are composed of two or more PMSAs within these most populous MSAs. More than one-third of Americans live in the country's twenty-two CMSAs.

For the marketer, metropolitan areas represent geographically concentrated target segments which hold great market potential. They are the keys to allocation of not only advertising dollars, but also federal funds. Figure 4-2 presents the nation's metropolitan areas. This diagram shows that metropolitan areas have begun to merge as suburbs of one spill over into suburbs of another. Such a development gives rise to the concept of a new type of supercity termed "megalopolis" or "interurbia." This process will continue in the years ahead.

NONMETROPOLITAN POPULATION IN THE UNITED STATES

An almost unnoticed population trend occurring in the United States during the 1970s was the growth of small towns and rural areas. Then, for the first time in U.S. history, nonmetropolitan areas grew faster than the cities (metropolitan areas) did, by 15.5 percent, or 8.4 million persons.[58] In fact, public opinion polls showed that more than half of the American people preferred to live on a farm or in a small town.[59] Yet during the early 1980s metropolitan areas again led the nation's growth, not due to their own resurgence, but because of the slowing growth of nonmetropolitan areas. The average annual metropolitan growth rate in the 1980s has been about what it was in the 1970s, 1 percent; but the annual growth rate of nonmetropolitan areas has dropped from 1.3 percent to 0.8 percent. However, among the 877 nonmetropolitan counties that reversed at least two decades of population loss, 628 of them are still growing, although 64 percent are growing more slowly than they did in the 1970s.[60] There are also significant variations in growth patterns by region and state.

Why the growth in small towns? Authorities include the following among major reasons: (1) a stabilizing farm population, (2) industrial migration to rural areas, and (3) a desire by some for a simpler, safer living environment.[61] Marketers should continue to be aware of this migration pattern and understand the implications it may have for marketing programs. For example, to reach consumers in less-populated areas, major chain retailers such as K mart, Sears, Wal-Mart, and J. C. Penney, are opening approximately 50 percent of their new stores in small towns of 8,000 to 20,000 population, outside of metropolitan areas. These stores are typically in the 30,000- to 40,000-square-foot category rather than the 60,000- to 90,000-square-foot variety found in big cities. The rationale for this move is that metropolitan centers are saturated with large retail stores, which contributes to slow sales growth for these companies. Marketing research indicates that the ten largest metropolitan areas are expected to post an inflation-adjusted 37 percent increase in retail sales between 1978 and 1990, while the ten smallest metropolitan areas should increase sales by 54 percent.[62]

GEOGRAPHIC MOBILITY OF THE POPULATION

Another characteristic of our population and one that is a potentially useful segmentation dimension is geographic mobility. The average American will move at least eleven times in his lifetime, compared to, for example, five times for the average Japanese. Counting those Americans who move more than once in a year leads to an average of twenty-nine times in their lives.[63] About 17 percent of the U.S. population moves annually, down from the all-time high of 21 percent from 1960 to 1961. During 1984, 39 million Americans changed their place of residence at least once. Of those who moved, 24 million moved within the same county, 8 million moved to a different county in the same state, 6 million moved to a different state, and 1 million moved from abroad. Such movement adds up to a significant shift in our demographic geography.[64]

People move for the following reasons: a job change, 23 percent; a job transfer, 20 percent; a larger residence, 13 percent; a better location, 11 percent; to own a home, 10 percent; to be closer to relatives, 5 percent; for retirement, 3 percent; for health, 2 percent.[65] Mobility varies from region to region. For example, the northeast has had about one-half the percentage of its families moving as

METROPOLITAN STATISTICAL AREAS (CMSAs, PMSAs, and MSAs)
JUNE 30, 1986

FIGURE 4-2

Metropolitan areas in the United States.
Source: U.S. Office of Management and Budget, Statistical Policy Division, *Metropolitan Statistical Areas,* 1986, rev. ed., Washington, D.C., 1986.

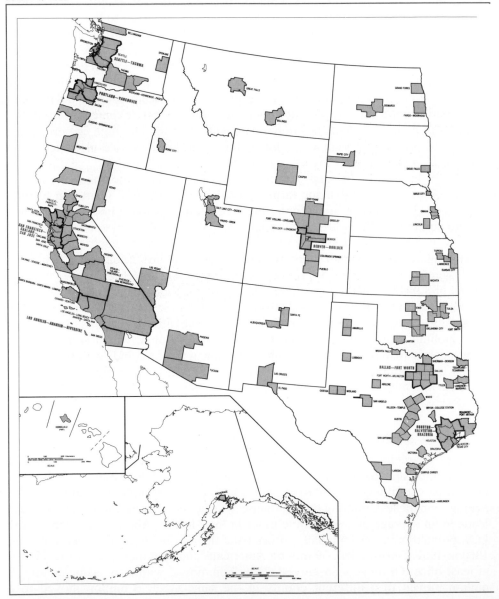

has the west. There are indications, however, that the game of musical houses is slowing down in the United States, particularly because of recent increases in energy and housing costs.

In spite of the decreases in mobility in the United States, those who do continue to move are seen as a very attractive segment to be cultivated by many marketers because they generally have more income and live in costlier homes. Studies of mobile consumers have demonstrated that people varying in degree of

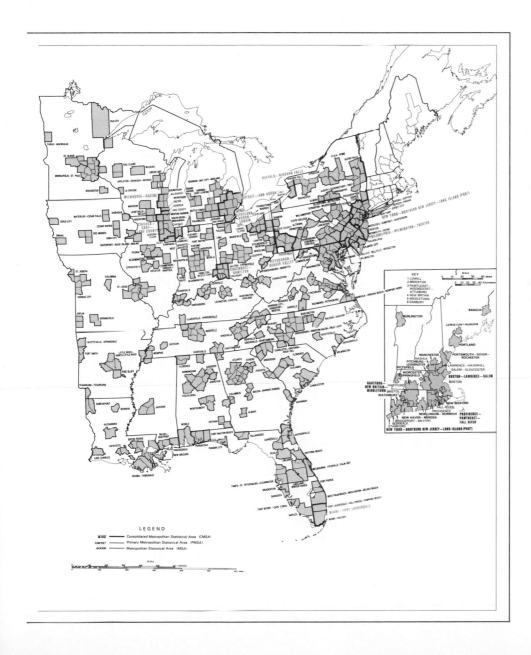

LEGEND

Consolidated Metropolitan Statistical Area (CMSA)
Primary Metropolitan Statistical Area (PMSA)
Metropolitan Statistical Area (MSA)

mobility constitute distinct market segments.[66] One study found the following profiles for low- and high-mobile consumers.[67]

Low mobiles	High mobiles
■ Infrequently shop outside their community of residence.	■ Frequently shop outside their community of residence.
■ Are infrequent convenience store shoppers, purchasing relatively few convenience store products.	■ Are frequent convenience store shoppers, purchasing relatively more convenience store products.
■ Are older.	■ Are younger.
■ Have lower educational level.	■ Have higher educational level.
■ Are most satisfied with life.	■ Are least satisfied with life.
■ Have most traditional family ideology.	■ Have least traditional family ideology.

The mobile segment has been found to be a potentially superior market for such products as furniture, clothing, drapes, slipcovers, other dry goods, and consumer durables such as automobiles and appliances.[68] Once relocated, mobiles must rebuild shopping patterns in their new community.[69] They learn about new suppliers primarily from word-of-mouth communication with friends, neighbors, and coworkers. However, mass-media sources such as newspapers and the yellow pages are also important, as is personal observation while driving around. Mobiles tend to rebuild shopping patterns rapidly, in part because of holding charge accounts with national retailers, which allows them to transfer their store and brand loyalty to the new community.

Because of the value of this segment, retailers in particular should be cognizant of the efforts necessary to attract the geographically mobile market. For example, a retailer could benefit from setting up a newcomer program to identify new arrivals and make contact with these families before their shopping habits have been rebuilt. Such a program could include (1) offering to extend check-cashing or credit privileges, (2) delivering a gift to the home, (3) providing coupons redeemable in the store, and (4) offering a price cut or refund on items purchased.[70] Thus, geographic mobiles are often a worthwhile target segment because they can be identifiable, accessible, and substantial. Concentration of marketing effort on this segment, particularly by retailers, should pay great dividends.[71]

SOCIOECONOMIC CHARACTERISTICS AND MARKET SEGMENTATION

A final dimension for market segmentation to be examined in this chapter involves socioeconomic characteristics. Included within this category are the variables of education, occupation, and income. Closely related to income are consumers' past and future spending patterns.

EDUCATION

The future generation of adults is acquiring considerably more schooling than the present generation.[72] This trend has been occurring as a result of affluence, changing social values, and the shifting employment needs of industry. In 1980,

approximately 32 percent of adults aged 25 years and older had at least some college training. By 1990, the figure is expected to reach 35 percent. The younger age categories are the key college-educated groups. For example, approximately 45 percent of those aged 25 to 34 have some exposure to college, compared to only 15 percent of those older than age 65. A large share of the college-student increase is accounted for by women who now outnumber men on many campuses.

Households headed by those with some college education comprise a lucrative market segment. For example, the college graduate household head tends to be young; approximately half are under age 40. Over two-thirds of the households are a husband-wife unit, and in many instances both of them work. Income in households headed by someone who has had at least some exposure to college runs approximately 10 percent above the norm, while college graduate households are 50 percent above the norm. As a group, those who have spent at least some time in college account for approximately 45 percent of the total U.S. spending power.

The relative importance of the educated segment of consumers will continue to expand. Their above-average discretionary income and desire for new products will make them more attractive to many marketers as their size approaches mass-market status.

In addition to the aspects of income associated with increasingly educated consumers, there are also a number of unique characteristics that further differentiate them from the average consumer. They are more sophisticated in their product and store choices, for example. They are also more alert to quality, packaging, and advertising messages. Moreover, they have differing needs from those of the typical consumer, tending to spend somewhat more (after allowing for the income difference) on clothing, home furnishings, medical and personal care, entertainment, travel, and many other items. Thus education does make a difference not only in what the consumer buys but often probably in the brand selected.

OCCUPATION

Just after World War II, the U.S. labor force contained more blue-collar than white-collar workers. However, rising industrial productivity and the shifting needs of business have brought about a substantial rise in white-collar workers. In the mid-1960s, approximately 45 percent of the nation's labor force was white-collar workers, whereas today the figure is approximately 51 percent. Blue-collar workers have steadily decreased as a percentage of the work force, while service occupations have increased during this period.

There are some important differences in households headed by blue- and white-collar workers.[73] First, workweeks typically differ, with 40 hours the standard in blue-collar trades, while 35 hours is usual in white-collar occupations. Second, the household size is smaller for white-collar workers compared with blue-collar workers. Third, substantial income variations exist among the two groups. For example, the average income of the white-collar household is 30 percent larger than that of the blue-collar household, and although the white-collar group accounts for 34 percent of all households, they receive 47 percent of all income. This compares with approximately 27 percent of the nation's households headed by blue-collar workers who receive only 29 percent of all income. Thus,

higher average earnings in conjunction with smaller household sizes add up to a much better than average living standard for the white-collar worker's family.

Another important dimension of the changing work force relates to our previous discussion of age. By 1995 nearly half of the labor force will be aged 35 to 54, up from slightly over one-third of workers in 1986. On the other hand, the number of younger and older workers will decline during the decade. Also, the participation rate of women in the labor force should rise to 60 percent by 1995, when women are expected to represent 46 percent of the total labor force.[74]

INCOME

The marketer is highly interested in the second part of our formula concerning what constitutes a market: what people have available to spend. Before we examine income levels, however, we need to understand what is meant by "income" because there are several concepts of this term, not all of which are equally important in evaluating a market.

> *Personal income* is the income from wages, salaries, dividends, rent, interest, business and professions, social security, and farming.

> *Disposable personal income* is the amount available, after deducting taxes, for personal-consumption expenditures and saving.

> *Discretionary income* is the income available for spending after deducting expenditures for necessities or fixed items such as food, clothing, transportation, shelter, and utilities. The Census Bureau and the Conference Board have defined discretionary income as income at least 30 percent greater than the average income of households grouped by comparable size, location, and age. Overall, more than 26 million, or 31 percent, of the nation's 84 million households had discretionary income in 1982, amounting to $10,525 (in 1984 dollars).[75]

Operationalism of the concept of discretionary income, however, has been difficult because of the word "necessities." Specification of this amount requires arbitrary decisions as to exactly what is necessary. For example, how much of your money spent on food is "necessary" and how much is "luxurious"? Also, complex adjustments are necessary for household size, area of residence, and other demographic characteristics. Not only are these decisions and adjustments difficult, but they may require information not available and uncollectible. Consequently, a more useful concept may be that of subjective discretionary income (SDI), which incorporates the idea of how satisfied people are with their life and with their perceived economic well-being.[76] It can be measured by obtaining people's agreement or disagreement to such statements as the following:

- We have more to spend on extras than most of our neighbors do.
- Our family income is high enough to satisfy nearly all our important desires.
- No matter how fast our income goes up, we never seem to get ahead.

People who score high on this scale are saying that they have enough money to buy what they think they need, and then some. Those scoring low are indicating that they have a tough time just making ends meet. In an application of this concept, researchers found that (1) SDI, as opposed to total family income (TFI), was more highly correlated with life satisfaction, and (2) SDI could contribute beyond demographic factors to predictions of consumer purchases. In addition, researchers were able to characterize lifestyles of individuals with varying levels of SDI and TFI. Table 4-5 presents profiles of male consumers' lifestyles according to their TFI and SDI, illustrating how this psychological concept adds a useful dimension to marketers' understanding of consumer behavior.

One of the most significant developments of this decade and beyond is the changing nature of income levels in the United States. Our nation is becoming a

TABLE 4-5
Male Consumer Lifestyles According to Total Family Income (TFI) and Subjective Discretionary Income (SDI)

High TFI; Low SDI

Makes a good salary, but still has to struggle to get by
Spends money faster than he earns it
Has difficult time saving money
Heavy user of bank charge cards and credit unions
Investments typically require smaller amounts of liquid capital: IRAs, retirement accounts, and common stock
More likely to read *The Wall Street Journal* than are members of the two lower income groups
Not a very happy individual
Openly admits the desire to leave his present life behind
Feels more pressure than most
Does not believe that his neighbors perceive him as a leader
Believes that his greatest achievements are ahead of him
Likely to own relatively expensive and nonessential items

High TFI; High SDI

Most "well off," economically and subjectively.
More likely to invest in money market funds, mutual funds, common stocks, and certificates of deposit.
Less likely to spend for today and let tomorrow take care of itself.
An economic optimist.
Least likely to believe it's difficult to find a good job.
Believes he will make more money next year.
Price conscious to the point of paying attention to food prices.
Feels less pressure than most.
Doesn't dread the future, wish for the "good old days," or feel that things are changing too fast today.
Well educated (often post-graduate).
Believes in making detailed plans.
Most likely to read *The Wall Street Journal* and the business section of his local newspaper.
Least likely to live in a two-person household.
Most likely to own relatively expensive and nonessential items.

Low TFI; Low SDI

Not well off and doesn't feel well off.
An economic pessimist.
Not good at saving money.
Shopping is no fun.
Outlook on life is negative.
Feels under pressure.
Doesn't feel influential.
Least satisfied with his current situation.
Dreads the future.
Wishes for the good old days.
Doesn't like to make detailed plans.
Has few interests.
Money market funds, common stock, certificates of deposit or even IRAs are not part of his investment portfolio (if, indeed, he has one).
Not particularly concerned about stylish clothes.
The most likely to purchase sportswear at K-Mart.

Low TFI; High SDI

More than a third are over age 65.
Likely to be retired.
Believes his greatest accomplishments in life are behind him.
Has a comfortable nest egg.
Believes one shouldn't spend for today and not worry about tomorrow.
Greater use of savings stamps.
Conservative.
Some views seem old-fashioned when compared with those of his younger counterparts.
Tends to watch what he eats and prefers natural foods.
Likes to read advertising supplements and *Reader's Digest*, and to watch the *Today Show* and *Real People*.

Source: Adapted from William D. Wells, Thomas C. O Guinn, and Martin L. Horn, "The Micawbar Connection: Subjective Discretionary Income," in Richard J. Lutz (ed.), *Advances in Consumer Research*, vol. 13, Association for Consumer Research, Provo, Utah, 1986, pp. 350–351.

more affluent country, with the pattern of income distribution becoming an inverted pyramid as shown in Figure 4-3. In other words, there will be relatively fewer poor families and more wealthy families in future years than there are at present.

The number of families that have moved into the affluent income levels has increased dramatically in recent years. It has been estimated that the top 5 percent of U.S. families hold over 40 percent of all wealth, while the top 20 percent of families have three times the net worth of the lower 80 percent.[77] Less than one-fourth of U.S. households account for almost one-half of all income. For many business people, this higher-income group is a market of considerable significance. This group is an important audience for a wide array of quality goods and services that appeal to the needs and fancies of the very well-heeled (sometimes referred to as the "carriage trade"). In fact, many industries are heavily dependent on this market's patronage. Such items as boats, second homes, quality photographic and audio equipment, gourmet foods, elegant cars, and top-of-the-line products in general are aimed at this income class.

The income elite market is of increasing interest to businesses because there are many more households in this bracket than there were a few years ago. In 1970, approximately 6.5 million households had an annual income of $50,000 or more (in 1985 dollars), while in 1985 there were over 11 million such households, a 70 percent increase.[78]

Who are these income elite, sometimes referred to as the American "super-class"? Basically they are likely to be households containing the middle-aged, with older children, working wives, and those who are college-educated and working in managerial and professional jobs.

The upscale market is growing rapidly, such that some predict the "class" market will become a "mass" market.[79] Companies are adopting strategies to deal with such a market. For example, General Electric Co. faces a mature life-cycle stage in many of its home appliances. To counter the basic problem of replacement demand, GE is extending its top-of-the-line offerings in product categories by upgrading the devices with electronic features to appeal to more upscale customers.

FIGURE 4-3
The changing income pyramid.
Source: Fabian Linden, "The Great Reshuffle of Spending Power—1," *Across the Board,* November 1978, p. 62.

The Changing Income Pyramid
Projected percent distribution of households based on 1978 dollars

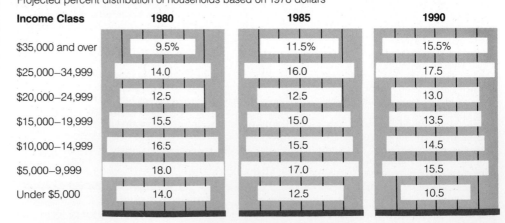

Income Class	1980	1985	1990
$35,000 and over	9.5%	11.5%	15.5%
$25,000–34,999	14.0	16.0	17.5
$20,000–24,999	12.5	12.5	13.0
$15,000–19,999	15.5	15.0	13.5
$10,000–14,999	16.5	15.5	14.5
$5,000–9,999	18.0	17.0	15.5
Under $5,000	14.0	12.5	10.5

During recent years, many American marketers particularly of luxury goods have focused on attracting the expenditures of a portion of the baby boomer market known as "yuppies," an acronym for young, urban professionals. But only 4.2 million individuals (5 percent of baby boomers) or 2.2 million households (6 percent of baby boomer households) are considered yuppies—that is, people aged 25 to 39 who live in metropolitan areas, work in professional or managerial occupations, and have an income of at least $30,000 if they live alone, or a household income of at least $40,000 if they live with someone else.[80]

Who are the yuppies? They are described by one research organization as confident, happy with their lives, and interested in financial success and its rewards. They view themselves as well-organized, and tend to be socially liberal but economically conservative. They not only buy more consumer products, but they are willing to spend more for them than both nonyuppies and the general population. For example, yuppies:

■ Would pay over $2000 more than nonyuppies and $1600 more than the general population for a new car.

■ Have twice the number of Japanese or European cars owned by their age-group counterparts as the general population.

■ Have higher-than-average use of credit cards, automatic teller machines, personal computers, financial planning services, and merchandise catalogs.

■ Don't savor bologna, instant potatoes, or presweetened cereals, but instead prefer croissants, fresh coffee beans, and imported wines and beers.

But even within the yuppie segment there are additional subsegments.[81]

Marketers have viewed the yuppie group as a lucrative market for all sorts of upscale products. However, despite the current image of a spending binge occurring, studies show that this group's spending rate on basic goods and luxury items has barely fluctuated over the past 30 years. Moreover, in this group, until age 45 median mortgage and consumer debt combined exceeds median family income. Thus, the much-heralded uniqueness of yuppies' consumption patterns turns out to be more about style than volume.[82] Millions of baby boomers follow the trends that the yuppies set; in fact, some estimate that half of baby boomers think and act like yuppies even though they don't meet the financial criteria.

Expenditures Spending patterns of the average American household and how they change over time are matters of great importance to marketers.[83] The most comprehensive source of data on both the spending habits and the social, demographic, and economic characteristics of American consumers is the Consumer Expenditure Survey of the Bureau of Labor Statistics. Comparisons between studies reveal useful insights. For example, the decade from 1972–1973 to 1982–1983 was one of the most tumultuous periods in recent U.S. economic history. It included two major oil-price shocks, several years of double-digit inflation, stagnant productivity, record-high interest rates, and the most severe recession since the great depression. In spite of this, however, there was little overall change in how Americans divided their budgets among expenditure categories. But within categories, considerable reshuffling was done as consumers worked to maintain their standards of living. Just as stagnant incomes, soaring prices, and shifting demographics formed the pattern of household expenditures in the last decade, the same factors of income, prices, and demographics will determine future spending.

Table 4-6 presents recent spending patterns by age and income. The largest spending categories are housing, transportation, food, personal insurance and pensions, and clothing (accounting for about 80 percent of expenditures) with health care, entertainment, and cash contributions constituting the remainder (20 percent). Comparison of recent expenditures with those a decade earlier shows that as a percentage of total spending (and after adjusting for inflation):

■ Spending declined for food, gasoline and motor oil, health care services and products, cash contributions, and tobacco.

■ Spending increased on home furnishings and equipment, entertainment, reading, food away from home, and alcoholic beverages.

Data on consumer spending suggests that when their incomes are falling, consumers try to keep their standard of living at the same level by taking out loans or by using their savings. Although income is certainly the most important determinant of household spending, the strength of consumer demand during the last decade was not due to high family incomes, but rather to the growth in the number of households as a result of the baby boom generation's maturing. During the next fifteen to twenty years, however, the pattern will reverse as consumer spending is based more on the increasing affluence of households rather than on a large growth in numbers.

Since spending on many items varies strongly by age, household size, and composition, demographic shifts will affect spending patterns of the future. It is known, for example, that the average age of the American consumer will continue to rise, that the percentage of single-person households will decrease as some of those who have postponed marriage will now marry, and that two-income families will continue to grow. Such changes may shift expenditure patterns, leading to more growth in spending on entertainment, housing, health care, food away from home, and appliances and services that allow these households to increase the value of their leisure time. Such a pattern may, in turn, lead to growth in mail-order companies, one-stop shopping malls, home computers to track bills and finances, ''room service'' for house and apartment dwellers, and new options in home entertainment.

Of course, economic upheavals have a very important influence on consumer expenditures. One of the characteristics of the U.S. economy during the 1970s was *stagflation,* a term describing a stagnant economy in a time of inflation or a combination of inflation, recession, shortage, and high unemployment. As a result of stagflation in the 1970s consumers felt worse off financially than they had before; they were afraid of increasing inflation, were avoiding debt and credit, were delaying home and car purchases, were staying at home more often, and were taking steps to save money. However, with economic conditions changing worldwide, a new problem emerged by the mid-1980s. No longer was inflation the problem; instead, deflation had taken its place for many Americans. A downward

TABLE 4-6

Spending and Age

Index of spending, 1985	Under 25	25–34	35–44	45–54	55–64	65 and over
Households (in 000s)	$5,438	20,014	17,481	12,628	13,073	18,155
Average household size	2.3	2.9	3.4	3.2	2.4	1.8
Average household income	$16,643	$26,177	$33,389	$36,002	$30,516	$18,279
Relative expenditures (average = 100.0)						
Total expenditures	63.4	102.8	126.1	130.9	99.6	61.6
Food	60.2	94.4	127.9	132.5	102.0	67.1
Food at home	56.3	91.8	129.2	131.1	102.5	70.6
Food away from home	72.2	102.4	124.0	136.4	100.8	56.8
Alcoholic beverages	114.0	125.7	115.7	117.2	97.2	42.6
Tobacco, smoking supplies	68.8	96.3	124.4	139.1	114.6	52.3
Housing	62.3	112.3	125.3	115.9	90.4	69.3
Shelter	69.5	122.9	127.6	111.9	82.6	61.6
Utilities, fuels, public services	46.8	87.7	119.4	130.6	108.9	83.2
Telephone	75.0	103.6	120.1	125.7	98.2	67.6
Fuel oil	18.2	53.7	91.8	129.1	128.1	142.6
House furnishings and equipment	70.1	115.8	130.2	119.7	96.4	51.5
Furniture	87.6	133.4	139.7	100.1	83.2	40.8
Major appliances	63.7	113.8	115.0	133.6	89.2	65.7
Apparel	71.1	104.0	143.1	133.8	93.2	44.2
Men's and boys'	65.0	106.4	152.1	140.4	86.0	35.4
Women's and girls'	64.4	87.6	145.8	140.9	100.1	51.8
Footwear	69.1	103.8	152.3	125.8	89.8	44.2
Transportation	74.0	105.4	124.1	141.2	102.2	48.6
Vehicles	83.2	112.6	127.4	146.6	94.4	36.6
New cars	60.0	103.0	119.6	149.9	109.8	48.1
Gasoline	70.5	104.6	124.8	137.4	103.2	51.6
Vehicle insurance	61.1	96.2	112.1	152.5	109.5	60.8
Airline fares	49.2	82.6	115.4	131.5	133.9	73.1
Health care	33.8	67.9	99.2	116.4	112.6	135.3
Health insurance	32.4	65.5	83.8	106.8	124.4	151.4
Prescription drugs	26.5	48.1	78.5	112.2	130.4	169.1
Personal care	48.0	73.9	114.8	135.3	123.1	88.8
Recreation	75.2	115.8	143.4	118.8	93.4	40.0
Fees and admissions	72.8	95.1	148.3	133.8	98.8	44.5
TVs, radios, sound equipment	95.8	117.8	125.2	123.3	91.2	47.6
Life and personal insurance	26.7	87.6	129.9	151.1	127.5	51.4

Source: Fabian Linden, ''Spending Boom and Bust,'' *American Demographics*, October 1986, p. 4

spiral in raw-material prices (farm crops, minerals, and crude oil), real wages, and asset values caused significant economic upheavals in the twenty-odd contiguous states across middle America that contain most of the country's natural resources.[84] The important point for the marketer is that these economic shifts have significant impact on consumer buying patterns.

Willingness to Buy   The last portion of our equation (page 87) regarding what constitutes a market is the consumer's willingness to buy. As George Katona stated, "Consumers' discretionary demand is a function of both ability to buy—primarily income—and of willingness to buy."[85] Katona maintained it is the combination of these two elements that holds the key to future buying. One indication of willingness to buy is the consumer's plans for future spending.

Probably the most important organization presently active in the quest to determine consumer spending plans is the University of Michigan's Survey Research Center, which polls consumers and attempts to blend psychology and economics to achieve an accurate estimate of consumers' willingness to buy. Each monthly survey contains approximately forty core questions covering three broad areas: personal finances, business conditions, and buying conditions (Two sample questions were presented in Chapter 2). The surveys are not intended to establish the absolute level of consumer sentiment at any given time, but to measure the direction and degree of change. Analysis is also made of why these changes in consumer attitudes and expectations occur and how they relate to later shifts in consumer behavior.[86]

Reports provided by such consumer surveys are closely watched by such major companies as General Motors, RCA, and General Electric, and by major banks. The surveys not only help businesses to anticipate trends in the economy, but also provide help in understanding the past.[87] For example, during one year, auto sales had an unexpected spurt in the third quarter, despite the addition of a 10 percent income-tax surcharge for that period. It was found that consumers expected new car prices to be higher and were trying to beat the increase.[88]

LIMITATIONS OF DEMOGRAPHICS IN PREDICTING CONSUMER BEHAVIOR[89]

There has been much discussion in recent years about the role of demographic factors as determinants or even correlates of consumption behavior of people. A number of researchers have expressed skepticism that such factors can be effectively used.[90] For example, there are some undeniable demographic patterns to purchasing, such as that razor blades are purchased mainly for men. However, except for specific products aimed directly at specific demographic groups, evidence indicates that demographic measures, outside of education, are not an accurate predictor of consumer behavior.[91]

One limitation of demographics in explaining consumer behavior is based on the claim that while demographic factors may have been very relevant in the past (even up until World War II), they are now obsolete because of the narrowing differences in income, education, and occupational status. Nevertheless, there is much evidence showing that group differences among *categories* of income,

education, and occupation are large and statistically significant in spite of a large number of within-group differences. It should also be noted that demographic factors include numerous other variables (such as age, sex, race, and religion) which are much less subject to influence from environmental change. For example, older people tend not to listen to rock music, per capita consumption of liquor is three times higher among blacks than whites, and Catholics still tend to use contraceptives much less than the rest of the population.

A second and more basic argument against demographics is that they have generally failed to explain and predict consumption behavior. However, although demographics have failed to explain brand-choice behavior, they seem to succeed in explaining buying behavior at the broad product-class level of such items as durable appliances, automobiles, and housing. Thus, before demographics are abandoned because of their lackluster performance, it has been suggested that several past problems with demographic research be subjected to further study. These problems are mainly associated with techniques for measuring demographic variables, assumptions underlying their relationship to consumer behavior, inclusion of a small group of people in such studies who do not have a consistent pattern of behavior, and techniques of statistical analysis that are performed on the data.

Important reasons exist for the continued use of demographics in segmenting markets. First, they are easier to collect, easier to communicate to others, and often more reliable in measurement than many of the competing approaches to segmentation. Moreover, only through demographic factors is the researcher able to project results to the country's population, because the Bureau of the Census collects and updates only demographic profiles.

For these reasons, discarding demographics would seem to be premature. Instead, they should continue to be used as one element along with numerous other variables in the puzzle of explaining consumer behavior. In any event, demographics will continue to be used for projection, identification, and segmentation of markets as long as our census data are limited to a socioeconomic-demographic profile of citizens.

MANAGERIAL REFLECTIONS

For our product or service situation . . .

1   Is market aggregation or market segmentation more appropriate?

2   Is segmentation effective? That is, does one or more market groups appear to be identifiable and measurable, accessible, substantial, and responsive?

3   How does the growth in total population affect our sales prospects?

4   What are the implications of the changing age mix of potential consumers?

5   Are there regional trends in consumption that can be effectively used for geographic segmentation?

6   Are there differences in terms of metropolitan and nonmetropolitan buyers?

7   How does geographic mobility influence market segments and sales?

8 What education levels have potential buyers achieved and how may this influence our marketing?

9 What occupational categories are represented by buyers?

10 How do income and expenditure patterns of our market affect demand?

11 To what extent can consumers' buying intentions or willingness to buy be forecasted?

DISCUSSION TOPICS

1 Cite products (brands) in addition to those mentioned in the text that have followed a policy of market aggregation, concentrated marketing, and market atomization.

2 What are the benefits and costs of market segmentation?

3 Why are the following segmentation approaches or groups not very effective?
   a   Segmenting a market on the basis of personality
   b   Advertising to skeet shooters in *Time*
   c   Developing an insurance plan for all quadruplets born in the United States

4 What are the major population changes taking place in the United States? What implications are there for the marketer of (*a*) baby furniture, (*b*) insurance, (*c*) electronic products, (*d*) sporting goods, and (*e*) food.

5 Distinguish between MSA, PMSA, and CMSA.

6 What are the directions of consumer movement? Discuss the implications of these trends to (*a*) Allied Van Lines, (*b*) Pizza Hut, (*c*) J. C. Penney, and (*d*) General Electric.

7 What products might effectively segment their market on the basis of education? Occupation? Income?

8 Find a recent article from *The Wall Street Journal, Business Week,* or *U.S. News & World Report,* and report on the current mood of consumers and their willingness to buy.

PROJECTS

1 Interview a local retail-store owner and determine what demographic and socioeconomic segment(s) the store appears to satisfy. How did the owner select this segment or segments?

2 Interview a local retailer of one of the products listed in Discussion Topic 4 and determine his or her perceptions of how the major population changes of recent years have affected sales and the store's marketing activities.

NOTES

[1] "Merry Maids Clean Up," *American Demographics*, March 1986, p. 20.

[2] Theodore Levitt, "Marketing Success through Differentiation—of Anything," *Harvard Business Review*, **58**:83–91, January–February 1980.

[3] "Marketing: The New Priority," *Business Week*, November 21, 1983, p. 96.

[4] A. R. Morden, "Market Segmentation and Practical Policy Formulation," *The Quarterly Review of Marketing*, Winter 1985, pp. 1–12.

[5] Daniel Yankelovich, "New Criteria for Market Segmentation," *Harvard Business Review*, **42**:83–84, March–April 1964.

[6] John Koten, "Giving Buyers Wide Choices May Be Hurting Auto Makers," *The Wall Street Journal*, December 15, 1983, p. 29.

[7] "Name Game," *Time*, August 31, 1981, pp. 41–42.

[8] Frederick W. Winter, "A Cost-Benefit Approach to Market Segmentation," *Journal of Marketing*, **43**:103–111, Fall 1979.

[9] Shirley Young, Leland Ott, and Barbara Feigin, "Some Practical Considerations in Market Segmentation," *Journal of Marketing Research*, **15**:405–412, August 1978.

[10] James F. Engel, Henry F. Fiorillo, and Murray A. Cayley, *Market Segmentation: Concepts and Applications*, Holt, New York, 1972, p. 8.

[11] John M. McCann, "Market Segment Response to the Marketing Decision Variables," *Journal of Marketing Research*, **11**:399–412, November 1974; and Arch G. Woodside and William H. Motes, "Sensitivities of Market Segments to Separate Advertising Strategies," *Journal of Marketing*, **45**:63–73, Winter 1981.

[12] Young, Ott, and Feigin, "Some Practical Considerations," p. 405.

[13] This section is based on Yoram Wind, "Issues and Advances in Segmentation Research," *Journal of Marketing Research*, **15**:321–322, August 1978; and Art Weinstein, "Ten-Point Program Customizes Segmentation Analysis," *Marketing News*, May 23, 1986, p. 22.

[14] See Douglas MacLachlan and Johny K. Johansson, "Market Segmentation with Multivariate AID," *Journal of Marketing*, **45**:74–84, Winter 1981; and Henry Assael and A. Marvin Roscoe, Jr., "Approaches to Market Segmentation Analysis," *Journal of Marketing*, **40**:67–76, October 1976.

[15] Wind, "Issues," pp. 330–332.

[16] Wind, "Issues," p. 320.

[17] E. M. Tauber, "Stamp Out the Generic Segmentation Study," *Journal of Advertising Research*, **23**:7, April/May 1983.

[18] Russell I. Haley, "Benefit Segmentation—20 Years Later," *Journal of Consumer Marketing*, **1**(2):9, 1984.

[19] "Population Changes That Help for a While," *Business Week*, September 3, 1979, pp. 180–187.

[20] "The Geopolitics of Population," *Public Opinion*, December/January 1986, p. 22.

[21] "Those Missing Babies," *Time*, September 16, 1974, pp. 56, 61.

[22] James C. Hyatt, "Costs of Being a Parent Keep Going Higher," *The Wall Street Journal*, October 2, 1980, p. 27.

[23] "Baby Boomlet: Its Impact on the '80s," *U.S. News & World Report*, June 15, 1981, pp. 51–52.

[24] "Decade's Boom in Prime-Age Consumers Will Offer Vast Opportunity for Business," *The Wall Street Journal*, June 26, 1980, p. 23.

[25] William Lazer, "The 1980s and Beyond: A Perspective," *M.S.U. Business Topics*, Spring 1977, pp. 21–35.

[26] See Fred D. Reynolds and Joseph D. Rentz, "Cohort Analysis: An Aid to Strategic Planning," *Journal of Marketing*, **45**:62–70, Summer 1981, for an illustration of the examination of age-consumer behavior relationships in strategic planning decisions.

[27] "How the Changing Age Mix Changes Markets," *Business Week*, January 12, 1976, pp. 74–75.

[28] Joan Berger, "Breadwinners Are Still Running to Stay in Place," *Business Week*, June 23, 1986, pp. 68–70.

[29] Richard Kern, "The Mommy Boom," *Sales and Marketing Management*, April 1, 1985, p. 14.

[30] Thayer C. Taylor, "We the People: Older, Smarter, Liberated, Richer," *Sales & Marketing Management*, The Marketer's Complete Guide to the 1980s/A Special Report, December 10, 1979.

31 Paul B. Brown et al., "Bringing Up Baby: A New Kind of Marketing Boom," *Business Week,* April 22, 1985, pp. 58–65; and Leo J. Shapiro and Dwight Bohmbach, "Outlook Brightened by Boomer's Babies," *Advertising Age,* May 13, 1985, p. 96.

32 "Household Growth Could Spurt in '80s, But Much Hinges on Lifestyle Choices," *The Wall Street Journal,* July 1, 1980, p. 23.

33 "The Divorced Generation," *American Demographics,* July 1986, p. 11.

34 Earl C. Gottschalk, Jr., "Disney to Shift Target of Some Parks, Movies, to Teen-Agers, Adults," *The Wall Street Journal,* January 26, 1979, p. 1.

35 "Gerber: 'Selling More to the Same Mothers Is Our Objective Now," *Business Week,* October 16, 1978, pp. 192–194.

36 Gail Bronson, "Baby Food It Is, But Gerber Wants Teen-Agers to Think of It as Dessert," *The Wall Street Journal,* July 17, 1981, p. 21.

37 "The Graying of the Soft-Drink Industry," *Business Week,* May 23, 1977, pp. 68–72.

38 Brad Edmonson, "Merrill Lynch Invests in Demographics," *American Demographics,* February 1986, p. 18.

39 This section is drawn largely from "How the Changing Age Mix Changes Markets," pp. 74–75.

40 "Research Profiles 'Mature Mothers,' " *Marketing News,* January 4, 1985, p. 49.

41 "Dual Targets," *American Demographics,* October 1986, p. 22.

42 Leland L. Beik and Scott M. Smith, "Geographic Segmentation: A Fund-Raising Example," in Neil Beckwith, Michael Houston, Robert Mittlestaedt, Kent B. Monroe, and Scott Ward (eds.), *1979 Educator's Conference Proceedings,* American Marketing Association, Chicago, 1979, pp. 485–488.

43 "Regional Growth," *American Demographics,* November 1985, p. 58.

44 John D. Kasarda, Michael D. Irwin, and Holly L. Hughes, "The South Is Still Rising," *American Demographics,* June 1986, p. 39.

45 Samuel E. Krug and Raymond W. Kulhavy, "Personality Differences Across Regions of the United States," *The Journal of Social Psychology,* **91**:73–79, October 1973.

46 Lawrence Rout, "Regional Architecture Revives, Spurred by Expensive Energy," *The Wall Street Journal,* March 22, 1981, p. 25.

47 Thomas Moore, "Different Folks, Different Strokes," *Fortune,* September 16, 1985, pp. 65–68.

48 Del I. Hawkins, Don Roupe, and Kenneth A. Coney, "The Influence of Geographic Subcultures in the United States," in Kent B. Monroe (ed.), *Advances in Consumer Research,* vol. 8, Association for Consumer Research, Ann Arbor, Mich., 1981, pp. 713–717.

49 Joel Garreau, *The Nine Nations of North America,* Avon, New York, 1981.

50 "Ogilvy & Mather's Eight Nations of the United States," *Listening Post,* December 1983.

51 Lynn R. Kahle, "The Nine Nations of North America and the Value Basis of Geographic Segmentation," *Journal of Marketing,* **50**:37–47, April 1986.

52 James W. Gentry, "The Development of Boundaries of Geographic Subcultures," in Richard Lutz (ed.), *Advances in Consumer Research,* vol. 13, Association for Consumer Research, Provo, Utah, 1986, p. 664.

53 Kahle, "The Nine Nations" p. 44.

54 Robert Selwitz, "Have It Their Way," from *Madison Avenue,* abstracted in SCAN, **32**:15–17, December 1984.

55 "Regions," *The Wall Street Journal,* November 4, 1980, p. 25.

56 Fabian Linden, "A Decade of Suburban Growth," *The Conference Board Record,* September 1971, pp. 49–50.

57 Jim L. Grimm and Paul R. Winn, "A Ten-Year Study of Urban-Rural Market Penetration Patterns for Consumer Nondurables," in Robert S. Franz, Robert M. Hopkins, and Alfred G. Toma (eds.), *Proceedings: Southern Marketing Association 1979 Conference,* Southern Marketing Association, Lafayette, Louisiana, 1979, pp. 333–336.

58 Richard L. Forstall and Maria Elena Gonzalez, "Twenty Questions: What You Should Know About the New Metropolitan Areas," *American Demographics,* April 1984, pp. 22–31; and "America's Small Town Boom," *Newsweek,* July 6, 1981, pp. 26–37.

59 Courtenay Slater, "Population Growth Slows; Shift to Open Spaces Speeds Up in 70's," *Commerce America,* June 5, 1978, p. 19.

60 Richard A. Engels and Richard L. Forstall, "Nonmetropolitan Areas—Growth Again," *American Demographics,* April 1985, pp. 22–25, 45.

61 "Out of the Cities, Back to the Country," *U.S. News & World Report,* March 31, 1976, p. 46.

[62] Steve Weiner, "Branching Out," *The Wall Street Journal*, May 28, 1981, pp. 1, 20.

[63] William Dunn, "Americans on the Move," *American Demographics*, October 1986, pp. 49–51.

[64] Fabian Linden, "Geography is Destiny," *Across the Board*, May 1981, pp. 54–57.

[65] Dunn, "Americans on the Move," p. 50.

[66] W. Thomas Anderson, Jr., and Linda L. Golden, "Life Trajectory: Population Migrations and Lifestyle Over Time," in Neil Beckwith, Michael Houston, Robert Mittlestaedt, Kent B. Monroe, and Scott Ward (eds.), *1979 Educators' Conference Proceedings*, American Marketing Association, Chicago, 1979, pp. 291–296.

[67] Linda L. Golden, W. Thomas Anderson, Jr., and Nancy M. Ridgway, "Consumer Mobility: A Life History Approach," in Jerry C. Olson (ed.), *Advances in Consumer Research*, vol. 7, Association for Consumer Research, Ann Arbor, Mich., 1980, pp. 460–465.

[68] "Movers Could Be Shakers," *Chain Store Age, General Merchandise Trends*, June 1986, p. 9.

[69] See Alan R. Andreasen, "Geographic Mobility and Market Segmentation," *Journal of Marketing Research*, 3:341–348, 1966; and James E. Bell, Jr., "Mobiles—A Neglected Market Segment," *Journal of Marketing*, 33:37–44, April 1969.

[70] James E. Bell, Jr., "Mobiles—A Possible Segment for Retailer Cultivation," *Journal of Retailing*, 46:13–14, Fall 1970.

[71] Gerald Albaum and Del I. Hawkins, "Geographic Mobility and Demographic and Socioeconomic Market Segmentation," *Journal of the Academy of Marketing Science*, 11:97–113, Spring 1983.

[72] Fabian Linden, "Per Capita-ism," *Across the Board*, June 1980, pp. 65–69.

[73] Fabian Linden, "Keys to the '80s—Youth and Affluence," *Across the Board*, December 1979, pp. 33–37; and Linden, "Per Capita-ism," p. 66.

[74] "The Middle-Aged Work Force," *American Demographics*, March 1986, p. 58.

[75] Martha F. Riche, "Big Spenders," *American Demographics*, April 1986, pp. 40–42.

[76] William D. Wells, Thomas C. O'Guinn, and Martin L. Horn, "The Micawber Connection: Subjective Discretionary Income," in Richard J. Lutz (ed.), *Advances in Consumer Research*, vol. 13, Association for Consumer Research, Provo, Utah, 1986, pp. 349–353.

[77] "Who Has the Wealth in America?" *Business Week*, August 5, 1972, p. 54.

[78] Fabian Linden, "The Income Elite," *American Demographics*, August 1986, p. 4.

[79] Bruce Steinberg, "The Mass Market Is Splitting Apart," *Fortune*, November 28, 1983, p. 82.

[80] "The Big Chill (Revisited) or Whatever Happened to the Baby Boom?" *American Demographics*, September 1985, p. 29.

[81] Yuppies: The Big Boon of the Baby Boom," *Marketing News*, June 7, 1985, pp. 10–11.

[82] Maria Fisher, "The Last Yuppie Story You Will Ever Have to Read," *Forbes*, February 25, 1985, pp. 134–135.

[83] David E. Bloom and Sanders D. Korenman, "The Spending Habits of American Consumers," *American Demographics*, March 1986, pp. 22–54; Fabian Linden, "Spending Boom and Bust," *American Demographics*, October 1986, pp. 4, 6; and Bryant Robey, "How Consumers Spend," *American Demographics*, October 1983, pp. 17–21.

[84] James R. Norman, et al., "America's Deflation Belt," *Business Week*, June 9, 1986, pp. 52–59.

[85] "How Good Are Consumer Pollsters?" *Business Week*, November 8, 1969, p. 108.

[86] Richard T. Curtin, "Indicators of Consumer Behavior: The University of Michigan Surveys of Consumers," *Public Opinion Quarterly*, 46:340–352, 1982.

[87] Fabian Linden, "The Consumer as Fortune Teller," *Across the Board*, June 1981, p. 62; and Edward Meadows, "The Unhealthy Glow on Retail Sales," *Fortune*, July 3, 1978, pp. 46–48.

[88] "How Good Are Consumer Pollsters?" p. 110.

[89] Much of this section is based on Jagdish N. Sheth, "Demographics in Consumer Behavior," *Journal of Business Research*, 5:129–138, June 1977.

[90] See, for example, Franklin B. Evans, "Psychological and Objective Factors in the Prediction of Brand Choice," *Journal of Business*, 33:340–369, October 1959; and Arthur Koponen, "Personality Characteristics of Purchasers," *Journal of Advertising Research*, 1:6–12, September 1960.

[91] John C. Bieda and Harold W. Kassarjian, "An Overview of Market Segmentation," in Bernard A. Morin (ed.), *Marketing in a Changing World*, American Marketing Association, Chicago, 1969, p. 250.

MARKET SEGMENTATION: ADDITIONAL DIMENSIONS

LEARNING OBJECTIVES
After studying this chapter, you should understand . . .

■ How use of lifestyle and psychographic information enhances an understanding of market segments and leads to effective marketing-strategy decisions

■ The various facets of consumer usage that are relevant to the marketer and how these bases may be used for segmentation

■ The role of benefit segmentation in helping analyze why consumers purchase different brands

■ Why product positioning decisions are important in the segmentation process, and which positioning bases are frequently used

■ Why market segmentation and product positioning will continue to be important functions for marketers

After spending several years trying to assess how consumers feel about the cars they buy and drive, researchers have found that basic demographics like age, sex, and income do not describe the market sufficiently. Instead of using only demographics, one study divided car buyers into the following six groups, depending on their attitudes and buying habits:

Auto-philes (24 percent) are driving enthusiasts who like to service their own cars. They belong to the lowest income group but spend a greater percentage of their income on cars. They prefer sports and sporty cars such as Pontiac Fiero.

Necessity drivers (13 percent) hate cars and would just as soon do without one. The best educated group, they prefer low-end cars such as Chevette.

Auto-phobes (12 percent) prefer to let someone else do the driving. Safety is important, and they prefer large cars such as Chevrolet Caprice.

Auto-cynics (14 percent) think driving is fun. Sporty looks are important to them, but they don't admit to liking anything. Independent types, they prefer small, middle, and sporty cars such as Ford Mustang.

Comfort-seekers (17 percent) like cars, particularly comfortable, well-equipped, luxury models such as Lincolns and Cadillacs.

Sensible-centrists (20 percent) like cars, but they look for small and midsize functional, economical models such as Toyota Corolla and Ford Tempo. Fuel economy and price are important.[1]

5

The example above illustrates that auto marketers may better understand consumers when they look beyond simple demographics to segment markets. This chapter will expand on the discussion of Chapter 4 by further examining the concept of market segmentation. In addition, the associated concept of product positioning will be explored. As will be seen in this chapter, the marketer has available numerous additional dimensions by which markets may be segmented. Each of these approaches builds on the demographic, socioeconomic, and/or geographic bases described Chapter 4. The ultimate goal is not merely the definition of market segments and product positions, but the use of this information to develop marketing programs that appeal more strongly to chosen target groups.

LIFESTYLE AND PSYCHOGRAPHIC SEGMENTATION

One of the major problems of demographic segmentation is its lack of "richness" in describing consumers for market segmentation and strategy development. It lacks color, texture, and dimensionality when describing consumers, and it often needs to be supplemented by something that fills in the bare statistical picture. Consequently, many firms are looking for a better way to define markets. One of the newest, most exciting, and promising approaches to selecting target markets is *lifestyle* and *psychographic segmentation*. Although the concepts of lifestyle and psychographics are often used interchangeably, they are not equivalent but are complementary.

The term "lifestyle" is not new, but its application to marketing has been rather recent. Alfred Adler coined the phrase "style of life" over 50 years ago to refer to the goal a person shapes for himself, and the ways he uses to reach it. From our perspective, lifestyle can be viewed as a unique pattern of living which influences and is reflected by one's consumption behavior.[2] Therefore, the way in which marketers facilitate the expression of an individual's lifestyle is by "providing customers with parts of a potential mosaic from which they, as artists of their own lifestyles, can pick and choose to develop the composition that for the time seems best."[3] Many products today are "lifestyle" products, that is, they portray a style of life sought by potential users.

How does the concept of psychographics relate to lifestyle? Unfortunately, it is not an easy matter to define psychographics because there is no general agreement as to exactly what it is. It has to do with mental ("psycho") profiles ("graphics"), or the profiling of psychological processes or properties of consumers. Thus it pertains to the consumer's cognitive style.[4] One of the more precise statements about its nature is the following: *psychographics* is the systematic use of relevant activity, interest, and opinion constructs to quantitatively explore and explain the communicating, purchasing, and consuming behaviors of persons for brands, products, and clusters of products.[5]

Thus, psychographics may be viewed as the method of defining lifestyle in measurable terms. It should be noted, however, that there is some question about the use of psychographic instruments as a precise measure of the lifestyle of the individual consumer.[6] Nevertheless, the basic premise underlying lifestyle research is that the more marketers understand their customers, the more effectively they can communicate and market to them.[7] In many cases the primary targets of such marketing efforts are heavy users. Heavy users have traditionally been looked at demographically, but by incorporating lifestyle characteristics the marketer obtains a better, more true-to-life picture of such customers.

THE TECHNIQUE OF LIFESTYLE SEGMENTATION

Lifestyle-segmentation research measures (1) how people spend their time engaging in activities, (2) what is of most interest or importance to them in their immediate surroundings, and (3) their opinions and views about themselves and the world around them. Together, these three areas are generally referred to as *Activities, Interests, and Opinions,* or simply *AIOs*. Table 5-1 indicates the lifestyle dimensions (particularly AIOs) that may be investigated among consumers.

In a typical large-scale, lifestyle research project, questionnaires are mailed to members of a nationwide consumer panel. The questionnaires solicit traditional demographic information, average usage rates for as many as 100 different products, media habits, and respondents' activities, interests, and opinions. Approximately 300 AIO statements may be included, to which respondents indicate the extent of their agreement or disagreement on six-point Likert scales ranging from "definitely disagree" to "definitely agree." The following illustrate the nature of typical AIO statements employed:

I like gardening.

I do not get enough sleep.

I enjoy going to concerts.

A news magazine is more interesting than a fiction magazine.

There should be a gun in every home.

Instant coffee is more economical than ground coffee.

I stay home most evenings.

There is a lot of love in our family.[8]

TABLE 5-1

Lifestyle Dimensions

Activities	Interests	Opinions	Demographics
Work	Family	Themselves	Age
Hobbies	Home	Social issues	Education
Social events	Job	Politics	Income
Vacation	Community	Business	Occupation
Entertainment	Recreation	Economics	Family size
Club membership	Fashion	Education	Dwelling
Community	Food	Products	Geography
Shopping	Media	Future	City size
Sports	Achievements	Culture	Stage in life cycle

Source: Joseph T. Plummer, "The Concept and Application of Life Style Segmentation," *Journal of Marketing*, **38**:34, January 1974, published by the American Marketing Association.

Where do AIO items originate? They may come from intuition, hunches, conversations, research, reading, and group or individual in-depth interviews.[9]

Armed with these three sets of data (AIOs, demographics, and product usage), the marketer constructs user profiles. The analysis involves relating levels of agreement on all AIO items with the levels of usage of a product and with demographic characteristics. Typically, a pattern emerges in which AIO statements cluster together; that is, similar respondents are grouped together from a lifestyle perspective.[10]

Generally, then, the process of lifestyle segmentation involves two steps. First, a determination is made of which lifestyle segments will efficiently produce the greatest number of profitable customers. Often heavy users are sought, but as we have seen, other segments also have potential. The second step involves defining and describing the selected target customers in more depth to understand how they may be attracted and communicated with more efficiently and relevantly.[11]

APPLICATIONS OF LIFESTYLE SEGMENTATION

Lifestyle may be used as a basis for segmentation in four possible ways. These approaches are discussed below, and examples are provided for each situation.[12]

Segmentation Based on General Lifestyle Characteristics   In this approach the marketer seeks to classify the consumer population into groups based on general lifestyle characteristics, so that consumers within the groups have similar lifestyles. Using the research approach described above, a representative sample of consumers respond to a questionnaire containing AIOs, product usage, media consumption, and demographic items. Through statistical routines (clustering and others) the marketer attempts to find out if people can be grouped together into distinct groups. Each group represents a different pattern of needs for and consumption of products and services. Once these groups are identified, the marketer is able to direct his product to appeal to one or several segments.[13]

As an example of this approach, a major study by DDB Needham Worldwide Inc. advertising agency categorized almost 3300 respondents into ten different lifestyle types—five female and five male. To help clients understand the lifestyle data, the ten consumer composites were even given names as shown in Table 5-2.

From these profiles, indexes of product usage for some items of interest can then be developed showing how the groups differ in their consumption. For example, Eleanor, Candice, and Mildred are heavy cosmetics users. Given their varying psychographic profiles, however, quite different strategies will be necessary to reach the different groups. By also understanding the media patterns of these groups, marketers can select appropriate advertising vehicles. For example, magazines such as *Glamour, Cosmopolitan,* and *True Story,* and radio stations playing heavy rock are much more likely to reach Mildred, while publications such as *Vogue, Cosmopolitan,* and *Better Homes and Gardens,* and radio stations playing classical music tend to appeal to Eleanor and Candice.[14]

A general segmentation study was successfully used by a manufacturer of intimate apparel for women, to diversify its product lines. The maker had been selling a line of old-fashioned, traditional lingerie that appealed to the Thelmas and Cathys of the United

States. As a result of a segmentation study, the company uncovered an opportunity to design and market two new lines of intimate apparel, one to appeal to people resembling Eleanor and Candice, and the other to be aimed at people such as Mildred.[15]

Segmentation Based on Product-Specific Lifestyle Characteristics   In this approach, the marketer seeks to understand consumer behavior related to a particular product or service. That is, in order to obtain more meaningful data the marketer tailors the general AIO questions to make them more product-specific. For example, the general AIO statement "I like to exercise" may be modified to "I like to play tennis." The advantage of this approach is that groups emerge that are more sharply defined in terms of their usage of a particular product or service.

Such a segmentation study of the leisure travel market led Air Canada to develop new vacation packages to meet the needs of some segments which were identified. For example, the largest segment, a group identified as "cautious homebodies," were found to want safety, security, and a predictable environment on their vacation. Their desire to be led around and made to feel secure was recognized and translated into a vacation package based on a guided coach tour of England. Many other vacation package concepts were designed based on the demographic and vacation-specific lifestyle attributes of the market.[16]

Profiling Based on General Lifestyle Characteristics   The marketer, instead of segmenting to find the most appropriate number of meaningful homogeneous groups into which a heterogeneous population can be divided, may need to profile a homogeneous group of respondents according to the "typical" individual in the group. This use of general AIO items may allow the marketer to define more adequately a segment of interest. For instance, although insurance companies have traditionally relied on demographic characteristics to identify accident-prone drivers, use of general lifestyle characteristics to profile these individuals is also helpful. One study shows that the accident-prone driver is more likely than the safe driver to be a risk taker and an impulse buyer, is restless, feels pressured, has money problems but is optimistic, has a cosmopolitan outlook, is interested in movies (especially X-rated and disaster ones), and is less likely to be socially or politically conservative. Knowledge that such lifestyle characteristics correlate with the propensity to have driving accidents can lead an insurance company to develop more effective communication and other programs as part of its marketing strategy.[17] Even its accident, or risk-rating, program may be influenced by such data.

Profiling Based on Product-Specific Lifestyle Characteristics   In the previous approach, the marketer developed the psychographic profile for the segment of interest from a large set of general lifestyle items. When a psychographic study is devoted to a single product category, however, the researcher can focus instead on a limited group of relevant, product-related dimensions.

Colgate Palmolive undertook a psychographic segmentation study of soap users and uncovered three clearly defined consumer groups—*independents, rejuvenators,* and *compensators*—with the following characteristics:

TABLE 5-2

Psychographic Profiles   **The Female Segments**

Thelma, the old-fashioned traditionalist (25 percent)
This lady has lived a "good" life—she has been a devoted wife, a doting mother, and a conscientious housewife. She has lived her life by these traditional values and she cherishes them to this day. She does not condone contemporary sexual activities or political liberalism, nor can she sympathize with the women's libbers. Even today, when most of her children have left home, her life is centered around the kitchen. Her one abiding interest outside the household is the church which she attends every week. She lacks higher education and hence has little appreciation for the arts or cultural activities. Her spare time is spent watching TV, which is her prime source of entertainment and information.

Mildred, the miltant mother (20 percent)
Mildred married young and had children before she was quite ready to raise a family. Now she is unhappy. She is having trouble making ends meet on her blue-collar husband's income. She is frustrated and she vents her frustrations by rebelling against the system. She finds escape from her unhappy world in soap operas and movies. Television provides an ideal medium for her to live out her fantasies. She watches TV all through the day and into late night. She likes heavy rock and probably soul music, and she doesn't read much except escapist magazines such as *True Story*.

Candice, the chic suburbanite (20 percent)
Candice is an urbane woman. She is well educated and genteel. She is a prime mover in her community, active in club affairs and working on community projects. Socializing is an important part of her life. She is a doer, interested in sports and the outdoors, politics and current affairs. Her life is hectic and lived at a fast clip. She is a voracious reader, and there are few magazines she doesn't read. However, TV does relatively poorly in competing for her attention—it is too inane for her.

Cathy, the contented housewife (18 percent)
Cathy epitomizes simplicity. Her life is untangled. She is married to a worker in the middle of the socioeconomic scale, and they, along with their several preteen children, live in a small town. She is devoted to her family and faithfully serves them as mother, housewife, and cook. There is a certain tranquility in her life. She enjoys a relaxed pace and avoids anything that might disturb her equilibrium. She doesn't like news or news-type programs on TV but enjoys the wholesome family entertainment provided by *Walt Disney, The Waltons,* and *Happy Days*.

Eleanor, the elegant socialite (17 percent)
Eleanor is a woman with style. She lives in the city because that is where she wants to be. She likes the economic and social aspects of big city living and takes advantage of the city in terms of her career and leisure time activities. She is a self-confident on-the-go woman, not a homebody. She is fashion conscious and dresses well. She is a woman with panache. She is financially secure; as a result she is not a careful shopper. She shops for quality and style, not price. She is a cosmopolitan woman who has traveled abroad or wants to.

Independents. Forceful leaders concerned about getting ahead, confident, self-assured, calm and unflappable, practical, realistic, rugged, and self-reliant people who don't pamper themselves

Rejuvenators. Outward-directed, basically insecure people who need the social reassurance of those around them

Compensators. Inward-directed, passive, and withdrawn people

In terms of soap preferences, the independents were on one end of the spectrum, oriented toward cleaning and refreshment in a toilet soap, while compensators were on the other end, desiring luxury and comfort in the bath. Independents were found to have a disproportionate number of men and were shown to be a group ready for something

The Male Segments

Herman, the retiring homebody (26 percent)

Herman is past his prime and is not getting any younger. His attitudes and opinions on life, which are often in conflict with modern trends, have gelled. And he is resistant to change. He is old-fashioned and conservative. He was brought up on "motherhood and apple pie" and cherishes these values. Consequently he finds the attitudes of young people today disturbing. He realizes he cannot effect any change, and has withdrawn into a sheltered existence of his own within the confines of his home and its surroundings. Here he lives a measured life. He goes to church regularly, watches his diet, and lives frugally. He longs for the good old days and regrets that the world around him is changing.

Scott, the successful professional (21 percent)

Scott is a man who has everything going for him. He is well educated, cosmopolitan, the father of a young family, and is already established in his chosen profession. He lives a fast-paced active life and likes it. He is a man getting ahead in the world. He lives in or near an urban center and seems to like what a big city has to offer—culture, learning opportunities, and people. He also enjoys sports, the out-of-doors, and likes to keep physically fit. He is understandably happy with his life and comfortable in his lifestyle.

Fred, the frustrated factory worker (19 percent)

Fred is young. He married young and had a family. It is unlikely that he had any plans to get a college degree; if he did, he had to shelve them to find work to support his family. He now is a blue-collar worker having trouble making ends meet. He is discontented, and tends to feel that "they"—big business, government, society—are somehow responsible for his state. He finds escape in movies and in fantasies of foreign lands and cabins by quiet lakes. He likes to appear attractive to women, has an active libido, and likes to think he is a bit of a swinger.

Dale, the devoted family man (17 percent)

Dale is a wholesome guy with a penchant for country living. He is a blue-collar worker, with a high school education. The father of a relatively large family, he prefers a traditional marriage, with his wife at home taking care of the kids. His home and neighborhood are central in his life. He is an easygoing guy who leads an uncomplicated life. Neither worry nor skepticism are a part of him. He is relaxed and has a casual approach to many things. He is a happy, trusting soul who takes things as they are.

Ben, the self-made businessman (17 percent)

Ben is the epitomy of a self-made man. He was probably not born wealthy, nor had he the benefit of higher education, but through hard work and shrewd risk-taking he has built himself a decent life. He has seen the system work. He believes if you work hard and play by the rules you will get your share (and perhaps some more). Therefore he cannot condone hippies and other fringe groups whom he sees as freeloaders. He embraces conservative ideology and is likely to be a champion of business interests. He is a traditionalist at home, and believes it is a woman's job to look after the home and to raise a family. He is gregarious and enjoys giving and attending parties. And he likes to drink.

Source: Sunil Mehrotra and William D. Wells, "Psychographics and Buyer Behavior: Theory and Recent Empirical Findings," in Arch G. Woodside, Jagdish N. Sheth, and Peter D. Bennett (eds.), *Consumer and Industrial Buying Behavior*, Elsevier North-Holland, New York, 1977, pp. 54–55.

new and fresh in bar-soap benefits. They wanted a long-lasting, hard soap that would keep them clean, fresh, and odor-free and could be used by the whole family.

To fulfill the needs of this vacant market niche, Colgate assessed many possibilities for a product name, shape, color, and scent which best fulfilled the concept of a deodorant soap for men yet would be mild enough for the rest of the family. Emerging from this search was the product Irish Spring, with an advertising appeal aimed primarily at men. A rugged-looking, self-assured spokesman matched the independents' characteristics. However, in order to broaden the appeal to the household purchasing

agent, women were also brought into the commercial with the selling phrase, "Manly, yes, but I like it too." In addition, the Irish setting for the advertisements created a sense of outdoors and freshness. Three years after national introduction, Irish Spring was the third leading bar soap on the market.[18]

USES OF LIFESTYLE INFORMATION

As stated before, the purpose of using lifestyle or any other variable to segment a market is not as an end in itself, but to help successfully develop and target marketing mixes. To elaborate on some of the marketer's key uses for lifestyle information in this regard, we will examine several areas of application.

Developing New Products   Psychographic research can often be used as a springboard to development of new products based on the identification of unserved market segments.

New York Telephone found that psychographics could not only help the marketer highlight unsatisfied customer needs, but also aid in strategic life-cycle planning by revealing situations where marketing activities must be redesigned to match current market conditions. The company faced a decision regarding its decorator telephone line in which they needed to find the most appropriate market for their existing products. They used an understanding of lifestyle to suggest which telephone might appeal to which type of lifestyle. It was found that several sets of telephones were competing for the same customers, while there were no sets aimed at certain lucrative target lifestyle groups. As a result, one telephone product was dropped, which made the others directed at that same market segment more competitive and much more profitable. Also, product voids were filled with a number of new decorator telephones.

A new model, the Rendez-vous, was launched to appeal to a sizeable lifestyle group consisting of achievement-oriented people and those who emulated these achievers. The achievement-oriented group was a very affluent segment who tended to be society's important decision makers. Their purchasing was oriented toward buying the best-quality merchandise and services, and they were relatively unattracted by low price. Those who emulated the achievers were a younger and less-affluent group who consumed similar, but less-high-quality products because they could not afford them. The model aimed at this group became the number-three-selling set in New York Telephone's line. Two other new sets aimed at smaller lifestyle segments also sold well.[19]

Developing Promotion Strategy   Probably the most extensive use of lifestyle information is in connection with development of advertising campaigns. Here, the marketer can particularly benefit from an understanding of lifestyle as it relates to consumer media usage and as a source of ideas for advertising approaches. Lifestyle, along with other sources of information, can be useful to advertisers in suggesting new or changed advertising characters, settings, moods, and themes.

SELECTING MEDIA   It has been suggested that lifestyle measures have been most useful for media selection and scheduling.[20] Use of lifestyle profiles for different media can suggest appropriate vehicles to use in reaching target markets. For instance, examination of the *Playboy* reader lifestyle profile will reveal a vast difference between that and the lifestyle of readers of many other magazines. To illustrate, Table 5-3, comparing heavy readers of *Playboy* and *Reader's Digest* on only a few lifestyle statements, indicates very different orientations regarding optimism, religion, conservatism, and permissiveness.

The *Playboy* readers' lifestyle profile points to selection of this medium as a good vehicle for such products as liquor, air travel, sports cars, mutual funds, beer, credit cards, moving companies, and new products in general. Their lifestyle profile also suggests a swinging, permissive, light, and rather youth-oriented approach to advertising copy. Such a copy approach—and many of the products appropriate for *Playboy*—may not be appropriate for *Reader's Digest*. Before including *Playboy* in the media set for a campaign, however, the marketer will need to look at audiences of other relevant media and, particularly, at the cost per thousand of reaching the appropriate audience.

DETERMINING CREATIVE STRATEGY   Lifestyle information is frequently used when developing advertising campaigns. A classic case of the use of lifestyle research to develop a national advertising campaign is illustrated by Schlitz beer.[21] Schlitz had been running a successful ad campaign formulated around the copy line of "When you're out of Schlitz, you're out of beer." There was a general feeling that a new, fresh approach was needed. The advertising director visited neighborhood taverns to observe and talk with target customers—heavy beer drinkers. In addition, one element emerged from past Schlitz advertising—the word "gusto." Research showed it to have strong connotations, conveying relevant meanings about beer, taste, and life, and it also turned out to be "owned" by Schlitz. Another element emerging from the review process was that Schlitz is sold almost everywhere in the world—in fact, the world was used as a symbol on the label.

The "tavern tour" of the advertising director yielded the following informal lifestyle portrait of the heavy beer drinker as:

. . . the man who belongs to the 20 percent of the population that drinks 80 percent of the beer. A man who drinks a case a weekend or even a case a day. . . . He is a guy who is not making it and probably never will. He is a

TABLE 5-3

Differences in Readers' Lifestyles for Two Media

	Percent who definitely agreed among:	
	Heavy **Playboy** readers, %	Heavy **Reader's Digest** readers, %
My greatest achievements are still ahead of me.	50	26
I go to church regularly.	18	40
Movies should be censored.	14	40
Most men would cheat on their wives if the right opportunity came along.	27	12

Source: Douglas J. Tigert, "Life Style Analysis as a Basis for Media Selection," in William D. Wells (eds.), *Life Style and Psychographics*, American Marketing Association, Chicago, 1974, p. 179.

dreamer, a wisher, a limited edition of Walter Mitty. He is a sports nut because he is a hero worshipper. . . . He goes to the tavern and has six or seven beers with the boys. . . . If we are to talk to this man where he lives, in terms he respects and can identify with, we must find for him a believable kind of hero he inwardly admires.[22]

Next, formal research on the lifestyle of the heavy beer drinker was completed. It was found that the heavy user:

■ Had a middle-class income level derived primarily from blue-collar occupations.

■ Was young, with at least a high school education.

■ Was more hedonistic and pleasure-seeking toward life than the nondrinker was.

■ Had less regard toward family and job responsibilities than nondrinkers did.

■ Had a preference for a physical, male-oriented existence and was inclined to fantasize.

■ Had a great enjoyment of drinking, particularly beer, which was seen as a real man's drink.

Using the lifestyle portrait of the heavy beer drinker, it was decided that the "gusto man, and gusto life" approach would strongly appeal to the heavy user's sense of masculinity, hedonism, and fantasy. From this research Schlitz built a successful ad campaign around imagery of the sea to glamorize the adventure of seamen who lived their lives with gusto and enjoyed a "gusto brew." The copy for the ads stated, "You only go around once in life. So grab for all the gusto you can."

Schlitz subsequently sank from its number two position in the industry to fourth place, behind Anheuser-Busch, Miller, and Pabst, as a result of an unsuccessful product-taste modification in which its brewing cycle was accelerated and as a result of numerous substantial changes in the industry, particularly those centering on new products and strong, effective advertising by Busch and Miller.[23]

When more than one segment is targeted, different advertising strategies may be needed for each one, based on their lifestyle, demographic, and media-usage profiles. For example, the state of South Carolina employed five distinct advertising strategies using different creative approaches, media schedules, and direct-mail literature in order to appeal to five different vacation market segments.

BENEFITS OF LIFESTYLE SEGMENTATION

Lifestyle segmentation has been the object of increasing research and application in marketing because of its potential benefits. Although the problems involved in getting, analyzing, and interpreting lifestyle data are not to be minimized, the examples presented above are good testimony of the technique's ability to assist the development of marketing strategy. Thus, the marketing manager may be able to develop improved multidimensional views of key target segments, uncover new product opportunities, obtain better product position, develop improved advertising communications based on a richer, more lifelike portrait of the target consumer, and generally improve overall marketing strategies.[24]

Additional benefits of psychographics are being realized by consumer-behavior researchers, who tend to have a more esoteric view than does the practicing marketer. For these researchers, psychographic methods are leading to enhanced general knowledge of consumer behavior in at least three ways. First, they have contributed to a better understanding of numerous consumer behavior facets such as opinion leadership, retail shopping, private-brands buying, consumerist activism, and other attributes. Second, with the repetition of studies, trend data may be accumulated to show how consumers may be changing. Third, general segmentations of consumer groups are creating new typologies for more efficiently describing and understanding consumer behavior.

Thus the result of psychographic research findings such as those presented here may lead marketers to think routinely in terms of segments marked off by common sets of activities, interests, needs, and values and to develop products, services, and media schedules specifically to meet those segments.[25]

USAGE SEGMENTATION

Another segmentation approach often used by marketers is based on product or brand usage by consumers. Usage segmentation can take a number of directions. For example, the marketer may want to identify various segments of users for a particular product category or users of the company's brand. In other cases, one may want to segment users into those who buy frequently versus those who only buy occasionally (either product or brand), or into those users who usually purchase the same brand versus those who switch from brand to brand. It may also be useful for the marketer to understand how segments arise based on different product-usage situations. Any usage segmentation approach needs to specify the relevant dimensions of interest.

BRAND-USER SEGMENTATION

The marketer is generally most interested in determining whether those who purchase the company's brand are different, either demographically or psychographically, from those buying competitors' brands. If characteristics can be distinguished, then marketing programs can perhaps be developed to attract more buyers who resemble the preferred buyer.

Avon conducted a research study to identify its buyers, and it found them likely to be somewhat older than average, high school but not college graduates, living outside metropolitan areas, having husbands with blue-collar jobs and relatively low incomes, and having large families. Their lifestyles and attitudes tended to be conservative, and they had old-fashioned tastes. They were cost-conscious, centered around their homes and families, and didn't like to buy beauty products in stores because of the lack of privacy and personal attention. The best feature was that they spent 92 percent of their beauty-aid dollars with Avon. Since there was not a strong need to build their acceptance level, the company sought to identify other groups with a high potential for purchasing Avon products. Close analysis of the data indicated a sizable group of

women with a high potential for increased sales. They were like Avon's loyal customers in their attitudes toward in-home buying and personal service and they spent much money on cosmetics. However, they differed in other ways. For example, they were more up-scale, less conservative and family-oriented, more interested in being up-to-the-minute in fashion, and less inclined to believe that Avon products could give them whatever look they wanted. Avon's resulting advertising campaigns designed to attract these high-potential customers featured the themes "You Never Looked So Good," and "We're Going to Make You Feel Beautiful."[26]

A related approach that may be profitable to pursue is to develop new products to appeal to nonusing segments. Such a move may make it difficult for a company to maintain a consistent image, however. If such an image is critical, the marketer may need to work only with buyers similar to present users. Cadillac faced this problem in the launch of its Cimarron (a lower-priced, small luxury car model), which appealed not to the traditional Cadillac buyer, but to those who were younger and had been buying expensive, sporty imported cars. The result may have been a diffused image among customers as to what the Cadillac brand meant.

PRODUCT-USER SEGMENTATION

Although buyers of different *brands* may not be found to have different characteristics, the marketer nevertheless will be interested in segmenting *product* users on the basis of any such distinguishing demographic or psychographic characteristics in order to reach them effectively. Within a product category such as soft drinks, for example, it may be found that those who consume low-calorie drinks differ demographically and psychographically from regular soft-drink users, although perhaps Diet Pepsi and Tab drinkers are virtually the same.

Of course, for many products nonusers may represent a significant marketing opportunity. Mercury Outboards, for example, is attempting to expand the boating universe by attracting nonusers—people who like boating but have never owned a boat. Also, public goods and nonprofit-organization specialists are continually confronted with the reality of the need to convert nonusers to users. For example, consider the following marketing problems:

> Convincing nonusing men and women to avail themselves of cancer check-ups.

> Attracting nonriders to mass transportation.

> Attracting nonsubscribers to symphonies, lectures, and other cultural events.

Each of these problems represents a marketing opportunity to convert nonusers to users. Obviously, the past rate of success for such projects has not been great, but with increased application of marketing research to understanding the motivations of different segments, greater success should occur in the future.

LOYALTY SEGMENTATION

Marketers are often interested in attracting not just brand users, but perhaps more importantly, those who consistently purchase the company's brand. When these

brand-loyal buyers are identified (assuming they differ on certain characteristics from the nonloyal buyer), appropriate marketing strategies may be developed to attract competitors' buyers who have similar characteristics or to increase the loyalty rate among current less-loyal buyers. Loyalty segmentation can also be successfully applied to retail store customers.[27]

Marketers of new national brands are often advised to target toward those segments that exhibit considerable brand switching. However, one research study of the introduction of a new national brand (Puffs facial tissue) indicated that marketing efforts could actually be successfully targeted toward brand switchers as well as toward households that were loyal to existing national brands and toward purchasers of private-label brands.[28]

VOLUME SEGMENTATION

Volume segmentation attempts to identify frequent users of a product category or brand. Marketers often refer to the "20–80" thesis, that is, that 20 percent of the market accounts for 80 percent of sales of their product. Although the exact proportions may vary and the rule may not universally apply, it does indicate the importance of a relatively small group of consumers to the health of a firm's product or service.

The Technique of Volume Segmentation   Research has shown that purchase concentration is not always a simple function of obvious demographic factors such as income or household size. Thus, the marketer must measure consumption and identify the characteristics that are useful in distinguishing the various purchase intensities.

Frequently, this is accomplished by dividing the market into heavy, light, and nonusers of the product and then examining their distinguishing characteristics. At one time this was an extremely difficult process for most companies, but today several marketing research organizations are able to provide such data. For example, Axiom Market Research Bureau, Inc., conducts periodic national studies of product usage, personal characteristics, and media habits of a sample of over 30,000 adults and 8000 teenagers. They regularly analyze 900 product categories and subcategories and publish Target Group Index (TGI) to assist the marketer in identifying potential audiences.

Figure 5-1 is based on analysis of household consumption data from a panel of *Chicago Tribune* newspaper subscribers and indicates the importance of the heavy user. Notice in Figure 5-1 that relatively few households account for the bulk of sales in these products. For instance, 39 percent of the households purchase 90 percent of cola beverages, while an additional 39 percent of the households in the market account for only 10 percent of colas consumed. Also of importance is the finding that 22 percent of the market are nonusers of colas.

Application of Volume Segmentation   Marketers of a broad range of goods and services utilize volume as a fundamental segmentation criterion. The following example illustrates one area of application.

Target markets are often categorized in terms of their lucrativeness. This was the case with Quaker Oats Company when it segmented the market for its breakfast cereal Life.

The firm determined that family size and the age of the housewife were the two characteristics that distinguished intensity of product use. Consequently, Quaker ranked its target segments in the following hierarchy:

Families with above-average consumption ("extremely important" and "important" targets) were characterized by housewives under age 40, families of four or more members, in metropolitan areas of 50,000 to 500,000 population, with moderate incomes.

Families with average consumption ("average" targets) were characterized by housewives 40 to 49, living in cities of 2 million or more population.

Families with below-average consumption ("unimportant" and "very inferior" targets) were characterized by housewives 50 and over, with less than four family members, low and high incomes, and in small towns or rural areas.[29]

It is probably for this reason that advertising for Life cereal (see Figure 5-2) often shows three children at the breakfast table, thus reflecting the large-family-size characteristics of their most important target segment.

Research by TGI for packaged consumer goods indicates that the best way to increase sales of a product is to persuade present users to use more of that product, rather than to attract new users. This suggests that marketing efforts should generally be aimed at light to heavy users rather than at nonusers.[30]

One of the real attractions of the usage approach to market segmentation is the ease with which the technique can be employed by so many firms. Most

FIGURE 5-1
The "heavy user" annual purchase concentration in selected product categories.
Source: Adapted from Dik Warren Twedt, "How Important to Marketing Strategy Is the 'Heavy User'?" *Journal of Marketing,* **28**:72, January 1964, published by the American Marketing Association.

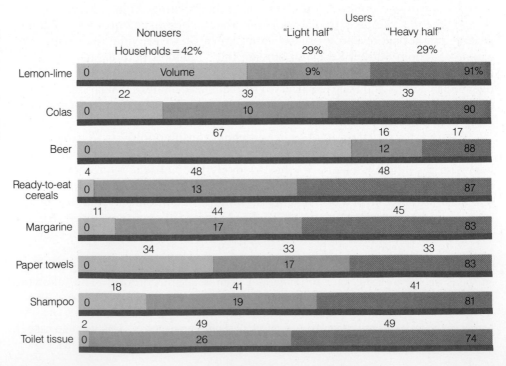

FIGURE 5-2
An advertisement for Life
cereal, aimed at heavy users.
Courtesy of the Quaker Oats Co.

companies are able to segment consumers by usage rates because of access to marketing-research services and data-processing systems that can quickly categorize and analyze consumers by purchase activity. Thus, department stores are able to analyze charge account customers' purchases with regularity; banks can assess their customers' banking usage; and, as mentioned previously, many

packaged-consumer-goods firms can subscribe to syndicated services to provide the same usage information.

SITUATION SEGMENTATION

Marketers often become complacent after identifying their market by demographics and psychographics (''who'' buys) and may go no further to understand ''how'' the product is used and enjoyed, whether the consumer is at work, play, or home. Actually, a manufacturer's or retailer's product line can be seen as a range of items appealing to the needs of diverse person-situation market segments.[31] This segmentation approach divides the market by groups of consumers within usage situations. For example, Holiday Inns, Inc., has established categories on the basis of situational needs of travelers. The various Holiday Inn brands might be chosen by travelers in different situations, as follows:

> *Holiday Inn (midscale).* On a business trip to Chicago, you need to be close to the airport and have to meet clients for dinner.

> *Crown Plaza (upscale).* On a business trip to Chicago, you need to be downtown.

> *Hampton Inn (budget).* You and the family are visiting Grandma for Thanksgiving.

> *Embassy Suite (all suites).* You are traveling to Memphis on business and plan to stay for one week.

> *Residence Inns (residence hotel).* You are relocating to San Francisco on a temporary business assignment of a few weeks or months.[32]

Thus, consumers often select products on the basis of usage situations they expect to encounter.[33]

The steps involved in this situation approach are shown in Table 5-4, and an illustrative person-situation matrix for suntan lotion is shown in Table 5-5. Any special features that might be desired in particular usage situations or by particular groups of users are shown in the row and column margins. Products designed for a particular person-situation submarket should meet the needs listed at the end of the row and bottom of the column for that segment. Any unique needs for certain person-situation combinations are shown in the individual cells (for example, a perfumed winter lotion for female snow skiers). The cells should also include an estimate of the size of the market and list any company and competitive brands designed to meet the specific needs of that market. This may be very helpful in identifying market opportunities, selecting target markets, and developing marketing mixes. For instance, placing in the matrix the company's current product line and the competition's brands and lines will show whose needs are not being currently met.

BENEFIT SEGMENTATION

The approaches to market segmentation discussed so far are all helpful to the marketer. However, they suffer from an underlying disadvantage—all are based on an ex post facto analysis of the kinds of people who make up specific segments of a market. That is, emphasis is on *describing* the characteristics of different segments rather than on learning what *causes* these segments to develop. However, proponents of benefit segmentation claim that the *benefits* that people are seeking are the basic reason for purchase and therefore the proper basis for market segmentation.[34]

Marketers have learned, for example, that knowing people's interest in alternative benefits is helpful in predicting the attention paid to advertising copy developed around those benefits. In one study, air travelers who indicated being more interested in "fun while flying" than in "travel-planning help" were more attentive to advertising focused on the fun benefit, while those interested in travel planning were more attentive to advertising featuring that theme. This relationship held true even though both segments were exposed to both themes. Thus people are more likely to attend to commercials and buy brands that center on benefits of interest to them.[35]

THE TECHNIQUE OF BENEFIT SEGMENTATION

The technique of benefit segmentation typically involves a three-step process:

1 Exploratory research to develop a complete listing of benefits of possible value in segmenting the relevant market.

TABLE 5-4

Person-Situation Segmentation Procedure

1 Use observational studies, focus group discussions, and secondary data to discover whether different usage situations exist and whether they are determinant, in the sense that they appear to affect the importance of various product characteristics.

2 If step 1 produces promising results, undertake a benefit, product perception, and reported market behavior segmentation survey of consumers. Measure benefits and perceptions by usage situation as well as by individual characteristics. Assess situation usage frequency by recall estimates or usage situation diaries.

3 Construct a person-situation segmentation matrix. The rows are the major usage situations, and the columns are groups of users identified by a single characteristic or combination of characteristics.

4 Rank the cells in the matix in terms of their submarket sales volume. The situation-person combination that results in the greatest consumption of the generic product would be ranked first.

5 State the major benefits sought, important product dimensions, and unique market behavior for each nonempty cell of the matrix. (Some person types will never consume the product in certain usage situations.)

6 Position your competitors' offerings within the matrix. The person-situation segments they currently serve can be determined by the product feature they promote and other marketing strategy.

7 Position your offering within the matrix on the same criteria.

8 Assess how well your current offering and marketing strategy meet the needs of the submarkets compared with the competition.

9 Identify market opportunities on the basis of submarket size, needs, and competitive advantage.

Source: Peter R. Dickson, "Person-Situation: Segmentation's Missing Link," *Journal of Marketing*, **46**:61, Fall 1982, published by the American Marketing Association.

2   Development of sensitive and reliable scales to measure major attitude dimensions.

3   Quantitative measurement of the market, usually involving a national sample, resulting in clustering of respondents by their attitude. Individual clusters (or segments) are described in terms of their behavior, lifestyles, demographics, and other relevant characteristics. Segments, therefore, are discriminated by their attitudes, and differences in their behavior are analyzed through cross tabulations.[36]

Although the concept appears simple, its implementation is very complex, often requiring computers and sophisticated multivariate attitude-measurement

TABLE 5-5
Speculative Person-Situation Segmentation Matrix for Suntan Lotion

Situations	Young children Fair skin	Young children Dark skin	Teenagers Fair skin	Teenagers Dark skin	Adult women Fair skin	Adult women Dark skin	Adult men Fair skin	Adult men Dark skin	Situation benefits/features
Beach/boat sunbathing	Combined insect repellent				Summer perfume				**1** windburn protection **2** formula and container can stand heat **3** container floats and is distinctive (not easily lost)
Home-poolside sunbathing					Combined moisturizer				**1** large pump dispenser **2** won't stain wood, concrete, or furnishings
Sunlamp bathing					Combined moisturizer and massage oil				**1** designed specifically for type of lamp **2** artificial tanning ingredient
Snow skiing					Winter perfume				**1** special protection from special light rays and weather **2** antifreeze formula
Person Benefit/ features	Special protection **1** protection critical **2** nonpoisonous		Special protection **1** fit in jean pocket **2** used by opinion leaders		Special protection Female perfume		Special protection Male perfume		

Source: Peter R. Dickson, "Person-Situation: Segmentation's Missing Link," *Journal of Marketing*, **46**:62, Fall 1982, published by the American Marketing Association.

techniques. The statistical methods employed relate the responses of each consumer to those of every other respondent and then develop clusters (typically three to seven segments) of consumers with similar rating patterns. Each of these segments represents a potentially profitable and different opportunity for marketing effort.

APPLICATIONS OF BENEFIT SEGMENTATION

One example of benefit segmentation involves the restaurant industry. The data presented in Table 5-6 are illustrative of segmentation research results that might be obtained for an "adult-fun" dinner house. Suppose that this dinner house is struggling in a highly competitive market and has experienced declining sales. In Table 5-6, the dinner house is restaurant X, and, as shown in the table, its customers are drawn from segments 1 and 3. So far, management's strategy has focused on segment 3, called "Entertainers." Other data from the study show that patrons of this segment perceive few distinguishing features between restaurants

TABLE 5-6
Restaurant Benefit Segments

Characteristic	Segment 1 Family diners	Segment 2 Romantics	Segment 3 Entertainers
Market share:			
Patrons	25%	50%	25%
Dollars	35%	25%	40%
Valued ideal-restaurant factors	Seek food variety and value	Fun and social	Discriminating
	Not interested in entertainment	Food variety and value	Seek quality food and service
		Good drink value	Not interested in food variety or value
		Entertainment	
Key lifestyle factors	Traditionalists	Uninhibited morals	Socially secure
	Restaurant loyalists	Bar drinkers	Not restaurant loyalists
	Not bar drinkers	Untraditional	Traditional morality
	Traditional morality	Not restaurant loyalists	Opinion leaders
Typical restaurant usage patterns	Dinners, no drinks	Dinners, wine	Lunches and dinners, drinks
Number in party	Three to five people	Two people	Four people
Consideration choices	Restaurants A, B, X	Restaurants C, D, E, F	Restaurants F, G, H, I, X
Preference choices	A	D, F	F, G, H, I
Size of check	Food $32	Food $19	Food $55
	Drinks $2	Drinks $7	Drinks $20
Occasion of use	Family dining	Dating	Entertaining
Demographic description			
Sex	Equally male and female	Preponderantly male	Preponderantly male
Age	35 to 50	Under 30	Over 40
Education	Some college	Some college	Advanced degrees
Marital status	Married	Single	Married
Income:			
Personal	Over $35,000	Under $20,000	Over $40,000
Family	Over $45,000		Over $75,000

Source: William R. Swinyard and Kenneth D. Struman, "Market Segmentation: Finding the Heart of Your Restaurant's Market," *Cornell Hotel and Restaurant Administration Quarterly,* May 1986, p. 95.

in this market and that this initially lucrative segment has attracted a disproportionately large share of strong competitors. Such findings might cause management of restaurant X to search for other segments less satisfied with available restaurants. Segment 1 may offer potential. Consumers in this group are relatively dissatisfied with available restaurants and seek a country atmosphere; fine, home-style food promptly served; and waitresses who enjoy their work and are courteous to the point of being familiar.

Detailed segment profiles guide the marketing group in redirecting operations and marketing strategies. Restaurant management may decide to focus entirely on segment 1 and not to dilute its effort by also trying to compete in segment 3. If the firm makes this change, it needs to continue to track the needs of the market segments, checking periodically for changes in market needs and changes in the way the market perceives restaurants as meeting these needs.[37]

This example demonstrates the advantage of benefit segmentation. The greatest difficulty in applying the approach exists in choosing the benefit to be emphasized. For example, the company must be certain that buyers' stated motives are their real motives for purchase, which is not an easy task because of the complexity of human motivation. Consequently, the number of consumers in each benefit segment is difficult to estimate; moreover, the proportions shift over time, presenting further complications. Thus, considerable research is needed to ascertain product benefits and the size of consumer segments for each.

LIMITATIONS OF BENEFIT SEGMENTATION

Segmentation based on benefits desired can be a meaningful approach from a marketing standpoint because it directly facilitates product planning and marketing communications but may be most useful for brand positioning.[38] The approach is not relevant for all situations, however. Here are three cases in which it may not be appropriate:[39]

1 Traditional price lines have developed so that all marketing activities are based on price levels. For certain products such as clothing, cosmetics, automobiles, and appliances, traditional price lines have developed to the extent that markets have become segmented into price lines. Because all product offerings and marketing activities are contingent upon the price line offered, marketing considerations dictate that the market be segmented at least initially by price lines. For many product categories, the size of the market for any price line is too low to permit further segmentation.

2 The benefits desired are determined by the situation or purpose for which the product is used. The desires of consumers can vary by the type of occasion for which the product is used. For example, clothes suitable for some occasions will not be suitable for other occasions. For effective marketing, consumer desires must be segmented by usage occasion to determine which products will be most suitable for each occasion. In many complex markets, this type of segmentation is necessary to derive the underlying competitive framework. Conventional segmentation questioning about the product without a specific usage occasion will provide meaningless information.

3   The style or appearance of the product is the overriding criterion of success. If fashion appeal is the major consideration in marketing success, the marketer must segment markets on the basis of styling preference in order to market a successful line of styles to each segment. Some examples of style-oriented lines are silverware, small appliances, fashion accessories, apparel, furniture, and automobiles.

Perhaps the greatest difficulty in applying the approach exists in choosing the correct benefits to be emphasized and making certain that buyers' stated motives are their real motives. Failure to understand the benefits which consumers may be seeking can prevent marketing success. For example:

When General Foods introduced Shake 'n' Bake—a bread coating for chicken and pork that simulated frying but was prepared untended in the oven rather than using deep fat in a frying pan—its competitor, Best Foods, saw this new product as a threat. Because Best Foods produced Mazola Oil, a product often used in frying chicken and pork, the company decided that it needed to counter Shake 'n' Bake with a similar product that would still entail the use of their oil. The result was Tasti-Fry, a seasoned breading mix used to coat the food, which was then fried. The product was taste-tested against Shake 'n' Bake, and in every instance won, leaving no doubt that food prepared with Tasti-Fry that was fried tasted better than food coated with Shake 'n' Bake that was baked. Based on these tests, Best Foods rushed the product to the test market where, despite heavy marketing expenditures, it was a miserable failure. What Best Foods neglected to research and understand were the other product benefits it was competing against—not just the product's taste, but also the product concept and promise. What General Foods successfully offered the housewife was an easier untended cooking convenience that resulted in an acceptable flavor, which was not placed in a spattering frying pan, and would not be viewed unfavorably as fried food and therefore fattening and possibly harmful to health.[40]

ANALYSIS OF CONSUMER PROBLEMS

The situation above also illustrates the need for a system that can supplement benefit analysis. When marketers ask consumers what benefits or attributes they want in a product, consumers often parrot back to researchers what they have already been told. For example, asking consumers what benefits they want in a toothpaste would likely elicit such benefits as ''decay prevention,'' ''whitening,'' ''fresh breath,'' and so forth—which is what they have heard though advertising. Thus, because consumers are often not highly introspective when asked, they are not likely to provide new information about product benefits which will move the company's brand to the top in market share.

If benefit information is supplemented with information about consumer problems, however, new insights may be developed. One approach to this is problem-inventory analysis in which consumers are provided with a list of problems and for each one are asked what products come to mind as having that problem.

Once general problems are determined, the marketer may proceed to perform more in-depth research for specific new product concepts.[41] For example, one

advertising agency uses a research technique known as "problem detection" to identify important problems for a particular product, how frequently those problems occur, and whether the solution to the problem has been preempted by some existing product or service. The "problem score" received by a product is expressed numerically with a larger score indicating a larger opportunity. The contribution of problem analysis to a company is illustrated in the following situation:

Surveys on dog food indicated three most-wanted attributes: (1) balanced diet, (2) good nutrition, and (3) containing vitamins. This information was not very helpful to the manufacturer because these benefits were already being served by other dog-food companies. However, when purchasers were asked what their dog-food problems were, the top three mentioned were: (1) it smelled bad, (2) it cost too much, and (3) it did not come in different sizes for different dogs. Three successful new product introductions resulted from these findings: (1) a dog food that smelled good enough to be called stew; (2) mixing chunks used in conjunction with dry food, which made it inexpensive; and (3) different size cans for different size dogs.[42]

PRODUCT POSITIONING

Effective product positioning is a key ingredient of successful marketing today. This section discusses the importance of positioning as it relates to the segmentation process, and discusses several approaches to the process.

THE INTERRELATIONSHIP OF MARKET SEGMENTATION AND PRODUCT POSITIONING

Segmentation is essentially the accommodation of different consumer groupings in a marketing plan or strategy. Knowing that different consumers respond differently to products, promotions, prices, and channels means that the marketer should not consider just the overall population's reaction to, say, a product, but also the reaction among different market segments. Market segmentation, therefore, is both the process of defining the characteristics of various segments in the marketplace, as well as the allocation of marketing resources among these segments. *Product positioning* is closely linked with market segmentation. A product's position is the place that it occupies in a given market as perceived by the relevant group of customers, that is, by the target-market segment. Positioning involves determining how consumers *perceive* the marketer's product and also developing and implementing marketing strategies to achieve the desired position in the market. Product, price, distribution, and promotional ingredients should all be viewed as potential tools for positioning a company and its offerings. Positioning, therefore, has no value in itself, only in its effect on the target-market segment. Marketers must look at segmentation and positioning in tandem. The process may start either by selecting a target-market segment and then trying to develop a suitable position, or by selecting an attractive product position and then identifying an appropriate market segment.

Whether the product is new or old, positioning is a key ingredient for achieving successful market results. For example, even radio stations find that proper positioning can help them carve out a profitable niche in tight competition.

Radio station KRXV focuses its signals on a narrow audience as competition in radio grows. The average listener to KRXV eats out eighteen times a month, owns a $93,000 house, has a MasterCard credit card, and is about to spend at least $423 in five days—much of it on gambling. The 23 million yearly listeners are almost all southern Californians on their way between Los Angeles and Las Vegas along Interstate 15. The station features programming designed to make its gambling-bound listeners happy—music by entertainers that listeners will see in Las Vegas, advisories on road conditions, and advertisements for Las Vegas hotels, casinos, and restaurants.[43]

Although business people have long been positioning their products to appeal to target-market segments, these decisions have not always been made consciously or successfully. To increase the chances of success, a systematic approach to the decision is needed. The remainder of this chapter will discuss various strategies and techniques used in a systematic approach to positioning.

STRATEGIES TO POSITION PRODUCTS[44]

Many ways exist for positioning a product or service (or even an organization). The following illustrate some of these approaches. It should be noted that combinations of these approaches are also possible.

Position On Product Features The product may be positioned on the basis of product features. For example, an advertisement may attempt to position the product by reference to its specific features. Although this may be a successful way to indicate product superiority, consumers are generally more interested in what such features mean to them, that is, how they can benefit by the product.

Position on Benefits This approach is closely related to the previous method. Toothpaste advertising often features the benefit approach, as the examples of Crest (decay prevention), Close-Up (sex appeal through white teeth and fresh breath), and Aqua-fresh (a combination of these benefits) illustrate. The difference between this and the features approach is illustrated by the adage, "Don't sell the steak, sell the sizzle."

Position on Usage This technique is related to benefit positioning. Many products are sold on the basis of their consumer usage situation. For instance, with the slogan "Weekends are made for Michelob," Michelob was traditionally positioned as the weekend beer. Such a limited position restricted the brand, however, by making new usage situations seem inappropriate. Michelob, therefore, has sought to expand the appropriate usage time with its recent slogan, "The night belongs to Michelob."

Other companies have sought to broaden their brand's association with a particular usage or situation. Campbell's Soup for many years was positioned for use at lunchtime and advertised extensively over noontime radio. It now stresses a variety of uses for soup (recipes are on labels) and a broader time for consumption, with the more general theme "Soup is good food."

Products can have multiple positioning strategies, but increasing the number may prove risky and difficult. Such approaches may be useful in expanding the market for a product, however. Gatorade, for example, was originally a summer

beverage for athletes who needed to replace body fluids; but it has also tried to develop a positioning strategy during the cold or flu season as the beverage to drink when the doctor recommends consuming plenty of fluids. Arm & Hammer very successfully added a position to its baking soda—as an odor-destroying agent in refrigerators—and sales jumped tremendously.

Position on User This approach associates the product with a user or a class of users. Some cosmetic companies seek a successful, highly visible model as their spokesperson (Christie Brinkley for Cover Girl) as the association for their brand. Other brands may pick a lesser known model to portray a certain lifestyle in its ads (Revlon's Charlie cosmetic line, for example). With its humorous sports personalities Miller Lite beer has been very successful in positioning itself as a beer for the heavy user who dislikes that filled-up feeling. A company may sometimes need to appeal to new users as it shifts markets. Johnson & Johnson baby shampoo now presents adult users as well as babies in its ads.

Because users and usage situations are related, they may often be linked in an ad. Figure 5-3 presents an ad for Sony in which different users and usage situations for the product are shown to consumers.

Position against Competition Often, success for a company involves looking for weak points in the positions of its competitors and then launching marketing attacks against those weak points.[45] In this approach, the marketer may either directly or indirectly make comparisons with competing products. For example, the famous ''Uncola'' campaign successfully positioned 7-Up as an alternative to Coke, Pepsi, and other colas (since almost two-thirds of soft drinks consumed in the United States are colas). Notice too, how this brand confronted a situation of special-usage positioning. For instance, it was originally thought of as a hangover cure, and it is still viewed as a special-occasion beverage, for an occasion other than a cola time.[43] Other classic positioning examples following this strategy include Burger King and McDonald's (over broiling versus frying) and Hertz versus Avis.

Corporations as well as products may be positioned, and can, in fact, serve to strongly reinforce the chosen product position. For instance, Neiman Marcus has positioned itself at the opposite end of the retailing spectrum from K mart. When companies fail to position themselves clearly, product sales may likely suffer from confusion in the consumer's mind. Perhaps the best illustration of this situation is the case of Goodyear and Goodrich tire companies. B. F. Goodrich faces a situation in which their name is similar to that of a larger company (Goodyear) in the same industry. Attempts by Goodrich to position themselves as ''the other guys'' and ''the ones without a blimp'' have not found great success with the tire-buying public. In this case, a name change might produce a better position than an approach which calls attention to the confusion with its competitor Goodyear.[46]

Another competitive positioning situation which may arise for the marketer of a new product is to disassociate older or typical products in an established category from the new product. In this case, the marketer may seek to distance the innovation from other perhaps similar products so that consumers more clearly recognize the uniqueness and superiority of the new item. Sometimes, seeming disadvantages may be turned into advantages for new products when the right position is determined. For example:

L'Oreal, a major European hair-care producer, faced the problem of establishing credibility of its name among U.S. women and making its company a dynamic factor in the U.S. hair-color market, which was dominated by Clairol. Research showed that hair-color users were not vulnerable to brand switching because a woman chooses a particular shade and fears she will not obtain that same tint if she switches brands. In addition, because hair color offers a cosmetic benefit, it cannot be positioned solely on a nonemotional basis. L'Oreal decided to position Preference, the highest-priced product within its color line, as "the most expensive hair color in the world." Consumers were to interpret this position to mean superior ingredients and a quality product. In addition, the ad copy line "because I'm worth it," appealed to self-esteem. This positioning resulted in dramatic market-share gains and moved L'Oreal into the number 2 position in the marketplace.[47]

POSITIONING ANALYSIS

The marketer may use several techniques for determining the appropriate positioning for a brand. Whether the brand is new or old, focus groups and depth interviews may be helpful in providing insights from consumers. In addition, survey and experimental research approaches such as those discussed in Chapter 3 may provide useful positioning data. Lifestyle information and a technique known as perceptual mapping can also be helpful in positioning decisions.

Lifestyle Positioning   Consumer AIOs can be used in designing a marketing strategy for potential markets. This approach is illustrated by positioning for the volunteer army. The army found dramatic differences between young men favoring and those not favoring the army as a career. Data suggest that it may be a mistake to position the army as a continuous party in which discipline is relaxed and nobody is required to stand in line, clean rooms, follow orders, or shoot guns. Young men and women who agree that the army is a good career appear to be unusually patriotic and conservative and are willing to accept hard work, discipline, and direction.[48] Figure 5-4 illustrates the creative response to such findings.

Perceptual Mapping   The above discussion suggests that consumers' perceptions of products are developed in a complex way and are not easily determined by the marketer. However, a technique known as perceptual mapping may be used in exploring consumers' product perceptions. Since products can be perceived on many dimensions (such as quality, price, and strength) the technique is *multidimensional* in nature. That is, it allows for the influence of more than one stimulus characteristic on product perceptions. Typically, consumers fill out measuring scales to indicate their perceptions of the many characteristics or similarities of competing brands. Computer programs analyze the resulting data to determine those product characteristics or combination of characteristics which are most important to consumers in distinguishing between competing brands. Results of this analysis can be plotted in terms of perceptual "maps," which display how consumers perceive the brands, and their differences, on a coordinate system.

FIGURE 5-3
Advertisement for a product
positioned on different usage
situations.
Courtesy of Sony.

Figure 5-5 presents a brand image map created by Chrysler Corp. to understand consumers' actual perception of car brands. Chrysler draws up a series of maps several times a year, using responses to customer surveys. The surveys ask owners of different car brands to rank their autos on a scale of one to ten on such attributes as "youthfulness," "luxury," and "practicality." The answers ultimately result in a mathematical score for each model, which is plotted on a graph showing broad criteria for evaluating buyer appeal.

The map in Figure 5-5 measures the images of the major divisions of U.S. auto makers and several imported brands. It shows, for instance, that the position held by the Plymouth brand is generally a practical, but somewhat stodgy, image. The Chrysler brand, on the other hand, is perceived as more luxurious, but not nearly as luxurious as its main competition—Cadillac and Lincoln.

By plotting strong areas of consumer demand on the map, a car maker can determine whether its autos are aimed at the right target. And from the concentration of dots representing competitive brands, a marketer can tell how much competition will be met in a particular segment on the map. As a result of such analysis, Chrysler executives decided that Plymouth, Dodge, and Chrysler all needed to present a more youthful image and that Plymouth and Dodge should also move up significantly on the luxury dimension. Such a map can also be used to position individual models (both current and future). Sometimes, changing the styling, price, or advertising can move a model into an unoccupied space on the map, thus carving out a distinctive market niche.[49]

THE FUTURE OF SEGMENTATION AND POSITIONING

The various bases for segmenting markets discussed in this and the previous chapter have underscored the need to understand consumers. Each segmentation approach has merit, and although not all have exhibited the ability to predict consumers' purchasing habits, they do enable marketers to understand better their target markets. When combinations of approaches are used in aiming at the total marketing problem, segmentation research can be very meaningful.[50] With enhanced understanding comes the ability to develop more tailored marketing programs. The need to segment markets and position products effectively is increasingly being recognized by marketing managers. For instance, a recent survey of top marketing executives showed that developing market segmentation strategies was one of the key pressure points they had to deal with in a recent year.[51]

The great deal of attention and interest generated by the concept of market segmentation is sure to become even more significant in the future. Three environmental factors are expected to lead to this growth. First, the advance of the consumerism movement will foster market segmentation, since critics have pointed to segments they believe are neglected in our present system. The result of these critic pressures is that managers become more attentive to previously unrecognized consumer needs.

A second factor encouraging market segmentation is intensified competition. With increasingly competitive markets (domestic and worldwide) in the future, business people will seek untapped segments to gain an advantage over rivals.

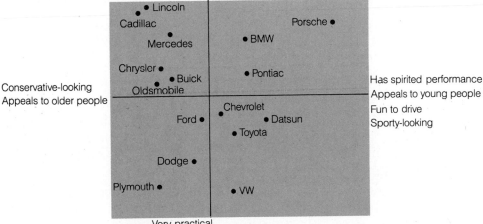

FIGURE 5-5
Perceptual map-auto brand images.
Source: John Koten, ''Car Makers Use 'Image' Map as Tool to Position Products,'' *The Wall Street Journal,* March 22, 1984, p. 33. Used by permission of *The Wall Street Journal.* Copyright © 1984 by Dow Jones & Company, Inc. All Rights Reserved.

The third factor stimulating market segmentation is the growing awareness of nonbusiness applications of the technique. It will be increasingly utilized for marketing in nontraditional areas such as politics, religion, and public issues.[52]

MANAGERIAL REFLECTIONS

For our product or service situation . . .

1   Can customer groups be segmented by lifestyle?

2   How may relevant segments' lifestyles be characterized in terms of their activities, interests, and opinions?

3   What differences exist between users of different brands or product types that may lead to effective segmentation?

4   Who are the loyal and heavy-user consumers in this product category, and how may they be attracted?

5   Are there differences in usage situations among consumers that may be identified and used as the basis for appeals?

6   What benefits are consumers seeking and/or what problems are they trying to avoid with this purchase?

7   What product position is most appropriate among chosen market segments, and what strategy will be used to secure it?

DISCUSSION TOPICS

1   What is the significance to the marketer of the heavy user?

2   Suggest a marketing strategy to convert nonusers of the following goods and services into users: (*a*) cancer detection checkups for women aged 40 to 50; (*b*) bus, mass-transit, and carpools for geting to work; (*c*) unit price information in a supermarket; (*d*) a symphony series; (*e*) paper towels; and (*f*) home permanents.

3   Determine the primary benefits that might be sought by consumers of the following products: (*a*) hair coloring, (*b*) mouthwash, (*c*) barbecue grill, (*d*) compact car, and (*e*) bread.

4   How is lifestyle segmentation useful to developing promotion campaigns?

5   For the following goods and services, suggest an appropriate segmentation strategy: (*a*) a dinner theater in a medium-sized city, (*b*) a church on campus, (*c*) your university, (*d*) sailboats, (*e*) coffee, and (*f*) *Cosmopolitan* magazine. How would you determine the size and behavioral attributes of the segments? What marketing strategy might be appropriate?

6   Attempt to determine how each of the following products is positioned: (*a*) Apple personal computer, (*b*) Radio Shack color computer, (*c*) Kodak films, (*d*) Wrangler jeans, (*e*) Calvin Klein jeans, (*f*) Sony radios and TVs, and (*g*) General Electric radios and TVs.

PROJECTS

1 Find three advertisements of products segmented on a lifestyle basis and describe the lifestyle portrayed.

2 Select a product category and find three advertisements directed at different benefit segments. Explain how the benefits are depicted in the ad.

NOTES

[1] Betsy Sharkey, "Will Today's Auto Marketing Go the Way of Model T?" *Adweek,* February 25, 1985, p. 6; and "Why You're Driven to Buy That Special Car," *USA Weekend,* October 18–20, 1985, p. 18.

[2] William Lazer, "Life Style Concepts and Marketing," in Stephen Greyser (ed.), *Toward Scientific Marketing,* American Marketing Association, Chicago, 1963, p. 130.

[3] Harper W. Boyd, Jr., and Sidney J. Levy, *Promotion: A Behavioral View,* Prentice-Hall, Englewood Cliffs, N.J., 1967, p. 38.

[4] W. Thomas Anderson, Jr., and Linda L. Golden, "Lifestyle and Psychographics: A Critical Review and Recommendation," in Thomas Kinnear (ed.), *Advances in Consumer Research,* vol. 11, Association for Consumer Research, Provo, Utah, 1984, pp. 405–411.

[5] Fred D. Reynolds and William R. Darden, "An Operational Construction of Life Style," in M. Venkatesan (ed.), *Proceedings of the Annual Conference of the Association for Consumer Research,* 1972, p. 482.

[6] Alvin C. Burns and Mary Carolyn Harrison, "A Test of the Reliability of Psychographics," *Journal of Marketing Research,* **16**:32–38, February 1979.

[7] Joseph T. Plummer, "The Concept and Application of Life Style Segmentation," *Journal of Marketing,* **38**:33, January 1974; and Philip Meyer, "The ABC's of Psychographics," *American Demographics,* November 1983, p. 25.

[8] Reprinted from Joseph T. Plummer, "Life Style and Advertising: Case Studies," in Fred Allvine (ed.), *AMA Proceedings 1971 Conference,* American Marketing Association, Chicago, 1971, p. 291.

[9] William D. Wells and Douglas J. Tigert, "Activities, Interests and Opinions," *Journal of Advertising Research,* **11**:31, August 1971.

[10] Plummer, "Life Style and Advertising," p. 291.

[11] Plummer, "The Concept and Application of Life Style," pp. 35–36.

[12] This section is based on Sunil Mehrotra and William D. Wells, "Psychographics and Buyer Behavior: Theory and Recent Empirical Findings," in Arch G. Woodside, Jagdish N. Sheth, and Peter D. Bennett (eds.), *Consumer and Industrial Buying Behavior,* Elsevier North-Holland, New York, 1977, pp. 49–65; and William D. Wells, "Psychographics: A Critical Review," *Journal of Marketing Research,* **12**:196–213, May 1975.

[13] Peter W. Bernstein, "Psychographics Is Still an Issue on Madison Avenue," *Fortune,* **97**:78–80, January 16, 1978.

[14] Mehrotra and Wells, "Psychographics and Buyer Behavior," p. 53.

[15] Mehrotra and Wells, "Psychographics and Buyer Behavior," p. 53.

[16] Mehrotra and Wells, "Psychographics and Buyer Behavior," p. 56.

[17] Mehrotra and Wells, "Psychographics and Buyer Behavior," p. 57.

[18] "How Colgate Brand Manager Applied Psychos to Market and Media for Irish Spring," *Media Decisions,* December 1976, pp. 70–71, 104, 106.

[19] Leon G. Schiffman and Michael D. Jones, "Four Case Histories: The Reality of Psychographic Segmentation in the Marketing Mix," *Marketing Review,* December 1982–January 1983, pp. 27–28.

[20] William L. Wilkie and Joel B. Cohen, "An Overview of Market Segmentation: Behavioral Concepts and Research Approaches," *Marketing Science Institute Working Paper,* June 1977.

[21] Plummer, "Life Style and Advertising," pp. 292, 294.

[22] Reprinted from Plummer, "Life Style and Advertising," p. 292, published by the American Marketing Association.

[23] Jacques Neher, "What Went Wrong," *Advertising Age*, April 13, 1981, pp. 61–64; and "Lost at Sea," *Advertising Age*, April 20, 1981, pp. 49–52.

[24] Plummer, "The Concept and Application of Life Style," pp. 36–37.

[25] Wells, "Psychographics: A Critical Review," p. 209.

[26] "Ad Creatives Need Relevant, Honest Attitudinal Data from Researchers," *Marketing News*, May 15, 1981, p. 3.

[27] Kenneth E. Miller and Kent L. Granzin, "Simultaneous Loyalty and Benefit Segmentation of Retail Store Customers," *Journal of Retailing*, 55:47–60, Spring 1979.

[28] Robert C. Blattberg, Thomas Buesing, and Subrata K. Sen, "Segmentation Strategies for New National Brands," *Journal of Marketing*, 44:59–67, Fall 1980.

[29] "Quaker Oats Life Cereal (A)," Harvard Business School Case M-220R, p. 26.

[30] Bernice Finkleman, "Ads Should Reinforce Current Users, Not Necessarily Convert Nonusers of Products," *Marketing News*, January 15, 1974, p. 1.

[31] Peter Dickson, "Person-Situation: Segmentation's Missing Link," *Journal of Marketing*, 46:56–64, Fall 1982.

[32] "A Variety of Lodging 'Brands' Enables Holiday Inns to Cater to Independent-Minded People," *Marketing News*, October 25, 1985, p. 29.

[33] Russell W. Belk, "An Explanatory Assessment of Situational Effects in Buyer Behavior," *Journal of Marketing Research*, 11:156–163, May 1974; and Russell W. Belk, "Situational Variables and Consumer Behavior," *Journal of Consumer Research*, 2:157–164, December 1975.

[34] Russell I. Haley, "Benefit Segmentation: A Decision-Oriented Research Tool," *Journal of Marketing*, 32:31, July 1968.

[35] Russell I. Haley, "Benefit Segmentation—20 Years Later," *Journal of Consumer Marketing*, 1:6, No. 2, 1984.

[36] Russell I. Haley, "Benefit Segments: Backwards and Forwards," *Journal of Advertising Research*, 24:21, February/March 1984.

[37] William R. Swinyard and Kenneth D. Struman, "Market Segmentation: Finding the Heart of your Restaurant's Market," *The Cornell Hotel and Restaurant Administration Quarterly*, May 1986, p. 96.

[38] Wilkie and Cohen, "An Overview. . . ."

[39] Reprinted from Shirley Young, Leland Ott, and Barbara Feigin, "Some Practical Considerations in Market Segmentation," *Journal of Marketing Research*, 15:405, August 1978, published by the American Marketing Association.

[40] Robert S. Wheeler, "Marketing Tales with a Moral," *Product Marketing*, April 1977, p. 42.

[41] Vithala R. Rao and Frederick W. Winter, "An Application of the Multivariate Profit Model to Market Segmentation and Product Design," *Journal of Marketing Research*, 15:361–368, August 1978; and Allan D. Shocker and V. Srinivasan, "Multiattribute Approaches for Product Concept Evaluation and Generation: A Critical Review," *Journal of Marketing Research*, 16:159–180, May 1979.

[42] E. E. Norris, "Your Surefire Clue to Ad Success: Seek Out the Consumer's Problem," *Advertising Age*, March 17, 1975, pp. 43–44.

[43] Laurel Leff, "As Competition in Radio Grows, Stations Tailor Programs for Specific Audience," *The Wall Street Journal*, November 18, 1980, p. 48.

[44] This section is based on Yoram Wind, "Going to Market: New Twists for Some Old Tricks," *The Wharton Magazine*, vol. 4, no. 3, 1980; and David A. Aaker and J. Gary Shansby, "Positioning Your Product," *Business Horizons*, May–June 1982, pp. 56–62.

[45] Paul Brown, "Forget Satisfying the Consumer—Just Outfox the Other Guy," *Business Week*, October 7, 1985, p. 55.

[46] Jack Trout and Al Ries, "The Positioning Era: A View Ten Years Later," *Advertising Age*, July 16, 1979, p. 40.

[47] Virginia Miles, "Research Is Key in Changing Your Brand Strategy," *Advertising Age*, July 12, 1976, p. 39.

[48] William D. Wells, "Life Style and Psychographics: Definitions, Uses and Problems," in William D. Wells (ed.), *Life Style and Psychographics*, American Marketing Association, Chicago, 1974, pp. 322–325.

[49] John Koten, "Car Makers Use Image Map as Tool to Position Products," *The Wall Street Journal*, March 22, 1984, p. 33.

[50] Nariman K. Dhalla and Winston H. Mahatoo, "Expanding the Scope of Segmentation Research," *Journal of Marketing,* **40**:34–41, April 1976.

[51] "Segmentation Strategies Create New Pressure Among Marketers," *Marketing News,* March 28, 1986, p. 1.

[52] James F. Engel, Henry Fiorillo, and Murray A. Cayley (eds.), *Market Segmentation: Concepts and Applications,* Holt, New York, 1972, pp. 459–465.

CASES FOR PART TWO

CASE 2-1
LADY INDIAN BASKETBALL*

Benny Hollis, Athletic Director at Northeast Louisiana University (NLU), was very interested in the results of a survey he had just received. The research had been conducted by his staff in response to his request for information about the women's basketball program at the university. Although the team was becoming very successful, growth in fan attendance was lagging behind. Hollis hoped that the results of a survey to find out what type of person attends women's basketball games might be used to develop a better program for marketing the sport at NLU.

The Lady Indians were gaining much success. They were undefeated in the 1982–83 season in Southland Conference play. In the same season they were ranked among the top twenty teams in the nation in four of the eight team-statistics categories compiled by the NCAA, and they were third in the nation in scoring. However, Hollis was not sure that they had been adequately marketed to the relevant groups of fans who might be attracted. This was true not only at NLU, but also around the country as women's sports were just beginning to grow.

Hollis believed the greatest return for the cost, at that time, was to be found in the promotion of women's basketball. The quality of competition and the level of interest had increased to the point that if the sport were effectively marketed, it could have a significant impact on university athletic income. Additionally, most conferences, including the Southland Conference, had now incorporated women's programs into their conference structures, thus enhancing image

and interest. Most of these changes had occurred in just the past three to five years.

It was also apparent to Hollis that there was tremendous room for attendance growth in women's basketball. For instance, the average attendance for all NCAA Division I women's basketball games (excluding doubleheaders with men) was only 555—up 9.25 percent over the previous year. Yet, a few teams did better: Louisiana Tech (located 30 miles from NLU), Iowa, and Southern California averaged 5285, 3381, and 3159, respectively, during their seasons. NLU averaged only 2441 at home for the season. However, as recently as five years before, a crowd of 200 was considered good.

Although the potential for increased attendance appeared to be present, Hollis realized that women's basketball had to be properly marketed. Before an effective marketing plan could be developed, however, the market for women's basketball had to be defined and selected. Then a marketing program could be assembled to attract this target market. Thus, the sports information department planned a survey aimed at learning some things about women's collegiate basketball fans to help establish appropriate marketing strategies.

A questionnaire was developed to administer to patrons at one of the well-attended games during the season. The single-page, two-sided questionnaire was designed to obtain general demographic information as well as to gauge what attracts women's fans to the game.

The questionnaire was distributed at the home game between the NLU women and Louisiana Tech University. Almost everyone entering the arena was offered a questionnaire to complete for usher pickup at half time. To assure maximum participation, a pencil was supplied with each questionnaire. A total of 2200 questionnaires were distributed and 717 were returned. Questionnaires completed by half time were collected by ushers; those not completed by half time could be deposited in boxes provided at all exits.

The questionnaires for nonstudents were tabulated and summarized as shown in Table 1. All responses are expressed as percentages. As Hollis evaluated the responses, he now had the challenging job of interpreting their meaning for the future marketing direction of the Lady Indian basketball program.

---

*This case was prepared by David Loudon, C. W. McConkey, and Maynard M. Dolecheck, all of Northeast Louisiana University. Copyright © 1986 by David Loudon, C. W. McConkey, and Maynard M. Dolecheck. Reprinted with permission.

TABLE 1

Dear Fan:

To learn more about the growing interest in *women's* college basketball please help us by completing this questionnaire. It will take you less than 10 minutes to complete . . . *Thank you*.

SECTION 1

For *each* of the statements below, *circle* the number that best describes how much you *agree* with that statement. Please give careful thought to each of the statements.

TABLE 1 *(Continued)*

	Strongly disagree	Disagree	Neither	Agree	Strongly agree
1. *Women's* basketball should be the preliminary game to the *men's* game so the fans can view two games for a single admission.	11.5	22.6	11.7	24.4	29.9
2. Sufficient tax dollars should be spent on athletics to produce a winning program.	9.2	14.8	14.4	34.2	27.5
3. *Women's* basketball is more entertaining that *men's* basketball because it displays more finesse than physical dominance.	6.8	19.5	33.0	19.9	20.8
4. I select basketball games to attend on the basis of the reputation and ranking of the visiting team.	11.7	22.1	23.4	30.4	12.5
5. *Women's* basketball is one of the best entertainment values available.	2.9	7.3	18.8	45.4	25.6
6. I attend *women's* basketball because of the urging of my spouse or children.	24.2	21.9	42.5	7.5	4.0
7. I usually attend *women's* basketball games with a friend or neighbor.	6.7	7.0	30.5	38.7	17.1
8. I am personally acquainted with one or more players in tonight's game.	18.6	17.6	38.7	14.7	10.4
9. I would be inclined to attend more *women's* basketball games when my team is ranked nationally.	6.5	14.1	15.0	33.5	31.0
10. I listen to the away games on the radio when I an unable to attend.	9.1	17.1	19.5	34.3	20.0
11. I enjoy participation in recreational activity.	2.9	5.9	8.2	42.2	40.8
12. Special event nights (such as T-shirt night) are important to my attending *women's* basketball.	22.3	29.5	32.6	9.7	5.9
13. Quality education is more important for *women* athletes because of the lack of professional sports opportunities.	7.6	12.7	14.6	34.2	30.8
14. A successful athletic program is important for a positive University image in the community.	3.6	5.3	6.8	35.5	49.0

SECTION 2

Please supply the following information by either filling in the blanks or circling the number of the appropriate reply:

1. *Sex:* 1. Male 2. Female
   50.1 49.9
2. *Marital status:* 1. Single 22.3 2. Married 77.7
3. *Number of children:* 0 1 2 3 4 5 or more
   24.2 17.7 32.3 18.3 9.2 3.5
4. The age of my youngest child is _____.
   Under 6 18.6 7–14 25.4 15–19 19.1 20 or more 36.8
5. *Education:* (highest level of education attained):
   1. Grade School 0.2 2. High School 20.8 3. Vo-Tech 3.0 4. Attended College 28.5 5. College Graduate 47.4
6. My age is _____.
   Under 25 11.5 25–34 21.3 35–44 30.2
   45–54 20.9 55–59 5.6 60 and over 10.5
7. *Race:* 1. Black 2. White 3. Other
   3.0 96.8 0.2
8. *Employment status:*
   1. Retired 7.0 2. Home-maker 8.9 3. Self-employed 12.3 4. Employed (not self) 50.9 5. Student 20.9
9. I have attended the following universities:
   1. NLU 2. Tech 3. Other 4. Both
   51.5 18.3 20.8 9.4
10. I am a graduate of the following university:
    1. NLU 2. Tech 3. Other 4. Both
    47.2 26.4 25.3 1.1
11. My children have attended the following universities:
    1. NLU 2. Tech 3. Other 4. Both
    51.7 17.4 20.8 10.2
12. Circle all of the following that describe you:
    1. College Athletic Club Member 16.7 2. College Alumni Association Member 23.7 3. Civic Club Member 21.8
    4. Country/Tennis Club Member 15.0 5. Fitness Club Member 17.6 6. Union Member 5.1

TABLE 1 *(Continued)*

13. How many miles have you traveled to see tonight's game?
    1. 10 or less   2. 11–20   3. 21–50   4. More than 50
        45.1   11.5   22.9   20.5
14. How many *women's* basketball games will you attend this season? _____.
    0–1 14.6   2–5 39.5   6–10 21.7   11 or over 26.2
15. How many *men's* basketball games will you attend this season? _____.
    0 27.5   1 8.0   2–5 29.9   6–10 12.4   11 or over 22.2
16. My interest in *women's* basketball started when I was exposed via
    1. Newspaper 13.5   2. T.V. 12.9   3. Radio 3.2   4. Game Attendance 51.4   5. Discussion of friends 19.0
17. For sports information, I depend on:
    6.2 KTVE-TV   1.1 Quachita Citizen   51.7 KNOE-TV   2.8 Ruston News Leader
    0.8 KARD-TV   29.2 Monroe News-Star World   1.9 KNLU radio   6.3 Word of Mouth
18. Which radio format do you listen to most often?
    1. Country   2. Soft rock   3. Hard rock   4. Easy listening
        46.1   21.4   4.4   28.1
19. Other than basketball, which *women's* sport would you most enjoy viewing?
    1. Softball   2. Tennis   3. Swimming   4. Track   5. Volleyball
        40.0   23.7   10.8   13.6   12.0
20. Do you plan to attend the NLU vs. Tech *men's* basketball game on Feb. 9?
    1. Yes   2. No   3. Undecided
        41.1   32.6   26.2
21. Which team are you "rooting" for tonight?
    1. Tech   2. NLU
        27.5   72.5

Please pass the completed questionnaire to the end of the row for collection as instructed by the public address announcer. . . . Thank you.

Questions

1 Evaluate the research project conducted to improve attendance at Lady Indian basketball games.
2 Suggest a marketing strategy for Hollis based on the results of the Lady Indian survey.
3 What additional consumer behavior research and information would be helpful to Hollis?

CASE 2-2
CIRCLE K CORPORATION*

INDUSTRY BACKGROUND

The convenience store industry has been the retail sector with the best growth record in the 1980s, hitting $55 billion dollars in sales in 1985 compared to less than $6 billion in 1975. Approximately 36 million people shop in this country's

58,000 convenience stores (c-stores) daily, and the industry is expected to double in size over the next fifteen years. Convenience stores are generally defined as small (1200 to 3000 square feet) retail outlets offering staple groceries and snacks quickly and conveniently. Convenience stores generally open early and close late—if they close at all—and are located along heavily traveled streets and intersections. Consumers are drawn to them because there are no long lines, crowded parking lots, or out-of-the-way locations. Convenience stores have assumed some of the characteristics of the old general store. Some experts see c-stores evolving into compact centers for neighborhood activity. The 3500 c-stores nationwide in 1962 expanded to over 11,600 by 1970.

Convenience stores began as a response to four suburban phenomena: (1) the growth of the supermarket (and the growing inconvenience of shopping at such large stores), (2) the establishment of suburban shopping centers which concentrated retail facilities along major thoroughfares, (3) the decline of "mom-and-pop" grocery stores which left neighborhoods without local food stores, and (4) the desire to save personal time because of greater time being spent driving to and from work.

Convenience stores have been dependent upon the automobile and developed first in mild-climate areas where the

*Jeremy Schlosberg, "The Demographics of Convenience Stores," *American Demographics,* October 1986, pp. 36–42; Jennifer Pendleton, "Circle K Aiming for Tops in Convenience," *Advertising Age,* April 2, 1984, pp. 4, 55; Lisa Tubernick, "Stores for Our Times," *Forbes,* November 3, 1986, pp. 40–42; and Faye Brookman, "Convenience Outlets Expanding Customer Base," *Advertising Age,* April 18, 1985, pp. 36–39.

population was most mobile (see Table 1). Today convenience stores are concentrated primarily in the warm weather states of the south and southwest. In cold weather climates people tend to avoid venturing out for one or two items, particularly late at night, and in the snow. In addition, significant tourist traffic leads to c-store success. Consequently c-stores have done well in Florida. When people travel, price is not important, their shopping habits become unstructured.

Convenience stores have attracted a customer base of largely blue-collar men aged 18 to 34. A recent Gallup report done for the National Association of Convenience Stores (NACS) found that 43 percent of the c-store customers surveyed had blue-collar jobs, while only 30 percent had white-collar jobs. Thirty-four percent of the convenience store customers surveyed in the NACS study were from one- and two-person households. The Gallup report also showed that the women's share of convenience store customers in 1985 was no greater than in the previous two years. Thus, the industry has not yet attracted working women or upscale customers. Table 2 summarizes some of the characteristics of convenience-store customers.

If the 11 percent of customers who are infrequent shoppers could be attracted to come in about twice a month, it would result in 1200 more visits, or $29,000 added revenue per outlet (beyond the $500,000 business an average 4000 square foot unit does each year). Women make up two-thirds of those who do not frequent convenience stores.

Observers blame this inability to attract certain segments on an image that may be out of date. For some people, c-stores have had a stereotyped image of being purveyors of last-minute party supplies and snacks. Others have shied away from patronizing c-stores because of their image of having a crime problem. Over 50 percent of all c-stores are open twenty-four hours in order to meet changing work and shopping schedules. Because they are open late hours or around the clock and have some cash in the drawer, they have attracted more than their share of violent crime, which has frightened away potential customers, making them still mostly male. Some potential shoppers have viewed the stores

TABLE 1

The south and southwest have the greatest concentration of convenience stores while states in the midwest have the lowest concentration.

Where the Stores Are, and Aren't (Number of households per convenience store)

	Households per c-store
Eight most saturated markets:	
Oklahoma	985
Florida	1183
Texas	1213
South Carolina	1252
New Mexico	1335
Georgia	1363
Mississippi	1377
Tennessee	1560
Eight least saturated markets:	
New York	6389
Illinois	5002
California	3936
Michigan	3528
Indiana	3185
Wisconsin	3157
Washington	3060
Missouri	3003

Source: Alex, Brown & Son, Inc., June 1985. From Jeremy Schlosberg, "The Demographics of Convenience," *American Demographics,* October 1986, p. 39.

as being dirty. Another image problem has been the view that c-stores have high prices. A final problem has been lack of employee service to patrons.

To attract the desired clientele of infrequent shoppers, stores are adding such things as more fast foods, including freshly prepared dishes, more health and beauty products, and better services.

C-stores were traditionally mainly in competition with food stores, and today they are giving both supermarkets and other food stores strong competition. C-stores now account for 8 percent of total food dollars spent compared with only 3.8 percent a decade ago. It is predicted that their sales increase will outpace other food retailers through 1987. They are slowly changing food shopping patterns. In 1980, over one-half of consumers shopped for groceries in conventional supermarkets. But by 1984, because many consumers had switched to superstores and convenience stores, the number was down to 39.2 percent and has fallen still further since.

Drug chains are another competitor for convenience stores. Drug chains have been enlarging their convenience food selections. For example, one chain now has a 1000-square-foot section offering 800 of the most wanted items. Oil companies are also competing with convenience stores as they have opened their own versions of them. Likewise, c-stores have bought out many of the old full-service gas stations in prime locations and have added more self-service gas pumps and a variety of other merchandise.

One of the important new products to be added by convenience stores is fast food. Although c-stores average a 30 percent gross profit margin, fast food produces a margin as high as 60 percent. And stores are adding everything from French bread pizza to hamburgers for microwaving. Thus fast food is the biggest growth segment in the industry. C-stores are now even bringing threats to the Golden Arches as they begin selling hamburgers. A growing number of c-stores are

TABLE 2

Customers of Convenience
(Customers of convenience stores in a given day, in percent)

Convenience-store customers are likely to be men aged 18 to 34.

	C-store customers	U.S. population
Sex:		
Male	57%	48%
Female	43	52
Age:		
18 to 24	21%	15%
25 to 34	31	24
35 to 49	25	25
50+	23	35
Education:		
Less than high school	19%	18%
High school graduate	62	60
College	19	22
Annual household income:		
< $10,000	14%	13%
$10,000 to $14,999	11	10
$15,000 to $19,999	12	10
$20,000+	48	48
Unknown	15	19
Race:		
White	83%	87%
Nonwhite	17	13

Source: The Gallup Organization, December 1985, for the period of January to June 1985. Jeremy Schlosberg, "The Demographics of Convenience," *American Demographics*, October 1986, p. 38.

providing sit-down room in their stores for fast-food customers. Nevertheless, a recent NACS study indicated that fast food has not yet attracted new types of customers in any important, industry-wide way. Except for buyers of single beverages and coffee or tea, fast-food patrons in c-stores are largely blue-collar workers or students. Households with low incomes (under $15,000) tend to be average or slightly above average purchasers of the fast foods.

Another significant new product carried by convenience stores is videocassettes for rent. The benefit of videocassette rental is that customers must come in at least two times—once to rent and another to return. One report shows that in addition to video rental, these customers are spending about $8 on the first visit and $3 on the second, which is considerably higher than the average convenience store transaction of around $2.

Although the convenience store industry has national trend data, it lacks local trend information. This is a problem for an industry in which individual retail units cater to households within a mile of their location. Doing something with such information—if it were available—is another matter, however. C-store chains, like most other national chains, require member stores to standardize from location to location—which doesn't always make sense, even within the same town.

CIRCLE K CORPORATION

Broadly, it appears that convenience stores offer an undifferentiated product because of all the copying that goes on when one chain finds something that is successful. But the strategic implementation of these things varies widely among the companies. Generally, convenience stores offer just what the name implies—convenience. Whatever can be sold through the massive distribution system will be tried.

At a Circle K store in downtown Phoenix you can use an automated teller machine to get $100 from your bank account, buy groceries, get a roast beef sandwich, pick up a Dunkin' Donut, rent the latest videocassette, fill your gas tank, and charge it all to your bank debit card.

Circle K now owns 3435 stores and is in a distant second place behind the 7-Eleven chain of 8200 stores. But Circle K believes it can outperform its larger rival, 7-Eleven, by providing more and better services. When Circle K was acquired by its chairman, Karl Eller, it was a company good in systems but not so good in marketing. When Eller took over, the chain:

■ Began marketing research to identify its customer base and understand public attitudes about c-stores, generally, and Circle K in particular. Many respondents, particularly women, said they avoided c-stores because they believed they were dark, cluttered, and carried high-priced merchandise.

■ Remodeled stores to give them better lighting, cleaner and brighter interiors, and improved shelf placements and walk-in spaces. Exteriors were repainted from red, white, and green to a lively red, orange, and purple. Employee uniforms adopted the same color scheme.

■ Upgraded and merchandised fast-food products. In 1984 Circle K had gas pumps at 60 percent of its stores, making it the largest single item the company sold, accounting for 38.4 percent of actual sales. But with its new emphasis, fast-food sales were projected to rise from 8 percent of Circle K's business to 15 percent within five years. Circle K now carries twenty-two items of fast food, including a variety of sandwiches, Mexican food, and breakfast items. Its new fast food products are said to be among the most important offerings in Circle K stores. The items are geared toward the types of people Circle K wants to attract. For example, the chain has introduced a low-calorie sandwich line aimed directly at working women. In addition, Circle K is placing Hooker's hamburgers franchises next to some outlets in order to serve the fast-food market.

■ Expanded international operations. Franchises were added in Hong Kong, Singapore, Australia, and Malaysia, on top of the 126 stores already open in Japan.

■ Launched a new TV, print, and radio advertising campaign with the theme, "We'll save you time." This was the element research had shown was the single most important reason people shop at convenience stores. Customers do not feel much loyalty about convenience stores. They will pay higher prices to save time.

■ Also quickly launched a videotape rental program, renting tapes on weekdays for 99 cents and on weekends for $1.99. Circle K's research showed that 55 percent of tape rentals were to new customers and that 45 percent were to women.

Eller is bullish on the convenience store business and intends for the Circle K chain to become a major retailing force that will eventually challenge 7-Eleven as the world's premier convenience store company.

Questions

1 What demographic changes have affected the rapid growth of convenience stores?

2 What consumer benefits are relevant to the success of c-stores?

3 Evaluate the characteristics of the c-store approach as a shopping innovation which will affect its spread and success.

4 Evaluate the marketing strategy of Circle K corporation.

CASE 2-3
THE NUTRITION-CONSCIOUS CONSUMER*

The popular press and marketing publications abound with articles about the new health-conscious consumer and the profound effect she will have on the food industry. Here are just a few of the headlines:

GOOD NUTRITION IS POSITIVE FALLOUT FROM FITNESS CRAZE

MARKETERS FEED ON HEALTH-NUTRITION TREND

FIRM EXPLORES SNACK MARKET CHANGES AS CONSUMERS LOOK FOR HEALTHY FOODS

NUTRITION KEY FACTOR IN FOOD TRENDS

The picture one gets of the "new consumer" is that of a modern, physically fit young woman who is knowledgeable about nutrition and carefully monitors the amount of fiber, cholesterol, salt, sugar, calories, and additives in the foods she eats and serves her family.

Food manufacturers have been quick to respond with new health-oriented products that are designed, positioned, and advertised with this picture of the health-conscious consumer in mind. In order to determine whether this is an accurate picture of the health-conscious consumer, and whether health and nutrition concerns are the primary forces behind consumer purchase patterns, a food attitude segmentation study was conducted by DDB Needham Worldwide, Inc. The survey used a representative sample of 2000 married women from the Market Facts mail panel. The results of the study are based on the replies of 1730 respondents representing a return rate of 86 percent.

A food attitude segmentation was carried out based on cluster analysis of thirty separate food-related items found by factor analysis to be representative of ten food attitude areas (food concerns, cooking attitudes, scratch cooking, brand loyalty, fast food interest, price sensitivity, new product interest, meal consumption, and overeating).

The segmentation analysis produced three groups, each with a distinctive pattern of food-related attitudes, behaviors, and values.

*Kay L. Satow, "The Nutrition Conscious Consumer: A Segmentation Approach," in David W. Stewart (ed.), *Proceedings of the Division of Consumer Psychology, 1984 Annual Convention of the American Psychological Association, Division of Consumer Psychology,* San Antonio, 1985, pp. 25–26. Reprinted with permission.

HELEN THE HEALTH-CONSCIOUS CONSUMER (57 PERCENT)
Helen is the most concerned about healthful eating. She carefully monitors her intake of sugar, salt, cholesterol, fiber, additives, and calories. And, she eats breakfast, lunch, and dinner every day. She is a name brand buyer who believes that a known name is a guarantee of high quality.

By far the oldest of the three (45 percent are 50 or older), Helen's food concerns are probably due in large part to age-related medical considerations. And because she is older, she is least likely to have children at home.

CONNIE THE CONVENIENCE FOOD FAN (20 PERCENT)
Connie is the heaviest user of convenience foods and fast food. With the exception of items like layer cake mixes, which are closer to baking from scratch, Connie is most likely to use a wide variety of mixes, ready-to-eat, and frozen convenience foods. She is also the heavy user of fast food.

Connie's reliance on convenience foods is explained, in part, by her hectic lifestyle. She is most likely to work outside the home and to feel pressed for time. Meals in her household tend to be eaten on an irregular schedule. Yet another reason for her reliance on convenience foods is the fact that she dislikes cooking and baking and is least likely to hold traditional attitudes towards woman's role in the kitchen.

Connie has the poorest eating habits of the three. She skips breakfast and sometimes lunch as well, then eats snack foods to make up for it. She is least concerned of the three about food ingredients. Salt, sugar, cholesterol, fiber, caffeine, additives, and calories are all relatively unimportant considerations in her choice of foods to eat and serve her family.

The most upscale of the three, Connie is not a price shopper or brand-loyal consumer, but rather tends to be an impulse buyer. If a product appeals to her, she will buy it without worrying much about the price, the brand name, or the ingredients.

SUSAN THE SCRATCH COOK (23 PERCENT)
Susan is characterized by her cooking and baking from scratch. One explanation for her involvement in the kitchen is her enjoyment of cooking and baking activities. Another is her desire to cut costs.

Susan is a careful, controlled shopper, unlikely to spend more for fancy packaging or for added convenience and she is least likely to be among the first to try a new product. She has the largest family of the three segments.

Questions

1 What do the study results suggest for food manufacturers, particularly for their product and advertising decisions?

2 What additional information would be helpful?

THE PERFORMING ARTS MARKET*

The fundamental marketing goal of any arts organization is to make its offerings more responsive to the needs of the various publics it serves. However, it has been suggested that performing artists often seek unquestioned acceptance of their "new products" by audiences, and they fail to adequately consider the reasons that individuals might attend their performances. Although the use of market research by performing arts organizations has increased sharply in recent years, many of the studies have limited their definitions of arts audiences to attendance patterns or demographic characteristics.

*Adapted from Margery Steinberg, George Miaoulis, and David Lloyd, "Benefit Segmentation Strategies for the Performing Arts," in Bruce J. Walker et al. (eds.) *An Assessment of Marketing Thought and Practice, 1982 Educators' Conference Proceedings,* American Marketing Association, Chicago, 1982, pp. 289–293. Reprinted with permission.

Benefit segmentation, an approach to identifying markets based on similarities among consumers with respect to purchase motives and preference patterns, has potential as a tool for designing effective marketing strategies and positioning for artistic programs. Combining a benefit-oriented analysis of segments with demographic and utilization data can give the arts administrator a more complete picture of target audiences for understanding arts consumption behavior and making artistic programming decisions. Benefit segmentation responds directly to the underlying purpose for conducting marketing research—to assist the arts community in the design and delivery of marketing programs which consider the needs and wants of various groups—by identifying benefits sought. Thus, benefit segmentation assists in developing fine-tuned strategies which relate the limited available marketing resources to potential audiences. Atten-

TABLE 1
Segmentation Grid for Arts Attenders

Name of segment	Segment #1 Cultural aspirants	Segment #2 Temporary diversion	Segment #3 Peak aesthetic experience
Benefits sought	Enlightenment: cultural exposure Intellectual expansion Identification with the "Cognoscenti"	Passive entertainment: relaxation Noncognitive diversion A social medium An evening out	Emotional and intellectual involvement/stimulation Professional excellence; creativity and beauty
Category beliefs	Arts attendance helps provide the intellectual sophistication of the "cognoscenti" with whom I identify	Arts performances should offer entertainment and diversion, a relaxing atomsphere while enjoying the company of friends and family	Arts performances should offer a high level of artistic excellence and permit complete emotional and intellectual involvement
Preferred leisure activities	Reading, crafts, antiquing "Serious" arts performances felt to be attended by segment #3	Dining out, movies; skiing, biking, sightseeing Lighter arts performances	Crafts, sailing, reading, skiing, etc. "Professional" arts performances of particular merit
Participation	Frequent	Infrequent to moderate	Moderate to frequent
Occasions of participation	Evenings, weekends—whenever programs offered	Predominantly weekends	Evenings, weekends: performances and activities of special interest
Media habits	Printed media: Local/national newspapers Posters, mailers, handbills	Printed media: Local newspapers, posters and handbills Broadcast Media: Moderate TV and radio	Printed media: Local/national newspapers Posters, mailers, handbills Broadcast Media: Light TV and radio
Personality/ lifestyle	Other-directed Impressionable	Other-oriented and socially active	Sophisticated and well educated Inner-directed Socially active
Demographics	Age: Younger, 21–35 College education Beginning professional career	Age: 25–49 High school or some college education Income: $10–15,000	Sophisticates of all ages College educated, professional Income: $15,000 and over

dance patterns, subscription purchases, and contribution behaviors can all be related to benefits sought.

In order to demonstrate the linkage between benefit-oriented market segmentation and the development of marketing strategies for the performing arts, research was performed in rural New Hampshire and in Dayton, Ohio. The goal of the research was to identify benefit segments for the performing arts and to recommend marketing strategies for

the achievement of four main objectives of arts organizations. These objectives are:

1 To increase awareness of arts programs and the potential benefits they offer to the community.
2 To clarify misconceptions about the arts, particularly on the part of nonattenders, and induce trial attendance.
3 To increase overall attendance at arts programs.
4 To increase support of current funding sources and attract new contributors.

The research process employed to identify benefit segments

TABLE 2
Segmentation Grid for Arts Nonattenders

Name of segment	Segment #1 Security seeker	Segment #2 Hedonist	Segment #3 Pragmatist	Segment #4 Children-oriented
Benefits sought	Relaxation, security of family and friends Peer approval To feel at ease	Entertainment Excitement Action	Convenience Diversion Feeling of productivity and involvement	Upward mobility for children; well-rounded education for children
Category beliefs	Arts are designed for more sophisticated group Would feel insecure, uncomfortable and out of place	Arts are too formal, serious, and passive	Arts are for snobbish, nonactive people Don't understand or relate to arts—find them boring, uninteresting	Children should have the educational and social opportunities needed for a successful life
Preferred leisure activities	Television, dining out, family outings Peer and family-oriented activities	Hunting, fishing, boating, sports, etc. Action-oriented activities	Gardening, hunting, woodworking, sewing Productive activities	Family activities: Outings, camping, sports, etc. Scouting, school clubs encouraged
Volume of activity involvement	Low to moderate	High	Moderate to high	Moderate to high
Occasions of leisure activity involvement	Weekends, holidays, vacations	Evenings, weekends, whenever possible	Evenings, weekends, vacations	Encouraged to become involved frequently
Media habits	Local newspapers Heavy radio and TV	Local/national newspapers, Moderate radio and TV, special interest magazines, posters	Local newspapers Low to moderate TV Special interest magazines Posters, mailers	Local newspapers Mailers Moderate radio and TV
Personality/ lifestyle	Reticent, insecure, conforming Oriented toward family and friends	Outgoing, active Fast-paced lifestyle	Practical, organized Family- and work-oriented	Conservative, practical, hardworking Family-oriented
Demographics	Age: 25–64; unskilled or semi-skilled High school education or less Income: Below average	Age: 25–49; technician, white collar High school or college education Income: Above average	Age: 35–64: tradesperson High school or technical school education Income: Above average	Age: 35–49; semi-skilled or clerical High school education Income: Average

involved 400 in-depth interviews, each approximately one-half hour in length, conducted over a one-month period with performing arts attenders and nonattenders (defined as during a given one-year period), adult men and women, in the Dayton, Ohio, MSA and the Monadnock Region of Southwestern New Hampshire. This sample design provided the opportunity to identify the (leisure time-related) benefits sought by a diverse actual and potential performing arts audience.

Seven benefit-oriented market segments were identified: three segments among performing arts attenders and four

among the nonattenders. Tables 1 and 2 present a detailed accounting of both the benefits sought and descriptive factors for each of the seven identified benefit segments.

Question

Suggest specific recommendations for strategy design in marketing the arts by relating the seven benefit-oriented segments to the four main objectives cited.

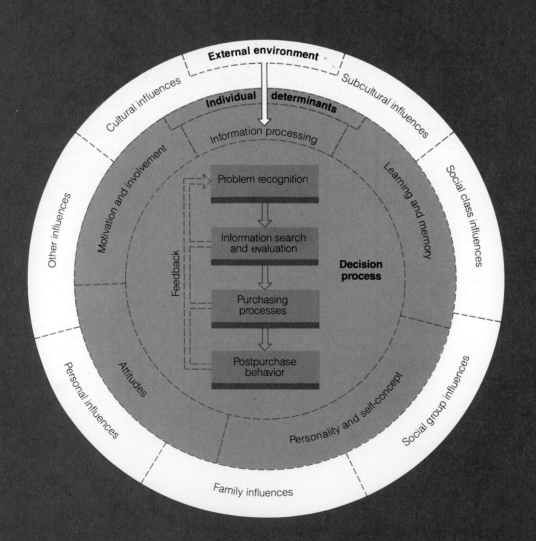

ENVIRONMENTAL INFLUENCES ON CONSUMER BEHAVIOR

CULTURE

LEARNING OBJECTIVES

After studying this chapter, you should understand . . .

■   The meaning of culture and its most important characteristics

■   The nature of cultural values in general, as well as the core values held by American consumers

■   That cultural values do influence consumer behavior

■   That because culture changes, marketers must monitor and be prepared to take advantage of these shifts

■   The importance of cross-cultural knowledge of consumer behavior in developing effective marketing programs internationally

It is 3:29 A.M. Harvey Reeves fell asleep over two hours ago, during David Letterman's second guest, and his television set is still on. The station is now signing off with the national anthem.

In a few hours, Harvey awakes to the sound of an electronic household alarm and, like millions of other individuals, performs a personal ritual that transports him from "the land of Nod" to the office. First, Harvey shuffles into the kitchen to start the coffee. Then he turns on the radio. In about ten minutes he's through with the newspaper and into the shower. Harvey is spending a little more time grooming these days and has just recently added a skin moisturizer to his morning routine. At 7:03 he turns on his phonemate, exits his apartment, and slips into his 300-ZX and onto the freeway. En route to work Harvey attends an early mass at St. Vincent's and afterwards mails a birthday card to his Aunt Helen.

At the office the morning is particularly trying because of interminable negotiations with a Japanese business team. The highly formal and slow-paced Japanese bargaining style is driving Harvey crazy. Lunch is a real snooze: a retirement luncheon for the head of the accounting department. Harvey's attention begins to wander. "What am I going to buy Mother for Christmas? Will we stay in town or go someplace? After an afternoon of formal personnel reviews, Harvey begins to think about his blind date tonight.

He meets Susan at the Red Onion for an early getting-to-know-you dinner; then they drive to the sports arena to drink beer, shake their pompons, shout "Defense! Defense!" for two hours, and watch the Los Angeles Clippers. Susan decides that Harvey is a bore, so the basketball game is followed by the awkward rituals of social disengagement.

Preparing for bed, Harvey does his fifty sit-ups, pumps some iron, and consumes a bowl of cereal with Johnny Carson. Across town, Susan sets her hair and her alarm clock, applies a facial mask, says her prayers, and falls asleep with Agatha Christie.[1]

6

We begin our study of environmental elements impinging upon consumers by first looking at the very broad, basic, and enduring factor of culture. The scenario above illustrates the pervasiveness in modern life of the ritual behavior which is an important part of our culture. The activities described are associated with various types of rituals: media, patriotic, household, grooming, religious, gift-giving, business, eating, rite of passage, holiday, romantic, athletic, and bedtime. Notice how such ritual behavior often also involves significant aspects of consumer behavior processes in obtaining goods and services, exchanging them, or using and disposing of them. Consumption has even been interpreted as the essential ritual of modern life.[2]

Ritual behavior is only one dimension of a culture. In this chapter we shall investigate the role and usefulness of cultural analysis in the development of marketing strategies. After defining and characterizing culture, the basic cultural values of American consumers shall be outlined. This will be followed by an examination of cultural change and its effect on consumer behavior. Finally, cross-cultural consumer behavior and its implications for international marketing will be discussed.

CULTURE DEFINED

It is difficult to present only one definition of culture and expect it to portray the richness of the field and its relevance to understanding consumers. However, the following two are representative:

That complex whole that includes knowledge, belief, art, morals, law, custom, and any other capabilities and habits acquired by man as a member of society[3]

The distinctive way of life of a group of people, their complete design for living[4]

Therefore, culture is everything that is socially learned and shared by the members of a society. Culture consists of material and nonmaterial components. Nonmaterial culture includes the words people use; the ideas, customs, and beliefs they share; and the habits they pursue. Material culture consists of all the physical substances that have been changed and used by people, such as tools, automobiles, roads, and farms. In a marketing and consumer behavior context, artifacts of the material culture would include all the products and services which are produced and consumed; marketing institutions such as Safeway supermarkets, K mart discount houses, and 7-11 convenience stores; and advertisements. Nonmaterial culture would include the way in which consumers shop in supermarkets, our desire for newer and better products, and our responses to the word "sale."

The significance of culture in understanding human behavior (of which consumer behavior is a subpart) is that it extends our understanding of the extent to which people are more than just chemistry, physiology, or a set of biological drives and instincts.[5] The implication is that although all customers may be biologically similar, their views of the world, what they value, and how they act differ according to their cultural backgrounds.

CULTURAL RELEVANCE TO MARKETING DECISIONS

It has long been recognized that culture influences consumers. For example, Duesenberry observed in 1949 that all of the activities in which people engage are culturally determined, and that nearly all purchases of goods are made either to provide physical comfort or to implement the activities that make up the life of a culture.[6] Thus, an understanding of culture enables the marketer to interpret the reaction of consumers to alternative marketing strategies. Sometimes guidance from *cultural anthropologists* (those social scientists who study people and their culture) is sought in order to gain a better understanding of the market.

Anthropologists are able to assist the marketer in understanding a number of cultural facets of behavior, such as the following:

National character, or the differences that distinguish one national group from another. These are the obvious as well as the more subtle cultural differences that distinguish Americans, Swedes, Germans, and Brazilians.

Differences in *subcultures* such as blacks, Jews, and Puerto Ricans.

The *silent language* of gesture, posture, food and drink preferences, and other nonverbal clues to behavior.

The significance of *symbols* in a society.

Taboos or prohibitions in a culture, relating to various things such as the use of a given color, phrase, or symbol.[7]

Ritualized activities in which people participate at home, work, or play, both as individuals and as members of a group. Such behavior is expressive and symbolic, occurs in a fixed episodic sequence, and tends to be repeated over time.[8] Rites of passage are ritual events marking significant points in a person's life as that person passes from one status to another, as in graduation, marriage, retirement, and death.

Anthropologists have also helped marketers recognize that consumer goods have a significant ability to carry and communicate cultural meaning. This occurs through a process in which cultural meaning is drawn from a particular cultural world and is transferred to a consumer good through advertising and the fashion system and then from these goods into the life of the individual consumer through certain consumption rituals.[9]

THE CHARACTERISTICS OF CULTURE

Although the definitions of culture presented earlier are excellent, they seek to characterize culture in only a few words. It is evident that the concept is difficult to convey clearly in any definition. As one writer notes, "It's like putting your hand in a cloud."[10] This section, therefore, will expand on these definitions by discussing the significant characteristics or features of culture. Many characteristics of culture may be cited to describe its nature, but most social scientists agree on the following features.

CULTURE IS INVENTED

Culture does not simply "exist" somewhere waiting to be discovered. People invent their culture. This invention consists of three interdependent systems or elements: (1) an *ideological system* or mental component that consists of the ideas, beliefs, values, and ways of reasoning that human beings learn to accept in defining what is desirable and undesirable; (2) a *technological system* that consists of the skills, crafts, and arts that enable humans to produce material goods derived from the natural environment; and (3) an *organizational system* (such as the family system and social class) that makes it possible for humans to coordinate their behavior effectively with the actions of others.[11]

CULTURE IS LEARNED

Culture is not innate or instinctive, but is learned early in life and charged with a good deal of emotion. The great strength of this cultural stamp handed down from one generation to another is such that at an early age, children are firmly imbued with their culture's ways of acting, thinking, and feeling. This obviously has important implications for the behavior of consumers, because these preconditions are molded by their culture from birth.

CULTURE IS PRESCRIPTIVE

Culture involves ideal standards or patterns of behavior so that members of society have a common understanding of the right and proper way to think, feel, and act in any given situation. Ideal patterns of behavior, thought, and feeling which groups share are termed *norms*. When actual behavior deviates from the ideal patterns, or norms, of society, *sanctions* are frequently taken. That is, certain types of pressures are brought to bear on deviant individuals so that they will conform their behavior to what society expects.

CULTURE IS SOCIALLY SHARED

Culture is a group phenomenon, shared by human beings living in organized societies and kept relatively uniform by social pressure. The group that is involved in this sharing may range from a whole society to a smaller unit such as a family.

CULTURES ARE SIMILAR BUT DIFFERENT

All cultures exhibit certain similarities. For example, each of the following elements is found in all societies: athletic sports, bodily adornment, a calendar, cooking, courtship, dancing, education, family, gestures, government, housing, language, law, music, religious ritual, and numerous other items. There is, however, great variation from society to society in the nature of each of these elements, which may result in important consumer behavior differences around the world.

CULTURE IS GRATIFYING AND PERSISTENT

Culture satisfies basic biological as well as learned needs. It consists of habits that will be strengthened and reinforced as long as those who practice them are gratified. Because of this gratification, cultural elements are handed down from

generation to generation. Thus, people are comfortable doing things in the customary way.

Our thorough inculcation of culture causes it to persist even when we are exposed to new cultures. No matter where we go or what we do, we cannot escape our cultural heritage. Its persistence means that change although not impossible, is often quite difficult because resistance to it may be strong.

CULTURE IS ADAPTIVE

In spite of our resistance to change, cultures are gradually and continuously changing. Some societies are quite static with a very slow rate of change, while others are more dynamic, with very rapid changes taking place.

CULTURE IS ORGANIZED AND INTEGRATED

A culture "hangs together"; that is, its parts fit together. Although every culture has some inconsistent elements, it tends to form a consistent and integrated whole.

CULTURAL VALUES

Cultural values are important to the organized and integrated nature of culture. A *cultural value* can be defined in a sociological perspective as "a widely held belief or sentiment that some activities, relationships, feelings, or goals are important to the community's identity or well-being."[12] In a psychological vein, Milton Rokeach defines values as centrally held and enduring beliefs which guide actions and judgments across specific situations and beyond immediate goals to more ultimate end-states of existence. Values, therefore, produce inclinations to respond to specific stimuli in standard ways.[13] That is, a specific behavior is expected to either help or hinder the attainment of some value or group of values. Consumers, then, are motivated to engage in behaviors designed to enhance the achievement of certain values and to avoid those behaviors which are perceived to hinder the attainment of certain value states.[14]

Chapter 16 will discuss the concept of attitudes and their relationship to consumer behavior. However, because there often is confusion over the concepts of attitude and value, it may be useful at this point to clarify these terms. Attitudes can be viewed as the individual's positive or negative evaluations of objects, situations, or behaviors, which predispose the individual to respond in some manner. Values, on the other hand, transcend specific objects and situations. They deal with modes of conduct (termed *instrumental values*) and end-states of existence (called *terminal values*). That is, an individual who has a "value" has an enduring belief that a particular mode of conduct or end-state of existence is preferable to some other mode of conduct or end-state of existence. Values serve as standards or criteria that tell us how to act, what to want, and what attitudes to hold, and they allow us to judge and compare ourselves with others. Compared to attitudes, which focus directly on specific objects, situations, or actions, values transcend specific circumstances. In addition, values act as standards or yardsticks guiding attitudes, actions, and evaluations of ourselves and others. Whereas individuals may possess thousands of attitudes, they are likely to possess less than a hundred values.[15]

Since values are culturally determined, this means that they are learned from social interaction, largely from our families and friends in settings such as schools and churches. Values strongly influence consumer behavior; even though the specific situation may dictate slightly different actions, overall there is much similarity in consumer behavior within a given culture, such as in tastes, methods of shopping, and so forth.

It is crucial for the marketer to understand society's basic value structure so that strategy decisions do not fly in the face of ingrained cultural patterns. It is much easier to harmonize with the culture than to attempt to change fundamental cultural values.

U.S. CULTURAL VALUES

Each culture has what may be termed *core values,* which are the dominant or basic cultural values that people accept with little question. In America, although values are not always obvious or easy to analyze, there are major patterns that can be identified. This is not to say that "American values" are exclusive to the United States, or that all Americans share them. However, the American value system is appreciably different from those of some other cultures, and most Americans do subscribe to the cultural pattern described below.

The following discussion of our cultural values may seem somewhat obvious to the reader, but this simply underscores the fact that Americans accept these values as "givens." The values to be discussed represent abstracted dominant themes which are ideal types, and thus may be subject to some exceptions.

Individualism This value is complex and closely interrelated with a number of other facets such as freedom, democracy, nationalism, and patriotism. It is founded on a belief in the dignity, worth, and goodness of the individual. People have freedom; that is, they are independent from outside constraint. However, they are not freed from all social restraints but are to act as responsible agents. Figure 6-1 illustrates how Plymouth advertising has used a patriotic theme in appealing to consumers.

The stress on individualism has been reinforced by the trend widely referred to during the 1970s as the "Age of Me." The "Me" decade emphasized self-fulfillment, self-actualization, inner motivation, and a focus on self, and it is exemplified by such slogans as "I want to be me," "I did it my way," and "I'm looking out for number one." Some have described the 1980s as the "We Decade" in which self-interest is focused in terms of collective action, societal effort, and security in numbers—spurred on by economic conditions of recession and inflation.[16]

Equality Americans believe in the intrinsic equality of man, that is, that each person is an individual (all are equal before God). Everyone has an equal right to life, liberty, and the pursuit of happiness, and an equal opportunity for social and economic rewards.

During recent decades there has been an increasing push for social and economic equality in America. One of the most profound impacts during this period has been women's demand for equality, which has brought about changes in the marriage relationship and the American family. The women's liberation movement represents a value structure that has resulted in greater independence and equality of women. It has been expressed in numerous ways, such as more women having careers outside the home, changing sex roles within the home, and some women opting for lifestyles other than marriage. Virginia Slims cigarettes has, in a series of ads, successfully related to this equality movement.

Activity   Our culture stresses activity, especially work, as a predominant value. This derives largely from the Puritan or Protestant ethic, which stressed that idleness was evil. An individual was expected to work hard, save money, and be thrifty. Thus, work was conceived as a means of religious discipline.

Today Americans believe not only in working hard but also in playing hard. Increased productivity and affluence have resulted in replacing long hours of hard work with longer vacation periods, shorter workweeks, and more paid holidays. This has generated increased leisure time in which activity is still stressed, but it is manifested in numerous leisure pursuits, as evidenced by the boom in participant sports such as tennis and golf. Often the activity is a competitive one, and marketers frequently use such appeals as the basis for ads.

Progress and Achievement   Americans believe in progress for society and in achievement and success for the individual. We are oriented toward the future rather than the past, and believe in change and forward movement. Personal achievement is stressed, as evidenced by the "success story" and by our desire to master the physical world. We also prize the characteristics of self-reliance and initiative. Figure 6-2 illustrates how Baldwin incorporates achievement values in its advertising to parents.

FIGURE 6-1
Advertisement for Plymouth Voyager.
Courtesy of Plymouth Division of Chrysler Corporation.

FIGURE 6-2
Advertisement for Baldwin.
Courtesy of Baldwin Piano & Organ
Company.

One manifestation of our emphasis on progress in America is the sometimes wasteful use of material possessions and resources. Contemporary America stresses continuous style changes and the discarding of still functionally useful products in order to buy what is new. Of course, the marketer benefits from an environment which is so conducive to innovation and in which consumers are eager to have the most up-to-date items.

An indication of our culture's orientation toward achievement, from a marketing perspective, is the importance placed on certain symbols in our society. Because achievement often has a materialistic aspect to it, Americans grant to owners of certain products the stamp of having "arrived." For example, a Cadillac or Mercedes tells something about the achievement of its owner, as does a large house in the "right neighborhood," and expensive clothing. These products are symbols to their owners as well as to others, and their meanings are usually unmistakable.[17]

Efficiency and Practicality Americans greatly appreciate technical values and constantly search for better ways of doing things. Our entire economic system is founded on these ideals and emphasizes mass production and mass consumption.

Americans are interested in performance features of products, such as speed, economy, safety, and durability. This appreciation of the practical as opposed to the intellectual also helps explain why certain advertising messages are very successful. Advertising-effectiveness tests consistently show that using "How to . . . " oriented headlines does better than using a non-problem-solving approach. Similarly, there is a far more widespread market for *Reader's Digest* and *Popular Mechanics* than for *Smithsonian* and *Omni*.

Another example of our culture's value of practicality concerns the orientation toward informality. We have moved away from the formal traditions (long associated with the eastern United States) and have adopted more informal habits in manners, dress, speech, and social relationships. Moreover, the United States has never placed as much emphasis on formality, ceremony, and tradition as has Europe. Consequently, Americans tolerate, in fact welcome, less structure and rigidity and more comfort in the way they work and relax. Certain regions of the country are particularly high on this scale of informality. For example, the celebrated Southern California lifestyle of casual dress, informal entertaining, and outdoor living is a prime example.

Mastery over the Environment Americans do not like to be controlled by their environment; rather, they seek to control it. This not only includes controlling the weather and harnessing the sun and tides as energy sources, but it also extends to areas like genetic engineering. Even the nature of products introduced in America is indicative of this underlying cultural value. For instance, there seems to be a product answer for every chore the consumer might face. During each Christmas season our television sets bring us news of products that knit our clothes, attach our buttons, and spin, chop, slice, and dice our vegetables. All of these items attest to our desire to provide an engineered answer for almost every situation we face.

We also desire to master our own bodies and the surrounding environment. Because of this value, we spend tremendous amounts of money on deodorants, shampoos, colognes, and cosmetics in order to improve or hide our true bodily features, while we buy detergents, cleansers, waxes, rug shampoos, room deodorizers, and electric bug killers to conquer the dirt, germs, pests, and odors that surround us.

Another aspect of this value is that we have long viewed the world and its resources as there to use as we saw fit. In so doing, however, we have encountered numerous environmental and diminishing-resource problems. On the positive side, a growing ecological orientation can be seen in the marketplace. Some manufacturers are using recycled materials to produce new items (such as glass and paper products) and more biodegradable products are being marketed (such as laundry detergents).

Religious and Moral Orientation According to one Gallup poll, 94 percent of Americans believe in God and 64 percent believe in life after death. In fact, the

United States is found to be more religious than any other industrialized country in the world. More than twice as many adult Americans consider religion to be very important to them, compared to western Europeans, for example. According to one recent study which investigated major aspects of American life—community involvement, political and moral beliefs, personal relationships, and work—the level of religious commitment was found to be the factor that most consistently and dramatically affects the values and behavior of Americans.[18]

Thus, we are a religious people, and our Judeo-Christian heritage has imbued us with a strong moral and ethical quality. Consequently, we tend to view the world in absolute terms and tolerate few gray areas—that is, we judge things in terms of good or bad, right or wrong, ethical or unethical. This value results in a strong evangelistic spirit among Americans. We are rather *ethnocentric*, believing that our culture and way of life is the best and feeling that it is our duty to bring others around to our way of thinking and acting.

One implication of the religious and moral orientation of Americans is our receptivity to the "marketing" of certain religious views and social causes. For example, some very effective marketers of Christianity include Billy Graham and Pat Robertson.

Humanitarianism Americans have a strong sense of personal concern for the rights and welfare of others. We provide aid in mass disasters, have a large philanthropic system, and feel that we should give our money and/or our time to such organizations as the United Fund, Red Cross (see Figure 6-3), CARE, and the Peace Corps. The operation of religious and other charitable institutions is a huge business and draws good support even in unfavorable economic times.

Youthfulness Young people set much of the tone of our culture and have been a growing force in our society as their proportion has risen. Because Americans want to look and act young, we consume great quantities of those products that hold promise for achieving these ends. For instance, hair colorings for men and women are very much in demand, as are preparations to do away with wrinkles, flab, and spots caused by the aging process. The available array of vitamins and other supplements (such as Geritol) is another indication of our youth orientation.

Marketers have played up the theme of youthfulness in numerous product and service promotions with slogans such as "You're as young as you feel" and "For those who think young." An effective twist on this approach, but accomplishing the same result, was a successful slogan for Clairol's Loving Care hair coloring: "You're not getting older. You're getting better."

Underlying the youth theme pervading our culture is the implication of romance. The younger you look, presumably the more attractive you are, especially to the opposite sex. The weakening of sexual prohibitions in our society has led to product promotions with more playful, thinly disguised appeals to romantic and sexual motives. This *creative eroticism* is reflected in many products and promotional slogans. For instance, Love Cosmetics' choice of the product name "Love" suggests that the items are "love potions."

Other evidence of the strong romantic emphasis in our culture is the fact that more than 20 million Americans weekly follow the dozen or more daytime television soap operas. In addition, more than 1200 romantic novels are published each year to be pored over by avid readers.

Materialism The U.S. culture is materialistic, and Americans are the world's most voracious consumers, each year buying millions of color TV sets, washing machines, refrigerators, vacuum cleaners, lawn mowers, radios, and other items. Material progress has made America a land of abundance where more than half of all families own their homes, and two cars per family is the standard.

Materialism seems to be on the rise. One study of the growing materialism found in American advertising indicated that ads increasingly stress the good life of luxury and pleasure.[19] In addition, a content analysis of popular literature since World War II indicates that we are increasingly preoccupied with brands having strong value expressiveness.[20]

Marketing's role in fostering materialism and any consequent unhappiness and dissatisfaction which results is an important social issue needing further study.[21]

FIGURE 6-3
Advertisement for the Red Cross.
Courtesy of the American Red Cross.

Related to the core culture value of materialism is the growing trend toward *hedonism,* or devotion to pleasure. We desire maximum pleasurable sensation with minimum effort. Our culture's increasing devotion to hedonism is reflected in the sale of all sorts of products ranging from luxury cars and homes to many foods and such pastimes as electronic video games. In addition, we are more willing to admit the existence of this situation to ourselves and others. For example, a classic L'Oreal hair color ad states, "It costs a little more, but I'm worth it." This and many similar ads stress how good the feeling is that comes from using a certain product.

Social Interaction and Conformity   These values seem in contrast to our emphasis on individualism, but some amount of conformity is necessary for a smoothly functioning society. Americans seem to be especially sensitive to group pressure. For example, David Riesman suggests that America can be characterized as a country of *inner-directed* and *other-directed* persons. Inner-directed individuals have their principles firmly instilled by their elders while other-directed persons receive their direction from contemporaries, directly or indirectly, either personally or through the mass media. Although the majority of the population of this country would have to be categorized as inner-directed, there is a trend in the metropolitan areas of America toward other-directedness.[22]

The trend of other-directedness suggests that people are seeking satisfaction of some need through greater social involvement with each other. Much of the advertising we are exposed to incorporates this theme. Promotions for products as diverse as motorcycles ("You meet the nicest people on a Honda"), clothing, recreation equipment, cigarettes, and beverages of all kinds incorporate the theme of how beneficial these products are in achieving pleasurable social interaction.

DO VALUES INFLUENCE CONSUMER BEHAVIOR?

Intuitively we can see that culture is a strong force in the consumer's milieu affecting his or her choice of behavior. Thus, marketers have long recognized the importance of appealing to consumers' values in marketing. For instance, Marlboro's theme ("The Marlboro Man") may attract people who value the respect connected with rugged and independent cowboys, while Camel's theme ("Where a man belongs") appeals to a sense of belonging. Salem stresses warm relationships with others ("Share the spirit"); and Merit, in its appeal, promotes fun and enjoyment in life ("The pleasure is back").[23] Unfortunately, little research has been conducted assessing the usefulness of cultural values in understanding or predicting consumer behavior, although there seems to be ample evidence that values do generally influence behavior.[24] Rokeach believes that values guide actions, attitudes, and judgments and that the consequences of people's values are evident in practically any phenomenon that social scientists may think worthy of study and understanding. Even though the influence of values may be pervasive on much human (and consumer) behavior, relatively little research has been conducted on the subject (and especially when compared to the great amount of investigation with regard to attitudes).[25] In order to create a meaningful objective research instrument to improve the value measurement process, Rokeach created the Rokeach Value Survey (RVS) consisting of two sets of values, eighteen instrumental and eighteen terminal values, each of which is

ranked by subjects in order of the value's importance or is responded to with an
agree-disagree scale. Table 6-1 presents these thirty-six values.

However, researchers at the University of Michigan have created an alternative value-measurement scale and procedure. Their List of Values (LOV) may
be better for establishing important relationships between values and consumption and may relate more closely to the values of life's major roles (such as
marriage, parenting, work, leisure, and daily consumption). Table 6-2 shows that
LOV has a higher percentage of terms that people say influence their daily lives,
according to one research study.

Some recent studies have found that commonly held cultural values do shape
consumption choices to a certain extent.[26] For example, a study examined the
ownership of generic categories of automobiles (such as full-size, intermediate,
compact, and subcompact-size cars) and concluded that culture is an underlying
determinant of the type of car purchased.[27] Another study found that car owners'
values can also be used to differentiate between owners of small, domestic cars,
owners of small, foreign cars, and owners of large, domestic cars.[28]

In addition, an investigation of homemakers' purchases of household appliances has used terminal and instrumental value lists to discover an important
relationship between purchase and values. Women were interviewed who planned
to make a purchase of one or more of eight major household appliances. Terminal
values were found to be related much more strongly than were instrumental
values to the product-class level of choice (for example, when deciding between
clothes washers such as full-size automatics, "mini" automatics, or compact

TABLE 6-1

Cultural Values

Terminal values (end states of existence)	Instrumental values (modes of conduct)
A comfortable life (a prosperous life)	Ambitious (hard-working, aspiring)
An exciting life (a stimulating, active life)	Broadminded (open-minded)
A sense of accomplishment (lasting contribution)	Capable (competent, effective)
A world at peace (free of war and conflict)	Cheerful (lighthearted, joyful)
A world of beauty (nature and the arts)	Clean (neat, tidy)
Equality (brotherhood, equal opportunity)	Courageous (standing up for your beliefs)
Family security (taking care of loved ones)	Forgiving (willing to pardon others)
Freedom (independence, free choice)	Helpful (working for others' welfare)
Happiness (contentedness)	Honest (sincere, truthful)
Inner harmony (freedom from inner conflict)	Imaginative (daring, creative)
Mature love (sexual and spiritual intimacy)	Independent (self-reliant, self-sufficient)
National security (protection from attack)	Intellectual (intelligent, reflective)
Pleasure (an enjoyable, leisurely life)	Logical (consistent, rational)
Salvation (saved, eternal life)	Loving (affectionate, tender)
Self-respect (self-esteem)	Obedient (dutiful, respectful)
Social recognition (respect, admiration)	Polite (courteous, well-mannered)
True friendship (close companionship)	Responsible (dependable, reliable)
Wisdom (a mature understanding of life)	Self-controlled (restrained, self-disciplined)

portables). At the brand-choice decision level (such as deciding between Maytag and General Electric), instrumental values were found to be related, while terminal values were not related at all. Thus, terminal values would seem to guide choice among product classes, while instrumental values would seem to guide choice among brands.[29] This concept is diagramed in Figure 6-4. As we can see, each set of values is thought to influence choice criteria (product or brand)—that is, the standards used to judge various alternatives. The choice criteria are, in turn, seen as having an influence on the consumer's formation of attitudes toward products or brands. These research findings are useful for directing the positioning of the brand so that advertising may communicate to the prospective buyers how the marketer's offering is superior to its competition.[30]

Researchers using both the LOV and RVS have examined several consumption questions and found that differences exist based on values held by consumers. For example, people more highly endorsing a sense of belonging tend to be heavily involved with individual and group leisure activities with others. In other words, they search for activities which enable them to fulfill their important values or needs. Consumers endorsing fun and excitement in life apparently desire more exciting media, such as police dramas, and engage in more exciting activities, such as sports like jogging and skiing. Conversely, those who more heavily stress security seem to like passive activities more, such as watching sporting events and having hobbies, and they have different media preferences.

Both the Rokeach Value Survey and the List of Values can prove helpful to the marketer in understanding important consumption facets. Knowing that consumers who endorse certain values more highly than other values have different lifestyles may be extremely useful in determining promotion appeals, product positioning and design, channels of distribution, and pricing approaches. In market segmentation decisions, knowledge of personal values can significantly en-

TABLE 6-2

Percentage of Respondents Checking Each Value as Influencing Their Daily Lives

LOV	%	RVS	%
Warm relationship with others	87.4	Self-respect	86.0
Self-respect	84.8	Happiness	83.1
Sense of accomplishment	84.6	True friendship	82.3
Fun and enjoyment in life	80.3	Freedom	79.2
Self-fulfillment	76.7	Sense of accomplishment	77.2
Being well respected	69.7	Family security	76.1
Security	67.7	Mature love	71.6
Sense of belonging	67.1	Pleasure	70.8
Excitement	59.0	Exciting life	69.7
		Comfortable life	68.0
		Inner harmony	68.0
		Wisdom	66.0
		World of beauty	62.1
		Equality	57.0
		Social recognition	56.5
		World at peace	49.2
		Salvation	34.3
		National security	28.4

Source: Sharon E. Beatty, Lynn R. Kahle, Pamela Homer, and Shekhar Misra, ''Alternative Measurement Approaches to Consumer Values: The List of Values and the Rokeach Value Survey,'' *Psychology & Marketing*, 2:192, Fall 1985. Copyright © 1985, John Wiley & Sons, Inc. Used with permission of John Wiley & Sons, Inc.

hance demographic understanding. For example, one study involving a national chain of family restaurants and its leading competitor found that brand preference was not differentiated with respect to demographic characteristics of consumers who ate at both chains and had a stated preference for one or the other. However, market segments based on value orientations of these fast-food restaurant customers did reveal differences that predisposed consumers' brand preferences. This kind of information is useful in designing effective advertising campaigns and developing products that incorporate salient product attributes, thereby enhancing the competitive posture of the brand.[31] Values have also been used to relate to contributions to charitable causes,[32] to help explain automobile importance ratings,[33] to predict mass-media usage,[34] and to relate mass-media vehicles to promotional messages.[35] However, more research is needed on the subject of values as they relate to purchasing behavior. There is still much disagreement on how widely and how intensely held values must be among consumers. A greater understanding is also needed on the origins and consequences of values. In addition, more research is necessary to understand cultural value influences on consumer behavior across a broader range of products than has so far been investigated.[36]

Several companies are pursuing such a goal of broadening the application of consumer values to users of a wide range of products. For example, SRI International combines value and lifestyle (termed VALS) information with available demographic data.[37] The purpose of VALS is to create a general psychographic framework that can be used to understand consumers of a variety of products, from deodorants to television sets.

By using this information, SRI has isolated and labeled nine types of consumers, each type so distinctive in its behavior and emotional makeup that it is held to constitute a specific market segment. The three major categories and nine subcategories are identified in Table 6-3.

Based on information gathered by SRI on dozens of products, the VALS program appears to have much usefulness for understanding the purchase habits for each category of consumer. For example, experientials and societally conscious individuals tend to buy foreign cars, while belongers tend to buy American cars. Media habits also differ among the groups. For instance, in print media, tabloids appeal to sustainers; business magazines are popular with achievers; sports magazines are frequently bought by I-am-me's; and literary magazines are preferred by experientials and societally conscious people. Marketing strategies

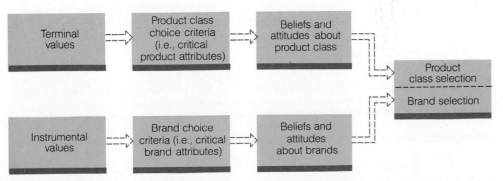

FIGURE 6-4
The nature of cultural value influence in purchase decisions.

of client firms have been influenced by such research. For example, Merrill Lynch & Co., Inc., changed the thrust of its "Bullish on America" advertising campaign after finding that its prime customers were "achievers," while its bull-herd had greatest appeal to "belongers." Merrill Lynch kept the bull, but deftly shifted the focus by showing a single animal, with the headline reading "A Breed Apart."[38]

Further research into the VALS categories has sought to identify these consumers' spouses so that advertisers, particularly, will have more insight as they try to reach the nearly 64 percent of the adult population that is married (see Table 6-4). Findings from this research indicate that:

■ Among married couples, 44 percent are "mixed," having two different VALS types with two different sets of needs. Thus, an achiever husband may want a minivan for his buddies and their golf clubs, while his belonger wife needs it for

TABLE 6-3

Consumer Value Categories

1 *Need-driven* (11 percent of adult population). "Money restricted"; struggling just to buy basics. Buy more out of need than choice or whim. Sometimes splurge on luxury items.
   a *Survivors* (4 percent). The most disadvantaged; old, poor, depressed, and far removed from the cultural mainstream.
   b *Sustainers* (7 percent). Relatively young, angry, and crafty; struggling on the edge of poverty, and willing to do anything to get ahead.

2 *Outer-directed* (66 percent). Middle America. Conduct their lives so that others will think well of them. Buy on the basis of what others will think. Purchase is dominated by outer rather than inner measures.
   a *Belongers* (35 percent). Traditional, conservative, conventional, nostalgic, sentimental, puritanical, and unexperimental. Buy to fit in, not stand out. Conforming and traditional in spending. Prime drive to belong.
   b *Emulators* (9 percent). Trying to make it big. Highly visible lifestyle. Ambitious, upwardly mobile, status conscious, and competitive. Distrustful and angry. Little faith they will get a fair shake from the Establishment. Imitate buying patterns of their models, the Achievers.
   c *Achievers* (22 percent). Driven, oriented to success. Leaders in business, politics, professions. Characterized by efficiency, fame, status, the good life, comfort, materialistic values. Pragmatic believers in rugged individualism and the traditional American system, and have formed the core of America's leadership elite for the last 100 years. Spend on the good things of life, and dominate top-of-the-line luxury markets.

3 *Inner-directed* (21 percent). Idealistic and conservation-oriented. Value the artistic and spiritual. Many are well-educated and form avant garde markets. Buy to meet their own inner wants and pleasures, rather than to respond to norms of others. Only group expected to grow in the 1980s.
   a *I-am-me's* (5 percent). A small group, fiercely individualistic, flamboyant, young, zippy, exhibitionistic, narcissistic, dramatic, impulsive, and inventive. Many fads originate here.
   b *Experientials* (7 percent). Concerned with inner growth and naturalism. Seek direct experience, intense involvement, a rich inner life. Mature vareity of I-am-me's. Important to various here-and-now markets such as outdoor sports, creative home pursuits, arts and crafts, etc.
   c *Societally conscious* (9 percent). Acutely aware of social issues. Live in a socially responsible way. Stress simplicity, frugality, conservation, ecological soundness, consumerism. Lean toward items made via appropriate technology. Fastest growing segment.

4 *Integrated* (2 percent). Highly developed psychologically. Live in accord with what is fitting, self-fulfilling, releasing, and balanced. Tolerant, assured, self-actualizing. Often have world perspective. Practical dreamers. Evolve from either an inner- or other-directed set of values and represent a synthesis of both power and sensitivity.

Source: "Information on Values and Lifestyles Needed to Identify Buying Patterns," *Marketing News*, October 5, 1979, pp. 1, 4, 7; and Niles Howard, "A New Way to View Consumers," *Dun's Review*, August 1981, pp. 42–46.

getting the kids around and shopping. Advertising copy would have to satisfy both needs.

■ There is at least one achiever in 44 percent of all marriages, which is important since the dominant partner tends to make the buying decisions. They are the most active buyers or users of videocassette recorders, automatic teller machines, disc cameras, and pay TV. Achiever marrieds spend more and spend more often as they dominate family buying.[39]

Researchers involved with the LOV system claim that it is a better methodology and works better than does VALS.[40] Nevertheless, SRI's pioneering work in the values and lifestyles of consumers has achieved much notoriety and success within the business community.

CULTURAL CHANGE AND COUNTERCULTURES

The core values just discussed are not fixed or static but instead are dynamic, changing elements of our culture. Cultural change may come about slowly in an

TABLE 6-4

What Will and Won't Sell to the Four Biggest Married VALS Groups

---

Belonger husband/belonger wife
25 percent of the married population

The steamy Diet Pepsi commercials, with a lens that seems to visually caress bodies, won't work with this couple. And they're probably not going to like Paco Rabanne ads much better. Belonger couples simply aren't comfortable with that sort of personal intimacy. These couples have traditional values and traditional lifestyles. And while the interaction between a ''him'' and a ''her'' won't work, the implied intimacy of a family dinner, a vacation, the emotion of a team, will.

Achiever husband/achiever wife
20 percent of the married population

They've already made it. They've worked hard, they've succeeded and they know they deserve the best—but they don't want ads to tell them that. Ads that work with this incredibly confident couple—the most active buyers—assume success and build a story from there. BMW ads, ''The Ultimate Driving Machine,'' using the image of the car as a singular statement—the car (and its driver) in control of the road, in control of life—tell the quintessential achiever/achiever story.

Achiever husband/belonger wife
13 percent of the married population

He has worked hard climbing the corporate ladder. She has stayed at home raising the kids and keeping his dinner warm. Ads that work with this group reflect these roles—making her feel comfortable as a homemaker and him feel good about his constant climb. The American Express ads, with assertive women and secure men, would leave this duo cold. She not only hasn't come a long way, baby—she doesn't want to. Ads that promise to take her there won't work either.

Emulator husband/belonger wife
5 percent of the married population

These couples like reinforcement—he's trying to jump on the fast track and she's helping him get there. Products and advertising that pave the way to success, or create the illusion of success, are what this couple reacts to. She still worries about ring around the collar, and he's ready to mortgage the house for a Cadillac. Where they're going, it's Michelob.

Source: Betsy Sharkey, ''News VALS Study Identifies Consumers' Spouses,'' *Adweek*, February 11, 1985, p. 58. Reprinted with permission of ADWEEK.

evolutionary manner, or it may change rapidly, which tends to place more stress on the system. The marketer needs to understand that cultures do change and to appreciate the implications which this may have for consumer behavior.

CHANGING CULTURAL VALUES IN THE UNITED STATES

In the book *Megatrends,* author John Naisbitt cites ten fundamental changes sweeping America today:

1   We are shifting from an industrial to an information-based society.

2   High technology can no longer be forced on the population without the human element or "high-touch" reaction it causes being considered.

3   Our economy is increasingly part of a global structure.

4   Managers are beginning to think about the long run rather than just the next quarter.

5   Centralized structures are becoming decentralized.

6   Our traditional sense of self-reliance is once again replacing reliance on institutions.

7   Citizens, workers, and consumers have a greater voice in government, business, and the marketplace.

8   The computer has allowed us to move from pyramidal hierarchies to networks.

9   Population, jobs, government power, and wealth are moving irreversibly from North to South.

10   Our either/or world has become one of a multitude of options.[41]

As the world around us is transformed, American values are undergoing some major shifts.[42] Opinion research shows that since the 1960s some fundamental and widely shared cultural views have changed in the United States. Only 20 percent of the public now cling to traditional values of hard work, family loyalty, and sacrifice.

Approximately 17 percent of the population cite self-fulfillment as their principal life goal. But the majority (63 percent) embrace some traditional values and also espouse views that would have been considered heretical only a generation ago.[43] Thus, the marketer faces a situation in which new value trends coexist with long-standing values still deeply rooted in the country. This pluralism is one of the characteristics of our emerging society.[44] Evidence of these changing patterns shows up among baby boomers. A survey conducted among those born between 1946 and 1964 produces picture of a new brand of traditionalism: a distinct longing for more traditional values in some areas, values including hard work, strong family and religious ties, and respect for authority, but these values being coupled with an increasing acceptance of nontraditional ideas in other areas—a tolerance of changing sexual mores and a desire for less materialism.[45]

Philip Kotler suggests that, generally, the following changes are taking place in American cultural values:[46]

From	To
Self-reliance	Government reliance
"Hard work"	The "easy life"
Religious convictions	Secular convictions
Husband-dominated home	Wife-dominated home
Parent-centered household	Child-centered household
Respect for individual	Dislike of individual difference
Postponed gratification	Immediate gratification
Saving	Spending
Sexual chastity	Sexual freedom
Parental values	Peer-group values
Independence	Security

The values listed above may be characteristic of intergenerational differences, but differences can also be found between various groups of the same age. For example, noncollege youths appear to be about five years behind the college population in adoption of new social values and moral outlooks.[47]

IMPLICATIONS OF CULTURAL CHANGE FOR THE MARKETER

Changes in norms such as those cited above signal a new American value pattern emerging whose impact will be felt by marketers in many ways.[48] Just a few such areas are cited here.

First, the search for a new work ethic will mean that leisure activities will occupy a more important place in people's lives. Thus, new opportunities will continue to open up in travel, entertainment, sports, leisure-oriented products, and also in the education and information industries.

Related to the work/leisure situation is the fact that time is becoming a more precious commodity and those items that save time are becoming greatly valued by consumers. Time-saving goods and services include convenience foods, microwave ovens, disposable diapers, fast-drying paints, fast-food restaurants, supermarket deli operations, professional lawn- and household-care services, and special airline and rental car procedures to eliminate waiting.

Another factor connected to the work/leisure situation is the role of the home as a focal point of social activities, long-term investment, and personal expression.[49] Inflation has caused people to evolve a new economic logic, and the home is increasingly being seen as an investment. Coupled with changing lifestyles, there is, consequently, more of a focus on obtaining items for the home and spending time in the home, which helps to spur the do-it-yourself market and the sales of home-technology items such as videocassette recorders and computers, as well as recreational or leisure assets such as exercise machines, swimming pools, and spas.

Second, as people shift their notions about individual rights and responsibilities and increasingly expect that they are entitled (regardless of their ability to pay) to such things as adequate retirement income, comprehensive health care, decent housing, and college educations, consumerism may be expected to expand. This entitlement psychology will lead to an escalation in people's insistence on having their "rights" to safe, proven, nonpolluting products and packaging. More informative and truthful labeling and advertising may also be expected.

Third, the trend toward self-fulfillment and self-realization, with its emphasis on inner- rather than other-directed satisfactions, means that consumers will want to live life to the fullest.[50] There is an unprecedented degree of interest in spending time, money, and effort on maximizing looks and feelings of vigor, vitality, and well-being. Studies have shown that 80 percent of consumers are concerned with "being good to myself" and "improving myself."[51] Consequently, marketing opportunities abound for new products and services aimed at self-fulfillment and improvement. The success of self-help books testifies to this movement, as does the fact that the adult sector is the fastest-growing portion of the education market. Opportunities ranging from hobbies (to satisfy personal creativity needs) to weight watching and whirlpool baths (to satisfy health and personal care needs) should remain strong. The broad-based growth in the elite market will foster an increased interest in elegance, in sales of certain kinds of high-end products that people associate with the very wealthy, in more home decorating, and generally in more concern with status among the "haves" who desire to flaunt it.

Fourth, the new morality of the market reflects changing attitudes toward sex. Implications of this trend range from acceptance of "anatomically correct" dolls in the toy industry to ads with sexually explicit and frank appeals.

Fifth, the back-to-nature or "simple is better" trend has been influential in the rejection of the artificial and the acceptance of the natural. This has found expression in many product areas including apparel (natural fabrics), toiletries (natural makeup and herbal fragrance shampoos), pharmaceuticals (stressing simple ingredients with no harmful side effects), food (natural ingredients, health foods, and home preserving), and housing (earth tones and indoor plants).[52]

As these cultural changes mold a new American consumer, they have significant implications for many aspects of marketing strategy, including product-planning, distribution, advertising, and market-segmentation decisions.

Product Planning   Assessing consumers' present and emerging value orientations can help the marketer identify new product opportunities and achieve better product positioning among consumer segments.[53] For example, as values such as "pleasure," "an exciting life," "a comfortable life," and "self-respect" increase in importance, the marketer may find a need for having products with brand names, colors, and designs that enhance these important values. Consider a furniture manufacturer who might link these changing values with a growing demand for furniture style and design that incorporate bright colors, bold designs, unique materials of construction, and unusual comfort features.

Value segments containing many consumers suggest that products can be positioned by designing them with attributes which are related to the global values distinguishing that particular market segment. For example, a segment of consumers who regard the values "imaginative," "an exciting life," and "independent" as important might be defined as that group which is concerned with individuality and self-expression. The group might be a reliable segment for marketers of products which are partially finished (such as furniture, and homes) and products which can be tailored to the individual needs of consumers through the use of accessories, styling, chemical formulation, and so on. Marketers of homes, automobiles, clothing, cosmetics, and fast foods have successfully used this approach.[54]

Therefore, contemporary marketing offerings require periodic audits of product and service lines to determine how well they satisfy the complex needs and wants of changing consumers.

Distribution Channels Changing consumer-value systems may lead to different shopping patterns, and new outlets may be necessary to reach consumers. For instance, the "ego-involved," self-gratifying values of the marketplace offer many retailing challenges and opportunities.[55] For time-pressured consumers, retailers may offer in-home catalog shopping or toll-free telephone ordering of merchandise. Stores may use discounts and special offers to shift nonemployed consumers to off-peak hours in order to expedite shopping by the most time-impoverished consumers. Even drive-in churches and funeral parlors exist for those who don't have time to get out of their cars.

Promotion New approaches in copy and artwork are called for in communicating memorably and persuasively with changing consumers. There are a number of ways that advertising is moving to appeal to the values of this new society: (1) defiance of social taboos; (2) more informative copy; (3) more true-to-life vignettes; (4) more advertising that names and debates competitors; (5) more advertising segmented toward the higher-educated, higher-income groups; (6) more advertising that frankly acknowledges mounting public cynicism about advertising; (7) greater stress on ecology; (8) more advertising that realistically, not paternalistically, acknowledges women's changing role in our society; and (9) more advertising that breaks with tradition.[56]

Market Segmentation Knowledge of consumer value orientations provides a measurable set of variables, related to needs, which gives the marketer insight beyond merely demographic and psychographic dimensions. The growing diversity of individual tastes, coupled with a hedonistic philosophy and increasing incomes are contributing to ever greater segmentation of the market. Thus, understanding such value shifts in American society could be useful in predicting changing consumption patterns for products. Also, the marketer might be able to identify large market segments on the basis of value profiles and then develop programs that would enhance those values important to each consumer segment. For example, when one group views a product in terms of status and another views it in a more functional way, then different promotional messages are likely to be needed for each group, as well as, perhaps, tailored products.

It will be necessary for marketers to assess the changes in size and composition of value segments in the marketplace and to understand the implications of these shifts for company activities. Here, marketing research will be useful for conducting broad-based longitudinal studies to identify changes in value orientations. Such research may be helpful to uncover smaller blocs of consumers within the overall U.S. culture who emphasize significantly different cultural values than do the dominant cultural patterns. Such groups are often referred to as *counter-cultures*.

For example, the very nature of consumption activity may be shifting as a different value pattern emerges. Futurist Alvin Toffler, in his book *The Third Wave,* argues that *consumers* are a phenomenon of the industrial age. As society

moves toward the *postindustrial age* some of the pure consumers will be replaced by *prosumers,* who produce many of their own goods and services.[57] Why will people move toward more prosumption activity? Several reasons are advanced by Toffler. First, a decline in the workweek will continue. More leisure time may be applied to self-reliant production activities. Second, people's higher education level will result in their not accepting boring work as readily, allowing them to use their time in other ways. Third, the rising cost of skilled labor, such as of plumbers, electricians, and carpenters, will push more people to do their own work. Fourth, people engaging in increasingly mental work in our technologically advanced society will seek more physical activities, including self-reliant production. Fifth, some people will feel that their own production is of higher quality than what is generally available in the market. Sixth, people will seek individualization by producing their own goods and services in order to avoid mass-produced items.[58]

If Toffler is correct about the growth of prosumption activities, marketers will face a challenge but also an opportunity. Prosumers should be viewed as another market segment to be identified and helped to meet its product or service needs.

TRACKING CULTURAL CHANGE

Alvin Toffler discusses the corporate mind-set necessary for adequate understanding of and dealing with changes in the future:

Simply tracking trends is not an adequate way to understand an environment and upheaval. Straight-line predictions are treacherous. . . . I think the starting point is to assume that tomorrow will be different, maybe radically different. That may sound obvious, but there are many executives who really believe that the future will be pretty much like today. They feel that if they continue doing what was successful until now, it will work tomorrow. As long as that assumption guides the major actions of the company, the company will be a candidate for destruction. . . . Also, the company can't rely on a group of geniuses at the top of the tower to anticipate everything. Everyone in the organization must become a futurist who senses change in his particular specialty. Look at changes overseas, look at technologies in other industries, build scenarios. . . . I think marketers are probably more alert to change than most people. If you look at the other functions of the corporation, they tend to be less aware of the fragility of the present.[59]

Several information services are available to track the changing cultural pattern of values, attitudes, and lifestyles. One of these is SRI International, which has over seventy major companies supporting its research in the area of values and lifestyles described above. SRI also publishes a report that identifies society's newest trends so that corporations will have insight into the sort of economic and social conditions in which they will have to do business in the future.[60]

A second approach to identifying social changes uses a technique known as content analysis, developed during World War II by the forerunner of America's Central Intelligence Agency (CIA). It is a scientific, objective, systematic, quantitative, and generalizable description of communications content.[61] Taking this

approach, the Naisbitt Group scans each issue of over 200 daily newspapers around the country and categorizes every local news article into one of eleven major topics—consumer affairs, energy, housing, transportation, environment, employment, health, education, law and justice, social relations, and government and politics—and into fifteen subtopics. The company's newsletter *Trend Report* is subscribed to by such major corporations as American Broadcasting, Arco, Beatrice, Dow, and Holiday Inns who pay $15,000 a year to receive Naisbitt's insights.

Numerous pollsters and survey researchers are at work taking the pulse of American consumers in a third approach to determining the direction of cultural trends. Those active in the field are such names as Louis Harris and George Gallup. Perhaps the best-known survey research service keeping up with social changes while working for over 100 sponsoring companies, however, is Yankelovich Clancy Shulman. The company produces ''Monitor,'' which annually tabulates the responses of 2500 people surveyed nationwide, about, for example, how important they think it is to plan in advance and how much they enjoy doing things at the spur of the moment. The in-depth interviews take approximately ninety minutes and are conducted in respondents' homes. The survey covers fifty value categories affecting shifts in cultural trends. Another service examines how the public and a cross section of the leadership community feel toward thirty widely discussed public issues such as pollution control, truth in advertising, and business regulation. The goal of these research services is to provide useful data on broad social trends and changes in values that affect demand for companies' products and services. Such a need is increasingly recognized by business people.[63]

Assessing cultural change still remains a difficult task, however, and marketers are likely to continue to face problems when attempting to understand, appreciate, and reflect changing cultural values. First, these changes are elusive and hard to define, and their practical effects are frequently indirect. Second, the marketer may tend to ascribe fundamental cultural changes simply to the ''generation gap'' and incorrectly assume that they are only fads which will quickly disappear. Finally, because change often generates complexity, marketers may resist changing cultural values rather than trying to take advantage of them.[64]

CROSS-CULTURAL UNDERSTANDING OF CONSUMER BEHAVIOR

More and more companies have adopted a global outlook in which the world becomes their market. For example, numerous major corporations such as Coca-Cola, Hoover, IBM, Pfizer, and Gillette receive over half of their earnings from foreign operations, while many others also have significant international markets. Such situations require the marketer's appreciation both of cultural differences that exist among international markets and of their influence on consumer behavior. In this section some of the marketing implications of these cultural subtleties will be discussed. Unfortunately, there have been rather few published cross-cultural studies of consumer behavior that the marketer may use in making strategy decisions. There have been some important recent examples of research in this area, however.[65]

THE NEED FOR CROSS-CULTURAL UNDERSTANDING

When American managers venture abroad, they experience what anthropologists call *culture shock,* that is, a series of psychological jolts when they encounter the wide variety of customs, value systems, attitudes, and work habits, which thus reduces their effectiveness in foreign commercial environments.[66] Therefore, it is crucial to effective operations that the manager be well-schooled in the host culture. A lack of understanding of the host culture will lead the manager to think and act as he would in his home culture. Such a *self-reference criterion,* that is, the unconscious reference to one's own cultural values—has been termed the root cause of most international business problems abroad. The goal should be to eliminate this cultural myopia.[67]

The marketer needs a frame of reference with which to understand and evaluate the range of cultural values which may be encountered. A useful conceptualization of the possible range of variations in values found in different cultures has been offered by Kluckhohn. Table 6-5 presents a classification of value orientations which might be encountered by the international marketer. This model suggests five basic orientations which are thought to be common to all human groups. These relate to human nature, relationship of man to nature, sense of time, activity, and social relationships. The marketer's task then becomes one of seeking to understand what type of value system predominates in any culture, and relating effectively to that system through marketing activities. Thus, the international marketer would benefit from doing the same. Americans would fall on the right-hand side of this value range. Nevertheless, it has been observed that even in our modern value system there are some primitive aspects of consumption that serve as an outlet for spiritual expression and the preservation of ethnic heritage.[68]

TABLE 6-5
Variations in Value Systems

Orientation	Range		
Human nature	*Evil* (changeable or unchangeable): Most people are basically evil and can't be trusted.	*Mixture of good and evil* (changeable or unchangeable): There are evil and good people in the world.	*Good* (changeable or unchangeable): Most people are basically good and can be trusted.
Man-nature relationship	*Subjugation-to-nature*: Life is largely controlled by outside forces.	*Harmony-with-nature*: Live in harmony with nature.	*Mastery-over-nature*: Man should challenge and control nature.
Time-sense	*Past-oriented* (tradition bound): Man should learn from and emulate the glorious past.	*Present-oriented* (situational): Make the most of the present moment. Live for today.	*Future-oriented* (goal-oriented): Plan for the future in order to make it better than the past.
Activity	*Being*: The spontaneous expression of impulses and desires. Stress on who you are.	*Being-in-becoming*: Emphasizes self-realization, development of all aspects of the self as an integrated whole.	*Doing*: Stressing action and accomplishment.
Social relations	*Lineal* (authoritarian): Lines of authority are clearly established with dominant-subordinate relationships clearly defined and respected.	*Collateral* (group-oriented): Man is an individual as well as a group member participating in collective decisions.	*Individualistic*: Man is autonomous and should have equal rights and control over his own destiny.

Source: Adapted from Florence R. Kluckhohn, ''Dominant and Variant Value Orientations,'' in Clyde Kluckhohn and Henry A. Murray (eds.), *Personality in Nature, Society, and Culture*, 2d ed., New York, Alfred A. Knopf, 1953, p. 346.

When a company is marketing products internationally, a thorough understanding of cultural practices is useful in determining whether a single strategy can be effective in different national environments, or whether several strategies must be adopted, with each geared to the distinctive cultural setting. Global marketing with a single approach has its champions.[69] There are others, however, who consider trying to sell products around the world with only one marketing strategy a dangerous approach for naive marketers.[70] For example, potential global marketers must consider such issues as the following:

■ Has the market developed in the same way from country to country? Kellogg's Pop Tarts failed in Britain because toasters weren't widely owned. Similarly, there was little demand in Europe for fabric softener sheets used in dryers because most people still have clotheslines.

■ Are consumer targets similar in different countries? Canon's American advertising of 35-mm cameras has to appeal to people fearful of complex technological products, whereas its Japanese advertising relates to consumers who tend to seek sophisticated, high-tech products.

■ Do consumers share the same wants and needs in different countries? In America, General Foods successfully positioned Tang as a substitute for orange juice at breakfast. But in France people consume little orange juice and virtually none at breakfast; hence, Tang was positioned as a refreshment for any time of day.

Some companies have been successful with a single marketing strategy or have at least reduced some of the duplication that existed in their efforts. For example:

Playtex developed a global advertising approach to sell its new Wow bra in twelve countries—a departure from the forty-three different versions of ads it had running throughout the world a few years ago. But there were difficulties in accomplishing the task. The company came up with appropriate names for the product in each language (such as ''Traumbugel'' in German and ''Alas'' in Spanish). Dozens of models were screened before final selection of a blonde and two brunettes (said to have universal appeal). One hundred fifty popular-style bras were used to film the commercials (because, for example, the French like lacy bras while Americans prefer plain, opaque styles). TV standards at the time in the United States and South Africa didn't allow women to be shown modeling bras, and so models held the bra on a hanger; but in other countries models wore the bras. In all ads, though, a single Wow feature having universal appeal was stressed: underwire support and shape achieved without the uncomfortable wires, because of a new plastic. A monumental editing job was necessary to produce the commercials to each country's requirements. Nevertheless, the campaign allowed Playtex to present one unified message and save money at the same time.[71]

DECISION AREAS FOR THE INTERNATIONAL MARKETER

The outline presented in Table 6-6 is suggested for use by the international marketer in conducting cultural analysis. It should also be noted that this outline is perhaps as helpful a framework to the domestic marketer as to the international marketer.

Gaining a better understanding of the host culture is made difficult, however, by problems confronting consumer research abroad. Researchers in under-developed foreign markets encounter numerous difficulties in obtaining satisfactory consumer interviews because of a mistrust of strangers asking questions. Moreover, certain subjects may be taboo and thus are not to be discussed, especially with strangers. In a number of countries even the subject of consumption habits is considered inappropriate.[72] In such an environment, it is clear that the marketer will have a difficult time piecing together information on which to base the company's strategies. The following discussion of several marketing-decision areas reveals some of the cultural barriers that may be present.

Market Segments It is critical to recognize that just as in domestic marketing, there will be market segments that must be identified and understood in order to develop successful marketing programs internationally. For example, a study of Canadian women revealed two broad groups—those who focus on home life and those who focus on work involvement—but five segments:

1 *Contented, striving.* This is the largest segment, usually over age 40 and a homemaker. She is content with that role. She believes it is unwise to buy on credit (other than house and car). She reads ads and uses coupons.

2 *Independent, self-confident.* This is the youngest segment, with an average age of 32. She thinks she is a leader, is ambitious, and has initiative. She doesn't spend a lot of time talking with friends about brands or products. She is not one to save and redeem coupons, shop by catalog, or take advantage of special offers on packages. She is not overly price-conscious or likely to buy brands on sale.

TABLE 6-6

Elements of Consumer Behavior Analysis in a Cross-Cultural Setting

1 Determine underlying values and their rate of change within the relevant market: What values are generally held strongly within the general market and the intended market segment? What is the rate and direction of value changes taking place within the relevant culture?

2 Evaluate the product concept as it relates to this culture: Is this product concept one that harmonizes with current and evolving values? If there are value conflicts with ownership of this product, can the product be changed to fit these values? How can the product be effectively identified with positive values? What needs does this product satisfy for members of the culture? Are these needs important? How are competitive products and brands currently satisfying these needs?

3 Determine characteristic purchase decision-making patterns: How do consumers make decisions for this product? Which family members are involved in purchase decision making and use of this product? What role does each member typically play in the process? What purchase criteria and sources of information do consumers use in making buying decisions for this product? What is the cultural attitude toward acceptance of innovations? What cultural values might be congruent with or conflict with purchase and use of this product?

4 Determine appropriate promotion methods: What means of communication exist for advertising to consumers? How is advertising perceived among those in the culture? Must different languages be used to reach various cultural groups? What are the most relevant appeals for this product among the culture? What taboos (such as words, themes, colors, or pictures) exist which may impinge on our sales or advertising strategy? What is the role of the salesperson in this culture?

5 Determine appropriate distribution channels: What are the characteristic distribution channels for this product? Are capable institutions available for handling this product? Might new channel opportunities exist which would be readily accepted by consumers? What is the nature of the shopping process for this product?

3 *Insecure*. This is the third largest segment, with an average age of 35. She is not satisfied with herself or her role in life and tends to feel lonely and inadequate. She believes generics are as good as nationally advertised brands, and is not brand-loyal. She values price over convenience and quality.

4 *Traditional*. This segment, predominant in Quebec and rural areas, has an average age of 42. She believes the best values are from the past; she is strongly committed to the belief that a man should head the family and women belong in the home. She's a comparison shopper but seeks quality and convenience over price. She is loyal to stores and brands, and reluctant to buy new brands unless recommended by someone. She prefers paying cash and shops on the basis of a budget.

5 *Career-oriented*. This segment, with an average age of 39, is similar to independents but more committed to work and opinionated about role. She prefers doing things other than shopping. She views brands as homogeneous, pays cash, is not price-conscious, and will pay more for convenience.[73]

Thus, separate marketing mixes and programs may need to be targeted at Canadian segments. Sometimes they can be language-based (French/English) or even determined on metropolitan geographical factors. Especially for food items—where the French and English subcultures show differences in food-preparation motives, brand- and store-loyalty patterns, and usage patterns of convenience products—separate ad themes, media, and distributional policies may be developed and maintained to appeal to each segment.[74]

Product Considerations   Each country has a different mix of consumption. Therefore, the types of products that are salable in each culture vary. For example, household appliance ownership data for several neighboring western European nations show quite differing consumption patterns, even though these countries are at similar levels of economic development. Such a pattern of consumer behavior can be attributed more to cultural differences than to economic differences.

A product being considered for marketing in a foreign country should be assessed for its "fit" with that country's value system. One study indicates that 80 percent of imported products require some adaptation.[75] There are numerous examples in the history of international business of products that succeeded here yet sputtered abroad because they failed to take account of differences between American and other countries' value systems. The following examples are representative:

Mr. Donut's entry into the Japanese market encountered a host of problems such as counters that people said were too high, pastry that was too big, cups that were too heavy, and donuts that had too much nutmeg. But the company succeeded by making the necessary cultural adaptations.[76]

A Japanese toy maker selling Barbie dolls had near-zero sales for decades until he persuaded Mattel, Inc., to allow a change in the westernized look of the doll. When the toy maker reduced the doll's bosom, changed her blue eyes to brown, and darkened her blonde hair, sales zoomed.[77]

Even such seemingly simple elements as package and product color have played havoc with many international marketers.

Promotion Considerations   Promotion represents another area of marketing strategy that must be culturally tempered. Promotion failures have occurred abroad because of lack of understanding of the foreign culture.

Some marketers have committed fatal bloopers in their zeal simply to export intact their product's brand name or advertising themes to a foreign market or to attempt direct translation of such words:

> Coca Cola's first attempt to translate its trademark into Chinese characters resulted in something that sounded like Coca-Cola but meant "bite the wax tadpole."

> "Body by Fisher" became "Corpse by Fisher" in Flemish.

> Colgate-Palmolive's "Cue" toothpaste is a pornographic word in French.

> Enco means "stalled car" in Japanese—a good reason for changing to Exxon, which is meaningless in any language.

Entire promotion campaigns may even fail due to cultural barriers encountered, unless an adjustment is made. The following example illustrates how one marketer was able to overcome the self-reference criterion.

> Avon Products, Inc. had to reshape its personal selling program for Hong Kong. In the United States, the Avon saleswoman was accustomed to being greeted at the door by the woman of the house and led into the living room where she could sell over a cup of coffee. In Hong Kong, however, it was likely to be a servant peering through a metal gate who met the visitor and announced that the mistress of the household wasn't home. Because of this difference, Avon began recruiting special saleswomen for Hong Kong. They tended to be well-to-do housewives or women at a certain professional level, such as travel consultants or executive secretaries, who were thought to be able to sell to their acquaintances or gain access to women in their neighborhoods who would invite them to stop by.[78]

Distribution Channel Consideration   Failure to understand the foreign culture when making channel decisions often causes problems, as the following case indicates:

> The cultural influence on retailing may be seen in the development of supermarkets in the United Kingdom. Although supermarkets in Britain have substantially increased their share of food sales, the stores are rather small by U.S. standards. Because British housewives lack cars and shop on foot in the neighborhood, each store attracts customers from a relatively small area. In addition, the British housewife is not yet completely attuned to all aspects of typical supermarket shopping. She likes the modern convenience of the supermarket, but she still expects the social relationships which are traditional among small shopkeepers and their customers. In order to maintain this formalized daily shopping and social relationship, many have scheduled their purchases so that they may buy fats and oils on Monday, flour and sugar on Tuesday, and so on. Therefore, executives of U.S. food manufacturers doing business in the United Kingdom

must realize that British culture assigns a role to supermarkets that differs from their role in the United States. Successful channel management must take that role into account through the marketing strategies used.[79]

MANAGERIAL REFLECTIONS

For our product or service situation . . .

1   Which core cultural values (using the RVS or LOV approaches) are of greatest importance to our chosen market in this purchase?

2   Which VALS segments appear to be appropriate target markets?

3   Are changes occurring in the cultural values of the market that will have an affect on its purchase?

4   If foreign marketing exists or is planned, how do these various markets differ in cultural values and systems that might affect our success?

5   What significant market segments may be distinguished within the foreign culture?

6   Can our marketing mix be transplanted or must it be adapted or a new mix developed to satisfy target cultural segments?

DISCUSSION TOPICS

1   Define culture. What are the most important characteristics of culture that describe its nature?

2   Why is the study of culture important to the marketer?

3   What is the function of culture?

4   What are the core cultural values held by members of the American culture?

5   How have core cultural values changed in the United States over the past generation? What shifts do you expect in these core values over your own generation? What effects are likely on consumer behavior and marketing?

6   Cite examples of marketing practices that either conform to or actively take advantage of core cultural values.

7   Name three products that are presently culturally unacceptable. What marketing strategies would you use to overcome their cultural resistance?

8   Why is an understanding of the foreign cultural environment especially important to the international marketer?

PROJECTS

1   Locate two articles on marketing failures by companies operating in a foreign market. Could an improved cultural understanding have prevented these failures? How?

2 Select a specific product and foreign market and perform the cross-cultural analysis outlined in Table 6-6.

NOTES

[1] Adapted from Dennis W. Rook, "The Ritual Dimension of Consumer Behavior." *Journal of Consumer Research,* **12**:251, December 1985.

[2] David E. Wright and Robert E. Snow, "Consumption as Ritual in the High Technology Society," in Ray B. Browne (ed.), *Rituals and Ceremonies in Popular Culture,* Bowling Green University Popular Press, Bowling Green, Ohio, 1980.

[3] Edward B. Tylor, *Primitive Culture,* Murray, London, 1891, p. 1.

[4] Clyde Kluckhohn, "The Study of Culture," in Daniel Lewer and Harold D. Lasswell (eds.), *The Policy Sciences,* Stanford University Press, Stanford, Calif., 1951, p. 86.

[5] R. P. Cuzzort, *Humanity and Modern Sociological Thought,* Holt, New York, 1969, p. 356.

[6] James S. Duesenberry, *Income, Saving and the Theory of Consumer Behavior,* Harvard University Press, Cambridge, Mass. 1949, p. 19.

[7] Charles Winick, "Anthropology's Contributions to Marketing," *Journal of Marketing,* **25**:55–56, July 1961.

[8] Rook, "The Ritual Dimension," p. 251.

[9] Grant McCracken, "Culture and Consumption: A Theoretical Account of the Structure and Movement of the Cultural Meaning of Consumer Goods," *Journal of Consumer Research,* **13**:71–84, June 1986.

[10] "Corporate Culture," *Business Week,* October 27, 1980, p. 149.

[11] Richard T. LaPiere, *Sociology,* McGraw-Hill, New York, 1946.

[12] Leonard Broom and Philip Selznick, *Sociology, A Text with Adapted Readings,* 4th ed., Harper & Row, New York, 1968, p. 54.

[13] Milton J. Rokeach, *Beliefs, Attitudes, and Values,* Jossey Bass, San Francisco, 1968, p. 161.

[14] Jonathan Gutman and Donald E. Vinson, "Value Structures and Consumer Behavior," in William L. Wilkie (ed.), *Advances in Consumer Research,* vol. 6, Association for Consumer Research, Ann Arbor, Mich. 1979, pp. 335–336.

[15] Milton J. Rokeach, "The Role of Values in Public Opinion Research," *Public Opinion Quarterly,* **32**:550–551, Winter 1969–1970.

[16] Daniel Yankelovich, *New Rules: Searching for Self-Fulfillment in a World Turned Upside Down,* Random House, New York, 1981.

[17] For examples of the symbols we buy, see Sidney J. Levy, "Symbols for Sale," *Harvard Business Review,* **37**:117–124, July–August 1959.

[18] *The Connecticut Mutual Life Report on American Values in the 80s: The Impact of Belief,* Connecticut Mutual, Hartford, Conn., 1981, pp. 6–7, 17.

[19] Russell W. Belk and Richard W. Pollay, "Images of Ourselves: The Good Life in Twentieth-Century Advertising," *Journal of Consumer Research,* **11**:887–897, March 1985.

[20] Monroe Friedman, "Are Americans Becoming More Materialistic? A Look at Changes in Expressions of Materialism in the Popular Literature of the Post-World War II Era," in Elizabeth Hirschman and Morris Holbrook (eds.), *Advances in Consumer Research,* vol. 12, Association for Consumer Research, Provo, Utah, 1985, pp. 385–387.

[21] Russell W. Belk, "Materialism: Trait Aspects of Living in the Material World," *Journal of Consumer Research,* **12**:265–280, December 1985.

[22] David Riesman, Nathan Glazer, and Reuel Denny, *The Lonely Crowd,* abr. ed., Yale University Press, New Haven, 1961.

[23] Sharon Beatty, Lynn Kahle, Pamela Homer, and Shekhar Misra, "Alternative Measurement Approaches to the Rokeach Value Survey," *Psychology & Marketing,* **2**:199, Fall 1985.

[24] R. M. Williams, Jr., "Change and Stability in Values and Value Perspectives: A Sociological Perspective," in M. Rokeach (ed.), *Understanding Human Values: Individual and Societal,* Free Press, New York, 1979; and Yankelovich, *New Rules. 1981.*

[25] Royce Anderson and David Brinberg, "The Rokeach Value Survey and Consumer Behavior: Theory, Method and Guidelines," in Richard J. Lutz (ed.), *Advances in Consumer Research,* vol. 13, Association for Consumer Research, Provo, Utah, 1986, p. 662.

[26] See, for example, R. E. Pitts and A. G. Woodside (eds.), *Personal Values and Consumer Psychology*, Lexington Books, Lexington, Mass. 1984; Walter A. Henry, "Cultural Values Do Correlate with Consumer Behavior," *Journal of Marketing Research*, **13**:121–127, May 1976; Joseph F. Hair, Jr., and Rolph E. Anderson, "Culture, Acculturation, and Consumer Behavior," in Helmut Becker and Boris Becker (eds.), *Combined Proceedings*, American Marketing Association, Chicago, 1972, pp. 423–428; Roy A. Herberger and Dodds I. Buchanan, "The Impact of Concern for Ecological Factors on Consumer Attitudes and Buying Behavior," in Fred C. Allvine (ed.), *Combined Proceedings*, American Marketing Association, Chicago, 1971, pp. 644–646; Donald E. Vinson, Jerome E. Scott, and Lawrence M. Lamont, "The Role of Personal Values in Marketing and Consumer Behavior," *Journal of Marketing*, **41**:44–50, April 1977; and Kent L. Granzin and Kenneth D. Bahn, "Do Values Have General Applicability to Retail Market Segmentation?" in Robert H. Ross, Frederick B. Kraft, and Charles H. Davis (eds.), *1981 Southwestern Marketing Proceedings*, The Southwestern Marketing Association, Wichita, Kan. 1981, pp. 146–149.

[27] Henry, "Cultural Values," pp. 121–127.

[28] Glenn S. Omura, "Cultural Values as an Aid in Understanding Domestic Versus Foreign Ownership," in John H. Summey and Ronald D. Taylor (eds.), *Evolving Marketing Thought for 1980*, Southern Marketing Association, Carbondale, Ill. 1980, pp. 141–144.

[29] R. E. Pitts and A. G. Woodside, "Personal Value Influences on Consumer Product Class and Brand Preferences," *Journal of Social Psychology*, **119**:37–53, 1983; and Alfred S. Boote, "Psychographics: Mind Over Matter," *American Demographics*, April 1980.

[30] Alfred S. Boote, "An Exploratory Investigation of the Roles of Needs and Personal Values in the Theory of Buyer Behavior," unpublished doctoral dissertation, Columbia University, 1975.

[31] Alfred S. Boote, "Market Segmentation by Personal Values and Salient Product Attributes," *Journal of Advertising Research*, **21**:29–35, February 1981; and Kenneth D. Bahn and Kent L. Granzin, "Alternative Means of Marketing Segmentation in the Restaurant Industry," in Terrence A. Shimp et al. (eds.), *1986 AMA Educators' Proceedings*, American Marketing Association, Chicago, 1986, pp. 321–326.

[32] L. L. Manzer and S. J. Miller, "An Examination of the Value-Attitude Structure in the Study of Donor Behavior," presented at annual meeting of American Institute for Decision Sciences November 1978.

[33] L. Bozinoff and R. Cohen, "The Effects of Personal Values and Usage Situations on Product Attribute Importance," in B. J. Walker et al. (eds.), *An Assessment of Marketing Thought and Practice*, American Marketing Association, Chicago, 1982, pp. 25–29.

[34] B. W. Becker and P. E. Conner, "The Influence of Personal Values on Attitude and Store Choice Behavior," in B. J. Walker et al. (eds.), *An Assessment of Marketing Thought and Practice*, American Marketing Association, Chicago, 1982, pp. 21–24.

[35] John S. Wagle and William O. Hancock, "Matching Values Presented in Mass Media Vehicles to Promotional Messages: A Shortcut to the Marketing Concept," in Paul Thistlethwaite, Dorrie Billingsly, and John Berens (eds.), *Proceedings*, Midwest Marketing Association, Macomb, Ill., 1985, pp. 35–40.

[36] Francesco M. Nicosia and Robert N. Mayer, "Toward a Sociology of Consumption," *Journal of Consumer Research*, **3**:65–75, September 1976.

[37] Niles Howard, "A New Way to View Customers," *Dun's Review*, August 1981, pp. 42–46.

[38] Howard, "A New Way," p. 46.

[39] Betsy Sharkey, "New VALS Study Identifies Consumers' Spouses," *Adweek*, **35**:58, February 11, 1985.

[40] Lynn R. Kahle, "Social Values in the Eighties: A Special Issue," *Psychology & Marketing*, **2**:234, Winter 1985.

[41] John Naisbitt, *Megatrends*, Warner Books, New York, 1982.

[42] "American Values: Change and Stability," *Public Opinion*, December/January 1984, pp. 2–8; and Susanna McBee, "The State of American Values," *U.S. News & World Report*, December 9, 1985, pp. 54–58.

[43] Daniel Yankelovich, "New Rules in American Life: Search for Self-Fulfillment in a World Turned Upside Down," *Psychology Today*, April 1981, p. 60.

[44] "Smith Outlines Eight Trends to Watch," *Advertising Age*, August 24, 1981, p. 22.

[45] Barbara A. Price, "What the Baby Boom Believes," *American Demographics*, May 1984, pp. 30–33.

[46] Philip Kotler, *Marketing Management: Analysis, Planning and Control,* 3d ed., Prentice-Hall, Englewood Cliffs, N.J., 1976, p. 43.

[47] "Changing Attitudes of Youth on Sex, Patriotism and Work," *U.S. News & World Report,* June 3, 1974, pp. 66–67.

[48] Daniel Yankelovich, "New Rules: Some Implications for Advertising," *Journal of Advertising Research,* **22**:9–14, October/November 1982.

[49] "Prepare for the Future: Explore These Six Trends," *Marketing News,* January 4, 1985, p. 26.

[50] "Managers Should Position Products for Emerging Uninhibited Consumers," *Marketing News,* February 1, 1985, p. 28.

[51] Roger D. Blackwell, "Successful Retailers of 80s Will Cater to Specific Lifestyle Segments," *Marketing News,* March 7, 1980, p. 3.

[52] "Urgent: Greater Sensitivity to Social Change," *Grey Matter,* 1976.

[53] "Analyze Lifestyle Trends to Predict Future Product/Market Opportunities," *Marketing News,* July 10, 1981, p. 8.

[54] Vinson, Scott, and Lamont, "The Role of Personal Values," p. 49.

[55] Blackwell, "Successful Retailers," p. 3.

[56] E. B. Weiss, "Creative Advertising Moves Toward the New Society," *Advertising Age,* **4**:27–28, July 2, 1973.

[57] Alvin Toffler, *The Third Wave,* Morrow, New York, 1980.

[58] Philip Kotler, "The Prosumer Movement: A New Challenge for Marketers," in Richard J. Lutz (ed.), *Advances in Consumer Research,* vol. 13, Association for Consumer Research, Provo, Utah, 1986, pp. 510–513.

[59] Reprinted from "Toffler on Marketing," *Marketing News,* March 15, 1985, p. 31, published by the American Marketing Association.

[60] "A Dip Into a Think Tank," *Time,* November 30, 1981, p. 65.

[61] Harold H. Kassarjian, "Content Analysis in Consumer Research," *Journal of Consumer Research,* **4**:110, June 1977.

[62] B. G. Yovovich, "His Crystal Ball: The Daily Newspaper," *Advertising Age,* October 11, 1982, pp. M-4-M-5.

[63] "Information on Values and Lifestyles Needed to Identify Buying Patterns," *Marketing News,* October 5, 1979, p. 1.

[64] Lee Adler, "Cashing-In on the Cop-Out: Cultural Change and Marketing Potential," *Business Horizons,* February 1970, pp. 21–27.

[65] See, for example, Hans B. Thorelli, Helmut Becker, and Jack Engledow, *The Information Seekers,* Ballinger, Cambridge, Mass. 1975; Jagdish N. Sheth and S. Prakash Sethi, "Theory of Cross-Cultural Buyer Behavior," *Faculty Working Papers,* University of Illinois, May 31, 1973; Robert T. Green and Eric Langeard, "A Cross-National Comparison of Consumer Habits and Innovation Characteristics," *Journal of Marketing,* **39**:34–41, July 1975; and Susan P. Douglas, "Cross-Cultural Comparisons: The Myth of the Stereotype," Marketing Science Institute, Cambridge, Mass. 1975.

[66] Lawrence Stessin, "Incidents of Culture Shock Among American Businessmen Overseas," *Pittsburgh Business Review,* November–December 1971, p. 1.

[67] James A. Lee, "Cultural Analysis in Overseas Operations," *Harvard Business Review,* **44**:106, March–April 1966.

[68] Elizabeth C. Hirschman, "Primitive Aspects of Consumption in Modern American Society," *Journal of Consumer Research,* **12**:142–154, September 1985.

[69] Theodore Levitt, "The Globalization of Markets," *Harvard Business Review,* **83**:92–102, May–June 1983.

[70] Ronald Alsop, "Efficacy of Global Ad Projects Is Questioned in Firm's Survey," *The Wall Street Journal,* September 11, 1984, p. 31.

[71] Christine Dugas and Marilyn A. Harris, "Playtex Kicks Off a One-Ad-Fits-All Campaign," *Business Week,* December 16, 1985, pp. 48–49.

[72] Harper W. Boyd, Ronald Frank, William Massy, and Mostafa Zoheir, "On the Use of Marketing Research in the Emerging Economies," *Journal of Marketing Research,* **1**:23, November 1964.

[73] "When Fragmenting Works Better Than Segmenting," *Marketing News,* January 3, 1986, p. 56.

[74] Charles M. Schaninger, Jacques C. Bourgeois, and W. Christian Buss, "French-English Canadian Subcultural Consumption Differences," *Journal of Marketing,* **49**:82–92, Spring 1985.

[75] Alice Rudolph, "Standardization not Standard for Global Marketers," *Marketing News,* September 27, 1986, p. 3.

[76] "Global Approach Seeks Similarities in Markets," *Marketing News,* October 11, 1985, p. 13.

[77] Rudolph, "Standardization," p. 3.

[78] Nicole Seligman, "Be Sure Not to Wear a Green Hat if You Visit Hong Kong," *The Wall Street Journal,* May 10, 1979, p. 41.

[79] Jac Goldstucker, "The Influence of Culture on Channels of Distribution," in Robert L. King (ed.), *Marketing and the New Science of Planning,* American Marketing Association, Chicago, 1968, p. 470.

SUBCULTURES

LEARNING OBJECTIVES
After studying this chapter, you should understand . . .

■ The nature of subcultures and the variety of possible subcultural targets for the marketer

■ The types of ethnic subcultures of significance to marketers

■ Important demographic and psychographic features of the major racial and nationality ethnic categories within the United States

■ How consumer behavior within black and Hispanic subcultures may differ from that of whites and non-Hispanics, as well as possible marketing mixes to target each effectively

■ Characteristics of both youth and elderly subcultures and their consumer-behavior patterns

■ Marketing-mix guidelines for attracting young and old-age subcultures

New Coke is out to break Pepsi's hold on teenagers, those who drink more cola than anybody. The company has developed an imaginative campaign featuring a British cult figure called Max Headroom, a computer-generated personality known as TV's ''ultimate talking head.'' Max is played by an actor who spends four hours being made up and appears to have a face made of plastic. His act is taped, then run through a computer to achieve an enhanced visual image and a synthesized voice that sometimes stutters and is often out of sync with his lips. Max's appearances as America's leading ''Cokeologist'' in his ''Catch the Wave'' spots have become the hit of the airwaves—especially among the 12 to 24 age group being targeted by Coke.[1]

7

This is an example of how marketers may achieve success by properly understanding subcultural behavior patterns. The youth market—the largest consumers of soft drinks—may be viewed by Coca-Cola as a subculture and thus segmented accordingly. The result is a successful marketing program to appeal to this group.

THE NATURE OF SUBCULTURE

We learned in Chapter 6 that one's cultural heritage has a very basic and lasting influence on his or her consumer behavior. Culture was seen to consist of basic behavioral patterns which exist in a society. However, as we saw from the discussion of countercultures, not all segments of a society have the same cultural patterns. Perhaps, therefore, the marketer can distinguish more homogeneous subgroups within the heterogeneous national society.

We refer to these groups as *subcultures* because they have values, customs, traditions, and other ways of behaving that are peculiar to a particular group within a culture. This means that there are subcultures of students, professors, professional football players, prison inmates, rock musicians, marketers, and other groups. Moreover, individuals may be members of more than one subculture at the same time. Thus, it is imperative that marketers understand who constitutes the most relevant subculture for their particular product or service. By knowing the characteristics and behavioral patterns of the segment they are trying to reach, they are in a better position to refine the marketing mix required to satisfy that target segment properly.

Although subcultures may be categorized along seemingly infinite dimensions, this chapter will examine only a few of the less-understood, but important, subcultures that exist in the United States. The fact that these groups are among the most easily identifiable subcultures in the United States makes their segmentation feasible. This chapter examines consumer behavior within two broad subculture categories: ethnic and age. A final point must be made before proceeding to a discussion of these subcultures, however. The groups to be discussed in this chapter should not be considered monolithic. That is, in spite of numerous similarities within any subculture a subculture is not merely one homogeneous market, but instead consists of various subsegments.[2]

Ethnic is the generic term used to describe the approximately 106 groups in America characterized by a distinctive origin. Generally, it refers to the minority groups of a society. Ethnic identification is based on what a person is when he or she is born, and it is largely unchangeable after that.[3] Members of a given ethnic group (1) generally descend from common forebearers, (2) tend to reside in the same locale—and one that is distinct from another ethnic group—over generations, (3) tend to marry within their own group, (4) give certain objects meanings unique to their ethnic group over generations, and (5) share a common sense of peoplehood—of kindredness.[4]

Consumers may be subdivided into the following three types of ethnic dimensions, only the first two of which will be examined further in this chapter:

1 *Race.* Racial subcultures are made up of people with a common biological heritage involving certain physical distinctions. The two most significant minority races in the United States for the marketer are blacks and Orientals. We will examine only the black market, however. While Asians are the fastest growing minority in the United States, they represent only 2 percent of the population and will reach just 3 percent by 2000.[5]

2 *Nationality*. People with a common national origin constitute another ethnic subculture. The nationality grouping is usually characterized by a distinctive language or accent. The minority market segment to be discussed in this category will be the Hispanics.

3 *Religion*. Religious subcultures are composed of people with a common and unique system of worship. Two important minority religious segments are Jews and Catholics. However, useful knowledge about the consumer behavior of these groups is presently quite limited and will not be discussed in this chapter.[6]

The power of subcultures and their impact on potential marketing plans is evident when it is considered that in more than half of the cities of 100,000 population or more, at least 25 percent of the residents are minorities. And twenty-five of the nation's largest cities—including Chicago, Detroit, Baltimore, New Orleans, San Antonio, Atlanta, Miami, Los Angeles, and Washington, D.C.—have *majority* populations of Asians, blacks, Hispanics, and other minorities.[7]

The ethnic dimensions will now be illustrated by discussing two examples of important U.S. subcultures. Then two subcultures based on age will be discussed to illustrate better how consumer behavior varies among such groups.

THE BLACK SUBCULTURE

There are four reasons that the black market exists and is important: (1) the people making up this market are identifiable, (2) they have definable purchase patterns, (3) the market is very large, and (4) the market is concentrated in certain locations within the United States. This section will review some unique aspects of black consumer behavior and its relevant marketing strategy implications.

DEMOGRAPHIC CHARACTERISTICS

Generally, blacks may be described as disadvantaged compared with whites, in terms of education and occupational attainment. They are also more likely than whites to live in the crowded, poorer neighborhoods of large cities.

Size The black market, America's largest racial minority market, amounts to 30 million people, or about 12 percent of the total U.S. market. The market size is increasing over twice as fast as the white population and is projected to comprise 36 million people by the year 2000.

Location Although the percentage of blacks in the total U.S. population has remained rather constant since 1900, their geographic distribution has changed significantly during the last few decades. The percent living in the south has decreased slowly until 1980 when reverse immigration began to occur, yet the south still accounts for about half of all blacks in the United States and for

approximately 20 percent of the region's population (compared with a less-than-10-percent share of the population in the north and west).

Income and Employment Patterns Black buying power stands at approximately $150 billion. However, while the ratio of black family income to that of whites has increased, the median figure is still only 57 percent that of whites.

The proportion of blacks in each occupational category is beginning to approximate more closely their share of the total labor force. Thus, more members of this group have moved into skilled, better-paying jobs.

Education On this factor, blacks have steadily improved their position. The college enrollment of blacks has increased greatly, as has the number of black college graduates. Nevertheless, the proportion of whites who have completed four or more years of college is over 2½ times the percentage of blacks.

Family and Age Patterns One of the most striking patterns of the black family is its tendency toward matrilinealism. Almost 34 percent of all black families are headed by a female, compared to only about 10 percent of white families.

A final characteristic that distinguishes this group is its age distribution. It is considerably younger than the white population—with a median age of 25 compared to 31 for whites.

PSYCHOGRAPHIC CHARACTERISTICS

Recent lifestyle and psychographic segmentation research on the black market has led to numerous interesting and useful findings, some of which are presented in Table 7-1. The Leo Burnett advertising agency has concluded that black female lifestyle patterns, particularly in an urban setting, indicate a stronger interest in style and fashion than those of whites.[8] There is also less mobility and less involvement in traditional civic and community organizations, greater reliance on the electronic media, and a stronger sense of alienation than with the average white American. Black women also have a stronger commitment to the importance of work and a clearer career orientation than do white women. Their lifestyle patterns and attitudes generally reveal the importance of money and budgeting and the need to be conservative, smart shoppers. As reflects their generally lower incomes, black women are more value conscious, more expectant of future income gains, and are heavier advertising readers. In spite of this orientation, there appears to be little advertising directed toward the black woman, acknowledging her needs and attitudes in this area of price and value.[9]

There also are important differences between middle-class black and middle-class white women in the area of the home. Black women have a stronger self-perception about neatness and traditional home pride. They work hard to keep their home neat and clean, and they have a strong desire to live even better in the future and to make improvements such as installing better fixtures and dependable appliances.

Although lifestyle research has found that there are really more similarities than differences between black and white women, there are still a number of implications from findings such as those cited above. First, since black families are larger than white ones, with more working mothers, this group could be an

excellent target for many convenience foods and home appliances. Second, be-cause of the unrealized aspirations among black women, advertisers should be careful not to "overpromise" them. Third, their shopping patterns suggest that advertising to black women could stress price and value. Finally, this group appears to be a promising market for home cleaning and personal hygiene products.

CONSUMER BEHAVIOR AND MARKETING IMPLICATIONS

The following examples illustrate some of the differences between black consum-ers and the general market:

How would you advertise liquor and automobiles to blacks? According to a New York advertising executive, not without carefully understanding men's and women's roles in black families. In white families, wives have become increasingly influential in the selection of liquor brands. However, the black male has remained much more dominant in brand selection than his white counterpart. Thus, effective promotion of scotch relies on appealing to black masculinity. Scotch is known as the "black man's martini," whereas gin is perceived by blacks as a woman's drink. Failing to understand such perceptions, a major scotch brand and several bourbon brands have hurt their standing

TABLE 7-1

Black and White Lifestyle Differences

	Percent agreed	
	White	**Black**
Strong pride toward home		
I take great pride in my home.	73	77
I get satisfaction out of cleaning because that is what people notice.	29	46
I am a very neat person.	50	66
A house should be dusted and polished at least three times a week.	23	41
A desire to improve it		
I would like to move to a larger house.	33	47
I like ultra-modern style furniture.	14	34
When buying appliances, it pays to get the best even though it's more expensive.	61	73
I like to own the most expensive things.	14	25
Attitudes toward money management		
Our income is satisfactory.	48	27
Our family is too heavily in debt today.	15	32
I wish we had more money.	46	71
Five years from now our income will be a lot higher.	39	48
Grocery shopping for my family means following a strict budget.	34	43
I watch the advertisements for sales.	66	70
I study the grocery store ads in the newspaper each week.	66	74

Source: Leo Burnett Company.

by depicting women in ads to blacks. Similarly, marketers must be careful about depicting families in car ads aimed at blacks. Among blacks, cars are more an individual, ego-oriented product. Unlike white consumers' idea of a "family car," for black men automobiles are a "man's car" that the family just happens to use.[10]

Now let us examine some specific consumer-behavior findings regarding this market. We shall look at the most important elements and see how they relate to marketing-strategy variables.

Product Purchase Patterns   Research studies show that there are important differences between black and white purchasing patterns.[11] For example, with regard to the general spending behavior of blacks versus whites, the following three major findings have emerged:

1   Total consumption expenditures are less for blacks than for comparable-income whites; that is, blacks save more out of a given income than do whites.

2   Black consumers spend more for clothing and nonautomobile transportation and less for food, housing, medical care, and automobile transportation than do comparable-income whites.

3   There is no consistent racial difference in expenditures for either recreation and leisure or for home furnishings and equipment at comparable income levels.[12]

There are some rather obvious reasons that account for these consumption differences, as well as some reasons that are more subtle.[13] For example, with regard to owning major home appliances, low ownership appears to be primarily related to low income, substandard housing, and lack of proper utility connections. Another reason behind the different black and white consumption patterns is the blacks' narrower spectrum of choice due to their history of being discriminated against. That is, blacks have had less selection in the purchase of homes, vacations, travel, dining, entertainment, and so on, which has resulted in a greater expenditure per unit on other things that are available to them.[14] Nevertheless, the pattern is changing so that today blacks are spending more for such things as housing, recreation, travel, and education. Effective marketing and public relations campaigns by such companies as American Airlines, PepsiCo, and Greyhound have both influenced and benefited from such changing patterns.[15]

Another factor that may cause different consumption patterns is thought to be the tendency by minority groups to engage in *compensatory consumption,* that is, an attempt to purchase the material goods that are reflective of their achievement of full status in American society. Results of product-usage research, in fact, support this general pattern and suggest that blacks spend more on socially visible products than do whites of the same income class.

Studies have consistently shown that blacks are prone to buy brands that are nationally advertised, those that have a prestige connotation, and those about which they can feel confident.[16] In fact, as prices increase, the movement of black consumers toward private labels and generics is slower than it is for the general population.[17] It has been found that blacks in some shopping situations remain loyal to some national brands even when prices are raised 45 percent or more.[18]

Black consumers are open to trying new products if these products are appropriately presented as items that can perhaps help them live better, save time, or achieve more status. For example, pop wines were positioned as a new, stylish drink to enjoy when having fun, and they immediately became popular with blacks.

One factor affecting new-product adoption has been found to be the social visibility of the product. Blacks appear to be less innovative than whites with respect to appliances and food—two nonsocially visible items. They are more innovative than whites, however, with respect to socially visible fashions and clothing.[19] Blacks appear to be trend-setters in fashion, hair styles, shoes, and evening apparel.[20] The understanding that black fashion innovation may have different characteristics than that for whites, however, offers opportunities for developing appropriate marketing strategies to deal with those variations. For instance, black female innovators place greater emphasis on the area of credit/billing policies offered by retailers than do whites. They also possess fewer credit cards, have different media patterns (for example, they are much more likely to prefer rock/jazz radio programming as opposed to white's easy-listening music preferences), and have significantly less participation in formal group memberships and organized social activities than do whites.[21]

Shopping Behavior   The black market has also been researched on the basis of its shopping patterns. Here, too, differences have been found between whites and blacks. While much of the research deals with food-purchasing habits, other product shopping patterns have also been investigated.

A study by *Progressive Grocer* of factors influencing store choice found that blacks' assessments of supermarkets generally match those of the population at large. There are several differences, however, that could prove useful to supermarket managers when planning marketing strategy. Although brand loyalty is generally high, store loyalty is not as strong. One study showed that only 59 percent of blacks are always or almost always satisfied with the food stores where they do most of their shopping, compared to 72 percent of whites.[22]

Firm conclusions cannot yet be drawn about black shopping patterns in nonfood stores. However, one study did find that blacks frequented discount stores (as opposed to department stores) more often than did whites (although this finding tends to vanish where upper-income blacks are concerned).[23] A probable reason for this patronage is the emphasis on price by black shoppers. Another reason could be related to the atmosphere of large department stores, which has been found to cause some feelings of insecurity among black shoppers.[24]

Clothing purchases by black women have also been the subject of some research studies. A general pattern appears to be the frequent use of department, discount, and chain stores by black women and of department and specialty stores by white women. Findings seem to differ, though, depending on factors such as age, geographic location, social class, and fashion consciousness.[25]

Promoting to Blacks   The lack of fuller understanding of black consumer behavior has probably perplexed marketers most in the area of promotion. For instance, marketers have wondered whether they should promote in a specialized way through specialized media to reach the black market or whether they should

expect to reach it through their general appeal to the broad market of consumers. In addition, concern exists regarding whether advertisements should be all-black in content, or mixed, or all-white. These questions are addressed in this section.

MEDIA PATTERNS   The issue of specialized versus general advertising programs cannot be resolved easily, but one can obtain a better understanding of the problem by looking at the alternatives. There are three main avenues that may be taken in a specialized appeal to blacks—radio, magazines, and newspapers aimed specifically at the black market. Television, a fourth approach, has been tried, but only to a limited extent. The big advantage of black media is that blacks know the advertisement is meant for them, while in other media they may not always be sure.

Black media have developed mainly since World War II, and they include dozens of magazines, several hundred newspapers and radio stations, and one TV channel. Only a very small amount of all advertising, however, is placed in those media. Of the more than $14 billion spent in advertising each year, barely 1 percent is spent in black media, and slightly more than that is spent in advertising specifically created for the black consumer.[26]

The major black-oriented medium is radio, since research shows that blacks spend more time listening to radio than do whites. Moreover, approximately one-half of all listening done by blacks is to black radio stations.[27] Black magazines are read widely by both black men and women and have substantially higher readership than general-market magazines. Blacks have a strong attachment to such media because they emphasize black achievements in government, business, sports, and the arts. For example, *Ebony* and *Jet* are the two most widely read magazines among both black men and women.[28]

Although there are numerous black-oriented radio and magazine vehicles, black television programming is less widespread. There have been a few network shows featuring blacks and their lifestyles, with black situation comedies being the most popular. Daytime soap operas, news, and game shows also have high viewership among blacks. There is also an increase in the amount of syndicated television programming being developed for this audience. However, television is primarily a white-oriented medium, and as such, many marketing experts doubt that sole reliance on television can effectively sell this ethnic market. In fact, reliance on black-oriented prime-time network series programming to deliver massive tune-in by blacks may not even be justified. An Arbitron television study provides data indicating that in some markets, more blacks would be reached with commercials on some white-oriented programs than on the top black-oriented shows.[29]

Outdoor advertising should also be mentioned as an attractive vehicle by which blacks can be reached, because of their geographic concentration. Alka-Seltzer, for example, has used two versions of the same billboard ad. The words are the same on both, but black models are used in black areas and white models in other areas. Liquor, beer, soft-drink, and cigarette manufacturers are other frequent users of outdoor ethnic advertising.

EFFECTIVE MESSAGES   The use of both black and white models in integrated ads for general-coverage media has been fairly recent. Most research on integrated

advertising has shown that both races react favorably to such ads,[30] although one recent study of print ads indicates that blacks considered "black-only" ads to be more realistic, stimulating, and indicative of their social reality than "white-only" and integrated ads.[31] "Tokenism" in advertising is viewed unfavorably among blacks. Therefore, the marketer must take care to avoid such an impression.

Even advertising themes or appeals may need tailoring to special market segments, as the following examples show:

A&P developed its "Price and Pride" campaign for the general market. However, the company was under a great deal of pressure because of its lack of attention to the black consumer. In tone and approach, Mr. Price and Mr. Pride reaffirmed A&P's negative position as far as the black consumer was concerned. Thus, for the black community, A&P came up with the "We're Going to Make Your Bag Our Bag" campaign. In its first phase, the campaign told black consumers that A&P heard their dissatisfaction and was going to change. Subsequent advertising featured foods purchased more heavily by blacks, and black health and beauty aids. The company chose TV, black radio, and black magazines such as *Ebony* and *Essence* to reach its desired segment.[32]

Thus, companies should test different appeals among market segments to find which one works best.

Blacks have a distinctive way of looking at ads. They tend to view advertising as doing two things—selling the product and contributing to the overall process of building the image of black people in general. Thus, the marketer should carefully attempt to accomplish both goals. The use of a black celebrity is one way that companies can mount effective promotion programs. A recent survey found that 49 percent of the blacks surveyed said they would be more likely to purchase a product featuring a black ad representative.[33] Consequently, a number of highly regarded blacks have been used in ad campaigns by major companies. For instance, Bill Cosby advertises Del Monte vegetables and Jell-O Puddings (see Figure 7-1), O. J. Simpson advertises Hertz car rentals, Muhammad Ali has appeared in some public service advertisements, and Reggie Jackson was featured in Volkswagen commercials.

THE HISPANIC SUBCULTURE

Hispanics are the nation's second-largest and its fastest-growing minority market. In spite of their potential as a consumer goods market, however, Hispanics are not well understood by marketers. This is a segment with which the marketer should be familiar. Moreover, the future impact of this group on the United States and on the marketer is expected to be even greater. Here, the important demographic characteristics of this market will first be presented in order to bring this market more clearly into focus. This will be followed by a discussion of the most significant consumer-behavior and marketing implications.

DEMOGRAPHIC CHARACTERISTICS

The Hispanic market differs radically from other ethnic segments and mainstream America in that it is continually infused with new immigrants from the Spanish-

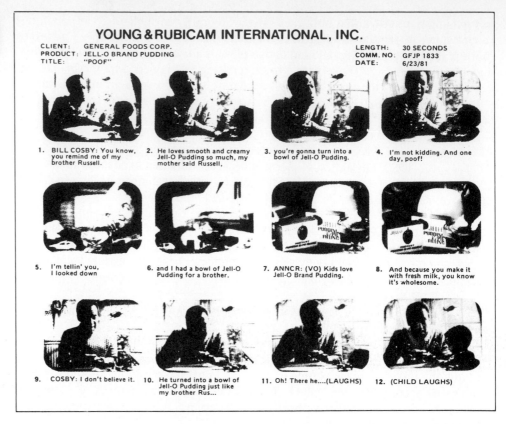

FIGURE 7-1
Advertisement for Jell-O Brand Pudding. Courtesy of General Foods Corporation.

speaking world. The old country is never far away, either symbolically or geographically. This group also clings tenaciously to the Spanish language, the Catholic church, and the family unit, and it generally defies the melting-pot concept. Many Hispanics, although they like the idea of living in America, want to keep their culture and language. For example, almost half consider themselves "Hispanic first, American second." Of the remainder, almost all say "Hispanic and American equally."[34]

Size This market consists of approximately 18 million people. Between 1970 and 1980, the Hispanic segment increased by 61 percent (partially due to a more complete census count of all Hispanics, including the very large number of illegal Hispanic aliens in the United States). This segment should number 21 million by 1990 and nearly 30 million by 2000.[35] A large portion of this market's growth comes from immigration. More than six in ten Hispanic-American adults were born outside the United States.

The U.S. Hispanic population is largely of Mexican origin (61 percent of the total), with Puerto Ricans (15 percent) and Cubans (7 percent) comprising the other significant categories of origin.

Location The Spanish subculture is largely an urban population segment. For example, in 1980 about 82 percent of all Hispanics lived in metropolitan areas, compared to 67 percent of the non-Hispanic population. Moreover, the Hispanic population is concentrated heavily in comparatively few metropolitan areas such as Los Angeles, New York, and Miami, and in a few states—Texas, New Mexico, Arizona, California, Colorado, New York, Pennsylvania, New Jersey, and Florida.

Income and Employment Patterns   Hispanic buying power approaches $100 billion, but the income level of Hispanic families is significantly lower than for families of non-Hispanic origin. The median income for Hispanic families is approximately 66 percent of that for white families, generally. In higher-income brackets this disparity continues with only half the percentage of Hispanic families earning more than $25,000, compared to families of non-Hispanic origin.

Occupations of men of Hispanic origin are predominantly blue-collar in nature. Approximately 58 percent of Hispanic men are blue-collar workers, while only 24 percent work at white-collar occupations.

Education   Hispanics generally attain a slightly lower level of education than do blacks and other non-Hispanics. Among Hispanic people 25 to 29 years of age, approximately 57 percent have completed high school as compared to more than 87 percent of persons of non-Hispanic origin. However, Hispanics believe *saber es poder* (knowledge is power), and younger Hispanics are rapidly closing the education gap.

Family and Age Patterns   Hispanic families are, on the average, larger than non-Hispanic families, with the mean number of persons in the Spanish-origin family being 3.85 as compared to 3.28 for non-Spanish-origin families. The family unit also appears to be stronger than does the family unit for non-Hispanics.

The Hispanic market is a much younger market than is the non-Hispanic market. The median age for Hispanics is 23, with approximately 41 percent of the Hispanic market being less than 18 years of age, as compared to 28 percent for the non-Spanish-origin population.

PSYCHOGRAPHIC CHARACTERISTICS

In spite of the background, migration, and socioeconomic differences among the Hispanic nationality subgroups, there is a great degree of homogeneity in their lifestyle patterns. In comparison with others, some interesting results show up. Table 7-2 presents data comparing the general U.S. population with Hispanics on several lifestyle and product-ownership dimensions.

CONSUMER BEHAVIOR AND MARKETING IMPLICATIONS

More and more companies are recognizing the importance of the Hispanic-American market. In this section, several of the marketing-mix variables will be examined to understand the major implications of Spanish-American consumer behavior on these decision areas.

Product Purchase Patterns   The marketer should be aware that the Hispanic market is highly individualistic in its product and brand preferences, which are often reflective of cultural differences. For some products, particularly food

purchases, this market is very significant. Partly because of their larger-than-average families, they spend about 10 percent more per week on food purchases than do other groups. In addition, more Hispanic households visit fast-food restaurants frequently than do non-Hispanic consumers. For example, 20 percent of those from Hispanic homes visit such outlets more than once per week, versus 9 percent of those from non-Hispanic homes.[36] They are also much heavier consumers of beverages such as soft drinks and beer. The Schaefer Brewing

TABLE 7-2
Hispanic Lifestyle and Product Ownership Characteristics

	Hispanics					United States total
Percent who agree/strongly agree with statements	**Total**	**Puerto Rico**	**Mexico**	**Cuba**	**Other**	
Optimism in improved standard of living It is becoming harder to be optimistic that our standard of living in the future is going to be better than it is now.	61	67	58	60	66	77
Pleasure from work I don't expect to get much pleasure from my work. Work is just what you do to earn a living.	41	46	37	35	52	24
Materialism/tangibles I prefer to spend money on tangible things that I can keep rather than on things that give me temporary enjoyment like a vacation and so on.	61	75	55	51	74	48
Live for today I try to have as much fun as I can now and let the future take care of itself.	36	29	36	29	41	47
Feelings of despair I often feel there is nothing in this world worth striving for.	24	27	22	12	37	16
Interest in change I need to satisfy my hunger for new experiences.	62	55	61	65	68	62
Physical attractiveness I need to keep up with the new styles.	49	51	42	69	64	46
Physical fitness We are all getting soft; it is more important today than ever to take special measures to maintain our health.	86	92	85	79	86	90
Individualism People should be free to look, dress, and live the way they want to whether others like it or not.						
1 Fits me very well.	47	50	42	47	55	43
2 Fits me pretty well.	33	24	35	39	33	31
3 All right for others.	14	12	17	10	8	17
4 Don't approve at all.	6	14	6	4	4	9
Nonconformity *Many people are puzzled by the changing values of this country. They feel it's difficult to know whether something that is wrong today will still be wrong a year from now. Other people are not at all influenced by changing values; they have their own long-standing personal standards of right and wrong to guide them.*						
1 Puzzled by changing values.	28	45	25	35	30	27
2 Uncertain.	25	30	23	37	21	16
3 Guided by personal standards.	47	25	52	28	49	57

Company, for example, estimates Spanish beer consumption to be 1.5 times greater than the national average.

Hispanic-Americans are highly brand-loyal, trusting well-known, high-quality, and familiar brands. For example, Sears has learned that Hispanics tend to buy more of its DieHard batteries and Craftsman tools than does the population in general. Thus, the U.S. Hispanic population is more likely than the U.S. Anglo population to stress product quality, to value name or advertised brands, and to be brand-loyal, yet, at the same time, to seem receptive to new products.[37] Such strong Hispanic brand loyalty can be a significant resource for a company. For example, a marketing research study within the Los Angeles market shows that Hispanics prefer U.S. autos over imports by a 9 percent margin. Thus, they have a greater likelihood of purchasing U.S. cars than do Anglo new-car buyers. This finding should be of much interest to U.S. car manufacturers, such as Chrysler, in

Percent who agree/strongly agree with statements	Hispanics					United States total
	Total	Puerto Rico	Mexico	Cuba	Other	
Attitude toward family *There should be less emphasis on family togetherness and more on the individual.*						
1 Fits me very well.	14	11	10	9	31	13
2 Fits me pretty well.	19	20	19	13	23	19
3 All right for others.	23	21	23	44	14	24
4 Don't approve at all.	44	48	48	34	32	44
Attitude toward sex roles *Being masculine means:*						
A good provider to his wife and family.	55	67	57	58	37	36
Someone you can depend on in times of need	15	10	17	13	12	23
Just a person who happens to have been born a male rather than a female.	9	6	9	7	11	18
A leader, not a follower.	5	4	3	3	12	10
Sexually attractive to women.	3	1	—	4	12	9
Makes the important decisions for the family.	10	9	11	12	7	4
Careers for women *Suppose a married woman with children wants to work and is able to handle her home and family while pursuing a career. How do you feel about it?*						
Such a woman should definitely be given the opportunity to have a career.	48	46	49	56	45	48
Even if she wants to and can work, a woman with children and home responsibilities should only consider part-time work while her children are in school.	29	30	29	15	30	35
Unless the extra money is needed, a woman with children should not have an outside job, even if she wants one.	23	24	22	26	25	17
Luxury product ownership (percentage who own):						
Color TV	83	82	83	94	80	83
Stereo equipment	71	81	66	83	73	63
Sewing machine	50	42	54	63	38	57
Tape recorder	47	46	42	62	60	51
TV videogame	11	4	13	20	7	18

Source: Yankelovich, Skelly, and White, Inc., *Spanish U.S.A: A Study of the Hispanic Market in the United States*, The SIN National Television Network, New York, June 1981, pp. 10, 11, 13.

their battles with foreign imports. Despite this favorable Hispanic predisposition toward domestic cars, however, Chrysler has only recently begun to advertise specifically to this group via Spanish-language ads.[38] Hispanics, according to a New York study, concentrate their influence on a relatively few brands. Although comprising only 12 percent of metropolitan New York's population, their highly concentrated purchasing can change a brand's overall market share considerably. For example, about 4 percent of non-Hispanics cite Tang as their most-often-used brand of powdered drink, but among Hispanics, 33 percent name Tang, leading to an overall share of 11 percent.[39]

The market is also interested in status symbols. Because most Hispanics have come to the United States from poorer countries to seek a better life, they are often interested in purchasing those things that demonstrate that they have "arrived." Bulova watches offer a good example of this attitude:

The Bulova image among Hispanics was once that of a cheap American product. To counter this attitude, the company began to position itself among this segment as an expensive, but affordable, piece of jewelry. Bulova stressed its use of gold and accentuated the fact that it had an extensive line of 18-karat gold watches—because to Hispanics "14-karat" is synonymous with "gold-plated." The result was that Bulova gained a 40 percent share of the Hispanic market.[40]

This subculture generally exhibits more new-product openness than do U.S. consumers as a whole. For example, compared with non-Hispanic consumers, a greater percentage of Hispanic shoppers say they seek:

- New foods to eat at home
- New supermarkets and department stores to shop in
- New laundry and household cleaning products to use
- New types of beer, liquor, and cocktails to drink
- New magazines to read
- New TV programs to watch[41]

Because of value differences between Hispanics and mainstream Americans, different product benefits may need to be stressed when selling to the Hispanic segment compared to the non-Hispanic segment.[42] Product and package adaptations are also sometimes advisable in attracting Hispanics. Whirlpool, for example, has introduced Spanish-language controls and instructions on some of its washers and dryers.

Shopping Behavior   With regard to store selection, research has shown that some Spanish-speaking housewives feel lost in giant supermarkets where they are surrounded by many unfamiliar products and are inhibited about asking questions. Because such uneasiness exists with regard to large stores, these Hispanics do much of their shopping in bodegas, which are small neighborhood stores where only Spanish may be spoken. For example, in New York, bodegas account for 30 percent of the grocery volume among Spanish-speaking residents, in spite of markups at least 13 percent higher than the supermarket average.[43]

Although bodegas and other small retailers are important with some Hispanics, both full-service department stores such as J. C. Penney, Sears, and Macy's, and discount department stores such as Zayre's, K mart, and Target also play an important role in shopping patterns. A New York research study in 1985 showed that 68 percent of Hispanic respondents said they shop at department stores—63 percent of those shop most often at discounters, and 36 percent most often at full-service stores.[44]

Among national retailers J. C. Penney is "luciendo mejor que nunca" (looking smarter than ever) with one of the most sophisticated Hispanic marketing programs. It started with a Spanish booklet telling Hispanic shoppers how to buy from its catalog. This was followed by a credit application in Spanish. The basis of the Penney effort consists of regional Hispanic marketing teams in key cities and including important store management, sales promotion staff, and Hispanic associates. These teams have implemented in-store bilingual directories, service signage, local promotional efforts using Spanish-language television and radio commercials as well as Sunday newspaper preprints. Advertising campaigns start from scratch and commercials are developed to carefully avoid stereotypes and literal translations. Corporate involvement in community activities is also strong.[45]

Promoting to Hispanics The Hispanic market, although concentrated geographically and in urban areas, is sometimes difficult to reach because of the language barrier. A 1981 survey found that approximately 90 percent of the adult Hispanic population speak Spanish and 43 percent speak "only enough English to get by."[46] Therefore, in order to reach this market effectively, Spanish-language media frequently must be used.[47] In fact, 70 percent of Hispanics watch, listen to, or read Spanish media every week. Half of them use Spanish media primarily (that is, 50 percent or more of the time). Of the Spanish media, television is used most, followed closely by radio, and print is a distant third.[48]

MEDIA PATTERNS Television has developed into an important medium for Spanish advertising, with thirteen stations in the United States and four more just across the Mexican border. One study found that 64 percent of Hispanic households in the New York City area were tuned in to a Spanish television station during one weekday evening at prime time.[50] With Hispanic television ownership at approximately the same level as that of the general population, and with the increase in UHF television penetration and the addition of Mexican stations to cable network, the marketer is increasingly able to reach the Hispanic segment by using this medium. Spanish television generally costs much less per thousand viewers reached than does general-market television.

Radio is also an important medium for the Hispanic-American market. There are at least 180 U.S. radio stations that present Spanish-language programming on a full- or part-time basis. Radio ownership in this market is comparable to that for all U.S. households. Moreover, Hispanic-Americans are frequent listeners. A survey of New York Spanish-speaking radio households showed median daily listening of more than 4 hours per day, compared to the average adult listening of

2.5 hours per day for all U.S. radio households. In addition to being frequent listeners, about 60 to 80 percent of Hispanic listeners' time is devoted to Spanish-language programming.[51] Hispanic teens, on the other hand, devote 61 percent of their listening time to contemporary music stations, versus only 14 percent for Spanish stations and almost as much time for black radio stations.[52] Radio is a very effective medium for several reasons: It is inexpensive and flexible, it is accessible when Spanish television may not be on the air (such as mornings), it reaches Hispanics as they engage in day-to-day mobility, and it is often played in the small stores where many Hispanics shop.[53] Both Spanish-language television and radio audiences appear to be composed of less acculturated Hispanics of lesser economic means.[54]

Print media, including magazines and newspapers, are also used to reach the Hispanic-American market. These, however, tend to have much less widespread impact than other media because of the lower literacy rates in the Hispanic population. Nevertheless, this medium cannot be overlooked for the wealthier, better-educated Hispanics.

EFFECTIVE MESSAGES   In order for advertising to the Hispanic-American market to be successful, the communication must fit the people's subculture. Sometimes a general market message may work with Hispanics. For example, the humorous ad shown in Figure 7-2 may be effective without translation into Spanish. However, ads that are authentically Hispanic in setting and language and highly personal in approach are perceived as most meaningful. Even mass-appeal commercials can be used by substituting a Spanish voice-over, but the marketer should be sure that the video portion is appropriate. Some well-known advertising personalities are effectively used in this market. For instance, the late Colonel Sanders and also Frank Perdue have appeared speaking Spanish in commercials for their chicken products.

Numerous language bloopers have been made by firms in advertising to Hispanics. For example, a Spanish-language television commercial for an adhesive bandage recommended for helping *conquitos* on a child's injured knee encountered translation difficulties. Although the word correctly meant "little scratches" to Cubans, to Mexicans it meant "little coconuts"—not exactly what was intended. Several major tobacco companies have advertised low-tar cigarettes with the Spanish word *brea*. Although *brea* translates literally into "tar," it is the type of tar used on streets. Thus, the companies were actually advertising "low-asphalt" cigarettes.[55]

As tailored promotions appear, advertising agencies must keep cultural differences in mind to attain credibility with their Hispanic audiences.[56] The following example illustrates such an acculturated approach:

Budweiser radio advertising has been subsegmented into four styles of music to correspond with the different ethnic types of Hispanics around the country. The music running in Los Angeles has a mariachi sound that appeals to Mexicans living there; in Texas, a polka Nortena is a familiar sound to Texas Hispanics; in Florida, the Cubans listen to a version of their charanga; and in New York, there is a Puerto Rican salsa. The accent used throughout is broadcast Spanish, a sound with no regional ties.[57]

A family tie-in can often be appealing because of this group's large family sizes and their high regard for strong family bonds. Figure 7-3 presents a successful family-oriented approach for Johnson & Johnson.

The marketer will have to conduct research to find out what appeals are best for this segment. It may be found that appeals used in the general market are not as successful in the Hispanic segment. For example, Mazola ads don't even mention cholesterol, but stress how good the oil tastes.

FIGURE 7-2
Advertisement for Miller Lite Beer.
Courtesy of Miller Brewing Company.

AMERICA'S BEST KNOWN BEER DRINKERS TALK ABOUT **Lite** BEER...

TITLE: "CARLOS PALOMINO"

COMM'L NO.: MOTI 1230

CARLOS: Y'know, one of the best things about coming to America was that I got to try American Beers.

I tried them all.

And the one I like best is Lite Beer from Miller.

It's got a third less calories than their regular beer.

It's less filling.

And it really tastes great.

That is why I tell my friends from Mexico,

"When you come to America, drink Lite Beer.

But,

don't drink the water."

ANNCR: (VO) Lite Beer from Miller. Everything you always wanted in a beer.

And less.

In addition to consumer-behavior differences based on ethnic factors, marketers also recognize distinct patterns based on age categories. There are two significant age subcultures in which many marketers should be vitally interested, yet which marketers often fail to understand and appreciate fully. These two groups are the *youth* market and the *older* American market. The characteristics and marketing significance of each of these subcultures will be discussed in this section.

FIGURE 7-3
Advertisement for
Johnson's Baby Powder.
Courtesy of Johnson & Johnson.

JOHNSON'S BABY POWDER

TITLE: "COMPARTA SU BIENESTAR" :30
TITLE: "SHARE THE WELL-BEING" :30

COMM'L. NO.: JJYP 3010
DATE: FEBRUARY 1981

(MUSIC UP)

ANNCR: (VO) Por generaciones...
ANNCR: (VO) For generations...

...las familias han compartido...
...families have shared...

el bienestar del talco Johnson.
the well-being of Johnson's Powder.

SONG: Es un toque que perdura,
SONG: A touch that lasts,

de suavidad
gives softness

y frescura.
and freshness.

El talco Johnson
Johnson's Powder

es carino que haz gozado
is a warm feeling that you have enjoyed

desde nino.
since you were a child.

ANNCR: Johnson's Baby Powder solo de
Johnson y Johnson.
ANNCR: Johnson's Baby Powder...only from
Johnson & Johnson.

Comparta su bienestar.
Share the well-being.

THE ¡BRAVO! GROUP: HISPANIC MARKETS DIVISION OF YOUNG & RUBICAM INC.

THE YOUTH SUBCULTURE

The youth market is a significant subculture for the marketer. Youth are often considered to be those between the ages of 14 and 24, although we will concentrate on teenagers. The youth market is important to marketers not only because it is lucrative, but also because many consumption patterns held throughout life are formed at this time, and also because of the public policy implications of marketers' activities directed at younger people during their formative years.[58]

DEMOGRAPHIC CHARACTERISTICS

There are many important characteristics of the youth market with which marketers should be familiar. The following is a summary of these factors.

Size In 1985, there were about 26 million persons between the ages of 13 and 19, or less than 10 percent of the population. The teenage group will bottom out at 23 million by 1991, but then increase to 27 million by 2000.

Income and Spending There is no market without income, and the youth segment qualifies on this important dimension. Their spending reached about $50 billion in 1985, with approximately $10 billion put in savings. Because many jobs are available in fast-food restaurants and other businesses that need young people for labor, over 30 percent of high school senior boys and nearly 25 percent of senior girls say they average over 20 hours of work a week during the school year.

Many youths are earning over $200 a month. The most important facet of these incomes is that they are almost entirely discretionary; that is, there are few, if any, fixed obligations such as taxes, rent, insurance, and utilities that these youths must meet. A notable result of increasing youth income is the increasing tendency of youths to buy more durable and high-priced products, from radios to designer jeans, cosmetics, and footwear. According to the president of a youth-research company, "Products which were considered luxuries a few years ago are deemed necessities by youths and parents alike."[59] Thus, some youths are experiencing "premature affluence"—they have a lot of spending money but will not be able to sustain that level of discretionary spending once they have taken on the burdens of paying for their own necessities.[60]

Why do youths have such a strong consumption orientation? According to one researcher, three significant forces have molded their attitudes and consumer behavior. First, the experience of growing up in a period of almost unbroken prosperity has produced a widely shared feeling of economic optimism. A second factor is permissive child rearing, which has been linked by researchers to a reduced capacity for initiative and independence. Third, the new generation has a higher educational level and heavier exposure to the mass media.

These environmental forces have had a significant influence on their consumer-behavior orientations. The result has been that youths tend to be rather optimistic about their future financial situations and levels of living. For example, almost all young people look forward to what has been labeled the "standard package"—the set of durable goods, clothing, food products, and services en-

joyed by the majority of Americans.[61] Although they used to be told to save their money, young people in America today are being raised to spend, according to an authority who conducts a yearly youth poll. In 1981, 65 percent of teenagers said thrift was seldom if ever discussed at home or in school, compared with 1956 when 69 percent said thrift was mentioned "a great deal." Similarly, in 1981, 67 percent of teens said their parents were not thrifty, whereas in 1956, 56 percent of the teenagers said their parents were thrifty.[62]

PSYCHOGRAPHIC CHARACTERISTICS

The gap between young people and the rest of the population is closing in some areas of attitude and behavior, such as appearance, according to a recent advertising agency report. It finds that today's youths want to look young, healthy, and refreshing, but, unlike their counterparts of the 1960s, they are willing to use artificial means (such as cosmetics, hair coloring, and beauty treatments) to obtain that look.[63] There is more interest in dress among youth today. Even *Rolling Stone* carries ads for status brands of jeans. Nevertheless, though there are likenesses, there are some areas in which substantial differences may still be found between youths and older segments.

Teenagers, themselves, are no more alike than are adults. Teen consumers can be segmented into four attitudinal groups:

Socially driven. They have the highest disposable incomes, are the most brand-conscious, and spend heavily on personal grooming and clothing to give them status.

Diversely motivated. They are the most energetic, adventurous, and cultured, and are equally as comfortable in solitary activities as in group ones.

Socioeconomically introverted. They like solitary activities and spend money on products and services for use in these pursuits.

Sports-oriented. They represent the biggest market for sports and home video equipment.

Young & Rubicam ad agency conducted an in-depth study of teens and found that they all crave peer acceptance and parental noninfluence. Beyond this, they were an enigma. Y & R found that teens:

■ Want to learn things but don't want to be told.

■ Want independence yet want to be taken care of.

■ Want to be treated as adults but don't want too much responsibility.

■ Want to be active yet spend endless hours relaxing.

■ Want to try new things but only acceptable things.

■ Want to be individuals but also members of the group.

■ Can be very critical yet are very sensitive to criticism.[65]

This section explores the nature of consumer behavior within the youth market of the United States. However, it should be emphasized that many of the findings presented below are for teens. Thus, there may be substantial differences between this group and older youths. The three marketing variables to be discussed are product decisions, shopping patterns, and promotion.

Product Purchase Patterns   Marketers are interested in understanding what products will sell well in the youth market. Moreover, it is important to appreciate the influence which youths exert on purchases by others, such as parents. This secondary influence may be more significant to most marketers than is youth's role as primary purchaser of certain items.

How do youths spend their incomes? Both female and male teenagers spend most of their money on clothes, records, stereo equipment, entertainment, and travel. Young women spend most on cosmetics, followed by clothes, health and beauty aids, and jewelry. Young men spend the most on dates and autos, followed by sporting goods, cameras, records, stereo equipment, bicycles, athletic shoes, jeans, hobby-type products, musical instruments, and electronic games. The following purchase patterns give an indication of the importance of certain products: 16 percent of teens own a car, 66 percent a record player, 86 percent a camera, 34 percent a television, 12 percent a home computer, and 14 percent stocks and bonds.

As members of a highly consumption-oriented society, teenagers have become increasingly aware of new products and brands. They are natural "triers" and spend hours shopping for themselves.

In addition to their direct impact on the marketplace, youths exert secondary influence on many of their parents' product and brand choices. For example, research studies reveal the following patterns:

■ Three out of four teens influence their parents' purchasing decisions.[66]

■ A study of university students' influence on their families' purchases of television sets and automobiles has found that many students not only provided opinions and information about both products, but also participated in shopping.[67]

For major purchases, teens' highest influence occurs in the initiation stage of the decision-making process and is strongest for aesthetic considerations such as style, color, and make or model of the product but weakest for decisions such as where and when to purchase and how much money to spend.[68]

Apple computer's research showed that teens are influencing family decisions about buying computers. As a result, one of its recent model introductions used contemporary hit radio and youth-skewed computer enthusiast magazines to encourage teens to convince their parents to buy the product or, as a joking last resort, to tell teens they can always get a paper route if mom and dad won't budge.[69]

With the large growth in the number of families of two working parents,

youths are doing more of the food shopping and other shopping for parents. For example:

■ It was found that 49 percent of teenage girls and 26 percent of boys had shopped for family groceries the previous week. Six of every ten teen supermarket shoppers help make up the family shopping list, and 40 percent select the brands to be bought. Boys spend over half an hour grocery shopping for the family, while girls spend an hour and a quarter. Both spend about an hour a week doing other family shopping.[70]

■ Teen girls spend 40 percent of the family's food budget, or $16 billion.[71]

Kraft has recognized the importance of teenage grocery shopping and is advertising on MTV, in network syndication, in selected teen magazines, and on contemporary hit radio, emphasizing recipes containing Kraft products. Tied in with the ad campaign is an educational kit on "Food Buymanship" provided to home-economics teachers to distribute to teenagers in school.

Thus, it is clear that this market also occupies an important position in terms of its secondary influence on parents' buying decisions.

Another factor emphasizing the market importance of the youth group is that this is the time when brand loyalties may be formed that could last well into adulthood.[72] For example, a brand-loyalty study prepared by the Yankelovich organization for *Seventeen* magazine found that at least 30 percent of adult women were using the same brands they first chose as teenagers.[73] Translated into total market figures, the findings would mean, for instance, that 6,760,000 women still are using the same brand of mascara and 8,900,000 still are eating the same kind of packaged cheese that they first bought.[74]

During the process of making their buying decision, to what extent are teens influenced by parents, friends, sales clerks, media, or other sources? For many product decisions, friends are the most significant influence. Nevertheless, parents are still an important factor affecting many buying decisions. The important point for the marketer is that although peer pressure is quite strong, family influences are also significant.[75] Thus, the marketer should attempt to keep up with which group predominates at any period in order to orient merchandising strategies properly.

Shopping Behavior Teenagers spend much time engaged in shopping activities. One study learned that more than one-fourth of teenagers questioned spent more than two hours shopping on weekends, while another one-fifth spent between one and two hours.[76] The fact that teens are doing more shopping may result in their spending more money in stores they patronize.

Although the popular belief is that young people buy products impulsively and are less rational than the market as a whole, surveys indicate a different pattern. One study of persons aged 14 to 25 showed that 74 percent of the respondents compare prices and brands before buying.[77] Research on adolescent shopping behavior has produced the following tentative conclusions:[78]

■ Adolescents tend to rely more on personal sources for information on products of high socioeconomic and performance risk, and on most media for information on products perceived as low for such risk.

■ At the product-evaluation stage of the decision process, price (''sales'') and brand name are perceived as the most important evaluative criteria, with a relatively low social influence coming from parents and peers.

■ As teenagers mature, they use more sources of consumer information prior to decision making, rely more on friends and less on parents for information and advice in buying, and prefer to purchase products without parental supervision.

In addition, youths often have a great deal of authority in store-selection decisions. For example, one study found that 89 percent of the girls and 80 percent of the boys claimed to have all or most of the say in the choice of a clothing store.[79]

Promoting to Youth   A final marketing element that is very important in appealing to youth is promotion. There are many effective media available to reach the youth market—radio, television, direct mail, magazines, and newspapers. However, the marketer should be aware that use of these media varies with family socioeconomic conditions. For instance, teenagers in higher income and higher education families view fewer hours of television than those with lower income and education.[80] Let's examine the media habits of youth and potential promotional strategies that might be successful in appealing to this group.

MEDIA PATTERNS   Nearly all teenagers own radios, and they spend considerable time listening to them.[81] Surveys show that 75 percent of teens listen on a daily basis and average almost three hours per day—about one-fifth of their waking hours. In addition, radio reaches more than 90 percent of all teenagers in the course of a week. These listening patterns vary significantly by the time of day, exhibiting heavy nighttime listening, particularly during winter months when apparently the radio is used while studying.

Teen radio-listening preferences are clearly toward contemporary or rock music stations. In addition, almost three-fourths of all teen listening is to stations on the FM dial. They tend to select one or two favorite stations, and they listen to them repeatedly day after day. Consequently, massive teen audiences are available with relatively concentrated station schedules. Hence, radio is probably the fastest, easiest, and most effective way to reach teens.

In contrast to adults, who spend much of their leisure time watching television, teens are relatively light viewers, although virtually all have access to sets and 90 percent of them can be reached this way during one week.[82] Teens appear to be too busy to spend a lot of time watching television; however, they do have preferred programs, and they may watch these quite regularly. Young teens are significantly heavier viewers than are older teens. Television programming that has proved popular with teens includes music-dance shows, movies, sports, situation comedies, and suspense-mystery shows.

Print media also are important in promoting to the youth market.[83] Magazines, for example, are viewed by young people as being primary sources of

information on a number of different subjects. Newspapers also have heavy youth readership.

Direct mail may also be effective in reaching the youth market. This is one medium that probably will attract more attention than some other alternatives, because youths receive little mail and are likely to be quite receptive to advertising in this form.[84] Other effective promotional efforts are utilized by marketers. For example, some companies hire student representatives on many college campuses whose job may include selling or renting merchandise, putting up posters, or distributing advertisements and product samples.

Some companies reach youth with their own media. For example, Kimberly-Clark uses a publication, *Young Woman,* in which Kotex feminine products is the single advertiser. The magazine is targeted to high school senior women and is designed to entice more female consumers when they are making brand decisions they may stick with over the years. Tie-in promotions or "events marketing" is also increasingly used by marketers to reach the youth group. For example, Expo-America takes advantage of the spring-break influx of students into Florida resort towns such as Daytona Beach by offering companies such as Anheuser-Busch, McDonald's, and Bristol-Myers the chance to make their pitch to the youth with exhibit-hall presentations, pool-side programs, specially delivered samples, and dance and fashion shows.

EFFECTIVE MESSAGES   Promotional messages must be carefully designed for today's youth because they are becoming increasingly skeptical about such communications. For example, a recent youth poll found that 24 percent of the respondents said ads directed at them were not believable; 19 percent found them uninformative; 28 percent thought they were silly; and only 7 percent viewed them as sincere. Nevertheless, 87 percent of youths 14 to 25 years old would rather buy advertised than nonadvertised products.[85]

When developing effective sales appeals to the youth market, the advertiser should keep in mind the following rules:[86]

1   Never talk down to youths.

2   Be totally, absolutely, and unswervingly straightforward.

3   Give youths credit for being motivated by rational values.

4   Be as personal as possible.

The successes of certain promotional campaigns aimed at youth indicate several ingredients which marketers should consider incorporating:

■ *Sports themes.* Coca-Cola has introduced Mello Yellow, a low-carbonated drink, to sell to young people who like sports. Its commercials feature sports competition, such as auto racing, basketball, and football.

■ *A "gimmick."* Department and specialty stores around the country use music, blinking lights, and space-age displays to lure youths.

■ *Celebrities.* Converse features Larry Bird and "Magic" Johnson in its basketball shoe commercials.

■ *Humor.* Many advertisers believe humor has a stronger appeal than factual accounts when advertising to high school and college groups. Examples include Bubble Yum gum and *Time* magazine.

There are two additional factors that should be cited in order to ensure greater success in the youth market. The first is that the youth group is a *perpetually* new market. As consumers move into this market, the advertiser needs to attract them, since every brand is a new brand to someone who has never used it before. This stream of young consumers moves along in age and finally drifts into an older pool of householders. Thus, a marketer must not neglect young consumers who come "on stream" if the company's brand is to have continued success in the older-age market. Two companies utilizing this approach to attract youths successfully are presented below:

American Express has developed a special plan to lure graduating college students as card holders. The usual application requirements are reduced and the program is promoted with a special campaign in college newspapers (see Figure 7-4). The company has even adapted its familiar slogan to reach the youth market. The tag line is "The American Express Card. Don't leave school without it."

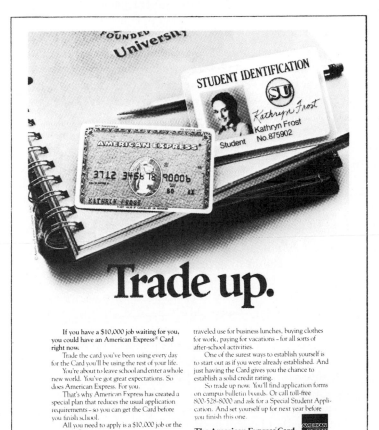

FIGURE 7-4
Advertisement for American Express.
Courtesy of American Express Company.

Schick has been able to outflank Gillette, the dominant company in the razor-blade market, by consistent and specific efforts to win young shavers. Through various means it offers young men the opportunity to receive Schick razors, either free or at nominal expense. In some wild, crazy ads featuring college students and dormitories, the company has sought to capture the aged 16 to 34 young shaver through portraying them in ads. The result has been that Schick has gained a significant presence in this market.[87]

A second point to remember is that companies may be able to utilize youth appeals to a market broader than the traditional age boundary would indicate. Marketers today are defining "youth" more in terms of a state of mind than of a specific age. The result of this is that many companies, ranging from retailers to manufacturers, are broadening their emphasis to include the mature and more affluent customers who "think young."

THE OLDER SUBCULTURE

Although business people have painted a glowing picture of the opportunities in the youth market, the opposite end of the age spectrum has been largely neglected by marketers and frequently by society itself.[88] Many people feel that American marketers have gone overboard in courting the youth market. As one advertising executive explained in *Business Week,* "As I watch television and read magazines and attend movies these days, I sometimes wonder if anybody besides myself is over 30. There seems to be a conscious denial of middle age—and certainly of old age."[89] Another advertising executive observed that marketers have long concentrated only on consumers below the age of 49. He noted that "beyond 49 the world ceases to exist, you fall off the edge."[90]

Why the neglect? One writer explains, "Youth suggests excitement and glamour; the no-longer-young are considered dowdy and uninspiring."[91] Although this situation may be understandable psychologically, it may make poor economic sense, because middle-aged consumers hold considerably more promise for a wide range of consumer goods and services than do the young.[92]

DEMOGRAPHIC CHARACTERISTICS

This section summarizes several important demographic characteristics of older consumers, concentrating on those over age 65. This is actually only one segment of the so-called mature market. Those 55 to 64 are called the "older" population; those 65 to 74 are "elderly," those aged 75 to 84 are called the "aged," and those 85 and over are the "very old."

Size In 1984, 32 million people in 18 million households in the United States were 65 years of age or older, or almost 14 percent of our total population. Each census during this century has found the elderly to make up an increasingly larger share of the total population generally, and if present trends continue, those 55 and over are expected to account for 20 percent of the population by 1995. Thus, statistics negate a long-held concept that the United States is a nation of young people and is getting younger.

Location The largest group of elderly consumers lives in the central cities of our metropolitan areas. This characteristic differs from the population as a whole, in which suburbanites outnumber residents of central cities.

States with the largest populations also have the largest numbers of senior citizens. For example, New York, California, Pennsylvania, and Illinois account for nearly one-third of the elderly. However, many states with the highest proportions of older people are those which have had heavy out-migration by younger people. This is especially true of much of the midwestern farm belt—Iowa, Kansas, Missouri, Nebraska, Oklahoma, and South Dakota.

Many older people who have the means move toward the ''gerontopolises'' of the Sunbelt when they retire. Florida has the highest proportion of elderly of any state.

Marital and Family Status A large majority of the elderly are women, most of whom are widowed, and many of whom live by themselves. However, most elderly men are married and live with their wives. Household size of older prospects is much smaller than for other groups in the population because their children have grown up and moved away, and because many of them are widowed. For example, more than 73 percent of all households in which the head is over 65 consist of only one or two individuals. Contrary to the general impression, very few of the American elderly live in homes for the aged. Only 3 percent of men and 5 percent of women are in such arrangements. The percentage of men and women living as dependent ''other relatives'' in family groups may also be lower than commonly believed (7 percent and 17 percent, respectively).

Income People over 50 comprise a market worth over $800 billion. An economic profile of the mature market is presented in Table 7-3. The picture of the average senior citizen as poor, entirely dependent on social security, who is much worse off than the general population and than when he or she was working is very outdated, as shown by this profile. Slightly over 12 percent of the 65-and-over population is classified at the poverty level, but the proportion is little higher than that for all adults.[93] Thus, a very significant number of elderly persons live at ''comfortable'' levels of income. In fact, average income per household member for the elderly is higher than for the young.

Even where the incomes of elderly may be low, these incomes are often able to go farther than those of younger customers because of fewer obligations. For example, there may be no children to educate, clothe, or support; work-related expenses are curtailed; double exemptions are granted on income tax returns; Medicare helps pay for medical expenses; and three-fourths of the aged own their own homes, with 84 percent of these homes being mortgage-free.

Some workers can look forward to perhaps 30 years in retirement, with incomes at approximately the same level as their preretirement, after-taxes income. This market will in the future be one with even more discretionary income and more ways to spend it, because the problem of security will be being taken off the individual's shoulders and placed in the hands of bodies beyond ourselves—such as the government, insurance, pensions, and the like.

PSYCHOGRAPHIC CHARACTERISTICS

The segment aged 55 and over has in many cases a different set of activities, interests, and opinions from those of younger groups. A few of their patterns involve a tendency toward seasonal migration to warm climates, earlier bedtimes, less physical activity, more leisure-time activities, and positive identification with their age, shunning the public's sometimes negative stereotype. Actually our opinions in America about when "getting old" occurs are shifting as we age—40 percent of people over 60 say "old" is over 75. People over 60 commonly say they feel ten years younger.[94] This subjective age, or how old we feel, is related to health and financial conditions.

It has also been shown that the way in which senior citizens adjust to old age provides a useful classification system for differentiating market segments among them.[95] This, in turn, may lead to more appropriate strategies for marketing to these segments.

CONSUMER BEHAVIOR AND MARKETING IMPLICATIONS

The lack of attention by marketers to the senior market shows in the dearth of research findings on this group's behavior as consumers.[96] This section distills

TABLE 7-3
Economic Profile of the Mature Market, 1984

Characteristic	Total	Household head <50	Household head aged 50 and over			
			Total	50–64	65–74	75+
Total households (in millions)	85.4	48.2	37.2	19.3	10.7	7.2
Percent distribution	100.0%	56.4%	43.6%	22.7%	12.5%	8.4%
Average household size	2.7	3.1	2.2	2.6	1.9	1.6
Total persons (in millions)	230.6	148.5	82.1	50.2	20.4	11.5
Percent distribution	100.0%	64.4%	35.6%	21.8%	8.8%	5.0%
Male labor force participation rates	76.4%	87.9%	51.2%	75.4%	20.9%	7.4%
Female labor force participation rates	53.6%	67.4%	28.6%	47.5%	11.0%	2.5%
Total income (in billions)	$2,153.2	$1,287.3	$865.9	$573.3	$195.0	$97.6
Percent distribution	100.0%	59.8%	40.2%	26.6%	9.1%	4.5%
Average household income	$25,211	$26,723	$23,255	$29,655	$18,220	$13,547
Income per household member*	$9,338	$8,677	$10,549	$11,432	$9,553	$8,467
Total discretionary income (in billions)	$262.0	$131.5	$130.5	$84.0	$32.5	$14.0
Percent distribution	100.0%	50.2%	49.8%	32.1%	12.4%	5.3%
Average financial assets†	$28,290	$11,630	$49,270	$44,900	$65,340	$37,060
Percent distribution	100.0%	23.0%	77.0%	37.2%	29.1%	10.7%
Percent distribution of net worth	100.0%	30.5%	69.5%	37.0%	23.4%	9.1%
Incidence of homeownership	64.6%	54.7%	77.4%	79.4%	77.3%	72.3%
Average net equity of homeowners	$55,800	$45,800	$64,900	$71,400	$63,670	$47,760
Percent of homeowners with mortgage debt	57.0%	80.0%	33.0%	49.0%	20.0%	5.0%
Percent of households with installment debt	41.0%	53.0%	25.0%	37.0%	14.0%	6.0%

* Average household income divided by average household size.
† Includes only households that hold such assets.
Source: Fabian Linden, "The $800 Billion Market," *American Demographics*, February 1986, p. 4.

some of the most important findings and presents some useful insights for the marketer.

Product Purchase Patterns Significant marketing potential appears to be available to those who provide the proper kinds of products to meet the needs of the senior market. Some have ventured into this market to sell specially designed products more attuned to elderly needs. The following examples illustrate the awakening of the "new world" of the older consumer by marketers:

FOOD   Coca-Cola, concerned that the 13 to 24 age group which accounts for such an important part of its soda market (consuming 1½ times as much per capita as the general public) will shrink by 8 percent in the 1980s, has moved more heavily into wine, orange juice, coffee, and tea—beverages more popular with older consumers. In addition, a new reduced-acid orange juice has been marketed. Procter & Gamble is offering High Point, a decaffinated coffee, which is a product older consumers buy much more than regular coffee. Kellogg markets Special K, Product 19, and Smart Start to provide more vitamins for older consumers (who are the second highest group in consumption of cereal, behind only the under-12 market).

COSMETICS   Estée Lauder, Elizabeth Arden, Revlon, Helena Rubenstein, Oil of Olay, and others are now marketing skin-care products which are designed to appeal to older women. Other companies are offering hair care designed to meet the special needs of consumers over 40 or 50. The approach is a delicate one from an industry that has long been based strictly on its youth image. Companies are searching for ways to overcome the age taboo by referring only to "maturing skin" and the like—everything but age.

SERVICES   Airlines such as American and United and many lodging chains such as Ramada have offered discounts to older travelers. Southwestern Bell Corp. is publishing a successful series of telephone directories aimed at senior citizens, with ads offering them discounts. Sears, Roebuck & Co. formed the Mature Outlook Club to woo customers over 50 with discounts up to 25 percent on everything from lawn mowers to eyeglasses. ARA Services and Marriott have opened life-care nursing facilities. Colonial Penn Group aims life insurance at the elderly.

Older consumers appear to place great importance on manufacturers' brand names. They tend to buy fewer private labels and appear to demand guarantees and warranties more often than do average consumers.[97] Because many over-65 shoppers are on fixed or low incomes, however, there is a trend toward increased acceptance of private labels and generic items among this shopper group.[98]

There is also an impression that older buyers are generally less inclined to try new products, especially those that involve adopting new technologies.[99] One study, however, found that the group aged 65 and over was more inclined than the middle-aged, 55 to 64 years old, to say that they buy products for the fun of it or just to try them once. It was also found that there is little self-initiated experimenting; instead, new product and service acceptance often comes as a response to a recommendation by others.[100] This has important promotional implications for the marketer, and it means that messages must be well planned to take advantage of this word-of-mouth communication.[101] Another study among the elderly found

strong interest in new generic products.[102] However, given the apparent high brand loyalty of this group, manufacturers and retailers who properly serve those in this group can expect them to be loyal, dependable customers.

Shopping Behavior   Most of the research on older citizens' shopping patterns has been conducted in an exploratory manner with limited samples. Therefore, the findings must be interpreted with caution. There are a number of helpful insights, however, emerging from expanded research on the topic. One national study on store choice for apparel found that the elderly generally base their patronage decisions on the same attributes as younger counterparts do.[103] Another study of elderly shoppers indicates that there are subsegments who can be identified by unique shopping orientations.[104]

Business Week provides perspective regarding the general shopping patterns of senior citizens by observing that they "tend to be more cautious than younger consumers, more set in their preferences, and shrewder comparison shoppers. They favor larger chain stores and shun small specialty outlets, especially those that gain a name for catering just to the elderly."[105]

Another study found that the primary sources of product information were newspapers and personal observations while shopping. Shopping appeared to be a major part of their lifestyle and provided more of a pleasure than a burden.[106]

Other studies have shown that older consumers shop near their residences since many lack personal transportation. In addition, substantial store loyalty has been exhibited by this group with regard to low-cost items or products about which the store owner may give advice (such as drugs and medicines). Store loyalty disappears as unit value of an item increases and frequency of purchase decreases (such as when shopping for appliances). Greater store loyalty, however, is exhibited by senior citizens at higher income and age levels.[107]

Some of this country's important retail institutions, such as shopping centers and supermarkets, have features that make them quite attractive to older shoppers. The generally favorable prices and the safe, comfortable atmosphere of these stores contribute to their appeal. At the same time, however, other features of these institutions inhibit older consumers and prevent them from taking advantage of the stores. First, they are generally located away from older neighborhoods where many aged and most poor live. Moreover, the right merchandise assortment to satisfy the needs of older consumers frequently cannot be found. For these and other reasons, such retail institutions have not adequately met the needs of senior citizens.[108] One retailer has long been concerned about this segment:

Publix Super Markets Inc. is a Florida chain that makes shopping easier for the elderly. They do this by placing benches in front of their stores, providing restrooms, and teaching employees how to make things easier for the elderly, such as giving customers two light bags during checkout instead of a single heavy one.

Promoting to the Older Market   Even developing the right product and getting it to the right place is no guarantee of success among older consumers. It must also be matched with the proper promotion. Marketers who have succeeded in this market have done so largely because of effective promotion.

MEDIA PATTERNS The marketer must select appropriate media for promoting to the senior-citizen market. There are some difficulties, however, when effectively segmenting the senior-citizen market by media. Television programming, for instance, is largely youth-oriented. Nevertheless, viewership by older consumers is above average during certain times of the day. Television viewership for those aged 55 to 64 is heaviest between 7 and 10 A.M. and 5 and 11 P.M., and for those 65 and over it is from 7 A.M. to 7:30 P.M. Thus, daytime and syndicated programming appealing to older adults is the mainstay for the television advertiser. New avenues for reaching older consumers are also opening up. For example, Cineamerica offers programming for people over age 50 as part of its satellite-linked cable TV package.

Radio is an effective medium to reach older buyers. Formats such as all news, talk shows, beautiful music, and sports are traditionally strong among those over 55. Nostalgic approaches are also useful for finding success, with formats such as big-band music and radio drama.

With regard to print media aimed directly at this market, the choices were, until recently, rather limited. Now, however, there are several specialty magazines for older people, in addition to the general audience magazines (such as *Reader's Digest* and *TV Guide*, which historically have found a large market among this segment). Magazines such as *Prime Time, 50 Plus,* and *Modern Maturity* are useful vehicles for aiming messages at those over 45. In addition, many newspapers around the United States aimed at older consumers allow the marketer to more effectively reach this group. It should also be noted that newspapers may be the most appropriate media if the objective is to have older consumers learn new information. They are frequent users of this medium, and they consider it their most important mass-media source of information. Because their information processing with print media is self-paced, there are liable to be fewer difficulties in learning new information.[109]

EFFECTIVE MESSAGES Poor promotion, especially advertising, appears to have contributed to the alienation of older consumers.[110] Much advertising today stereotypes older Americans (often negatively), and thereby insults them. For example, *The Wall Street Journal* states that "Older people in TV ads are recognizable most often by their stereotypes: half-deaf codgers, meddling biddies, grandfatherly authority figures or nostalgic endorsers of products that claim to be just as high-quality as they were in the good old days. Rarely are older people shown just as ordinary consumers."[111] Although those over age 55 comprise approximately 29 percent of U.S. adults, several studies have shown that they account for only about 10 percent of TV-commercial characters—usually those in need of laxatives, denture adhesives, and sleeping pills—but are significantly used in magazine ads.[112]

Advertisements which are not sensitive to older consumers may be perceived as offensive. For example, a denture adhesive ad once showed an older couple perched in infant high chairs to indicate that people with loose dentures need easy-to-chew food. More recently, a General Foods ad for Country Time powdered lemonade mix featured a hard-of-hearing grandfather who kept asking his family to repeat the product's name as a device for gaining repetition. However, the ad was perceived very negatively, and because of the protests received, it was quickly withdrawn from broadcast. On the other hand, advertisements such as Clairol's, ''You're not getting older, you're getting better,'' can be very useful in building older consumers' self-esteem.

As indicated previously, older citizens are a prime market and thus promotions should be directed to them in a way commensurate with their value. Many business people, however, are reluctant to solicit trade from the elderly. A study by the National Council on Aging found that local store managers, even when convinced that elderly consumers represented a sizable market, refused to direct any advertising or promotion efforts toward the aged for fear it would ''hurt their public image'' and tend to keep away their most desirable age group—the youth.[113]

On the other hand, companies should be careful about blatantly singling out senior citizens as the target. Many older consumers do not want to be reminded that they are old, and therefore they tend to react against advertising and marketing programs that separate them from the rest of the population; nor do they want to be treated as kids. An approach which works for many companies is the ''transgenerational'' strategy, or ''fence straddling.''[114] In this case, ads feature both youngsters and oldsters using and enjoying the product. The key is to present older characters in a matter-of-fact, realistic, way. Advertisements for Greyhound, McDonald's, Coca-Cola, AT&T, and Kellogg are examples of this strategy. Thus, the marketer must be careful not to alienate any age group. Other marketers catering to the senior market have found success by using well-known senior citizens as spokesmen for their products. For example, Joe DiMaggio, Lorne Greene, Robert Young, and Andy Griffith have been particularly effective in this role.

Another facet of advertising to the older market concerns the way in which messages are presented. It is important to understand that older consumers process information differently from younger buyers because of changes in vision, hearing, and memory, for example. Consequently, marketers should follow certain guidelines when communicating with older buyers. First, ads and packages should not be cluttered with too much visual information. Second, action in commercials should be relevant and not distracting. Humor may also distract and clutter the message. Third, fast-speaking characters and those who don't enunciate clearly should be avoided. Fourth, pictures should be clear, bright, and sharp. Fifth, the language and message should be simple, focusing on one or two selling points. Finally, new information should relate to something with which they are already familiar.[115]

The marketer should not, however, automatically run the same ads in specialized media (such as older-oriented magazines) as those run in the general-audience media. Such unadapted advertising is liable to be largely ineffective with the older group.

Marketers who want to develop successful advertising for this group should consider the following suggestions: (1) include older buyers in focus-group research in order to learn of their motivations and attitudes; (2) hire older copywriters to provide new perspectives on this segment; (3) incorporate older models in advertisements in a genuine and typical way; (4) let the older buyers know the product will appeal to them, but do so subtly.

In summary, the older market represents a powerful economic force that is certain to grow even stronger. Although the youth market has become almost a "religion" to many companies, some are beginning to feel that the senior market is really the "now" generation, because older consumers don't know how long the "now" will last. Thus, there is substantial opportunity in this subculture for the marketer not only to satisfy the goals of his firm, but at the same time to help accomplish some of society's aims as well. However, in order for these goals to be effectively realized, marketers will need to know much more about this neglected segment.

MANAGERIAL REFLECTIONS

For our product or service situation . . .

1 What relevant subcultures exist that may be targeted?

2 How may these subcultures be described demographically and psychographically?

3 What identifiable consumer-behavior patterns exist among target subcultures?

4 How should the marketing mix elements be adapted to appeal effectively to chosen subcultures?

DISCUSSION TOPICS

1 What is a subculture?

2 Describe some important subcultures that exist in the United States. Why are these important? Are all subcultures equally important to, or usable by, the marketer?

3 Prepare a report on the current demographic picture of one of the subcultures discussed in this chapter.

4 Assume that you are the product manager in charge of marketing for Tide detergent and you are developing an advertising campaign. Use the knowledge you gained in this chapter to put together an effective campaign for the black and Hispanic subcultures.

5 What are the most important considerations in marketing to the Hispanic segment?

6 Why are the youth and senior-citizen markets characterized as "subcultures"?

7 Illustrate with food products and automobiles how the marketer might promote to youths in order to take advantage of their secondary influence on family-purchase decisions.

8 What improvements can you suggest for the retail environment in order to better meet the needs of today's senior citizens?

PROJECTS

1 Look through some black-oriented magazines (such as *Ebony*) and select three advertisements that are similar, except for the models, to those appearing in predominantly white-oriented media (bring in white ads, too). Are there any other differences between the ads, such as language or situation? Explain why or why not.

2 Select two product areas that appear to have good potential in the older market but are at present being poorly marketed. Present a plan for more effective marketing in order to take advantage of this opportunity.

NOTES

[1] "'Ultimate Talking Head' C-C- Catches Fancy of Youth," *Marketing News,* September 26, 1986, p. 1; and Scott Scredon, "Brian Dyson Takes the New Coke Challenge," *Business Week,* May 26, 1986, p. 81.

[2] See "New Survey Reveals Five Lifestyle Segments of Age 18–49 Black Women," *Marketing News,* August 21, 1981, p. 6; "Views from the Inside," *Advertising Age,* April 6, 1981, pp. S-6–S-9; "U.S. Firms Must Act Now to Tap Chicano Market," *Marketing News,* August 22, 1980, pp. 1, 6; Mary C. LaForge, Warren A. French, and Melvin R. Crask, "Segmenting the Elderly Market," in Jerry R. Reeves and James R. Sweigart (eds.), *Proceedings,* vol. 1, 13th Annual Meeting of the American Institute of Decision Sciences, Boston, 1981, pp. 248–250; and Jeffrey G. Towle and Claude R. Martin, Jr., "The Elderly Consumer: One Segment or Many?" in Beverlee B. Anderson (ed.), *Advances in Consumer Research,* vol. 3, Association for Consumer Research, Cincinnati, 1976, p. 467.

[3] Bernard Berelson and Gary Steiner, *Human Behavior: An Inventory of Scientific Findings,* Harcourt, New York, 1964, p. 494.

[4] Elizabeth C. Hirschman, "Primitive Aspects of Consumption in Modern American Society," *Journal of Consumer Research,* **12**:145, September 1985.

[5] Leon F. Bouvier and Anthony J. Agresta, "The Fastest Growing Minority," *American Demographics,* May 1985, p. 46.

[6] Jewish consumer behavior is discussed in the following: Elizabeth C. Hirschman, "American Jewish Ethnicity: Its Relationship to Some Selected Aspects of Consumer Behavior," *Journal of Marketing,* **45**:102–110, Summer 1981; Dan Lionel, "How to Reach the Jewish Market," *Editor & Publisher,* December 8, 1979, p. 30; Larry A. Rubin, "Jewish Media Problem: Combating Stereotypes," *Advertising Age,* April 16, 1979, p. S-32; and Richard A. Jacobs, "Jewish Media Provide What Others Don't," *Advertising Age,* April 16, 1979, p. S-28.

[7] *Marketing News,* January 4, 1985, p. 38.

[8] Leon Morse, "Black Radio Market Study," *Television/Radio Age,* February 28, 1977, pp. A-1–A-31.

[9] "Use Different Ad Tack for Blacks, Meet Urged," *Advertising Age,* February 14, 1977, p. 66; and Kelvin A. Wall, "Trying to Reach Blacks? Beware of Marketing Myopia," *Advertising Age,* May 21, 1979, p. 60.

[10] "Use Different Ad Tack," p. 66 and Wall, "Trying to Reach Blacks?" p. 60.

[11] Simon Bensimon, "Buying Patterns Different," *Advertising Age,* April 7, 1980, pp. S-10, S-24.

[12] Marcus Alexis, "Some Negro-White Differences in Consumption," *American Journal of Economics and Sociology,* **21**:11–28, January 1962.

[13] James E. Stafford, Keith K. Cox, and James B. Higginbotham, "Some Consumption Pattern Differences Between Urban Whites and Negroes," *Social Science Quarterly,* **49**:629, December 1968.

[14] "Is There Really a Negro Market?" *Marketing Insights,* January 29, 1968, p. 14.

[15] "Marketing Observer," *Business Week,* December 18, 1978, p. 103.

[16] "The Negro Market: 23 Million Consumers Make a $30 Billion Market Segment," *Marketing Insights,* January 29, 1968, p. 11.

[17] Alphonzia Wellington, "Traditional Brand Loyalty," *Advertising Age,* May 18, 1981, p. S-2.

[18] Bernard F. Whalen, "Study Measures Impact of Inflation on Blacks' Product, Brand Choices," *Marketing News,* March 20, 1981, pp. 1, 4.

[19] Donald E. Sexton, Jr., "Black Buyer Behavior," *Journal of Marketing,* **36**:38, October 1972; and "Consumer Dynamics in the Supermarket," *Progressive Grocer,* 1969.

[20] Al Harting, "Cultural Differences Offer Rewards," *Advertising Age,* April 7, 1980, p. S-21.

[21] Elizabeth C. Hirschman, "Black Ethnicity and Innovative Communication," *Journal of the Academy of Marketing Science,* **8**:100–119, Spring 1980.

[22] Robert F. Dietrich, "Know Your Black Shopper," *Progressive Grocer,* June 1975, p. 46.

[23] Lawrence P. Feldman and Alvin D. Star, "Racial Factors in Shopping Behavior," in Keith K. Cox and Ben M. Enis (eds.), *A New Measure of Responsibility for Marketing,* American Marketing Association, Chicago, 1968, pp. 216–226.

[24] Henry Allen Bullock, "Consumer Motivations in Black and White," part I, *Harvard Business Review;* May–June 1961, pp. 99–100.

[25] A. Coskun Samli, Enid F. Tozier, and Doris Y. Harps, "Social Class Differentials in the Store Selection Process of Single Black Professional Women," *Journal of the Academy of Marketing Science,* Spring 1980, pp. 138–150.

[26] Keith E. Lockhart, "Missing the Mark on the Black Market," *Broadcasting,* **95**:22, September 25, 1978.

[27] Morse, "Black Radio," p. A-24.

[28] Wally Tokarz, "Minority Marketing Looks to the 80s," *Advertising Age,* April 7, 1980, p. S-22.

[29] James P. Forkan, "Arbitron Study Charts Ethnic TV Viewing Habits," *Advertising Age,* October 22, 1979, p. 20.

[30] See Arnold M. Barban and Edward W. Cundiff, "Negro and White Response to Advertising Stimuli," *Journal of Marketing Research,* **1**:53–56, November 1964; Arnold M. Barban, "The Dilemma of Integrated Advertising," *Journal of Business,* **42**:477–496, October 1969; B. Stuart Tolley and John J. Goett, "Reactions to Blacks in Newspaper Ads," *Journal of Advertising Research,* **11**:11–17, April 1971; Lester Guest, "How Negro Models Affect Company Image," *Journal of Advertising Research,* **10**:29–34, April 1970; Mary Jane Schlinger and Joseph T. Plummer, "Advertising in Black and White," *Journal of Marketing Research,* **9**:149–153, May 1972; William V. Muse, "Product-Related Response to Use of Black Models in Advertising," *Journal of Marketing Research,* **8**:107–109, February 1971; and James W. Cagley and Richard N. Cardozo, "White Response to Integrated Advertising," *Journal of Marketing Research,* **10**:35–40, April 1970.

[31] David M. Klein, William Lesch, and Allen E. Smith, "Integrated Advertising: Changing Times, Changing Perspectives," in Naresh K. Malhotra (ed.), *Proceedings,* Academy of Marketing Science, Miami Beach, Fla., 1985, pp. 288–293.

[32] Lockhart, "Missing the Mark," p. 22.

[33] Leah Rozen, "Black Presenter Makes a Difference: Study," *Advertising Age,* October 13, 1980, p. 20.

[34] Yankelovich, Skelly and White, Inc., *Spanish U.S.A.: A Study of the Hispanic Market in the United States,* The SIN National Spanish Television Network, New York, June 1981, p. 4.

[35] Thomas G. Exter, "Focus on Hispanics," *American Demographics,* August 1985, pp. 29–33.

[36] Joseph M. Aguayo, "Latinos: Los Que Importan Son Ustedes," *Sales and Marketing Magazine,* July 11, 1977, p. 29.

[37] Yankelovich, Skelly and White, Inc., *Spanish U.S.A.,* p. 12; and Joel Saegart, Robert J. Hoover, and Marye T. Hilger, "Characteristics of Mexican American Consumers," *Journal of Consumer Research,* **12**:104–109, June 1985.

[38] "Chrysler Sets Hispanic Test," *Advertising Age,* November 24, 1980, p. 66; and "So They All Speak Spanish," *Media Decisions,* May 1977, pp. 68–71, 117–118.

[39] Elisa Doriano and Dale Dauten, "Hispanic 'Dollar Votes' Can Impact Market Shares," *Marketing News,* September 13, 1985, p. 45.

[40] Luis Diaz-Albertini, "Brand-Loyal Hispanics Need Good Reason for Switching," *Advertising Age,* April 16, 1979, pp. S-22, 23.

[41] Yankelovich, Skelly and White, Inc., *Spanish U.S.A.,* p. 13.

[42] Marco Rosales and Sylvia Rosales, "If You Don't Sell Hispanics in Spanish, You Don't Sell," *Advertising Age,* April 16, 1979, p. S-2.

[43] Terry Agins, "Latin Oases: To Hispanics in U.S., A Bodega Or Grocery Is Essential," *The Wall Street Journal,* March 15, 1985, pp. 1, 17.

[44] Hilary Marsh, "Por Fin, National Retailers Are Thinking Hispanic," from *Madison Avenue,* abstracted in SCAN, April 1986, pp. 14–15.

45 "Say 'Si' to Untapped Market," *Chain Store Age Executive*, March 1984, p. 36.

46 Yankelovich, Skelly and White, Inc., *Spanish U.S.A.*, p. 4.

47 Karen Rothmyer, "A Spanish Accent is Very 'In' These Days on Madison Avenue," *The Wall Street Journal*, January 24, 1975, p. 1.

48 Yankelovich, Skelly and White, Inc., *Spanish U.S.A.*, p. 18.

49 For a discussion of Hispanic media see the following: "Minority Potential Big, But Still Unrealized," *Advertising Age*, April 16, 1979, pp. S-8, 10; Bob Marich, "Broadcast: Los Angeles Espanol," *Advertising Age*, April 6, 1981, pp. S-10–S-14; Jaclyn Fierman, "Meal Foulups Lead to Hunger for Radio," *Advertising Age*, April 6, 1981, pp. S-14–S-15; Steven Reddicliffe, "Print: Magazines Put Accent on Miami," *Advertising Age*, April 6, 1981, pp. S-16–S-17; Robert Flood, "Outdoor and the Hispanic Market OLÉ!" *Marketing & Media Decisions*, May 1981, p. 82; and Yankelovich, Skelly and White, Inc., *Spanish U.S.A.*, pp. 17–23.

50 Rothmyer, "A Spanish Accent," p. 1.

51 Richard P. Jones, "Spanish Ethnic Market Second Largest in U.S.," *Marketing Insights*, November 27, 1976, p. 11.

52 "Latino Media: Available in Any Mood from Conservative to Salsa," *Sales and Marketing Magazine*, July 11, 1977, p. 25.

53 "So They All Speak Spanish," p. 117.

54 Thomas C. O'Guinn, Ronald J. Faber, and Timothy P. Meyer, "Ethnic Segmentation and Spanish-Language Television, *Journal of Advertising*, **14**:63–66, No. 3, 1985.

55 Wayne E. Green, "Firms Seek to Tighten Links with Hispanics as Buyers and Workers," *The Wall Street Journal*, November 10, 1981, pp. 1, 14.

56 Aguayo, "Latinos," p. 29.

57 "Advertising's Missed Opportunity: The Hispanic Market," *Marketing & Media Decisions*, January 1981, p. 134.

58 George P. Moschis and Gilbert A. Churchill, Jr., "An Analysis of the Adolescent Consumer," *Journal of Marketing*, **43**:40, Summer 1979.

59 "Special Interest Group: Teenagers Continue to Set Spending Records," *The Wall Street Journal*, November 6, 1975, p. 1.

60 Doris L. Walsh, "Targeting Teens," *American Demographics*, February 1985, p. 22.

61 Robert O. Herrmann, "Today's Young Adults as Consumers," *Journal of Consumer Affairs*, **4**:23, Summer 1970.

62 Jane See White, "Study Shows What Teens Do Best—Spend Money," *The Evening Bulletin*, June 12, 1981, p. A-8.

63 "Youth Market Growing More Conventional," *Advertising Age*, May 16, 1977, p. 84.

64 Walsh, "Targeting," p. 23.

65 Rebecca Fannin, "Marketing to Teens: All Talk, No Action," *Marketing & Media Decisions*, July 1984, pp. 201–202.

66 "Teenagers Are Spending More Than Ever," *Chain Store Age General Merchandise Trends*, May 1986, p. 7.

67 William P. Perreault, Jr., and Frederick A. Russ, "Student Influence on Family Purchase Decisions," in Fred C. Allvine (ed.), *Combined Proceedings*, American Marketing Association, Chicago, 1971, pp. 386–390.

68 George E. Belch, Michael A. Belch, and Gayle Ceresino, "Parental and Teenage Child Influence in Family Decision Making," *Journal of Business Research*, **13**:163–176, April 1985.

69 Fannin, "Marketing to Teens," p. 204.

70 Walsh, "Targeting," pp. 23–24.

71 Aimee Stern, "Companies Target Big-Spending Teens," *Dun's Business Month*, March 1985, pp. 48–52.

72 George P. Moschis and Roy L. Moore, "A Study of the Acquisition of Desires for Products and Brands," in Kenneth Bernhardt et al. (eds.), *The Changing Marketing Environment: New Theories and Applications*, American Marketing Association, Chicago, 1981, pp. 201–204.

73 "Seventeen Makes a Sales Call," *Madison Avenue*, November 1980, pp. 85–95.

74 Jaclyn Fierman, "Reaching Teens: Less Emphasis on the Product," *Advertising Age*, April 28, 1980, p. S-24.

75 See, for example, George P. Moschis and Gilbert A. Churchill, Jr., "Consumer Socialization: A Theoretical and Empirical Analysis," *Journal of Marketing Research*, **15**:599–609, November 1978;

George P. Moschis and Gilbert A. Churchill, Jr., "Consumer Socialization: A Theoretical and Empirical Analysis," *Journal of Marketing Research*, **6**:101–112, September 1979; and Gilbert A. Churchill, Jr., and George P. Moschis, "Television and Interpersonal Influences on Adolescent Consumer Learning," *Journal of Consumer Research*, **6**:23–25, June 1979.

[76] Dennis H. Tootelian and H. Nicholas Windeshausen, "The Teen-Age Market: A Comparative Analysis, 1964–1974," *Journal of Retailing*, **52**:56–58, Summer 1976.

[77] "Youth Market Growing More Conventional," p. 84.

[78] Moschis and Moore, "Decision Making," pp. 101–112; and Moschis and Churchill, Jr., "Consumer Socialization," pp. 599–609.

[79] Paul E. Smith, "Merchandising for the Teenage Market," *Journal of Retailing*, **37**:12, Summer 1960.

[80] George P. Moschis, "Socialization Perspectives and Consumer Behavior," in Ben M. Enis and Kenneth J. Roering (eds.), *Review of Marketing 1981*, American Marketing Association, Chicago, 1981, pp. 48–49.

[81] Edward Papazian, "Teenagers . . . and Broadcast Media," *Media/Scope*, **11**:111–115, December 1967; and Wally Tokarz, "Radio Considered Teen Medium," *Advertising Age*, April 28, 1980, pp. S-10, S-15.

[82] Papazian, "Teenagers," pp. 110–111; and Mark Kirkeby, "Youth TV Viewing Habits Vary," *Advertising Age*, April 28, 1980, p. S-6.

[83] "Youth Media Market Diverse," *Advertising Age*, April 28, 1980, p. S-2; and Ellis I. Folke, "Teenagers . . . and Print Media," *Media/Scope*, **11**:118, December 1967.

[84] Kate Stoker, "Catching Up with the College Crowd," *Sales and Marketing Management*, October 6, 1980, p. 44.

[85] Frank Reysen, "Youth Markets: A Psychedelic Maze," *Media/Scope*, **14**:40, February 1970.

[86] George W. Schiele, "How to Reach the Young Consumer," *Harvard Business Review*, **52**:85–86, March 1974.

[87] Schiele, "How to Reach the Young Consumer," pp. 83–84; and Patricia Winters, "Schick Targets Young Shavers," *Advertising Age*, March 17, 1986, pp. 3, 103.

[88] Ganesan Visvabharathy and David Rink, "The Elderly: *Still* the 'Invisible and Forgotten' Market Segment," *Journal of the Academy of Marketing Science*, **13**:81–100, Fall 1985.

[89] "The Power of the Aging in the Marketplace," *Business Week*, November 20, 1971, p. 52.

[90] Mark Kirkeby, "The Maturity Market is Coming of Age," *Advertising Age*, August 25, 1980, p. S-11.

[91] Fabian Linden, "The $200 Billion Middle-aged Market," *Conference Board Record*, December 1972, p. 17.

[92] William Lazer, "Inside the Mature Market," *American Demographics*, March 1985, pp. 22–25, 48–49.

[93] Joan Berger, " 'The New Old': Where the Economic Action Is," *Business Week*, November 25, 1985, p. 140.

[94] Paul B. Brown, "Last Year It Was Yuppies—This Year It's Their Parents," *Business Week*, March 10, 1986, p. 74.

[95] Warren A. French and Richard Fox, "Segmenting the Senior Citizen Market," *Journal of Consumer Marketing*, **2**:61–74, Winter 1985.

[96] Charles D. Schewe, "Buying and Consuming Behavior of the Elderly: Findings from Behavioral Research," in Richard J. Lutz (ed.), *Advances in Consumer Research*, vol. 13, Association for Consumer Research, Provo, Utah, 1986, p. 558.

[97] "Don't Overlook the $200 Billion 55-Plus Market," *Media Decisions*, **12**:122, October 1977.

[98] Jo-Ann Zbytniewski, "The Older Shopper: Over 65 and Overlooked?" *Progressive Grocer*, November 1979, pp. 109–111.

[99] Mary C. Gilly and Valarie A. Zeithaml, "The Elderly Consumer and Adoption of Technologies," *Journal of Consumer Research*, **12**:353–357, December 1985.

[100] Consumer Interests of the Elderly (Remarks by Professor John A. Howard, Hearing before the Subcommittee on Consumer Interests of the Elderly of the Special Committee on Aging, United States Senate, 90th Congress, 1st Session, January 17–18, 1967), Washington, D.C.: U.S. Government Printing Office, 1967, p. 128.

[101] R. Eugene Klippel and Timothy W. Sweeney, "The Use of Information Sources by the Aged Consumer," *The Gerontologist*, April 1974, pp. 163–166.

[102] Marilyn Fox, A. Marvin Roscoe, Jr., Alan Feigenbaum, "A Longitudinal Analysis of Consumer Behavior in the Elderly Population," in Thomas C. Kinnear (ed.), *Advances in Consumer Research,* vol. 11, Association for Consumer Research, Provo, Utah, 1984, pp. 563–568.

[103] James Lumpkin, Barnett Greenberg, and Jac Goldstucker, "Marketplace Needs of the Elderly: Determinant Attributes and Store Choice," *Journal of Retailing,* 61:75–105, Summer 1985.

[104] James Lumpkin, "Shopping Orientation Segmentation of the Elderly Consumer," *Journal of the Academy of Marketing Science,* 13:271–289, Spring 1985.

[105] "The Power of the Aging in the Marketplace," p. 56.

[106] Joseph Barry Mason and Brooks E. Smith, "An Exploratory Note on the Shopping Behavior of the Low Income Senior Citizen," *The Journal of Consumer Affairs,* 8:204–210, Winter 1974.

[107] A. Coskun Samli, "The Elusive Senior Citizen Market," *Business & Economic Dimensions,* 3:7–16, November 1967; and A. Coskun Samli and Feliksas Palubinskas, "Some Lesser Known Aspects of the Senior Citizen Market—A California Study," *Akron Business and Economic Review,* Winter 1972, pp. 47–55.

[108] John A. Reinecke, "Supermarkets, Shopping Centers and the Senior Shopper," *Marquette Business Review,* 19:106, 1975; and Zarrell V. Lambert, "An Investigation of Older Consumers' Unmet Needs and Wants at the Retail Level," *Journal of Retailing,* 55:35–37, Winter 1979.

[109] Lynn W. Phillips and Brian Sternthall, "Age Differences in Information Processing: A Perspective on the Aged Consumer," *Journal of Marketing Research,* 14:450, November 1977.

[110] Troy Festervand and James Lumpkin, "Response of Elderly Consumers to Their Portrayal by Advertisers," in J. H. Leigh and C. R. Martin, Jr., (eds.), *Current Issues and Research in Advertising,* University of Michigan, Ann Arbor, 1985, pp. 203–226.

[111] Bill Abrams, "Advertisers Start Recognizing Cost of Insulting the Elderly," *The Wall Street Journal,* March 5, 1981, p. 25.

[112] Anthony C. Ursic, Michael L. Ursic, and Virginia L. Ursic, "A Longitudinal Study of the Use of the Elderly in Magazine Advertising," *Journal of Consumer Research,* 13:131–133, June 1986.

[113] Virginia Knauer, "The Aging Alienated Consumer," in *The Aging Consumer,* "Occasional Papers in Gerontology, No. 8," Institute of Gerontology, Ann Arbor, Mich., p. 20.

[114] "The Power of the Aging in the Marketplace," p. 55.

[115] Abrams, "Advertisers Start," p. 25; Phillips and Sternthall, "Age Differences," p. 450; and "A Biting Analysis on Reaching Elderly," *Advertising Age,* March 15, 1982, pp. 55, 60.

SOCIAL CLASS

LEARNING OBJECTIVES

After studying this chapter, you should understand . . .

- The process of social stratification in societies

- Characteristics of the social-class system

- How social class standing is measured and categorized

- The lifestyles of the three broad social classes in the United States—upper, middle, and lower Americans

- The role of social class in market segmentation

- How social-class membership affects consumer behavior

Sea Goddess Cruises, acquired by Cunard in 1986, was created to fill a market opportunity in the upper-class segment of the market. The concept is simple: custom build an ocean liner which offers understated elegance, visits ports where other cruise ships can't enter, and—most importantly—ferries a silk-stocking crowd that blanches at the thought of a mass-market cruise which caters to Aunt Millie and Uncle Ted from Heartland, U.S.A.

At about $1000 a day per couple (with a maximum capacity of fifty-eight couples), a cruise on the *Sea Goddess* caters to an audience that understands gracious living and is prepared to pay for it. All of the cabins boast a view and measure about 200 square feet, or about half again the size of the typical cruise ship cabin. With beautiful woodwork, wool carpets, designer fabrics, and quiet colors, each cabin also has climate control, a color TV, teletext, a video player, stocked bar, and ship-to-shore telephone.

Clients typically earn upwards of $100,000 a year, are active in business or the professions, may own their own business or derive their income from investments, have an average age in the upper 40s, and are socially active.

Exclusivity is what its passengers want, and *Sea Goddess* aims to deliver it. The ambience of a private club on a private yacht is emphasized throughout the *Sea Goddess* promotional brochure. It describes the *Sea Goddess* as offering a way for a small number of people with similar background and interests to travel together, receive the finest of personalized service, and not be bothered by mass tourism, bus excursions, and regimented schedules that characterize traditional cruise ships.

8

In this chapter we shall examine the influence of social class on consumer behavior. In a sense, we may think of social classes, or strata, as being sub-cultures, for each class has its distinguishing mode of behavior or lifestyle. We shall first discuss what is meant by social stratification and how social-class divisions are determined. This will be followed by a discussion of differences in the values of each class and their lifestyle differences. Finally, the nature of consumer behavior within each class will be described as it is determined by these values and lifestyle differences. The concept of social class can be useful to the marketer for understanding consumer behavior and plotting a marketing strategy. In order to use it wisely, however, one must first understand its meaning.

The term "social class" is used here in the descriptive, not normative, sense. That is, we are not implying that one class is better than another. We are simply describing the class structure as we know it to be. Some may resent such a discussion or be uncomfortable about it, feeling that it is undemocratic. However, social classes exist and their patterns must be understood if the marketer is to be successful.

THE PROCESS OF SOCIAL STRATIFICATION

As much as we Americans like to think that all people are created equal, we are aware that some are "more equal" than others; that is, there are some people who stand high in the community, while others rank low on the totem pole. We refer to these levels as social strata, or classes. "Social stratification," then, is the general term whereby people in a society are ranked by other members of a society into higher and lower social positions, which produces a hierarchy of respect or prestige.[2]

THE NATURE OF SOCIAL CLASS

The term "social class" has been defined as a group consisting of a number of people who have approximately equal positions in a society. These positions may be achieved rather than ascribed, with some opportunity existing for upward or downward movement to other classes.[3] The following are six basic characteristics of social class.

SOCIAL CLASSES EXHIBIT STATUS

Social class and status are not equivalent concepts although they do have an important relationship. *Status* generally refers to one's rank in the social system, as perceived by other members of society. An individual's status, therefore, is a function not only of the social class to which he belongs but also of his personal characteristics. For example, the fact that an individual is a scientist means that she has a high rank in the total social system (as seen in Table 8-1). However, a scientist employed by a prestigious research institute earning $75,000 a year will have higher status or rank than a scientist employed by a small firm and earning $35,000, even though both may be members of the same social class. Moreover, an individual's personal contributions to society will help determine his or her status. A scientist who discovers a breakthrough in laser technology, for example, will have higher status than another who has made no such significant contribution.

Each society subjectively establishes its set of values. These values are reflected in the ideal types of people in that society. That is, those who more nearly conform to the ideal are accorded more respect and prestige, while those who conform less nearly are ranked lower by the society. In one country, members of the armed services may be accorded the greatest prestige; in another, politicians, educators, or business people may be selected. The particular criteria used, as well as their relative weights, are determined by the values which that society stresses. Factors that seem to be important in determining status are: authority over others, power (political, economic, military), ownership of property, income, consumption patterns and lifestyle, occupation, education, public service, ancestry, and association (ties and connections).[4]

Symbols of Status People buy products for what the products mean as well as what they can do. That is, products and services are seen to have personal and social meanings in addition to their purely functional purpose. This idea was expressed long ago by Thorstein Veblen, who suggested that there is a tendency by some members of each social class to engage in *conspicuous consumption* while others spend more conservatively.[5] By conspicuous consumption Veblen

TABLE 8-1

The Ratings of Occupations

White-collar groups	
350 and up	Very high status occupations: presidents and chairmen of boards; the most highly successful lawyers and physicians
250–349	Successful business and professional people: top managers; owners of substantial but not mammoth businesses; professors at universities and high-prestige colleges; reasonably successful doctors, lawyers, and architects
175–249	Moderately successful people: persons in the less prestigeful professions; managers at lower levels; owners of smaller businesses
130–174	Middle managers; small-business owners (retail only); manufacturers' representatives; wholesale salesmen; and some technicians
115–129	The lowest level of managerial, professional, and kindred workers
95–114	Entry-level clerical and salespeople; managers of quite small, mainly blue-collar enterprises
Under 95	Clerks in low-status retail and wholesale establishments

Blue-collar groups	
115 and up	Foremen and craftsmen where the craft requires quite special skills
110–114	Typical craftsmen and skilled manual and service workers
85–99	Ordinary working-class jobs
70–84	Less securely rewarded working-class jobs
55–69	Marginal blue-collar and service jobs
Under 55	Very poor jobs

Source: From *Social Standing in America: New Dimensions of Class* by Richard P. Coleman and Lee Rainwater with Kent A. McClelland. Copyright © 1978 by Basic Books, Inc. By permission of Basic Books, Inc., Publishers, New York.

referred to consumers purchasing things that they do not really need so that others can see what they have done. The things consumers buy become "symbols," telling others who they are and what their social class is. In some states, even license plates convey great status—so much so that one auto dealer offered to exchange a new car in return for a low-numbered license plate in his state, while others have been offered $15,000 to $30,000 for the plate they have.[6]

In a complex society in which financial wealth dictates status, one's possessions become a substitute indicator of the individual's worth, value, wealth, and so forth. Possessions, therefore, take the place of income as an indicator of status, since we aren't likely to know how much others are paid. Consequently, there may be members of a society at each social-class level who seek to achieve a certain higher status by virtue of their possessions. It should be noted, however, that others at the same level may be content to save more and spend much less extravagantly.

Marketers have always catered to consumers who were looking for something to give them an edge, whether real or imagined, over their peers. The key to status symbols is their scarcity and social desirability. As such, they are marks of distinction, setting their owners apart from others.

Blurring of Symbolism   At one time, class differences in status and its symbols were an accepted fact of life in clothing, housing and furnishings, food, drink, speech, and even religious affiliation. Today, however, views of status symbols are changing.[7] Rapid advances in technology and communications have spread the desire for and availability of these material pleasures through all social classes. And as Americans have become more affluent, even those with moderate incomes are able to own their own homes, color televisions, boats, and all sorts of home appliances, and to take exotic vacations. Consequently, if "perfectly ordinary" people can display expensive cars and fancy appliances, then these things obviously have lost much of their effectiveness as status symbols.

A recent fashion phenomenon is the designer label and status emblem on everything from shirts, dresses, sweaters, underwear, and socks to luggage, cologne, and automobiles. Products marketed by LaCoste (Izod), Gucci, Pierre Cardin, Gloria Vanderbilt, Calvin Klein, Ralph Lauren, Halston, and Oleg Cassini, among others, exact high prices, yet they find ready buyers. The mass marketing of these items results in less-than-clear distinctions between the social classes. Thus, people today cannot be sure of who is dramatizing what sort of status with what sort of symbol. According to one writer, "Order Gucci loafers and you only risk winding up shod the same as the boy who delivers them. A Cadillac today signifies nothing about the owner except that he might well pull in at the next Burger King."[8]

Such a situation usually results in new symbols being adopted by higher social classes. In addition, many Americans have lost interest in showing off status. Others have picked unconventional symbols to reflect values other than social rank. For instance, some professional and artistic Americans have downplayed the traditional symbols of economic standing.

In addition, many of the status symbols of today have not filtered down from the upper class to the middle and working classes, but instead have percolated up from the bottom. Recent styles such as blue jeans are indicative of this. Another

confusing element is that traditional status symbols are available today even to those who are not wealthy. For instance, art and sculpture can be rented, inexpensive opera and ballet offerings are available, and tennis, skiing, and sailing can be pursued on a low budget.

Thus, traditional status symbols are no longer the clear indicator of social class they once were, and marketers must understand these trends in order to take advantage of consumers' changing values. It should also be noted that what is "in" in one region of the United States may be "out" in another. Consequently, status symbols can vary geographically.

SOCIAL CLASSES ARE MULTIDIMENSIONAL

Social classes are multidimensional, being based on numerous components. They are not equivalent to, or determined solely by, occupation or income or any one criterion; however, they may be indicated by, or be related to, one or more of these measures. It is important for the marketer to realize that some of these variables are more reliable "proxies" (substitutes) than others. As we shall discuss later, income is often misleading as an indicator of social-class position. Yet money, far more than anything else, is what Americans associate with the idea of social class.[9]

On the other hand, occupation generally provides a fairly good clue to one's social class; in fact, some believe it is the best single indicator available, because certain occupations are held in higher esteem than others by Americans. Table 8-1 illustrates the hierarchy of prestige accorded to many occupations in the United States. The numerical scores indicate the level of status for the occupational category. Thus, the higher the score, the higher the status is perceived to be. Notice also that both blue- and white-collar groups are included, with some overlap of status between high-blue-collar groups and low-white-collar groups.

Housing is another key social-class ingredient, according to most theories. The Johnnie Walker Black Label advertisement in Figure 8-1 illustrates the relationship of housing to that product's consumption image. Most marketers believe "Birds of a feather flock together" and thus "You are where you live." Consequently, some researchers cluster U.S. postal zip-code areas together on the basis of key demographic factors. For example, one company characterizes those at the top of the hill as "the blue-blood estates," followed in descending order by "furs and station wagons," and "money and brains," to "blue-chip blues," and "Bunker's neighbors," to "down-home gentry," and "hard scrabble."[10] Such information can be used for market segmentation and strategy decisions. For instance, Colgate-Palmolive used this approach to pick neighborhoods for a drop of 7 million samples of Fresh Start detergent.

SOCIAL CLASSES ARE HIERARCHICAL

Social classes have a vertical order to them, ranging from high status to low status. They exist as a position on the social scale. Individuals may be placed within a class on this hierarchy, based on status criteria.

SOCIAL CLASSES RESTRICT BEHAVIOR

Interaction between the classes is limited because most of us are more comfortable and find reinforcement with those "like us" in terms of values and behavior

You can tell from the outside which Scotch they serve on the inside.

Johnnie Walker Black Label Scotch

12 YEAR OLD BLENDED SCOTCH WHISKY. 86.8 PROOF. BOTTLED IN SCOTLAND. IMPORTED BY SOMERSET IMPORTERS, LTD., N.Y. © 1981

Figure 8-1
Advertisement for Johnnie
Walker Black Label.
Created by Smith/Greenland Inc. for
Somerset Importers Ltd., importers of
Johnnie Walker Black Label Scotch.

patterns. Consequently, members of the same social class tend to associate with each other and not to any large extent with members from another social class because they share similar educational backgrounds, occupations, income levels, or lifestyles. The factor of limited interaction impedes interpersonal communication between different classes about advertising, products, and other marketing elements.

SOCIAL CLASSES ARE HOMOGENEOUS

As indicated above, social classes may be viewed as homogeneous divisions of society in which people within a class have similar attitudes, activities, interests, and other behavior patterns. For the marketer this means that groups of people are exposed to similar media, purchase similar products and services, and shop in similar stores. This homogeneity allows the marketer in many cases to effectively segment the market by social class and to develop appealing marketing mixes.

SOCIAL CLASSES ARE DYNAMIC

Social stratification systems in which people have some opportunity for upward or downward movement are known as *open systems*. People in *closed systems* have inherited or ascribed status; that is, they are born into one social level and are unable to leave it. Thus, the difference between a system based on earned or achieved status versus one based on inherited status is significant with regard to social mobility. The United States illustrates a social-class, or open, system which offers moderate opportunity for mobility. Although such a change can occur, it is usually not large and generally takes place over an extended time. Sometimes an entire occupational category seeks to raise its status through public relations efforts, as evidenced by attempts in many fields to attach the term ''professional'' to their work activities (for example, law enforcement officers, accountants, and even truck drivers). Parts of rural India illustrate a caste, or closed, system which has existed for thousands of years, in which social inequality is rigidly enforced, creating a permanent social position assigned at birth and preventing any social mobility by the individual.

SOCIAL-CLASS MEASUREMENT AND CATEGORIZATION

Research studies have attempted to stratify social classes in the United States using various measurement approaches. Generally, three methods have been utilized: the subjective method, the reputational method, and the objective method.

THE SUBJECTIVE METHOD

In this approach, individuals are asked to rank themselves in the social-class hierarchy. However, because most people are reluctant to categorize themselves as either lower or upper class, the middle class ends up with an unrealistically large share. Today, file clerks earning as little as $8000 and lawyers making as much as $80,000 think of themselves as middle class, although sometimes with ''upper'' and ''lower'' as modifiers.[11]

THE REPUTATIONAL METHOD

This approach asks members of a community to rank each other in the status system. Because citizens must know each other in order to rank each other, this approach is limited to small communities and, therefore, cannot be widely used by marketers.

THE OBJECTIVE METHOD

Individuals are ranked on the basis of certain objective factors and are positioned accordingly in the social-status hierarchy. For the marketer who is seeking only suggestive evidence of class's impact on a product area, a simplified, proxy measure is acceptable. An example of such a measure is presented in Table 8-2. The Computerized Status Index (CSI) was developed by Social Research, Inc., and has been used successfully since the late 1960s. In this recent version, occupation is weighted double when computing the total score. For unmarried respondents, education as well as occupation would be given double weight. Status interpretation of the total score for conventional married-couple cases with male household heads aged 35 to 64 would be as follows:

TABLE 8-2
Example of a Computerized Status Index (CSI)

Interviewer circles code numbers (for the computer) which in his/her judgment best fit respondent and family. Interviewer asks for detail on occupation, then makes rating. Interviewer often asks respondent to describe neighborhood in own words. Interviewer asks respondent to specify income—a card is presented the respondent showing the eight brackets—and records R's response. If interviewer feels that this is over-statement or under, a "better-judgment" estimate should be given along with explanation.

EDUCATION:	Respondent	Respondent's spouse
Grammar school (8 years or less)	−1	−1
Some high school (9 to 11 years)	−2	−2
Graduated high school (12 years)	−3	−3
Some post high school (business, nursing, technical, 1 year college)	−4	−4
Two, three years of college; possibly Associate of Arts degree	−5	−5
Graduated four-year college (B.A./B.S.)	−7	−7
Master's or five-year professional degree	−8	−8
Ph.D. or six/seven-year professional degree	−9	−9

R's age: ⬚   Spouse's age: ⬚

OCCUPATION PRESTIGE LEVEL OF HOUSEHOLD HEAD: *Interviewer's judgment of how head-of-household rates in occupational status.*

(Respondent's description—ask for previous occupation if retired, or if R. is widow, ask husband's: _____)

Chronically unemployed: "day" laborers, unskilled; on welfare	−0
Steadily employed but in marginal semiskilled jobs; custodians, minimum pay factory help, service workers (gas attendants, etc.)	−1
Average-skill assembly-line workers, bus and truck drivers, police and firefighters, route deliverymen, carpenters, brickmasons	−2
Skilled craftsmen (electricians), small contractors, factory foremen, low-pay salesclerks, office workers, postal employees	−3
Owners of very small firms (2 to 4 employees), technicians, salespeople, office workers, civil servants with average level salaries	−4
Middle management, teachers, social workers, lesser professionals	−5
Lesser corporate officials, owners of middle-sized businesses (10 to 20 employees), moderate-success professionals (dentists, engineers, etc.)	−7
Top corporate executives, "big successes" in the professional world (leading doctors and lawyers), "rich" business owners	−9

AREA OF RESIDENCE: *Interviewer's impressions of the immediate neighborhood in terms of its reputation in the eyes of the community.*

Slum area: people on relief, common laborers	−1
Strictly working class; not slummy but some very poor housing	−2
Predominantly blue-collar with some office workers	−3
Predominantly white-collar with some well-paid blue-collar	−4
Better white-collar area: not many executives, but hardly any blue-collar either	−5
Excellent area: professionals and well-paid managers	−7
"Wealthy" or "society"-type neighborhood	−9

TOTAL FAMILY INCOME PER YEAR:

Under $5,000	−1	$20,000 to $24,999	−5
$5,000 to $9,999	−2	$25,000 to $34,999	−6
$10,000 to $14,999	−3	$35,000 to $49,999	−7
$15,000 to $19,999	−4	$50,000 and over	−8

TOTAL SCORE _____

Estimated status _____

(Interviewer's estimate: _____ and explanation: _____)

R's MARITAL STATUS: Married ___ Divorced/Separated ___ Widowed ___ Single ___ (CODE: ___)

Source: Richard P. Coleman, "The Continuing Significance of Social Class to Marketing," *Journal of Consumer Research*, **10**:277, December 1983. Used with permission.

Remember, such an abbreviated scale will not produce a "correct" social-class placement for each household. As one writer cautions, "Social class is a conceptual tool, and lacking precise definition, is ultimately not susceptible to perfect measurement nor to absolute standards of validity in case placements."[12] Perhaps the best known early study using an objective approach was done by W. Lloyd Warner and his associates.[13] Warner discerned a six-class system of stratification based upon research conducted in several small communities. He categorized the six classes as follows: upper-upper, lower-upper, upper-middle, lower-middle, upper-lower, and lower-lower.

Warner's categorization of classes remained popular for decades, until the 1970s when dramatically changing demographic and social trends lessened its applicability to current society. Two recent views of the status structure are presented in Table 8-3. The views appear to have much in common since they both acknowledge three main groupings of Americans—upper, middle, and lower—and assign almost identical proportions of population to each. However, the two views are based on different classificatory principles. Gilbert and Kahl give much attention to capitalist ownership and to occupation, with prestige, association, and values as derivatives. Coleman and Rainwater take the social-psychological approach of Warner to construct a national status hierarchy. It is based on personal and group prestige and reflects how people interact with one another—as equals, superiors, or inferiors. In the Coleman-Rainwater view, class identification is influenced most heavily by educational credentials and occupation (including income as its success measure), but ultimately relates to a person's social circle of acceptance.

PROBLEMS IN SOCIAL-CLASS MEASUREMENT

In spite of the many approaches used to measure and categorize social classes, there are a number of problems with the concept of doing this. An analysis of the major research done on this topic has found important shortcomings.[14] The following are a few of the problem areas often associated with social-class measurement done by marketers.[15]

1   The ranking of social class is based simply upon an average of the person's position on several status dimensions. This ignores the inconsistencies which arise from an individual ranking high on one dimension (such as income) but low on another (such as education).

2   A person's social class is assumed to be stable, and thus the effects of mobility are ignored.

3   An individual identifies only with the social class in which she or he is categorized, thus ignoring reference-group effects from other classes.

4   The social class of an entire family may be measured by examination of characteristics of only the adult male wage earner, thus ignoring characteristics of

TABLE 8-3
Two Recent Views of the American Status Structure

The Gilbert-Kahl New Synthesis Class Structure:* A situations model from political theory and sociological analysis	The Coleman-Rainwater Social Standing Class Hierarchy:† A reputational, behavioral view in the community study tradition
Upper Americans	**Upper Americans**
The capitalist class (1 percent). Their investment decisions shape the national economy; income mostly from assets, earned, inherited; prestige university connections	*Upper-upper* (0.3 percent). The "capital S society" world of inherited wealth, aristocratic names
Upper middle class (14 percent). Upper managers, professionals, medium business people; college educated; family income ideally runs near twice the national average	*Lower-upper* (1.2 percent). The newer social elite, drawn from current professional, corporate leadership
	Upper-middle (12.5 percent). The rest of college graduate managers and professionals; lifestyle centers on private clubs, causes, and the arts
Middle Americans	**Middle Americans**
Middle class (33 percent). Middle-level white collar, top-level blue collar; education past high school typical; income somewhat above the national average	*Middle class* (32 percent). Average-pay white-collar workers and their blue-collar friends; live on the "the better side of town," try to "do the proper things"
Working class (32 percent). Middle-level blue collar; lower-level white collar; income runs slightly below the national average; education is also slightly below	*Working class* (38 percent). Average pay blue-collar workers; lead "working class lifestyle" whatever the income, school background, and job
Marginal and Lower Americans	**Lower Americans**
The working poor (11 to 12 percent). Below mainstream America in living standard, but above the poverty line; low-paid service workers, operatives; some high school education	*"A lower group of people but not the lowest"* (9 percent). Working, not on welfare; living standard is just above poverty; behavior judged "crude," "trashy"
The underclass (8 to 9 percent). Depend primarily on welfare system for sustenance; living standard below poverty line; not regularly employed; lack schooling	*"Real lower-lower"* (7 percent). On welfare, visibly poverty-stricken, usually out of work (or have "the dirtiest jobs"); "bums," "common criminals"

* Abstracted by Coleman from Gilbert, Dennis and Joseph A. Kahl (1982). "The American Class Structure: A Synthesis," Chapter 11 in *The American Class Structure: A New Synthesis*. Homewood, Ill. The Dorsey Press.
† This condensation of the Coleman-Rainwater view is drawn from Chapters 8, 9, and 10 of Coleman, Richard P. and Lee P. Rainwater, with Kent A. McClelland (1978). *Social Stranding in America: New Dimensions of Class*, New York: Basic Books.
Source: Richard P. Coleman, "The Continuing Significance of Social Class to Marketing," *Journal of Consumer Research*, **10**:267, December 1983. Used with permission.

other family members, particularly the employment and education of the adult female in the family.[16]

Resolution of these and other problems would make the concept of social class a more useful one for marketers.[17]

Although the size of different classes may vary depending on the classification method used and may shift over time, it is nevertheless quite important to realize that the bulk of the market for most products exists in the broad upper- and middle-class groups. The very highest class is made up of only about 1 percent of the population; because of its wealth, it is important to the marketing of certain luxury items. However, this group is too small in number to provide the focal point for most marketers. On the other hand, at the lowest end of the class spectrum one generally finds a market that, even though sizable, does not have sufficient income for many products. Therefore, most consumer-goods marketers concentrate their major attention on the remaining groups.

SOCIAL-CLASS LIFESTYLES

The significance of social stratification for the marketer is that there are differences in values, attitudes, and behavior of each of the classes. These differences provide a basis on which to segment markets and obtain an enhanced understanding of the behavior of consumers. Some of the major findings from research on general social-class differences are summarized in this section, which discusses class variations and lifestyle differences. As we describe the lifestyles of each of the major social-class groups, it should be kept in mind that we are not implying that all members of the same class have homogeneous behavior. As Coleman observes, "A diversity of family situations and a nearly unbelievable range in income totals are contained within each class"[18] and "There is a considerable variation in the way individual members of a class realize these class goals and express these values."[19] Moreover, it is impossible to point to a clear line of demarcation where one class changes to another. There is some blurring and overlapping of the social strata. Nevertheless, we will attempt to make some major distinctions between each of the social classes.[20]

UPPER AMERICANS

The lifestyles of this group have changed more over the last twenty years than have those of people in the classes below them. This group is an interesting mix of many lifestyles: postpreppy, luxurious, countercultural, conventional, intellectual, political, and the like. They account for 14 percent of the market and are the segment of our society who most value quality merchandise, pay special attention to prestige brands, and believe it is important to spend with good taste.

Grouping these people together makes sense for the marketer because their motives and goals in consumption for most mass-marketed items are similar. However, luxury and specialty items may require differential treatment among the groups.

Upper-Upper Class This is the "Social Register" class composed of old, locally prominent families—the aristocracy of birth and wealth with at least three generations in the community and class. It is the smallest class group, international in residence, friendships, and relationships. Its members have occupations as large merchants, financiers, and in the higher professions. Their reference group is the British upper class. They are oriented toward living graciously, upholding the family reputation, reflecting the excellence of one's breeding, and displaying a sense of community responsibility.

This group is sometimes known as "old money," because of its inherited wealth status. Even though this small group is not a significant factor in America's overall consumption system, it wields much of our country's wealth and power. For certain luxury markets this group is important.

Lower-Upper Class This is the nouveau riche, or "newly rich" class, composed of those who have recently arrived at their wealth and are not quite accepted by the

upper-uppers. They are the "executive elite," founders of large businesses, and wealthy doctors and lawyers. They have the highest incomes of all the classes and their goals are a blend of the upper-uppers' pursuit of gracious living and the upper-middles' success drive.

Many of the nation's millionaires fit this category. In 1979, an estimated 520,000 Americans, or about one in every 424 citizens, had a net worth of $1 million or more. Historically, the greatest proportion of millionaires had inherited wealth (upper-uppers). In recent years, that proportion has sharply diminished. Many of the new millionaires come from the ranks of entrepreneurs, especially those who have founded technological businesses; skilled professionals in fields such as neurosurgery and the law; top corporate executives; and professional entertainers and sports stars.[21]

Upper-Middle Class   This class consists of moderately successful professional men and women, such as doctors, lawyers, and professors; owners of medium-sized businesses; and "organization men" at the managerial level. It also includes younger men and women who are expected to reach those occupational-status levels within a few years. Most members are college-educated; hence, this group is sometimes referred to as "the brains and eyes" of our society.

The motivations of this group are toward achieving success in their careers, reaching a higher income level, and achieving social advancement for themselves and their children. They strive to cultivate charm and polish and handle a broad range of civic and/or cultural interests. They play bridge and Scrabble; go to plays, museums, symphonies, and art galleries; and are members of golf clubs, yacht clubs, and college clubs. Their possessions are usually new and their reference group is the upper class.

MIDDLE AMERICANS

This group accounts for seven out of ten Americans and represents a large segment of the American mainstream. Here, the middle class and working class are worth separate attention by marketers because there are significant differences in values and lifestyles between these groups even though there is considerable overlap in income levels.

Middle Class   This class is at the top of the "common man" or "average man" level. It is composed of nonmanagerial workers, small-business owners, and highly paid blue-collars. These lower echelon white-collar workers and small-business owners are at the bottom of the white-collar status ladder while their blue-collar counterparts are at the top of theirs.

The key motivations for this group are "respectability" and "striving." Men and women want to be judged respectable in their personal behavior by their fellow citizens; that is, they desire to live in well-maintained homes which are neatly furnished and are located in neighborhoods that are on the right side of the tracks. They strive to do a good job at their work. Home is their focus and much time and effort is spent in it, especially keeping it clean and tidy.

This group is recognized as one in which people want to "do the right thing" and "buy what's popular." They are concerned with fashion and follow the recommendations of "experts" in the media. With increasing incomes they have spent more money on "worthwhile experiences" for their kids, pushed them toward a college education, and shopped at more expensive stores for clothing with better brand names. Their reference orientation toward upper Americans distinguishes them from the working class. They are big supporters of dinner theater; are lifting themselves up by enrolling in universities and community colleges; are eating out more; dressing more casually; and enjoying vacations. Possessions and pride have given way somewhat to activities and pleasure.

Working Class   These are "poor but honest" and "family folks." The largest of all classes, it is composed of skilled and semiskilled workers and small business tradespeople. Contrary to what may be expected, many of these class members make very good money; they simply don't use it to become "respectable" the way the middle class does. Working class people are oriented toward living well and enjoying life from day to day rather than saving for the future or being concerned about what the middle classes think of them. They want to be modern, to keep up with the times rather than the Joneses.

The working-class family's world view is one of great anxiety. They value the present, the known, and the personal, while avoiding the competitive, the impersonal, and the uncertain. They indulge rather than invest. They are preoccupied with stable human relationships in their everyday lives. Moreover, because they see themselves as being quite restricted in their ability to rise in social status, those with whom they identify are largely chosen from their own class. The working-class woman tends to be part of a tightly knit social group composed primarily of female kin. Thus, more than in any other class, the working-class family generally looks horizontally for its norms and standards rather than up to the next class. Here are some additional characteristics of the women in this group:[22]

■   Although the necessity of working has expanded the social horizons of many working-class women, the traditional female jobs which most of them hold are not intrinsically rewarding.

■   These expanded horizons are reflected in the decreasing propensity of working-class women to define family responsibilities, especially child care, as the central focus of their lives.

■   Wives' employment is often viewed as threatening by the working-class husband, whose ability to provide for the family is often the major source of his sense of self-worth.

■   Working-class husbands and wives tend to adhere to traditional household roles and to engage in sex-segregated leisure activities, even if wives work.

■   While feelings of lack of self-worth and competency in dealing with the world outside the home have decreased among working-class women, they have decreased more slowly than have the same feelings among middle-class women. The result is an increasing disparity in feelings of self-worth and self-confidence between the two social-class groupings.

■   Working-class women are more likely than their middle-class counterparts to feel that their adult life is better than their childhood was. Since part of the

perceived improvement is due to acquisition of desired material goods, working-class women are more positive toward business in general and specific products, and toward the media in general and advertising in particular, than are middle-class women.

This group's emphasis on family ties is one sign of their limited social, psychological, and geographical horizons when compared to the middle class. Their parochial view extends to other areas, however. They tend to live within a mile of a relative, follow local sports heroes, watch local TV news rather than national or world news, vacation at home or within two hours' distance, and buy large domestic cars, not small, foreign ones.[23]

Although this group has become much more affluent over the last thirty years, there has been essentially no value change. This group's basic characteristics—limited horizons, focus on family, and sharp family sex-role divisions—have been relatively unchanged. They have sought change through using modern possessions, not through human relationships or new ideas.

This class together with the middle class enjoys canasta, rummy, poker, TV, movies, and bowling. The men belong to unions, lodges, and fraternal orders.

LOWER AMERICANS

This group contains 16 percent of the population and is generally referred to as "disadvantaged" and outside the mainstream. It is composed of mostly unskilled workers, unassimilated ethnics, and those who are sporadically employed. They may be subdivided into two groups: those who are working and those who are on welfare. The two segments total less than one-fifth of the adult population and account for less than one-tenth of the disposable income.

Upper-Lower Class   This class is the working poor who have not escaped the marginal sector of the labor market. Although above the poverty level, they cannot count on steady employment. Because they may have only some high school education, they are relegated to low-paying, unskilled-labor positions. Unable to advance to the working class because of their low education level, they fear slipping to the lowest class.

Lower-Lower Class   This class amounts to 7 percent of the population. Living below the poverty line, they receive most of their income from illegal activities or from welfare. This group is categorized as the "American underclass" whose environment is often a "junk heap of rotting housing, broken furniture, crummy food, alcohol and drugs."[24] They are apathetic and fatalistic in their outlook, and their behavior generally, and as consumers, is toward "getting their kicks wherever they can." They have a bad reputation among higher classes who view them as lazy, shiftless, against work, and immoral.

THE ROLE OF SOCIAL CLASS IN SEGMENTING MARKETS

It is evident that the concept of social class should help us to understand better the behavior of the various market segments. However, the marketing practitioner wants to know if segmentation on the basis of social class is an advantageous approach.

Social-class segmentation involves two basic issues.[25] First, opinions differ concerning which procedures are best for identifying social classes. This issue is beyond the scope of our discussion. However, it should simply be noted here that there are various approaches to social-class measurement, with each one offering certain advantages and disadvantages. A second and more fundamental problem is whether even to use social class (which is, in effect, a composite index consisting of several variables) in segmenting markets, or whether to use a single proxy variable such as income (for which data more readily exist). Thus, the basic question here is, Which approach better explains consumer behavior?

SOCIAL CLASS AND INCOME RELATED TO LIFESTYLE PATTERNS

While we are addressing this issue, it may be useful to examine the results of a study that correlated more than 200 lifestyle items with both social class and income. Although none of the correlations was as high as might be desired in order to clearly support the contention that lifestyle is the "essence" of social class, those correlations obtained for social class were generally higher than those obtained for income. The most meaningful lifestyle statements and their correlation coefficients for social class (r_{SC}) and income (r_i) are presented in Table 8-4. Two conclusions from this study should be cited:[26]

1 Many lifestyle items show significant correlations with the index of social class, indicating definite but small differences between the social classes in terms of lifestyles.

2 Some items show a much greater correlation with social class than with income, suggesting that social class is a better predictor of consumers' living patterns than is income.

Those items that were more related to social class than to income seemed to comprise two "clusters": one representing "cultural" activities; the other representing a group of social-interaction items. Cultural activities (such as concerts,

TABLE 8-4

Correlations of Lifestyle Items with Social Class and Income

Item	r_{SC}	r_I
I enjoy going to concerts	.26	.11
I enjoy going through an art gallery	.25	.18
I attend a bridge club regularly	.24	.18
I am usually an active member of more than one service organization	.24	.16
I like ballet	.24	.14
I think I'm a pretty nice-looking person	.23	.12
I am a homebody	−.22	−.13
I feel I can do things as well or better than most people	.21	.11
My children are the most important thing in my life	−.19	−.08
I think I have less self-confidence than most people	−.18	−.07
I often take an active part in some local civic issue	.17	.09
I am usually the center of attention in a group	.15	.08

Source: James H. Myers and Jonathan Gutman, "Life-Style: The Essence of Social Class," in William D. Wells (ed.), *Lifestyle and Psychographics*, American Marketing Association, Chicago, 1974, pp. 250–251.

ballet, and bridge games) are available to people of almost any income level. The fact that some people choose to engage in them and others do not is one of the things that makes social class a meaningful concept. Social interaction items (such as confidence, outgoingness, or good looks) may result from higher-class people feeling a sense of belonging and recognition from having a secure place higher up in the social structure. However, upper-social-class people also seem to have less interest in the home in general, and in children in particular, than do upper-income/lower-class individuals.

How may the marketer use such information?[27] General lifestyle items that correlate well with product usage might well explain characteristics of the markets' activity, interest, and opinion to the seller. Such findings could give the marketer some direction for product, promotion, channel, and pricing decisions. A preferred approach, however, would be to design a lifestyle study especially for the particular firm or its product line.[28]

SOCIAL CLASS AND INCOME RELATED TO CONSUMER BEHAVIOR PATTERNS

The previous section assessed the relationship of social class and income to lifestyle and patterns and consumers' interests as a basis of segmenting markets. A fundamental question not specifically addressed above, however, is whether social class or income is more closely associated with specific consumer activity, particularly with product purchase patterns.

Those who believe that social class is much better than income for market segmentation claim that income categories are quite often irrelevant in analyzing markets and explaining consumers' shopping habits, store preferences, and media usage. An example of the superiority of social class to income is the following comparison of three families, all earning approximately the same amount per year (that is, $25,000), but belonging to different social classes with radical differences in their spending patterns.[29]

An *upper-middle-class* family headed, perhaps, by a young lawyer or a college professor is likely to spend a relatively large share of its income on housing in a prestige neighborhood, on expensive furniture, clothing from quality stores, and on cultural amusements or club memberships.

A *middle-class* family headed, let's say, by an insurance salesman or a successful grocery store owner probably has a better house, but in not as fancy a neighborhood; as full a wardrobe, although not as expensive; more furniture, but none by name designers; and a much bigger savings account.

A *working-class* family headed, perhaps, by a welder or cross-country truck driver, is likely to have less house and less neighborhood than the others; however it will have a larger, newer car, more expensive kitchen appliances, and a larger TV set in the living room. This family will spend less on clothing and furniture, but more on food and sports.

Nevertheless, most of the research that has been conducted has found income to be more useful than social class for segmenting markets. One study showed that for a number of low-priced consumer packaged goods, both income and social class were found to correlate with buying behavior. However, product usage generally proved to be more closely related to income than to social class.[30]

A follow-up study included certain durable-goods items plus a few services and confirmed the earlier study by showing income to be superior to social class in segmenting the market for nearly all items.[31] Thus, some products appear to be classless in their appeal. For example, in the hot southwest, income, not social class, largely determines whether a family buys air conditioning. If the family can afford to purchase air conditioning, it does so. On the basis of such findings, it would appear that social class, although useful as a concept, has often not been as successful as other approaches in segmenting markets.

Much of the earlier research, however, based its findings on *use* or *nonuse* of a product or service rather than on *how often* that product or service was used. Since there are many products or services that a broad spectrum of consumers would buy or use at least once, one research study examined the role of *frequency of use* in selecting the superior segmentation bases among income, social class, age, and stage in family life cycle for various entertainment activities. This research showed that income and stage in the life cycle were more highly related to *use* of all the entertainment activities than were age and social class. However, all four variables—especially social class—showed strong associations with the *frequency of use* of these entertainment activities.[32] More research is needed on a broad variety of products before a generalization of this finding is made.

Several explanations have been suggested for the apparent lackluster performance of social class as a basis for market segmentation.[33] One factor is the recent and dramatic changes which have taken place in our society's economic, social, and cultural climate and which have diminished the differences in consumer behavior between the classes.

Another explanation for the poor showing of social class is that researchers have failed to account for the diversity within classes. That is, individuals, although in the same social class, may show considerable discrepancy in their ratings on the variables the class consists of. For example, some may have high education with low income or vice versa, yet be members of the same social class. This inconsistency in strata variables, known as *status incongruency* or *low status crystallization,* presents difficulties not only in ranking individuals but also in understanding their behavior.

The diversity within social classes is particularly evident with income level variations. For example, it has been suggested that there are *overprivileged* and *underprivileged* members within each class. The overprivileged families in each class are those with incomes 25 to 30 percent above the class median, who have money left over to spend after acquiring the standard package of shelter, clothing, and transportation for their class. Some families are in the middle of the class income range for their situations. Other families are underprivileged, having incomes at least 15 percent below the class median. While not really poor (unless in the lower classes), they find it difficult to exhibit the standard of living expected from people of their status and must scrimp, save, and sacrifice to have the proper appearance. In 1983 the income minimums for "class-average" status were $100,000 for the upper class, $45,000 for the upper-middles, $24,000 for middle class, $16,000 for working class, and almost $10,000 for lower-class Americans.[34] Thus, an upper-class family earning $80,000 a year is "underprivileged" by the standards of its level. That family can't own a mansion and a second home and obtain private schooling. It has to sacrifice.

This concept is believed to explain the purchase of certain consumer durables. For example, the dominant market for high-priced domestic cars has been the overprivileged buyers from each social class rather than high-income Americans as a group. On the other hand, small cars have been bought by the underprivileged segments of each class. Thus, a struggling young lawyer, as an underprivileged member of the upper-middle class, may purchase a Toyota as a temporary transportation solution until her income rises, then buy a new Buick when she gets to be overprivileged. Similarly, costly household appliances and recreational activities tend to have been consumed by the overprivileged members of each class. Color television sets, for instance, were first bought primarily by this segment.

Based on a recent, thorough research study, the following tentative generalizations are possible regarding when social class, income, or their combination is superior as a segmentation variable:[35]

1   Social class is superior to income for areas of consumer behavior that do not involve high-dollar expenditures, but do reflect underlying lifestyle, value, or homemaker role differences. Relevant products in this situation might include instant, frozen, and canned convenience foods and beverages; snack foods; and imported and domestic wines, for example. Social class is also superior for both method and place of purchase of highly visible, symbolic, and expensive living-room furniture.

2   Income is generally superior for products which require substantial expenditures, and which may no longer serve as symbols of status within a class or as status symbols to the upper-lower class (such as major kitchen and laundry appliances).

3   The combination of social class and income is generally superior for product classes that are highly visible, serve as symbols of social class or status within class, and require either moderate or substantial expenditure (such as clothing and makeup, automobiles, and television sets).

Before attempting to use social class to segment markets, the marketer should remember three guidelines:

1   Social class may not always be a relevant consideration; that is, segmentation by other criteria, such as age and sex, is frequently more appropriate.

2   Benefits from social-class segmentation for undifferentiated products may be less than the costs incurred to achieve such segmentation.

3   Social-class segmentation is frequently most effective when used in conjunction with such additional variables as life-cycle stage and ethnic group.[36]

However, even for cases in which social class may have only limited application, it does provide the marketer with helpful insights—some of which may be specifically used in developing marketing strategies, and others of which at least offer an improved general understanding of consumer behavior.[37]

In the remaining section of this chapter, we will present some of the research findings on the relationship of social class, consumer behavior, and the development of marketing mixes.

SOCIAL CLASS AND CONSUMER BEHAVIOR

This section examines the most significant findings concerning various classes' behavior with regard to the products they buy, the places they shop, and the promotions and prices they respond to.

For many products the groups of interest to the marketer are the middle and working classes—by far the largest segment of the market. Because of this, the bulk of our attention in this section will be focused on these two categories in order to provide a more complete understanding of these groups. Where possible, special emphasis will be given to the working class because of the marketer's inherent difficulty in understanding this market, a difficulty which springs from the fact that most marketing managers are members of the middle or upper classes. These are the groups that form the basis of their *self-reference criterion;* that is, they tend to assume that everyone else is like themselves in values, attitudes, tastes, lifestyle, and so forth. Such a premise is very likely to result in marketing strategy failure.

PRODUCTS AND SERVICES CONSUMED

Product choice and usage differ among the social classes. There are items that are bought mainly by the upper classes, such as bonds and exotic vacations, and others that are purchased mainly by lower classes, such as roller derby tickets and cheap wine. Not only are there between-class purchasing differences but also within-class variations. As mentioned previously, each class level has its conspicuous consumers and its more conservative buyers—that is, its overprivileged and its underprivileged members. Illustrating the consumption differences between underprivileged Upper Americans and overprivileged Middle Americans of the same income level, Coleman observes that the latter have a much greater frequency of ownership of motorboats, RVs, campers, pickup trucks for sport or work, tractor lawnmowers, snowblowers, remote-control TVs, backyard swimming pools, lakeside homes, late-model sports cars for their teenage college children, and large, expensive cars for themselves. In contrast, Upper Americans at the same income level spend a greater percentage of time and money on private club memberships, unique educational experiences for their kids, high-culture objects and events, and civic affairs. Their houses may be no more expensive but have the "proper" address.[38]

However, many products are purchased by a wide variety of consumers so it becomes difficult to distinguish class differences in purchasing patterns. For example, all people purchase food, clothing, and shelter items. The differences come into view when we examine not just generic categories but types of products and particular brands, and frequency of purchase.

Although our understanding and appreciation of social class differences and similarities in product choice and usage is limited, we can make some rather general statements regarding the product and service orientations of the classes.

Upper-Uppers   The consumption patterns of upper-uppers are quite different from those of other classes. Although expense is frequently no object, they do not purchase in order to impress others. Therefore, they may be content to wear 20-year-old sportcoats and drive 10-year-old cars. They tend to be conservative in their consumption, buying relatively few goods, and use more services than goods. One reason for their low consumption of goods is that many of their belongings are passed on from generation to generation.

Lower-Uppers   The consumer behavior of lower-uppers may be characterized as oriented strongly toward conspicuous consumption. Their purchase decisions are geared toward demonstrating wealth and status through such items as expensive cars, large estates, expensive jewelry, and so forth. This group is the prime target for some outlandish gifts offered by Texas retailer Neiman-Marcus.

While the upper class may be a significant market for many high-priced luxuries, for most new-product introductions this group can be largely ignored. However, they may be used effectively as reference groups in advertising to those below them and sometimes their use of certain products will "trickle down" to the other social-class groups. This approach has been used by France's Perrier mineral water and Lenox china and crystal.

The upper classes are effectively used in advertising for Lenox. The ads (see Figure 8-2) show beautiful women in elegant surroundings, which is a very image-conscious and upscale approach. The china is prominent, but not at the center of attention. The aim is to convey the idea that Lenox is the sign of a hostess with excellent taste. The company is selling dreams. If the potential Lenox buyer can't have the model's sophistication or beauty, at least they can have her Lenox.[39]

Upper-Middles   This group purchases a far greater number of products than any other class. Because they are successful, their purchase decisions reflect strong social implications. Through their consumption they want to project an image of success and achievement. Their purchases emulate higher strata and are a display of their success, not only for their peers but for others lower on the social scale. Because they purchase higher-quality products and attempt to display good taste, they are frequently termed the "quality market."

Because this group is so important as a market, many businesses are broadening their appeal to include upper-middles. Country clubs, for example, long considered to be plush, snobby, and oriented mainly to the upper class, have changed their image. Today many of them appear to have a more democratic image and a growing middle-class orientation where members tend to be younger, more informal, and where women and minorities are increasingly included.

The high education level of this group strongly influences the kinds of expenditures they make. As cited earlier their desired consumption pattern is heavily "experience" centered, that is, spending where one is left typically with memories rather than tangible assets.

Middle Class   Social acceptability is an important guideline in the consumption activity of this group also. They are more interested in a product's giving them social acceptance than in the luxuriousness or functionality of the item. Products, especially home furnishings, are bought on the basis of what is "pretty" and stylish and will suit the housewife and win praise from her friends and neighbors. Product choices are made along safe and conservative lines rather than on the basis of original and imaginative thoughts.

Working Class   Rainwater reports that there are five basic goals that activate the consumer behavior of the working-class housewife:

1   The search for social, economic, and physical security

2   The drive for a ''common man'' level of recognition and respectability

3   The desire for support and affection from the people important to her

4   The effort to escape a heavy burden of household labors

5   The urge to decorate, to ''pretty up,'' her world[40]

The working-class world tends to be more limited in both direct and vicarious experiences, which is reflected in consumption patterns. Expenditures are concentrated into fewer categories of goods and services. The working class are more concerned with immediate gratification than are middle-class families, but avoid

Figure 8-2
Advertisement for Lenox china and crystal.
Courtesy of Lenox, Inc.

spending their money in ways that are considered "out-of-place." Their spending is centered more on the interior-exterior interest of their house than on the size and location of the house itself. Since their upward social mobility is quite limited, they are not concerned about socially elite addresses. Instead, their housing tastes are very practical and utilitarian with "decent," "clean," "new," and "safe" characterizing their outlook. An example of this orientation, in spite of an income that would allow other alternatives, is illustrated by Michigan's first million-dollar lottery winner, who collects $50,000 a year for the next 20 years. Although he retired from his manual labor job, he did not move his family from their one-bedroom bungalow. Instead he installed aluminum siding, central air-conditioning, storm windows, a sun porch, double-oven gas stove, color television, and finished his basement recreation room with dark green paneling and indirect lighting.[41]

Although working-class consumers' behavior resembles middle-class behavior in hard goods spending, their expenditures for services lag behind and are also lower than their own expenditures for durables. Some of the reasons suggested for the lack of service-oriented consumption among the working class in comparison with the middle class are (1) they tend to be do-it-yourselfers; (2) their expenditures for children's education are much smaller; (3) they are more likely to spend their vacation at home or visiting relatives, saving on motel and transportation costs; (4) they do not frequent expensive restaurants, but tend to consume their meals away from home with relatives, or at a franchised drive-in.[42] Thus, the tremendous boom in the service sector of our economy is largely a middle-class phenomenon.

Lower Americans Contrary to what might be expected, some members of this group may represent an attractive segment for manufacturers of food products or other frequently purchased items, and for certain durables. For example, one study found that such families are consumers of many major consumer durables, frequently the new, more expensive models.[43] Another researcher found that the prevailing market value of the lower-class family's car, television set, and basic appliances average almost 20 percent higher than the average value of similar possessions for the working class, despite a median income which was one-third lower than the working-class group.[44] Lower-class spending behavior can be described as "compensatory consumption." The lower-lower class family's pessimistic outlook on life causes them to spend for immediate gratification. Thus, through their purchasing they try to emulate the "good life." This group's purchasing patterns also reveal a tendency to buy on impulse with little planning. Low educational level appears to be a primary cause of this.

SHOPPING BEHAVIOR

Shopping behavior also varies by social class. For example, a very close relation between store choice and social-class membership has been found, indicating that it is wrong to assume that all consumers want to shop at glamorous, high-status stores. Instead, people realistically match their values and expectations with a store's status and don't shop in stores where they feel out of place.

Thus, no matter what the store, each shopper generally has some idea of the social-status ranking of that store and will tend not to patronize those where they feel they do not "fit," in a social-class sense.[45] The result is that the same products and brands may be purchased in different outlets by members of different social classes.[46] Therefore, an important function of retail advertising is to allow the shopper to make a social-class identification of stores. This is done from the tone and physical character of the advertising.

One research study of the shopping behavior of a group of urban women has provided a number of valuable insights into the influence of social class on the shopping process:

> Most women enjoy shopping regardless of their social class; however, reasons for enjoyment differ. All classes enjoy the recreational and social aspects of shopping, as well as being exposed to new things, bargain hunting, and comparing merchandise. However, lower classes found acquiring new clothes or household items more enjoyable, while upper-middles and above more frequently specified a pleasant store atmosphere, display, and excitement.
>
> Middle- and upper-class women shopped more frequently than those in the lower class.
>
> The higher a woman's social class the more she considered it important to shop quickly.
>
> Middle and working classes had a greater tendency to browse without buying anything.
>
> The lower the social status, the greater the proportion of downtown shopping.
>
> A greater percentage of lower-class women favored discount stores than did women in the middle or upper classes. The attraction to high-fashion stores was directly related to social class. Broad-appeal stores were more attractive to the middle class.[47]

Let us examine more closely the nature of social-class variations in shopping patterns in order to better understand marketing-strategy decisions.

Uppers and Upper-Middles   Women of this group organize shopping more purposefully and efficiently than those of lower status. They tend to be more knowledgeable about what they want, where and when to shop for it; their shopping is both selective and wide-ranging. These consumers are more likely to search for information prior to purchase. They are more likely to read brochures, newspapers, and test reports before buying appliances.[48]

There is also an emphasis by this group on the store environment. Stores must be clean, orderly, and reflect good taste. Moreover, they must be staffed with clerks who are not only well-versed in their particular product line, but also well aware of their customers' status. This attitude indicates a leaning toward urban and suburban specialty stores and away from larger, more general outlets. For example, women from this group have been characterized as usually buying most of their public appearance clothes at specialty shops or in specialty departments of the town's best department stores.[49]

Is there a paradox between consumer status and discount-house patronage among this group? Actually, the extent of patronage depends on the nature of the product sought. This group apparently has few qualms about buying appliances in discount houses because they feel they cannot "go wrong" with nationally advertised brand names. A furniture purchase, however, is another matter, and the same consumer is likely to go to a status store which can act as an "authority" on tasteful home furnishings.

Middle Class   Women of this class "work" more at their shopping. They exhibit more anxiety, particularly when purchasing nonfoods, which they feel can be a demanding and tedious process filled with uncertainty. They are value-conscious and try to seek out the best buy for the money. Such an orientation would indicate a strong tendency to patronize discount houses.

Working Class   Because of this group's strong concern with personal relationships, there is a tendency to shop along known, local friendship lines. This attitude also explains their loyalty to certain stores in which they feel at home. Martineau describes situations in which lower-status women who shopped in high-status department stores felt clerks and higher-class customers in the store "punished" them in various subtle ways. One woman expressed her feeling that in a higher-status store "the clerks treat you like a crumb." Another related how she had vainly tried to be waited on, finally to be told, "We thought you were a clerk."[50]

The shopping behavior of this group has been described as a pattern of routine standardized purchasing, usually of national brands, having infrequent impulsive or unplanned purchases. The factors contributing to this behavior are thought to be limited perspective, short-time horizons, and frustrations.[51]

The working classes buy with less prepurchase deliberation than do middle and upper classes. They are much more likely to use in-store information sources, such as displays and salespeople.[52] The routinized nature of their shopping suggests for the marketer an emphasis on the use of enticing point-of-purchase displays and easy availability of items. It is clear that this group is a prime target for discount houses, and in fact it has been a potent force in the development of suburban discount retailing.[53]

Lower Americans   This group is one that buys largely on impulse. This tendency results in the necessity to rely heavily on credit, since money that might have been spent for big-ticket items has been drained off in impulse buying of small things. At the same time, however, these people can be poor credit risks because of their low-income status. This often forces them into a pattern of dealing with local merchants who offer tailor-made (yet sometimes quite exorbitant) credit terms.

PROMOTIONAL RESPONSE PATTERNS

Important class differences exist with regard to promotional response. The social classes have differing media choice and usage patterns. For example, readers of *National Geographic* and *The New Yorker* are typically of a higher class than the readers of *Police Gazette, True Confessions*, and *The Star*. Even magazines in the same topic area may be aimed at different social classes as target audiences. The

social classes also have different perceptions and responses to advertising and other promotional messages, responses which are significant in the development of proper marketing strategies. The basis of advertising differences directed at the various classes should be founded on the differing communication skills and interests of these groups. For example, sophisticated and clever advertising such as that appearing in *The New Yorker* and *Esquire* is almost meaningless to lower-class people who don't understand the subtle humor and are baffled by the bizarre art. This certainly does not imply that they lack intelligence or wit, but merely that their communication skills or experiences have been oriented in a different way. Thus, their symbol systems are different, and they have a quite different approach to humor.[54]

Beer producers segment markets by social class, with different brands and advertising aimed at each group. For instance, Miller and Lowenbrau, produced by the same company, appeal to different social classes. Miller with its "Made the American way" theme presents a strong working class, masculine image by featuring people in various tough, physical jobs, whereas Lowenbrau appeals on the basis of more-refined sociability by featuring upscale groups with the theme "Here's to good friends."

The marketer must also cautiously select key advertising words because of their different perceptions among the classes which could cause problems. Consider, for example, potential class reactions to an advertisement for a soap product used to wash baby clothes. In a motivation study of soaps and detergents it was learned that middle-class women associated the words "darling," "sweet," or "mother" with the word "baby," while lower-class women, reacted with such terms as "pain in the neck," "more work," or "a darling but a bother."[55]

In addition, certain voice and speech patterns may be more influential than others for specific consumer segments. Thus, speakers with "upper-class" voices and speech patterns can appear more credible to higher classes than "low-status" sounding speakers.[56] This supports such spokesperson choices as Sir John Gielgud for Paul Masson wines, John Houseman for Smith Barney, and Sir Laurence Olivier for Polaroid.

Consequently, marketers must understand their market thoroughly and communicate meaningfully to it within the range of their skills. The media patterns of each class are described below as well as some possible promotional appeals.

Uppers   The upper classes tend to buy more newspapers, read more of the newspaper, see more magazines, and watch less television than other classes. They also listen to FM radio.

Upper-Middles   The media choices of this group tend toward FM radio, particularly classical music stations; magazines such as *Time, Fortune, Vogue, The New Yorker, Consumer Reports,* and *House & Garden;* and newspapers. The upper-middle class does not fully embrace television, worrying about its effect on their children. Nevertheless, they do watch significant amounts, with their programming tastes tending toward current events and drama. Because of later dinner hours and bedtimes, they have a high exposure to late-night television shows, such as the *Tonight Show* and *Nightline.*

This group and the upper classes represent challenging targets to the mar-

keter in developing promotion appeals. They tend to be more critical of advertising, are suspicious of its emotional appeals, and question its claims. They usually display an attitude of sophisticated superiority to it. This is not to say, however, that they are unresponsive to advertising. They can be attracted by approaches that are different, individualistic, witty, sophisticated, stylish, that appeal to good judgment and discriminating taste, and that offer the kinds of objects and symbols that are significant to their status and self-expression goals.

Middle Class　This group tends to read morning newspapers and magazines such as *Reader's Digest, Sports Illustrated, Esquire, Good Housekeeping,* and *Ladies' Home Journal* and watches a good deal of television. This group, as well as the working class, takes a rather straightforward, literal-minded, and pragmatic approach to advertising. Effective promotion appeals are those portraying the home and relating use of the product to success as a housewife and mother. Labor-saving products such as instant foods, for example, are best promoted in a way that also satisfies conscientiousness.

Although attracted by discount coupons, this group is careful in the use of them. They want to be sure that the incentive is worth the effort, that they are being sensible in their use of them.

Working Class　The media choices of this group tend toward AM radio, heavy television viewing, especially soap operas, game shows, situation comedies, variety shows, and late movies, magazines such as *True Story,* and afternoon and tabloid newspapers. For example *The Star, The National Enquirer,* and *Midnight Globe* sell 11 million copies a week, primarily to women who are over age 46, in blue-collar households, who are high school graduates of slightly lower income than average, and with larger-than-average households. Psychographically, such readers believe miracle cures are fascinating, politicians are dishonest, Laetril should be legalized, UFOs are real, and abortions should be outlawed.[57]

A study made by Social Research, Inc., of the women in this group found that some interesting changes are taking place, which could have relevance to the marketer's promotional strategy:

> Although they are no longer captives of husband, children, and home and have a new desire for independence, these women resent efforts to "put down" the role of wife, mother, and homemaker.
>
> Most have new interests in their communities and jobs.
>
> They want products that will free them from housework or contribute to their comfort or gratification.[58]

This class is also the most receptive group to sales promotion offers. They are eager to take advantage of many of the offers that come their way, to cut costs or get something extra.

Lower Americans　The media habits of this group are similar to those of the working class except that they have even lower readership of magazines and newspapers. They are more audio(AM radio)- and video(television)-oriented.

Both groups have early dinner hours and thus have heavier exposure to early-evening television than do higher social classes. This group comprises a large segment of the heavy television viewers, who tend to be under 30, high school dropouts, removed from the job market, with personal income below the poverty level.[59]

Promotion directed to this class is constrained as a result of their lower education and intelligence levels and the difficulty they have in thinking abstractly. For these reasons it is suggested that simple, concrete appeals be used, with greater visual stimulation, such as the use of color and heavy reliance on symbols.

PRICE-RELATED BEHAVIOR

Research on these variables is extremely limited and most of what exists relates to the poor. Lower-class consumers are more poorly informed about price and product alternatives.[60] They are also more likely to buy products on sale or priced lower.[61] Regarding price perceptions among the middle and working classes, a shopping simulation showed that working-class housewives have a greater reliance on the general belief that there is a price/quality association; that is, the higher the price of a product is, the higher the quality. They perceive that they have an inability to discriminate between products and are therefore forced to fall back on a general belief in order to handle this problem of which product to buy. Although the better-educated housewives in both classes had stronger beliefs that price and quality are related, they preferred lower-priced product alternatives. They apparently felt capable of judging the product alternatives on their own merits rather than having to rely on general beliefs in price/quality to make a decision.[62]

Research on commercial-bank credit-card holders has uncovered social-class variations in card use patterns. For example, members of the lower class tend to use their cards for installment purchases and seek out stores that honor their cards, while upper classes use them for convenience and do not seek stores accepting the card.[63]

ARE CLASS DIFFERENCES DISAPPEARING?

The marketer is vitally interested in changes occuring in the social-class system. If this construct is indeed becoming less important as a means of identifying markets, then it will be less effective as a segmenting variable. Unfortunately, the issue addressed here cannot be answered unequivocally. There is some evidence supporting both views: That is, social class seems to continue as a permanent fixture in America, yet there is some blurring of class boundaries. Our country is becoming less of a rigid and fixed-by-birth system.

Evidence for the decreasing importance of social class comes from the study by Coleman and Rainwater who found that more than two-thirds of their respondents—including nearly 90 percent of those under 30 years of age—viewed social class as becoming less important in America than it used to be. Social mobility has increased as many barriers have fallen. The end of job discrimination by race and minority is one contributing factor. Decline in prejudice related to

ancestry and religion is another element. Educational opportunity is much broader today so that all classes have access to higher education to become doctors, lawyers, and so forth. In addition, the changing income distribution and changes in the comparative standing of occupational groups have resulted in less disparity between white- and blue-collar workers.[64] These are some of the factors involved in the decline of the social-class system.

Others suggest that the mass media have had a leveling influence on the values and lifestyle aspirations of all people. As a result, it is argued, differences in product preferences among social classes may have disappeared.[65] Research on this topic, however, has not supported this contention.[66]

It has also been claimed that the development of mass merchandising and the sale of mass-produced consumer goods means that most people buy the same brands in the same stores. The thousands of McDonald's, Sears, and Goodyear stores offer consumers standardized quality and sameness. Thus, the market seems to have become more "massified"; that is, the broad middle class seems to typify the nation's lifestyle.

In spite of these signs, other evidence points to continued differentiation between the classes. For example, survey research such as that done by the Gallup organization indicates that responses are linked to class, and that class differences do still exist.[67] In addition, there is other evidence that occupational and educational differences are still strong between the classes, as are differences in lifestyle patterns.[68] Class value systems have maintained continuity in spite of thirty years of economic cycles of inflation and recession and numerous changes in consumption of cars, clothing, and food.[69] Thus, the marketer should be cognizant of a broadened middle-class pattern in the marketplace. Nevertheless, the social-class system is still a factor with which to be reckoned in segmenting markets, developing marketing programs, and understanding consumer behavior.

MANAGERIAL REFLECTIONS

For our product or service situation . . .

1 What is the predominant social class of buyers?

2 Is there an important symbolism affecting its purchase?

3 What are the demographic and socioeconomic characteristics within social-class segments chosen as target markets?

4 How may the lifestyle of our social-class market be described?

5 Is social class a useful way to segment buyers?

6 What patterns are exhibited by target social-class segments with regard to product choice, shopping behavior, and promotion and price responsiveness?

7 To what extent are social-class differences disappearing among our market segments?

DISCUSSION TOPICS

1   What is meant by the term "social stratification"?

2   Discuss the use of social class as a market-segmentation approach.

3   Select one of the social-class categories and prepare a report on its lifestyle.

4   How might a marketer have a problem with his "self-reference criterion" when making marketing decisions involving social-class ramifications?

5   Find at least two manufacturer's ads for the same generic product (such as, clothing) that you think are aimed at different social classes. Explain the differences in the ads.

6   Find three newspaper advertisements by local retailers that you think reach the different social classes. Explain the differences in the ads.

7   Classify the major department stores in your area according to your estimation of the social class of their customers. How do the marketing features of these stores differ?

8   What social class would you choose for initial marketing efforts if you were to introduce home computers? Suggest a marketing strategy.

9   Discuss the relationship of social class and consumption.

10   Are social-class differences diminishing? Prepare a report supporting your position.

PROJECTS

1   Choose two sections of your town—one where residents are professional and business people and one where residents are mostly working class. How do the housing values differ? Does the appearance, architecture, or decoration of homes differ? Are there stores in each area that differ in terms of merchandise and promotional policies?

2   Bring to class copies of magazines which were described in the chapter as appealing to certain social classes. Discuss their differences and similarities.

NOTES

[1] Kevin Higgins, "Ship Commandeers Cruise Industry's Affluent Niche," *Marketing News*, February 1, 1985, pp. 1, 18.

[2] Bernard Berelson and Gary Steiner, *Human Behavior: An Inventory of Scientific Findings*, Harcourt, Brace & World, New York, 1964, p. 453.

[3] David Dressler and Donald Carns, *Sociology: The Study of Human Interaction*, 2d ed., Knopf, New York, 1973, p. 370.

[4] Berelson and Steiner, *Human Behavior*, p. 454.

[5] Thorstein Veblen, *The Theory of the Leisure Class*, Macmillan, New York, 1899.

[6] M. Charles Bakst, "Police Probe Dealer's Offer to Swap Car for Status Plates," *Providence Journal-Bulletin,* December 6, 1986, pp. A1–A2.

[7] "Flaunting Wealth: It's Back in Style," *U.S. News & World Report,* September 21, 1981, pp. 61–64; and "An Authority Tells Why Status Symbols Keep Changing," *U.S. News & World Report,* February 14, 1977, pp. 41–42.

[8] Frank Trippett, "Hard Times for the Status-Minded," *Time,* December 21, 1981, p. 90.

[9] Richard P. Coleman and Lee Rainwater, *Social Standing in America: New Dimensions of Class,* Basic Books, Inc., New York, 1978, p. 29.

[10] Christy Marshall, "Prizm Adds ZIP to Consumer Research," *Advertising Age,* November 10, 1980, p. 22.

[11] Robert C. Yeager, "Caught in the Middle—I," *Across the Board,* November 1980, p. 24.

[12] Richard P. Coleman, "The Continuing Significance of Social Class to Marketing," *Journal of Consumer Research,* **10**:276, December 1983.

[13] W. Lloyd Warner, Marchia Meeker, and Kenneth Eells, *Social Class in America,* Science Research Associates, Chicago, 1949, pp. 11–15.

[14] Luis V. Dominguez and Albert L. Page, "Use and Misuse of Social Stratification in Consumer Behavior Research," *Journal of Business Research,* **9**:151–173, 1981.

[15] Gerald Zaltman and Melanie Wallendorf, *Consumer Behavior: Basic Findings and Management Implications,* Wiley, New York, 1979, pp. 86–87.

[16] Marie R. Haug, "Social Class Measurement and Women's Occupational Roles," *Social Forces,* **52**:86–93, 1973.

[17] See Terence A. Shimp and J. Thomas Yokum, "Extensions of the Basic Social Class Model Employed in Consumer Research," in Kent B. Monroe (ed.), *Advances in Consumer Research,* vol. 8, Association for Consumer Research, Ann Arbor, Mich. 1981, pp. 702–707; and Dominguez and Page, "Use and Misuse," for suggestions to overcome some of these problems.

[18] Coleman, "The Continuing Significance," p. 268.

[19] Richard P. Coleman, "The Significance of Social Stratification in Selling," in Martin L. Bell (ed.), *Marketing: A Maturing Discipline,* American Marketing Association, Chicago, Winter 1960, p. 175.

[20] This section is drawn from Coleman, "The Continuing Significance"; Coleman, "The Significance of Social Stratification," pp. 171–184; Warner, Meeker, and Eells, *Social Class,* pp. 11–21; Margaret C. Pirie, "Marketing and Social Classes: An Anthropologist's View," *Management Review,* **49**:45–48, September 1960; Kim B. Rotzoll, "The Effect of Social Stratification on Market Behavior," *Journal of Advertising Research,* **7**:22–27, March 1967; Ronald E. Frank, William F. Massy, and Yorman Wind, *Market Segmentation,* Prentice-Hall, Englewood Cliffs, N.J., 1972, pp. 44–48; and James M. Patterson, "Marketing and the Working-Class Family," in Arthur B. Shostak and William Gomberg (eds.), *Blue-Collar World,* Prentice-Hall, Englewood Cliffs, N.J., 1964, p. 78.

[21] "The Ranks of the Rich Get Richer," *Time,* July 9, 1979, p. 54.

[22] Mary Lou Roberts, "Women's Changing Roles—A Consumer Behavior Perspective," in Kent B. Monroe (ed.), *Advances in Consumer Research,* vol. 8, Association for Consumer Research, Ann Arbor, Mich., 1981, p. 594.

[23] Coleman "The Continuing Significance," p. 270.

[24] The American Underclass," *Time,* August 19, 1977, p. 14.

[25] Frank, Massy, and Wind, *Market Segmentation,* p. 45.

[26] James H. Myers and Jonathan Gutman, "Life-Style: The Essence of Social Class," in William D. Wells (ed.), *Life Style and Psychographics,* American Marketing Association, Chicago, 1974, p. 252.

[27] This section is adapted from Myers and Gutman, "Life Style," pp. 253–254.

[28] A. Marvin Roscoe, Jr., Arthur LeClaire, Jr., and Leon G. Shiffman, "Theory and Management Applications of Demographics in Buyer Behavior," in Arch G. Woodside, Jagdish N. Sheth, and Peter D. Bennett (eds.), *Consumer and Industrial Buying Behavior,* North-Holland, New York, 1977, pp. 67–76.

[29] Coleman, "The Significance of Social Stratification," pp. 176–177.

[30] James H. Myers, Roger R. Stanton, and Arne F. Haug, "Correlates of Buying Behavior: Social Class vs. Income," *Journal of Marketing,* **35**:8–15, October 1971.

[31] James H. Myers and John F. Mount, "More on Social Class vs. Income as Correlates of Buying Behavior," *Journal of Marketing,* **37**:71–73, April 1973.

[32] Robert D. Hisrich and Michael P. Peters, "Selecting the Superior Segmentation Correlate," *Journal of Marketing,* **38**:60–63, July 1974.

[33] Frank, Massy, and Wind, *Market Segmentation*, p. 49.

[34] Coleman, "The Continuing Significance," p. 274.

[35] Charles M. Shaninger, "Social Class Versus Income Revisited: An Empirical Investigation," *Journal of Marketing Research*, **18**:206–207, May 1981.

[36] Thomas S. Robertson, *Consumer Behavior*, Scott, Foresman, Glenview, Ill., 1970, p. 129.

[37] Roscoe et al., "Theory," p. 75.

[38] Coleman, "The Continuing Significance," p. 274.

[39] Lenox's Spending Spree in Print," *Marketing & Media Decisions*, August 1981, p. 75.

[40] Lee Rainwater, Richard P. Coleman, and Gerald Handel, *Workingman's Wife*, Oceana Publications, Inc., New York, 1959, p. 205.

[41] William Mitchell, "First Lottery Millionaire Settles into Easy Living," *Detroit Free Press*, July 8, 1973, p. 3a.

[42] Gerald Handel and Lee Rainwater, "Persistence and Change in Working-Class Life Style," in Shostak and Gomberg (eds.), *Blue-Collar World*, p. 41.

[43] David Caplovitz, *The Poor Pay More*, Free Press, New York, 1963.

[44] Patterson, "Marketing and the Working-Class," p. 79.

[45] Pierre Martineau, "Social Classes and Spending Behavior," *Journal of Marketing*, **23**:126–127, October 1958.

[46] Sidney J. Levy, "Social Class and Consumer Behavior," in Joseph W. Newman (ed.), *On Knowing the Consumer*, Wiley, New York, 1966, p. 153.

[47] Stuart U. Rich and Subhash C. Jain, "Social Class and Life Cycle as Predictors of Shopping Behavior," *Journal of Marketing Research*, **5**:41–49, February 1968.

[48] Gordon R. Foxall, "Social Factors in Consumer Choice," *Journal of Consumer Research*, **2**:60–64, June 1975.

[49] Coleman, "The Significance of Social Stratification," p. 177.

[50] Martineau, "Social Classes," p. 121.

[51] Frank, Massy, and Wind, *Market Segmentation*, p. 47.

[52] Foxall, "Social Factors," p. 62.

[53] David J. Rachman and Marion Levine, "Blue Collar Workers Shape Suburban Markets," *Journal of Retailing*, **42**:5–13, Winter 1966–1967.

[54] Martineau, "Social Classes," p. 127.

[55] Pierre Martineau, *Motivation in Advertising*, McGraw-Hill, New York, 1957, p. 166.

[56] L. S. Harms, "Listener Judgments of Status Cues in Speech," *Quarterly Journal of Speech*, **47**:164–168, April 1961.

[57] "The Supermarket Tabloids," *Media Decisions*, May 1979, pp. 69, 98.

[58] "Blue Collar Wives Seek Convenience: MacFadden," *Advertising Age*, October 8, 1973.

[59] Marilyn Jackson-Beeck and Jeff Sobal, "The Social World of Heavy Television Viewers," *Journal of Broadcasting*, **24**:5–11, Winter 1980.

[60] Andrew Gabor and S. W. J. Granger, "Price Sensitivity of the Consumer," *Journal of Advertising Research*, **4**:40–44, December 1964; and Caplovitz, *The Poor Pay More*.

[61] Frederick E. Webster, Jr., "The Deal-Prone Consumer," *Journal of Marketing Research*, **1**:32–35, August 1964.

[62] Joseph N. Fry and Frederick H. Siller, "A Comparison of Housewife Decision Making in Two Social Classes," *Journal of Marketing Research*, **7**:333–337, August 1970.

[63] H. Lee Mathews and John W. Slocum, Jr., "Social Class and Commercial Bank Credit Card Usage," *Journal of Marketing*, **33**:71–78, January 1969.

[64] Coleman and Rainwater, *Social Standing*, pp. 294–296.

[65] J. C. Bieda and H. H. Kassarjian, "An Overview of Market Segmentation," in Bernard A. Morin (ed.), *Marketing in a Changing World*, American Marketing Association, Chicago, 1969, pp. 249–253.

[66] J. Michael Munson and W. Austin Spivey, "Product and Brand User Stereotypes Among Social Classes," in Kent B. Monroe (ed.), *Advances in Consumer Research*, vol. 8, Association for Consumer Research, Ann Arbor, Mich., 1981, pp. 696–701.

[67] Norval D. Glenn, "Massification vs. Differentiation: Some Trend Data From National Surveys," *Social Forces*, **46**, December 1967.

[68] Coleman and Rainwater, *Social Standing*.

[69] Coleman, "The Continuing Significance," p. 278.

SOCIAL GROUPS

LEARNING OBJECTIVES

After studying this chapter, you should understand . . .

- What is meant by the term "group" and how different group types may have relevance for consumer behavior
- The nature of status, roles, norms, and socialization properties exhibited by groups
- How groups exert power over members' behavior
- How reference-group influence varies under differing conditions
- The nature of reference-group influence on consumer behavior

UndercoverWear, Inc., the innovator of home lingerie parties, offers women the opportunity to treat themselves to something special by shopping for intimate apparel in the privacy of their own homes. The sales technique has blossomed into a multimillion-dollar company with over 40,000 salespeople (called UndercoverWear Agents) covering fifty states and Canada. The product, of course, is not new. Clothes of a seductive nature have long been sold through the mail. But now they have been brought out of their plain brown wrappers to a new market segment comprising solid middle-class suburbanites. Manufacturers have successfully used home sales parties to sell a variety of household goods such as plastic storage containers and cosmetics, but UndercoverWear uses them to market lingerie.

The parties attract women of all ages, from their twenties to their sixties. Some are homemakers, and others are career women. Friends gather to enjoy a little wine and cheese; then they all take a "sensuality test" to break the ice. There are about twenty questions on the test, such as "If you've ever read *The Sensuous Woman,* give yourself 10 points." A lingerie prize is given to the winner.

When the group is in the right mood to inspect the line of conservative to sexy lingerie, the living room is turned into an UndercoverWear boutique, with a "soft sell." As the saleswoman holds up a pastel-colored wisp of diaphanous material—actually a nightie with a supersheer look—the women gasp, giggle, and shriek. Then the moment of truth comes as guests are invited to try anything on. Some of the younger, slimmer, and bolder guests may dash to a bathroom or bedroom, close the door, and try on an armful of negligees. The teenage daughter of the hostess and her friends may be unabashed enough to model the lingerie before the living room crowd; but others will only let one or two close friends see theirs.

By the end of the party, the saleswoman is likely to have sold $300 worth of supersheer, baby doll, lacy, satiny, backless, frontless, sideless, and very sexy lingerie.[1]

9

This example illustrates some of the many influences social groups may have on buyers. As we continue to narrow our discussion of environmental variables, this chapter examines ways in which groups impinge on consumer decision making. This is an important ingredient in the marketer's understanding of consumer behavior.

Our first task will be to define several group concepts essential to our discussion. Next, the major characteristics of groups and group types will be examined. Finally, we shall discuss reference groups and their special relevance for the marketer in understanding consumer behavior.

WHAT IS A GROUP?

Not every collection of individuals is a group, as the term is used by sociologists. Actually, we can distinguish three different collections of people: aggregations, categories, and groups. An *aggregation* is any number of people who are in close proximity to one another at a given time. A *category* is any number of people who have some particular attributes in common. A *group* consists of people who have a sense of relatedness as a result of interaction with each other.[2]

To illustrate these concepts, consider four people sitting on a bench at a university. They are an "aggregation" since they are in close proximity. They may be a "category" if they share some attribute such as being majors in the College of Business Administration. They may also be a "group" if they have a shared sense of relatedness through interaction, that is, if they are all friends or classmates in a consumer-behavior course, for example.

Although our emphasis in this chapter is on groups, this does not mean that the marketer is not interested in aggregations and categories. These collections are frequently the focus for developing marketing strategies. For example, market segmentation typically does not involve social groups but instead uses categories, since the people are not all interacting with one another.

CLASSIFICATION OF GROUPS

Groups may be classified according to a number of dimensions, including function, degree of personal involvement, and degree of organization.

CONTENT OR FUNCTION

Most of us view the content of groups in terms of their function. For example, we categorize them along such lines as students, factory workers, church members, and so on. Actually, these are subtypes of the major kinds of groups that we encounter in a complex society, which could generally be categorized along such lines as family, ethnic, age, sex, political, religious, residential, occupational, educational, and so forth.

DEGREE OF PERSONAL INVOLVEMENT

By using this criterion, we can identify two different types of groups: primary and secondary. The hallmark of a *primary group* is that interpersonal relationships

take place usually on a face-to-face basis, with great frequency, and on an intimate level.[3] These groups have shared norms and interlocking roles. Families, work groups, and even recreational groups (if individuals have some depth of personal involvement) are examples of such groups.

Secondary groups are those in which the relationship among members is relatively impersonal and formalized. This amounts to a residual category that includes all groups that are not primary, such as political parties, unions, occasional sports groups, and the American Marketing Association. Although such groups are secondary, the interpersonal relationships that occur may nevertheless be face-to-face. The distinction lies in the lack of intimacy of personal involvement.

DEGREE OF ORGANIZATION

Groups range from those that are relatively unorganized to highly structured forms. We usually simplify this continuum into two types: formal and informal. *Formal* groups are those with a definite structure (for example, they may have a president, vice president, secretary, and treasurer). They are likely to be secondary groups designed to accomplish specific goals, whether economic, social, political, or altruistic. The United Way, the Miss America Pageant, and the local Republican party are examples. *Informal* groups are typically primary groups, characterized by a relatively loose structure, a lack of clearly defined goals or objectives, unstructured interaction, and unwritten rules. Because of the extent of their influence on individuals' values and activities, informal groups are probably of greater importance to us in seeking to understand consumer behavior.

It should be evident from this discussion that the term "group" is multifaceted and that groups have important influences on individuals, including on their activities as consumers. Primary informal groups have the greatest degree of impact on consumers and are therefore most important to marketers. From such groups, consumers develop their product-consumption, shopping, and media patterns. Consequently, these groups are generally most influential on consumers' buying behavior. As a result, advertisers normally present their products within a primary group setting such as among friends (Coca-Cola, Pizza Hut), family (Pillsbury, Johnson's Baby Powder, Cheer detergent), or work groups (Dial soap, Haggar suits).

Secondary informal groups probably are the next most influential to consumers and, therefore, are sometimes used in advertising efforts. For example, a new type of golf club, racquetball racket, or snow ski may be featured in the appropriate friendly, competitive, but professional-looking surroundings in which the product and user may be shown excelling and being rewarded with admiration. Or, in the case of other sponsors, the product itself may be the reward (such as Michelob Light beer for the winners of a racquetball match). Primary and secondary formal groups are much less widely used by marketers because they have far less direct, intimate influence on consumer behavior. In specialized situations, however, certain marketers may find them useful. For example, travel or insurance agents may develop specific offerings for members of an organization, such as state employees or university alumni.

GROUP PROPERTIES

In order to understand the nature of groups better, we need to examine several other important concepts, including status, norms, role, socialization, and power, and their significance for consumer behavior.

STATUS

Status refers to the achieved or ascribed position of an individual in a group or in society, and it consists of the rights and duties associated with that position. In Chapter 8, we referred to status in a prestige sense; however, this is only one of several different ways in which statuses may be classified. Status also may refer to some grouping on the basis of age or sex, family, occupation, and friendship or common interest.[4]

NORMS

Norms are the rules and standards of conduct by which group members are expected to abide. For informal groups, norms are generally unwritten but are, nevertheless, usually quite well understood. For example, as a salesperson for a large business machines company, you might be expected to live in a certain area of town, drive a certain type of car (perhaps a midsize Oldsmobile), and dress conservatively (such as in a navy-blue suit and striped tie). Behavior deviation outside these latitudes might result in slower advancement in the organization. Thus, as employees or consumers, we often readily know what we can and cannot wear, drive, say, eat, and so on, in order to be well accepted within the relevant group.

ROLE

This term is used to designate all of the behavior patterns associated with a particular status. Role is the dynamic aspect of status and includes the attitudes, values, and behavior ascribed by the society to persons occupying this status. The social structure partially prescribes what sort of role behavior is acceptable and thus what is expected. For instance, an upper-class husband who is a successful physician may feel that in his position he is expected to drive an expensive car, live in an exclusive neighborhood, dress in fashionable clothes, attend country club activities, and give generously to charities. Conversely, a lower-class husband who is an assembly-line worker may feel comfortable in a role in which he drives a pickup truck, lives in a bungalow, wears jeans and boots, and fishes, hunts, and drinks beer with his friends.

Essentially, role theory recognizes that an individual carries out life by playing different roles. This concept was expressed in a poetic way by Shakespeare in the following well-known passage:

All the world's a stage,
And all the men and women merely players.
They have their exits and their entrances;
And one man in his time plays many parts.
His acts being seven ages.

This means that each consumer enacts many roles, which may change over time, even during the course of a day. For example, a woman may have the role of wife, mother, employee, family financial officer, lover, Sunday School teacher, and many others. Her behavior in each of these roles will differ as she keeps "switching hats," depending on her role at each moment.

Carrying the concept of playing a role further, Goffman suggests that the individual must not only learn his lines (the group's special language) but he needs a costume (the group's accepted dress), props (the group's equipment or accoutrements), a set (where the group interacts), and a team or cast of players (the group members).[6]

Roles in groups (just as those in a play) are learned, but not every individual learns a given role in the same way.[7] Society allows some variation in role performance, but if too much latitude is taken, sanctions of some sort will be imposed. Thus, other people expect us to behave in a certain way and will reward conformity and punish nonconformity to those expectations.

Roles have a strong, pervasive influence on our activities as consumers. For example, other people have expectations regarding the products we buy to meet the needs of our roles. Just a few of the many consumption decisions directly affected include the places we shop, the clothes we wear, the cars we drive, the houses in which we live, and the recreational activities we engage in. Marketers, therefore, help individuals play their roles by providing the right costumes and props to be used in gaining acceptance by some group. Again, it's the symbols of products that provide so much of the satisfaction that accrues from a product.

Because of the many roles we try to fulfill, whether at different times or simultaneously, we may develop *role conflict,* which means that two or more of our roles are incompatible with each other. The strain may often be evidenced in the behavior of consumers. For example, a working wife may feel that the demands on her time may be more easily met by fixing her family quick and easy meals, particularly by using frozen TV dinners. However, in her role as a loving wife and the family's gourmet cook, such product usage may be abhorrent. Thus, some resolution of this conflict will be necessary. A creative advertiser may suggest a solution through showing her purchasing the company's TV dinners because, although easily prepared, when served on her regular china, seasoned to taste, and garnished attractively, they resemble a gourmet meal.

SOCIALIZATION

Socialization refers to the process by which a new member learns the system of values, norms, and expected behavior patterns of the group being entered. When a new student arrives on a college campus, she or he soon learns from fellow students what is expected in the way of dress, eating patterns, class attendance, extra-curricular activities, and so on. Residents new to a neighborhood soon learn what patterns are expected in the group concerning home maintenance, lawns and landscaping, interior decoration, entertaining, and so on. Thus, individuals are continually engaging in the process of socialization (although it is more intense at an early age) as they encounter new groups that have an impact on their lives. Consumer socialization, therefore, is the process by which individuals acquire skills, knowledge, and attitudes relevant to their effective functioning as consum-

ers in the marketplace.[8] This is particularly relevant to young people, although it has usefulness in other situations, too, as was indicated above.

POWER

Groups have power to influence their members' behavior. Various sources of social power may be operative in different social group situations, however: reward power, coercive power, legitimate power, expert power, and referent power.[9] Marketers also seek to use these forms of power to influence consumers.

Reward Power   This is based on the perception one has of another's ability to reward him. The strength of reward power increases with the size of the rewards which an individual perceives another can administer. Rewards might include either tangible items such as money or gifts, or intangible things such as recognition, praise, or other nonmaterial satisfaction.

Social groups often have a great deal of reward power which they may dispense to their members. This "carrot" approach can often result in the desired behavior being exhibited by members. For example, Amway Products, which uses direct-selling methods for its line of household products, makes effective use of reward power in motivating its sales force, by holding large sales rallies where young salespeople, usually middle-class couples, watch a 20-minute color film that features family scenes of successful Amway couples enjoying the fruits of their labors—swimming pools and motor homes.[10]

Marketers also use reward power directly and indirectly in order to influence consumers. Of course, they are able to reward consumers directly by providing high-quality products and services. In other situations marketers promise (implicitly, at least) the rewards of group acceptance, such as love, through use of a product. For example, some brands of beer (such as Lowenbrau and Old Milwaukee) and liquor attempt to show how group acceptance takes place through purchase and consumption of their product.[11] The Johnny Walker ad in Figure 9-1 illustrates another approach in the direct use of reward association for the product.

Coercive Power   This is the power to influence behavior through the use of punishment or the withholding of rewards. Punishment, for our purpose, does not refer to the physical kind, but the more subtle, psychological sanctions. For example, students may readily conform to the dress code of some group on campus such as a sorority or fraternity and purchase the accepted clothing of this group in order not to be ridiculed by it.

Marketers are also able to use coercive power effectively in certain situations. Inducing fear is one approach that may be taken by advertisers of some items such as life insurance, mouthwash, weight-reducing products, dishwashing detergents, cat litter, and deodorants. Coercion occurs through showing the unfortunate consequences that could befall a consumer who fails to own or use such products. For example, the embarrassment of having loose dentures is brought to our attention by Poligrip and other denture adhesive manufacturers. Similarly, the group ridicule which comes from having "b.o." is humorously but effectively illustrated in a Dial soap ad in which several car-pool members all ride

in the rear seat of a car while the driver, alone in the front seat, gets the message that she needs to use Dial.

Tupperware and other products sold in social group situations also make effective use of group coercive power. Group pressure may be strong because some attendees at these sales parties tend to feel that if others are buying something they do not want to be embarrassed by not also making a purchase. They may feel that such an action would let the hostess and her friends down.[12]

Legitimate Power   This power stems from members' perception that the group has a legitimate right to influence them. We speak of such behaviors with expressions like "should," "ought to," and so on. Many of these feelings have been internalized from parents, teachers, and religious institutions. Thus, there is some sort of code or standard that the individual accepts, and by virtue of which the group can assert its power. One small group in which legitimate power can be seen to operate is the family. Each member has a set of roles to carry out which is legitimized by the other members.

FIGURE 9-1
Advertisement for Johnnie Walker Black Label.
Created by Smith/Greenland Inc. for Somerset Importers Ltd., importers of Johnnie Walker Black Label Scotch.

Marketers are able to utilize this type of power in many situations by appealing to consumers' values. Appeals from charitable organizations (such as the United Way and Red Cross) exert legitimate power, as do those for patriotic and nationalistic causes such as "Buy American" or "See America First."

Expert Power   This influence results from the expertise of the individual or group. Consumers regularly accept influence from those they perceive to have superior experiences, knowledge, or skill. For instance, we may accept the recommendation of another person for a purchase we are about to make if we view that person as more knowledgeable than ourselves. Salespeople make effective use of this approach with their own product expertise.

Many advertisements rely on an expert's opinion about the product. For instance, Schlitz has used the company's president, who is a master brewer, to promote the product's taste in comparison with other brands; Jimmy Connors promotes Wilson tennis equipment; and A. J. Foyt advertises Goodyear tires. Manufacturers may even "create" experts when no one else seems suitable. For example, General Motors' Mr. Goodwrench, General Mills' Betty Crocker, and A&P's Ann Page are all fictitious, but effective, endorsers.

Information power, often related to expert power, stems from the "logic," "reasoning," or importance of the communication provided by the influencing agent.[13] Ads which use information power may explain why the product is good, often citing available evidence such as price, quality of ingredients, performance specifications, and so forth.

Referent Power   This influence flows from the feeling of identification an individual has with the group. As a consequence of this feeling of oneness or desire for such an identity, the individual will have a desire to become a member or gain a closer association with the group. The individual's identification with the group can be established or maintained if he or she behaves, believes, or perceives as the group does. The stronger this identification with the group, the greater its referent power. In this chapter and Chapter 11 we will look more closely at the use of referent power.

Advertisers often use referent power in promotions by encouraging consumers to be like or do the same thing as the individual advertising the brand. For instance, with many status-oriented products consumers are encouraged (either subtly or not so subtly) to obtain a similar status to that of the recommender by purchasing the item advertised. Colognes, clothing, automobiles, and stereo equipment often use such an approach. Use of celebrities is especially popular in these situations, whereby consumers may aspire to have hair or skin like Christie Brinkley. In other approaches, marketers may use slice-of-life commercials or testimonials from "ordinary" consumers to show that other people experience the same problems and have found satisfaction with the recommended brand. Therefore, the individual advertised to may readily identify with that situation and be highly receptive to the brand. Products such as Oil of Olay, Extra Strength Anacin, Crest gel toothpaste, and Allstate insurance have been promoted with such an approach.

REFERENCE GROUPS

Having discussed some important group concepts necessary for our interests, let us further examine the topic of reference-group influence.

TYPES OF REFERENCE GROUPS

Reference groups are those an individual uses (that is, refers to) in determining his judgments, beliefs, and behavior. These may be of a number of types, as explained by the following classification system.[14]

Membership versus Nonmenbership *Membership* groups are those to which the individual belongs. Membership in some groups is automatic by virtue of the consumer's age, sex, education, and marital status. Before acting, a consumer might consider whether purchase or use of a product would be consistent with his or her role as a member of one of these groups.

Nonmembership groups are those to which the individual does not presently belong. Many of these groups are likely to be *anticipatory* or *aspirational* in nature, that is, those to which the individual aspires to belong. Such aspirational groups can have a profound influence on nonmembers because of their strong desire to join the group. This pattern of behavior is evident among upwardly mobile consumers who aspire to join higher-status clubs and social groups.

Positive versus Negative Reference groups can also be classified as to whether they attract or repel the individual. For instance, a *positive* reference group for the upwardly mobile consumer may be the "country club crowd" in that city. There are *negative* groups, however, that a person attempts to avoid being identified with. For example, an individual who is trying to succeed as a new management trainee may attempt through her speech, dress, and mannerisms to disassociate herself from her lower-social-class background in order to have a greater chance of success in her job.

REASONS FOR ACCEPTING REFERENCE-GROUP INFLUENCE

Generally, consumers accept reference-group influence because of the perceived benefits in doing so. It has been suggested that the nature of social interactions between individuals will be determined by the individual's perception of the *profit of the interaction*. An interaction situation may result in *rewards* (such as friendship, information, satisfaction, and so on) but will also exact *costs* (lost time, money expended, alternative people and activities sacrificed). The difference between these rewards and costs, that is, the net profit from the social exchange, individuals will attempt to maximize. Thus, individuals will choose their groups and interact with members based upon their perception of the net profit of that exchange, rather than rewards or costs alone.[15]

At a more specific level, consumers may be seen to accept reference-group influence because of its role in providing informational, utilitarian, and value-expressive benefits.[16] Table 9-1 presents a series of statements that typify these three types of reference-group influence situations.

Informational Benefits One reason reference-group influence is accepted (or internalized) is that the consumer perceives that his knowledge of his environment and/or his ability to cope with some aspect of it (such as buying a product) is enhanced. Consumers most readily accept those information sources that are thought to be most credible. A consumer using an informational reference group may (1) actively search for information from opinion leaders or some group with the appropriate expertise or (2) come to some conclusion through observing the behavior of other people. Therefore, actual physical interaction with the group is not necessary in this type of information search.

In this situation, then, the marketer may be able to appeal to consumers through the use of advertising testimonials from experts or even "men in the street," or by encouraging consumers to find out more about the brand from friends, neighbors, or work associates. This personal source of information is often more influential in purchasing than are commercial sources such as advertising and salespeople as studies of food, small appliances, and other products

---

TABLE 9-1

Typical Reference-Group
Influences on
Brand Decisions

Informational influence

1 The individual seeks information about various brands of the product from an association of professional or independent group of experts.
2 The individual seeks information from those who work with the product as a profession.
3 The individual seeks brand-related knowledge and experience (such as how brand A's performance compares to brand B's) from those friends, neighbors, relatives, or work associates who have reliable information about the brand.
4 The brand which the individual selects is influenced by observation of a seal of approval of an independent testing agency (such as *Good Housekeeping*).
5 The individual's observation of what experts do influences his or her choice of a brand (such as observing the type of car which police drive or the brand of TV which repairmen buy).

Utilitarian influence

1 To satisfy the expectations of fellow work associates, the individual's decision to purchase a particular brand is influenced by their preferences.
2 The individual's decision to purchase a particular brand is influenced by the preferences of people with whom he or she has social interaction.
3 The individual's decision to purchase a particular brand is influenced by the preferences of family members.
4 The desire to satisfy the expectations which others have of him or her has an impact on the individual's brand choice.

Value-expressive influence

1 The individual feels that the purchase or use of a particular brand will enhance the image which others have of him or her.
2 The individual feels that those who purchase or use a particular brand possess the characteristics which he or she would like to have.
3 The individual sometimes feels that it would be nice to be like the type of person which advertisements show using a particular brand.
4 The individual feels that the people who purchase a particular brand are admired or respected by others.
5 The individual feels the the purchase of a particular brand helps to show others what he or she is, or would like to be (an athlete, successful business person, good mother, etc.).

Source: C. Whan Park and V. Parker Lessig, "Students and Housewives: Differences in Susceptibility to Reference Group Influence," *Journal of Consumer Research*, 4:105, September 1977.

indicate. One of the key linkages in this process is the credibility of the influencer. A consumer contemplating a major appliance purchase will rely on friends, salespersons, or even product-rating magazines if the information obtained is perceived as credible. Thus, consumers accept such expertise because of its informational benefits.

Utilitarian Benefits This reason refers to pressure on the individual to conform to the preferences or expectations of another individual or group. In a product-purchasing situation, the consumer will comply if (1) she believes that her behavior is visible or known to others, (2) she perceives that the others control significant sanctions (rewards or punishments), and (3) she is motivated to realize the reward or avoid the punishment.

Visibility is very important in order for this normative influence to operate. As will be shown later in this chapter, in situations in which the product is visible or the effects from its use or nonuse are visible, reference groups are able to exert strong normative influence. Thus, products such as clothing and furniture are highly visible to others and therefore are quite susceptible to normative group influence. Even for items which are not themselves visible to others when in use (such as antiperspirant deodorants), normative influence is still likely to be strong, because the effects of nonuse will be rather evident (for example, body odor and a stained dress or shirt underarm area). Consequently, fear of group reaction will influence the product's use.

Thus, an individual accepts influence from the group because she hopes to attain certain specific rewards or avoid certain punishments controlled by the group. In effect, the individual learns to say or do the expected thing in certain situations, not because she necessarily likes it, but because it is instrumental in producing a satisfying social effect.

Value-Expressive Benefits This relates to an individual's motive to enhance or support his self-concept by associating himself with positive reference groups and/or disassociating himself from negative referents. Value-expressive reference-group influence is characterized by two different processes. First, an individual may utilize reference groups to express himself or bolster his ego. Second, an individual may simply like the group and therefore accept its influence. Thus, an individual adopts behavior derived from the group as a way of establishing or maintaining the desired relationship to the group and the self-image provided by this relationship. The individual may say what the group members say, do what they do, and believe what they believe in order to foster the relationship and the satisfying self-image it provides.

THE VARIABILITY OF REFERENCE-GROUP INFLUENCE

Reference groups can be very potent influences on behavior in general, and they may also be very influential on consumer behavior. For example, before making a decision about purchasing a product, consumers often consider what a particular group would do in this situation, or what they would think of the consumer for purchasing the product. This commonsense notion, however, has been difficult to apply meaningfully in specific marketing situations. The basic problem is one of

determining which kinds of groups are likely to be referred to by which kinds of individuals under which kinds of situations in making which decision, and of measuring the extent of this influence. Nevertheless, a start has been made in understanding this process. This section discusses some of what we now know about the variability of reference-group influence on consumers.

VARIABILITY AMONG PRODUCTS

Charles Glock[17] first studied the influence of reference groups on the purchase of a number of consumer goods and found that the "conspicuousness" of a product is a strong determinant of its susceptibility to reference-group influence. Conspicuousness may be of two forms, however. First, the item must be exclusive in some way. If virtually everyone owns it, it is not conspicuous in the first sense, even though it may be highly visible. Operationally, we may think of this as the distinction between luxuries (having a degree of exclusivity) and necessities (possessed by virtually everyone). Second, the item must be seen or identified by others. Thus, where an item is consumed has great relevance. In this situation, a distinction may be made between publicly consumed products (which are seen by others) and privately consumed items (not seen by others). Reference groups may influence either the purchase of a product or the choice of a particular brand, or both.

Because of several defects in Glock's work, as well as its age, other consumer researchers have investigated the role of reference-group influence on product and brand choice for several product categories. One of these studies is summarized in Figure 9-2. It combines the concepts of public-private consumption and luxury-necessity items and, when applied to product and brand decisions, offers the following set of eight relationships:[18]

1 *Publicly consumed luxury.* A product consumed in public view and not commonly owned or used (such as golf clubs). In this case, whether or not the

FIGURE 9-2
Combining public-private and luxury-necessity dimensions with product and brand purchase decisions.
Source: William O. Bearden and Michael J. Etzel, "Reference Group Influence on Product and Brand Purchase Decisions," *Journal of Consumer Research,* **9**:185, September 1982. Used with permission.

Brand \ Product	Public — Weak reference group influence (−)	Public — Strong reference group influence (+)
Strong reference group influence (+)	*Public necessities* Influence: Weak product and strong brand Examples: Wristwatch, automobile, man's suit	*Public luxuries* Influence: Strong product and brand Examples: Golf clubs, snow skis, sailboat
Weak reference group influence (−)	*Private necessities* Influence: Weak product and brand Examples: Mattress, floor lamp, refrigerator	*Private luxuries* Influence: Strong product and weak brand Examples: TV game, trash compactor, icemaker

Necessity — Luxury

Private

product is owned and also what brand is purchased is likely to be influenced by others.

Relationships with reference-group influence:

a Because it is a luxury, influence for the *product* should be *strong*.
b Because it will be seen by others, influence for the *brand* of the product should be *strong*.

2 *Privately consumed luxury*. A product consumed out of public view and not commonly owned or used (for example, a trash compactor). In many cases, the brand is not conspicuous or socially important and is a matter of individual choice, but ownership of the product does convey a message about the owner.

Relationships with reference-group influence:

a Because it is a luxury, influence for the *product* should be *strong*.
b Because it will not be seen by others, influence for the *brand* of the product should be *weak*.

3 *Publicly consumed necessity*. A product consumed in public view that virtually everyone owns (such as a wristwatch). This group is made up of products that essentially all people or a large proportion of people use, although they differ as to what type of brand to use.

Relationships with reference-group influence:

a Because it is a necessity, influence for the *product* should be *weak*.
b Because it will be seen by others, influence for the *brand* of the product should be *strong*.

4 *Privately consumed necessity*. A product consumed out of public view that virtually everyone owns (such as a mattress). Purchasing behavior is largely governed by product attributes rather than by the influences of others. In this group, neither products nor brands tend to be socially conspicuous, and the products are owned by nearly all consumers.

Relationships to reference-group influence:

a Because it is a necessity, influence for the *product* should be *weak*.
b Because it will not be seen by others, influence for the *brand* of the product should be *weak*.

More refinement is needed for understanding such reference influence, however. Research indicates, for example, that consumers perceive their own personal preferences to strongly outweigh reference groups' in arriving at their product and brand decisions. Table 9-2 presents evidence of the extent of reference-group influence for several product categories. It is clear that the perceived influence of reference groups is substantially underestimated by the consumer. The consumer views herself as largely independent of the implicit social pressures exerted on her product and brand selection by reference groups. For major durables or "family products," the greatest group influence comes from the family. Other reference groups are more influential in the case of products linked to social visibility or social status.

The marketer should also be aware that some shifting of product perceptions may occur over time. For example, a product may shift from a category in which

reference-group influence is weak to another in which it is strong, especially through the use of heavy promotional efforts designed to create a favorable image and make a product or brand socially conspicuous. Of course, products may also slip in their degree of reference-group influence as they near saturation levels of ownership. Thus, attention to changing perceptions over a product's life cycle is important.

How may the kind of information presented in Figure 9-2 and Table 9-2 be used when making marketing decisions? The following advertising strategies may be adopted depending on the degree of reference-group influence found for the product or brand:

TABLE 9-2
Reference-Group Influence

Product	Referent on product usage				Referent on brand choice			
	Family	Friends	Work associates	Personal preference	Family	Friends	Work associates	Personal preference
Air conditioner	38.7%	29.7%	17.9%	51.4%	40.0%	32.9%	20.5%	52.7%
Beer	11.0	26.9	8.3	74.7	7.6	29.0	6.2	79.5
Canned peaches	36.2	3.4	.7	72.6	35.6	4.1	1.4	73.8
Cars	43.2	28.3	17.2	82.2	44.5	31.0	18.6	82.9
Cigarettes	5.5	9.0	7.6	75.3	3.4	11.0	6.2	80.8
Clothing	27.4	34.5	17.2	80.8	27.2	35.2	11.0	86.3
Drugs	31.7	17.9	6.8	67.1	33.8	19.3	6.9	72.6
Furniture	50.7	13.1	6.2	81.5	45.9	22.1	9.0	78.8
Instant coffee	35.6	15.2	5.5	67.6	34.9	15.9	4.8	70.3
Laundry soap	37.7	9.0	2.8	86.2	40.4	9.7	2.1	68.3
Magazines	24.7	19.3	11.7	85.6	30.1	26.2	13.8	87.7
Radio	30.3	26.2	6.9	80.1	23.4	7.6	1.4	76.6
Refrigerators	45.2	24.8	16.6	52.7	41.4	30.1	13.0	61.0
Soap	29.5	13.1	4.8	80.1	34.9	7.6	1.4	76.6
Toilet soap	32.2	4.8	0	72.4	32.2	2.8	0	74.5
TV (color)	44.5	26.2	12.4	69.9	46.2	35.6	15.1	71.2

Overall perceived group influence

Influence agent	Perceived group influence	Most important choice criterion	Influence agent	Perceived group influence	Most important choice criterion
Product usage:			*Brand choice:*		
Family	33.2%	24.7%	Family	32.6%	22.6%
Friends	18.8	6.2	Friends	21.4	14.4
Work associates	8.9	.7	Work associates	8.7	0
Personal preference		68.4	Personal preference		63.0
		100.0%			100.0%

Source: William G. Lundstrum, William G. Zikmund, and Donald Sciglimpaglia, ''Reference Group Influence on Product and Brand Choice: Update of a Classic Study,'' in Robert S. Franz, Robert M. Hopkins, and Alfred G.Toma (eds.), *Proceedings: Southern Marketing Association 1979 Conference,* Southern Marketing Association, Lafayette, La. 1979, p. 264.

1   Where neither product nor brand appear to be associated strongly with reference-group influence, advertising should emphasize the product's attributes, intrinsic qualities, price, and advantage over competing products.

2   Where reference-group influence is operative, the advertiser should stress the kinds of people who buy the product, reinforcing and broadening where possible the existing stereotypes of users. The strategy of the advertiser should involve learning what the stereotypes are and what specific reference groups enter into the picture, so that appeals can be "tailored" to each main group reached by the different media employed.[19]

VARIABILITY AMONG GROUPS

Reference-group influence has been shown to vary according to characteristics of the group or its type. For example, comparison of reference-group influence scores for students and homemakers across twenty products showed that there are significant differences between the groups in terms of the influence of reference groups on brand selection and that students are generally more susceptible to reference-group influence. Why? Perhaps differences in needs or motivations among the groups result in different responses to reference-group influence. First, the lower age of students perhaps results in their having less familiarity with products and less product information and in their facing greater purchase risk than homemakers would. Second, social surroundings and daily activity differences exist between the groups. Students have more frequent social contacts, more interaction within groups (such as sororities, fraternities, and dormitory residents) which impose more rules and norms and more visible behavior subject to group pressure than do homemakers. Third, hedonism may be stronger among students than among homemakers, so that they are more highly ego-involved in their purchases.[20] Thus, we see that different groups exhibit different reference influences. Let's briefly examine a few of these group factors that seem to influence conformity.

First, conformity may be related to *group cohesiveness*. One study of brand-choice behavior found group cohesiveness and brand similarities to be positively related.[21] However, not all researchers have found group cohesiveness to be associated with group influence. Conformity also appears to be related to group size. One set of experiments showed that increasing the number of influencing members up to three increased the pressure toward conformity on the experimental subject, but beyond three, the influence was found to be no greater.

Proximity to group members can influence conformity. For example, a study of elderly consumer social-interaction patterns found that more than 80 percent of the exchange of information and advice about a new product occurred between persons living on the same floor.[23] This and other studies have indicated that influencers and influencees live close to each other.

The *individual's relationship* to the group is another factor that determines its influence on conformity. His or her social integration (such as the level of acceptance by other group members) and his or her group role are factors that generally are positively related to the degree of group influence on the individual.[24] However, social comparison processes are at work even in socially distant reference groups.[25]

Similarity to the group's characteristics, outlooks, and values is also important. For example, consumers are more likely to seek product information, to trust this information, and to choose the same products as do friends who have similar attributes. This suggests that a new product can be diffused fastest when the market possesses similar value orientations about similar types of products, because the likelihood of interpersonal communication and influence is greatest.[26]

Although similarity is likely to be important, one research study indicates that the single most important element of referent selection for fifteen products commonly purchased by undergraduate males is *stage presence*.[27] The persuasive charisma resulting from this attribute may be very relevant in certain marketing situations. For instance, the marketer may often want to choose a model or potential referent having this attribute when promoting through advertising or personal selling. James Garner as the spokesperson for Mazda appears to fulfill this criterion. For example, Garner has been rated as the top advertising spokesperson and as the most liked celebrity advertiser.

VARIABILITY AMONG INDIVIDUALS

The strength of reference-group influence not only varies among products and group type, but also among different consumers. That is, some individuals are more susceptible to reference-group influence than others are. What individual characteristics seem to be associated with a consumer's susceptibility to reference-group influence? It appears that both demographic and psychological factors are relevant.

First, *personality* factors are important. Conformity has been found to vary by personality type and is positively related to the following personality traits: low intelligence, extroversion, ethnocentrism, weak ego, poor leadership, authoritarianism, need for affiliation, being a firstborn or only child, and feelings of personal inferiority or inadequacy.[28]

The type of *social character* of consumers may also affect reference-group influence. An important consumer typology related to this is Riesman's inner-directed and other-directed individual.[29] This theory describes inner-directed individuals as those who turn to their own inner standards and values to guide their behavior. Early in childhood they are taught by parents, the church, and other cultural institutions to accept and internalize these standards and to use them as a frame of reference for future behavior. These internalized values are relatively durable and change little over the individual's lifetime.

Other-directed individuals depend on others around them for direction and guidance. They have been taught to look to other people for correct standards of behavior and to be sensitive to the values and attitudes of their respected reference groups and associates. An analogy which distinguishes these two social character groups is to think of inner-directeds as being equipped with a gyrocompass, while other-directeds are guided by radar.

A second set of factors relating to reference-group susceptibility is the consumer's *demographic* attributes. For example, differences in reference-group influence have been found between males and females, married couples and singles, younger and older people, and between different nationalities.[30]

VARIABILITY BY TYPE OF INFLUENCE

A study of reference-group influence on brand decisions of students and house-wives investigated the relevance of three types of reference-group influence (informational, utilitarian, and value-expressive) to a consumer's selection of a brand or model.[31] The consumer was assumed to have already decided to buy the product but was undecided on the brand or model.

The study showed, for example, that among students, ratings of informational influences were most important for half of the products studied, followed by utilitarian influences, with value-expressive influences least important for the products studied. Those products most likely to be subject to informational influence generally were items with greater technological complexity (like color TVs). Those products most subject to utilitarian and value-expressive influences were products that were important means of conforming to group norms or obtaining group identification and support through self-expression (such as auto-mobiles and clothing). This study, therefore, indicates that for these subjects and products, informational benefits appear to outweigh the role of utilitarian and value-expressive benefits from the group.

Often, therefore, consumers buy products that others in their groups buy, not to establish some self-fulfilling role relationship to others, nor to obtain reward or avoid some punishment from the group, but simply to acquire what they perceive as a good product. In a similar way, an individual in a shopping situation may use the reactions of other shoppers as a basis for inferring the value of products that she or he is unable to assess completely from direct observation.[32]

Other research studies support the idea that groups may be used by consum-ers more for the information they provide than for the reward and identification they offer.[33] The consequence of such findings for the marketer may be that more information-oriented advertising can be utilized with groups or referent individ-uals. In particular, the use of "typical consumers" in advertising to impart in-formation to influencees seems to be in order. Current industry practice empha-sizing "hidden" camera interviews with consumers appears to support this.

VARIABILITY BY SITUATION

Several of the research studies cited previously related the variability of refer-ence-group influence to a behavioral situation. That is, reference-group influence was seen to be related in some cases to the type of product, the item's social visibility, and so forth. Several other research studies also indicate that the nature of the consumer situation has an important impact on the nature of reference influence.[34] For example, investigation of group influence on brand usage of inexpensive grocery items, on patronage among various retail stores, and on utilization of certain services (such as a plumber or a physician) has shown that the areas of retail-store patronage and service utilization are perhaps more suscep-tible to group influence than is brand usage of group products. Apparently, too, the amount of pressure exerted by a group in one behavioral context is not necessarily likely to be exerted in another context. That is, conformity influence appears to be a situation-specific phenomenon.[35]

Marketers should, therefore, carefully assess the extent to which reference-group influence exists for their product, what type of influence appears to be more pervasive, and how customer segments may differ in their responsiveness to such influences. The situational nature of such influence also needs to be understood. From such knowledge, more effective marketing strategies may be developed incorporating referent power.

WHICH REFERENCE GROUP DOMINATES?

We see, then, that reference groups are highly relevant and potent influences in consumer decision making. But how do we identify the specific individual, group, or groups who are most relevant to the consumer's behavior? Unfortunately, at this stage we are unable to answer this question definitively; we simply are not sure which reference groups will be most important in a given buying decision. Thus, when a young woman goes to the store to buy a new outfit, the ultimate choice may reflect her sorority, her family, her church group, her boyfriend and his friends, or any other group. It is very difficult for the marketer to know which reference group generally dominates.

MANAGERIAL REFLECTIONS

For our product or service situation . . .

1 What classification of groups (primary/secondary, informal/formal) is most important in its purchase and consumption and how may these be incorporated in promotional messages?

2 How may it be related to various roles that consumers enact?

3 What types of social-group power are operative and how may we use that power to influence purchasers?

4 Is reference influence an important factor?

DISCUSSION TOPICS

1 What is meant by the term "group"? What are some types of groups?

2 On what bases may groups be classified?

3 Distinguish between the following types of groups: (*a*) primary versus secondary, (*b*) formal versus informal, (*c*) social group versus aggregation.

4 Discuss the basic properties of a group. How do these properties relate to consumer behavior?

5 What is a reference group? Name two reference groups that are important to you. In what way do they influence your consumer behavior?

6 What groups do you belong to that you feel are not influential on you and your behavior as a consumer?

7 Suggest a product not listed in Figure 9-2 over which reference groups would exert a strong or weak influence with regard to the purchase of the product and its brand or type. Explain.

8 Decide which of the consumer's reference groups would appear to be most important for the following purchase decisions: (*a*) a formal evening gown, (*b*) selection of a physician, (*c*) a new home, (*d*) a basketball and warm-up suit.

9 What factors appear to influence reference-group influence?

10 Bring in ads illustrating the marketer's use of each type of group power influence.

PROJECTS

1 Interview managers of clothing departments of several department stores. Ask whether the departments seek to attract any specific reference or social group. How were the groups identified? What promotional or merchandising policies attempt to attract these groups?

2 Interview someone who has attended a "home party" where products were sold (Amway, Tupperware, Sarah Coventry jewelry, and so on). What types of group power (such as reference, coercive, and the like) are you able to identify, based on the description of this party?

NOTES

[1] Adapted from Manli Ho, "Peddling Naughty Lingerie . . . In Suburban Livingrooms," *Boston Globe,* March 2, 1976.

[2] David Dressler and Donald Carns, *Sociology: The Study of Human Interaction,* Knopf, New York, 1973, p. 259.

[3] Charles H. Cooley, *Social Organization,* Scribners, New York, 1909, p. 23.

[4] Ralph Linton, *The Cultural Background of Personality,* Appleton Century Crofts, New York, 1945.

[5] William Shakespeare, *As You Like It,* act 2, scene 7, lines 140–143.

[6] Erving Goffman, *The Presentation of Self in Everyday Life,* University of Edinburgh Social Sciences Research Centre, London, 1958.

[7] David Krech, Richard S. Crutchfield, and Egerton L. Ballachey, *Individual in Society,* McGraw-Hill, New York, 1962, p. 313.

[8] Scott Ward, "Consumer Socialization," *Journal of Consumer Research,* 1:1–14, September 1974.

[9] John R. P. French and Bertram Raven, "The Bases of Social Power," in D. Cartwright (ed.), *Studies in Social Power,* Institute of Social Research, Ann Arbor, Mich., 1959, pp. 150–167.

[10] "Soft Soap and Hard Sell," *Forbes,* September 15, 1975, pp. 72, 78.

[11] Scott B. MacKenzie and Judy L. Zaichkowsky, "An Analysis of Alcohol Advertising Using French and Raven's Theory of Social Influence," in Kent B. Monroe (ed.), *Advances in Consumer Research,* vol. 8, Association for Consumer Research, Ann Arbor, Mich., 1981, pp. 708–712.

[12] Ellen Graham, "Tupperware Parties Create a New Breed of Super-Saleswoman," *The Wall Street Journal,* May 21, 1971, pp. 1, 18; and Flavia Krone and Denise Smart, "An Exploratory Study Profiling the Party-Plan Shopper," in Robert H. Ross, Frederick B. Kraft, and Charles H. Davis (eds.), *1981 Proceedings, Southwestern Marketing Association,* Wichita State University, 1981, pp. 200–203.

[13] John L. Swasy, "Measuring the Bases of Social Power," in William L. Wilkie (ed.), *Advances in Consumer Research,* vol. 6, Association for Consumer Research, Ann Arbor, Mich., 1979, p. 341.

[14] Francis S. Bourne, "Group Influence in Marketing and Public Relations," in Rensis Likert and Samuel Hayes, Jr., (eds.), *Some Applications of Behavioral Research,* UNESCO, Paris, 1957, pp. 208–209; and Tamotsu Shibutani, "Reference Groups as Perspectives," *American Journal of Sociology,* **60**:562–569, May 1955.

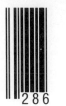

ENVIRONMENTAL
INFLUENCES ON
CONSUMER
BEHAVIOR

286

[15] George Homans, *Social Behavior: Its Elementary Forms,* Harcourt, Brace & World, New York, 1961; and Michael J. Ryan and E. H. Bonfield, "The Fisbein Extended Model and Consumer Behavior," *Journal of Consumer Research,* **2**:118–136, September 1975.

[16] C. Whan Park and V. Parker Lessig, "Students and Housewives: Differences in Susceptibility to Reference Group Influence," *Journal of Consumer Research,* **4**:102–110, September 1977; Herbert C. Kelman, "Processes of Opinion Change," *Public Opinion Quarterly,* **25**:57–78, 1961; and M. Deutsch and H. B. Gerard, "A Study of Normative and Informational Social Influences Upon Individual Judgment," *Journal of Abnormal and Social Psychology,* **51**:624–636, 1955.

[17] Glock's research results were written by Francis S. Bourne in "Group Influence."

[18] William O. Bearden and Michael J. Etzel, "Reference Group Influence on Product and Brand Purchase Decisions," *Journal of Consumer Research,* **9**:184–185, September 1982.

[19] Bourne, "Group Influence," pp. 221–222.

[20] Park and Lessig, "Students and Housewives," pp. 103–104.

[21] Robert E. Witt, "Informal Social Group Influence on Consumer Behavior," *Journal of Marketing Research,* **6**:473–476, November 1969.

[22] John H. Murphy and William H. Cunningham, "Correlates of the Extent of Informal Friendship-Group Influence on Consumer Behavior," in Subhash C. Jain (ed.), *Research Frontiers in Marketing: Dialogues and Directions,* American Marketing Association, Chicago, 1978, pp. 130–133; and Jeffery D. Ford and Elwood A. Ellis, "A Reexamination of Group Influence on Member Brand Preferences," *Journal of Marketing Research,* **17**:125–132, February 1980.

[23] Leon G. Schiffman, "Social Interaction Patterns of the Elderly Consumer," in Boris W. Becker and Helmut Becker (eds.), *Combined Proceedings of the American Marketing Association,* American Marketing Association, Chicago, 1972, p. 451.

[24] Thomas S. Robertson, *Consumer Behavior,* Scott, Foresman, Glenview, Ill., 1970, p. 74.

[25] Benton A. Cocanougher and Grady D. Bruce, "Socially Distant Reference Groups and Consumer Aspirations," *Journal of Marketing Research,* **8**:379–381, August 1971.

[26] George Moschis, "Social Comparison and Informal Group Influence," *Journal of Marketing Research,* **13**:237–244, August 1976.

[27] W. Thomas Anderson, Jr., Linda L. Golden, and Joel Saegert, "Reactional Analysis of Referent Selection in Product Decisions," in Subhash C. Jain (ed.), *Research Frontiers in Marketing: Dialogues and Directives,* American Marketing Association, Chicago, 1978, pp. 134–138.

[28] Lyman O. Ostlund, "Role Theory and Group Dynamics," in Scott Ward and Thomas S. Robertson (eds.), *Consumer Behavior: Theoretical Sources,* Prentice-Hall, Englewood Cliffs, N.J., 1973, p. 245.

[29] Harold H. Kassarjian, "Riesman Revisited," *Journal of Marketing,* **29**:54–56, April 1965; and Richard W. Mizerski and Robert B. Settle, "The Influence of Social Character on Preference for Social Versus Objective Information in Advertising," *Journal of Marketing Research,* **16**:552–558, November 1979.

[30] Donald W. Hendon, "A New and Empirical Look at the Influence of Reference Groups on Generic Product Category and Brand Choice: Evidence From Two Nations," in *Proceedings of the Academy of International Business: Asia-Pacific Dimensions of International Business,* College of Business Administration, University of Hawaii, Honolulu, 1979, p. 757; and Robert T. Green, Joel G. Saegert, and Robert J. Hoover, "Conformity in Consumer Behavior: A Cross-National Replication," in Neil Beckwith et al. (eds.), *1979 Educator's Conference Proceedings,* American Marketing Association, Chicago, 1979, pp. 192–194.

[31] Park and Lessig, "Students and Housewives," pp. 102–110.

[32] Robert E. Burnkrant and Alain Cousineau, "Informational and Normative Social Influence in Buyer Behavior," *Journal of Consumer Research,* **2**:214, December 1975.

[33] Fleming Hansen, "Primary Group Influence and Consumer Conformity," in Philip R. McDonald (ed.), *Marketing Involvement in Society and the Economy,* American Marketing Association, Chicago, 1969, pp. 300–305; and Moschis, "Social Comparison."

[34] Bobby J. Calder and Robert E. Burnkrant, "Interpersonal Influence on Consumer Behavior: An Attribution Theory Approach," *Journal of Consumer Research,* **4**:29, 37, June 1977; and James H. Leigh and Claude R. Martin, Jr., "A Review of Situational Influence Paradigms and Research," in Ben M. Enis and Kenneth J. Roering (eds.), *Review of Marketing 1981,* American Marketing Association, Chicago, 1981, p. 68.

[35] Murphy and Cunningham, "Correlates."

FAMILY

LEARNING OBJECTIVES

After studying this chapter, you should understand . . .

- The importance of family influences on consumer behavior

- The meaning of ''family'' and ''household'' and their importance to marketing decisions

- The nature of traditional and modern family life cycles

- How families make purchase decisions

- The nature of significant changes occurring among contemporary families

Club Med, the international vacation village resort giant which established its reputation in America as a free-spirited summer camp for swinging singles in the mid-60's, is widening its appeal to the family market. Although its European resorts have had children's and babies' programs for over twenty years, Club Med is increasingly gearing itself to families in its western hemisphere villages, due to the large growth in new parents from the current baby boomlet. Club Med is aiming at a market of 5 to 8 million Americans, many of whom are two-income families with children who can afford a $3000 week of complete family relaxation. A number of its resorts in the Americas offer Mini Clubs for children aged 2 to 11. The Paradise Island Club in the Bahamas and the Sandpiper, Port St. Lucie, Florida, have Baby Clubs with a staff who will warm bottles, mix baby food, and take care of children from 4 months to 23 months of age. Such an atmosphere appeals to many new parents who can play tennis or water ski while their kids learn scuba diving or the high trapeze.'

10

As marketers at Club Med understand the changing family structure of the marketplace and those factors that influence family decisions in purchasing vacation packages, they are better able to develop effective marketing strategies.

SIGNIFICANCE OF THE FAMILY IN CONSUMER BEHAVIOR

In Chapter 9 we examined the topic of social groups in order to understand their relevance to individuals and how marketers could use this knowledge. Now we turn to the family, not just as a type of small group, but one that is often predominant in its influence over consumer behavior. The family is both a *primary* group (characterized by intimate, face-to-face interaction) and a *reference* group (with members referring to certain family values, norms, and standards in their behavior). These two factors, however, are not the sole reasons accounting for the strength of the family's influence. Rather it is, first, the fact that the bonds within the family are likely to be much more powerful than those in other small groups. Second, contrary to most other groups to which the consumer belongs, the family functions directly in the role of ultimate consumption. Thus, the family operates as an economic unit, earning and spending money. In doing this, family members must establish individual and collective consumption priorities, decide on products and brands that fulfill their needs, and also decide where these items are to be bought and how they are to be used in furthering family members' goals. Also, consumers' attitudes toward spending and saving and even the brands and products purchased have been molded, often quite indelibly, by the families they grew up in. Thus, marketers need to understand the nature of the family's influence on its members and the way in which purchase decisions are made by members so that they may effectively program their marketing mix.

The thrust of this chapter will first be to review several terms important in understanding this subject. Second, we shall describe the basic functions of the family. Next, we shall examine the family life-cycle concept and assess its meaning for the marketer. Family organization and decision-making roles will then be discussed, also incorporating marketing implications and examples. Finally, the changing nature of the family, especially here in America, will be discussed along with implications for marketers who face this changing scene.

FAMILIES AND HOUSEHOLDS

It is important to understand the difference between various terms that are frequently encountered when discussing the concept of family. First, we should distinguish between the terms "family" and "household," since market statistics may be gathered on either of these bases. A *household* includes the related family members and all the unrelated persons who occupy a housing unit (whether house, apartment, group of rooms, or other). The term "family," however, is more limited and refers to a group of two or more persons related by blood, marriage, or adoption and residing together in a household. In 1980 there were approximately 80 million households and 58 million families. Table 10-1 presents data on household changes in the United States.

It should be noted that marketers are interested not only in the concept of families but also of households, since both may form the basis or framework of much consumer decision-making and buying behavior. The marketer will use the concept that seems most relevant for segmenting markets. For instance, manufacturers of refrigerators, dishwashers, ranges, and other kitchen appliances would probably find households to be the most relevant dimension in estimating market size since purchase and replacement of these appliances would depend more on household formation than family formation. On the other hand, sellers of children's clothing and toys would probably be more interested in data on families.

FAMILY LIFE CYCLE

The concept of family life cycle has proven very valuable for the marketer, especially for segmentation activities. This section will describe the concept and discuss its application to consumer behavior and marketing strategy.

TRADITIONAL LIFE-CYCLE STAGES

The term "life cycle" refers to the progression of stages through which individuals and families proceed over time. In the United States, the following stages are typical of the family life-cycle progression:

1   The Bachelor Stage: young, single people

2   Newly Married Couples: young, no children

3   Full Nest I: young married couples with youngest child under 6

TABLE 10-1

Household Change

Married couple households with children will decline in this decade while less traditional household types will rapidly increase

	1981	Projection 1990	Percent change 1981–1990
All households (in 000s)	82,368	95,076	15.4
Percent	100.0%	100.0%	
Married couple households	59.8%	55.1%	6.2
With children under 18	30.2	25.8	− 1.9
No children under 18	29.6	29.3	14.2
Other, woman as householder	26.5%	29.0%	26.0
With children under 18	6.8	7.9	33.0
No children under 18	19.7	21.1	23.6
Woman living alone	14.2	15.4	25.0
Other	5.5	5.7	19.6
Other, man as householder	13.6%	15.9%	35.4
With children under 18	0.8	0.9	32.7
No children under 18	12.8	15.0	35.5
Man living alone	8.8	10.3	34.4
Other	4.0	4.7	35.6

Source: Paul C. Glick, "How American Families Are Changing," *American Demographics*, January 1984, p. 23.

4   Full Nest II: young married couples with youngest child 6 or over

5   Full Nest III: older married couples with dependent children

6   Empty Nest I: older married couples with no children living with them and household head in labor force

7   Empty Nest II: older married couples with no children living with them and household head retired

8   Solitary Survivor I: older single people in labor force

9   Solitary Survivor II: older retired single people

With the life-cycle concept the marketer is able to appreciate better how the family's needs, outlooks, product purchases, and financial resources vary over time. The major family life-cycle stages are further described below.[2]

Bachelor Stage   At this stage of the life cycle, earnings are relatively low because the individual is often just beginning a career. In spite of a low income, there are also few financial burdens which must be assumed; consequently, discretionary income is quite high. This group is generally recreation-oriented and high on fashion-opinion leadership. As a result, purchase patterns consist of vacations, cars, clothing, and various other products and services needed for the mating game. In addition, the establishment of their own residences away from their family usually requires the purchase of some basic furniture and kitchen equipment.

Newly Married Couples   This group is generally better off financially than when they were single because both spouses are likely to be working. They are also healthier financially than they will be in the next stage, which brings added demands on their resources. But for now this family has the highest purchase rate and the highest average purchase of durable goods, especially furniture and appliances. They also spend heavily on cars, clothing, and vacations.

Full Nest I   When the first child is born most wives have traditionally stopped working, which causes a reduction in family income. At the same time, new demands are added to the family's purchasing requirements. For example, the increased family size may necessitate more space, so the family moves into a new home and purchases items necessary to fill their new environment. Furniture for the baby's room and other furnishings are bought, as well as such appliances as a washer, dryer, and television set. In addition, many child-related expenses are now added, including baby food, baby medicines, doctor's visits, and toys of all sorts. The parents are quite interested in new products and are susceptible to things they see advertised; however, they also grow more dissatisfied with their financial position and the amount of money available for savings.

Full Nest II   In this stage, the family's financial position has improved with the husband's advancement and perhaps, too, the wife's return to work. Families in this stage are still new-product-oriented, but tend to be less influenced by advertising because they have more buying experience. Products heavily purchased during this time include many foods (especially in larger packages and multiple-unit deals), cleaning materials, bicycles, and musical instruments and lessons.

Full Nest III   During this stage, the family's income continues to advance, more wives return to work, and even the children may be employed. Although they are more resistant to advertising, this type of family has a high average expenditure for durable goods, primarily because of their need to replace older items. They purchase new, more tasteful furniture, luxury appliances, boats, and automobiles. They also do more traveling and spend more on dental bills and magazines.

Empty Nest I   At this stage, the family is most satisfied with its financial position and savings accumulation. Home ownership is at a peak, and major expenditures are necessary for home improvement. Although the couple is not interested in new products, they do show an interest in travel, recreation, and self-education. This spending pattern emphasizes gifts and contributions, vacations, and luxuries.

Empty Nest II   During this stage the couple's income is drastically cut. They stay at home more and spend more for medical appliances, medical care, and products that aid their health, sleep, and digestion.

Solitary Survivors   If these individuals are still active in the labor force, their income is likely to continue to be good. However, the home is likely to be sold, and more money will be spent for vacations, recreation, and health-oriented items. Those who are retired will suffer a drastic cut in income but will continue to have the same medical and product needs as other retired groups. During this stage, individuals also have a special need for attention, affection, and security.

A MODERNIZED FAMILY LIFE CYCLE

During recent years, many changes in the family have occurred, particularly in smaller family size, postponement of marriage, and rising divorce rates. Thus, another conception of the life cycle, which includes the stages of divorced and middle-aged married without children, has been offered. This modernized version is shown in Figure 10-1. It helps to visualize the possible variety of different family life-cycle stages by presenting a diagram of the flow. Both the traditional and modernized conceptualizations are shown in this figure.

RELATIONSHIP BETWEEN FAMILY LIFE CYCLE AND CONSUMER BEHAVIOR

Although nine distinct stages were suggested above, there is no unanimity among research studies as to the most appropriate categorization of life cycle. For example, the dividing line for terms such as "young" and "older" might be 40 years of age in one study and 45 in another, which makes it difficult to compare results among various research studies. In spite of these definitional difficulties there is, nevertheless, widespread agreement on the relationship between life cycle and consumer behavior.

Sears & Roebuck, Inc., did a large study recently to find out who purchased what at what stage of life. They found that people leaving the "young single" stage and entering

the "young family" stage were far more likely to buy and own all types of appliances. Such information helps Sears's corporate buyers, marketers, advertisers, and sales staff. For instance, salespeople are encouraged to identify the customer's position in the life cycle—how many kids, what their ages are, and so forth—to sell products to appropriate prospects.[3]

Further evidence is provided by a cross-national research study, in which the sizes and compositions of household expenditures were found to be systematically related to the stage of the family life cycle.[4] Such findings are relevant to marketing managers when developing forecasts, for example. Demand for different product and service categories may be estimated from knowledge of the relationship between demand and stage in life cycle and the predicted number of households in the various stages. A number of other studies have related shopping behavior to life-cycle stage.[5]

LIFE CYCLE VERSUS AGE IN SEGMENTING MARKETS

The reader may wonder whether the life-cycle concept offers a richer explanation of consumer behavior than a single variable such as age does. You will recall that we raised a similar question earlier when considering the merits of social class versus income in segmenting markets. The evidence heavily favors the use of life cycle as a way of segmenting markets.[6] One in-depth study on this subject found that for most items investigated, life cycle was more sensitive to product consumption than was age.[7] It should be noted, however, that for several categories of products and services the reverse was true. One category for which this was the case was products tied to age-related physical difficulties (such as medical ap-

FIGURE 10-1
Family life-cycle flows.
Source: Patrick E. Murphy and William A. Staples, "A Modernized Family Life Cycle," *Journal of Consumer Research* **6:**17, June 1979.

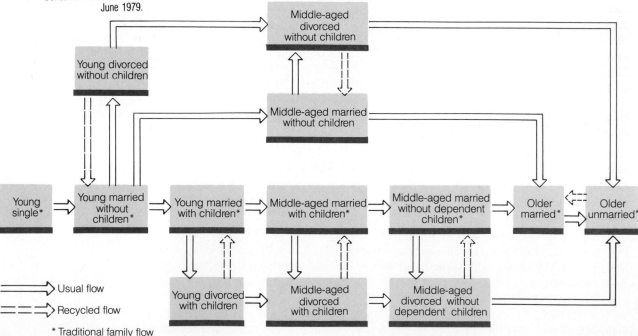

pliances and other medical-care items). Age was also more sensitive for products and services classified mainly as luxuries, and for a diverse catchall category.

For most products, however, life-cycle analysis allows the marketer to achieve a richer understanding of the market. A summary overview of life-cycle stages for all family members and their consumer behavior is presented in Table 10-2.

FAMILY PURCHASING DECISIONS

This section probes more deeply into the nature of the decision-making process within the family and its implications for consumer behavior and marketing. Family purchasing decisions will be examined from four perspectives: (1) role structure, (2) power structure, (3) stage in the decision-making process, and (4) family-specific characteristics. It is very important that the marketer understand who influences whom, and how, in the family buying process, so that the proper marketing strategy may be developed.

ROLE STRUCTURE

In our earlier discussion of the concept of roles, we described how society is structured of roles that are occupied (or played) by its members. So, too, does the family have its own structure, with each member playing his or her role. Although several theories have been used to describe the structure of marital roles in decision making, from the standpoint of those interested in consumer behavior, the following role categorizations appear to be perhaps the most helpful.

Instrumental and Expressive Roles   Generally, in traditional families among societies throughout the world the husband is more likely to provide material support and primary leadership authority within the family, and the wife is more likely to provide affection and moral support. This distinction relates to what are known as instrumental and expressive needs of all small groups (including the family); that is, the need for leadership and fulfillment of the task on the one hand, and the need for morale and cohesion on the other.[8]

This differentiation of roles is known to result from small-group interaction. Leaders are produced who specialize in either *instrumental* functions (known as functional or task leaders) or *expressive* functions (social leaders). The former concern themselves with the basic purpose or goal of the group, while the latter attempt to reduce tension and give emotional support to members in order to maintain intragroup cohesion.[9] Within the family, the instrumental role has typically been played by the father and the expressive role by the mother. That is, men tend to be task-oriented leaders, while women lead in social-emotional behavior. The result of this is that in purchasing decisions husbands tend to concern themselves with functional product attributes and to exert more influence in deciding whether to buy and in closing the sale. The wife concerns herself more with aesthetic product attributes and with suggesting the purchase.[10]

Although the general role pattern cited above has been historically true, these roles are undergoing some degree of change today, particularly as more women enter the labor force. Much more will be said on changing roles in a later section of

TABLE 10-2
Consumer Elements by Consumer Life-Cycle Stage

Consumer element	Childhood	Adolescence	Early singlehood	Mature single	Newly married couples (young, no children)
Consumer characteristics	All needs provided by parents Little or no understanding of marketplace Marketplace limited to that of parents Limited cognitive ability Limited and unorganized product knowledge	Basic needs provided by parents Luxuries increasingly provided through part-time work Tastes and preferences evolving Susceptible to peer pressure to conform Limited product knowledge Limited understanding of marketplace Marketplace not solely limited to that of parents	Values and priorities unclear ∴ experimentation in lifestyle and associated consumption Highly mobile Few financial burdens Few assets Recreation oriented Fashion opinion leaders Marketplace not limited by parents or legal restrictions due to age Wide product knowledge but little depth	Expectations of financial support by near relatives possible Discretionary income typically high Full marketplace accessible Wide product knowledge in depth likely Independent decision making	Resolution of lifestyle and values concerning consumption Lack of financial planning Financial condition better now than for near future High purchase of durables Wide product knowledge
Typical products and services	Toys Clothes Sweet treats Games Comic books	Records Bicylces Some personal care products Toys Clothes Sporting goods	First car Basic home furnishings Home electronic equipment Vacations Sport equipment Education Personal care products First use of credit Groceries	Tasteful home furnishings Appliances Travel Hobby related purchases Better restaurants Savings for retirement House/condominium	Home equipment Durable furniture Cars Vacations Insurance

Source: Ronald W. Stampfl, "The Consumer Life Cycle," *Journal of Consumer Affairs*, **12**:214–215, Winter 1978.

this chapter. For now it should merely be noted that wives may be just as likely to perform certain instrumental roles as their husbands do."

Internal and External Roles Another differentiation of roles occurs in the family with regard to the husband's primary concern with matters *external* to the family and the wife's concern largely with *internal* matters.

The interaction of the two basic types of roles discussed above is presented in Figure 10-2. This matrix indicates that when expressive-external and instrumental-internal roles are involved in a purchase decision, both husband and wife will

	Full nest				Empty nest			
	I	II	III	IV	I	II		
	Youngest child under six	Youngest child six or older	Older married couples with dependent children	Single parenthood	Older married couples; no children at home, head in labor force	Older married couples; no children at home, head retired	Older solitary survivor, in labor force	Solitary survivor, retired
	Home purchase of primary concern Low liquid assets Conversion to one income likely Most susceptible to advertising and new products Dissatisfied with financial condition Change in lifestyle due to children Expansion of family influences on purchasing	Change in family risk patterns and concern for security Needs still expanding faster than income Consumption time scheduling difficult Some wives working Less susceptible to advertising Larger unit purchases	Aging parents Recycling of products to younger siblings while protecting individual needs Heavy replacement of durables More wives working Hard to influence with advertising Wide product knowledge in depth likely Some children get jobs	Administration of consumption difficult Product knowledge of spouse lost Dissatisfaction with dual parent role	Pre-retirement planning Home ownership at peak Typically in best financial position Not interested in new products Financial assistance to children	Drastic drop in income Want to keep home Product knowledge becoming obsolete	Income still good but likely to sell home Independent decisions now required due to absence of spouse	Drastic drop in income Independent decisions now required due to absence of spouse
	First house Day care Community services more important—schools, hospitals Baby food Toys Fast food Energy use high Bikes Baby furniture	Assortment increases due to expressed preferences Rapid usage of clothing Larger house or remodeling Larger size packages Music lessons and instruments Fast food	Food expense at peak Dental services New furniture Coats Magazines Nonnecessary appliances Boats Recreational vehicles College expenses	Home security devices Buyable recreation for children Housekeeping services Day care Education for reentry to job market	Travel Recreation Contributions Self education Vacations Home improvements Savings for retirement Home security devices Hobby related purchases	Medical care and products which aid sleep, health, digestion Leisure time equipment not formerly owned due to time constraints Household services for aging Vacation home Restaurants	Household services Restaurants Similar to mature singlehood except for gifts to grown children Hobby related purchases	Mass transportation Same product needs as other retired

be involved; that is, joint decision making will be the case. For product decisions involving expressive-internal and instrumental-external roles, wives and husbands, respectively, will be more heavily involved. We shall elaborate on the nature of each spouse's decision-making input to purchasing processes for various products in a later section of this chapter.

Purchase Process Roles There are several ways of viewing family member roles as they relate to the purchase decision and consumption process. In this context, there are six roles that may be performed by various family members.

First, one or another family member may be the *initiator* (for example, the individual who recognizes the problem or need for the item). In this role, the suggestion may be made by the wife, for example, that the household needs a food processor in order to prepare meals more easily. A second role is that of *influencer*, which is the person who informs or persuades others in a purchase situation. He may also be thought of as an *opinion leader* in that he exerts personal influence on other family members with regard to a particular purchase situation.

A third and related role is that of *information gatherer*, in which one or more individuals will secure information related to the possible purchase. This information may pertain to products or places of shopping. Often, the individual most knowledgeable in the product category will gather information. For example, a husband may well gather information about a possible lawn tractor purchase while the wife may gather information about new financial services offered by a local bank.

The role of *decision maker* involves having authority to make the buying decision. The individual who makes this decision might be the same as the influencer or information gatherer, although not necessarily so. For instance, the wife may make the decision to purchase a microwave oven as well as the decision on which brand to buy, after having gathered information about various models available. Often the decision is a joint or shared one in which more than one family member participates.

The *purchaser* role involves the act of purchase by one of the family members. In other words, the individual who buys the item in the store or, perhaps, places a telephone order for merchandise is acting in the role of purchasing agent for the family. The decider and purchaser need not necessarily be the same individual. For example, a teenage son or daughter may merely execute his or her parents' supermarket shopping list. In this situation (in which brands, sizes, and the like are specified), the youth is only a purchaser, not a decision maker. At other times, however, the purchaser may occupy a very strategic role in the brand decision. One study, for instance, found that nearly one-third of beer drinkers delegated the brand decision to the purchaser (usually the wife) and that the purchaser was aware of the consumer's preferences nine out of ten times.[12]

Sometimes, the purchaser may be referred to as the *gatekeeper*, that is, a family member who is able to control the flow of products into the family. In other words, the purchase may be consummated or blocked by this individual. The role of gatekeeper is well-illustrated in a study of children's purchase influences on parents. In this research, children were found to suggest which cereal brands their

FIGURE 10-2
Role interaction.
Source: Adapted from James H. Myers and William H. Reynolds, *Consumer Behavior and Marketing Management*, Houghton Mifflin Co., Boston, 1967, p. 245.

	External	Internal
Expressive	Both	Wife
Instrumental	Husband	Both

mothers should purchase when shopping. The mothers, however, were in the gatekeeper position, frequently disagreeing with their children as to what cereal should be purchased, and hence controlling the flow of this product into the family.[13]

Users are those who consume the product or service. A user may be the same person who performs each of the other roles, or it may be another person. The latter situation is often possible, for instance, in the case of a child for whom products such as clothing, toys, and so forth are purchased.

For the marketer, it is important to distinguish each family member's role in order to develop an optimum marketing strategy. Assumptions made about such roles should be checked through consumer research so that the marketer is certain that the correct mix is aimed at the right individual. Knowledge of who generally performs which purchase and consumption process role within the family unit will aid in product planning and development, providing promotion messages, determining distribution decisions, and so forth. More will be said about this topic in the following section.

POWER STRUCTURE

This factor has to do with which family member is dominant or considered to be the family's head. A family may be *patriarchal,* in which case the father is considered to be the dominant member. In a *matriarchal* family, the woman plays the dominant role and makes most of the decisions, while in the *equalitarian* family, the husband and wife share somewhat equally in decision making. Although the American family is still generally patriarchal and our society is male-dominated, egalitarianism is a continuously emerging pattern.

The United States is also moving increasingly toward a child-centered family in which children have a strong influence on their parents' consumption decisions. For example, parents often yield to their children's television-viewing preferences (such as watching *Sesame Street* rather than an afternoon movie), recreation or entertainment requests (a vacation to Disney World rather than Europe), and product choices (Kellogg Frosted Flakes rather than Special K).

Purchase Influence Pattern   Research on power relationships in the family has taken several directions. One approach to understanding the marital power structure in consumer decision making categorizes the possibilities for dominance in the following way: (1) *autonomic,* in which an equal number of decisions is made by each spouse, (2) *husband dominant,* (3) *wife dominant,* and (4) *syncratic,* in which most decisions are made by both husband and wife.[14]

A study using this concept measured the relative influence of Belgian husbands and wives in purchase decisions for twenty-five representative products.[15] Figure 10-3 positions these decisions according to the four marital decision-making categories of autonomic, husband dominant, wife dominant, and syncratic. Each decision is positioned in this figure according to two axes. The vertical axis is a scale of the relative influence between husband and wife. Decisions can range along a continuum from 1 (if respondents report husband specialization) to 3 (if respondents report wife specialization). The horizontal axis is a scale of the extent of role specialization as measured by the percentage of

families reporting that a decision is made jointly. Syncratic decisions, therefore, are those in which more than half the respondents reported that the decision was joint, while in the autonomic case, less than half the respondents indicated the decision was joint but there was no consensus among respondents as to whether the decision was dominated by husband or wife. Thus, autonomic decisions, as well as husband-and-wife dominant decisions, represent role specialization. In reading the figure, it may be seen that the relative influence score for household cleaning products is approximately 2.9, with only 6 percent of the families decid-

FIGURE 10-3
Marital roles in
twenty-five decisions.
Source: Adapted from Harry L. Davis
and Benny P. Rigaux, "Perception of
Marital Roles in Decision Processes,"
Journal of Consumer Research,
1:54, June 1974.

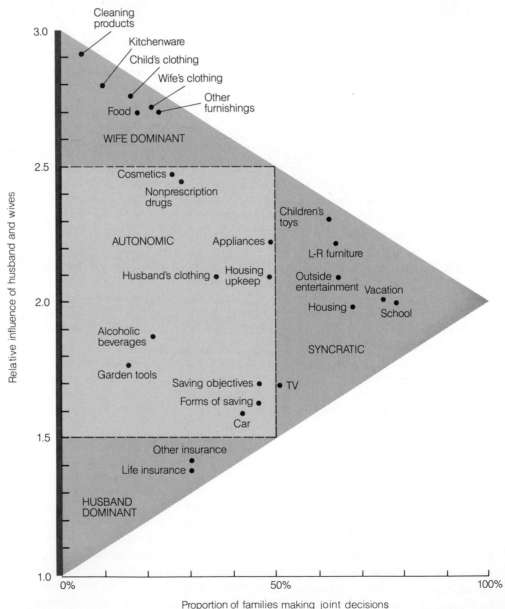

ing jointly on this item's purchase. Thus, the wife dominates this purchase decision. Similarly, the relative influence score for vacations is approximately 2.0, with 78 percent of families deciding jointly (a syncratic role structure). A similar study of U.S. couples' perceptions of marital roles in consumer decision processes found that the Belgian results were generally supported.[16]

These and other studies have found that marital role specialization in the consumer decision-making process varies significantly across product categories.[17] Results of these studies lead to the conclusion that joint decision making is most likely to occur for purchases that represent significant economic outlays; whereas routine expenditures for items viewed as necessities will probably be delegated to one of the spouses.

Table 10-3 presents selected data from a thorough analysis of husband-wife relative purchase influence covering 108 different products and services ranging from packaged products to durable goods and services.[18] The study was conducted among both husbands and wives and measured purchase patterns and direct and indirect influences. For all products, measures were made of influence on both the decision to buy the product and on the decision to select the particular brand purchased. Spousal influence was defined as "a state of mind recalled by the purchaser which affected a specific recent purchase," and was categorized for packaged products as direct (that is, consciously recalled) and indirect (that is, consideration given to satisfaction of the wants and preferences of each spouse by the purchaser). For durables, however, no important distinction was made between direct and indirect influence, since the purchase is discussed and deliberately decided on, thus satisfying both spouses' wants and preferences. Information was also gathered on relative influence on two aspects of prepurchase activity: initiation of the purchase and information gathering prior to the purchase decision.

Strategies to Resolve Conflict Family purchase decisions are often characterized by conflict over differences between the parties on several factors concerning the decision. For example, family members often have different views of who should make the purchase decision, how that decision should be made (such as how much information should be gathered), and who should implement the decision. Thus, the family purchasing-decision process is not always characterized by stability and easy agreement. Instead, conflict is quite likely, with families engaging in bargaining, compromising, and coercing in order to arrive at a joint decision.

Several strategies for resolving such conflicts may be adopted. These are illustrated in Table 10-4. In this view of family decision-making patterns, members may either agree or disagree about the goals or desired outcomes of a decision. If agreement on such matters exists, *consensus* is said to occur. For example, family members may agree that a winter vacation to Disney World should be taken. On the other hand, *accommodation* may be necessary because of disagreement over goals and outcomes. Thus, such a conflict situation will require accommodation or compromises by one or more family members. It should be recognized that family buying decisions are not totally consensual or accommodating. Yet, we will simplify it to this level in order to describe the various options.

In the *role structure strategy,* the need for family discussion may be reduced or eliminated by having one or perhaps two people responsible for the decision.

TABLE 10-3
Purchase Influence of Husbands and Wives in Buying Decisions (in percent)

	Relative Influence											
	Purchased by		Direct influence				Indirect influence				
			Product		Brand		Product		Brand		
	W	H	W	H	W	H	W	H	W	H
Cereals:										
Cold (unsweetened)	84	16	74	26	71	29	65	35	67	33
Hot	84	16	67	33	67	33	63	37	59	41
Packaged lunch meat	73	27	60	40	64	36	65	35	68	32
Peanut butter	81	19	70	30	74	26	65	35	68	32
Scotch whiskey	35	65	18	82	18	82	22	78	23	77
Bar soap	85	15	65	35	64	36	60	40	61	39
Headache remedies	67	33	67	33	67	33	64	36	65	35
Cat food (dry)	66	34	75	25	81	19	80	20	80	20
Dog food (dry)	76	24	60	40	59	41	60	40	61	39
Fast-food chain hamburgers	68	32	55	45	55	45	53	47	52	48
Catsup	75	25	68	32	68	32	60	40	62	38
Coffee:										
Freeze-dried	68	32	57	43	62	38	56	44	59	41
Regular ground	74	26	65	35	65	35	58	42	60	40
Mouthwash	72	28	56	44	56	44	52	48	53	47

	Share of influence											
	Purchase decision influence				Initiation				Information gathering			
	Product		Brand		Product		Brand		Product		Brand	
	W	H	W	H	W	H	W	H	W	H	W	H
Vacuum cleaner	60	40	60	40	80	20	69	31	66	34	65	35
Electric blender	59	41	53	47	67	33	50	50	53	47	52	48
Broadloom carpet	60	40	59	41	82	18	74	26	72	28	69	31
Automobiles	38	62	33	67	22	78	21	79	18	82	18	82

Source: ''Purchase Influence Measures of Husband/Wife on Buying Decisions,'' Haley, Overholser & Associates, Inc., New Canaan, Conn., January 1975; and ''Buying Study Called Good Support Data,'' *Advertising Age,* March 17, 1975, p. 52. Percentages reflect relative purchase activity, direct and indirect influence of husbands and wives in the sample. For durables and services, percentages reflect relative activity in purchase decision, initiation of idea to purchase and the gathering of information.

Frequently, a *specialist* develops who assumes or is delegated the primary responsibility for decision making in a particular product or service decision area. This expertise comes to be accepted by other family members.

In the *budget strategy,* the decision responsibility is controlled by a set of rules that have been decided upon and established by the family. Thus, the

controller in the family becomes an impersonal budget determined by family members. Once the size and allocation of the budget is set, say, for a new car, decisions are then made only on the basis of the various models available for that price.

A *problem-solving strategy* is likely when agreement exists about which goals are desirable. Various modes of decision making are possible in this situation. First, an *expert* from within or outside the family may be relied on to help determine the best alternative. Second, family discussion may evoke a *better solution* than that originally suggested by any one family member. Third, a *multiple purchase* may be decided upon that resolves or avoids conflict. For example, a husband and wife may decide to purchase two $6500 subcompact cars instead of one $13,000 family sedan as a way of minimizing conflict over use of a single car.

Persuasion strategies involve attempts to force someone to make a decision that she or he would not otherwise make. For example, generally the spouse who has authority for a decision gets the credit or blame for that decision's outcome. The other spouse, freed from this responsibility, may try to dominate by becoming an *irresponsible critic* who freely criticizes and offers ideas without having to worry about how realistic they are. If the other spouse's decision was right, the critic has lost nothing; if it was wrong, the critic can say "I told you so." The other spouse may increasingly concede decision areas to the critic to avoid this situation.

Intuition is a second strategy in which one spouse learns to identify the moods in which the other spouse is most susceptible to new ideas or persuasion, as well as types of appeals that are most effective with that spouse. A third persuasive strategy is to take another family member along when shopping for a product. *Shopping together*, therefore, can secure a decision commitment that may be difficult to reverse later. Fourth, *coercion* is an extreme form of persuasion which secures unwilling agreement through threats. Finally, *coalitions* may

TABLE 10-4

Alternative Decision-Making Strategies

Goals	Strategy	Ways of implementing
"Consensus" (family members agree about goals)	Role structure	"The Specialist"
	Budgets	"The Controller"
	Problem solving	"The Expert" "The Better Solution" "The Multiple Purchase"
"Accommodation" (family members disagree about goals)	Persuasion	"The Irresponsible Critic" "Feminine Intuition" "Shopping Together" "Coercion" "Coalitions"
	Bargaining	"The Next Purchase" "The Impulse Purchase" "The Procrastinator"

Source: Harry L. Davis, "Decision Making Within the Household," *Journal of Consumer Research*, **2**:255, March 1976. Reprinted with permission from the *Journal of Consumer Research*.

be formed within the family in order to force other members to go along. These latter two persuasive approaches—coercion and coalitions—have been described as the least desirable forms of conflict resolution, because they imply not only disagreement between family members over buying goals, but also over fundamental attitudes and lifestyles. Such fundamental conflicts are more difficult to resolve.[20]

Bargaining represents an alternative approach to resolving disagreements about family goals in purchasing situations. In contrast to persuasion, which represents more short-run efforts to win a specific decision, bargaining leads to willing agreement and involves longer-term considerations. Family members must engage in mutual give and take. This approach can occur in several ways. First, certain family members may have their way in a current purchase as long as others get their choice in the *next purchase*. For instance, the wife may buy new clothes now if the husband will later be able to purchase a new boat. In a second approach, a family member may make an *impulse purchase* and then bargain. For example, the husband may bring a newly purchased boat home and then try to convince his wife that she will love it. Finally, *procrastinating* can continue the bargaining process after a selection has been made. By delaying the purchase, new information may develop or the situation may be changed so that a new choice is made.

Different decision-making strategies are likely for different situations. That is, depending on the family members, the product, the stage in the decision process, and so forth, the strategies selected will vary.

Changing Roles and Family Purchase Decisions Changing role patterns of husbands and wives are having numerous effects.[21] Previous marriage patterns meant that there were generally no decisions to be made regarding the wife's chief life interest and sphere, nor the husband's. She concentrated on domestic activities, and he concentrated on occupational efforts. Today, however, sex-role shifts toward egalitarianism mean that there is less inevitability of such a pattern, and many new and critical decisions must be made. Increasing numbers of younger and better-educated men and women are bargaining with each other about their chief life interests. And this is occurring not only among those soon-to-be or newly married, but also among couples married for some time. There are virtually no nonnegotiable issues among such modern marriages, for example, where to live (near his work or hers), how many children to have and when, who will perform child care and domestic chores, how to spend *their* incomes, and so forth.

In addition to the number of issues to be decided, there is also the matter of how this is negotiated. Women who have more traditional roles in marriage tend to negotiate with their husbands and try to persuade them to compromise on the basis of *collective* interest—what is best for the family group, for their marital relationship, for the children. A woman who has adopted modern roles tends to negotiate more in terms of her own *individualistic* interests—what is best for her. Such a strategy seems to result in achieving more equitable compromises in terms of reaching her goals.

Although purchase influence may change over a period of time as the American family structure adapts, it is difficult to judge whether, and if so, how far purchase-influence roles have shifted.[22]

STAGE IN THE FAMILY PURCHASE-DECISION PROCESS

The marketer is interested not only in the physical act of purchasing a product or brand, but also in the stages leading up to that decision. The research study on family participation and influence in purchasing behavior described above and presented in Table 10-3 also found that roles and influence vary throughout the buyer decision-making process. Such knowledge can be of great help in formulating product, promotion, channel, and pricing strategies. As shown in Table 10-3, for most of the products wives are involved more heavily in the initiation, information-seeking, and purchasing stages than are husbands. At all stages, however, there is a greater tendency for husbands to participate in the decision process when the product is high-priced and technically or mechanically complex.

Other studies have examined products not included in the study cited above, with similar findings. Their data support the contention that the extent of husband-wife involvement varies considerably from product to product throughout the decision-making process.[23]

Figure 10-4 graphically illustrates the changes in marital roles occurring among a sample of U.S. husbands and wives as decision-making proceeds (after

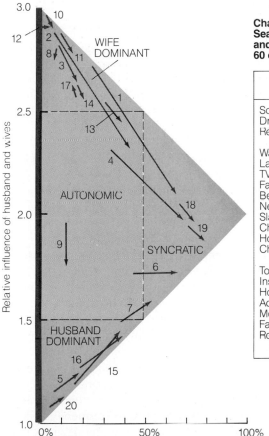

Changes in Marital Roles between Search for Information (Phase 2) and Final Decision (Phase 3) 60 couples (n = 120)

Decision	Key number
Sofa for living room or family room	1
Drapes for living room or family room	2
Replacement or addition of pots and pans for the kitchen	3
Washing machine	4
Lawnmower	5
TV for living or family room	6
Family car (primary)	7
Beef roast	8
Necktie for the husband	9
Slacks for the wife	10
Children's shoes	11
Household cleaning products	12
Children's toys for birthdays and holidays	13
Toothpaste	14
Insurance on the husband's life	15
Homeowner's or renter's insurance	16
Adhesive bandages	17
Movies	18
Family vacation	19
Replacement tires for the family car (primary)	20

FIGURE 10-4
Marital role changes in the decision process for twenty products.
Source: Adapted from E. H. Bonfield, "Perception of Marital Roles in Decision Processes: Replication and Extension," in H. Keith Hunt (ed.), *Advances in Consumer Research,* vol. 5, Association for Consumer Research, Ann Arbor, Mich., 1978, pp. 302, 303, 305.

phase 1—problem recognition) from phase 2 (search for information) to phase 3 (final decision).

FAMILY-SPECIFIC CHARACTERISTICS

There are a number of additional variables that have been found to influence the nature of purchasing decisions made within the family. The influencing factors to be discussed below include culture, subculture, social class, reference groups and social interaction, stage in life cycle, mobility, geographical location, and children.

Culture   The roles of husbands and wives may differ dramatically from culture to culture, which may result in numerous differences in consumer decision making. The basic family systems encountered by the marketer around the world fall into three general patterns, illustrated as follows: (1) in Moslem cultures, the wife is generally in a subordinate and secluded role, with few rights and little control over the affairs of the family; (2) in the Latin American culture, the wife is freer but is still definitely a junior member of the partnership, with the husband having the final authority in all but minor matters; and (3) in European and North-American cultures the basic pattern is equality.[24] This latter region, for instance, evidences substantial similarity with regard to husband-wife involvement for a number of household activities.[25]

Subculture   In addition to cultural variations from one country to another, there are also subcultural or ethnic variations in consumer behavior within a country's heterogeneous population. For example, in the United States joint decision making is most pronounced among white families, with husband dominance strongest among Japanese-Americans, and wife dominance strongest among black families.[26]

Social Class   Several studies on the relationship of socioeconomic class and joint participation in purchase decision making have indicated that a curvilinear relationship exists. That is, autonomy in decision making is most likely at upper and lower social classes, while joint decision making is most common among the middle class.

Reference Groups and Social Interaction   Although no research has been conducted on the role of reference groups in family purchase decisions, it is thought that such relationships are influential. Some authors indicate that the greater the extent to which spouses have social ties or connections with relatives or friends, the less the amount of joint or shared decisions. This is because some decisions may be made in consultation with friends or relatives rather than only with one's spouse.[27]

Stage in Life Cycle   The nature of family decision making changes over the life cycle. For example, wives with pre-school-age children have considerably less independent responsibility for economic decisions than do other wives. In addition, families in early stages of the life cycle show a very high frequency of joint decisions.[28] However, evidence indicates that joint decision making declines over the life cycle. This tendency has been explained in terms of an increased efficiency or competence that people develop over a period of time in making purchasing decisions that are acceptable to their spouses. Such competence eliminates the need for extensive interaction.[29]

Mobility   Mobility, both social as well as geographic, tends to increase the extent of intrafamily communication and the degree of joint decision making. One researcher attributes this to the fact that movement away from stable primary groups such as family and close friends "throws spouses upon each other."[30]

Geographical Location   Limited research on the influence of place of residence on family decision making indicates that rural families have a higher frequency of joint decisions than do urban families. Also, the wife occupies a less influential role in rural families.[31]

Children   Based on a study of purchase-decision processes by families as opposed to couples without children, husbands tended to dominate decision making more in families, while joint decision making was more prevalent among couples. Also, greater variability in the relative influence of husbands and wives across different elements of the decision process was found in family decision-making units.[32]

MARKETING IMPLICATIONS OF FAMILY PURCHASING DECISIONS

It should be clear by now that the marketer's strategy is influenced at almost every turn by the nature of family role and decision-making patterns. Whether the marketer is concerned with product, promotion, channel, or pricing decisions, family household purchase patterns must be well understood. Consider the following implications for promotion strategy.

The development of advertising and personal selling messages is strongly impacted by family roles and decision-making patterns. For instance, the evaluative criteria by which a family will decide which brand of major appliance to purchase must be understood in developing the sales message. However, these criteria may vary among husbands and wives. For those decisions in which one spouse (such as the wife) dominates, then messages may be developed with that segment in mind. However, where joint decision making prevails, the marketer may need to develop separate messages attuned to each party's buying criteria.

Similarly, differences in use of media among family members may necessitate using various message channels in order to reach influential or dominant family members. Reaching the purchaser may require one communication medium, while reaching the user may require another. For example, wives often are the purchasers of their husband's clothing. Consequently, a men's clothing manufacturer may use one campaign to reach men through male-dominated media and another campaign to reach women through female-oriented media, to encourage their purchase of the brand. Appealing to both segments with specific media and with appeals that are appropriate for each would be ideal, but this approach assumes a rather large budget.

A similar strategy is often called for when advertising products for which children are significantly involved in the purchase decision. For example, because children directly influence the choice of which fast-food establishment to patronize, Burger King, McDonald's, and other chains find it necessary to appeal to

children as well as to their parents. As a result, ads often feature people of all ages, with particular emphasis on families. Toy companies, likewise, often aim their ads at children as well as at parents.

The next section will examine ways in which changes are occurring among families in our culture, and how these changes may be expected to affect the marketer.

THE CHANGING AMERICAN FAMILY

It should come as no surprise to the reader that families in America and other parts of the world are changing. It is important to understand what the major changes are and what these shifting patterns mean for marketers in the 1980s. This section provides some insight into these issues.

Perhaps the most important change occurring today is the shifting view of the roles of marriage partners. Over the last several years, the number favoring shared roles in marriage (in which both work, share homemaking, and child raising) has surpassed those favoring a traditional marriage (in which the husband is the breadwinner and the wife is homemaker) by a ratio of 48 percent to 43 percent. However, the small remaining number favoring alternative living arrangements (such as unmarried couples) reinforces the basic and continuing strength of Americans' belief in the nuclear family system.[33] In addition, it should also be noted that the American norm is still a family including children. More than 94 percent of women are in favor of having at least one child. The real shift has come, however, in attitudes toward the ideal number of children to have, which has decreased over the past twenty years.[34]

Let us examine more closely changing female and male roles, particularly as they exist within the family structure today. In addition, we will discuss some marketing implications of these changes.

CHANGING FEMALE ROLES

One of the most significant areas of change to occur in the American family concerns the role of the wife. More than that of either the husband or children, the role of the wife has undergone the greatest transformation in the past few decades. More and more women are opting for a shared role situation rather than the traditional approach in marriage. To a large extent, what this means is that the wife has accepted a job outside the home in addition to her job within the home. But fewer than one-third of the men surveyed in a national study approve of the changes in the role of women in American society.[35] Married men were concerned about how these changes may affect their personal comfort and well-being. The biggest drawback to these men is that they have to spend more time on household chores they don't like.

These changing female role patterns will be examined in this section in terms of two dimensions, both of which may be fruitful from a segmentation standpoint. First, it is useful to view women in terms of their traditionalist/feminist orientation. Second, wives may also be categorized along a working dimension which may be partially reflective of their traditional/feminist orientation. Each of these concepts may be helpful in achieving a better understanding of how family patterns are changing today. First, let us look at the traditionalist/feminist lifestyle orientation.

Traditionalists and Feminists There are significant variations today between women on their lifestyle and demographic characteristics.[36] One study evaluated the attributes of women who were characterized as having either a traditional or a modern feminine lifestyle. Some significant differences between the segments appeared as shown in Table 10-5. From this and other research, it appears that, compared to other groups, feminists tend to be younger and better-educated with a greater sense of independence in terms of how they perceive themselves within the household. They are more liberal in their attitudes toward life, events, and business; have more cosmopolitan interests; are financially optimistic; are very interested in personal appearance; are opposed to sex stereotyping; are more accepting of risk behavior and physically demanding leisure activities; and are more self-confident. Feminists also perceive that role portrayals in ads depict women as sexual objects and do not reflect the market changes that are taking place.

Although the modern role segment has been growing, the marketer should also remember that there is still a sizable group of American men and women who prefer traditional roles in marriage (37 and 43 percent, respectively, according to a recent survey).[37] Studies indicate that most nonworking mothers are happy with their choice to remain at home with their children and even exhibit signs of a superiority complex. Compared to their wage-earning counterparts, they more often describe themselves as family-oriented, faithful to their husbands, fun-loving, sexy, and romantic. Consequently, appealing to this group on the basis of its own value system may be very rewarding to many companies. Yet, many advertisements that glorify working women risk turning off millions of full-time homemakers. One-third of the homemakers in one national study said working women are emphasized too much in TV commercials.[38] Thus, advertisers must look beyond the employment dimension and address the many other facets of today's woman.

Even traditional women are changing in some of the ways they view their lives, and they are adopting different strategies. One of the basic lifestyle changes has been the way full-time homemakers blend family responsibilities with outside activities. What is different about this is that they feel it is legitimate, even essential, that they spend time outside the home and family. Thus, for many housewives, "family" is no longer the central focus or concern in life.[39]

Because of these changing perspectives, they are also changing housework strategies (as are women with jobs outside the house). They are trying to spend this reduced time differently, and they have modified their standards and adopted pragmatic approaches for dealing with their at-home roles.[40]

Another dimension on which the female market may be segmented is that of working versus nonworking women. The next section will discuss certain important facets of the working-wife segment.

Working Wives Historically, women have been viewed by marketers in the roles of wife, mother, and homemaker. Roles outside the family, such as of career

TABLE 10-5

Lifestyle Profile of the Traditional and Modern Woman

Statement	Percent agreeing[a]	
	Traditional	**Modern**
Traditional roles: home and work		
A woman's place is in the home.	68	30
The working world is no place for a woman.	28	9
I am a homebody.	77	62
Traditional roles: family relations		
Men are smarter than women.	29	18
The father should be the boss in the house.	81	59
A wife's first obligation is to her husband, not her children.	74	67
Children are the most important thing in a marriage.	60	45
Orientation toward housekeeping activities		
Our home is furnished for comfort, not style.	92	88
My days seem to follow a definite routine (eating meals at the same time each day, etc.).	70	62
Meal preparation should take as little time as possible.	37	44
Satisfaction with life		
I wish I could leave my present life and do something entirely different.	22	30
My greatest achievements are still ahead of me.	56	70
Physical attractiveness		
I like to feel attractive to members of the opposite sex.	79	89
I want to look a little different from others.	66	72
All men should be clean shaven every day.	76	67
I like to think I am a bit of a swinger.	18	39
Travel proneness		
I would feel lost if I were alone in a foreign country.	75	64
I would like to take a trip around the world.	59	74
I would like to spend a year in London or Paris.	25	39
Mobility		
We will probably move at least once in the next five years.	32	41
Attitudes toward transportation		
I have often thought of buying a subcompact car.	42	50
I like sports cars.	30	47
Financial outlook		
Five years from now our family income will probably be a lot higher than it is now.	60	70
I am considering buying life insurance.	13	22

Statement	Percent agreeing[a]	
	Traditional	**Modern**
Views toward events and situations		
Everything is changing too fast today.	69	62
There is too much emphasis on sex today.	90	81
I think the Women's Liberation movement is a good thing.	41	61
Activity patterns		
I have somewhat old-fashioned tastes and habits.	91	81
I went to the movies at least once in the past year.	68	79
I attended school at least once during the past year.	22	32
I went to a pop concert at least once last year.	7	18

Source: Fred D. Reynolds, Melvin R. Crask, and William D. Wells, "The Modern Feminine Life Style," *Journal of Marketing*, **41**:42–43, July 1977, published by the American Marketing Association.
[a]$P \leq .05$

women and professional workers, were given little or no attention. Yet, these latter roles are assuming considerable importance today, particularly due to the women's movement in the United States. Women now account for 45 percent of the labor force. The predictions are that women will continue to go to work at an unprecedented rate, increasing from approximately 48 percent of all women in 1980 to 51 percent by 1990.[41] The greatest increase in the participation rates of wives has generally been among mothers of children under 3.

A woman works outside the home for one or more of the following reasons:

1 To add to the family's economic security

2 To join the mainstream of worldly endeavor

3 To get acquainted with people who are achievers and to sharpen her own talents and skills

4 To escape the dullness of housework

5 To prepare for the time when she might again be single or the children may be grown[42]

Thus, there are both socioeconomic and social-psychological reasons for wives working. Moreover, these determinants or reasons are different for those in higher-income families versus those in lower-income families. It is important to know the reasons wives work, because it may help in understanding their consumer-behavior patterns.[43]

An important consideration for the marketer is whether working women behave as consumers in the same way as do their nonworking counterparts. In general, the answer is that there are some important distinctions between the two groups. For example, working women's media behavior differs from that of nonworking women. They watch less television (particularly daytime) and read more magazines. Working women also spend somewhat more time listening to radio and reading newspapers.[44]

Research results also show that working women respond differently to advertising and that their responses reflect their interests, lifestyle, and usage patterns. For example, products and product categories with higher advertising recognition scores by working women include cigarettes, major appliances, personal hygiene products and hair products, passenger cars, pet supplies, and surprisingly, soaps, cleansers, and polishes.[45] Working versus nonworking women also exhibit some differences in product usage patterns. It should be noted, however, that for some durable goods and other products and services the existence of a working wife does not appear to be a determinant of whether the goods and services are purchased or of how much is spent, according to one recent study. Thus, though the wife's earnings raise family income, families with working wives do not spend any more or less frequently or heavily on some items than do families without working wives.[46] It might also be expected that employed wives, who report greater time pressures than nonemployed wives, should more intensively use strategies to economize on time (such as purchase of microwave ovens), but we find that income and life-cycle stage are more salient determinants of time use than is employment status.[47]

Marketing Implications   Mountains of statistical data could be cited regarding the changing role of women. However, what are some of the fundamental marketing implications suggested by these trends? The following list includes some of the more important ones:

1   Working women can justify economic expenditures for, and psychologically accept, expensive appliances and household equipment, such as microwave ovens and prepared foods, which may even reduce the wives' roles in important household tasks.

2   Working wives are often unable to shop during regular retailing hours. They might prefer that sales be held in the evening.

3   Some shopping may be done by wives' surrogates—daughters and sons. Shopping also becomes more of a shared husband and wife activity, or even a family venture. Saturdays, Sundays, and evenings become very important shopping times.

4   The distinction between men's and women's work in the home has blurred and a sense of shared household duties prevails. Appliances that formerly had an image of being a female appliance, such as a vacuum cleaner, tend to take on a unisex image.

5   Working women place a premium on a youthful appearance and on the "maintenance of self." Advancement in business is often associated with being young.

6   Working wives tend more to become equal decision makers in the home. This change is particularly noticeable among lower social classes where wives were very subordinated.

7   The availability of household services beyond the usual morning and afternoon household hours, such as repair services during weekends, will become increasingly important.

8   Price for some products may become less important than convenience, availability, service, and time savings.[48]

One area of marketing that is likely to be strongly influenced by women's changing roles is advertising. As one writer observes, "If advertising to the new woman is to persuade, it must treat women as intelligent adults who will respond to a reasonable and believable presentation of the product's case."[49] Many have been critical about the treatment of women in advertisements, particularly their limited role portrayal.[50] Role portrayal of females in television commercials, for instance, was found in the early 1970s to be quite different from their actual roles in the population. By the mid-1970s, research indicated considerable improvement in role portrayals of women.[51] However, by 1980 other research indicated that sexual stereotyping in television commercials had continued and even increased in some instances.[52] A study of magazine advertising over a twenty-year period revealed that although the percentage of women portrayed in working positions had not increased significantly since 1958, the kinds of roles they were associated with had been upgraded.[53]

Regarding the way in which women should be portrayed in advertisements, several suggestions have been offered:[54]

1   Ads for health and beauty products should appeal to a woman's sense of well being *for her own sake*—not to enhance her status as a sex object.

2   Whether a woman works or not, she should be shown as competent and creative in using products which help her to perform the tasks she perceives her roles and lifestyle necessitate.

3   If the target market is men, portraying women as decorative or alluring is appropriate. If the target market is traditional women or both women and men, portraying the women as equal partners or participants is appropriate. If the target market is contemporary women, portraying the women as successful or dominant is appropriate.

4   Show women as congenial and supportive of one another in a setting appropriate to the lifestyle of the target market.

5   Traditional women will attribute higher credibility to an authoritative male figure. This is especially true in product categories such as major appliances or those products which represent new technological developments. Contemporary women will prefer a female figure who has the necessary level of technical expertise. In promoting nontechnical products, including home and personal care products, all women will find a female with whose lifestyle they can identify to be the most credible.

Although these ideas have not been fully tested to determine their validity, they do offer the marketer some reasonable guidance in this area.

As advertisers seek to appeal to the changing woman, particularly the woman who works, some are breaking away from the stereotypes by showing dual roles, role switching, and role blending.[55] The use of *dual roles* portrays women in roles that are in addition to a more traditional role in the house, such as a wife/manager or mother/professional. For example, in a campaign aimed at getting female passengers to fly on Boeing aircraft, Boeing shows a businesswoman poring over paper work on a night flight, with the caption, "A woman's work is never done."[56]

The pressures of the various roles that many women play today have brought about advertisements pitched along dual role lines such as the TV jingle for Enjoli, "the 8-hour perfume for the 24-hour woman," which suggests:

I can put the wash on the line, feed the kids,
Get dressed, pass out the kisses,
And get to work by 5 of 9,
'Cause I'm a wo-man.

With *role switching,* purchase or use of the product is portrayed by persons of the sex opposite that of the traditional stereotype. For example, a recent "give-me-the-Campbell's-life" commercial showed a husband home from work dancing around the kitchen fixing soup and sandwiches just in time for his working wife to arrive home from the office.

Role blending obscures the role stereotype of purchaser or user by showing scenes in which no sex dominates. For example, car manufacturers often show a man and woman (or even the entire family) engaged in decision-making activity. In addition, food manufacturers sometimes show a man and woman shopping in the supermarket.

Market Segments Although we have been treating working and nonworking women as different homogeneous groups, it should be recognized that there are also variations within each group. In other words, segmentation of both markets reveals some important differences in orientations among the subsegments.

Recent large samples of U.S. adult females have identified two types of working wives and two types of homemakers. These four groups have been described as: (1) the working woman who thinks her work is a career; (2) the working woman who says it's just a job; (3) the homemaker who plans to work; and (4) the stay-at-home homemaker.[57] The most important characteristics of each group are shown in Table 10-6.

From the research, we summarize here a few of the consumer-behavior differences between these groups. The plan-to-work segment appears to be the most active and sophisticated in terms of shopping behavior; they are more actively involved in shopping and devote more skill and attention to it than other groups. The career segment is most concerned with shopping for clothes and is not oriented toward budgeting or shopping for specials. The stay-at-home group appears to be the most economy-minded of the segments. The least sophisticated and involved in shopping behavior is the just-a-job group.

Additionally, it appears that career women shop at specialty stores more than do either women who view their work as just a job or homemakers. Career and working women tend to shop more in the evenings and on weekends than do homemakers. These three groups also seem to use substantially different criteria for selecting retail stores in which to shop.[58]

Other research has found that career women and women who view their work as just a job display greater usage of print media (for example, newspapers and magazines), whereas homemakers rely more heavily on television (but not radio).[59]

Descriptions of market characteristics such as those above enable the marketer to tailor distribution approaches, promotional appeals, and product charac-

TABLE 10-6

Segments of Working Wives and Homemakers

Career working woman	Working woman who feels "It's just a job"
Is future- (vs. present-) oriented in terms of both her personal and her work life. Is relatively highly educated. Virtually 20 percent of the segment is non-white. Is youngest of the four in terms of age. Has the largest income of the four segments. Has the largest number of single females of all four segments. (Note that this includes divorced, widowed, and separated women) Tends not to live in a single-family dwelling. Most actively involved in shopping for clothes and household articles. Has the highest frequency of return rates for unsatisfactory products. Has the strongest positive self-image. Sees self as broad-minded, dominating, frank, efficient, independent, self-assured, and very amicable.	Views her work as dull. Believes that women's place is really "in the home." Has the lowest income of all four segments. Is the second highest in terms of percentage of the single women. Spends the least time in shopping for household articles.

Plan-to-work homemaker	Stay-at-home homemaker
Is interested in acquiring tangible products which additional income could provide. Is extroverted and visits others as well as entertains in her own home. Tends to reside in rural vs. urban locations. Tends to be younger in age. Highest percentage of married women are in this segment. Tends to have a larger household size. Actively involved in shopping for household articles. High usage of newspaper ads and sales announcements used in shopping for specials. Highest usage of a budget in grocery shopping. Tends to be tense, stubborn, and feels awkward. Describes herself as creative and affectionate.	High homemaker role orientation. High agreement with traditional attire (white gloves). Lowest educational attainment. Most live in rural residences. Oldest of all segments. Ranks second in terms of incomes over $15,000. Most are married. Largest percentage of households larger than four. Largest percentage of single-family dwellings. Least inclined to shop for clothes. Tends to utilize ads and sale announcements for shopping. Thinks of herself as kind, refined, and reserved. Much below the norm in feeling brave, stubborn, dominating, or egocentric.

Source: Dan H. Robertson, Danny H. Bellenger, and Barnett A. Greenberg, "Helping Marketers Understand the Female Markets," in Robert S. Franz, Robert M. Hopkins, and Alfred G. Toma (eds.), *Proceedings: Southern Marketing Association 1979 Conference*, Southern Marketing Association, Lafayette, La. 1979, pp. 319–320; and Rena Bartos. "What Every Marketer Should Know About Women," *Harvard Business Review*, May–June 1978, p. 81.

teristics to one of the segments, based on knowledge of their behavioral and attitude characteristics.

CHANGING MALE ROLES

I'm really knocked out. I have to take care of three children, prepare the food for them, do their laundry, bring them to school, pick them up. At the same time, of course, I have to make a living and try to hold on to my job.[60]

This quote does not seem too unusual until we push aside our stereotypes and realize that it comes, not from a woman, but from a 38-year-old divorced man. Such is the nature of changing roles for men in American society. A growing number of men in the 1980s will become single, "mother/father" combinations. Yet, this is only one facet of the nature of these role shifts.

Additional insight into changing men's roles comes from recent studies of the married male segment. An important finding is that large numbers of married men are assuming a wide variety of nontraditional family roles. For example, during a given two-week period: 32 percent do the main food shopping, 80 percent take care of the children (in households with children under age 12), 47 percent help cook a family meal, 33 percent cook an entire meal for the family, 39 percent vacuum the house, 29 percent do the laundry, 74 percent take out the garbage, 53 percent wash the dishes, and 28 percent clean the bathroom.[61] Not only are men increasingly pushing the shopping carts, but they are exhibiting shopping behavior that differs from that of women. For instance, when husbands do the grocery shopping they may well choose a brand different from the one the wife would have picked.[62]

Segmenting Husbands   As we have noted, there is an important segment of husbands who help a great deal around the house. This group is only one of the categories of married men, however. For instance, one study divides husbands into the following five segments:[63]

1   New Breed Husbands, representing 32 percent of all married men, willingly share with their wives household chores such as cooking, cleaning, and grocery shopping. They are usually under age 40 and are mostly white-collar workers and well-educated. Their wives work full-time, and they probably have young children.

2   Classics, representing 25 percent, believe women shouldn't work unless it's an economic necessity. They'll share responsibilities, but insist on having the final word.

3   Retired, 16 percent of the total. Typically over age 40, they are less involved in decision making and are remote from their families.

4   Bachelor Husband, 15 percent of all married men, is usually under age 30 and a "bachelor at heart." He normally doesn't make decisions with his wife or ask for her advice, and he is less inclined to feel that the family comes first.

5   Strugglers, 12 percent of total, think of themselves as ship captains. They demand that their wives keep the house clean, and they want the final say. Strugglers are usually in lower-income brackets and are middle-aged.

Although the modern role segment represents only one of the married male markets, the size of this group, combined with those who appear to be moving in that direction, offers some interesting possibilities for the marketer.

Marketing Implications   There are a number of implications that flow from the finding that a significant group of married men are much less traditional in their roles. First, increased male use of once traditionally female household products will mean that male users' product needs will have to be increasingly considered, more product testing among men will have to occur, and packaging will have to project an image compatible with men's use. Second, advertising for household products will portray men more often in domestic activities, with the potential for interesting and memorable situations. In fact, people are much more likely to remember commercials that show new roles for men and women than those that perpetuate stereotypes.[64] However, exaggerated and unreal presentations of men or women, whether traditional or progressive in style, cause significant consumer irritation.[65] Advertising of household products to men in a way that does not alienate them may be done by portraying the houseworking husband as a no-nonsense person knocking off a job because it has to be done—the pleasure coming from the accomplishment or completion, not the esthetic fulfillment. Also, advertisers should be careful not to portray husbands as just helping out their wives. Such an approach might alienate women who expect the sharing of household tasks as a right and obligation, not as a favor on the part of their mates.[66]

Product advantages significant to men will also become part of the advertising message for household products. Thus, ads must reassure men that the product meets their criteria of advantages and carries the appropriate brand image, while simultaneously supporting female selection of the brand. In addition, nontraditional advertising media for household products will be more widely used.[67]

GROWTH OF THE SINGLES MARKET

In the rotunda at New York's Madison Square Garden some 34,000 men and women recently plopped down $10 each to attend a trade show for the unattached, called Single in New York. Run by Everything for Singles, Inc., an $8-million-a-year company, the convention featured lots of lonely hearts eyeing each other while listening to the pitches of dating services, hotels, travel agents, and other less obvious participants in the getting-people-together industry. The most successful dating service companies are small, local, entrepreneurial outfits, though many are now expanding nationally via franchises or company-owned branches. A few already trade their shares publicly. But marketing a mate-service is tricky. Firms must strive for respectability; advertising must be sensitive and high-toned, with word-of-mouth endorsements being the best ads of all.[68]

The singles market in the United States consists of 60 million adults over 18 (56 percent female, 44 percent male), with most under 40, and relatively affluent. The tremendous rise of singles, especially among the young has been one of the

important market developments to occur in the last decade. The singles segment is growing over five times as fast as the nation as a whole, according to the U.S. Census Bureau, and it is estimated to account for over $1 out of $8 of total consumer spending for goods and services.[69] This growing segment of the American market has not been ignored by marketers. New product and service opportunities have opened up in a wide range of categories geared to this market. For example, consider the following:

BUILDING AND HOME FURNISHING   The smaller household of the future—both families and singles—means more apartments and condominiums and fewer homes. More furniture will be suitable for apartments. Practicality rather than status and prestige will be stressed. Mobility of furniture will be important, giving added emphasis to new design and styles, such as modular arrangements.

AUTOS   Smaller cars are the big seller here, but with emphasis on sporty styling and plenty of pleasure-oriented options, such as stereo. For example, Porsche estimated that in a recent year about half of their autos were bought by singles.

FOODS   More single and dual-serving packages, cans, plastic bags, and so on will be marketed, with convenience and disposability rather than economy being the prime benefits.

APPLIANCES   General Electric Co. expects 21 million new households in the 1980s, and it gleefully notes that each will need three to six major appliances plus one or more television sets. Magic Chef Inc. is stressing production of microwave ovens partly because of the numbers of single and divorced people who are setting up houses.[70]

MANAGERIAL REFLECTIONS

For our product or service situation . . .

1   Are families or households the target of greatest interest to us in marketing efforts?

2   Which family life-cycle stage is likely to be the most important in its consumption?

3   How does the family role structure play a part in its purchase and consumption?

4   What general patterns of purchase influence are exhibited among family members, and how do these influences change as the decision process continues?

5   How are changing female or male family roles influencing the marketing approaches necessary to reach and sell our prospects effectively?

DISCUSSION TOPICS

1   Distinguish between families and households. In what ways is each important to the marketer in analyzing consumer behavior?

2 Discuss the significance of the family in consumer behavior.

3 Describe the traditional and more modern family life-cycle stages. What influence does life cycle have on consumer behavior?

4 Explain how marketers of the following items would use the life-cycle concept in their strategies: (*a*) mutual funds, (*b*) pianos, (*c*) motor homes, (*d*) camping equipment.

5 Describe the meanings of the following family roles: (*a*) instrumental and expressive, (*b*) internal and external, (*c*) purchase-process. What is their significance in terms of consumer behavior and marketing strategy?

6 Referring to Figure 10-4 showing U.S. family decision-making power structures, explain how a marketer could use this information in developing marketing strategies (especially advertising and personal selling activities) for the following products: (*a*) living room furniture, (*b*) life insurance, (*c*) kitchenware, (*d*) automobiles.

7 Describe how family-specific characteristics influence the nature of purchasing decisions within the family.

8 Who is the gatekeeper in your family or household for product or brand decisions involving (*a*) furniture, (*b*) foods, (*c*) clothing, (*d*) financial services, (*e*) toys? Who is the opinion leader?

9 Write a report on one of the following subjects, indicating specifically what some of the effects on consumer behavior and marketing might be: (*a*) changing family values, (*b*) changing role of women, (*c*) women in advertisements, (*d*) divorce and alternative "family" arrangements.

10 Discuss the role of children in family decision making.

PROJECTS

1 Visit three local restaurants and assess how each attracts clientele in different stages of the family life cycle.

2 Interview salespeople who sell the following products: kitchenware, alcoholic beverages, life insurance, and living room furniture. Ask who mostly makes the purchasing decision for these items, the husband or wife? How do the observations of the salespeople compare to Figure 10-3?

NOTES

[1] Adapted from "Club Med in a Family Way," *American Demographics,* January 1987, pp. 24–25.
[2] This summary of life-cycle stages has been adapted from the following sources: William D. Wells and George Gubar, "Life Cycle Concept in Marketing Research," *Journal of Marketing Research,* **3:**355–363, November 1966; S. G. Barton, "The Life Cycle and Buying Patterns," in Lincoln H. Clark (ed.), *Consumer Behavior,* **2:**53–57, New York University Press, New York, 1955; John B. Lansing and James N. Morgan, "Consumer Finances Over the Life Cycle," in Clark (ed.), *Consumer Behavior,* pp. 36–51; and John B. Lansing and Leslie Kish, "Family Life Cycle as an Independent Variable," *American Sociological Review,* **22:**512–519, October 1957.

[3] Brad Edmondson, "How Big Is the Baby Market?" *American Demographics,* December 1985, p. 27.

[4] Johan Arndt, "Family Life Cycle as a Determinant of Size and Composition of Household Expenditures," in William L. Wilkie (ed.), *Advances in Consumer Research,* vol. 6, Association for Consumer Research, Ann Arbor, Mich., 1979, pp. 128–132.

[5] Stuart U. Rich and Subhash C. Jain, "Social Class and Life Cycle as Predictors of Shopping Behavior," *Journal of Marketing Research,* **5:**41–49, February 1968; Ben M. Enis and Keith K. Cox, "Demographic Analysis of Store Patronage Patterns: Uses and Pitfalls," in Robert L. King (ed.), *Marketing and the New Science of Planning,* American Marketing Association, Chicago, 1968, pp. 366–370; and Barton, "The Life Cycle."

[6] George P. Moschis, "Socialization Perspectives and Consumer Behavior," in Ben M. Enis and Kenneth J. Roering (eds.), *Review of Marketing, 1981,* American Marketing Association, Chicago, 1981, p. 49.

[7] National Industrial Conference Board, *Expenditure Patterns of the American Family,* Life, New York, 1965.

[8] Bernard Berelson and Gary Steiner, *Human Behavior: An Inventory of Scientific Findings,* Harcourt, New York, 1964, p. 314.

[9] R. F. Bales, "In Conference," *Harvard Business Review,* **32:**44–50, March–April 1954.

[10] William F. Kenkel, "Husband-Wife Interaction in Decision-Making and Decision Choices," *The Journal of Social Psychology,* **54:**260, 1961.

[11] Robert Ferber and Lucy Chao Lee, "Husband-Wife Influence in Family Purchasing Behavior," *Journal of Consumer Research,* **1:**43–50, June 1974.

[12] John S. Coulson, "Buying Decisions Within the Family and the Consumer Brand Relationship," in Joseph W. Newman (ed.), *On Knowing the Consumer,* Wiley, New York, 1967, p. 60.

[13] Lewis A. Berey and Richard Pollay, "The Influencing Role of the Child in Family Decision-Making, *Journal of Marketing Research,* **5:**72, February 1968.

[14] P. G. Herbst, "Conceptual Framework for Studying the Family," in O. A. Oeser and S. B. Hammond (eds.), *Social Structure and Personality in a City,* Routledge, London, 1954.

[15] Harry L. Davis and Benny P. Rigaux, "Perceptions of Marital Roles in Decision Processes," *The Journal of Consumer Research,* **1:**51–62, June 1974.

[16] E. H. Bonfield, "Perception of Marital Roles in Decision Processes: Replication and Extension," in H. Keith Hunt (ed.), *Advances in Consumer Research,* vol. 5, Association for Consumer Research, Ann Arbor, Mich., 1978, pp. 300–307.

[17] See for example, Arch G. Woodside, "Dominance and Conflict in Family Purchasing Decisions," in M. Venkatesan (ed.), *Proceedings of the Third Annual Conference,* Association for Consumer Research, Chicago, 1972, pp. 650–659; and Elizabeth H. Wolgast, "Do Husbands or Wives Make the Purchasing Decisions?" *Journal of Marketing,* **22:**151–158, October 1958.

[18] Haley, Overholser & Associates, Inc., *Purchase Influence,* New Canaan, Conn., January 1975.

[19] This section is based on Harry L. Davis, "Decision Making Within the Household," *Journal of Consumer Research,* **2:**254–256, March 1976; and Michael A. Belch, George E. Belch, and Donald Sciglimpaglia, "Conflict in Family Decision Making: An Exploratory Investigation," in Jerry C. Olson (ed.), *Advances in Consumer Research,* vol. 7, Association for Consumer Research, Ann Arbor, Mich., 1980, pp. 475–479.

[20] Jagdish N. Sheth, "A Theory of Family Buying Decisions," in Jagdish N. Sheth (ed.), *Models of Buyer Behavior,* Harper & Row, New York, 1974, p. 33.

[21] John Scanzoni, "Changing Sex Roles and Emerging Directions in Family Decision Making," *Journal of Consumer Research,* **4:**185–188, December 1977.

[22] Isabella C. M. Cunningham and Robert T. Green, "Purchasing Roles in the U.S. Family, 1955 and 1973," *Journal of Marketing,* **38:**64, October 1974; "Marketing Observer," *Business Week,* September 28, 1974, p. 18; and Haley, Overholser & Associates, Inc., *Purchase Influence.*

[23] See for example, Arch G. Woodside and John F. Willenborg, "Husband and Wife Interactions and Marketing Decisions," *Southern Journal of Business,* **7:**55, May 1972; and "A Pilot Study of the Roles of Husbands and Wives in Purchasing Decisions," conducted for *Life* magazine by L. Jaffe Associates, Inc., 1965.

[24] John Fayerweather, *International Marketing,* 2d ed., Prentice-Hall, Englewood Cliffs, N.J., 1970, p. 25.

25 Susan P. Douglas, "A Cross-National Exploration of Husband-Wife Involvement in Selected Household Activities," in William L. Wilkie (ed.), *Advances in Consumer Research,* vol. 6, Association for Consumer Research, Ann Arbor, Mich., 1979, pp. 364–371.

26 Douglas J. Dalrymple, Thomas S. Robertson, and Michael Y. Yoshino, "Consumption Behavior Across Ethnic Categories," *California Management Review,* **14:**64–70, Fall 1971.

27 James F. Engel, David T. Kollat, and Roger D. Blackwell, *Consumer Behavior,* 2d ed., Holt, New York, 1973, pp. 199–200; and Mira Komarovsky, "Class Differences in Family Decision-Making on Expenditures," in Nelson Foote (ed.), *Household Decision-Making,* New York University Press, New York, 1961, p. 258.

28 Wolgast, "Do Husbands or Wives Make the Purchasing Decisions?" p. 154.

29 Donald H. Granbois, "The Role of Communication in the Family Decision-Making Process," in Stephen A. Greyser (ed.), *Toward Scientific Marketing,* American Marketing Association, Chicago, 1963, pp. 44–57.

30 Komarovsky, "Class Differences," pp. 255–265.

31 Wolgast, "Do Husbands or Wives Make the Purchasing Decisions?" p. 154.

32 Pierre Filiatrault and J. R. Brent Ritchie, "Joint Purchasing Decisions: A Comparison of Influence Structure in Family and Couple Decision-Making Units," *Journal of Consumer Research,* **7:**131–140, September 1980.

33 "Poll Shows Shared Roles in Marriage Are Gaining," *Providence Sunday Journal,* November 27, 1977, p. A-20.

34 "Sex . . . Marriage . . . Divorce—What Women Think Today," *U.S. News & World Report,* October 21, 1974, p. 107.

35 "Males Don't Like New Woman: DDB," *Advertising Age,* October 20, 1980, p. 60.

36 Alladi Venkatesh, "Changing Roles of Women—A Life-Style Analysis," *Journal of Consumer Research,* **7:**189–197, September 1980.

37 Shirley Wilkins and Thomas A. W. Miller, "Working Women: How It's Working Out," *Public Opinion,* October/November 1985, p. 47.

38 "Ads Glorifying Career 'Superwomen' Can Alienate Full-time Housewives," *Marketing News,* May 1, 1981, pp. 1–2.

39 "Research Profiles Pragmatic, Unliberated Woman Segment; Suggests Marketing Appeals," *Marketing News,* May 15, 1981, pp. 1, 7.

40 "Research Profiles," pp. 1, 7.

41 Rena Bartos, "The Moving Target: The Impact of Women's Employment on Consumer Behavior," *Journal of Marketing,* **41:**31, July 1977.

42 "The Working Woman," *Media Decisions,* February 1976, pp. 53–54.

43 Jeanne L. Hafstrom and Marilyn M. Dunsing, "Socioeconomic and Social-Psychological Influences on Reasons Wives Work," *Journal of Consumer Research,* **5:**169–175, December 1978.

44 "The Working Woman," p. 54.

45 "Marketers Told How to Reach Working Women," *Editor & Publisher,* June 9, 1979, p. 48.

46 Myra H. Strober and Charles B. Weinberg, "Working Wives and Major Family Expenditures," *Journal of Consumer Research,* **4:**141–147, December 1977.

47 Myra H. Strober and Charles B. Weinberg, "Strategies Used by Working and Nonworking Wives to Reduce Time Pressures," *Journal of Consumer Research,* **6:**338–348, March 1980.

48 Reprinted from William Lazer and John E. Smallwood, "The Changing Demographics of Women," *Journal of Marketing,* **41:**21–22, July 1977, published by the American Marketing Association.

49 E. B. Weiss, "New Life Styles of 1975–1980 Will Throw Switch on Admen," *Advertising Age,* September 18, 1972, p. 62.

50 See for example Michael B. Mazis and Marilyn Beuttenmuller, "Attitudes Toward Women's Liberation and Perception of Advertisements," in M. Venkatesan (ed.), *Proceedings of the Third Annual Conference,* Association for Consumer Research, Chicago, 1972, p. 428; Alice E. Courtney and Sarah W. Lockeretz, "A Woman's Place: An Analysis of the Roles Portrayed by Women in Magazine Advertisements," *Journal of Marketing Research,* **8:**95, February 1971; and Louis C. Wagner and Janis B. Banos, "A Woman's Place: A Follow-up Analysis of the Roles Portrayed by Women in Magazine Advertisements," *Journal of Marketing Research,* **10:**213–214, May 1973.

51 Kenneth C. Schneider and Sharon B. Schneider, "Trends in Sex Roles in Television Commercials," *Journal of Marketing,* **43:**79–84, Summer 1979.

[52] Michael F. d'Amico and John W. Hummel, "Sex Role Portrayals in Television Commercials: 1971, 1976, 1980," in John H. Summey and Ronald D. Taylor (eds.), *Evolving Marketing Thought for 1980,* Southern Marketing Association, Carbondale, Ill., 1980, pp. 396–399.

[53] Marc G. Weinberger, Susan M. Petroshius, and Stuart A. Westin, "Twenty Years of Women in Magazine Advertising: An Update," in Neil Beckwith et al. (eds.), *1979 Educator's Conference Proceedings,* American Marketing Association, Chicago, 1979, pp. 373–377.

[54] Mary Lou Roberts and Perri B. Koggan, "How Should Women Be Portrayed in Advertisements?— A Call for Research," in William L. Wilkie (ed.), *Advances in Consumer Research,* vol. 6, Association for Consumer Research, Ann Arbor, Mich., 1979, pp. 66–72.

[55] William J. Lundstrom and Donald Sciglimpaglia, "Sex Role Portrayals in Advertising." *Journal of Marketing,* **41**:78, July 1977.

[56] Ellen Graham, "Advertisers Take Aim at a Neglected Market: The Working Woman," *The Wall Street Journal,* July 5, 1977, pp. 1, 5.

[57] Dan H. Robertson, Danny N. Bellenger, and Barnett A. Greenberg, "Helping Marketers Understand the Female Markets," in Robert S. Franz, Robert M. Hopkins, and Alfred G. Toma (eds.), *Proceedings: Southern Marketing Association 1979 Conference,* Southern Marketing Association, Lafayette, La., 1979, pp. 317–320; and Rena Bartos, "What Every Marketer Should Know About Women," *Harvard Business Review,* May–June 1978, p. 81.

[58] Elizabeth C. Hirschman, "Women's Self-Ascribed Occupational Status and Retail Patronage," in Kent B. Monroe (ed.), *Advances in Consumer Research,* vol. 8, Association for Consumer Research, Ann Arbor, Mich., 1981, pp. 648–654.

[59] Elizabeth C. Hirschman, "Women's Role Perceptions and Usage of Information Sources," in Robert S. Franz, Robert M. Hopkins, and Alfred G. Toma (eds.), *Proceedings: Southern Marketing Association 1979 Conference,* Southern Marketing Association, Lafayette, La., 1979, pp. 313–316.

[60] Ernest Dichter, "New Roles and Interests for Men in the 1980s," *Marketing Communications,* in SCAN, July 1980, p. 21.

[61] Benton & Bowles, *American Consensus: Men's Changing Role in the Family of the '80s,* Benton & Bowles, Inc., New York, September 1980, pp. 2–3.

[62] Jo-Ann Zbytniewski, "The Men Who Man the Shopping Carts," *Progressive Grocer,* May 1979, p. 44; and Jo-Ann Zbytniewski, "Consumer Watch," *Progressive Grocer,* March 1980, p. 37.

[63] Reprinted from "New Research Identifies Five Subsegments of Married Men," *Marketing News,* November 14, 1980, p. 7, published by the American Marketing Association.

[64] Cyndy Scheibe, "Sex Roles in TV Commercials," *Journal of Marketing Research,* **19**:23–27, February 1979.

[65] Thomas W. Whipple and Alice E. Courtney, "How to Portray Women in TV Commercials," *Journal of Advertising Research,* **20**:53–59, April 1980.

[66] "Males Don't Like New Woman: DDB."

[67] Benton & Bowles, *American Consensus: Men's Changing Role;* and Gay Sands Miller, "Change of Pitch: More Food Advertisers Woo the Male Shopper as He Shares the Load," *The Wall Street Journal,* August 26, 1980, pp. 1, 21.

[68] Edward C. Baig, "Making Money Helping Singles Mingle," *Fortune,* February 18, 1985, pp. 98–103.

[69] Fabian Linden, "Singular Spending Patterns," *Across the Board,* July 1979, p. 31.

[70] "Household Growth Could Spurt in '80s, But Much Hinges on Lifestyle Changes," *The Wall Street Journal,* July 1, 1980, p. 23.

PERSONAL INFLUENCE AND DIFFUSION OF INNOVATIONS

LEARNING OBJECTIVES

After studying this chapter, you should understand . . .

■ The nature and significance to marketers of personal and word-of-mouth communications

■ How the communication and influence process operates between marketers and consumers

■ The characteristics of opinion leaders, reasons that they influence others, and reasons that their leadership is accepted

■ The nature of an innovation

■ How individuals move through stages in a process of product adoption

■ The characteristics of groups or categories of adopters making up the diffusion process by which an innovation spreads through a market

■ What factors influence the rate of diffusion for an innovation

■ What marketing strategies are appropriate in utilizing the personal influence process

When it comes to consumer electronics, "Taffies" should be watched carefully because they have been found to be a critical part of the success of new electronic products. No, Taffies are not some unusual components made of silicon; they are the gadget freaks who enjoy snapping up the latest gee-whiz electronic products—even if it means skipping lunch for the next two months to pay for them. These people, sometimes considered oddballs, are almost infallible bellwethers of a new electronic product's chances for great success. According to the new head of one consulting firm who has studied them, "if you fail with this group, you're doomed. . . . If you succeed, your chances are very good, though not guaranteed, because other consumers view these people as the innovators—the experts they turn to for advice." These Technologically Advanced Families—TAFs, or Taffies, for short—are almost seven times more likely to have a

11

personal computer than the general public is (81 percent versus 12 percent, respectively) and more than three times as likely to own a videocassette recorder.

Taffies are integrating consumer electronics into their lifestyles by planning their schedules on personal computers, waking up to digital alarms, cooking in microwave ovens, listening to portable stereos while headed to work or school and to their high-fidelity components during the evening, or using VCRs to watch time-shifted programs on their large-screen TVs. In contrast to the electronics buffs who used to lead the consumer electronic field, this group buys practical products that have mass-market potential. They investigate and make the decision as to whether a product offers enough performance for the price. Their actions determine the direction of the mass market, since their homes become the showcases for the products. They account for about 11 percent of American families, or about 9.2 million households, twice as many as a decade ago, but they are not all affluent yuppies. Most Taffies have incomes ranging from $25,000 to $40,000. As marketers learn about the lifestyles and attitudes of Taffies, future electronic products may be enhanced in ways that will generate strong Taffie appeal.[1]

This chapter further investigates the way in which individuals influence each other's behavior as consumers. We shall first describe the nature of influence and then discuss its significance as evidenced by word-of-mouth communication among individuals. Next, models of the flow of communication will be examined to better understand how personal influence occurs. Then we shall discuss the nature and significance of opinion leadership in marketing and the characteristics of leaders as well as followers. The concept of personal influence is strongly embodied in the process of adoption and diffusion of innovations; thus this topic will also be examined to understand better its significance to the marketer. Finally, we shall see how the marketer can use the concept of influence to his or her advantage by incorporating opinion leadership as a cornerstone of promotional programs.

THE NATURE AND SIGNIFICANCE OF PERSONAL INFLUENCE

Personal influence is best described as the effect or change in a person's attitudes or behavior as a result of communication with others. It can occur in a number of ways. The following distinctions can be made to indicate the multidimensional nature of this communication phenomenon:

1 Communication leading to influence may be *source-initiated* (by the influencer) or *recipient-initiated* (by the influencee).

2 Communication may result in *one-way* or *two-way* influence. That is, the individual may influence while being influenced.

3 Communication resulting in influence may be *verbal* or *visual*.[2]

Personal influence is frequently used synonymously with the term ''word-of-mouth'' advertising or communication, even though the above classification indicates that they are not the same. Since word-of-mouth is oral communication, it is actually a subset of personal influence; however, we shall use the terms synonymously in this chapter.

Promotional activities conducted by the marketer are not the only or necessarily the most important influences on purchasing behavior. There is evidence that favorable word-of-mouth communication can actually have more influence than the huge sums spent on advertising. Consequently, many companies advertise little and depend, instead, on word-of-mouth promotion. Here are some examples of word-of-mouth advertising's impact:

In-depth interviews on buyer motivations, done by one research organization, frequently found that friends, experts, or relatives told the individual about the product—and that is why the product was purchased. At times, the influence of "recommenders" ran as high as 80 percent.[3]

A study of durable goods purchases found that word-of-mouth was the major information source, with over 50 percent of the sample turning to friends for advice.[4]

Among male and female students at a large southern university, nearly 50 percent discussed clothing brands, styles, retail outlets, and prices with their friends.[5]

Word-of-mouth advertising is very important in the motion-picture industry.

The marketer frequently tries to create a "synthetic" word-of-mouth program by using celebrities in advertising campaigns. These spokespeople enter our homes via the media and speak to us as if it were a one-to-one conversation. This simulated personal influence may nevertheless be very effective. There are two excellent illustrations of the way in which celebrities may affect our behavior as consumers:

When Clark Gable took off his shirt in a 1934 movie *It Happened One Night,* he revealed a bare chest. As a result, undershirt sales are said to have dropped 75 percent that year.[6]

Johnny Carson once suggested in his *Tonight Show* monologue that there was an acute shortage of toilet paper in the United States. (His source was a Wisconsin congressman who had actually been referring only to the cheaper federal government issue of toilet paper.) As a result, people dashed to their supermarkets to stock up; within one week, there actually was a shortage of the better toilet paper.[7]

It is clear that personal influence—whether actual or synthetic—can be quite convincing. The marketer is vitally interested in this process because a product's success appears dependent on it. It is very important, therefore, that mostly favorable, not unfavorable, communications take place. As one study of the spread of usage in a new food product in a married students' housing complex showed, exposure to favorable word-of-mouth communication increased the probability of purchase, while exposure to unfavorable comments decreased the probability.[8]

Why is word-of-mouth communication so strong? There seem to be three main reasons for its dominant position in relation to impersonal media:

1 Consumers view word-of-mouth as reliable and trustworthy information which can help people to make better buying decisions.

2 In contrast to the mass media, personal contacts can provide social support and give a stamp of approval to a purchase.

3 The information provided is often backed up by social-group pressure to force compliance with recommendations.[9]

In order to understand better the way in which personal influence and word-of-mouth advertising occur, several models of the communication process will be presented.

MODELS OF COMMUNICATION AND INFLUENCE FLOW

Personal influence is necessarily dependent upon the process of communication. The marketer may view the situation in several ways: as a one-step process; as a two-step flow of communication; or as a multiple-step model of interaction. Let's examine these various interpretations of the way in which influence results from communication.

THE ONE-STEP MODEL

For years, marketers operated under the assumptions contained in the one-step or one-way model of communication. In this model, portrayed in Figure 11-1, communication is represented as a one-way process flowing from the marketer to consumers. Notice that this model of communication assumes the marketer is directing the appeal to *each* consumer expecting that the consumer will (1) notice the advertisement, (2) be informed, persuaded, or reminded by it, and (3) buy the product or service.[10]

This model has been criticized, however, for its oversimplification. First of all, few messages actually reach consumers, and those that do are not likely to elicit a response directly. Product sales are influenced by many other marketing and extraneous variables in addition to the promotional communication.

Because of these drawbacks, communications researchers turned to a more

FIGURE 11-1
The one-step model of communication.

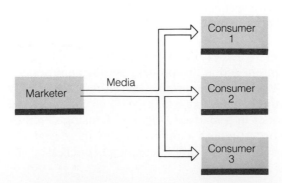

sophisticated explanation of the influence process—one that recognized the influence not only of impersonal channels (such as radio, television, and magazines), but also personal channels of communication and influence. This was the development of the two-step flow theory of communication.

THE TWO-STEP FLOW MODEL

The process of communication and influence has been found not to be an exclusively direct flow as had been originally supposed. Instead, it appears that influence occurs in a two-step flow, moving first from the mass media directly to influentials, or *opinion leaders,* who then through interpersonal networks pass on to their associates what they have seen or heard. The two-step model is illustrated in Figure 11-2.

The two-step model represents an improvement over the one-step scheme because it recognizes the influence of interpersonal contact. However, it also has certain limitations. Among the biggest problems are (1) it suggests that an absolute leader exists for each informal group, when actually all group members have some amount of opinion leadership; (2) information is assumed to flow only from the mass media to opinion leaders who disseminate it to followers—actually followers are also in touch with mass media, but perhaps not to the same degree as leaders; and (3) it is not always *influence* that is transmitted interpersonally, but in some cases simply information, which may be relatively free of influence.[11]

Thus, the two-step communication model has merit, but it implies a passive audience and active, information-seeking opinion leaders. Because of these limitations, many communications researchers now suggest a multistep interaction model as a more accurate representation of personal influence.

MULTISTEP MODELS

Researchers have shown that audiences are not simply passive receivers of communication. Instead, they have been found in several studies to be active seekers and important links in the flow of market information. Many audience members act as transmitters and receivers of information. One study found a similarity between opinion leaders and opinion seekers. In fact, almost two-thirds of opinion seekers also viewed themselves as opinion leaders in a product category, underscoring the view that opinion leadership is more of an exchange of opinion and information than a one-way flow of influence.[12] It has, furthermore,

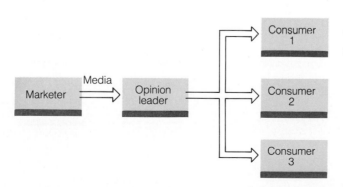

FIGURE 11-2
The two-step model of communication.

been suggested that the flow of communication may take place through three or more stages. Figure 11-3 presents a model of this process.

Consider the following examples of the different directions that a verbal flow of communication and personal influence may take between a source and a receiver:

1 Source-initiated, one-way influence (this is most typical of the two-step flow model): "Jim told me how good his B. F. Goodrich radials are, so I decided to buy a set."

2 Receiver-initiated, one-way influence: "I asked Jim what kind of tire he recommends."

3 Source-initiated, two-way influence: "I showed Susan our new Jenn-Air range. She really wants to buy one when her old stove gives out. Her interest made me feel better about our range's higher price."

4 Receiver-initiated, two-way influence: "I asked Carol what she knew about electric ranges. We had an interesting discussion of the features of different brands."

Of course, we could add additional levels to the flow and a visual mode of communication as well. The point is that obviously the communication process and flow of influence is much more involved than previously imagined. In the next section, we will more closely examine the nature of personal influence as effected through opinion leadership.

OPINION LEADERSHIP IN MARKETING

Opinion leaders were defined in Chapter 10 as those people who are able, in a given situation, to exert personal influence. They are the ones to whom others look for advice and information. Now, let us describe these people more specifically.

The term "opinion leader" is perhaps unfortunate because it tends to connote

FIGURE 11-3
A multistep model of communication.

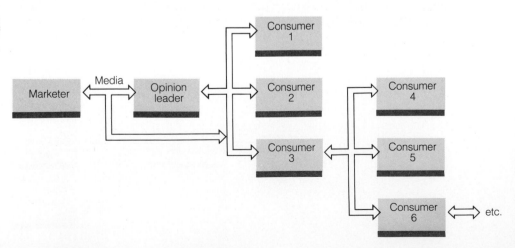

people of high status who make major decisions for the rest of us. In the marketing context, such a designation is unfortunate because it erroneously suggests an absolute leader whom others seek to follow. In effect, opinion leadership is a relative concept, and the opinion leader may not be much more influential than his followers.[13]

Nevertheless, opinion leaders can informally and subtly affect the behavior of others toward products, either positively or negatively. If they like a product or service, they can help to assure its success; if they do not like it, they can contribute to its failure. It all depends on the verbal and/or visual communication that flows between them and others whom they influence.

For communication of marketing information through two- or multistep flow models, opinion leadership is important and is found at all levels in society. That is, consumers tend to be influenced by those who are members of the same groups, people very much like themselves. Thus, every status level and every group will have opinion leaders, with the flow of influence being generally horizontal within them. However, the fact that opinion leaders are found in all strata of society does not necessarily mean that they are equally effective or important to the marketer at each social level. In fact, personal influence appears to be more operative and to have greater importance and effectiveness at higher-income and status levels.[14] These, then, are the levels which the marketer is often more concerned about reaching. Such opinion leaders may have an important impact on markets, as follows:

Influential Americans—one of every ten adults—are the trendsetters of the marketplace according to one research organization. They are among the first to try new products. They are better educated and earn more money than the average American and are typically married and in their 30s or 40s. They are categorized as influential if they have engaged in at least three public activities within the last year—such as running for political office, attending a public meeting, or making a speech. They are attracted more than the average citizen to civic, local, and national affairs and are ''addicted'' to TV newscasts and newspapers. They seek product quality at a reasonable price, enjoy shopping in specialty stores and by mail, but do not like telemarketing sales calls.[15]

WHO ARE OPINION LEADERS?

Because personal influence of opinion leaders is quite significant, marketers are obviously interested in trying to reach such influentials. To do so, however, requires that they first be identified and segmented. Perhaps they may then be reached with promotional messages and may then participate in additional communication and influence with their fellow group members.

Characteristics Numerous studies have been conducted attempting to identify opinion leader characteristics. The research is not conclusive, but we have some understanding of the opinion leader's profile:

1 Opinion leaders have approximately the same social-class position as nonleaders, although they may have higher social status within the class.[16] This does not mean that personal influence does not flow across different class lines, but it is likely to be infrequent and of a visual nature rather than verbal.

2   Opinion leaders have greater exposure to mass media that are relevant to their area of interest.[17] For example, opinion leaders for women's fashions could be expected to have higher exposure to such magazines as *Vogue* and *Glamour*. Similarly, automobile opinion leaders might be expected to read *Motor Trend* or *Hot Rod*. Exposure to relevant mass media provides them with information useful in enhancing their leadership potential.

3   Opinion leaders have greater interest and knowledge of the area of influence than do nonleaders. This finding is closely related to their greater media exposure. Of course, knowledge is not a prerequisite for opinion leader influence. Undoubtedly, much influence takes place by those who are ignorant of the topic of conversation.

4   Opinion leaders are more gregarious than nonleaders are. This finding is logical, given that they must interact with those whom they influence. Thus, opinion leaders are generally more sociable or companionable.

5   Opinion leaders have more innovativeness than do nonleaders. This does not mean, however, that they are *innovators* (the first people to purchase a new item). In fact, innovators and opinion leaders have been found in several studies to have differing characteristics and lifestyles. In the fashion market, for instance, the innovator is seen as an adventurer who is the earliest visual communicator of the newest styles aimed at the mass of fashion consumers.[18] The opinion leader, however, may be characterized more as an "editor" of fashions, who defines and endorses appropriate standards.

6   Opinion leaders are also more familiar with and loyal to group standards and values than are nonleaders. This refers to the fact that opinion leaders are vested with leadership authority by group members, and in order to maintain this position, the individual has to reflect underlying norms and values for that area of consumption leadership. The clothing influential, for instance, cannot be too far ahead of or behind fashion, but must reflect the current norms in clothing.

"General" Opinion Leaders   The question of whether generalized opinion leaders exist for a wide variety of products as opposed to specialized opinion leaders for each product has been the subject of much debate. Although research is often conflicting, it appears that there is *moderate* opinion leadership overlap across product categories; that is, general opinion leaders do appear to exist to some extent. One of the keys to this question seems to be the interest patterns of opinion leaders, with highest overlap existing among product categories involving similar interests.[19]

   The existence of generalized opinion leaders, or more precisely, opinion leadership overlap, does not mean, however, that such individuals are opinion leaders for *all* product categories. One study of seven product-interest areas, for example, found that only about 3 percent of the respondents were opinion leaders for at least five of the items.[20]

Situational Opinion Leaders   In the absence of a standardized, clear-cut opinion leader profile applying across all products, and where influencers and influencees seem to be so much alike, how is the opinion leader distinguished from those who follow? It has been suggested that influence is related to the following factors:

1 *The personification of certain values* (who one is). Thus, individuals who closely represent or personify group values are likely to be opinion leaders. For example, if some particular clothing style is valued by the group, the individual most closely representing this is likely to be influential.

2 *Competence* (what one knows). An individual who is very knowledgeable about some topic valued by the group will probably be influential.

3 *Strategic social location* (whom one knows inside and outside the group). For example, an individual who is available and active in the interpersonal communication process in her sorority will have a better chance for a leadership position.[21]

Thus, influence takes place because opinion leaders personify group norms, exhibit competence, and are accessible with active communication between themselves and others.

Because such leadership is situational and does not have a consistent pattern of characteristics across products, marketers might investigate the three characteristics cited above with regard to those who consume particular goods or services. In this way, they may uncover specific patterns which could then guide marketing strategies.

WHY OPINION LEADERS ATTEMPT TO INFLUENCE OTHERS

Consumers, generally, do not speak about products or services unless they expect to derive some kind of satisfaction from the activity. We can categorize four reasons that opinion leaders engage in word-of-mouth communication about products or services:

1 *Product-involvement*. Use of a product or service may create a tension that may need to be reduced by way of talk, recommendation, and enthusiasm to provide relief. For example, consumers often are fascinated by new items and feel they must tell someone about how good a product they've found.

2 *Self-involvement*. In this case, the emphasis is more on ways the influencer can gratify certain emotional needs. Product talk can achieve such goals as the following:

Gaining attention. People can have something to say in a conversation by talking about products rather than people or ideas.

Showing connoisseurship. Talk about certain products can show one is "in the know" and has good judgment.

Feeling like a pioneer. The speaker likes to identify with the newness and uniqueness of products and their pioneering manufacturers.

Having inside information. The speaker is able to show how much more he or

she knows about the product and its manufacturer than the listener (and thus how clever the speaker is).

Suggesting status. Talking about products with social status may elevate the speaker to the level of its users.

Spreading the gospel. The speaker may be able to convert the listener to using the product.

Seeking confirmation The more followers accept his or her advice about the product, the more assured the speaker feels about his or her own decision.

Asserting superiority. Recommending products to listeners can help the speaker gain leadership and test the extent to which others will follow.

3 *Other-involvement*. In this case, product talk fills the need to "give" something to the listener, to share one's happiness with the influencee, or to express care, love, or friendship.

4 *Message-involvement*. Talking may also be stimulated by great interest in the messages used to present the product. For example, advertising that is highly original and entertaining may be the topic of conversation, especially since most of us feel we are experts on effective advertising and can thus speak as critics.[22]

WHY FOLLOWERS ACCEPT PERSONAL INFLUENCE

The marketer would certainly want to know the situational attributes under which opinion leadership will most likely occur so that he or she could actively cultivate the process. There are numerous product, individual, and group characteristics that can be expected to influence the acceptance of opinion leadership by followers. Only a few of these will be cited here.[23]

Product characteristics are important in judging the significance of personal influence. For example, when products are highly visible or conspicuous (such as clothing as opposed to laundry detergents), they are more susceptible to personal influence. Products that can be tried or tested and compared against objective criteria are less susceptible to personal influence than those that cannot be tried. Product complexity may also give rise to the occurrence of personal influence, as would a product that is high on the amount of risk which consumers perceive to be associated with its purchase.

Using these four factors to evaluate products helps the marketer to determine when opinion leadership is apt to be strong. For example, most food products would be expected to have little opinion leadership while small appliances would be thought to have much more personal influence. However, one research study indicates that opinion seeking is not limited to particular types of goods but ranges across nondurables and durables, with the highest incidence occurring in the food category. Perhaps the process involves consumers' use of social communications more as a means of acquiring product information than as a means for reducing risk or evaluating complex products.[24]

Individual consumer characteristics and group influences are also important in determining the extent to which opinion leadership will be operative. For example, individuals who are other-directed look to other people for behavioral guidance, in contrast to those who are inner-directed and rely on their own value systems for direction. Also, individuals who face new life experiences (such as newlyweds or retirees) may be very receptive to information and consequently be quite susceptible to personal influence. In addition, those who aspire to membership in particular groups are receptive to personal influence and may emulate the behavior of group members. A final factor to be mentioned that affects acceptance of opinion leadership is the individual's personality. For example, some individuals are more persuasible than others.

THE MARKET MAVEN

A view that broadens the concept of opinion leaders is that of the market maven. The term ''maven'' is Yiddish and connotes a neighborhood expert who has information ranging over several topics. ''Market mavens,'' therefore, are defined as individuals having information about many kinds of products, places to shop, and other facets of markets, who initiate discussions with consumers and respond to their requests for market information.[25] This definition is similar to that of the opinion leader in that influence is derived from knowledge and expertise. However, it differs in that the market maven's expertise is of a more general market, rather than one of a product-specific nature. Market mavens do not have to be early purchasers of products or necessarily even users of products about which they have information.

Although there has been no clear demographic or psychographic profile identified for these influencers, they do appear to be aware of new products earlier; provide information to other consumers across product categories; engage in general-market information seeking; have greater participation in market activities, couponing, and reading advertisements; and have higher than average general media usage. They enjoy shopping and use browsing and shopping as an important way of learning about new products.[26]

While opinion leaders and early purchasers of products may be important prospects when diffusing information about new products, their usefulness may be limited in communicating other information such as changes in prices, availability of products, new stores, and the like. Here, mavens may be useful targets for marketers because they appear to have knowledge about a wide array of goods and services and about the process of acquiring them, and they are also active in providing other people with information and advice. Retailers and producers of low-involvement items (such as convenience goods), particularly, may find these influences very important in the spread of information. Unfortunately, until more is known about market mavens, targeting them with communications will be difficult.

ADOPTION AND DIFFUSION OF INNOVATIONS

The innovation adoption and diffusion processes will be discussed in this section to illustrate the way in which communication and interpersonal influence work with new products.

WHAT IS AN INNOVATION?

New-product innovation is an essential element of the dynamic American economy and a critical activity for the marketer. As new and better products are

developed, they are launched in the marketplace and their fate is determined by votes of consumers through their purchase or rejection of the products. New-product introductions are becoming more expensive, and the chances of product success are less than in previous years.[27] Thus it is important to understand the nature of an innovation and how individuals and groups of consumers adopt them.

The term "innovation" can be defined in several ways. One view based on consumer perceptions defines it as "any idea, practice, or material artifact perceived to be new by the relevant adopting unit."[28] Another view establishes a continuum or range of newness based on the product's effect on established consumption patterns. Under this conception three categories of innovation are classified as described below:

1 *Continuous innovations* have the least disrupting influence on established consumption pattersn. Product alteration is involved, rather than the establishment of a totally new product. Examples of products that are representative of this situation are fluoride toothpaste, new-model automobile changeovers, and menthol cigarettes.

2 *Dynamically continuous innovations* have more disrupting effects than do continuous innovations, although they do not generally alter established patterns. These may involve the creation of new products or the alteration of existing items. Examples of this would include electric toothbrushes, electric autos, wall-sized television screens, and video telephones.

3 *Discontinuous innovations* involve the establishment of new products with new behavior patterns. Examples of these situations would include television, computers, and automobiles.[29]

THE ADOPTION PROCESS

Before we examine how products spread among population groups, we need to look at the process as it relates to individuals. The acceptance and continued use of a product or brand by an individual is referred to as "adoption." Figure 11-4 presents a simplified diagram of the adoption process. This model consists of the following stages:

1 *Awareness*. At this stage the potential adopter finds out about the existence of a product but has very little information and no well-formed attitudes about it.

2 *Comprehension*. This stage represents the consumer's having knowledge and understanding of what the product is and can do.

3 *Attitude*. Here, the consumer develops favorable or unfavorable behavioral predispositions toward the product. Termination of the adoption process is likely at this stage if attitudes are not favorable toward the product.

4 *Legitimation*. Here, the consumer becomes convinced that the product should be adopted. This stage is predicated upon favorable attitudes toward the innovation, and the consumer may use information already gathered as well as additional information in order to reach a decision.

5 *Trial.* If possible, the consumer tests or tries the product to determine its utility. Trial may take place cognitively, that is, whereby the individual vicariously uses the product in a hypothetical situation or it may be actually used in a limited or total way, depending on the innovation's nature.

6 *Adoption.* At this stage, the consumer determines whether or not to use the product in a full-scale way. Continued purchase and/or use of the item fulfills the adoption process.[30]

Thus, adoption is seen to be a sequence of events through which individual consumers pass over a period of time. Some consumers pass through these stages early in a product's life while others may do so much later. In addition, the adoption process describes consumers who are actively involved in thinking about and considering a product.

The significance of the adoption process to the marketer is twofold. First, not all consumers pass through the adoption process with the same speed—some move swiftly, while others proceed more slowly. Second, the marketer's communication forms vary in their effectiveness over the different stages in the adoption process. These points can be important in assisting the marketer to develop an effective promotional program. It has been found, for example, that for early stages of the adoption process, the mass media appear to be most effective in creating awareness; thus, the marketer would design awareness- and interest-generating messages to be transmitted by such impersonal sources. At later stages in the adoption process, however, personal sources of information appear to become more important so the marketer would desire to have effective personal selling and word-of-mouth communications at these points. This indicates then, that as consumers move through the adoption process, the amount of mass-media advertising might be decreased while the amount of personal selling is increased.

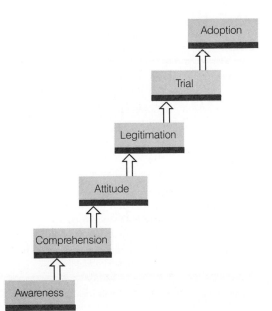

FIGURE 11-4
The adoption decision process.
Source: Adapted from Thomas S. Robertson, *Innovative Behavior and Communication,* copyright © 1971 by Holt, Rinehart and Winston, New York, p. 75. Used with permission of Holt, Rinehart and Winston, CBS College Publishing.

The adoption process also may not be completed by the individual, which means that the innovation will not be adopted. Several factors that may lead to an incomplete adoption process are listed in Table 11-1. The marketer should take care to minimize the marketing problems leading to consumer failure to complete the adoption process.

THE DIFFUSION PROCESS

In this section, we shall discuss the nature of the process by which innovations spread. The marketer is vitally interested in this because it determines the success or failure of any new product brought to market. The marketer usually desires to secure the largest amount of adoption within the shortest period of time. Whether such an accelerated strategy is chosen (as is the case for most continuous innovations), or one that moves more slowly is chosen (as might be taken with discontinuous innovations), the marketer needs to understand the diffusion process so that he can properly manage the spread of the new product or service.[31] Although there are many limitations and weaknesses in much of the diffusion research that has been conducted by scholars, the research has helped us understand the communication process for innovations and the social structure within which this occurs.[32]

We should first distinguish the concept of diffusion from that of adoption. As we saw earlier, the adoption process is an *individual* phenomenon relating to the sequence of stages through which an individual passes from first hearing about a product to finally adopting it. The diffusion process, however, refers to a *group* phenomenon, indicating how an innovation spreads among consumers. The diffusion process, of course, necessarily involves the adoption process of many individuals over time.

TABLE 11-1

Potential Causes of Incompleted Adoption Process

Acceptance process stage	Marketing-organization causes of incompleted processes	Consumer causes of incompleted processes
Awareness	Poorly used or too little communication	Selective exposure Selective perception
Comprehension	Communication hard to understand	Selective retention
Attitude	Communication not persuasive	Complacency Suspended judgment
Legitimation	Poor source effect of communications	Peer-group pressure against adoption Laws regulating use of innovation
Trial	Behavioral response not specified in communications Poor distribution system	Alternative equally good Innovation not available
Adoption	Failure to develop new products and improve old products	Replaced by another innovation

Source: Adapted from Gerald Zaltman and Ronald Stiff, "Theories of Diffusion" in Scott Ward and Thomas S. Robertson (eds.), *Consumer Behavior: Theoretical Sources,* copyright © 1973, p. 451. Reprinted by permission of Prentice-Hall, Inc., Englewood Cliffs, N.J.

Perhaps the best marketing-oriented definition of the diffusion process is "the adoption of new products and services over time by consumers within social systems as encouraged by marketing activities."[33] This definition recognizes the various components of the process which are important in the spread of an innovation.

How does diffusion occur? Analysis of fashion life cycles and their diffusion provides some insights into the process. Several theories of fashion diffusion have been suggested.[34] First, the theory of upper-class fashion leadership postulates that fashions are initially adopted by the upper class and are then imitated by each succeeding lower class until they have "trickled-down" to the lowest class. The fashion industry has long emphasized elite-oriented fashion, and lesser fashion designers and producers frequently copy the designs of their more famous counterparts. A second theory proposes that mass production combined with mass communications make new styles and information about new styles available simultaneously to all socioeconomic classes. Fashion diffusion, therefore, has the potential to start at essentially the same time within each class. This mass-market view is sometimes referred to as the horizontal flow or "trickle-across" theory. A third and newer theory of fashion diffusion recognizes that many new fashions have been initiated by subcultural groups such as youths, blue-collar workers, and ethnic minorities such as Indians and blacks. These innovations may range from new ideas (such as miniskirts), to customary artifacts of a culture or subculture, to styles resurrected from the past, or even to homemade inventions (such as the tie-dyed products pioneered by youth, which appeared in the 1960s). Whether a fashion is new or customary, the unique subculture style becomes admired and diffuses into the mass population where it is selectively assimilated into the dominant culture. The fourth and most general theory of leadership suggests that nearly all creative or innovative individuals can become leaders of fashion trends if their innovative choices are reasonably in line with the social climate and lifestyles of the times. In this view, fashion leadership is not confined to the upper class but can emerge by a process in which collective tastes are formed by many people. Styles that most closely represent existing trends in consumers' tastes will slowly gain acceptance as the preferred fashion. Prestigious innovators who select this fashion will help to better define the public's tastes toward what should be the appropriate fashion and to legitimize their choices. There is evidence to support each of these theories of fashion diffusion.

The fashion-conscious or fashion-change–agent sector of the population can be important to the spread of a new fashion. This group is a large and broadly fashion-oriented market segment. Many of the people in the population are interested in or oriented toward fashion monitoring, if not necessarily toward changing their wardrobes. For example, data consistently show that as much as half the female population and 25 percent of the male population have an active fashion consciousness. This group enjoys monitoring fashion magazines, fashion trends, and new style offerings, and is broadly innovative and communicative. For a new style to obtain mass endorsement, fashion-change agents are important. This group, working across geographical regions and within personal social networks, is significant in the acceptance or rejection of a fashion object.[35]

Now, let's look more closely at the general process of diffusion and what it means for the marketer. We must remember that marketing actions should be

designed to change the diffusion process to the firm's advantage. Table 11-2 suggests how the proactive nature of marketing and competitive actions relates to various diffusion concepts.

Categories of Adopters Because we know that people will not all adopt an innovation at the same time, we might classify consumers on the basis of time of adoption. In so doing, we will also discover that those who adopt new products at approximately the same time have similar characteristics. Armed with such knowledge, the marketer may thus be able to segment a market by adopter type and aim strategies, in turn, at each group over time. Five adopter categories have been identified: innovator, early adopter, early majority, late majority, and laggard. Each of these groups' characteristics is summarized below.[36] The percentages that follow represent the proportion of all who adopt an innovation, which may be only a small proportion of the total market.

Innovators (2.5 percent of a market) are the first to adopt new products. They are quite venturesome and are eager to try new ideas. They have more risk capital (both material and social) and can afford to take calculated risks. Innovators are well-educated, come from well-established families, and are cosmopolitan, having friends outside the community. Their sources of information also transcend the local community, incorporating other innovators and impersonal and scientific sources. They may belong to state, regional, or national organizations and are respected by local community members for their success.

Robertson has distilled twenty-one studies of new-product diffusion and

TABLE 11-2

Marketing Impact on Diffusion

Diffusion concept	Marketing impact
The innovation	Marketing actions in product design and positioning are critical in the consumer perception of the innovation and its characteristics.
The diffusion process	Marketing actions can influence the pattern and speed of diffusion for the total market and by segment based on pricing, promotional expenditures, and distribution intensity. Competitive marketing actions have a similar effect.
The adoption process	Marketing actions can modify the speed of adoption and the form of the adoption process; for example, via sampling programs which take consumers from awareness to trial.
The communication process	Marketing change agents bear distinguishing characteristics from those in farming: they are inherently self-serving and biased. Advertising, personal selling, and sales promotion are the dominant communication sources and can lead to purchase without "objective, scientific authority."
Opinion leadership and personal influence	Marketing actions can both preclude the importance of personal influence and influence the occurrence of personal influence depending on objectives.
Adopter categories	Marketing actions can be instrumental in determining who the innovator will be based on market segmentation decisions.

Source: Thomas S. Robertson, "Marketing's Potential Contribution to Consumer Behavior Research: The Case of Diffusion Theory," in Thomas C. Kinnear (ed.), *Advances in Consumer Research*, vol. 11, Association for Consumer Research, Provo, Utah, 1984, p. 486.

developed a profile of the innovative consumer. Because the studies span various product categories, sampling populations, research methodologies, and definitions of innovation, the picture they provide of the consumer innovator must be viewed with caution. Nevertheless, Table 11-3 summarizes these characteristics.

Early adopters (13.5 percent of a market) are the second group to adopt an innovation. This group is more socially integrated locally than are innovators, and it has the greatest degree of opinion leadership in most social systems. They are likely to hold positions of leadership within the community and are respected as good sources of information and advice about the innovation. For this reason, they are very important in speeding the diffusion process. They watch the innovators and adopt when the innovation appears successful. They are just ahead of the average individual in innovativeness, so they are able to serve as role models for others in the market.

Early adopters have less risk capital than do innovators. They are younger than later adopters, higher in social status, and above average in education. Early adopters subscribe to more magazines than later adopters (yet not as many as innovators). They also have been found to have the greatest contact with salespeople.

How important are innovators and early adopters in the success of new products? Quite significant, as General Electric has found in studies of its appliances. One study of a new cordless electric clothes brush, for example, obtained data from warranty cards for the new product and through personal interviews with early buyers. GE found that these early buyers directly influenced other consumers by talking about the product and by having it in their homes.[37]

Moreover, when the early adopters begin buying something new, retailers see the product moving and are likely to advertise it more heavily and feature it prominently in stores. This can enhance the retailer's image as an innovative store by handling "hot" new products.

The *early majority* (34 percent of a market) is the next group to adopt an innovation and is the most deliberate of all adopter categories. Those in the early majority may consider an innovation for some time before adopting; thus, their adoption period is longer than that of the two previous groups. They adopt an

TABLE 11-3

A Profile of the Consumer Innovator

Findings for the innovator vs. noninnovator	
Demographic factors Higher income levels Often younger Better educated Higher occupational status	*Attitudinal and perceptual factors* More venturesome and perceives less risk in buying new products Perceives himself as an innovator Has favorable attitudes toward new products
Social interaction factors Greater participation in friendship and organizational groups An opinion leader Socially mobile Favorably disposed to innovation	*Consumption patterns* Higher usage rate for the innovative product category Marked willingness to buy new products *Communication behavior* Reads more print media

Source: Thomas Robertson, *Innovative Behavior and Communications*, Holt, New York, 1971, pp. 100–110.

innovation just before the average member of a social system, which puts them in a crucial position to legitimize the new idea for others.

Those in the early majority are slightly above average in age and education and in social and economic status. Although they belong to formal organizations, they are likely to be active members rather than leaders. They rely more heavily on informal sources of information than do earlier adopters. The early majority subscribe to fewer magazines and journals than do previous adopters, but they have considerable contact with salespeople. They are frequently the neighbors and friends of early adopters.

The *late majority* (34 percent of a market) adopts an innovation just after the average consumer in the market place. This group can be described as "skeptical" about new ideas and may yield only because of economic necessity or increasing social pressures. Those in the late majority are above average in age and below average in education, social status, and income. They belong to few formal organizations and exhibit little opinion leadership with communication patterns oriented primarily toward other late majority members in their neighborhood. There is little use of the mass media (for example, fewer magazines are taken) but heavy reliance on informal sources of information and influence.

Laggards (16 percent of a market) are the last group to adopt an innovation. They are tradition-bound, with decisions based on what has been done in the past. Laggards are suspicious of innovations and perhaps of those who offer them. The length of the adoption process for this group is quite long; when adoption finally comes, a new innovation has likely superseded the previous innovation.

Laggards have the least education, the lowest social status and income, and are the oldest of any adopter category. They are the most local in orientation, which tends to be their immediate neighborhood, and they communicate mostly with other laggards, who are their main sources of information. Laggards possess almost no opinion leadership, have little participation in formal organizations, and subscribe to few magazines.

Although these categories and descriptions may vary for different products, they do provide the marketer with a helpful framework for managing an innovation's diffusion. One of the most important facets of the work in this regard will be the development of a sound promotional strategy. Clearly, adopter characteristics differ greatly among categories, and this requires that the marketer tailor promotions to appeal to each group over time. Table 11-4 illustrates the kinds of promotional approaches that appear to be most effective for each adopter category.

Factors Influencing the Rate of Diffusion The rate of an innovation's diffusion could range from several weeks to several decades, depending upon consumers' acceptance of the item, which, in turn, is determined by how the innovation is perceived by consumers. There appears to have been, over time, a general increase in the rate of adoption of innovations.[38] Thus, a rapidly shortening product life cycle appears to be occuring. This trend has importance to marketers, public policymakers, and consumer researchers because it may represent a significant change in consumption patterns. For example, more and more rapid adoption rates may preclude involved decision processes, so that other purchase approaches may be increasing, such as conformity, imitation, and recommendation.

Even the meaningfulness of adopter category distinctions may lose their usefulness as these cycles are decreased.

The marketer, too, is generally interested in understanding how an innovation may be spread more rapidly among a relevant market. There are six product characteristics that seem to influence the rate and extent of adoption of an innovation: (1) relative advantage, (2) compatibility, (3) complexity, (4) trialability, (5) observability, and (6) cost. These characteristics are described below:[39]

Relative advantage is the degree to which an innovation is perceived as superior to preceding products or those with which it will compete. This might be reflected in longer life, easier maintenance, or other measures. Products that have a strong relative advantage will be adopted more rapidly.

Compatibility is the degree to which an innovation is consistent with existing consumer values and past experiences of adopters. Acceptance will be retarded for new products that are not compatible with consumers' norms.

Complexity refers to how difficult the innovation is to understand and use. Diffusion will tend to be slowed for more complex items.

Trialability (or divisibility) is the extent to which an innovation may be tried on a limited basis. Where an item cannot be sampled on a small, less-expensive scale, diffusion is retarded.

TABLE 11-4

How Promotion Varies by Stage in the Diffusion Process

Adopter category	Promotional approach
Innovator	Technical or scientific information about the innovation is made available in special-interest or professional media and at trade meetings.
	Appeals should stress the excitement of trying something completely new and revolutionary.
	Salespeople should concentrate on people who are relatively young and who have high social status, incomes, and education.
Early adopters	Advertisements should emphasize the prestige of owning the item.
	Testimonials by respected people may be particularly effective.
Early majority	Appeals should concentrate on materials designed for this group's evaluation stage in the adoption process.
	Salespeople should stress that others, especially the relevant opinion leaders, have adopted the innovation.
	Make use of peer social pressure with the "house party" sales technique.
Late majority	Advertising appeals should overcome skepticism by making liberal use of such reassuring terms as: "Guaranteed by *Good Housekeeping*," "Produced by the makers of . . . ," or "Tested and approved by the . . . Laboratory."
	Salespeople are important and should concentrate on consumers whose income and social status are below average.
	Proper product demonstration is a must when this group is at the trial stage.
Laggards	Best to ignore them, in most instances.

Source: Adapted from Gerald Zaltman, *Marketing: Contributions from the Behavioral Sciences*, pp. 51–53, copyright © 1965 by Harcourt Brace Jovanovich, Inc. Reprinted by permission of the publisher.

Observability (or communicability) refers to the conspicuousness of the innovation. New products that are highly visible in social situations are those that will be communicated most readily to other adopters.

Cost refers to the magnitude of the financial resources required to obtain and operate this innovation. Innovations high in cost would be expected to diffuse more slowly. However, one study indicates that cost does not appear to be significantly correlated with rate of adoption.[40]

The marketing implications of these characteristics are readily apparent. First of all, an innovation should exhibit some clear-cut advantages. In addition, products might be designed so that they could be evaluated on a limited basis (for example, small trial sizes of a new toothpaste). With some products, however, such as automobiles and air conditioners, trial is more difficult. Nevertheless, auto test drives (or in some cases even extended car loans) and free home trials for appliances have been offered. Products should also be designed with minimum complexity and maximum compatibility (these also may make up part of the product's relative advantage). These features should then be stressed in promotional messages to potential adopters. If complexity and noncompatibility are inherent in the innovation, promotion should seek to overcome these limitations (for example, by stressing warranties or product-servicing facilities).

"General" Innovators   It was concluded earlier that there is a moderate amount of opinion leadership overlap across product categories, with the greatest extent involving related product areas. A similar conclusion can be made with regard to innovators. There is no "superinnovator" who plays this part across a host of products. However, within a product category and perhaps between related product categories some innovative overlap can be expected to occur.[41]

MARKETING IMPLICATIONS OF PERSONAL INFLUENCE

In this section, we shall suggest various marketing strategies that effectively use the process of personal influence. Two cautions are in order, however. First, it should be remembered that opinion leadership is not equally active for all products—some products are very prone to personal influence, while others are not. Opinion leaders are more likely in product categories in which pleasure or satisfaction is derived from product usage or in which association with the product provides a form of self-expression. Consequently, using opinion leaders may be effective to diffuse information about such products as automobiles and personal computers but may be ineffective for products like refrigerators and dehumidifiers. Second, it may be difficult and expensive to control the process of personal influence.

The marketer will want to address several questions when targeting prospects for a new product: (1) the target market's innovative and early adoption propensities, (2) its heavy volume potential, (3) its susceptibility to influence, and (4) the cost of reaching this group. This will require a systematic procedure utilizing information from concept testing, product testing, test marketing, and so forth.[42] If the marketer finds that personal influence is potentially strong for the product, then he or she may desire to guide the process. There are several strategies which might be adopted: (1) identifying and using opinion leaders directly, (2) creating opinion leaders, (3) simulating opinion leaders, (4) stimulating opinion leadership, and (5) stifling opinion leadership.

IDENTIFYING AND USING OPINION LEADERS DIRECTLY

There are two major difficulties in pursuing this strategy. First of all, locating opinion leaders who are influential over a particular product is most complicated. Characteristics of opinion leaders, which were discussed earlier in this chapter, make it clear that they are not easy to isolate. Moreover, for the consumer-goods marketer the task is likely to be hard because of the large number of consumers. In order to identify the leaders, the marketer would need to conduct difficult and expensive research on his own product. Second, there is evidence that in some cases opinion leaders may not be reached by certain advertising media any more effectively than the average consumer in a market would be.[43] Thus, direct appeal to personal influence may not always be the most effective approach.

If the direct approach is decided upon, however, the first step is to identify opinion leaders. There are several ways in which this may be done. One set of techniques involves measuring the degree of opinion leadership among consumers. Table 11-5 presents a questionnaire that has been effectively used to ascertain the degree of consumers' opinion leadership through survey research. In this instance, individuals would evaluate themselves on this characteristic. Another approach to measuring opinion leadership involves the *sociometric* technique, which consists of asking group members to whom they go for advice and information about an idea. Finally, *key informants* in a group may be asked to designate the opinion leaders.

One of the best ways to identify those who may be influential for a company's product is to examine purchase records. For instance, many products today use a

TABLE 11-5

Opinion Leadership Scale

1 In general, do you like to talk about _____ with your friends?

2 Would you say you give very little information, an average amount of information, or a great deal of information about _____ to your friends?

3 During the past six months, have you told anyone about some _____?

4 Compared with your circle of friends, are you *less likely, about as likely,* or *more likely* to be asked for advice about _____?

5 If you and your friends were to discuss _____, what part would you be most likely to play? Would you *mainly listen* to your friends' ideas or would you *try to convince them* of your ideas?

6 Which of these happens more often? Do *you tell your* friends about some _____, or do *they tell you* about some _____?

7 Do you have the feeling that you are generally regarded by your friends and neighbors as a good source of advice about _____?

Source: Adapted from Charles W. King and John O. Summers, "Overlap of Opinion Leadership Across Consumer Product Categories," *Journal of Marketing*, 7:45, February 1970, published by the American Marketing Association.

warranty card return system whereby the marketer can identify specific individuals who are early adopters of the product and identify the characteristics of these buyers. Of course, one disadvantage of relying exclusively on this approach is that not all buyers return these cards. Nevertheless, identifying and communicating with present owners may lead to effective incorporation of personal influence in marketing strategy.

Vermont Castings, Inc., a maker of wood- and coal-burning cast-iron stoves, generates affectionate word-of-mouth advertising. Owners of Vermont Castings' Defiant, Vigilant, and Resolute stoves boast about how many friends they have converted to them. When the company asked owners whether they would be willing to show curious strangers how their stoves worked, 3000 owners volunteered. The company's showroom has a bulletin board covered with testimonial letters and proud customers' snapshots of installed stoves. On one August weekend 10,000 people showed up at an owners' outing in a central Vermont town of 4500 to take plant tours and listen to lectures on wood and coal burning, insulation, and stove safety.[44]

Study of past purchases may indicate which consumers are most likely to adopt new products. For example, by knowing that the most likely adopter of new telephone-system services, such as the videophone, would occur among those who had previously bought such equipment as pushbutton phones, extension phones, and color phones, the telephone company might assess available records to determine the households in the service area which would have the greatest likelihood of adopting the new equipment.

It is also significant to realize that early product triers also tend to be heavy users.[45] Thus, the marketer of a new product might engage in a two-step consumer identification program. First, heavy users of products within the same category as the to-be-introduced item should be characterized in terms of relevant background and behavioral variables so that a marketing program which appeals to these persons can be developed. Second, once the product is introduced, description of the earliest triers should be obtained quickly so that the marketer may develop inducements for consumers with similar backgrounds.

Names and addresses of potential opinion leaders might be gathered not only from purchase records, but also from sponsorship of consumer contests, use of reader-service cards in magazines, and similar activities. To illustrate, Campbell Soup Company received over 94,000 entries in a recent "Creative Cooking Contest," in which original recipes were submitted. Once names of potential opinion leaders have been secured, the marketer is in a position to utilize their influence effectively. The opinion leaders may be reached through direct-mail advertising, if the cost is not prohibitive. They can also be provided with inside information about new products so that they are in a strategic position to pass along this information to others.

One approach that may work well is to obtain mailing lists containing names of people who have a high level of interest in a particular product category. In other words, identify the "enthusiast" for this product. These people are quite likely to be heavy readers of magazines relating to the product—for instance, the automobile buff:

Readers of the automotive enthusiast press—such as *Road & Track, Car and Driver,* and *Motor Trend*—tend to be the "hardcore car buffs," according to an executive at Chevrolet's advertising agency. "They're the guys who live, breathe, and sleep cars." These media reach the core driver group which really enjoys cars, and they are also read with a certain sense of intensity by the car buff. Manufacturers attempt to establish credibility with this segment, particularly if the new product is dramatically different. Therefore, the enthusiast press is a very important part of any car advertising campaign. One of the basics of automotive advertising is keeping the person who's informed, informed. They consider themselves automotive experts, and people call on them for advice. For instance, 39 percent of *Road & Track*'s readers are asked about cars one or more times a week, and one of every two readers is considering the purchase of a new car in the upcoming year. Thus, even if the enthusiast isn't a potential buyer for a new car immediately, he can talk it up and spread information around via word-of-mouth. Therefore, it is good to have your name and message before them because of this amplifying effect in which buffs have an influence beyond their own purchases.[46]

Opinion leaders could also be provided with free samples (if it were an inexpensive product),[47] discounts off the price of new products, or loan of the item (in the case of expensive durables).[48] Zack's Famous Frozen Yogurt shops give samples of the product to grammar schools in hopes of winning the kids over from ice cream. For certain product categories, providing sampling for an even broader audience than simply opinion leaders is achieved through advertising. Fragrance strips providing a whiff of perfume or cologne have displaced sampling in stores for some companies, while cosmetics inserts carrying several shades of eye shadow, makeup and lipstick have been used by Cover Girl, L'Oreal, and Revlon.

Another approach that has been successfully used is to have opinion leaders model or sell the product. For example, many clothing stores have established "fashion advisory boards" on which high school or college opinion leaders are placed. These fashion leaders may act as retail salespeople for the store, model the store's newest fashions for customers, and also appear in store advertising.

CREATING OPINION LEADERS

When opinion leaders cannot be easily identified or used, it may be possible to "create" them. Such an approach is frequently attempted by aluminum siding and swimming pool manufacturers. Companies will typically select homeowners (especially those with central locations in their neighborhoods) and induce them to buy the product at a very low price if they will then demonstrate the product to others. The homeowner opinion leader is, in efect, being created by the company.

Another successful use of this technique was reported in the introduction of a new pop record. The task was to transform an unknown song recorded by an unknown singer into a hit. The initial step was to seek out social leaders among the relevant buying public—high school students. Names of class presidents, class secretaries, sports captains, and cheerleaders selected from geographically diverse high schools were obtained. Although these were social leaders, prior to the project these students would not likely have been classified as opinion leaders for records because of their low ownership of this item. Next, the students were contacted by mail and invited to join a select panel to assist a manufacturer in

evaluating new records. They were to receive free records and were encouraged to discuss their choices with friends. This inexpensive experiment provided very successful results. Several records reached the top ten charts in the trial cities while failing to make the top ten selections in any other cities. Thus, without promoters contacting any radio stations or record stores, records were pulled through the channels of distribution and made into hits.[49]

A number of companies have attempted to create opinion leadership by getting the product into the hands of people who have a great deal of public contact or exposure. Ford Motor Company has successfully utilized this approach. For example, when the Mustang was introduced, college newspaper editors, disc jockeys, and airline stewardesses were loaned Mustangs, largely on the presumption that they were influentials with regard to automobiles.

SIMULATING OPINION LEADERSHIP

In this approach, personal influence is simulated by various means, especially advertising. Advertisers frequently simulate opinion leadership by approximating the position of the disinterested and noncommercial speaker who would engage in word-of-mouth communication. By taking such a position, the need for personal influence may be replaced to a certain extent by advertising.

There are several ways in which the marketer can simulate opinion leadership. One approach is that taken in promotions for many detergents, foods, laxatives, and other products, in which a person (the simulated opinion leader) tells another person about the virtues of the sponsored item. Visual communication also is frequently used in commercials simulating opinion leadership, whereby one shopper watches to see what another shopper (the opinion leader) purchases, and then is seen to buy the same item based on this visual recommendation. Commercials of the sort in which a friend recommends the product to another often use nonprofessionals to enhance the believability and use a script which is written in authentic consumer language based on focus-group research.

Often, the advertiser simulates personal influence by using a *testimonial* approach, in which the user of the product conveys a favorable experience or opinion about the item. One testimonial approach uses typical people in a seemingly unsolicited recommendation for the product. Commercials featuring man-on-the-street recommendations, hidden camera interviews, and similar techniques may serve to influence viewers through a simulation of opinion leadership. Other testimonials often feature a famous actor or athlete as the endorser.

What effectiveness do celebrity endorsers have?[50] Not the automatic influence many marketers probably expect of them.[51] Celebrities will be most effective when there is a close match of personalities with products and advertising copy. A review of hundreds of celebrity commercials over a twelve-year period indicates that only 41 percent obtained above-average scores in either brand awareness or attitude shift tests, and only 19 percent were above-average in both categories.[52] It appears that women, athletes, and veteran actors scored best, while younger dramatic actors, comedians, and nonentertainment personalities scored poorly. The effectiveness varies depending on the situation. For instance, a laboratory experiment of print advertising indicated that for the products of costume jewelry, vacuum cleaners, and cookies the best endorsers were celebrities, experts, and typical consumers, respectively. Furthermore, these particular product-endorser combinations resulted in better overall attitude toward the product, greater intent to purchase the advertised product, and more credibility for the endorser. However, regardless of the type of product, the celebrity endorser was most effective in sustaining brand-name recall and recall of the advertisement in the viewer.[53] Thus, if the advertiser most desires brand-name and advertisement recall, then a celebrity endorser is appropriate. If, on the other hand, believability of the endorsement, overall attitude toward the advertised product, and initial intent to purchase the advertised product are desired, celebrities may be best when the product purchase involves psychological or social risk. When the product involves financial, performance, and/or physical risk, the advertiser might utilize an expert endorser. For products with little inherent risk, a typical-consumer endorser should be chosen.

Marketers who use celebrities in their advertising must be careful to follow certain regulations. Federal Trade Commission (FTC) guidelines require, for instance, that celebrity or expert endorsers must actually use the product if the advertisements represent that they do and that the copy must represent the endorser's honest view of the product, with product claims substantiated.[54]

Because of the potential problems of using celebrities (cost, death, scandal, and the like), companies often create characters to star in their ads, with some achieving highly effective results.[55] Maytag's Old Lonely, Charmin's Mr. Whipple, Folger's Mrs. Olson, and even animated characters such as Pillsbury's Doughboy and Kellogg's Tony the Tiger provide instant identification for the company's products and set them apart from the competition. Maytag's Old Lonely commercials regularly score twice as high as other appliance commercials in consumer-awareness surveys. Mr. Whipple, often cited in surveys as one of the most obnoxious characters in TV ads, nevertheless, has made Charmin the top-selling toilet paper. Sometimes, it may be better to be noticed and disliked than not to be noticed at all.[56]

The success of the testimonial approach depends on several things, therefore. First, the customer must believe that the speaker is talking to the interviewer spontaneously and disinterestedly (that is, the speaker is not simply being paid to speak about a product). Second, the speaker needs a believable relationship to the product. Third, the language which is used must sound authentic. In any event, it has been claimed that the use of a testimonial can increase advertising recall by 18 percent, while a celebrity's testimonial will boost it 75 percent.[57]

A final approach to simulating opinion leadership is to use a company's chief executive as the spokesperson for the product or service. It is claimed that commercials featuring company spokespersons generate three times the response of those using actors.[58] Examples of this practice abound in the media. Consider the following recent ''stars'': Lee Iacocca (Chrysler), Frank Perdue (Perdue Farms Chicken), and Victor Kiam (Remington Products). More major companies are featuring bosses as pitchmen because the public tends to believe them. They can also be good motivators of the sales force, distributors, and employees around the country.[59] Although credibility can be a major plus, the drawback is that the public may also perceive the company to be in bad financial or other shape. The ads may be seen as spreading unfavorable personal influence, because many

corporations put their chief executives on the air when they are fighting an image problem. As the famous advertiser David Ogilvy advised, "Only in the gravest cases should you show the clients' faces."[60]

STIMULATING OPINION LEADERSHIP

This strategy is designed to get people to talk about the product and thereby exert personal influence. One way this may be encouraged is by using a *teaser* promotional campaign. Such a technique provides only enough information about the new item to pique the customer's curiosity.

A second advertising strategy is to develop such highly entertaining or emotional campaigns that consumers engage in discussions about the product and its advertising. A recent campaign for California raisins—"Heard It Through the Grapevine"—was an outstanding success in this regard. Some advertisers are even successful in having their slogans become adopted as part of the everyday language, such as Alka-Seltzer's "I can't believe I ate the whole thing," and Miller's "It's Miller Time." The increase in zany TV commercials by regional businesses trying to peddle their products with goofy, whimsical, and sometimes downright obnoxious approaches is an attempt to get people to talk about and shop at these stores for their electronics, waterbeds, appliances, and autos.[61]

Other advertising strategies encourage consumers to talk about the product. For example, Firestone's ads prompt the reader to "Ask a friend about Firestone." This attempts to instigate personal influence through having users disseminate product information and potential users request product information. Obviously, the marketer would desire only favorable word-of-mouth communications to be imparted about the product. This suggests that a monitoring system is needed to find out what present and potential customers are saying about the product and to help in the formulation of advertising strategies designed to react to word-of-mouth communication.

A final strategy is for the marketer to secure high visibility of the item. One approach is to use in-store demonstrations and displays at favorable locations. For example, Fiberfab kit cars are displayed fully assembled in selected airports around the country. Another approach is to have the product placed in a movie or television show.[62] Hershey's Reese's Pieces gained instant fame when in the movie *E.T. the extraterrestrial* was lured out of hiding by a trail of the candy.

Contests and sweepstakes are another way to build visibility and interest and to get consumers talking about products and services. Similarly, when brand names are linked with athletes or athletic events in media coverage, corporate sponsors may score points in the marketplace. That is why 2400 U.S. companies are now involved in sports marketing. They act as official sponsors of a variety of athletic events hoping to boost brand awareness among armchair and arena audiences and to reinforce the product image created from advertising. Such events also offer the chance for consumer product sampling.[63]

STIFLING OPINION LEADERSHIP

There may be times when the marketer desires to stifle personal influence rather than encourage it. Generally negative personal influence may be the result of rumor, a poor product, or misunderstandings among consumers. When consumers spread negative word-of-mouth communication over dissatisfaction with a product or over a question or complaint that is ignored or unsatisfactorily resolved by the marketer, the effect may be quite damaging.[64] For example:

Although less than 3 percent of a sample of communications received by Coca-Cola from consumers in a recent year were complaints, customers who complained and weren't satisfied with the response typically told nine or ten friends or associates about their experience, and in 12 percent of the cases, they told more than twenty people. In addition, 30 percent said they stopped buying Coca-Cola products, while another 45 percent said they would buy less in the future.[65]

Another study indicated that 34 percent of those dissatisfied with a personal care product told others about their dissatisfaction.[66]

One condition under which unfavorable personal influence should be retarded exists when a damaging rumor surfaces about the company or its product. Rumors abound in our society; they are part of people's fascination with the grotesque. For example, the following unfounded business rumors have circulated among the public recently:[67]

■ McDonald's adds worms to hamburger meat.

■ R. J. Reynolds Tobacco owns marijuana fields in Mexico.

■ False teeth dissolve if left overnight in a glass of Coca-Cola.

■ General Foods' Pop Rocks Crackling Candy makes your stomach explode.

■ Wearing Jockey shorts makes men sterile.

■ Procter & Gamble, whose century-old trademark is a man in the moon, is owned by the Reverend Sun Myung Moon's Unification Church. Others have claimed that the trademark is satanical.

■ Life Savers' Bubble Yum bubble gum causes cancer and/or has spider eggs in it.

In unfortunate cases such as these, the marketer must take immediate action to stop negative word-of-mouth communication and must build up a positive image. However, the traditional theoretical and intuitive strategy of directly refuting a rumor appears to be rather ineffective. Instead, information-processing strategies that attempt to influence the way a rumor is stored and retrieved by consumers may produce much more favorable results.[68] Whatever the theoretical approach, the marketer should stand ready to formulate promotional and public relations responses capable of diffusing the negative publicity.[69]

A final factor requiring slowing of personal influence results from consumer misunderstandings and could lead to poor word-of-mouth communication if not corrected. For example, consumers may be operating the product incorrectly, leading to malfunctions. Perhaps the item needs to be redesigned or instruction manuals need rewriting to make them clearer. When the product is radically new, such problems are very likely to exist. In these cases demonstrations may be

called for in stores, and more explicit commercials may be necessary, showing the product in use. Once again the necessity of a system to monitor personal influence and word-of-mouth communication—both good and bad—is underscored.

MANAGERIAL REFLECTIONS

For our product or service situation . . .

1   What communication and influence flows are exhibited between us and our customers?

2   Who are the opinion leaders relevant in this product category?

3   To what extent do our customers seek to influence others about the item?

4   What type of innovation is it considered to be, based on behavioral changes required of consumers?

5   Are there marketing or consumer barriers that may lead to an incompleted adoption process?

6   Which adopter category are we seeking in the diffusion process and how may the group be effectively marketed to?

7   Are there characteristics of the product that need modifying in order to encourage its rate and extent of adoption?

8   How may opinion leaders be identified and used directly?

9   Can additional opinion leaders be created?

10   Should attempts be made to simulate personal influence?

11   What techniques can be adopted to stimulate the process of personal influence?

12   Are we prepared to stifle negative opinion leadership?

DISCUSSION TOPICS

1   Describe the nature of personal influence. Why is it important to the marketer?

2   Describe the three models of communication discussed in the text. Which appears to be the most complete model of communication and influence?

3   Who are marketing opinion leaders? How do they differ from those they influence?

4   Think of a product or service about which you communicated by word-of-mouth recently. Were you the influencer or influencee? Which of the reasons for opinion leadership discussed in the text apply to this communication situation?

5   Locate several examples of new products (you might look in *Advertising Age, Business Week,* and the like) How would you classify each of these innovations in terms of their "newness"?

6 Pick one of the products discovered from question 5 and describe how you would market the item.

7 How might promotion differ as consumers move through the adoption process?

8 Describe the adopter categories.

9 Categorize your friends according to their position among the adopter categories. Which tend to be innovators, opinion leaders, laggards?

10 Suggest a plan for using the process of personal influence in the following marketing situations: (*a*) a campus clothing store, (*b*) a new food product, (*c*) a new, sophisticated stereophonic receiver, (*d*) a new sports car, (*e*) a new novel.

PROJECTS

1 Develop for a local retailer a promotional campaign that takes advantage of the personal influence process. Present it to the class.

2 Select three recent innovations and assess each on the basis of the six factors in the chapter which influence the rate of diffusion. Do you predict each will be adopted quickly? Why or why not?

NOTES

[1] Len Strazewski, "Families Tune In For Efficiency, Entertainment," *Advertising Age*, January 9, 1986, pp. 9–10; and Otis Port, "The Gadget Freaks Who Can Make or Break a Product," *Business Week*, August 19, 1985, p. 81.

[2] Thomas S. Robertson, *Innovative Behavior and Communication*, Holt, New York, 1971, p. 170. Deborah Sue Yeager, "Markdown Mecca," *The Wall Street Journal*, July 6, 1976, p. 1.

[3] Ernest Dichter, "How Word-of-Mouth Advertising Works," *Harvard Business Review*, **44**:147, November–December 1966.

[4] George Katona and Eva Mueller, "A Study of Purchasing Decisions," in Lincoln H. Clark (ed.), *Consumer Behavior: The Dynamics of Consumer Reaction*, New York University Press, New York, 1955, pp. 30–87.

[5] John R. Kerr and Bruce Weale, "Collegiate Clothing Purchasing Patterns and Fashion Adoption Behavior," *Southern Journal of Business*, **5**:126–133, July 1970.

[6] Dale M. Elsner, "The Story in Brief Is Men's Underwear, and It's Full of Holes," *The Wall Street Journal*, June 3, 1975, p. 1.

[7] Ralph Schoenstein, "It Was Just a Joke, Folks," *TV Guide*, May 8, 1974, pp. 6–7.

[8] Johan Arndt, "Role of Product-Related Conversations in the Diffusion of a New Product," *Journal of Marketing Research*, **4**:291–295, August 1967.

[9] Johan Arndt, *Word of Mouth Advertising: Review of the Literature*, Advertising Research Foundation, New York, 1967, p. 25.

[10] James H. Myers and William H. Reynolds, *Consumer Behavior and Marketing Management*, Houghton Mifflin, Boston, 1967, pp. 302–303.

[11] Robertson, *Innovative Behavior*, pp. 126–127.

[12] Lawrence F. Feick, Linda L. Price, and Robin A. Higie, "People Who Use People: The Other Side of Opinion Leadership," in Richard J. Lutz (ed.), *Advances in Consumer Research*, vol. 13, Association for Consumer Research, Provo, Utah, 1984, pp. 301–305.

[13] Robertson, *Innovative Behavior*, p. 175.

[14] Myers and Reynolds, *Consumer Behavior*, p. 306.

[15] "Are You a Trendsetter?" *American Demographics*, October 1986, pp. 74–75.

[16] Everett M. Rogers, *Diffusion of Innovations*, Free Press, New York, 1962, p. 241.

[17] John O. Summers, "The Identity of Women's Clothing Fashion Opinion Leaders," *Journal of*

Marketing Research, **7**:178–185, May 1970; and Fred D. Reynolds and William R. Darden, "Mutually Adaptive Effects of Interpersonal Communication," *Journal of Marketing Research,* **8**:449–454, November 1971.

[18] Charles W. King, "Fashion Adoption: A Rebuttal to the Trickle Down Theory," in Stephen A. Greyser (ed.), *Toward Scientific Marketing,* American Marketing Association, Chicago, 1964, pp. 108–125.

[19] Charles W. King and John O. Summers, "Overlap of Opinion Leadership Across Consumer Product Categories," *Journal of Marketing Research,* **7**:43–50, February 1970.

[20] David B. Montgomery and Alvin J. Silk, "Patterns of Overlap in Opinion Leadership and Interest for Selected Categories of Purchasing Activity," in Philip R. McDonald (ed.), *Marketing Involvement in Society and the Economy,* American Marketing Association, Chicago, 1969, pp. 377–386.

[21] Elihu Katz, "The Two-Step Flow of Communication: An Up-to-Date Report on an Hypothesis," *Public Opinion Quarterly,* **21**:73, Spring 1957.

[22] Dichter, "How Word-of-Mouth Advertising Works," pp. 148–152.

[23] Robertson, *Innovative Behavior,* pp. 191–209.

[24] Feick, Price, and Higie, "People Who Use People," p. 304.

[25] Lawrence F. Feick and Linda L. Price, "The Market Maven: A Diffuser of Marketplace Information," *Journal of Marketing,* **51**:85, January 1987.

[26] Feick and Price, "The Market Maven," pp. 93–94.

[27] "Firm: Consumers Cool to New Products," *Marketing News,* January 3, 1986, pp. 1, 45.

[28] Gerald Zaltman and Ronald Stiff, "Theories of Diffusion," in Scott Ward and Thomas S. Robertson (eds.), *Consumer Behavior: Theoretical Sources,* Prentice-Hall, Englewood Cliffs, N.J., 1972, p. 426.

[29] Thomas S. Robertson, "The Process of Innovation and the Diffusion of Innovation," *Journal of Marketing,* **31**:15–16, January 1967.

[30] Robertson, *Innovative Behavior,* pp. 76–77.

[31] Peter C. Wilton and Edgar A. Pessemier, "Forecasting the Ultimate Acceptance of an Innovation: The Effects of Information," *Journal of Consumer Research,* **8**:162–171, September, 1981; and Raymond J. Lawrence, "The First Purchase: Models of Innovation," *Marketing Intelligence and Planning,* **3**:37–72, Number 1, 1985.

[32] Everett M. Rogers, "New Product Adoption and Diffusion," *Journal of Consumer Research,* **2**:290–301, March 1976; Vijay Mahajan and Eitam Muller, "Innovation Diffusion and New Product Growth Models in Marketing," *Journal of Marketing,* **43**:55–68, Fall 1979; V. Solomon, E. Little, and T. Parker, "A Demonstration of a Theoretical Model For the Diffusion of Information Through Word-of-Mouth Communication," in P. Thistlethwaite, D. Billingsly, and J. Berens (eds.), *Proceedings,* Midwest Marketing Association, Macomb, Ill., 1985, pp. 111–118, and Herbert Gatignon and Thomas Robertson, "A Propositional Inventory for New Diffusion Research," *Journal of Consumer Research,* **11**:849–867, March 1985.

[33] Robertson, *Innovative Behavior,* p. 32.

[34] George B. Sproles, "Analyzing Fashion Life Cycles—Principles and Perspectives," *Journal of Marketing,* **45**:116–124, Fall 1981.

[35] Charles W. King and Lawrence J. Ring, "The Dynamics of Style and Taste Adoption and Diffusion: Contributions from Fashion Theory," in Jerry C. Olson (ed.), *Advances in Consumer Research,* vol. 7, Association for Consumer Research, Ann Arbor, Mich., 1980, pp. 13–16.

[36] See Rogers, *Diffusion of Innovations,* pp. 168–171; *The Adoption of New Products: Process and Influence,* Foundation for Research on Human Behavior, Ann Arbor, Mich., 1959, pp. 1–8; and Gerald Zaltman, *Marketing: Contributions from the Behavioral Sciences,* Harcourt, New York, 1965, pp. 45–51.

[37] "Early Adopters an Aid in New Product Success, GE Finds," *Marketing Insights,* April 24, 1967, p. 14.

[38] Richard W. Olshavsky, "Time and the Rate of Adoption of Innovations," *Journal of Consumer Research,* **6**:425–428, March 1980.

[39] Everett M. Rogers and F. Floyd Shoemaker, *Communication of Innovations,* Free Press, New York, 1971, pp. 137–157; and Gerald Zaltman and Melanie Wallendorf, *Consumer Behavior: Basic Findings and Management Implications,* Wiley, New York, 1979, p. 470.

[40] Olshavsky, "Time and Rate of Adoption."

[41] Thomas S. Robertson and James H. Myers, "Personality Correlates of Opinion Leadership and Innovative Buying Behavior," *Journal of Marketing Research,* **6**:164–168, May 1969; Robertson, *Innovative Behavior,* pp. 110–112; and James W. Taylor, "A Striking Characteristic of Innovators," *Journal of Marketing Research,* **14**:104–107, February 1977.

[42] Philip Kotler and Gerald Zaltman, "Targeting Prospects for a New Product," *Journal of Advertising Research,* **16:**7–18, February 1976.

[43] Douglas J. Tigert and Stephen J. Arnold, *Profiling Self-Designated Opinion Leaders and Self-Designated Innovators Through Life Style Research,* University of Toronto School of Business, Toronto, June 1971, pp. 28–29.

[44] William L. Bulkeley, "Woodstove Maker Has Hot Love Affair with Its Customers," *The Wall Street Journal,* September 9, 1981, pp. 1, 19.

[45] Fred W. Morgan, Jr., "Are Early Triers Heavy Users?" *Journal of Business,* **52:**429–434, 1979.

[46] Stuart Elliot, "How to Reach the Automobile Buff," *Advertising Age,* June 22, 1981, pp. S-16–S-18.

[47] Alix Freedman, "Free Product Samples . . . As Sales Tool," *The Wall Street Journal,* August 28, 1986, p. 19.

[48] Myers and Reynolds, *Consumer Behavior,* p. 309.

[49] Joseph R. Mancuso, "Why Not Create Opinion Leaders for New Product Introductions?" *Journal of Marketing,* **33:**20–25, July 1969.

[50] John C. Mowen, Stephen W. Brown, and Meg Schulman, "Theoretical and Empirical Extensions of Endorser Effectiveness," in Neil Beckwith et al. (eds.), *1979 Educators' Conference Proceedings,* American Marketing Association, Chicago, 1979, pp. 258–262; Jack Kaikati, "The Current Boom in Celebrity Advertising," in John H. Summey and Ronald D. Taylor (eds.), *Evolving Marketing Thought for 1980,* Southern Marketing Association, Carbondale, Ill., 1980, pp. 68–70; and Arthur J. Bragg, "Celebrities in Selling," *Sales and Marketing Management,* February 4, 1980, pp. 30–36.

[51] Robert A. Swerdlow, "Star Studded Advertising: Is It Worth the Effort?" *Journal of the Academy of Marketing Science,* **12:**89–102, Summer 1984; and Charles Atkin and Martin Block, "Effectiveness of Celebrity Endorsers," *Journal of Advertising Research,* **23:**57–61, February/March 1983.

[52] James P. Forkan, "Product Matchup Key to Effective Star Presenters," *Advertising Age,* October 6, 1980, p. 42.

[53] Hershey H. Friedman and Linda Friedman, "Endorser Effectiveness by Product Type," *Journal of Advertising Research,* **19:**63–71, October 1979.

[54] Dorothy Cohen, "FTC Issues Guidelines on Endorsements, Testimonials," *Marketing News,* March 21, 1980, p. 3.

[55] Bourne Morris, "Will a Personality Sell a Product Better? Pros and Cons," *Advertising Age,* February 5, 1975, pp. 43–44; and Bill Abrams, "When Ads Feature Celebrities, Advertisers Cross Their Fingers," *The Wall Street Journal,* December 4, 1980, p. 25.

[56] Lawrence Ingrassia, "As Mr. Whipple Shows, Ad Stars Can Bring Long-Term Sales Gain," *The Wall Street Journal,* February 12, 1981, p. 27.

[57] "Ads Should Focus on Products, Not Themselves," *Marketing News,* August 12, 1977.

[58] Leslie Schultz, "Not Quite Ready for Prime Time President," *Inc.,* April 1985, pp. 156–160.

[59] Judith Dobrzynski and J. E. Davis, "Business Celebrities," *Business Week,* June 23, 1986, pp. 100–107.

[60] Ann M. Morrison, "The Boss as Pitchman," *Fortune,* August 25, 1980, pp. 66–73.

[61] Gordon M. Henry, "And Now a Gag from Our Sponsor," *Time,* May 19, 1986, pp. 71, 74.

[62] Kevin Higgins, "There's Gold in Silver Screen Plugs," *Marketing News,* October 11, 1985, p. 6.

[63] Cheryl Waixel, "Score One for the Sponsor!" *World,* May–June 1986, pp. 38–42.

[64] Marsha L. Richins, "Negative Word-of-Mouth by Dissatisfied Consumers: A Pilot Study," *Journal of Marketing,* **47:**68–78, Winter 1983.

[65] "Marketing," *The Wall Street Journal,* October 22, 1981, p. 29.

[66] Betty Diener and Stephen Greyser, "Consumer Views of Redress Needs," *Journal of Marketing,* **42:**21–27, October 1978.

[67] Jim Montgomery, "Rumor-Plagued Firms Use Various Strategies to Keep Damage Low," *The Wall Street Journal,* February 6, 1979, pp. 1, 22; Michael Waldholz, "Of Gingerbread Men With Pigtails, Rumor Problems at Entenmann's," *The Wall Street Journal,* October 1, 1980, p. 31; and John E. Cooney, "Bubble Gum Maker Wants to Know How the Rumors Started," *The Wall Street Journal,* March 24, 1977, p. 1.

[68] Alice M. Tybout, Bobby J. Calder, and Brian Sternthal, "Using Information Processing Theory to Design Marketing Strategies," *Journal of Marketing Research,* **18:**73–79, February 1981.

[69] Daniel Sherrell and R. Eric Reidenbach, "A Consumer Response Framework for Negative Publicity: Suggestions for Response Strategies," *Akron Business and Economic Review,* Summer 1986, pp. 37–44.

CASES FOR PART THREE

CASE 3-1
DOMINO'S PIZZA*

The clock is ticking. Up drives a car with a blue sign strapped on top of it. Out jumps the driver in a red, white, and blue polyester uniform carrying in an insulated bag the cardboard carton containing a Domino's pizza. He hurries up the sidewalk while the customer times him to the second, since the 2000-outlet chain guarantees the pizza will arrive at its destination within thirty minutes or the purchaser gets a discount of at least $3; if delivery takes over forty-five minutes, the pizza is free.

Domino's is the nation's second largest pizza chain behind only Pizza Hut. As a result of a partnership split-up with his brother when the company was struggling, Thomas Monaghan began to implement his business concepts in 1965. He removed all food items except pizza from his small restaurant's menu, went exclusively to take-out and delivery, and changed the name to Domino's, selecting as a logo a red domino with three dots—one for each of his stores. The name Domino's had immediate identification with a known symbol, thus helping its recognition.

Although most other fast-food operations are diversifying their menus, Domino's has stressed one of its basic principles—"keep it simple." This means, generally, that only pizza and colas are offered, with only two sizes of pizza available, with a choice of ten toppings. Monaghan believes the thirty-minute free delivery within a store's delivery zone was the greatest thing Domino's ever did.

The stores are small, compact units composed of ovens, work space, and storage space. Taking inventory at the end of the day requires only about five minutes.

The biggest challenge for Domino's is getting people used to ordering dinner by phone. The keys to Domino's success have been convenience and a competitive product. Also, inclement weather helps sales. Domino's fast growth to over $1 billion in sales has been impressive and has produced a bunch of imitators featuring various menus, all of them

working to develop their particular niche. Now that baby boomers, who grew up on fast foods, have their own children, it is not hard for them to make the switch to ordering pizza for dinner rather than eating hamburgers. As parents they may also find comfort in not having to deal with recalcitrant children in a restaurant. With more couples working, everything is leaning toward convenience, especially in the home.

Only 20 percent of all pizzas are now delivered; thus it is expected that this factor will be a very important element in the future of fast food. Many expect to see hamburgers, chicken, fish, and Mexican food chains moving toward home delivery, since consumers appear willing to pay for the convenience. In fact, it has been suggested that all food items that can be packaged well enough to stand the ten- to fifteen-minute travel time will be home delivered.

Initially Domino's stores were concentrated around college campuses and military bases. But with urban markets now being targeted, more consumer awareness is necessary. Until recently the company was not well known in the fast-food industry because they only spent money in their immediate delivery area for direct mail, door hangers, and local radio. Now corporate Domino's and franchisees spend over $60 million on merchandising, promotions, and advertising. The company even sponsors a professional team-tennis league and enters a number of car-racing events including the Indianapolis 500.

With the chain strongly established in lucrative suburban markets across the United States, it is now looking at major metropolitan areas for expansion potential. But, in metropolitan areas the cost of expansion is high and the competition is tough.

Another market for Domino's is overseas. It offers at least double the potential of the U.S. market. However, starting up abroad requires a lot of effort but produces small results. The company has a goal of 1000 international stores by 1990. Domino's biggest international marketing task is to sell the idea of home delivery in areas where there is no such tradition. In other countries, too, Domino's guarantees thirty-minute delivery or else a rebate if that goal is not met.

---

*Kevin T. Higgins, "Home Delivery Is Helping Pizza to Battle Burgers," *Marketing News*, August 1, 1986, pp. 1, 6; Aimee Stern, "Domino's: A Unique Concept Pays Off," *Dun's Business Month*, May 1986, pp. 50–51; Raymond Serafin, "Domino's Pizza Finds Global Going Slow," *Advertising Age*, January 6, 1986, p. 12; and Raymond Serafin, "Domino's Pizza Delivers on the Basics," *Advertising Age*, July 8, 1985, pp. 4, 60.

Questions

1 What cultural values are important in this situation?
2 Describe other businesses or products that cater to such values in the United States.
3 What are some important demographic characteristics influencing the success of these situations in the United States?
4 Why is Domino's delivery concept more difficult to sell abroad?

As Dick Richards speaks, the soft, familiar sounds of the Texas plains pepper his conversation. Familiar, too, are the 830 stores the Tandy vice-president operates in five European countries. "Basically," Richards says, "the merchandise is the same; the concept is the same; the different categories—from the hi-fi stereo to the different parts and pieces—are the same. I think you would probably recognize a Radio Shack store of a few years back."

What distinguishes Tandy's European stores (operated under the Tandy name) from American Radio Shack stores is unprofitability. European operations have reported losses both in local currencies and in U.S. dollars for each of the last three fiscal years. Stores in the Netherlands and West Germany have never turned a profit. "From 1979 to 1982," Richards says, "we were highly successful—and profitable—in Belgium, France, and the United Kingdom. As the U.S. dollar strengthened, it eroded a lot of things. As the Belgians like to call it, the crisis of Europe hit, and the economy was pretty stagnant." Yet, what troubles Tandy-Europe is more than just unfavorable currency conversions, and Richards is among the first to admit it. "I think that contributes to it," he says, "but I don't think that's the total problem. There've been some real problems other than the dollar effect."

Before Tandy-Europe can be turned around, volume per store must be increased. Currently, Tandy-Europe stores average only $140,000 in annual sales, compared to U.S. Radio Shack's $355,000 per store average. Sales per square foot are under $200 in Europe, compared to over $300 in U.S. stores. In addition, Richards must find a way to increase gross margins, which have been slipping for the last two years. At the same time he must trim operating expenses. Within the confines of European retailing, the winning combination will be difficult to achieve.

Upping store volume will be a troublesome task, since the typical Tandy store in Europe is only a little over half the size of the average 1200-square-foot Radio Shack store in the United States. With a proportionately fewer number of SKUs (stock-keeping units) to merchandise, the mix in Europe will have to be further fine-tuned to provide more dramatic one-of-a-kind values to boost sales. Also, Richards will have to do without at least one of Radio Shack's best-selling categories—telephones. In the United States, Radio Shack claims a market share for telephones second only to AT&T Phone Stores. With a still largely regulated market for phones over most of Europe, the option to create similar success is

impossible. Richards, in some markets, will also have to increase store volume without some of the promotional tools that are standard in the United States. In West Germany, for example, promotional battery or flashlight giveaways are deemed illegal inducements to buy.

Tandy-Europe, then, will be forced to develop its own strategies distinct from those that work for Radio Shack back home. In the United Kingdom, Tandy is experimenting with both different categories of merchandise and an incremental move away from private label brands. The mix in British stores now includes up to 20 percent popular-branded goods. As the British market heated up for microwave ovens, Tandy brought in Sharp microwaves at first and now have added Tandy-labeled ovens. But the need to maintain gross margins in the face of price-increase restrictions in some European markets will hamper the amount of experimentation. The cheapest way for Tandy-Europe to achieve buying clout will be continuing to piggyback onto orders U.S. Radio Shack president Bernard Appel makes from Fort Worth.

"We'll still try to basically merchandise the line as much as possible along the same lines, so that we have economy of purchasing," Richards says. "At one time we would follow right along behind Bernie, and when he made a purchase, we would try to tag along and get the better price. That was great to start off with, and we will do that in some cases, but where we can, we go to a more European styling," says Richards.

There is also a recognition that the customer in Antwerp is different from the customer in Altoona. For one, Europeans prefer less bass sound from their audio systems. And while pastel colors are all the rage this year in the United States, Europeans fancy what Tandy is calling "Le Black Power," or stark, black surfaces. And while the buyer in Fort Worth will also sell goods in Dallas, the comparisons in Europe do not always hold true, further fragmenting buying power. For instance, videocassette recorders are a hit in Britain, but their sales on the Continent are less astounding. Also, the British prefer mini and rack stereo systems, the Belgians less so, and the French least of all. In addition, from place to place in the European system the customer watches a completely different television receiving system. Then there are computer keyboards which must be rearranged according to the language custom of the user. As annoyingly small a detail as what plugs into the electrical outlet at the end of the cord must be adjusted market by market, adding cost to every buying decision.

Not only do cultural differences limit efficient buying, but also they make efforts to reduce operating costs all that more

---

* Rick Gallagher, "Tandy Faces Troubled Operations in Europe," *Chain Store Age, General Merchandise Trends,* May 1986, pp. 41, 43. Reprinted with permission.

difficult. "Because of the changes of language, because of the changes of currency, and because everybody's got to do everything a little bit different, it creates challenges," says Richards. Though Tandy-Europe spends the same 9 to 10 percent of sales on advertising that U.S. Radio Shack does, expensive European advertising rates mean less promotion for the same money. In an international environment, even the basic Tandy catalog is more expensive. "The language difference is the big thing," Richards says, "because instead of putting out one catalog like they do in the U.S., on the Continent here we put out two versions for Belgium—the Dutch and the French with the same Belgian franc pricing— we put out one for Germany, one for Holland. In France it's different, too, even in your basic advertising, because Belgian French is different from French French."

Equally demanding, and expensive, is the need to tailor merchandise presentations to individual national markets. "The United Kingdom stores will have the same color schemes as the French stores, but they'll look different because the French want a store that looks different," Richards says. "The United Kingdom is more flamboyant in their merchandising. In France and Holland and Belgium and Germany, it's a little bit more conservative. You have the same color scheme—the reds and the grays—but it's not the kind of thing that hits you like a United Kingdom store, where the image is 'Here's the place to get some bargains.'"

Tandy-Europe will also have to increase its number of stores to achieve further economies. Though its current 830 stores is below the 1984 high of 852, Tandy plans an aggressive rollout of new stores. Immediate expansion is planned for both Britain and France. "There's a lot of truth to the fact that what makes Radio Shack really big is that they're on every block, and they're convenient," says Richards. In the United States there is a Radio Shack store for every 35,000 people. In contrast, there is only one Tandy store for every 1.5 million West Germans.

Despite all the obstacles, Richards thinks he can turn Tandy-Europe into a profit maker. "There's business to be done here," he says, "and money to be made—big money."

Questions

1 How have cultural differences affected Tandy's success in Europe?

2 In what ways can an understanding of these cross-cultural patterns help in developing an appropriate marketing strategy for Tandy-Europe?

CASE 3-3
METROPOLITAN LIFE INSURANCE*

Metropolitan Life is the top insurance company in market share and consumer awareness in seven Hispanic markets in the United States. The company discovered Hispanics by accident when it was looking for overseas markets in 1982. Met Life was looking for other countries but found a country within a country, called Hispanic America, a market of 15 million people.

Research showed that recent immigrants were prime life insurance customers. Hispanics were seen as stable, hard-working, family-oriented, and interested in savings, their children's education, and making it in America—similar in those respects to immigrants of earlier eras.

Metropolitan embarked on a nationwide marketing effort tailored to the needs of Spanish-speaking Americans. The company uses bilingual managers and sales representatives supported with Spanish language sales promotion material, advertising, direct mail, and special telemarketing programs. It established a bilingual toll-free number for questions and new orders. In 1982, Metropolitan Life was fourth in the market penetration of Hispanics. In 1986 they were first.

In 1985 a door-to-door survey was conducted of 1400 Hispanics in Chicago, Houston, Los Angeles, Miami, New York, San Antonio, and San Francisco. The study ranked Metropolitan first in the three categories it measured: top-of-mind awareness, total unaided awareness, and consumer life insurance ownership as a measure of market share.

Metropolitan has programmed its nationwide computerized sales system to print out information in Spanish and English, to serve Hispanic customers. In addition, the Metropolitan Life Foundation, the philanthropic arm of the company, plans to award scholarships through the National Hispanic Scholarship Fund to Hispanic students in colleges and universities in areas where Metropolitan has offices.

Less than a year after its marketing rollout, Metropolitan had doubled its life insurance market share in some parts of the country. In others its share was tripled. The company now intends to strengthen and increase its leadership in the Hispanic market. As a result of Metropolitan's success in that market, the company recently expanded operations to the Caribbean by opening an office in San Juan, Puerto Rico.

The company's experience with Hispanic customers changed the way senior management looked at the United States and started them thinking about marketing to different

---

* Adapted from "Metropolitan Life Tops with Hispanics," *Marketing News,* November 8, 1985, p. 4, published by the American Marketing Association; and "Met Life Mines Minority Market," *American Demographics,* July 1986, pp. 18–19.

groups. Asian Americans stood out as the next undiscovered market. Metropolitan life already had 300 Asian salespeople in 1985, and the company's top sales offices, in Los Angeles and Houston, were headed by Asians.

Life insurance salespeople expect that about 15 percent of their customers will let their insurance lapse in an average year. However, Asian customers have a lapse rate of between 5 and 10 percent. And Asian families routinely save as much as one-fifth of their income.

Focus group research with Asian salespeople uncovered special qualities in Asian American consumers. Recently arrived Asian householders may be well-educated and hold down skilled jobs, but they usually choose conservative savings and investment plans because security is of critical importance. They follow powerful traditions of respect for elders and love of children. Chinese consumers purchase insurance to protect the family and pay for education, so they choose plans that offer high cash value. Korean consumers, although still interested in security, express more interest in plans that provide a maximum return on investment. To sell insurance to a Korean, an agent must first be introduced by a mutual acquaintance because few will buy from strangers. Filipino consumers are most interested in education, while Vietnamese consumers, the newest group of immigrants, are "survival oriented."

These profiles were used to develop marketing plans for Boston, Chicago, Houston, Los Angeles, New York City, Philadelphia, San Francisco, and Washington, D.C. The company has translated sales and promotional literature into Chinese and Korean, and they have hired a small agency in New York that specializes in the Chinese market, to develop ads. After Metropolitan Life establishes itself among Chinese and Korean Americans, it plans to begin selling insurance to Vietnamese, Filipino, Laotian, and Indian consumers.

Questions

1 Based on Metropolitan Life's success, what general guidelines are suggested for subcultural marketing by other companies?
2 What other influences may be important factors in understanding these markets for insurance purchasing?

CASE 3-4
FAMILY DOLLAR STORES*

Many discount stores serving the blue-collar market have been "upscaling," that is, they have opened fancy new stores in higher income suburban areas and changed their emphasis toward higher priced merchandise lines. Not Family Dollar Stores, Inc., headquartered in Charlotte, North Carolina. Started in 1959, Family Dollar has grown to 1000 stores in twenty states located as far north as Pennsylvania and Ohio, as far south as Florida, and as far west as Arkansas and Louisiana. The company has found that there is big money to be made in meeting the needs of those with little money to spend or those intent on spending what they have more wisely. Although such downscale buyers may each spend less than the much-touted upscale shoppers, they still spend billions of dollars each year on the basics, because they have to. Family Dollar has zeroed in on this segment and succeeded, because of its commitment to downscale marketing.

Discount pioneers such as J. C. Penney, K-mart and Wal-Mart have attempted to broaden their appeal and reach middle-income Americans as well as less affluent buyers. A visit in 1986 by England's Prince Charles and Princess Diana to a Penney's in suburban Washington, D.C., was clear evidence that the chain was no longer just for bargain hunters. Although K-mart, Penney, Sears, and others have moved upscale, Family Dollar has stayed in its original blue-collar niche. "We've always had a working-man base. We broadened that base during the recession. Then middle-class shoppers had to look for better values," states the company's president.

Approximately 65 percent of Family Dollar Stores are located in towns and rural areas with a population of 15,000 or less. Some of the stores are free-standing, but most are located in strip shopping centers. When the company's real estate staff checks out the 500 to 600 potential locations available at any given moment, they look for oil spots and cheap shoes. These telltale signs say much about their potential customers. Apparently they drive old cars that drip a lot of oil. The stores don't cater to people who wear old clothes but have on $50 running shoes. Thus it is shoes, not clothes, that are the tipoff. The stores have to be placed in

* Steve Lawrence, "The Green in Blue-Collar Retailing," *Fortune,* May 27, 1985, pp. 74–77; Liz Murphy, "Watch Out America, Here Comes Family Dollar," *Sales and Marketing Management,* October 8, 1984, pp. 64–67; and William Dunn, "In Pursuit of the Downscale," *American Demographics,* May 1986, pp. 26–33.

low- and lower-middle income areas, since the typical customer has a family income under $17,000 a year, or about $7580 below the U.S. median.

Each 6000-to-8000 square-foot store handles approximately 5000 SKUs (stock-keeping units), or approximately one-fifth the items found in large discount stores. Apparel and footwear account for 45 percent of sales, while 50 percent comes from health and beauty items, gifts, toys, and household items. Less than 4 percent of Family Dollar's merchandise is seconds or irregulars. Anything priced above $16.99 must be approved by the company's policy committee, who must be convinced that their customers need the product. Price has been a critical factor in developing customer loyalty.

Because Family Dollar's customers tend to live from paycheck to paycheck the stores carry the smallest size of toiletries and beauty aids, which match tight budgets. Customers have learned to shop Family Dollar every week. The average customer spends slightly more than $6 each shopping trip, all in cash since Family Dollar has no charge accounts and honors no credit cards.

Stores are laid out with hard goods on one side, soft goods on the other, and an alley of tables with promotional goods in between. Stores are nearly identical: they are brightly lit, air-conditioned, and clean. They have no piped-in music and practically shout "bargain."

The basic floor plan dictated from Charlotte calls for women's wear to be at the right of the front door because most customers are women and most shoppers walk to the right when they enter a store. Toys are placed at the back right corner so that traffic is drawn through the store. Impulse and sale items are found at the ends of aisles.

The chain advertises in 800 newspapers each week (such as the *Elba Clipper, Choctaw Advocate,* and *Jeff Davis County Leader*). Sixteen million color circulars that are the same in every area are distributed monthly through mailings, newspaper inserts, and by hand delivery. Weekly newspaper advertising in the chain's market area stresses Family Dollar's good-value-at-low-prices theme. Direct mail is increasing because Family Dollar shoppers are not regular newspaper subscribers.

Knowing that poor quality merchandise won't sell to their customers, the stores "offer plain, not fancy, good-quality merchandise at moderate prices." Brand names account for about 30 percent of merchandise at Family Dollar Stores. All stores now sell the same mix of products, but the chain may need to consider adapting to preferences as it expands its locations to the north and west.

Expansion doesn't mean a change of focus. "We know the

customers and their needs. We don't try to be all things to all people. We see ourselves as sort of a convenience store, like 7-Eleven," says the company's president. He states, "We do not sell fashion. It doesn't matter whether miniskirts are in or out. We sell basic skirts in basic colors. It is our competition that keeps going upscale, and all they have done is left us a bigger gap to fill. We do not want to be like Wal-Mart, where you have to walk 40 yards to find something and then wait in long lines to pay for it."

Some retail analysts question whether Family Dollar is well positioned for further expansion, particularly because of the recent economic recovery in the United States. But the chain headquarters believes that because so many large discount houses have moved to higher-priced merchandise, an even larger market niche has been created for them.

Questions

1 Which social-class segment(s) is Family Dollar Stores seeking to attract?
2 Is their marketing approach in appealing to the segment(s) appropriate?
3 Are they positioned well for further expansion?

CASE 3-5
HALLMARK CARDS*

Americans bought 7 billion greeting cards in 1983, cards for everything from birthdays to barbecues. Greeting cards were half the personal mail sent last year, with a total of 2.3 billion names on our cumulative Christmas list, 1.5 billion birthday greetings amounting to 6.3 cards for each of us, and 900 million hearts on Valentine's Day, 1983. The remainder announced events private and public, secret desires, and personal woes. Because of its "communication needs," the public spends approximately $3.4 billion each year on cards, not counting postage.

One sociologist notes that cards may not be the convenience item they are perceived to be, since it takes much more time to drive to the store and pick out a card than it does to write a letter. Cards represent, therefore, not a substitute for letters, but a new form of brief communication. Although cards are unnecessary, effective marketing has turned them into an imagined necessity, as with cake mixes and deodorant soaps.

With growing access to telephones and lower rates, it was feared by card producers that the public would not mail as many greeting cards. But while telephones may have de-

* Jeffrey P. Rosenfeld and Susan Rodin, "Lifestyle: It's In the Cards," *American Demographics,* December 1984, pp. 31–37; Robert McGough, "Pansies Are Green," *Forbes,* February 10, 1986, pp. 89–92; and Laurie Freeman, "Card Marketers Getting the Message," *Advertising Age,* February 27, 1986, pp. 18–20.

stroyed the letter, they have not hurt the greeting card. A telephone call cannot be held in the hands or put on the mantel. The mass greeting card industry grew as it became linked to Christmas messages. Even during World War II, when the U.S. government threatened paper and ink rationing for greeting cards, this frivolity was made to appear necessary because of a Hallmark official's claim that greeting cards were a major factor in building the morale of the people. The ink and paper were not rationed.

Eleven million cards a day are produced by Hallmark and sent to 37,000 outlets—22,000 independent specialty retail stores and 15,000 of Hallmark's Ambassador outlets. Computers keep track of all cards and two huge automated warehouses ship reorders based on the past sales of each card in each store. Over 90 percent of cards are replaced with new designs every year. With 32,000 card types, there is a message for every occasion.

Increasingly, the card business is finding itself controlled by the whims of fashion. Changes in taste are accelerating in the United States. New companies have entered the market to provide "alternative" cards (such as unusual, humorous, risqué, or goofy) and have become a serious threat to major companies such as Hallmark. Hallmark refuses to produce risqué cards. While aiming for the big segment of the market rather than small niches, Hallmark has fought back against alternatives with its Lite line of cards ("a third less serious than regular greeting cards"). This product line has grown faster than the rest of the company, leading Hallmark to add other alternative lines as well.

Card companies, large and small, adapt to our changing communication needs by following the behavior of a so-called modal buyer. Statistically speaking, she is in her late forties, married, suburban, and traditional. Apparently she keeps the cash registers humming, too. Hallmark and American Greetings, together, sell half of all cards purchased in the United States every year. These industry giants work on the assumption that women buy 85 percent of all greeting cards. Other companies disagree, however. The demographics of the alternate market are anything but traditional, suburban, and female. An estimated 35 percent of people buying cards from Paper Moon, Rock Shots, and California Dreamers are men living in gentrifying urban areas. In general, "alternate" card buyers are better educated, less traditional, and more cosmopolitan than card buyers from Hallmark country. The industry divides card buyers into two markets based on age. The first is the older American—the 25 million people aged 65 and older. The other is the age-conscious people aged 35 to 64.

Card shops are stocking greater numbers of cards for older Americans because there are more four-generation families and more social situations involving older people. Cards intended for older people include the expected ones to commemorate birthdays, anniversaries, and retirements. New

additions include grandparent announcements for older people to send and birthday wishes for great-grandchildren. Hallmark created variety packs of cards for older people—packages of cards for different occasions—after learning that older Americans wanted to minimize their trips to the stationery store.

Cards for and about grandparenting make good demographic sense because 75 percent of older Americans have living children and 90 percent of these Americans have grandchildren.

The greeting cards older Americans give and get are respectful and friendly in tone. They reconfirm traditional roles and celebrate the part that older people play in American family life. This celebration of old age is different from greeting cards that deal with aging—cards pitched at a younger market.

The greeting card industry—with a large female work force of its own—has been giving special attention to women. It has successfully capitalized on the subject of work, and also on the fact that working women want to save time. Greeting cards are a quick fix.

Cards for working women can be serious, sarcastic, or just plain nice. They are rarely floral or frilly. Hallmark has avoided the floral look in promoting its Modern Woman line of cards. Working women enjoy the humor but shy away from the frills.

Housework, child care, and job obligations are not easy to juggle. Hallmark understands that working women can overlook dirty laundry now and then, but they will never compromise on child care. As a result, working women now have cards that read, "Thanks for all your help" or "You have such a way with children" and "Can't thank you enough for doing so much."

Working women are more likely than working men to send cards to the people who work for them. They also send more cards to coworkers and supervisors. Examples of women's business greetings include, "Congratulations on your promotion" and "Good luck in your new job," as well as a simple "Thanks for a good job." Greeting cards confirm what so many of us know from thumbing through our personal address books: relationships in the 1980s are changeable and complex. This fact only increases the opportunities for greeting card manufacturers, who see new relationships and remarriages as a way to sell more cards.

Divorce is still a sensitive subject but is socially acceptable enough for Hallmark to be marketing a number of cards for divorced people, including Hallmark's "Thinking of you as you're starting over." Hallmark also helps the recently divorced with packaged divorce announcements.

The greeting card industry appreciates children whose

parents are divorced or remarried—a delicate topic. An estimated 8 percent of American households are single-parent households, which is why American Greetings will offer a card that reads, ''Because you do the work of two people, you're appreciated twice as much.''

There are greeting cards for the live-in lover or new spouse. Gone are the days of the wicked stepmother, especially since 1300 new step-families are created each day. This is why Drawing Board Greeting Cards in Dallas now markets greetings ''To my dad and his wife'' and ''To my other mother.'' The company also has cards for the step-grandparents that any divorce or remarriage will generate. An estimated 65 percent of grandparents will be step-grandparents by the year 2000—a legacy of all the divorcing and remarrying their children have done.

There are currently 1.9 million couples living together unmarried, more than triple the 1970 figure. Cohabitants are a prime market for greeting card manufacturers. Paper Moon's display rack in one Manhattan card shop on the Upper West Side has more slots for Friends/Lovers cards than for Wedding or Anniversary Greetings.

Cards for cohabitants are based on the relationship itself and not on the milestones that a married couple celebrates. Hallmark's line of New Relationships cards explores such themes as coping, support, and friendship. ''Happy anniversary on your special day'' is a Hallmark card that sells briskly, because the card never specifies what the special day is.

There are now greeting cards for people of all social and sexual persuasions: cards as prim as the Just Desserts line with its sundae-shaped greetings, and cards as naughty as those from Rock Shots. ''A poem for your birthday'' reads the front of one card by The Maine Line Company. ''Hip Hip Hooray! I'm glad you're gay!'' says the inside. No one can accuse greeting cards of not keeping up to date. Like any other profit-oriented industry, greeting card companies can't afford to be locked into today's ideas. Two trends are already emerging that show signs of reshaping the industry in years to come.

The first is a growing health consciousness. Daniel Yankelovich, a public opinion researcher who has studied this trend, says interest in health and fitness will intensify, and with it will come more self-expression. Even now this is translating into subjects and occasions for card sending. Everything from weight loss to good wishes on an upcoming marathon shows up in greeting cards.

The shift from acute to chronic illness that has already reshaped American health care will soon affect the greeting card industry. Along with the ''Get well soon'' wishes for

acutely ill people will be ''Feel better'' cards for the chronically ill.

Ethnic cards are becoming big sellers, especially for Hispanics who number 16 million. Hallmark's Plaza Press is a rapidly expanding line of cards geared to these buyers. Ethnic consumers are different. They have a higher demand for Mother's Day and Christmas cards and lower demand for Valentine's Day cards. Cards for important Hispanic cultural events such as a girl's 15th birthday (*Quince Ano*), first Holy Communion, and birthday cards for godparents are also much demanded. Hispanics also place much more emphasis on quality than on price in card selection. Moreover, once a card brand is accepted, they are highly loyal.

In the 1960s Hallmark tried a Spanish-language card line designed primarily for distribution in Latin America, but it did not work well and was abandoned. The rapid increase in Hispanic population caused Hallmark to try again; thus, in 1982 it reentered the market with a line that concentrates on the United States, although the cards are also available in Latin America. More than 350 Spanish-language all-occasion and seasonal cards are marketed by Hallmark, but not in all outlets. There are few low-price points in the line since buyers seem more concerned with high quality and value. They are more likely to trade up in price for a greeting card. The oversized cards are of high-quality finishes, such as satin, embellished designs. Although the same cover art may be used for English and Spanish-language cards, captions are never translated into Spanish. Spanish-speaking writers start from scratch and use Castilian or ''generic'' Spanish to avoid the problems of translating into regional dialects spoken by those of Mexican, Puerto Rican, or Cuban backgrounds. So far, no card has been recalled because of embarrassing words or because of something offensive. Hallmark is trying to add humorous cards into the line to be aimed at younger consumers.

Hallmark does not advertise its Spanish-language line but relies instead on point-of-purchase materials and word of mouth. However, the company's old corporate campaign ''When you care enough to send the very best'' has had some carryover benefit with Hispanic buyers.

Greeting cards for other ethnic groups such as Asian Americans—particularly Chinese, Japanese, and Koreans—could become much more visible, at least in some cities. Asians' educational and income levels make them prime greeting card consumers.

Whatever demographic changes lie ahead, the industry that was once based on eternal verities like love and marriage will continue to adapt. Roses may still be red and violets, blue, but greeting cards, more than ever, will reflect you.

Questions

1 How have greeting card makers segmented the market?

2 What demographic and lifestyle trends are reflected in greeting card themes?

3 What cultural values are relevant to greeting card success?

4 Evaluate the ethnic strategy of greeting card makers.

5 Visit a card store or drugstore and examine the greeting cards. Write down the copy from five cards that are a clear reflection of demographic trends and from five that exhibit support for certain core values.

CASE 3-6
CODE-A-PHONE*

After years of slow growth, telephone answering devices (TADS) have suddenly piqued consumer interest. From 1981 to 1984, market research tracked a leisurely 25 percent increase in the number of households that said they expected to buy an answering machine. During the period from 1985 to mid-1986, however, the number who said they would buy an answering device jumped another 54 percent. The latest survey records the highest level of consumer interest in the five years of consumer polling.

THE TAD INDUSTRY

Industry analysts are attributing the sudden support of consumer interest to everything from more working women to more single-person households. Code-A-Phone marketing vice president Paul Newman postulates a simpler answer—the product's time has come. Newman says that with telephone answering devices now exceeding a 10 percent household penetration, the devices have hit a crucial point in the marketing cycle where they will begin to create wider demand as more people are exposed to their benefits.

Thus far, though, interest in telephone answering machines is most heavily concentrated in certain geographic areas. According to the poll, buying intentions are highest in the south Atlantic, south central, mid-Atlantic, and Pacific states. Consumer buying plans are lowest in North Carolina and the mountain states, as well as in New England.

Code-A-Phone has a number of competitors in the TAD market. One of these is AT&T. In telephones, the communications giant enjoys both tremendous market share and considerable top-of-mind consumer awareness. In a 1986 survey, 51.1 percent of the households that expected to buy a telephone in the next year said that they wanted to buy an AT&T phone. Though undeniably the biggest player to be reckoned with in telephones, AT&T's strength doesn't seem

---

* Adapted from Rick Gallagher, "AT&T Is Not Answering the Phone," *Chain Store Age, General Merchandise Trends,* May 1986, p. 46; Rick Gallagher, "TAD's Intention to Buy Jumps 54%," *Chain Store Age, General Merchandise Trends,* May 1986, p. 46; and Rick Gallagher, "TAD's Message Needs Clarification," *Chain Store Age, General Merchandise Trends,* August 1986, pp. 28, 30. Reprinted with permission.

to carry over into telephone answering machines. According to one poll, only 13 percent of those who intend to buy an answerer expect to buy AT&T. Panasonic, named by 26.1 percent of prospective consumer buyers, unspecified brand name (23.9 percent), and store brands (17.4 percent) all beat out AT&T in the survey.

On the whole, consumers have a pretty good idea of what they will be spending for answerers. The average amount cited by prospective buyers in a recent survey is $127. Retailers reflect this thinking in their assortment. Macy's New York, for example, offers one brand at $119 and tops out with another at $229, which meets the price expectations of 68 percent of potential customers. Adding an addtional unit priced just under $100, however, would up that number to 84 percent.

CODE-A-PHONE

In order to identify ways of strengthening its marketing strategy, Code-A-Phone conducted consumer research to better understand its market. One Code-A-Phone focus group found that potential telephone answering device customers understand the major benefits of TAD but think the machines are overpriced. The research also reveals potential customers as confused about many of the marketing and advertising terms the industry takes for granted.

When the focus group, one of several Code-A-Phone interviewed in the San Francisco area during 1986, was asked what features a telephone answering device should have, its members ticked off a pretty standard list of what's on the market. Answering and screening calls is at the top of their list. In addition, the group said the machine should record any length message, have automatic shutoff at the end of the caller's message, record at least 10 to 15 messages, and have some sort of remote message playback.

Yet when the group was asked to define the very terms the industry uses to identify these same features, they drew a blank. One of the group confused "beeperless remote" with paging devices. Given the term "remote turn-on" one group member, after barely containing a giggle, felt obliged to apologize, "Sorry, I had to laugh at that one." "It would be fine," quipped another group member, "as long as it didn't open your garage door." However, all the focus group members immediately and correctly understood what a PIN (Personal Identification Number) is, suggesting at least one way to explain to customers what beeperless access really means. But, as with the terms the industry uses to define other features, the focus group was equally befuddled about "voice-activated recording" and "one-touch message playback."

Asked about "long distance toll-saver," one group member asked, "Would it save when you call or when someone calls you?" Another remarked, "I'd like to know how they'd do that." The group had an easier time understanding what "indefinite length message" meant, but preferred the term "unlimited length message." Given the choice between a compact unit and a larger machine, the group opted for smaller TADs. Yet, they showed some hesitation about the microcassettes which the smaller devices use. "I would wonder if they hold the same amount of data," asked one member. Another group participant worried that the smaller cassettes would be easier to lose, or even to step on. They also showed concern for how much a microcassette machine would cost. "I don't see many of those small ones," said one. "I wouldn't know where to buy them. They're more expensive, too."

In the end, the group continually returned to the issue of price. Once they overcame some of their confusion over what particular features are correctly called, the group again questioned expense. Worse yet, they said they are not willing to spend even $5 more for any feature. The group's consensus was that telephone answering devices retail for about $150. A more reasonable price, according to one group member, would be equal to what a telephone itself costs. "I think that's kind of expensive," he said, "because your average telephone from AT&T is only $70, and you use that just as often as you do your answering machine." Even at $70, the focus group demanded packaging which clearly describes the product's features and benefits. "For 70 bucks, I want a lot of information," said one. "I want to figure out what it does before I even decide if I want to consider buying it. I want to clearly understand: OK, you can do this and this."

When it comes to just what a TAD does, the focus group had a firm grip on their function. "When you're not home, you're not home," summed up one group member. "I'm not usually at home," said another. "I work late at night, so about 12 or 1, I get off. I get a lot of calls, so I can get them. All my friends call me, so I know what they have to say."

The focus group also revealed that its members clearly understood the benefit of—and the term—"call screening." In fact, the group saved much of its enthusiasm for the idea that they can avoid unwanted calls. "Some nights we get so many calls," lamented one group member, "we wish we had a machine so we could have it on and we could answer it whenever we wanted to."

On the negative side, some of the focus group still harbored resentment toward those who use the telephone answering devices. "I don't like it," said one, "when you call somebody and just get the answering service. It's kind of irritating." But other group members disagreed. "I get a lot of dial tones on my machine from people who refuse to leave a message," said one member. "I find that they're rare or just being weird."

In fact, at least one of the focus group considered a telephone answering machine preferable to leaving a message with a human answerer. "I never mind leaving a message on a machine," he said, "because usually you can trust they're going to get the message. Believe it or not, it's better than leaving it with a person, who either will forget or give you the wrong message."

Questions

1 Evaluate Code-A-Phone's consumer research.
2 Suggest ways Code-A-Phone and other manufacturers can accelerate diffusion of TADs.

CASE 3-7
COMPACT DISCS*

COMPACT DISC TECHNOLOGY

Compact disc (CD) players are giving the audio business its first hit since stereo. In 1983 laser-read CD records were an untested and expensive new technology whose acceptance by consumers was the music industry's great question mark. Today the CD is challenging the supremacy of the long-playing record. In 1985 CDs accounted for 8.9 percent of the sales of the $4.4 billion recording industry which also includes LPs and tapes. In 1986 analysts expected CD sales of nearly 50 million discs.

Defenders of LPs have been striking back at the shiny, aluminum-and-plastic CDs. One writer calls them "metallic, gritty, grainy, and unnatural." Others call the claims for superiority of CDs "hype," and some audio retailers believe that LPs are not going to vanish.

In traditional analog recording, sound waves are transcribed as grooves onto a vinyl disc. A diamond-tipped stylus in the turntable's tone arm then traces the grooves to reproduce the sound. But with the new digital recording for compact discs, the music is sampled by a microchip at the rate of 44,100 times a second and recorded as a series of ones and zeros. The numbers, encoded in invisible "pits," are read by a laser-beam player, which sends the information to a microcomputer that converts the numbers back to sound.

---

* Adapted from Michael Walsh, "The Great LP vs. CD War," *Time,* August 25, 1986; Rick Gallagher, "A Shot In the Arm for CD Players," *Chain Store Age, General Merchandise Trends,* January 1987, pp. 40–41; and Rick Gallagher, "Looming Entry Could Cause Problems," *Chain Store Age, General Merchandise Trends,* October 1986, pp. 60–61. Reprinted with permission.

Critics claim that digital recordings lack the warmth and ambience of the top analog recordings when played on the best equipment. They contend, for example, that there is nothing wrong with LPs that cannot be cured by a $1000 Linn Sondek turntable, a $1200 tone arm and an $850 rosewood cartridge. But few ordinary music buffs will want to spend the $10,000 or more to experience the hidden delights of LPs. Despite any problems, CDs have a number of advantages. The sound is clear and bright with no surface noise, no turntable rumble, and no pitch fluctuation. Although recorded on only one side, CDs also have more potential playing time (75 minutes) than the average LP. In addition, songs can be programmed to play in any order, or skipped entirely, allowing listeners to customize their music programming.

THE COMPACT DISC MARKET

Although LPs have an emotional appeal, CDs appear to be here to stay. Feature-loaded players are available for $350 to $500, and the price of the discs has dropped from an average $20 to around $14. Retailers discovered some time ago that the nice thing about razors were razor blades. They are now happily discovering the same relationship with CD players and compact discs. After plunking down $391 for a CD player, the average owner spends another $198 for discs—or about half the cost of the player itself. According to a recent *Chain Store Age* poll, there are 12.4 discs in the average collection. Customers report spending about $15 for each recording. A significant number of CD-player owners—1 in 10—say that they own 25 or more discs already.

Customers with big disc collections are the best prospects for buying a second CD player. In the poll, those who both already own a CD player and who say that there is at least some chance that they will buy an additional player in the next year have twice as many discs as those who say they will not buy a second player this year.

The problem for most retailers will be figuring a way to sell both. Most general merchandise chains—as well as the electronics specialists—have adopted top-seller only merchandise strategies in records and tapes. The best customer for both compact discs and CD players is still a more serious music fan for whom these selections might prove inadequate.

Other findings from the *Chain Store Age* survey reveal that about seven out of ten households say that they have heard of a compact disc player. A little over one-third of households say they actually have listened to a CD recording. And they like what they hear. About seven out of ten in the group that has heard a CD recording report that they can detect a difference between CDs and black vinyl. The hands-down winner is digital—by a margin of over 100 to 1. When asked to rate how much better CD sounds, customers in the survey say, "a lot better" by a 2 to 1 margin. Of those who say that there is at least some chance that they will buy a CD player

within the next twelve months, 60 percent have actually heard a digital recording. Only 45 percent who say that there is no chance they will buy this year have ever heard a CD.

Twelve percent of current CD player owners say that they definitely will buy another player in 1987. Another 12.2 percent report that they maybe or probably will purchase a second CD player this year. And among the 4.5 percent of the sample who say there is at least some chance they will buy a CD player for their car in 1987, all of those who say they definitely will buy are current CD player owners.

The industry's very success in establishing CDs' benefits, however, may be driving the market into price competition as the only way to distinguish players. The effect of price competition over the last year is evident in the survey. While those who already own a CD player report having spent an average $391, those who plan on buying this year expect to pay almost one-fourth less, or only $300.

But despite the industry's tendency to turn to price competition over all others, the poll clearly shows that there are factors other than price which affect the customer's buying decision.

Asked to rank the importance of construction, warranty length, brand name, and cosmetics, customers rated how well a CD player is made as the most important criterion in choosing a specific product to buy. In the sample, 58 percent rank construction as very important. Warranty length is rated as very important by 54 percent; brand name, by 30 percent; and cosmetics, by 20 percent.

When asked what brand they intend to buy, "no answer" is the top choice among those who say there is at least some chance they will buy a CD player this year. Among potential buyers who do have a brand preference, Sony is the first choice, followed by Fisher, Panasonic, Pioneer, RCA, Sharp, Zenith, and Yamaha.

Almost one-fourth of customers cannot give an estimate of what they think they should pay for a CD player. Of those who do know what they expect to pay, there appear to be four prime price points. At the low end, $150 to $179 is the answer for about 5 percent of those polled. Another 11.7 percent think $200 to $249 is the right price, while 14 percent say $300 to $349. There is a healthy upper end, composed of 15 percent of the sample, which expects to pay over $500. Given the choice between a home CD unit and a portable disc player, customers in the survey pick home units by a 2 to 1 margin.

Average income for households which already own a digital disc player stands at $36,500, but falls to $34,000 for those who say they might buy in 1987. Age and education levels of those who will buy this year are also falling. Current

CD player owners are 31.7 years old, but this year's buyers will be a few months younger at 31.4. While last year's buyer was more likely to have a college or postgraduate degree, this year's buyer will include a healthy chunk of those with high school educations.

Men still account for a disproportionate share of those who plan to buy digital players in 1987. Put all together, the best customer for CD players this year will be a white male in his early thirties with an income of $34,000, a high school education or better, and who lives in the suburbs of a metropolitan area with a population of 1 million plus.

DAT MAY BE NEXT

The next important product to be launched in this market could be digital audio tape (DAT) players, which are the magnetic version of compact disc players, just as cassette tapes are the magnetic counterpart to black vinyl records. A DAT delivers the same flawless sound reproduction as a CD, but with one important difference—owners can do their own recording at home. And that is where the controversy begins.

"It creates severe potential problems for the industry," says a Record Industry Association of America (RIAA) spokesperson. "It would enable people to make better and more copies of compact discs." Already, the RIAA estimates that the record industry loses $1.5 billion in income from those who make tape copies of records at home for personal use.

Though none of the DAT player prototypes currently will record off of a compact disc, the technical changes required to accomplish CD to DAT recording would not be difficult to overcome. The legality of taping records for personal use has never been tested in court. Nonetheless, the RIAA has campaigned to add a royalty onto the sale of DAT players to compensate artists for lost revenues.

But disagreement with the record industry is nothing new to the electronics industry, and most manufacturers brush off the taping question for DATs, just as they have for dual cassette recorders. The important question for them continues to be whether or not DATs' introduction now would stifle the still fledgling market for compact disc players.

Both Hitachi and Yamaha look like good bets to introduce DAT players in the near future, and it is unlikely that other companies will let them run away with the market, regardless of its potentially small size. Hitachi, with no major presence in CD players, has little to lose. Yamaha is looking to bolster its high-end image.

Should DAT players reach the market, even some of their detractors think their impact has been overstated. Some think DATs and CDs are compatible—that there are people who will only want discs and people who will only want tapes and people who will want both.

A recent marketing survey in Japan conducted by Sharp seems to confirm this view. According to the study, CD player sales will continue to grow, even after a DAT player introduction. The survey projects that CD player unit sales would grow from 9 million in 1986 to 14 million in 1988, compared to sales of only 800,000 DAT players in 1988.

Though right now the industry looks unwilling to kill the goose that laid the golden egg, DAT players still have their proponents. "DAT could become a real product in the future," says Sharp's national marketing manager, "but I'm not going to say when." He cites the lack of software as still another stumbling block in the path for DAT's debut. "You have to have the software out there to feed the hardware," he says. "The two industries do not always work side by side."

Questions

1 How would you classify these recording innovations?
2 For CD and DAT players, evaluate the product characteristics that influence their rate and extent of adoption. Do you think that both will survive?
3 Does the CD player fit any pattern of diffusion?
4 How may the process of personal influence be used to spread diffusion of CDs and DATs?

CASE 3-8
FORD THUNDERBIRD*

When Ford Motor Co. introduced the 1983 Thunderbird, it tried to rekindle the love affair of former T-Bird owners who had shunned recent models. Those who had bought the car in the mid-to-late 1960s because of its sportiness had abandoned the classic during the 1970s. One owner described how many felt: "I had three T-Birds, the '65, the '67, and the '69—then they changed the styling, and I didn't like it at all anymore. It looked bigger, less European, and they cheapened the insides." Many of these buyers switched to Japanese cars.

Then Ford restyled the 1983 Thunderbird, and the problem came in dealing with skeptics. As one visitor to a Ford showroom remarked to the salesperson, "This car looks so good, it looks like you guys didn't build it." Once Ford gave its boxy Thunderbird an aerodynamic styling overhaul, it had to get its target market of prosperous, performance-oriented professionals into showrooms and convince them that the sporty two-door was a high-quality car made for accurate handling.

Ford decided to offer more than just a quick test drive to

---

* Adapted from Meg Cox, "Ford Pushing Thunderbird with VIP Plan," *The Wall Street Journal,* October 17, 1983, pp. 33, 53.

disarm the skeptics. It developed a "VIP Program" that included invitations sent to 406,720 executives and professionals to drive a Thunderbird for a day. From nationwide lists of business leaders, Ford selected prospects on the basis of salary and profession. The prospects received a candid letter inviting them to try the new car for twenty-four hours. During the three-month program approximately 14,000 people borrowed T-Birds for day-long drives. Ford's surveys found that 10 percent said they planned to buy a T-Bird, and 84 percent said they would recommend the car to a friend. Many of the respondents said they would never have entered a Ford dealership without the unique offer. Thunderbird sales jumped 200 percent in the nine months after introduction of the new model.

Many of the triers were knowledgeable car buffs with a "prove it" attitude. The twenty-four-hour drive gave these people a chance to really put the car through its paces. One prospect—an engineer who had regularly read *Consumer Reports* and studied cars diligently before buying a Toyota the previous year—gave the car a critical eye as he drove it. While not in the market for a car himself, he felt he might recommend the T-Bird to a friend. Other foreign car owners seemed to be pleased and tempted.

Some receiving the letter accepted the loaner because they were flattered to be included, and they used the additional time to show the T-Bird to their friends. Fifty Boeing engineers strolled out to the company parking lot to look at the Thunderbird one of their colleagues had borrowed. He thought they were impressed with the car. This was part of Ford's plan—to have T-Birds seen being driven by influential people showing up at the right restaurants, theaters, and country clubs.

Not everything went according to plan, however. One prospect drove his T-Bird to a memorial service. Another let his 12-year-old son's friends sit in it for five hours playing the radio and adjusting the power seat. One woman with four kids of driving age was concerned that they might get carried away driving such a "cool" car. And a Mercedes owner was nearly embarrassed to be seen in a T-Bird. Some of his friends asked him if he'd lost his job.

Questions

1 Is this marketing approach appropriate for any year new-model car?

2 Evaluate the VIP program as a way of using the personal influence process.

3 What additional personal influence approaches might have been used?

4 What group influences can be identified in this situation?

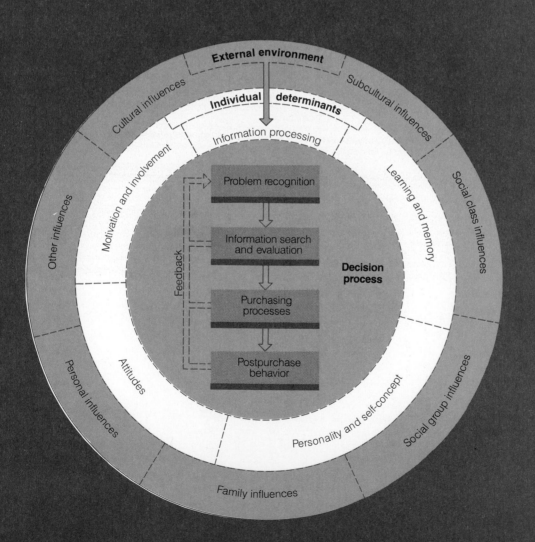

INDIVIDUAL DETERMINANTS OF CONSUMER BEHAVIOR

PART 4

MOTIVATION AND INVOLVEMENT

LEARNING OBJECTIVES

After studying this chapter, you should understand . . .

■ The nature of motives and their role in influencing consumers

■ Some of the basic categories of motives

■ How motives energize consumers and give direction to their activities

■ How motives interact with each other to affect consumers' behavior

■ The use of motivation research methods for discovering consumers' motives and the problems associated with their use

■ The nature of consumer involvement and its influence on consumers

Why eat a cookie? Some reasons might be to satisfy your hunger, to increase your sugar level, or just to have something to chew on. However, recent success in the packaged-cookie market suggests that these may not be the only, or perhaps even the most important, reasons. It appears that cookie-producing companies have realized some other motives and, as a result, are delivering to the market—and with a vengeance—products resulting from their awareness.

These relatively new product offerings are usually referred to as "soft" or "chewy" cookies, to distinguish them from the more typical crunchy varieties. Why all the fuss over their introduction? Apparently much of their appeal has to do with childhood memories of sitting on the back steps devouring those melt-in-your-mouth confections that were delivered by Mom straight from the oven, while they were still soft. This *emotional* appeal of soft cookies is apparently at least as strong as are the physical cravings that the product satisfies.

Market statistics testify to the success of the emotional appeal—Nabisco's brand far exceeded sales expectations and was the most significant factor in boosting its 1984 total cookie-sales volume by 20 percent. Also it is no mistake that their brand is named *Almost Home,* and they use the nostalgic slogan, "Like Mom used to bake."

Other firms have also tried to capture market share. For example, Procter & Gamble introduced their Duncan Hines version ("Crispy, Chewy, Homemade Goodness"), and Frito-Lay also has an offering. Even though Nabisco has been the clear leader, P&G is exploring additional ways of appealing to emotion-based consumption motives. Their Blue Ribbon Recipe cookies are less uniform in size and texture, to make them resemble the old-fashioned, home-made type even more.[1]

12

Anyone interested in consumers soon becomes concerned with what "turns them on"—the forces that activate and direct their behavior. As our example shows, this is more than a subject of idle curiosity for marketing managers, since many of their decisions are based on knowledge or assumptions about the general forces activating consumers.

It would be surprising if any one variable could fully explain what initiates and guides consumers' actions. Nevertheless, the concept of motivation plays an essential role in any such understanding. This chapter begins by defining motives, indicating their importance and influence, and discussing some methods of classifying them. Attention then turns to what arouses motives and what factors influence how they are structured together. Next, several particular aspects of motivational influences are discussed, and we then turn to a brief review of the somewhat controversial subject of motivation research. The topic of involvement is addressed next. After characterizing the concept, we review its dimensions and indicate how it is related to motivation. Finally, some of the marketing implications of involvement are discussed.

THE NATURE AND ROLE OF MOTIVES

THE NATURE OF MOTIVES

A number of writers have drawn distinctions between motives and other related concepts such as needs, wants, and drives.[2] For our purposes, these distinctions are not very helpful and will be avoided. We will view a *motive* as an inner state that mobilizes bodily energy and directs it in selective fashion toward goals usually located in the external environment. This definition implies that motives involve two major components:

1 A mechanism to arouse bodily energy

2 A force that provides direction to that bodily energy

The arousal component activates general tension or restlessness but does not provide direction for release of this energy. It could be compared to the random thrashing about that newborn babies often show. The directive aspect of motives focuses such aroused energy toward some goal in the individual's environment. Thus, when our hunger is aroused, we are usually directed toward particular foods.

It is useful to note that various concepts have been offered to explain how motives exert their directional influences on consumers. Earlier views held that inborn instincts beyond the control of individuals provided the direction for their behavior. Later it was stressed that basic needs (hunger, thirst, and the like) impelled people toward action. This view also held that behavior instrumental in satisfying a need would become associated with it and have a higher likelihood of occurring in future situations involving the same need arousal.

Many behavioral scientists have found these views of motivation lacking because they imply that people are impelled by various forces and have very little conscious control over the direction of their own actions. For this reason, a *cognitive* orientation has gained in popularity.[3] It emphasizes the role of mental processes such as planning, evaluation, and goal selection in directing behavior. This suggests that consumers have a very active role in selecting their goals, evaluating the relative usefulness of products in terms of these goals, and consciously orchestrating their behavior in terms of these products.

THE ROLE OF MOTIVES

As has already been noted, the role of motives is to arouse and direct the behavior of consumers. The arousal component activates bodily energy so that it can be used for mental and physical activity. In their directive role, motives have several important functions for guiding behavior.[4] These are discussed below.

Defining Basic Striving   Motives influence consumers to develop and identify their basic strivings. Included among basic strivings are very general goals such as safety, affiliation, achievement, or other desired states which consumers seek to achieve. They serve to guide behavior in a general way across a wide variety of decisions and activities.

Identifying Goal Objects   Although there are exceptions, people often view products or services as a means by which they can achieve their motives.[5] In fact, consumers often go one step further and think of products as their actual goals, without realizing that they really represent ways of satisfying motives.

This motivational push that influences consumers to identify products as goal objects is of great interest to marketers, particularly since it appears that it can be influenced. Certainly, the features designed into a product can affect the degree to which consumers may accept it as a goal or means for achieving some goal. Much effort is also spent on developing promotions that persuade consumers to consider products as objects useful for achieving some motive. For example, the advertisement in Figure 12-1 effectively suggests that use of the product may lead to pleasant motive satisfactions.

Influencing Choice Criteria   Motives also guide consumers in developing criteria for evaluating products. Thus, for a car buyer strongly influenced by the convenience motive, features such as electronic speed control and easy-servicing requirements would become more-important choice criteria than would styling or mileage.

It appears that marketers are also capable of influencing consumers' choice criteria. In some cases, this occurs because consumers are not consciously aware of their own motives. For example, a salesperson for air conditioners may remark that one model is more efficient than others, thereby making the consumer realize that operating economy is important to his choice. In other cases, people are aware of their motives but unsure of the specific criteria to use in their product evaluations. In this case, the marketer can inform consumers of the importance of particular criteria and how well her product meets these criteria. Figure 12-2 shows one such example.

FIGURE 12-1
An example of motive
directional influence.
*Reproduced by permission of
Shulton, Inc.*

Directing Other Influences   At a more fundamental level, motives affect the individual determinants of perception, learning, personality, attitudes, and how people process information. This also results in directional influences on behavior. For example, motives influence information processing, which in turn regulates how we interpret and respond to our environment. These influences are discussed in greater detail in the remaining chapters of this section.

CLASSIFYING MOTIVES

Since the early 1900s many thousands of motive concepts have been suggested to account for the great diversity of human behavior.[6] The need to group so many suggestions into a more-manageable set of general categories soon became apparent. A variety of classification schemes ranging from the simplified to the complex have been proposed.

FIGURE 12-2
A L.a. Gear advertisement informing consumers of specific choice criteria. Reprinted by permission of L.a. Gear.

SIMPLIFIED SCHEMES

A number of classification methods are simplified so that they group motives on the basis of one unique characteristic of interest. Several of particular relevance to understanding consumers are highlighted as follows.

Physiological versus Psychogenic   One scheme categorizes motives according to their underlying sources. *Physiological* motives are oriented toward directly satisfying biological needs of the individual, such as hunger, thirst, and pain-avoidance. Conversely, *psychogenic* motives focus on the satisfaction of psychological desires. Examples include the seeking of achievement, affiliation, or status. It is interesting to note that consumers often can satisfy physiological needs at the same time they are satisfying psychogenic motives. For example, sharing a favorite drink with friends after a touch football game satisfies affiliation needs as well as one's thirst.

Although general agreement exists about the number and nature of physiological motives, there is less consensus about their psychogenic counterparts. However, a common characteristic of such psychological motives is that they are learned. This learning can occur throughout life, but the childhood socialization process probably accounts for a majority of these acquired motives. The nature of this learning will be explored in Chapter 14.

Learned or *secondary motives* exert a very important influence on people. In fact, many argue that in economically advanced societies, psychogenic motives dominate over physiological ones in affecting consumers' goals and acquisition of products to attain or express these goals. This is a significant consideration to marketers involved in the design of products and advertising appeals.

Primary versus Selective   Motives may also be classified according to how they influence buying decisions. A *primary* influence involves initiating buying behavior and directing it toward certain generic product categories such as televisions or health spas. Conversely, *selective* influences guide choices between stores or brands and models within a generic product class. As noted earlier, this can occur through development of choice criteria that serve as standards for evaluating brands.

Motivational concepts are certainly useful for understanding consumer behavior at both the primary and selective level. However, some suggest that the generalized nature of their influence makes them more useful for understanding consumer choices among generic product classes.[7] Preference and attitude concepts discussed in Chapter 16 may be more appropriate for understanding final choices between brands.

Conscious versus Unconscious   Motives also differ in the degree to which they reach consumers' awareness. Conscious motives are those of which consumers are quite aware, whereas a motive is said to be unconscious when the consumer is not aware of being influenced by it.

It has been suggested that people are not conscious of some motives because they don't want to confront the true reason for their purchase. To illustrate, purchases of expensive clothes are frequently justified in terms of the clothes' "fit" or durability rather than the status they are expected to display. In other cases, consumers simply may not be aware of the true motives behind many of their purchases. For example, we really don't understand why we prefer certain colors over others.

Positive versus Negative   Motives can exert either positive or negative influences on consumers. Positive influences attract consumers toward desired goals, while negative ones direct them away from undesirable consequences. Positive attractions exert the predominant influence, but a few very important cases of negative forces do exist. One example of a negative force is fear, which can play an important role in some purchases such as toothpaste for decay prevention and insurance to protect loved ones.

A COMPREHENSIVE SCHEME

Although the above distinctions provide useful perspective, they are limited because only one characteristic serves as the basis of classification. Recently, a more comprehensive method using four two-pole motive tendencies has been suggested by McGuire.[8] As shown in Table 12-1, the relevant distinctions are cognitive/affective (mental deliberation versus emotional reactions), preservation/growth (maintenance of equilibrium versus self-development), active/passive (self-initiated action versus reactive tendencies) and internal/external (achievement of new internal states versus new relationships with the environment). These four means of classification are not intended to be mutually exclusive. In fact, when used together they provide an interesting basis for appreciating sixteen major motivational influences on consumer behavior. Each is briefly characterized in Table 12-2.

The description and classification of motives provide useful perspectives for understanding consumers. However, it must be remembered that motives have only a general influence on behavior. Their exact effect is modified by environmental conditions and the consumer's existing states, such as attitudes and knowledge. Consequently, although we may know that a given motive *can* activate and guide behavior toward a particular direction, this does not necessarily

TABLE 12-1
A Comprehensive Classification of Major Motive Influences

		Active		Passive	
		Internal	**External**	**Internal**	**External**
Cognitive	Preservation	1 Consistency	2 Attribution	3 Categorization	4 Objectification
	Growth	5 Autonomy	6 Exploration	7 Matching	8 Utilitarian
Affective	Preservation	9 Tension-reduction	10 Expressive	11 Ego-defensive	12 Reinforcement
	Growth	13 Assertion	14 Affiliation	15 Identification	16 Modeling

Source: Adapted from William J. McGuire, "Some Internal Psychological Factors Influencing Consumer Choice," *Journal of Consumer Research*, 2:302–319, March 1976.

TABLE 12-2

Sixteen Major
Motivational Influences
Identified by McGuire

1 *Consistency.* Motivation to maintain a coherent and organized view of the world. *Example*: When a consumer learns that the cereal he considered nutritious really is not very high in food value, he feels "uncomfortable" and attempts to find an explanation for this inconsistency.

2 *Attribution.* Motivation to understand or infer *causes* for various occurrences. This is focused in three major directions: *(a)* inferences as to the causes of various *events*; *(b)* attempts by people to understand their *own* attitudes, values, and so on, from the behavior they see themselves engaging in; and *(c)* inferences about the reasons *other people* act the way they do. *Example*: The meaning consumers derive from information in their environment, such as promotional messages, being strongly influenced by attribution inferences.

3 *Categorization.* Motivation to categorize complex information in order to organize and deal with it more easily. *Example*: Clothing, which is frequently categorized into formal, casual, and "hang-around" categories.

4 *Objectification.* Motivation to use "objective," external information instead of internal reflection to draw conclusions about one's values, attitudes, and the like. This is similar to attribution but more passive in nature. *Example*: A consumer using the amount of ski equipment purchased as her measure of the degree she enjoys the sport.

5 *Autonomy.* Motivation to seek individuality and personal growth through self-actualization and development of a distinct identity. *Example*: Reading various self-help books in order to improve oneself.

6 *Exploration.* Motivation to seek stimulation through new events or circumstances. *Examples*: Impulse purchases or switching from favorite to other brands to generate some excitement in one's life.

7 *Matching.* Motivation to develop mental images of ideal situations and regularly compare (match) perceptions of actual situations to these ideals. *Example*: Comparison of a new car model to one's ideal car rather than to other brands. A strong matching motive implies that internal standards, not characteristics of other brands, are more important criteria for judging products.

8 *Utilitarian.* Motivation to use the external environment as a valuable resource for information and skills to solve life's problems. *Example*: Doing a lot of "window shopping" to see how available products can help around the home.

9 *Tension reduction.* Motivation to reduce or avoid any tension that is generated when needs are not being satisfied. *Example*: Avoiding new brands because they generate uncertainty (and tension) regarding how well they will perform.

10 *Self-expression.* Motivation to project one's identity to others. *Example*: Purchase of a Corvette to reflect one's enjoyment of the sporty life in the fast lane.

11 *Ego-defensive.* Motivation to protect oneself from social embarrassment and other threats to feelings of self-worth. *Example*: Purchase of underarm deodorant, dandruff shampoo, strong denture adhesive, or carpet freshner to avoid the potential of social disgrace.

12 *Reinforcement.* Motivation to act in ways that have previously resulted in rewarding situations. *Example*: Consistently arguing with one's auto mechanic because such behavior was necessary in the past to get the car fixed properly.

13 *Assertion.* Motivation to strive for competition, power, and success. *Example*: As Figure 12-3 suggests, consumers using of some products as a means to be competitively successful.

14 *Affiliation.* Motivation to seek acceptance, affection, and warm personal contact with others. *Example*: As Figure 12-4 presents, one of the many instances where AT&T has linked its services to the affiliation motive.

15 *Identification.* Motivation to develop new identities and roles to enhance one's self-concept. Acting these roles out in social settings allows expression of values and development of feelings of importance. *Example*: Patronizing certain "gathering spots" frequented by young professionals in an attempt to belong or identify with that group.

16 *Modeling.* Motivation to *imitate* other individuals with whom one identifies or empathizes. *Example*: G.I. Joe, Rambo, wrestling figures, or similar toys.

Source: Based on William J. McGuire, "Some Internal Psychological Factors Influencing Consumer Choice," *Journal of Consumer Research*, 2:302–319, March 1976.

enable us to predict that it *will* do so. Also, any given behavior, such as the purchase of a particular product, can be influenced by many motives. This means that by merely observing consumers' actions we are often not in a good position to specify the motives that are influencing them. These comments demonstrate the need for marketers to understand more about the structuring and operational characteristics of motives, such as how they are aroused, what influences their strength, and why they persist over time. It is to these and similar issues that we now turn.

MOTIVE AROUSAL

The arousal concept concerns what energizes consumers. Remember from our earlier discussion that although arousal activates bodily energy, it provides little, if any, direction to behavior.

TRIGGERING AROUSAL

A variety of mechanisms can trigger the arousal of motives and energize consumers. The following may work alone or in combination to activate behavior.[9]

Physiological Conditions   One source of arousal acts to satisfy our biological needs for food, water, and other life-sustaining necessities. Depriving such a bodily need

FIGURE 12-3
An appeal to the assertion motive category.
Courtesy of BMW of North America, Inc.

generates an uncomfortable state of tension. When this tension is sufficiently strong, arousal occurs to provide energy necessary to satisfy the need. The consumer's previous experience and present situation will strongly influence the directions any heightened activity will take.

Cognitive Activity Humans engage in considerable cognitive activity (thinking and reasoning) even when the objects of their thoughts are not physically present. This thinking, considered by some to be daydreaming or fantasy, can also act as a motive trigger. One way this occurs is when consumers deliberate about unsatisfied wants. For example, thinking about one's lack of physical activity can arouse energy to remedy the situation.

Situational Conditions The particular situation confronting consumers may also trigger arousal. This can occur when the situation draws attention to an existing physiological condition, as when noticing an advertisement for Slice soda suddenly makes you aware of being thirsty. Here, the need for liquids may have been present, but not yet strong enough to trigger arousal. Seeing the advertisement draws attention to the condition and leads to activity.

FIGURE 12-4
An appeal to the affiliation category of motives.
Courtesy of AT&T.

Situational conditions can also work alone to generate motive arousal. This appears to occur when circumstances draw consumers' attention to the disparity between their present state and something viewed as a better condition. For example, a car owner may see an advertisement stressing how a new type of spark plug will result in considerable fuel economy. Such a message might, by itself, be responsible for triggering the aroused state.

Stimulus Properties A number of behavioral scientists have noted that certain properties of external stimuli themselves also seem to have the power to generate arousal.[10] These *collative properties* include the characteristics of novelty, surprisingness, ambiguity, and uncertainty. Stimuli possessing a sufficient amount of these properties have the potential of drawing attention to themselves by arousing an individual's curiosity or desire for exploration. As such, they represent a special type of situational condition.

Stimuli with arousal potential are important for marketers because they can be used to attract and focus consumers' attention. This represents an opportunity to present information, facilitate consumers' processing of that information, and increase involvement and interest in the product. Therefore, a great deal of effort is devoted to incorporating stimuli with arousal potential into promotions and packaging. An important aspect of this effort is to choose stimuli that will also draw sufficient attention to the marketer's message or product as well as to themselves.[11]

OPTIMAL STIMULATION AND AROUSAL

Historically, consumers have been viewed mainly as tension avoiders. Similar to the operation described for physiological triggers, events creating tension were seen as generating arousal which initiated tension reduction activity. From this, it might be tempting to conclude that since external variables can also generate tension, consumers might *consistently* seek to minimize such environmental stimulation. However, at best, this conclusion only describes certain activity patterns. Casual observation and research evidence both suggest that in many situations consumers do not act to minimize external sources of stimulation. Sudden purchases of different brands "just for a change," window shopping activity, and the trial of many new products have been cited as examples. Another is the great interest many consumers show in various intriguing products such as Rubik's Cube.[12]

We do not presently know a great deal about the exact causes underlying such behavior. However, several theories suggest the existence of a motivation to seek variety or novelty, or to explore stimuli that are seemingly inconsistent with expectations.[13] This was noted in McGuire's motive classification scheme reviewed earlier. One element common to most of these explanations is that consumers' *optimum* stimulation level is at a moderate (not minimum) magnitude. Therefore, depending on conditions, consumers may seek increases or reductions in their external stimulation.

The theory proposed by Streufert and Driver serves to explain such behavior.[14] In this scheme, the stimulation a consumer derives from the environment is determined by the amount of incongruity or disparity existing between his stored

knowledge about the environment and the information that he actually receives from it. For example, a large disparity between what the consumer "knows" about a brand and the experiences he actually has while using it would generate considerable stimulation. However, if the consumer's beliefs and knowledge are confirmed through use of the brand, little stimulation is likely to occur.

Based on past experiences, each consumer is seen as adapting to and expecting certain average levels of incongruity or stimulation from his environment.[15] This level, called the *General Incongruity Adaptation Level* (GIAL), becomes the optimum amount of stimulation derived from the environment. Therefore, more or less than the optimum amount will be uncomfortable and is likely to motivate behavior designed to return to the optimum. The type of behavior that will be engaged in is influenced by the magnitude and direction of the difference between present levels of environmental stimulation and the GIAL.

These relationships are shown in Figure 12-5. The degree of incongruity or stimulation generated by differences between stored knowledge about the environment and actual experiences is represented on the *x* axis. The amount of affect (degree of liking) of the stimulation is represented on the *y* axis. This ranges from negative levels through zero, which is represented by the horizontal line, to positive levels. The parabolic-shaped curve shows the relationship between levels of stimulation and the degree of liking or affect that the consumer will exhibit. Note that the optimum level of stimulation (GIAL), shown on the *x* axis, corresponds to the greatest degree of consumer satisfaction. Also, note that this value is somewhat *above* the zero point on the *x* axis, showing that the optimum amount of environmental stimulation is at a moderate level.

Figure 12-5 also shows that very low and very high levels of stimulation produce negative affects, while moderate deviations from the GIAL produce positive affects. In fact there are four ranges or zones of stimulation values that a given stimulus might generate for a consumer. If the stimulus falls into Zone 1 the resulting stimulation will be very low, generating the negative affect of consider-

FIGURE 12-5
A diagram based on Streufert and Driver's theory of the relationship between optimum stimulation and affect.

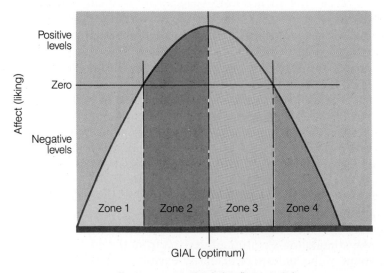

able boredom. A rather active search for completely new, more stimulating experiences is to be expected in this situation. This behavior is quite descriptive of a consumer who has become extremely familiar with and actually bored by a brand that she has purchased repetitively for a considerable period of time.

In Zone 2 stimulation is still below optimum, but not enough to generate negative affects. Consequently, new stimulus experiences will not be sought. Instead, the consumer will be passively receptive to new stimulus situations and will probably devote some effort to exploring existing stimuli in greater depth. Both of these activities are taken to yield moderate increases in stimulation. Consumers facing Zone 2 levels of stimulation include those that are only slightly bored by their existing brands. As such, they may be susceptible to negative information about these brands coming from other consumers or producers of competitive brands.

Zone 3 levels of stimulation are slightly above optimum but still within levels that the consumer perceives favorably. Therefore, the motivation to seek new sources of stimulation is not high. Passive reception of other stimuli and examination in greater depth of existing stimuli are likely to occur. In both cases, the goal is to reduce stimulation levels. Consumers who have purchased a new product or brand and then learn that it is a little too different, novel, or complex are likely to experience Zone 3 levels of stimulation.

In the fourth zone, present levels of stimulation are so high above optimum that they are quite uncomfortable to the consumer, and they yield negative affects. Additional stimulation certainly will not be sought. In fact, the consumer will be motivated to escape from the uncomfortable state and actively seek other more familiar stimuli that will bring him or her closer to optimum. People in this situation are frequently seen as avoiding unfamiliar or novel brands and preferring known, standard brands. They are also susceptible to advertisements that make brands appear less novel.

To summarize, the theory suggests that the types of information a consumer will seek and be receptive to are a function of the present level of stimulation being received from the environment. If stimulation levels are below optimum, the consumer will be disposed to increase them, and if levels are above optimum, action will be directed toward reducing the stimulation. The nature of the actions will depend on the particular stimulation zone the consumer is facing.

EFFECTS OF AROUSAL

We have already seen that several mechanisms can trigger arousal to release energy for consumers' actions. Factors influencing the extent and direction of aroused behavior will be discussed shortly. What is important to note here is that the intensity of arousal acts to regulate the amount of effort consumers will devote to a particular motivating situation. This can take a variety of forms. One aspect is the degree to which attention mechanisms are sensitized to receive information from the environment. Higher amounts of arousal result in greater attention to stimuli that may have been previously ignored. This increases the chances that the consumer will become aware of information useful in dealing with the motivational situation.

The process just described is quite passive in nature, because the consumer's increased attention is only focused on stimuli that happen to be available. Another

effect of arousal can expand the consumer's available information by energizing an active search process. This can involve asking questions of salespeople, reading *Consumer Reports,* or making a point to have a conversation with a friend. Of course, the exact nature of information desired and methods used to obtain it will be strongly influenced by the situation and the consumer's existing behavior patterns. However, active search processes generally include the purposeful seeking of information as well as an increased awareness of stimuli.

Arousal also influences the cognitive activity (thinking and evaluating) devoted to decision making about alternative goods and services. This involves regulating the effort allocated to interpreting potentially informative stimuli such as the EER rating for an air conditioner. It also involves allocating effort to reviewing stored knowledge about brands by using decision rules to evaluate and choose among purchase alternatives. Each of these activities can be accomplished with a great deal of deliberation or with hardly any conscious effort. Aroused energy is an important factor in influencing the extent of such decision making.

MOTIVE STRUCTURING

Motives do not act on consumers in an arbitrary manner. They fit together in a unified pattern. This suggests the existence of a priority scheme or structuring mechanism. The structuring of motives also provides a central theme or organization for the consistency of influence over time.

MOTIVE HIERARCHY

The concept of a hierarchy underlies many schemes offered to explain the structuring of motive influences. The most influential motive is seen as enjoying the most dominant position in the hierarchy, the second most influential holds the second most dominant position, and so on through the entire list. To be useful, however, the hierarchy concept must also help explain what factors influence the relative ordering of motives.

Maslow's Hierarchy   Perhaps the most widely known hierarchy was proposed by A. H. Maslow. His scheme classified motives into five groupings and suggested the degree to which each would influence behavior.[16] Although this theory certainly is relevant to the topic of motive classification discussed earlier, its treatment has been reserved until now because of its importance to the structuring concept.

Maslow proposed that motives could be classified into five basic categories: physiological, safety, belongingness and love, esteem, and self-actualization. As depicted in Figure 12-6, he also suggested that these groupings are arranged in ascending order with physiological motives occupying the first position on the hierarchy and self-actualization occupying the last step. The degree to which each motive category is essential to existence and survival was seen to define its *prepotency* or initial importance. The first ordering of motives is then determined by their relative prepotency. The most prepotent motives (physiological) would have the greatest influence on behavior until they are adequately satisfied. At that point the next most prepotent motive—safety—would begin to dominate behavior. We would expect this to influence various purchase behaviors, such as concern with auto smoke, burglar alarms, studded snow tires, and other similar features or products. If the consumer is capable of adequately satisfying each succeeding motive category, self-actualization will finally tend to dominate behavior. The pattern of succeeding motive influence is depicted in Figure 12-6. Points A through D define the places where higher level motives will begin to assume dominance over more prepotent, but adequately satisfied, motives.

It is also important to note that even after being passed on the hierarchy, a motive can assume temporary dominance over behavior. This will occur as a result of *deprivation*—the extent to which the motive is not being adequately satisfied. The degree to which deprivation can affect the structuring of motives and assume temporary dominance over consumers' actions is easily appreciated if you recall the last time you were extremely hungry.

Maslow also argued that as individuals progress from being dominated by physiological motives toward self-actualization, they grow psychologically and come to develop more wants and to seek a greater variety of ways to satisfy particular motives. Thus, in our economy, consumers dominated by the "higher" motives of esteem or self-actualization will be expected to show interest in a greater variety of products and services than consumers dominated by "lower" order motives. Of course, this focus on goods and services does not necessarily hold for individuals or peoples from other cultures with less materialistic tendencies.

FIGURE 12-6
A diagram of Maslow's motive hierarchy depicting the relative predominance of motives and the number and variety of wants recognized for each motive.
Source: David Krech, Richard S. Crutchfield, and Egerton L. Ballachey, *Individual in Society,* McGraw-Hill, New York, 1962, p. 77.

Key:
Physiological: motives which seek basic body requirements including water, food, and oxygen

Safety: motives for security, protection, and stability in one's life

Belongingness and love: those motives oriented toward affection and affiliation with others

Esteem: motives oriented toward achievement, prestige, status, and self-confidence

Self-actualization: those motives relating to self-fulfillment and maximizing one's potential

Although Maslow's scheme is useful for a general understanding of motives, it has limited use in attempting to predict specific behavior.[17] Of particular concern is that consumers are continually influenced by motives that they apparently passed on the hierarchy. For example, even in our economy, safety (second on the hierarchy) still appears to motivate many consumer decisions. Some suggest that the theory accounts for this because even though the focus is on dominant motives, the hierarchy still allows for the influence of other motives not in a dominant position. This is said to explain fluctuating behavior under conditions of a stable hierarchy. However, the mechanism regulating this process has not been well defined.

Hierarchy Dynamics   Difficulties in explaining changing behavior patterns using a relatively stable motive hierarchy have led some to suggest a goal hierarchy to help bridge the gap between motives and behavior.[18] Motives can then be viewed as exerting a relatively stable influence on goals. Opportunities, constraints, and changing conditions in the consumer's environment may be seen as a dynamic influence. The interaction of these two forces can then lead to changes in goal importance and flexible behavior patterns.

Aspiration levels also help to explain how dynamic consumer goals can occur under the influence of relatively stable motives. A level of aspiration may be thought of as a goal that can be influenced by a number of factors to change either up or down over time. Therefore, as consumers approach achievement of a goal, they can still be influenced by the same motive structure to strive for even higher levels of achievement. Similar to Alice in Wonderland, the goal moves upward so that we run faster and faster to reach it. For example, hunger can easily be satisfied by very basic foodstuffs such as beans and milk, but most American consumers set their sights "higher" for foods such as Whoppers and tacos. Influences on consumers' levels of aspirations include:

1   *Achievement.* Success yields rising aspiration levels, while failure tends to result in a decline in such goals.

2   *Reality orientation.* Usually aspirations are set to reflect the individual's assessment of what levels of achievement are within reach.

3   *Group influences.* Consumers' aspirations are influenced by individuals in membership and reference groups. In addition to pressures to "keep up with the Joneses," this provides consumers with reference points as to what levels of achievement exist for various activities and interests.[19]

These characteristics of aspiration levels demonstrate that wants are insatiable and that consumers' attempts to achieve them through purchases in the marketplace have led to a very advanced economic system in the United States. However, some suggest that it also has created serious resource shortages, a degradation of our environment, and various other problems.[20]

A further influence on motive and goal structuring is learning. As indicated earlier under the discussion of classifying motives, consumers can acquire (learn) new motives from dealing with their environment. Much of this occurs during the childhood socialization process. The acquisition of these *secondary* motives results in restructuring the hierarchy. This occurs because secondary motives are often quite strong and therefore can significantly influence behaviors. Consider, for example, how the learned needs for social approval so strongly influence purchase decisions from personal-care products to automobiles.

MOTIVE COMBINATIONS

It is convenient to discuss motives separately, as if they influence consumers independently and one at a time. Actually, they often interact, leading to a combined influence or to situations in which they conflict and exert opposing influences on behavior.[21]

Motive Linking Because motives can differ in how specific they are, it is possible for a linking to occur at various levels of generality. For example, safety may actually be made up of more specific motives, including those relating to security and protection. Therefore, achievement of a specific motive can be a means of approaching a more general motive which is viewed as the goal.[22] This is referred to as the means-end linking of motives. A linking that might exist to influence purchase of a door lock is depicted in Figure 12-7. Here, we see that safety has been linked to the more specific motives of protection and security. In turn, these have been linked to strength, dependability, and durability properties of the product. All of these factors can exert a combined influence on the consumer.

Motive Bundling It is very important to realize that a given product can satisfy various motives at the same approximate level of specific influence. This results in the bundling or combining of influences on consumers' decisions. To illustrate, for an automobile purchase, a desire for transportation can bundle with motives for achievement, social recognition, safety, and economy.

Motive bundling and linking allow development of product and promotional strategies to increase or sustain consumers' interest over a period of time. For example, the diminishing supplies and increasing prices of gasoline resulted in changing both automobiles and their promotions to emphasize fuel economy. Also, Sears has promoted their radial tires at various times as appealing to the economy motive (long-lasting), safety motive (superior handling), and again later in terms of economy (better mileage).

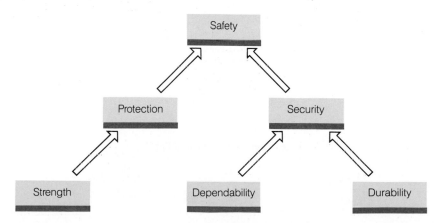

FIGURE 12-7
A means-end linking for a door-lock purchase.
Source: John A. Howard and Jagdish N. Sheth, *The Theory of Buyer Behavior,* Wiley, New York, 1969, p. 107.

Motive Conflict   Motives can also conflict with each other to affect how consumers interact with the marketplace. A major contributor to the topic of motive conflict is Kurt Lewin.[23] He viewed motives as influencing the attracting or repelling forces of goals in the individual's environment. The degree to which a product or service satisfies a motive will therefore determine its attracting (positive) force, and how adverse it is to a motive will influence its repelling (negative) force.

In Lewin's view, conflict is most likely when motives are of approximately equal strength. Three principal cases are possible: approach-approach, avoidance-avoidance, and approach-avoidance conflict. Actually, these terms refer to psychological tendencies for attraction or repulsion, not necessarily actual physical movement.

APPROACH-APPROACH CONFLICT   This is a situation in which conflict exists between two desirable alternatives, such as when a consumer must decide how to allocate purchasing dollars between a home exercise center and a microcomputer (see Figure 12-8). These situations can lead to a period of temporary indecision and vacillation between alternatives. Permanent indecision is rare, however, because approach-approach conflict is said to be unstable. This occurs because the pull toward a positive goal increases as one approaches it, and declines as one moves away. Therefore, a slight tendency to accept one alternative can lead to resolving the conflict quickly. Such resolution can occur through exposure to information useful in evaluating the alternatives. Promotional literature and salespeople's comments play a crucial role in this process.

Resolution of approach-approach conflict can also occur through reassessment of goals that might lead to a decision that achieving one goal is more important than the other. Again, comments of salespeople can be quite influential.

FIGURE 12-8
A typology of motive conflict situations.
Source: Kurt Lewin, *A Dynamic Theory of Personality,* McGraw-Hill, New York, 1935.

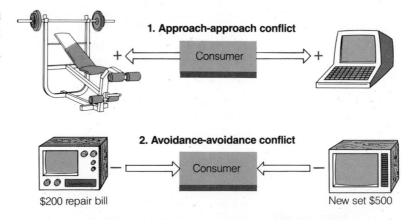

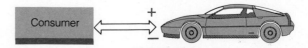

Of course, a third resolution involves attempts to achieve modified versions of both goals. In our example, this could occur through purchase of less-expensive models of a microcomputer and home exercise center.

AVOIDANCE-AVOIDANCE CONFLICT   This situation occurs when consumers face choices between two alternatives, both of which are perceived as being negative in nature. For example, when the television set with which a family has been perfectly happy becomes seriously "ill," the alternatives may be a hefty repair bill or the large expense of a replacement set (see Figure 12-8). Such situations are characterized as being stable because consumers tend to vacillate between undesirable alternatives. This occurs because approaching a negative alternative leads to a stronger repulsion by it. Such situations often lead to considerable search for information (window shopping, reading ads, and making inquiries) but often stop short of a purchase commitment.

APPROACH-AVOIDANCE CONFLICT   Situations in which consumers are in conflict between a positive and negative alternative make up this category. Such situations often occur when making decisions on a single product in which both positive and negative aspects are involved in the purchase. For example (see Figure 12-8), to acquire an attractive product such as a car, consumers must part with a sizable amount of scarce purchasing dollars. These types of cash outflows can generate considerable amounts of purchase avoidance, as demonstrated by the frequent auto sales slumps that occur.

Approach-avoidance conflict also tends to be stable, because both attracting and repelling forces increase as the goal object is approached; but the repelling force increases more sharply. This results in the consumer being attracted by goal objects but experiencing increasing resistance to them as they are approached. Marketers have recognized this problem, and they have developed means to reduce the avoidance aspect of such conflicts. Banks offer loans in which you "borrow in June and start paying in September" and major airlines offer "Fly Now, Pay Later" programs. The availability of credit cards and financing arrangements also contribute to the ease of making large expenditures.

Approach-avoidance conflict also happens in more subtle ways such as when consumers must choose between alternative brands of a given product in which, compared to one another, each brand has both positive and negative features. As a case in point, choosing a Ford over a Chevrolet because of its styling also means sacrificing the traditionally higher trade-in value of Chevrolets. When faced with such important choices, consumers frequently exhibit considerable conflict and indecision. Consequently, salespeople have developed closing techniques to encourage customers to make a decision. The following is just a sampling of such methods:

Advantage/disadvantage close. Negative and positive features of each alternative are summarized to assist the customer in determining which alternative appears to be the better choice.

Critical feature close. Stress is placed on one or a few "critical" features of one brand that the other does not possess.

Critical time close. In cases in which one brand is in short supply, or in which a special sale is about to end, emphasizing the immediacy of the decision can convince a consumer to purchase.

SELF-CONCEPT

Although a consumer's motive structure exhibits some flexibility over time, there remains a central theme or organization to the structure. One factor influencing this organization is the individual's self-concept. That is, consumers possess a certain image of themselves, and this self-concept exerts an organizing influence on their motives.

One important effect of this influence on motives is reflected in the types of goods purchased, since consumers appear to prefer some products and brands that are consistent with their self-concepts. Thus, we would expect to see individuals who view themselves as successful business persons drive cars, own homes, join clubs, and interact with social groups that reflect this self-image. These points will be more fully discussed in Chapter 15. However, the topic of self-concept is introduced here because of its relationship to consumer involvement, which will be discussed shortly.

MOTIVATION RESEARCH

We have noted that many consumers are unaware of the motives influencing their purchase behavior. That is, some motives may not reach the consumer's consciousness, and others may be repressed because to deal with them may be uncomfortable. This presents difficulty to the marketer who needs to understand consumers in order to design the most effective mix of marketing offerings. Any direct attempts to determine such motives, say by interviewing consumers, may only yield "surface" explanations or rationalizations that hide true strivings.

The concept of *motivation research* has been offered as a means of identifying consumers' true, underlying purchase motives. The term is typically not used to describe just any type of research on motivational issues. It refers to certain research techniques and, to some extent, ways of interpreting information about motivation generated by these techniques. An introduction to this field and its methods was made in Chapter 3, and it would be useful to refer to it at this point. Briefly stated, the methods involve disguised and indirect techniques in an attempt to probe consumers' inner motives without arousing defense mechanisms which can generate misleading results.

In practice, motivation research has yielded provocative and sometimes strange conclusions. For example, earlier findings included:

Many men don't like to fly because they fear that if the plane crashes they will be blamed by their family for not being killed in a decent fashion, such as in a car crash.

When she is baking, a woman is unconsciously and symbolically reenacting the process of giving birth.

Men who use suspenders have an unresolved castration complex.[24]

The novelty of these interpretations is at least partially explained by the central role of fantasy, unconscious antisocial strivings, and sex in Freudian psychology, which has apparently strongly influenced conclusions drawn from many motivation-research studies. There have also been a number of other criticisms leveled at motivation researchers.[25] First, sample sizes are frequently small because of the costly nature of depth interviewing. This has created problems with regard to making conclusions about the entire population of consumers. Second, motivation-research studies have generated inconsistent findings, and this leaves the marketer in a quandary as to what action should be taken. Further, some findings are difficult for the marketer to capitalize on. For example, of what practical use is it to know (assuming it is true) that suspender wearers have a castration complex? Finally, and perhaps most importantly, motivation researchers have been criticized for improperly employing research techniques borrowed from psychologists. In psychology, these techniques are used in conjunction with knowledge of a patient's history and normal standards of behavior to serve as references. The lack of such standards in marketing make it difficult to determine whether many motivation-research findings are truly representative of most consumers.

Despite its potential limitations, motivation research has been a valuable research tool in a number of situations. For example, in a now-classic study, Haire discovered evidence suggesting that initial resistance to Nescafé instant coffee may have been due to more than just its taste characteristics. Projective methods revealed that women believed users of the instant product were lazy and not particularly good wives. Thus, it was argued, they would not be quick to adopt it themselves.[26] Other studies have provided data for marketing decisions of major industrial giants such as Alcoa, Colgate-Palmolive, General Mills, and Chrysler Corporation. Therefore, it appears that when properly conducted motivation-research studies are employed with other information, they can provide valuable information about consumers.

INVOLVEMENT

Consider a consumer facing two different buying situations. The first involves purchasing a new pair of running shoes. Because this consumer runs an average of 50 miles per week, she is really "into" the sport and quite interested in her footwear. Recent talks with another runner resulted in consideration of a change in brands. This led to a careful reading of many advertisements in several issues of *Runners World* magazine. She also closely studied the special issue that rated all major shoe brands according to a variety of criteria. Based on detailed evaluation of her own running characteristics and the magazine's ratings of shoes, she decided that a top-of-the-line model of New Balance shoes was her best choice. Discussion of this decision with fellow runners and salespeople at a sports store confirmed the choice and led to a purchase. The decision-making process took two weeks.

In the second situation, this same consumer decided it was time to restain the deck of her house. Although she had seen numerous television commercials for California Storm Stain, they had not captured her interest or attention. Conse-

quently, the brand was not on her mind during the trip to a local hardware store. Upon finding three different brands on display, she began looking at the labels and recognized the California name. She was not aware of any previous exposure to this brand, but since a glance revealed no drastic price differences she purchased three gallons of California in a brown color. The entire process occupied only a portion of one Saturday afternoon and involved little effort.

These two buying situations differ considerably in terms of the energy devoted to purchase decisions. Unfortunately, many marketers assume that typically, consumers are actively involved to the extent described in the first example. Although this view may be appropriate for many situations, it appears lacking for a wide variety of other cases that more resemble our second example—consumers having little concern about their consumption activities and adopting a rather detached, reactive stance to stimuli that reach their awareness.

Herbert Krugman proposed the concept of *involvement* to characterize differences in the intensity of interest with which consumers approach their dealings with the marketplace.[27] A major concern is how the level of involvement affects attention given to advertisements, and how it influences the extent to which consumers will actively evaluate or passively accept the information contained in these communications. Special focus is also on low-involvement situations, because they appear to evoke different mental processes than those generated under conditions of high involvement. For example, under low involvement the consumer may learn product information even when not attempting to do so, and his brand attitudes may actually not be a very strong influence on his purchase decisions.

Recently, consumer researchers have become quite interested in the topic of consumer involvement. As one might expect for a relatively new concept, full agreement has not yet been reached regarding its nature.[28] Some definitions emphasize the degree to which the consumer makes personal connections between a product and herself. Others focus on changes in arousal levels or on how involvement affects consumers' processing of information contained in marketing communications. However, most definitions acknowledge that involvement:

1 Is related to the consumer's values and self-concept, which influence the degree of personal importance ascribed to a product or situation.

2 Can vary across individuals and different situations.

3 Is related to some form of arousal.

On the basis of a review of these and other characteristics, it has been suggested that involvement has the critical properties of (1) intensity—degree of arousal, and (2) directional influence.[29] Therefore, although involvement as characterized above may not be identical to motivation, the two concepts appear closely related in important aspects.

DIMENSIONS OF INVOLVEMENT

The concept of involvement is multifaceted in that it appears to have a number of important dimensions. The following paragraphs describe several of these dimensions to encourage a fuller appreciation of this potentially important influence on consumers.

Involvement Levels   Typically, involvement has been viewed in terms of two broad categories—high and low. More recently, some have suggested that additional levels may exist to influence how consumers act with regard to product and brand information in their environment.[30] An important contribution of these schemes is their implication for an understanding of how consumers process information. However, for our purpose here it is sufficient only to draw distinctions between high and low involvement levels.

Traditionally, a highly involved consumer is defined as one who is very interested in differences between particular brands of a product and is willing to invest considerable energy in decision making about purchasing them. Similar to the example about buying running shoes, this interest often generates a sizeable amount of active search for information, as well as increased attention to relevant brand advertisements. In addition, highly involved consumers, rather than just passively accepting information, tend to critically evaluate the negative and positive implications of received information. Attitudes are formed about specific brands from the beliefs that consumers develop from such critical evaluations.

When consumers operate under low-involvement conditions, they are described as passive receivers of information who engage in virtually no active information search about alternative brands. Also, advertisements or other information actually reaching attention will only be processed at a very superficial level, receiving little meaningful evaluation. Very low levels of brand awareness and comprehension will be the result. Further, consumers do not appear to develop distinct attitudes about brands from such information.

Involvement Types   A second involvement dimension deals with factors influencing its nature or intensity.[31] One factor appears to be consumers themselves. A given product class will have more or less importance to various consumers, that is, due to consumers' individual values, self-concepts or experiences. For example, some consumers are very involved with stereo equipment while others are much more concerned about skiing, cars, or clothes. This type of involvement has been referred to as *enduring involvement* since it defines the consumer's baseline or long-term level of interest in a given product.[32]

A second factor is characterized as *situational involvement*. This refers to the *temporary* involvement in a product that occurs as a result of the situation a consumer finds himself in: the situation, rather than some long-term interest in the product itself, defines the product's relevance. For example, the purchase situation (gift for a close friend, feelings of low knowledge about brands, the amount of pleasure to be derived from purchase, and so on) can significantly influence the consumer's involvement in the purchase decision he is confronting. Therefore, situational factors can temporarily lead to high levels of involvement even for products generating low levels of enduring involvement for the consumer.

Recently, researchers have proposed that there are five major antecedents or sources influencing both enduring and situational involvement:

1   Perceived importance (personal meaning) of the product

2   Perceived risk of the purchase influenced by the perceived importance of negative consequences stemming from a poor purchase choice

3   Perceived risk of the purchase influenced by the perceived likelihood of making a poor purchase choice

4   The symbolic value (social embarrassment and the like, as opposed to physical gain or harm) perceived in the product

5   The perceived ability of the product to provide pleasure and emotional rewards

These factors not only influence the degree of involvement in a product but also seem to affect how consumers respond. We now turn to this topic.

Response Characteristics   The response dimension characterizes how a consumer behaves under different involvement conditions. That is, it describes the mental and physical actions or reactions the consumer engages in. Therefore, the response dimension is really a function of the type of involvement generated by enduring and situational influences.

Some response characteristics have already been mentioned in our earlier discussion of involvement levels. However, it is useful to provide a fuller view of their nature here. Generally, we can view the response dimension as including different patterns of information search and acquisition, the mental processing of information to evaluate products and make decisions about them, and post-decision behavior.

As already mentioned, some research has indicated that high involvement generates rather intense efforts on the part of the consumer for attending to and actively searching out sources of product and brand information. In fact, one study found that consumers high in *enduring* involvement for a product engaged in a regular, *ongoing* search for information about it.[33] This is to be contrasted with the search activity that may increase shortly before purchasing a product.

Conversely, low involvement is said to result in a passive consumer who engages in little if any active search for information. Here, exposure to products occurs mainly through advertisements and other information which the consumer happens to confront as a result of engaging in other activities (such as watching TV). Also, because of this lack of interest, little attention is devoted to these sources. Consequently, only modest amounts of information may be acquired about a specific brand even after many exposures to advertisements for it.

After acquiring information, consumers process it to determine its meaning. The steps undertaken in this information-processing stage have been viewed in terms of a *hierarchy of effects* because they appear to describe the mental processes that lead to a purchase. A variety of hierarchies have been proposed under one common assumption—the consumer is highly involved. More recently, a different hierarchy of effects has been proposed for low-involvement conditions.[34] The essence of each hierarchy that is relevant to our present discussion is presented in Figure 12-9.

Cognition in the high-involvement hierarchy refers to the knowledge and beliefs about brands that consumers derive from evaluating information. Active

search and attention to information fosters learning about advertisements and other product information. In addition, the consumer engages in considerable thinking about this information to determine its consistency with his existing brand knowledge and beliefs. Critical evaluation and rejection of information inconsistent with existing beliefs are likely to occur. This can happen through the consumer's use of arguments to counter information or advertising claims ("the price is low, but I'll bet the service is bad") and through attempts to discredit the source of the information. Alternatively, consistent information is likely to generate strong supportive arguments. The result is a new or modified set of beliefs about alternative brands.

As the second stage in the high-involvement hierarchy suggests, evaluation of beliefs in a positive and negative sense leads the consumer to form attitudes about the brands and their relative desirability. Resulting behavior is believed to be strongly influenced by the attitudes that the consumer holds.

Cognition in the low-involvement hierarchy differs considerably from its counterpart under conditions of high involvement. Attention levels are low because the consumer has little desire to process information for the purpose of evaluating brands. Despite exposure to many advertisements, knowledge about brands is also very low. In fact, the consumer may not even be consciously aware of the brand name. Consequently, beliefs about brands are not well founded and will not be strong enough to support the formation of brand attitudes.

Another consequence may occur after numerous exposures to advertisements about a particular brand. The brand name can become sufficiently familiar to the consumer so that she recognizes it when shopping for the product. Because the consumer has no strong attitude about any of the specific brands, this familiarity may be a sufficient reason for purchase of the brand. Therefore, as the second stage in the low-involvement hierarchy shows, purchase behavior occurs before strong brand attitudes have developed. After the consumer purchases and experiences the product through direct use, it is likely that she will develop some attitudes about it. However, these attitudes may never become very strong because of the low importance of the product to the consumer.

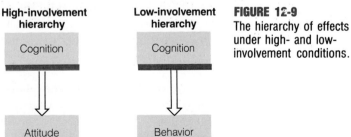

FIGURE 12-9
The hierarchy of effects under high- and low-involvement conditions.

MARKETING IMPLICATIONS

Two essential conclusions emerge from the above review:

1   For numerous products or situations, many consumers are quite uninterested in learning about alternative brands and their characteristics.

2   Consumers may make many purchase decisions without first developing clear brand attitudes or even having much knowledge about alternative brands.

Given that involvement can vary across consumers and situations, these conclusions have a number of marketing strategy implications.[35] A primary consideration is to determine whether any strategy should account for different levels of involvement. If only a small proportion of the market operates on a low-involvement condition for the brand in question, it may not be economical to consider changing strategies. However, if sizable portions of the potential market might relate to the company's offerings at either level of involvement, then some manner of coping with these different levels would seem highly desirable. One strategy might be to differentiate marketing communications for each condition. For example, high-involvement messages would entail longer advertisements and considerable amounts of more-complex information. In addition, because of its higher involvement demands, print media may be the more appropriate choice for advertising insertions.[36] For the low-involvement advertisements, short visually oriented messages with little information content could be frequently repeated to foster brand awareness. Many of these might be placed on television because of its lower demands for viewer concentration and the potential for frequent advertising insertions.

The picture may even be slightly more complicated. Earlier we suggested that five antecedents of involvement may influence the *nature* of consumers' responses. This seems to be the case. For example, very recent evidence suggests that the amount of risk perceived in a purchase will more strongly influence how extensive the decision process will be than will other antecedents, such as the product's perceived pleasure value. Also, the consumer's tendency to allow exposure to advertising messages does not seem highly related to risk importance but is strongly influenced by the product's perceived pleasure value.[37] Of course such results need to be verified by additional research. If they are confirmed, these findings imply that marketers will benefit from discovering the sources of consumer involvement before designing marketing strategies for their products or services.

A second involvement-related strategy would be an attempt to move low-involvement consumers to higher levels.[38] Of course, the specific situation will determine the feasibility of this alternative. If conditions appear favorable, various methods may be considered. These could include creating controversy (the Pepsi challenge, live taste tests for Schlitz beer, and so on), linking the product to a highly involving issue (air fresheners related to the problem of social disgrace), or changing the product to add features which might increase involvement levels, like the producers of VitaGum did when they added vitamins to chewing gum.

A third strategy option is also possible—segmenting consumers into high- and low-involvement groups and tailoring marketing programs for each.[39] An example might be writing pens. Low-involvement consumers could be catered to with inexpensive models that are rather nondescript and disposable. Frequent television commercials could remind mass audiences of the brand name. Conversely, those concerned with conveying an image with their pen might be willing to spend more than $30 and even as much as $9000.[40] These instruments would have distinctive materials, styling, and craftsmanship. Promotions detailing many product features might be placed in exclusive magazines such as the *New Yorker* or *Smithsonian* to attract high-income readers.

This section has introduced the involvement concept, suggested its general potential for influencing the behavior of consumers, and indicated its implications for marketing strategy. We will build on this introduction in subsequent chapters to show the relevance of involvement to the variables under discussion.

MANAGERIAL REFLECTIONS

For our product or service situation . . .

1   What motives might be influencing choice criteria?

2   What factors are likely to trigger arousal and how can they be influenced?

3   What motives may be combining to influence purchases? Which may put the consumer into conflict and how might we be able to help resolve such conflict?

4   How might motivation research methods help to give us insight into consumers?

5   To what degree are consumers influenced by enduring involvement?

6   Should segmentation be based on involvement levels?

DISCUSSION TOPICS

1   What is a motive? Indicate the various roles motives play in influencing behavior.

2   Find three examples of advertisements that appeal to psychogenic motives. Be prepared to discuss the appropriateness of the association between the product and the motive.

3   Discuss the problems unconscious motives pose for implementing the marketing concept.

4   What general factors can trigger motive arousal? Cite at least two examples of each type.

5   It has been argued that at times consumers actually seem to increase levels of environmental stimulation as well as strive to reduce them. Review this argument, and suggest situations, as well as marketing strategies that could relate to such situations.

6   Briefly review Maslow's motive hierarchy and the concept of prepotency. Cite at least three products that might appeal to an individual at each stage of the

hierarchy. Can you suggest any product for which a marketer might be able to appeal to at least three of the stages at the same time?

7 Of what interest is the concept of "levels of aspiration" to the marketer? What relevance does this concept have to the problem of energy shortage and depletion of resources?

8 Review the concepts of motive linking and motive bundling. Show how they can apply to the purchase of a jogging suit.

9 Define each of the major types of motive conflict and cite a personal experience that fits each of these situations. Be sure to indicate the specifics involved, including any relevant products, the duration of the conflict, and how it was resolved.

10 Construct two high-involvement and two low-involvement consumer scenarios, and suggest marketing strategies to accommodate them.

PROJECTS

1 Conduct a focus group interview in an attempt to discover the motives influencing purchases of some type of electronics equipment.

2 Interview several consumers and attempt to identify different situations which can be categorized into at least two of the four zones of environmental stimulation as identified in Figure 12-5. Develop marketing strategies to appeal to behavior that could be expected from consumers in such situations.

3 Interview several consumers and attempt to discover products or situations leading to high-involvement conditions for them. Can you discover the antecedents (review the section on involvement types) of these different involvement situations? Can you identify any implications for marketing to such consumers?

NOTES

[1] Based on "Chewy Cookies," *AdWeek,* November 4, 1985, p. H.P. 16; and Laurie Freeman, "Cookie Marketers Keep Mixing It Up," *Advertising Age,* February 24, 1986, p. 12.
[2] See Joe Kent Kerby, *Consumer Behavior: Conceptual Foundations,* Dun-Donnelly, New York, 1975; Johan Arndt, "How Broad Should the Marketing Concept Be?" *Journal of Marketing,* **42**:101–103, January 1978; and Gerald Zaltman and Melanie Wallendorf, *Consumer Behavior: Basic Findings and Management Implications,* Wiley, New York, 1979.
[3] See Abraham K. Korman, *The Psychology of Motivation,* Prentice-Hall, Englewood Cliffs, N.J., 1974.
[4] Portions of this section follow the discussion in John Howard and Jagdish Sheth, *The Theory of Buyer Behavior,* Wiley, New York, 1969, pp. 105–118.
[5] One exception is the case of anxiety in which consumers suffer from a lack of direction to their arousal.
[6] See G.W. Allport and H. S. Odbert, "Trait-Names: A Psychological Study," *Psychological Monographs,* **47**(1), 1936.
[7] W. Fred van Raaij and Kassaye Wandwossen, "Motivation-Need Theories and Consumer Behavior," in Keith Hunt (ed.), *Advances in Consumer Research,* vol. 5, Association for Consumer Research, Ann Arbor, Mich., 1978, pp. 590–595.
[8] See William J. McGuire, "Some Internal Psychological Factors Influencing Consumer Choice," *Journal of Consumer Research,* **2**:302–319, March 1976; and William J. McGuire, Psychological

Motives and Communication Gratification,'' in J. G. Blumer and E. Katz (eds.), *The Uses of Mass Communications: Perspectives on Gratifications Research,* Sage Publications, Inc., Beverly Hills, Calif., pp. 167–196.

[9] Some of this section follows David Krech, Richard S. Crutchfield, and Egerton L. Ballachey, *Individual in Society,* McGraw-Hill, New York, 1962, pp. 84–87.

[10] See, for example, D. E. Berlyne, *Conflict, Arousal and Curiosity,* McGraw-Hill, New York, 1960; Werner Kroeber-Riel, ''Activation Research: Psychobiological Approaches in Consumer Research,'' *Journal of Consumer Research,* **5**:240–250, March 1979; and P. S. Raju and M. Venkatesan, ''Exploratory Behavior in the Consumer Context: A State of the Art Review,'' in Jerry C. Olson (ed.), *Advances in Consumer Research,* vol. 7, Association for Consumer Research, Ann Arbor, Mich., 1979, pp. 258–263.

[11] For factors to consider in this decision see Werner Kroeber-Riel, ''Activation Research'' and Kathy A. Lutz and Richard J. Lutz, ''The Effects of Interactive Imagery on Learning: Application to Advertising,'' University of California, Los Angeles Center for Marketing Studies, Paper No. 40, March 1976.

[12] Based on Gail Bronson, ''Turn for the Worse: 'Simple' Little Puzzle Drives Millions Mad, *The Wall Street Journal,* March 5, 1981, pp. 1, 20; Jane Carmichael, ''Figure This One Out,'' *Forbes,* April 27, 1981, p. 34; and ''Hot-Selling Hungarian Horror,'' *Time,* March 23, 1981, p. 83.

[13] See M. Venkatesan, ''Cognitive Consistency and Novelty Seeking'' in Scott Ward and Thomas S. Robertson (eds.), *Consumer Behavior: Theoretical Sources,* Prentice-Hall: Englewood Cliffs, N.J., 1973, pp. 354–384; and P. S. Raju, ''Theories of Exploratory Behavior: Review and Consumer Research Implications,'' in Jagdish N. Sheth (ed.,), *Research in Marketing,* vol. 4, JAI Press, Greenwich, Conn., 1981, pp. 223–249.

[14] S. Streufert and M. J. Driver, ''The General Incongruity Adaptation Level (GIAL),'' Technical Report 32, Dorsey Press, Homewood, Ill., 1971.

[15] This discussion follows Raju, ''Theories of Exploratory Behavior''; and P. S. Raju and M. Venkatesan, ''Exploratory Behavior in the Consumer Context.''

[16] A. H. Maslow, ''A Theory of Human Motivation,'' *Psychological Review,* **50**:370–396, 1943.

[17] See Frederick Herzberg, ''Retrospective Comment,'' in Howard A. Thompson (ed.), *The Great Writings in Marketing,* Commerce, Plymouth, Mich., 1976, pp. 180–181; and van Raaij and Wandwossen, ''Motivation-Need Theories and Consumer Behavior'' for critiques of Maslow's contributions.

[18] As an example, see James R. Bettman, *An Information Processing Theory of Consumer Choice,* Addison-Wesley, Reading, Mass., 1979.

[19] George Katona, *The Powerful Consumer,* McGraw-Hill, New York, 1960, p. 130.

[20] See John Kenneth Galbraith, *The Affluent Society,* Houghton Mifflin, Boston, 1958.

[21] Some of this section follows Howard and Sheth, *The Theory of Buyer Behavior,* pp. 105–118.

[22] See Bettman, *Information Processing,* pp. 19–22, for an illustration.

[23] Kurt Lewin, *A Dynamic Theory of Personality,* McGraw-Hill, New York, 1935.

[24] See Ernest Dichter, *Handbook of Consumer Motivations,* McGraw-Hill, New York, 1964, for these and other interesting motivation research findings.

[25] See N. D. Rothwell, ''Motivational Research Reinstated,'' *Journal of Marketing,* **19**:150–154, October 1955.

[26] Mason Haire, ''Projective Techniques in Marketing Research,'' *Journal of Marketing,* **14**:649–656, April 1950.

[27] H. E. Krugman, ''The Impact of Television Advertising: Learning Without Involvement,'' *Public Opinion Quarterly,* **29**:349–356, Fall 1965.

[28] Anthony G. Greenwald, Clark Leavitt, and Carl Obermiller, ''What is Low Consumer Involvement?'' in Gerald J. Gorn and Marvin E. Goldberg (eds.), *Proceedings, Division 23 Program of the 88th Annual Convention,* American Psychological Association, Montreal, 1980, pp. 65–74.

[29] Andrew A. Mitchell, ''Involvement: A Potentially Important Mediator of Consumer Behavior,'' in William L. Wilkie (ed.), *Advances in Consumer Research,* vol. 6, Association for Consumer Research, Ann Arbor, Mich., 1979, pp. 191–196.

[30] See Andrew Mitchell, ''The Dimensions of Advertising Involvement,'' in Kent B. Monroe (ed.), *Advances in Consumer Research,* vol. 8, Association for Consumer Research, Ann Arbor, Mich., 1981, pp. 25–30; and Greenwald, Leavitt, and Obermiller, ''What is Low Involvement?'' for two different views of the three-level scheme.

[31] See Harold H. Kassarjian, "Low Involvement: A Second Look," in Kent B. Monroe (ed.), *Advances in Consumer Research,* vol. 8, Association for Consumer Research, Ann Arbor, Mich., 1981, pp. 31–34; and Michael J. Houston and Michael L. Rothschild, "Conceptual and Methodological Perspectives on Involvement," in Subhash C. Jain (ed.), *Research Frontiers in Marketing: Dialogues and Directions,* American Marketing Association, Chicago, 1978, pp. 184–187.

[32] Houston and Rothschild, "Conceptual and Methodological Perspectives on Involvement"; and Marsha L. Richins and Peter H. Block, "After the New Wears Off: The Temporal Context of Product Involvement," *Journal of Consumer Research,* 13:280–285, September 1986.

[33] Peter H. Bloch, Daniel L. Sherrell, and Nancy M. Ridgway, "Consumer Search: An Extended Framework," *Journal of Consumer Research,* 13:119–126, June 1986.

[34] See Michael L. Ray, "Marketing Communication and the Hierarchy of Effects," in Peter Clark (ed.), *New Models for Mass Communication Research,* Sage Publications, Inc., Beverly Hills, 1973, pp. 147–176; and Krugman, "Television Advertising: Learning Without Involvement," pp. 349–356.

[35] See Michael L. Rothschild, "Advertising Strategies for High and Low Involvement Situations," in John C. Maloney and Bernard Silverman (eds.), *Attitude Research Plays for High Stakes,* American Marketing Association, Chicago, 1979, pp. 74–93; Tyzoon T. Tyebjee, "Refinement of the Involvement Concept: An Advertising Planning Point of View," in John C. Maloney and Bernard Silverman (eds.), *Attitude Research Plays for High Stakes,* American Marketing Association, Chicago, 1979, pp. 94–111; Richard Vaughn, "How Advertising Works: A Planning Model," *Journal of Advertising Research,* 20:27–33, October 1980; and Greenwald, Leavitt, and Obermiller, "What Is Low Involvement?"

[36] Herbert E. Krugman, "The Measure of Advertising Involvement," *Public Opinion Quarterly,* 30:583–596, Winter 1966.

[37] Gilles Laurent and Jean-Noel Kapferer, "Measuring Consumer Involvement Profiles," *Journal of Marketing Research,* 22:41–53, February 1985.

[38] Rothschild, "Advertising Strategies for Involvement."

[39] See Tyzoon T. Tyebjee, "Refinement of the Involvement Concept," pp. 107–108.

[40] Mitchell C. Lynch, "How're Ya Fixed for Fountain Pens?" *The Wall Street Journal,* June 12, 1981, p. 23.

INFORMATION PROCESSING

LEARNING OBJECTIVES

After studying this chapter, you should understand . . .

■ Characteristics of consumers' information acquisition processes and their implications for marketing

■ How consumers' sensory processes influence their behavior

■ The role and marketing implications of consumers' attention mechanisms

■ How consumers derive meaning from information in their environment

■ The direct relevance of consumers' information processing activities to marketing decisions in the areas of product, price, channels, and promotion

It was expensive—costing in the neighborhood of $1.4 million. It was lavish—one of the better known firms in the ad industry, Chiat/Day, had developed it. Its coming was heralded—newspaper ads teased the public into looking for its appearance. And, according to many, it went over like a sour lemon.

This probably summarizes a large part of the advertising industry's analysis of the much-touted Apple Computer advertisement shown during the last minutes of the 1985 Super Bowl. Apple was attempting to live up to the excitement and attention it had generated with its 1984 Super Bowl advertisement—appropriately named "1984." Unfortunately, it appears that something was lost in the translation. The 1985 "Lemmings" ad was designed to stimulate interest in new offerings for the Macintosh computer that Apple claimed would revolutionize methods and efficiency. The ad did this by showing a macabre death march, characteristic of how lemmings inexplicably rush into the sea to drown. But here the scene depicted blindfolded business people chanting a somber funerallike version of "Hi-ho, hi-ho, it's off to work we go" and marching in lock-step fashion off a cliff to their certain death. However, as one man neared the edge, he raised his blindfold, saw what was happening, and refused to walk any further. The voiceover in the ad indicated that Apple would soon introduce new Macintosh products and that viewers should look into them or go on with business as usual—a line that many interpreted to mean that a strategy of continuing to purchase IBM products was akin to blindly walking off a cliff.

What impact did this lavish production have? It appears that results were quite underwhelming. Many felt it had a depressing tone, and others reacted with aversion to the death scene. However, what seemed to hurt most of all was that this grandiose effort went unnoticed by multitudes of viewers. An independent telephone survey of 300 television viewers revealed that just 54 percent recalled seeing an Apple Computer advertisement during the Super Bowl, and only 10 percent were able to describe it

13

correctly. Also, fewer than 17 percent of those surveyed could identify correctly the product being advertised. What were perhaps the most frustrating responses of all were those mentioning a Charlie Chaplin look-alike—the character used in IBM microcomputer advertisements![1]

As this example illustrates, it is important for the marketer to understand how consumers acquire and handle the information available from stimuli in their environment. This chapter introduces the nature and role of information processing. It begins with a brief overview of the concept. Major aspects of information acquisition, selective attention to stimuli, and the task of deriving meaning from these stimuli are then discussed in greater depth. The application of these concepts to a number of actual marketing decision problems is then reviewed. Additional information-processing topics are also treated later in the learning and attitude chapters as well as in Part Five of the text.

OVERVIEW

It is often helpful to view consumers as problem solvers who use information in an attempt to satisfy their consumption goals. From this perspective, *consumer information processing* may be thought of as the acquisition of stimulus inputs, the manipulation of these inputs to derive meaning from them, and the use of this information to think about products or services. More specifically, five of the major ways in which consumers use information derived from their environment are:

1 To understand and evaluate products and services.

2 To attempt to justify previous product choices.

3 To resolve the conflict between buying or postponing purchases.

4 To satisfy a need for being informed about products and services in the marketplace.

5 To serve as a reminder to purchase products that must be regularly replenished (soap, beverages, and the like).[2]

It is important to realize that, as its definition implies, information processing is not the end result of an activity, but the actual process itself that consumers engage in when dealing with their environment. Figure 13-1 shows the basic components of information processing and will serve as a framework for our overview.

It should be noted that this model is more descriptive of processing activities that consumers engage in under conditions of high involvement, particularly with regard to stimulus-acquisition activities. Processing under conditions of low involvement was briefly described in Chapter 12. That discussion can be used as a guide to draw material from this chapter that is relevant to the low-involvement condition. Future sections will also address this topic. However, because a great deal is not yet known about low-involvement processing, our treatment of it will be brief.

The basic components shown in Figure 13-1 can be arranged into four groupings: (1) stimuli which serve as the raw material to be processed, (2) the stages of processing activities which are linked by arrows and are mainly internal to the consumer, (3) situational and consumer characteristics which can influence the nature of these processing activities, and (4) an executive system which guides the process by regulating the type and intensity of processing activities engaged in at any time. Each of these is briefly characterized below.

Stimuli may be thought of as units of energy such as light and sounds which can excite our sensory receptors. We have receptors for internally produced stimuli such as hunger pangs, as well as receptors for the commonly known five senses of taste, touch, smell, vision, and hearing. Typically, a given stimulus does not exist in isolation but is part of a larger stimulus situation which comprises many individual stimuli.

The *acquisition process* enables consumers to confront certain stimuli in their environment and begin to process them. *Exposure,* which is part of the acquisition process, occurs in a wide variety of ways, but two major categories exist: active search and passive reception. In *active search*, the consumer's executive system serves as a guide to seek out specific types of stimuli, such as the nutritional content per serving in a can of soup. As Figure 13-1 shows, this information may already exist in memory, or it can be part of the external environment. The way in which the search process is conducted will be influenced by the consumer's motives, and it is mainly within conscious control. Conversely, in *passive reception,* consumers confront stimuli in the process of living their daily lives. Exposure to many advertisements, news reports on various products, and in-

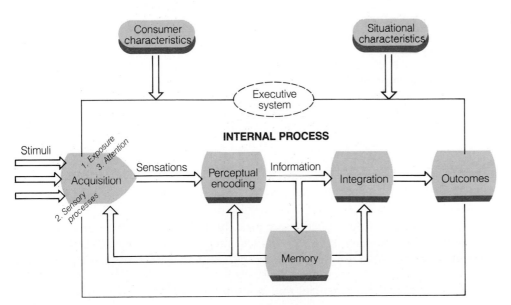

FIGURE 13-1
An information-processing framework.

formation acquired as a by-product of normal shopping activities are all examples of the passive reception mode of stimulus acquisition.

The exposure process, through both active search and passive reception, is capable of acquiring an almost infinite number of stimuli. Because the consumer has limited capacity to process this amount of data, two major mechanisms reduce the number of stimuli to manageable proportions. First, sensory receptors have limited sensitivity, which means that our *sensory processes* produce sensations for only a specific range of stimulus values. Second, we selectively devote *attention* to only a small proportion of the resulting sensations, and we literally ignore the rest. Therefore, with certain exceptions to be discussed later, stimuli that are capable of producing sensations and then attracting the consumer's attention are the main focus of further processing efforts.

Sensations may be thought of as electrical impulses with no innate meaning that are produced by our receptors. A *perceptual encoding* process involves several activities that allow the consumer to interpret these raw inputs. The process can be thought of as constructing mental symbols to represent sensations in order to derive meaning from them. Various symbols such as words or mental images can serve as representations. Of course, characteristics of the stimulus itself will strongly influence how it will be represented. As Figure 13-1 shows, however, another major influence is the information already stored in memory. That is, the meaning we derive from stimuli is greatly affected by our previous experiences. It is for this reason that the perceptual encoding process is said to develop personal meaning called *information* from raw stimulus inputs. Thus, consumers act on their own interpretation of the world, as opposed to what actually may exist.

Figure 13-1 indicates that information generated by perceptual encoding can be stored in *memory* for future use, and it can also be directly transferred to the *integration* stage of processing. Here, the consumer combines and arranges various informational inputs to reach conclusions about the environment. For example, information on the package size, number of servings, price, and brand name of several supermarket products could be arranged in various ways to be meaningful in the consumer's mind. Information available from memory, as well as material obtained directly from the environment, represent inputs to this integration process.

A major goal of information processing is to deal effectively with the environment. Therefore, *outcomes* of information-processing activities are likely to affect evaluation and attitudes. Information that has been integrated involves *attitudes* when the consumer's beliefs or feelings about a particular object (brand, product, purchasing action, and so on) are developed or changed. These attitudes can be held by the consumer to influence later actions toward the object. For example, if the consumer's attitudes toward purchasing Haggar slacks are positively influenced by an advertisement, this is likely to increase the probability of a later purchase.

A second outcome can occur more directly. Information can be processed for the purpose of product *evaluation*, choice, and immediate purchase. Here, the consumer, rather than forming attitudes to influence later decisions, makes a brand choice as the information is processed.

In some cases, the consumer may not think the evaluation or choice task has

high importance. This usually results in a brief process of review. Here, various rules of thumb (select the lowest-priced alternative, and so on) may be employed to minimize choice effort. However, when the evaluation and choice situation is perceived to be quite important, considerable effort is likely to be devoted to the process.

Information processing is strongly influenced by *consumer characteristics*. For example, previous attitudes can affect how the consumer will evaluate a particular brand, and the evaluation process can in turn result in attitude change or development of new brand attitudes. Other consumer characteristics exerting a major influence on information processing are the consumer's motives, personality attributes, and learning. *Situational characteristics* can also play a role. For example, the consumer's environment is sometimes overloaded with potential information, and some selection of stimuli for processing must be made. At other times, the environment may actually generate such little stimulation that the consumer begins looking for more.

Information-processing activities do not act independently of each other. Rather, each activity needs to be coordinated with others so that intelligible meaning can be derived from stimuli. The *executive system* is the mechanism that coordinates various information-processing activities. It also serves as a command center that directs attention and organizes processing energies toward those stimuli that are potentially more relevant to the consumer's goals.

The vast majority of information-processing activities are internal to the consumer and therefore are unobservable. Two notable exceptions are portions of the stimulus-acquisition process (the number of stores shopped, salespeople consulted, and so on) and certain overt responses (such as brands purchased). Figure 13-1 recognizes these overt activities by showing that stimulus acquisition and outcomes are not completely encompassed within the internal framework (lines of the box). Although such overt actions can be directly observed, the majority of information-processing activities must be studied by determining their influence on other variables and measures.

The preceding paragraphs presented a brief overview of the major activities involved in information processing. The chapter now turns to a more-detailed review of two of these components—acquisition and perceptual encoding. Subsequent chapters will treat other activities in greater depth.

INFORMATION ACQUISITION

The term *information acquisition* describes the set of activities or means by which consumers are exposed to various environmental stimuli and begin to process them. As mentioned in the overview, exposure occurs in two major ways: when consumers are motivated to actively seek information and when they passively receive these stimuli that are confronted in daily activities. We will discuss aspects of the active search process first.

ACTIVE SEARCH

Consumers often actively seek and selectively acquire information that has potential usefulness for achieving their consumption goals. The first stage in this process appears to be *internal search*, because of the relative ease with which it

can be accomplished compared to external search. Internal search involves scanning memory for stored information that is relevant to the purchase situation under consideration. This available information has been previously acquired from passive reception experiences as well as through active external searches.[3] Consequently, it can include information derived from advertising claims, personal experiences, product test reports, previous solutions to similar purchase problems, and interactions with other consumers.

Internal search will tend to be rather deliberate and comprehensive when the consumer views a situation as important, when the purchase decision is a difficult one, and when the amount of information in memory is considerable or complex. In other cases, such as during the regular replenishment of one's usual brand of bath soap, the memory scan may be so automatic that it never even reaches conscious awareness

In what actually appears to be the majority of cases, information acquired from an internal memory scan is sufficient for the consumer's needs. Consequently, a decision will be made without seeking any external information. For the remaining situations, the consumer is not satisfied with his existing knowledge and becomes sufficiently motivated to engage in external search.

The amount of external search varies considerably across individuals and different purchase situations. Factors affecting this amount include (1) market conditions such as price and feature differences between brands, (2) situational factors including conditions of store crowding and the urgency of need, (3) buying strategies that consumers may adopt such as brand or store loyalty patterns, and (4) individual factors including the level of involvement and self-confidence. Chapter 19 will explore these factors in greater depth.

PASSIVE RECEPTION

The preceding section focused on active search, which consumers use when deliberately seeking information relevant to a consumption goal or special interest. As mentioned earlier, the passive reception process is another means of information acquisition. In this mode, consumers confront and acquire information in the process of living their daily lives. For example, when watching a TV program, casually talking to a friend, or searching for literature about house paints, one could be exposed to information about aluminum house siding. This information might be stored away for a future time when the need to address the issue of house siding arises. As this situation demonstrates, passive reception occurs when consumers acquire information that they are not presently seeking. Instead of having a plan of search, the individual responds to environmental stimuli to which she is exposed.

Although virtually any type of stimulus may be passively acquired, substantial amounts of certain types of information are likely to be received in this manner.[4] For example, consumers frequently become aware that various products exist without actively seeking such knowledge. A significant amount of learning about product attributes and their advantages can also be acquired passively. In addition, it is likely that consumers obtain at least some of their knowledge about the quality of products through conversations with friends or other passive means.

The way in which passive reception occurs has important practical implications, because consumers' daily living patterns selectively influence their exposure to advertisements and other sources of consumption-related information. For this reason, marketers spend considerable time and effort on studies of consumers' selective media habits (magazine readership, TV programs watched, and so on) and activity patterns (such as shopping habits, and so on) that lead to exposure opportunities.

SENSATION

The exposure mechanisms of active search and passive reception produce many more stimuli than the consumer is capable of processing. Two of the gatekeeping mechanisms that reduce this "blooming confusion" to more manageable proportions involve consumers' physiological limitations: awareness thresholds and differential thresholds.

Awareness Thresholds   Any given stimulus may be either too small or weak to notice, or so great that it also escapes awareness. Consumers' zones of stimulus awareness can therefore be identified by defining two thresholds:

Absolute threshold. The minimum value of a stimulus capable of being consciously noticed

Terminal threshold. The maximum value of a stimulus capable of being consciously noticed

To illustrate, the average person's absolute and terminal thresholds for sound pitch are about 20 and 20,000 cycles per second, respectively. Those familar with audio equipment will notice that this is the exact range stereo manufacturers concentrate on when designing their equipment.

The threshold concept implies that we can determine precise values which mark the boundaries of stimulus awareness. This is actually misleading, since these limits for any given stimulus differ among individuals and even for the same individual over a period of time. Therefore, thresholds must be viewed as being somewhat variable and are usually defined by the stimulus value that goes undetected 50 percent of the time.

Consumers' absolute thresholds are often of more interest to marketers than are terminal thresholds because of their greater relevance to product designs. For example:

■ Common household light bulbs pulsate at 60 cycles per second but appear to have a constant intensity.

■ Television sets produce an apparent full-screen image by rapidly scanning the entire screen with a narrow beam of light.

■ In another application, because adults differ significantly in their taste sensitivity to beer, experts have segmented the consuming public into three distinct groupings: (1) discriminating individuals mainly concerned with the taste of beer, (2) discriminating individuals influenced by price and other variables, and

(3) nondiscriminating consumers.[5] Marketing strategies directed at such segments could differ significantly.

Differential Thresholds   Many sellers have made changes in their offerings only to find that they went unnoticed in the marketplace. This suggests that consumers also have limited sensitivity for noticing differences between different stimulus values. The *differential threshold* defines this sensitivity as the smallest detectable difference between two values of the same stimulus. For example, if the Coca-Cola Company were interested in whether consumers could detect a difference in sweetness between two different sugar concentrations of a drink it would need to examine consumers' differential threshold for sweetness.

To measure the differential threshold for a stimulus, one commonly changes its intensity in very small amounts, as in a hearing test. The consumer's threshold exists when he first notices that the stimulus has changed. The difference between this value and the starting value is often referred to as the *just noticeable difference (jnd)*.

WEBER'S LAW   As in the case of absolute thresholds, consumers also differ in their ability to detect differences between stimulus values, and this sensitivity varies with conditions. However, numerous studies have revealed a general relationship known as *Weber's Law,* which states that the stimulus change needed to reach the differential threshold (produce a just noticeable difference) is a constant *proportion* of the starting stimulus value. Weber's Law can be expressed as:

$$\frac{\Delta s}{S} = K$$

where S = the initial stimulus value

Δs = the smallest change in the stimulus capable of being detected: the just noticeable difference (jnd)

K = the constant of proportionality

Expressing the equation as $\Delta s = K \cdot S$ suggests that if we know the values of K and S, we could predict how large a change in the stimulus is necessary before consumers detect the change. To illustrate, assume that through testing we found that 1 ounce ($\Delta s = 1$) had to be added to a 10-ounce package ($S = 10$) before consumers detected a change in its weight. This would yield a constant of proportionality of $K = 1/10 = 0.1$, allowing us to predict that: (1) consumers will not detect a change in the weight of a 50-ounce box of detergent unless at least 5 ounces are added to or removed from it or (2) consumers will be able to detect a 3-pound addition to a 20-pound portable television.

Two points should be noted with regard to Weber's Law: (1) there are different constants of proportionality for different stimuli such as weight, color, and size, and (2) the law is not universal in its applicability because individuals differ and because it does not predict well near absolute or terminal thresholds. However, refinements have been made to the basic law and it appears to hold fairly well over the majority of stimulus range.

APPLYING WEBER'S LAW Marketers can apply Weber's Law to predicting how consumers will respond to differences between marketing variables or changes in these variables.[6] Sometimes the goal is to have consumers detect differences, and in other cases it is to have differences escape their attention. For example, because the cost of candy ingredients fluctuates widely there is a constant search for more stably priced substitutes. According to one report, this led to the discovery by Peter Paul, Inc., that tasters could not distinguish between one type of chocolate made with vegetable oil and another made with traditional cocoa butter.[7] However, a second firm found that most consumers could detect a difference between a chocolate substitute and the real thing.

A second way to hold prices constant in times of changing costs is to change the size or amount of the product slightly. For example, during a twenty-three-year period the Hershey Foods Corporation changed the price of its basic milk chocolate bar only three times, but varied its weight fourteen times.[8] It should be noted that many of these changes escaping consumers' awareness were weight *increases* allowed by declining costs. Similar changes (increases as well as decreases) have occurred in numerous packages and products, including newspapers, bathroom tissues, and soft drinks.

Another application of Weber's Law lies in the battleground of brand competition. Here producers of major brands such as A. T. Cross pens and Green Giant canned vegetables seek to distinguish their products as quite different from those of private competitors. However, some competing firms seek to produce similar products using less costly ingredients that might escape consumers' notice, thereby obtaining a differential price advantage. Also, packages of some privately labeled grocery products bear a striking resemblance to those of major brands.[9] Presumably, this discourages shoppers from detecting any noticeable differences existing between the brands. Figure 13-2 presents examples of this situation.

Pricing decisions may also make use of Weber's Law. For example, many merchants have noted that price reductions of at least 15 percent are usually needed to attract consumers to sales. This experience is supported by experimental evidence suggesting that consumers do possess awareness thresholds for price changes.[10]

ATTENTION

A research study conducted some time ago suggested that the average American adult is aware of seeing less than 100 major media advertisements per day.[11] However, the daily advertising exposure rate for a typical consumer has been estimated to range as high as 3000 or more. This suggests that although exposure and sensory processes both selectively filter stimuli for information processing, additional points of selectivity must also exist. One such filtering mechanism is *attention,* which can be viewed as the allocation of processing capacity to stimuli. That is, attention regulates the amount of additional processing that a stimulus will receive. Generally, the more processing capacity that is devoted to a stimulus, the greater will be the consumer's awareness and comprehension of it.

Voluntary and Involuntary Attention Consumers allocate their attention on both a voluntary and an involuntary basis. For voluntary attention, stimuli are deliber-

Checkout-Counter

Some supermarket and drugstore house brands are becoming masters of disguise.

Cheaper than national-brand products and often comparable or even identical in quality, the house brands of supermarkets and other big retailers have long appealed to the thrifty. Now, as these photographs suggest, some house-brand distributors also seem to be seeking the business of the merely careless.

Chains around the country have begun to feature private-label packages that look remarkably like proven name brands. Sometimes the similarity goes beyond the box. By definition, all petroleum jellies have to be much the same. And labels divulge that Safeway's Town House hominy, for example, has the same ingredients as the regional Burbank brand. On the other hand, Grand Union adds preservatives to its potato chips (69¢ for ten ounces in the New York market where *Money* bought them), while its owlish counterpart (79¢ for eight ounces) doesn't.

A few companies have gone to the courts to stop the lookalikes. Bristol-Myers, which makes Excedrin, has sued to force Dart Drug, a Washington-area discount chain, to change the package and name of Dart's Extracin. Others are unhappy. "We do not want anyone to have the opportunity to confuse or dupe the consumer," says a spokesman for Chesebrough-Pond's, maker of Vaseline.

The chain stores, however, contend that any lookalikes are only in the eye of the beholder. Says John Prinster, a Safeway vice president, "We are very careful not to copy; we don't want to confuse the consumer." A Grand Union spokesman asserts that "even if the consumer bought the wrong thing, he would get more for less." Well, not necessarily. An A&P clerk in Manhattan mistakenly charged one recent shopper the 55¢ Wonder bread price for a similar-looking 43¢ loaf of A&P's own Jane Parker. —*Candace E. Trunzo*

FIGURE 13-2
Examples of package similarity.
Source: Candace E. Trunzo, "Checkout-Counter Lookalikes." Reprinted from the May 1976 issue of *Money* magazine, pp. 71–72, by special permission; copyright © 1976, Time Inc. All rights reserved.

ately focused on because of their relevance to the task at hand. Carefully reviewing the manufacturer's specifications on a microwave oven that one is about to purchase is an example. The consumer's motives, knowledge, and expectations about what information will be found serve to guide this selective attention.

Lookalikes

Money MAY 1976 71

Conversely, involuntary attention occurs when the consumer confronts novel or unexpected stimuli that seem interesting or distinctive in some way, even though they may be unrelated to the current goal or activity at hand. Funny, "catchy," or otherwise unusual advertisements often fall into this category. Also,

many other stimuli consumers confront in living their daily lives are handled by the involuntary attention process. In fact, most of the stimuli that consumers process reach awareness via involuntary attention.

Both types of attention play a useful role for the consumer. Voluntary attention facilitates progress toward immediate goals by concentrating processing capacity on the most task-related stimuli and filtering out others. On the other hand, involuntary attention allows the consumer to be generally knowledgeable about the environment by keeping him or her in touch with stimuli that are potentially relevant to a variety of his or her interests.

Characteristics of Attention   We have already noted that the consumer's attention is selectively allocated to only certain stimuli. Before turning to factors influencing this process, three characteristics of attention having important implications for marketers should be mentioned.[12] First, consumers can only attend to a limited number of items at any one time. This limit appears to be from five to seven "chunks" of information, in which a chunk is an organized grouping of data or informational inputs. An example would be how telephone numbers are arranged into three major chunks to facilitate their retention—area code, prefix, suffix. This five-to-seven-chunk capacity shows that consumers' span of attention can be quite limited.

Second, many stimuli require attention to be processed, while others that are very familiar to the consumer do not.[13] Because the span of attention is limited, those stimuli that require attention cannot all be processed at the same time. The consumer must allocate this limited resource to them in some type of sequence or order; while one is being processed, others cannot be attended to. A case in point is when we are unable to both read something and listen to a radio message at the same time. Conversely, stimuli not requiring attention can be received *simultaneously* from several channels and will be automatically transferred to the next stage of processing. To illustrate, when exposed to a television advertisement for Amtrak trains, consumers might be able to visually process physical attributes of the train (color, shape, and size of the interior, and the like) and how much people seem to enjoy the ride at the same time that they are listening to the tune which accompanies the visual presentation.

A third characteristic is that attention can be allocated to stimuli on a rapid basis. One set of studies found that processing occurred at the rate of twenty-six items per second.[14] This speed tends to compensate for consumers' limited span of attention.

Marketers should give serious consideration to these attention characteristics because they can significantly influence the effectiveness of various efforts to communicate with consumers. Of course, another area of concern is the many factors, both within and outside the marketer's control, that influence how consumers allocate their attention among stimuli. These influences mainly affect involuntary attention, and they can be categorized into stimulus and individual factors.

Selective Attention: Stimulus Factors   Certain characteristics of stimuli themselves attract attention. Generally, these include emotion-arousing properties (like colors, pleasant phrases), physically intense values (such as loud noises, bright colors), and novel or surprising characteristics.[15] More specifically, the following are mentioned because of their particular importance to promotional campaigns.

COLOR   Historically, color advertisements have been found to attract more attention than those presented in black and white. However, the higher cost of using color may result in capturing less attention per advertising dollar spent.[16] Also, because the attraction power of color may be a result of its novelty, common use of it in any medium such as television may reduce its attention-attracting power unless more intense or unusual hues are employed—a practice finding increased use lately.[17]

NOVELTY AND CONTRAST   Stimuli that stand out against their background attract attention. Novel stimuli achieve this through unique images, shapes, sounds, and colors; Figure 13-3 presents an illustration. Novelty can also be achieved through messages that seem at odds with commonly held beliefs; Figure 13-4 is an example.

Contrast also attracts attention through its distinctiveness. Reversals (white printing on black background) in print media and changes in volume levels (louder

FIGURE 13-3
Novelty used to attract attention.
Courtesy of Lennox Industries, Inc.; photo courtesy of the American Gas Association.

or softer) for television or radio advertisements are examples of contrast effects used to capture attention.

SIZE AND POSITION   In print media, attention increases with the size of an advertisement but appears to grow in proportion to the square root of the ad's area. Thus, to double its attention-attracting power, the size of an advertisement would have to be quadrupled.

Position also is an important influence as the following findings illustrate. First, in terms of layout, ads with vertical splits (pictures on one side and copy on the other) and haphazard arrangements of pictures appear to discourage at least some readers.[18] Second, in terms of placement on a page, position does not seem to have an effect unless many ads share the page, in which case the upper righthand corner appears advantageous.[19] Third, there appears to be an attention advantage for magazine ads placed in the first ten pages or next to related editorial matter, but due to high page traffic, position within a newspaper is not as critical.[20]

HUMOR   Television announcers are frequently shown in strange or embarassing situations, cracking jokes, getting pies in the face, being bitten by dogs or doused

FIGURE 13-4
Achieving novelty through a
message that is at odds with
commonly held beliefs.
Courtesy of The Potato Board.

with water or colored liquids, and crashing into various objects. All of these situations, plus more subtle approaches, are attempts to employ humor in advertising. In fact, estimates are that between 15 and 42 percent of television and radio advertising employs some form of humor, usually designed to attract attention.[21]

Although practioners generally appear to believe that humor can attract attention, there has not been a great deal of research conducted in an advertising context to test this belief.[22] Based on the evidence that is available, a tentative conclusion appears to be that humorous messages in advertising can generally attract audience attention. However, it also appears that the effectiveness of humor depends on the characteristics of audience members. For example, the attention attracted by humorous messages appears to vary depending on the sex and racial background of audience members.[23]

A wide variety of other stimulus factors have been employed to attract consumers' attention. These include "scratch and sniff" strips in printed promotions, inflatable sections of billboards, and signs with moving parts. Because a detailed treatment of each is beyond the scope of this chapter, we now turn to individual factors influencing attention.

Selective Attention: Individual Factors   In addition to stimulus characteristics, individual attributes of consumers themselves also influence whether a given stimulus will receive attention. Some of these individual factors are discussed below.

ATTENTION SPAN   We have already noted that consumers' attention span, as measured by the number of items processed at any time, is quite limited. An important implication of this for advertisers is to "keep the message simple." The time that stimuli can hold the consumer's attention also appears to be rather short—perhaps only a matter of seconds. Therefore, attention must be repeatedly captured, even for something as brief as a fifteen-second spot commercial on television. This is one reason advertisers use a variety of stimulus factors to not only capture, but also to hold consumers' interest.[24]

ADAPTATION   Prolonged exposure to constant levels of stimulation results in consumers not noticing the stimuli. This gradual adjustment to stimuli is called *adaptation*. For example, an air-conditioned building first appears quite cool to us, but a short time later we adapt to the temperature and become less aware of it. Similarly, consumers adapt to various marketing stimuli such as price levels and advertising messages. This helps to explain why marketers search for fresh advertising approaches and try to offer new and improved products.

PERCEPTUAL VIGILANCE AND DEFENSE   The concept of *perceptual vigilance* explains consumer's heightened sensitivity to stimuli that are capable of satisfying motives. This suggests that consumers will pay increased attention to marketing stimuli relevant to an aroused motive. Based on this concept, it has been suggested that less expensive, small- or medium-sized print advertisements may be more economically effective than large ones for reaching the attention of motivated consumers.[25]

Individuals are also capable of *perceptual defense*, that is, decreasing their awareness of threatening stimuli. For example, one study found that only 32

percent of a sample of smokers consistently read articles relating smoking to lung disease, while 60 percent of a group of nonsmokers read the articles.[26] Apparently, smokers feel threatened by such information, and their perceptual defense mechanisms allow them to ignore it.

The topic of perceptual defense has relevance in advertising, particularly to the use of fear appeals to promote products such as burglar alarms and smoke detectors. Of course, the danger of fear appeals is that they may be so threatening to consumers that they lead to perceptual defenses against the entire message. For example, an advertisement showing burned children to draw viewers' attention to the need for home fire alarms would probably fail because consumers want to avoid thinking of such a tragedy.

Our discussion of the acquisition process has focused on three major subcomponents: (1) exposure—the means by which consumers come in contact with stimuli, (2) sensation—the means by which only certain stimulus values produce messages for further processing, and (3) attention—the means by which processing capacity is allocated to stimulus sensations. Focus turns now to how consumers derive meaning from these raw sensory inputs.

PERCEPTUAL ENCODING

Because sensations generated by stimuli are only a series of electrical impulses, they must be transformed into a type of language that is understandable to the consumer. This is accomplished by *perceptual encoding,* which is the process of assigning mental symbols to sensations. These symbols can be words, numbers, pictorial images, or other representations that consumers use to interpret or assign meaning to their sensations. They are also used to remember stimuli and do any subsequent thinking about them.

Much of the encoding process is automatic and not within the consumer's conscious control. That is, the individual typically does not make deliberate decisions as to what type of symbols will be used to represent sensations. Nevertheless, the process is highly individualistic, and a given stimulus is unlikely to be represented in exactly the same way by different consumers. A major reason for this is that each person's previous experiences, as stored in memory, strongly influence the symbolism used. The way different people view a four-wheel-drive Jeep Wagoneer illustrates this rather well. A contractor may consider it as a piece of construction equipment, someone living in a rural area might think of it as an all-purpose family vehicle, and a young adventurer may consider it as an off-the-road recreation vehicle. As we might expect, each individual's reactions toward the vehicle will be influenced by the different mental symbols each uses to represent it. The important point here is that perceptual encoding is a symbol-assigning process that each individual uses to derive personal meaning from stimulus experiences. Any actions or subsequent thoughts will be based on interpretations derived from stimuli rather than on the actual stimuli themselves.

STAGES IN THE ENCODING PROCESS

Two major activities involved in encoding appear to be feature analysis and a synthesis stage.[27] In *feature analysis,* the consumer identifies main stimulus features and assesses how they are organized. In the *synthesis stage,* organized

stimulus elements are combined with other information available in the environment and in memory to develop an interpretation of the stimulus. Our previous example of how consumers reacted to the Jeep Wagoneer illustrates these stages. First, each person assessed the basic size, shape, color, and other prominent features of the vehicle. These characteristics were then organized into a unified whole and appreciated as a type of motorized vehicle rather than as separate components of glass, steel, rubber, and so on. However, even in the unlikely event that all three consumers developed the same unified whole during the feature analysis stage, each would interpret it differently depending on her or his individual experience. In fact, it can be said that there are three major influences on the synthesis stage: (1) stimulus features, (2) contextual influences, and (3) memory factors.[28]

We have already mentioned that major aspects of the stimulus will influence the interpretation process. To this must be added the stimulus context. That is, the stimulus being focused on in any particular situation is surrounded by a wide variety of other stimuli which form a context for interpreting the focal stimulus. Marketers are well aware of this influence and frequently use it to promote and position their offerings. The use of highly active and dynamic dancers in Bounce fabric softener commercials or the bright blue water scenes in Bel Air cigarette ads are cases in point.

The consumer's experiences stored in memory will also strongly influence how a stimulus is represented. The more closely that major features of a stimulus resemble situations stored in memory, the greater the likelihood that it will be represented in the same way as these experiences. In fact, a major influence on interpretation is derived from *expectations* the consumer has as a result of previous experiences. If other elements remain constant, strong expectations are likely to reduce the consumer's attention to actual stimulus features. Meaning will then be assigned to the stimulus on the basis of its expected characteristics, rather than on the basis of what exists in reality.[29] This has the potential advantage of efficiency, because the consumer can respond to very similar stimuli in much the same way and not expend effort treating each one as a unique case. However, there also is a potential problem of incorrect interpretation as demonstrated by the following message:

PARIS
IN THE
THE SPRING

Many readers do not notice that the message involves repetition of a word. Consumers who mistakenly purchase one of the look-alikes in Figure 13-2 or who realize their favorite brand has been "new and improved" only after bringing it home are other examples of such problems. Conversely, when a stimulus is quite novel and has features considerably different than expected, more attention will be allocated to it, and greater effort will be given to its interpretation.

Earlier, it was mentioned that the attention mechanism regulated the amount of processing a stimulus receives. Current thought is that this effort can be devoted to increasing the spread of processing, or increasing the depth of processing.[30] Increased *spread of processing* occurs when effort is devoted to further elaboration of the stimulus at the same depth of meaning. Consumers do this when generally reviewing additional physical features (shape, size, and so on) of a stimulus. This would be exhibited by a consumer casually examining a radio, touching its tuning controls, and turning it in different directions to "take in" its basic features. Although many aspects of the product are noted, very little is done in terms of considering the meaning of these features. The term *depth of processing* refers to the degree of effort the consumer expends in developing meaning from stimuli. If little effort is expended, a great deal of meaning will not be derived. However, at deeper levels of processing the stimulus is represented with symbols that are more meaningful to the consumer. For example, reading the ingredients listed on a type of snack-food package could lead the consumer to the relatively shallow interpretation "it's mainly sugar" or to the deeper level "it's a fattening and unhealthy food." Here, we can see that the deeper level of processing results in a more personally relevant representation and interpretation of the stimulus. We will return to this depth-of-processing concept in the next chapter when we consider its relevance to learning and memory.

INFLUENCES ON ENCODING

A wide variety of factors influence the encoding process. Although some were briefly mentioned above, it is useful to give more-detailed treatment to several major influences. The first group of influencing factors is more relevant to feature-analysis activities, while the second group has its primary influence on the synthesis stage.

Factors Influencing Feature Analysis   Much of feature analysis involves mentally arranging sensations into a coherent pattern which is often called a *gestalt* (pronounced guh-shtált). In fact, this process has been the prime interest of gestalt psychologists, and much of this section is based on their work. Although visual examples are primarily used here, many of the principles can also be applied to other stimuli.

FIGURE-GROUND   This is one of the most basic and automatic organizational processes perceivers impose on their world. Two properties of this innate perceptual tendency are (1) the figure appears to stand out as being in front of the more distant background and (2) the figure is perceived to have form and to be more substantial than the ground. An example of the way in which the figure-ground process operates is shown in Figure 13-5. Most individuals organize this stimulus situation as a white goblet (figure) on a black ground rather than as two faces (figure) with a white ground separating them.

Print advertisements frequently employ figure-ground techniques to assist readers in organizing symbols and other material that the marketer deems most important.

PROXIMITY In this organization process, items close to each other in time or space tend to be perceived as being related, while separated items are viewed as being different. The uses of proximity in promotions are many. Mentholated cigarettes are shown in beautiful green, springlike settings or against a deep blue sky to suggest freshness. Soft drinks and fast foods are usually shown being enjoyed in active, fun-oriented settings, and sporty cars are frequently pictured at race-tracks or in other competitive situations. Also, in comparative advertising, the promoted brand is usually shown in the good company of other respected brands and separated from presumably inferior alternatives.

SIMILARITY Assuming that no other influence is present, items that are perceived as being similar to one another will tend to be grouped together. This, in turn, can influence the pattern one perceives in a conglomeration of items.

The principle of similarity has been used in various ways to influence consumers' perceptions. For example, some auto manufacturers have attempted to develop certain style similarities between their products and the BMW in the hope that consumers will conclude that the cars are also similar in other important respects. This must have led to concern at BMW, because they responded with advertising messages stressing that their car is a standard that other auto makers have tried to copy but have done so unsuccessfully, since similar looks do not necessarily mean similar cars.

CLOSURE Frequently, consumers organize incomplete stimuli by perceiving them as complete figures. In other words, a figure such as an opened circle, would tend to be filled in by the individual to result in perception of a whole.

FIGURE 13-5
An example demonstrating figure-ground perception.

Research suggests that under certain conditions this tendency toward closure can be an effective advertising device, because it motivates consumers to mentally complete the message.[31] This can focus attention and facilitate learning and retention. In fact, the closure concept has been employed by leading producers of consumer products. For example, Salem cigarettes were first advertised heavily in television employing the often quoted jingle: "You can take Salem out of the country but—You can't take the country out of Salem." The verse was repeated several times with a bell ringing between the two halves of the message. Finally, only the first half of the jingle was sung, ending with the bell and leaving the listener compelled to complete the message. Figure 13-6 shows another use of the closure concept to facilitate retention of an important message.

It should be mentioned that not all incomplete advertising messages appear to be remembered better than completed ones. Further investigation of closure is needed to determine both the nature and effectiveness of its role in advertising.

Factors Influencing Synthesis Stage   Many additional factors influence how consumers develop meaning from stimuli that have undergone feature analysis. The major effect of these influences is to predispose the individual toward interpreting stimuli in a certain way. Five major categories of influences are learning, personality, motivation, attitude, and adaptation levels.

LEARNING   Learning influences consumers to categorize stimuli by developing their abilities to identify stimulus attributes used in discrimination and leveling. In *discrimination,* consumers learn those attributes useful in distinguishing between items in order to categorize them differently. For example, we learn to distinguish fresh from stale bread, and traditional from contemporary furniture. Of course, there is no guarantee that all consumers will learn valid methods of discrimination. It depends on their prior experiences, as in the case where consumers rejected a new, quiet food mixer because they incorrectly perceived it as having less power than older, noisier models.[32] This was perhaps a result of their experience with powerful and noisy appliances in the past.

Learning also influences perceptual *leveling* whereby similar but not identical stimuli are classified into the same perceptual category and therefore generate the same response. For example, when instant coffee was first introduced, many families made clear distinctions between it and perk or drip coffee. However, over time, leveling has taken place to the extent that when coffee is now offered, no distinction is usually made as to its type.

Marketers are interested in these learning influences because they want to provide consumers with information, product cues, and promotional symbolism designed to influence how their product is categorized. In terms of product cues, consider the case in which a major producer of chickens for the Northeast feeds his poultry marigold petals and corn so that they develop the yellow skin that consumers of the region have learned to associate with succulent chicken.[33] The strategy of *positioning* as discussed in Chapter 5 can also influence consumers' interpretation process by manipulating symbols, slogans, and other variables. The goal is to establish a unique perceptual category for the brand in consumers' minds. Examples are promotions that categorize Canadian-brewed Molson Ale as an "imported" ale and Honda motorcycles as transportation for typical people instead of for cycle-gang members.

PERSONALITY AND MOTIVATION   Consumers' personality characteristics also influence the meaning they derive from stimuli. To illustrate, one study found that individuals who find it difficult to tolerate uncertain situations tend to be influ-

FIGURE 13-6
Promotional use of the closure concept. Courtesy of the Advertising Council, Inc.

enced by seals of approval, such as those of Good Housekeeping or Underwriters Laboratory, to a greater degree than do other consumers.[34] In addition, the meaning individuals derive from stimuli is also influenced by their motivational state. This has been demonstrated in one study in which hungry subjects "saw" more food-related items in ambiguously shaped stimuli than did subjects who were not hungry. Such findings help explain why certain products may be highly valued by some groups of consumers and deemed rather useless by others.

ATTITUDES   For our present purpose, consumers' attitudes may be thought of as predispositions to understand and respond to objects and events in consistent ways. That is, attitudes act as frames of reference which affect consumers' tendencies to interpret stimuli from the environment. These references are influenced by the consumers' values and beliefs that have developed from previous processing experiences.

The greater the consistency of a given stimulus with currently held attitudes, the more likely will the consumer be to interpret it in a way consistent with these attitudes. Thus, if a consumer having negative attitudes toward Mazdas sees one stalled on the roadside, she is more likely to interpret the situation as evidence of an inferior product rather than as an isolated problem with a quality car. However, a neighbor's high praise during an eight-year period for his Mazda will be very difficult for this consumer to interpret in the same light.

Because attitudes predispose consumers to interpret stimuli in consistent ways, they often lead to efficient processing. That is, many stimuli can be quickly interpreted without a great deal of processing effort being allocated to them. In addition, it must also be realized that the resulting meaning the consumer derives from these stimuli is very strongly influenced by his predispositions as well as by characteristics of the stimuli themselves. Chapters 16 and 17 will discuss these issues in greater depth.

ADAPTATION LEVEL   Our discussion of selective attention noted that consumers tend to adapt to rather constant stimulus levels. This process leads to the formation of *adaptation levels,* which are standards of reference used to judge new stimulus situations. To demonstrate, assume that two individuals must judge the heaviness of this textbook. Prior to the test, however, one is required to sort envelopes and the other is assigned to moving office furniture. It seems reasonable that, due to their different standards of reference, the mail sorter will judge the text to be heavier than would the furniture mover. In fact, results of many experiments have verified this expectation.[35] They have also demonstrated that adaptation levels can be influenced to *move* by exposing the individual to different stimulus values. This means that the standard of reference for judging stimuli is a sliding scale which can change over time.

The concept of an adaptation level serving as a *sliding* frame of reference suggests that consumers adapt to levels of service, products, and other marketing variables, and these become standards by which new situations are judged. As a case in point, consider how some of the advertisements employing sexual themes are accepted today compared to how they would have been judged just fifteen years ago. Another case in point is the U.S. energy problem and its effect on gasoline prices. In the early 1970s, when gas prices averaged between 30 and 40

cents a gallon, a price of 50 cents would have been judged extremely expensive. However, after we have adapted to gradually increasing gasoline prices, 50 cents would now be judged as a great bargain![36]

A basic conclusion of the above discussion is that perceptions are *subjective*. Consumers derive meaning from stimuli only by interpreting them in relation to the present situation, their experiences, and their physical and psychological states. This presents both problems and opportunities to the marketing manager. Problems are encountered because it cannot be assumed that consumers will perceive products and other marketing variables in the same way that the marketer does. Opportunities arise from determining how consumers perceive these variables and using this insight to design more competitive offerings.

INFORMATION LOAD

Earlier in the chapter, it was shown that the environment produces many more stimuli than consumers are capable of dealing with. Awareness thresholds, attention, and other mechanisms were mentioned as means consumers have for reducing the number of stimuli to more manageable proportions. Of course, at any time there is no guarantee the consumer will be able to handle all stimuli that succeed in passing through these filtering mechanisms. Some contend, based upon research they have conducted, that another threshold exists—an upper limit on the amount of information that consumers can effectively deal with in their decision-making process.[37]

Consumers' "information load" can be defined here in terms of the number of brands and/or the number of attributes per brand that are available for processing. The position of these researchers, then, is that a consumer's exposure to an amount of information that exceeds his threshold point will generate conditions of information *overload*. Further, when he is experiencing information overload, the consumer will make poorer decisions (ones that can benefit him less) than he would have made under conditions of less information. This may occur despite the possibility that the consumer will feel more confident with decisions based on large amounts of information. Of course, the implication here is that an overload condition not only involves attention and other information-acquisition mechanisms, but it also may influence perceptual encoding, integration, and evaluation processes.

The research and data on this topic have been the subject of considerable reanalysis, criticism, and debate.[38] Because of this, we are not in a position to conclude positively that information overload can occur. However, some recent additional evidence lends support to the contention.[39] We will return to this topic in Part Six when consumerism issues are considered.

MARKETING IMPLICATIONS

To this point, the information-processing activities involved in acquiring and interpreting stimulus experiences have been discussed. Soon to be treated in as much depth are memory factors, the information integration stage, and evaluation and choice activities. These processing components will be discussed in subsequent chapters along with related material. At this point, however, it is useful to review briefly some marketing applications of the material already examined.

PRODUCT FACTORS

The relevance of information processing to consumers' product evaluations has already been mentioned in this chapter. We would expect that product evaluations are at least in part based on consumers' attempts to *directly* evaluate physical product attributes, often called *intrinsic cues,* such as size, shape, and grade of ingredients. However, evidence suggests that, for many goods, buyers can have difficulty in distinguishing between different offerings on the basis of such direct product attributes. For example, one study found that subjects could discriminate between Pepsi-Cola and Coca-Cola in "blind" taste tests (a taste test where brand identification is hidden from the subjects) but they had difficulty distinguishing each of them from Royal Crown Cola.[40] In 1976, such evidence led to a serious promotional war when Pepsi attempted to gain market share from Coke by using an advertising focus stressing taste differences between the brands. The strategy was to show large numbers of cola drinkers, many with Coke as their favorite brand, actually preferring Pepsi over Coke in blind taste tests called the "Pepsi Challenge." Early advertising responses from Coca-Cola just encouraged consumers to stick to the "real thing." However, since the Pepsi challenge had considerable success, Coke responded more strongly, and hostilities broke out between the two soft-drink giants. Coke aggressively criticized and ridiculed Pepsi's testing methods, and the advertising debate that ensued became quite intense—so much so that some believe the promotional war, which has not completely subsided, left damaging effects on brand images in the soft-drink industry.[41] Despite such dangers, the apparent success of Pepsi, as measured by sales increases, has led other companies to attempt similar strategies. For example, Schlitz ran live taste tests of their beer against competing brands during halftime on televised pro-football playoff games. Burger King has also advertised results of taste tests in which its hamburgers "won" over McDonald's offering. Furthermore, Taylor has advertised how its wines have been judged by wine tasters as superior to competing brands such as Almaden and Gallo. It is interesting that this latter case began to stir strong negative reactions from Taylor's competitors because the company was then owned by Coca-Cola—the company that responded so negatively to the Pepsi Challenge!

A very important issue raised by the above discussion is whether consumers' differential thresholds are typically sensitive enough to discriminate between brands. If differences between some brands go undetected in taste tests in which consumers attempt to "tune in" their discriminatory powers, perhaps even larger differences escape notice in everyday consumption activity.

For other nonfood products, consumers may be capable of using intrinsic cues to discriminate between brands, but not be able to determine whether these differences are important in predicting which brand will provide greater satisfaction. For example, how many would be capable of identifying the "best" grade of carpeting without expert help? Given these problems, it is not surprising to find that product perceptions are often influenced by other factors. That is, in order to form impressions of products, consumers process additional stimuli that are not actual physical characteristics of the product itself. These features, often called *extrinsic cues,* could be packaging characteristics, advertising messages, statements of friends, and many other pieces of information from a wide variety of sources.[42] To illustrate, studies have shown that adding a faint, not consciously noticeable perfume scent to women's hosiery can lead consumers to strongly prefer them over identical but unscented alternatives.[43] Another finding is that bread wrapped in cellophane was judged by consumers to be fresher than identical bread wrapped in waxed paper.[44] Figure 13-7 shows how an advertisement might be designed to address both specific product features and general image characteristics in an attempt to influence consumers' brand perceptions. As we noted in Chapter 5, this is a major goal of positioning.

Some evidence suggests that consumers' product perceptions are more likely

Dannon Yogurt may not help you live as long as Soviet Georgians. But it couldn't hurt.

Bagrat Topagua, age 89.

His mother.

There are two curious things about the people of Soviet Georgia. A large part of their diet is yogurt. And a large number of them live to be well over 100.

Of course, many factors affect longevity, and we are not saying Dannon Yogurt will help you live longer. But we will say that all-natural Dannon is high in nutrients, low in fat, reasonable in calories. And quite satisfying at lunch or as a snack.

Another thing about Dannon. It contains active yogurt cultures (many pre-mixed or Swiss style brands don't). They make yogurt one of the easiest foods to digest and have been credited with other healthful benefits.

Which is why we've been advising this: If you don't always eat right, Dannon Yogurt is the right thing to eat.

By the way, Bagrat Topagua thought Dannon was "dzelian kargia." Which means he loved it.

Dannon Milk Products, 22-11 38th Ave. Long Island City, N.Y. 11101.

FIGURE 13-7
Reference to both extrinsic and intrinsic product cues to influence product perceptions.
Courtesy of the Dannon Company, Inc.

to be influenced by extrinsic cues when the product is complex in nature.[45] Generally, however, little is known about how consumers select such cues to form interpretations, or what the conditions are which influence this process. What is known suggests four propositions that are worthy of consideration:

1   Certain extrinsic cues are more likely than others to be selected for use in judging products. The selection will be influenced by the consumer's experience as well as the type of cues available.

2   The way in which extrinsic cues are encoded can strongly influence consumers' product evaluations. For example, the cellophane wrapping on a food item could be encoded as "packaging," but it also could be encoded as "freshly kept food," "protected food," or something similar. Each is likely to have a different influence on product perception.

3   Certain extrinsic cues may not be encodable in a meaningful way by the consumer. These would then have little if any subsequent effect on how the product is interpreted. The listing of certain packaged-food ingredients such as *sodium ascorbate, calcium propionate,* and *propyl gallate* might fit this description.

4   Available extrinsic cues may lead the consumer to develop additional *inferential beliefs* or interpretations of the product. An inferential belief is one formed without a direct basis in the existing stimulus situation. For example, an advertisement that only mentions the whitening ability of a laundry detergent might also lead some consumers to interpret the brand as having clothes-softening properties. This could occur because ads for other brands claim to have both properties, and consumers have associated the two in their minds. However, since the present advertisement makes no softening claim, such interpretations are based on inference and do not have a basis in the stimulus situation.[46]

We now turn to a special example of cue utilization in the discussion of how consumers process the information content of price. That is, the question of interest here is what meaning do consumers derive from the price variable?

PRICE CONSIDERATIONS

Traditional microeconomic theory as reviewed in Chapter 2 has apparently influenced many marketers to assume that consumers use price only as an indicator of product cost. Consumers' use of price in this way will generate the classic down-sloping demand curve as portrayed in Figure 13-8a. Here, lower prices result in greater quantities of the product being demanded. However, considerable evidence suggests that the meaning consumers derive from the price variable is much more complex in nature.[47]

Psychological Pricing   Much discussion of how consumers encode price information has focused on the concept of "psychological pricing"; this suggests that there is greater consumer demand at certain prices and that this demand decreases at prices above *and below* these points. Such a situation is described by the ratchet-type demand curve in Figure 13-8b. Prices $p_1, p_2,$ and p_3, respectively, are seen to generate a greater quantity demanded than other prices in their immediate range.

One aspect of psychological pricing is the frequently observed retail practice of odd-pricing. Here, it is said that prices ending in an odd number (such as 5, 7, or 9) or just under the round number (such as 96 or 98 as opposed to 100) generate significantly higher demand than related round-numbered prices. However, this argument is usually based on retailers' experiences and has not yet been confirmed by rigorous testing.

Price and Product Quality Another important price-perception topic is what has become known as the price-quality proposition, which holds that consumers tend to use price as an indicator of the quality or the satisfaction potential of a product. The use of price as an extrinsic product cue in this way is not unreasonable when consumers lack confidence or ability to judge product attributes directly. For example, previous purchase experiences may lead to an awareness that higher quality products tend to cost more. Adages such as "You get what you pay for" and messages such as the one in Figure 13-9 also act to reinforce this association. Given the uncertainty arising from attempts to evaluate today's technically complex products directly, consumers may rely on these previous experiences to conclude that higher-priced products are of higher quality. This, in turn, suggests that consumers may suspect the quality of some products that bear very low prices.

Based on the above argument, we can see how price may actually hold a dual informational role for consumers—as an indicator of product cost and as an indicator of product quality. Therefore, consumers' demand for a product will depend on the relative degree to which they use price as a measure of cost and quality. This can be shown by the unusually shaped demand curve in Figure 13-8c. The upper portion of the curve has a rather traditional shape reflecting consumers' use of price primarily as a measure of cost: lower prices generate greater quantity demanded. However, when the use of price as an indicator of product quality begins to dominate consumers' purchase decisions, lower prices can actually lead to a drop in quantity demanded. This situation is reflected in the backward-bending portion of the demand curve in Figure 13-8c.

Given such an important implication, a number of researchers have sought to determine the extent to which consumers might actually use price as an indicator

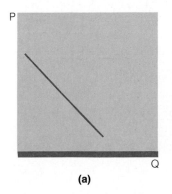
(a)

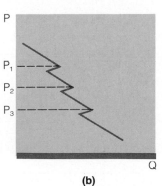
(b)

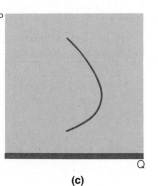
(c)

FIGURE 13-8
Potential shapes of the demand curve under conditions of different consumer perceptions of the price variable.

of product quality. To do this, experimental situations were developed in which only the price of a product was allowed to change across various testing situations. These studies found that respondents tended to prefer the higher-priced alternative, especially when brands were expected to differ considerably in terms of quality. Further studies determined that the price-quality relationship varied across products, and it was highest when consumers faced risky situations and when their confidence in directly judging the quality of products was low.[48]

More recent investigations have researched a variety of products and perhaps more realistic shopping situations. These findings are more complex in nature since they suggest that price is not always the most important influence on quality perception, especially when brand names are known and experience with the product is great.[49] Further, the importance of price in influencing perceptions may depend on the specific product-quality aspects being evaluated.[50] Therefore, overall product perceptions are probably the result of a combination of information

FIGURE 13-9
An advertising message
reinforcing price-quality
perceptions.
Courtesy of Jean Patou, Inc.

derived from price, other extrinsic cues, and judgments of intrinsic product characteristics.[51]

Several other conclusions have been derived from studies of how consumers react to the price variable. A review of this research offers the following summary:

1   Consumers appear to use price as an indicator of product quality as well as an indicator of purchase cost.

2   Consumers also tend to develop reference prices as standards for judging prices that they confront in the marketplace.

3   Reference prices are not constant, but are modified by market experiences. Therefore, the consumer's exposure to prices somewhat higher than her reference price is likely to result in an upward adjustment of the reference price. The opposite is likely for exposure to prices somewhat below the reference price.

4   Buyers appear to develop a range of acceptable prices around the standard or reference price. Prices outside the range (above, or *below*) are likely to be judged as inappropriate for the product in question and may result in a decreased willingness to purchase.

5   Certain factors (such as brand name, store image) can mitigate the strength of the perceived price-quality relationship and actually overshadow it for some products.

6   When prices are perceived as similar for various alternatives, then price is unlikely to be influential in choices between these alternatives.[52]

COMPANY AND STORE IMAGE

Astute marketers have long realized that, in addition to brand image, their company's image can strongly influence consumers' behavior toward their enterprise and its products. A company's image is the perception consumers have of its character as a result of their experiences with it and their knowledge of and beliefs about it.

Importance of an Image   A strong and clear company image can increase consumers' confidence in its products and their predisposition to purchase them. This is demonstrated by results of a study in which a sample of women were 14 percent more likely to try a new product offered from Heinz than from a large but unspecified food company.[53] Such evidence has encouraged many firms to change their name or company logo in an effort to refine their image. In addition, as companies diversify, merge, or acquire new operations, it often appears appropriate to rename the organization to reflect its new dimensions or make a break with its old identity. Thus, United Aircraft became United Technologies, California Packing became Del Monte, Ligget & Myers was changed to the Liggett Group, and Mobil Oil Corporation is now called Mobil Corporation. Such changes can be quite expensive—it has been reported that in the early 1970s Humble Oil spent more than $100 million to change its name to Exxon![54]

Because the way in which consumers perceive a company can influence their reactions to its offerings, managers are very concerned with their firm's image, even when a name change is not being considered. For example, the negative way in which business people can be portrayed in various entertainment shows is thought by many executives to create a general image problem for business.

Consumers' patronage of a particular retail store can also be significantly influenced by their perception of its image or "personality."[55] Store image may be defined as "the way in which the store is defined in the shopper's mind, partly by its functional qualities and partly by an aura of psychological attributes."[56] This implies that perception of store image is derived not only from so-called functional attributes of price, convenience, and selection of merchandise, but also from the influence of variables such as architecture, interior design, colors, and advertising. Therefore, consumers can develop images of stores regardless of whether retailers consciously attempt to project a specific image. In addition, recent research suggests that the type of store attributes that consumers use when constructing images varies according to the image component being developed. For example, brand name seems the most important cue for forming impressions about the quality of merchandise while the number of salespersons per department appears to most strongly influence images about the quality of service.[57]

For these reasons, it can be very important for retailers to measure their image as consumers perceive it. If consumers' choice criteria for stores can also be identified, the retailer can then determine how the store is evaluated on those factors that are most important in influencing patronage. Strategies for modifying the store image where appropriate can then be considered.

Measuring Store Images   Although a variety of methods (including perceptual mapping) exist to measure store images, one frequently used is the semantic differential profile that was described in Chapter 3. First, a list of important tangible and intangible store image attributes are identified. Then, for these attributes, a sample of consumers can indicate their perceptions of the store on semantic scales. This can also be done for competing stores in the same study. Average or median responses can then be calculated to yield an *image profile* for each store. Figure 13-10 serves as an illustration by portraying image profiles actually found for two competing department stores in the Los Angeles area.

These profiles indicate that store A is perceived more favorably than store B, although not by a great degree. Store A appears to have a rather high-price image but, compared to store B, consumers still perceive it as providing good value for the money. Ratings on attractiveness and neatness also reveal a potential problem to which managers of store B may wish to address their attention.

It should not be concluded from the above discussion that measurement of store image reveals only positive/negative image information. For example, one store may be perceived as progressive and another as conservative, neither of which is necessarily a good or bad trait. Research has also revealed some other interesting findings, particularly the fact that stores do have distinguishable images or personalities. Also, different stores appear to attract specific socio-economic segments, and consumers in different social classes, stages of family life cycle, or other market segments are likely to perceive a given store differently.[58] All of these findings suggest that stores may be more successful in appealing to specific target segments as opposed to the mass market.

ADVERTISING ISSUES

Applications of information processing to advertising have been cited throughout the chapter. However, two other areas that draw considerable attention are the use of sex in advertising and the controversy over subliminal advertising.

Sex in Advertising   The use of sexually attractive models and sexually suggestive themes in advertising has a long history. It is therefore surprising that little is generally known about specific consumer reactions to these methods of promoting products. Because the recent promotional trend has been toward a dramatic increase in the use of more explicit sexual themes and pictures, the need for research in this area is even greater.[59] Of course, it should be kept in mind that the findings of such research may pertain only to the culture in which the investigation was conducted.

The small number of investigations that have been generally published suggest that, in at least some circumstances, the use of sexual themes or nudity in promotions may have significant limitations. For example, some studies indicate that a majority of the public say that they believe that too much use is made of sexual appeals in advertising.[60] Further, because feminists and older individuals appear to hold this belief to a greater degree than do others, an advertiser's use of

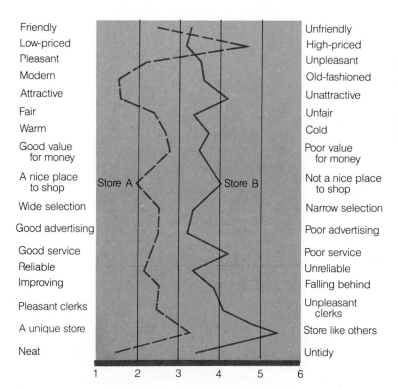

FIGURE 13-10
Semantic differential profiles of two competing department stores.
Source: Burton H. Marcus, "Image Variation and the Multi-Unit Retail Establishment," *Journal of Retailing,* **48**:39, Summer 1972. Adapted with permission of the *Journal of Retailing,* New York University.

sexual themes could generate negative reactions from substantial portions of the market.

One purpose for incorporating sexual themes or pictorial material into advertisements is to attract consumers' attention to the ad. However, evidence suggests that use of such material may not always have an easily predictable or desired effect. This is demonstrated by one study that found nonsexual and sexual-romantic themes to have a greater influence on consumers' attention than did nudity.[61] Also, an actual print advertisement for an office copier received much greater reader response when the bikini-clad model standing beside it was removed. One explanation is that the model that was employed to attract attention actually drew attention *away* from the advertising message.[62]

Of course, attracting attention is only one purpose of advertising. Consumers must also remember the brand name and advertising message in a favorable manner. It is interesting to note that studies have found that although consumers' recognition or recall of an advertisement may increase through the use of sexual illustrations, at best, no positive influence could be detected for the brand being advertised.[63] Other research indicates that even the higher recognition of advertisements may be confined mainly to the visual material and not to the verbal content of the ad.[64]

A further concern is how the use of sexual content influences consumers' perceptions of the advertisement and advertised brand. Here again, evidence does not consistently favor the use of sexual content in ads. For example, one study found that ads employing female nudity were perceived by consumers as being less appealing than ads without nude models. Also, the products advertised using nude models were actually perceived as being of lower quality.[65] However, results of this and other studies suggest that several other factors can influence how consumers will react to products advertised using sexual content. First, and quite predictably, consumers' predispositions toward sexual themes appear to be an important determinant of their reaction to ads containing such material. Second, reactions to nudity seem to be negative when a member of the same sex is used as the nude model.[66] Third, the use of sexual themes may be perceived as acceptable for certain products such as those that are designed to increase one's allurement (perfume, aftershave, body oil, and the like).[67] Furthermore, the people present in the viewing situation may also influence how consumers react to a given sexual theme.[68] Apparently, this occurs because the presence of certain people presents an uncomfortable situation for the viewer.

Thus, the decision to use sexual themes in advertising is not a simple, straightforward one. The product to be advertised, the situations involved, and the predispositions (attitudes toward sexual themes and sexual exploitation) of various market segments are all important considerations when making such a decision. This points to the need for a sound evaluation of advertising content and market characteristics before employing sexual themes to promote any specific product.

Subliminal Advertising   The technique called subliminal advertising has sparked considerable controversy in promotional and scientific fields. You may recall from earlier discussions that the absolute threshold identifies the minimum value of a stimulus capable of being consciously noticed. Because this is also referred to as a *limen,* the term "sub*liminal* perception" actually means perception of stimuli that are below the level needed to reach conscious awareness. Potentially, this could be achieved in at least three major ways: (1) presenting visual stimuli for a very brief duration, (2) presenting auditory messages through accelerated speech at low volume levels, and (3) imbedding or hiding images or words in pictorial material.[69] The purported benefit of using such techniques in advertising is that a subliminal message will not be strong enough to arouse consumers' selective attention and defense mechanisms, but it will have enough strength to influence them at an unconscious level.

The first widely known test of subliminal advertising was conducted by Vicary during the 1950s.[70] During movie theater tests more than 45,000 unsuspecting viewers were presented with filmed messages every five seconds at speeds said to be 1/3000 of a second in duration. The two messages employed were "Eat Popcorn" and "Drink Coca-Cola." By comparing sales receipts during the test period to those from a previous period, it was reported that popcorn sales increased 58 percent and Coca-Cola sales rose 18 percent.

These results quickly generated considerable concern regarding unethical uses of subliminal methods. However, closer examination of Vicary's research raised questions as to its validity. As one review stated, "There were no reports . . . of even the most rudimentary scientific precautions, such as adequate controls, provisions for replication, etc."[71] The lack of information on these provisions does not generate much confidence in the validity of the results.

Other efforts to influence audiences subliminally have not been able to document the strong positive effects reported by Vicary.[72] Nevertheless, a number of actual applications of subliminal or nearly subliminal messages in print and audio media have been reported. These range from attempts to deter shoplifting and influence purchases, to efforts at reducing radio audience stress and increasing the motivation of employees.[73] Popular books on the subject have also charged that effective subliminal images are embedded in many print advertisements, and that messages are also subliminally incorporated into movies and pop music.[74] Unfortunately, because careful steps have not been taken to measure the influence of these messages on the intended audience, their effects have not been well documented.

More carefully controlled experiments suggest that although subliminal messages may be capable of arousing basic drives such as thirst and hunger, evidence of their influence on attitudes or specific motives directing consumers toward particular brands has not been shown to be strong.[75] However, a review of studies from the field of psychology suggests that subliminal messages might possibly be capable of influencing consumers' specific but unconsciously held desires.[76]

In conclusion, some evidence suggests that under certain conditions subliminal perception may occur. However, considerable technical problems result when attempting to capitalize on this perceptual process by developing subliminal advertising messages in a commercial setting. First, the speed of the message must be determined. This may be especially difficult when one considers that the absolute thresholds of various consumers may differ by a considerable amount. Second, the message itself must be brief and simple, since anything more than a few words would probably be too complex to comprehend. Furthermore, we have seen how consumers' motives, personality, and other individual determinants influence selective perception of stimuli above the absolute threshold. There is no guarantee that these factors would not operate on subliminal stimuli. Thus, the subliminal message, "Drink Coke" could be distorted into "Stink Coke" or some other meaning not highly desired by the marketer.

Furthermore, because subliminal messages may arouse only basic drives, they may initiate behavior that is not always beneficial to the advertiser. Thus, a subliminal message for Pepsi may increase a consumer's thirst enough for a trip to the refrigerator for a glass of Dr. Pepper or another liquid refreshment that is on hand. Also, if such messages can actually appeal to consumers' unconscious motives, the problems of identifying and dealing with such motives appear to be quite large. Therefore, it seems safe to conclude that at present, subliminal advertising does not hold the threat of turning consumers into automatons who are at the mercy of marketers. In fact, minimal evidence regarding its effectiveness, technical difficulties associated with its use, and unknown consequences of employing it give little reason for advertisers to wholeheartedly embrace subliminal advertising.[77]

MANAGERIAL REFLECTIONS

For our product or service situation . . .

1 How much do consumers engage in active search for, as opposed to passive reception of, information?

2 To what degree are differential and absolute thresholds an important consideration?

3 How can we be creative in capturing consumers' attention to our advertisements?

4 In what ways can we influence how consumers interpret our products and advertisements?

5 To what extent is information overload a problem for consumers?

6 To what extent are intrinsic product cues important in consumers' perceptions of the product?

7 To what degree is there a price-quality perception among consumers?

8 What is our company's image? Are we satisfied with this image? What factors might be changed in an attempt to alter this image?

DISCUSSION TOPICS

1 What is information processing? Distinguish between the various activities that comprise the information-processing function.

2 It is often said that the information-acquisition activity is selective in nature. In what ways is this so? What implications does this have for understanding consumer behavior?

3 Review that portion of the chapter dealing with consumers' attention processes and then select several advertisements from various media (print, TV, and so on). Describe these advertisements and evaluate them in terms of their potential for attracting consumers' attention. If possible, include examples of the advertisements.

4 The resemblance of certain private-brand packaging to the packaging of nationally known brands has been so close at times that they have been described as lookalikes. Visit a supermarket and bring back two packaged products to demonstrate this. Also, while you are there, make an effort to determine the prevalence of this phenomenon. In what ways might it influence the behavior of consumers?

5 Assume that consumers have heightened awareness of the following prices for various models in a product line: $11.70, $15.21, and $19.77. Using Weber's Law, predict the next highest price in the line which would generate heightened awareness.

6 Bring to class two print advertisements which use each of the following techniques for influencing perceptual encoding: (*a*) similarity, (*b*) figure-ground, (*c*) proximity. Be prepared to assess how effectively these techniques have been employed.

7 Write up a procedure that you would employ for conducting a taste test to determine (*a*) if your fellow students can discriminate between three brands of cola and (*b*) if they have a preference for any particular cola based on taste alone. Indicate the variables that might influence the results and how you would design an experiment to minimize their influence.

8 Choose any two restaurants or pubs that are frequented by students at your school. Measure their image profiles by designing a number of semantic differential items and administering them to a random sample of your fellow students. What conclusions can you draw from your data?

9 Find several examples of magazine advertisements that employ sexual themes or illustrations to capture readers' attention or influence perceptual encoding. How appropriate do the methods appear to be for the target market involved? How effectively do the devices appear to accomplish their apparent goals? Can you foresee any possible problems the advertiser might encounter as a result of using the methods?

PROJECTS

1 Call or visit a local motel or hotel and record their room rate schedule. Is the fee structure in keeping with Weber's Law?

2 Interview a sample of ten friends, neighbors, or relatives to determine their attitudes regarding the use of sexual themes in advertising. How, if at all, do attitudes differ based on age, sex, and education? (Record this information for each respondent.)

NOTES

[1] Fred Danzig, "Super XIX Ad Winners, Losers," *Advertising Age,* January 24, 1985, p. 2; Stewart Alter and Cleveland Horton, "Lemmings Didn't Take Off," *Advertising Age,* January 24, 1985, pp. 1, 49; and Joseph M. Winski, "Apple Fails to Register," *Advertising Age,* January 28, 1985, pp. 1, 98.

[2] Jagdish N. Sheth, "How Consumers Use Information," Faculty working Paper No. 530, College of Commerce and Business Administration, University of Illinois at Urbana-Champaign, 1978, pp. 14–18.

[3] See Howard Beales et al., "Consumer Search and Public Policy," *Journal of Consumer Research,* 8:11–22, June 1981, for a more comprehensive discussion of this issue and its implications for public policy.

[4] See Beals et al., "Consumer Search and Public Policy," p. 13.

[5] "Does Taste Make Waste?," *Forbes,* June 1, 1974, p. 24.

[6] Some of the following discussion follows Richard Lee Miller, "Dr. Weber and the Consumer," *Journal of Marketing,* 26:57–61, January 1962; and Steuart Henderson Britt, "How Weber's Law Can Be Applied to Marketing," *Business Horizons,* 18:21–29, February 1975.

[7] L. Paul Gilden, "Sampling Candy Bar Economics," *The New Englander,* 22:32, January 1976.

[8] "Hidden Costs," *The Wall Street Journal,* February 15, 1977, p. 1.

[9] See "Checkout Counter Look-alikes," *Money,* May 1976, pp. 71–72.

[10] Joseph Uhl, "Consumer Perception of Retail Food Price Changes," paper presented at First Annual Meeting of the Association for Consumer Research, 1970.

[11] Raymond Bauer and Stephen Greyser, *Advertising in America: The Consumer's View,* Havard University Press, Cambridge, Mass., 1968, p. 178.

[12] Much of this section follows the discussion in Andrew A. Mitchell, "An Information Processing View of Consumer Behavior," in Subhash C. Jain (ed.), *Research Frontiers in Marketing: Dialogues and Directions,* American Marketing Association, Chicago, 1978, pp. 189–190.

[13] Walter Schneider and Richard M. Sheffrin, "Controlled and Automatic Human Information Processing: I. Detection, Search and Attention," *Psychological Review,* 84:1–66, 1977.

[14] S. Sternberg, "High Speed Scanning in Human Memory," *Science,* 153:652–654, 1966.

[15] See Geraldine Fennell, "Attention Engagement," in James H. Leigh and Claude R. Martin Jr. (eds.), *Current Issues and Research in Advertising,* University of Michigan Press, Ann Arbor, Mich., 1979, pp. 17–33, for a much fuller discussion of these factors.

[16] J. W. Rosenberg, "How Does Color, Size, Affect Ad Readership," *Industrial Marketing,* 41:54–57, May 1956.

[17] Rafael Valiente, "Mechanical Correlates of Ad Recognition," *Journal of Advertising Research,* 13:13–18, June 1973.

[18] Stephen Baker, *Visual Persuasion,* McGraw-Hill, New York, 1961.

[19] "Position in Newspaper Advertising: 1," *Media/Scope,* February 1963, p. 57. This finding is contrary to much previous research; see Melvin S. Hattwick, *How to Use Psychology for Better Advertising,* Prentice-Hall, Englewood Cliffs, N. J., 1950, pp. 145–150.

[20] See Hattwick, *How to Use Psychology for Better Advertising,* p. 155; and "Position in Newspaper Advertising: 1," p. 57.

[21] See Pat Kelly and Paul J. Soloman, "Humor in Television Advertising," *Journal of Advertising,* 4:33–35, Summer 1975; Peter Lubalin, "Humor in Radio," ANNY, November 4, 1977, p. 22; and Dorothy Markiewicz, "Effects of Humor on Persuasion," *Sociometry,* 37:407–422, 1974.

[22] See Markiewicz, "Effects of Humor on Persuasion" and Brian Sternthal and Samuel Craig, "Humor in Advertising," *Journal of Marketing,* 37:12–18, October 1973.

[23] See Sternthal and Craig, "Humor in Advertising"; and Thomas J. Madden and Marc G. Weinberger, "The Effects of Humor on Attention in Magazine Advertising," Working Paper 81-19, School of Business Administration, University of Massachusetts, Amherst, Mass., 1981.

[24] Allan Greenberg and Charles Suttoni, "Television Commercial Wear-out," *Journal of Advertising Research,* 13:47–54, October 1973.

[25] See Alvin J. Silk and Frank P. Geiger, "Advertisement Size and the Relationship between Product Usage and Advertising Exposure," *Journal of Marketing Research,* 9:22–26, February 1972, which credits this hypothesis to Leo Bogart.

[26] Charles F. Cannell and James C. MacDonald, "The Impact of Health News on Attitudes and Behavior," *Journalism Quarterly,* 33:315–323, July–September 1956.

[27] See Bettman, *An Information Processing Theory*, pp. 79–82; and Peter H. Lindsay and Donald A. Norman, *Human Information Processing*, Academic Press, New York, 1972, pp. 115–147.

[28] Bettman, *An Information Processing Theory*, p. 79.

[29] Lindsay and Norman, *Human Information Processing*, pp. 131–133.

[30] Jerry C. Olson, "Theories of Information Encoding and Storage: Implications for Consumer Research," in Andrew A. Mitchell (ed.), *The Effect of Information on Consumer and Market Behavior*, American Marketing Association, Chicago, 1978, p. 52.

[31] Norman Heller, "An Application of Psychological Learning Theory to Advertising," *Journal of Marketing*, **20**:248–254, January 1956; and Dev Pathak, Gene Burton, and Ron Zigli, "The Memory Impact of Incomplete Advertising Slogans," in Henry Nash and Donald Robin (eds.), *Proceedings of the Southern Marketing Association Conference*, 1977, pp. 269–272.

[32] Robert Froman, "You Get What You Want," in J. H. Westing (ed.), *Readings in Marketing*, Prentice-Hall, Englewood Cliffs, N. J., 1953, p. 231.

[33] William Copulsky and Katherin Marton, "Sensory Cues, You've Got to Put Them Together," *Product Marketing*, January 1977, pp. 31–34.

[34] Thomas L. Parkinson, "The Use of Seals of Approval in Consumer Decision-Making as a Function of Cognitive Needs and Style," in Mary Jane Schlinger (ed.), *Advances in Consumer Research*, vol. 2, Association For Consumer Research, Chicago, 1975, pp. 133–140.

[35] Harry Helson, *Adaptation-Level Theory: An Experimental and Systematic Approach to Behavior*, Harper & Row, New York, 1964.

[36] See Albert J. Della Bitta and Kent B. Monroe, "The Influence of Adaptation Levels on Subjective Price Perceptions," in Scott Ward and Peter Wright (eds.), *Advances in Consumer Research*, vol. 1, Association for Consumer Research, Urbana, Ill., 1973, pp. 359–369; and Anthony N. Doob et al., "Effect of Initial Selling Price on Subsequent Sales," *Journal of Personality and Social Psychology*, **11**:345–350, April 1969.

[37] See Jacob Jacoby, Donald E. Speller, and Carol A. Kohn, "Brand Choice Behavior as a Function of Information Load," *Journal of Marketing Research*, **11**:63–69, February 1974; Jacob Jacoby, Donald E. Speller, and Carol A. Kohn, "Brand Choice Behavior as a Function of Information Load: Replication and Extension," *Journal of Consumer Research*, **1**:33–42, June 1974; and Jacob Jacoby, Donald E. Speller, and Carol A. K. Berning, "Constructive Criticism and Programmatic Research, Reply to Russo," *Journal of Consumer Research*, **2**:154–156, September 1975. See also Debra L. Scammon, "Information Load and Consumers," *Journal of Consumer Research*, **4**:148–155, December 1977, for additional relevant evidence.

[38] See Edward J. Russo, "More Information Is Better: A Re-evaluation of Jacoby, Speller and Kohn," *Journal of Consumer Research*, **1**:68–72, December 1974; John O. Summers, "Less Information is Better?," *Journal of Marketing Research*, **11**:467–468, November 1974; William L. Wilkie, "Analysis of Effects of Information Load," *Journal of Marketing Research*, **11**:462–466, November 1974; and Naresh K. Malhotra, Arun K. Jain, and Stephen W. Lagakos, "The Information Overload Controversy: An Alternative Viewpoint," *Journal of Marketing*, **46**:27–37, Spring 1982.

[39] Naresh K. Malhotra, "Information Load and Consumer Decision Making," *Journal of Consumer Research*, **8**:419–430, March 1982.

[40] F. J. Thumin, "Identification of Cola Beverages," *Journal of Applied Psychology*, **46**:358–360, October 1962.

[41] See "Coke-Pepsi Slugfest," *Time*, July 26, 1976, pp. 64–65; "The Cola War," *Newsweek*, August 30, 1976, p. 67; "One Sip Not a Taste Test, Coke Tells New Yorkers," *Advertising Age*, August 16, 1976, p. 6; and Peter W. Bernstein, "Coke Strikes Back," *Fortune*, June 1, 1981, pp. 30–36.

[42] See Donald F. Cox, "The Sorting Rule Model of the Consumer Product Evaluation Process," in Donald F. Cox (ed.), *Risk Taking and Information Handling in Consumer Behavior*, Harvard Business School, Cambridge, Mass., 1967, pp. 324–369; Jerry C. Olson and Jacob Jacoby, "Cue Utilization in the Quality Perception Process," in M. Venkatesan (ed.), *Proceedings, 3rd Annual Conference of the Association for Consumer Research*, Association for Consumer Research, College Park, M. D., 1972, pp. 167–179; Jerry C. Olson, "Inferential Belief Formation in the Cue Utilization Process," in H. Keith Hunt (ed.), *Advances in Consumer Research*, vol. 5, Association for Consumer Research, Ann Arbor, Mich., 1978, pp. 706–713; Robert E. Burnkrant, "Cue Utilization in Product Perception," in H. Keith Hunt, (ed.), *Advances in Consumer Research*, vol. 5, Association for Consumer Research, Ann Arbor, Mich., 1978, pp. 724–729; and John Wheatley and John S. Y. Chiu, "The Influence of Intrinsic and Extrinsic Cues on Product Quality Evaluations of Experts and Non Experts," in Neil Beckwith

433

et al. (eds.), *1979 Educators' Conference Proceedings,* American Marketing Association, 1979, pp. 205–209. See also, Allison and Uhl, "Influence of Beer Brand Identification on Taste Perception," for an excellent example of how marketing efforts can influence brand perceptions.

[43] D. A. Laird, "How The Consumer Estimates Quality by Subconscious Sensory Impressions," *Journal of Applied Psychology,* **16**:241–246, June 1932; and *Women's Wear Daily,* January 28, 1961, p. 15.

[44] Robert L. Brown, "Wrapper Influence on the Perception of Freshness in Bread," *Journal of Applied Psychology,* **42**:257–260, August 1958.

[45] Burnkrant, "Cue Utilization in Product Perception."

[46] See Olson, "Inferential Belief Formation," for a discussion of this topic.

[47] For excellent reviews of this evidence see Kent B. Monroe, "Buyers' Subjective Perceptions of Price," *Journal of Marketing Research,* **10**:70–80, February 1973; Jerry C. Olson, "Price as an Informational Cue: Effects on Product Evaluations," in Arch G. Woodside, Jagdish N. Sheth, and Peter D. Bennett (eds.), *Consumer and Industrial Buyer Behavior,* North-Holland, New York, 1977, pp. 267–286; and Kent B. Monroe and Susan M. Petroshius, "Buyers' Perceptions of Price: An Update of the Evidence," in Harold H. Kassarjian and Thomas S. Robertson (eds.), *Perspectives in Consumer Behavior,* 3d ed., Scott, Foresman, 1981, pp. 43–55, upon which much of this section is based.

[48] See Benson Shapiro, "Price as a Communicator of Quality: An Experiment," unpublished doctoral dissertation, Harvard University, 1970; and Zarrel Lambert, "Price and Choice Behavior," *Journal of Marketing Research,* **9**:35–40, February 1972.

[49] See, for example, Robert A. Peterson, "Consumer Perceptions As A Function of Product, Color, Price, and Nutrition Labeling," in William D. Perreault, Jr. (ed.), *Advances in Consumer Research,* vol. 4, Association for Consumer Research, Atlanta, 1977, pp. 61–63.

[50] Michael Etgar and Naresh K. Malhotra, "Determinants of Price Dependency: Personal and Perceptual Factors," *Journal of Consumer Research,* **8**:217–222, September 1981.

[51] Jacoby, Olson, and Haddock, "Price and Product Composition Characteristics."

[52] Monroe and Petroshius, "Buyers' Perceptions of Price."

[53] National Probability Sample in Great Britain, Market and Opinion Research International Cooperative Image Study, Spring 1970, reported by Robert Worcester, "Corporate Image Research," in Robert Worcester (ed.), *Consumer Market Research Handbook,* McGraw-Hill, London, 1972, p. 508.

[54] "Humble Exxon in; Esso Out," *National Petroleum News,* June 1972.

[55] See, for example, Ponpun Nickel and Albert I. Wertheimer, "Factors Affecting Consumers' Images and Choices of Drugstores," *Journal of Retailing,* **55**:71–78, Summer 1979; B. Rosenbloom, *Retail Marketing,* Random House, New York, 1981; and James M. Kenderdine and Jack J. Kasulis, "The Relationship Between Changes in Perceptions of Store Attributes and Changes in Consumer Patronage Behavior," in Robert F. Lusch and William R. Darden (eds.), *Retail Patronage Theory: 1981 Workshop Proceedings,* Center for Economic and Management Research, University of Okalahoma, Norman, OK, 1981, pp. 100–105.

[56] Pierre Martineau, "The Personality of the Retail Store," *Harvard Business Review,* **36**:47–55, January-February 1958.

[57] David Mazursky and Jacob Jacoby, "Exploring the Development of Store Images," *Journal of Retailing,* **62**:145–165, Summer 1986.

[58] See William Lazer and Robert G. Wyckham, "Perceptual Segmentation of Department Store Marketing," *Journal of Retailing,* **45**:3–14, Summer 1969; and William D. Haueisen, "Market Positioning: A New Segmentation Approach," in Robert F. Lusch and William R. Darden (eds.), *Retail Patronage Theory: 1981 Workshop Proceedings,* Center for Economic and Management Research, University of Oklahoma, Norman, Okla., 1981, pp. 86–92.

[59] See, for example, Gail Bronson, "King Leer: Sexual Pitches in Ads Become More Explicit and More Pervasive," *The Wall Street Journal,* December 18, 1980, pp. 1, 14; and Christopher Rowley, "Sex in Advertising," *Scan,* **29**:12–15, April 1981.

[60] See, for example, Gordon L. Wise, Alan L. King, and J. Paul Merenski, "Reactions to Sexy Ads Vary With Age," *Journal of Advertising Research,* **14**:11–16, August 1974; and Deborah K. Johnson and Kay Satow, "Consumers' Reactions to Sex in TV Commercials," in Keith H. Hunt (ed.), *Advances in Consumer Research,* vol. 5, Association for Consumer Research, Ann Arbor, Mich., 1978, pp. 411–414.

[61] Bruce John Morrison and Richard C. Sherman, "Who Responds to Sex in Advertising?" *Journal of Advertising Research,* **12**:15–19, April 1972.

[62] See Baker, *Visual Persuasion;* and Gordon Patzer, *The Physical Attractiveness Phenomena,* Plenum Press, 1985.

[63] See Robert Chestnut, Charles LaChance, and Amy Lubitz, "The Decorative Female Model: Sexual Stimuli and the Recognition of Advertisements," *Journal of Advertising,* 6:11–14, Fall 1977; Major Stedman, "How Sexy Illustrations Affect Brand Recall," *Journal of Advertising Research,* 9:15–19, March 1969; and Raymond L. Horton, "The Effects of Nudity, Suggestiveness, and Attractiveness on Product Class and Brand Name Recall," in Vinay Kothari (ed.), *Developments in Marketing Science,* vol. 5, Academy of Marketing Science, Nacogdoches, Tex., 1982, pp. 456–459.

[64] Leonard N. Reid and Lawrence C. Soley, "Another Look at the 'Decorative' Female Model: The Recognition of Visual and Verbal Ad Components," in James H. Leigh and Claude R. Martin, Jr. (eds.), *Current Issues and Research in Advertising—1981,* Graduate School of Business Administration, Division of Research, University of Michigan, Ann Arbor, Mich., 1981, pp. 123–133.

[65] Robert A. Peterson and Roger A. Kerin, "The Female Role in Advertisements: Some Experimental Evidence," *Journal of Marketing,* 41:59–63, October 1977.

[66] See Donald Sciglimpaglia, Michael A. Belch, and Richard F. Cain, Jr., "Demographic and Cognitive Factors Influencing Viewers Evaluations of 'Sexy' Advertisements," in William Wilkie (ed.), *Advances in Consumer Research,* vol. 6, Association for Consumer Research, Ann Arbor, Mich., 1979, pp. 62–65; and Michael A. Belch et al., Psychophysiological and Cognitive Responses to Sex in Advertising," in Andrew Mitchell (ed.), *Advances in Consumer Research,* vol. 9, Association for Consumer Research, Ann Arbor, Mich., 1982, pp. 424–427.

[67] Sciglimpaglia, Belch, and Cain, "Demographic Factors Influencing Evaluations of 'Sexy' Advertisements"; and Deborah K. Johnson and Kay Satow, "Consumers' Reactions to Sex in TV Commercials," in Keith H. Hunt (ed.), *Advances in Consumer Research,* vol. 5, Association for Consumer Research, Ann Arbor, Mich., 1978, pp. 411–414.

[68] Sciglimpaglia, Belch, and Cahn, "Demographic Factors," and Johnson and Satow, "Consumers' Reactions."

[69] Timothy E. Moore, "Subliminal Advertising: What You See Is What You Get," *Journal of Marketing,* 46:38–47, Spring 1982.

[70] See H. Brean, "What Hidden Sell is All About," *Life,* March 31, 1958, pp. 104–114.

[71] James V. McConnell, Richard L. Cutter, and Elton B. McNeil, "Subliminal Stimulation: An Overview," *American Psychologist,* 13:230, May 1958.

[72] See M. Mannes, "Ain't Nobody Here but Us Commercials," *Reporter,* October 17, 1957, pp. 35–37; and "Subliminal Ad Okay if it Sells: FCC Peers into Subliminal Picture on TV," *Advertising Age,* 28, 1957.

[73] See, for example, "Secret Voices," *Time,* September 10, 1979, p. 71; Neil Maxwell, "Words Whispered to Subconscious Supposedly Deter Thefts, Fainting," *The Wall Street Journal,* November 25, 1980, p. 25; Fred Danzig, "Relaxed Radio Soothes—But Subliminally," *Advertising Age,* September 15, 1980, p. 34; and Bernie Whalen, "Threshold Messaging Touted as Antitheft Measure," *Marketing News,* March 15, 1985, pp. 5–6; and "Subliminal Ad Tactics: Experts Still Laughing," *Marketing News,* March 15, 1985, pp. 6–7.

[74] See Wilson Bryan Key, *Subliminal Seduction,* Prentice-Hall, Englewood Cliffs, N. J., 1973; Wilson Bryan Key, *Media Sexploitation,* Prentice-Hall, Englewood Cliffs, N. J., 1976, and Wilson Bryan Key, *The Clamplate Orgy,* Prentice-Hall, Englewood Cliffs, N. J., 1980.

[75] See Del Hawkins, "The Effects of Subliminal Stimulation on Drive Level and Brand Preference," *Journal of Marketing Research,* 7:322–326, August 1970; John G. Caccavale, Thomas C. Wanty III, and Julie A. Edell, "Subliminal Implants in Advertisements: An Experiment," in Andrew Mitchell (ed.), *Advances in Consumer Research,* vol. 9, Association for Consumer Research, Ann Arbor, Mich., 1982, pp. 418–423; William E. Kilbourne, Scott Painton, and Danny Ridley, "The Effect of Sexual Embedding on Response to Magazine Advertisements," *Journal of Advertising,* 14:48–56, 1985; and Larry T. Patterson and Mary Ann Stutts, "Subaudible Radio Messages: Did I Hear What I Think I Heard?" in David Klein and Allen Smith (eds.), *Proceedings,* Southern Marketing Association Conference, Southern Marketing Association, 1985, pp. 20–22.

[76] Joel Saegert, "Another Look at Subliminal Perception," *Journal of Advertising Research,* 19:55–57, February 1979.

[77] See Moore, "Subliminal Advertising."

LEARNING AND MEMORY

LEARNING OBJECTIVES

After studying this chapter, you should understand . . .

■ The principal elements of learning

■ The various means by which learning is likely to occur and their implications for understanding consumer behavior

■ The role of behavior modification in consumer behavior

■ Factors influencing consumers' rate and degree of learning and loss of learned information

■ The major characteristics and operations of memory systems and their impact on consumers' behavior

Children of parents who grew up during the Vietnam era, which began our most recent peace movement, have been receiving quite a bit of hard sell for what some like to describe as ''action toys.'' These include Masters of the Universe and Transformer figures, as well as more humanoid characters such as Rambo, G.I. Joe, and Chuck Norris.

Some claim that the popularity of many of these toys follows a rebound in national mood that began after our ill-fated attempt to rescue hostages in Iran. The 1984 Olympics, the Granada invasion by our forces, and our air attack on Lybian targets appear to have changed our post-Vietnam national depression and influenced the positive take-charge mood of Americans. This resulted in acceptance of characters, such as Rambo, which would have generated very negative reactions during the Vietnam era.

What has some parents and child psychologists concerned, however, is that TV cartoon shows based on such toy figures may have an effect on young people's acceptance of war and violence. Some have suggested strongly that children who watch war-related cartoons come away believing that war can be won and the good guys will always win it—an unlikely event in the nuclear age. A professional researcher on television violence also argues that the 250 TV episodes of war cartoons shown per year equate to twenty-two days of classroom instruction on war—in essence teaching that war is fun. His recent research on aggressive tendencies in children seems to lend some support to his concerns. The 1982 National Institute of Mental Health report also concluded that violence on TV leads to aggressive and violent behavior on the part of children. However, others in the field of education disagree, arguing that such programming and toys can actually provide socially acceptable and safe outlets for children to work out aggressive feelings without hurting others.

14

Of course, no one is claiming that toy manufacturers and TV producers are intent on teaching aggression and violence. The real question is what are the unintended effects of their efforts? Are they unintentionally resulting in learned behavior which is undesirable and potentially dangerous?[1]

As this example indicates, consumers' learning is an important component of their behavior. Learning occurs intentionally, as when a problem is recognized and information is acquired about products which might solve the problem. And, as our example suggests, consumer learning also can occur unintentionally.

One benefit of the learning mechanism is that consumers are able to adapt to a changing environment. Consequently, knowledge of learning principles can be useful in understanding how consumers' wants and motives are acquired and how their tastes are developed. Also, appreciation of learning and memory processes can aid our understanding of how frequently to repeat advertising messages; how visual symbols, songs, and other techniques can facilitate consumers' learning and memory regarding products and promotions; and how consumers develop habitual purchase patterns for some goods.

This chapter begins by defining learning and describing what it is that we learn. Second, major elements of the learning process are reviewed. Next, several ways by which consumers can learn are described and characterized, followed by a number of additional learning topics particularly useful for understanding the behavior of consumers. Finally, consumers' memory and the process of forgetting are addressed.

CHARACTERIZING LEARNING

Before going further, it is useful to adopt a definition of learning. Several introductory comments concerning the nature of learned material will also provide a beneficial foundation.

LEARNING DEFINED

Very simply, learning can be viewed as a relatively permanent change in behavior occurring as a result of experience. The implications of this definition are fairly subtle and, therefore, require some explanation.

First, as before, the term "behavior" is used to refer to nonobservable cognitive activity as well as to overt actions. Therefore, it is very possible for learning to occur without any change in observable behavior. Changes in consumers' attitudes resulting from exposure to new information about a brand demonstrate this point. Second, learning results in relatively permanent changes in behavior. This excludes changes brought about by fatigue or other short-lived influences such as drug-induced behavior. Third, since our definition of learning stresses experience, we must exclude the effects of physical damage to the body or brain and of natural human growth. It is interesting to note, however, that much of our early learning experiences are controlled by the degree of physical development needed to make practice of an activity possible.

TYPES OF LEARNED BEHAVIOR

Nearly every type of behavior we exhibit as humans has been learned. The following paragraphs provide some specific examples.

Physical Behavior   Generally, we learn many physical behavior patterns useful in responding to a variety of situations faced in everyday life. For example, all healthy humans learn to walk, talk, and interact with others. As consumers, we also learn methods of responding to various purchase situations. These may take the forms of learning to act dissatisfied when hearing the first price quote on a car, or learning to read closely the fine print in purchase contracts. Consumers may also learn certain physical activity through the process termed *modeling,* in which they mimic the behavior of other individuals, such as celebrities. This suggests the important influence of learned physical behavior.

Symbolic Learning and Problem Solving   People learn symbolic meanings that enable highly efficient communication through the development of languages. Symbols also allow marketers to communicate with consumers through such vehicles as brand names (Kodak and Sony), slogans (''Coke is it''), and signs (McDonald's Golden Arches). As mentioned previously, the marketer intends for these symbols to connote positive images of the company to consumers in addition to keeping the firm's name familiar to them.

One can also engage in problem-solving learning by employing the processes of thinking and insight. *Thinking* involves the mental manipulation of symbols representing the real world to form various combinations of meaning. This often leads to *insight,* which is a new understanding of relationships involved in the problem. As we have noted, many consumer efforts can be viewed as problem-solving behavior. For example, consumers are constantly engaged in deliberating about how satisfaction of their various wants and needs can be improved by acquiring new or different products or services. Thinking and problem-solving behavior, therefore, enable consumers to evaluate mentally a wide variety of products without having to purchase them.

Affective Learning   Humans learn to value certain elements of their environment and dislike others. This means that consumers learn many of their wants, goals, and motives as well as what products satisfy these needs. Learning also influences consumers' development of favorable or unfavorable attitudes toward a company and its products. These attitudes will affect the tendency to purchase various brands.

As we discovered in earlier chapters, consumers' interactions within a social system can have a significant influence on their learning of tastes. This is quite obvious for products such as scotch and tobacco, in which it is said that one has to ''acquire a taste'' for the product. However, the same process is at work regarding the vast majority of foods, clothes, and other goods. The process that influences such learning includes sanctions and social pressure by group or family members.

The discussion of what we learn could easily fill the remaining pages of this chapter. It is more appropriate, however, that we now direct our attention toward

the principal elements of learning and other issues of importance to the understanding of this process.

PRINCIPAL ELEMENTS OF LEARNING

As will be demonstrated shortly, consumers learn in several basic ways. However, four elements seem to be fundamental to the vast majority of situations: motive, cue, response, and reinforcement.[2] The exact nature and strength of these components influence what will be learned, how well it will be learned, and the rate at which learning will occur.

Motive   As noted in Chapter 12, motives arouse individuals, thereby increasing their readiness to respond. This arousal function is essential, since it activates the energy needed to engage in learning activity. In addition, any success at achieving the motivating goal, or avoiding some unpleasant situation, tends to reduce arousal. Because this is reinforcing, such activity will have a greater tendency to occur again in similar situations. Thus, marketers strive to have their brand or its name available when relevant consumer motives are aroused because it is expected that consumers will learn a connection between the product and motive. For this reason, we see advertisements for Prestone antifreeze shortly before winter and Coppertone suntan lotion during the summer.

Cues   A cue may be viewed as a weak stimulus not strong enough to arouse consumers, but capable of providing *direction* to motivated activity. That is, it influences the manner in which consumers respond to a motive. The shopping environment is packed with cues, such as promotions and product colors, which consumers can use to choose between various response options in a learning situation. For example, when we are hungry we are guided by certain cues, such as restaurant signs and the aroma of food cooking, because we have learned that these stimuli are associated with food preparation and consumption.

It is interesting to note that consumers frequently learn such strong bonds between certain cues and products that they are highly reluctant to purchase when these cues are absent. For this reason, sellers make sure that the appropriate cues are present in their products. For example, many prepared foods have artificial coloring added to stimulate purchase. Also, an orange coloring is frequently added to whole oranges because consumers have learned to expect oranges to have such coloring.

Response   A response may be viewed as a mental or physical activity the consumer makes in reaction to a stimulus situation. Responses appropriate to a particular situation are learned over time through experience in facing that situation. As we have noted, the occurrence of a response is not always observable. Therefore, it must again be emphasized that our inability to observe responses does not necessarily mean that learning is not taking place.

Chapter 12 introduced the concept of a motive hierarchy, and a similar situation exists for responses. Before learning occurs, our innate characteristics order responses to a stimulus from the most likely to least likely response. Thus, a hungry baby is more likely to cry or exhibit sucking behavior than other responses. Over time, learning will modify the response hierarchy so that other responses have a greater chance of occurring. In this way, consumers are able to adapt to changing environmental conditions which confront them.

Reinforcement   Perhaps the most widely acceptable view of reinforcement is anything that follows a response and increases the tendency for the response to reoccur in a similar situation.[3] Because reinforced behavior tends to be repeated, consumers can learn to develop successful means of responding to their needs or changing conditions.

One important type of reinforcement is achieved through reducing motive arousal. This occurs through removing a *negative reinforcer* (something that generates discomfort and is avoided) or receiving a *positive reinforcer* (something that generates pleasure and is sought). In either case, reducing motive arousal is reinforcing to the consumer. For example, drinking 7-Up on a hot day or purchasing a Norelco smoke detector to lessen the dangers of a home fire can both reduce motive arousal for the consumer.

In still other situations, punishment through mental or physical discomfort is applied as a negative reinforcer. Such circumstances can result in learning to avoid something or to discontinue some behavior pattern. All of these situations demonstrate that reinforcement is a general term that involves more than just receiving or giving rewards.

It should be noted here that a number of learning experiments have not involved the introduction of positive or negative reinforcers.[4] In many cases, it appears that just the accomplishment of a learning task is by itself a reinforcing experience. Thus, consumers may learn about products merely by mentally evaluating their relevance to solving consumption problems. Window-shopping activity and informal discussions with friends or salespeople may be aspects of such learning behavior.

Another point to consider is that our behavior can be reinforced so subtly that we may not even be aware that it has occurred.[5] Simple social gestures such as a nod, smile, or frown are often deceptively powerful in their influence. This type of behavior can be observed in certain television commercials featuring a lead character that speaks directly to viewers while one or more other characters are seen engaged in some activity behind this spokesperson. Close observation of these background players will sometimes reveal that they nod approval or use other body language to support important points the lead character is making. This suggests that consumers can be encouraged to develop attitudes and patterns of behavior toward brands without becoming aware that such changes are occurring.

CLASSIFYING LEARNING

Various theories have been developed to explain different aspects of learning.[6] These theories, however, can be grouped into several major categories for the focus of our present discussion. As Figure 14-1 depicts, the first major division is between the connectionist and cognitive schools of thought. While *cognitive* interpretations place emphasis on the discovery of patterns and insight, *connec-*

tionists argue that humans learn connections between stimuli and responses. The connectionist school can be further subdivided on the basis of the type of conditioning employed. Each of these subdivisions will be discussed in turn.

LEARNING CONNECTIONS

Some learning theorists maintain that learning involves the development of *connections* between a stimulus and some response to it. That is, the association of a response and a stimulus is the connection that is learned.

A portion of this group minimizes the importance of reinforcement to learning, while others stress its crucial role. We shall sidestep this debate by adopting the reinforcement viewpoint because of its attractiveness in explaining consumers' learning behavior.[7] Reinforcement is employed in conjunction with two fundamentally different methods of learning connections: classical and instrumental conditioning.

Classical Conditioning   Essentially, classical conditioning (sometimes called respondent conditioning) pairs one stimulus with another that already elicits a given response. Over repeated trials, the new stimulus will also begin to elicit the same or a very similar response.

To appreciate the process involved, it is useful to review the experiment conducted by Pavlov, who pioneered study of classical conditioning.[8] Pavlov reasoned that because food already caused his dog to salivate, it might be possible to link a previously neutral stimulus to the food so that it too would be able to make the dog salivate. This would demonstrate that the dog had learned to associate the neutral stimulus with the food. Pavlov used a bell as the neutral stimulus. His experiment is diagramed in Figure 14-2.

The term "unconditioned stimulus" is used for the food because conditioning is not required for it to cause the dog to salivate. This built-in stimulus-response connection is represented by the solid arrow. Because the salivating response also does not require learning, it is termed the "unconditioned response." The bell is

FIGURE 14-1
A classification of
learning theories.

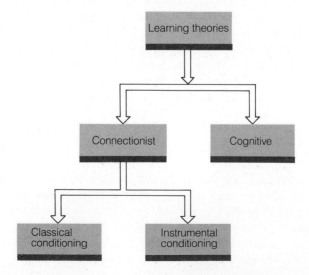

referred to as the "conditioned stimulus," because conditioning is required to learn a connection between it and the food. Pavlov accomplished this by ringing the bell every time he presented the dog with food. After a significant number of conditioning trials, the dog learned a connection between the bell and the food. In fact, the association was strong enough for the bell alone to then become capable of causing the dog to salivate. The dotted arrow connecting the bell and the food symbolizes the learned connection between these stimuli, and the second dotted line indicates that the bell can now cause the dog to salivate.

In this situation, a natural reflex of salivating to food was employed as the unconditioned stimulus. It is important to note, however, that classical conditioning does not require use of reflexive stimuli, and the dog could now be conditioned to a new stimulus by using the bell as the unconditioned stimulus. Learning new associations between stimuli in this manner is termed "second order conditioning." Because evidence suggests that humans are capable of even further levels of conditioning, this concept is more generally referred to as higher-order conditioning.[9]

Higher-order conditioning can be useful for understanding how consumers acquire secondary motives that were described in Chapter 12.[10] Here, goals that once had no motivating abilities can become associated with reinforcing stimuli and take on motivating properties themselves. For example, the achievement motive may be acquired by a child because rewarding praise was given to him or her for accomplishing certain tasks. Later, this achievement motive can influence the purchase of various products to assist in accomplishing tasks.

Instrumental Conditioning   The method of instrumental conditioning (also called operant conditioning) also involves developing connections between stimuli and responses, but the process involved differs from classical conditioning in several important respects. Although classical conditioning relies on an already established stimulus-response connection, instrumental conditioning requires the learner to discover an appropriate or "correct" response—one that will be reinforced.

The principles of this type of learning can best be illustrated by employing the same "box" that B. F. Skinner made famous with his pioneering work in the area.[11] Assume that we place a pigeon in a box. On one wall is a button which when pressed will deliver food to the pigeon. In this case, the button is the conditioned stimulus. When placed in the box, the pigeon can respond in a variety

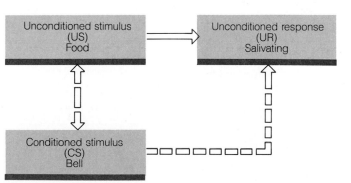

FIGURE 14-2
A representation of classical conditioning.

of ways shown as R_1 through R_n in Figure 14-3. Eventually, it will push button R_3, receive the food, and eat it with great enjoyment. Here, the food, which represents a positive reinforcer, is the unconditioned stimulus.

Most likely, the pigeon will not immediately associate pushing the button with receiving the food. Other responses will occur, but only a push of the button will lead to reinforcement. Therefore, over a number of reinforced trials the pigeon will learn a connection between the stimulus (button) and response (pushing). This can lead to very rapid repetition of the process—perhaps until the bird becomes ill from consuming too much food—which, as we know, also leads to learning.

Distinctions between Conditioning Methods A number of distinctions can be made between classical (respondent) and instrumental (operant) conditioning. Three of the most important ones are summarized in Table 14-1. Note that while classical conditioning is dependent on an already established connection, instrumental conditioning requires the learner to discover the appropriate response. For this reason, instrumental conditioning involves the learner at a more conscious and purposeful level than does classical conditioning.

A second distinction between these two methods concerns the outcome of the learning situation. In classical conditioning, the outcome is not dependent on the learner's actions, but with instrumental conditioning a particular response can change the learner's situation or environment. The response then is actually *instrumental* in producing reinforcement or making something happen in the environment, hence the name for this type of conditioning.

Because of the above differences, each conditioning method is suited to explaining different types of learning. Learning to adapt and control one's environment is better explained by instrumental conditioning because it requires

FIGURE 14-3
A representation of
instrumental conditioning.

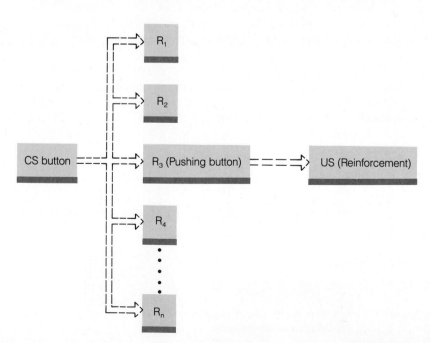

that the learner discover the response that leads to reinforcement. Alternatively, classical conditioning is often more useful in explaining how consumers learn brand names and acquire or change their opinion, tastes, and goals. That is, the material to be learned in such cases is associated with stimuli that already elicit favorable or unfavorable experiences.

COGNITIVE INTERPRETATIONS

Instead of viewing learning as the development of connections between stimuli and responses, cognitive theorists stress the importance of perception, problem solving, and insight. This viewpoint contends that much learning occurs not as a result of trial-and-error or practice but through discovering meaningful patterns which enable us to solve problems. These meaningful patterns are termed *gestalts,* and cognitive theories of learning rely heavily on the process of insight to explain the development of gestalts.

Wolfgang Kohler's work with apes provides an interesting example to understand better this view of learning.[12] In one experiment, a chimpanzee was placed in a cage with a box, and bananas were hung from the top of the cage beyond reach, even if the ape jumped. After failing to reach the food, the problem was solved when suddenly the chimp placed the box under the bananas and jumped from it to reach the food. This suggested that the ape's learning was not a result of trial-and-error, but a consequence of deliberation and sudden insight into a problem solution. This feeling of insight is familiar to all of us when we suddenly "see" the solution to a problem situation (the "ah ha" effect).

Although the chimp in Kohler's experiment was able to get rewarded by reaching the bananas, the reward is not so apparent in many cognitive learning situations. For example, no observable reward is present when the student solves a difficult problem in statistics. However, the concept of *closure* is viewed as having important reinforcing properties in the cognitive viewpoint. As long as an individual has not solved a problem, a state of incompleteness produces tension to motivate continued search for a solution. Problem solution results in closure, which reduces the motivating tension and is reinforcing.

APPLYING ALTERNATIVE LEARNING CONCEPTS TO CONSUMER BEHAVIOR

We should not be dismayed by alternative explanations of how consumers learn. In fact, it is useful to have these alternatives, since the nature of what consumers learn probably influences the method they use to learn it.

TABLE 14-1

Important Distinctions between Classical and Instrumental Conditioning

Classical (respondent) conditioning	Instrumental (operant) conditioning
1 Involves an already established response to another stimulus.	No previous stimulus-response connection necessary. Learner must discover appropriate response.
2 The outcome is not dependent on learner's actions.	The outcome is dependent on learner's actions.
3 Influences development and changes in opinions, tastes, and goals.	Influences changes in goal-directed behavior.

Source: Based on David Krech et al., *Psychology: A Basic Course,* Knopf, New York, 1976, pp. 50–61.

As we have noted, cognitive interpretations stress problem-solving behavior and the learner's active understanding of situations confronting her. It is not "blind" or rote behavior, as the learning of connections can be. This view is therefore most useful in understanding how consumers learn which stores, methods of shopping, or products will best meet their needs. For example, it can take the form of learning about the uses and benefits of products new to the market, especially if they represent significant innovations. It can also explain how consumers learn about existing products for which they have developed a recent interest or need.[13] In either case, the learning that is involved is purposeful and goal directed, requiring conscious problem-solving involvement on the part of the consumer.

Connectionists' theories of learning are appropriate to understanding a variety of other aspects of consumer behavior. As has already been noted, classical conditioning is useful for explaining how consumers acquire tastes and motives. Advertisers also employ the concept by showing their brands in pleasant, exciting, or otherwise emotionally positive surroundings. For example, home computers are shown being enjoyed in interesting settings, Lipton iced tea is depicted in refreshing swimming pool settings, and fast-food products are often shown being consumed in fun-filled social gatherings. Here, the concept of classical conditioning applies to the advertiser's plan for repeated association of a brand with the positive surroundings, which will lead to consumers developing a preference toward the brand. Figure 14-4, which parallels Figure 14-2, suggests how this would occur using a happy situation as the unconditioned stimulus. The setting (such as a family gathering) is selected because it already elicits pleasant feelings from consumers—the unconditioned response. Repeated association of the brand with this setting, such as picturing its use during a family gathering, will enable the brand itself to generate similar pleasant feelings. This should increase consumers' preferences for it. Figure 14-5 shows an advertisement that is consistent with the above explanation.

Recent consumer research has demonstrated that this type of advertising strategy has considerable potential for influencing consumers' brand preferences.[14] However, additional research is needed to more fully explore the influence of the classical conditioning process in a marketing setting and how it could be adequately utilized by advertisers.[15]

Certain types of habitual behavior are also explained through classical or respondent conditioning. For example, many consumers automatically purchase

FIGURE 14-4
How classical conditioning can be used to develop pleasant feelings toward an advertised brand.

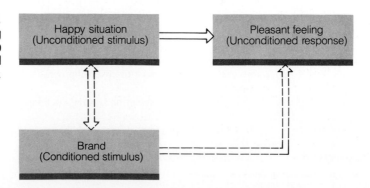

particular brands such as Scotch tape and Bayer aspirin because they have developed strong associations between the brand name and the generic product. This is often an advantage accruing to marketers who first develop a product that dominates the market. In still other cases, consumers habitually purchase particular brands such as Campbell's soups merely because their parents did. Here, such a strong association has been made between a particular brand and an activity or a need that little consideration may be given to its actual suitability.

Instrumental or operant conditioning is useful for understanding consumer learning where conscious choices resulting in positive or negative reinforcement are made. The obvious case is consumers' purchase and evaluation of products. Favorable experiences will result in positive reinforcement of the particular choice. Of course, learning to avoid certain products due to negative reinforcement from bad experiences with them is also possible. This is strong justification for the marketer's stress on satisfying the customer.

Advertisements depicting satisfied buyers can also result in consumers learning a connection between a brand and favorable experiences. Other types of promotional efforts, including cash rebates, free product samples, trial periods, or low introductory prices, also make use of instrumental conditioning. The goal in

FIGURE 14-5
An advertising example of the use of classical conditioning.
Courtesy of Hershey Foods Company.

these cases is to structure a situation so that consumers are given rewards as a consequence of having performed an activity that is desired by the marketer.

Many other applications of both cognitive and connectionist learning could be cited. However, we now turn our attention to other useful concepts of consumer learning.

ADDITIONAL CONSUMER LEARNING TOPICS

A number of other aspects of learning have importance for those interested in the behavior of consumers. Although the following topics by no means exhaust the list of useful concepts, they are representative of the potential applications of learning to understanding consumers.

THE BEHAVIOR MODIFICATION PERSPECTIVE

The emphasis in a behavior modification perspective (BMP) of learning is on a set of intervention techniques designed to influence the behavior of individuals. That is, focus is placed on how environmental events (stimuli, reinforcements, and the like) can be modified to bring about changes in the way people act. In fact, a segment of BMP advocates, containing those who are referred to as behavioralists, completely discards the role of internal psychological processes (such as needs, attitudes) and the concept of learning when studying behavioral changes in people. Behavioralists argue that it is sufficient to just consider changes in behavior and the environmental events that appear capable of influencing such behavior, rather than also attempting to *explain* what internal forces within the individual relate these two events together. A less radical view, which is adopted here, proposes retaining explanations of internal processes and blending them with consideration of environmental influences.[16] Therefore, we will view the BMP as having a distinct focus but sharing certain principles such as conditioning and reinforcement with theories of learning that also incorporate internal psychological processes to explain behavior.

Several areas of environmental influence can be considered as within the BMP domain: classical (respondent) conditioning, instrumental (operant) conditioning, modeling, and ecological design. Both classical and instrumental conditioning have already been discussed. The examples given for classical conditioning were sufficient to demonstrate how environmental variables could be used to influence consumers' behavior. Although examples were also provided for instrumental conditioning, it is useful to discuss three additional topics in this area (reinforcement schedules, shaping, and discrimination) to show how they can be used to influence behavior change.

Reinforcement Schedules   It is not necessary to reinforce every "correct" response in order for learning to occur. Different reinforcement schedules, however, lead to different patterns of learning. *Continuous reinforcement* schedules, which reward every "correct" response, yield rapid changes in behavior. Conversely, *partial reinforcement* schedules yield a slower rate, but also result in learning that is more permanent in nature. This may at least partially explain why consumers' negative attitudes toward brands are usually very difficult to reverse.

That is, negative attitudes can be acquired through partial reinforcement because a few unsatisfactory experiences with a brand can occur over a period of time. This can result in consumers being highly resistant to positive information about the brand, especially if the marketer is the source of such information.

In a different vein, partial-reinforcement schedules can also represent an economical alternative for marketers. Because many marketing forms of reinforcement (like advertisements, sales) can cost considerable sums of money, finding a way to cause changes in consumers' behavior without having to reward every learning experience represents an attractive opportunity.

Shaping The term "shaping" refers to influencing a large change in behavior over time by reinforcing successively closer approximations to that behavior. The thinking behind the idea of shaping is described by an ancient proverb: "A journey of a thousand miles is started with but a single step." That is, although it might be very difficult to achieve a rather large or complex change in consumers' behavior in one step, a series of smaller changes leading to the same end point may be much less difficult.

An example of shaping would be to offer consumers special prizes to visit a retail store over several weeks and, while they are there, encouraging them to purchase items by using discounts, special sales, or rebates. The behavior of traveling to the store is rewarded, and purchasing at the store is also reinforced. In this way, it is expected that consumers will adopt the behavior of regularly shopping at the store after the special reinforcements are withdrawn. Many similar examples of shaping exist in the selling and consumer-behavior area.

Discrimination Learning to discriminate between various objects or events is important for consumers, because it helps them adapt to their environment. Discrimination is learned over time when the same response to two similar but noticeably different stimuli leads to different consequences (reinforcement). Stimuli which the consumer can use to distinguish between various items in their environment are often termed *discriminative stimuli*.

Consumers make frequent use of discrimination learning. New or different brands as well as different models within the same producer's line must be distinguished, even though they might differ by only a few features. Products that provide rewarding service must also be distinguished from those that are relatively inferior. Of course, a great deal of marketing effort encourages such discrimination learning. Here, the goal is to reinforce consumers' attention to the uniqueness of a brand. In fact, brand names, logos, and trademarks are quite useful discriminative stimuli, but unique colors, shapes, and packages also have utility. In another quite different and interesting case, patrons of a small retail shop were personally telephoned and thanked for shopping at the store. Reaction to this distinctive reinforcement was quite favorable—sales increased 27 percent during the test period.[17] This attests to the impact of reinforcement in consumers' discrimination learning.

Modeling The term "modeling" refers to learning which occurs as a result of the individual observing both the behavior of others and the consequences of that

behavior. This can lead to (1) the learning of new behavior, (2) a change or strengthening of existing behavioral tendencies, or (3) the facilitation of previously learned responses. The potential for modeling in the marketing discipline is considerable because demonstrations, advertisements, and other promotional means can be used to develop the appropriate modeling scenarios. In fact, the technique is actually employed quite extensively for some of today's most successful products.[18] The usual procedure is to produce a TV advertisement that depicts one or more individuals engaging in certain behavior and receiving a reinforcement. The reinforcement can be in the form of social approval or embarrassment, or in the form of direct product benefits or dissatisfactions. Examples include consumers suffering problems because they had their car brakes repaired by someone other than Midas and people eliminating the social embarrassment caused by slipping dentures after they started using Poligrip.

Ecological Design The concept of ecological design involves a deliberate attempt to manipulate aspects of the environment to achieve changes in behavior. Building and landscape architects have made extensive use of ecological principles for the purpose of directing traffic patterns, focusing office workflow, and achieving crowd control. However, similar principles have also been used in the field of marketing. Consider the efforts made to design nightclubs and discos as exciting environments, as well as the placement of displays and demonstrations in central areas of shopping malls to attract shoppers' attention and influence their purchase behavior. Perhaps more obvious examples would include the physical layout of supermarkets to encourage high shopper exposure to a wide variety of merchandise, and the use of racks at checkout counters to display a variety of convenience or so-called "impulse" items to the waiting customer. The potential of ecological design for affecting the behavior of consumers is considerable. For example, in one study the tempo of background music was found to influence the pace with which consumers walked through the store—faster music resulted in a faster pace. Also, the consumers treated to slower paced music were found to spend significantly more than those treated to music with a faster tempo.[19] We can expect other advances in this field, especially those directed at the use of design to influence consumers' moods, perceptions, and attitudes.

The above comments have provided only a brief review of the BMP which grew out of work by B. F. Skinner and other behaviorally oriented psychologists. A few examples were given of its application to the field of marketing. Table 14-2 presents an excellent summary of additional areas of application and methods for their achievement.

It should be mentioned that the BMP has not enjoyed a high level of awareness and appreciation among those interested in marketing or the behavior of consumers. Despite this, many of the practical marketing tactics that have been developed without knowledge of the field appear to be quite consistent with it. As the perspective achieves wider exposure and additional effort is devoted to exploring its marketing applications, additional insights should lead to the development of more effective tactics. In addition, when combined with more internally oriented viewpoints, the perspective could prove quite beneficial in describing how the purchase-consumption process works.[20]

STIMULUS GENERALIZATION

When a given response to a stimulus has been learned, it will tend to be elicited not only by the original stimulus involved in the learning situation but also by stimuli that are similar to it. This process, called *stimulus generalization,* appears to occur *automatically* unless stopped by discrimination learning.[21] Stimulus generalization simplifies the consumer's life, because it means that learning a unique response to every stimulus is not necessary. One response can be used for similar stimuli unless there is some important reason to learn to discriminate between them.

The *gradient of generalization* relates the degree of similarity between two stimuli to the likelihood that both will generate the same response. It has been found that the greater the resemblance between a given stimulus and another that already causes a response, the greater the chance that it will also generate the same response.[22] Conversely, the more dissimilar two stimuli are, the smaller the likelihood of stimulus generalization occurring. As noted in Chapter 13, some producers of private brands make use of the gradient concept by packaging products to closely resemble national brands in appearance. In other cases, firms "ride the coattails" of success of pioneering companies by offering highly similar products. The sudden appearance of various caffeine-free soft drinks and sugarless gums are cases in point.

The generalization gradient also helps us understand the marketing approach of introducing "new" products that often bear a considerable resemblance to their predecessors. This encourages consumers to generalize learned attitudes and preferences from the old product to the new model. The *family brand* strategy employs similar methods. Here, the family brand name is prominently associated with the new product, as in the case of a General Motors car, a Wilson football, or a Panasonic radio. The intention is that consumers' favorable perceptions and attitudes about the family name will be generalized to the new product. Of course, the danger of such a strategy is that unfavorable experiences on the part of consumers with one product in the family line may lead to generalizing poor impressions toward the entire group of products.

RATE AND DEGREE OF LEARNING

In general, learning of all but the simplest tasks appears to follow a rather common pattern which has become known as a *learning curve*. A typical curve is displayed in Figure 14-6, where the amount learned is measured on the *y* axis and the number of practice trials is shown on the *x* axis. The characteristic shape of this curve demonstrates that the rate of learning is quite rapid during initial stages. However, in later stages, as the amount learned accumulates, the *rate* of additional learning per trial decreases. This demonstrates the highly effective nature of practice in early stages of learning and its diminishing effect in later trials. It also demonstrates that even though the rate of learning is high initially, many practice trials are needed to ensure a large amount of total learning.

It is important to note that repetition of an advertisement appears to lead to a learning curve similar to the one in Figure 14-6.[23] In these cases, the number of times the advertising message is repeated is measured along the *x* axis and the

TABLE 14-2

Some Illustrative Applications of the Behavior Modification Perspective in Marketing

I. Some applications of respondent conditioning principles

A. Conditioning responses to new stimuli:

Unconditioned or previously conditioned stimulus	Conditioned stimulus	Examples
Exciting event	A product or theme song	Gillette theme song followed by sports event
Patriotic events or music	A product or person	Patriotic music as background in political commerical

B. Use of familiar stimuli to elicit reponses:

Conditioned stimulus	Conditioned response(s)	Examples
Familiar music	Relaxation, excitement, "good will"	Christmas music in retail store
Familiar social cues	Excitement, attention, anxiety	Sirens sounding or telephones ringing in commercials

II. Some applications of operant conditioning principles

A. Rewards for desired behavior (continuous schedules):

Desired behavior	Reward given following behavior
Product purchase	Trading stamps, cash bonus or rebate, prizes, coupons

B. Rewards for desired behavior (partial schedules):

Desired behavior	Reward given following behavior
Product purchase	Prize for every second, or third, etc., purchase
	Prize to a fraction of people who purchase

C. Shaping:

Approximation of desired response	Consequence following approximation	Final response desired
Opening a charge account	Prizes, etc., for opening account	Expenditure of funds
Trip to point-of-purchase location	Loss leaders, entertainment, or event at the shopping center	Purchase of products
Product trial	Free product and/or some bonus for using	Purchase of product

D. Discriminative stimuli:

Desired behavior	Reward signal	Examples
Entry into store	Store signs	50% off sale
	Store logos	K mart's big red "K"
Brand purchase	Distinctive brandmarks	Levi tag

III. Some applications of modeling principles

Modeling employed	Desired response
Instructor, expert, salesperson using product (in ads or at point-of-purchase)	Use of product in technically competent way
Models in ads asking questions at point-of-purchase	Ask questions at point-of-purchase which highlight product advantages
Models in ads receiving positive reinforcement for product purchase or use	Increase product purchase and use
Models in ads receiving no reinforcement or receiving punishment for performing undesired behaviors	Extinction or decrease undesired behaviors

IV. Some applications of ecological modification principles

Environmental design	Specific example	Intermediate behavior	Final desired behavior
Store layout	End of escalator, end-aisle, other displays	Bring customer into visual contact with product	Product purchase
In-store mobility	In-store product directories, information booths	Bring consumer into visual contact with product	Product purchase
Noises, scents, lights	Flashing lights in store window	Bring consumer into visual or other sensory contact with store or product	Product purchase

Source: Adapted from Walter R. Nord and J. Paul Peter, "A Behavior Modification Perspective on Marketing," *Journal of Marketing*, **44**:42–43, Spring 1980, published by the American Marketing Association.

extent of consumers' learning of the message is measured along the y axis. Of course, marketers must determine whether this general pattern actually fits their particular products and situations.[24] For example, it may not describe learning in some low-involvement situations in which fewer repetitions might be necessary for storing simple facts, such as brand names, away in memory.[25] For cases in which the curve is appropriate, there are several implications regarding the use of advertising to encourage consumer learning. First, as the curve demonstrates, a

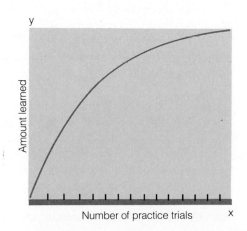

FIGURE 14-6
A typical learning curve.

marketer must be willing to repeat an advertising message a significant number of times. This is also why a brand name may be repeated several times in just one advertisement. Second, the curve demonstrates that after repeating messages many times, the marketer is paying for small increases in consumer learning. Further, evidence suggests that advertising messages are subject to *wearout* and manipulation by audience members. That is, as the number of message repetitions increases, boredom can result, inattention can increase, and audience members may switch from rehearsing the message to generating and attending to their own less-positive thoughts about the message.[26] This type of evidence might tempt the marketer to stop advertising after time. However, as will be demonstrated shortly, if a message is not repeated, consumers tend to forget most of it quite rapidly. This indicates the need to repeat advertisements merely to *maintain* consumers' level of learning. One strategy that might reduce wearout and other negative consequences of repetition is to repeat the basic content of an advertising message while periodically changing the method of doing so, to maintain consumers interests. An additional advantage of such variety is that it could encourage consumers to engage in deeper processing of the basic message in order to facilitate learning and memory.[27] It actually may also encourage positive feelings toward the brand.[28] Means of accompanying such a strategy include using different spokespeople, employing various beginnings and endings to the ads, and adopting different themes, scenarios, or backgrounds for the message. Close attention to advertisements on television will reveal that such techniques are actually being employed.

Although the above general patterns of consumer learning appear to exist, a number of variables influence the rate and strength of the process. Two of these factors are briefly reviewed below.

Learning Ability Individuals differ considerably in their abilities to learn, and intelligence is a primary factor influencing this ability. Intelligence appears to be normally distributed within the population with some consumers being much higher than average and others being considerably below average. Highly intelligent consumers are capable of learning more quickly and are often interested in learning different types of information about products than consumers of lower intelligence. In addition, they tend to be more critical of unsubstantiated advertising claims and often have different readership habits than do other consumers. For example, readers of *National Geographic, Scientific American,* and *Saturday Review* tend to have higher intelligence levels than readers of many other magazines. Such differences in learning abilities require marketers to consider carefully intelligence levels of their target market before designing the content of promotional messages.

Practice Schedules If only the time actually spent at a learning task is considered, periods of practice separated by rest intervals achieve much more efficient learning in many situations than do learning periods with no rest. The term *distributed practice* refers to learning sessions with rest periods, while learning without rest periods is known as *massed practice*. Aside from its obvious relevance to students' study habits, practice schedules have implications regarding the proper scheduling of advertising messages over time. Given that distributed practice is an effective learning technique, the marketer is interested in the optimum time interval to plan between advertising repetitions in order to generate the greatest amount of consumer learning. This has sparked a considerable amount of research in the advertising field.[29]

EXTINCTION

We can "unlearn" material or behavior that has been previously learned. This unlearning process is termed *extinction* and occurs when, over time, a learned response is made to a stimulus but reinforcement does not occur. The greater the number of nonreinforced trials, the less likely the response is to occur; but complete extinction is rare. Also, *spontaneous recovery*—the sudden reappearance of an extinguished response—reduces the chance of complete extinction. Resistance to extinction also increases when: (1) impelling motives are strong, (2) the number of previously reinforced trials are large, (3) the amount of reward during learning is large, (4) reward is delayed during the learning process, and (5) a partial reinforcement schedule is used in the learning process.

change many tastes, shopping patterns, and consumption habits. For example, many find it difficult to reduce or eliminate sweets, coffee, or smoking. Similarly, others who have developed strong brand or store loyalties over time resist making changes, even if their regular brands or stores are not currently providing the rewards they once did. This poses a great challenge to marketers attempting to draw patronage away from competition.

FORGETTING

It is important to distinguish extinction from the process of forgetting. Extinction will occur when a previously learned response continues to be made but is no longer reinforced. *Forgetting* can be defined as the loss of retained material due to nonuse or interference from some other learning task. As can be inferred from this definition, *retention* is the amount of previously learned material that is remembered.[30]

The process of forgetting, and how it can be minimized, has been of more concern to marketers than has extinction. This is so not only because it is a more significant problem, but also because marketers can influence the process by repeating advertising messages to encourage consumers' retention. To determine the extent of their success, various measures of advertising retention are employed. The two most commonly used methods are:

Recall. The consumer tells an interviewer the advertisement she remembers seeing recently. She may not be prompted at all (unaided recall), or may be given some guidance (aided recall), such as the product category involved.

Recognition. The consumer is presented with an advertisement or series of advertisements and is asked to indicate which ones he has seen recently.

Both methods of measuring retention are used frequently, but as shown in Figure 14-7 the level of retention as measured by recognition is typically greater than indicated by the recall method. Of course, the most appropriate technique will depend on promotional goals and the specific situation, such as the type of

product involved. However, the marketing manager must be aware of which technique is being employed to evaluate properly the success of the promotional effort.

Note from Figure 14-7 that regardless of the measure of retention used, the fastest rate of forgetting occurs soon after learning has occurred. As the time since the last learning trial increases, forgetting continues, but its rate slows considerably. This was dramatically demonstrated in one marketing experiment in which the percentage of people who could remember a specific advertisement dropped by 50 percent only 4 weeks after the last repetition.[31]

This characteristic shape of retention curves demonstrates the marketer's concern for repeating advertisements to combat the forgetting process. However, designing effective methods to minimize forgetting requires some understanding of human memory. We now turn our attention to this topic.

MEMORY

As everyone's experience has demonstrated, material that consumers have "learned" is not always readily retrievable by them. Some information, such as popular brand names or the location of merchandise in a supermarket, is easily "remembered." Other information appears to end up lost, or at least it does not appear to be readily obtainable. This section of the chapter focuses on the structure and operation of consumers' memory. The discussion picks up where we left off in the information-processing chapter. Here we are concerned with the storage and retrieval of information after it has been acquired and has undergone initial processing.

Memory processes are of considerable importance to the understanding of consumers. Basically, this is so because, to a large extent, consumers act on the basis of their *cognitions,* or their knowledge or beliefs about the world. These cognitions are stored in memory and, as we saw in Chapter 13, they influence how incoming stimuli are interpreted. They also form the basis for attitudes and

FIGURE 14-7
A graph showing loss of retention as measured by recognition and recall methods.
Source: C. W. Luh, "The Conditions of Retention," *Psychological Monographs,* **31**:1–87, 1922. Copyright 1922 by the American Psychological Association. Reprinted by permission.

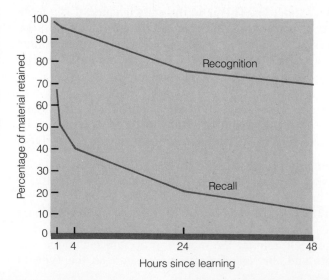

behavioral intentions which are the subject of the next two chapters. On a more concrete level of illustration, consider the goal of marketers who strive to have consumers retain their brand name or information about it. The challenge is great when one realizes that approximately 23,000 different brands are advertised on a national or regional scale in the United States alone.[32] In a very real sense, each of these brands, as well as many local ones, vie for a prominent place in consumers' memory.

CHARACTERISTICS OF MEMORY SYSTEMS

Several views exist regarding the structure of memory and its operation.[33] One, termed the *multiple store* approach, views memory as being composed of three distinct storage registers (sensory, short-term, long-term) which differ in capacity, storage duration, and functioning. A second perspective which has been quite popular is that there is only one memory and distinct storage registers do not exist in a physical sense. Different storage registers appear to exist because different *levels of processing* are involved. That is, stimuli can receive shallow processing, such as an analysis of basic sensations, as well as deeper processing, such as when people interpret incoming information and relate it to existing knowledge. Different levels of processing exist because humans have limited processing capacity to allocate across a variety of incoming stimuli. Also, information receiving deep levels of processing will enjoy a more complex and longer-lasting memory, while shallow processing is likely to result in only temporary storage.

A third conception of memory, called the *activation model,* also makes use of the single-memory-store concept. However, in this view humans are seen as having only a limited ability to activate their memory. The result is that at any time only a portion of memory can be activated to deal with incoming information. Consequently, the remaining portions are not available for processing. Also, activation is only temporary, which means that the portion of memory that is dealing with incoming information will not stay active unless effort is expended to maintain it.

It has been argued that although these three models of memory are distinct in terms of their emphasis, they are not necessarily incompatible.[34] For example, one could view short-term memory in the multiple-store model as that part of memory which is being *activated* and performing a certain function at a given *level* of processing. Other points of commonality can also be found. Therefore, for purposes of exposition we shall discuss memory in terms of the three-component model. We must be careful to note, however, that each component should *not* be viewed as a physically separate entity, but as a distinct process or *functioning* of memory which has certain unique characteristics. The diagram in Figure 14-8 showing the three components of sensory memory, short-term memory, and long-term memory will facilitate our discussion.

Sensory Memory As Figure 14-8 shows, information is first received by sensory memory. Input is in the form of sensations that have been produced by the sensory receptors. Memory registers exist for sensations being produced through the visual, auditory, and other sense organs. The capacity of these registers is very large—capable of storing all that the sensory receptors transmit. They also appear to represent this information faithfully in a form that closely resembles the actual stimuli. A good illustration of the nature of these representations is the after-image we ''see'' in our ''mind's eye'' immediately after observing an object and closing our eyes. This example also illustrates the duration of sensory memory. Information is stored for only a fraction of a second and will be lost through decay (fading away) unless sufficient attention is allocated to it so that it can be analyzed and transferred to short-term memory for further processing. This initial information analysis is conducted in terms of physical characteristics (such as size, color, shape, and so on), which is the process of feature analysis described in Chapter 13.

Short-Term Memory To a large extent, short-term memory can be viewed as the workspace for information processing. That is, it is a portion of memory activated to temporarily store and process information in order to interpret it and comprehend its meaning. This is accomplished by combining incoming information with other information (past experiences, knowledge, and the like) stored in long-term memory.

Although the duration of this memory register is considerably longer than that of sensory memory, it still is quite brief, lasting less than one minute. In addition, the capacity of short-term memory is quite limited. Approximately seven items or groupings of items are all that can be sorted at any one time.[35]

Material residing in short-term memory does not bear a one-to-one correspondence with the real world. Instead, the process of *coding* is used to organize information into a more easily handled and remembered format. The primary method of this coding is termed *chunking,* which can be defined as the method of assembling information into a type of organized unit having a more understandable or familiar form to the individual. For example, consider how the numbers 62895091963 could be more easily utilized if they were grouped into the configurations 628-9509 1963, which most of us would code as a telephone number and a date.

Brand names as well as symbols, trademarks, and other representations also can serve as chunks to organize material. Thus, the word Campbell or the Mercedes symbol are able to bring forth a large number of informational items or thoughts the consumer may have about those companies. Also, when we realize that a chunk can be among the approximately seven items a person can simultaneously hold in short-term memory, we should appreciate that the capacity of seven items or chunks is not as limited as one might initially suspect.

FIGURE 14-8
A representation of memory systems.

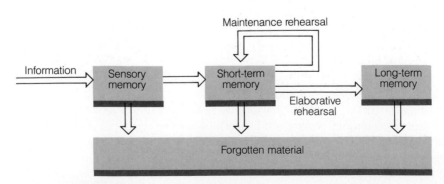

It appears that to employ the chunking process an individual must be prepared to receive the incoming information. For example, a radio advertisement involving a telephone number should alert consumers that a number will be mentioned so that they will be prepared to chunk it into an exchange plus a four-digit number. Without such preparation, the material may be forgotten before chunking can be used. In addition, the telephone number should be announced in chunked form to facilitate memory.

As Figure 14-8 demonstrates, rehearsal is required to maintain information in short-term memory or to transfer it to long-term memory. If rehearsal does not occur, the information will be forgotten through the process of decay. However, it appears that the type of rehearsal involved differs depending on whether the goal is to retain material in short-term memory for additional processing or to transfer it to long-term memory. The process of *maintenance rehearsal* involves the continual repeating of information so that it can be held in short-term memory.[36] For example, after hearing a new brand name of interest, the consumer might keep on repeating it silently until she could write it down. The type of rehearsal used to transfer information to long-term memory is frequently called *elaborative rehearsal,* because it appears to involve relating the new information to prior experiences and knowledge in order to derive meaning from it. This is considered to involve "deeper" levels of processing rather than mere repetition of the information.

Long-Term Memory This memory system can be thought of as the relatively permanent storehouse for information that has undergone sufficient processing. Material can be maintained in long-term memory for as little as a few minutes to as long as many years. In addition, this system has the capacity to store an almost unlimited amount of information.

A predominant key to coding material for storage in long-term memory is *meaningfulness,* the personal understanding an individual can derive from the information. That is, through elaborative rehearsal the individual uses his existing knowledge to interpret incoming information and code it in a way that is consistent with his existing cognitive structure (knowledge base). The degree of success in accomplishing this will affect how well the new information can be retained and made available for future use.[37]

Some people claim that we never really forget anything that has been transferred to long-term memory.[38] Instead, they argue, what is forgotten is the key which tells us where the material is located in our memory. Of course, such a position is difficult to prove or disprove. We therefore will side-step this issue by expanding the term "forgetting" to refer to a general inability to access material that has been stored in long-term memory. Given this, we can now state that material, instead of just decaying over time, appears to be forgotten from long-term memory as a result of other learning *interfering* with retention of the material. The interference concept holds that material can be forgotten in two basic ways. In *retroactive inhibition,* new learning interferes with material already in long-term memory, and the material in memory is forgotten. This could occur, for example, when studying concepts in this chapter results in forgetting material studied in the chapter on information processing. In *proactive inhibition,* material already in memory interferes with the remembering of new material. In either

case, the greater the similarity between two sets of different material, the more they will interfere with each other.

The above paragraphs presented an overview of the sensory memory, short-term memory, and long-term memory systems. Their duration, capacity, type of coding, and major forgetting mechanisms were noted. These characteristics are also summarized in Table 14-3. At this point, it is useful to explore long-term memory in somewhat greater depth. Our attention is focused on this system because of its central role in interpreting new stimulus situations and its functioning as a storehouse for what consumers know about their world.

CONTENT OF LONG-TERM MEMORY   Because long-term memory is a depository for the wide variety of material that a person can learn, it stands to reason that different ways should exist for storing or coding this information. Evidence suggests that this is the case.[39] As indicated in the previous section, one heavily used method of coding involves semantic concepts and the associations between them. By *semantic concepts* we mean one's general abstracted knowledge about facts, objects and their attributes, and other aspects of the world. Therefore, the individual does not perform semantic coding by directly representing an object in memory. Instead, it is stored in a generalized form which has meaning for the individual. Because of this, each of us may store an object in a different way. For example, some people might conceptualize an Apple computer as a powerful method of performing business or household tasks, while others might conceptualize it primarily as a home-entertainment device. Still others might think of it as a learning tool for their children. In each case, the same object will be represented in memory differently, and each representation is likely to be associated with emotions and other already-existing memory concepts that are similar to it.

Other material coded into memory includes chronological representations of events that have occurred in the past. That is, we often store information about happenings by coding them as a sequence of events that occur in a certain time order. The notion of scripts appears to be one example of such coding.[40] A *script* is a representation in memory of a series of actions occurring in some particular type of past situation. What seems to be important is that a well-defined script tends to

TABLE 14-3

Characteristics of
Memory Systems

Memory system	Duration	Capacity	Type of coding	Major forgetting mechanism
Sensory memory	Fraction of a second	All that perceptual sensors can deliver	Quite direct representation of reality	Decay
Short-term memory	Less than one minute	Approximately seven items	Indirect—chunking	Decay
Long-term memory	Up to many years	Almost unlimited	Indirect—clustering via meaningfulness	Interference

Source: Adapted from David Krech et al., *Psychology: A Basic Course,* Knopf, New York, p. 83. Copyright © Alfred A. Knopf, Inc.

influence the consumer's expectations about what actions will occur at a future time when a similar situation occurs. As a result, it tends to guide behavior. Therefore, we can see that the name "script" was chosen because the representation in memory resembles an outline of actions that actors follow in a play or movie. An example might be the script that guides behavior when purchasing a new pair of slacks: find an appropriate size, choose a color, make a comparison to other available brands with similar prices and quality, select a brand, try on two different sizes to select the best fit, and so forth.

Scripts are believed to be useful to consumers because they can be activated automatically when the consumer confronts a familiar situation, and because they guide behavior without requiring much thought or deliberation from the consumer.[41] This relatively automatic behavior also has a number of implications for marketing strategy. For example, it suggests that for many products consumers may not be highly conscious of some of their purchasing patterns. Also, these patterns may be resistant to influence attempts because they are so well established in long-term memory.

A third method of coding information into long-term memory appears to be visual in nature. That is, people appear to use mental images to represent certain information, especially when something tangible such as a physical object is involved.[42] To demonstrate this, we only have to try to remember what is hung on a given kitchen wall in our home. Most people will accomplish this by recalling a "mental picture" of the wall and its contents. It has been shown that using such mental images to store information often leads to a very strong long-term memory for the material.[43]

The strong memory potential for visually coded information has important implications for those who design packaging, company logos, and promotional messages.[44] However, evidence suggests that more is involved than just the old conclusion that "a picture is worth a thousand words." This is so because certain types of verbal stimuli which are not associated with any visual presentations also appear capable of influencing consumers to develop distinct mental images.[45] In addition, some methods of designing pictures, graphics, and similar presentations appear more effective than others for facilitating consumers' visual memory. For example, research has shown that interactive images are more effective for influencing consumers to remember brand names than are normal visual presentations.[46] In this context, an *interactive image* is one that actually becomes part of the brand name or visually integrates the brand name with the product or service being provided. Figure 14-9 presents examples of such interactive images for two hypothetical retail firms. In order to use interactive imagery to its full potential, marketers will have to design their visual presentations carefully.

Ron's Tire Service   Mercury Lawnmowing Service

FIGURE 14-9
Examples of interactive imagery in advertising.

There is also evidence that other formats are used for coding information into long-term memory, including auditory (coding by sounds), taste, and olfactory (coding by smells) methods of representation.[47] These various methods do not appear to be completely independent. Instead, they interact to influence the retention and retrieval of information.

It has been suggested that the various methods of long-term memory coding can be grouped into three general categories which interact with each other: episodic memory, procedural memory, and semantic memory.[48] In *episodic memory,* a record of events in one's personal life is stored according to the time order in which the events occurred. Facts are stored independent of each other and more in terms of how and when they occurred, rather than in terms of the meaning they have. Therefore, retrieval of such information requires that we "play back the tape" from a starting point. For example, when asked how much liquid we had to drink today, most of us would probably try to remember by tracing our steps from when we got up in the morning. Statements reflecting episodic memory include: "I bought that sweater during the fall," "M*A*S*H reruns are on Channel 12 right before dinner," and "That store always has a sale right after Valentine's Day."

Our *procedural memory* holds knowledge about skills and methods for dealing with facts, concepts, and episodes. Therefore, it is a memory for knowing *how* to perform certain functions or tasks, and it plays an important role in problem-solving behavior. Statements reflecting procedural memory include: "When buying a car, always offer the seller less than the stated price," "A new coat of paint adheres better if the old coat is lightly sanded first," and "Always check unit prices before buying packaged food products."

Our *semantic memory* contains general knowledge we have about the world—facts and concepts, as well as objects and their attributes. It seems that this knowledge is not linked to the means or the time period in which it was obtained. For example, most of us have stored information about Kellogg's Corn Flakes, but we usually cannot remember when or how we acquired this information. Because of this, retrieval of material from semantic memory can be direct without the need to "replay" a sequence of events as in episodic memory. Another important characteristic of semantic memory is that it is *associational* in nature. That is, new information is related to existing stored knowledge so that associations are formed between elements and they develop into a type of meaningful cognitive structure. Statements reflecting semantic memory include: "Stereo systems can be expensive," "Cassette players produce better sound than 8-track systems," and "Craig car stereos have a good reputation." How such knowledge can be associated in a memory structure is addressed next.

STRUCTURE OF SEMANTIC MEMORY   It is currently believed that memory is organized into numerous groupings or packets of information. Various types of packets have been suggested by researchers.[49] However, one of the most frequently mentioned schemes is the associative network model of semantic memory. We have already described aspects of this model, but it is useful to look at it a little more closely.

The network model depicts semantic memory as an interconnected system of "nodes" representing the concepts being stored. Figure 14-10 shows how that

portion of a consumer's memory for a Craig car stereo system might be represented using the model. The first thing to note is that a hierarchical structure is involved. That is, the general category of stereos is shown at the top of the figure, and car stereos installed after a car is purchased (retrofit) are seen as only one type of system. Next, we see that the Craig system is one of several types of retrofit brands of which the consumer is aware. Finally, the consumer's knowledge of various characteristics of the Craig system are shown.

We can also see from the figure that each concept in semantic memory is integrated into an organized structure involving one or more other concepts. This is shown by the connecting lines which also represent the strength of the indicated relationship—the darker the line the stronger the association between concepts. Specifically, the lines show that the consumer has remembered the Craig system as one type of auto retrofit stereo system. She also has associated performance, durability, construction, and convenience concepts with the Craig system. The performance concept is most strongly linked to the Craig, followed by the con-

FIGURE 14-10
An illustration of
a memory network.

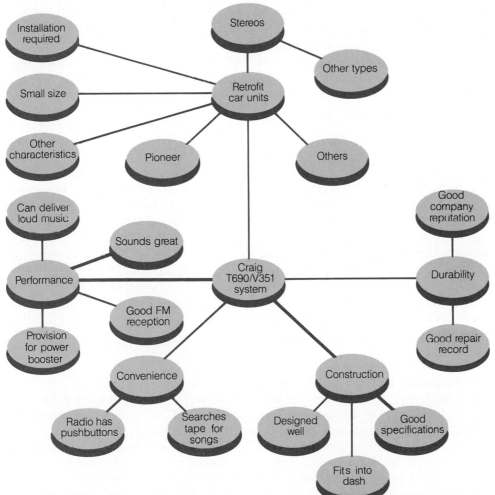

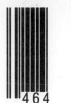

struction concept. Each of the concepts also has particular characteristics which have made enough of an impression on the consumer to be remembered.

It should be clear that semantic memory is viewed as a highly organized structure of knowledge and beliefs. Progressive marketers have shown interest in this conclusion because it implies that an awareness of consumers' memory structures is useful in predicting how they will interpret and respond to new inputs such as product information and promotions. However, as discussed below, evidence has been accumulating recently which adds additional importance to the need to understand consumers' cognitive structures.

Surprisingly, it is possible for semantic memory to contain more than what was received from the environment. That is, associations between concepts in memory are not part of the environment, but are actively *formed* by consumers when they attempt to interpret and store incoming information. One consequence of this is that consumers can develop beliefs about a specific product without ever receiving information directly relevant to that belief.[50] As an example, assume that our consumer examined several Craig models and found that all of these units had good FM reception. It is then quite possible that when introduced to a new Craig unit, this consumer might just infer that it also has good reception, even if she never directly evaluates the new model. Because of the way in which they are formed, such beliefs are termed *inferential beliefs*.

Another closely allied process also occurs while consumers are rehearsing new material and attempting to interpret it for storage in long-term memory. This involves what has become known as *cognitive response,* or positive or negative thoughts generated by the consumer as a result of being exposed to information.[51] When information is in the form of advertising messages, the major forms of cognitive response are generated thoughts that support the message, refute or diminish the message, or degrade the source of the message so that its impact can be minimized. We will examine this in greater detail when dealing with consumers' attitudes. What is important to understand here is that these self-generated thoughts can also be stored in long-term memory along with the information that generated them. This means that they also become part of long-term memory and can be retrieved to influence the interpretation of future information. For example, while a consumer is watching a TV commercial for a brand of personal computer, she or he might think "Basically, they just look like fancy game machines to me." If this concept is associated with personal computers in long-term memory, it could be retrieved at some future date to have a strong influence on the interpretation of additional messages about personal computers. How this could occur is the subject of the next section.

RETRIEVAL OF INFORMATION

Retrieval is the process of accessing information in long-term memory and bringing it into consciousness. The retrieved data may then be combined with other material available in short-term memory, elaborated on, and formed into a coherent package of meaningful information. Therefore, retrieval may be viewed as the means of transferring information from long-term memory into the activated workspace of short-term memory so that it can be processed further.

Several factors are important influences on the process of retrieval. One is the extent of original learning—the more thoroughly material is learned, the eas-

ier it should be to retrieve. As we have seen, the thoroughness of learning is a function of the degree of elaborative processing used to fit material into a cognitive structure, as well as the amount of rehearsal involved. A second factor influencing retrieval appears to be the goals involved in the original learning situation. For example, evidence suggests that consumers have better recall for information when their original purpose is to commit it to memory rather than to use it to choose between various brands.[52] A third major influence on retrieval is the context of the situation. Context is important because it contains cues providing guidance as to which portion of long-term memory should be accessed. For example, assume that we hear the word "ring" mentioned. It is quite possible that this word is stored in several parts of our cognitive structure to represent (1) something a telephone does, (2) a dirt line on a shirt collar, (3) something worn on a finger, or (4) a layer of scum in the bathtub. The context in which the word is used will strongly influence what aspects of memory will be retrieved.

Because concepts in long-term memory are associated or linked with other concepts, retrieval typically involves bringing an interrelated packet of information to consciousness. Usually an environmental event will trigger a search of long-term memory, and elements of the context will influence which node or nodes will be activated. Other concepts that are strongly linked to the activated nodes are themselves likely to be activated. However, concepts that are weakly linked or not linked at all are unlikely to be activated. The result is that when a situation initiates a search of long-term memory, activated concepts as well as material they are linked to are likely to be retrieved and reach conscious attention. These interrelated informational items may then be combined with other material in short-term memory and be modified or expanded upon for use in a variety of ways.

An example can help to explain the interrelationships involved. Assume that while shopping in a department store a customer asks some salesperson about a particular Zenith color television set. He is told that the set is a 19-inch table model of all solid-state design. The salesperson also mentions that the set is mostly hand crafted and it has an excellent warranty. As shown in Figure 14-11, this information represents environmental input into the initial stage of short-term memory. The term "initial" is being used here to indicate the status of memory stores at the start of some event.

As we know, information can only be maintained if it is rehearsed. The arrow from initial short-term memory to expanded short-term memory represents maintenance of a portion of the information through rehearsal. Specifically, information about the size of the set and its warranty has been maintained, while the remaining items have been lost from memory.

On the basis of previous experience, the consumer has retained certain beliefs and knowledge about Zenith television sets. The figure shows that this material is stored in initial long-term memory along with other information that is not relevant to the situation. The dotted line entering this part of the figure indicates that information from the salesperson has activated long-term memory. The solid line leading from this part to expanded short-term memory shows that activation has resulted in three items of information being transferred from long-term memory to the consumer's conscious attention.

The salesperson's comments are also shown by a dotted line as activating the

consumer's inferential and cognitive responses. Thus, even though the salesperson never really stated it, the consumer has inferred that the 19-inch measurement actually represents screen size as measured on the diagonal. We also see that the salesperson's comments have stimulated the consumer to generate a supportive cognitive response—the set is well made. The line leading from initial long-term memory to these conclusions suggests that they are at least partially influenced by what resides in memory as well as by what transpires in the situation at hand. The inference and cognitive response are then transferred to expanded short-term memory to be combined with other material.

We can now see that short-term memory is "where it all comes together." To use a cooking analogy, a pinch of this is added to a measure of that and a dash of something else. Elaborative rehearsal develops a meaningful pattern from material received from the environment, from inferences and cognitive responses, and from the retrieval of information in long-term memory. As shown in Figure 14-11, the result is that long-term memory now holds an expanded and coherent packet of information about the Zenith television set. This is available for immediate use, such as deciding on a purchase, and it is also available in long-term memory for future reference.

ADVERTISING APPLICATIONS

Numerous memory concepts have significant implications for the field of advertising. The following conclusions represent only a sampling of the useful guidelines that are available. While some are drawn directly from our previous discussion, others represent extensions of that material.[53] Of course, in all cases these conclusions are generalizations which will not apply in every specific case.

FIGURE 14-11
A representation of retrieval and the interrelationship between memory elements.

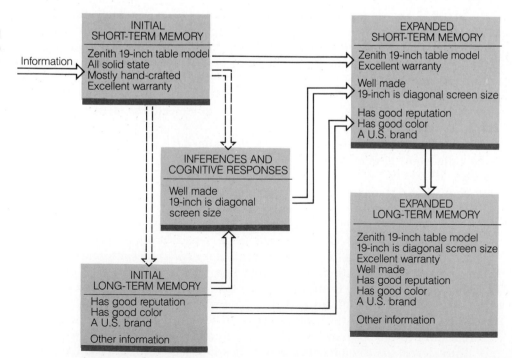

1 *Advertising messages with unique aspects have a greater potential for being remembered.* This occurs because material with unusual aspects is least affected by the interference process of forgetting. This is one factor that motivates advertisers to seek novel approaches and themes for their messages.

2 *The order in which material is presented seems to influence how well it will be retained, with the middle portion being most easily forgotten.* This apparently occurs because the beginning and ending of messages stand out the most and interfere with remembering material in-between (retroactive and proactive inhibition). The implication is that the most important parts of advertising messages should be placed at the beginning or end, or both. Conversely, some direct-mail advertisers bury the price of their merchandise in the middle of a long letter so as to minimize its negative impact on a purchase decision.

3 *Messages that encourage immediate rehearsal of material stimulate its retention.* Maintenance rehearsal keeps material in short-term memory. Elaborative rehearsal will encourage the transfer of material to long-term memory. This is why some radio and television advertisers encourage listeners to repeat a telephone number or address several times, and also attempt to develop some meaningful pattern to the numbers.

4 *The amount of information that can be transferred to long-term memory is a function of the time available for processing.* When recall of a message will be required, approximately five to ten seconds is required to transfer one chunk of information to long-term memory through memorization. The amount of information that an advertiser presents should therefore be tailored to the amount of time available for processing and the way the information can be packaged.[54]

5 *More information can be processed and retained if it is chunked.* Because the capacity of short-term memory is approximately seven items, chunking can be viewed as a way to package a greater amount of information efficiently. This suggests that advertisers should attempt to find appropriate methods of chunking information for consumers so that they can deliver a greater amount of message content in the limited time or space at their disposal.

6 *Memory is cue-dependent, and presentation of relevant cues will stimulate recall.* Apparently, certain cues present during the learning context become associated with the material in memory. Their presentation at a later date facilitates recall of the learned material. This process can be very effectively employed by designing packages and point-of-purchase displays to contain the same cues used in advertisements for the product. For example, a picture of a snow-capped mountain reminds some consumers of Busch beer, and just the word ''blimp'' reminds others of Goodyear.

7 *Material retained in long-term memory can be quite different than the information presented in a learning situation.* This is so because some information will be lost from short-term memory, the consumer may generate inferences and cognitive responses, and material will also be drawn from long-term memory. It is important for advertisers to understand these activities and their potential in any specific situation for influencing the meaning that consumers derive from promotional messages.

8 *Material that is meaningful to the individual is learned more quickly and therefore has a greater chance of being retained than does nonmeaningful material.* Apparently, meaningful material actively involves the individual's mental capacities, and this leads to its greater retention. Therefore, the strong recommendation that has been made for some time is to design advertisements that stimulate consumers' mental involvement, thereby making messages meaningful to them. However, the marketer should develop the specific meaning desired for the message rather than relying on chance for consumers to determine what meaning they will derive from it themselves. Some methods of accomplishing this are listed below. Of course, the specific situation will dictate the degree to which they are appropriate.

a *Visual material.* Information presented as visual content is frequently more memorable than verbal content. This suggests that, where possible, advertisers find ways to "say it with pictures" rather than conveying information with advertising copy.[55]

b *Interactive imagery.* Use of pictures, symbols, and other visual devices that depict how two concepts or properties relate to each other can be a highly effective aid to consumers' memory. Such imagery can be used to link a specific brand to particular needs or to a general product group. A splendid example is using the image of the sun kissing an orange for the Sunkist brand of oranges.

c *Showing mistakes.* During demonstration of mechanical skills, performance, or decision making, it is often useful to show how things should *not* be done, as well as how they should be done. The Midas muffler commercial that depicts a car owner's trauma when attempting to get his muffler replaced at service stations is such an example. An additional technique, which also heightens involvement, is to simulate situations as if the viewer were actually experiencing them.

d *Incomplete messages.* Leaving some messages open-ended so that consumers must become involved to complete them has been found to increase retention.[56] This may be quite overtly done by simply not completing the entire message, as in the advertisement for preventing forest fires cited in the last chapter, or it may be more subtly accomplished by having the announcer ask a question or pose a decision problem for the viewer to answer.

e *Mnemonic techniques.* The art of mnemonics (ne-mon'-ics) involves the development of a pattern for a series of seemingly unrelated facts so that they can be more easily remembered. Therefore, any technique that allows consumers to "see" some pattern for associating otherwise meaningless facts will usually be helpful. When possible, you should provide word associations for telephone numbers. For example, some cities have reserved the telephone number HELP (4357) for their emergency hotlines. A number of private firms have employed a similar technique. In other cases, a melodic pattern can be employed. The singing jingle Sheraton hotels devised to promote consumers' memory of their toll-free reservation number (800-325-3535) is a good illustration. In a similar fashion, a narrative or song can sometimes be devised to promote retention of other information. An excellent example is the jingle using the lyrics of "Two all-beef patties, special sauce, lettuce, cheese, pickles, onions on a sesame-seed bun." The proportion of Americans that remember these product characteristics for the Big Mac hamburger is probably astounding.

Again, it should be stressed that the above list of general guidelines regarding consumers' memory is not by any means exhaustive. In addition, the specific situation must be considered before employing any of them. However, the list is illustrative of the potential benefits of applying such concepts to the design of marketing communications.

MANAGERIAL REFLECTIONS

For our product or service situation . . .

1   What is the potential for using classical conditioning in our advertising?

2   How might an attempt to structure product trials or introductions make effective use of instrumental conditioning?

3   What implications do stimulus generalization and discrimination have for our marketing efforts?

4   What are the major potential uses of the behavior modification perspective?

5   What are the practical implications for the major memory system characteristics summarized in Table 14-3?

6   What are the common characteristics of consumers' semantic memory structure for our offerings?

7   What types of inferential beliefs are consumers likely to form from our marketing communications?

DISCUSSION TOPICS

1   What is learning? Briefly indicate its importance to understanding consumer behavior.

2   What method of learning (classical conditioning, instrumental conditioning, or cognitive) seems best able to explain (*a*) smoking cigarettes, (*b*) purchasing an air conditioner primarily for reducing the humidity in a hot, humid room, and (*c*) writing Scotch tape on a shopping list instead of cellophane tape?

3   What are stimulus generalization and discrimination learning, and how are they important to the marketer?

4   Draw a learning curve, and discuss its implications for repeating a given advertising message to consumers.

5   Add a typical retention curve to the end of the learning curve drawn for question 4. Discuss the implications of these curves for advertisers.

6   Design examples of how a marketer could employ the following behavior modification elements: (*a*) shaping, (*b*) modeling, and (*c*) classical conditioning.

7   Suggest some circumstances in which an advertiser might be more interested

in using the recall method for measuring retention rather than the recognition method. Do the same for the recognition method as opposed to the recall method.

8   Officials of the federal government once decided that the United States would "go metric." They became concerned with how to promote learning of the metric system among the citizenry. Suggest methods and programs to assist in accomplishing this goal.

9   Compare and contrast the sensory memory, short-term memory, and long-term memory systems. Indicate the relevance of each to advertising strategies.

10   Cite some suggestions you would give to advertisers who were concerned with consumers remembering the following:

   a   The instructions to start a rotary lawn mower safely. One should make sure that (1) the deflector chute or grass bag is attached, (2) no objects or debris are next to the mower, (3) the left foot is placed on the mower, and (4) the right foot is placed well back.

   b   A brand name for earth-moving equipment, one which contractors will remember and associate with their need for such equipment.

   c   How to pronounce the airline name Alitalia so that they will not be reluctant to ask for it on their trips to Europe.

11   Choose a brand name for a particular product. Develop *your* semantic network (as in Figure 14-10) for this brand. Be sure to include where the specific brand fits into a hierarchical structure of the product class and where it fits into the set of alternative brands.

PROJECTS

1   Select a product and develop three advertising or product introduction or trial scenarios that would make use of learning or memory principles discussed in the chapter. Be specific in discussing how the particular principles are being applied.

2   Develop a number of environmental or ecological design suggestions for a department store manager to use to encourage shopping and purchase behavior in the store.

3   Select three willing participants and choose a brand that is familiar to all three. Using the free-association technique (you mention key words and subject relates what comes to his or her mind) attempt to discover the semantic network for this brand.

NOTES

[1] Based on Cynthia Kooi, "War Toy Invasion Grows Despite Boycott," *Advertising Age*, March 3, 1986, p. 44.
[2] Much of this section is based on John Dollard and Neal Miller, *Personality and Psychotherapy*, McGraw-Hill, New York, 1950, pp. 25–47.
[3] Winfred F. Hill, *Learning: A Survey of Psychological Interpretations*, Chandler, San Francisco, 1963, p. 225.
[4] Hill, *Learning*, pp. 100–112.

5 Leonard Krasner, "Studies of the Conditioning of Verbal Behavior," *Psychological Bulletin,* **55**:148–170, 1958.

6 See Ernest R. Hilgard and Gordon H. Bower, *Theories of Learning,* 3d ed., Appleton-Century-Crofts, New York, 1966, for a comprehensive review of these theories.

7 The two schools of thought are referred to as the reinforcement and contiguity advocates. See Hill, *Learning,* pp. 31–89, for a review of their differences and many similarities.

8 Ivan Pavlov, *Conditioned Reflexes. An Investigation of the Psychological Activity of the Cerebral Cortex,* edited and translated by G. V. Anrep, Oxford University Press, London, 1927.

9 Clark L. Hull, *Principles of Behavior,* Appleton-Century-Crofts, New York, 1943, p. 94.

10 See Francis K. McSweeney and Calvin Bierley, "Recent Developments in Classical Conditioning," *Journal of Consumer Research,* **11**:619–631, September 1984.

11 B. F. Skinner, *The Behavior of Organisms: An Experimental Analysis,* Appleton-Century-Crofts, New York, 1938.

12 Wolfgang Kohler, *The Mentality of Apes,* Harcourt, Brace & World, New York, 1925.

13 See Alan R. Andreasen and Peter G. Durkson, "Market Learning of New Residents," *Journal of Marketing Research,* **5**:166–176, May 1968.

14 See Gerald J. Gorn, "The Effects of Music in Advertising On Choice Behavior: A Classical Conditioning Approach," *Journal of Marketing,* **46**:94–101, Winter 1982; and Calvin Bierley, Francis K. McSweeney, and Renee Vannieuwkerk, "Classical Conditioning of Preferences for Stimuli," *Journal of Consumer Research,* **12**:316–323, December 1985.

15 See Chris T. Allen and Thomas J. Madden, "A Closer Look at Classical Conditioning," *Journal of Consumer Research,* **12**:301–315, December 1985.

16 See Walter R. Nord and J. Paul Peter, "A Behavior Modification Perspective on Marketing," *Journal of Marketing,* **44**:36–47, Spring 1980; Michael L. Rothschild and William C. Gaidis, "Behavioral Learning Theory: Its Relevance to Marketing and Promotions," *Journal of Marketing,* **45**:70–78, Spring 1981; and J. Paul Peter and Walter R. Nord, "A Clarification and Extension of Operant Conditioning Principles in Marketing," *Journal of Marketing,* **46**:102–107, Summer 1982, upon which much of this discussion is based.

17 J. Ronald Carey et al., "A Test of Positive Reinforcement of Customers," *Journal of Marketing,* **40**:98–100, October 1976.

18 See Rom J. Markin and Chem L. Narayana, "Behavior Control: Are Consumers Beyond Freedom and Dignity?" in Beverlee B. Anderson (ed.), *Advances in Consumer Research,* vol. 3, Association for Consumer Research, Ann Arbor, Mich., 1976, p. 225.

19 Ronald E. Milliman, "Using Background Music to Affect the Behavior of Supermarket Shoppers," *Journal of Marketing,* **46**:86–91, Summer 1982.

20 Nord and Peter, "A Behavior Modification Perspective."

21 Bernard Berelson and Gary A. Steiner, *Human Behavior: An Inventory of Scientific Findings.* Harcourt, Brace & World, New York, 1964, pp. 138–139.

22 C. I. Hovland, "The Generalization of Conditioned Responses: I," *Journal of General Psychology,* **17**:125–148, 1937.

23 See Hubert A. Zielske, "The Remembering and Forgetting of Advertising," *Journal of Marketing,* **23**:239–243, January 1959; and Julian L. Simon and Johan Arndt, "The Shape of the Advertising Response Function," *Journal of Advertising Research,* **20**:11–28, August 1980.

24 Michael L. Ray, Alan G. Sawyer, and Edward C. Strong, "Frequency Effects Revisited," *Journal of Advertising Research,* **11**:14–20, February 1971.

25 See Herbert Krugman, "What Makes Advertising Effective?" *Harvard Business Review,* **53**:96–103, March–April 1975; and Howard Kamin, "Advertising Reach and Frequency," *Journal of Advertising Research,* **18**:21–25, February 1978.

26 See Bobby Calder and Brian Sternthal, "Television Commercial Wearout: An Information Processing Perspective," *Journal of Marketing Research,* **17**:173–186, May 1980; and George E. Belch, "The Effects of Television Commercial Repetition on Cognitive Response and Message Acceptance," *Journal of Consumer Research,* **9**:56–65, June 1982.

27 See Joel Saegert and Robert Young, "Comparison of Effects of Repetition and Levels of Processing in Memory for Advertisements," in Andrew Mitchell (ed.), *Advances in Consumer Research,* vol. 9, Association for Consumer Research, Ann Arbor, Mich., 1982, pp. 431–434.

28 See Alan G. Sawyer, "Repetition and Affect: Recent Empirical and Theoretical Developments," in

Arch Woodside, Jagdish Sheth, and Peter Bennett (eds.), *Consumer and Industrial Buyer Behavior,* North-Holland, New York, 1977, pp. 229–242; and Belch, "Effects of Television Commercial Repetition."

[29] See Edward C. Strong, "The Use of Field Experimental Observations in Estimating Advertising Recall," *Journal of Marketing Research,* **11**:369–378, November 1974, for one such investigation.

[30] Howard H. Kendler, *Basic Psychology: Brief Version,* W. A. Benjamin, Menlo Park, Calif., 1977, p. 448.

[31] Zielske, "Forgetting of Advertising."

[32] Leo Bogart and Charles Lehman, "What Makes A Brand Name Familiar?" *Journal of Marketing Research,* **10**:17, February 1973.

[33] See James Bettman, *An Information Processing Theory of Consumer Choice,* Addison-Wesley, Reading, Mass., 1979, pp. 139–143.

[34] Bettman, *An Information Processing Theory.*

[35] See George A. Miller, "The Magical Number Seven, Plus or Minus Two: Some Limits on Our Capacity for Processing Information," *Psychological Review,* **63**:81–97, 1956.

[36] Peter H. Lindsay and Donald A. Norman, *Human Information Processing: An Introduction to Psychology,* 2d ed. Academic Press, New York, 1977, p. 319.

[37] See Joel Saegert, "A Demonstration of Levels-of-Processing Theory in Memory for Advertisements," in William L. Wilkie (ed.), *Advances in Consumer Research,* vol. 6, Association for Consumer Research, Ann Arbor, Mich., pp. 82–84; Leonard N. Reid and Lawrence C. Soley, "Levels-of-Processing in Memory and the Recall and Recognition of Television Commercials," in James H. Leigh and Claude R. Martin, Jr. (eds.), *Current Issues and Research in Advertising, 1980,* The University of Michigan, Ann Arbor, Mich., 1980, pp. 135–145; and Joel Saegert, "Comparison of Effects of Repetition and Levels of Processing in Memory for Advertisements," in Andrew Mitchell (ed.), *Advances in Consumer Research,* vol. 9, Association for Consumer Research, Ann Arbor, Mich., 1982, pp. 431–434.

[38] See Allan G. Reynolds and Paul W. Flagg, *Cognitive Psychology,* Winthrop Publishers, Cambridge, Mass., 1977, pp. 144–147.

[39] Reynolds and Flagg, *Cognitive Psychology,* pp. 139–144, 163–170.

[40] See R. P. Abelson, "Psychological Status of the Script Concept," *American Psychologist,* **36**:715–729, 1981.

[41] See Lorne Bozinoff, "A Script Theoretic Approach of Information Processing: An Energy Conservation Application," in Andrew Mitchell (ed.), *Advances in Consumer Research,* vol. 9, Association for Consumer Research, Ann Arbor, Mich., 1982, pp. 481–486, for an elaboration and some examples.

[42] Different methods of storing information do not necessarily require different storage registers. Rather, material processed in different ways (visual, verbal, etc.) may just be represented in different ways in long-term memory. See, for example, Zenon W. Pylyshyn, "What the Mind's Eye Tells the Mind's Brain: A Critique of Mental Imagery," *Psychological Bulletin,* **80**:1–24, July 1973; and John R. Anderson and Gordon H. Bower, *Human Associative Memory,* Winston, Washington, D.C., 1973.

[43] See Allan Paivio, *Imagery and Verbal Processing,* Holt, New York, 1971.

[44] For more information on the effects of visual information see Terry Childers and Michael Houston, "Conditions for a Picture-Superiority Effect on Consumer Memory," *Journal of Consumer Research,* **11**:643–654, September 1984; Terry Childers, Susan Heckler, and Michael Houston, "Memory for the Visual and Verbal Components of Print Advertisements," *Psychology & Marketing,* **3**:137–150, Fall 1986; Meryl Gardner and Michael Houston, "The Effect of Verbal and Visual Components of Retail Communications," *Journal of Retailing,* **62**:64–78, Spring 1986; and Ruth Smith, Michael Houston, and Terry Childers, "The Effects of Schematic Memory on Imaginal Information Processing: An Empirical Assessment," *Psychology & Marketing,* **2**:13–29, Spring 1985.

[45] See, for example, Kathy A. Lutz and Richard J. Lutz, "Imagery-Eliciting Strategies: Review and Implications of Research," in H. Keith Hunt (ed.), *Advances in Consumer Research,* vol. 5, Association for Consumer Research, Ann Arbor, Mich., 1978, pp. 611–620; Larry Percy, "Psycholinguistic Guidelines for Advertising Copy," in Andrew Mitchell (ed.), *Advances in Consumer Research,* vol. 9, Association for Consumer Research, Ann Arbor, Mich., 1982, pp. 107–111; and Morris B. Holbrook and William L. Moore, "Feature Interactions in Consumer Judgments of Verbal Versus Pictorial Presentations, *Journal of Consumer Research,* **8**:103–111, June 1981.

[46] Kathy A. Lutz and Richard J. Lutz, "Effects of Interactive Imagery on Learning: Applications to Advertising," *Journal of Applied Psychology,* **62**:493–498, 1977.

[47] See Reynolds and Flagg, *Cognitive Psychology,* pp. 163–170.

[48] Lyle E. Bourne Jr., Roger L. Dominowski, and Elizabeth F. Loftus, *Cognitive Processes,* Prentice-Hall, Englewood Cliffs, N.J., 1979, pp. 10–11.

[49] See Andrew A. Mitchell, "Models of Memory: Implications for Measuring Knowledge Structures," in Andrew A. Mitchell (ed.), *Advances in Consumer Research,* vol. 9, Association for Consumer Research, Ann Arbor, Mich., 1982, pp. 45–51.

[50] See Jerry C. Olson, "Inferential Belief Formation in the Cue Utilization Process," in H. Keith Hunt (ed.), *Advances in Consumer Research,* vol. 5, Association for Consumer Research, Ann Arbor, Mich., 1978, pp. 706–713; and Philip A. Dover, "Inferential Belief Formation: An Overlooked Concept in Consumer Behavior Research," in Andrew Mitchell (ed.), *Advances in Consumer Research,* vol. 9, Association for Consumer Research, Ann Arbor, Mich., 1982, pp. 187–189.

[51] Peter L. Wright, "The Cognitive Processes Mediating Acceptance of Advertising," *Journal of Marketing Research,* **10**:53–62, February 1973.

[52] See Gabriel Biehal and Dipanker Chakravarti, "Information-Presentation Format and Learning Goals as Determinants of Consumers' Memory Retrieval and Choice Processes," *Journal of Consumer Research,* **8**:431–441, March 1982.

[53] For additional guidelines see Steuart Henderson Britt, "How Advertising Can Use Psychology's Rules of Learning," *Printer's Ink,* **252**:74+, September 1955; and Steuart Henderson Britt, "Applying Learning Principles to Marketing," *MSU Business Topics,* **23**:5–12, Spring 1975.

[54] James R. Bettman, "Memory Factors in Consumer Choice: A Review," *Journal of Marketing,* **43**:37–53, Spring 1979.

[55] See John R. Rossiter, "Visual Imagery: Applications to Advertising," in Andrew Mitchell (ed.), *Advances in Consumer Research,* vol. 9, Association for Consumer Research, Ann Arbor, Mich., 1982, pp. 101–106.

[56] See, for example, James T. Heimbach and Jacob Jacoby, "The Zeigarnik Effect in Advertising," in M. Venkatesan (ed.), *Proceedings of the Third Annual Conference,* Association for Consumer Research, College Park, M.D., 1972, pp. 746–757.

PERSONALITY AND SELF-CONCEPT

LEARNING OBJECTIVES
After studying this chapter, you should understand . . .

■   The major theories of personality and their potential for understanding consumers

■   Limitations of previous personality studies in the consumer-behavior field and their implications for future research

■   The nature and role of psychographic research for understanding consumer behavior

■   The nature of self-concept theory including how the self-concept develops

■   The major ways that self-concept research can improve our understanding of consumer behavior and marketing

Who rides a motorcycle? Are these people alike and are they all attracted to their bikes for the same reasons? Such questions are important to those involved in producing and marketing motorcycles to the American public. At least some people in the industry believe that standard research techniques such as surveys and focus groups do not provide sufficient answers to such questions. This led one advertising executive in Los Angeles to go undercover. Basically she borrowed a technique from anthropologists: she actually became part of the group and directly inter-acted with them to learn characteristics which might explain their behavior and tastes. To do this she hung around a local café frequented by many motorcyclists.

The project generated very interesting findings. For example, cyclists appear to come from quite diverse backgrounds, including medical and accounting professions as well as from the more stereotyped manual-labor crowd. However, further probing also revealed that this diverse mixture of people seems to fall into only two major groups, or segments, which are distinguished by their personality characteristics. One group, called the Outer-Directed, comprises about two-thirds of the market. They can be characterized as achievement-oriented, and they also tend to emulate others with whom they identify in some manner. Outer-directed cyclists were found to be mainly interested in so-called "touring bikes" because these machines are perceived as projecting images of success, strength, and virility to others. On the other hand, the Inner-Directed segment comprises about one-third of the market. These people are concerned with living life to the max. They seek a great deal of pleasure from the riding experience. Therefore, they tend to evaluate motorcycles according to how well the machines contribute to the

15

cycling experience; the inner-directed group is less interested in projecting some type of image to others. These are the cyclists who lean forward while riding, in an intense and focused manner.

On the basis of findings regarding these and other distinguishing personality characteristics, the advertising agency was able to develop unique appeals, directed at each of the two groups, for Kawasaki motorcycles.[1]

This example reflects a belief that most people seem to share: the behavior of an individual is organized into a coherent pattern. That is, although a person's behavior changes somewhat to deal with many different circumstances, there is a tendency to behave in a consistent manner throughout various situations. This view emphasizes the *totality* of a person's makeup rather than focusing on specific actions that he or she will take in any particular instance.

Personality and self-concept are two psychological notions that have been used by those studying consumer behavior to account for the organized totality of the consumer's makeup. Our purpose in studying these variables is to determine their usefulness in understanding consumers' basic orientations and their brand and store preferences, media usage patterns, susceptibility to persuasion, and other facets of consumer behavior. The hope is that knowledge of consumers' personalities and self-concepts will allow us to appreciate the underlying consistency or pattern reflected in their product choices and other behavior.

This chapter begins with a fuller characterization of the term personality and a short description of some methods used to measure it. Next, several of the many theories that have been offered to explain the concept are reviewed briefly. One concept that has seen extensive marketing application is then assessed in terms of its usefulness in predicting and understanding consumer behavior. After relating personality theory to psychographics and its consumer-behavior relevance, attention then turns to the topic of consumers' self-concept. Finally, the importance of self-concept to understanding the motivations and behavior of consumers is addressed.

PERSONALITY THEORIES AND APPLICATIONS

The study of personality and its relationship to human behavior can be traced back to the earliest writings of the Europeans, Greeks, Chinese, and Egyptians. Also, people have always made judgments about the personalities of others in terms of the degree to which they are aggressive, adventuresome, sociable, charismatic, and so on. Despite this long history of interest, and even though most of us believe that we have an intuitive grasp of what constitutes personality, behavioral scientists have been unable to agree on a precise definition of the concept. However, it has been noted that there are three major aspects of similarity among the various definitions:

1 They focus on unique characteristics that account for differences between individuals rather than on how people are alike.

2 They stress the consistency of an individual's *dispositions* rather than changes in his or her actual behavior across different situations.

3 Each definition includes a behavioral tendency to reflect how an individual's personality will tend to influence his or her actions and reactions to environmental situations.[2]

Most theories of personality also stress how it is integrative in nature, encompassing various processes that interact with each other. That is, among other factors, personality is usually considered to include the interactions of an individual's moods, values, attitudes, motives, and habitual methods of responding to situations.

Within this general framework, a number of methods for measuring personality have evolved, as have a variety of alternative theories of the exact nature of the concept. We will first look briefly at the general methods of measurement, and then we will provide a short review of several major personality theories.

MEASURING PERSONALITY

It should be clear from the above discussion that personality is not a concept that has a single characteristic. Instead, it is multidimensional in nature, with many interacting elements. Therefore, measurement methods have to account in some way for this variety, rather than focusing solely on only one aspect of the complex whole. Four general approaches to measurement that have had popularity and can accommodate the multidimensional nature of personality are rating methods, situational tests, projective techniques, and inventory schemes.

Rating Methods Typically, the rating method involves one or more evaluators assessing predetermined personality characteristics of a subject on a number of standardized rating scales. In some cases, the basis of the evaluation is a somewhat informal interview with the subject. In other cases, observation of the subject's behavior is used in place of an interview. This observation may be accomplished in a setting designed for the purpose, or it may take place in a portion of the subject's everyday environment. Of course, the type of scale employed for evaluation (five point versus six point, definitions of each category provided versus no definitions provided, and so on), the personality characteristics chosen for study, and the skills of evaluators can all have an influence on final results.

Situational Tests With this technique, a situation is devised that closely resembles a typical real-life situation. Usually, several people are allowed to interact with each other in a group setting. A topic or scenario is provided to them as a focus of discussion, and the behaviors of the subjects are observed and measured. This may take the form of tabulating the frequency of occurrence for specific activities (such as aggression, submissiveness) or rating the intensity of certain

behaviors on standard scales. A special form of situation technique is the stress test which places an individual in a pressure-type situation; his methods of acting in the situation are assessed to reveal aspects of his personality.

Projective Techniques   The objective behind development of most projective methods is to uncover the basic organization of an individual's personality, as well as his underlying conflicts and motives. Typically, the individual is presented with a vague visual image and is asked to explain it or relate any meaning it has to him. The assumption is that because the stimulus itself is vague, the individual is actually projecting his own interpretations onto it, and in the process he reveals aspects of his own personality. One popular type of projective technique is called the *Rorschach test* which consists of ten inkblots similar to the one shown in Figure 15-1, but varying in color, shape, and shading. Another frequently used projective technique is the *Thematic Apperception Test* (TAT) which typically involves presentation of twenty pictures showing different vague situations. The subject is asked to develop a story that is based on each picture. The stories are assessed by a trained evaluator for basic interpretations the individual appears to relate about the pictures and, therefore, about himself.

Inventory Schemes   A potential limitation of rating methods, situational tests, and projective techniques is subjective scoring. That is, the measurement of an individual's personality is largely dependent upon the evaluator's subjective interpretation of the information obtained. In addition, these methods require a considerable amount of time and effort to set up, administer, and evaluate. The

FIGURE 15-1
A Rorschach-type inkblot.

personality inventory is designed to minimize these potential problems by exposing subjects to a large number of standardized questions with prespecified answer options from which they can select. Usually, the inventory is in written form, and a subject responds to the instrument much in the same way as he would to an "objective" test. For example, one popular inventory, the Minnesota Multiphasic Personality Inventory (MMPI), consists of 550 statements such as "I like to try new things." If the subject feels a statement describes her, she will mark the "true" answer option. "False" and "cannot say" options are also available.

The same personality characteristics are addressed through a variety of different statements contained in such inventories. This minimizes the danger of a subject being able to manipulate the results of her or his testing, and enables one to assess personality aspects from different perspectives. As a consequence, the number of items included in the inventory is much larger than the number of personality dimensions being measured. For example, the MMPI's 550 statements assesses ten personality characteristics.

Scoring of personality inventories is standardized and based on norms which have been established from previous testings of large numbers of individuals. Because of their ease of administration and the availability of standardized scoring, the inventory method has been the most popular approach to personality measurement in the field of consumer behavior. Inventories that have been commonly employed by consumer-behavior researchers include the Edwards Personal Preference Schedule, Gordon Personal Profile, and the California Personality Inventory. We now turn our attention to several of the major concepts of personality that have enjoyed considerable popularity.[3]

SOME MAJOR PERSONALITY THEORIES

It certainly is not possible in the scope of this text to review all major concepts of personality. It should also be appreciated that to fully characterize even a few of the major theories would require a great deal of space. Therefore, the following paragraphs are offered as brief "thumb-nail" sketches of only some of the important aspects of several major personality theories.

Psychoanalytic Personality Theory   Freud, the father of psychoanalytic theory, proposed that every individual's personality is the product of a struggle among three interacting forces—the id, the ego, and the superego. According to Freud, the *id* is the source of strong inborn drives and urges such as aggression and sex. The id operates on what is called the *pleasure principle,* that is, it acts to avoid tension and seeks immediate pleasure. However, it tends to operate at a very subjective and unconscious level and is not fully capable of dealing with objective reality. Also, many of its impulses are not acceptable to the values of organized society. For example, when an individual is hot and thirsty his id would urge him to grab something cold to drink. There would be no concern about how the drink was acquired or whether it belonged to someone else.

The *ego* comes into being because of the limitations of the id in dealing with the real world. Through learning and experience, the ego develops the individual's capabilities of realistic thinking and ability to deal appropriately with his environment. It operates on what is called the *reality principle,* which is capable of

postponing the release of tension until that time when it will be effectively directed at coping with the external environment. To illustrate, although the hungry individual's id would encourage him to just take food away from his friend, the ego might reason that asking for the food may take longer but may also result in getting a greater portion. Because it serves in this way as the organized focal point for effective action in the environment, the ego is said to be the executive of the personality.

The *superego* is the third component of personality. It constitutes the moral part of the individual's psychic structure through internalizing the values of society. It represents the ideal by defining what is right and good, and it influences the individual to strive for perfection. Therefore, it acts to control basic strivings of the id which could disrupt the social system and influences the ego to strive for socially approved goals rather than purely realistic ones. As an example, people often compliment their friends on their taste in selecting new clothes or other products. The ego might influence such behavior, because it is instrumental in maintaining a friendship. However, the superego would also have an influence, because the activity is something that our society has accepted as proper and good behavior. This may be happening while the id is actually fostering feelings of jealousy. However, because these feelings will not be very effective for dealing with the environment, the ego will act to suppress them.

According to Freud, the individual's total personality develops and is defined by the relationships among the id, ego, and superego. The ego serves to administer the interaction between moral standards of the superego and the often socially unacceptable desires and attempted expressions of the id. This usually results in realistic compromises between very basic strivings and accepted behavior. Many of these compromises are said to be accomplished at the unconscious level. In fact, Freudian psychology argues that a vast portion of our behavior is unconsciously motivated or affected by subconscious factors that only occasionally reach the individual's conscious level of awareness. Therefore, to fully understand the causes of behavior and the interactions of personality, one must appreciate what factors are influencing the consumer at unconscious and subconscious levels.

Although the ego is capable of resolving many of the conflicts that arise between the three personality components, on some occasions no resolution is achieved, and the individual is placed under considerable tension. It is usually at this time that defense mechanisms are enacted to deal with the tension. *Defense mechanisms* can be thought of as unconsciously determined techniques for avoiding or escaping from high levels of tension brought about by unresolved conflict between components of the personality.

Many defense mechanisms have been characterized, but only a few will be described here to give an impression of their general nature. One very basic form is called *repression*. Basically this mechanism allows the individual to forget aspects of the conflicting situation so that the conflict is no longer apparent. For example, a consumer might be in conflict about going to sporting events that are violent but also entertaining. If the ego cannot reach some sort of compromise, it is possible that the consumer may diminish and forget the violent aspects of these sports. In this way, he has avoided the conflict and can continue to watch the events.

Projection is the term used to describe the defense mechanism, in which feelings generated by the individual's id or superego are ascribed by her to another person or group. In this way, she escapes the tension generated from realizing that the feelings are her own. For example, a person's disdain for how others are constantly purchasing various products and displaying them for others to see may actually be a mask for her own desire to engage in the same behavior.

In *identification,* the individual unconsciously imitates the behavior of another person whom he believes has successfully handled the conflict with which he is currently dealing.

Finally, the last defense mechanism to be mentioned here is *reaction formation,* in which unconscious feelings held toward others are consciously expressed as opposites. For example, a consumer with hostile feelings toward a friend might actually purchase many gifts for this person.

APPLICATIONS OF PSYCHOANALYTIC THEORY Marketers have sometimes used Freudian psychoanalytic theory as a basis for attempts at influencing consumers. One such application is the appeal to fantasy, which plays an important role in the operation of the pleasure principle of the id. Fantasy has been used in promotions for various products including perfume (Chanel No. 5), men's cologne (Old Spice), and jeans (Levi's).

In another area of application, Freudian proponents suggest that various appeals can assist in resolving the conflict which can develop between the id, ego, and superego in some purchase situations. Appeals directed to the id, but disguised by a veiled appeal to the superego, are said to result in a situation that can be satisfactorily resolved by the ego. In this way, the ego directs behavior that is also acceptable to the id and superego. The idea has been translated into advertising themes such as those found for the Playtex Free Spirit bra. Here, a young woman, shown above the waist wearing only a bra, is pictured in the intimate company of a young man. However, rings that appear to be wedding bands are prominently displayed on the left hand of both models to satisfy moral concerns of the superego. The ego then reasons that sex is socially acceptable behavior under conditions of marriage, and therefore the sexual innuendo of the ad is acceptable. In advertising, this approach is sometimes referred to as the *triple appeal,* because the id is sexually stimulated and allowed to engage in fantasy while the moral requirements of the superego are placated. The ego arbitrates the acceptability of these two forms of expression among both the id and superego.

Marketers have made many other uses of sexual and aggressive symbols that appeal to the id while avoiding those that are directly offensive to the superego. For example, many people have argued that the shape of containers for various personal-care products (such as Macho cologne for men) are clearly phallic. Also, the bottles for Jóvan men's and women's cologne have quite discernible male and female shapes.

Although most people believe that Freudian applications to marketing are restricted to sex, we have already shown that there are many themes which are not. Wish fulfillment, fantasy, aggression, and escape from life's pressures are Freudian themes upon which some appeals are based. For example, a suburban real estate company might advertise to city dwellers with the theme, ''Escape to country living.'' Also, sporting events are often promoted by showing aggression

or violent scenes. Previews for racing events and boxing matches as well as the ''agony of defeat'' befalling a ski jumper in the introduction to *The Wide World of Sports* are excellent illustrations. In other cases, promotions for Bermuda, Las Vegas, the Bahamas, and other vacation resorts frequently employ themes stressing escape, freedom, and a chance to ''let it all hang out.'' Figure 15-2 presents yet another example of a fantasy appeal.

Finally, an understanding of the operation of defense mechanisms can assist the marketer in developing marketing and promotional strategies. For example, knowledge that a group of consumers have repressed aspects of a conflicting situation would alert the marketer that such topics should probably not be addressed in a promotional message. Because the topics have been repressed, consumers would not be aware of the issues. Consequently, a promotion raising such issues would have little meaning to these consumers. In a similar vein, knowing that a group of consumers have employed the defense mechanism of identification can also be of considerable potential benefit. For example, many men and women experience conflict arising from hostile feelings they hold toward their spouses, for whom they believe they should have strong affection. A well-

FIGURE 15-2
A fantasy appeal.
Courtesy of the Mercury Outboard
Division of the Brunswick Company.

known celebrity who has had marital problems and has publicly reconciled with his or her spouse could therefore be a source of strong identification for these people. Use of such a person to promote and endorse various products could be even more effective than the use of other spokespeople.

Social Theories Among those who rejected Freud's id-based theory of personality, some reasoned that the individual develops a personality through numerous attempts to deal with others in a social setting. These social theorists, sometimes collectively called the neo-Freudian school, viewed individuals as striving to overcome feelings of inferiority and searching for ways to obtain love, security, and brotherhood. Their argument minimized the role of id-based instincts that Freud emphasized. Instead, they stressed that childhood experiences in relating to others produce feelings of inferiority, insecurity, and lack of love. These feelings motivate individuals to perfect themselves and also to develop methods to cope with anxieties produced by such feelings of inferiority.

The first major consumer-behavior study using a neo-Freudian approach was based on the theoretical scheme of Karen Horney.[4] Horney identified ten major needs which are acquired as a consequence of individuals attempting to find solutions to their problems in developing a personality and dealing with others in a social environment. These ten needs were then classified into three major orientations which describe general strategies for relating to others:

1 *Compliant orientation*. Those who move toward people and stress the need for love, approval, and affection. These individuals tend to exhibit large amounts of empathy and humility, and are unselfish.

2 *Aggressive orientation*. Those who move against people and stress the need for power, strength, and the ability to manipulate others.

3 *Detached orientation*. Those who move away from people. These individuals stress the need for independence, freedom, and self-reliance in their dealings with others. An important consideration is that no strong emotional ties develop between themselves and others.

A CAD (Compliant, Agressive, Detached) instrument was developed to measure people's interpersonal orientations within a consumer context. Results of the study indicated that different products and brands were used by individuals having different personality types. For example, it was found that "compliant" types prefer known brand names and use more mouthwash and toilet soaps; "aggressive" types prefer to use razors instead of electric shavers, use more cologne and after-shave lotions, and purchase Old Spice and Van Heusen shirts; and "detached" types appear to have the least awareness of brands. Although such findings are interesting, social personality theories have found little application in the consumer-behavior area. Additional research is necessary to generate a wider base of findings from which to develop marketing strategies.

Stimulus-Response Theories Stimulus-response personality theories are grounded on contributions from notable learning theorists such as Pavlov, Skinner, and Hull. Although there are differences among these theorists there is agreement that

personality results from habitual responses to specific and generalized cues. Theorists believe that complex behavior patterns, attitudes, and so on, are learned from stimulus-response situations that are continually reinforced, either positively or negatively. The personality, therefore, is created and changed by reinforcement of these stimulus-response associations. However, because of the lack of measuring instruments to study these propositions critically, few if any consumer-behavior studies have been conducted relating stimulus-response concepts of personality to purchase behavior.

Trait and Factor Theories   The most popular personality concepts used to explain the behavior of consumers have been trait and factor theories. The concept of a *trait* is based upon three assumptions or propositions: (1) individuals possess relatively stable behavioral tendencies, (2) people differ in the degree to which they possess these tendencies, and (3) when identified and measured, these relative differences between individuals are useful in characterizing their personalities. Therefore, we see that traits are general and are relatively stable personality characteristics which influence tendencies to behave.

Factor theories are based on the quantitative technique of *factor analysis,* which explores the interrelationship between various personality measures across a large number of individuals. Basically, the underlying logic is that if responses to certain personality-inventory items are correlated across many different testing situations, then these responses are probably each related to some underlying personality characteristic or trait. If the measures are highly correlated with each other, they probably tend to measure the same dimension of the trait, and if their correlation is lower, they probably reflect somewhat different aspects of the same trait. Therefore, a factor can be viewed as a general-level variable that is based on a combination of test items and is used to identify personality traits.

Various traits or factors are identified when subgroups of measures form. That is, factors emerge when certain measures show higher levels of correlation within themselves but quite low degrees of correlation across other subgroups of items. The task of the researcher is to use factor analysis to assist in identifying these interrelated groups of variables. The actual number of factors that will be identified depends on how well the variables in different subgroups correlate among themselves. Once factors are identified, each one can be quantified with a factor score—a weighted combination of the measures that have correlated together to identify the factor.

A second task is to label or describe the factors that have been identified. This is accomplished by interpreting the factor loadings—correlations between the original measures and the factor score that is based on these measures. For example, consider a factor score that had strong loadings (correlations) with the personality measures of despondency, moodiness, and pessimism. The researcher might use this information to label the factor as "depression." It is important to note that even though the naming of factors is guided by reference to the factor loadings, a considerable amount of subjective interpretation is still involved in this process.

After doing years of careful research, some theorists have proposed that most personalities can actually be described by a small number of factors. In essence, this view is that factor analysis of the results of many test situations has identified core personality traits.[5] Therefore, results of an individual's testing using a personality inventory enables the researcher to compare the individual's raw score and factor scores to the results of other subjects. This assists in the interpretation of the individual's personality.

APPLICATIONS OF TRAIT AND FACTOR THEORIES   In terms of their use in studying consumers, the advantage of trait and factor theories is that they are based on a number of readily available and standardized personality inventories and evaluative techniques. Using these techniques, a large number of researchers have tried to find a relationship between personality and the behavior of consumers. These attempts have met with various degrees of success. Several representative studies are reviewed below to give the reader some appreciation of the nature of research in this area.

One researcher, using the Edwards Personal Preference Schedule (EPPS), collected data from almost 9000 consumer panel participants.[6] His results indicate a positive relationship between cigarette smoking and the traits of sex dominance, aggression, and achievement needs among males. He also found personality differences between smokers of filter and nonfilter cigarettes and among readers' preferences for certain magazines. However, a later reanalysis of this data suggested that personality traits accounted for only a small number of the differences among these groups.[7]

Another study using the Gordon Personal Profile found associations between certain personality traits and use of alcoholic beverages, automobiles, chewing gum, mouthwash, and other products.[8] Unfortunately, in this as in many other studies, the associations were not very strong.

In what has now become a classic study, the EPPS was employed to determine if personality differences could be found between Ford and Chevrolet owners. Findings were that measurable personality differences were of little value in predicting whether a consumer would own a Ford or a Chevrolet.[9] Many studies have reexamined this research, and the basic conclusion appears to be that personality traits are not very helpful in predicting consumers' brand choice for automobiles. However, some evidence indicates that they may be useful in predicting preferences for the type of automobile (sedan versus convertible, for instance).[10]

Other more recent studies have attempted to relate personality differences to innovativeness and to other consumer characteristics. As in previous cases, these studies have met with varying degrees of success.[11]

After reviewing more than 200 personality studies that have been conducted in consumer research, Kassarjian concluded that the results can be described by a single word, "equivocal."[12] Although a few studies indicate a strong relationship between personality and aspects of consumer behavior, some studies indicate no relationship, and the vast majority of studies suggest that if a relationship does exist, it is so weak that it is of little practical value to the marketer. Yet, experts still contend that personality is a critical variable in influencing consumers' purchasing processes. They argue that the lackluster performance of previous studies is due to inappropriate research methods and an inadequate understanding of the role of personality in influencing consumers. Some of these criticisms are reviewed below to provide guidelines for evaluating future personality studies:

1   Personality tests have frequently been inappropriately employed in consumer studies. Often, a standard test designed by psychologists to detect general personality traits, or to use in clinical studies for understanding abnormal behavior, is used to predict consumers' product or brand purchases. Because the test was not designed for such predictions, it is not surprising to find a low success rate in this type of use. Future efforts should employ tests that are designed for the specific needs of a consumer investigation.[13]

2   Personality tests have not always been carefully administered when used in consumer studies. Also, in a number of consumer investigations, standardized inventories have been arbitrarily shortened or modified.[14] Because such changes can seriously alter the validity and usefulness of a test, future modifications should be validated prior to their actual use.[15]

3   Many studies have searched for a relationship between personality and specific aspects of consumer behavior (such as brand choice, brand loyalty over time, amount of product use). In many cases, the analysis was performed without much prior thought regarding why or how one should expect personality to relate to such behavior.[16] In fact, as mentioned earlier, personality usually interacts with a variety of other variables to influence general tendencies to behave. Specific actions will be strongly affected by the particular consumer situation as well as this general influence.[17] Therefore, it is more likely that personality would show stronger relationships with broad strategies and procedures that people adopt to deal with various consumer situations. Recent studies investigating such relationships between personality and general patterns of information acquisition and brand choice have tended to support these expectations.[18]

4   A sizable number of consumer studies have focused on specific personality traits (like tolerance for ambiguity, rigidity, self-actualization, need for affiliation) and their relationship to certain types of behavior. This has led some to lose sight of the importance of the whole personality for understanding consumer behavior. It must be remembered that each trait is only a partial component of the entire personality. Therefore, because traits can interact to result in a personality that is different from the sum of its parts, individuals are best understood through appreciation of the entire personality structure. Future investigations should be more strongly influenced by this perspective.[19]

One review of the status of personality investigations concludes that because of the above limitations, it is actually surprising that many previous studies were able to find *any* relationship between personality and consumer behavior.[20] Future research must be more carefully designed and must employ more relevant tests of consumers' personalities. One development in this regard is the use of the personality concept as part of a larger research ''package'' to understand consumers. This reorientation has resulted in the psychographic profiling of consumers.

PSYCHOGRAPHICS

Some studies demonstrating the nature and use of psychographics for understanding consumers were reviewed in Chapter 5. Major areas of application included segmentation research, developing profiles of target markets, exploring the potential for new products, and devising promotional strategies. A return to Chapter 5 at this point to briefly review the methods and applications of psychographics is recommended.

The reader may have noticed a strong resemblance between the nature and form of psychographic test items and those used in personality inventories. Review of the material in Chapter 5 may also have revealed that some psychographic items appear to address aspects of consumer motivation. Actually, these resemblances are not the result of coincidence. In fact, the field of psychographics is said to have originated from a merger of the areas of personality assessment and motivation research.[21] The merger yielded potential benefits in overcoming two limitations that had been noted about personality inventories and motivation research: (1) psychographics promise to be less abstract and more directly related to consumer situations than standardized personality testing, and (2) psychographic tests allow more efficient and apparently objective measurement of consumers' desires than do the long interview methods of motivation research. Also, psychographics yields quantitative results which can be easily submitted to statistical analysis. This is not true of the long narratives produced by motivational research interviews.

A variety of applications for psychographics were also mentioned in Chapter 5. Notable among these were the uses in developing advertising strategy and copy. For example, one researcher has demonstrated that, based on extensive investigations, psychographic profiles of media users can be more important to advertisers' selection of media than can traditionally used demographic variables. He successfully argues that lifestyles of product and brand users cut across demographic and socioeconomic segments. Media selection should therefore be based upon the appeal directed toward the selected target audience and its lifestyle.[22]

Psychographic studies have also benefited other consumer-related decisions including the design of marketing channels. Getting the goods and services consumers want to the best place for a profit is a goal of distribution systems. However, with changing lifestyles affecting channels of distribution, psychographics can provide useful data for channel designs. For example, because women are increasingly desirous of employment, they have less free time for shopping, and they therefore demand more convenience in their purchase activity. It has been suggested that many purchase decisions will become more routine for reasons of efficiency. Therefore, strong advertising programs designed to build a brand's reputation can assist in moving certain sales transactions away from stores and toward more automatic order systems that can be used in the home.[23]

Psychographic data also has been shown to be useful to industrial designers in creating product designs to satisfy consumer wants. For instance, one study involving industrial design compared the usefulness of demographics versus psychographic data to the styling of a clock radio. A class of industrial design students was given a paragraph describing either the demographic characteristics or the psychographic characteristics of a given market and asked to create the radio's design based solely on the paragraph of information given them. Interviewers returned to the subjects from whom they had originally obtained the demographic and psychographic data and asked them to state their preferences for

each of the radio designs. They found that the radios designed from psychographic data were preferred to those designed from demographic data.[24]

As these and the previous examples in Chapter 5 illustrate, psychographic information can be useful in a variety of ways, including market segmentation, creation of advertising strategy and copy, media selection, and product design.

PERSONALITY AND MARKETING: A SUMMARY

Personality research in general, and those studies related to consumer behavior in particular, have evolved through various stages and in several directions. The application of personality measurements to studying consumer behavior has produced many contradictory findings and often disappointing relationships. Ironically, of all the personality concepts available, the one that has probably enjoyed the greatest popularity and use among business practitioners is psychoanalytic theory, especially as used in one of the most highly subjective and least scientific areas—motivation research.

Of the remaining personality viewpoints, trait theory has been used in research on consumers more than has any other concept. As noted previously, however, its ability to predict or explain consumer behavior has often met with lackluster success. Some new and promising directions regarding the use of personality in understanding general consumer strategies or behavior patterns were mentioned. In addition, personality concepts have made significant contributions to the area of psychographics. Instead of being used alone, personality traits are combined with information on activities interests, opinions, demographics, and other measures to *profile,* not predict, consumers and their behavior.[25] Therefore, psychographics has emerged in the last decade as an approach to developing composite "pictures" of consumer types and to "humanizing" the data that are collected from consumers. In the next section we look at another theory which takes a total view of consumers and attempts to relate it to their behavior.

SELF-CONCEPT

Self-concept (or self-image) has become a popular approach in recent years to investigating possible relationships between how individuals perceive themselves and what behavior they exhibit as consumers. An advantage of studying consumer behavior using the theory of self-concept is that consumers provide descriptions of themselves, as opposed to having descriptions made by outside observers. That is, each consumer describes his or her own view of himself or herself, which is in contrast to personality tests that fit consumer responses into predetermined categories or traits. This distinction is important, because the way in which a consumer perceives himself or herself might differ substantially from the way in which the researcher sees or categorizes that same consumer.

As defined by Newcombe, *self-concept* is "the individual as perceived by that individual in a socially determined frame of reference."[26] More simply, the self-concept may be thought of as the person's perception of himself. This self-perception is not confined just to the physical being but includes such characteristics as strength, honesty, good humor, sophistication, justice, guilt, and others.[27] In short, it refers to the totality of an individual's thoughts and feelings about himself.[28]

Although the self-concept is highly complex, it is well organized and works in a consistent way. To the outside observer, a person may appear irrational and inconsistent in her behavior, but the individual taking such action is behaving in the only way she knows, given her frame of reference. When this individual's point of view is known, it usually becomes clear that she is not acting in an inconsistent way. For example, we may think a consumer is irrational to patronize a store that charges higher prices than its competition does for identical products. However, the consumer may show this loyalty because of the good service or because the salespeople make her feel important. Therefore, when viewed through her eyes, the slightly higher cost for her store loyalty may be well worth the money.

HOW THE SELF-CONCEPT DEVELOPS

Behaviorists have formed various theories of how people develop their self-concepts. Social interaction provides the basis for most of these theories. Four particular views of self-concept development are presented below.

Self-Appraisal Some theorists believe that a person fashions a self-concept by labeling his own dominant behavior patterns according to what is socially acceptable and unacceptable behavior. For example, certain behaviors are classified as "social," and others are labeled as "antisocial." By observing his own behavior, a person might begin to develop an awareness that his behavior falls into the general category "antisocial." With repeated confirmation of this label, a portion of the person's self-concept emerges, playing a dominant role in how he views himself.

Reflected Appraisal A second theory of self-concept development is termed reflected appraisal or the "looking-glass self." Basically, this theory holds that appraisals a person receives from others mold the self-concept. The extent of this influence depends upon characteristics of the appraiser and his or her appraisal. Specifically, greater impact on the development of a person's self-concept is said to occur when: (1) the appraiser is perceived as a highly credible source, (2) the appraiser takes a very personal interest in the person being appraised, (3) the appraisal is very discrepant with the person's self-concept at the moment, (4) the number of confirmations of a given appraisal is high, (5) the appraisals coming from a variety of sources are consistent, and (6) appraisals are supportive of the person's own beliefs about himself or herself. Appraisals from "significant others" such as parents, close friends, trusted colleagues, and other persons the individual strongly admires influence self-concept development.

Social Comparison The reflected appraisal theory gives a rather depressing picture of self-concept development because it emphasizes that people are passive and merely reflect the appraisals of others. The social comparison theory, however, states that peoples' self-concepts depend on how they see themselves in relation to others. Thorstein Veblen, the major proponent of this theory, was curious as to why people so strongly desired to acquire more goods and services than were necessary to meet their physical needs. The absolute amount of products, property, and services was not as important, he felt, as the *relative* amount accumulated; that is, in comparison with others. "The end sought by accumulation is to rank high in comparison with the rest of the community. . . . So long as the comparison is distinctly unfavorable to himself, the normal, average individual will live in chronic dissatisfaction."[29]

This theory has much more direct bearing upon the development of marketing strategies than have the theories discussed so far. In particular, this view of how people perceive themselves is dependent upon their perception of their relative status as compared to social class, reference groups, and other groups important to them. By determining which groups a person compares himself or herself to in the consumption of products and services, marketers can develop messages that communicate the group referent's use of particular products and brands. Purchases would then be seen by the person as a means to increase relative position in the group.

Festinger improved upon the social comparison theory by arguing that people need to affirm continuously that their beliefs and attitudes are correct and that they compare their beliefs and attitudes with others to determine the validity of their own.[30] If, for example, a person is asked whether she is conservative, romantic, or sociable, the answer will depend to a large extent on how the person perceives himself in comparison with others.

Biased Scanning   The last theory we shall discuss is concerned with motivation and biased scanning. In essence, this theory views self-concept development in terms of identity aspirations and biased scanning of the environment for information to confirm how well the person is meeting his or her aspirations. It suggests that a person who aspires (is motivated) to be a good lawyer, for example, will seek out information that helps to confirm this aspiration and filter out information that contradicts it. Thus, perceptual scanning is biased toward seeing ourselves as we would like to be (that is, it is biased toward self-gratification).

As we can see, these theories of self-concept development take somewhat different views of how people see themselves. In reality, probably all of the theories are working to some extent. Our self-concepts are very likely shaped to varying degrees according to how we perceive ourselves relative to others, our levels of aspirations and biased selection of information about ourselves, the labeling of ourselves according to how we perceive society categorizes us, and the reflected appraisals of significant others.[31]

CONSISTENCY OF THE SELF

Although theories vary on the development of a self-concept, psychologists agree that a person's conception of self displays a high degree of consistency, particularly in the short run. This relatively fixed structure of self is due to two conditions. First, as with many systems, self has an inertial tendency, that is, it tends to resist change. Second, after the self has become established, change becomes less likely because of selective perception of environmental information. That is, the self tends to interpret concepts in terms of the self.[32] Thus, ideas formed from a new experience are easily absorbed into the existing organization of self when the experience is perceived as consistent with the existing structure. In contrast, ideas perceived as inconsistent with the present structure are either rejected or altered to fit into the self, since they pose a threat to the individual.

SELF-CONCEPT AND CONSUMER BEHAVIOR

Consumers' self-perceptions can have a strong influence on their behavior in the marketplace. For example, the way an individual perceives various products could be affected by the image he has of himself. In fact, preferences might actually develop for certain brands because the consumer perceives them as reflecting his own self-image. Certain other brands may be desired because the consumer views them as projecting an image that he presently does not possess but aspires to have. Because of these and other possible influences, consumer researchers and marketers have developed a strong interest in self-concept theory. The following sections address some main concerns of those who have studied self-concept and its influence on consumer behavior.

Alternative Views of the Self   Up to this point, self-concept has been discussed as if total agreement existed regarding its exact nature. Actually, as implied in our discussion of self-development, this is not the case. Especially in the field of consumer behavior, a wide variety of philosophies regarding the self have emerged. These viewpoints can be generally divided into two groups: single- and multiple-component theories.[33] Those using a single-component perspective have focused on the *actual self*—the perception of oneself as one believes she actually is.[34]

Other researchers subscribe to multiple-component perspectives, which argue that a full understanding of the self is best obtained by using schemes that account for two or more components or dimensions. The simplest multiple-component model proposes that the self is two-dimensional, having an ideal as well as an actual component. The *ideal self* may be defined as the perception of oneself as one would ideally like to be.[35] Other multiple-component advocates have suggested additional aspects which would extend views of the self into three or more dimensions. Among several viewpoints, these newer perspectives include the *social self*—the perception of oneself as one believes others actually perceive him to be; the *ideal social self*—the perception of one's image as he would like others to have of him; and the *expressive self*—the ideal self or the social self, depending on situational and social factors.[36] Figure 15-3 graphically portrays these components of the self.

While this wide variety of perspectives on self-concept has led to a degree of confusion in the field, some researchers have recently argued that the various definitions should be viewed as complements to each other rather than as competing viewpoints to choose among. One recent argument along this line is that the self has a variety of dimensions (actual, ideal, social, and the like), and the consumer's goals, as well as the situation she confronts at any particular time, will determine which aspect of the self will influence her behavior.[37] For example, the

ideal self may be the predominant influence on an individual when she is purchasing sweaters, while the actual self may exert a strong influence when she is purchasing an automobile.

Major Areas of Investigation A comprehensive review of the self-concept area identified five major types of research investigations relating consumer behavior to self-concept:

1 Attempts to determine if specific types of self-concepts are related to socioeconomic or psychological factors such as social stratification and personality type

2 Studies of whether the behavior of consumers is related to the degree of congruity between their self-concepts and their perception of product and brand images

3 Investigations of the degree to which consumers' behavior is consistent with their perceptions of themselves (such as, do consumers who perceive themselves as innovative tend to act as innovators in their purchasing patterns?)

4 Studies relating to the possibility that consumers attribute their self-images to products that have similar images, or to products that they regularly purchase (''I purchase this product, so it must be like me.'')

5 Research focused on whether product images that are consistent with the consumer's self-concept influence his self-perceptions (''this product resembles me in a number of ways, so I probably am like it in many other ways.'')[38]

Although a comprehensive treatment of each area is beyond the scope of this chapter, we turn our attention to one major focus of investigation as described in item two above: how the behavior of consumers is related to the degree of

FIGURE 15-3
Various viewpoints of self-concept.

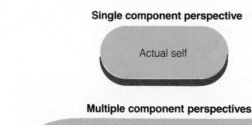

Single component perspective

Actual self

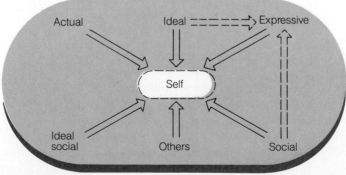

Multiple component perspectives

Actual   Ideal ====> Expressive

Self

Ideal social   Others   Social

congruity between their self-concepts and their perception of products and brands.

Consumer Behavior and Self-Concept/Product Image Congruence   As noted in previous chapters, consumers appear to hold images of various products, and these images can be viewed as symbols that communicate meaning about those who purchase them. Therefore, an area of considerable practical interest is the degree to which a consumer might actually prefer certain products or brands because she perceives their images as consistent with her view of herself, what she would like to be, or some other aspect of self-concept. An explanation of this behavior can be summarized as follows:

1   Consumers form their self-concepts through psychological development and social interaction. Because the individual's self-concept has value to him, he will act to define, protect, and further it.

2   Products and brands are perceived by consumers as having images or symbolic meaning.

3   Because of their symbolic role, selective possession, display, and use of these good-symbols assist an individual in defining and enhancing his self-concept for himself and for others.

4   Therefore, the behavior of individuals will be motivated toward furthering and enhancing their self-concept through the consumption of goods as symbols.

5   The brands that will be preferred are those that the consumer perceives as having images which are most consistent with his self-concept.[39]

Figure 15-4 shows this process whereby the consumer's preferred brands are identified through a matching between her self-image and her perception of various brand images. Congruity theory proposes that the greater the brand/self-image congruence, the more a brand will be preferred. It should again be noted that congruity can exist along a number of self-concept dimensions. For example,

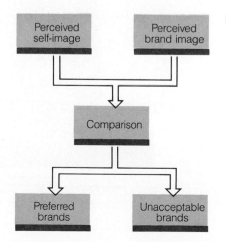

FIGURE 15-4
A model of the brand choice process as a function of self-image and brand image.

the consumer may not perceive a strong match between the brand's image and her actual self-concept, but she may perceive a close match with her ideal self. The theory would still predict that the consumer can have a strong preference for this brand because of the degree of congruity existing between the brand image and what she aspires to become. Also, the degree of congruence to both the actual and ideal self may join to exert a combined influence on consumers' attraction toward a brand.[40] The ideal self-concept appears to be a motivating force behind the design of advertisements such as the one shown in Figure 15-5. Here, we see that the brand is effectively linked to a handsome model whom many males might aspire to look like.

MEASUREMENT ISSUES   It is not difficult to envision that if self-concept theory has validity it could be very useful in such areas as product design, positioning of product images, and predicting consumers' behavior toward various brands. To achieve its potential, however, adequate measures of products and self-images are required. As one might suspect, various measurement methods have been developed. A frequently chosen technique is the semantic differential that was first described in Chapter 3. Recall that the semantic differential typically consists of seven-point scales, with bipolar adjectives or antonym phrases (happy-sad, reserved-outgoing, and so on) labeling the two scale endpoints. To employ this

FIGURE 15-5
An advertisement useful in appealing to ideal self-image.
Courtesy of the Arrow Company.

If lean, mean fit and great new looks are what you're after,
Arrow is the answer.

Arrow's **Brigade** shirt collections include great looking new colors, hot new styles, sensational stripes and plaids, wonderful weekend looks, all with the slim, trim fit you want.

Worn by half the men in America and reaching for the rest.

Company, 530 Fifth Avenue, New York, N.Y. 10036

technique, the researcher must first identify the most important personality/image attributes to measure and then develop semantic scales for these attributes. Consumers are next asked to reveal the dimension of their self-concept under investigation (real, ideal, and the like) by marking the scales in order to most appropriately describe themselves. A second set of scales are used to measure the same consumers' perceptions of brand images. If numbers are assigned to each response option on the semantic scales, it is then possible to determine the numerical distance between consumers' self-perceptions and their brand images. This numerical distance is used to represent the degree of congruence that exists for each brand.

To use a specific example, assume the goal is to measure the degree of congruence between womens' actual self-concepts and three different brands of perfume. Assume further that five personality/image components are thought to influence perfume purchases, and seven-point semantic scales are developed for each component. Numbers 1 through 7 are then assigned to the response options. Each consumer in the study would next indicate on the scales her image of each brand and her own self-image.

Adjectives used to describe scale endpoints, and one woman's numerical evaluation of herself and three brands, are shown in Table 15-1. One method of determining "how close" the woman perceives each brand image to her own self-image is the general distance formula found in solid geometry.[41] Here, it is referred to as the D measure and is represented as

$$D_{Kj} = \sqrt{\sum_{i=1}^{n} (S_{ij} - P_{ij})^2}$$

where D_{Kj} = the overall linear discrepancy between the jth consumer's self-image and her perception of the image of the Kth brand

i = the specific image components used to assess both brand and self-image

S_{ij} = the jth consumer's self-perception on the ith image component

P_{ij} = the jth consumer's brand perception on the ith image component

The various D measures can be calculated to represent the degree of congruity between a consumer's self-image and her image of each brand. For example, calculations for the distance between self-image and the image of brand B for the woman described in Table 15-1 would be:

$$D_{Bj} = \sqrt{(2 - 1)^2 + (1 - 2)^2 + (6 - 7)^2 + (2 - 1)^2 + (2 - 1)^2}$$
$$= \sqrt{1 + 1 + 1 + 1 + 1}$$
$$= \sqrt{5} = 2.2$$

Similar calculations for the discrepancy between self-image and the image of brands A and C would yield measures of $D_{Aj} = 8.4$ and $D_{Cj} = 5.9$ respectively. Our prediction would then be that the woman would prefer brand B, because her image of it best matches (has lowest discrepancy with) her own self-image.

Developing these *D* measures across many consumers could enable prediction of general market behavior.

RESEARCH EVIDENCE   More than thirty research efforts have examined the possible relationship between brand/self-image congruity and various aspects of consumer behavior. A review of most of these studies found that although research has produced a number of inconsistencies and areas of confusion, several generalizations can still be made:[42]

1   Many findings support the argument that consumers prefer, intend to purchase, or actually use brands with images they see as being congruent with their actual self-concept. To illustrate, one of the earliest studies found that a sample of car owners had self-perceptions more closely matching their image of their own car than that of eight other brands.[43]

2   A number of studies have also found that consumers are more likely to prefer, intend to purchase, or use brands with images that they see as being congruent with their ideal self-concept.

3   The relationship between consumers' brand/social self-image congruity and their brand preferences, purchase intentions, or loyalties has not been strongly supported by research evidence. However, the relationship with brand/ideal social self-image congruity has been moderately supported.

4   A moderate amount of evidence also supports the argument that consumers perceiving themselves as feminine (or masculine) more frequently use products that they perceive as having feminine (or masculine) images.

5   Whether or not a product is conspicuous (that is, displayed or consumed in social settings) has not been found to generally influence the relationship between brand/self-image congruence and brand preference or choice. However, some research has suggested that product conspicuousness may influence the brand preferences of upper social classes.

6   Some evidence suggests that several other variables may affect the relationship between brand/self-image congruence and various aspects of consumers' behavior toward brands. Included are the type of decision (routine versus nonroutine), personality type, and the degree to which a product has an image that is

TABLE 15-1

A Woman's Numerical Ratings of Self-Image and Three Brands of Perfume

Scales	Concepts			
	Self-Image	Brand A	Brand B	Brand C
Sexy-reserved	2	7	1	3
Unadorned-sophisticated	1	2	2	6
Innocent-flirty	6	1	7	4
Sensitive-insensitive	2	4	1	3
Daring-cautious	2	6	1	4

strongly stereotyped with a particular type of user—as Calvin Klein jeans, Brut cologne, or Jaguar automobiles might be.

PERSONALITY AND SELF-CONCEPT

497

Marketing Applications It has been noted that several limitations of the self-concept notion can impede its usefulness in marketing applications. In addition to problems of measurement common to many concepts, there is also lack of a clear-cut agreement on what is specifically meant by the "self." Different interpretations of the concept can create uncertainty regarding its use in understanding consumers. Further, the self-image concept stresses consumers' self-awareness at the conscious level and tends to minimize the importance of subconscious or unconscious levels of influence. As we noted in Chapter 12 and earlier in this chapter, such deeper mainsprings of behavior can have an important influence on consumers' behavior.

In spite of these potential limitations, self-image is a powerful concept which has many implications and applications in the field of consumer behavior. The concept has been used in market segmentation, advertising, packaging, personal selling, product development, and retailing.

Some people have suggested that companies can segment markets into more homogeneous sets of self-image profiles. These self-descriptions could then serve as "blueprints" useful to marketers in designing total marketing programs. It is argued that decisions based on markets segmented by consumer self-images operationalize the marketing concept by viewing the consumer from the consumer's own point of view.[44]

The self-image concept is quite heavily used in a variety of aspects of promotion. This is clearly demonstrated in the area of clothing. For example, certain types of men's suits are shown being worn by distinguished, conservative-looking models, often with a touch of gray in their hair. Such suits are usually seen on bankers and businessmen who have achieved considerable success. Other suits, frequently those with continental styling, are shown being worn by younger men with longer hair, who appear much more contemporary. The setting for these advertisements frequently involves active, informal social settings where the model often is shown without a tie. Salespeople will often emphasize such self-image messages by telling customers they know that items are either consistent or not consistent with their self-images ("that suit is just not you").

In another promotional area, notice the differences between advertisements showing women using Dial and Camay bath soaps. Women using Dial are depicted as having very active days with a great deal of excitement and exercise. They are shown using Dial in invigorating, refreshing showers, and they generally seem to live life with gusto. Conversely, women who use Camay tend to be portrayed as considerably more feminine in nature. They seem to embrace the product for the delicate way in which it will treat their skin and the softness that it will yield. As opposed to taking refreshing showers they appear to desire the sensual experience of long, warm, relaxing baths. It is interesting to note how packaging of each product appears to support such distinctions in the image of each product.

In Chapter 13, we noted the importance for retailers to know the image of their store as perceived by customers. It should again be emphasized here that consumer segments with various self-images will probably exist within the trading

area of any given store. It is quite possible that the store's image may not be consistent with some consumers' self-images. Therefore, it is essential for the retailer to determine the market segment to which the store is appealing.[45] Decisions must then be made on the appropriate target segments. This could entail adjustments of the store's image in order to coincide better with the self-images of target patrons.

Analysis of consumers' self-images and their images of brands can also aid marketers in developing products. New brands can be created based on consumer self-image profiles for which there are no "matching" brand images existing. Product categories having particular promise in this area include those that generate high ego involvement and have high social visibility among the upper social classes. Examples include home furnishings, clothing, and automobiles, as opposed to such products as fingernail clippers and light bulbs. Therefore, measurement of consumers' product-image perceptions would involve more than just the assessment of product attributes as described in the perceptual mapping example in Chapter 5. Consumers' perceptions of nonphysical image components and the degree of their correspondence to self-image perceptions must also be assessed.

One final comment regarding the self-image concept is important to mention. Studies have suggested that self-image can be an important predictor of consumers' brand preferences. However, brand preferences are not necessarily translated directly into purchases. Constraining factors such as price and other individual or environmental influences can modify these brand preferences before they are acted upon.

MANAGERIAL REFLECTIONS

For our product or service situation . . .

1 What methods and problems exist for measuring the personality types of our consumers or consumer segments?

2 How might personality be expected to relate to consumers' behavior toward our offerings and marketing efforts?

3 How might the field of psychographic research benefit our marketing activities?

4 In what areas does it appear reasonable to expect consumers' self-concept to be related to their behavior toward our offerings?

5 Does the real self or ideal self appear to be more useful in understanding our consumers' behavior?

6 How might we practically determine the extent of congruence between consumers' self-image and their image of our offerings?

DISCUSSION TOPICS

1 Distinguish between the id, ego, and superego in the Freudian personality scheme. Suggest the basic influence each might exert on a purchase decision.

2 Of what relevance is the personality concept to understanding consumer behavior?

3 Describe the major characteristics of trait theories of personality, indicating their major advantages and disadvantages. Review their usefulness in explaining consumer behavior.

4 Find at least three examples of promotions that appear to be using Freudian concepts. Be specific in describing which concepts are involved and how you think they are being used.

5 Cite at least two product examples in which it would appear that an understanding of consumers' psychographic profiles would be useful in describing their reaction to the products involved.

6 What are the significant limitations of the self-concept in explaining consumer behavior?

7 Of what usefulness is it for a marketing manager to know that the self tends to be consistent?

8 Why is it important for the marketer to understand the distinction between consumers' self-image and ideal self-image?

PROJECTS

1 Choose two brands within the same product category that appear to be projecting different images. Characterize each image being projected by comparing and contrasting them. What methods or techniques are being used to project these images?

2 Interview the managers of three retail clothing stores. Determine the degree to which they believe that consumers' personality and self-image are important to the marketing activities of the store.

3 Develop a set of scales to measure consumers' self-image and their image of the Pontiac Fiero. Administer your scales to twenty people between the ages of 18 and 22. To what degree did you find image congruence?

NOTES

[1] Based on Brad Edmondson, "Living with Kawasakis," *American Demographics,* October 1985, p. 18.

[2] Gerald Zaltman and Melanie Wallendorf, *Consumer Behavior: Basic Findings and Management Implications,* Wiley, New York, 1979, p. 357.

[3] Some of the following discussion follows Harold H. Kassarjian, "Personality and Consumer Behavior: A Review," *Journal of Marketing Research,* **8**:409–418, November 1971.

[4] Joel B. Cohen, "An Interpersonal Orientation to the Study of Consumer Behavior," *Journal of Marketing Research,* **4**:270–278, August 1967. Also see Joel B. Cohen, "Toward an Interpersonal Theory of Consumer Behavior," *California Management Review,* **10**:73–80, Spring 1968.

[5] Seymour Epstein, "Traits Are Alive and Well," in David Magnusson and Norman Endler (eds.), *Personality at the Crossroads: Current Issues in Interactional Psychology,* Lawrence Eribaum Associates, Hillsdale, N.J., 1977, pp. 83–98; and David Krech et al., *Psychology: A Basic Course,* Knopf, New York, 1976, pp. 322–323.

[6] Arthur Koponen, "Personality Characteristics of Purchasers," *Journal of Advertising Research,* **1**:6–12, September 1960.

[7] Robert Brody and Scott Cunningham, "Personality Variables and the Consumer Decision Process," *Journal of Marketing Research,* **5**:50–57, February 1968.

[8] William T. Tucker and John Painter, "Personality and Product Use," *Journal of Applied Psychology,* **45**:325–329, October 1961.

[9] Franklin B. Evans, "Psychological and Objective Factors in the Prediction of Brand Choice," *Journal of Business,* **32**:340–369, October 1959.

[10] See Alan S. Marcus, "Obtaining Group Measures from Personality Test Scores: Auto Brand Choice Predicted from the Edwards Personal Preference Schedule," *Psychological Reports,* **17**:523–531, October 1965; Gary A. Steiner, "Notes on Franklin B. Evans' 'Psychological and Objective Factors in the Prediction of Brand Choice,'" *Journal of Business,* **34**:57–60, January 1961; Charles Winick, "The Relationship Among Personality Needs, Objective Factors, and Brand Choice: A Re-examination," *Journal of Business,* **34**:61–66, January 1961; and Ralph Westfall, "Psychological Factors in Predicting Product Choice," *Journal of Marketing,* **26**:34–40, April 1962.

[11] See Charles M. Schaninger and Donald Sciglimpaglia, "The Influence of Cognitive Personality Traits and Demographics on Consumer Acquisition," *Journal of Consumer Research,* **8**:208–216, September 1981; Raymond L. Horton, "Some Relationships Between Personality and Consumer Decision Making," *Journal of Marketing Research,* **16**:233–246, May 1979; Thomas S. Robertson, *Innovation and the Consumer,* Holt, New York, 1971; and Louis E. Boone, "The Search for the Consumer Innovator," *Journal of Business,* **43**:135–140, April 1979, for representative findings.

[12] See Kassarjian, "Personality and Consumer Behavior"; and Harold H. Kassarjian and Mary Jane Sheffet, "Personality and Consumer Behavior: One More Time," in Edward M. Mazze (ed.), *1975 Combined Proceedings,* American Marketing Association, Chicago, 1975, pp. 197–201.

[13] See William D. Wells, "General Personality Tests and Consumer Behavior," in Joseph W. Newman (ed.), *On Knowing the Consumer,* Wiley, New York, 1966, pp. 187–189; and Kathryn E. A. Villani and Yoram Wind, "On the Usage of 'Modified' Personality Trait Measures in Consumer Research," *Journal of Consumer Research,* **2**:223–228, December 1975.

[14] Ibid.

[15] See George Brooker, "Representativeness of Shortened Personality Measures," *Journal of Consumer Research,* **5**:143–144, September 1978; and Villani and Wind, "On the Usage of 'Modified' Personality Trait Measures."

[16] Kassarjian, "Personality and Consumer Behavior," p. 416.

[17] See Robert A. Peterson, "Moderating the Personality-Product Usage Relationship," in Ronald C. Curhan (ed.), *1974 Combined Proceedings,* American Marketing Association, Chicago, 1975, pp. 109–112.

[18] See Shaninger and Sciglimpaglia, "Personality and Information Acquisition"; and Horton, "Personality and Consumer Decision Making."

[19] See Stewart Bither and Ira Dolich, "Personality as a Determinant Factor in Store Choice," in M. Venkatesan (ed.), *Proceedings of the Third Annual Conference,* Association for Consumer Research, College Park, M.D., 1972, pp. 9–19; Robert A. Peterson and Louis K. Sharpe, "Personality Structure and Cigarette Smoking," in Barnett A. Greenberg (ed.), *Proceedings: Southern Marketing Association 1974 Conference,* Southern Marketing Association, 1975, pp. 295–297; and Larry Percy, "A Look at Personality Profiles and the Personality-Attitude-Behavior Link in Predicting Consumer Behavior," in Beverlee B. Anderson (ed.), *Advances in Consumer Research,* vol. 3, Association for Consumer Research, Ann Arbor, Mich., 1976, pp. 119–224.

[20] Kassarjian and Sheffet, "Personality and Consumer Behavior."

[21] Sunil Mehrotra and William D. Wells, "Psychographics and Buyer Behavior: Theory and Recent Empirical Findings," in Arch G. Woodside, Jagdish N. Sheth, and Peter D. Bennett (eds.), *Consumer and Industrial Buying Behavior,* Elsevier North-Holland, New York, 1977, pp. 49–65.

[22] Douglas J. Tigert, "Life Style Analysis as a Basis for Media Selection," in William D. Wells, (ed.), *Life Style and Psychographics,* American Marketing Association, Chicago, 1974, pp. 173–201.

[23] Calvin Hadock, "Use of Psychographics in Analysis of Channels of Distribution," in Wells (ed.), *Life Style and Psychographics,* pp. 215–216.

[24] Robert W. Frye and Gary D. Klein, "Psychographics and Industrial Design," in Wells (ed.), *Life Style and Psychographics,* pp. 225–232.

[25] William D. Wells, ''Personality as a Determinant of Buyer Behavior: What's Wrong? What Can Be Done About It?'' in David Sparks (ed.), *Broadening the Concept of Marketing,* American Marketing Association, Chicago, 1970, p. 20.

[26] Theodore M. Newcombe, *Social Psychology,* Holt, New York, 1950, p. 328.

[27] Donald Snygg and Arthur W. Combs, *Individual Behavior,* Harper, New York, 1949, p. 57; and William James, *Psychology,* Henry Holt and Company, New York, 1892, p. 176.

[28] Morris Rosenberg, *Conceiving the Self,* Basic Books, New York, 1979, p. 7.

[29] Thorstein Veblen, *The Theory of the Leisure Class,* Mentor Books, New York, 1958, p. 42, a reprint from Thorstein Veblen, *The Theory of the Leisure Class,* Macmillan, New York, 1899.

[30] Leon A. Festinger, ''A Theory of Social Comparison,'' *Human Relations,* **14**:48–64, 1954.

[31] For additional views on principles influencing the development of the self, see Rosenberg, *Conceiving the Self,* pp. 62–77.

[32] Snygg and Combs, *Individual Behavior,* p. 57.

[33] M. Joseph Sirgy, ''Self-Concept in Consumer Behavior: A Critical Review,'' *Journal of Consumer Research,* **9**:287–300, December 1982.

[34] See, for example, Edward L. Grubb and Gregg Hupp, ''Perception of Self, Generalized Stereotypes, and Brand Selection,'' *Journal of Marketing Research,* **5**:58–63, February 1968; G. Hughes and P. Naert, ''A Computer Controlled Experiment in Consumer Behavior,'' *Journal of Business,* **43**:354–372, 1970; and Edward L. Grubb and Bruce L. Stern, ''Self-Concept and Significant Others,'' *Journal of Marketing Research,* **8**:382–385, August 1971.

[35] See Curtis B. Hamm and Edward W. Cundiff, ''Self Actualization and Product Perception,'' *Journal of Marketing Research,* **6**:470–472, November 1969; George E. Belch and E. Laird Landon, Jr., ''Discriminant Validity of a Product-Anchored Self-Concept Measure,'' *Journal of Marketing Research,* **14**:252–256, May 1977; and George E. Belch, ''Belief Systems and the Differential Role of the Self-Concept,'' in Keith H. Hunt (ed.), *Advances in Consumer Research,* vol. 5, Association for Consumer Research, Ann Arbor, Mich., 1978, pp. 320–325, for examples.

[36] See, for example, M. Joseph Sirgy, ''Self-Concept in Relation to Product Preference and Purchase Intention,'' in V. V. Bellur (ed.), *Developments in Marketing Science,* vol. 3, Marquette, Mich., Academy of Marketing Science, 1980; G. David Hughes and Jose L. Guerrero, ''Automobile Self-Congruity Models Reexamined,'' *Journal of Marketing Research,* **8**:125–127, February 1971; and J. Michael Munsen and W. Austin Spivey, ''Assessing Self-Concept,'' in Jerry C. Olson (ed.), *Advances in Consumer Research,* vol. 7, Association for Consumer Research, Ann Arbor, Mich., 1980, pp. 598–603.

[37] Carolyn Turner Schenk and Rebecca H. Holman, ''A Sociological Approach to Brand Choice: The Concept of Situational Self Image,'' in Jerry C. Olson (ed.), *Advances in Consumer Research,* vol. 7, Association for Consumer Research, Ann Arbor, Mich., 1980, pp. 610–614.

[38] Sirgy, ''Self-Concept in Consumer Behavior.''

[39] Edward L. Grubb and Harrison L. Grathwohl, ''Consumer Self Concept, Symbolism and Market Behavior: A Theoretical Approach,'' *Journal of Marketing,* **31**:25–26, October 1967.

[40] M. Joseph Sirgy, ''Using Self-Congruity and Ideal Congruity to Predict Purchase Motivation,'' *Journal of Business Research,* **13**:195–206, 1985.

[41] For a review of alternative models of self/brand image congruity and their predictions of product preference and purchase intention, see M. Joseph Sirgy and Jeffrey E. Danes, ''Self-Image/Product-Image Congruence Models: Testing Selected Models,'' in Andrew Mitchell (ed.), *Advances in Consumer Research,* vol. 9, Association for Consumer Research, Ann Arbor, Mich., 1982, pp. 556–561.

[42] The following list of generalizations follows closely the review, in Sirgy, ''Self Concept and Consumer Behavior.''

[43] A. Evans Birdwell, ''Influence of Image Congruence on Consumer Choice,'' in George South (ed.), *Reflections on Progress in Marketing,* American Marketing Association, Chicago, 1965, pp. 290–303.

[44] Wayne DeLozier and Rollie Tillman, ''Self Image Concepts—Can They Be Used to Design Marketing Programs?'' *The Southern Journal of Business,* **7**:11, November 1972.

[45] For two endeavors of this nature, see Joseph Barry Mason and Morris L. Mayer, ''The Problem of the Self-Concept in Store Image Studies,'' *Journal of Marketing,* **34**:67–69, April 1970; and Ira J. Dolich and Ned Shilling, ''A Critical Evaluation of 'The Problem of Self-Concept in Store Image Studies,''' *Journal of Marketing,* **35**:71–73, January 1971.

ATTITUDES

LEARNING OBJECTIVES

After studying this chapter, you should understand . . .

■ The nature and characteristics of consumers' attitudes

■ The major functions that attitudes provide for the consumer

■ How attitudes develop

■ Some of the major theories that have been constructed to understand attitudes

■ Significant characteristics of Fishbein's multiattribute attitude model and behavioral intentions model and their potential for understanding consumers' behavior

For 103 years the Procter & Gamble Company had used a stylized drawing as its logo. In it, a bearded man's face is the main portion of a quarter moon all within a circle. The face gazes at thirteen five-pointed stars shown against a dark background. The company explains that when the logo was developed in the late 1800s, the stars were chosen to represent the original colonies, and the human face in the crescent moon was a popular figure of that time (as illustrated by the photo of antique jewelry).

Not so, says a rumor mill that surfaced in 1981 and then reappeared with a vengeance in 1984. According to the rumors, these images are satanic in nature and reflect that the company is in some way connected with devil worship. A laughable situation not to be concerned with? Far from it—P&G executives treated the rumor mill as a serious problem. They realized that such rumors could affect many consumers' attitudes toward the company, and this would have a very strong impact on sales volume.

Evidence supported their fears: between 1981 and 1985 the company handled more than 100,000 telephone calls and letters from consumers concerned with the alleged satanism connection. Hotbeds of consumer concern included, geographically, the northeast, mid-Atlantic states, and Michigan, as well as California and Florida.

The company fought back with threats of lawsuits against those starting rumors and other activities in an effort to retain positive consumer attitudes that it had generated over the years across all consumer segments. However, costs for the war in terms of expenses and lost sales revenues were huge. Finally, the company gave up the fight; it announced in 1985 that it would remove its logo from all product labels. Apparently, the potential damage inflicted by the rumor mill on consumers' attitudes toward the company and its products was too much of a cost to bear.[1]

This example demonstrates marketers' concern with a central issue of consumers' behavior—attitudes. In fact, the topic of attitudes has been one of the most important subjects of study in the field of consumer behavior. Widespread investigations of attitudes among academicians and practicing marketers supports this statement. Attitude research forms the basis for developing new products, repositioning existing products, creating advertising campaigns, and predicting brand preferences as well as general purchase behavior. Understanding how attitudes are developed and how they influence consumers is a vital ingredient to the success of any marketing program.

Material presented in Chapters 12 and 13 provides useful perspective for our discussion in this chapter. Recall from Chapter 12 that the role of attitudes differs depending on the level of consumer involvement in a purchase situation. It was argued that in low-involvement situations, attitudes toward a brand are formed *after* a purchase has been made, when the brand is being evaluated through actual use. However, in high-involvement situations consumers are seen as forming attitudes about brands and then making a purchase decision based on these attitudes. This means that in high-involvement cases, attitudes are formed on the basis of product evaluations that are made *prior* to purchase. Therefore, they represent one outcome of the information-processing activities that are shown in Figure 13-1.

The high-involvement perspective is most relevant to our discussion of attitudes in this chapter. That is, the sequence of steps an involved consumer takes can be thought of as (1) processing information, (2) forming attitudes, and then (3) making choices in the marketplace, guided by these attitudes.

In this chapter, we explore how attitudes are formed and organized. The functions of attitudes in our daily lives and their relationship to purchase behavior are then discussed. Additionally, we describe several well-known attitude models and theories which help us to measure and predict consumer behavior. These principles form a foundation for Chapter 17, which treats attitude change and the role of marketing communications in influencing consumers.

DEFINITIONS OF ATTITUDE

Social psychologists, unfortunately, do not agree on the precise definition of an attitude. In fact, there are more than 100 different definitions of the concept.[2] However, four definitions are more commonly accepted than others. One conception is that an attitude is how positive or negative, favorable or unfavorable, or pro or con a person feels toward an object.[3] This definition views attitude as a feeling or an evaluative reaction to objects.

A second definition represents the thoughts of Allport, who views attitudes as "learned predispositions to respond to an object or class of objects in a consistently favorable or unfavorable way."[4] This definition is slightly more complicated than the first because it incorporates the notion of a readiness to respond toward an object.

A third definition of attitude popularized by cognitively oriented social psychologists is: "an enduring organization of motivational, emotional, perceptual, and cognitive process with respect to some aspect of the individual's world."[5] This views attitudes as being made up of three components: (1) the *cognitive*, or knowledge, component, (2) the *affective,* or emotional, component, and (3) the *conative,* or behavioral-tendency, component.

More recently, theorists have given more attention to a new definition of attitude which has generated much research and has been useful in predicting behavior. This definition explicitly treats attitudes as being multidimensional in nature, as opposed to the unidimensional emphasis taken by earlier definitions. Here, a person's overall attitude toward an object is seen to be a function of (1) the strength of each of a number of beliefs the person holds about various aspects of the object and (2) the evaluation he gives to each belief as it relates to the object.[6] A *belief* is the probability a person attaches to a given piece of knowledge being true.

This last definition has considerable appeal, because it has been shown that consumers perceive a product (object) as having many attributes, and they form beliefs about each of these attributes. For example, a consumer may believe strongly that Listerine mouthwash kills germs, helps prevent colds, gives people clean, refreshing breath, and prevents sore throats. If this consumer evaluates all five of these attributes as favorable qualities, then according to the definition he would have a strongly favorable overall attitude toward the brand. On the other hand, a second consumer might believe just as strongly as the first consumer that Listerine possesses all five of these traits; however, she may not evaluate all attributes as favorably as the first consumer does. Therefore, her overall attitude toward the brand would be less favorable. This idea will be discussed in more detail later in the chapter.

It has been important to provide all four attitude definitions because the majority of attitude studies have been based upon them. In fact, results of this research serve as the basis of this chapter and Chapter 17.

CHARACTERISTICS OF ATTITUDES

Attitudes have several important characteristics or properties; namely, they (1) have an object; (2) have direction, intensity, and degree; (3) have structure; and (4) are learned.

ATTITUDES HAVE AN OBJECT

By definition, attitudes must have an object. That is, they must have a focal point. The object can be an abstract concept, such as "consumerism," or it can be a tangible item, such as a motorcycle. The object can be a physical thing, such as a product, or it can be an action, such as purchasing a product. In addition, the object can be either one item, such as a person, or a collection of items, such as a social group; it also can be either specific (Chevy Camero) or general (General Motors, Inc.).

ATTITUDES HAVE DIRECTION, DEGREE, AND INTENSITY

An attitude expresses how a person feels toward an object. It expresses (1) direction—the person is either favorable or unfavorable toward, or for or against the object; (2) degree—how much the person either likes or dislikes the object; and (3) intensity—the level of sureness or confidence of expression about the object, or how strongly a person feels about his or her conviction. Although degree and intensity might seem the same and are actually related, they are not synonymous. For example, a person may feel that an Ariens riding mower is very unreliable. This indicates that his attitude is negative and the *degree* of negative feeling is quite extensive. However, the individual may have very little *conviction* or feeling of sureness (intensity in attitude) that he is right. Thus, his attitude could be more easily changed in a favorable direction than a person who feels a strong conviction that Ariens mowers are very unreliable.

The direction, degree, and intensity of a person's attitude toward a product has been said to provide marketers with an estimate of his or her readiness to act toward, or purchase, the product. However, a marketer must also understand how *important* the consumer's attitude is vis-à-vis other attitudes, and the situational constraints, such as ability to pay, that might inhibit the consumer from making a purchase decision.

ATTITUDES HAVE STRUCTURE

As explained below, attitudes display organization, which means that they have internal consistency and possess interattitudinal centrality. They also tend to be stable, to have varying degrees of salience, and to be generalizable.

The structure of human attitudes may be viewed as a complex Tinker Toy set erected in a type of circular pattern. At the center of this structure are the individual's important values and self-concept. Attitudes close to the hub of this system are said to have a high degree of *centrality*. Other attitudes located farther out in the structure possess less centrality.

Attitudes do not stand in isolation. They are associated (tied in) with each other to form a complex whole. This implies that a certain degree of *consistency* must exist between them. That is, because they are related, there must be some amount of "fit" between them, or conflict will result. Also, because the more central attitudes are related to a larger number of other attitudes, they must exhibit a greater degree of consistency than more peripheral attitudes do.

Because attitudes cluster into a structure, they tend to show *stability* over time. The length of time may not be infinite, but it is far from being temporary. Also, because attitudes are learned, they tend to become stronger, or at least more resistant to change, the longer they are held.[7] Thus, newly formed attitudes are easier to change and less stable than are older ones of equal strength.

Attitudes tend to be *generalizable*. That is, a person's attitude toward a specific object tends to generalize toward a class of objects. Thus, a consumer who purchases a Porsche which develops mechanical difficulties may believe that all Porsches and Volkswagen products, and possibly all German-made products, are poorly constructed. Consumers tend to generalize in such a manner in order to simplify their decision making.

Among all of the attidues in a person's attitudinal structure, some are more important or salient to her than others. For example, a U.S. consumer might feel that "buying American" is more important than saving energy. Therefore, she might purchase an American car that consumes more gasoline than a comparable foreign car that uses less. Also, the "buy American" attitude can be closely tied to attitudes of creating American jobs, keeping money at home, and the like, which thereby support the "buy American" attitude and increase its salience.

507

ATTITUDES ARE LEARNED

Just as a golf swing, a tennis stroke, and tastes are learned, so are attitudes. They develop from our personal experiences with reality, as well as from information from friends, salespeople, and news media. They are also derived from both direct and indirect experiences in life. Thus, it is important to recognize that learning precedes attitude formation and change, and that principles of learning discussed in Chapter 14 can aid marketers in developing and changing consumer attitudes.

FUNCTIONS OF ATTITUDES

Attitudes serve four major functions for the individual: (1) the adjustment function, (2) the ego-defensive function, (3) the value-expressive function, and (4) the knowledge function.[8] Ultimately, these functions serve people's need to protect and enhance the image they hold of themselves. In more general terms, these functions are the motivational bases which shape and reinforce positive attitudes toward goal objects perceived as need-satisfying, and/or negative attitudes toward other objects perceived as punishing or threatening. These situations are diagramed in Figure 16-1. The functions themselves can help us to understand why people hold the attitudes they do toward psychological objects.

THE ADJUSTMENT FUNCTION

The adjustment function directs people toward pleasurable or rewarding objects and away from unpleasant, undesirable ones. It serves the utilitarian concept of maximizing reward and minimizing punishment. Thus, the attitudes of consumers depend to a large degree on their perceptions of what is need satisfying and what is punishing. Because consumers perceive products, services, and stores as providing need-satisfying or unsatisfying experiences, we should expect their attitudes toward these objects to vary in relation to the experiences that have occurred.

THE EGO-DEFENSIVE FUNCTION

Attitudes formed to protect the ego or self-image from threats help fulfill the ego-defensive function. Actually, many outward expressions of such attitudes reflect the opposite of what the person perceives himself to be. For example, a consumer who has made a poor purchase decision or a poor investment may staunchly defend the decision as being correct at the time or as being the result of poor advice from another person. Such ego-defensive attitudes help us to protect our self-image, and often we are unaware of them.

THE VALUE-EXPRESSIVE FUNCTION

Whereas ego-defensive attitudes are formed to protect a person's self-image, value-expressive attitudes enable the expression of the person's centrally held values. Therefore, consumers adopt certain attitudes in an effort to translate their

FIGURE 16-1
Attitude development and function based on perceived need satisfaction or harm avoidance.

values into something more tangible and easily expressed. Thus, a conservative person might develop an unfavorable attitude toward bright clothing and instead be attracted toward dark, pin-striped suits.

Marketers should develop an understanding of what values consumers wish to express about themselves, and they should design products and promotional campaigns to allow these self-expressions. Not all products lend themselves to this form of market segmentation, however. Those with the greatest potential for "value expressive" segmentation are ones with high social visibility. Cross pens, Saks Fifth Avenue clothes, Ferrari automobiles, and Bang & Olufsen stereo systems are examples.

THE KNOWLEDGE FUNCTION

Human beings have a need for a structured and orderly world, and therefore they seek consistency, stability, definition, and understanding. Out of this need develop attitudes toward acquiring knowledge. In addition, the need to know tends to be specific. Therefore, an individual who does not play golf or wish to learn it is unlikely to seek knowledge or an understanding of the game. Out of the need to know come attitudes about what we believe we need or do not need to understand.

SOURCES OF ATTITUDE DEVELOPMENT

The preceding section not only discussed the functions of attitudes but also provided us with an initial understanding of how and why attitudes develop. All attitudes ultimately develop from human needs and the values people place upon objects that satisfy those perceived needs. This section discusses sources that make us aware of needs, their importance to us, and how our attitudes develop toward objects that satisfy needs.

PERSONAL EXPERIENCE

People come into contact with objects in their everyday environment. Some are familiar, while others are new. We evaluate the new and reevaluate the old, and this evaluation process assists in developing attitudes toward objects. For example, consider a gourmet cook who has searched two months for a new food processor only to have it break down three months after purchase. Through direct experience, she will then reevaluate her earlier attitude toward the processor.

Our direct experiences with sales representatives, products, services, and stores help to create and shape our attitudes toward those market objects. However, several factors influence how we will evaluate such direct contacts:

Needs. Because needs differ and also vary over time, people can develop different attitudes toward the same object at different points in their life.

Selective perception. We have seen that people operate on their personal interpretation of reality. Therefore, the way people interpret information about products, stores, and so on, affects their attitudes toward them.

Personality. Personality is another factor influencing how people process their direct experiences with objects. How aggressive-passive, introverted-extroverted, and so on, that people are will affect the attitudes they form.

GROUP ASSOCIATIONS

All people are influenced to one degree or another by other members in the groups to which they belong. Attitudes are one target for this influence. For example, our attitudes toward products, ethics, warfare, and a multitude of other subjects are influenced strongly by groups that we value and with which we do or wish to associate. Several groups, including family, work and social groups, and cultural and subcultural groups, are quite important in affecting a person's attitude development:

Family. The family is perhaps the most influential group in shaping a person's attitudes. Parents orient a child's early thinking, and this influence on attitudes is often so strong that it carries over to adult life.

Peer groups. The norms, standards, and influence attempts of important groups in the consumer's work and social life make a strong impact on a wide variety of the person's attitudes.

Culture and subculture. Cultural and subcultural inheritances are a result of the socialization process. This legacy results in a sense of identification about who we are, and it strongly affects attitudes about a variety of objects in our environment.

INFLUENTIAL OTHERS

A consumer's attitude can be formed and changed through personal contact with influential persons such as respected friends, relatives, and experts. Opinion leaders are examples of people who are respected by their followers and who may strongly influence the attitudes and purchase behavior of followers.

To capitalize on this type of influence, advertisers often use actors and actresses who look similar to or act similar to their intended audiences. People tend to like others who are similar to themselves, because they believe that they share the same problems, form the same judgments, and use the same criteria for evaluating products.[9] Another application which advertisers use to influence audience attitudes is the so-called "slice of life" commercial. These ads show "typical" people confronting "typical" problems and finding solutions in the use of the advertised brand. Examples include ads for Head and Shoulders shampoo (to solve dandruff problems), Crest toothpaste (to fight cavities), and Midas mufflers.

Although sales representatives are sometimes viewed with a certain amount of suspicion, they can also positively influence consumers' attitudes when they express opinions similar to the consumer's viewpoint. A second condition for effective influence, however, usually is that the salesperson is also perceived by the customer as having some degree of expertise regarding the product.[10]

A pictorial summary of what we have learned so far is depicted in Figure 16-2. The model is a simple representation of the concepts that have been discussed in the previous sections. It shows that several sources provide consumers with

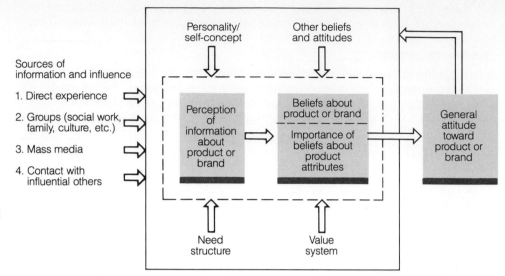

FIGURE 16-2
A simple model of the interrelationships of attitude and other psychological processes.

information and influence about products, services, retail stores, and other objects. The individual selectively receives and distorts the information according to her individual needs, values, and personality, and according to how well the information "fits" with currently held beliefs and attitudes. This processed information initiates either development, change, or confirmation in the consumer's beliefs about the product and the importance of each of the product's attributes to her and her current needs. Out of this process is synthesized a general attitude toward a product. Admittedly, this model is an oversimplification. However, it reflects current understanding of attitudes and presents a concise picture of the psychological and external elements involved in the process of forming attitudes toward products. Also, it should be pointed out that the process is dynamic; it continues to change over time.

ATTITUDE THEORIES AND MODELS

This section describes several attitude theories and models.[11] Although at first glance some may appear to be somewhat complicated, their essence is usually quite simple and useful in understanding the role of attitudes in consumer behavior.

Attitude theories primarily are concerned with how attitudes develop and change. Three of the more popular viewpoints are founded on the general principle that *the human mind strives to maintain harmony or consistency among currently perceived attitudes*. If the mind perceives an inconsistency within its attitude structure, mental tension develops to return the structure to a consistent state. The three classical theories based upon the consistency principle are congruity, balance, and cognitive dissonance. Newer multiattribute attitude theories are discussed after a consideration of these traditional views.

A basic understanding of the congruity model can be gained through consideration of the following examples. Assume that a consumer holds attitudes toward entertainer Cliff Robertson (positive attitude of scale value +2) and AT&T (negative attitude of scale value −2), as illustrated in Figure 16-3. Also assume that the consumer sees Robertson in a television advertisement in which he makes positive statements about AT&T. Given this situation, the consumer will have inconsistent attitudes: "Robertson, whom I like, said something nice about AT&T, which I don't like." In this case, the consumer is in a state of *incongruity*. This condition produces uncomfortable tension which must ultimately resolve the incongruous state. The congruity model would predict that a person in this situation would reduce his favorable attitude toward Cliff Robertson and decrease his unfavorable attitude toward AT&T, as shown in part (*b*) of Figure 16-3. The model would predict a movement of two units of each concept toward each other (the center in this case), because the consumer perceives both objects as being of equal strength but in opposite directions of the neutral point of zero.

Most of the time, the resulting equilibrium point is not determined so simply. Figure 16-4 presents another situation of a consumer's perceived attitudes toward Cliff Robertson and AT&T. Note that the scale distance between the two concepts is four units as before. However, resolution is not the midpoint between the two concepts (+1), as we might expect. Instead, the model would predict that resolution would occur at +2, reducing the consumer's perceived attitude of Robertson by only one scale unit and increasing his attitude toward AT&T by three scale units.

Although the mathematics used to predict the resolution point will not be presented here, the greater shift for AT&T than for Robertson is intuitively understandable.[12] Strong attitudes are more difficult to change than are weak or moderate ones. Thus, the consumer's stronger positive attitude toward Robertson exerts greater pull on his weaker negative attitude toward AT&T. This idea suggests that when consumers develop a strong dislike toward a brand, company efforts to improve consumer attitudes will require a tremendous marketing effort, which may not be worth the cost. The company may be better off in many cases either to (1) drop the brand and reintroduce it under another name, if promotional

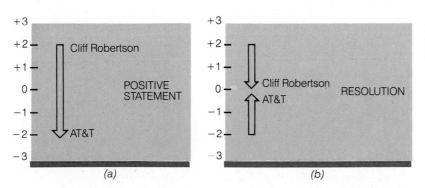

FIGURE 16-3
A simple example of resolving incongruity.

positioning has been the problem or (2) introduce a new reformulated brand, if product quality, design, or formulation has been the problem. Conversely, if the consumer holds an extremely positive attitude toward the brand, considerable unfavorable experiences and word-of-mouth influence would be required to deteriorate the attitude significantly.

It should be noted that although the model predicts resolution at a value of +2 in Figure 16-4, there are qualifications. First, if the consumer perceives the information he had heard to be totally unbelievable, he can reject it, and no attitude change will occur. In this instance, the information would be totally discounted. Second, if the consumer experiences only some disbelief instead of total disbelief, his attitudes will change only slightly.[13] This qualification for disbelief adds further strength to the marketing examples previously mentioned. Specifically, consumers who hold extremely negative attitudes toward a brand will not only be difficult to change, but will ignore or discount information to the contrary.

The congruity principle is used frequently in marketing.[14] Advertisers often use hired celebrities to endorse brands, services, organizations, and causes. Athletes speak against drug use among young people; movie actresses endorse various kinds of beauty aids; and race-car drivers promote brands of tires, spark plugs, and other automobile accessories. Of course, the intent is to have consumers who hold positive attitudes toward a source (the person making such favorable statements about an object) to develop a positive value association between the source and the object.

BALANCE THEORY

Several balance models have been developed, all of which are based upon the pioneering work of Fritz Heider.[15] According to balance theory, a person perceives her or his environment in terms of *triads*. That is, a person views herself or himself as being involved in a triangular relationship in which all three elements (persons, ideas, and things) have either positive (liking, favorable) or negative (disliking, unfavorable) relationships with each other. This relationship is termed *sentiment*.

Unlike the congruity model, there are no numerical values used to express the degree of unity between elements. Instead, the model is described as *unbalanced* if the multiplicative relationships among the three elements is negative, and *balanced* if the multiplicative relationship is positive. To illustrate, consider the

FIGURE 16-4
A more complex example of
the resolution of incongruity.

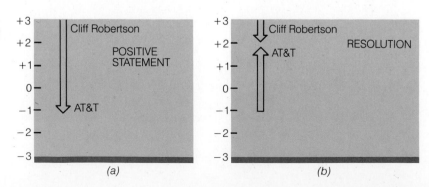

consumer situation expressed as three statements: (1) "I like large luxurious cars," (2) "I don't like energy-wasting products," (3) "I believe large, luxurious cars waste energy." This situation is described by the triad shown in Figure 16-5. Notice that the structure is not in balance, because there is a positive relationship on two sides of the triad and a negative relationship on the third side, and this results in a negative multiplicative product.

Because the relationship presented in the example is unbalanced, it will produce tension for the consumer. It may be possible for her to "live with" the tension and do nothing to resolve it. However, if sufficient tension exists, it is likely that attitude change will occur regarding at least one element in the triad in order to restore balance to the system. These attempts at resolution can result in the consumer: (1) disliking large, luxurious cars; (2) believing that large, luxurious cars are not really energy-wasting products; or (3) liking energy-wasting products (they create jobs and provide psychological satisfaction, for example). As we can see, rationalization can help to change our perceptions of relationships and thus our attitudes.

COGNITIVE DISSONANCE

The theory of cognitive dissonance was developed in 1957 by Leon Festinger.[16] Festinger describes cognitive dissonance as a psychological state which results when a person perceives that two cognitions (thoughts), both of which he believes to be true, do not "fit" together; that is, they seem inconsistent. The resulting dissonance produces tension, which serves to motivate the individual to bring harmony to inconsistent elements and thereby reduce psychological tension.

Dissonance can arise in three basic ways. First, any *logical inconsistency* can create dissonance. For example, "all candy is sweet; my candy is sour." Second, dissonance can be created when a person experiences an *inconsistency either between his attitude and his behavior or between two of his behaviors*. For example, Michael actively compliments Nike running shoes on many occasions and then purchases a pair of Adidas running shoes. This is an example of an inconsistency between two behaviors. On the other hand, a discrepancy between an attitude and behavior would exist when David strongly dislikes gambling but bets on the outcome of football games. Third, dissonance can occur when a strongly held *expectation is disconfirmed*. To illustrate, Margaret expects to find

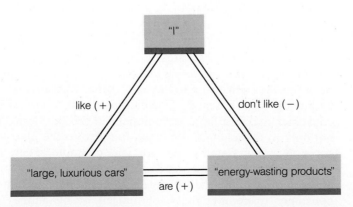

FIGURE 16-5
A graphic representation of an unbalanced attitudinal structure.

significant savings at a sidewalk sale but finds only unstylish and damaged merchandise.

In all three cases, it is necessary for a person to perceive the inconsistency; otherwise, no dissonance will occur. Some people are very capable of holding an attitude that contradicts their behavior without perceiving the contradiction. Therefore, they suffer no dissonance.

Regardless of its source, cognitive dissonance arises *after* a decision has been made. The decision, in effect, *commits* the person to certain positions or attitudes, when prior to that time that person was capable of adjusting her attitudes or behavior to avoid dissonance.

A person experiencing cognitive dissonance has three major ways to reduce it. They are (1) rationalization, (2) seeking additional information that is supportive of or consistent with his behavior, and (3) either eliminating or altering some of the dissonant elements, which can be accomplished by either forgetting or suppressing dissonant elements or by changing his attitude so that it is no longer dissonant with another attitude or behavior. Each of these strategies may be used alone or in combination.

To illustrate these methods, consider Diane who has purchased a Nikon 35-mm, single-lens reflex camera outfit for $560 after seriously considering other brands, such as Pentax, Canon, and Minolta, in the same general price range. Besides the investment of $560, she also has invested much thought and searching time and a considerable amount of ego in the purchase decision. Therefore, the amount at stake in this purchase is considerable. After evaluating the pros and cons of each brand of camera, she has selected the Nikon. Subsequent to the purchase, Diane finds her camera hard to focus and the lenses difficult to change. Furthermore, the strap broke on the carrying case. She now begins to doubt the wisdom of her purchase. A tension arises from her two beliefs that (1) Nikons are well-constructed, precision cameras and (2) "my Nikon is difficult to focus for clear pictures, it takes too much time and effort to change lenses, and the strap on the carrying case has broken."

Diane can reduce the tension arising from these two cognitions by *rationalizing* that any fine camera can have its faults and that the retailer probably treated the carrying case with abuse which caused the eventual strap break. Or she might *seek information* which reinforces her belief that Nikon cameras are among the very best in the world, thereby amplifying the strong points of the camera, such as rapid film advancement, nice styling, and a solid shutter click, indicating durability. Finally, a third option is to *change her opinion* toward Nikon cameras: "They are not good cameras. I should have purchased a Canon."

This example illustrates a very common type of marketing related phenomenon—*postpurchase dissonance*. Postpurchase dissonance occurs when a person makes a decision to buy one brand from among several alternative brands within a product category. The dissonance becomes particularly strong when the consumer makes a large commitment in the purchase. Such commitment refers not only to the amount of money, but also to the investment of time, effort, and ego as was illustrated in the previous example. Therefore, a purchase decision involving choice among brands of chewing gum at a supermarket checkout counter is unlikely to produce much perceptible dissonance. Goods requiring the consumer to commit much of himself or his money, however, are likely to generate considerable postpurchase dissonance. In general, therefore, durable and luxury goods are more likely to produce dissonance than are convenience goods, because they usually require larger consumer investment in time, ego, and money.

During purchase decisions, dissonance can result when the consumer recognizes that alternative brands have both positive and negative characteristics. Therefore, after making a decision, the consumer realizes that he has acquired some *relatively* undesirable traits of the selected brand while foregoing some relatively desirable traits of the alternative brands. At this point, the consumer may even rate the unchosen alternatives higher than the brand purchased. In the consumer's mind, positive attributes of unchosen brands and negative characteristics of the chosen brand are emphasized. This period of postpurchase process is called the *regret* phase, and it usually is very brief. The next phase is termed the *dissonance reduction period*. In this stage, the consumer is very likely to evaluate the chosen brand more positively than at the time of purchase, and he may evaluate the unselected brands less positively.

MULTIATTRIBUTE MODELS

In recent years, the adequacy of earlier attitude theories and models has come under question. An important criticism has been the lack of attention to the complexity and interactions of attitude components. In fact, early work employed only one-component definitions of attitude by focusing exclusively on a person's overall feelings or evaluative reactions toward objects. Later theories expanded on this view by stressing that attitudes have three major components: (1) the *cognitive* component, which accounts for the individual's perceptions and knowledge about an object; (2) the *affective* component, which describes the individual's feelings or emotional reactions (like/dislike) toward the object; and (3) the *conative* component, which encompasses a tendency to act in certain ways toward the object. Unfortunately, although the importance of the three component view of attitudes was widely recognized, many marketers continued to employ measures that only focused on the affective component for determining an individual's overall evaluation of an object. As a consequence, it was difficult to determine the basis of a person's overall attitude and how it might be possible to influence this attitude to change.[17] Of course, as we might expect, the basis or reasons for holding an attitude, and the factors which might influence it to change over time are two considerations of high importance for the design of marketing strategies. Therefore, attitude measures that continued to focus only on the affective component were of limited usefulness to marketers.

Rosenberg and Fishbein pioneered new models of attitudes which have overcome many of the shortcomings of previous theories.[18] Because marketers and consumer behaviorists have given more attention to the Fishbein model, it will be reviewed here as an example of multiattribute attitude models.[19]

Fishbein's Attitude Model   Fishbein's position is that people form attitudes toward objects on the basis of their *beliefs* (perceptions and knowledge) about these objects. Beliefs are in turn acquired by processing information which is obtained from direct experiences with objects and from communications about them received from other sources. Therefore, to understand consumers' attitudes adequately we must determine the beliefs that form the basis of these attitudes. Notice how this view is consistent with the flow of high-involvement consumer activities that has been presented in this text: information processing leads to cognitions or beliefs about products which in turn, lead to attitudes that are involved in the evaluation of products.

Because any object such as a product has numerous attributes (size, features, shape and the like), an individual will process information and form beliefs about many of these individual attributes. Positive or negative feelings are also formed on the basis of the beliefs held about these attributes. Therefore, Fishbein's model is constructed so that a person's overall attitude toward some object is derived from his beliefs and feelings about various attributes of the object. This is why we refer to it as a *multiattribute* attitude model.

Fishbein's attitude model can be expressed in equation form as:

$$A_o = \sum_{i=1}^{n} b_i e_i$$

where A_o = the person's overall attitude toward the object

b_i = the strength of his belief that the object is related to attribute i (such as the strength of the belief that Wrangler jeans are durable)

e_i = his evaluation or intensity of feelings (liking or disliking) toward attribute i

n = the number of relevant beliefs for that person

We can see that the model explicitly incorporates the cognitive (belief) and affective (evaluation) components of attitudes. It also accounts for the strength or intensity of these elements. The conative component, to be discussed in more depth shortly, is related to these two components.

The model states that to determine a person's overall attitude toward some object, it is first necessary to determine those beliefs that have the most influence on her attitude. These most relevant beliefs, called *salient* beliefs, frequently do not exceed nine in number.[20] The overall attitude toward an object can then be obtained by multiplying the belief score by the evaluation score for each attribute and then summing across all relevant beliefs to obtain the value A_o.

An example will reinforce our understanding of the model. Assume that we want to determine a consumer's overall attitude toward a certain brand of wristwatch and that through questioning we have been able to identify five beliefs that appear to be salient for this consumer. The strength of each belief can be measured on a bipolar scale such as the following:

The wristwatch is high in price

likely								unlikely
	(+3)	(+2)	(+1)	(0)	(−1)	(−2)	(−3)	

By responding to this scale, the consumer is indicating the degree to which she believes that the wristwatch possesses the attribute in question—in this case, a high price. If we were attempting to assess the attitudes of more than one consumer, we could question a sample of them and then select as salient beliefs those that are most frequently mentioned. The entire group of consumers would then be asked to respond to these salient beliefs, as indicated above.

After obtaining belief scores, the consumer would be asked to indicate her evaluation of each product attribute for which a salient belief exists. This is frequently accomplished on the following type of scale:

A high price for the wristwatch is:

good _____ _____ _____ _____ _____ _____ _____ bad
　　　 extremely　 moderately　 slightly　 neither/nor　 slightly　 moderately　 extremely
　　　　(+3)　　　　(+2)　　　　(+1)　　　　 (0)　　　　 (−1)　　　　 (−2)　　　　 (−3)

Be careful to note that these evaluation scores measure the consumer's feelings about each attribute itself (high price, accurate time, and so on). They do *not* measure how much the consumer is pleased or displeased that the brand in question possesses the attribute.

Table 16-1 presents hypothetical results of these data collection efforts. As the model requires, each of the consumer's belief scores are now multiplied by their respective evaluation scores to obtain the last column of the table. Adding all of the products in this column reveals that the consumer's overall attitude toward the brand stands at +5. This represents a slightly positive attitude toward the brand when compared to a maximum attainable attitude score of +45. The consumer's attitude toward other wristwatch brands could also be calculated and compared to this brand. For the additional brands, it would only be necessary to obtain new belief scores because, as mentioned, the evaluation score measures feelings toward general product attributes and therefore does not vary across brands.

It is important to note how differences in belief scores and evaluation scores can influence the consumer's overall attitude toward the product. For example, note in Table 16-1 that the first two salient beliefs both have the same evaluation score of +2. However, because the consumer is more confident that this brand of wristwatch keeps good time (+3) than she is that it has a waterproof case (+2), the time-accuracy attribute contributes more to her attitude toward the brand.

TABLE 16-1

Calculating a Consumer's Attitude Toward a Brand of Wristwatch

Salient beliefs	Belief strength (b_i)	Evaluation score (e_i)	Product ($b_i e_i$)
Keeps accurate time	+3	+2	+6
Has waterproof case	+2	+2	+4
Has day/date calendar	+1	+3	+3
Is high in price	+3	−2	−6
Has digital display	+2	−1	−2

Overall attitude score: $(A_o) = \sum_{i=1}^{5} b_i e_i = +5$

Conversely, notice that the first and fourth salient beliefs both have the same belief strength, but they differ considerably in terms of evaluation scores ($+2$ versus -2), yielding *offsetting* contributions to the consumer's overall attitude. This points out an important characteristic of this type of attitude model—in addition to being multiattribute in nature, it is also a *compensatory* model. This means that the product of belief and evaluation scores on one brand attribute can be offset or *compensated* for by the products derived from one or more other attributes. The implication is that a poor response of the consumer to one feature of a brand does not necessarily cancel this brand out in her eyes.

These last comments demonstrate an important potential of multiattribute models. As has been stated:

The potential advantage of multi-attribute models over the simpler "over-all affect" approach (unidimensional model) is in gaining understanding of attitudinal structure. Diagnosis of brand strengths and weaknesses on relevant product attributes can then be used to suggest specific changes in a brand and its marketing support.[21]

That is, information regarding consumers' beliefs and evaluations generated by a multiattribute model provides important knowledge relevant to marketing strategy. The information can be used to suggest changes in brand attributes, modifications of promotional messages to better acquaint consumers with existing brand attributes, and the identification of new market opportunities. More will be said about these strategies in the next chapter.

MODEL LIMITATIONS   Many marketers were quick to capitalize on the potential of Fishbein's model and similar multiattribute models for predicting the behavior of consumers. Consequently, numerous studies were undertaken to establish the strength of this attitude-behavior linkage. Unfortunately, these studies did not yield a consistently positive relationship. Several reasons have been offered for these lackluster results:

1   Consumption situations can vary, and this will influence the strength of the attitude-behavior relationship.[22] In fact, evidence suggests that consumers' attitudes toward a given brand can actually vary depending on the situation.[23]

2   Time usually elapses between when consumers form attitudes and when they are ready to act on these attitudes. During that time, many variables, both expected and unexpected, can intervene to also influence behavior. For example, an unexpected need for a new family car could quickly postpone or cancel plans to purchase a home video recorder.

3   A distinction must be made between attitudes toward objects and attitudes toward behaving in a certain way toward these objects. For example, many consumers could have a favorable attitude toward Chevrolet Corvettes, but, because of their cost, few would realistically have a favorable attitude toward purchasing one. The consumer's attitudes toward some type of behavior are influenced by his evaluation of the perceived consequences (positive and negative) of taking such action. Therefore, these attitudes are more relevant for predicting consumers' actions than are attitudes toward the objects themselves.

4   Consumers are often influenced by their *perceptions* of what others will think of their actions. Therefore, even though a consumer may have a favorable attitude toward making some purchase, he may refrain from doing so because of his perception that others who are important to him may not approve of the action. This influence is referred to as a *subjective norm*.

These considerations convinced attitude theorists that it is inappropriate to expect attitude-toward-object models to successfully predict behavior. New modeling efforts were necessary to account for the additional complexity introduced by such factors. Fishbein responded with the behavioral intentions model.[24]

Fishbein's Behavioral Intentions Model   The new model offered by Fishbein, and contributed to by Ajzen, can be presented in diagram form as shown in Figure 16-6. Here, we see that a person's behavior is a function of his intention to behave in a certain manner and other intervening factors. This means that intention to behave cannot be expected to be a perfect predictor of behavior.

Two factors are seen to influence the person's intention to act in a certain manner: (1) his attitude toward acting in that manner and (2) subjective norms, which we said are the individual's perceptions of how others who are important to him will react to such behavior. The relative influence of each of these factors will determine the exact nature of the person's behavioral intentions. The figure also shows that attitudes toward behavior are determined by beliefs and evaluations that the consumer holds about the consequences of behavior. Subjective norms are determined by the consumer's beliefs about reactions of others regarding his intended behavior, and his motivations to comply with their standards for behavior.

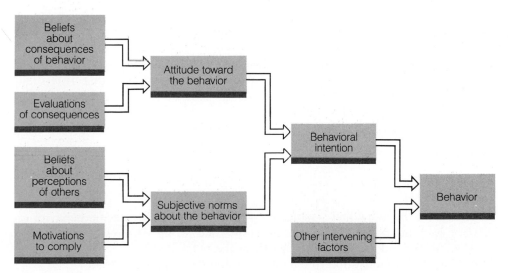

FIGURE 16-6
The relationship of components in Fishbein's behavioral intentions attitude model.

Fishbein expressed these relationships in equation form as:

$$B \approx BI = w_1(A_B) + w_2(SN)$$

where B = the person's actual behavior, which is approximately equal to BI
  BI = his intention to behave in a specific manner
  A_B = his attitude toward performing that behavior
  SN = the subjective norm regarding this behavior
  w_1, w_2 = weights representing the relative influence of A_B and SN, respectively, on the behavioral intention

As the model shows, to predict behavior one must determine the individual's attitude toward the specific behavior in question (A_B), and his subjective norm (SN) regarding that behavior. Each of these would then be weighted by w_1 and w_2 respectively (which add up to 1.0) to reflect their relative importance in influencing the behavioral intention. Such weights would be derived by regression analysis from a preliminary study. The weighted components would then be combined to yield a measure of behavioral intention to be used for prediction. We can see, therefore, that use of the model requires determination of its two components—A_B and SN. Each of these is discussed, in turn, below.

The individual's attitude toward performing the specific behavior (A_B) is expressed as:

$$A_B = \sum_{i=1}^{n} b_i e_i$$

where A_B = the individual's overall attitude toward performing the specific behavior
  b_i = the person's belief that performing that behavior results in consequence i
  e_i = the person's evaluation of consequence i
  n = the number of relevant behavioral beliefs

It will be noticed that the *structure* of this component is identical to the model for attitude toward objects that was discussed earlier. As was stated before, relevant beliefs must be determined and then these beliefs and the accompanying evaluations must be measured on scales. The important change here is that beliefs and evaluations are about certain *actions* and the consequences of these actions, rather than about attributes of an object.

The subjective norm component of the behavioral intentions model can be expressed as follows:

$$SN = \sum_{i=1}^{k} b_i m_i$$

where SN = the individual's subjective norm regarding the specific behavior
  b_i = his normative belief that reference group or person i thinks he should or should not perform the behavior
  m_i = his motivation to comply with the thoughts of referent i
  k = the number of relevant referents

An example will provide more meaning to these formulas. Assume that a consumer is considering the purchase of a chartered vacation package for a two-week period during the first half of July. To simplify the situation, also assume that she is only interested in choosing between two vacation packages—one to England and one to Japan. The consumer's behavioral intention toward these alternatives will be a function of her attitude toward purchasing each and of the subjective norms she holds about each purchase. These components are each examined in turn below.

As our formula for A_B shows, to determine the consumer's attitude toward purchasing either vacation package we must first identify the salient beliefs she holds toward the consequences of a purchase. Often these can be obtained through a questioning process. However, if the attitudes of a large number of consumers needed to be measured, questioning a sample of them would identify the most frequently held salient beliefs. In either case, once consumers' salient beliefs regarding the consequences of actions have been identified, we would need to measure their belief strengths and their evaluations of these consequences. The difference between the scales that would measure these variables and the ones used for Fishbein's earlier attitude model is that now focus is on the *consequences* of purchase *behavior* rather than on the attributes of the object.

Table 16-2 presents results that we could have been obtained from our consumer. The first column identifies six salient beliefs this consumer holds about the consequences of purchasing the two chartered vacation packages. Notice that the statements refer to a specific time interval for the actions. The second and third columns represent the degree to which the consumer believes these consequences describe the England trip and Japan trip, respectively. The third column represents the consumer's evaluation of the consequences described in column 1. Notice that these evaluations would be the same for the various trips, because

Salient beliefs about consequences	Belief strengths (b_i)		Evaluation score (e_i)	Product ($b_i e_i$)	
	England trip	Japan trip		England trip	Japan trip
Taking the England/Japan vacation package in July will:					
■ Increase my social contacts	+2	+2	+3	+6	+6
■ Provide a restful vacation	+2	+1	+1	+2	+1
■ Improve my mental attitude	+1	+3	+2	+2	+6
■ Be expensive	+2	+3	−2	−4	−6
■ Make me a more interesting person	+1	+3	+2	+2	+6
■ Involve difficult language skills	−2	+2	−3	+6	−6
Overall attitude toward purchase: $A_B = \sum_{i=1}^{6} b_i e_i =$				+14	+7

they reflect feelings about consequences and not feelings about the extent to which such consequences would result from particular trips.

The last two columns present the product of belief and evaluation scores for each trip; the sum of these columns shows that the consumer holds a more favorable attitude toward taking the England trip ($+14$) than she does the Japan trip ($+7$).

Now, in order to determine the consumer's subjective norm for purchasing either vacation package, we must first identify the groups and individuals who have the most influence on her regarding the behavior in question. These are called the *salient referents*. Often, this information can be obtained through a questioning process. Assume for our purposes that there are three individuals who are salient referents for this consumer: her brother, a special friend, and her boss.

We next must identify the consumer's beliefs about thoughts or reactions of these people regarding her purchase of each of the vacation trips. Her motivation to comply with these thoughts must also be measured. This information could be obtained from the following types of measurement scales:

My brother thinks that I

| should | ____ | ____ | ____ | ____ | ____ | ____ | ____ | should not |
| | (+3) | (+2) | (+1) | (0) | (−1) | (−2) | (−3) | |

take the charter trip to England in July

How much do you want to do what your brother thinks
that you should do?

_____	Not at all	(0)
_____	Slightly	(+1)
_____	Moderately	(+2)
_____	Strongly	(+3)

Table 16-3 summarizes results of our data collection regarding the subjective norm component in much the same way as previous tables have done. It is useful to notice how the consumer's motivation to comply weights the perceptions of salient referent opinions. For example, she believes that both her special friend

TABLE 16-3

Calculating a Consumer's Subjective Norm Toward Purchasing Different Vacation Packages

Salient referents	Normative belief strength (b_i)		Motivation to comply (m_i)	Product ($b_i m_i$)	
	England trip	Japan trip		England trip	Japan trip
Brother	+2	+1	+1	+2	+1
Special friend	−1	+2	+3	−3	+6
Boss	+1	+2	+2	+2	+4
Subjective norm: SN $= \sum_{i=1}^{3} b_i m_i =$				+1	+11

and her boss hold the same opinions about the Japan trip, but because she is more motivated to comply with her friend's opinion, it carries more weight in influencing her subjective norm. Overall, we see from a summation of the last columns that the subjective norm considerably favors the Japan trip ($+11$) over the England trip ($+1$).

The last ingredients needed to determine our consumer's behavioral intentions are weights that reflect the relative importance of her attitude toward behavior and her subjective norm. Recall that these weights would have to come from regression analysis of a preliminary study. Assume that such an investigation generated weights of .4 and .6 for the attitude and subjective norm components respectively. We now can substitute these weights and information from Tables 16-2 and 16-3 into the equation that was presented earlier and is repeated below:

$$BI = w_1(A_B) + w_2(SN)$$

For the England trip we find that $BI = .4(14) + .6(1) = 6.2$ and for the Japan trip $BI = .4(7) + .6(11) = 9.4$. We see that, in this case, even though the consumer's attitude strongly favors the England trip, her subjective norm strongly favors the Japan trip. Because the subjective norm carries more weight in her decision making on this issue (.6 versus .4), the prediction is that she intends to purchase the Japan trip. However, recall from our earlier discussion and Figure 16-6 that because of other influencing factors the consumer's behavioral intentions will only be an approximation of her actual behavior.

MODEL EVALUATION   A number of issues and limitations of the Fishbein behavioral intention model still need to be resolved.[25] Nevertheless, evidence accumulating from tests of the model has been quite encouraging.[26] Our ability to predict the behavior of consumers has improved when compared to the earlier attitude-toward-object model. However, what appears to be just as important are the implications this model has for marketers in terms of factors influencing consumers' intentions to behave. These attitudinal and subjective norm components can enable diagnosis of reasons for behavior, and also suggest alternative marketing strategies for effecting changes in consumers' attitudes and intentions to behave. These practical implications will have much of our attention in the next chapter.

ATTITUDE TOWARD THE AD

The reader should be aware that Fishbein's models are belief-based. That is, the models assume that consumers will first develop beliefs about individual attributes of a brand and then use these beliefs to form an overall attitude about the brand. Notice that the focus here is on *conscious* attitude development, with stress on the processing of *verbal* information in the form of cognitions (thoughts or beliefs) about the brand.

A short time ago several researchers began to question whether such a process is the only way consumers form brand attitudes.[27] This led to a proposal for an additional source of brand attitudes: *attitude toward the ad*. Essentially, the argument is that if consumers develop positive reactions to an advertisement itself

(its visual images, music, and the like), then this might also have a favorable impact on their attitudes toward the brand being advertised.

One way this might occur is that consumers translate their favorable reactions toward the ad into verbally represented beliefs about the brand being advertised. These beliefs would be the same as those we discussed in Fishbein's models. The implication would then be that those interested in consumers' brand attitudes would have to be concerned with the nature of the advertisement itself (pictures, models used, background music) as well as the *verbal content* or copy of the ad that specifically addresses brand attributes.

However, a more intriguing possibility has also been proposed: Consumers may process the visual and other nonverbal elements of an ad directly, rather than translating them into verbal thoughts or beliefs. Recall that our discussion in the early part of the information processing chapter suggested that humans appear to have separate channels for processing visual and other nonverbal stimuli. Therefore, the proposal is consistent with some of what we know about consumers' information-processing activities. A recent study provides additional evidence to support this line of reasoning.[28] Separate groups of subjects were shown different advertisements for four fictitious brands of facial tissue. Three ads contained no verbal information beyond the fictitious name of the facial tissue (identified only by a letter of the alphabet) but did contain a half-page color photograph. One ad showed a soft, fluffy kitten with the facial tissue box, one used a sunset over an ocean, and another showed a presumed neutrally evaluated abstract painting. The fourth ad contained a verbal claim about softness of the tissues, but no picture. Study results indicated that subjects formed significantly different impressions of the advertised tissues. Both the kitten and sunset ads created more positive brand attitudes than the verbal message or the picture of the abstract painting did. Also, subjects exposed to the ad showing the soft, fluffy kitten rated the facial tissues significantly more soft than did any of the other groups. Fishbein's attitude model did not successfully predict these attitude scores of the subjects. Given such results, one implication is that those who would employ Fishbein's belief-based model to assess consumers' brand attitudes might stand the risk of misrepresenting these attitudes to some degree.

Why do consumers act in this way? What mechanism might be involved? Actually, we have already discussed a leading contender for explaining such results—*classical conditioning*. We saw in Chapter 14 that repeated pairing of a neutral stimulus with one that evokes positive reactions can lead to the neutral stimulus evoking similar reactions. Therefore, the classical conditioning explanation would suggest that if advertisers repeatedly show their brand with stimuli such as fluffy kittens, pleasant music, people having good times, and so on, then the positive reactions generated by these stimuli will tend to become associated with the advertised brand. This might then increase consumers' positive evaluations of the brand more than their cognitive beliefs alone would account for. Figure 16-7 presents one type of advertisement that appears capable of accomplishing this.

Additional research has generated further support for the classical conditioning explanation of attitude-toward-the-ad effects.[29] However, other plausible mechanisms do exist, and recent evidence reveals that they may also have an important influence.[30] Also, one study suggests that the effects may be much more

525

Looks like a
Dinty Moore day.

Dinty Moore Beef Stew makes any day better.
Serve your family America's favorite.
Make It A Dinty Moore Day with A Real Meat
And Potatoes Meal.

FIGURE 16-7
An advertisement potentially
capable of generating
positive attitude-toward-the-
ad effects.
Courtesy of George A. Hormel &
Company.

important under conditions of low involvement.[31] However, what is clear is that
given the large number of advertisements which stress the visual presentation and
often convey little verbal information, those interested in consumers' attitudes
should be quite eager to learn more about these fascinating new proposals on the
effects of advertisements.

MANAGERIAL REFLECTIONS

For our product or service situation . . .

1   What experiences are likely to be influential in forming attitudes toward our
offering?

2   How might congruity theory and balance theory be useful in understanding
consumers' attitudes?

3   What are likely sources of dissonance related to our offerings, and how might
we influence the dissonance process?

4   Of what potential benefit is Fishbein's attitude model? What are its potential
limitations?

5   How might we successfully employ Fishbein's behavioral intentions model?

6   What are some of the ''other intervening factors'' that might result in a
difference between consumers' intentions to behave and their actual behavior?

7   What are the potential implications of consumers' attitudes toward our advertisements?

DISCUSSION TOPICS

1   A variety of definitions of attitude exist. What appears to be the emphasis of the more recent definitions?

2   What are the major characteristics of attitudes? Assume an attitude regarding a specific product, and use this as an example to demonstrate each characteristic.

3   What are the functions of an attitude? Can you cite specific personal experiences that demonstrate each of these functions?

4   What are the sources of attitude development? Can you foresee how these sources might conflict with one another in their influence on developing attitudes? If so, cite an example to demonstrate your point.

5   Review the attitude theories of congruity, balance, and cognitive dissonance. Highlight their major characteristics.

6   Some advertisements make highly exaggerated claims for a brand, claims which probably cannot be fulfilled. Using your knowledge of cognitive dissonance, assess the wisdom of this technique.

7   Distinguish between the Fishbein attitude model and earlier attitude theories. What implications does this have for predicting consumer behavior?

8   It has been argued that the consequences of action referred to in Fishbein's behavioral intentions model can be linked to the concepts of consumers' perceived benefits and benefit segmentation. Discuss this argument.

9   Think of a product, or action toward a product, about which you hold an attitude. Did you use a compensatory method in formulating this attitude? If so, explain how. If not, explain why you think this is the case.

PROJECTS

1   Select some subjects and a brand that they might reasonably be expected to purchase relatively frequently. Attempt to determine their behavioral intentions for such a purchase within the next two weeks.

2   Interview a friend and analyze two of his or her recent experiences within the context of the congruity, balance, and Fishbein models.

3   Identify at least four advertisements that might have the characteristics for evoking favorable effects from positive consumer attitudes toward the ad. What are their characteristics?

NOTES

[1] Based on Lisa Phillips, ''Devil Rumor Still Hounds P & G,'' *Advertising Age,* April 22, 1985, p. 127; and ''The Man in the Moon Disappears,'' *Time,* May 6, 1985, p. 63.

[2] Martin Fishbein, "The Relationship between Beliefs, Attitudes, and Behavior," in Shel Feldman (ed.), *Cognitive Consistency*, Academic, New York, 1966, pp. 199–223.

[3] The term "object" is used here to include abstract concepts such as enjoyment, as well as physical things.

[4] Gordon W. Allport, "Attitudes," in C. A. Murchison (ed.), *A Handbook of Social Psychology*, Clark University Press, Worcester, Mass., 1935, pp. 798–844.

[5] D. Krech and R. Crutchfield, *Theory and Problems in Social Psychology*, McGraw-Hill, New York, 1948.

[6] Martin Fishbein, "A Behavior Theory Approach to the Relations between Beliefs about an Object and the Attitude Toward the Object," in Martin Fishbein (ed.), *Readings in Attitude Theory and Measurement*, Wiley, New York, 1967, p. 394.

[7] T. M. Newcomb, R. H. Turner, and P. E. Converse, *Social Psychology*, Holt, New York, 1965, p. 115.

[8] Daniel Katz, "The Functional Approach to the Study of Attitudes," *Public Opinion Quarterly*, **24**:163–204, 1960.

[9] M. Wayne DeLozier, *The Marketing Communications Process*, McGraw-Hill, New York, 1976, p. 81.

[10] Arch G. Woodside and J. William Davenport, "The Effect of Salesman Similarity and Expertise on Consumer Purchasing Behavior," *Journal of Marketing Research*, **11**:198–202, May 1974.

[11] This section is based largely upon the works of Charles E. Osgood, George J. Suci, and Percy H. Tannenbaum, *The Measurement of Meaning*, University of Illinois Press, Urbana, Ill., 1957; Milton J. Rosenberg et al., *Attitude Organization and Change*, Yale University Press, New Haven, Conn., 1960; Leon A. Festinger, *A Theory of Cognitive Dissonance*, Stanford University Press, Stanford, Calif., 1957; Roger Brown, *Social Psychology*, Free Press, New York, 1965; and Martin Fishbein and Icek Ajzen, *Belief, Attitude, Intention and Behavior*, Addison-Wesley, Reading, Mass., 1975.

[12] For a thorough treatment of the mathematics involved in predicting the resolution of such cases, see Osgood, Suci, and Tannenbaum, *Measurement of Meaning*, pp. 199–207.

[13] See Jonathan L. Freedman, Jr., Merrill Carlsmith, and David O. Sears, *Social Psychology*, Prentice-Hall, Englewood Cliffs, N.J., 1970, p. 263; and Charles E. Osgood and Percy H. Tannenbaum, "The Principle of Congruity in the Prediction of Attitude Change," *Psychological Review*, **62**:42–55, 1955.

[14] Some of the ideas in this section are attributable to Brown, *Social Psychology*, pp. 566–670.

[15] Fritz Heider, "Attitudes and Cognitive Organizations," *Journal of Psychology*, **21**:107–112, January 1946.

[16] See Festinger, *Cognitive Dissonance*.

[17] See Fishbein and Ajzen, *Belief, Attitude, Intention and Behavior*, pp. 11–13; and Icek Ajzen and Martin Fishbein, *Understanding Attitudes and Predicting Social Behavior*, Prentice-Hall, Englewood Cliffs, N.J., 1980, pp. 18–20.

[18] See Milton J. Rosenberg, "Cognitive Structure and Attitudinal Affect," *Journal of Abnormal and Social Psychology*, **53**:367–372, November 1956; Martin Fishbein, "An Investigation of the Relationship between Beliefs about an Object and the Attitudes toward That Object," *Human Relations*, **16**:233–240, 1963; and Martin Fishbein, "Attitude and the Prediction of Behavior," in Martin Fishbein (ed.), *Readings in Attitude Theory and Measurement*, Wiley, New York, 1967, pp. 477–492.

[19] Some examples are Arch G. Woodside and James D. Clokey, "Multi-Attribute/Multi-Brand Models," *Journal of Advertising Research*, **14**:33–40, October 1974; Frank M. Bass and W. Wayne Talarzyk, "An Attitude Model for the Study of Brand Preference," *Journal of Marketing Research*, **9**:93–96, February 1972; Michael B. Mazis, Olli T. Ahtola, and R. Eugene Klippel, "A Comparison of Four Multi-Attribute Models in the Prediction of Consumer Attitudes," *Journal of Consumer Research*, **2**:38–52, June 1975; and James R. Bettman, Noel Capon, Richard J. Lutz, "Multi-attribute Measurement Models and Multi-attribute Theory: A Test of Construct Validity," *Journal of Consumer Research*, **1**:1–14, March 1975.

[20] Ajzen and Fishbein, *Understanding Attitudes and Predicting Social Behavior*, p. 63.

[21] William L. Wilkie and Edgar A. Pessemier, "Issues in Marketing's Use of Multi-Attribute Attitude Models," *Journal of Marketing Research*, **10**:428, November 1973.

[22] See William O. Bearden and Arch G. Woodside, "Interactions of Consumption Situations and Brand Attitudes," *Journal of Applied Psychology*, **61**:764–769, 1976.

[23] See Kenneth E. Miller and James L. Ginter, "An Investigation of Situational Variation in Brand Choice Behavior and Attitude," *Journal of Marketing Research*, **16**:111–123, February 1979.

[24] See Martin Fishbein, "Attitude and the Prediction of Behavior"; and Ajzen and Fishbein, *Understanding Attitudes and Predicting Social Behavior*.

[25] See, for example, Paul R. Warshaw, "Predicting Purchase and Other Behaviors from Generally and Contextually Specific Intentions," *Journal of Marketing Research,* **17**:26–33, February 1980; and Michael J. Ryan and E. H. Bonfield, "Fishbein's Intentions Model: A Test of External and Pragmatic Validity," *Journal of Marketing,* **44**:82–95, Spring 1980.

[26] See, for example, Richard L. Oliver and Philip K. Berger, "A Path Analysis of Preventive Health Care Decision Models," *Journal of Consumer Research,* **6**:113–122, September 1979; and Ryan and Bonfield, "Fishbein's Intentions Model."

[27] See Terence A. Shimp, "Attitude toward the Ad as a Mediator of Consumer Brand Choice," *Journal of Advertising,* **10**:9–15, 1981; and Andrew A. Mitchell and Jerry C. Olson, "Are Product Attribute Beliefs the Only Mediator of Advertising Effects on Brand Attitude?" *Journal of Marketing Research,* **18**:318–332, August 1981.

[28] Mitchell and Olson, "Are Product Beliefs the Only Mediator on Brand Attitude?"

[29] Andrew A. Mitchell, "The Effect of Verbal and Visual Components of Advertisements on Brand Attitudes and Attitude toward the Advertisement," *Journal of Consumer Research,* **13**:12–24, June 1986.

[30] See Larry G. Gresham and Terence Shimp, "Attitude toward the Advertisement and Brand Attitudes: A Classical Conditioning Perspective," *Journal of Advertising,* **14**:10–17, 49, 1985; and Scott B. MacKenzie, Richard J. Lutz, and George Belch, "The Role of Attitude toward the Ad as a Mediator of Advertising Effectiveness: A Test of Competing Explanations," *Journal of Marketing Research,* **23**:130–143, May 1986.

[31] C. Whan Park and Mark Young, "The Effects of Involvement and Executional Factors of a Television Commercial on Brand Attitude Formation," Report No. 84-100, Marketing Science Institute, Cambridge, Mass., 1984.

CHANGING ATTITUDES

LEARNING OBJECTIVES

After studying this chapter, you should understand . . .

■ The role of persuasive communications in influencing consumers' attitude development or attitude change

■ The influence of consumer involvement on marketing strategies which are designed to change attitudes

■ The sources available to marketers for encouraging attitude change and conditions influencing their effectiveness

■ How various message characteristics can influence the effectiveness of marketing communications

■ How certain traits of audience members may make them more or less susceptible to persuasive communications

As one business executive stated: "You gotta have sizzle." This was his justification for spending $250 per year in 1984 to use the newly introduced American Express Platinum charge card. The executive was referring to benefits of possessing what has come to be known as a "prestige card." In essence, his argument, which is subscribed to by many others, is that business people who do a significant amount of job-related entertaining need more than fancy suits and briefcases to create favorable impressions among their clients. The image boost provided by flashing this prestige credit card, which is only available by invitation from American Express, is also quite helpful.

The lesson that image "sells" was learned well by American Express, since the 1966 introduction of its Gold Card created the "prestige" market. From that time the company has concentrated on encouraging the "image" attitude among consumers with advertising slogans such as, "It takes more than income to earn it." In fact, the Platinum Card actually represents an extension of the prestige concept into even higher levels of the image market.

All of this success certainly did not go unnoticed by executives of MasterCard and Visa. These companies introduced their equivalents of the Gold Card in 1982. Promotional messages for these cards also attempted to develop favorable consumer attitudes by focusing on image and prestige issues. For example, for five years MasterCard promotions revolved around the "So worldly so welcome" theme. Ads featured James Coburn, Christie Brinkley, Shari Belafonte-Harper, and others touting their standard card as a means of securing trendy and upscale pleasures throughout the world.

17

However, efforts of MasterCard and Visa have not made strong inroads into American Express' hold on the status market. This appeared to be an important reason for MasterCard's recent promotional about-face. Their next advertising theme attempted to generate favorable attitudes toward MasterCard by returning to a focus on "practicality" rather than on image. Its theme: "Master the possibilities." Promotions stressed functionality and also featured a frontal attack on image. For example, in one ad actress Angela Lansbury asks, "Have you ever been really impressed by a person's credit card?" In another, film star Robert Duvall states, "Possibilities and personal choice. That works for me—I choose it because I use it." Hopes at MasterCard ran high that this $30 million campaign would influence consumers' attitudes enough to increase MasterCard's market position significantly.'

The situation faced by MasterCard involves considerations commonly faced by many marketers who are attempting to change consumer attitudes through use of persuasive messages. Consideration must be given to various characteristics of the audience that will receive communications, the type of spokespeople or other sources to use in these communications, and the content of messages that will be delivered. In addition, care must be taken to understand the nature of situations surrounding consumer decisions to purchase the advertised product or service.

As we have just suggested, the persuasive communication process appears capable of influencing attitude change among consumers. It should also be kept in mind, however, that many of the methods for influencing attitude change that will be discussed in this chapter are also useful for encouraging the development of new attitudes—as in the case of consumers' attitude formation for new products. The reader should also note that the degree of success in changing consumers' attitudes depends on how strongly existing attitudes are held. Those that are strongly entrenched are difficult to change, while neutral and weakly held attitudes are much easier to influence.

The chapter begins by discussing strategies for changing consumers' attitudes and reviewing the general nature of the communication process used to accomplish these strategies. Several major components of such communications are discussed next in terms of their influence on attitude change. First, various communication sources and their potential effects are addressed. Different properties of the message itself are then treated. Finally, characteristics of the intended audience which affect their receptivity to persuasive communications are examined.

STRATEGIES FOR CHANGING ATTITUDES AND INTENTIONS

Some strategies for influencing changes in consumers' attitudes toward certain behaviors have already been identified. Other strategies exist, however, that accomplish changes in behavioral intentions without directly affecting attitudes. Because Fishbein's behavioral intentions model links these concepts so closely together, the various change strategies are discussed collectively below. Although many factors can influence the marketer's choice among these alternatives, one fundamental consideration should be the degree of involvement that consumers are experiencing with the product.

LOW-INVOLVEMENT STRATEGIES

In Chapter 12, we noted that under low-involvement conditions consumers are not likely to make brand choices on the basis of well-formed attitudes. In essence, their interest is too low for evaluating product attributes and forming beliefs about various brands. Given this, it is generally unproductive for the marketer to develop communications designed to modify prepurchase attitudes. One potential exception to this was noted in Chapter 16. We indicated that recent research suggests consumers' attitudes may not be completely based on their beliefs or cognitions. Recall that attitudes also might be changed as a result of consumers developing favorable reactions to the *advertisements* used to promote the brand. It was also indicated that this may occur as the result of classical conditioning, which would operate quite well under low-involvement situations. Therefore, although we do not yet know a great deal about the mechanisms involved, one potential low-involvement strategy may be to change consumers' attitudes by encouraging favorable reactions toward the advertisements used to promote the brands. The options that remain stress capitalizing on a means to transform the situation into one characterized by high involvement. For example, remember that the low-involvement hierarchy of effects model (review Figure 12-10) indicates that consumers may form attitudes on the basis of *postpurchase* brand evaluations. This highlights the importance for marketers of delivering quality products that will receive positive evaluations during use, which will result in favorable consumer attitudes. If such postpurchase attitudes are sufficiently formed, they will guide subsequent purchases. The marketer would then be able to employ attitude-change strategies developed for high-involvement situations.

A second attitude-change strategy option for low-involvement situations entails encouraging consumers to increase their prepurchase involvement levels. Success here would allow use of high-involvement attitude-change methods to influence brand choices. How can this increase in prepurchase involvement be accomplished? A list of options suggested by various researchers has been compiled:[2]

1 *Link the product to an involving issue*. Because issues are often more involving than are products, this linkage could increase involvement regarding the product. Linking a breakfast cereal to problems of deficient performance among school-children who have not had a wholesome breakfast would be one example.

2 *Link the product to a presently involving personal situation*. On some occasions, a message can be targeted to audiences at the time they are engaged in an activity related to the product. At this time, their interest could be sufficiently high to qualify as high involvement. An example might be radio advertisements for a suntan lotion during midday hours of summer weekends.

3 *Develop high-involvement advertisements*. Because consumers' involvement in a product is low, it does not necessarily mean that they cannot become involved

in advertisements for the product. The use of humor, dramatic events, or other methods can create an involving advertisement to which the product could then be linked. Examples might include the active scenes of Slice soft drink commercials and other television ads showing the humorous woes of people who failed to use the advertised brand.

4 *Change the importance of product benefits.* This option is quite difficult to pursue, because it attempts a frontal attack on consumers' perceptions of product benefits. To illustrate, if consumers could be convinced that the fiber content in dried cereal is very important to their health, they might become more involved in their choice of cereal. The brands that possess this attribute are then likely to be the recipient of favorable consumer attitudes.

5 *Reveal or introduce important product characteristics.* New attributes can be associated with a product, and consumers can also be made aware that some favorable attributes have been product characteristics for a long time. These have the potential for increasing involvement levels. The absence of caffeine and sugar or the addition of calcium in a number of soft drinks certainly appears to capture the interest of many consumers because of their implications regarding the health and appearance of the body. Fortification of milk and other foods with vitamins represents another example.

In all of these cases, the attempt has been to increase involvement levels among consumers to the point where they will form attitudes prior to purchase and use these attitudes to influence their purchase decisions. We now turn to strategies designed for conditions in which these prepurchase attitudes are likely to be formed.

HIGH-INVOLVEMENT STRATEGIES

Potentially, a variety of strategies are available for changing consumer attitudes under high-involvement conditions. Before implementing such strategies, however, the marketer must be clear on whether the attempt is to change consumer attitudes about the brand, or whether it is to change attitudes about behaving toward the brand. As we found in Chapter 16, consumer attitudes about behaving toward a brand are more closely related to their intentions to purchase. Therefore, we will focus on attitudes toward behavior in the following discussion.

Figure 17-1 is based on Fishbein's behavioral intentions model and closely parallels portions of Figure 16-6. It suggests a variety of potential strategies for influencing change in consumers' attitudes toward behavior.[3] Employing the same reasoning as Fishbein used to develop his model, we can argue that behavioral change is a function of changes in behavioral intentions and other intervening factors. Changes in behavioral intentions are related to changes in attitudes toward the behavior and changes in subjective norms about the behavior. Each of these, in turn, are functions of their components. These relationships suggest the following potential strategies:

1 *Change existing beliefs about the consequences of behavior.* Consumers often hold incomplete or incorrect beliefs about the consequences of purchasing and using particular brands. Modification of those beliefs that will positively influence attitudes can increase intentions to purchase. One way to accomplish this is for advertisements to focus on *brand benefits*. Here, the message would be that purchase of the brand will yield certain beneficial results (consequences) for the consumer. As an example, consider the following message: "Users of Top Flight golf balls get up to 14 more yards per drive than users of other brands." Of course, a second option is for advertisements to suggest that few negative consequences will result from purchasing the brand. Stress on a low price is one such method.

2 *Change consumers' evaluation of the consequences of a particular action.* In many cases, consumers may believe that using a brand will lead to certain consequences, but these consequences are not evaluated very positively. Measures taken to increase evaluations of the consequences can have positive results. For example, an advertisement for Listerine mouthwash has stressed that its strong taste is associated with effectiveness in killing germs and giving fresh breath—"It tastes strong because it is strong." Potential results are more positive evaluations of the strong taste and enhancement of attitudes toward the brand.

3 *Introduce new belief/evaluation combinations.* In some cases, marketers can add or delete product attributes and generate positive consequences for the consumer. In other cases, the presence or absence of existing product attributes can be stressed in terms of their favorable consequences for the consumer. The former case is exemplified by the addition of Floristat to Crest toothpaste. This ingredient was advertised as being more effective in preventing tooth decay than its previous fluoride compound known as Fluoristan. An example of the latter strategy was used by Canada Dry when in 1982 it announced that its ginger ale does not have caffeine and it never did. This was important information to consumers who wanted to minimize their caffeine intake.

4 *Change existing normative beliefs.* In some situations, consumers may hold favorable attitudes toward certain behaviors but be reluctant to take action

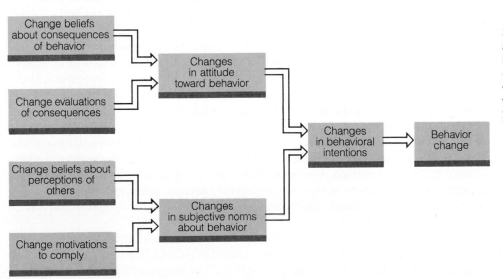

FIGURE 17-1
Some strategy options for attitude change in high-involvement conditions.
Source: Martin Fishbein and Icek Ajzen, *Belief, Attitude and Behavior: An Introduction to Theory and Research,* Addison-Welsey, Reading, Mass., 1975, p. 407.

because of an unfavorable reaction on the subjective norm component. Such a situation could occur when the consumer holds a belief that others who are important to her will not react favorably to the actions in question. This can be an important consideration with regard to the purchase of certain clothing items and other socially visible products. Although it may be difficult, the possibility exists that changes in such beliefs can be achieved. For example, promotions may simulate group settings in which people with whom the consumer might identify express favorable reactions to purchasing the advertised brand. Given sufficient realism, such advertisements may weaken the consumer's beliefs that people important to her will have negative reactions to purchase of the brand.

5 *Change motivations to comply with subjective norms.* A second strategy to modify the subjective norm component of behavioral intentions is to alter consumers' motivations to comply with the influences of people important to them. One way this can be accomplished is to diminish or increase the perceived importance or status of these influential others for at least the decision in question. For example, advertisements for a particular brand might stress the importance of being an individual and not always heeding the opinions of friends or important others.

6 *Introduce new normative components.* Subjective norms can also be influenced by the addition of new normative components which will be strong in their influence on the consumer. This can occur through the introduction of additional salient referents to the subjective norm component of the behavioral intentions equation. Promotions showing how family members, friends, and so on, react to certain purchase decisions, and why these reactions might be important to the consumer, are possibilities.

The above review suggests that a variety of potential strategies exist for influencing attitude change among consumers in high-involvement situations. Selection of one or more strategies will be affected by the competitive environment, consumers' existing conditions, knowledge and beliefs, characteristics of the product, and related factors. A few comments are useful on several of these issues.

Experience has shown marketers that it is much easier to change the intensity of attitudes than it is to change their direction. For example, if consumers have negative attitudes toward a brand, it would be a difficult task to transform these attitudes into positive ones. Efforts may be successful in reducing the intensity of negative attitudes, but the payoff involved in such endeavors would be questionable. In such cases, the frequent recommendation is to "Go with the Flow," which could mean withdrawing the brand or redesigning or reformulating it and introducing it to consumers under another name so that it will be given a fighting chance in the marketplace. For brands that receive generally favorable consumer acceptance, the strategy is typically to identify and concentrate on those components that yield the most positive change in attitudes for a given amount of investment in promotion.

Related to this discussion is the point that weakly held attitudes are easier to change than ones that are strongly held. Attitude strength has a variety of sources. One is the strength of the consumer's beliefs. The more confident a consumer is

about his or her brand beliefs, the more difficult they are to change. For example, two consumers may believe that Michelin tires will yield only moderate levels of tread wear. However, the strength of one's beliefs may be much greater than the other. It would be more difficult to convince the consumer with strong beliefs that Michelins give excellent tread wear. Strong beliefs are formed through personal experience and from information about products that is clear and readily available for a period of time. Weaker beliefs tend to exist under opposite conditions.

A second influence on attitude strength is the degree of involvement a consumer has with the product in question. Greater involvement reflects more personal relevance of the product to the consumer. Consequently, an involved consumer is likely to hold stronger beliefs about the brands in question. Additional evidence suggests that more-involved consumers will be less willing to accept statements that diverge from beliefs held about a brand.[4] The degree of divergence that will be accepted is referred to as the consumer's *latitude of acceptance*. Conversely, statements that the consumer does not accept will fall into his *latitude of rejection*. The implication of this is that highly involved consumers are likely to hold strong beliefs about a brand and accept only those advertising claims that deviate very little from these beliefs. On the other hand, consumers who are not highly involved will have wider latitudes of acceptance, and their attitudes can be changed by more-discrepant advertising claims. As a consequence, more advertising dollars will probably have to be expended to gradually change the brand beliefs of highly involved consumers, while more rapid change with fewer resources may be possible for less-involved consumers.

A final point to mention here is that typically it appears to be easier to change consumers' beliefs than to change their evaluations of the consequences of certain actions. This is probably so because evaluations are based on the consumer's need structure, which is more enduring and central to his values and self-concept than are beliefs about purchasing a particular brand.

Discussion in the previous paragraphs has focused on strategies for making absolute changes in consumers' brand or purchase attitudes. Of course, in most situations consumers face competing brands and perceive them relative to each other. Therefore, a potential strategy not yet mentioned would be for the marketer to increase her brand's *relative* attitude standing by encouraging consumers to develop more negative attitudes toward competing brands. This would require communications that directly attack competing brands, initiate or encourage damaging rumors about these brands, or utilize similar measures. Generally speaking, there has been very little of this type of behavior in the marketplace. In addition to the ethical issues that speak against it, such efforts are likely to result in damaging counterattacks from competitors. The ensuing battle would probably hurt all those involved. Therefore, we will not discuss such strategies further.

THE COMMUNICATION PROCESS

The primary means available to marketers for influencing attitude change is the design and implementation of persuasive communications. Properly designed communications benefit from an appreciation of the general nature of the communication process. A simplified model of this process is shown in Figure 17-2 and described below.

The sender initiates a communication message. This individual or group has as an objective the transmission of an intended message to one or more individuals acting as receivers. In marketing, the sender usually represents a company or its brand, and the intended message is usually conceived of as a mechanism to change consumers' attitudes toward the brand or toward purchasing it.

An intended message is the meaning a sender wishes to convey to receivers. In order to deliver this intended meaning, however, the message must be suitably formed for transmission in the channel selected for its delivery. That is, the intended message must be *encoded* into symbols making up the actual message which represent thoughts of the sender. These symbols are usually words, but often they involve pictures and actions of the sender.

The sent (actual) message is transmitted over a channel of communication. In marketing, the potential channel alternatives are varied, ranging from radio to in-store displays and personal messages. Therefore, considerable deliberation must be taken to select the channel with characteristics most appropriate to the message involved.

The sent message is acquired by one or more receivers. However, received messages are rarely identical to sent messages. Characteristics of the channel of transmission are one set of factors accounting for this difference. For example, it is very difficult to accurately reproduce product colors and textures on television or in newspapers. Consequently, the received message can differ significantly from the sent message.

The received message is transformed into a perceived message through the receiver's information-processing activities. That is, the message is *decoded*—received symbols are transformed back into meaning or thoughts by the receiver. As we have seen, an individual's experiences, as well as the context in which she perceives the message, will influence any meaning she derives from it. Attitude change and/or actions will then be based on this perceived message.

The feedback loop in Figure 17-2 recognizes that the communication process involves a two-way flow. That is, individuals or groups are both receivers and senders of messages, and they interact with each other. Therefore, feedback can

FIGURE 17-2
A simplified model of the
communication process.

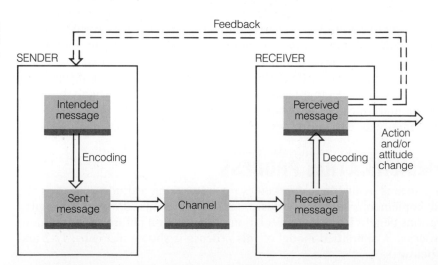

be viewed as the initiation of another communication in which the receiver can now be construed as a message sender. This feedback process enables the original sender to monitor how well her intended meaning was conveyed and received. In many marketing situations, communications are transmitted via mass media to widely distributed consumers; therefore, accurate feedback information is very rare and difficult to obtain.

The concept of *noise* is frequently used to refer to a type of disruption in the communication process. We have seen that a variety of noise sources exist. The sender may have difficulty with formulating an intended message, and further problems can occur while attempting to encode a message for transmission. The channel of communication itself is also capable of interfering with a message. The receiver may also introduce noise through the decoding process. Of course, the feedback loop may contribute additional noise. Therefore, each state of the communication process is susceptible to message distortion.

In order to appreciate the persuasive communication process, it is necessary to understand three general kinds of factors that operate to influence beliefs, attitudes, and behavior. They are source, message, and receiver factors.[5] These three sets of factors interact to produce intended and unintended communication effects. For simplicity, each set of factors is next examined one at a time. However, the reader should continually bear in mind that these factors are interactive.

SOURCE FACTORS

What characteristics do certain individuals, companies, or groups possess that facilitate their effectiveness in changing views and attitudes of others? This section discusses major characteristics of persuasive communication sources. The major types of marketing communication sources are reviewed first, and factors influencing their persuasiveness are discussed next.

MARKETING COMMUNICATION SOURCES

In a marketing context, several sources can be employed in an attempt to reach consumers with persuasive communications. These can be used alone or in combination to produce a combined source effect on consumers. Six prominent marketing source influences are briefly described below.

The Company   Consumers perceive companies as sources of information, and some are seen as highly credible but others are viewed with suspicion. Most consumers feel that Procter & Gamble, for example, is a trustworthy company, because P&G has built an excellent reputation by developing good products and spending considerable sums of money on advertising and consumer research. Because of its highly credible image, P&G can have more success than some other firms in introducing new brands to the market.

Sales Representatives   Because of their face-to-face contacts with current and prospective customers, sales representatives are viewed by consumers as information sources. Also, salespeople who are viewed as knowledgeable (expert) and trustworthy often are more persuasive than those not so highly regarded.[6] In

addition, evidence suggests that consumers are more receptive to salespeople from highly credible companies such as the Prudential Insurance Company and Colgate-Palmolive than from unknown or low-credibility companies.[7] Thus, sales representatives from a well-known company can have an advantage over those from less well-known or less-respected companies.

The Media   Consumers use the media extensively for product information. Although media are actually channel links between companies and consumers (receivers), people view them as sources; thus, it is important to understand their effects on persuading consumers to purchase products. *Good Housekeeping* and *Parents' Magazine* are examples of media that consumers perceive as credible sources of product information. Because of their product-screening processes and "seals of approval," they have built reputations as expert and trustworthy sources upon which consumers can rely.

Hired Promoters   Companies typically employ individuals as representatives in advertising. In fact, on-camera spokespeople appear in a significant portion of television advertising. Effective hired promoters are ones who have established reputations for themselves, often in occupations unrelated to the advertised product. For example, Bob Hope over the years has established himself as an honest, sincere, and likable person. He has tremendous credibility among many consumers, particularly since people perceive that he has virtually nothing to gain financially from his commercial recommendations.

Retailers   At the local level, retailers often act as sources for marketing communications. A department store that has a good local reputation may more easily sell unknown brands than less-reputable stores might. Also, specialty shops are successful in selling unknown brands because of their perceived expertise in the product line, such as with cameras and stereo equipment. Thus, a manufacturer who produces brands with low consumer awareness can benefit from using specialty outlets if he can convince the retailers to carry his line.

Combined Source Effects   Although we have described each of the above marketing sources separately, in reality there are combined source effects that interact to produce a persuasive impact on consumers. Therefore, producers must carefully select hired promoters, media, and retailers to deliver persuasive brand messages. One bad selection can cancel the positive effects of other message sources used. All source components must be reviewed from a system's point of view to gain maximum effectiveness.

INFLUENCES ON SOURCE EFFECTIVENESS

A variety of factors can influence the persuasiveness of those who transmit marketing communications. Among many factors influencing the ability of a source to change attitudes are his credibility, his similarity to audience members, and his attitudes toward himself, the message, and audience members. This section reviews these major influences.

Credibility and Its Effects   Perhaps the most investigated source factor in persuasion is credibility (believability). A long-held conclusion from numerous research studies has been that highly credible sources achieve greater attitude change in consumers than those having less credibility. One important aspect of this finding is that credibility rests in the eyes of receivers. That is, receivers must *perceive* a source as credible, regardless of whether or not he *actually* is honest, trustworthy, and so on.

This general finding about the effectiveness of highly credible sources for generating attitude change reflects common sense to many of us. However, recent evidence suggests that the impact of source credibility is complex, depending on a number of specific conditions. Some of these are addressed below. In this discussion, we are assuming that conditions of high involvement exist, so that consumers are actively attending to the communications being sent.

INFLUENCE OF RECEIVER'S OPINION   The initial opinion of audience members appears to be one important influence on the impact of source credibility. Specifically, when receivers already hold opinions that are opposite to those presented in a message, a highly credible source is likely to generate more attitude change than will sources of lower credibility. However, when audience opinions already favor positions to be presented in a message, then highly credible sources have not been found more effective than sources of lower credibility in generating attitude change. In fact, some research even suggests that sources of lower credibility will actually be *more* effective in generating attitude change.[8]

To appreciate why these statements may have validity, we must understand that communications can generate cognitive responses among consumers. Recall from the section on memory in Chapter 14 that *cognitive response* refers to thoughts a consumer will retrieve from long-term memory upon exposure to a communication such as an advertising message. Those responses most relevant to our discussion here are (1) *counterarguments*—thoughts stored in long-term memory that are used to contradict aspects of the message being received, and (2) *support arguments*—thoughts stored in long-term memory that are used to support aspects of the received message. Counterarguments are generated by receivers when messages oppose their initial opinions, and support arguments are developed for messages consistent with initial positions. One interesting finding is that highly credible sources appear to have such significant believability that they tend to block cognitive responses.[9] This means that when receivers are initially opposed to information in a message, highly credible sources will tend to block counterarguments. The message is therefore likely to be accepted without much modification, yielding a considerable change in attitudes. However, the same message received from sources having lower credibility will be critically reviewed. This will generate counterarguments, tending to neutralize points made in the message. Therefore, the amount of attitude change will be less than what a highly credible source could achieve.

What happens when receivers' initial opinions or beliefs are consistent with the content of a message? The message transmitted from a highly credible source will again be accepted without much critical examination. However, because it is

consistent with the receiver's existing position, a large amount of attitude change is unlikely. Conversely, as before, the same message received from a less-credible source will be critically reviewed and will generate cognitive responses. Because the cognitive responses will now be in the form of support arguments, the resulting attitude change can be greater than that achieved by the highly credible source.

Important practical implications can be drawn from this analysis. First, marketers may usually want to avoid developing communications that oppose consumers' opinions because of their requirements for a highly credible source. Since the task of achieving very high credibility in a marketing context is quite difficult, often expensive, and sometimes impossible, an alternative to consider carefully is using communications consistent with consumers' positions. However, when fighting rumors, bad publicity, and various other forms of unwarranted consumer beliefs, the design of such opposing communications may be necessary. In these cases, it would be quite important to carefully identify and use sources that will have high credibility for the specific situation at hand.

MESSAGE DISCREPANCY CONDITIONS   A topic closely related to the above discussion is message discrepancy. Highly discrepant messages do not oppose receivers' initial opinions, but are quite deviant from the receivers' beliefs. Marketers encounter such situations when they wish to demonstrate extraordinary products such as Super Glue or to make claims about their offerings that differ considerably from current beliefs in the target market. Similar to the situation of negative initial opinions, very credible sources are most effective in achieving attitude change for highly discrepant messages. As before, the explanation appears to be that high credibility minimizes cognitive responses, which are likely to be counterarguments in cases of high discrepancy.[10] For messages of little discrepancy, counterarguments are less likely, while support arguments will be more prevalent. Therefore, under such conditions less-credible sources can be effective in achieving attitude change.

What are the strategy implications of these findings? If the marketer can achieve a high-credibility standing in the target market, discrepant promotional claims can be employed to yield considerable attitude change. However, as we have noted, very high levels of credibility are often difficult to achieve. In such cases, the suggestion has been to design only mildly discrepant messages.

LOW-CREDIBILITY EFFECTIVENESS   Are there situations in which highly credible sources can actually *inhibit* attitude change in an audience? Research suggests that this may be the case. In fact, we have already mentioned one such situation—when audience members hold initial opinions that are in agreement with points to be made in the message. A second situation appears to be when the marketer wishes to change consumers' behavior directly and have this lead to later attitude change.[11] Such a case could occur when free brand samples or trials are offered to encourage development of favorable attitudes.

In other situations, high credibility may be most effective in changing attitudes, but using a less-credible source is more feasible. Here, a potential strategy is to improve the amount of attitude change that can be achieved with a low-credibility source. One method to accomplish this is to develop a situation in which the source will argue against her own self-interest. By doing so, the communicator appears to establish credibility, because it becomes obvious to an audience that she has nothing to gain by arguing for someone else's position. For example, in one advertisement the spokesperson states that he is not getting "one red cent" for endorsing the advertised product.

A low-credibility source also can increase his persuasiveness if he is identified *after,* rather than *before* presenting his message. The reason is that an audience will attend to the message if they do not know he is a low-credibility source. Otherwise, they will selectively ignore the presentation if they strongly suspect his credibility.

Care must be taken in using these strategies. Their implementation can be difficult and can cause problems for other aspects of the message. Therefore, it probably would be wise to consider other options before embracing such strategies.

THE SLEEPER EFFECT The above review suggests that under certain circumstances highly credible communicators can influence significant attitude change. However, a very valid question is whether we can expect this change in attitudes to be long-lasting. Research evidence suggests that the initial effect can dissipate rather rapidly, which is not completely surprising given our understanding of the learning curve. However, a startling finding of early research was that an audience exposed initially to a low-credibility source develops opinions *more* closely in line with the source as time passes.[12] This result became known as the "sleeper effect." Consideration of both findings would lead one to predict that as time passes, opinion change achieved by high- and low-credibility sources would tend toward equality. Figure 17-3 graphically illustrates this conclusion, which drew the attention of astute marketers interested in long-run attitude change.

The explanation offered for these findings is that receivers tend to forget message sources more rapidly than they forget message content. Thus, as the "enhancing" and "depressing" effects of high- and low-credibility sources dissipate, what will tend to remain is message content, which is the same in both cases.

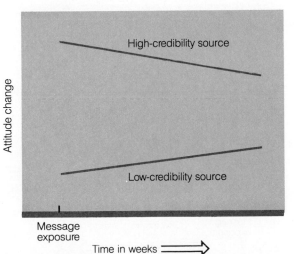

FIGURE 17-3
An illustration of attitude change convergence predicted by early research evidence on source credibility effects over time.

Unfortunately, additional research has not shown consistent support for the sleeper effect.[13] This means that we cannot unquestioningly accept that small amounts of initial attitude change achieved by using a low-credibility source will increase over time. A further finding adds one more piece to the puzzle: If original sources are reinstated (allowed to reintroduce their position), the effect is to restore audience opinion levels to nearly the points they were right after initial message exposure.[14] In effect, reintroduction of a source tends to yield the same effect as when it was initially used. Figure 17-4 graphically summarizes these points. Note how the dashed lines duplicate the situation shown in Figure 17-3. Therefore, the assumption being used here is that other things being held constant, (1) the sleeper effect is valid and (2) a decline in attitude change will occur over time for the highly credible source. The new solid lines in this figure now indicate that reinstatement of each source tends to hold attitude change levels near their original conditions. If one were to assume that the sleeper effect was not valid, the dashed and solid lines for the low-credibility source would coincide and run horizontally.

The evidence presented above and summarized in Figure 17-4 tends to favor use of a high-credibility source when situations discussed in the previous sections warrant. Typical marketing applications, such as advertising repetition, could easily involve source reinstatement, which would act to maintain initially favorable attitude change levels achieved with a highly credible source. Therefore, whether or not a sleeper effect does exist would only influence the *degree* to which a highly credible source would generate more long-run attitude change than one of low credibility. Combined conditions favoring a low-credibility source would be (1) the existence of a valid sleeper effect, (2) a relatively large expense involved in identifying and using a highly credible source and, (3) as suggested in Figure 17-4, a strategy that does not involve source reinstatement.

BASES OF CREDIBILITY   Our conclusion is that in a number of circumstances, using a highly credible communicator can benefit the persuasiveness of marketing

FIGURE 17-4
An illustration of the effects of reinstatement on long-run attitude change. Conditions of a sleeper effect are assumed.

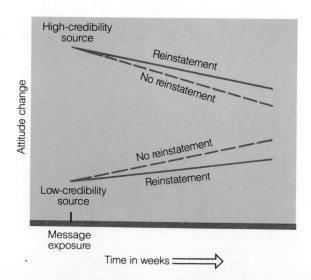

messages. Practically speaking, therefore, many marketers may wish to identify sources that have high credibility in communicating to an audience about a particular brand. But what factors influence the credibility of a source in the eyes of an audience? Five major bases are (1) trustworthiness, (2) expertise, (3) status or prestige, (4) likability, and (5) an assortment of physical traits. Each of these is discussed below.

A source will be perceived as more credible if her audience views her as honest or trustworthy, and this is related to the degree she is perceived as having an *intention to manipulate*. If the audience believes that the communicator, no matter how generally honest, has something to gain personally by her message, then her persuasive attempts will lose effectiveness.

This idea suggests one reason why advertising and personal selling are generally less effective than the advice of a trusted friend for changing consumer attitudes. Advertisers have attempted to overcome this problem to some extent by using "candid interviews" with consumers who were not aware that they were giving testimony to a company's brand. Other similar approaches, such as disguised brand tests, have been used by advertisers to reduce their perceived "intention to manipulate." This technique has been used for Ivory Snow, Pepsi, Schlitz, Anacin, and Mercury automobiles.

Another basis of source credibility is perceived expertise. That is, when an audience views a communicator as having higher qualifications than others to speak on a topic, he will be more persuasive than a person viewed as less qualified. This is why experts in a field related to a company's product often are used to promote its brands. An example would be Larry Bird promoting Converse basketball shoes.

A communicator whom an audience perceives as high in status or prestige is often more credible than one perceived as low in these attributes. As we have learned, society "confers" status and prestige upon individuals according to the roles they occupy. For example, a physician is generally regarded as having higher status and prestige than a nurse, and a scientist usually has more prestige than an engineer. Marketers often attempt to obtain as endorsers of their products individuals who have obtained high status. Examples include using former President Gerald Ford to endorse the Boy Scouts and former test pilot Chuck Yeager as a spokesman for automotive products. It should be noted that although the concepts of prestige and expertise overlap, they are not synonymous.[15]

Finally, the physical characteristics and other features of communicators can influence their credibility. For example, age, sex, color, dress, likability, and voice inflections, as well as general attractiveness can affect source credibility.[16] Regarding age, older people tend to be influential on younger people in many cultures. The tendency for youth to accept their elders' advice and influence might be due largely to the younger generation's perception of their elders' experience in life, thus viewing them as more "expert."

This discussion has focused on the influence of source credibility in achieving attitude change. Two other groups of source factors that can also be important are briefly reviewed in the following sections.

Attitude of the Communicator   A communicator is more persuasive when she has a positive attitude toward herself, her message, and her receiver.[17] Within a market-

ing context, a sales representative who has a positive attitude toward herself is one who has self-confidence. Her self-confidence is perceived by the prospective buyer and can influence the decision to buy.

Sales representatives are trained to show a positive attitude toward their product and sales presentation (their message). That is, they are trained to *believe* in the product they are selling and what they say about it. Thus, many sales training programs are designed to develop representatives' confidence in their company and the products they sell.

The marketer must demonstrate respect and admiration toward his prospective buyers to be successful. Consumers quickly realize when they are being "talked down to," and in such cases they will quickly react negatively to the presentation and brand involved.

Similarity with Audience   Another finding regarding communication sources is that people are persuaded more by a communicator they perceive to be similar to themselves.[18] That is, people seem to be influenced by others who are like themselves. Similarity can be perceived in a variety of ways, such as personality, race, interests, self-image, and group affiliations. This has led marketers to use so-called slice-of-life advertisements in many cases. For example, ads for Maxwell House coffee, Calgon dishwasher detergent, and Crest toothpaste, as well as many other brands, attempt to show "typical" people finding satisfaction with their products.

MESSAGE FACTORS

It is important to understand what components make up a persuasive message. This section discusses three sets of message factors: (1) message structure, (2) message appeal, and (3) message code.

MESSAGE STRUCTURE

Message structure refers to how the elements of a message are organized. Three structures that have been extensively studied are message sidedness, order of presentation, conclusion drawing, and repetition.

Message Sidedness   A message can be either one-sided or two-sided. A *one-sided message* is one in which only the strengths of the communicator's position are described. For example, advertisements for Chevrolet automobiles often only address their advantages and don't mention any of their possible weaknesses or the possible advantages of Fords. A *two-sided message,* on the other hand, presents the strengths of the communicator's position as in the one-sided message, but it also either admits to weaknesses in the communicator's position or to some strengths in the opposite position. In a marketing context, the typical method of implementing the two-sided approach would be for the spokesperson to mention one or two weaknesses in her company's products or to admit to one or two strong features of competitor's products. Cases include Listerine, which claims effectiveness but admits to less than perfect taste. Another example of a two-sided message is presented in Figure 17-5, a direct-mail advertisement sent by Publishers Clearing House.

545

Two questions arise regarding message sidedness. First, why would anyone want to admit to weaknesses in his or her own product or mention the strengths of competing products? Second, which approach is more effective? The answer to the first question lies in discussion of the second. Either approach can be more effective than the other depending upon conditions under which the message is presented. The relevant conditions are (1) the audience's initial opinion on the issue, (2) their exposure to subsequent counterarguments, and (3) the audience's educational level.[19]

In the first condition, a one-sided argument appears to be more effective when the audience is already in agreement with the communicator's position, and a two-sided message is more effective when the audience initially disagrees with the communicator's position. The one-sided message is more effective for an audience in agreement because it reinforces what they already believe. A two-sided message under this condition would serve only to place doubt in their minds. However, the use of a one-sided message for an audience *not* in initial agreement with the communicator's stance tends to be relatively less effective, because the audience will perceptually resist a view counter to its own. In this case, a two-sided message is more effective, because the audience tends to view the communicator as more objective and honest (credible) since he admits to the merits of their position. The approach allows a communicator to get through the audience's perceptual filters, to present his views, and thereby to increase the likelihood of gaining some measure of attitude change.

A second condition influencing the relative effectiveness of one-sided and two-sided messages is the kind of information that receivers will be exposed to at a later date. If an audience is likely to receive counterarguments in the future, such as when competitors make counteradvertising claims, some theorists would suggest using two-sided messages. This suggestion is derived from what has

FIGURE 17-5
A two-sided message.
Courtesy of Publishers Clearing House.

become known as *inoculation* or *immunization* theory. In essence, this theory holds that just as people are inoculated with vaccines (weakened disease cultures) to increase their resistance to diseases, exposure of an audience to weakened forms of counterarguments will tend to immunize them from more strongly stated opposing arguments that they will confront at a later time. Therefore, by using this technique, salespeople could take the "wind out of their competitors' sails" (and sales) by presenting buyers with two-sided messages. Although we cannot yet say for sure that inoculation theory is completely valid, research evidence tends to support it as a justification for using two-sided messages.[20]

A third condition for determining whether to use a one-sided or two-sided message is the educational level of an audience. A two-sided message appears to be more persuasive on better-educated audiences, whereas a one-sided message is more effective in changing the opinions of less well-educated audiences. Because better-educated people generally are more capable of seeing both sides of an argument anyway, a communicator should either admit the strengths of opposing views or weaknesses in his own position. In this way, the communicator is established as being more objective and credible in the minds of his audience. Less-educated people are not as capable of seeing another side of an issue and therefore are more likely to accept the argument they hear. To present both sides might confuse them, and they would find it difficult to know which side to accept.

The effectiveness of one- and two-sided messages in an advertising context comes from a study where half of a 500-subject sample group listened to one-sided radio commercials for an automobile, a gas range, and floor wax. Each commercial was "conventional" in the sense that it presented only positive product features. The second half of the sample was presented with two-sided commercials comparable to the one-sided messages, except that some negative features were also included. Findings included the following:

1 Two-sided advertisements were more effective on higher-educated subjects, whereas one-sided advertisements were more effective on less-educated subjects.

2 Two-sided messages were more effective on subjects who used competing brands, whereas one-sided commercials were more effective on subjects using the brand featured in the commercial. In this case, a subject who used the advertised brand is similar to one who has initial agreement with the communicator. A subject who used the competing brand is similar to one who does not have initial agreement with the communicator.

3 The commercials' effectiveness in changing opinions appeared to be influenced by characteristics of the product being promoted. For example, greater attitude change was created for the low-cost floor wax than for the high-priced automobile. This finding can be explained in terms of the amount of commitment (or investment) a person has made in the product in terms of money, search time, and effort. With greater commitment involved, consumers hold more tightly to their purchase decision.

4 After four to six weeks, subjects showed no diminishing effects on their attitudes toward the advertised brands. In fact, subjects exposed to the two-sided advertisements actually showed an increase in attitude toward the advertised brand.[21]

Perhaps unfortunately, many companies have generally rejected the idea of their spokespeople ever admitting to either a competitor's product's strengths or to their own product's weaknesses. However, in a number of situations this could be a very viable approach. First, where it is possible to segment consumers into loyal and nonloyal groups, it may be useful to direct one-sided messages toward loyal customers and two-sided ads toward the nonloyal group.[22] Of course, this strategy requires that each group is capable of being isolated enough so that they are not inadvertently exposed to both messages. Salespeople may also find it to their advantage to use a two-sided sales pitch, either by admitting to minor weaknesses in their companies' brands or by mentioning one or two strengths of competitors' brands. Such a tactic may create a resistance in prospects' minds toward competitors' sales claims. Additionally, in an industrial selling situation, sales representatives usually are confronted by well-educated purchasing agents, consulting engineers, and others of similar education. In these cases, a two-sided sales pitch should prove more effective than a one-sided message. However, for door-to-door salespeople in a low-income (and therefore very likely poorly educated) neighborhood, a one-sided argument should be more effective.

Message Order   What is the best order in which to present persuasive arguments in an advertising message? Should the most important parts to the communicator be presented at the beginning, middle, or end? If a two-sided message is used, should the marketer use a pro-con or con-pro order? For a series of advertisements in a medium such as television, does the first or last ad have an advantage in influencing attitude change? This section briefly addresses these questions and reviews some of the evidence relevant to them.

CLIMAX VERSUS ANTICLIMAX ORDER   A *climax order* refers to ordering message elements whereby the strongest arguments are presented at the end of a message. An *anticlimax order* refers to the presentation of the most important points at the beginning of a message. When the most important materials are presented in the middle of a message, it is referred to as a *pyramidal order*. Figure 17-6 graphically describes these three alternatives.

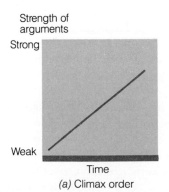

(a) Climax order

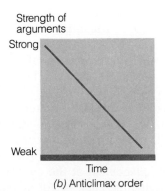

(b) Anticlimax order

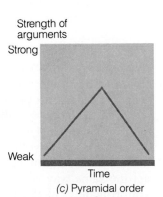

(c) Pyramidal order

FIGURE 17-6
Three orders of message presentation.

On the basis of research findings, the following tentative guidelines can be offered regarding the ordering of messages:

1 An anticlimax order tends to be most effective for an audience having a low level of interest in the subject being presented.

2 A climax order tends to be most effective for an audience having a high level of interest in the subject being presented.

3 The pyramidal order is the least effective order of presentation.

The first two generalizations can be explained in terms of audience interest. Where interest is low, the stronger, more interesting points in a message have the greater potential for gaining audience attention, and therefore they should be placed first (anticlimax order). In this way, a communicator is better able to get her message across and thus effect change in the audience. However, with this approach the communicator also must be careful of avoiding an audience "let down" when the weaker points in a message follow.

When audience interest in the subject is high, there is no need to present the stronger points first, because the message will be attended to out of interest. Therefore, the climax order should be used, because points made at the end of the message exceed expectations created by the points initially presented.[23]

The lesson marketers must learn from these statements is that for low-interest products an anticlimax order appears effective. In addition, in some cases each method can perhaps be strengthened by presenting the important points at *both* the beginning and end of the message—in the form of an introduction and summary of important points. However, very little if any justification exists for a pyramidal order.

RECENCY AND PRIMACY EFFECTS   Two additional questions were raised above. When presenting a two-sided message, should the points favorable to the advertiser's brand be presented first or second? If many competing messages are involved, as they are in magazines and during commercial breaks on television, does the first or last communication tend to have the advantage? Both of these issues involve the subject of primacy and recency effects. When the material presented first produces the greater opinion or attitude change, a *primacy effect* has occurred. When material presented last produces the greater change, then a *recency effect* has been observed.

Research into the question of which presentation of order is more effective when using a two-sided message has not been very conclusive. It appears that sometimes a primacy and sometimes a recency effect is observed. The reasons for these contradictory findings is not at all clear. Therefore, we will not even offer tentative guidelines on this subject.

The evidence on whether it would be better for a promotional message to appear first or last in a series of messages is also not clear. However, many advertisers who favor evidence suggesting a primacy effect are willing to pay a premium for early placement in a magazine or during a commercial break. Others act the same way regarding placement at the end of a series of advertisements. Unfortunately, at the present time each set of advocates can point to research evidence supporting their position. More investigation of the factors accounting for such contradictory findings is certainly needed.

Conclusion Drawing   Is it better to draw a conclusion for your audience at the end of a message or let them draw their own conclusion? Investigations of this question have shown that a conclusion must often be drawn to achieve attitude change among less-intelligent audience members. If this is not done, they may draw either the ''wrong'' conclusions or no conclusions and therefore the intended opinion change will not occur. For audiences of higher intelligence, it usually makes no difference whether a conclusion is drawn, because they have the ability to reach the ''correct'' conclusion. Therefore, although the answer to this question is dependent upon several conditions, the most useful safe generalization is that communicators appear to be more effective in changing opinions of an audience if they draw a conclusion for them.[24]

Repetition   In Chapter 14, we saw that repetition of persuasive messages can be beneficial in encouraging rehearsal, transferring information to long-term memory, and forestalling forgetting. Other benefits were also suggested. That is, some research evidence indicates that increased repetition of an advertising message can, by itself, encourage consumers to develop positive feelings toward the brand.[25] This suggests that consumers' attitudes can be changed in a positive direction through frequent advertising exposures. Conditions which appear to produce such an effect are (1) when the audience initially favors the message position and (2) when a soft-sell (as opposed to a hard-sell) is employed.

Even under the conditions just cited, marketers should not expect continuous positive attitude change from increased repetitions of a communication. At some point, message *wearout* occurs. Here, the positive effects of repetition diminish as repetition occurs because of audience boredom, inattention, and increased cognitive response activity that is less positive in content than the message.[26] The conclusion from these studies is that moderate levels of advertising repetition over time appear to positively influence attitudes as well as rehearsal and memory. The effects of wearout can probably be forestalled by employing a series of messages having a central theme with unique components to provide different information and some novelty to maintain audience interest.

MESSAGE APPEALS

The above review summarized some major conclusions regarding the structuring of messages to achieve maximum attitude change. We now turn our attention to message appeals and how they can be used to enhance the persuasiveness of messages.

Fear Appeals   In some situations, it seems reasonable for marketers to consider using fear in their attempts to persuade consumers. That is, fear of physical danger, social disapproval, or other consequences seem potentially useful in influencing consumers' attitudes and/or behavior toward the advertised brand. In fact, fear appeals have been employed to promote the use of a wide range of goods from toothpaste to life insurance. Figure 17-7 presents an example of an advertisement capable of evoking fear among at least some readers.

The earliest fear research appeared to suggest that as the intensity of a fear appeal increases, its effectiveness in persuading audiences will decrease.[27] One explanation is that strong fear-evoking components of a message cause consumers to set up perceptual defenses, and in so doing they also reject the rest of the message. The result of these and other early findings was that most advertisers become highly reluctant to use fear appeals for promoting their products or services.

Several years later, other investigations began to uncover additional results.[28] The conclusion then appeared to be summarized as follows: low fear appeals generate little motivation for attitude change; high fear appeals also yield little attitude change, because they activate *defense mechanisms* against feared aspects of the message, which also screen out other parts of the message. Moderate fear appeals, which provide sufficient motivation but do not activate perceptual defenses, appear most effective in generating attitude change.

More recently, others have argued that it is probably inappropriate to draw general conclusions about any given level of fear, because numerous factors may influence how audiences will respond to the appeal. For example, factors that

FIGURE 17-7
A fear-evoking
advertisement.
Courtesy of Lever Brothers Company.

appear to influence the persuasiveness of fear appeals include (1) source credibility, (2) audience characteristics, (3) the type of fear appeal used, and (4) the context of the message presentation.[29] Generally, the following conclusions appear warranted:

1   Highly credible sources are more effective in employing fear to change attitudes, because their credibility tends to block counterarguments consumers use to protect themselves from fear-evoking messages.

2   Characteristics of an audience can influence the degree to which they are persuaded by fear appeals. Receivers who are high in self-esteem, are effective in coping with tension, and do not perceive themselves as particularly vulnerable to the feared consequences appear to be more persuaded by high fear appeals than receivers who do not have these characteristics. This suggests that marketers must investigate their target audience in order to determine whether a high fear appeal is warranted. For example, people who perceive themselves as having very risky occupations might not be receptive to high fear appeals for occupational related disability insurance. More moderate fear appeals can be employed for such target groups.

3   Some evidence suggests that fear appeals are more effective when they focus audience attention on the specific danger or threat and practical steps that may be taken to avoid any undesirable consequences. Messages that dwell on the unpleasant circumstances, without suggesting practical ways to avoid them, will tend to be less persuasive.

4   Certain conditions in the environment (such as humor) which can distract audience attention away from a strong fear appeal can increase message persuasiveness. Some evidence also suggests that fear of social disapproval may be more effective in influencing actual behavior change than will an appeal based on fear of physical harm.

Certain promotional messages appear to be using some of these more recent findings regarding fear appeals. In many cases, the technique often appears to involve a means that makes it easier for the audience to deal with the fear-arousing message. This may include making light of the object involved, presenting it in a humorous way, or using an indirect technique such as making some third party bear the brunt of the feared consequences. An example of a message using both humor and the third-party technique is shown in Figure 17-8.

Distraction   Some evidence suggests that pleasant forms of distraction can often work to increase the effectiveness of persuasive appeals in encouraging attitude change.[30] Sales representatives often practice this principle when they take clients out to dinner. Advertisers can also use such pleasant forms of distraction as music or background activity.

The explanation for the effectiveness of distraction on attitude change has been that it retards counterargumentation. That is, distraction tends to make the receiver lose his train of thought or forget to argue against the message. This, according to the explanation would, result in greater message acceptance.

Studies have shown conflicting evidence on the distraction concept.[31] Also, in some cases distraction may actually reduce receivers' attention to the message. Therefore, evidence is still not clear regarding the effectiveness of this method of increasing attitude change and the conditions that influence it.

Participation   As was discussed earlier in the text, active audience participation is a means of gaining attention to and enhancing the learning of a message. Similarly,

FIGURE 17-8
Use of humor and a third-party technique to reduce negative effects of a fear-evoking message.
Courtesy of New England Mutual Life Insurance Company.

participation can increase the effectiveness of a persuasive appeal.[32] Marketers have learned the value of giving product samples to prospective customers, encouraging trial use of their products, and providing coupons for trial purchase. In addition, they often develop television advertisements that place the viewers in the position of vicariously "trying" a product by using well-developed camera angles and other production techniques that make them feel a part of the commercial.

Humor Estimates are that between 15 and 42 percent of radio and television advertising employs humorous appeals. Print media also contain many similar messages. To a considerable extent, much of this humor is designed to attract audience attention. However, in other cases the intent is to moderate the perceived threat of fear appeals or to assist message persuasiveness in some manner.

Some advertisers, such as Volkswagen and Isuzu, have developed extensive campaigns based on humor, while others never give it serious consideration, arguing that amusing circumstances are not universal in appeal, they wear out quickly, and they consume too much valuable advertising time or space. Daily experience and research evidence seems to support the contention that humor is not universal in its appeal. For example, studies investigating reactions to three basic types of humor (hostile, sexual, and nonsensical) find that females and males differ in their perception as to what is amusing.[33]

Certainly, universal agreement does not exist on the benefits of this message factor. However, a review of the relevant research included the following conclusions:[34]

1 Humorous messages can attract attention, but they may also have a detrimental effect on message comprehension. (In an advertising context, one can sometimes counter this potential problem by focusing the humor on product attributes expected to be instrumental in influencing attitudes. Figure 17-9 provides an illustration.)

2 Humorous appeals appear to increase the credibility of a source and may also increase audience liking for the source, as well as create a positive mood toward it.

3 Although humorous appeals appear to be persuasive, they do not seem to be more persuasive than serious appeals.

These and other findings indicate that more needs to be generally known about the effectiveness of humor and conditions which affect its ability to influence attitude change.

Emotional versus Rational Appeals Should marketers use emotional or rational appeals in promoting their products? As the reader might guess neither approach has been shown to be generally superior to the other. This seems understandable, because the effectiveness of appeals is likely to be a function of the underlying motives consumers have for considering the product.

When emotional appeals appear to be appropriate, the following points have been offered as guidance for constructing the appeal:

1   Use emotionally charged language, especially words that have a high personal meaning to the target consumers.

2   If the brand or message is unfamiliar to the audience, associate it with well-known ideas.

3   Associate the brand or message with visual or nonverbal stimuli that arouse emotions.

4   The communication should be accompanied by nonverbal cues, such as hand motions, which support the verbal message.[35]

Comparative Appeals   The term "comparative advertising" refers to advertising messages that make some form of comparison between the promoted brand and some other brand or brands. In a stricter sense, this would involve comparisons with one or more *specifically* named or recognized brands of the same generic product in terms of one or more *specific* products or attributes.[36] Figure 17-10 presents a good example of an ad that meets these criteria.

Although comparative ads are now fairly popular, prior to the 1970s they

Figure 17-9
Use of humor to focus audience attention on product attributes expected to be instrumental in attitude formation or change.
Courtesy of the American Tourister Company.

were quite rare, especially on television. However, in 1979 the Federal Trade Commission formally encouraged the practice, based of the belief that such ads would provide consumers with more and better information for making brand comparisons. Some of the more widely known comparative campaigns include the Avis Corporation stating, "We try harder," compared to Hertz and showing service attributes as their claim to superior performance. Schick also confronted Norelco, Remington, and Sunbeam in a direct comparison of electric shaver performance. And of course, in 1975 Pepsi met Coke head-on in the now famous "Pepsi Challenge" comparative campaign. In all of these cases, and in a number of others, quite favorable sales results accrued to the company initiating the comparative appeal.

However, although many advertising practitioners extol the benefits of comparative appeals, research evidence has suggested a number of potential problems. These include the following:

1 Comparative ads have not been shown to be significantly more effective in increasing brand awareness.

2 Comparative ads may result in information overload for consumers.

Figure 17-10
A comparative appeal.
Courtesy of Software
Publishing Corporation.

3 Comparative ads may be perceived as offensive, and the sponsoring company may be perceived as less trustworthy.

4 Comparative themes may encourage consumers' involvement and, as a consequence, lead to more counterarguments against the message. This can generate a so-called "boomerang" effect and depress brand attitudes rather than generating more favorable ones. However, use of two-sided comparative ads (where some minor disadvantages for the brand are mentioned) appear to reduce such counterarguments.

5 The effect of comparative ads may be influenced by various situations. For example, those loyal to the advertised brand may tend to respond more favorably than others. Also, some evidence suggests that such ads may be more effective for the brand that is not the present market leader.[37]

These situations suggest that more still needs to be known about the effects of comparative ads on consumers' attitudes and other response variables.

MESSAGE CODES

The way in which marketers assemble and use message codes can have an impact on the persuasiveness of their messages. Three broad classes are (1) verbal codes, (2) nonverbal codes, and (3) paralinguistic message codes.

Verbal Codes   The verbal code is a system of word symbols that are combined according to a set of rules, as in the English language. Although a variety of alternatives exist for devising verbal code structures, advertisers tend to use modifier words, such as adjectives and adverbs, to elicit favorable emotions within a consumer. For example, the same factual information is conveyed by using either of the following advertising messages, but one conveys the facts with words higher in emotion:

1 The new plastic product resembling leather will soon be available to shoe manufacturers.

2 The fabulous new plastic product which out-leathers leather will soon replace all other products used in the manufacture of superior quality shoes.[38]

The advertiser is likely to use the second statement, because it expresses the same idea but with more highly charged modifiers.

Nonverbal Codes   Nonverbal codes are extremely important in persuasive communication, and they have not been given the attention they deserve in published research.[39] For example, a communicator's facial expressions, gestures, posture, and dress can affect how a receiver responds to a message.

Sales representatives have found the study of nonverbal communications extremely helpful in better understanding prospective customers and in meeting sales resistance. Astute representatives can tell when a client is bored, receptive, doubtful, critical, interested, and so forth by observing nonverbal cues such as crossed legs, body lean, hand gestures, and mannerisms. Advertisers also are aware of the importance of nonverbal communications in television and print advertisements, particularly those that use models.

Paralinguistic Codes   Paralinguistic codes are those which lie between the verbal and nonverbal codes. They primarily involve two components—voice qualities and vocalizations.[40]

Voice qualities refer to such speech characteristics as rhythm pattern, pitch of voice, and precision of articulation. They can communicate urgency, boredom, sarcasm, and other feelings. *Vocalizations,* on the other hand, are sounds such as yawns, sighs, and various voice intensities which reflect certain emotions.

Advertisers are very careful to select models whose tonal qualities match the product message. For example, when facial soaps, body creams, and shampoos that are soft and gentle are being promoted, the model's voice tends to be quite soothing. However, advertisements for pick-up trucks, tools, and some heavy-duty cleansers typically employ low, powerful-sounding voices.

RECEIVER FACTORS

To be a persuasive communicator and an effective marketer, it is important to adopt a ''know your audience'' position. In our discussion throughout this chapter, we have already focused on a number of receiver factors that affect the persuasiveness of communications. For example, we have noted that the effectiveness of fear and humor appeals depends on characteristics of audience members. This section briefly deals with two remaining general receiver characteristics that deserve mention. These are the receiver's personality traits and belief types.

PERSONALITY TRAITS

Behavioral research has shed light on the relationship between personality traits and persuasibility. Among these traits are (1) self-esteem, (2) rich imagery, and (3) intelligence.

Self-Esteem   Self-esteem refers to a person's feelings of adequacy and self-worth. In general, research has suggested that people who have low self-esteem tend to be more persuasible than those with high self-esteem.[41] This generalization appears to be particularly true in situations in which people are motivated by social approval. Researchers believe that people who feel inadequate are more persuasible because they lack confidence in their judgments and therefore tend to rely upon the opinions of others.

In a marketing study concerning the persuasibility of women subjects in a personal selling situation, it was found that women with medium self-esteem showed the greatest opinion change, while women at the high and low ends of the self-esteem spectrum were low in their susceptibility to the persuasive sales pitch. The researchers suggested that women with low self-esteem acted in an ego-defensive manner, such as to say ''I don't need help in making up my mind,'' while those with high self-esteem behaved as had subjects in previous experiments.[42] The apparent contradiction of these findings to previous research may be due to the broader range of self-esteem of subjects in this sample. Also, differences in experimental settings may have influenced the results. Earlier studies used social approval to motivate subjects to change opinions, whereas this study and other later studies involved subjects in problem-solving situations.[43]

Rich Imagery   People who are high in rich imagery, or who live out much of their lives through dream worlds and fantasy, are more persuasible than those who are not high in rich imagery. With this information, companies such as Schlitz have developed successful advertising themes, which stressed a number of situations that audience members could fantasize about. The brand was then associated with these situations.

Intelligence   People of both high and low intelligence are susceptible to persuasion, depending upon the message approach a communicator uses. Two general principles which emerge from behavioral research on audience intelligence are the following:

1   Persons with high intellectual ability will tend, mainly because of their ability to draw valid inferences, to be more influenced than will those with low intelligence when exposed to persuasive communications that rely primarily on impressive logical arguments.

2   Persons with high intelligence will tend, mainly because of their superior critical ability, to be less influenced than will those with low intelligence by unsupported generalities or false, illogical, irrelevant arguments.[44]

A person's intellectual capacity is made up of three interacting components: (1) learning ability, which is the mental capacity to acquire and recall information; (2) critical ability, which is the ability to assess the rationality of information and to accept or reject it on a logical basis; and (3) ability to draw inferences, which refers to the ability to interpret information and to use facts to make sound implications. In the first principle stated above, the relationship between intelligence and persuasibility is based upon a person's ability to draw correct inferences; in the second principle, the relationship is based upon a person's critical ability.

In marketing, audiences can be segmented according to levels of intelligence, often by inference rather than through data collection. Physicians, engineers, business leaders, and other similar occupations generally are made up of people with high intellectual ability. Specialized media are available to advertise products that are pertinent to their fields and to them personally.

BELIEF TYPES

As indicated in Chapter 16 and in the introduction of this chapter, a receiver's existing attitude and belief structure can be an opportunity for, or an obstruction to, persuasive marketing communications.[45] The direction of attitudes and the strength of beliefs are two factors that were mentioned as particularly important in influencing change. Three basic belief types influence the commitment that the consumer will have regarding his knowledge. Of course, these in turn will influence the difficulty in changing attitudes. *Central beliefs* form the core of a person's cognitive structure. Because they are deeply rooted to so many other beliefs, they are quite resistant to change. This was suggested in our discussion of memory structure in Chapter 14. *Derived beliefs* are an outgrowth of central beliefs. For example, "Retailers should be free to charge whatever prices they feel are appropriate" is a belief derived from a central belief about freedom. As the name implies, *central-free beliefs* exist separate and apart from other beliefs in the consumer's cognitive structure. "I believe that Al's market is the best in town" is an example.

In order of difficulty, central beliefs are the hardest to change, derived beliefs are the next most difficult, and central-free beliefs the easiest to change. Marketers should avoid attacking central beliefs and instead should see them as opportunities. That is, messages that are aligned with central beliefs are readily acceptable, because they reinforce already strongly held attitudes. Similarly, beliefs derived from more central ones may be used as a basis for an advertising theme. In this way, the beliefs are not attacked, but instead are used as a means of enhancing the value of the advertised brand. The lesson to be learned is that a consumer's psychological barriers should be avoided and turned into opportunities.

MANAGERIAL REFLECTIONS

For our product or service situation . . .

1   What low or high involvement strategies appear to have the greatest potential for changing consumers' attitudes toward purchasing our brands?

2   What insights does the communication-process model described in Figure 17-2 provide for our promotional efforts?

3   What are the major marketing communication sources for our organization?

4   What are the implications of source credibility for our firm's communications?

5   Do two-sided messages have potential benefits for our marketing communications?

6   Do fear, humor, or emotional appeals appear to have any significant potential for our promotional messages?

7   Do comparative appeals appear beneficial for our advertisements?

8   Which types of message codes appear appropriate for our broadcast advertisements?

9   What are the unique characteristics of our consumers which may influence how they respond to our promotions?

DISCUSSION TOPICS

1   Who are the major marketing communicators of a firm?

2   What major factors assist a source in being perceived as credible? Cite specific advertising examples of the use of each factor.

3 What is the so-called sleeper effect, and, if it were shown to exist, what implications would there be for the communicator?

4 What recommendations would you make to a communicator regarding the following aspects of message structure: (*a*) message sidedness, (*b*) order of presentation, and (*c*) message code?

5 What suggestions would you offer regarding drawing a conclusion in a marketing communication? Watch a number of TV advertisements and try to determine the extent to which these suggestions are being followed.

6 What conclusions can you offer regarding the effective use of message appeals? Can you point out any specific advertisements that might not be following these conclusions?

7 Under what conditions might a highly credible source detract from the persuasiveness of a message?

8 If you were going to present a speech to United States business leaders on "The Declining Quality of America's Goods and Services," what guidelines could you employ from this chapter?

9 Suggest the characteristics of some fear appeals that might be used for (*a*) the American Heart Association attempting to get people to regularly check their blood pressure, (*b*) Goodrich steel-belted radial tires, (*c*) Prudential disability insurance, and (*d*) a Sears burglar alarm system for the home.

10 When might a manager want to employ comparative appeals?

PROJECTS

1 Select an existing product or service, and design several advertisements which make use of the various principles discussed in the chapter. Explain why you believe they would be effective.

2 Sample advertisements from the print or broadcast media. To what extent do the following appear to be used: (*a*) two-sided appeals, (*b*) fear appeals, (*c*) humor, (*d*) methods to generate credibility, and (*e*) comparative appeals? How effectively do you think these are being accomplished?

NOTES

[1] Based on Christine Douglas, "Plastic Prestige: Credit Cards That Make You Somebody," *Business Week,* November 11, 1985, p. 62; and Brian Moran, "MasterCard Shuns Status," *Advertising Age,* February 24, 1986, pp. 3, 83.

[2] Henry Assael, *Consumer Behavior and Marketing Action,* Kent, Belmont, Calif., 1981, p. 91.

[3] Richard J. Lutz, "Changing Brand Attitudes Through Modification of Cognitive Structure," *Journal of Consumer Research,* **1**:49, March 1975, has discussed some of these strategies.

[4] See John L. Lastovicka and David M. Gardner, "Components of Involvement," in John C. Maloney and Bernard Silverman (eds.), *Attitude Research Plays For High Stakes,* American Marketing Association, Chicago, 1979, pp. 53–73; and C. W. Sherif, M. Sherif, and R. E. Nebergall, *Attitude and Attitude Change: The Social Judgment Involvement Approach,* Yale University Press, New Haven, Conn., 1965.

[5] One might validly suggest that channel factors should be included in this list. However, for purposes

of this chapter, these effects are included within the source, because consumers frequently view a medium as a source of information and influence.

6 Arch G. Woodside and J. William Davenport, "The Effect of Salesman Similarity and Expertise on Consumer Purchasing Behavior," *Journal of Marketing Research,* **11**:198–202, May 1974.

7 Theodore Levitt, "Communications and Industrial Selling," *Journal of Marketing,* **31**:15–21, April 1967.

8 See, for example, Brian Sternthal, Ruby Dholakia, and Clark Leavitt, "The Persuasive Effects of Source Credibility: Tests of Cognitive Response," *Journal of Consumer Research,* **4**:252–260, 1978; D. Bock and T. Saine, "The Impact of Source Credibility, Attitude Valence, and Task Sensitization on Trait Error in Speech Evaluation," *Speech Monographs,* **37**:342–358, 1975; and Robert R. Harmon and Kenneth A. Coney, "The Persuasive Effects of Source Credibility in Buy and Lease Situations," *Journal of Marketing Research,* **14**:255–260, May 1982.

9 See Sternthal, Dholakia, and Leavitt, "The Persuasive Effects of Source Credibility."

10 See Brian Sternthal, Lynn Phillips, and Ruby Dholakia, "The Persuasive Effect of Source Credibility: A Situational Analysis," *Public Opinion Quarterly,* **42**:285–314, 1978; and Daniel R. Toy, "Monitoring Communication Effects: A Cognitive Structure/Cognitive Response Approach," *Journal of Consumer Research,* **9**:66–76, June 1982.

11 See Ruby Dholakia and Brian Sternthal, "Highly Credible Sources: Persuasive Facilitators or Persuasive Liabilities?" *Journal of Consumer Research,* **3**:223–232, March 1977.

12 See Carl Hovland and Walter Weiss, "The Influence of Source Credibility on Communication Effectiveness," *Public Opinion Quarterly,* **15**:635–650, 1951–1952; Herbert Kelman and Carl Hovland, " 'Reinstatement' of the Communicator in Delayed Measurement of Opinion Change," *Journal of Abnormal and Social Psychology,* **48**:327–335, 1953; and Carl Hovland, Arthur A. Lunsdaine, and Fred D. Sheffield, *Experiments on Mass Communications,* Princeton University Press, Princeton, N.J., 1949, pp. 188–189.

13 See, for example, N. Capon and J. Hulbert, "The Sleeper Effect: An Awakening," *Public Opinion Quarterly,* **37**:333–358, 1973; and C. Gruder et al., "Empirical Tests of the Absolute Sleeper Effect Predicted from the Discounting Cue Hypothesis," *Journal of Personality and Social Psychology,* **36**:1061–1074, 1978.

14 Kelman and Hovland, "Reinstatement of the Communicator."

15 For a more complete discussion, see E. P. Bettinghaus, *Persuasive Communication,* 2d ed., Holt, New York, 1973, p. 10.

16 See, for example, E. Aronson and B. Golden, "The Effect of Relevant and Irrelevant Aspects of Communicator Credibility on Opinion Change," *Journal of Personality,* **30**:135–146, 1962. Also see Peter Bennett and Harold Kassarjian, *Consumer Behavior,* Prentice-Hall, Englewood Cliffs, N.J., 1972, p. 89; and Gordon Patzer, *The Physical Attractiveness Phenomena,* Plenum, 1985.

17 David K. Berlo, *The Process of Communications,* Holt, San Francisco, 1960, pp. 45–48.

18 M. Karlins and H. I. Abelson, *Persuasion,* 2d ed., Springer, New York, 1970, p. 128.

19 See C. Hovland, A. Lumsdaine, and F. Sheffield, *Experiments in Mass Communication,* vol. 3, Princeton University Press, Princeton, N.J., 1948; also see Linda Golden and Mark Alpert, "The Relative Effectiveness of One-Sided and Two-Sided Communication for Mass Transit Advertising," in H. Keith Hunt (ed.), *Advances in Consumer Research,* vol. 5, Association for Consumer Research, Ann Arbor, Mich., 1978, pp. 12–18.

20 See Stewart W. Bither, "Resistance of Persuasion: Inoculation and Distraction," in Arch Woodside, Jagdish Sheth, and Peter Bennett (eds.), *Consumer and Industrial Buying Behavior,* North-Holland, New York, pp. 243–250; Michael Etgar and Stephen A. Goodwin, "One-Sided versus Two-Sided Comparative Message Appeals for New Brand Introductions," *Journal of Consumer Research,* **8**:460–465, March 1982; and Michael A. Kamins and Henry Assael, "Two-Sided versus One-Sided Appeals: A Cognitive Perspective on Argumentation, Source Derogation, and the Effect of Disconfirming Trial on Belief Change," *Journal of Marketing Research,* **24**:29–39, February 1987.

21 E. W. J. Faison, "Effectiveness of One-Sided and Two-Sided Mass Communications in Advertising," *Public Opinion Quarterly,* **25**:468–469, 1961.

22 M. Wayne Delozier, *The Marketing Communications Process,* McGraw-Hill, New York, 1976, p. 95.

23 C. I. Hovland, I. L. Janis, and H. H. Kelley, *Communication and Persuasion,* Yale University Press, New Haven, Conn., 1953, p. 119.

24 See Hovland, Janis, and Kelley, *Communication and Persuasion,* pp. 103–105, and D. L. Thistle-

thwaite, H. de Haan, and J. Kamenetzky, "The Effects of 'Directive' and 'Nondirective' Communication Procedures on Attitudes," *Journal of Abnormal and Social Psychology,* **51:**107–113, 1955.

[25] See Alan G. Sawyer, "Repetition and Affect: Recent Empirical and Theoretical Developments," in Arch Woodside, Jagdish Sheth, and Peter Bennett (eds.), *Consumer and Industrial Buyer Behavior,* North Holland, New York, 1977, pp. 229–242; and George E. Belch, "The Effects of Television Commercial Repetition on Cognitive Response and Message Acceptance," *Journal of Consumer Research,* **9:**56–65, June 1982.

[26] See Bobby Calder and Brian Sternthal, "Television Advertising Wearout: An Information Processing View," *Journal of Marketing Research,* **17:**173–186, May 1980.

[27] I. Janis and S. Feshbach, "Effects of Fear-Arousing Communications," *Journal of Abnormal and Social Psychology,* **48:**78–92, 1953.

[28] See L. Berkowitz and D. R. Cottingham, "The Interest Value and Relevance of Fear-Arousing Communication," *Journal of Abnormal and Social Psychology,* **60:**37–43, 1960; A. S. DeWolf and C. N. Governale, "Fear and Attitude Change," *Journal of Abnormal and Social Psychology,* **69:**119–123, 1964; H. Leventhal, R. P. Singer, and S. Jones, "Effects of Fear and Specificity of Recommendation upon Attitudes and Behavior," *Journal of Personality and Social Psychology,* **2:**20–29, 1965; C. A. Insko, A. Arkoff, and V. M. Insko, "Effects of High and Low Fear-Arousing Communications upon Opinions toward Smoking," *Journal of Experimental Social Psychology,* **1:**254–266, August 1965; and Michael L. Ray and William L. Wilkie, "Fear: The Potential of an Appeal Neglected by Marketing," *Journal of Marketing,* **34:**54–62, January 1970.

[29] See Brian Sternthal and C. Samuel Craig, "Fear Appeals: Revisited and Revised," *Journal of Consumer Research,* **1:**22–34, December 1974; John J. Burnett and Robert E. Wilkes, "Fear Appeals to Segments Only," *Journal of Advertising Research,* **20:**21–24, October 1980; and John J. Burnett and Richard L. Oliver, "Fear Appeal Effects in the Field: A Segmentation Approach," *Journal of Marketing Research,* **16:**181–190, May 1979.

[30] M. Karlins and H. I. Abelson, *Persuasion,* 2d ed., Springer, New York, 1970, p. 15.

[31] See Stewart W. Bither, "Effects of Distraction and Commitment on the Persuasiveness of Television Advertising," *Journal of Marketing Research,* **9:**1–5, February 1972; and David Gardner, "The Distraction Hypothesis in Marketing," *Journal of Advertising Research,* **10:**25–31, December 1970.

[32] See Hovland, Janis, and Kelley, *Communication and Persuasion,* pp. 228–237; also see W. Watts, "Relative Persistence of Opinion Change Induced by Active Compared to Passive Participation," *Journal of Personality and Social Psychology,* **5:**4–15, 1967.

[33] See Thomas W. Whipple and Alice E. Courtney, "How Men and Women Judge Humor: Advertising Guidelines for Action and Research," in James H. Leigh and Claude R. Martin Jr. (eds.), *Current Issues and Research in Advertising,* University of Michigan, Ann Arbor, 1981.

[34] Brian Sternthal and C. Samuel Craig, "Humor in Advertising," *Journal of Marketing,* **37:**12–18, October 1973.

[35] E. P. Bettinghaus, *Persuasive Communication,* 2d ed., Holt, New York, 1973, pp. 160–161.

[36] William L. Wilkie and Paul W. Farris, "Comparison Advertising: Problems and Potential," *Journal of Marketing,* **39:**7–15, October 1975.

[37] See Stephen B. Ash and Chow-Hou Wee, "Comparative Advertising: A Review with Implications for Further Research," in Richard Bagozzi and Alice Tybout (eds.) *Advances in Consumer Research,* vol. 10, Association for Consumer Research, Ann Arbor, Mich., 1983, pp. 370–376; "George E. Belch, "An Examination of Comparative and Noncomparative Television Commercials: The Effects of Claim Variation and Repetition on Cognitive Response and Message Acceptance," *Journal of Marketing Research,* **18:**333–349, August 1981; William R. Swinyard, "The Interaction between Comparative Advertising and Copy Claim Variation," *Journal of Marketing Research,* **18:**175–186, May 1981; Terence A. Shimp and David C. Dyer, "The Effects of Comparative Advertising Mediated by Market Position of Sponsoring Brand," *Journal of Advertising,* **3:**13–19, Summer 1978; and Gerald J. Gorn and Charles B. Weinberg, "The Impact of Comparative Advertising on Perception and Attitude: Some Positive Findings," *Journal of Consumer Research,* **11:**719–727, September 1984.

[38] Bettinghaus, *Persuasive Communication,* pp. 121–122, in reference to G. L. Trager, "Paralanguage: A First Approximation," *Studies in Linguistics,* **13:**1–12, 1958; also see Larry Percy, "Psycholinguistic Guidelines for Advertising Copy," in Andrew Mitchell (ed.), *Advances in Consumer Research,* vol. 9, Association for Consumer Research, Ann Arbor, Mich., 1982, pp. 107–111, for some practical guidelines for using verbal codes.

[39] For a recent exception, see Patrick L. Schul and Charles W. Lamb, Jr., ''Recoding Nonverbal and Vocal Communications: A Laboratory Study,'' *Journal of the Academy of Marketing Science,* **10:**154–164, Spring 1982.

[40] Bettinghaus, Persuasive Communication, pp. 121–122, in reference to G. L. Tragar, ''Paralanguage: A First Approximation,'' *Studies in Linguistics,* **13:**1–12, 1958.

[41] See I. L. Janis, ''Personality Correlates of Susceptibility to Persuasion,'' *Journal of Personality,* **22:**504–518, 1954; F. J. Divesta and J. C. Merivan, ''The Effects of Need-Oriented Communications on Attitude Change,'' *Journal of Abnormal and Social Psychology,* **60:**80–85, 1960; and I. L. Janis and C. I. Hovland (eds.), *Personality and Persuasibility,* Yale University Press, New Haven, Conn., 1959, pp. 55–68.

[42] D. F. Cox and R. A. Bauer, ''Self Confidence and Persuasibility in Women,'' *Public Opinion Quarterly,* **28:**453–466, Fall 1964.

[43] R. A. Bauer, ''Games People and Audiences Play,'' paper presented at seminar on Communications in Contemporary Society, University of Texas, March 17, 1967.

[44] Hovland, Janis, and Kelley, *Communication and Persuasion,* p. 183.

[45] This discussion is based in part upon Bettinghaus, *Persuasive Communication,* pp. 59–61.

CASES FOR PART FOUR

CASE 4-1
DOODLE, DAZZLE, AND SPARKLE*

A California dentist tries to amuse his young patients by dressing up in a red cape with blue tights and calling himself "Plaque Invader." Actually, he uses a total of twelve different

*This case is based on information appearing in "Drilling for New Business," *Time,* December 1, 1980, p. 110; "Retail Dentistry," *Newsweek,* November 27, 1978, p. 63; Elizabeth Bailey, "The Department Store Dentist," *Forbes,* March 19, 1979, pp. 112–114; and Darolyn Lendio, "Dentists Ponder Case of the Missing Patients as Appointments Lag." *The Wall Street Journal,* October 10, 1980, pp. 1, 14.

costumes in his practice. This same dentist drives to work in a white Volkswagen that has a top formed in the shape of a molar. The vehicle is called a "Plaquemobile." For adults, a hot tub and choice wines are available while waiting for an appointment, or after a visit. In addition, chances to win record albums, free dinners, and turkeys are given away.

Is this a professional that has gone off the deep end, or is he an entrepreneur with particularly good insight into consumers? A little information on the dental-care industry provides some perspective. For decades, dentists have been in the tooth-repair business while being almost evangelistic in promoting good oral hygiene to reduce the risk of additional cavities and other dental problems. At the same time, dental schools have been training a growing number of professionals to repair teeth that have fallen victim to decay. Nevertheless, until the 1970s, demand for dental services in the United States continued to exceed the supply of dentists significantly. However, during the 1970s the number of active dentists increased 21 percent to about 124,000 while the population

FIGURE 1
An advertisement focusing on the concept of sparkle.
Courtesy of the American Dental Association.

SPARKLE:

Get it for her at the dentist regularly.

It's a look. It's a feeling. Mostly it's an attitude, one kids will keep for the rest of their lives: the self-assurance that comes with strong, beautiful teeth. Advances like fluoride toothpaste mean a lot, but not without an early program of regular dental visits. So start them out young, yes, even before they're three. A checkup takes just a few minutes of your time. And it costs less than what it takes to keep a child in shoes for a year.

Sparkle. It's a quality you've admired in others. It's something you can give your kids for a lifetime.

The American Dental Association

increased only 8.8 percent. The consequence has been that average patient loads per dentist have declined perceptively. This is especially noticeable in California, where the number of dentists per 1000 persons is higher than in any other state.

Factors other than changing demographics have also contributed to declines in the demand for dental chairs. Better oral hygiene practices promoted by dentists actually have reduced the need for corrective dentistry. Also, fluoridation of drinking water for about one-half of the nation's population has had a similar effect. One study showed that a child who drinks fluoridated water from infancy to 14 years of age develops 60 percent fewer cavities than others who drink unfluoridated water. More efficient dentistry has also had a dramatic impact. High-speed, diamond-tipped drills and other advances have reduced the duration of appointments for some procedures by two-thirds or more.

Of course, there also is a negative side to these statistics and trends. In many areas of the country, dentists are becoming concerned about declines in revenues as a result of fewer and shorter patient visits. Some critics, who have referred to the profession as "Drill, Fill, Bill, and Coupe DeVille" have not shown a great deal of sympathy. But dentists, and the associations that represent them, are quite concerned.

Because of this, one portion of the marketplace has become the focus of considerable attention—those people who do not visit a dentist on a regular basis. Surprisingly, about one-half of the U.S. population falls into this category. Therefore, there is considerable potential demand for dentistry services among these residents. Some dentists, like the one described earlier, have focused on novelty, humor, and extras to lure potential customers. Others have constructed elaborate offices with wood paneling and stained glass windows. Still others have offered unique features such as a disco called the "waiting room" for those that come early for their appointments. In addition, a dentist in California actually offers special tattoo work on new caps. He features the slogan "Get Drilled at Ernie's" on T-shirts and other displays.

The American Dental Association has also become involved by sponsoring a variety of promotional messages on behalf of member dentists. In contrast to previous messages that educated the public on proper dental hygiene, current focus is on encouraging people to visit their dentist. One theme has been referred to as "Dazzle" because its basic message is "Dazzle. When your teeth have it, you have it. So go get some at your dentist's." An offshot of this is the "Sparkle" theme as shown in Figure 1. Another recent message is referred to as "Doodle" because it focuses on the consequences of tooth decay and warns: "Don't doodle around with your teeth. Call your dentist today."

Still other dentists have concluded that the high cost of dental work serves as a deterrent to regular office visits. One

response has been dental care centers installed in department stores and in shopping malls. Because of the high volume of business, these centers are often capable of offering a fee structure that is 20 to 40 percent below regular dental rates. In addition, an added bonus of such centers is convenience, because they are usually open ten to twelve hours, Monday through Saturday, and six hours on Sunday.

Still others point to evidence suggesting that cost ranks seventh out of eleven "barriers" to regular dental visits. Fear and concern about pain are the major factors to deal with according to this group. However, little has been done to address this issue. Some progress has been made to make dentists' offices look less imposing through changes in decor. Also, some claim that locating offices in more typical surroundings, such as at a shopping mall, and placing chairs out in an open area have resulted in reduced patient anxiety. The use of nitrous oxide to relax patients and the availability of more effective pain killers have also been communicated to the public in low-key ways to help dispel anxiety. However, to date, the magic key has not yet been found to encourage the majority of the public to make regular dental appointments.

Questions

1 Suggest motivating influences that might be involved in the decision to visit a dentist. How would you categorize these and how do they relate to one another?
2 In what ways might the motives that actually influence use of a dentist be determined?

CASE 4-2
JOLT COLA*

In the world of colas, two stand out in our minds and have dominated the cola industry for many users—Coke and Pepsi. Therefore, if you want to enter the cola wars, you had better have something unique about your cola that attracts people's attention. The cola's name had better jump out at the audience so they will not forget that it is not Coke or Pepsi.

How about JOLT Cola? The name JOLT (with a lightning bolt going through the O) should stand out in everyone's mind. The name is symbolic of the contents in JOLT. "Loaded with sugar and caffeine" is the claim that JOLT producers make in their promotions.

Some in the industry think that there are consumers who need a "kick" in a good-tasting soft drink. JOLT was proudly

---

*Adapted from, "Jolt Gets Lightning Fast Start," *Advertising Age*, July 28, 1986, p. 46E.

introduced as an alternative cola with substantial amounts of sugar and caffeine.

In selecting the name JOLT, the management team considered many things. One important factor was that every cola has been concerned about caffeine since 7-Up made famous the slogan: "Never had it, never will." Coke and Pepsi have also introduced and promoted the no-caffeine brands to the market. It occurred to JOLT management that these cola giants were taking their soda concepts too seriously. Too much emphasis was being placed on the ideas of less sugar and no caffeine.

JOLT's philosophy was that all cola consumers are not highly concerned about the sugar and caffeine levels of their cola. In fact, it was thought that many people probably drink their colas to get an added "boost." Therefore, the philosophy was that at least one group of consumers need a good-tasting soft drink without such a serious attitude about its ingredients. Consequently, instead of taking such a serious approach, the people at JOLT took a fun-loving, crazy approach. They emphasized the fact that their cola had lots of sugar and a heavy dose of caffeine. The ingredients and the advertising led to the name JOLT. The lightning bolt through the O in JOLT gave it that extra pow!

Advertisements feature such themes as dancing JOLT cans and people having a good time at a beach party. Each version includes a high-energy jingle emphasizing the sugar and caffeine that JOLT possesses.

JOLT is sold in six-packs and 2-liter plastic bottles at prices that are competitive with Coke and Pepsi. Everyone knows that it is extremely difficult to carve a niche in the cola market dominated by Coke and Pepsi. Therefore, the people at JOLT are hoping that at least a portion of the market will be attracted to the name JOLT and what it represents.

Questions

1 What type of segmentation strategy does JOLT appear to be using?

2 Is there any research that you could suggest to JOLT managers?

3 What motives might be important influences on consumers interested in JOLT?

4 Can you suggest any advertising appeals based on these motives?

CASE 4-3
OLD COLONY BANK*

For some time the Old Colony Bank management team had believed that advertisements for the institution should focus on its product offering. The philosophy seemed to be that in a changing financial-institution market, consumers had to be aware of the new product offerings available to them. Therefore, the bank's advertisements focused on providing consumers with information about such things as money market accounts, interest rates, and new financial alternatives for combined checking and savings accounts.

A recently conducted marketing research study revealed some surprising findings that focused management's thinking in a new direction. The study, which concentrated on consumers' reactions to the bank and its offerings, suggested that people in the market area (Rhode Island and nearby Massachusetts) did not have a clear concept or image of the bank. That is, people did not think of the bank in one way or another in terms of a variety of image criteria. Instead, the bank appeared to have a rather bland "no image" in the consumers' minds.

Given these results, management decided to turn to an advertising agency for assistance in determining how to build the bank's new image. As a first step, the advertisements of competing banks in the market area were reviewed. The interesting finding was that most of these financial institutions were touting their size. However, since the state was relatively small, these campaigns did not seem to leave consumers with a clear idea that the banks were primarily focused toward customers in the state, as opposed to customers both within and outside the state. That is, no bank seemed to be clearly identified with only Rhode Island. Therefore, it seemed that an opportunity existed for Old Colony to claim itself as a bank for the people of Rhode Island.

This concept led to a search for a vehicle to associate the bank with the state or some characteristic of the state. In addition, a campaign that attracted a great deal of attention would be preferable, since it would be likely to increase consumers' awareness of the advertisements and, therefore, of the image characteristics being portrayed.

One result was a decision to use the creative talents of a cartoonist who had gained notoriety by concentrating on Rhode Island and its unique characteristics in a humorous manner. This cartoonist's work often appeared in local and state newspapers and had also been published in such books as *Beware of the Quahog*. A quahog is the name locally given to clams found in the salt waters of the state.

The head of the advertising agency's creative staff believed

---

*Adapted from William J. Donovan, "A Bank's Search for an Identity Translated into an Ad Campaign," *Providence Journal,* p. F-6, September 1, 1985.

that the cartoonist's work was a "natural" for the bank's new image campaign. He believed that the cartoonist's concept was completely unique to the state and the humor carried in his cartoons would be a good attention-getter for the advertising campaign. The result was what some have termed "Rhode Island Gothic." The characters in these cartoons, which appeared in both print and television advertising, were in a style very typical of the cartoonist. A man and woman, who appeared to be married, were drawn with very rotund body shapes, small heads, and not highly attractive faces. The woman typically wears a floral-patterned dress with beads and large earrings—a style that is very grandmotherlike in design. The man is often portrayed wearing chest-high waders, a flannel shirt, and a knit hat popular with fishermen in the state. In a style reminiscent of Grant Wood's American Gothic painting of the elderly farm couple standing side-by-side, the male cartoon character is shown holding a clam rake while the woman is holding a basket filled with clams, or quahogs as they are called in Rhode Island.

As the two figures are shown in various scenes with their basket of clams, the television advertisement features a voice-over that describes why the bank is the best place to stash your "clams"—also known as money. Each time the announcer mentions the word clams the woman corrects him in a shrill voice by saying "quahogs." In this way the point is driven home that especially in Rhode Island are clams called quahogs.

The advertising agency was hoping that this quahogs-not-clams line would catch on among residents of the state in a way that the "Where's the beef?" ad did so well for Wendy's. In that way humor would be used to attract the attention of viewers, and use of the word quahogs, as well as the unique style of the cartoonist, would identify the bank with something that was uniquely Rhode Island.

Questions

1 How would you evaluate the use of humor in this situation?
2 What are the potential image benefits which may accrue from this campaign?
3 Are their any potential drawbacks to the campaign?
4 If you were interested in assessing the bank's advertising and image sometime after the campaign, what specific elements would you measure and how would you measure them?

CASE 4-4
EASY LIFE, INC.*

Michael Evans, a marketing manager in the kitchen products division for Easy Life, a leading small household appliance manufacturer, regularly attends conferences where the latest research evidence on consumer behavior is discussed. Consequently, Mike's awareness of different methods for studying how consumers process information is quite high. He believes that investigations of consumer information-processing yield insights into how consumers make purchase decisions. These insights can have an important impact on the design of advertisements and other aspects of Easy Life's marketing strategy.

One method of learning about how consumers process information is sometimes called the *thought protocol method.* This technique basically requires that consumers "think aloud" as they engage in some task, such as choosing which of several brands they will purchase. Typically, a brand-choice situation is set up by displaying several competing brands as they might appear in a retail store. The consumer is asked to make a purchase decision and speak out loud the thoughts that he or she has during the decision process. These verbalized thoughts are recorded and then converted into a typed transcript for further analysis. Although many subjects do not verbalize a high proportion of their thoughts initially, they soon become at ease with the process and the number of thoughts that are mentioned increases considerably.

After analyzing written protocols with his staff, Mike has concluded that they provide useful insights into, among other things, the images consumers have of various brands, how consumers process the information presented with a product, and what features of a product elicit positive responses among consumers. Of course, considerable effort is required to analyze just a small number of consumers' thought protocols. For this reason, large samples of consumers cannot be studied using this method. Consequently, any insights gained must be examined further to determine how representative they are of a wider group of consumers.

Another method of investigating how consumers process information is *eye movement analysis.* Use of this method requires that a consumer view a stimulus display (such as a

*This case is based on Raymond J. Smead, James B. Wilcox, and Robert E. Wilkes, "An Illustration and Evaluation of a Joint Process Tracing Methodology: Eye Movement and Protocols," in Jerry C. Olson (ed.), *Advances in Consumer Research*, vol. 7, Association for Consumer Research, Ann Arbor, Mich., 1980, pp. 507–512. Figures 1 and 2 from this source are reproduced here with permission of the Association for Consumer Research.

product or an advertisement) while the movement of his or her eyes is being recorded by a very sophisticated piece of equipment. The result of this process can be a picture of the stimulus display that the consumer was viewing with a series of dots, numbered consecutively, superimposed on the picture. The dots show exactly where the consumer's eyes fixated on the display, and the numbers show the sequence in which each fixation occurred. A limitation of this method is that it typically requires the consumer to remain motionless during the stimulus presentation so that equipment can track eye movements. However, valuable information can be gained about which aspects of the stimulus presentations (product feature, advertising element, and so on) attract viewer attention and when they do so. For example, Mike learned that when viewing a display of the company's food mixer and its accessories, very few consumers looked at the special paddles used to knead bread dough.

At a recent conference Mike was intrigued by a rather novel suggestion. The author of one paper was proposing that by combining the methods of thought protocols and eye movement analysis one could learn more about how consumers decide among alternative brands than when either method is used alone. In this approach, thought protocols are used in traditional fashion but eye movement analysis is used at a more macro-level to show which of several alternative brands

the consumer is looking at. The combined method was referred to as *joint process tracing* (JPT) by the researcher.

One of the professed benefits of the JPT method for studying brand-choice situations is that it allows a rather natural simulation of in-store choice environments. An experimental situation might be set up as follows. A moderator would accompany an experimental subject into the testing room where a shelf several feet in front of a wall containing a mirror displays several alternative brands of a given product. A microphone in the room would be connected to a tape recorder using a two-track (stereo) sound system. Anything said by either person would be recorded on one track of the tape. The moderator would instruct the subject regarding the choice situation and encourage the subject to say out loud all thoughts he or she has as the brands are reviewed.

A second researcher is seated behind the mirror wall and is able to see the subject through the mirror. This researcher's task is to speak into a second microphone and indicate the brand name the subject is viewing during each second of the experiment. A metronome audibly clicks off each second of time to assist the researcher in accomplishing this task. Therefore brand names are recorded on the second track of the stereo tape. The result of this data collection effort is one tape which has recorded which brand is being viewed and the verbalized thoughts of the subject that are occurring while the brand is being viewed. The recorded information is then transformed into a typed transcript called a protocol-graph.

Figures 1 and 2 contain portions of protocol-graphs from

FIGURE 1

Time	Brand code		Time	Brand code	
1	6		24	2	
2	6		25	2	
3	6		26	1	
4	1		27	1	
	SCAN 1		28	1	
6	2		29	1	
7	1		30	1	1) this one is 19.99
8	1		31	1	
9	1		32	1	
10	1		33	1	2) price is always a
11	1				consideration of
12	1				course
13	1		34	1	
14	1		35	2	
15	2		36	2	
	PAUSE 3		37	2	3) $26.64, Sunbeam
19	1		38	2	
20	1		39	2	
21	1		40	2	
22	1		41	2	4) I am acquainted with
23	2				quality

FIGURE 1
(continued)

Time	Brand code		Time	Brand code	
42	2		93	6	15) which I don't have much of
43	2		94	1	
44	2	5) it's usually pretty good in my experience	95	1	
45	2		96	1	
46	2		97	6	
47	2	6) Mr. Coffee, I guess was one of the first ones that went this way	98	3	
48	3		99	6	
49	3		100	6	
50	3		101	6	16) (Mod.-what are you thinking?)
51	3		102	5	
52	3		103	6	
53	4		104	1	17) well, I'm thinking that probably everything else was equal in quality
54	4		105	1	
55	4		106	2	
56	4	7) Flav-o-fresh I don't know	SCAN 1		18) I'd rule those two out just on size
57	4		108	5	
58	4		109	5	
59	4		110	5	
SCAN 1			111	6	19) because I have such a limited amount of counter space
61	4		112	6	
62	2		113	5	
63	4	8) dial-a-brew I would assume would give you more choice	114	4	
64	4		115	3	
65	5		PAUSE 1		20) if Proctor-Silex was equal in quality
66	5		117	6	
67	5		118	6	
68	5		119	6	
69	5		PAUSE 1		21) which I have no way of knowing
70	5	9) strength etc.	121	6	
71	5		122	5	22) except I have had a Proctor iron which was very good
72	4		123	4	
73	5	10) than any of these others	124	1	
74	5	11) judging by looks	125	1	
PAUSE 1			126	1	23) its cost is least
76	5		127	1	
77	5		128	4	
78	5	12) GE same price approximately	129	5	
79	4		130	1	24) as I said, at my house we always look at the price tag
80	6		131	1	
81	6		132	4	
82	6		133		25) sometimes before other things which isn't necessarily good
83	6		134	5	
84	5		135	6	
SCAN 1			136	6	26) but I think for my purposes
86	1		137	5	
87	1	13) well, at my house GE	138	5	
88	2				
89	3				
90	3				
91	6				
92	1	14) and Mr. Coffee would take more room			

FIGURE 1
(continued)

Time	Brand code		Time	Brand code	
139	5		189	5	
140	6	27) being as how I really am not making a lot of coffee nowadays	190	5	
141	6		191	5	
142	6		192	5	
143	6		193	5	
144	6		194	5	
145	5		195	5	
SCAN 1			196	5	
147	3	28) and because of the limited amount of space	197	5	
148	3		198	5	
149	5		199	5	
150	5		200	5	
151	5		(BREAK)		
152	5	29) I'd probably rule out GE and Mr. Coffee sizewise	PAUSE 3		
			309	3	
PAUSE 1			310	3	
154	5		311	3	
155	5		312	3	
156	2	30) GE certainly because that is the biggest one	313	3	
			314	1	
157	5		315	2	
158	5		PAUSE 2		
159	5		318	4	47) I ruled out GE
PAUSE 2			319	4	
162	6		320	4	48) and I ruled out Mr. Coffee
PAUSE 2			321	4	
165	6		322	4	
166	6		323	4	
SCAN 2		31) (Mod.-yes?)	324	4	
169	1		325	5	49) because I'm prejudiced
170	6	32) well, I was just trying to figure out maybe what all this does	326	5	
			327	6	
171	6		328	4	50) because of a past experience with a Sears electrical product
172	5		329	6	
173	5		330	4	
174	5		331	2	
175	5		332	2	
176	5		333	1	
177	5	33) that has nothing to do with strength, apparently, or does it?	334	1	
			335	2	51) I would probably rule against this one when I see a Sears
178	5		336	5	
179	5		337	4	
180	5		338	4	
181	5	34) that number of cups or is that the kind of brew?	339	4	52) that's prejudiced, I realize it is
182	5		340	4	
183	5		341	4	53) but we all are that way are we not?
184	5		342	4	
185	5		343	4	
186	5		344	4	
187	5		345	4	
188	5		346	4	
			347	4	

FIGURE 1
(continued)

Time	Brand code			Time	Brand code		
348	4			401	2		
349	4			402	2		
350	4			403	2		
351	4			404	2		62) which may or may not be true under the circumstances but
352	4						
353	4						
354	4			405	2		
355	4			406	2		
356	4			407	2		
357		5			PAUSE 1		
358		5		409	2		63) it does have warm
359		5		410	2		
360		5		411	2		64) now let's see about
361		5		412	2		
	SCAN 1			413	2		
363		5		414	2		
364	2			415	2		
365	2			416	2		
366	2			417	2		
367	2			418	2		65) this is just off and on I guess
368	2						
369	2		54) ok, that one tells you to clean it twice a year	419	2		
				420	2		
370	2			421	2		
371	2				PAUSE 2		66) this one has a different switch to brew than warm, looks like
372	2						
373	2		55) this one doesn't tell you what to do	424		5	
374	2			425		5	
375	2			426		5	
376	2			427		5	
377	2			428		5	
378	2		56) yes, maybe it does	429		5	
379		5		430		5	
380		5		431		5	
381		5		432		5	
382		5	57) clean according to instructions	433		5	
383		5	58) ok, so somewhere its got to tell you	434		5	
				435	2		
384		5		436	2		
385		5		437	2		67) no it doesn't have a different switch
386	2			438	2		
387	2			439	2		68) it just has a different light
388	2			440	2		
389	2			441	2		
390	2			442	2		69) that one comes on when it's done probably
391	2		59) stainless steel				
392	2			443	1		
393	2			444	1		
394	2		60) well that's maybe nicer	445	1		
395	2			446	1		
396	2			447	1		
397	2			448	1		
398	2		61) oh you might say it's more permanent etc. than plastic	449	2		
				450	2		
399	2			451	2		
400	2			452	2		

FIGURE 1
(continued)

Time	Brand code		Time	Brand Code	
453	2	70) well, let's see, Sunbeam		PAUSE 1	
454	2		479	2	
455	2		480	2	
456	2	71) yeah, that's the kind of mixer I've got	481	2	
457	2		482	2	
458	2		483	1	
459	2		484	1	76) $26, that one's $28
460	2		485	1	
461	2		486	2	
462	2		487	2	
463	2		488	2	
464	2		489	2	
465	2		490	2	77) I wish I had a little more information on both of them
466	2				
467	2		491	2	
468	2		492	2	
469	2	72) it's worked for 30 years		PAUSE 4	78) but since I don't
470	2	73) it's worked beautifully	497	5	
471	2		498	5	
472	2		499	2	
473	2		500	5	
474	3	74) so if their other products are as good as that	501	2	79) say that probably today I would buy the Sunbeam
475	3		502	2	
476	4		503	2	
477	5	75) well there again I might be prejudiced because of good experience with a Sunbeam	504	2	
			505	2	
			506	2	

FIGURE 2

Time	Brand code		Time	Brand code	
11	4	1) the first thing that would come into my mind	25	3	
			26	3	
12	3			PAUSE 1	6) I've talked to friends
13	4	2) if I were buying a coffee maker	28	3	7) whose element has gone out totally
	SCAN 1	3) is that I already have a Mr. Coffee	29	3	
	PAUSE 3	4) and I consider that the brand name in coffee makers	30	3	8) mine doesn't keep my coffee very hot anymore
			31	3	
18	3		32	3	9) so I've gone back to using instant coffee
19	3				
20	3	5) the problem is that the heating element seems to go bad on the	33	3	
				PAUSE 1	
			35	4	10) this doesn't look like Mr. Coffee though:
21	3		36	4	
22	2		37	3	11) so probably if I were going to start all over
23	3				
	PAUSE 1		38	3	

FIGURE 2
(continued)

Time	Brand code		Time	Brand code	
39	3		84	1	28) but now that I've had a Mr. Coffee
40	3	12) I would look at another Mr. Coffee:	85	1	
41	3	13) and I would ask a salesperson	86	1	29) I think I would start down here with Proctor-Silex
42	3		87	1	
43	SCAN 1	14) if they had improved the heating element		PAUSE 1	
44	3		89	1	
45	3	15) and if they don't have problems with them any more	90	1	
			91	1	30) and readily consider them all
46	3		92	1	
47	3		93	1	
48	3		94	1	
49	3	16) mine was an older model	95	1	
50	3		96	1	
51	3		97	1	
52	3		98	1	
52	3		99	1	
53	3	17) so that wouldn't keep me from considering it	100	1	
			101	2	
54	3		102	3	
55	3		103	3	31) Okay, because I have a basis of comparison
56	3		104	3	
57	4	18) but I think I wouldn't be so prejudiced	105	3	32) I'll probably keep going back to Mr. Coffee
58	3		106	3	
59	3		107	3	
	SCAN 1	19) as I was the first time around	108	3	
61	3	20) I thought well Mr. Coffee invented these machines	109	3	33) it looks to me like they've improved.
62	3		100	3	
63	4	21) so I'll just go with the best I can find	111	3	
			112	3	34) their pot looks different
	SCAN 4	22) also this is kind of funny		SCAN 1	35) another problem we've had
	PAUSE 2	23) the higher prices seem to me to be good			
70	3		114	3	
71	3		115	3	36) is that you always spill your coffee as you pour it
72	3				
73	3	24) and the fact that you think well	116	3	
			117	3	37) maybe its the lip design that causes that
74	3		118	3	
75	3	25) I'm paying for more quality	119	3	
			120	3	38) but it is very embarrassing for guests
	SCAN 1	26) so sometimes I tend to rule out the lowest priced thing	121	3	
77	1		122	1	39) because they always wind up drinking their coffee over the counter
78	1				
79	3		123	1	
	SCAN 1	27) I think, well, that couldn't be as good as the highest priced	124	1	
81	6		125	1	
82	6		126	1	
83	3		127	1	

FIGURE 2
(continued)

Time	Brand code	
128	1	40) this pot looks very different and it feels very heavy
129	1	
130	1	
131	1	41) so I would probably be impressed with the Proctor-Silex
132	1	
133	1	
134	1	
135	1	
136	1	
137	1	
138	1	
139	1	
140	1	
141	1	
142	1	
143	1	
144	1	
145	1	42) the whole machine on the Mr. Coffee always felt a bit flimsy
146	1	
147	1	
148	1	43) evidently it doesn't take a lot of mechanism in it
149	3	
150	3	
151	3	
152	3	
153	3	
154	3	44) the Proctor-Silex doesn't wiggle on its base like my old Mr. Coffee
155	3	
156	3	
157	3	
158	3	
(BREAK)		
377	6	98) okay, after looking at all three
378	6	
SCAN 1		
380	6	99) I think I would go back to the first two
381	6	
382	6	
383	2	
384	1	100) I don't know
385	1	101) I like the heavy feel of the pot
386	1	
387	1	102) on the Proctor-Silex
388	1	
389	1	

Time	Brand code	
390	1	103) something else that happened to my Mr. Coffee pot is
391	1	
392	1	104) that the handle got loose and you have to get out a knife
393	1	
394	3	
395	3	
396	3	105) because I didn't have a screwdriver to tighten it up
397	3	
398	3	
399	3	
400	3	
401	3	
402	3	
403	3	
404	1	
405	1	
406	1	
407	1	
SCAN 4		
412	1	106) (Mod. what are you thinking?)
413	3	
414	3	
415	1	107) well, I'm thinking that everything is so relative
SCAN 1		
417	4	
PAUSE 3		108) that there is no perfect truth
421	6	109) and even though I didn't like the GE
422	6	
423	5	
424	5	110) I would probably consider that
PAUSE 3		111) I thought it was gimmicky
428	6	112) that it had extra painted things on it
429	6	
430	6	113) that it didn't need
431	6	114) but it has an overall good look
432	6	115) it looks neater than the others
433	6	
434	6	
435	3	
436	6	

FIGURE 2
(continued)

Time	Brand code		Time	Brand code	
437	1	116) okay, I'm thinking if I were going to buy one right now	444	3	
			445	3	
			446	1	
438	1		447	3	
439	1		PAUSE 2		
440	1	117) having the experience I had with Mr. Coffee	450	3	
			451	3	
441	1		SCAN 1		
442	3		453	1	119) I'd probably spend the least and buy the Proctor-Silex
443	3	118) and knowing it wasn't the great thing I thought it was going to do			

two subjects who participated in an experiment involving six different brands of coffee makers. Each brand was coded as indicated below:

Code	Brand
1	Proctor Silex
2	Sunbeam
3	Mr. Coffee
4	Sears
5	Norelco
6	General Electric

Certain conventions are used in producing protocol-graphs. Typically the leftmost column (see Figure 1) provides a running count of time in seconds. As the figures show, time progresses *down* the page of a graph. Columns 2 through 6 indicate the code number of the brand being observed at the time indicated in column 1. Multiple eye fixations are recorded as a SCAN, which may be thought of as the subject's eyes wandering over various points of the display. If a scan lasts longer than one second it is coded as SCAN 2, SCAN 3, and so forth. Also, in Figures 1 and 2, two scans separated by a one second fixation are treated as a single scan. If at any time the subject takes his or her eyes off the brand display, it is recorded as a PAUSE on the protocol-graph. The length of the pause is coded by its duration if it lasts longer than one second (for example, PAUSE 2 represents a 2-second pause). Finally, the protocol-graph also displays the thought protocol of experimental subjects. These comments, listed in numerical order are positioned at the correct time-position on the graph.

Mike obtained the two protocol-graphs (shown in Figures 1 and 2) from the conference paper. He was reviewing them to learn what insights about consumer decision making they might yield. He also wondered in what way this new JPT method might represent an improvement over singular methods of studying consumer decision making.

Questions

1 What insights about consumer decision making can be gained from this investigation into how consumers behave?
2 Does there seem to be any evidence to indicate that the joint process method produces more insights into consumer information-processing than either method taken alone?
3 If the experimental findings were generally representative of consumers' reactions to coffee makers, would there be any marketing implications for producers of the product?

CASE 4-5
PURITEEN COSMETICS, INC.*

Puriteen, a cosmetics company based in Atlanta, recently acquired a faltering perfume and cologne company located in Orangedale, Florida (a suburb of Jacksonville). The small producer, Henri's, was started by Henri and Marie Depuy in 1972, but local and area business was not enough to keep alive the dreams of the married couple to develop their own perfume and cologne business.

BACKGROUND ON HENRI'S

Henri and Marie came to the United States in 1965 from Grasse, France, the world's chief center of perfume manufacture. Having become naturalized U.S. citizens, the well-educated Depuys decided to sink their life savings, if necessary, into their new business venture. Both had worked in a Grasse perfume company and had gained the necessary technology and skills to manufacture perfume.

The Depuys began in their garage producing two fragrances, "Henri's" and "Marie," named after themselves. Henri's was a special formulation handed down from generation to generation through the Depuy family in France. (Such practices are quite common among the French.)

However, after struggling for four years producing and selling the two fragrances, the Depuys realized the coming demise of their business and decided to seek a buyer for their family-heirloom formula.

Raymond L. "Pete" Dozier, vice president of marketing at Puriteen, learned of the Depuys' situation through a friend, Mitchell R. Morris, while in Jacksonville on a business trip. Morris, a district sales manager for Puriteen, had bought a bottle of Henri's for his wife Jil and was recently made aware of the Depuys' situation. Jil and Mitch were impressed with the fragrance of Henri's and were saddened that the Depuys were planning to sell their business.

Speaking with Dozier, Morris learned of Puriteen's interest to expand into the perfume and cologne business to complement its cosmetic lines. During the conversation, Morris told Dozier of the Depuys' business and strongly urged Dozier to discuss a business deal with Henri.

After six weeks of negotiations with the Depuys, the Puriteen Company agreed to pay Henri and Marie a 10 percent royalty on the net sales of the two perfumes and to hire the Depuys to supervise the manufacture of the per-

*This case was written by M. Wayne De Lozier. Permission to reprint granted by the author.

fumes. The success of the negotiations for the Depuys was largely due to Marie's idea of sending a bottle of each fragrance to the wives of Puriteen's top management.

BACKGROUND ON PURITEEN

Puriteen was founded in 1946 by William D. "Son" Grimsley and Raymond L. "Pete" Dozier. Son and Pete met in the Navy during World War II and found that they had a mutual interest in developing a business at the war's end. Son, who had earned a B.S. degree in chemistry at Georgia Tech, took his first job in a cosmetics firm before the war. During his three years with the cosmetics company, Son advanced to assistant director of research before volunteering for military service.

Pete received a degree in economics at a well-known northeastern university and after graduation spent four years in the sales division of a regional pharmaceutical company.

Before the war's end, Son had received legal notice that his Aunt Jeanette had died and left him $26,000 in cash, seventy-five acres of land near Covington, Georgia, and forty hogs, ten horses, and twenty-five milk-producing cows. His inheritance provided the major portion of capital for starting up a business, and in 1946 Son and Pete created Puriteen.

Son took on the responsibilities of production and development of several cosmetic lines, while Pete handled sales and finance.

By year-end 1975, Puriteen had become a leader in cosmetics in the Southeast with $125 million in sales. Distribution of Puriteen products stretched from Virginia south to Florida and west to the Mississippi River.

THE NEW PRODUCT

In mid-1975, Puriteen's top management had decided to expand their lines by entering the perfume and cologne market. Long-range plans were to enter the shaving cream and deodorant markets as well. Dozier had defined their business as a personal care business and believed that these and other products were essential to long-term growth.

In February 1976, Puriteen acquired Henri's, and Dozier began to consider plans for marketing the two newly acquired perfumes.

Henri's and Marie perfumes were fresh, new fragrances to the market. Both rated very high in consumer smell preference tests and certainly had tremendous potential. However, Dozier knew from his experiences and those of other companies that the success of such products depended upon the creation of an appealing image for the brand.

The Generic Product

Perfume is a fragrant substance which has been used since prehistoric times. The essence of many fragrances comes from the oils in the petals of fresh flowers, such as the rose, carnation, and orange blossom. However, fragrances are not limited to the petal, but can come from the leaves of lavendar, peppermint, and geranium. Also, the oils of cinnamon and balsam are derived from bark, while the oils of cedar come from its wood. The fragrance of ginger and sassafras comes from roots, whereas that of orange, lemon, and nutmeg comes from fruits and seeds. Thus, there are many sources from which to derive fragrances for perfume.

Certain materials must be added to the perfume fragrances to prevent evaporation by a process called *fixation*. Ambergris, musk, and castor are fixatives which are often used in the production of perfumes.

Artificial perfumes have been created at a lower cost through the use of synthetics and semisynthetics. They generally are classified under the categories of aldehydes, esters, and ethers, and are rapidly growing in use.

Henri's and Marie are produced with natural ingredients and are therefore more expensive to produce and higher priced than many of the more popular brands of perfume on the U.S. market.

ENTERING THE PERFUME MARKET

Pete Dozier had recently taken several evening courses in marketing at Georgia State in Atlanta to keep track of the current developments in marketing. One of the courses he took was Consumer Behavior. He became very interested in the notion of developing brands which were based upon consumer self concepts.

In March of 1976, Dozier decided to use his understanding of self theory to develop a marketing program for Henri's. By June, he had developed a semantic differential to measure the self and ideal-self images of female consumers and the images they held for three unfamiliar perfume brands (the brand names were fictitious).

The tests were conducted in New Orleans, Tallahassee, Atlanta, Raleigh, and Memphis. Four hundred ninety-six personal interviews were conducted (approximately 100 inter-

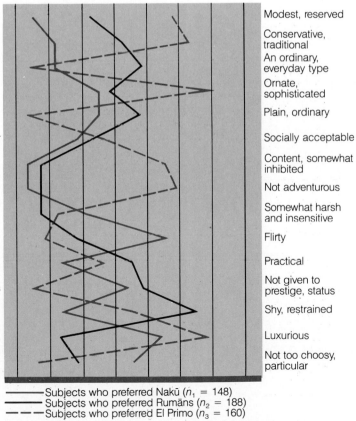

1 Appealing, sexy — Modest, reserved
2 Individualistic, nonconforming — Conservative, traditional
3 Fashionable, vogue — An ordinary, everyday type
4 Natural, unadorned — Ornate, sophisticated
5 Aristocratic, refined, dignified — Plain, ordinary
6 One of the most popular — Socially acceptable
7 Youthful, exciting, vibrant — Content, somewhat inhibited
8 Adventurous — Not adventurous
9 Delicate, sensitive — Somewhat harsh and insensitive
10 Innocent — Flirty
11 Free-spirited — Practical
12 Given to prestige, status — Not given to prestige, status
13 Bold, daring — Shy, restrained
14 Economical, thrifty — Luxurious
15 Choosy, particular — Not too choosy, particular

Subjects who preferred Nakū ($n_1 = 148$)
Subjects who preferred Rumäns ($n_2 = 188$)
Subjects who preferred El Primo ($n_3 = 160$)

FIGURE 1
Perfume images.

views per city). Subjects were given a semantic differential scale on which to describe their self and ideal-self concepts, and their perceptions of each of three perfume advertisements presented them. Each perfume advertisement was a videotaped version of a proposed Henri's advertisement. However, fictional names were used in each case. The order of presentations of the ads and self concepts were randomized. Subjects were asked at the end of the session to select which of the brands they preferred. They were offered the brand they selected as a prize if their numbers were selected at a later drawing.

The advertised "brands" were given three different themes. One used a sensual theme, the second a romantic theme, and the third a prestigious, regal theme. The following is a partial reproduction of each theme:

Nakū. "Nakū—the naked scent. Unadorned, primitive, sensuous Nakū. Nakū is for the woman who has a mind of her own; for the woman who goes her own free and feminine way. It's for the woman who understands that perfume is feminine power! Nakū—the naked scent. It is the essential you!" (Sensual theme.)

Rumäns. "Fragrance admittedly triggers emotions, but science doesn't know why. The whole wide world of scents is full of mysteries. However, Rumäns has captured the one scent that can make your world come alive with excitement and romance.

"Rumäns is a word of endearment, full of affection. Like dew sparkling, brooks babbling, stars smiling, lovers meeting, Rumäns goes about its business of making its wearer feel spirited, airy, romantic.

"Wear Rumäns day and night. Because love comes without warning!" (Romantic theme.)

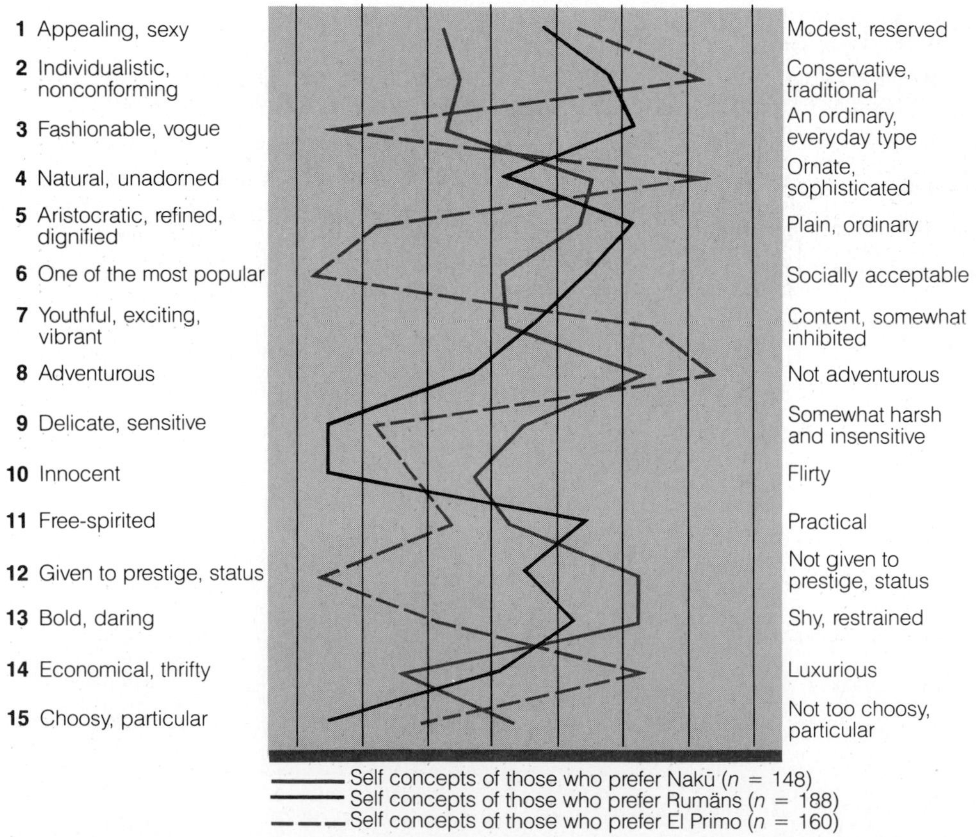

FIGURE 2
Self concepts.

1 Appealing, sexy — Modest, reserved
2 Individualistic, nonconforming — Conservative, traditional
3 Fashionable, vogue — An ordinary, everyday type
4 Natural, unadorned — Ornate, sophisticated
5 Aristocratic, refined, dignified — Plain, ordinary
6 One of the most popular — Socially acceptable
7 Youthful, exciting, vibrant — Content, somewhat inhibited
8 Adventurous — Not adventurous
9 Delicate, sensitive — Somewhat harsh and insensitive
10 Innocent — Flirty
11 Free-spirited — Practical
12 Given to prestige, status — Not given to prestige, status
13 Bold, daring — Shy, restrained
14 Economical, thrifty — Luxurious
15 Choosy, particular — Not too choosy, particular

—— Self concepts of those who prefer Nakū (n = 148)
—— Self concepts of those who prefer Rumäns (n = 188)
– – – Self concepts of those who prefer El Primo (n = 160)

El Primo. "Once she was the *only* woman in the world allowed to wear this perfume. The Queen of Navarre commissioned the most famed alchemist in Paris to create a perfume of magical potency and bewitching powers. A perfume so irresistable, it disarmed her competitors. A perfume so feminine, it intensified her legendary appeal, drawing the great and the glorious to her court. This magical perfume was El Primo. Unchanged since 1572, it casts its spell for great women today. El Primo, the perfume made for a queen!" (Prestigious, regal theme). Each script was provided with an appropriate model and picture sequence to match the theme.

The results of the test are presented in Figures 1 through 3 and Table 1.

DEVELOPING THE MARKETING PROGRAM

Dozier feels sure that the quality of the two perfumes is the best on the market. But he also knows that product quality alone does not sell a product. It requires a sound communications program. He feels that matching brand image to consumer self image is a sound approach. He must recommend a plan to the Puriteen board next week.

Questions

1 A portion of self theory holds that individuals try to protect or enhance their self concept; that is, they make decisions which are most consistent with their self or ideal-self images. Given this theory, what marketing plan should Dozier recommend to the Board of Directors of Puriteen?

2 What analyses might you perform on the data?

3 What additional information would you want in developing a program for Puriteen?

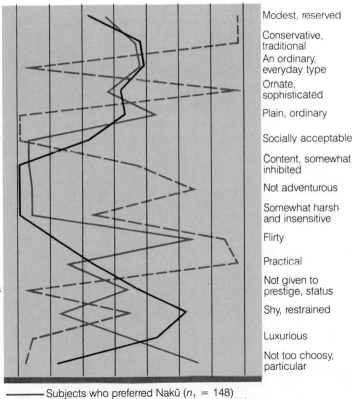

1 Appealing, sexy	Modest, reserved
2 Individualistic, nonconforming	Conservative, traditional
3 Fashionable, vogue	An ordinary, everyday type
4 Natural, unadorned	Ornate, sophisticated
5 Aristocratic, refined, dignified	Plain, ordinary
6 One of the most popular	Socially acceptable
7 Youthful, exciting, vibrant	Content, somewhat inhibited
8 Adventurous	Not adventurous
9 Delicate, sensitive	Somewhat harsh and insensitive
10 Innocent	Flirty
11 Free-spirited	Practical
12 Given to prestige, status	Not given to prestige, status
13 Bold, daring	Shy, restrained
14 Economical, thrifty	Luxurious
15 Choosy, particular	Not too choosy, particular

——— Subjects who preferred Nakū ($n_1 = 148$)
——— Subjects who preferred Rumäns ($n_2 = 188$)
– – – Subjects who preferred El Primo ($n_3 = 160$)

FIGURE 3
Ideal-self concepts.

TABLE 1
Ages and Family Incomes of Subjects Preferring Each Brand

Family income	Nakū				Rumäns				El Primo				Totals
	Age categories				Age categories				Age categories				
	18–25	26–35	36–49	50+	18–25	26–35	36–49	50+	18–25	26–35	36–49	50+	
$6000–9999	2	22	2	—	18	12	1	—	3	—	—	1	61
$10,000–14,999	5	30	15	—	33	8	15	1	2	6	2	4	121
$15,000–19,999	3	15	17	4	29	14	14	3	18	6	14	22	159
$20,000 and over	1	27	2	3	15	6	13	6	19	8	19	36	155
Totals	11	94	36	7	95	40	43	10	42	20	35	63	
Grand total	148				188				160				496

4 Evaluate the dimensions used in Dozier's semantic differential. How would you improve it?

5 Which self concept is most useful—self or ideal-self concept—in developing marketing programs? Defend your answer.

6 How does the use of consumer self concept differ from the use of consumer personality traits as a basis for developing brand images? Explain.

CASE 4-6
EASTERN STATE UNIVERSITY*

Shana Birk, chief admissions officer of Eastern State University, a school with current enrollment of 10,000 full-time students, was reviewing a research report on the college choice process. Her level of interest was particularly high because recent trends suggested rather significant declines in the number of college-age students.

Shana had been the prime mover behind this study because, in her opinion, maintaining enrollment at ESU through the 1980s and 1990s was going to be somewhat of a challenge. She convinced the university's president to fund the study and had approached two professors in the marketing department to serve as principal investigators. These professors suggested that the college choice process is most likely based on fairly careful consideration of how well various educational alternatives match certain choice criteria of prospective students.

The first step was a review of existing literature to determine what could be learned from previous research into the college choice process. Results of this stage were informative but Shana found them limited in at least two respects. First, most previous studies had only surveyed recently enrolled or recently admitted students. Therefore, they did not sample students in the process of making a choice regarding college attendance, or those who had gone to other institutions. Second, research to date had been mainly associational rather than predictive in nature. That is, the studies had focused on discovering what demographic variables and other student characteristics are related to college enrollment, rather than targeting on what variables might *predict* the enrollment choices of prospective students. Shana felt that predictive studies were needed so that groups of students representing the best prospects for ESU could be targeted, contacted, and supplied with appropriate information about the university.

After a discussion of these thoughts, the principal investigators suggested that the Fishbein A-act multiattribute attitude model might represent a useful conceptual approach to explaining how prospective students proceed in the decision process regarding college enrollment. Further work led to a study involving 2000 randomly selected junior and senior high school students in the state. In-state students were focused on because they represent the most important pool of potential enrollees.

*This case is based on material appearing in Robert E. Spekman, James W. Harvey, and Paul N. Bloom, "The College Choice Process: Some Empirical Results," in Jerry C. Olson (ed.), *Advances in Consumer Research*, vol. 7, Association for Consumer Research, Ann Arbor, Mich., 1980, pp. 700–704. Adapted with permission of the Association for Consumer Research.

STUDY DESIGN

The basic approach was to define components of the A-act model, measure respondents on these components, independently measure their overall attitude toward enrollment, and then determine how well the component measures were able to predict the independently measured attitude toward enrollment. However, discussions led to two modifications which made this basic approach even more interesting to Shana. Located in the state was a nationally recognized private university and a state-supported four-year college. These institutions also competed with ESU for in-state students. Therefore, it was decided that all three institutions should be addressed in the attitude study. In this way, it might be possible to determine whether some attitude components vary in their influence on enrollment attitudes for the different in-state institutions. Second, the research team (Shana and the two principal investigators) reasoned that by including measures of certain respondent characteristics, they might be able to identify different subgroups or segments of the applicant pool. That is, certain attitude components might vary in their influence across these potentially different segments.

As a result, the study design involved collection of a number of pieces of information. First, the dependent variable was defined as attitude toward the act of enrolling at each of the three institutions. This was measured independently on a seven-point scale ranging from ''very favorable'' to ''very unfavorable.''

Next, exploratory research with prospective students and previous research suggested seventeen school attributes which might be potentially relevant to attitudes toward enrolling at the institutions. These attributes are shown in the left column of Table 1. As can be seen in the table, the first thirteen belief statements refer to attributes of the college or university in question, while the last four were identified as potentially relevant normative beliefs. Each survey participant was asked to respond to all seventeen beliefs for each of the three institutions being studied. Responses were made on seven-point scales (ranging from ''very likely to have'' to ''very unlikely to have'') indicating how certain the individual was that the school in question possessed each of the seventeen attributes.

For measurement of the affect component (e_i) relevant to these attributes, respondents were asked to express their feelings along a seven-point scale as to how desirable (''very good'' to ''very bad'') it would be for them if the school they enrolled in had each of the seventeen attributes described in Table 1.

Demographic information collected from respondents included academic potential as measured by current grades and SAT scores, race, geographical location in the state, and current class (junior or senior in high school). In addition, attention focused on how serious each respondent appeared to be regarding the college choice decision. The research team concluded that this level of seriousness resembled the concept of involvement because more involved prospects were more likely to engage in a more intensive search process. This involvement was quantified by combining, with equal weights, respondents' answers regarding the number of schools applied to, the number of schools visited, the length of the decision process, the degree of care being taken in the decision, how important the respondent felt the decision was, and how certain the respondent was of his or her intended area of study.

The survey generated 583 usable responses, which represented a 29 percent response rate. The split between juniors and seniors was about even. In addition, the racial composition and reported SAT scores closely matched data available from census and educational testing service reports. Other information suggested that although response rates were rather low, no significant bias had been introduced into the study because of the low rate of returns.

ANALYSIS AND RESULTS

The first major data analysis step was to determine the product of belief and evaluation scores ($B_i e_i$). The second step was to use these data to determine whether all seventeen items in Table 1 were independent and important determinants of attitudes toward the enrollment decision, or whether some were highly related and could be combined to define a new, smaller set of composite variables. This was accomplished through use of a technique called factor analysis which is helpful in identifying how a set of measures may group together to form more aggregate variables which are termed factors. Table 1 presents results of this analysis step.

The research team concluded that factor analysis had identified six composite variables or factors. These were identified and named by the researchers (see column headings in Table 1) after consideration of the manner in which the initial measures grouped together to form the composite variables. The degree of correlation between composite variables and the initial measures are shown in each column of Table 1. Also, the underscored correlations in any one column indicate which initial measures were combined to form the composite variables. Thus, we see that $B_i e_i$ scores for the first six attribute items listed in the table all combined to identify the new composite variable (factor) which was named ''college environment.'' Components of the other five factors are also denoted with underscores in the table. As in the case of the first factor, study of the initial measures that were most related to the remaining five composite variables

TABLE 1

Attribute Descriptions and
Factor Analysis Results

	Factors					
Attribute descriptions	College environment	Authority recommendations	Size	Cost	Social aspects	Friends
1 Quality academics	.71	.13	.08	−.09	.05	.06
2 National reputation	.68	.07	.06	.06	−.05	.01
3 Friendly people	.60	.05	−.02	.04	.29	.22
4 Opportunities for part-time work	.58	.15	.00	.11	.05	−.30
5 Fair treatment of minorities	.57	.14	−.10	−.02	.27	.17
6 Athletic team I could play for	.39	.09	.27	−.06	.13	−.04
7 Recommendations of teachers	.17	.85	−.04	−.03	−.08	.06
8 Recommendations of counselors	.16	.83	.04	−.02	−.00	−.06
9 Recommendations of parents	.29	.56	.33	.11	.04	.12
10 Large classes	−.01	.07	.86	−.01	−.05	−.00
11 Many students	.08	.00	.80	.05	.19	.04
12 Near home	.04	.07	.16	.78	−.12	.01
13 Low cost of education	−.04	−.07	−.13	.74	.15	.05
14 Many parties	.16	−.07	.16	−.10	.70	.01
15 Location near city	.24	.02	.00	.29	.56	.01
16 Old friends from home	.32	−.02	.10	.12	−.23	.72
17 Recommendations from friends	−.28	.43	−.08	−.04	.31	.57

guided the research team in naming those composite variables.

Given that attitudes toward enrollment at three different institutions were being studied, it is reasonable to expect that the composite variables identified for one school might not be the same as those identified for another school. However, this was not the case. The same set of composite variables were identified in the same way for all three institutions. Therefore, Table 1 can be used to characterize results for each school.

Next, the research team explored how important each of the six factors were in predicting attitudes toward enrollment at the three schools. This was accomplished using regression analysis where the six factors were used as predictor variables and the independently measured attitude toward enrollment was used as the dependent variable. Table 2 presents results of this analysis by showing the relative importance-ranking of each predictor variable. Thus, for ESU size was the most important predictor, followed by authority recommendations and cost respectively. However, for the private university the top three predictors were authority recommendations, social, and cost, respectively. A different pattern emerged for the state college. But for each of the three institutions the total predictive ability of the six factors was quite high.

Study of the regression results revealed another interesting finding. For both the state university and the state college, one factor (size and environment, respectively) appeared to play a very important role in predicting attitudes toward enrollment. In fact, these factors (denoted with asterisks in Table 2) clearly dominated all other factors in influencing attitudes toward enrolling at the state schools. However, for the private university each factor had about equal predictive ability. These results suggest that a noncompensatory model may be most appropriate for describing the attitude formation process for the state schools, but a compensatory model might be best for the private university.

The last analysis step was to examine results across groups of respondents to determine whether distinct segments of prospective students appeared to exist. Table 3 summarizes the most significant results for the indicated groups. The second column of the table reveals those variables that were most influential in determining attitudes toward enrollment. The word "various" indicates that different attributes dominated, depending on the type of institution. The third column suggests the most likely type of attitude formation process. That is, it indicates (1) whether a given factor dominated prediction of attitudes toward enrollment (indicating a noncompensatory model), (2) whether no variable tended to dominate (indicating a compensatory model), or (3) whether a variable dominated for the state schools but did not dominate for the private university (indicating that the type of model depends on the type of institution being studied). As can be seen from columns 2 and 3, enrollment attitudes of blacks, high-involvement groups, and juniors all seemed to be most influenced by the authority recommendation factor. However, for blacks and high-involvement groups, this factor dominated all enrollment decisions investigated, while it only influenced attitudes on the public institutions among juniors. White students and seniors did not appear to be consistently influenced by any one variable, and students with high or low grade-point averages acted in similar ways. In addition, enrollment attitudes of low-involvement prospects were most influenced by the cost factor, but this was not a dominant variable for either the private or public institutions.

Shana was attempting to wade through these results in order to determine what would be an appropriate plan of action. She believed that the results were quite relevant to attracting in-state students to ESU university, but as yet she had not studied them enough to assess their implications.

Questions

1 How would you summarize the findings of the research conducted for ESU University?
2 Are there any suggestions you might make for improving the study or conducting additional research?
3 If the validity of these research findings were established, what implications might they hold for recruitment of in-state students to ESU University?

TABLE 2

Relative Importance of Six Composite Variables in Influencing Attitudes Toward Enrollment

	Environment	Authority recommendations	Size	Cost	Social	Friends
State university	4	2	1*	3	6	5
Private university	4	1	6	3	2	5
State college	1*	3	6	2	5	4

* Importance rating was considerably higher than other attributes.

TABLE 3

Summary of Group Differences

Groups	Attributes most determinant of A-act	Most likely attitude model
Race		
Black	Authority recommendations	Noncompensatory
White	Various	Depends on type of institution
Involvement		
Low	Cost	Compensatory
High	Authority recommendations	Noncompensatory
Grade point		
Low	Little difference	Depends on type of institution
High	Little difference	Depends on type of institution
Year		
Juniors	Authority recommendations	Depends on type of institution
Seniors	Various	Depends on type of institution

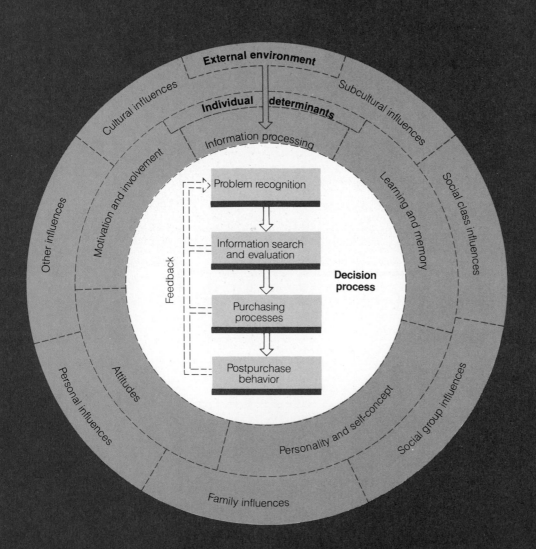

CONSUMER DECISION PROCESSES

PART 5

PROBLEM RECOGNITION

LEARNING OBJECTIVES

After studying this chapter, you should understand . . .

- The various types of decisions consumers must make

- The nature of consumer decision making as a process

- What problem recognition entails

- The various types of problem recognition and what outcomes may result from it

- How the marketer may measure problem recognition, activate it, and track it over time

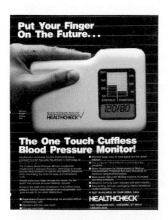

Until recently fitness fanatics worked out at local health clubs and gymnasiums. But now exercise has been brought out of the gyms and returned to the home. Many Americans are even retooling their basement or family room into a private gym, complete with rowing machines and exercise bicycles, to the tune of close to $1 billion a year.

As part of this at-home health movement, many consumers are taking the concept of the house call one step further. Since few physicians are willing to make house calls, patients are now more willing to assume responsibility for their health. Thus, more and more consumers are doing medical diagnostic tests in their own homes. There has been a dramatic rise in what one national magazine has dubbed "medicine chest labs." Increasingly, consumers are willing to diagnose on their own everything from pregnancy and colorectal cancer to hypertension and menopause. Tests also are marketed to help monitor blood sugar, identify venereal disease, or determine if someone has a urinary tract infection.

Sales of home health-test kits are expected to reach $500 million by 1990, compared to some $60 million in 1983. Experts identify three trends behind this boom. One is economic. As health-care costs have risen, consumers are tending to avoid visits to physicians. Advances in medical technology, making many of these kits more accurate, is another factor. And finally, the overall move toward fitness and "wellness" has made consumers that much more medically conscious.[1]

18

This example illustrates how many consumers have moved into the stage of problem recognition, the major topic of this chapter, for some of their health needs. They have become increasingly conscious of the need for fitness and wellness and have purchased various products that allow them to achieve this desired state of well-being. For all buying situations, consumers start at the place of problem recognition. Consequently, it is of great importance that the marketer understand this first step of the purchasing process.

In this chapter, we shall examine the types of consumer decisions which are possible and shall see that these may range from very simple to quite complicated processes. Next, the basic model of steps involved in consumer decision making will be highlighted to set the stage for the remainder of this section. The bulk of this chapter will then discuss the nature of problem recognition, its determinants, and implications of this particular consumer decision stage to marketers.

TYPES OF CONSUMER DECISIONS

There are a myriad of decision options possible for the consumer in today's market economy. These options, however, may be distilled into five main types of decisions: (1) what to buy, (2) how much to buy, (3) where to buy, (4) when to buy, and (5) how to buy.

Deciding *what* to buy is one of the consumer's most basic tasks. No buying activity may take place unless this fundamental decision is made. A consumer's product or service decision may encompass not only the generic category of products desired, such as appliances, but more specifically, the narrower range of items, such as kitchen appliances. Consumers must even make decisions on brands, prices, and product features. For example, a homemaker may decide to purchase an Amana Radarange 700-watt microwave oven, Model RR-1000, with electronic digital controls and stainless steel interior, for a price of $599. This is a specific decision as to what will be purchased, and with this particular decision finalized the consumer moves closer to completion of the overall purchase-decision process.

A second basic decision by the consumer relates to *how much* of the item will be purchased. For example, when shopping for groceries the consumer must determine whether three cans of Libby's green beans will be bought or perhaps a greater supply purchased.

Another determination to be reached by the consumer involves *where* the selected product or service will be purchased. This is a very important decision, which interacts thoroughly with the previous decision on what to buy. Two products, although physically the same, are likely to be perceived differently because of other facets associated with them. For example, consider an air conditioner sold with delivery, installation, and in-home servicing guaranteed by a full-service department store compared with the same model priced lower but sold on a no-frill basis in a discount house, with none of the above services. Consumers clearly are likely to perceive these same air conditioners in quite different ways, based on the nature of the prices and services attached.

Consequently, what one purchases is closely related to decisions of where one decides to purchase. Not all sales outlets are alike, and consumers have many options concerning location (such as downtown or suburban stores), services offered (discount or full-service), merchandise lines (full versus narrow), prices (high versus low), and so on. Consumers must decide not only on the general type of store to purchase from but also determine the particular outlet. In fact, buyers may decide not to even visit a store but to purchase from a catalog instead.

The consumer must also determine *when* to buy. Such a decision is influenced by such factors as urgency of the need and availability of the chosen item. Other elements such as store opening times, periods of sales and clearances, availability of transportation, and freedom of family members to shop all have a bearing on when one purchases.

Finally, the decision of *how* to buy is another complex issue. Many factors influence how the consumer buys. To indicate merely a few of the elements involved, consider some of the alternative strategies consumers use: shop extensively or buy from the first outlet, pay cash or charge it, have it delivered or take it home.

Numerous purchasing patterns occur in the marketplace, with each consumer relying on whatever strategy seems to work well for himself. The problems that consumers must solve, however, could benefit from the cold logic of a computer rather than the "hit or miss" decision approach taken by some consumers. The next section outlines the general purchase-decision process often followed by consumers, particularly for major purchases.

INTRODUCTION TO THE CONSUMER DECISION-PROCESS MODEL

Consumer decision processes vary considerably in their complexity. Most of the decisions consumers are required to make are probably rather simple ones such as the purchase of staple foods (although a disadvantaged consumer might argue persuasively that merely buying food is difficult when one is functionally illiterate). However, consumers also must make decisions that are comparatively complicated, such as when buying durable goods. The range of difficulty of consumer decision processes extends even further to problem solving that may be characterized as being highly complex, such as might well typify the consumer's purchase of a very expensive item like a home.

The examples of consumer decision making cited above may be generalized toward a typical consumer problem-solving model consisting of four basic types of activities in the process of purchasing. The consumer's four steps are (1) problem recognition, (2) information search and evaluation, (3) purchase decision, and (4) postpurchase behavior. The assumptions underlying this and other decision-process approaches to consumer behavior seem to be the following:[2]

1 Two or more alternatives exist, so that a choice must be made by the consumer.

2 Consumer evaluative criteria facilitate the forecasting of each alternative's consequences for the consumer's goals or objectives.

3 The consumer uses a decision rule or evaluative procedure to determine the chosen alternative.

4 Information obtained from external sources and/or memory is used in the application of the decision rule or evaluative procedure.

However, it has been suggested that for certain purchase situations some consumers do not engage in a prepurchase decision process. For example, they may not have stored information, it may not be retrieved or retrievable, and they may not search externally.[3] Thus, some purchases may occur as a result of approaches other than a decision process. They can occur out of necessity (such as allocation of income within certain categories of expenditures, food/beverage, housing, and medical care); they can be derived from certain culturally mandated lifestyles (for example, the "standard package" of goods desired throughout American society, including transportation, personal care, and household appliances and furnishings items); they can be interlocked with other purchases (such as gasoline, repair services, and insurance being interlocked with the purchase of an automobile); they can reflect purchase preferences acquired in early childhood (such as with food preferences and store choices); they can result from conformity to group norms or imitation of others (such as adoption of smoking behavior among teens); they can result from recommendations by personal or nonpersonal sources (such as often occurs in the adoption process); they can be made on the basis of various surrogates (such as price, manufacturer's reputation, or packaging); they can even occur on a more superficial basis (such as selecting a brand on the basis of convenience of the shelf height).[4]

Additional information will be provided in later chapters to indicate that a significant proportion of purchases appear not to be preceded by a decision process of any extensiveness. Nevertheless, the decision sequence discussed in this section represents a useful framework for integrating much of the material from earlier chapters in a pragmatic way for the marketer. In the remainder of this chapter, the first stage in this problem-solving model will be further examined. The other processes will be discussed in detail in the following chapters.

PROBLEM RECOGNITION

Problem recognition results when a consumer recognizes a difference of sufficient magnitude between what is perceived as the desired state of affairs and what is the actual state of affairs, enough to arouse and activate the decision process.[5] The "actual state" refers to the way in which a need is already being met and the "desired state" is the way a person would like for the need to be satisfied.

This process integrates many of the concepts that have been discussed in previous chapters. For example, consumer information processing and the motivation process are highly relevant here. Consumers must become aware of the problem or need through processing of information arising internally or externally. They then become motivated. Thus, the process of problem recognition means that the consumer becomes aroused and activated to engage in some purposeful purchase-decision activity.

This motivation to resolve a particular problem, however, depends on two factors: the magnitude of the discrepancy between the desired and actual states, and the importance of the problem.[6] For instance, a consumer may desire to own a new front-wheel-drive automobile of the same size and gas mileage consumption

as his current one-year-old rear-wheel-drive model. A discrepancy may exist between the consumer's actual and desired state, but it is not likely to be large enough to motivate him to proceed further in the decision process. In addition, the importance of the problem may be such that the consumer may not be motivated toward further decision-process behavior. Assume that the consumer in the previous example had a sufficient difference between desired and existing states of auto ownership. However, the importance of this particular problem may be low compared to other consumption needs the consumer faces, such as food, housing, and clothing. Thus, consumers facing time and/or budget constraints will attempt to solve only the most-significant problems as they perceive them (and not, incidentally, as an objective outsider might view them).

Problem recognition must also result in the problem being sufficiently defined if the consumer is to engage in meaningful behavior aimed at solving it. Sufficient problem definition occurs for the consumer to be able to act on it in many problem-recognition situations. For instance, the consumer who runs out of milk or bread has a clear definition of the problem. Other situations exist, however, in which the consumer may not have a clear definition of the problem, even though problem recognition has occurred. For example, the matter of self-image may lead to such an occurrence, such as when the consumer feels that her expression of a desired image is not quite right and yet she is unable to define exactly what is wrong. In such cases, information search may be engaged in to more clearly identify the problem. These cases of problem recognition and definition may often be complex.[7]

RESEARCH ON PROBLEM RECOGNITION

One recent stream of research on problem recognition has viewed the process as being a function of the congruity between the positive or negative valence values of some perceptual stimulus and the respective positivity/negativity values for some evoked referent.[8] For example, a consumer may see a friend's new car (perceptual stimulus) and compare it to his own old model (evoked referent). If the new car is perceived to be significantly better than his old one, then problem recognition would be expected to occur.

Another research direction taken has been to view problem recognition longitudinally.[9] Instead of focusing on one instance of problem recognition, the effect of repeated occurrence of similar problems is considered. For example, consumers may have problem recognition triggered in three ways: by the actual state changing, by the desired state changing, or by a combination of both changing. As the consumer experiences the problem several more times, a "style" of recognizing the need begins to develop. Thus for some consumers, problem recognition is triggered mainly by a change in the desired state (we may call these consumers a DS type). For others a problem would rarely be recognized unless their actual state changed (an AS type). These two types of problem recognition styles may operate among consumers for numerous products, such as clothing, cologne, shampoo, home decorations, appliances, and automobiles. With some needs, however, almost all consumers may be AS types. For a light bulb purchase, nearly all buyers would only recognize the problem when a bulb burns out. In the opposite way we are almost all DS types when it comes to recorded music because our motivation to purchase has more to do with novelty

seeking than it does with replacing a lost or damaged record. Limited research also indicates that DS and AS types have different shopping orientations and information-source usages.[10]

TYPES OF PROBLEM RECOGNITION[11]

Rather than viewing problem recognition as occurring in only one way, it is useful to understand that there may be varying types of problem-recognition processes. One approach has been to develop a classification system of situations based on the factors of immediacy of required solution and whether or not the problem was expected. The resulting matrix of problem types is shown in Table 18-1, consisting of routine, emergency, planning, and evolving situations. Immediacy of problem solution is a relevant factor in determining the decision time horizon; that is, how soon a problem solution is needed will affect the length of decision process and intensity of decision effort. Expectancy of the problem can affect such facets as the sources of information used in the decision process, for example, as well as the number of alternatives considered. It should be remembered, too, that importance of the problem will be a significant factor influencing decisions within each category of problem recognition. Thus, some decisions (in the same category or type of problem recognition situation) are more important to us than others and, as a result, we find different decision-process strategies being used.

Routine problems are those in which the difference between actual and desired states is expected to occur and an immediate solution is required. Typically, convenience goods are associated with this type of problem recognition, such as most grocery purchases made by consumers. In these cases, items are ordinarily used up and must soon be replaced.

Planning problems occur when the problem occurrence is expected but an immediate solution is not necessary. For instance, a consumer who expects that his car will only last one additional year may begin to engage in window shopping for autos, have discussions with friends about various brands, and pay closer attention to automotive ads.

Emergency problems are those that are unexpected in which immediate solutions are necessary. For instance, a consumer who is involved in an automobile accident and "totals" his car may need a quick solution to his transportation problem. Consequently, the individual may have little time to engage in shopping for the perfect replacement vehicle, but instead may purchase something that is reasonably satisfactory and available for immediate delivery. Notice that in

TABLE 18-1

Types of Problem
Recognition

Expectancy of problem	Immediacy of solution	
	Immediate solution required	Immediate solution not required
Occurrence of problem expected	Routine	Planning
Occurrence of problem unexpected	Emergency	Evolving

Source: Del I. Hawkins, Kenneth A. Coney, and Roger J. Best, *Consumer Behavior*, Business Publications, Inc., Dallas, 1980, p. 390.

such a case the vehicle may be viewed as a temporary solution, with a trade-in likely in the near future in order to obtain a better car. This now becomes a planning problem. Some retailers cater to customers facing emergency problems. Convenience stores such as 7-Eleven meet the needs of this segment by offering more extended shopping hours.

Evolving situations occur when the problem is unexpected but no immediate solution is required. The fashion-adoption process illustrates this case. Fashion adoption ordinarily occurs over a lengthy period of time for many consumers. Although one may become aware of the new fashion item's existence, there may be no initial desire to own that item. Over time, as the innovation spreads and more consumers buy the item, a discrepancy between the consumer's desired and actual state may develop and increase. At some point, the consumer may purchase the fashion innovation. Thus, the diffusion of an innovation often involves the situation of evolving problems.

SITUATIONS LEADING TO PROBLEM RECOGNITION

There are numerous situations that may cause consumer problem recognition to occur. Although discussion of all of the potential sources is impossible, we can present the most significant reasons and explain briefly how each one might arise.

Depleted or Inadequate Stock of Goods These are probably the most frequent reasons for consumers recognizing problems. In the first situation, the consumer uses up the assortment of goods she has and must repurchase in order to resupply her needs. As long as there still is a basic need for the item, problem recognition should result from its consumption. The most obvious purchasing situations which result from this are caused by consumers running out of groceries, gasoline, health and grooming aids, and other similar convenience goods.

Sometimes the consumer's stock of goods is inadequate for even her everyday needs and may require a purchase. For instance, she may want to install a bracket for a hanging planter but finds that she doesn't have the necessary tools such as a ruler, a drill, and a screwdriver.

Discontentment with the Stock of Goods Frequently, consumers become discontented with products they own, and this leads to problem recognition. For example, men's ties and jacket lapels narrow and widen as fashion cycles progress. Consequently, men may feel their clothing is no longer stylish, and they may desire to update their wardrobes. Even though the old clothes might be perfectly serviceable, they may be an embarrassment to wear. As a result, this problem is resolved by purchasing some of the latest fashions.

The consumer's dissatisfaction with her present assortment of goods can also arise as the result of other decisions. For instance, consider the case of a family that remodels their twenty-year-old home. After the work is completed and the house looks new again, then comes the letdown and dissatisfaction of having to move all the family's old hand-me-down furniture into the newly decorated rooms. The result of this problem recognition may be the purchase of new furniture to go with the remodeled house.

Finally, discontentment may lead the consumer simply to search for something new and different, to break out of a rut. Problem recognition in this case is

really founded on a desire to do something novel for a change. One research study on new-product adoption has shown, for example, that one-third of those switching to a new brand did so simply because they desired a change, not because they were dissatisfied with their present brand.[12]

Changing Environmental Circumstances

Consumers sometimes encounter changes in their environmental circumstances which lead to problem recognition. One of the most significant of these situations is the family's changing characteristics. As we learned in earlier chapters, different life-cycle stages produce needs for different products. Consequently, as the family evolves, new problems are continually being recognized which result in different assortments of goods over time.

Another important force in the consumer's environment which leads to problem recognition is the influence of reference groups. As we identify with different reference groups, their standards are likely to influence our consumption patterns. For example, the code of dress among a college student's fraternity or sorority group may cause that student to recognize a problem with his or her current wardrobe. Several items of new clothing may be purchased so that the person fits in with this reference group.

Changing Financial Circumstances

The financial status of the consumer has a very important relationship to problem recognition. The present or anticipated financial picture may trigger problem recognition as the consumer determines what purchases can be afforded. A consumer, for example, who inherits $50,000, or receives a $2000 salary increase, or receives an income tax refund of $800 may begin to consider new alternative ways of spending or saving the money. The person may substantially alter his or her desired state in a positive direction based on a financial windfall. Problem recognition, in this case, may lead to purchasing a new car, a new boat, a dishwasher, or taking a vacation. If, on the other hand, the consumer expects to lose his or her job and livelihood, then the financial expectations and desired state will be altered in a negative direction.

Marketing Activities

The marketer frequently attempts to precipitate problem recognition through promotional efforts aimed at the consumer. With such efforts, the marketer seeks to have the consumer perceive a difference of sufficient magnitude between her desired state (ownership of the product) and her actual state (not owning it) to engage in search, evaluation, and purchasing activity for the marketer's brand.

Although such marketing efforts may have some influence on problem recognition on the part of the consumer, it is ordinarily not an easy process to accomplish. As we learned in the discussion of information processing, consumers have the capability of filtering out any messages in which they are not interested or with which they disagree. Consequently, marketing activity may achieve its greatest effectiveness once consumer problem recognition has already occurred. For instance, large numbers of those who take home movies may be dissatisfied with currently available products utilizing film. As a result, this group may be highly receptive to videotape equipment having appropriate desirable features. The marketer's job, then, is to develop a marketing mix that appeals to these dissatisfied consumers. Decisions regarding product features, prices, dis-

tribution, and promotion may then be molded to suit particular desired segments of potential buyers. Thus, with many consumers having already engaged in problem recognition and accepted the merits of videotape, the marketer's promotion activity is much more likely to fall on fertile ground than when he is trying to convince uninterested and unbelieving consumers that there is a better product available.

RESULTS OF PROBLEM RECOGNITION

Once the consumer becomes aware of a problem, two basic outcomes are possible. One result is for the consumer, in effect, not to pursue any further problem-solving behavior, which might occur if the difference between the consumer's perceived desired and actual states is not great enough to cause him to act to resolve the difference. For example, assume that a consumer has a six-month-old, 19-inch color television set that works perfectly. One day he visits his neighbor who has just bought a 25-inch model, and sees how much larger the picture is compared to his set. Although our consumer's desired state may be to own a larger screen TV, there is not likely to be a difference of sufficient magnitude between that and his actual state (the 19-inch set) to cause him to purchase one. If, however, his set were to give out, then he might be motivated to purchase the larger model.

Another situation in which problem recognition may not lead to further stages of consumer decision-making occurs when certain environmental elements preclude it. For example, suppose the consumer from our previous illustration has his household belongings (including his TV) destroyed by a fire. In replacing his possessions, one of the first things he wants to buy is a new 25-inch television set, like his neighbor's. However, because his insurance policy does not cover the full replacement value of all his belongings, and other items are of greater urgency, he determines that he can get along well enough for a while without a TV. Thus, in spite of a difference of sufficient magnitude between the consumer's desired state (owning a TV) and actual state (not owning a TV), financial considerations restrict the consumer's ability to proceed further in the decision-making process.

Other constraints may similarly preclude further decision activity by the consumer. Factors such as time constraints, social-class values, and differing family desires may all impede the process.

The second type of response that may occur from the problem-recognition process is for the consumer to proceed into further stages of decision-making activity by engaging in information search and evaluation.

PROBLEM RECOGNITION UNDER LOW-INVOLVEMENT CONDITIONS

Much of what we have discussed so far relates to high-involvement buying decisions. If you refer to Chapter 12, you will recall that two purchasing conditions were summarized—high-involvement and low-involvement. High-involvement purchase situations are those which, because of their relevance and significance for the individual, are characterized by more extensive decision-process behavior. The consumer moves through the sequence of stages diagramed at the beginning of Part 5. However, when products have little relevance and importance to consumers, the decision process is quite different.

Problem recognition under low-involvement conditions is thought to be different from that under high-involvement conditions. Rather than being anything dramatic and highly goal-oriented, it is characterized more by point-of-purchase triggering or stimulation of problem recognition based on familiarity with the brand developed through repetitive advertising. Problem recognition, therefore, occurs in this case not as a result of first-time exposure to promotion, but perhaps because of a low level of appeal in which the consumer may develop a mild interest in checking out the product's suitability at some point in the future. If the product is purchased, tried, and then favorably evaluated, it may become a routine purchase because it is consumed and must be replenished from time to time. Most supermarket items fall into the category of low-involvement purchases, and they are bought in this way.

MARKETING IMPLICATIONS OF PROBLEM RECOGNITION

The significance to marketers of the problem-recognition stage of consumer decision making is that the process can be effectively measured and can be used to develop and evaluate marketing strategies.

MEASURING PROBLEM RECOGNITION

Consumer researchers have found that the best way to assess the problem-recognition process is through scaling techniques, which measure purchase intentions. Purchase intentions incorporate the consumer's attitudes toward the product and may be viewed as the mental forerunner of buying behavior. The continuum presented in Table 18-2 indicates attitudes that correspond to the various levels of buyer predisposition and are indicative (where positive) of a situation in which problem recognition has occurred and the consumer has some intention of resolving the problem.

TABLE 18-2

Range of Consumer's Predispositions

Category	Predisposition	Attitudes
1	Firm and immediate intent to buy a specific brand.	"I am going to buy some right away." "I am going to buy some soon."
2	Positive intention without definite buying plans.	"I am certain I will buy some sometime" "I probably will buy some sometime."
3	Neutrality: Might buy, might not buy.	"I may buy some sometime." "I might buy some sometime, but I doubt it."
4	Inclined not to buy the brand but not definite about it.	"I don't think I'm interested in buying any." "I probably will never buy any."
5	Firm intention not to buy the brand.	"I know I'm not interested in buying any." "If somebody gave me some, I would give it away, just to get rid of it."
6	Never considered buying.	"I have never heard of the brand."

Source: Adapted from William D. Wells, "Measuring Readiness to Buy," *Harvard Business Review*, **39**:82, July–August 1961.

ACTIVATING PROBLEM RECOGNITION

Promotion is an important vehicle used by marketers to cause problem recognition to occur among potential customers. Activities may be focused on the consumer's *desired state* and/or perceptions of the *actual state,* such that a difference of sufficient magnitude occurs between them.

Influencing the Desired State   Marketers often seek to influence consumers' desired states such as in much of the advertising stressing benefits of product ownership. Our discussion of consumers' motives in Chapter 12 indicated that consumers desire pleasure rather than pain. Therefore, advertising and personal selling efforts attempt to sell consumers on the positive features of product or service consumption. For example, Figure 18-1 illustrates a typical ad pointing out how ownership and use of the product solves the consumer's problem.

Influencing Perceptions of the Actual State   Consumers' actual states often develop into situations that are routine, habitual, or unnoticed patterns of behavior. For instance, the buyer may habitually purchase a brand without consideration of that brand's merits or of how alternative brands may be superior. Thus, marketers

FIGURE 18-1
An advertisement for
Palmolive Automatic.
Courtesy of Colgate-Palmolive Co.

may attempt to interrupt consumers' rather automatic decision-making sequence by having them consider other alternatives. Allstate Insurance uses an effective approach in its advertising by encouraging potential clients to compare policies before automatically renewing their insurance. Similarly, an aggressive new brand may use comparative advertising in order to have consumers of an established dominant brand become aware of that brand's deficiencies and the advantages of the new brand.

Consumers may also need to become aware of problem situations they have simply become accustomed to and have therefore ignored. Many companies' ads attempt to bring such problems out in the open for buyers' consideration. Figure 18-2 shows how one company has tried to make potential customers aware of a problem before it becomes critical.

UTILIZING PROBLEM-RECOGNITION INFORMATION

The marketer may find information on buyer intentions to be useful in the following ways.

Analyzing Purchase-Intention Categories   From measurement of the speed, direction, and size of shifts in buying likelihoods for a product over several periods in

FIGURE 18-2
An advertisement for
Custom Calling Services.
Courtesy of South Central Bell.

various market segments, the marketer may discover what trends are taking place as well as the timing and size of their potential impact on sales.[13] For example, consider the kinds of comparisons that may be made based on Table 18-2.[14] From this table, we can see that consumers who use either statement in category 1 to describe their intentions appear highly predisposed to buy. Consumers who describe their readiness in terms of statements from category 2 are favorably disposed but are without immediate purchasing intentions. Consequently, a low category 1–to–category 2 ratio means that there is a large reservoir of goodwill that needs to be converted into a stronger intention to buy. If this ratio increases over a period of time, it suggests that consumers holding favorable disposition toward the brand are increasing their intentions to purchase it. Deficiencies at the point of sale may be a reason for failure to convert predispositions into purchases. Perhaps price reductions or special promotional deals might be called for in such a situation.

Concentrations of respondents in category 3 may not be unfavorable since these consumers are still psychologically accessible because their intentions are not yet firmly set. Of course, the marketer would want to shift these respondents into higher categories over a period of time. A strong, effective promotion campaign may be called for in this instance.

A concentration of persons in category 5 is very undesirable. These respondents have strong, preformed negative intentions about the brand and are likely to be extremely difficult to convince to buy. If the marketer suspects that these attitudes could be the result of his promotion campaign, new and different appeals might be tried with this segment. Since laggards (the last adopter category) are likely to be in categories 4 and 5, such changed appeals will probably be necessary. Personal selling may also be more heavily needed for this group.

Failure to shift respondents out of category 6 (those who have never heard of the brand) into higher categories probably indicates lack of a sufficient program to establish ready brand recognition. Heavier advertising and free product sampling may be called for in this case in order to increase consumers' knowledge levels.

If the marketer fails to convince consumers that his brand is worth trying, this pattern will show up as a movement of respondents from category 6 into 5, 4, or 3, rather than into the top two categories. Product or package improvements may be called for in this case. Product improvements are almost certainly in order if the marketer finds a shift into lower categories by those who have already used the brand.

Analyzing Conversion of Purchase Intentions[15] The marketer may also find significant implications for his marketing strategy by investigating the relationships between purchasing intentions and buying behavior. Longitudinal analysis of intentions data allows the marketer to understand the dynamics of marketplace activity. He obtains a clearer picture of which brands are converting predispositions into buying action. This information can help him to determine the point at which marketing success or failure is occurring and isolate the reasons.

In order to conduct this analysis, data on purchase intentions and behavior over a period of time are necessary, such as those contained in Figure 18-3. Assume that there are three national brands in a particular appliance category for which such data have been gathered from interviews conducted twelve months

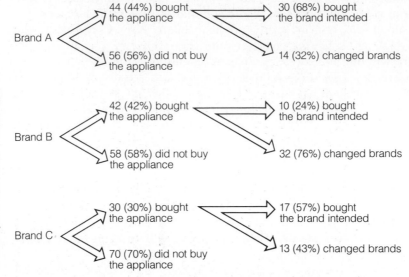

Of each 100 persons who stated
a definite intention to buy a (brand) appliance:

Brand A

44 (44%) bought the appliance
56 (56%) did not buy the appliance

30 (68%) bought the brand intended
14 (32%) changed brands

Brand B

42 (42%) bought the appliance
58 (58%) did not buy the appliance

10 (24%) bought the brand intended
32 (76%) changed brands

Brand C

30 (30%) bought the appliance
70 (70%) did not buy the appliance

17 (57%) bought the brand intended
13 (43%) changed brands

FIGURE 18-3

Comparison of buying intentions and behavior (12 months between interviews). *Source:* Adapted from Robert W. Pratt, Jr., "Understanding the Decision Process for Consumer Durable Goods: An Example of the Application of Longitudinal Analysis," in Peter D. Bennett (ed.), *Marketing and Economic Development,* published by the American Marketing Association, Chicago, 1965, p. 249.

apart. Figure 18-3 indicates that 44 percent of those who stated a definite intention to buy a brand A appliance actually bought an appliance during this period (we are not concerned at this moment with brand decisions, only generic product decisions). From Figure 18-3 it can be seen, therefore, that brand A had a higher percentage of intenders making purchases than either brands B or C.

A second very important aspect of these conversion patterns is the *brand intention-fulfillment rate.* Looking again at Figure 18-3 it may be seen that 68 percent of those who intended to buy brand A actually did so, while 32 percent bought an alternative brand. According to the brand-fulfillment data in Figure 18-3, brand A was most successful at converting brand-preference intentions, followed by brand C and brand B. Thus, brand A appears to have the most effective marketing strategy, while brand C is more effective than brand B. On the basis of information such as this, the manager of brand B might seek to determine the reasons for his brand's disappointing sales by assessing the various elements in its marketing program.

MANAGERIAL REFLECTIONS

For our product or service situation . . .

1 What types of problem-recognition situations typify our customers: routine, emergency, planning, and/or evolving?

2 What situations appear to lead most frequently to problem recognition among buyers?

3 What factors typically constrain further purchasing process activity by the consumer, and how may we help the removal of such barriers?

4 What intentions to purchase do consumers express?

5 How may we help activate the consumers' problem-recognition process by emphasizing their desired state, actual state, or the level of discrepancy between the two?

6 How are consumers' predispositions to buy shifting over time? To what extent are favorable intentions being converted to purchase?

DISCUSSION TOPICS

1 Why is it important to understand consumer decision making?

2 Describe the general types of consumer decisions. Illustrate them with a recent decision of your own.

3 What is consumer problem recognition?

4 Describe from your own recent experience what factors led to problem recognition in at least three different product or service situations (not necessarily purchases). Explain the similarities or differences that exist in these situations.

5 Distinguish between problem recognition under conditions of low involvement and under conditions of high involvement. What implications might each of these situations have for promotional plans?

6 How can the marketer use purchase-intentions data?

PROJECTS

1 Interview five students and learn what factors led to problem recognition (not necessarily purchase) by them for different products or services within the last two weeks. Explain the similarities or differences that existed in these situations.

2 Bring to class an advertisement that attempts to activate the problem-recognition process. Does it work on the consumer's actual state or desired state? How would you suggest the ad be improved in order to trigger problem recognition?

3 Interview ten consumers exiting a supermarket. Select the same purchased item (such as cereal) and gather the following information (as in Figure 18-3):

a For the purchased item, was the brand selected the same as that they originally planned to purchase?

b If brand switching occurred, what factors appeared to influence it?

c Were there any other items planned for purchase which were not purchased? Why?

What can you conclude from your findings? How could this information assist the retailer or manufacturer?

NOTES

[1] Merri Rosenberg, "The Hottest Products," *Adweek,* November 4, 1985, p. H.P. 20.
[2] Richard W. Olshavsky and Donald H. Granbois, "Consumer Decision Making—Fact or Fiction?" *Journal of Consumer Research,* **6**:93, September 1979.

[3] Harold H. Kassarjian, "Presidential Address, 1977: Anthropomorphism and Parsimony," in H. Keith Hunt (ed.), *Advances in Consumer Research,* vol. 5, Association for Consumer Research, Ann Arbor, Mich., 1978, pp. xii-xiv.

[4] Olshavsky and Granbois, "Consumer Decision Making," pp. 93–99; and Roger A. Formisano, Richard W. Olshavsky, and Shelley Tapp, "Choice Strategy in a Difficult Task Environment," *Journal of Consumer Research,* 8:474–479, March 1982.

[5] James F. Engel and Roger D. Blackwell, *Consumer Behavior,* 4th ed., Dryden Press, New York, 1982, p. 300.

[6] Del I. Hawkins, Kenneth A. Coney, and Roger J. Best, *Consumer Behavior,* Business Publications, Inc., Dallas, 1980, p. 388.

[7] Hawkins, Coney, and Best, *Consumer Behavior,* p. 389.

[8] M. Joseph Sirgy, *Social Cognition and Consumer Behavior,* Praeger Publishers, New York, 1983.

[9] Gordon C. Bruner, "Recent Contributions to the Theory of Problem Recognition," in Robert F. Lusch et al. (eds.), *American Marketing Association, Educators' Proceedings,* American Marketing Association , Chicago, 1985, pp. 11–15.

[10] Gordon C. Bruner, "Problem Recognition Styles and Search Patterns: An Empirical Investigation," *Journal of Retailing,* 62:281–297, Fall 1986.

[11] This section is based on Hawkins, Coney, and Best, *Consumer Behavior,* pp. 389–393.

[12] Elihu Katz and Paul Lazarsfeld, *Personal Influence,* Free Press, New York, 1955.

[13] C. Joseph Clawson, "How Useful Are 90-Day Purchase Probabilities?" *Journal of Marketing,* 35:43–47, October 1971.

[14] William D. Wells, "Measuring Readiness to Buy," *Harvard Business Review,* 39:81–87, July-August 1961.

[15] This section is drawn from Robert W. Pratt, Jr., "Understanding the Decision Process for Consumer Durable Goods: An Example of the Application of Longitudinal Analysis," in Peter D. Bennett (ed.), *Marketing and Economic Development,* American Marketing Association, Chicago, 1965, pp. 244–260.

SEARCH AND EVALUATION

LEARNING OBJECTIVES
After studying this chapter, you should understand . . .

■ The major types of consumer information-seeking activities

■ The types and sources of information used by consumers

■ How much external search consumers engage in and what factors influence it

■ How consumers evaluate information obtained during search by establishing choice criteria, narrowing the range of brands considered, and evaluating alternatives

■ What strategies marketers may use to influence the information search-and-evaluation process of consumers

After initial explosive growth in which consumers were lured with grandiose rhetoric and promises, the personal computer industry has slowed down and is faced with a market it does not know how to advertise to. The first wave of buyers has already bought computers. To attract the next wave, producers and distributors must determine how to reach buyers who don't know why they need a computer and are confused by the myriad of choices.

This consumer bewilderment and confusion are exacerbated by all the flashy advertising that has occurred. Some companies, such as Apple, have approached selling computers the same way as soap or automobiles, or as a high-tech version of Pepsi versus Coke. Value and lifestyle ads have been used to frame the conflict with IBM as a battle for the human soul rather than a battle for shelf space. Hardware and software companies seem to agree that vague image-building campaigns won't sell computers.

On the other hand, technical data about a product's capabilities has not been a big success either. Enthusiastic marketers telling the world about the technical wizardry of their new computers have, unfortunately, failed to explain why buyers need their product. They have assumed that the need for a computer was self-evident. Thus, nuts and bolts brand comparisons have filled the ad pages of computer magazines and have even been aimed at those who are less familiar with computers. These ads risk turning off computer illiterates who don't know the difference between bits and bytes. Lotus executives found that the more they talked about bells and whistles, the more they scared off buyers. Now they simply stress the security of buying the industry's best-selling program. Apple and others are stressing benefits more, trying to show potential buyers how a computer can help their work. However, critics of some computer advertising are concerned with the amount of license taken in demonstrating product

19

benefits and the tendency to gloss over the limitations of computers, which may cause some buyers to become disenchanted with the technology.

As expectations for computer advertising are lowered by many in the industry, one executive states that ''There are some dynamics of people reading, thinking and watching friends and coworkers making up their own mind on their own schedule. And I don't think advertising can speed them up.''

Once consumers have recognized the existence of a problem, and assuming there are no constraints preventing further behavior, they move to the next stage in the decision-making process. The situation above illustrates how important it is to producers and retailers to understand how consumers search for and evaluate information on possible purchases. Unless it is known what information they need in their decision making, that which is provided may be inappropriate and ineffective.

In this chapter, we shall first examine what the information-search process entails and the many ways it is influenced. Next, the process of evaluation will be discussed. Finally, some marketing implications will be presented to indicate how the marketer may seek to influence consumer search processes.

THE INFORMATION-SEARCH PROCESS

In this section, we shall examine the search process engaged in by consumers and the factors that influence it.

TYPES OF CONSUMER SEARCH ACTIVITIES

For our purposes here, *information* may be considered to be knowledge obtained about some fact or circumstance. And in the context in which we are dealing within this chapter, such knowledge is to be used in a consumer-behavior situation.

As discussed in Chapter 13, the term ''search'' refers to mental as well as physical information-seeking and processing activities which one engages in to facilitate decision making regarding some goal-object in the marketplace.[2] Consequently, search may be undertaken in order to find out about products, prices, stores, and so on, related to the product. Search may be categorized as prepurchase or ongoing (based on the purpose of search) and as internal or external (based on its source).

Prepurchase Search　This is the typical form of search we associate within the purchasing context. If the consumer has recognized a problem, then prepurchase search would be engaged in.

Ongoing Search　This is characterized as search activities independent of specific needs or decisions; that is, it does not occur in order to solve a recognized and immediate purchase problem. Thus if a consumer were searching with an interest in a product but with no demand for the product, the search would be ongoing rather than prepurchase.

Ongoing search for automobiles may include regularly reading automotive magazines. Prepurchase search, however, might involve use of the same magazines, but only reading them every few years when a new car purchase is about to occur. Notice that these search purposes are different but they involve the same activities; consequently, they are difficult to separate in practice. Table 19-1 offers a summary of the similarities and differences between these two types of search in terms of determinants, motives, and outcomes.

Internal Search This is the first stage to occur after the consumer experiences problem recognition. It is a mental process of recalling and reviewing information stored in memory that may relate to the purchase situation. For instance, a consumer may recall that a friend made very negative comments about a particular brand of coffee maker (which the consumer is now considering buying) while playing bridge several months ago. Notice that these derogatory comments were stored in the consumer's memory and now have come into play by affecting her attitudes unfavorably toward the brand. Thus, the consumer relies on any attitudes, information, or past experiences that have been stored in memory and can be recalled for application to the problem at hand. The recall may be immediate or may occur slowly, as a conscious effort is made to bring the information to mind. Once recalled, the information may be used in the evaluation process as the consumer seeks to resolve the purchase decision confronting her.

The reliance on internal search may be a very important part of shoppers' strategies. For instance, one study showed that most shoppers rely on experiential information sources in retail shopping trips.[3] That is, they turn inward to their previous shopping experiences for making decisions about where to shop. Only a limited number of people engage in any external information search (whether from

TABLE 19-1

A Framework for Consumer Information Search

	Prepurchase search	Ongoing search	
Determinants	■ Involvement in the purchase ■ Market environment ■ Situational factors	■ Involvement with the product ■ Market environment ■ Situational factors	
Motives	To make better purchase decisions	Build a bank of information for future use	Experience fun and pleasure
Outcomes	■ Increased product and market knowledge ■ Better purchase decisions ■ Increased satisfaction with the purchase outcome	■ Increased product and market knowledge leading to: —future buying efficiences —personal influence ■ Increased impulse buying ■ Increased satisfaction from search, and other outcomes.	

Source: Peter H. Bloch, Daniel L. Sherrell, and Nancy M. Ridgway, "Consumer Search: An Extended Framework," *Journal of Consumer Research*, **13**:120, June 1986.

family, friends, or advertisements) prior to making a major shopping trip. This situation makes it especially difficult to overcome a negative image or mistaken impression that people in the market may have of a retail store. Once the store has been removed from the consumer's mental set of acceptable alternatives it may be quite difficult to get that consumer to reconsider or reexperience the store.

The result or outcome of internal search and alternative evaluation may be that a consumer: (1) makes a decision and proceeds to engage in purchase behavior, (2) is constrained by certain environmental variables (such as a determination that his checking account cannot stand the purchase), or (3) determines that insufficient or inadequate information exists in his memory to make a decision now, so that external search is undertaken.

External Search   This refers to the process of obtaining information from other sources in addition to that which can be recalled from memory. Some sources from which such information might be obtained are advertisements, friends, salespeople, store displays, and product-testing magazines.

TYPES AND SOURCES OF INFORMATION

A great variety of information of potential interest to consumers exists in the external environment. Three general categories are (1) information about the existence and availability of various product and service offerings, (2) information useful in forming evaluative criteria—the standards which are employed to evaluate alternatives, and (3) information on the properties and characteristics of alternatives. In general, it appears that the type of information sought depends upon what the consumer already knows. For example, when the consumer has little knowledge about available offerings, search effort tends to focus on learning about the existence of alternatives and forming appropriate evaluative criteria. When she feels sufficiently informed in these areas, search is likely to be redirected toward learning more about the characteristics of available offerings in order to evaluate them.[4]

In addition to the direct experience of using products themselves, consumers gain information from three major areas: (1) marketer-dominated sources, (2) consumer sources, and (3) neutral sources. Information in marketer-dominated channels stems from salespeople, packaging, and other sources under the control of the marketer. Consumer sources include all those interpersonal communications not under the control of the marketer. Neutral sources include a portion of the mass media, government reports, and publications from independent product-testing agencies. These groups are not under the direct control of the marketer.

It appears that although marketer-dominated sources may be extensively used in the early stages of product awareness and initial interest, personal sources enjoy the most use in latter stages of the decision process.[5] The perceived trustworthiness of personal sources is usually cited as a reason for this finding.

AMOUNT OF EXTERNAL SEARCH ACTIVITY

Many studies have examined the amount of external search that consumers actually undertake. The majority of these have used only one measure of total search activity.[6] However, when viewed together they paint a rather consistent and somewhat surprising picture of consumers' external-search behavior. The following are representative of the general findings:

1 Research suggests that consumers typically consult few information sources (friends, articles, advertisements, and so on) before making a purchase. For example, one study showed that, prior to purchase, 15 percent of major appliance and car buyers consulted no information sources, while 30 percent consulted only one, and 26 percent consulted two.[7]

2 In terms of outlets visited, various studies suggest that approximately 40 to 60 percent of shoppers visit only one store before making a purchase. This appears to hold across both durable and nondurable goods.[8]

3 Evidence regarding the number of alternatives buyers consider again suggests limited search. For example, one study reported that 41 percent of refrigerator shoppers considered only one brand, while those considering only one brand of washing machine and vacuum cleaner were 61 percent and 71 percent, respectively.[8]

4 Shoppers also appear to acquire limited amounts of information about the brands actually under consideration. To illustrate, one study found that of the 560 items of readily available information to consider when choosing among sixteen brands of cereal, the median number of items reviewed was only seven.[10]

Because they are based only on single measures of behavior, the above findings each provide an incomplete picture of consumers' external search activity. However, taken together these results strongly suggest that the majority of consumers actually engage in quite limited amounts of external search. Also, other studies have used composite indexes of search by combining several measures together.[11] These studies confirm that many, perhaps even a majority of consumers, engage in little external search for information. Additional evidence suggests that consumers can be categorized according to their general tendency to engage in external search. For example, a recent investigation identified three different groups among car buyers: low searchers, high searchers, and selective searchers.[12] The latter group used intensively only certain sources of information (such as media, friends) and tended to ignore others.[13] Finally, a number of findings suggest that those who typically engage in considerable external-search activity—the so-called information seekers—are identified by a higher demographic profile (higher educational levels, income, occupational standing, and so on) than are low searchers.[14]

The amount of external search that consumers engage in varies considerably across individuals and different purchase situations. Although a number of explanations have been offered for this variability, the cost/benefit view appears to be the most popular one.[15] This explanation holds that external search will be undertaken and will continue as long as the consumer perceives the benefits of search to be greater than the costs involved. Included among the potential benefits of external search are (1) a more comfortable feeling about making an "informed" purchase, (2) an increase in the actual chances of making a choice that leads to greater satisfaction, (3) the positive feelings derived from being generally knowl-

edgeable about products and services, and (4) the pleasure that can result from engaging in shopping activities. Potential costs of external search include the commitment of time, foregoing other pleasant activities, and the frustrations or tensions involved, as well as any actual monetary expenditures (such as fuel and parking fees).[16] It is important to appreciate that the costs and benefits involved are those that are perceived by the consumer, even if they do not correspond perfectly with reality.

Table 19-2 summarizes many of the factors that can influence the amount of external search, either by directly affecting the consumer's cost/benefit perceptions or by indirectly acting as constraints on the process. Several of these categories are suggested below.[17]

Market Conditions   Characteristics of the marketplace can have a significant effect on external search behavior. Availability of information, the number of alternatives to consider, and the location of outlets are among the influencing factors. In addition, many market conditions lead consumers to attach importance to the purchase situation or to perceive differences between available alternatives. This appears to foster greater external-search activity. To illustrate, among the conclusions drawn from various studies are that external search is greater when:

- Prices are higher,[18] and price differences between brands are greater.[19]

- Style and appearance are perceived to be quite important.[20]

- It is suspected that substantial differences may exist between product alternatives.[21]

TABLE 19-2

Determinants of the Extent of Information Search

Market environment:
- Number of alternatives
- Complexity of alternatives
- Marketing mix of alternatives
- Stability of alternatives on the market (new alternatives)
- Information availability

Situational variables:
- Time pressure
- Social pressure (family, peer, boss)
- Financial pressure
- Organizational procedures
- Physical and mental condition
- Ease of access to information sources

Potential payoff/product importance:
- Price
- Social visibility
- Perceived risk
- Differences among alternatives
- Number of crucial attributes
- Status of decision-making activity (in family, organization, society)

Knowledge and experience:
- Stored knowledge
- Usage rate of product
- Previous information
- Previous choices (number and identity)
- Satisfaction

Individual differences:
- Ability
- Training
- Approach to problem solving (compulsiveness, open-mindedness, preplanning, innovativeness)
- Approach to search (enjoyment of shopping, sources of information)
- Involvement
- Demographics (age, income, education, marital status, household size, social class, occupation)
- Personality/lifestyle variables (like self-confidence)

Conflict and conflict-resolution strategies

Source: William L. Moore and Donald R. Lehman, "Individual Differences in Search Behavior for a Nondurable," *Journal of Consumer Research*, 7:298, December 1980. Reprinted by permission.

Buying Strategies Consumers often adopt various strategies which reduce the amount of external search. For example, pattterns of brand and store loyalty can develop through purchase experience over time. Also, evidence suggests that when the purchase decision is complex or when the available information is difficult to process, consumers tend to adopt simple choice rules (such as "pick the middle-priced one") and significantly curtail their external search.[22]

Individual Factors Of course, many of the consumer's own characteristics influence the degree of external-search activity. The following generalizations illustrate the variety of relevant findings:

1 Greater market experience with a product is associated with a lower degree of external search.[23]

2 Open-mindedness and self-confidence of consumers have been found to be positively related to greater search activity.[24]

3 Socioeconomic characteristics have been related to search. For example, higher educational levels and income have been associated with greater search, while a reduction in activity is related to increasing age.[25]

4 Some evidence suggests that consumers differ in their ability to process information, and if their processing limits are reached, the effect may be to decrease the extent of external search.[26]

5 As mentioned in Chapter 12, higher levels of consumer involvement with a product appear to be associated with a greater degree of external search.

6 Chapter 12 also suggested that consumers appear to require an optimum level of stimulation from their environment. When stimulation is sufficiently below this level, external search for novel and exciting stimuli is likely. Conversely, when stimulation is much greater than optimum, external search will tend to be toward less-novel stimuli. This will help the consumer return to the optimum stimulation level.[27] Notice that this process may be occurring quite independently of any specific purchase problem the consumer may be facing at the time.

Situational Factors A number of factors unique to the specific situation can also influence external search. Search may be reduced when:

■ The urgency of a need or the amount of available time exert pressure on the purchase decision.[28]

■ Store conditions are perceived as being crowded.[29]

■ Special opportunities arise to purchase at an especially attractive price.[30]

Perceived Risk Risk or uncertainty regarding the most appropriate purchase decision or the consequences of the decision is a significant variable influencing the total amount of information gathered by consumers.

It is important to recognize that risk is subjective. That is, the risk involved in a purchase decision is *perceived* by the consumer and may or may not bear a

strong relationship to what actually exists. For example, an objective observer may not evaluate the purchase of a canned ham as involving much risk. However, the choice may involve considerable risk in terms of the impression a person wishes to make when purchasing the ham for a dinner party involving his or her boss.

SITUATIONS INFLUENCING RISK   There are several situations that influence the consumer's perception of uncertainty or consequences and, thus, the perception of risk:

1   Uncertainty regarding buying goals. For example, should a new sport jacket be purchased for more formal occasions or for very informal get-togethers?

2   Uncertainty regarding which alternative (such as product, brand, or model) will best match or satisfy the purchase goals. That is, if private transportation to school is desired, what should be purchased: car or motorcycle; Ford, Chevrolet, or Plymouth; two-door or four-door?

3   Perceived possible undesirable consequences if the purchase is made (or not made) and the result is failure to satisfy buying goals.[31]

If any of these situations are sensed by the consumer, then he or she is said to perceive risk in the situation.

TYPES OF RISK   As one may expect, there are also several kinds of risk that consumers may perceive in a purchase situation.[32]

Financial risk. The consumer may lose money if the brand doesn't work at all or costs more than it should to keep it in good shape.

Performance risk. The brand may not work properly.

Physical risk. The brand may be or become harmful or injurious to one's health.

Psychological risk. The brand may not fit in well with the consumer's self-image or self-concept.

Social risk. The brand may negatively affect the way others think of the consumer.

Time-loss risk. The brand may fail completely, thus wasting the consumer's time, convenience, and effort getting it adjusted, repaired, or replaced.

Thus, overall risk is a combination of several factors as perceived by consumers when buying a product.

DEALING WITH RISK   Because most purchase behavior appears to involve at least some risk, consumers may take various steps to handle the problem. In most cases, this results in attempts to reduce risk. Consumers develop various strategies to relieve perceived risk, including the following:

1 Buy the brand whose advertising has endorsements or testimonials from typical consumers, from a celebrity, or from an expert on the product.

2 Buy the brand that the consumer has used before and has found satisfactory.

3 Buy a major, well-known brand, and rely on its reputation.

4 Buy the brand that has been tested and approved by a private testing company.

5 Buy the brand offering a money-back guarantee with the product.

6 Buy the brand that has been tested and approved by a branch of the government.

7 Buy the most expensive and elaborate model of the product.[33]

Thus, as some of the approaches on the above list indicate, consumers may reduce risk through information acquisition aimed at reducing uncertainty. Several consumer research studies have confirmed this process.[34] Information acquisition can also be used to help reduce the perceived consequences of a decision, as can reduction of the amount at stake (such as purchasing a smaller size), reducing expectations about how perfect the product will be, or minimizing the consequences (such as a cigarette lighter slogan that states, "For 99 cents it's a pretty good lighter").

THE INFORMATION-EVALUATION PROCESS

As the consumer is engaged in search activity, he or she is also actively engaged in information evaluation. Evaluation involves those activities undertaken by the consumer to appraise carefully, on the basis of certain criteria, alternative solutions to market-related problems. The search process determines what the alternatives are, and in the evaluation process they are compared so that the consumer is ready to make a decision.

EVALUATIVE OR CHOICE CRITERIA

A consumer evaluates a brand on the basis of a number of choice criteria. These criteria are the standards and specifications the consumer uses in evaluating products and brands. They define the preferred product/brand features that a consumer seeks in a purchase and may be either objective or subjective in nature.[35] Thus, a new car buyer may have in mind certain objective characteristics when purchasing, such as mileage and engine characteristics. There may be other criteria which are subjective, however, such as the social-class image projected with the car.

Evaluative criteria may vary from one consumer to another. For example, when purchasing a food processor, one buyer may be most concerned about electric motor horsepower, blade revolutions per minute, and safety. Another shopper, however, may use a different set of evaluative criteria, including color and style of the processor, durability, warranty, and versatility; still another shopper may use only price as a criterion.

No matter how many criteria are evaluated by the consumer, they are likely to differ in their importance, usually with one or two criteria being more important than others. Thus, while several evaluative criteria are *salient* (important) to the consumer, some are *determinant* (they are most important and are also perceived to differ among the alternatives). Some refer to a determinant attribute which meets both of these conditions for a consumer as a *critical* attribute. That is, a critical attribute is the most determinant attribute for that consumer. For instance, in the purchase of running shoes, brand name, quality, price, and comfort may all be important to a buyer, but comfort is likely to have determinance for most runners. Notice that in this case a subjective factor is considered to be most important.

The marketer should be careful in assuming, however, that a certain feature ranked as most important by consumers is actually determinant. For instance, in studies asking consumers to evaluate such automobile attributes as power, comfort, economy, appearance, and safety, consumers often rank safety as first in importance. However, safety is not a determinant attribute to these same consumers, because they do not see various makes of cars as differing widely with respect to safety. Without the knowledge that consumers see small difference among autos with regard to safety, the marketer might naturally conclude that safety *is* a crucial attribute in their purchasing decision, and may therefore stress this feature in promotion efforts. However, these funds might be more effectively used in promoting other attributes that actually determine brand choice. Of course, the marketer would not ignore safety considerations, because then the brand might become perceived as being so unsafe that its share of the market could slip. At that point, safety could achieve determinance until the ''unsafe'' company brought its product back in line with the others. Thus, determinance should be viewed as a dynamic concept, and marketers must conduct longitudinal research to stay informed of possible shifts in attitudes related to buying behavior.[36]

The number and type of evaluative criteria may vary by product. Consumers generally use few evaluative criteria when purchasing most grocery items. However, when one is purchasing a home, car, or other major durable item, more evaluative criteria would typically be used in the evaluation process. This also means that consumers would tend to use more evaluative criteria for high-involvement products than for low-involvement ones. Generally, however, the number of determinant evaluative criteria used in a consumer decision is six or fewer, although there is some evidence that the number may be as high as nine.[37]

Evaluative criteria may also change over time. As consumers gain new experiences and information, their evaluative criteria may shift. When innovations appear with previously unknown features, consumers may begin to incorporate these features into their evaluative criteria. As they learn from marketers or friends what features they should look for in a particular product purchase, there may be changes in their evaluative criteria. Of course, this has important implications for the marketer who seeks to influence the evaluative criteria favorably toward his brand. As will be mentioned later, however, it is often difficult to change such ingrained decision factors.

REDUCING THE RANGE OF ALTERNATIVES

During search, the brand alternatives to the buyer's product-choice decision are identified. Although there may be many brands in existence in the product category (which we may call the *total set* of brands), the consumer is not likely to be aware of all of them. Thus, some brands will not be considered by the consumer because of this unawareness. Consequently, the marketer seeks to make consumers aware of the availability of his brand and to supply them with sufficient information to evaluate it and, hopefully, purchase it.

Even among brands of which the consumer is aware, however, are some that he would not consider purchasing for several reasons:

1   He may feel they are beyond his financial reach.

2   They are not perceived as adequate for his motives.

3   He has insufficient information on which to evaluate them.

4   He has tried and rejected them.

5   He is satisfied with his current brand.

6   He has received negative feedback from advertising or from word-of-mouth communication.[38]

It has been suggested, therefore, that there actually exist three subsets of brands within the awareness set of alternatives: (1) evoked set, (2) inert set, and (3) inept set.[39]

The *evoked set* consists of the few select brands evaluated positively by the consumer for purchase and consumption. These are the brands the consumer would be willing to consider further. The *inert set* consists of those brands that the consumer has failed to perceive any advantage in buying; that is, they are evaluated neither positively nor negatively. Perhaps the consumer has insufficient information on which to evaluate them, or she simply may not perceive them as better than the brands in her evoked set. The *inept set* is made up of brands that have been rejected from purchase consideration by the consumer because of an unpleasant experience or negative feedback from others. Thus, the brands in this set are evaluated negatively by the consumer and will not be considered at all in their present form. Figure 19-1 diagrams the elimination process leading to brand acceptance or rejection.

Knowledge of consumers' awareness sets of brands is valuable to marketers because they are interested in moving their items into their evoked set. Only if consumers are aware of the brand and have evaluated it positively will it be purchased. Later in this chapter we will discuss alternatives for moving a brand into consumers' evoked sets.

EVALUATING ALTERNATIVES

The marketer is interested in knowing how consumers process the information gathered during the search process on their evoked set of brands. There are two broad approaches: brand processing or attribute processing. In brand processing, the buyer assesses one brand at a time. Thus, the consumer may decide to look at a particular brand, examine several attributes of that brand, then assess several attributes for a second and third brand, for instance. In attribute processing, the consumer examines a specific attribute and then compares several other brands

on that attribute. Then, a second attribute may be selected for comparison, and so on. These two information-processing strategies are referred to as choice by processing brands (CPB) and choice by processing attributes (CPA), respectively.[40]

Generally, a CPB strategy appears to be common, although research also indicates that consumers in early stages of the decision process use a CPA strategy, switching to a brand-processing approach in later stages. Perhaps those with considerable experience or knowledge regarding a product and its purchase can be expected to rely more on a brand-processing approach.[41]

Consumers may either use compensatory processes or noncompensatory processes as decision rules in evaluating product-alternative attributes. However, there may be occasions when the consumer does not make full use of either of these approaches stored in memory and instead, takes a build-up approach to the situation by utilizing only fragments or elements of these rules. Such an approach may occur when the consumer has little product experience[42] or when pertinent information is available at the point of purchase.[43] The noncompensatory and compensatory decision-rule formats are discussed below.

Before proceeding, however, assume that the consumer has evaluated four brands of basic electronic calculators along only six dimensions. These evaluative criteria are shown in Table 19-3, along with the consumer's rating of each dimension. Notice also that this shopper has some standards by which these criteria are being evaluated. These are shown as the acceptable levels of performance required on each dimension, that is, as minimum levels of performance which must be met by each brand. Keep in mind that these evaluations are the individual consumer's *perceived* assessments. A truly objective product evaluation might arrive at different results.

Noncompensatory Decision Rules   Decision rules are said to be noncompensatory when good performance on one evaluative criterion does not offset or compensate for poor performance on another evaluative criterion of the brand. Several varieties of noncompensatory rules may be used by consumers. The following sum-

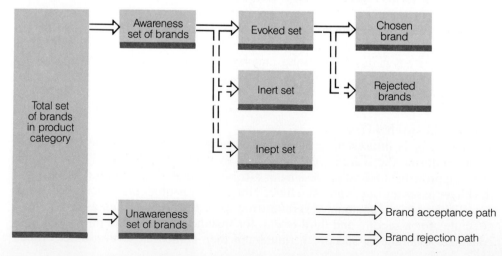

FIGURE 19-1
Brand elimination process.

mary of each type will be illustrated with data from the example provided in Table 19-3.

DISJUNCTIVE RULE   This approach is used when the consumer establishes minimum acceptable performance standards which each brand must meet. Any brand will be acceptable if it exceeds the minimum standard on any criterion. The decision rule will then be to select the brand that exceeds the others by the greatest amount on the criterion selected. For example, if the electronic calculator buyer with the evoked set presented in Table 19-3 were to use a price of less than $12 (see table) as the criterion, the disjunctive decision rule in this case would lead to the choice of the TI 1001, because (1) it is less than $12 and (2) it is the lowest-priced alternative in the acceptable group. Note that the Royal calculator would be eliminated immediately because its price is higher than $12.

CONJUNCTIVE RULE   The conjunctive decision rule requires the consumer to establish minimum levels of acceptability on each brand attribute. Thus, for each evaluative criterion of importance to the consumer a cutoff point will be set below which brand would not be considered further. Table 19-3 shows the minimum levels of acceptability for each evaluative criterion involved in this consumer's purchase of an electronic calculator (as determined by the consumer). Based on the conjunctive decision-rule process, every brand but the Canon LC-20 would be discarded from further consideration because each has one or more unacceptable attribute levels. For example, while the KMC 3000 has an acceptable price level and is rated as easy to use, it has a less-attractive warranty and does not offer as complete a range of functions/features as desired by this shopper. Thus, the Canon LC-20 would be the chosen brand if this buyer followed a conjunctive decision-rule process.

LEXICOGRAPHIC RULE   This extension of the disjunctive decision rule allows additional evaluative criteria to be incorporated in the decision if necessary. Thus, if a choice cannot be made by evaluating the most important criterion, other

TABLE 19-3

Electronic Calculators
In Evoked Set

Evaluative criteria	KMC 3000	Texas Instruments TI 1001	Royal LC-80	Canon LC-20	Acceptable level
Price	$9.00	$7.00	$13.75	$7.50	Less than $12
Ease of use	Very good	Very good	Fair	Very good	Good
Readability of display	Very good	Fair	Very good	Very good	Good
Warranty	90 days	1 Year	6 mos. parts, 3 mos. labor	1 year	6 mos.
Functions/features	Fair	Good	Very good	Good	Good
Battery life	Good	Fair	Very good	Very good	Good

evaluative criteria will be assessed in their order of importance. For instance, assume that the consumer's hierarchy of importance for the evaluative criteria presented in Table 19-3 were as follows: ease of use, functions/features, warranty, price, readability of display, and battery life. Using this decision approach, all brands would be first evaluated on the most important dimension—in this case, ease of use. A tie exists between the KMC 3000, TI 1001, and Canon LC-20, which are all rated as very good. Discarded from any further consideration would be the Royal LC-80 (even though it ranks highest on the next-most-important dimension). The three remaining brands are then assessed on the evaluative criterion of functions/features, and the KMC 3000 would now be dropped from further evaluation. The TI 1001 and the Canon LC-20 are evaluated equally on the next most important dimension, so an additional criterion must be assessed. On the fourth most important attribute, price, the TI 1001 as the lowest-priced brand would be the chosen alternative. Of course, each consumer may have a different hierarchy of importance for these criteria, which would result in other brands being selected by these shoppers.

SEQUENTIAL ELIMINATION RULE In this decision approach, the consumer has established acceptable performance minimums for each evaluative criterion and then proceeds to evaluate each brand and eliminate any which do not measure up to these minimums. This process is different from the lexicographic approach in that it does not require any specific ordering of attributes. To understand its operation, assume that our calculator shopper evaluated each criterion in the order in which they are shown in Table 19-3. First, price would be considered, and any brand whose price exceeded the acceptable limit would be eliminated. This leaves three remaining brands in consideration (KMC 3000, TI 1001, and Canon LC-20). Next, ease of use is evaluated, and all three brands exceed the minimum, with none being eliminated. Readability of display is assessed next, and the TI 1001 is eliminated because it does not meet the minimum acceptable performance standard. Warranty is the next criterion assessed, and one more model (KMC 3000) is eliminated from consideration. Therefore, the Canon LC-20 would be the brand chosen for purchase using the sequential elimination decision rule.

Comparative advertising strategies are sometimes designed along this approach in an attempt to convince consumers of the wisdom of a course of action. The advertiser may begin by showing all of the brand's competitors and then eliminating them from consideration as certain relevant evaluative criteria are considered. The sponsoring brand is then left as the "obvious" choice from among many competitors.

Compensatory Decision Rule Consumers using a compensatory decision rule will allow perceived favorable ratings or brand evaluative criteria to offset unfavorable evaluations. That is, brand strengths can compensate for brand weaknesses. This approach, therefore, uses more than one evaluative criterion for assessment by consumers. This decision rule should be recognized as similar to the Fishbein multiattribute model discussed in detail in Chapter 16. It evaluates brands individually along all dimensions, or attributes with the overall evaluation being the sum of the weighted ratings along each attribute. The brand obtaining the highest sum would be the brand purchased by the consumer. As an illustration of how this

decision rule might operate in the electronic calculator purchase situation, consider the information presented in Table 19-4. This carries the previous information in Table 19-3 one step further by providing a rating of the importance of each evaluative criterion (assigned a weight between 1 and 10) and a quantitative evaluation of how well each brand measures up on these evaluative dimensions (again, assigned a rating between 1 and 10). The evaluation scores are multiplied by the importance weights and summed to provide each brand's total score. The brand scoring highest in terms of total satisfaction contributed would be the alternative selected. In this case, the Canon LC-20 would be purchased.

While it should be emphasized that consumers do not calculate actual scores for brands as shown in Table 19-4, they do (1) determine the brands to be considered, (2) define their needs and rank them, (3) determine the degree to which brands meet their needs, and (4) select the brand that will best meet their most important needs, as they perceive them.[44]

Consensus A growing body of research on decision rules used by consumers indicates that compensatory strategies tend to be utilized under high-involvement conditions when the number of alternatives is small and the evaluative criteria may be large, and by those with greater education.[45] When the consumer is confronted with many alternatives, it appears that a conjunctive decision rule may be used to reduce the alternatives to a manageable number, and then a compensatory strategy may be used to assess the remaining brands for a final decision.

Only the lexicographic and sequential elimination approaches discussed above assume that consumers process information by attribute (CPA), while the remaining alternatives all assumed a processing by brand approach (CPB). The processing approach used by consumers has much to do with marketing strategies. For example, if consumers presently engage in a CPB approach and prefer

TABLE 19-4
Compensatory Model of Evaluation for Electronic Calculators

Evaluative criteria	Importance weight (*I*)	KMC 3000 Evaluation (*E*)*	*I* × *E*	Texas Instruments TI 1001 Evaluation (*E*)	*I* × *E*	Royal LC-80 Evaluation (*E*)	*I* × *E*	Canon LC-20 Evaluation (*E*)	*I* × *E*
Price	9	5	45	10	90	1	9	8	72
Ease of use	10	9	90	9	90	3	30	9	90
Readability of display	7	9	63	3	21	9	63	9	63
Warranty	3	3	9	10	30	6	18	10	30
Functions/ features	8	3	24	6	48	9	72	6	48
Battery life	2	6	12	3	6	9	18	9	18
		Σ =	243		285		210		321

* Assume the following evaluation scoring system:
  Very good = 9–10   Fair = 3
  Good   = 6   Poor = 1

this manner, then attribute information should continue to be provided in the context of the brand as it is normally now done in promotion and retail displays. However, if consumers prefer to process information by means of a CPA approach, then the attributes themselves might be more prominently featured, such as in retail displays which might group products and brands by salient attributes.[46]

FACTORS INFLUENCING THE AMOUNT OF EVALUATION

The same factors that were discussed earlier with regard to the extent of search activity will determine the amount of evaluation that occurs. For example, at least to some extent, the following guidelines are true:

1   The more urgent the need, the less evaluation will take place.

2   The more significant the product is to the buyer (for example, a house, car, boat), the greater the amount of evaluation.

3   The more complex the alternatives, the more evaluation will take place.

RESULTS OF EVALUATION

The appraisal of information produced during search may have several possible results, depending on the extent to which the buyer reconciles his desired and available alternatives. One outcome is for the consumer to stop searching because he has found an acceptable product which satisfies the recognized problem. At this point, assuming no further constraints, the consumer would purchase the item. A second possibility is for the consumer to discontinue search because no acceptable product has been identified. A third possible outcome is for the consumer to continue searching even though no acceptable alternative has yet been found. At this point, he obviously feels that the benefits of continued search outweigh the costs involved.

ALTERNATIVE EVALUATION IN LOW-INVOLVEMENT SITUATIONS

The information-evaluation process differs under low-involvement conditions because it mainly occurs after purchase, not before. That is, the consumer has some expectations, but not strong ones, about the product's anticipated performance. Purchase may occur based on name recognition (drilled in through advertising) of the brand in the store. Although the consumer perhaps has been exposed to the brand's name and attributes, no strong belief about the brand has been formed at this stage. Thus, the consumer makes a purchase anticipating that the brand will confirm certain expectations. As use occurs, the consumer evaluates the brand and develops attitudes toward it that may lead to repurchase, if favorable, or to brand switching, if unfavorable. Even though the consumer's attitudes toward the brand may be favorable based on usage of the item, brand switching is still likely to occur because several other brands may be seen to be relatively equal in quality, and any of these brands offering an incentive to purchase (coupon or price rebate) may get the consumer's nod.

MARKETING IMPLICATIONS

There are a number of marketing implications that flow from this exposition of search and alternative evaluation processes. In this section, we shall examine some of the significant ramifications of this process for the marketer's task.

STUDYING THE INFORMATION-SEARCH PROCESS

In order for the marketer to influence the process of search and alternative evaluation, he first must have information about it among his market segments. There are several pieces of the information-processing puzzle that he should seek to fill in (assuming that search activity is engaged in by a significant segment of his market). First, he needs to determine what sources of information are actually used by consumers. Next, he must determine each source's influence.

Determining Sources of Information   There are several useful approaches by which data may be gathered on information-source effectiveness. The following two research activities probably represent the easiest and most widely used approaches to date.

WARRANTY CARDS   Where appropriate, many marketers use warranty registration cards to gather data on the information-search activities of their customers. These questionnaires enable the respondent to check the source of information as well as the place of purchase for a product. However, these cards are often so small, in order to be machine-processed, that the amount of information obtainable on them is rather limited. Thus, such questions as where the consumer shopped (as opposed to purchased) and which information source was the most important are usually left for the company to speculate about. As a result, this type of research approach, although useful, leaves many unanswered questions for the marketer attempting to make distribution or promotion decisions.

IN-DEPTH RESEARCH   The marketer may also utilize cross-sectional or longitudinal research approaches to obtain information on consumer search processes. While cross-sectional approaches may be acceptable for products with relatively short decision times, longitudinal studies may be more useful, especially when the decision time for a product is long.

When formulating questionnaires to be used in such studies, it is suggested that the influence of information sources can be obtained by asking several types of questions:[47] (1) *specific influence* questions about the decision process itself (rather than specific sources), such as "How did you learn about this new product?" or "Why did you decide to buy this brand?" (2) questions *assessing overall influence,* such as, "Overall, what was the most important thing in causing you to purchase this product?" and (3) questions about *exposure* to various sources of information, such as checklists like those used on warranty cards.

Determining Source Influence   We learned in Chapter 18 that analysis of purchase intentions and fulfillment rates over time could help to pinpoint weaknesses in marketing strategy. One of the variables that needs to be assessed to determine its

strength or weakness is the influence of information sources on brand-purchase intentions and fulfillment.

Building on the discussion in Chapter 18, we can see the type of analysis that might be necessary in order for the marketer to secure greater intention-fulfillment rates. Several steps of analysis are required. First, the marketer should determine the effectiveness of information sources to which consumers of each brand are exposed. This necessitates gathering data for each brand and each information source with regard to whether that source was effective for consumers, and the degree of its effectiveness. Once this information is known, brands can then be compared on the basis of how effective each information source is. It may be found, for example, that one brand's word-of-mouth and television advertising is especially ineffective when compared to other brands.

One typology that has been suggested for comparing various information sources categorizes each one according to the following dimensions:[48]

1 *Decisive effectiveness.* The consumer evaluates this source as having a major or dominant impact on the decision process.

2 *Contributory effectiveness.* The consumer evaluates this source as playing a specific role in the decision process, although it is not among the most important sources.

3 *Ineffective.* This source is rated as having no particular role in the decision process, even though exposure to it did occur.

Several other facets of analysis would be helpful in isolating the problem. For example, analysis of information source effectiveness by type of customer (demographic or psychographic bases) would help to determine which consumers are being effectively or ineffectively influenced. Of course, once the weak link in the information search and evaluation process is known (such as poor word-of-mouth advertising), the reasons for the poor performance must still be determined and corrected.

INFLUENCING THE CONSUMER'S EVOKED SET

It is also beneficial for the marketer to determine whether his brand is perceived as being in the consumer's evoked, inert, or inept set.[49] The marketer can conduct research among a sample of consumers to determine all the brands they are aware of, the brand names that they do and do not consider buying, as well as the reasons for this. Using this approach, one can learn what percentage are aware of his brand and which awareness set it primarily falls into. From such study, one is likely to find that although consumers are aware of many brands in a product category they generally hold only a few brands in their evoked and inept sets. If the marketer determines that a large share of the market is unaware of his brand, this would indicate the need for an intensified advertising campaign. Reasons for a brand's position within consumers' awareness sets may also be learned by assessing information on their evaluative beliefs regarding the brand. This information may help explain why certain brands are in the evoked set while others are in the inept set. For instance, it may be learned that many consumers reject the marketer's brand because of its physical characteristics, or dislike of the brand's advertising, or lack of adequate information with which to evaluate the brand. Thus, the marketer might rectify these problems by modifying the physical features of the brand, changing the ad copy, or utilizing comparative advertising and free samples. As a result of such strategies, a brand currently in consumers' inept set may be able to move into their inert or evoked sets.

MEASURING EVALUATIVE CRITERIA

In order for the marketer to develop a successful marketing mix, there must be an understanding of what criteria are used by consumers in making a purchase decision for this product, as well as how important each criterion is, and how the consumer rates each brand on the various criteria. Each of these topics will be discussed below.

Determining Which Criteria Are Used by Consumers   The marketer will first need to determine which evaluative criteria are used by consumers in a purchase decision. This may be accomplished by *directly asking* consumers what factors they consider when they compare alternatives for purchase. It might be done in a survey questionnaire format, or perhaps through a focus group meeting. The greatest drawback to this approach is that it assumes that consumers know why they buy or prefer one product to another, and it assumes that they are willing to provide the requested information. Remember, however, that consumers may at times be unwilling or unable to answer such questions accurately. For example, they may provide the researcher with "socially acceptable" responses rather than their true feelings. In addition, they may have forgotten what the most important criterion was in a recent purchase. In order to secure valid data using this approach, the marketer should seek to develop questioning or measuring approaches that very carefully obtain the desired information.

If the marketer believes that consumers cannot or will not directly reveal their evaluative criteria, then an *indirect* approach may be utilized. In this situation, the marketer may, for instance, ask the consumer what evaluative criteria she thinks "someone else" would use. This type of questioning allows consumers to acceptably project their own attitudes through another individual.

Still another technique for determining evaluative criteria is *perceptual mapping*. One approach to this involves multidimensional scaling (MDS), in which consumers rate, two at a time, brand alternatives along a scale ranging from similar to dissimilar. The responses are processed by a computer, and a graphic output is produced revealing the extent to which consumers perceive these alternatives to be similar. The axes of such a map are assumed to be the evaluative criteria by which consumers made their judgments of similarity/dissimilarity. That, however, is one of the drawbacks to the approach. Because the marketer must infer the criteria and label these axes based on intuition or additional research conducted, there is great room for subjectivity and mistake in the process. (See Figure 5-5 for an example of a perceptual map.)

Determining the Importance of Criteria Used by Consumers   Once the evaluative criteria are known, a second measure that the marketer will find useful is the relative importance consumers place on these criteria. That is, the marketer is seeking to know the salience of each attribute in a purchase decision. A direct

method for researching this could involve the use of a *rating scale* method whereby consumers would be asked to evaluate the salience of each criterion on a six-point scale ranging from perhaps "unimportant" to "important." Another approach would be to use a *semantic differential,* with pairs of adjectives characterizing the criteria, such as "high price" and "low price." A third approach involves what is known as a *constant sum scale,* in which respondents typically allocate 100 points across the evaluative criteria according to their judgment of each one's importance. For example, a buyer of a ceiling fan might make the following allocation according to his perceived importance of each attribute:

Evaluative criteria	Importance (in points)
Motor quietness	20
Electricity consumption	5
Cubic feet per minute of air moved at high speed	25
Style	30
Price	10
Warranty period	10
	100

For this consumer, style is perceived as being most important, followed by ability to circulate air, quietness of motor, length of warranty and price (tied), and rate of electricity consumption.

Merely asking consumers which attributes are important in choosing a product may not be sufficiently meaningful to allow the focus to be narrowed to attributes which truly determine consumer behavior. Thus, a dual questioning approach may be much more useful. In this approach, consumers are first asked what factors they consider important in a purchasing decision. Next, they are asked how they perceive these factors as differing among the various brands. This

TABLE 19-5

Importance Ratings of Savings and Loan Characteristics

Benefit or claim	Average ratings*	Benefit or claim	Average ratings*
Safety of money	1.4	Compounding frequency	2.2
Interest rate earned	1.6	Branch location convenience	2.3
Government insurance	1.6	Time required to earn interest	2.3
Financial strength	2.0	Parking convenience	2.4
Ease of withdrawing money	2.0	Years in business	2.5
Management ability	2.0	Other services	3.1
Attitude of personnel	2.1	Building/office attractiveness	3.4
Speed/efficiency of service	2.2	Premiums offered	4.0

* 1—"extremely important" 2—"very important" 3—"fairly important" 4—"slightly important"
Source: James H. Myers and Mark I. Alpert, "Determinant Buying Attitudes: Meaning and Measurement," *Journal of Marketing,* **32**:15, October 1968, published by the American Marketing Association, Chicago.

approach is illustrated in Tables 19-5 and 19-6, which were developed from a survey of the general public in a major metropolitan area relative to attitudes towards savings-and-loan associations.[50]

These results illustrate that while some items rank high in importance (such as safety of money, government reassurance), they are not thought to differ much among the various savings-and-loan associations. Therefore, these attributes are not the most determinant, even though they are rated as being among the most important. Conversely, some elements differ greatly among the various associations (such as years in business and parking convenience) but have relatively little influence in determining the choice of a savings-and-loan association. Additionally, some attributes are viewed as being very important, and a large percentage of those responding said that there is a big difference (and a small percentage saying there is no difference) between associations. Thus, such features as interest rates and financial strength may be relatively determinant attributes.

Conjoint analysis is another technique that offers marketers the opportunity to determine the salience of consumers' evaluative criteria. Conjoint measurement starts with the consumer's overall judgments (expressed as preference or likelihood of purchase orderings, or as any other explicit judgmental criterion) about a set of complex alternatives (perhaps expressed as combinations of various potential attributes such as alternative package designs, prices, and brand names), and then proceeds to decompose these original evaluations into separate utility scales by which the original global judgments can be reconstituted. Computation of the utility scales of each attribute, which determines how important each is in consumers' evaluations, is accomplished by various computer programs. Such an

TABLE 19-6

Difference Rating of Savings and Loan Characteristics

Benefit or claim	Big difference	Small difference	No difference	Don't know
Years in business	52%	31%	10%	6%
Financial strength	40	32	22	6
Parking convenience	37	35	22	6
Safety of money	36	15	47	2
Management ability	35	26	27	12
Government insurance	35	11	51	3
Branch location convenience	34	36	28	2
Attitude of personnel	34	28	33	5
Interest rate earned	33	30	35	2
Speed/efficiency of service	32	28	35	5
Ease of withdrawing money	29	18	48	5
Compounding frequency	28	36	31	5
Time required to earn interest	26	34	33	7
Building/office attractiveness	24	44	30	2
Other services offered	21	34	29	16
Premiums offered	15	36	38	11

Source: James H. Myers and Mark I. Alpert, "Determinant Buying Attitudes: Meaning and Measurement," *Journal of Marketing*, **32**:16, October, 1968, published by the American Marketing Association, Chicago.

approach can provide managers with valuable information about the relative importance of various attributes of a product, as well as the value of various levels of a single attribute.[51]

Determining Consumers' Evaluations of Brand Criteria Performance   In this case, the marketer is seeking judgments by consumers relating to performance on various evaluative criteria by the brand. For instance, a sample of respondents, using a semantic differential, might rate the performance of various evaluative criteria found to be important for a particular brand of stereo receiver. A summary of the individual respondents' ratings could then be compiled. Such information allows the marketer to judge better the strengths and weaknesses of a brand on dimensions of importance to consumers.

INFLUENCING CONSUMERS' EVALUATION

The marketer may decide to change his brand's image upon finding that his brand suffers from continued existence in consumers' inept or inert sets. If he pursues this change, he has a choice between two main strategies. He may alter the characteristics of dominant cues and/or he may alter the information value of the cues.[52]

Altering Cue Characteristics   Changing the characteristics of a dominant cue can have a dramatic effect on the product image. This is particularly important in the many cases where brands are perceived very similarly. The marketer may be able to move her brand from the inert or inept set into the consumer's evoked set by a very minor change in a cue (for example, making an electric food mixer slightly noisier so that it seems more powerful to consumers). A "just noticeable difference" between brands can be accomplished by emphasizing a minor (but easy to evaluate with high confidence) difference in product, price, or package. Moreover, such changes appear to be more effective than claiming a large and nearly unbelievable (that is, difficult to evaluate with confidence) brand difference (such as, "This electric food mixer is powerful enough to churn concrete.").

Altering Information Value   Rather than changing characteristics of a cue, it may be possible to change the way consumers evaluate a product. For instance, rather than changing the sound of the mixer in the above example, one could educate consumers to base their evaluation of power on another cue (such as horsepower rating or wattage). Thus, this involves seeking to increase the degree of association in the mind of the consumer between horsepower rating and actual mixer power. One might accomplish this through advertising and personal selling efforts. At the same time, one may attempt to teach consumers how to be sure that a given horsepower rating was adequate or inadequate for a mixer (so that consumers could confidently evaluate the cue).

It should be carefully noted, however, that the marketer will generally find it difficult to change the evaluative criteria consumers use to assess products. Attempts to educate consumers or convince them of the "error of their ways" in terms of past product evaluation criteria they have used generally fall flat. Such evaluative criteria are so thoroughly embedded in consumers' minds (particularly in high-involvement purchasing conditions) that they are very resistant to con-

FIGURE 19-2
An advertisement for
the Ross bicycle.
Courtesy of Chain Bike Corporation.

version. As a result, consumers may selectively screen-out messages seeking to change these criteria, and they may continue to hold their previous views. Obviously, marketers will at times need to educate consumers as to the "proper" evaluative criteria to use in purchasing (see Figure 19-2). However, criteria that fly in the face of consumers' common-sense perceptions will find difficulty in gaining acceptance among large segments of the market.

MANAGERIAL REFLECTIONS

For our product or service situation . . .

1 What are the various types of search typically undertaken by our consumers?

2 What types of information are sought by buyers during the search process? How influential are these sources?

3 How much external search is generally made by consumers and what factors influence its extensiveness?

4   What evaluative or choice criteria have consumers established in its purchase? Which are salient, determinant, and critical?

5   To what extent is the brand perceived to be a member of consumers' evoked, inert, or inept sets? How may negative images be overcome and the brand moved into their evoked set?

6   Which decision rule is generally invoked for the purchase?

7   What types and amounts of information should be provided to buyers to help them make better decisions?

DISCUSSION TOPICS

1   Distinguish between prepurchase and ongoing, internal and external search.

2   "Consumers should read more advertisements and visit more retail stores during the information-gathering stage of the decision process." Evaluate this statement.

3   What are the benefits and costs of search activity?

4   What types of risk might consumers perceive in a purchase situation? How might consumers deal with these risks? How could the marketer seek to minimize each type?

5   Read several recent product rating reports contained in *Consumer Reports* and evaluate the rating system used. What other information would you find helpful?

6   Choose a product category and develop a table similar to Table 19-3. Show what decision each evaluation method discussed in the text would yield.

PROJECTS

1   Interview ten students and ascertain their awareness set of brands, evoked set, inert set, and inept set for the following products: computers, deodorants, cereals, and compact disk players.
   a   What evaluative criteria are important (ranked from most to least) to these students' brand evaluation?
   b   Determine the reasons for brands being in the inept set. What can you recommend to these marketers?

2   Visit a local supermarket and attempt to evaluate five brands of cereal by employing the processing-by-attribute model. What conclusions do you reach?

3   Select a product category and design a warranty registration card that you think would provide insight into the information search-and-evaluation process.

NOTES

[1] John Marcom, Jr., "Computer Firms Confused on How to Advertise to Changing Market," *The Wall Street Journal,* September 19, 1985, p. 34.

[2] Robert F. Kelly, "The Search Component of the Consumer Decision Process—A Theoretic Examination," in Robert L. King (ed.), *Marketing and the New Science of Planning*, American Marketing Association, Chicago, 1968, p. 273.

[3] Elizabeth C. Hirschman and Michael K. Mills, "Sources Shoppers Use to Pick Stores," *Journal of Advertising Research*, **20**:47–51, February 1980.

[4] See John A. Howard and Jagdish N. Sheth, *The Theory of Buyer Behavior*, Wiley, New York, 1969, pp. 26–27, 46–47.

[5] See Everett M. Rogers, *Diffusion of Innovations*, Free Press, New York, 1962; and Carol Kohn Berning and Jacob Jacoby, "Patterns of Information Acquisition in New Product Purchases," *Journal of Consumer Research*, **1**:18–22, September 1974.

[6] For an excellent and more extensive review of this subject see Joseph W. Newman, "Consumer External Search: Amount and Determinants," in Arch G. Woodside, Jagdish N. Sheth, and Peter D. Bennett (eds.), *Consumer and Industrial Buying Behavior*, North-Holland, New York, pp. 86–92, upon which much of this section is based.

[7] Joseph Newman and Richard Staelin, "Prepurchase Information Seeking for New Cars and Major Household Appliances," *Journal of Marketing Research*, **9**:249–257, August 1972.

[8] Newman, "Consumer External Search."

[9] William P. Dommermuth,"The Shopping Matrix and Marketing Strategy," *Journal of Marketing Research*, **2**:130, May 1965.

[10] Jacob Jacoby et al., "Prepurchase Information Acquisition: Description of a Process Methodology, Research Paradigm and Pilot Investigation," in Beverlee B. Anderson (ed.), *Advances in Consumer Research*, vol. 3, Association for Consumer Research, Ann Arbor, Mich., 1976, pp. 306–314.

[11] George Katona and Eva Mueller, "A Study of Purchasing Decisions," in Lincoln II. Clark (ed.), *Consumer Behavior: The Dynamics of Consumer Reaction*, New York University Press, New York, 1955; Newman and Staelin, "Prepurchase Information Seeking"; John D. Claxton, Joseph N. Fry, and Bernard Portis, "A Taxonomy of Prepurchase Information Gathering Patterns," *Journal of Consumer Research*, **1**:35–42, December 1974; and Geoffrey C. Kiel and Roger A. Layton, "Dimensions of Consumer Information Seeking Behavior," *Journal of Marketing Research*, **18**:233–239, May 1981.

[12] Kiel and Layton, "Dimensions."

[13] See Robert A. Westbrook and Claes Fornell, "Patterns of Information Source Usage Among Durable Goods Buyers," *Journal of Marketing Research*, **16**:303–312, August 1979, for a typology of selective search based on different research evidence.

[14] See Westbrook and Fornell, "Patterns of Information Source Usage"; Katona and Mueller, "A Study of Purchase Decisions"; Newman and Staelin, "Prepurchase Information Seeking"; Hans B. Thorelli, "Concentrations of Information Power Among Consumers," *Journal of Marketing Research*, **8**:427–432, November 1971; Hans B. Thorelli, Helmut Becker, and Jack Engledow, *The Information Seekers*, Ballinger, Cambridge, Mass., 1975; and Kiel and Layton, "Dimensions," for representative findings.

[15] See George Katona, *The Powerful Consumer*, McGraw-Hill, New York, 1960; Louis P. Bucklin, "Testing Propensities to Shop," *Journal of Marketing*, **30**:22–27, January 1966; and Allen Newell and Herbert Simon, *Human Problem Solving*, Prentice-Hall, Englewood Cliffs, N.J., 1972, for alternative perspectives.

[16] See Wesley C. Bender, "Consumer Purchase Costs—Do Retailers Recognize Them?" *Journal of Retailing*, **40**:1–8, 52, Spring 1964; and Thorelli, Becker, and Engledow, *The Information Seekers*, p. 16.

[17] See Newman, "Consumer External Search"; and James R. Bettman, *An Information Processing Theory of Consumer Choice*, Addison-Wesley, Reading, Mass., 1979, pp. 123–131, upon which much of this discussion is based.

[18] Newman and Staelin, "Prepurchase Information Seeking."

[19] Louis P. Bucklin, "Consumer Search, Role Enactment and Market Efficiency," *Journal of Business*, **42**:416–438, 1969.

[20] Claxton, Fry, and Portis, "A Taxonomy."

[21] Claxton, Fry, and Portis, "A Taxonomy."

[22] Edward J. Russo, "The Value of Unit Price Information," *Journal of Marketing Research*, **14**:193–201, May 1977.

[23] William L. Moore and Donald R. Lehman, "Individual Differences in Search Behavior For a Nondurable," *Journal of Consumer Research*, **7**:296–307, December 1980; and Newman and Staelin,

"Prepurchase Information Seeking." See also Kiel and Layton, "Dimensions," for results suggesting that specific experience may exert only a selective influence on search behavior.

[24] William B. Locander and Peter W. Hermann, "The Effect of Self-confidence and Anxiety on Information Seeking in Consumer Risk Reduction," *Journal of Marketing Research,* **16**:268–274, May 1979; and Paul Green, "Consumer Use of Information," in Joseph W. Newman (ed.), *On Knowing the Consumer,* Wiley, New York, 1966, pp. 67–80. For a recent contradictory finding see Kiel and Layton, "Dimensions."

[25] See Thorelli, Becker, and Engledow, *The Information Seekers;* Noel Capon and Marian Burke, "Individual, Product Class, and Task-Related Factors in Consumer Information Processing," *Journal of Consumer Research,* **7**:314–326, December 1980; Donald J. Hempel, "Search Behavior and Information Utilization in the Home Buying Process," in P. McDonald (ed.), *Marketing Involvement in Society and the Economy,* American Marketing Association, Chicago, 1969; and Newman and Staelin, "Prepurchase Information Seeking." See also Kiel and Layton, "Dimensions," for both supporting and divergent findings.

[26] See Jacob Jacoby, Donald Speller, and Carol Kohn Berning. "Brand Choice Behavior As a Function of Information Load: Replication and Extension," *Journal of Consumer Research,* **1**:33–42, June 1974; John T. Lanyetta and Vera T. Kanareff, "Information Cost, Amount of Payoff and Level of Aspiration as Determinants of Information Seeking in Decision Making," *Behavioral Science,* **7**:459–473, 1962; and J. Edward Russo, "More Information Is Better: A Reevaluation of Jacoby, Speller and Kohn," *Journal of Consumer Research,* **1**:68–72, December 1974, for information related to this topic.

[27] See P. S. Raju, "Theories of Exploratory Behavior: Review and Consumer Research Implications," in Jagdish N. Sheth (ed.), *Research in Marketing,* vol. 4, JAI Press, Greenwich, Conn., 1981, pp. 223–249.

[28] Findings have not been uniform on this issue. For two recent studies showing differing results see Moore and Lehmann, "Individual Differences" and Kiel and Layton, "Dimensions." Possible explanations for divergent findings include the use of different research products and whether the urgency stems from a felt need or an environmental pressure.

[29] G. D. Harrell and M. D. Hutt, "Crowding in Retail Stores," *MSU Business Topics,* **24**:31–39, Winter 1976.

[30] George Katona and Eva Mueller, "A Study of Purchasing Decisions," in Lincoln H. Clark (ed.), *Consumer Behavior: The Dynamics of Consumer Reaction,* New York University Press, New York, 1955.

[31] Donald F. Cox (ed.), *Risk Taking and Information Handling in Consumer Behavior,* Division of Research, Graduate School of Business, Harvard University, Boston, 1967, pp. 5–6.

[32] The first five risks listed were suggested in Jacob Jacoby and Leon Kaplan, "The Components of Perceived Risk" in M. Venkatesan (ed.), *Proceedings of the Third Annual Conference of the Association for Consumer Research,* Association for Consumer Research, Chicago, 1972, pp. 382–393. The sixth risk was suggested in Ted Roselius, "Consumer Rankings of Risk Reduction Methods," *Journal of Marketing,* **35**:56–61, January 1971.

[33] Roselius, "Consumer Rankings," pp. 57–58.

[34] See William P. Dommermuth and Edward W. Cundiff, "Shopping Goods, Shopping Centers and Selling Strategies," *Journal of Marketing,* **31**:32, October 1967; Dommermuth, "The Shopping Matrix," p. 130; and Jagdish N. Sheth and M. Venkatesan, "Risk-Reduction Processes in Repetitive Consumer Behavior," *Journal of Marketing Research,* **5**:307–310, August 1968.

[35] John A. Howard, *Consumer Behavior: Application of Theory,* McGraw-Hill, New York, 1977, p. 29.

[36] James H. Myers and Mark I. Alpert, "Determinant Buying Attitudes: Meaning and Measurement," *Journal of Marketing,* **32**:14, October 1968.

[37] James F. Engel and Roger D. Blackwell, *Consumer Behavior,* 4th ed., Dryden Press, New York, 1982, p. 418.

[38] Chem L. Narayana and Rom J. Markin, "Consumer Behavior and Product Performance: An Alternative Conceptualization," *Journal of Marketing,* **39**:2, October 1975.

[39] Narayana and Markin, "Consumer Behavior," p. 2.

[40] James R. Bettman, *An Information Processing Theory of Consumer Choice,* Addison-Wesley, Reading, Mass., 1979, pp. 132–133.

[41] James R. Bettman and C. Whan Park, "Effects of Prior Knowledge and Experience and Phase of the Choice Process on Consumer Decision Processes: A Protocol Analysis," *Journal of Consumer Research,* **7**:234–248, 1980.

[42] James R. Bettman and Pradeep Kakkar, "Methods for Implementing Consumer Choice in Product Class Experience," in Subhash C. Jain (ed.), *Research Frontiers in Marketing Dialogues and Directions,* American Marketing Association, Chicago, 1978, pp. 198–201; and James R. Bettman and Michael A. Zins, "Constructive Processes in Consumer Choice," *Journal of Consumer Research,* **4**:75–85, September 1977.

[43] James R. Bettman and C. Whan Park, "Implications of a Constructive View of Choice for the Analysis of Protocol Data: A Coding Scheme for Elements of Choice Processes," in Jerry C. Olson (ed.), *Advances in Consumer Research,* vol. 7, Association for Consumer Research, Ann Arbor, Mich., 1980, pp. 148–153.

[44] Henry Assael, *Consumer Behavior and Marketing Action,* Kent, Boston, 1981, p. 38.

[45] Michael L. Rothschild, "Advertising Strategies for High and Low Involvement Situations," in John C. Maloney and Bernard Silverman (eds.), *Attitude Research Plays for High Stakes* American Marketing Association, Chicago, 1979, pp. 74–93; and Denis A. Lussier and Richard W. Olshavsky, "Task Complexity and Contingent Processing in Brand Choice," *Journal of Consumer Research,* **6**:154–165, September 1979.

[46] Engel and Blackwell, *Consumer Behavior,* pp. 423–424.

[47] Engel and Blackwell, *Consumer Behavior,* p. 335.

[48] Engel and Blackwell, *Consumer Behavior,* p. 334.

[49] Narayana and Markin, "Consumer Behavior."

[50] Myers and Alpert, "Determinant Buying Attitudes," p. 16.

[51] Paul E. Green and Yoram Wind, "New Way to Measure Consumers' Judgments," *Harvard Business Review,* **53**:108–109, July/August 1975.

[52] Donald F. Cox, "The Sorting Rule Model of the Consumer Product Evaluation Process," in Donald F. Cox (ed.), *Risk Taking and Information Handling in Consumer Behavior,* pp. 365–368.

PURCHASING PROCESSES

LEARNING OBJECTIVES

After studying this chapter, you should understand . . .

- What motivates people to shop

- How consumers choose a store and the factors that influence the process

- How various merchandising techniques and personal selling efforts affect in-store purchasing behavior

- That consumer purchasing processes are heavily influenced by the situation surrounding the decision

- The nature of nonstore purchasing processes of consumers

- Why store and brand loyalty are important to marketers

- The implications of consumer impulse purchasing

Arthur Fletcher, marketing manager for the small appliance division of a major manufacturer, has covered all the bases. He has a new product which offers unique benefits and satisfies consumer needs. He has differentiated the product and is ready to build awareness and demand through advertising. He's conducted numerous marketing research and test marketing studies and has properly positioned the product to the target audience. The packaging is eye-catching. Promotion and sampling campaigns have been executed perfectly. The trucks have been loaded at the manufacturer's warehouse. According to the marketing concept, he should succeed. He sits back and waits for the sales figures to roll in. But they don't roll in—they trickle in. Advertising and promotion are beefed up and prices are cut, but to no avail. Eight months after introduction, the product is buried.

An autopsy establishes the cause of death as lack of effective in-store marketing. The product was poorly stocked and displayed and was poorly promoted by retailers. A certain amount of sales assistance was needed, but it wasn't delivered. Consumers required information and wanted to ask questions before buying the product. But the product was distributed to self-service discount stores.

The mistake was in not analyzing the in-store buying process. Fletcher should have worked more closely with the retailers to ensure a higher level of product visibility. If the product had to be sold in a self-service chain, the marketer should have put more buying information on the packaging to compensate for the lack of sales assistance. Special in-store displays may have been needed.

Moral: The marketer's job doesn't stop when the product is loaded on the truck, no matter how well the product has been presold. Today, you have to understand the

20

dynamics of the shopping experience; you have to know how your product is bought. People don't buy products in a vacuum. They buy products in stores, which have dozens of factors which influence sales. That's why marketers must take a more holistic approach and include the in-store environment in their research and strategies.[1]

In this chapter we shall be looking at the actual purchasing process of consumers, seeking to build a better understanding of how consumers make their purchases. Purchasing processes involve not only the purchase decision, but also activities directly associated with the purchase. The purchase-decision stage itself involves selecting a course of action based on the preceding evaluation process. Some of the elements of the purchasing process stage, such as choosing a store, may actually be viewed as part of search and evaluation activities. However, because they are more directly connected with making a purchase, they are best discussed at this point. Thus, we are considering in this chapter the various facets of the consumer purchase environment of which the marketer should be aware in order to attract the chosen segments successfully.

The first topics to be discussed in this chapter will be the motives consumers have for shopping and the matter of consumer store choice. This will be followed by a presentation of research findings regarding both in-store and out-of-store purchasing behavior. Finally, we shall examine some repeat purchasing patterns. Implications of these topics to the marketer will be discussed throughout the chapter.

WHY DO PEOPLE SHOP?

Before discussing the subject of why consumers shop where they do, a more basic question might be asked—Why do people shop? The obvious answer that "they need to purchase something" may not reflect the consumer's actual motivation in each circumstance. It has been suggested that both personal and social motives influence consumer shopping activities. The list in Table 20-1 has been suggested from exploratory research by means of individual in-depth interviews with men and women.

Thus, consumers' motives for shopping are a function of many variables, some of which are unrelated to the actual buying of products. Consequently, retailers need to understand the variety of shopping motives that may be present and incorporate this information into retailing strategy.

CHOOSING A STORE

We all like to think of ourselves as intelligent shoppers. But how do consumers actually make store-choice decisions? Basically, the consumer has certain evaluative store criteria established in her mind and compares these with her perception of a store's characteristics. As a result of this process, stores are categorized as either acceptable or unacceptable and, hence, will be patronized on that basis.

If the resulting shopping experience is favorable, the consumer is reinforced in her learning experience and the matter of store choice will become largely routinized over a period of time.

It is clear from this description that consumers engage in a decision-process approach for store choice as well as for product and brand choices. Thus, much of what we have already said regarding choice processes applies here also. For example, consumers may face complex store-choice decisions, or they may be able to routinize their store decisions. A couple new to an area may face a complex decision process as new store patronage patterns are being developed, particularly for clothing or durables. However, a long-time resident or one facing a convenience-good purchase will probably have the decision process refined to more of a habitual or routinized response.

A summary model of the store-choice process is presented in Figure 20-1. This flowchart depicts the relative directions of influences among variables involved in store-choice behavior. The model indicates that demographic characteristics, lifestyle characteristics, and other buyer characteristics lead to general opinions and activities concerning shopping and search behavior. These consumer characteristics also affect the importance consumers place on store attributes as

TABLE 20-1

Why People Shop

Personal motives

Role playing. Shopping activities are learned behavior and are expected or accepted as part of one's position or role, such as mother or housewife.

Diversion. Shopping can offer a diversion from the routine of daily life and is a form of recreation.

Self-gratification. Shopping may be motivated not by the expected utility of consuming, but by the utility of the buying process itself. Thus, emotional states or moods may explain why (and when) someone goes shopping.

Learning about new trends. Shopping provides consumers with information about trends and movements and product symbols reflecting attitudes and lifestyles.

Physical activity. Shopping can provide a considerable amount of exercise.

Sensory stimulation. Shopping can provide sensory benefits such as looking at and handling merchandise, listening to the sounds (e.g., noise, silence, soft background music) and smelling the scents.

Social motives

Social experience outside the home. Shopping can provide opportunities for seeking new acquaintances, encounters with friends, or just "people watching."

Communication with others having a similar interest. Shopping often affords an opportunity to interact with customers or salespeople having similar interests.

Peer group attraction. Certain stores provide a meeting place where members of a peer group may gather.

Status and authority. Shopping may provide an opportunity to attain a feeling of status and power by being waited on.

Pleasure of bargaining. Shopping may offer the enjoyment of gaining a lower price through bargaining, companion shopping, or visiting special sales.

Source: Adapted from Edward M. Tauber, "Why Do People Shop?," *Journal of Marketing*, **36**:47–48, October 1972, published by the American Marketing Association.

they evaluate store alternatives and the consumer's store perception or store image. The consumer's store attitudes then influence store choice and ultimately the product and brand-choice decision. Satisfaction with the process will lead through feedback to a reinforcement in the store's image, which will then increase the likelihood of continued patronage, that is, greater store loyalty.[2]

In selecting a store to shop, just as in selecting products and brands within stores, the consumer makes use of certain information sources. One research study which assessed the source shoppers use to pick stores found that previous shopping was more important than advertising. Table 20-2 illustrates, for two cities, the information sources consumers used for their last retail shopping trip. This finding suggests that only a limited number of consumers—generally less than half—engage in active external information search when making retail trips. Thus, most consumers appear to be using a routinized behavior pattern. This may mean that retail advertisers may be restricted in potential effectiveness to less than half of the target population.[3]

FACTORS DETERMINING STORE CHOICE

There are several important factors that influence consumer store-choice behavior. Although the influence of these elements differs, depending on such variables as the type of product purchased, the type of store (such as discount, department,

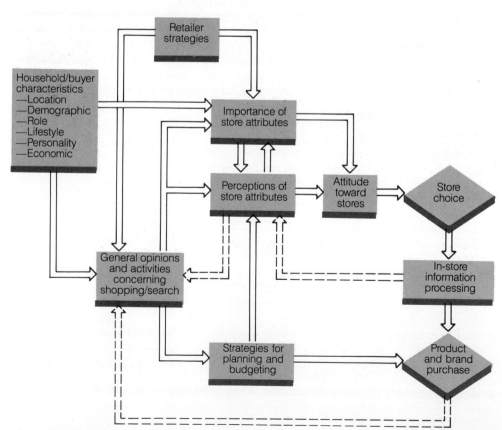

FIGURE 20-1
The sequence of effects in store choice.
Source: Kent B. Monroe and Joseph P. Guiltinan, "A Path-Analytic Exploration of Retail Patronage Influences," *Journal of Consumer Research,*, **2**:21, June 1975.

or other), and the type of consumer, the factors discussed in this section have been found to exert general influence on store choice. They include store location, physical design, assortment, prices, advertising, sales promotion, personnel, and services.

Store Location Location has an obvious impact on store patronage. Generally, the closer consumers are to a store, the greater their likelihood to purchase from that store. The further away consumers are from a store, the greater the number of intervening alternatives, and thus the lower the likelihood to patronize that store. Research on the influence of location on store choice has taken several directions described in the following sections.

INTERCITY CHOICE Marketers have long been interested in the factors that cause consumers outside metropolitan areas to choose city A rather than city B in which to shop. Reilly and Converse conducted research on the drawing power of urban areas on consumers located near these cities. Believing that population and distance were not the causes of consumer store choice but could be used as good substitute variables for all the factors influencing consumers, Reilly developed a "law of retail gravitation" to explain the strength of one city's attraction on consumers living near it.[4] In effect, this law states that two cities attract retail trade from an intermediate city or town in the vicinity of the breaking point (that is, where 50 percent of the trade is attracted to each city) approximately in direct proportion to their population and in inverse proportion to the square of the distances from these two cities to the intermediate town. Reilly tested this law by computing the breaking point between thirty pairs of cities. The predictions were very close to results of actual field studies in which the breaking point was measured.

In applying the laws of retail gravitation it should be kept in mind that they were meant to apply only to two large cities. In addition, the laws apply only to the division of shopping goods trade, and particularly to fashion goods (often referred to as style or specialty goods), because a large part of convenience and

TABLE 20-2

Information Sources Used for Last Retail Shopping Trip

	City A		City B	
	N*	%	N*	%
Habit	276	55.3	313	62.6
Newspaper advertisement	172	34.7	214	42.8
Friend or relative	38	7.6	51	10.2
Mail brochure	36	7.2	42	8.4
Television commercial	28	5.6	51	10.2
Radio commercial	5	1.0	10	2.0
	556	111.4	681	136.0

* Multiple responses allowed.
Source: Elizabeth C. Hirschman and Michael K. Mills, "Sources Shoppers Use to Pick Stores," *Journal of Advertising Research*, **20**:49, February 1980. Reprinted from *Journal of Advertising Research*. Copyright © 1980, by the Advertising Research Foundation.

bulk goods is purchased locally.[5] Although the work by Reilly and Converse has helped marketers to conceptualize intermarket behavior, these laws are incomplete as explanations for store-choice behavior because they ignore such factors as income levels, the character of retailing in the two cities, and consumer preferences.

While the above approach has taken a macro orientation to the examination of intermarket patronage, others have taken a micro approach, which rests on the assumption that consumers have different characteristics and therefore have a differential predisposition to forego secondary costs such as time, money, and effort in selecting one trade area over another. Studies have found that consumers frequently shop out-of-area (*outshoppers*), and they can be distinguished from nonoutshoppers by certain demographic and psychographic characteristics.[6]

INTRACITY CHOICE   As shopping centers developed during the period since 1950, researchers began to investigate their influence on the shopping behavior of consumers. These suburban alternatives to the central downtown shopping district introduced new wrinkles in explaining store choice.

To determine the factors that influence store choice within urban areas, some studies have examined the role of driving time on shopping center preference. Travel times longer than fifteen minutes appear to be a barrier to many shopping center patrons.[7] Those who are willing to drive longer times seem to be attracted by the size of the shopping center.[8] Another study indicates, however, that location of the shopping center is not nearly as important as other variables, such as price, value, variety of product and store, store quality and cleanliness, and friendly sales personnel.[9] This result is contrary to the emphasis placed on distance measures in most site location models.

Other work in the area of shopping center preference has been done by Huff, who developed a model to determine the retail trade area for a shopping center.[10] The model estimates the probability that shoppers in homogeneous geographical segments (such as census tracts or neighborhoods) will visit a particular shopping center for a particular type of product purchase. The two fundamental variables associated with probability of patronage are square feet of floor space in the shopping center and travel time to the center. These variables substitute for population and distance used in Reilly's model.

Although Huff's model achieves a higher level of sophistication than Reilly's, it nevertheless fails to adequately incorporate variables that may influence consumer store preferences.[11] The use of travel time and shopping center size, although important, are not the only factors that influence store choice. However, a model offering refinements to Huff's approach appears to outperform it substantially.[12] Also, Lusch has developed a model of patronage behavior which incorporates key concepts from geography, social psychology, and economics, and it appears to offer a more complete explanation of shopping behavior.[13]

INTERSTORE CHOICE   Store location can also be very influential in shopper choice among competing stores, especially through its effect on store image. For example, stores in attractive surroundings are more likely to be patronized than those in unattractive surroundings. The remainder of this section looks at other components of a store's image and the way in which these factors affect store choice.

Store Design and Physical Facilities   As we noted in Chapter 13, the design characteristics of a store visibly reflect its image and can dramatically influence patronage.[14] Many consumers appear to "size up" a store based on its outward appearance of architecture and signs and hence are drawn to the store or repelled by it, based on their perception of whether this store looks "right" for them. Interior design continues the image-fostering process. Such design features as store layout, aisle placement and width, carpeting, and architecture, as well as physical facilities in a store, including elevators, lighting, air conditioning, and washrooms, influence store assessment by consumers.[15]

Merchandise   This image element has to do with the goods and services offered by a retail outlet. There are five attributes considered to be important here: quality, selection or assortment, styling or fashion, guarantees, and pricing. For example, the product variety and assortment of a store have been found to influence store choice. Consumers prefer stores that offer either a wide variety of product lines, brands, and prices, or substantial depth to their assortment, such as in sizes, colors, and styles, over stores with only medium depth or breadth of assortment.[16]

Advertising and Sales Promotion   Within this category, such influences as advertising, sales promotion, displays, trading stamps, and even symbols and colors are considered important. Retail advertising does not have a consistent impact but instead appears to vary in influence, depending on product and store type. Nevertheless, it is certainly true that retail advertising can be important in fulfilling any of its three goals: (1) to inform consumers, such as for a new store opening, (2) to persuade consumers that they should patronize a certain store or buy a particular brand, and (3) to remind customers of the store that they are appreciated. As we also have learned, advertising can be highly influential in cultivating a store image in consumers' minds.

Personnel   Employees of a retailer also are very instrumental in influencing the store's image. Consumers generally desire to trade where store personnel, particularly salespeople, are perceived as helpful, friendly, and courteous.[17] For example, shopping center preference is strongly influenced by such factors, as demonstrated in one survey of five large metropolitan areas which found salesperson knowledgeability and helpfulness to be an important element in choice for more than 75 percent of those questioned.[18]

Customer Services   Retail stores may offer numerous services in order to attract customers. One scheme classifies services according to those which (1) increase product satisfaction (such as credit, alterations, installation, and shopper information), (2) increase convenience (such as delivery, telephone ordering, and parking), and (3) provide special benefits (such as gift wrapping, product returns, and complaint offices).[19]

Clientele   As we learned earlier, consumers' store choices have much to do with their social-class membership. Consumers will tend to patronize those stores where persons similar to themselves are perceived to be shopping. Thus, an important matching process occurs between the consumer's self-image and the

store's image to influence where people shop, with choices being made of stores that possess images which are similar to the images that consumers perceive of themselves.[20]

Store Atmosphere   This image attribute has to do with ecological design, that is, the quality of the store surroundings. Store atmospherics may affect the consumer's mood state at the point of purchase, which, in turn, may influence purchase behavior, brand evaluation, and information acquisition.[21] The importance of *atmospherics,* defined as the conscious designing of buying environments to produce specific emotional effects in buyers that enhance their purchase probability, is illustrated by the following:

Large department stores often operate a bargain basement selling lower-priced lines of merchandise or marked-down items for customers pursuing bargains. The atmosphere is typically stark and functional, with narrow aisles, harsh lighting, and counters loaded with chaotically arranged merchandise which reinforces the bargain image.[22]

Not only are the nonperson atmospheric elements of the retail store important (such as shelf space, in-store point-of-purchase promotion, lighting, noise, aisle design, and square footage), but also important are the atmospherics created by shoppers within the retail store.[23] One of the intended or unintended products of various current merchandising emphasis is retail crowding. This store atmosphere consequence is a result of high-density shopping environments, such as regional malls and super stores, as well as population shifts and concentrated shopping hours for working families. The result of such perceived crowding is to systematically affect shopping behavior and consumer feelings about retail outlets and shopping trips.[24]

THE IMPORTANCE OF STORE ATTRIBUTES

How important is each of these attributes when customers make store-choice decisions? It depends on the store type. Department store shoppers seem to be concerned about the quality of the store's merchandise, the degree of ease of the shopping process, and post-transaction satisfaction. Grocery shoppers are concerned about the store's merchandise mix, ease of the shopping process, and cleanliness of the store.

THE EFFECT OF STORE IMAGE ON PURCHASING

As indicated in Chapter 13, store image is a complex of tangible or functional factors and intangible or psychological factors that a consumer perceives to be present in a store. It is the way in which the store is defined in the consumer's mind.[25] The various determinants of store choice just discussed are intimately related to a store's image and influence its attracting power. Consequently, retailers need to understand what evaluative criteria consumers use in store choice, how important each criterion is, what image consumers have of the retailer's store, and how this image compares to an ideal image and to competitors' images. Store management must determine the unique market segments they want to attract and then develop a store image useful in influencing patronage by those segments.[26] There is also a need to periodically review desired market segments and the consistency of store image to those segments. Such activities should prove useful in satisfying consumer needs and in maintaining the vitality of the organization.

GENERAL SHOPPER PROFILES

It has been found that consumers tend to shop at different stores, depending partly on their demographic characteristics and their attitudes toward shopping. One useful approach to establishing a customer typology on this basis was that suggested by Stone who has identified four types of shoppers: (1) economic, (2) personalizing, (3) ethical, and (4) apathetic.[27] Although probably no single consumer is adequately described by any of the models, the models do represent composites of actual consumers and their characteristic role orientations.

The *economic consumer* is a close approximation to the classical economist's "economic man." She is quite sensitive to price, quality, and assortment of merchandise. Clerical personnel and the store are viewed merely as instruments of her purchase of goods.

The *personalizing consumer* shops where she is known by name. Strong personal attachments are formed with store personnel, and this personal, often intimate, relationship is crucial to her store-patronage decision.

The *ethical consumer* shops where she feels she "ought" to. That is, she is willing to sacrifice low prices or wide merchandise selection in order to "help the little guy out" or because "the chain store has no heart or soul." She sometimes forms strong attachments with personnel and store owners.

The *apathetic consumer* shops only because she "has" to. Shopping is viewed as an onerous task and one to be completed quickly. Convenient location is her crucial store-selection criterion, and since she is not interested in shopping, she minimizes her expenditure of effort in purchasing products.

What is particularly interesting is that each of these consumer types was characterized by a distinctive pattern of social position and community identification. For example, economic consumers were lower-middle-class housewives with little allegiance to the area. Personalizing consumers had lower social status and a positive allegiance to the local area. Ethical consumers were relatively high in social status and long-time residents in the area, while apathetic consumers were characteristically older women who were also long-time residents. Other consumer taxonomies have also been developed on the basis of shopping orientations, and research is continuing in this field.[28]

STORE-SPECIFIC SHOPPER PROFILES

It has been found that consumers tend to shop at different stores, depending on their demographic/socioeconomic and lifestyle attributes. For instance, one study has characterized those who shop most often at either traditional department stores (such as Foley's or Abraham & Straus), national chain department stores

(such as Sears or J. C. Penney), or discount department stores (such as K mart) with the following results.[29]

> Traditional department store shoppers are described as singles, under and over age 35; older couples with no dependent children; from higher social classes; higher in educational attainment; players of bridge or golf; innovative in apparel purchases; and placing high importance on store's layout and atmosphere, but less importance on merchandise pricing and the savings at sales.

> National chain department store customers were found to be described as most likely to carry credit cards for this type of store, attending movies more regularly, and emphasizing merchandise variety and pricing.

> Discount department store customers can be described as families with children over age 6; being lowest in having traditional or national chain department store credit cards; being from the lower social classes; having low educational attainment, being nonparticipants in social activities such as golf, bridge, or movies; and being most concerned with merchandise pricing and sale savings.

Shoppers may also be characterized in greater detail by retailers of each store type as a useful way of segmenting the market. For example, the marketer may desire to know more about his store's frequent customers and may be able to develop a portrait of the demographic, psychographic, and media patterns of store shoppers.

STORE LOYALTY

The term ''store loyalty'' refers to the consumer's inclination to patronize a given store during a specific period of time. Because consumer patronage results in revenue, store loyalty can be a very important factor influencing the company's profits. Loyal customers will tend to concentrate their purchases in the store and therefore may represent a very profitable market segment if they can be readily identified. Consequently, an important question for the marketer concerns the wisdom and ease of attracting this segment. Store loyalty among consumers can be measured. It varies by store type as well as consumer type. For example, some evidence indicates that loyalty may be higher for supermarkets than for department stores. However, store loyalty also appears to be diminishing.[30]

Several studies have examined the demographic, socioeconomic, and psychographic characteristics of store-loyal shoppers and found that there are patterns of personal characteristics.[31] The generally store-loyal consumer tends to be older and have a lower educational attainment and a lower family income than the store switcher. Psychographically, she tends not to be a fashion opinion leader, style conscious, venturesome in trying new products, urban-oriented, gregarious, or a credit user. However, she does tend to be time-conscious and a radio and television user. Thus, the store-loyal's profile is one of a relatively conservative, inactive, time-conscious, home-town oriented person. She expresses a positive attitude toward local shopping conditions but negative attitudes toward shopping in the nearest large city. Another study finds that highly store-loyal shoppers engage in less comparison search among stores before purchasing, know about the existence of and have visited fewer stores, and concentrate their purchases in a smaller subset of stores than do other consumers.[32]

Obviously, the financial benefit to the retailer of pursuing the store-loyal consumer may be very significant. Not only should the marketer seek to understand the store loyalty characteristics and patterns of customers but also of competitors' customers. Generally, it is important to learn as much as possible about why these families buy where they do. One element of the research should involve measuring the store's image in relation to the images of competitors. As a result of this kind of research, the marketer will be able to identify specific marketing programs to attract more store-loyal shoppers.[33]

IN-STORE PURCHASING BEHAVIOR

Once consumers have selected the stores they will patronize, they must then proceed to consummate the purchase. A number of factors influence consumers' behavior within the store environment. In this section, we shall examine some of the important variables affecting consumer shopping activities within stores.

MERCHANDISING TECHNIQUES

Merchandising techniques have an important influence on consumer shopping behavior.[34] This is particularly true for low-involvement purchase decisions. For example, nearly two out of three supermarket purchase decisions are not specifically planned.[35] Because there is generally little consideration of such purchases until the point of sale, merchandising techniques affecting the consumer in the store are often of great significance in securing purchase. A number of topics are discussed under the umbrella of merchandising techniques, including store layout, displays, product shelving, pricing strategies, branding, and promotional deals.

Store Layout and Traffic Patterns A store's interior is organized in such a manner as to accomplish the firm's merchandising strategy.[36] Retailers sometimes find, however, that their layout and design approach is failing to achieve company objectives. In such cases, a new store design may be necessary. A recent example of such a change is K mart:

K mart's growth through expansion has diminished due to its saturation of stores in all of the top metropolitan areas in the United States. Consequently, the chain is trying for more volume and more profitable volume per store from the cost-conscious consumers attracted to K mart. In order to get K mart customers to spend more, the cavernous buildings of plain design filled with racks, bins, and metal shelves are changing to emphasize the merchandise at least as much as the price signs. Clothing and other goods are now of a higher quality and are being displayed in ways that are intended to stimulate increased impulse buying. In addition, rather than having shoppers being greeted by a popcorn stand as many K marts used to do, shoppers in the new format are met by a jewelry and camera department. Besides cut-rate auto filters and folding lawn chairs, these K marts now handle German wines, designer eyeglass frames, and gourmet cookware.[37]

Traffic pattern studies are very popular with retailers in order to determine where good or bad sales areas are within the store. Supermarkets conduct such research in order to determine optimum layout and placement of goods. Shopper activity is diagramed on these layouts for both density and main direction of traffic for each aisle and for passing and buying rates within the aisles. These statistics show that customers shop a store in different ways. There are also differences in the times spent in the store among different patrons. Consequently, depending on the type of shopper and the length of time spent shopping, different expenditures result.[38] Although use of passing and buying ratios can be helpful in visualizing *what* consumers did, they fail to explain *why* these patterns exist. Thus, further research would need to be conducted by the retailer to understand why such passing and buying ratios exist and how a change in store layout could alter these patterns.

Displays With more than 80 percent of supermarket shoppers making their final buying decisions in the store, point-of-purchase activities by marketers assume an important role.[39] An effective combination of good store layout and attractive displays can change a humdrum retail environment into one that not only is more exciting but also produces more sales. Special displays are used in stores in order to attract shopper attention to one or more products.

The bulk of published research conducted on the effectiveness of displays has come from the supermarket and drugstore fields. Numerous examples of the effectiveness of displays in attracting consumer attention could be cited. The following are representative of the findings:

1 Of 2473 supermarket shoppers interviewed, 38 percent had purchased at least one brand or item they had never before bought. The reason cited most frequently (25 percent) for a first-time purchase was that it had been displayed.[40]

2 A study of 5215 customers in supermarkets, variety stores, drugstores, hardware stores, liquor stores, and service stations found that one-third had purchased at least one of the displayed items.[41]

3 K mart discovered a 251 percent sales increase for sports products featured on continuous loop film in point-of-purchase audiovisual displays.[42]

It is clear from these results that displays are effective in increasing sales.[43] A legitimate question by the reader may be whether the display takes sales away from ordinary shelf sales. It has been found that displays do tend to reduce normal shelf sales. However, net sales of display and shelf combined are usually so far above normal that use of displays appears to be strongly substantiated. Moreover, tests show that there is a rapid return to normal shelf sales once the item is removed from display. This would indicate that customers are not simply stocking up on the item but are actually consuming more. Thus, displays have much evidence to support their continued strong usage as a merchandising tool.

Product Shelving Product shelving has an important influence on consumer behavior. Both the height at which products are displayed and the number of rows presented (facings) can influence sales of products. In addition, the use of shelf signs and extenders can affect sales, as seen above.

SHELF HEIGHT   Because the average shopper selects only thirty-five of the available 7000 or more grocery products during the average twenty-seven-minute shopping trip, it is easy to see why manufacturers clamor for the most visible eye-level shelf position. Tests conducted by *Progressive Grocer* indicate that the most favorable shelf position is generally at eye level, followed in effectiveness by waist level, and knee or ankle level. It has been calculated from *Progressive Grocer* data that sales from waist-level shelves were only 74 percent as great and sales from floor-level shelves were only 57 percent as great as sales from equivalent space allocations on eye-level shelves.[44]

Beyond the physical impossibility of stocking all products at eye level, there are also valid arguments for placing products on lower shelves. Actually, the shelf height dictated for an item is a function of its package size, its normal movement, whether or not it is being advertised, and its market target.

SHELF SPACE   It is crucial for a product to be given enough shelf space to attract the buyer's attention. In order to help ensure this, the science and industry of packaging has mushroomed. Yet, all of the manufacturer's careful packaging efforts can be counteracted by an insufficient amount of shelf space in the store. Without adequate shelf facings, the item will be lost in the mass of 22,000 other facings lining the average supermarket's shelves.

There have been a number of experiments on *shelf space elasticity,* that is, the ratio of relative changes in unit sales to relative change in shelf space. The result of these experiments is that there is a small positive relationship between shelf space and unit sales. However, the relationship is not uniform among products or across stores or intrastore locations.[45] Supermarket tests have concluded that products can have too many as well as too few facings, with both situations resulting in wrong use of space.

An adequate number of facings is especially important for new products. Tests show that doubling shelf facings on new items during their first two to three weeks in stores produced sales increases from 85 percent to 160 percent over stores that stocked the items but did not make any facing adjustments. In addition, fast-moving items tend to react much more dramatically to changes in shelf space than do slow-moving products.

Pricing Strategies   We have already discussed the microeconomic view of consumer reactions (Chapter 2) and the way in which consumers' perceptual processes influence their evaluation of prices (Chapter 13). There are other elements of pricing which can affect consumers in their shopping activities. This section presents two of those influencing strategies.

PRICE AWARENESS   Although consumers have a critical attitude toward the general price level and supermarket prices in particular, they apparently have difficulty recalling the actual price paid for a previously purchased product. For example, only about one shopper in twelve can name the exact price of even one

out of a broad range of common food store items.[46] However, there has been some criticism of the method of such studies,[47] and recent research using a different approach suggests that shoppers are more knowledgeable about prices than earlier studies indicated.[48] Nevertheless, because price is one of the most important criteria in store choice, it is often important for store operations to achieve a low-price image. This is often accomplished by the use of *loss leaders*—products that are heavily advertised and sold at slightly above cost to draw traffic into the store and create an impression of low prices.

PROMOTIONAL PRICING   One form of promotional pricing involves multiple-pricing, the technique by which retailers price items in multiple quantities such as 2 for 25 cents, 3 for 49 cents, and so on. The basic idea of multiple-pricing is to offer the customer a lower price on a quantity purchase. However, the technique has long been complained about by some consumerists as a device that confuses customers more than it saves them money, and one that causes them to buy more than they had planned. Nevertheless, 74 percent of supermarket customers usually buy items priced in multiple-units.[49]

In addition to multiple-pricing, there are other pricing approaches in which the marketer merely cuts the price of an item, offers a "cents-off" special, or provides some sort of rebate on the product as a way of stimulating sales. One consideration in all such approaches, however, is the effectiveness of the price deal for accomplishing marketing objectives.[50] For example, it appears that price promotions can induce brand switching in favor of the dealt brand. It is not clear, however, that consumers remain with the brand once the deal is withdrawn (and, hence, the price is raised).[51] Thus, the marketer may not achieve lasting impact with price deals.

Can the "deal-prone" consumer be identified and segmented? That is, do certain consumers react more favorably than others to deals? Although research results are inconsistent,[52] recent studies indicate that for certain frequently purchased goods, deal-prone households can be identified, and that the key variables are household resource variables (such as home and car ownership). Buyers with higher incomes, and owners of cars and homes are more deal prone.[53]

COUPONING   This is a form of price dealing in which a cents-off coupon is redeemed during purchase, thus reducing the product's price. Couponing has had a sharp, continuing growth over the past few years.[54] In 1985, an estimated 180 billion coupons (2195 per household) were distributed by companies. The face value of these coupons averaged over 25 cents, representing a potential consumer savings of $45 billion.

Cents-off coupons have been criticized on several bases: (1) they discriminate against low-income and minority consumers and shoppers with high time costs, (2) they slow the checkout process, (3) they force food retailers to stock slow-moving items, (4) they impose costs on the food system by generating demand surges, and (5) they distort consumer choices between advertised and private labels.[55] In spite of these criticisms, the practice of couponing continues to grow, and more consumers are using them each year. At least four out of five households use them as an integral part of their shopping.[56] A consumer's decision to redeem a coupon is based on coupon characteristics, characteristics of the purchase, brand loyalty, and the present promotional conditions. Consumers attempt to strike a balance between their needs for economizing and reducing shopping time and effort.[57]

Although coupons are generally claimed to influence consumers to try new products or improve the position of older products, it is hoped they will result in long-term loyalty once trial occurs.[58] However, most coupons have been shown to result in short-term sales gains only,[59] although such gains may be impressive.[60]

Who uses coupons? Coupon usage is greater among middle- and upper-income groups and those with higher educational levels. Such refunds also attract larger and older families. In addition, redemption varies by region, with 81 percent of households in the northeast redeeming them, compared with only 68 percent in the southeast.[61]

Packaging   One of the most important point-of-sale influences is the package, including graphics, product information contained on the package, and the physical design of the package. In addition, the package can be extremely instrumental in the success of store displays. Thus, it is a basic ingredient in attracting the shopper's attention while in the store—the marketer's "silent salesman."

Brand Choice: National versus Private   For a number of years now, there has been a "battle" between manufacturers' national brands and distributors' private brands for brand predominance in certain product categories. To the winner go greater product sales and profits. Consequently, it is important, particularly from the marketer's viewpoint, to know whether there are any distinguishing characteristics between private- and national-brand customers which might make possible their effective market segmentation.

POSITION OF PRIVATE BRANDS   The competitive position of private brands differs from industry to industry. For example, although they account for less than 10 percent of sales in portable appliances, private brands control more than 50 percent of the market in shoes. In grocery and drug stores, private brands have less than a 30-percent share of the market. As for the number of consumers who purchase private label merchandise, the figures are quite large. Research by A. C. Nielsen found that 80 percent of buyers of grocery products have purchased private brands.[62] Nevertheless, based on the evidence available, no significant swing away from national brands to private brands is expected to occur.[63]

Although it has been shown that consumers view private and national brands differently, it is not clearly known what consumer characteristics differentiate between private- and national-brand users.[64] Thus, more research is needed to determine the extent to which such buyers are different, how they can be reached, and what the best marketing approaches might be.

GENERIC BRANDS   Generic or "no-name" brands are a relatively new feature in grocery retailing. Pioneered by the French supermarket chain, Carrefour, these products are easily distinguishable due to their basic and plain packaging characteristics coupled with the attribute of primary emphasis on the contents of the package rather than on brand name. Early introductions were often marketed in stark white packages with bold black content labeling. This approach contrasts

with private-label merchandise, which more closely resembles manufacturers' brands in that a brand name is stressed in the primary labeling with secondary emphasis given to content.[65]

Of course, price is an important factor in generics' success. They usually sell for 30 to 40 percent less than major advertised brand prices, and some sell for 20 percent less than supermarket private-label prices. As a result of this price difference, it appears that generics' gains have come more at the expense of name brands' market share than the private-label business.[66]

Who buys generic products? Studies tend to suggest the following general profile: larger families; shoppers with large weekly grocery expenditures; better-educated customers; those aged 35 to 44; those in middle stages of the family life cycle; less brand-loyal customers, and less one-store oriented, mildly innovative and venturesome customers; those who claim to be less-influenced by advertisements.[67] Compared to infrequent purchasers and nonpurchasers, however, high-volume generic buyers are a relatively burdened group, who tend to rent rather than to own their homes and who are likely to have a young child, a relatively low income, and restricted time for shopping trips, with a preference for discount stores.[68] Better economic conditions apparently result in a drop in generics' sales.[69]

Some retailers are dramatically increasing the selling power of generics by creating a ''brand'' identity and adding color to the package. The ''brand'' may be viewed as a cut above generics yet at a better price than private and national labels.

Other In-Store Merchandising Activities In-store merchandising is continually changing as marketers seek to discover new ways of reaching consumers with their promotional messages close to the point of purchase. In-store advertising is growing rapidly as marketers place messages on everything from shopping carts to store directories and shelves.[70]

PERSONAL SELLING EFFECTS

We have been primarily discussing in-store purchasing behavior for items that are sold via self-service. However, there are also many product purchase situations in which customers interact with salespeople.

Personal selling in which a salesperson interacts with a consumer is referred to as a ''dyad.'' Such an influence may be very strong, as seen in our earlier discussion of interpersonal influence and social group behavior. From a consumer-behavior viewpoint, however, little is known about what factors make this process a success. Studies of salespeople have generally sought to learn what main characteristics lead to success, and have assumed homogeneity among prospects. Usually, researchers point to a bundle of personality variables as predictors of good sales performance. More recently, however, researchers have begun to view selling as dyadic interaction in terms of the characteristics not only of the salesperson but also of the buyer, and how the two parties react to each other.[71]

As this recent research suggests, it appears that rather than focusing merely on the salesperson's traits, the marketer would do well to also consider the customer's traits. Careful research into market-segment characteristics and needs may result in more effective sales management. By hiring salespeople who more closely match desired customers and preparing them better to perform effectively in the dyadic interaction process, the firm may achieve more success in the market.[72]

THE SITUATIONAL NATURE OF CONSUMER DECISIONS

One of the most important factors influencing the choice and purchasing process is the situation surrounding the consumer's decision. Depending on the set of circumstances faced by the consumer in making a purchase, behavior may take any number of directions. Thus, consumer behavior may be said to depend largely on the situation. For instance, the type of car the consumer may purchase for commuting might well differ from the type of car bought for vacationing. The brand of canned ham bought to serve at a dinner party for one's boss may be different from the brand bought for everyday consumption. The type of clothes bought for gardening and landscape work at home are likely to be different from those worn at a neighborhood bridge party.

In these and countless other decisions, consumers may base their purchase acts on the situation attached to those acts. A *situation,* therefore, may be viewed as comprising all of those factors particular to a time and place of observation which do not follow from a knowledge of personal (intraindividual) and stimulus (choice alternative) attributes and which have a demonstrable and systematic effect on current behavior.[73]

Based upon this definition, five groups of situational characteristics may be identified:[74]

1 *Physical surroundings* are the most readily apparent features of a situation, including geographical and institutional location, decor, sounds, aromas, lighting, weather, and visible configurations of merchandise or other materials surrounding the stimulus object.

2 *Social surroundings* include such factors as other persons present, their characteristics, their apparent roles, and interpersonal interactions.

3 *Temporal perspective* is a dimension of situations which may be specified in units ranging from time of day to season of the year. Time may also be measured relative to a past or future event for the situational participant, such as time since the last purchase.

4 *Task definition* includes an intent or requirement to select, shop for, or obtain information about a general or specific purchase. It may also reflect different buyer and user roles anticipated by the individual. For example, a consumer shopping for a small appliance as a wedding gift for a friend is in a different situation than would be the case in shopping for a small appliance for personal use.

5 *Antecedent states* are momentary moods (such as acute anxiety, pleasantness, hostility, and excitation) or momentary conditions (such as cash on hand,

fatigue, and illness) rather than chronic individual traits, and they are immediately antecedent to the current consumer situation.

Patterns have been found among consumer segments in the type of products bought for certain situations, ranging across snack foods, beverages, leisure activities, fast foods, and numerous additional items.[75]

Although the situation is an important influence in the purchase and consumption decision, it may frequently be overriden by product considerations. For example, the degree of brand loyalty a consumer exhibits may be very influential in purchase decisions. A highly brand-loyal consumer will tend to purchase a favorite brand time after time no matter what the variation in the consumption situation. Thus, strong brand loyalty results in weaker situational influence. Another factor tempering situational influence is product involvement. Research indicates that when product involvement is low, the situation tends to determine behavior; however, in high-product-involvement cases, situational factors are not as important.[76]

NONSTORE PURCHASING PROCESSES

Although the vast bulk of consumer purchasing processes now take place in stores, there is a growing amount of in-home shopping. Marketers usually refer to this approach as *nonstore marketing* or *direct marketing*. It includes ordering via direct response TV, cable TV, catalogues, party and club plans, door-to-door selling, video cassettes, Teletext, direct mail, and other developing electronic technologies. One of the hottest trends is home shopping via TV.

Millions of American households have moved beyond one-stop shopping into nonstop shopping. These consumers are able to view a continuous stream of products on their TV sets from such sources as Home Shopping Network (HSN) or Cable Value Network (CVN). These live, twenty-four-hour, seven-day-a-week shopping programs use cable-TV channels or have their own UHF stations. The programs feature salespeople who promote all sorts of merchandise. Viewers can call toll-free numbers and charge to their credit card whenever the urge to buy strikes them, for such things as jewelry, clothing, tools, electronics, and Bibles, without ever leaving their TV set.[77]

THE SIGNIFICANCE OF NONSTORE BUYING

According to U.S. census retail trade statistics, in-home buying is increasingly urban and has been growing appreciably faster than total store sales and general merchandise sales for some time. Due to classification and measurement problems of the census, however, there is not a clear picture of the significance of this activity. Estimates of nonstore buying range from 2 to 12 percent of total retail sales. Mail-order retailers now distribute 20 to 25 billion catalogs each year. The 10,000 businesses of varying size in the mail order field account for an estimated $35 billion in sales annually.

The seeds of this change toward telecommunication-based merchandising are several:[78]

■ An increased emphasis on consumer self-identity, with individuality expressed through goods and services, which leads to a desire to consider more items than a store can display

PURCHASING
PROCESSES

■ A higher proportion of working women who have less time to shop

■ Increased leisure-time pursuits of self-development and creative expression, which allow less time to shop from store to store

■ Greater demand for specialty products and services that are difficult to get in most shopping centers

■ Rapid acceptance of new technology such as videotape recorders, home computers, and automated bank-teller machines, which means that more consumers are becoming technologically competent for new merchandising approaches

■ Increased popularity of such recent nonstore innovations as pay-by-phone, special-interest mail-order catalogs, and televised direct marketing, resulting in consumers who are becoming psychologically prepared for new shopping forms

However, in spite of these favorable conditions leading to a receptive environment for new video-based marketing approaches, the situation is not all positive.[79] A survey by Benton & Bowles, Inc. indicates that only 10 percent of consumers are very interested in shopping at home via two-way television. The major reasons consumers express in opposition to more active involvement in new video technologies are:[80]

1   They like to see products "in person" before they buy.

2   They "just don't need it."

3   They like to "go out" to shop.

4   They want to relax while watching TV and don't want to push buttons.

5   They feel they might be tempted to buy products they don't really need.

6   They fear that being "hooked up" to a computer would invade their privacy.

CHARACTERISTICS OF PURCHASERS[81]

There are a number of differences that are notable between in-home shoppers and other shoppers. These differences may be classified according to socioeconomic status, race, wife's employment status, and geographic location. It must be pointed out that, because of methodological differences between studies and the limited amount of research, these results are not conclusive.

1   *"Upscale" households.* With few exceptions, in-home shoppers are described as above-average in socioeconomic status. These differences increase with in-home shopping intensity and are especially pronounced among households utilizing several in-home shopping modes.

2   *Racial patterns.* It appears that black and white households differ little on total in-home shopping expenditures or frequency. However, shopping mode differences do exist. For example, blacks do less mail-order buying than do whites at similar income levels.

3 *Working wives*. It might be expected that working women restricted in shopping time flexibility would be especially likely to take advantage of in-home shopping. However, this relationship has not been supported so far. In fact, some studies have found employed women even more willing to shop in stores than women not employed outside the home.

4 *Geographic location*. There is limited evidence that geographical location within a trading area influences in-home shopping, with those in rural areas utilizing it more than their urban counterparts do. Its use seems to be higher where there is greater retail inaccessibility and inadequacy.

IN-HOME SHOPPING MOTIVATIONS

There are several motivational and lifestyle factors which influence in-home buying. The most important ones are discussed in this section.

Convenience   Shopping convenience is probably the most important motivator in consumer decisions to shop at home and is the one so often stressed by the industry. High convenience orientation does explain some but not all in-home shopping motivation. For example, phone shoppers seem especially convenience-oriented, while catalog buyers not only want shopping convenience, but also merchandise assortment and uniqueness, competitive prices, and useful descriptive shopping information. Mail order's strength today seems to lie less in its shopping convenience than its ability to offer new, unique, personalized products.

The Risk of Buying   In spite of the obvious advantages of shopping at home, the high perceived risk that is associated with buying by description partially explains why many consumers are hesitant to use this particular technique. Research on telephone and mail-order shopping supports this hypothesis.

Lifestyle   Active in-home buyers are more cosmopolitan, style- and value-conscious, convenience-oriented, and generally are more demanding shoppers than are other consumers. They are more flexible in shopping style, visit stores more frequently, and view shopping and shopping risk more positively. Their in-home buying is discretionary, often impulse- or convenience-oriented, and they use a variety of in-home buying methods and sources.

One advertising agency's lifestyle analysis of direct response purchasers found that those characterized as "impulse" buyers and those who found it "difficult to get to the store" were the most attractive.[82] For example, of the fifteen product categories in which direct response sales are significant, the "impulse" shopper ranks above average in nine of them.

Personality characteristics found among in-home shoppers indicate that they tend to be more self-assured, venturesome, and cosmopolitan in outlook and in shopping behavior.

MARKETING IMPLICATIONS

Designing a promotional mix appealing to at-home shoppers is a challenging task. The themes and copy should be consistent with this group's lifestyle, such as emphasizing their venturesome, self-assured, and cosmopolitan orientation. Both

in message design and layout, catalogs and circulars offered to this group should be carefully developed so as to be congruent with the images the marketer wants to project. To overcome hesitancy among buyers due to perceived risk associated with at-home shopping, promotional materials should provide buyers with sufficient information about products offered (perhaps including testimonials from satisfied users where appropriate) and safeguard the purchaser by offering easy, guaranteed return privileges.

PURCHASING PATTERNS

The final section of this chapter focuses on two important purchasing patterns. We shall examine (1) the extent to which consumers develop repeat purchasing patterns and (2) the extent to which purchases are unplanned. These subjects will be discussed in the context of brand loyalty and impulse purchasing.

BRAND LOYALTY

Brand loyalty is a topic of much concern to all marketers.[83] Every company seeks to have a steady group of unwavering customers for its product or service. Because research suggests that an increase in market share is related to improved brand loyalty, marketers are understandably concerned with this element. Thus brands that seek to improve their market positions have to be successful both in getting brand users and in increasing their loyalty.[84] The significance of brand loyalty is illustrated in the following examples:

In the cereal market, people switch brands as often as ten times a year, and a new brand has only six months to establish itself before losing out to a more popular competitor. Consequently, cereal brands scrap hard for shelf space and advertise loudly to catch consumer attention to be the one in three new brands that survives.[85]

Brand loyalty in big-ticket durable purchases is relatively low (only one out of three repurchases the same brand in a particular product category), although category repurchases comprise two of every three sales in a product category, on average.[86]

Thus, brand loyalty is a challenging goal each marketer seeks to attain; yet, many have been concerned over an apparent decrease in brand loyalty over the last decade, attributed to several factors:

- Sophisticated advertising appeals and heavy media support
- "Parity" of products in form, content, and communication
- Price competition from private and generic labels
- Sales promotion tactics of mass displays, coupons, and price specials that appeal to consumer impulse buying
- General fickleness of consumers in buying behavior
- High inflation of the late 1970s and early 1980s
- Growth of new products competing for shelf space and consumer attention

However, research indicates that overall brand loyalty has remained virtually stable over the past ten years, while many individual brands have had declines and gains in loyalty.[87] Table 20-3 illustrates categories of products having high, medium, and low loyalty.

The Nature of Brand Loyalty   A study of repeat purchase behavior for nine products based on a *Chicago Tribune* purchase panel suggested that there were four brand loyalty patterns, as follows:[88]

1   *Undivided loyalty* is exhibited by families purchasing brand A in the following sequence: A A A A A.

2   *Divided loyalty* is exhibited by the family purchasing brands A and B in the following sequence: A B A B A B.

3   *Unstable loyalty* is shown by the family buying brands A and B in the following sequence: A A A B B B.

4   *No loyalty* is shown by families buying brands A, B, C, D, E, and F in the following sequence: A B C D E F.

On the basis of the products studied, it was concluded that the majority of consumers tend to purchase a favorite brand or set of brands. Although the degree of loyalty varied by product, the percentage of consumers exhibiting some brand loyalty was rather high. A definite relationship was discovered between strength of brands and nature of the loyalty shown. Loyalty appears to be high for well-

TABLE 20-3

Who Can Be Loyal to a Trash Bag?

When generic products were coming on strong a few years ago, J. Walter Thompson, the New York–based ad agency, gauged consumer's loyalty to brands in eighty product categories. It found that the leader in market share was not necessarily the brand-loyalty leader. At that time, Bayer aspirin was the market share leader among headache remedies, but Tylenol had the most loyal following.

Thompson measured the degree of loyalty by asking people whether they'd switch for a 50% discount. Cigarette smokers most often said no, making them the most brand-loyal of consumers (see table). Film is the only one of the top five products that the user doesn't put in his mouth—so why such loyalty? According to Edith Gilson, Thompson's senior vice-president of research, 35-mm film is used by photography buffs, who are not your average snapshooter: "It's for long-lasting emotionally valued pictures, taken by someone who has invested a lot of money in his camera." Plenty of shoppers will try a different cola for 50% off, and most consumers think one plastic garbage bag or facial tissue is much like another.

High-loyalty products	Medium-loyalty products	Low-loyalty products
Cigarettes	Cola drinks	Paper towels
Laxatives	Margarine	Crackers
Cold remedies	Shampoo	Scouring powder
35-mm film	Hand lotion	Plastic trash bags
Toothpaste	Furniture polish	Facial tissue

Brand names matter more in some products than in others, researchers find.

Source: Anne B. Fisher, "Coke's Brand-Loyalty Lesson," *Fortune*, August 5, 1985, p. 46. Courtesy of FORTUNE Magazine, 1985.

established products in which little or no changes have occurred, and low where product entries are frequent.

Various other studies have used these and other measures of brand loyalty and have generally concluded that brand loyalty exists and is a relatively widespread phenomenon.[89] Most studies, however, suffer from a lack of comparability because of differing conceptions of brand loyalty. Until consumer-behavior researchers agree on a common definition, there will continue to be difficulty synthesizing results. Some researchers have suggested a useful definition of brand loyalty that recognizes that true brand-loyal consumers should exhibit not only a high degree of repeat purchasing but also a *favorable attitude* toward the purchased brand. Perhaps the most complete definition recognizing this position describes brand loyalty as (1) the biased (nonrandom) (2) behavioral response (purchase) (3) expressed over time (4) by a decision-making unit (5) with respect to one or more alternative brands out of a set of such brands, and is (6) a function of psychological (decision-making, evaluative) processes.[90]

Factors Explaining Brand Loyalty Although numerous studies attempting to explain brand loyalty have been largely inconclusive to this point, the following results appear to be indicated:

1 Some socioeconomic, demographic, and psychological variables are related to brand loyalty (when extended definitions are used) but tend to be product-specific rather than general across products.

2 Loyalty behavior of an informal group leader influences the behavior of other group members.

3 Some consumer characteristics are related to store loyalty, which in turn is related to brand loyalty.

4 Brand loyalty is positively related to perceived risk and market structure variables such as the extensiveness of distribution and market share of the dominant brand, but is inversely related to the number of stores shopped.[91]

The Effect of Out-of-Stock Conditions A potentially important influence on brand loyalty is the possibility of brand substitution. It has been found that between 19 percent and perhaps as much as 33 percent of shoppers presold by an advertising campaign change their minds and switch to another brand when they get inside the supermarket.[92] An important reason for brand substitution is an out-of-stock (OOS) condition. To appreciate the impact out-of-stock conditions may have on the retailer, consider that for a moderate-sized supermarket these costs have been estimated to run between $13,000 and $15,000 per year.[93]

Although the result of OOS conditions appears to be significant, little research has been done on its effect on brand loyalty. The A. C. Nielsen Company, however, has provided some indication of the extent of brand substitution in the supermarket. A large survey of shoppers found that 25 percent left the store with some portion of their wants unsatisfied because of OOS conditions among desired brands or package sizes. Although 42 percent of the consumers refused to accept a substitute brand, 58 percent were willing to do so. The proportion of consumers

refusing to accept a substitute brand varied among products studied, from 23 percent for toilet tissue to 62 percent for toothpaste. Among consumers who failed to find their desired package size, 52 percent bought another size of the same brand, while 30 percent bought another brand, and 18 percent would not accept a substitute.[94]

Thus, customer reactions to OOS conditions may be either short- or long-run in nature, including switching brands, substituting product class, shopping at other stores, postponing purchase, or altering choice behavior for later decisions.[95]

Marketing Implications Several marketing implications flow from our discussion of brand loyalty. The first question, of course, for the marketer attempting to attract more brand-loyal customers is the feasibility of segmenting this group. That is, are these consumers identifiable? As we have just seen from the correlates of brand loyalty, those customers generally do not appear to differ significantly from other customers on most segmentation bases. The marketer may be more successful, however, in discerning unique characteristics of customers loyal to his particular brand or product. The results of such an analysis may provide him with useful insights for developing attractive marketing strategies.

Wind has proposed the matrix, presented in Figure 20-2, incorporating attitudes and behavior by which the marketer may assess the brand's vulnerability. It provides some indication of the magnitude of exposure. In the first two rows, the more the brand is disliked, the greater its vulnerability. In the third row, the greater the brand is liked, the more vulnerable are customers to competitive brands. Of course, the marketer would need to identify the relevant reasons for consumers liking or disliking the brand. With such information, insights may be gained into not only the size of the loyal and vulnerable segments but also the magnitude and nature of customers' vulnerability. Marketing programs may then be developed aimed at reducing buyers' vulnerability while attracting customers of competing brands.[96]

These various goals of the marketer may necessitate different marketing

FIGURE 20-2
The vulnerability matrix.
Source: Adapted from Yoram Wind, "Brand Loyalty and Vulnerability," in Arch G. Woodside, Jagdish N. Sheth, and Peter D. Bennett (eds.), *Consumer and Industrial Buying Behavior*, North-Holland, New York, 1977, p. 314. Reprinted by permission. Copyright © 1977 by Elsevier Science Publishing Company, Inc.

		Attitude toward this brand		
		"Like" it	"Indifferent" to it and others	"Dislike" it
Purchase pattern with respect to this brand	Buy it regularly	"Loyal" to it 1	Customers of this brand who are vulnerable to competitors 2	3
	Buy it occasionally	Customers of this brand who are vulnerable to competitors 4	5	6
	Do not buy it	Customers of this brand who are vulnerable to competitors 7	8	Unlikely target for this brand 9

strategies. For instance, increasing brand loyalty of present customers may necessitate better after-sale service, while attracting new customers to become steady users may require certain inducements such as price discounts. Thus, the varying ranges of brand loyalty that the marketer faces point to different competitive actions. For less highly committed consumers, a catchy advertising message, coupon offer, free sample, point-of-purchase display, or attractive package could cause a switch to the marketer's brand. This is the reason we see so much of these sorts of activities and the resultant brand switching in certain product groups (such as foods, soaps, and detergents). The packaged consumer goods field can generally be considered highly dynamic in this regard.

In order to induce brand switching among customers who are more highly loyal, the marketer is likely to require more fundamental changes in consumer perceptions and attitudes. Therefore, significant revisions in product image are often necessary, frequently accomplished through revamped promotional programs.

Advertising decisions are usually geared to the loyalty situation that confronts the brand. It is suggested that if brand loyalty is high, the advertiser has a good case for "investment" expenditures where large amounts are expended over short periods of time to attract new users, because continued purchases after the advertising has been curtailed will "amortize" the advertising investment. Where a low degree of brand loyalty exists in the product class, advertising expenditures should be made at a fairly steady rate on a pay-as-you-go basis, with demonstrated returns in extra sales equal to or greater than the extra advertising costs.[97]

Finally, it is clear that both retailers and manufacturers need to strive to avoid out-of-stock conditions, which might lead not only to reduced sales but also to less store and brand loyalty.

IMPULSE PURCHASING

Impulse buying, or as some marketers prefer to call it—unplanned purchasing— is another consumer purchasing pattern. As the term implies, the purchase was not specifically planned. In this section, we will find that the process is rather widespread and may have significant implications for the marketer.

The Nature of Impulse Purchasing It is difficult for marketers to agree on a definition of impulse buying. Four types of impulse purchases have been cited:

1 *Pure impulse.* A novelty or escape purchase which breaks a normal buying pattern

2 *Suggestion impulse.* A shopper having no previous knowledge of a product sees the item for the first time and visualizes a need for it.

3 *Reminder impulse.* A shopper sees an item and is reminded that the stock at home needs replenishing, or recalls an advertisement or other information about the item and a previous decision to purchase.

4 *Planned impulse.* A shopper enters the store with the expectation and intention of making some purchases on the basis of price specials, coupons, and the like.[98]

While most marketing research has treated impulse purchasing simply as "unplanned," some maintain that it is an irrational process in which the urge to gratify an impulse triumphs over the rational parts of the mind. In this view, five critical elements seem to distinguish impulsive from nonimpulsive consumer behavior. First the consumer has a sudden and spontaneous desire to act, involving a marked divergence from previous behavior. Second, this sudden desire to buy puts the consumer in a state of psychological disequilibrium where he feels temporarily out of control. Third, the consumer may experience psychological conflict and struggle weighing the immediate satisfaction against the long-term consequences of the purchase. Fourth, consumers reduce their cognitive evaluation of product features. And fifth, consumers often buy impulsively without any regard for future consequences.

It has been suggested that the explanations of why consumers engage in such impulsive buying are that they do not realize the consequences of their behavior; that they are compelled by some force to buy even though they realize the dire consequences; and that in spite of the ultimate problems of buying, they are more intent on fulfilling present satisfaction.[99]

The Extent of Impulse Buying   There are several studies which have indicated the significant and growing trend toward unplanned purchasing. Here are some of the conclusions on the extent of impulse buying:

> More than 33 percent of all purchases in variety and drugstores are unplanned.[100]
>
> One-half of buying decisions in supermarkets are unplanned.[101]
>
> Thirty-nine percent of all department store shoppers and 62 percent of all discount store shoppers purchased at least one item on an unplanned basis.[102]

These statements are somewhat deceiving in that no distinction is made between the various kinds of impulse purchases possible for consumers. Although many consumers may not use a shopping list, their product and brand purchases are certainly rational (as we have defined it) and most probably fit into the reminder and planned impulse categories rather than the pure and suggestion impulse types.

The important point for marketers is that there is a large amount of decision making occuring at the point of purchase. Thus, as far as the retail decision maker is concerned, impulse buying can be pragmatically defined as purchasing resulting from a decision to buy after the shopper has entered the store (or perhaps simply turned on their television at home to shop via cable).[103]

Factors Influencing Impulse Purchases   The rather limited amount of research on unplanned purchases indicates that there are several product, marketing, and consumer characteristics which appear to be related to the process. Product characteristics that may influence greater impulse purchasing are those low in price, for which there is a marginal need, having a short product life, small in size or light in weight, and easy to store.

Marketing factors influencing impulse purchasing include mass distribution in self-service outlets with mass advertising and point-of-sale materials, and prominent display position and store location.[104] Few consumer personality, demographic, or socioeconomic characteristics have been shown to be related to the rate of impulse buying. However, the percentage of unplanned supermarket purchases appears to increase with (1) size of the grocery bills, (2) number of products purchased, (3) major shopping trips, (4) frequency of product purchase, (5) absence of a shopping list, and (6) number of years married.[105] Among department store shoppers, age and race may influence the amount of impulse purchasing.[106]

Marketing Implications   The unplanned nature of much purchasing behavior today places a greater burden on manufacturers and retailers. The extent to which shoppers buy on impulse and without written lists puts a strong emphasis on the various kinds of in-store merchandising and personal selling stimuli which the marketer may use.

Managers of retail outlets need to carefully understand the types and extent of occurrence of impulse purchases in order to better plan store layout, merchandise and display location and allocation, and so on. Manufacturers also could benefit from an improved understanding of impulse purchasing by determining how much in-store product information may be necessary to provide on or with their products.

MANAGERIAL REFLECTIONS

For our product or service situation . . .

1   What personal and social motives seem to be relevant in our consumers' shopping activities?

2   What factors are most important to buyers' store choice decisions and patronage behavior?

3   Are we utilizing the most effective in-store merchandising techniques to inform and attract shoppers?

4   Are personal selling efforts carefully planned to succeed with our chosen market target?

5   What circumstances (situational conditions) surrounding the buying decision have a systematic influence on consumers' purchasing process and choice behavior?

6   What is the nature of nonstore purchasing activities among our customers?

7   To what extent have we achieved brand loyalty among buyers, and what is our degree of vulnerability on this dimension?

8   Have we considered consumers' shopping environment for opportunities to influence impulse purchasing?

DISCUSSION TOPICS

1   Describe the types of personal and social motives consumers may have for shopping.

2   How does store image influence consumer purchasing?

3   What implications do the factors of store layout, displays, and product shelving have for customer shopping?

4   How may pricing strategies affect consumer purchases?

5   Describe the generic brand buyer.

6   Describe the five situational characteristics surrounding consumer-behavior decisions.

7   What are the characteristics and motivations of in-home shoppers?

8   What is the nature and significance of brand loyalty to the marketer?

PROJECTS

1   Visit competing discount houses, supermarkets, department stores, or specialty shops in your area and describe the image you have of each store. What factors account for the image differences? For the poorest image store, design a strategy for upgrading its image.

2   Bring to class two print advertisements illustrating different usage situations for the same product type. How may the market segments appealed to in these ads differ?

3   Keep a record of your product purchases for a period of time. How brand loyal are you? What factors seem to explain your degree of brand loyalty? How does your pattern and explanation differ from other students in the class?

NOTES

1 Adapted from Bernie Whalen, "Retail Customer Service: Marketing's Last Frontier," *Marketing News,* March 15, 1985, p. 16, published by the American Marketing Association.

2 Kent B. Monroe and Joseph B. Guiltinan, "A Path-Analytic Exploration of Retail Patronage Influences," *Journal of Consumer Research,* **2**:19–28, June 1975.

3 Elizabeth C. Hirschman and Michael K. Mills, "Sources Shoppers Use to Pick Stores," *Journal of Advertising Research,* **20**:47–51, February 1980.

4 William J. Reilly, *Methods for the Study of Retail Relationships,* University of Texas, Bureau of Business Research, Austin, Tex., Research Monograph, No. 4, 1929.

5 Paul D. Converse, "New Laws of Retail Gravitation," *Journal of Marketing,* **14**:379–384, October 1949.

6 See, for example, Robert O. Herrmann and Leland L. Beik, "Shoppers' Movements Outside Their Local Retail Area," *Journal of Marketing,* **23**:49–51, October 1968; John R. Thompson, "Characteristics and Behavior of Outshopping Consumers," *Journal of Retailing,* **47**:70–80, Spring 1971; and Fred D. Reynolds and William R. Darden, "Intermarket Patronage: A Psychographic Study of Consumer Outshoppers," *Journal of Marketing,* **36**:50–54, October 1972.

7 See, for example, James R. Lumpkin, Jon M. Hawes, and William R. Darden, "Shopping Patterns of the Rural Consumer: Exploring the Relationship between Shopping Orientations and Outshopping,"

Journal of Business Research, **14**:63–81, 1986; and James A. Brunner and John L. Mason, "The Influence of Driving Time upon Shopping Center Preference," *Journal of Marketing,* **32**:57–61, April 1968.

[8] William E. Cox, Jr. and Ernest F. Cooke, "Other Dimensions Involved in Shopping Center Preference," *Journal of Marketing,* **34**:12–17, October 1970.

[9] James W. Gentry and Alvin C. Burns, "How 'Important' Are Evaluative Criteria in Shopping Center Patronage?" *Journal of Retailing,* **53**:77, Winter 1977–1978.

[10] David L. Huff, "A Probabilistic Analysis of Consumer Spatial Behavior," in William S. Decker (ed.), *Emerging Concepts in Marketing,* American Marketing Association, Chicago, 1962, pp. 443–461. See also Art Palmer, "Survey Discloses Shifts in Shopping Center Choices," *Chain Store Age Executive,* May 1985, pp. 68–78; Art Palmer, "Retail Image Dimensions and Consumer Preferences," in Naresh K. Malhotra (ed.), *Proceedings,* Academy of Marketing Science, Miami Beach, Fla., 1985, pp. 11–15.

[11] For a discussion of problem areas in the Huff model, see David L. Huff and Richard R. Batsell, "Conceptual and Operational Problems with Market Share Models of Consumer Spatial Behavior," in Mary Jane Schlinger (ed.), *Advances in Consumer Research,* vol. 2, Association for Consumer Research, Chicago, 1975, pp. 165–172; Joseph Barry Mason, "Retail Market Area Shape and Structure: Problems and Prospects," in Schlinger (ed.), *Advances;* and Louis P. Bucklin, "The Concept of Mass in Intra-urban Shopping," *Journal of Marketing,* **31**:37–42, January–February 1958.

[12] Chow Hou Wee and Michael R. Pearle, "Patronage Behavior Toward Shopping Areas: A Proposed Model Based on Huff's Model of Retail Gravitation," in E. Hirschman and M. Holbrook (eds.), *Advances in Consumer Research,* vol. 12, Association for Consumer Research, Provo, Utah, 1985, pp. 592–597.

[13] Robert F. Lusch, "Integration of Economic Geography and Social Psychological Models of Patronage Behavior," in Kent B. Monroe (ed.), *Advances in Consumer Research,* vol. 8, Association for Consumer Research, Ann Arbor, Mich., 1981, pp. 644–647.

[14] See Pierre Martineau, "The Personality of the Retail Store," *Harvard Business Review,* **36**:47–55, January–February 1958.

[15] Jay D. Lindquist, "Meaning of Image," *Journal of Retailing,* **50**:31, Winter 1974–1975.

[16] Wroe Alderson and Robert Sessions, "Basic Research on Consumer Behavior: Report on a Study of Shopping Behavior and Methods for Its Investigation," in Ronald E. Frank, Alfred A. Kuehn, and William F. Massy (eds.), *Quantitative Techniques in Marketing Analysis,* Irwin, Homewood, Ill., 1962, pp. 129–145.

[17] Stuart U. Rich and Bernard D. Portis, "The 'Imageries' of Department Stores," *Journal of Marketing,* **28**:10–15, April 1964; and David J. Rachman and Linda J. Kemp, "Profile of the Discount House Customer," *Journal of Retailing,* **39**:1–8, Summer 1963.

[18] "Why They Shop Some Centers," *Chain Store Age Executive,* May 1978, pp. 31–35.

[19] C. Glenn Walters, *Consumer Behavior: Theory and Practice,* rev. ed., Irwin, Homewood, Ill., 1974, p. 425.

[20] Bruce L. Stern, Ronald F. Bush, and Joseph F. Hair, Jr., "The Self-Image/Store Image Matching Process: An Empirical Test," *Journal of Business,* **50**:63–69, January 1977.

[21] Meryl Paula Gardner, "Mood States and Consumer Behavior: A Critical Review," *Journal of Consumer Research,* **12**:292–293, December 1985.

[22] Philip Kotler, "Atmospherics as a Marketing Tool," *Journal of Retailing,* **49**:50, 56, Winter 1973–1974.

[23] Robert J. Donovan and John R. Rossiter, "Store Atmosphere: An Environmental Psychology Approach," *Journal of Retailing,* **58**:34–57, Spring 1982.

[24] Gilbert D. Harrell, Michael D. Hutt, and James C. Anderson, "Path Analysis of Buyer Behavior Under Conditions of Crowding," *Journal of Marketing Research,* **17**:45–51, February 1980.

[25] Martineau, "The Personality," p. 47.

[26] Leonard L. Berry, "The Components of Department Store Image: A Theoretical and Empirical Analysis," *Journal of Retailing,* **45**:18, Spring 1969.

[27] Gregory P. Stone, "City Shoppers and Urban Identification: Observations on the Social Psychology of City Life," *American Journal of Sociology,* **60**:36–45, 1954. See also William R. Darden and Fred D. Reynolds, "Shopping Orientations and Product Usage Rates," *Journal of Marketing Research,* **8**:505–508, November 1971; and Louis E. Boone et al., " 'City Shoppers and Urban Identification' Revisited," *Journal of Marketing,* **38**:67–69, July 1974.

[28] See, for example, P. Ronald Stephenson and Ronald P. Willett, "Analysis of Consumers' Retail Patronage Strategies," in Philip R. McDonald (ed.), *Marketing Involvement in Society and the Economy,* American Marketing Association, Chicago, 1969, pp. 316–322; William R. Darden and Dub Ashton, "Psychographic Profiles of Patronage Preference Groups," *Journal of Retailing,* **50**:99–112, Winter 1974–1975; and George P. Moschis, "Shopping Orientations and Consumer Use of Information," *Journal of Retailing,* **52**:61–70, 93, Summer 1976.

[29] Elizabeth C. Hirschman, "Intratype Competition Among Department Stores," *Journal of Retailing,* **55**:20–34, Winter 1979.

[30] Robert F. Dietrich, "Know Thy Consumer: A Quiz That Shows How Well You Do," *Progressive Grocer,* March 1975, p. 55.

[31] Ben M. Enis and Gordon W. Paul, " 'Store Loyalty' as a Basis for Market Segmentation," *Journal of Retailing,* **46**:42–56, Fall 1970; and Fred D. Reynolds, William R. Darden, and Warren S. Martin, "Developing an Image of the Store-Loyal Customer," *Journal of Retailing,* **50**:79, Winter 1974–1975.

[32] Reynolds, Darden, and Martin, "Developing an Image," p. 79.

[32] Arieh Goldman, "The Shopping Style Explanation for Store Loyalty," *Journal of Retailing,* **53**:33–46, 94, Winter 1977–1978.

[33] Ross M. Cunningham, "Customer Loyalty to Store and Brand," *Harvard Business Review,* **39**:137, November–December 1961.

[34] Francis Buttle, "Merchandising," *European Journal of Marketing,* **18**:104–123, Number 6/7, 1984.

[35] Louis J. Haugh, "Buying Habits Study Update," *Advertising Age,* June 27, 1977, p. 58.

[36] "Prototypes: A Step Beyond Whimsy," *Chain Store Age Executive,* February 1985, pp. 22–27; and Kevin T. Higgins, "Supermarket Designs Escape the Straight and Narrow," *Marketing News,* June 6, 1986, pp. 1, 18.

[37] Charles W. Stevens, "K mart Stores Try New Look to Invite More Spending," *The Wall Street Journal,* November 26, 1980, pp. 23, 28; and Charles W. Stevens, "K mart, Beset by Steady Drop in Earnings, Tries to Attract Higher Income Shoppers," *The Wall Street Journal,* August 10, 1982, p. 29.

[38] Consumer Behavior in the Super Market—Part I," *Progressive Grocer,* October 1975, p. 40.

[39] *POPAI Supermarket Consumer Buying Habits Study,* Point-of-Purchase Advertising Institute, Inc., Fort Lee, N.J., 1987.

[40] Howard Stumpf, "P-O-P State-of-the-Art Review," *Marketing Communications,* September 1976, p. 75.

[41] *Awareness, Decision, Purchase,* Point-of-Purchase Advertising Institute, New York, 1961, p. 14.

[42] "POP-AV Displays Boost Retail Sales," *Marketing News,* **2**:18, November 27, 1981.

[43] Jean Paul Gagnon and Jane T. Osterhaus, "Effectiveness of Floor Displays on the Sales of Retail Products," *Journal of Retailing,* **61**:104–116, Spring 1985.

[44] Ronald C. Curhan, "Shelf Space Allocation and Profit Maximization in Mass Retailing," *Journal of Marketing,* **37**:56, July 1973.

[45] Curhan, "Shelf Space," p. 56.

[46] Jo-Ann Zbytniewski, "Shoppers Cry 'Remember the Price'—But Do They Practice What they Screech?" *Progressive Grocer,* **59**:119–122, November 1980.

[47] Kent Monroe, Christine Powell, and Pravat Choudhury, "Recall Versus Recognition As A Measure of Price Awareness," in R. Lutz (ed.), *Advances in Consumer Research,* vol. 13, Association for Consumer Research, Provo, Utah, 1986, pp. 594–599.

[48] Jerry Conover, "The Accuracy of Price Knowledge: Issues in Research Methodology," in R. Lutz (ed.), *Advances in Consumer Research,* vol. 13, Association for Consumer Research, Provo, Utah, 1986, pp. 589–593.

[49] Multiple-Pricing Makes the Most of the Moment of Purchase, *Progressive Grocer,* March 1964, p. 128: and "How Multiple-Unit Pricing Helps . . . and Hurts," *Progressive Grocer,* June 1971, pp. 52–58.

[50] David Litvak, Roger Calantone, and Paul Warshaw, "An Examination of Short-Term Retail Grocery Price Effects," *Journal of Retailing,* **61**:9–25, Fall 1985.

[51] Robert W. Shoemaker, "An Analysis of Consumer Reactions to Product Promotions," in Neil Beckwith (ed.), *1979 Educator's Conference Proceedings,* American Marketing Association, Chicago, 1979, pp. 244–248; Robert G. Brown, "Sales Response to Promotions and Advertising," *Journal of Advertising Research,* **14**:33–39, August 1974; B. C. Cotton and Emerson M. Babb, "Consumer Response to Promotional Deals," *Journal of Marketing,* **42**:109–113, July 1978; J. A. Dodson, Alice M. Tybout, and Brian Sternthal, "Impact of Deals and Deal Retraction on Brand Switching," *Journal*

of Marketing Research, **15**:72–81, February 1978; Anthony N. Doob, J. Merrill Carlsmith, Jonathan L. Freedman, Thomas K. Landayer, and Tom Soleng, Jr., ''Effect of Initial Selling Price on Subsequent Sales,'' *Journal of Personality and Social Psychology,* **11**:345–350, No. 4, 1979; and Carol A. Scott, ''The Effects of Trial and Incentives on Repeat Purchase Behavior,'' *Journal of Marketing Research,* **13**:263–269, August 1976.

[52] William F. Massy and Ronald E. Frank, ''Short-Term Price and Dealing Effects in Selected Market Segments,'' *Journal of Marketing Research,* **2**:171–185, May 1965; Frederick E. Webster, Jr., ''The 'Deal-Prone' Consumer,'' *Journal of Marketing Research,* **2**:186–189, May 1965; and David B. Montgomery, *Consumer Characteristics and 'Deal' Purchasing,* Marketing Science Institute, Cambridge, Mass., 1970.

[53] Robert C. Blattberg, Thomas Buesing, Peter Peacock, and Subrata Sen, ''Identifying the Deal Prone Segment,'' *Journal of Marketing Research,* **15**:369–377, August 1978.

[54] Kevin Higgins, ''Sales Promotion Spending Closing In on Advertising,'' *Marketing News,* July 4, 1986, pp. 8, 10; and '''Pull' Promotions Gaining on 'Push,''' *Marketing News,* June 7, 1985, p. 16.

[55] J. N. Uhl, ''Cents-Off Coupons: Boon or Boondoggle for Consumers?'' *The Journal of Consumer Affairs,* **16**:162, Summer 1982.

[56] ''Recent Trends in Couponing,'' *The Nielsen Researcher,* Number 4, 1979, p. 10.

[57] Caroline Henderson, ''Modeling the Coupon Redemption Decision,'' in E. Hirschman and M. Holbrook (eds.) *Advances in Consumer Research,* vol. 12, Association for Consumer Research, Provo, Utah, 1985, pp. 138–143.

[58] ''Promotions in Advertising Contribute to Brand Identity,'' *Marketing News,* June 7, 1985, p. 16.

[59] K. C. Blair, ''Coupon Design, Delivery Vehicle, Target Market Affect Conversion Rate: Research,'' *Marketing News,* May 28, 1982, pp. 1–2.

[60] ''How Coupon Promotions Can Affect Sales,'' *The Wall Street Journal,* September 25, 1980, p. 31.

[61] ''Recent Trends in Couponing,'' p. 19; and Louis J. Haugh, ''How Coupons Measure Up,'' *Advertising Age,* June 8, 1981, p. 58.

[62] D. R. McCurry, ''Shifts in Supermarket Buying Patterns, 1975,'' *The Nielsen Researcher,* Number 2, 1975, p. 7.

[63] Joseph C. Cayce, ''Are Brand Names Losing Their Luster? A Respected Consumer Watcher Says 'No, But . . .,''' *Progressive Grocer,* October 1976, pp. 64–65.

[64] See, for example, John G. Myers, ''Determinants of Private Brand Attitude,'' *Journal of Marketing Research,* **4**:73–81, February 1967; Ronald E. Frank and Harper W. Boyd, Jr., ''Are Private-Brand-Prone Grocery Customers Really Different?'' *Journal of Advertising Research,* **5**:27–35, December 1965; and James T. Rothe and Lawrence M. Lamont, ''Purchase Behavior and Brand Choice Determinants,'' *Journal of Retailing,* **49**:19–33, Fall 1973.

[65] Jim L. Parks, *Generics in Supermarkets,* A. C. Nielsen Company, Northbrook, Ill., 1980, p. 2.

[66] Charles G. Burck, ''Plain Labels Challenge the Supermarket Establishment,'' *Fortune,* March 26, 1979, p. 71.

[67] T. J. Sullivan, ''Generic Products in Supermarkets,'' *The Nielsen Researcher,* Number 3, 1979, p. 3; Roger A. Strang, Brian F. Harris, and Allan L. Hernandez, ''Consumer Trial of Generic Products in Supermarkets: An Exploratory Study,'' in Neil Beckwith (ed.), *1979 Educators' Conference Proceedings,* American Marketing Association, Chicago, 1979, pp. 386–388; Dub Ashton and Larry Anvik, ''Generic Product Purchasers, A Discriminant Analysis,'' in Robert S. Franz, Robert M. Hopkins, and Alfred G. Toma (eds.), *Proceedings: Southern Marketing Association 1979 Conference,* Southern Marketing Association, Lafayette, La., 1979, pp. 234–237; and Joseph A. Bellizzi, Harry F. Krueckeberg, John R. Hamilton, and Warren S. Martin, ''Consumer Perceptions of National, Private, and Generic Brands,'' *Journal of Retailing,* **57**:56–70, Winter 1981.

[68] Kent L. Granzin, ''An Investigation of the Market for Generic Products,'' *Journal of Retailing,* **57**:39–55, Winter 1981.

[69] Dennis Rosen, ''Consumer Perceptions of Quality for Generic Grocery Products: A Comparison Across Product Categories,'' *Journal of Retailing,* **60**:64–80, Winter 1984; and Amy Dunkin, ''No-Frills Products: An Idea Whose Time Has Gone,'' *Business Week,* June 17, 1985, pp. 64–65.

[70] Christine Dugas, '' 'Ad Space' Now Has A Whole New Meaning,'' *Business Week,* July 29, 1985, p. 52; and Kevin Coupe, ''Invasion of the Instore Advertisers,'' *Supermarket Business,* March 1985, pp. 29–33.

[71] Irene Thorelli, ''Dyadic Interaction: A Theory of Interpersonal Compatibility,'' in P. Thistlethwaite, D. Billingsly, and J. Berens (eds.), *Proceedings,* Midwest Marketing Association, Macomb,

Ill., 1985, pp. 249–254; and Franklin B. Evans, *Dyadic Interaction in Selling: A New Approach,* Graduate School of Business, University of Chicago, Chicago, 1964, p. 25.

[72] Michael Solomon, Carol Surprenant, John Czepiel, and Evelyn Gutman, "A Role Theory Perspective on Dyadic Interactions: The Service Encounter," *Journal of Marketing,* **49**:99–111, Winter 1985.

[73] Russell W. Belk, "Situational Variables and Consumer Behavior," *Journal of Consumer Research,* **2**:158, December 1975.

[74] Belk, "Situational Variables," p. 149.

[75] For a summary of these research efforts, see James H. Leigh and Claude R. Martin, Jr., "A Review of Situational Influence Paradigms and Research," in Ben M. Enis and Kenneth J. Roering (eds.), *Review of Marketing, 1981,* American Marketing Association, Chicago, 1981, pp. 57–74.

[76] Keith Clarke and Russell W. Belk, "The Effects of Product Involvement and Task Definition on Anticipated Consumer Effort," in William L. Wilkie (ed.), *Advances in Consumer Research,* vol. 6, Association for Consumer Research, Ann Arbor, Mich., 1979, pp. 313–318.

[77] "Home Shopping Network," *American Demographics,* September 20, 1986, pp. 22–23.

[78] Larry J. Rosenberg and Elizabeth C. Hirschman, "Retailing Without Stores," *Harvard Business Review,* **58**:105, July/August 1980.

[79] George Moschis, Jac Goldstucker, and Thomas Stanley, "At Home Shopping: Will Consumers Let Their Computers Do the Walking?" *Business Horizons,* **28**:22–29, March–April 1985.

[80] "Research on New Video Technologies," *Marketing News,* May 29, 1981, p. 1, published by the American Marketing Association.

[81] This section is based largely on Peter L. Gillett, "In-Home Shoppers—An Overview," *Journal of Marketing,* **40**:81–88, October 1976.

[82] *A Look Before We Leap Into the 1980s,* Ogilvy & Mather, Direct Response, Inc., New York, 1979, p. 28.

[83] Thomas Exter, "Looking For Brand Loyalty," *American Demographics,* April 1986, pp. 32–33, 52–56.

[84] S. P. Raj, "Striking a Balance Between Brand 'Popularity' and Brand Loyalty," *Journal of Marketing,* **49**:53–59, Winter 1985.

[85] "Food in the A.M." *Time,* March 31, 1980, p. 53.

[86] "Big Ticket Buyers Seek Fulfillment, Not Utility," *Advertising Age,* July 4, 1977, p. 3.

[87] Tod Johnson, "The Myth of Declining Brand Loyalty," *Journal of Advertising Research,* **24**:9–18, February/March 1984.

[88] George H. Brown, "Brand Loyalty—Fact or Fiction?" *Advertising Age,* January 26, 1953, p. 75.

[89] See, for example, Ross M. Cunningham, "Brand Loyalty—What, Where, How Much?" *Harvard Business Review,* **34**:116–128, January-February 1956; Lester Guest, "A Study of Brand Loyalty," *Journal of Applied Psychology,* **28**:16–27, 1944; Lester Guest, "Brand Loyalty—Twelve Years Later," *Journal of Applied Psychology,* **39**:405–408, 1955; and Lester Guest, "Brand Loyalty Revisited: A Twenty-year Report," *Journal of Applied Psychology,* **48**:93–97, 1964.

[90] Jacob Jacoby and Robert W. Chestnut, *Brand Loyalty: Measurement and Management,* Wiley, New York, 1978, pp. 80–81.

[91] James F. Engel and Roger D. Blackwell, *Consumer Behavior,* 4th ed., The Dryden Press, New York, 1982, pp. 577–578.

[92] Gerald O. Caballo and M. Lewis Temares, "Brand Switching at the Point of Purchase," *Journal of Retailing,* **45**:27–36, Fall 1969.

[93] F. H. Graf, "The Logistics of Grocery Products," presented to the National Association of Food Chains, 55th Annual Meeting, A. C. Nielsen Co.

[94] J. O. Peckham, Sr., "The Wheel of Marketing," *The Nielsen Researcher,* 1973, pp. 9–11.

[95] Paul H. Zinszer and Jack A. Lesser, "A Behavioral Model of Customer Response to Stock-Out," in Robert S. Franz, Robert A. Hopkins, and Alfred G. Toma (eds.), *Proceedings: Southern Marketing Association 1979 Conference,* Southern Marketing Association, Lafayette, La., 1979, pp. 377–378.

[96] Yoram Wind, "Brand Loyalty and Vulnerability," in Arch G. Woodside, Jagdish N. Sheth, and Peter D. Bennett (eds.), *Consumer and Industrial Buying Behavior,* North-Holland, New York, 1977, pp. 313–319.

[97] Brown, "Brand Loyalty," p. 76.

[98] Hawkins Stern, "The Significance of Impulse Buying Today," *Journal of Marketing,* **26**:59–60, April 1962.

[99] Dennis W. Rook and Stephen J. Hoch, "Consuming Impulses," in E. Hirschman and M. Holbrook (eds.), *Advances in Consumer Research*, vol. 12, Association for Consumer Research, Provo, Utah, 1985, pp. 23–27; and Vic Pollard, " 'Impulse Shoppers' Say Shoes, Candy Call Out to Them," *News Star World*, April 27, 1986, p. 20.

[100] Vernon T. Clover, "Relative Importance of Impulse Buying in Retail Stores," *Journal of Marketing,* **15**:66–70, July 1950.

[101] *Consumer Buying Habits Studies,* E. I. Du Pont de Nemours and Co., Wilmington, Del., 1965.

[102] V. Kanti Prasad, "Unplanned Buying in Two Retail Settings," *Journal of Retailing,* **51**:3–12, Fall 1975.

[103] Danny N. Bellenger, Dan H. Robertson, and Elizabeth C. Hirschman, "Impulse Buying Varies by Product," *Journal of Advertising Research,* **18**:17, December 1978.

[104] Stern, "The Significance of Impulse," pp. 61–62.

[105] David T. Kollat, "A Decision-Process Approach to Impulse Purchasing," in Raymond M. Haas (ed.), *Science, Technology, and Marketing,* American Marketing Association, Chicago, 1966, pp. 626–639.

[106] Bellenger, Robertson, and Hirschman, "Impulse Buying," pp. 15–18.

POSTPURCHASE BEHAVIOR

LEARNING OBJECTIVES
After studying this chapter, you should understand . . .

- What additional behavior may occur by consumers beyond the purchase decision
- The nature of consumers' postpurchase evaluation process
- The factors influencing consumers' decisions to dispose of products

New-car buyers typically use dealership service until the car's warranty expires. Then they head off to the mass merchandiser or specialty service shop to get it fixed. But, increasingly, car dealers and manufacturers are using a marketing technique—the service contract—designed to attract those customers and keep them away from other aftermarket suppliers, until it's time to purchase another car.

One Ford dealer sounds a bit like an evangelist when he describes the Extended Service Plan his dealership sells. "We just believe in it," he says enthusiastically. "If you keep your customers coming back for three to five years, they'll always come to the floor here and talk to the salesman who sold the car originally. If you get them coming back in the dealership all that time, you've got another shot at them. The first couple of times they come in they'll tell you 'I'm using that Extended Service Plan you sold me.' After a while it's 'that Extended Service Plan I bought.' . . . With the high price of some repairs today you feel so much better when they have the plan."

As a rule, consumers would prefer to have their cars serviced by the dealership as the cars become more sophisticated, such as having computer technology on them. But research shows that there are a number of reasons why vehicles aren't serviced at the dealership where purchased: the most important being that it was perceived to be expensive, followed closely by the dealership being too far from the home or office. By having the service contract, customers know what the cost of the repair is going to be.

Ford's ESP marketing coordinator recognizes that "the name of the game is selling automobiles. . . . If I were a dealer I'd be delighted to have customers coming back so my salespeople would have a chance to expose them to new products. Cars are bought to replace wrecks, because one has worn out or been paid for, but also, in a surprising number of cases, because of exposure to new models."¹

21

This example illustrates the significance of consumers' experiences after the purchase is completed. Marketers must recognize that consumer decisions do not end with the act of purchase but continue as the consumer uses the product and evaluates his or her purchase decision and experience with the item, and may make related purchases, such as the service contract described above. In this chapter we shall examine the nature of consumer postpurchase behavior. We will first discuss the types of behavior that may be exhibited as a result of, and related to, the purchase. Next, the concept of postpurchase evaluation and the significant implications it holds for marketing strategy will be examined. Finally, the topic of consumer product disposition is discussed along with marketing implications.

BEHAVIOR RELATED TO THE PURCHASE

Once the consumer makes a decision to purchase a product, there can be several types of additional behavior associated with that decision. Three activities are of primary importance: (1) decisions on financing the purchase, (2) decisions on the product's installation and use, and (3) decisions on products or services related to the item purchased.

DECISIONS ON PRODUCT PAYMENT

Overall, American households pay for 57 percent of their expenditures with checks, 36 percent with cash, and 6 percent with credit cards. Only 14 percent of households use cash exclusively, and over one-third of these use money orders to pay for approximately 40 percent of their expenditures.[2] Although many small purchases are made for cash, our society is increasingly run on credit. The consumer's access to numerous credit avenues such as MasterCard, Visa, and oil company and department store credit cards means that for a vast number of purchases, especially expensive durables, a major decision involves the nature of payment to be used in the purchase. Such payment decisions may be very simple, reflexive decisions in which the consumer may instinctively pay cash or reach for her Visa card, for example. Other decisions to use credit may be classified as extended problem solving. For instance, a consumer may shop around for the most favorable credit terms, thus considering numerous alternatives.

DECISIONS ON PRODUCT SET-UP AND USE

All consumers who have purchased consumer durables are familiar with the need to have their product set up or installed. The product must be made ready for the buyer to use, as with a car, for example. Many other durables could be cited which necessitate some set-up in order for them to be properly used. Televisions, stereos, furniture, clothes washers, and air conditioners, for example, all must be carefully set up if the consumer is to find satisfaction from their use.

Many other types of products require very little in the way of set-up, however. Even apparently simple products, though, can be very complicated and frustrating in their set-up processes. For example, many a parent can tell Christmas Eve horror stories about all-night exercises in "simple assembly" of products for their children.

Of course, another element of product set-up and use concerns instructions given to the buyer for assembly and operation of the item. Products such as autos, calculators, microwave ovens, and so forth may require detailed explanations as to methods of operation. In order to ensure buyer satisfaction, such brochures (even books for some products) must be carefully developed to provide sufficient instructions.

DECISIONS ON RELATED PRODUCTS OR SERVICES

It often happens that a buyer of one item becomes a candidate for all sorts of options and related products or services. For example, Ford's Extended Service Plan described earlier is promoted to new-car buyers. As another illustration, consider a 35-mm-camera buyer who may become interested in numerous optional lenses, a camera bag, dust brush, filters, a slide projector and trays, photo developing equipment, and even photography lessons. In fact, many retailers have learned that the big profits are often in the optional extras that a consumer purchases, rather than in the original product itself. As a result, for example, many camera retailers sell 35-mm cameras close to cost or as a loss leader in order to draw customers into the store and sell accessories on which the markup runs much higher. Similarly, a camping enthusiast may begin with a tent and buy a wide range of related products such as a stove, lantern, sleeping bag, and back-pack.

MARKETING IMPLICATIONS

Some very important marketing implications flow from these consumer postpurchase decisions. First of all, marketers clearly must make the arrangement of payment as easy as possible. Retailers have moved to ease the payment decision in numerous ways. For instance, making store checkouts easier facilitates the consumer's payment process. The use of electronic scanners at the point of checkout combined with compatible credit cards should also make the payment decision process easier and quicker. Moreover, retailers generally offer numerous payment alternatives in order to meet consumers' needs.

Banks have also joined the move to facilitate purchase-payment decisions. Not only are numerous bank cards and loan plans available, but even after regular banking hours, electronic-funds transfers may be effected in order to obtain the necessary credit or cash with which to pay for purchases. Because consumers from different social classes use bank credit cards for different purposes (upper classes use them for convenience, while lower classes use them as installment credit), it may be helpful to incorporate appeals appropriate for each group in a bank's or retailer's advertising of its credit plans.[3] Certainly retailers and financial institutions need to research their chosen market segments to determine their desired financing alternatives and, if possible, to offer and promote these alternatives.

A second set of implications flows from decisions on product set-up and use. As mentioned previously, products such as televisions, ranges, washers, and so forth requiring set-up must be carefully installed and explained to the user. Unless such activities are conscientiously undertaken, consumer dissatisfaction is likely to result, and the consequence of consumer dissatisfaction, as we have seen, is likely to be poor word-of-mouth communications about the product, the retailer, or both. Thus, manufacturers need to select retailers carefully as members of their distribution team who will provide the kind of quality after-sale installation or warranty service that will enhance the manufacturer's image. The retailer needs to be considerate of such activities for the same reasons—that it can be an important factor in generating a favorable image and repeat customers.

The importance of information on product set-up and use becomes even more critical in today's self-service economy. Consumers are buying many complicated products from self-service discount outlets which may offer very little product knowledge or installation assistance. As a result, they must rely almost exclusively on whatever literature comes with the product. Such a situation provides an added impetus for manufacturers to assess their product literature and make sure it is readable and understandable. The consumer who fails to follow instructions with her microwave oven is likely to blame the manufacturer rather than herself.

Even more fundamental than the provision of information to consumers is the marketer's first understanding how his product is used by the consumer and how this product fits into the consumer's "consumption system." For example, the marketer needs to know how his product is used by consumers, not only to make improvements in its quality and functions, but also to suggest new uses for it (as done by Jell-O and Arm & Hammer Baking Soda). If marketers were to research more thoroughly the use-environment and behavior of their products prior to full-scale launching, we would undoubtedly see fewer failures and products more carefully attuned to consumers' lifestyles.

It is also important for the marketer to understand the user's consumption system, that is, the manner in which the consumer performs the total task of whatever she is trying to accomplish when using the product, whether it is washing clothes or cooking a meal.[4] By understanding how this product (let's say a washing machine) fits in with other products (such as a dryer, iron, and detergents) in terms of consumption behavior, new marketing opportunities may arise.

A third factor for the marketer to consider with regard to postpurchase activities concerns buyers' interests in related products and services. This is another area of potential profit that should be actively cultivated. An example of successful product linking is illustrated by a major oil company which, when replacing a customer's stolen credit card, distributes a flier offering a "pick-pocket-proof wallet" for sale.

Because buyers may become interested in related items, they need to be made aware of the potential products that exist. Thus, literature enclosed with a product could present other products in the line. For example, camera manufacturers do an excellent job of presenting their full line of attachments and accessories in this way. Also, appliance manufacturers such as Whirlpool and Hotpoint frequently feature a number of their major appliances in one advertisement, because the buyer who purchases a clothes washer may soon be interested in a matching dryer. It is known, for instance, that there is an underlying common order of acquisition for many durables. Thus, marketers of these as well as nondurable goods might cultivate the potential products that exist by linking products together.[5] Another example of this practice is the packing of Tide detergent and Bounce fabric softener in certain makes of washers and dryers. Buyers of these appliances may be very susceptible to brand switching at this time. Consequently, new customers may be gained through such sampling.

In order to capitalize on the sales potential of related items, many marketers have diversified their operations. Gillette sells razors, shaving cream, hair spray, and deodorants; Starcraft makes boats and motor homes; Coleman produces coolers, tents, trailers, and other camping gear. Thus, the marketer's task is to determine what product mix is most appropriate to the firm. This is largely a function of applying the marketing concept to identify products that may be related in nature and can be effectively marketed.

POSTPURCHASE EVALUATION

In addition to the overt types of behavior that result from purchase, the consumer also engages in an evaluation of the purchase decision. Because the consumer is uncertain of the wisdom of his decision, he rethinks this decision in the postpurchase stage. There are several functions which this stage serves. First, it serves to broaden the consumer's set of experiences stored in memory. Second, it provides a check on how well he is doing as a consumer in selecting products, stores, and so on. Third, the feedback that the consumer receives from this stage helps to make adjustments in future purchasing strategies.[6]

CONSUMER SATISFACTION/DISSATISFACTION

Satisfaction is an important element in the evaluation stage. According to Howard and Sheth, *satisfaction* refers to the buyer's state of being adequately rewarded in a buying situation for the sacrifice he has made. *Adequacy* of satisfaction is a result of matching actual past purchase and consumption experience with the expected reward from the brand in terms of its anticipated potential to satisfy the consumer's motives.[7] Figure 21-1 presents a diagram of the process.

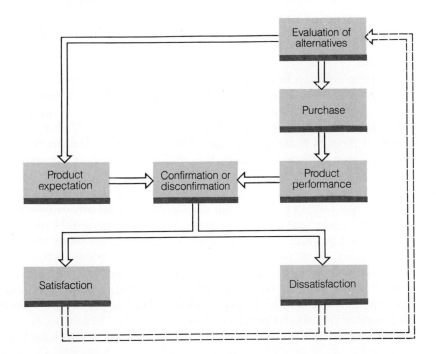

FIGURE 21-1
The purchase evaluation process.

The concept of satisfaction is one about which there are presently few agreed-upon definitions or approaches to measurement. Nevertheless, Hunt has summarized the concept in the following statement:

Satisfaction is a kind of stepping away from an experience and evaluating it. . . . One could have a pleasurable experience that caused dissatisfaction because even though pleasurable, it wasn't as pleasurable as it was supposed or expected to be. So satisfaction/dissatisfaction isn't an emotion, it's the evaluation of an emotion.[8]

Consumers form certain expectations prior to the purchase. These expectations may be about (1) the nature and performance of the product or service (that is, the anticipated benefits to be derived directly from the item), (2) the costs and efforts to be expended before obtaining the direct product or service benefits, and (3) the social benefits or costs accruing to the consumer as a result of the purchase (that is, the anticipated impact of the purchase on significant others).[9] Advertising may often be an important factor influencing these expectations, as we shall see later.

Once consumers purchase and use a product, they may then become either satisfied or dissatisfied. Research has uncovered several determinants which appear to influence satisfaction, including demographic variables, personality variables, expectations, and other factors. For example, older consumers tend to have lower expectations and to be more satisfied. Higher education tends to be associated with lower satisfaction. Men tend to be more satisfied than women. The more confidence one has in purchase decision making and the more competence in a given product area, the greater one's satisfaction tends to be. There is also greater satisfaction when relevant others are perceived to be more satisfied.[10] Higher levels of product satisfaction are also indicated by persons who are more satisfied with their lives as a whole, and by persons with more favorable attitudes toward the consumer domain, that is, the marketplace, business firms, and consumerism.[11]

The interaction between expectations and actual product performance produce either satisfaction or dissatisfaction. However, there does not appear to be merely a direct relationship between the level of expectations and the level of satisfaction. Instead, a modifying variable known as "disconfirmation of expectations" is thought to be a significant mediator of this situation. When a consumer does not get what is expected, the situation is one of disconfirmation. Such disconfirmation can be of two varieties: a *positive* disconfirmation occurs when what is received is better than expected, and a *negative* disconfirmation occurs when things turn out worse than anticipated. Thus, any situation in which the consumer's judgment is proven wrong is a disconfirmation.[12] Consumers' expectations from a product, as well as whether those expectations are met, are strong determinants, then, of satisfaction.

The result of satisfaction to the consumer from the purchase of a product or service is that more-favorable postpurchase attitudes, higher purchase intentions, and brand loyalty are likely to be exhibited. That is, the same behavior is likely to be exhibited in a similar purchasing situation. Thus, as long as positive reinforcement takes place, the consumer will tend to continue to purchase the same brand.

It is true, however, that consumers will sometimes not follow these established patterns but will purchase differently simply for the sake of novelty.[13] On the other hand, if consumers are dissatisfied, they are likely to exhibit less-favorable postpurchase attitudes, lower or nonexistent purchase intentions, brand switching, complaining behavior, and negative word-of-mouth.

POSTPURCHASE DISSONANCE

As we learned in Chapter 16, consumers may become dissonant over a purchase decision. As explained by Festinger, cognitive dissonance occurs as a result of a discrepancy between a consumer's decision and the consumer's prior evaluation. Consider the illustration in Chapter 16 of the Nikon camera buyer who encounters some problems with the brand he has purchased. This is a typical situation leading to postpurchase dissonance. Festinger's theory was derived from two basic principles: (1) dissonance is uncomfortable and will motivate the person to reduce it and (2) individuals experiencing dissonance will avoid situations that produce more dissonance. Let us examine this concept more closely to see what factors lead to dissonance, how the consumer deals with the conflict, and what marketing implications are embodied in the concept.

Conditions Leading to Dissonance   From a review of research findings on cognitive dissonance, Engel and Blackwell suggest that dissonance is likely to occur under the following conditions:[14]

1   Once a minimum threshold of dissonance tolerance is passed. That is, consumers may tolerate a certain level of inconsistency in their lives until this point is reached.

2   The action is irrevocable. For instance, when the consumer purchases a new car, there is little likelihood that he will be able to reverse his decision and get his money back.

3   Unselected alternatives have desirable features. In our camera example earlier, the Pentax, Canon, and Minolta (brands not selected), all had attractive features.

4   There are several desirable alternatives. Today's car buyer, for example, has an abundance of choices among similar attractive models. In fact, research indicates that those consumers who experience greater difficulty in making purchase decisions, or who consider a wider range of store and brand options, are more likely to experience greater magnitudes of postpurchase dissonance.[15]

5   Available alternatives are quite dissimilar in their qualities (there is little "cognitive overlap"). For instance, although there are many automobile models, each one may have some unique characteristics.

6   The buyer is committed to his decision because it has psychological significance. A large and important living room furniture purchase is likely to have great psychological significance to the buyer because of its dramatic reflection of one's decorating tastes, philosophy, and life style. Ego involvement will be quite high.

7   There is no pressure applied to the consumer to make the decision. If the

CONSUMER DECISION PROCESSES consumer is subjected to outside pressure, he will do what he is forced to do without letting his own viewpoint or preference really be challenged.

It is clear that dissonance is likely to be strongest for the purchase of durables, although it can exist for almost every purchase. The factors cited above and others are illustrated in Table 21-1, which presents conditions under which high or low dissonance would be expected.

Dissonance Reduction There are several major ways in which the consumer strives to reduce dissonance. He may (1) change his evaluation of the alternative, (2) seek new information to support his choice, or (3) change his attitudes.

CHANGING PRODUCT EVALUATIONS One of the ways consumers seek to reduce dissonance is to reevaluate product alternatives. This is accomplished by the

TABLE 21-1
Dissonance and Buying Situations

Factors affecting dissonance	Buying situations	Conditions with high dissonance expectation	Conditions with low dissonance expectation
1 Attractiveness of rejected alternative	A high school graduate decides which of several pictures to order.	Three of the proofs have both attractive and desirable features.	One of the proofs clearly is superior to the rest.
2 Negative factors in chosen alternative	A man chooses between two suits of clothing.	The chosen suit has the color the man wanted but not the style.	The chosen suit has both the color and style the man wanted.
3 Number of alternatives	A teacher shops for a tape recorder.	There are eight recorders from which to choose.	There are only two recorders from which to choose.
4 Cognitive overlap	A housewife shops for a vacuum sweeper.	A salesman offers two similarly priced tank types.	A salesman offers a tank type and an upright cleaner.
5 Importance of cognitions involved	A child buys a present for her sister.	The sister has definite preferences for certain kinds of music.	The sister has no strong tastes for certain records.
6 Positive inducement	Parents decide to buy a photo enlarger for their son.	The son already has hobby equipment and does not need the enlarger.	The son never has had a true hobby and needs something to keep him occupied.
7 Discrepant or negative action	A man purchases an expensive watch.	The man had never before paid more than $35 for a watch.	Fairly expensive watches had been important gift items in the man's family.
8 Information available	A housewife buys a detergent.	The housewife has no experience with the brand purchased—it is a new variety.	The housewife has read and heard a good deal about the product and has confidence in the manufacturer.
9 Anticipated dissonance	A small boy buys a model airplane.	The boy anticipates trouble at home because of the cost of the model.	The boy expects no trouble at home relative to the purchase.
10 Familiarity and knowledge	A family buys a floor polisher.	The item was purchased without much thought.	The item was purchased after a careful selection process.

Source: Robert J. Holloway, "An Experiment on Consumer Dissonance," *Journal of Marketing*, **31**:40, January 1967, published by the American Marketing Association.

consumers' enhancing the attributes of the products selected while decreasing the importance of the unselected products' attributes. That is, consumers seek to polarize alternatives in order to reduce their dissonance.[16]

Another approach to reducing dissonance is for the consumer to reevaluate product alternatives to view them as being more alike than was thought at the purchase stage, that is, to establish or imagine that cognitive overlap exists. As a result of viewing the alternatives as essentially the same, it makes little difference which one is chosen; hence, little dissonance would be experienced.

In addition, selective retention may operate to allow the consumer to forget positive features of the unselected alternative and negative features of the chosen product while remembering negative attributes of the unchosen item along with favorable features of the chosen alternative.

SEEKING NEW INFORMATION   A second way consumers may reduce dissonance is by seeking additional information in order to confirm the wisdom of their product choice. According to Festinger's theory, dissonant individuals would be expected to actively avoid information that would tend to increase their dissonance and seek information supporting their decision. It seems reasonable to assume that consumers would seek out advertisements for products they have purchased and tend to avoid competing ads. Research on this topic, however, has failed to support this hypothesis. Although it is widely documented that consumers experiencing dissonance do seek additional information, there is no evidence to substantiate either a general preference by consumers for supportive over nonsupportive information or a greater information-seeking/avoidance tendency by high-dissonance consumers. Consumers sometimes seek consonant information to support their choice, sometimes seek discrepant information to refute it, and sometimes look merely for useful information, no matter what the content. It appears to depend on the amount of information gathered before his decision and whether he perceives that he has made a wise choice. Thus, if the consumer gathered much evidence before purchase to support his decision and if he strongly believes he made a wise selection, he will feel free to seek out exposure to discrepant as well as consonant information.[17]

Unfortunately, the research findings in this area have numerous methodological problems; so at present it cannot be concluded that dissonance factors have any effect on the consumer's postpurchase information-seeking behavior.[18] Nevertheless, the fact that individuals do engage in selective exposure to marketing information and may at the same time be experiencing dissonance does have some implications for the marketing manager; these will be examined shortly.

CHANGING ATTITUDES   As a result of dissonance, the consumer may change his attitudes to make them consonant with his behavior. For example, when the marketer secures new-product trial among target customers who initially have an unfavorable attitude toward the item (let's say they purchased it because of a coupon offer, or were given a free sample), this situation is likely to produce dissonance. That is, unfavorable attitudes toward the product are inconsistent with the behavior of product trial. Motivation to achieve consonance will likely take the form of attitude change because that is easier than renouncing the purchase and returning the product. By reevaluating the product and adopting a

positive attitude toward it, attitudes and behavior are now consistent and consonance is achieved.

Marketing Implications There are several marketing implications that arise from our discussion of cognitive dissonance. Most of these suggestions relate to the promotional variable.

CONFIRMING EXPECTATIONS When the purchase confirms the consumer's expectations, reinforcement takes place. When expectations are not confirmed, however, cognitive inconsistency develops and the consumer will likely reduce the dissonance by evaluating the product (or store) somewhat negatively. Thus, where a product fails to measure up to the consumer's expectations or guidelines for evaluation, the result may be no initial sale, no repeat sale, or unfavorable word-of-mouth communication.[19]

It is important, therefore, for the product to confirm expectations. Similarly, it is imperative that the marketer not build up expectations unrealistically. Marketers should first design products that will fulfill consumers' expectations insofar as possible. As our scientific progress advances, people come to expect fewer technical deficiencies in products. These expectations may be set unrealistically high, with resultant dissatisfaction when they are not fulfilled, as when the product breaks down for some reason. In order to reduce this occurrence, products should be carefully developed with the consumer in mind. A clear understanding of how the product will be used and how it fits into the consumer's lifestyle is necessary.

Much of the advertising done today may appear to be harmless exaggeration or puffery, but it may actually be contributing unwittingly to less satisfaction on the part of buyers. Promotions that promise more than products can possibly deliver may be destined for problems. As a result, disconfirmed customers can spread unfavorable word-of-mouth communications and refuse to purchase the item again.

How can the advertiser counter this potential problem? One way is to develop promotions that are consistent with what the product can reasonably deliver. A number of recent ad campaigns have adopted this approach. Not only are positive product attributes mentioned, but some of the brand's deficiencies may also be cited. Such two-sided approaches to advertising may be very effective.

Packaging, too, can help present a more balanced picture of the product's attributes. As examples of how companies are seeking to foster lower expectations more in line with what the product will deliver, consider the case faced by Philip Morris:

Philip Morris launched Cambridge cigarettes as an ultra-low-tar brand. Cigarettes in the crushproof box variety of the brand, however, were difficult to keep lit and offered so little taste that the company printed a warning on the package that promised an "experience substantially different from other cigarettes you have smoked."[20]

For the marketer interested in conducting consumer analysis, surveys may be undertaken to find out what consumers like and dislike about a product. Ford

Motor Company conducts thousands of interviews with its buyers to learn what they like and do not like about their Fords. In addition, consumer expectations should be measured to determine how well the firm's product is meeting these expectations. Both manufacturer and dealer promotion should be assessed to determine if either is promising more than can be delivered.

A large-scale survey focusing on satisfied as well as unsatisfied product users might yield several important types of information:

- Areas for improvement of the physical product

- Ideas for promotional copy to create favorable attitudes toward the firm's brand

- Promotional copy illustrating why our brand is better, based on competitive product failures

- Guidelines for developing warranties or other kinds of guarantees[21]

Thus, to prevent cognitive dissonance from arising, marketers would be well advised not to create unrealistic expectations in the minds of consumers.

INDUCING ATTITUDE CHANGE   We saw earlier that when attitudes are inconsistent with purchase behavior, they are likely to change. Consequently, the marketer may seek to induce behavior changes in consumers through various means. Promotional tools including free samples and cents-off coupons are frequently used by the marketer to accomplish this. By offering these deals to consumers they may be enticed to try the item and as a result adopt the product or switch brands. However, the size and nature of the inducements should be carefully considered.

There is some evidence that the smaller the incentive, the greater the consumer's dissonance and the greater the attitude change.[22] That is, small inducements force the consumer to confront his purchase behavior without a ready explanation for it, whereas large inducements may allow the consumer to simply rationalize his behavior. Therefore, a coupon worth 25 cents off on an item may produce more attitude change than one for 50 cents off.

In the case of free samples, however, acceptance of the brand may never take place because the consumer could fail to expose herself fully to attitude change from use of the sample. Thus, there may very well be an optimum value range over which promotional techniques produce the desired attitude and behavior change; beyond that point (either too low or too high) they may be relatively ineffective.

REINFORCING BUYERS   Although it has not been proved that one reason consumers engage in postpurchase information-seeking behavior is to reduce dissonance, it may nevertheless be the prudent marketing approach to proceed on this supposition. Such an approach may pay handsome dividends to the company undertaking some promotion aimed at new buyers. It could be especially important in the case of a company launching an innovation.

The marketer may not have to develop special ads aimed at new buyers.

Much of his regular advertising may be sufficient to reinforce buyers about their decision. Maytag advertising is an excellent illustration of this approach (see Figure 21-2). The ads stress innovativeness in products to interest new buyers, but also convey a feeling of satisfaction among present Maytag owners. Nevertheless, if a sufficient advertising budget can be mustered, some ads specifically designed to reduce dissonance among buyers could be developed. Besides, the marketer may find that the kind of advertisement designed to attract customers may not be very effective in reducing dissonance among present buyers. Thus, ads more specifically tailored for new buyers may be necessary. Ford, for instance, for this reason has aimed certain advertisements specifically at new buyers.[23]

There are many illustrations of marketing strategies that appear to be logical approaches to reducing dissonance, in spite of the lack of substantiation in the

FIGURE 21-2
An advertisement for Maytag.
Courtesy of The Maytag Company.

The more things at Maytag change,

the more they stay the same.

At Maytag, no matter how innovative our new products are, we still build 'em like we used to.

We still build full-size washers, both regular and stacked, that last longer and need fewer repairs. We still make sure every Maytag dryer, dishwasher, range, microwave oven and disposer meets our rigorous standards. And we still manufacture many of our own parts to insure Maytag quality inside and out.

In fact, our standards are so high, we test each appliance before it leaves our door.

Which leaves a certain repairman quite lonely. But at Maytag, we would never have it any other way.

MAYTAG
THE DEPENDABILITY PEOPLE
One Dependability Square, Newton, Iowa 50208

©1986 The Maytag Company

published literature. For example, the marketer should supply sufficient dealer literature, which could provide new buyers with reinforcement. Moreover, instruction manuals should not only tell how to install and operate the product properly but also seek to convince the buyer of the wisdom of his selection. Information about warranties, guarantees, and where and how to secure service should help reduce postpurchase dissonance. These materials should be packed with the product. In addition, some firms spend huge sums to promote the availability and quality of their aftersales service in order to forestall dissonance.

Manufacturers and retailers may inaugurate correspondence with the new buyer as part of a dissonance-reducing campaign. For instance, auto companies publish magazines that are sent to new-car buyers, telling them how to gain more enjoyment from their purchase. Retailers have also learned that postpurchase messages to buyers can be beneficial. One study found that individuals receiving post-transaction letters from a retailer reinforcing their purchase decision experienced less dissonance.[24] Another study found that automobile buyers who received favorable postpurchase reinforcement from car salespeople had significantly lower back-out or cancellation rates.[25] Thus, marketers may develop several effective informational programs aimed at reducing cognitive dissonance in buyers.

PRODUCT DISPOSITION

A final topic of interest concerns the disposition of what the consumer has purchased. Most of the consumer-behavior literature has ignored this subject. However, it is important from a public policy perspective as well as from a marketing management orientation to better understand how consumers make disposition decisions for a product.

DISPOSITION ALTERNATIVES AND DETERMINANTS

There are various alternatives for disposing of a product. These are diagramed in Figure 21-3. In addition, the method of disposition may vary considerably across products. For example, while bicycles tend to be given away, this is not true of phonograph records, which are usually thrown away or stored. At present, little is known about the factors that influence the disposition choice made by the consumer. The following categories of factors have been suggested, however:[26]

1 *Psychological characteristics of the decision maker:* personality, attitudes, emotions, perception, learning, creativity, intelligence, social class, level of risk tolerance, peer pressure, social conscience, and so on. Although consumer demographic variables have not proved to be very enlightening in understanding disposition behavior, lifestyle factors have proved to be moderately useful.[27]

2 *Factors intrinsic to the product:* condition, age, size, style, value, color, power source of the product, technological innovations, adaptability, reliability, durability, initial cost, replacement cost, and so on.[28]

3 *Situational factors extrinsic to the product:* finances, storage space, urgency, fashion changes, circumstances of acquisition (gift versus purchase), functional

use, economics (demand and supply), legal considerations (giving to avoid taxes), and so on.

It has been suggested, too, that consumer product disposition is actually a process involving the steps of problem recognition, search and evaluation, disposition decision, and postdisposition outcomes.[29]

It is interesting for the marketer to speculate, using these reference frames, on the various possibilities for consumer product disposition, as in the following situation:

Consider a wristwatch which still runs but is no longer stylish. The consumer is faced with a first-level decision: keep it, get rid of it permanently, or get rid of it temporarily. Assume that he decides to keep it because of his thriftiness (psychological characteristic). He could have also decided to keep it because, although it was not stylish, it was still very reliable (product characteristic) or because he had no money for another one (situational factor). At some later time, the old watch is again brought to mind. He may decide to get rid of it permanently this time, because his status needs are no longer met by the watch (psychological characteristics), the band is worn (product characteristic), and/or he has too many old watches in his dresser drawer (situational

FIGURE 21-3
Product-disposition
alternatives.
Source: Jacob Jacoby, Carol K.
Berning, and Thomas F. Dietvorst,
"What about Disposition?" *Journal
of Marketing,* **41**:23, April 1977,
published by the American Marketing
Association.

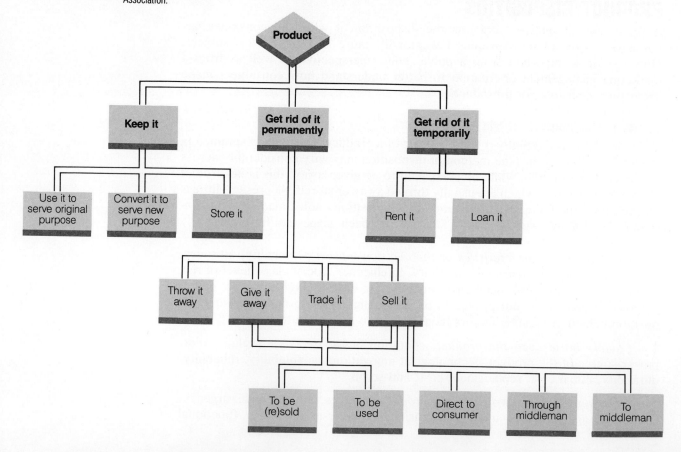

factor). At the second level, he may decide to give it away to a charitable institution so that he can claim a tax deduction.[30]

MARKETING IMPLICATIONS

The implications of the consumer product disposition process reflect on several areas of marketing. There are implications from a public policy perspective as well as from a strategy perspective.

The public policy effects of disposition are many. For example, the effects of disposition choice on the environment include the long-run effects of a throwaway lifestyle, the resources wasted when an item is discarded, and the resource depleted when it is replaced.[31] Thus, a study of the many problems of polluting and littering could be better addressed by considering consumer disposition.[32]

Habits of throwing away and littering might be changed by providing consumers with information about possible product uses or conversions (for example, having an automobile body shop inexpensively spray paint a refrigerator so that it will fit in with new decor). In addition, inappropriate disposition decisions might be discouraged through educational activities designed to change basic attitudes and values. More recycling centers might be established and consumers made aware of the significance of these centers for their own well-being.

Consumer disposition can influence a company's marketing strategy in several dimensions. First, marketers may have to become more involved in facilitating consumers' disposition processes if buyers are not to become discouraged and withdraw from the purchasing process. For instance, old products must often be disposed of before new ones can be purchased. This might be due to the need for money with which to make a down payment on the new item, or it could be a lack of storage space for both the old and new product that dictates its disposal. Second, forecasting sales of new products will have to take into account stocks of used goods which may also be on the market. For example, publishers and authors do not receive any income from college textbooks after the initial sale. The large used-book market for college texts in which old books are bought and then resold makes sales and income forecasting difficult for books in a publisher's line and substantially reduces the market for new titles.[33]

Third, the marketer can effectively use information on consumer disposition decisions in developing promotion strategy. For example, the marketer may learn the reason that consumers acquire new products even though their old ones are still performing satisfactorily (such as the new product has better features or fits better with perceived self-images). Identification of reasons such as these and their relative incidence by product can provide marketing and advertising managers with information useful for developing promotional strategies.[34]

MANAGERIAL REFLECTIONS

For our product or service situation . . .

1   What patterns of postpurchase behavior are engaged in by our customers as they make decisions on such factors as product financing, installation and use, and related items for purchase?

2   To what extent are our customers satisfied or dissatisfied?

3 How significant is postpurchase dissonance for our buyers and what strategies are in place for controlling it?

4 How do buyers dispose of the item and are there significant managerial or public policy implications to such disposition?

DISCUSSION TOPICS

1 Why should the marketer be concerned with postpurchase behavior?

2 Discuss the concept of satisfaction/dissatisfaction.

3 What is postpurchase dissonance, and what conditions lead to it?

4 How do consumers reduce cognitive dissonance?

5 Why should the marketer be concerned about consumer expectations in purchasing? What strategy implications are there in connection with expectation confirmation?

6 How can marketers reinforce buyers after the purchase?

PROJECTS

1 Develop a questionnaire to measure consumer satisfaction/dissatisfaction with a durable good (such as a car, computer, or stereo system) purchased within the last year. Survey ten students who bought that item and determine their level of satisfaction. What action was taken to resolve dissatisfaction? Discuss any marketing implications.

2 Select a consumer durable good and survey ten people to determine their disposition behavior. What is the significance of your findings to marketers of that product and to public policy formulation?

NOTES

[1] Adapted from Roger Rowand, "Dealers Shift to Service Contracts," *Advertising Age*, May 16, 1985, pp. 28–29.

[2] Martha F. Riche, "How Americans Pay," *American Demographics*, July 1986, pp. 46–47.

[3] H. Lee Mathews and John W. Slocum, Jr., "Social Class and Commercial Bank Credit Card Usage," *Journal of Marketing*, 33:71–78, January 1969.

[4] Harper W. Boyd, Jr., and Sidney J. Levy, "New Dimension in Consumer Analysis," *Harvard Business Review*, 41:129–140, November–December 1963.

[5] Jack Kasulis, Robert F. Lusch, and Edward F. Stafford, Jr., "Consumer Acquisition Patterns for Durable Goods," *Journal of Consumer Research*, 6:47–57, June 1979.

[6] C. Glenn Walters, *Consumer Behavior: Theory and Practice*, rev. ed., Irwin, Homewood, Ill., 1974, pp. 559–560.

[7] John A. Howard and Jagdish N. Sheth, *The Theory of Buyer Behavior*, Wiley, New York, 1969, p. 145.

[8] H. Keith Hunt, "CS/D—Overview and Future Research Directions," in H. Keith Hunt (ed.), *Conceptualization and Measurement of Consumer Satisfaction and Dissatisfaction*, Marketing Science Institute, Boston, 1977, pp. 459–460.

[9] Ralph L. Day, "Toward a Process Model of Consumer Satisfaction," in Hunt (ed.), *Conceptualization*, pp. 163–167.

10 Gerald Linda, "New Research Works on Consumer Satisfaction/Dissatisfaction Model," *Marketing News,* September 21, 1979, p. 8.

11 Robert A. Westbrook, "Intrapersonal Affective Influences on Consumer Satisfaction with Products," *Journal of Consumer Research,* 7:49–54, June 1980.

12 Linda, "New Research," p. 8; Richard W. Olshavsky and John A. Miller, "Consumer Expectations, Product Performance, and Perceived Product Quality," *Journal of Marketing Research,* 9:19–21, February 1972; Rolph E. Anderson, "Consumer Dissatisfaction: The Effect of Disconfirmed Expectancy on Perceived Product Performance," *Journal of Marketing Research,* 10:38–94, February, 1973; and Richard L. Oliver, "Effect of Expectation and Disconfirmation on Postexposure Product Evaluations: An Alternative Interpretation," *Journal of Applied Psychology,* 62:480–486, August 1977.

13 M. Venkatesan, "Cognitive Consistency and Novelty Seeking," in Scott Ward and Thomas S. Robertson (eds.), *Consumer Behavior: Theoretical Sources,* Prentice-Hall, Englewood Cliffs, N.J., 1973, pp. 354–384.

14 James F. Engel and Roger D. Blackwell, *Consumer Behavior,* 4th ed., The Dryden Press New York, 1982.

15 Michael B. Menasco and Del I. Hawkins, "A Field Test of the Relationship Between Cognitive Dissonance and State Anxiety," *Journal of Marketing Research,* 15:650–655, November 1978.

16 See William H. Cummings and M. Venkatesan, "Cognitive Dissonance and Consumer Behavior: A Review of the Evidence," in Mary Jane Schlinger (ed.), *Advances in Consumer Research,* 2d ed., Association for Consumer Research, Chicago, 1975, pp. 21–31; and Leonard A. LoSciuto and Robert Perloff, "Influence of Product Preference on Dissonance Reduction," *Journal of Marketing Research,* 4:286–290, August 1967.

17 Engel and Blackwell, *Consumer Behavior,* p. 507.

18 Cummings and Venkatesan, "Cognitive Dissonance." Also see William H. Cummings and M. Venkatesan, "Cognitive Dissonance and Consumer Behavior: A Review of the Evidence," *Journal of Marketing Research,* 13:303–308, August 1976, for a review of the methodological problems.

19 Richard N. Cardozo, "An Experimental Study of Customer Effort, Expectation, and Satisfaction," *Journal of Marketing Research,* 2:244–249, August 1965.

20 John Koten, "After String of Cigarette Hits, Philip Morris Finds Its Ultra-Low-Tar Entry a Poor Draw," *The Wall Street Journal,* August 18, 1980, p. 13.

21 John E. Swan and Linda Jones Combs, "Product Performance and Consumer Satisfaction: A New Concept," *Journal of Marketing,* 40:33, April 1976.

22 Thomas S. Robertson, *Consumer Behavior,* Scott, Foresman, Glenview, Ill., 1970, p. 58.

23 George H. Brown, "The Automobile Buying Decision within the Family," in Nelson N. Foote (ed.), *Household Decision-Making,* New York University Press, New York, 1961, pp. 193–199.

24 Shelby D. Hunt, "Post-Transaction Communications and Dissonance Reduction," *Journal of Marketing,* 34:46–51, July 1970.

25 James H. Donnelly, Jr., and John M. Ivancevich, "Post-Purchase Reinforcement and Back-Out Behavior," *Journal of Marketing Research,* 7:399–400, August 1970.

26 Jacob Jacoby, Carol K. Berning, and Thomas F. Dietvorst, "What About Disposition?" *Journal of Marketing,* 41:26, April 1977.

27 Marian Burke, W. David Conn, and Richard J. Lutz, "Using Psychographic Variables to Investigate Product Disposition Behavior," in Subhash C. Jain (ed.), *Research Frontiers in Marketing: Dialogues and Directions,* American Marketing Association, Chicago, 1976, pp. 321–326.

28 M. DeBell and R. Dardis, "Extending Product Life: Technology Isn't the Only Issue," in William Wilkie (ed.), *Advances in Consumer Research,* vol. 6, Association for Consumer Research, Ann Arbor, Mich., 1979, pp. 381–385.

29 James W. Hanson, "A Proposed Paradigm for Consumer Product Disposition Processes," *Journal of Consumer Affairs,* 14:49–67, Summer 1980.

30 Jacoby, Berning, and Dietvorst, "What About Disposition?" pp. 26–27, published by the American Marketing Association.

31 Burke, Conn, and Lutz, "Using Psychographic Variables," p. 321.

32 Hanson, "A Proposed Paradigm," pp. 64–65.

33 Del I. Hawkins, Kenneth A. Coney, and Roger J. Best, *Consumer Behavior: Implications for Marketing Strategy,* Business Publications, Inc., Dallas, 1980, p. 503.

34 Jacoby, Berning, and Dietvorst, "What About Disposition?" p. 26.

CASES FOR PART FIVE

CASE 5-1

THE CAMERA BUYER*

In order to gain greater insight into the photo/camera market, *Chain Store Age* commissioned several surveys covering such things as camera purchasing behavior, camera advertising effects, features consumers want in a camera, and what confuses the camera buyer. Findings from these studies are reported below.

CONSUMER PURCHASING PATTERNS

According to the *Chain Store Age* survey, women decide where to shop for instant, disc, and cartridge-film cameras. Women also make the decision as to which specific camera to buy for each of these formats. Only in 35-mm cameras do men take charge. Men also take charge in deciding where to buy 35-mm film. Women are the prime decision makers when it comes to buying other film sizes.

Two customers emerge: A man who does the buying for both 35-mm cameras and film and a woman who makes the decisions about purchasing instant, cartridge, and disc film and cameras. Men, certainly, are still the larger market. With the boom in automatic lens/shutter cameras, 35-mm has quickly become the standard for amateur photography.

Men make about 54 percent of the choices as to where 35-mm film is bought, according to the survey. For instant film, women make 56 percent of the buying decisions, says the study. Women account for 60 percent of the purchasing decisions for disc film and 62 percent for cartridge film.

Women are not only buying the film, they are buying the cameras, too. Families in the survey are reporting that women choose which instant camera to purchase 58 percent of the time. For cartridge film cameras it is 59 percent, and for disc cameras 68 percent. Women choose which store to shop 54 percent of the time for instant cameras, but 68 percent for disc cameras and 70 percent for cartridge film cameras.

*Adapted from Rick Gallagher, "The Image Is Shattered in 35-mm," *Chain Store Age, General Merchandise Trends,* February 1987, p. 65; Rick Gallagher, "For Photo Buyers It Pays to Advertise," *Chain Store Age, General Merchandise Trends,* February 1987, pp. 69–70; Rick Gallagher "Customers Want Fully-Automatic 35-mm Cameras," *Chain Store Age, General Merchandise Trends,* October 1986, pp. 53–54; and Rick Gallagher, "Camera Customers Confused," *Chain Store Age, General Merchandise Trends,* May 1986, p. 76. Reprinted with permission of *Chain Store Age.*

CAMERA ADVERTISING

According to the *Chain Store Age* research, camera advertising makes customers want to spend more for a camera—almost one-third more. For discount stores in particular, advertising brings more customers in the door. For manufacturers, advertising creates stronger brand preferences.

By far, newspaper advertising is the medium camera customers remember the most. Among the 40 percent of the sample who recall seeing camera advertising, 44 percent say they saw it in a newspaper. Another one-third report they watched it on television, while 28 percent say they saw ads in magazines. Catalogs and circulars get a 12 percent recall vote. Considering that newspapers get the lion's share of camera co-op dollars (ranging from 12 percent to 81 percent, depending on the manufacturer), it is no wonder that newspaper ads are the best remembered. Yet, according to the survey, customers recall circular and catalog advertising with little frequency.

Even fewer customers—only 3 percent—remember getting any direct-mail camera advertising. Direct mail accounts for only a tiny portion of all co-op programs. Though newspapers and television admittedly bring in a higher number of customers, direct mail does a more efficient job at turning advertising recall into actual sales.

In the survey, of households that remember seeing camera advertising in newspapers, 55 percent report that there is at least some chance they will actually buy a camera this year. This compares to 54 percent for the households that recall television advertising and 63 percent for those who remember magazine ads for cameras.

The single most effective medium, according to the poll, is direct mail. Of the small group in the survey which recalls direct-mail ads, every one of the households polled reports that there is at least some chance they will purchase a camera in the upcoming twelve months. Also effective is store or display-counter advertising. In the survey, 86 percent of those who remember seeing in-store advertising say that there is some chance they will buy a camera in 1987.

Catalogs, too, beat out TV, newspapers, and magazines in turning advertising recall into sales. Sixty-nine percent of households in the poll which recall catalog ads say they might purchase a camera this year. Families exposed to camera advertising are much more likely to want to buy a camera, pay more for it, and change where they will buy. They are also far more likely to be sure of the brand they want to buy.

Of those who remember some form of camera advertising, almost one in four (24.5 percent) say they probably or definitely will buy a camera within the next twelve months. Another 30.5 percent report that they may purchase this year. Only 42.1 percent absolutely rule out any chance of buying a camera in 1987. Compare these figures to those households who do not remember any camera advertising. More than three out of five (61.8 percent) report that they definitely will not buy this year. Another 18.2 percent rate their chances as only "maybe." Only 17.4 percent rank their chances of buying this year as "definite" or "probable."

In all, 55 percent of households that remember camera advertising say there is at least some chance they will purchase this year. Only 30 percent of those who did not see ads report the same. On the average, households which recall camera advertising say they will pay a median $218 the next time out. Families which did not remember camera ads report they expect to pay about one-third less, or a median of $150. The biggest difference occurs in those who expect to pay over $300 for their new camera. In that category, 16.4 percent of households that recall ads say they will pay over $300 the next time out, compared to only 11.5 percent of families who do not remember seeing advertising.

Families exposed to camera ads are more likely to say they want features like auto focus than are families who do not recall any advertising. Households remembering camera ads are also more likely to be attracted to 35-mm and are less likely to want cartridge-film cameras.

Though they expect to pay more for their next camera, families that recall camera ads still are looking for a bargain. And they are willing to shop at a discount store to find it, according to the survey. Among those who remember advertising, discount stores are the preferred place to shop. Almost three in ten, or 28.1 percent, say that a discount store is where they would most likely buy their new camera. Traditional camera dealers come in second, cited by 22.3 percent. For families who have not seen ads, however, camera dealers take the top spot, the choice of 24.8 percent of households in the poll. Discount stores pull in second, named by 18.7 percent. Among those who say they have seen camera advertising, K mart is the place to buy for 17.4 percent, more than for any other single retailer. Those who do not remember any camera ads choose K mart only 9 percent of the time, or about one-half the frequency.

As for manufacturers, camera advertising also provides a benefit. Of those who do not recall seeing any ads, three in ten say that they have no idea what brand of camera they will buy the next time out. Among those who do remember ads, the undecided group falls to only 11 percent. Among those who have seen ads, Polaroid's share of the market nearly doubles—from 3 percent to 6 percent—compared to those who have not seen ads. Minolta's standing also doubles—from 8 percent to 17 percent—as does Olympus's share. Kodak's share gains 20 percent due to advertising, according to the survey, and Canon records a 26 percent gain.

CAMERA FEATURES DESIRED

Asked what type of film their next camera would use if they were to buy one, 19.1 percent in the survey reported that it

would use instant film. This represents a doubling of the number recorded only a year ago and is about equal to levels of five years ago. The big losers, according to the latest study, are disc cameras, the choice of only 9 percent of households. Over the last three years, the number of households reporting that they will buy a disc camera has fallen by about one-half. Readings for prospective cartridge-film cameras sales are equal to last year's readings.

For 35-mm cameras, the poll shows a slight uptick in customer interest, with 42.9 percent saying their next camera would use 35-mm film. Of those who choose the 35-mm format, 52 percent report that they will buy a single lens reflex (SLR) camera. Of those interested in a 35-mm camera, 58 percent are not current 35-mm users. And of those who currently own a 35-mm camera, two out of three report that their next camera will be an SLR.

If there were a 35-mm camera which somehow could automatically arrange the kids around the birthday cake, snap a picture, and then blow out the candles, chances are customers would buy it. According to the survey, automatic cameras—and the more automated features, the better—have become the standard for amateur 35-mm photography. Whether they are first time 35-mm buyers or step-up customers, and regardless of whether they expect to pay $100 or $300, consumers in the poll say they expect their next 35-mm camera will include features such as auto focus, auto advance, auto load, and DX auto film-speed setting.

In the nationwide telephone poll, 76.3 percent say they have heard of automatic focusing, and 60.8 percent of that group also report that auto focus will be an essential feature on their next camera. This compares to the August 1984 survey where the number who were aware of automatic focusing was so small that it was considered statistically insignificant. In the poll, 73.7 percent report knowing about auto film advance, with 54.9 percent saying the feature is essential. Nearly two-thirds (64.6 percent) have heard of auto loading, with 49 percent rating it essential.

Of all the automated features studied, DX auto film-speed setting is the least known. Still, almost three out of five in the poll (57.8 percent) report some knowledge of DX coding, and 54.2 percent of those who know about it consider auto film-speed setting essential in a new camera. In absolute numbers, more potential customers say they want DX auto film-speed setting than say they want a more familiar feature, auto loading. In all, though, the trend toward buying automatic features holds equally, whether the customer is a first time 35-mm buyer or a customer trading up to a more sophisticated camera.

On the average, those in the survey who do not currently

own a 35-mm camera but who say there is a chance they will buy one within the next year, report that they expect to pay a median $195. Current owners say they will pay $300. Almost one in four of the nonowners (23.9 percent) think that they will spend under $125 for a 35-mm camera, compared to 4.8 percent of current owners. A majority (51.9 percent) of current owners report that they expect to pay over $275. Of nonowners, 28 percent think they will spend that amount. Perhaps the most interesting price expectations in the study, however, are those voiced by households which do not currently own a 35-mm camera and which say they definitely will not buy one within the next year. On the average, this group thinks they need to spend $281 for a 35-mm camera, 30 percent more than nonowners who do expect to buy.

Camera stores, according to the survey, are still the place where the greatest number of consumers expect to buy their next 35-mm camera. In the poll, 41.3 percent report that camera stores are the outlet of choice. Discount stores, however, are carving out a significant piece of the 35-mm market, as are catalog showrooms and department stores. Of those who think they will buy a 35-mm camera within the next year, 17.8 percent report they will buy at a discount store (9.3 percent say they will make their purchase at K mart). According to the survey, 11.3 percent say they will buy at catalog showrooms and 9.6 percent choose department stores.

Among respondents who say there is some chance that they will buy a camera in the next year, Canon, named by 27.9 percent in the poll, is the brand they most frequently mention they might purchase. Following are Minolta (20.9 percent), Nikon (13.2 percent), Kodak (10.4 percent), and Pentax (6.4 percent).

The potential customer's choice of a camera brand, however, changes when the survey's respondents are divided into current 35-mm owners and those who are buying a 35-mm camera for the first time. Among nonowners, Canon and Minolta run a dead heat, but current 35-mm camera users choose Canon by a 3 to 2 margin. Kodak's votes, meanwhile, come almost exclusively from those who do not yet own a 35-mm camera.

CAMERA CUSTOMER CONFUSION

According to *Chain Store Age* research, customers are awash on a sea of misinformation. Some disc and instant camera owners are confused about their purchase. For example, 5.6 percent of those who say they bought an SLR within the last year report buying Kodak, which has not even marketed a single lens reflex camera since 1970. Instead, they probably

bought one of Kodak's disc cameras. Similarly, 6 percent of those who say they bought a disc camera last year say they purchased from manufacturers such as Polaroid and Nikon, which do not market such cameras.

With more and more of the SLR business moving into self-service and low-service channels of distribution (20.1 percent of households in the poll report buying a camera at a discount store last year), the customer's lack of information could be hampering opportunities to move customers up the line to more sophisticated and more profitable cameras.

Potential customers have generally been divided into only two groups for advertising and marketing purposes: amateurs who are looking for snapshot cameras and hobbyists with more sophisticated requirements. However, Canon's success with its AE-1 series and Minolta's Maxxum success, point to a third market: advanced amateurs who are still snapshot photographers but who want the added quality and features of SLRs.

Questions

1 How do family roles play a part in camera purchase decisions?
2 What may be concluded about potential buyers' purchase plans for cameras?
3 What are consumers' evaluative criteria in a camera purchase?
4 How would you describe consumers' evoked set for this purchase?
5 What implications are there for retailers, based on consumers' store-choice plans in camera purchasing?
6 How can camera marketers use the research information presented to plan marketing strategies?

CASE 5-2
SHOPPER CRITERIA*

Chain Store Age surveyed consumers to find out what the most important elements were when buying hard or soft goods. Table 1 presents a summary of the results of the survey for each category of good analyzed. The values represent mean ratings for each criterion with 1 being not important and 9 being very important. Table 2 presents mean ratings by consumer respondent attribute.

Questions

1 How would you summarize the findings of this research?
2 How may manufacturers and retailers use this information?

*From Marsha Parker Cox, "Hard Goods Shoppers Prove Most Demanding," *Chain Store Age, General Merchandise Trends,* July 1985, p. 34. Reprinted by permission.

TABLE 1

	Major appliances	Furniture	Housewares	Electronics	Men's wear	Women's wear
Workmanship	5.66	5.80	5.44	5.77	5.26	5.26
Price	5.69	5.39	5.56	5.24	5.26	5.30
Material	5.17	4.73	5.18	4.52	4.96	5.10
Looks	4.38	5.17	4.38	4.71	4.89	5.13
Buy for less	4.69	4.52	4.84	4.88	4.76	4.82
Guarantee	5.34	4.87	4.70	4.91	4.28	4.62
Assortment	3.61	3.57	3.77	3.91	3.83	3.70
Brand name	3.95	3.61	4.03	3.84	3.79	3.58
Store	3.56	3.15	3.56	3.74	3.66	3.60
Country of origin	3.52	3.13	3.50	3.57	3.35	3.16
Advertising	2.94	2.91	2.91	3.25	3.24	3.03
Packaging	2.42	2.45	2.64	2.84	2.56	2.67

Average rating of importance on a scale of 1 (not important) to 9 (very important).
Source: *Chain Store Age*/Leo J. Shapiro & Associates.

TABLE 2

	Men	Working women	Working women with kids	Income			Age		
				$40K+	$20–$39K	Under $20K	Under 30	30–39	40+
Workmanship	5.54	5.52	5.54	5.78	5.47	5.08	5.36	5.60	5.44
Price	5.30	5.41	5.43	5.45	5.36	5.10	5.41	5.44	5.21
Material	4.93	5.01	4.91	5.25	4.93	4.77	4.81	5.05	5.09
Looks	4.75	4.88	4.78	4.81	4.87	4.83	5.14	4.67	4.75
Buy for less	4.64	5.00	5.01	4.76	4.78	4.88	4.80	4.96	4.72
Guarantee	4.51	4.81	4.97	4.60	4.72	4.55	4.60	4.71	4.72
Assortment	3.73	3.74	3.74	3.56	3.82	3.84	3.87	3.71	3.65
Brand name	3.68	3.75	3.70	3.59	3.65	3.90	3.74	3.52	3.71
Store	3.59	3.46	3.44	3.35	3.49	4.01	3.51	3.37	3.69
Country of origin	3.51	3.22	3.31	3.22	3.58	3.39	3.00	3.35	3.68
Advertising	3.10	2.93	2.98	2.82	3.06	3.35	2.90	3.06	3.06
Packaging	2.56	2.58	2.53	2.38	2.62	2.82	2.62	2.54	2.65

Average rating of importance on a scale of 1 (not important) to 9 (very important).
Source: *Chain Store Age*/Leo J. Shapiro & Associates.

CASE 5-3
JOHNSONS BUY A FOOD PROCESSOR*

At 4:52 P.M. on Friday, January 19, 1983, Brock and Alisha Johnson bought a food processor. There was no doubt about it. Any observer would agree that the purchase took place at precisely that time. Or did it?

When questioned after the transaction, neither Brock nor Alisha could remember which of them at first noticed or suggested the idea of getting a food processor. They do recall that in the summer of 1981 they attended a dinner party given by a friend who specialized in French and Chinese cooking. The meal was scrumptious, and their friend Brad was very proud of the Cuisinart food processor he had used to make many of the dishes. The item was quite expensive, however, at about $200.

The following summer, Alisha noticed a comparison study of food processors in *Better Homes and Gardens.* Four different brands were compared across a number of dimensions. At about the same time, Brock noticed that *Consumer Reports* also compared a number of brands of food processors. In both instances, the Cuisinart brand came out on top. Brock had even run his own weighting schemes on some of the results, using additive, conjunctive, and disjunctive weightings on the reports of the study to confirm the Cuisinart as the top-rated brand.

Later that fall, new models of the Cuisinart were introduced and the old standard model went on sale in department stores at $140. The Johnsons searched occasionally for Cuisinarts in discount houses or in "wholesale showroom" catalogs, hoping to find an even lower price for the product. The Cuisinarts simply were not offered there.

For Christmas 1982, the Johnsons traveled from Atlanta to the family home in Michigan. While there, the Johnsons received a gift of a Sunbeam Deluxe Mixer from a grandmother. While the mixer was beautiful, Alisha immediately thought how much more versatile a food processor would be. One private sentence to that effect brought immediate agreement from Brock. The box was (discretely) not opened, although many thanks were expressed. The box remained unopened the entire time the Johnsons kept the item.

Back home in Atlanta in January, Alisha again saw the $140 Cuisinart advertised by Rich's, one of the two major full-service department stores in Atlanta. Brock and Alisha visited a branch location on a Saturday afternoon and saw the item. The salesperson, however, was not knowledgeable of its features and not very helpful in explaining its attributes. The Johnsons left, disappointed.

Two days later, Alisha called the downtown location, where she talked to Mrs. Evans, a seemingly knowledgeable salesperson who claimed to own and love exactly the model that the Johnsons had in mind. Furthermore, Mrs. Evans said that they did carry Sunbeam mixers and would make an exchange of the mixer which had been received as a gift and for which no receipt was available.

On the following Friday morning, Brock put the mixer in his car trunk when he left for work downtown. That afternoon, Alisha and six-month-old Brock, Jr., rode the bus downtown to meet her husband and to make the transaction. After meeting downtown, they drove through heavy, rainy-day traffic to Rich's to meet Mrs. Evans, whom they liked as much in person as they did through telephone contact. After a brief "dry run" demonstration of the use and operation of the attachments for all of the models, the Johnsons confirmed their initial decision to take the $140 basic item. They then asked about exchanging the Sunbeam mixer that they had brought with them. "No problem," said Mrs. Evans.

After making a quick phone call, Mrs. Evans returned with bad news. Rich's had not carried that particular model of mixer. This model mixer, the I-73, was a single-color model that is usually carried at discount houses, catalog sales houses, and jewelry stores. The one carried by the better department stores, such as Rich's, was a two-tone model which allowed a two-tiered pricing structure through two different channels of distribution. Mrs. Evans was sorry she could not make the exchange but suggested that other stores such as Davison's, Richway Discount, or American Jewelers might carry the item. She even offered to allow the Johnsons to use her phone to verify the availability of the item. The Johnsons did exactly that.

Alisha dialed several of the suggested stores, looking for a retailer who carried both the Cuisinart and the Sunbeam model I-73, but she quickly learned that they were distributed through mutually exclusive distribution channels. The young man who answered the phone at American Jewelers, however, seemed friendly and helpful and Alisha was able to obtain his agreement to take the item as a return if she could get there that afternoon.

American Jewelers was about one-half mile away. Brock volunteered to baby-sit for Brock, Jr., at Rich's while Alisha returned the mixer. She took the downtown shopper bus to American Jewelers with the still unopened mixer box under her arm.

About an hour later, Alisha returned, cold and wet, with a $57 refund. Brock, having run out of ways to entertain a six-month-old, was very happy to see her. Together they bought the Cuisinart at 4:52 P.M. and proudly took it home.

Questions

1 Which of the Johnsons decided to buy a food processor? A Cuisinart? Defend your answer.

2 When was the decision to buy made? Discuss.

3 What, in your opinion, was the deciding factor in purchasing the item? The particular brand?

4 Would you consider this purchase process to be careful and deliberate? Was it an inefficient use of time? Is it a good model to follow?

5 Would your answer to question 4 change if you learned that

on February 19, 1983, discount stores began to sell the same model Cuisinart for $99.98?

6 You are suddenly granted perfect hindsight and are thrust into the role of Brock or Alisha (your choice) at the 1981 dinner party. How would your subsequent behavior differ from that reported here? (*Note:* The event described in question 5 may or may not happen.)

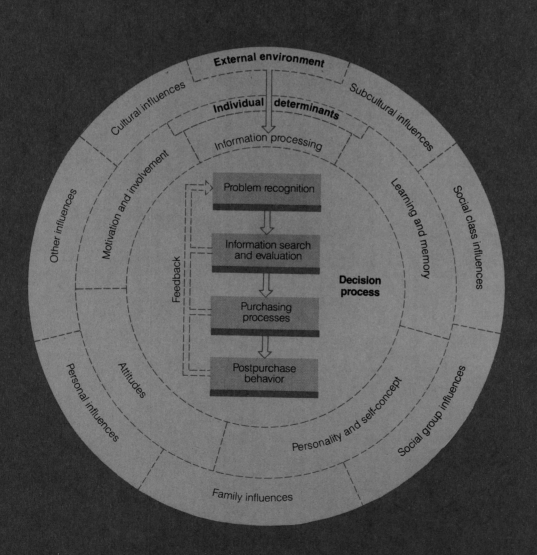

ADDITIONAL
DIMENSIONS

PART 6

CONSUMERISM

After studying this chapter, you should understand . . .

- The evolution of the consumerism movement in the United States

- The nature of consumerism and the consumer's bill of rights

- What ethical and social responsibility to consumers involves

- The nature of laws affecting consumers

- The responsibilities of consumers

- How the marketer can develop a marketing organization that is responsive to consumers

When several Chicago people died after taking Tylenol capsules laced with cyanide, the shock was felt by Johnson & Johnson, makers of Tylenol, and by all other pharmaceutical firms as well. Next it was the turn of the entire U.S. food industry to worry: if it happened with Tylenol capsules, who's to say someone wouldn't poison food products also?

Since the Tylenol incidents, safety seals around food products have become an increasingly common sight. The Closure Manufacturers Association, a trade group of manufacturers who produce plastic wrappers, shrink seals around lids, and pop-up caps for vacuum-packed jars, estimates that its business has grown 60 to 70 percent since 1982. A spokesperson says, "The food industry became frantic after Tylenol, fearful it would be next." Industry and governmental officials concede that although tampering may be made more difficult, no seals or lids are tamper-proof. The dilemma facing the food industry, like the drug industry, is that companies want to reassure consumers about product safety but do not want their actions to inspire hoaxers, attract copycat complaints, or goad a tamperer to act. Nevertheless, most of the food industry has concluded that product safety improvement is worth the risk of any possible negative side effect to sales.

Now packaging of products such as fruit juices, spaghetti and barbecue sauces, mayonnaise, and peanut butter is incorporating protective devices. Of course, the food industry has some advantages over the pharmaceutical business: Lethal contamination of food is harder to accomplish because people don't typically swallow it without tasting first, as they might with capsules. In addition, people know what the food should look or taste like, and so they should notice signs of poisoning because it generally affects color, appearance, odor, or taste.

One of the most publicized recent incidents of food tampering was the Gerber case. Consumers in thirty states reported finding glass fragments in more than 250 Gerber jars, and many grocery stores removed Gerber products from their shelves. After the

22

FDA opened and inspected 40,000 sealed jars of Gerber baby food, "harmless" glass specks no larger than grains of sand were found in nine of them. Although Gerber plants have excellent screening devices, it is supposed that glass fragments were planted by people seeking damages or publicity.

Quaker Oats, maker of Gatorade, had a bottle contaminated with urea, apparently tampered with after shipment from the bottling plant. The company met the problem head-on by distributing videotapes to local television stations informing people how to tell whether Gatorade's caps had been tampered with.

In other notorious cases, someone slipped razor blades into packages of Hormel hotdogs; and 800 cases were reported in 1984 of pins, needles, and other objects in Girl Scout cookies. Japan has an even more serious problem of food tampering: in 1985 at least eight people died drinking juice spiked with paraquat, a weedkiller.

As a response to the first Tylenol poisonings, U.S. federal law now protects consumers. Tampering with food, drugs, or cosmetics carries maximum penalties of life imprisonment and a $250,000 fine, with a five-year prison term just for a hoax.[1]

This is just one dimension of the types of problems encountered by consumers in today's society. Although the nature of the problems varies, the fundamental issues are the same: consumer dissatisfaction with or need for protection regarding some aspect of their position as consumers. Consumerism is one of the most popular social issues and is becoming increasingly publicized as time passes. The scope of the movement is so extensive that it draws attention from a variety of disciplines. Thus, an appropriate conclusion for our study of consumer behavior is an understanding of the consumer's position in society. Knowledge of the problems faced by consumers in the marketplace and the reality of their experiences is useful for interpreting many other topics that have been discussed.

The consumer of the future will be increasingly demanding, skeptical, and critical. Marketers who fail to understand the changes that are occurring in consumer behavior in today's marketplace are doomed to be less successful than they otherwise might be. Thus, the topic of consumerism is of prime importance for the marketer because it holds an important key to present and future success. Understanding consumers and being able to adapt to their changing demands will reward the innovative marketer.

The major issues discussed first in this chapter are consumerism's roots, business's ethical and social responsibility, consumer-oriented legislation, and the responsibilities of consumers. Attention is then focused on how to develop a sensitive marketing organization to deal with these issues and improve marketing's responsiveness to consumers.

THE ROOTS OF CONSUMERISM

The word "consumerism" has many connotations, depending on who is using the term. Business, government, consumer groups, and academic researchers have each developed their own definition of the term. These definitions span the gamut from challenging society's goals for material goods to reflecting people's desire for better values. One succinct definition is that ''Consumerism is a social movement of citizens and government to enhance the rights and powers of buyers in relation to sellers.''[2] Other authors have broadened this definition, stating that consumerism:

. . . encompasses the evolving set of activities of government, business, and independent organizations that are designed to protect the rights of consumers. . . . Consumerism is concerned with protecting consumers from all organizations with which there is an exchange relationship. There are consumer problems associated with hospitals, libraries, schools, police forces, and various government agencies, as well as with business firms.[3]

This broader definition will be used to reflect the many facets of the concept. Many organizations—business, government, consumer groups, and nonprofit groups—are concerned with ensuring consumers fair treatment in the exchange process.

There are numerous underlying roots of consumerism in the United States. The enduring problems which underlie the movement have been summarized as follows:[4]

1 *Disillusionment with the system.* All of our institutions have been subjected to increasing public scrutiny, skepticism, and loss of esteem. Many consumers think they get a worse deal in the marketplace than they used to. Thus, there is dissatisfaction with their bargaining position.

2 *The performance gap.* Many consumers express broad dissatisfaction with the goods they buy. Their expectation of product performance and reliability have risen (largely because of advertising touting the new improvements). Yet the increased product complexity brings about new possibilities for malfunction and a perception by consumers that the promise-performance gap is widening.

3 *The consumer information gap.* Amateur buyers lacking the time, interest, or capacity to process information adequately in order to make optimal marketplace decisions face literally thousands of complex products requiring evaluations along many dimensions relating to performance, convenience, or even societal concerns.

4 *Antagonism toward advertising.* Large segments of the population are very skeptical of the usefulness and truthfulness of advertising information. In addition, it is criticized for its intrusiveness and clutter, irritation factor, stereotyped role portrayals, and promotion of unrealistic or unsupportable expectations.

5 *Impersonal and unresponsive marketing institutions.* Such marketing factors as the rise of self-service retailing, reduced knowledge of sales employees, computerized impersonalness, and bureaucratic structures are contributors to a feeling that no marketer is listening

6 *Intrusions of privacy.* Development of the many consumer-information data bases made possible under our increasingly computerized society has caused

concern over the access to and use of such data and has led to attempts to protect the consumer's privacy.

7 *Declining living standards.* Recent reductions in consumers' real discretionary incomes has led to pessimism and disenchantment with the economic system and attempts to deal with the situation.

8 *Special problems of the disadvantaged.* The young, the old, and the poor are even more vulnerable than most other groups in society and face great difficulties coping in the marketplace.

9 *Different views of the marketplace.* Business people and their critics have radically different perceptions of the nature of the marketplace.

Such elements as these have fostered the rise of the consumer movement in the United States. The marketer of the 1980s and beyond faces a consumer who is better educated and informed, is more militant than previous generations were, is under great economic pressure, and tends to look at regulation as the cure-all.

HISTORY OF CONSUMERISM IN THE UNITED STATES

Consumerism is not new. Even in the Middle Ages, religious leaders such as Martin Luther and John Calvin attacked deceptive selling practices of business and advanced the concept of a just price rather than what the market would bear. In the United States three eras of consumerism have been identified. A description of these eras provides a historical perspective which aids in understanding the current movement and provides a background for analysis of future events.[5]

THE EARLY YEARS

The turn of the twentieth century brought about the first undercurrents of consumer unrest. *The Jungle* by Upton Sinclair was a 1906 exposé on the filth surrounding the Chicago meat-packing industry. This book created such a public outcry that Congress was compelled to pass the Meat Inspection Act of 1906. This act provided federal inspection of meat packing and processing. That same year the Food and Drug Administration was created as an agency charged with preventing misbranded and adulterated food and drugs in interstate commerce. The Federal Trade Commission (FTC) was established in 1914 to curb the growth of the use of monopolies and trade practices that might hinder competition. However, consumer protection was still not given prominence by business or government during this time.

THE FORMATIVE YEARS

The U.S. economy was undergoing substantial changes in the post–World War I years. The return of American troops from Europe brought about an awakening in our country of the goods and services available in other countries and a consumer anxious to buy new products. U.S. businesses responded with new products and new and bigger advertising campaigns. Books again stirred a consciousness of consumers' plight. *Your Money's Worth* attacked the manipulation and deceit of advertising and called for product standards and testing to give consumers information for making buying decisions. One result of this book was the establishment of the Consumers Union, which publishes *Consumer Reports*. The book *100,000,000 Guinea Pigs* pointed out loopholes in the Food and Drug Act which permitted the sale of dangerous medicines, unsafe cosmetics, and adulterated foods. This led to the passage of the Food, Drug and Cosmetic Act of 1938 and the Wheeler-Lea Act of 1938. The Wheeler-Lea amendment to the Federal Trade Commission Act increased the policing powers of the Federal Trade Commission. The FTC could now prosecute unlawful, deceptive, or unfair trade practices, thus providing some protection for consumers.

THE RECENT ERA

While a book by Vance Packard entitled *The Hidden Persuaders*, published in the late 1950s, again charged that consumers were being manipulated by advertising, the real impetus for the current consumerism movement came from President John F. Kennedy's speech to Congress in which he identified what has been referred to as the *consumer's bill of rights*. In 1962, Kennedy presented in a message to Congress the following four fundamental rights:[6]

1   The *right to safety*: to be protected against the marketing of goods which are hazardous to health or life.

2   The *right to be informed*: to be protected against fraudulent, deceitful, or grossly misleading information, advertising, labeling, or other practices, and to be given the facts needed to make an informed choice.

3   The *right to choose*: to be assured, wherever possible, access to a variety of products and services at competitive prices; and in those industries in which competition is not workable and government regulation is substituted, an assurance of satisfactory quality and service at fair prices.

4   The *right to be heard*: to be assured that consumer interest will receive full and sympathetic consideration in the formulation of government policy, and fair and expeditious treatment in its administrative tribunals.

Let's examine each of these rights and see how they are related to current issues for consumers. These rights are the foundation for the current interest in consumerism in the United States.

CONSUMER SAFETY

This is the oldest and least controversial of the consumer's rights and one which both business people and consumerists agree on and support. Consumers regularly complain about shoddy or defective merchandise and poor services. It is one thing to be cheated or deceived by a product, but it is quite another to be physically injured by an unsafe product. Several significant agencies are involved in the protection of consumer safety rights, but two of the most important are the Food and Drug Administration (FDA) and the Consumer Product Safety Commission (CPSC).

The Consumer Product Safety Commission has collected information about the most hazardous household products. The CPSC discovered that each year an estimated 20 million Americans are injured, with 30,000 of these victims killed and 110,000 permanently disabled, from 10,000 products under the commission's jurisdiction.[7] (Not even included under their authority are such potentially lethal products as motor vehicles, airplanes, boats, firearms, foods, drugs, cosmetics, medical services, and pesticides!) Among the most hazardous products are sports and recreation equipment, home structures, home furnishings, housewares, and personal use items.[8]

The CPSC has the power to set safety standards for products under its control, to recall products from the market, and to ban unsafe products. The commission began in 1972 and participated in the recall of over 1200 products in its first five years of operation.

Safety is still very much an issue for consumers, business, and government. The Tylenol poisoning episode brought to the forefront the need for tamperproof packages in medical products. Millions of dollars have been spent by producers to redesign packages to insure product safety.

CONSUMER INFORMATION

Consumer rights with regard to information relate to the marketer's provision of adequate information which neither deceives nor misleads.

DECEPTION OF CONSUMERS

Although numerous government agencies are involved in the area of preventing consumer deception, the Federal Trade Commission is probably the most active unit in this field. Charged with preventing unfair or deceptive acts or practices in commerce, the FTC has been most concerned with eliminating deceptive advertising. The FTC need not prove that deception actually occurred in an advertisement, but merely that the ad had the *capacity* to deceive. It should also be noted that the advertiser cannot escape liability simply because he did not know that the ad's claim was false.

Advertisements have long been designed on the basis of the accepted approach of puffery, that is, the use of exaggerated praise for an advertised item. The most difficult question to resolve, however, is the point at which puffery becomes deception. The FTC has generally taken the position that deception in advertising occurs when a false claim is presented or a false impression is created over a true claim, or that insufficient information is provided. A useful definition by which deception in advertising may be evaluated is as follows:

If an advertisement (or advertising campaign) leaves the consumer with an impression(s) and/or belief(s) different from what would normally be expected if the consumer had reasonable knowledge, and that impression(s) and/or belief(s) is factually untrue or potentially misleading, then deception is said to exist.[9]

On the basis of such a definition, three types of deceptive advertising may exist. First, the outright *lie* occurs where a claim is made that is completely false, even from an objective viewpoint. That is, it is impossible for consumers to achieve the claimed benefit. A claim that a new automobile carburetor device would increase gas mileage to over 100 m.p.g. could be such an example. Second, the advertiser may be guilty of *claim-fact discrepancy*, in which a claimed benefit of the advertised product must be qualified in some way for it to be correctly understood and evaluated (but this is not done in the ad). For example, an advertisement may claim that 60 percent of doctors recommend ''X.'' If the consumer knew what types of doctors, how many were surveyed, and what questions were asked, this claim could be more accurately evaluated. Third, the advertiser may deceive on the basis of *claim-fact interaction*. That is, the advertisement claim (while being neither explicitly nor implicitly deceptive) interacts with the accumulated belief and attitudes held by consumers in such a way that they are misled or deceived by it. For example, actor Robert Young, who played a medical doctor on the long-running television series *Marcus Welby,* may have been perceived by many consumers as acting in the role of a physician or recommending the product on the basis of medical knowledge when he appeared as a spokesperson in advertisements for Sanka brand decaffeinated coffee. Even though no mention is made of the fact, for some consumers, such a recommendation may interact deceptively with their beliefs.

Corrective Advertising While the FTC has been accused by some critics of a laissez-faire attitude toward deception, it has taken some actions to control the problem. It has, in some advertising situations, removed a message from the communications media. However, the problem with this is that consumers may have already stored this deceptive information in their memories. Consequently, the government has also adopted the position of requiring *corrective advertising*, in which past advertising transgressions are corrected.

The first case in which such a remedy was suggested concerned an advertisement by Campbell Soups. Campbell was alleged to have placed marbles at the bottom of the soup bowl in advertisements designed to indicate the large amounts of meat and vegetables in its soup bowl in advertisements. The marbles forced the solid ingredients to the surface, creating, according to the FTC, the false impression that there was more stock than actually existed. A group of law students, designating themselves as SOUP (Stamp Out Unfair Practices), recommended that the commission require Campbell to use corrective advertisements in order to dispel the memory trace resulting from its past advertising. The FTC accepted a consent agreement in which Campbell promised not to engage in such advertising in the future, but was not required to issue a correction.

The Listerine case is one of the most notable instances of corrective advertising. This situation involved advertisements which since the 1920s had cultivated the consumer belief that using Listerine would prevent or lessen the severity of sore throats and colds. The FTC required millions of dollars of corrective Listerine advertising which was intended to counter this mistaken belief. Unfortunately, it is not clearly known what the result of such corrective advertising is. For example, the FTC alleged that previous commercials for Bristol-Myers' Bufferin and Excedrin overstated their benefits and proposed that the company make certain remedial statements in future campaigns. However, research on the proposed statements revealed that remedial advertising statements may be miscomprehended as much as—or even more often than—the advertising they are supposed to remedy.[10]

Affirmative Disclosure   Affirmative disclosure is designed to eliminate the potential for deception in promotional material by providing consumer information on negative attributes of some products and services. Affirmative disclosure specifically requires a company to disclose in its advertising or labeling the deficiencies or limitations of its product or service. The warning notices in cigarette advertising are an example of affirmative disclosure.

The assumption being made with affirmative disclosure is that such information will affect consumers' attitudes or purchase behavior. This puts the consumer in a position of having both positive and negative information before purchase decisions are made.

AVAILABILITY OF SUFFICIENT INFORMATION

It is felt by many in legislative, regulative, and judicial circles that the consumer does not have adequate information on which to base decisions. Critics of current marketing practices claim that much factual information relevant to consumer choice is simply unavailable and that this results in higher prices, "artificial" brand differences, and a stress on frills that represent no real value to consumers. Marketers, on the other hand, rebut these claims by noting that in many of the cases in which product promotions contained numerous facts, there has been little positive effect on sales. In addition, marketers feel that if consumers really wanted and would use more product information, our system of competition would provide it.

In any event, there is growing pressure for businesses to provide more and better quality information so that more "rational" or better decisions can be made by consumers. A result of this belief has led to a number of consumer information programs.

Unit Pricing   Unit pricing means that the retailer not only displays the total price of the item, but also displays the price per relevant unit of the product (such as dollars per pound, fluid ounce, and so forth). The basis for this program arose from consumerists who alleged that consumers could not identify the most economical item in a product class because of the large variety of brands, package sizes, and quantity sizes (such as jumbo, super, giant, large economy size, and so on), and the poor presentation of quantity information on packages. Even better-educated shoppers sometimes find it difficult to identify the most economical items.

The results of studies on usage of unit pricing have not been consistent, however. Most have found higher usage among higher socioeconomic categories rather than among the lower-income groups who might appear really to benefit most from them. Research generally indicates a high awareness among consumers of unit pricing, but much variability with regard to claimed usage and effectiveness.[11] There are at least two reasons for such findings. First, even with access to unit-price information, consumers may not necessarily buy the most economical item because of such factors as brand quality differences and the convenience of smaller but more expensive sizes (such as to a single elderly buyer). Second, the method of unit-price information presentation varies considerably. Some unit-price programs have been very effectively introduced and run, while others meet the letter of the law without really facilitating consumers' usage.

Nutritional Labeling With the growing concern over dietary deficiencies among the American public (particularly among young people) and the increasing demand to know what really goes into the foods we eat, manufacturers have been under pressure to increase their nutritional labeling.[12] Yet, the extent to which consumers are able to understand and thus use such additional information is questionable. It has been shown that some consumers would refer to additional nutritional information and could buy more nutritious products as a result.[13] But just how much information should be provided is not clear. One study showed that consumers preferred labels with moderate levels of nutritional information, compared with those with either the least or the most information.[14]

As with research on unit pricing, most studies on nutrient labeling have found that consumers in lower socioeconomic categories are less likely to use such information.

Open Dating This is the practice whereby dates are printed on packaged food products to inform consumers of their freshness. Consumers appear to desire this information more than unit pricing or nutrient labeling. However, studies conducted on open dating indicate that only a small percentage of consumers are able to interpret the dates. Moreover, the system of dating used in most programs is the one least preferred by consumers.[15]

Truth in Lending The effects of federal truth-in-lending legislation (which requires full disclosure of the rate of finance charges and other aspects of a consumer credit transaction) are also unclear. One study showed that although the practice of making such information available apparently improves consumer knowledge of credit rates and charges, it has been found to do little to change credit behavior, because of the importance of the retailer in the credit decision. Moreover, it was shown that most consumers (particularly those with lower incomes and education) remained uninformed about interest rates; many did not even understand the concept of interest, nor could they calculate it in dollars. Thus, this study concluded that consumers must not simply be provided with information but should also be taught to understand it and use it.[16]

INFORMATION OVERLOAD?

Many of the foregoing research studies on consumer-information programs indicated that consumers do not heavily use them. What causes this lack of use? Some researchers suggest that the problem may be the result of information overload. That is, there are limits to the amount of information that consumers can process; hence, too much information is dysfunctional for them.[17]

In the first systematic study of information overload, subjects were asked to make decisions on product brands with varying quantities of information.[18] The researchers concluded that as the amount of information increased, consumers were less able to select the brand best for them. Yet, the information had beneficial effects on the consumer's degree of satisfaction, certainty, and confusion regarding her selection. That is, subjects appeared to feel better with more information while actually making worse purchase decisions! This result was taken to mean that an information overload phenomenon had been identified. Similar results were found in a succeeding study, in which information overload

was observed to be related to an increase in the number of brands. It was found, however, that increased information per brand resulted in better decisions.[19]

Critics of these two studies raised a number of conceptual and methodological issues.[20] Moreover, reanalysis of the data obtained in these research projects, with a more powerful analytical procedure, suggested that information overload may not have occurred in the experiments.[21] However, recent research of a more complex product-choice situation (house buying), incorporating four different means of information overload, with a more sophisticated analytical methodology, has again led to a finding of information overload.[22] Thus, additional replication is desirable across other decision-making situations in order to understand the nature and extent of information overload.

How does the consumer cope with information overload? There may be several strategies employed to reduce the amount of information actually used in purchase decision making so as not to be overwhelmed by the great amount available. It has been suggested that consumers base their decisions on the most important three to five product-attribute dimensions rather than on all of the information available.[23] Another suggestion is that consumers organize and integrate the separate information bits into larger information "chunks," as described in the learning chapter. For example, a brand name may serve as the consumer's basic device for summarizing the impressions and comparisons that exist among brand alternatives in the marketplace.[24]

Although few definitive statements can yet be made, the concept of information overload may become an extremely important issue among marketers, consumerists, legislators, regulators, and others who seek to provide even more information to the consumer. The "more information is better" argument, however, may result in American shoppers feeling better but making worse purchase decisions.

For the marketers to provide more information than they now do may also prove to be uneconomical. For instance, industry experience indicates that thirty- and fifteen-second television commercials are economically superior to a sixty-second ad, both in terms of recall and sales (except in the case of new products). Thus, if the marketer were compelled to run a longer commercial in order to provide more information to the consumer, this would be uneconomical from the brand's own standpoint, although perhaps justifiable from the position of industry's obligation to the consumer. Perhaps it is possible to restructure ads to provide more of the "right kind" of information within the same time limit. In order to resolve this potential problem, more advertising research will be needed.[25]

CONSUMER CHOICE

The American consumer, it would seem, has rather little restriction in choice within the marketplace. Some consumer activists argue, however, that the consumer actually has less choice than might be possible and desirable because of the economies of scale necessary in order to enter and compete effectively in certain industries. For example, in the cereal industry it is claimed that a small new producer of cereal would find it virtually impossible to enter and be successful. Therefore, some consumerists support expanded choice for the consumer through

regulations designed to control corporate power in the marketplace. Many of these controls are oriented toward breaking up larger corporate units into smaller and what are viewed as more freely competitive units. Major companies in industries involving computers, cereals, oil, and communications have been subjected to such attempts to dismember their operating units. It is not at all clear, however, that such a result would benefit consumers' rights to free choice. The issue of consumer choice also is related to U.S. international economic patterns. For example, in 1987 President Reagan placed a high tariff on some imported Japanese electronic products, making these products more expensive to U.S. consumers and encouraging them to buy competitive U.S.-made goods. Many consumerists have argued that such actions limit U.S. consumers' access to lower-priced foreign goods.[26]

In contrast to the view supporting more choice in the marketplace, consumerists sometimes support reduced choice by arguing that consumers should be given not simply what they want, but rather what is "best" for them. Thus, some consumerists support the notion that buyers are not able to adequately determine for themselves what is in their best interest and must instead be provided with the "right" products. This concept overlaps our earlier discussions of product safety and information disclosure. The government has mandated, for example, safer automobiles, lawn mowers, and other products.

Other laws have also been implemented in order to foster consumer safety in the usage of products (such as state laws requiring motorcycle riders to wear helmets). Increased disclosure of information is also an attempt to have consumers buy more wisely. Few would argue with some of these programs. Certainly consumers expect and demand safe products. However, much more debate will be forthcoming over the desirability of government intervention, decision, and control of consumer choice in order to guarantee that only product alternatives deemed by regulators as beneficial to consumers and society be allowed.

CONSUMER REDRESS

The consumer has the right to be listened to in the marketplace. That is, consumer input as a means of setting government policies should be available and consumer complaints directed to businesses should be facilitated and, more importantly, responded to in an equitable way.

There are numerous weapons at the consumer's disposal which may be used to obtain redress. Such activities include complaint letters, boycotts, class action suits, and other means. The remedies sought by these means include restitution and punishment. But the best way that the marketer can be protected from consumer redress is to *prevent* problems before they happen.[28] Listening to consumers, therefore, may warn of situations which can be remedied before they become problems. The marketer can establish codes of conduct, make better disclosures of information, and substantiate claims in order to forestall problems. Although prevention is a most desirable public policy, the history of consumer-protection activities indicates that it is insufficient as a sole remedial action.

A second way for consumers to obtain satisfaction from the marketer is through *restitution,* which means that the offender may have to engage in affirmative disclosure, corrective advertising, arbitration, or make refunds, for example.

Restitution is an area that has not been adequately explored by federal regulatory agencies. Arbitration, particularly, appears to hold much promise for resolving disputes. In this approach a dispute is referred to one or more impartial arbitrators for a final and binding decision. Although well known as a labor settlement device, arbitration has been much less widely used to resolve consumer controversies.

A final way for consumers to obtain redress is through *punishment* of the offending marketer. By means of fines, incarceration, class action law suits (in which a representative of a large group of people with similar claims against the same defendant sues on behalf of himself and others), and other legal processes the grievance may be remedied. For example, some view consumer fraud as a more harmful kind of social behavior than traditional crime. Therefore, punishment will continue to play a role in the consumer protection process. It will be used sparingly, however, in order to halt only the most abusive practices or to deter those who continually deceive despite the imposition of other remedial actions.

ENVIRONMENTAL CONCERNS

A fifth consumer right, not enumerated by Kennedy but which should be added, is stated as follows: The right to a *clean environment*—to be assured that the environment the consumer lives in is free from pollution. Widespread and large-scale pollution is a by-product of an economically developed society, but it is also an area of great concern for many consumers. The consumption of many products packaged in cans and in plastic—gasoline, detergents, and some aerosol sprays, for example—is directly linked to pollution. Marketing efforts aimed at increasing consumption of these products is in direct conflict with the desire for lower levels of pollution.

Earth Day, observed since 1970, is a consumer-led attempt to bring recognition to the need to conserve natural resources and protect the environment. Consumers have shown their awareness of environmental issues by their willingness to pay more for some pollution-reducing products and by buying products which are lower in pollutants.[28] Public demand for adequate programs for toxic waste management by the Environmental Protection Agency is another reflection of continuing consumer awareness and concern about environmental issues.

LEGISLATIVE RESPONSES TO CONSUMERISM

Consumerism has had an impact on legislative attempts to enhance consumer rights. Historically, legislation was oriented toward protecting competition and competitors rather than consumers. Since the 1960s, however, a large number of consumer-oriented bills have been enacted by Congress. This emphasis on consumer legislation was a result of heightened awareness by Congress of the widespread concern over consumer interest and environmental issues. Examples of this type of legislation include:

- Fair Packaging and Labeling Act
- Consumer Product Safety Act
- Cigar Labeling Act
- Truth-in Lending Act

These few examples of legislation indicate the thrust of recent consumerism in legislative circles. Advocates of this type of legislation feel that consumer rights can best be protected through governmental regulation of business practices.

BUSINESS RESPONSES TO SOCIAL AND ETHICAL ISSUES

The social and ethical responsibility of business has become a topic of much public debate. Many corporations have responded to their critics. These responses have three characteristics: changes in boards of directors, more emphasis on ethics, and use of social performance disclosures sometimes called social audits. Many boards of directors now include outside directors, such as influential academic, minority, and religious leaders, who give "society's" view during decision making.[29] Since marketing is usually the most visible activity of an organization, it must assume responsibility for developing useful products, fair pricing of products and services, and promoting them in an accurate manner.

Social responsibility and profits often complement each other. Some of the most profitable companies are often named as being the most socially responsible. *Business and Society Review,* which specializes in social responsibility issues, gives annual awards to the most socially responsible companies. Some of the recent recipients have been Mobil Oil, IBM, Bank of America, and Honeywell, which are also very profitable companies.

Corporate ethics are difficult to define and discuss because they are related to individual philosophies and values. But many large companies have written ethical codes to guide their employees. Some companies have even established industry standards with their well-developed codes of ethics.[30]

CONSUMERS' RESPONSIBILITIES

While the consumer's rights have been discussed in this chapter, nothing has been said about the obligations which accompany these rights. It has been suggested that consumer rights can only be achieved when accompanied by consumer responsibilities. Thus, consumers have the obligation to choose wisely, keep informed, sound off, put safety first, and help protect their environment.[31]

Although consumers may have certain responsibilities, they need to exercise these in an ethical fashion. For instance, the way in which consumers sound off their grievances should itself be responsible. But consider the following novel responses consumers have taken to resolve their perceived injustices:

■ One fellow burned his car on the front doorstep of the manufacturer because he was disappointed in it.

■ A Milwaukee citizen smashed a soda vending machine with a fire ax when it failed to function properly.

■ Many consumers fold, spindle, and mutilate their computer card bills because their complaint has not been resolved properly.

Such incidents as those above indicate that consumers also often fail to act totally responsibly. Moreover, consider the following all too typical consumer actions encountered in the marketplace:[32]

■ The shoppers who take the price tag from a cheaper item and put it on an expensive item before checking out

■ The shoppers who consume fruit, candy, and other goodies as they pass through the supermarket, and then don't pay

■ The woman who buys a fancy dress on the Friday before the country club dance and then returns it on Monday saying she changed her mind and who also gets very indignant if the sales clerk mentions that the dress looks as if it has been worn

■ The shoppers who scream loudly when they are overcharged but never utter a word when they are charged too little

■ The driver who brags about getting the "whole car repaired" on the insurance of the person who merely dented his fender

These are not examples of responsible marketplace behavior. Moreover, there are enormous costs for protecting business from consumers who shoplift, return goods for fictitious reasons, and in other ways take advantage of the system. Shoplifting itself is a multibillion-dollar-per-year business. While buyers complain about "excess packaging" on small items like batteries and razor blades (which are attached to much larger pieces of shrink-wrapped cardboard) the packaging was made necessary because it is bigger than the average shoplifter's pocket— where many of these small items used to go. Thus, it must be emphasized that consumers, just as business and other organizations, have an obligation to act responsibly in the marketplace in exchange relationships.

MARKETER RESPONSES TO CONSUMER ISSUES

Marketers face a twofold challenge in dealing with the issues discussed in this chapter. First, they must increase their level of knowledge of the nature of the issues, and second, they must design organizational elements to respond to consumers effectively.

UNDERSTANDING THE ISSUES

Many marketers are not aware of the issues and just how unfavorable situations are perceived to be by some consumers. Business people usually cite three possible defensive positions regarding consumer protection issues: (1) the number and seriousness of consumer problems suffered by the general population is not significant; (2) only a small, vocal minority of consumers complain about the problems they experience with products and services; and (3) the great majority of those complaints which are registered about products and services are resolved to the satisfaction of the consumer.

Data from a nationwide study of households do not support these contentions, however. Instead, there appears to be a need for the private sector to upgrade its complaint-handling capabilities. For example, among households which initiated complaint action about their most serious consumer problem, over 40 percent obtained completely unsatisfactory results.[33] Additional evidence indicates that consumers and business people are not on the same wavelength with regard to their perception of consumer problems and solutions. A report comparing opinions of executives and consumers on various consumer issues across several studies showed much consistency and indicated that a larger number of consumers disagree with executives about various issues. For example, there is disagreement over the adequacy of current levels of product quality and safety. Moreover, consumers lack confidence in advertising and look to government intervention to improve it. In addition, there are wide variations in executives' and consumers' views regarding the adequacy of product information, corporations' concerns for consumers, and the need for additional government regulation.[34]

This suggests that business must educate the public about the operation of the marketing system, the benefits of free enterprise, and the limitations of government intervention. Businesspeople also need to assess and modify their policies and practices in order to improve products and services offered to consumers.[35]

Businesses clearly have a responsibility to help protect the rights of consumers. Some business people are taking consumerism seriously and addressing the issues on a systematic and continuing basis. In the past, however, such action was not the first thing to occur when businesses were threatened with government regulation, according to *Business Week*.[36]

One recent study surveyed various corporate responses to consumerism. Overall, the results reflected a poor response to consumer needs:[37]

1 Few corporations had coordinated programs of response to consumerism.

2 Most industrial manufacturers believed consumerism did not influence their decisions.

3 Many firms claimed to have always been "consumer-oriented," so consequently, consumerism did not affect them. This seems to imply an apathetic attitude toward the movement.

4 Many firms were highly defensive about consumerism and viewed it as a "battle" between the seller and the buyer.

Today, most consumer affairs executives, at least, are convinced that consumerism can produce significant dividends for the company that works with it instead of against it.[38] That attitude must be spread throughout the company, however, if success is to be achieved.

DESIGNING A CONSUMER RESPONSE SYSTEM

But what does a company do? How should it respond to consumerism? First, companies should realize that the consumer is not a threat but an opportunity—an

opportunity because a satisfied customer is a repeat customer. And yet the history of American business seems to have been that companies generally have failed at the opportunity to exert leadership in this area, to set the public agenda, and, instead, have had to defend themselves against the public. Next, a program must be developed which will allow the company to communicate effectively with its customers and other publics, including government. There are numerous activities that businesses could adopt in responding to consumers. The important thing is that the company must be proactive rather than reactive in its approach. In other words, the firm must *manage* its consumer-response system. First, the company should conduct a consumer audit to determine its image among consumers and whether there is any need for change in its activities. Research on the public's image of the company should lead to an understanding of whether the company is viewed as progressive, honest, ethical, concerned, responsible, and responsive. Once consumer research identifies specific concerns, then the firm should formulate policies for dealing effectively with consumerism. A successful effort comprises several important elements: (1) understanding what consumers experience, (2) establishing a consumer advisory board, (3) listening to consumer complaints and responding effectively, (4) establishing a consumer affairs unit, and (5) helping to educate customers. Each of these will be discussed below.

Understanding What Consumers Experience

Many company executives are often not familiar with the world of the ordinary consumer. For example, the executives may not shop in the same places, and they are likely not to feel as much pressure from inflation as do the company's customers. Managers are often isolated in a corporate "cocoon" where they are shielded from contact with their customers.[39] It is necessary to break out of this cocoon and interact with buyers. As a result, many managers have begun riding repair trucks, answering telephones, waiting on shoppers, and standing in lines to seek out customers' opinions and experience firsthand what their customers experience. Thus, managers themselves must first be educated to what their "real-life" customer feels in the marketplace. It is beneficial if this can be obtained firsthand; however, it can also be obtained secondhand.

Establishing a Consumer Advisory Board

These customer councils are composed of a cross-section of perhaps ten to twenty of a firm's customers who meet every few months as a group with company executives to express their views, offer suggestions, react to company proposals, and listen to explanations of corporate conditions. For example, the Boston-based supermarket chain Stop & Shop has established a successful board with the following objectives:

- Make store personnel aware of what consumers are thinking.

- Elicit consumers' impressions of store operations, merchandising, and prices.

- Give consumers an opportunity to voice their complaints and to hear the experts explain the situation.

- Act as a sounding board for proposed products and policies.

- Glean ideas to improve operations at all levels.

Stop & Shop credits its advisory board with several successful operational and policy changes, such as decreasing the number of package sizes stocked and installing aisle warmers in the frozen food section.[40]

Listening to Consumers and Responding Effectively The public now finds it easier to complain, question, or compliment. Complaints may come not only from dissatisfied users of the product but also from those who are satisfied users of the product, nonusers of the product, and even nonpurchasers of the product.

Complaints from consumers to companies are one of the most important marketing assets available.[41] They are useful because they alert the company to a grievance that could lead to litigation or a government inquiry, and they act as an early warning system of problems whose quick solution could avert further complaints, brand switching, bad publicity, or product recalls.[42] Companies could actively solicit complaints by putting toll-free telephone numbers on packages and labels, for instance, and instructing consumers to call immediately with any problems they encounter.[43] Such information may lead to improvements in the physical product, its packaging, advertising, distribution, and in quality control programs of the company. For example, airlines, hotels, and restaurants use reply cards soliciting patrons' opinions; General Electric regularly conducts surveys on consumer dissatisfactions; and Whirlpool's use of its toll-free "cool line" telephone response system for customers has measurably reduced product and service complaints. Letters to Pillsbury and General Foods complaining about product problems have enabled these companies to quickly pinpoint product codes and dates and recall lots from store shelves. One study of the postpurchase attitudes and behavior of a home building company's customers indicated that the dollars spent on complaint handling may be more than repaid later in repurchase and referrals.[44] Questions from consumers can also be effective indicators that deficiencies may exist in advertising, labeling, or point-of-sale material.

Once received, complaints and questions must be dealt with effectively. Unfortunately, companies often fail to handle these properly. For example, one study found that 23 percent of consumer-complaint letters went unanswered, almost one-third of the responses were classed as "poor" overall, and the average length of time to receive an answer was over three weeks. Thus, business must respond in a swift, positive way.[45]

Proper complaint handling can be a marketing asset having the following bottom-line benefits: maintenance of market share, low-cost market research data base, lower warranty and service costs, improved employee productivity, and decreased government involvement in corporate affairs.

Establishing a Corporate Consumer Affairs Unit Part of the successful response necessary to the consumerism movement involves the company's making appropriate organizational changes. The establishment of a division for consumer affairs may be very beneficial to the company's relations with customers. Such a division could identify corporate practices that are perceived as deceptive or antagonistic by consumers. Review of such practices and resolution of problems would be conducted. Moreover, this group could have significant input to all corporate decisions having consumer implications. Consumer affairs units succeed, however, only when top management appreciates their involvement and

welcomes their special perspective in planning marketing decisions. Generally, the consumer affairs unit might have the following functions:[46]

- Resolve and analyze customer communication

- Develop and disseminate better information to consumers on the purchase and use of company products or services

- Serve as an internal consumer advocate and consultant

- Provide a liaison with consumer organizations

An example of the use of this type of approach is in Zayre Corporation, a large discount department store chain, which established an Office of Consumer Affairs in 1970 and has involved it in all consumer-related areas, from in-store customer contact, advertising practices, quality control, and merchandising, to participation in community consumer panels and working with both governmental agencies and consumer groups.[47]

Educating Consumers   Another area in which corporations may aid consumers is through education of the consumer, that is, providing them with greater knowledge about how to be effective consumers. Most consumers receive little education or training in how to shop wisely or manage their money intelligently. Doing more to remedy this situation would serve consumers' long-run interests better than increased legislation would.

Consumer education can be an effective competitive tool for the marketer. First, however, a company must determine what consumers need to know that will allow them to make the most satisfying purchases of the company's products and services. Next, the firm can integrate this consumer education material into its promotional program, utilizing creativity in this effort just as in its persuasive messages.[48]

MANAGERIAL REFLECTIONS

For our product or service situation . . .

1   Is the product or service safe for the consumer?

2   What information is being provided to the consumer and how can this process be improved?

3   Are there any parts of the marketing program which might be deceptive?

4   Are there environmental or pollution aspects of the product or service which need to be addressed?

5   Are the concerns of consumers fully understood by our personnel?

6   Has a system been established to respond effectively to consumerism issues?

DISCUSSION TOPICS

1   What is meant by the term "consumerism"?

2   Discuss the history of consumerism as it relates to current marketing practices.

3   Which of the consumer's rights are of most concern to you? Why?

4   What does the term "deceptive advertising" mean?

5   Find an ad you feel to be deceptive for a product or service, and explain how the ad should be altered to alleviate the deception.

6   Explain how consumer complaints can be a useful asset to a company.

7   What is meant by the term "consumer redress"?

8   What are the various forms of redress?

9   Why is it important for an organization to be responsive to consumers?

10   How is the responsiveness of firms to consumer problems related to consumer legislation?

PROJECTS

1   Visit a supermarket and select one aisle of products to obtain the following information: (*a*) number of products, (*b*) number of brands, (*c*) number of sizes in each brand. On the basis of this experience, do you think there is information overload? Why or why not?

2   Write a brief description of a system you would design for facilitating and effectively responding to students' complaints about university services such as food services or students' accounts.

NOTES

[1] Felix Kessler, "Tremors from the Tylenol Scare Hit Food Companies," *Fortune,* March 31, 1986, pp. 59, 62.

[2] Philip Kotler, *Marketing Management,* 5th ed., Prentice-Hall, Englewood Cliffs, N.J., 1984, p. 85.

[3] David A. Aaker and George S. Day, "A Guide to Consumerism," in David A. Aaker and George S. Day (eds.), *Consumerism: Search for the Consumer Interest,* 4th ed., Free Press, New York, 1982, pp. 8–15.

[4] David A. Aaker and George S. Day, *Consumerism: Search for the Consumer Interest,* 2d ed., Free Press, New York, 1974, p. xvii.

[5] Robert O. Herrmann, "Consumerism: Its Goals, Organizations, and Future," *Journal of Marketing,* **34**:56, October 1970.

[6] *Message from the President of the United States Relative to Consumers' Protection and Interest Program,* Document No. 364, House of Representatives, 87th Congress, 2d session, March 15, 1962.

[7] "Coming: A Rush of New Consumer-Safety Rules," *U.S. News & World Report,* July 18, 1977, p. 61.

[8] *Consumer Product Safety Commission Annual Report,* July 1, 1982–June 30, 1983, Washington, D.C., U.S. Government Printing Office, 1983.

[9] David M. Gardner, "Deception in Advertising: A Conceptual Approach," *Journal of Marketing,* **39**:42, January 1975.

[10] Jacob Jacoby, Margaret C. Nelson, and Wayne D. Hoyer, "Correcting Corrective Advertising," in Kent Monroe (ed.), *Advances in Consumer Research,* vol. 8, Association for Consumer Research, Ann Arbor, Mich., 1981, pp. 416–418.

[11] Kent B. Monroe and Peter J. La Placa, "What Are the Benefits of Unit Pricing," *Journal of Marketing,* **36**:16–32, July 1972; and Monroe P. Friedman, "Consumer Responses to Unit Pricing, Open Dating, and Nutrient Labeling," in M. Venkatesa/ (ed.), *Proceedings of the Third Annual Conference of the Association for Consumer Research,* Chicago, 1972, pp. 361–369.

[12] Warren A. French and Hiram C. Barksdale, "Food Labeling Regulations: Efforts Toward Full Disclosure," *Journal of Marketing,* **38**:14–19, July 1974.

[13] Raymond C. Stokes, "The Consumer Research Institute's Nutrient Labeling Research Program," *Food, Drug, and Cosmetic Law Journal,* **27**:263–270, May 1972.

[14] Edward H. Asam and Louis P. Bucklin, "Nutrition Labeling for Canned Foods: A Study of Consumer Response," *Journal of Marketing,* **37**:32–27, April 1973.

[15] Friedman, "Consumer Responses."

[16] George S. Day and William K. Brandt, "Consumer Research and the Evaluation of Information Disclosure Requirements: The Case of Truth in Lending," *Journal of Consumer Research,* **1**:21–32, June 1974.

[17] G. A. Miller, "The Magical Number Seven, Plus or Minus Two: Some Limits on Our Capacity for Processing Information," *Psychological Review,* **63**:81–97, 1956; and Richard N. Cardozo, "Customer Satisfaction: Laboratory Study and Marketing Action," in L. George Smith (ed.), *Reflections on Progress in Marketing,* American Marketing Association, Chicago, 1964, pp. 283–289.

[18] Jacob Jacoby, Donald E. Speller, and Carol A. Kohn, "Brand Choice Behavior as a Function of Information Load," *Journal of Marketing Research,* **11**:63–69, February 1974.

[19] Jacob Jacoby, Donald E. Speller, and Carol Kohn Berning, "Brand Choice Behavior as a Function of Information Load—Replication and Extension," *Journal of Consumer Research,* **1**:33–42, June 1974.

[20] J. Edward Russo, "More Information Is Better: A Reevaluation of Jacoby, Speller and Kohn," *Journal of Consumer Research,* **1**:68–72, December 1974; John O. Summers, "Less Information Is Better?" *Journal of Marketing Research,* **11**:467–468, November 1974; and William L. Wilkie, "Analysis of Effects of Information Load," *Journal of Marketing Research,* **11**:462–466, November 1974.

[21] Naresh K. Malhotra, Arun K. Jain, and Stephen W. Lagakos, "The Information Overload Controversy: An Alternative Viewpoint," *Journal of Marketing,* **46**:27–37, Spring 1982.

[22] Naresh K. Malhotra, "Information Load and Consumer Decision Making," *Journal of Consumer Research,* **8**:419–430, March 1982.

[23] Fleming Hansen, "Consumer Choice Behavior: An Experimental Approach," *Journal of Marketing Research,* **6**:436–443, November 1969; and Jerry Olson and Jacob Jacoby, "Cue Utilization in the Quality Perception Process," in M. Venkatesan (ed.), *Proceedings of the Third Annual Conference of the Association for Consumer Research,* Association for Consumer Research, Chicago, 1972, pp. 167–179.

[24] Jacoby, Speller, and Berning, "Brand Choice Behavior."

[25] John A. Howard, "Conceptualizing the Adequacy of Information," in M. Venkatesan (ed.), *Proceedings,* pp. 99–100.

[26] "Trade Face-Off," *Time,* April 13, 1987, p. 28.

[27] Dorothy Cohen, "Remedies for Consumer Protection: Prevention, Restitution, or Punishment," *Journal of Marketing,* **39**:24–31, October 1975.

[28] See George Fisk, "Product Planning and the Ecological Imperative," in Fred Allvine (ed.), *Combined Proceedings, Series No. 35,* American Marketing Association, Chicago, 1973, pp. 243–257; and Karl E. Henion, "The Effect of Ecologically Relevant Information on Detergent Sales," *Journal of Marketing Research,* **9**:10–14, February 1972.

[29] Patrick E. Murphy, "An Evolution: Corporate Social Responsiveness," *Michigan Business Review,* November 1978, pp. 19–25.

711

[30] Patrick E. Murphy and Gene R. Laczniak, "Marketing Ethics: A Review with Implications for Managers, Educators, and Researchers," in Ben M. Enis and Kenneth J. Roering (eds.), *Review of Marketing 1981*, American Marketing Association, Chicago, 1981, pp. 251–266.

[31] Hans Thorelli, "Consumer Rights and Consumer Policy: Setting the Stage," *Journal of Contemporary Business*, 7:3–16, Autumn 1978.

[32] Rose Dewolf, "Consumers Aren't All Angels Either," *DuPont Context*, 2:9–10, November 1, 1973.

[33] Marc A. Grainer, Kathleen A. McEvoy, and Donald W. King, "Consumer Problems and Complaints: A National View," in William L. Wilkie (ed.), *Advances in Consumer Research*, vol. 6, Association for Consumer Research, Ann Arbor, Mich., 1979, p. 498.

[34] Thomas J. Stanley and Larry M. Robinson, "Opinions on Consumer Issues: A Review of Recent Studies of Executives and Consumers," *The Journal of Consumer Affairs*, 14:207–220, Summer 1980.

[35] Hiram C. Barksdale and William R. Darden, "Consumer Attitudes Toward Marketing and Consumerism," *Journal of Marketing*, 36:35, October 1972.

[36] "Business Responds to Consumerism," *Business Week*, September 6, 1969, pp. 94–108.

[37] Frederick E. Webster, Jr., "Does Business Misunderstand Consumerism?" *Harvard Business Review*, 51:89, September 1973.

[38] E. Patrick McGuire, "Consumerism Lives! . . . And Grows," *Across the Board*, January 1980, pp. 57–62.

[39] "Corporate Cocoon?" *Wall Street Journal*, July 1, 1976, pp. 1, 20.

[40] Priscilla A. LaBarbera and Larry J. Rosenberg, "How Marketers Can Better Understand Consumers," *MSU Business Topics*, 28:31, Winter 1980.

[41] Robert C. Lewis and Philip L. Zweig, "The Positive Side of Guest Complaints," *Cornell Hotel and Restaurant Administration Quarterly*, 27:13, February 1987.

[42] Jacob Jacoby and James J. Jaccard, "The Sources, Meaning, and Validity of Consumer Complaint Behavior: A Psychological Analysis," *Journal of Retailing*, 57:4–24, Fall 1981.

[43] Robert B. Reich, "Business Can Profit from Consumer Protection," *Business and Society Review*, Fall 1980, pp. 60–63.

[44] Mary C. Gilly, "A Study of Post-Purchase Attitudes and Behavior of Consumers with Different Complaining Tendencies," in Kenneth Bernhardt et al. (eds.), *Proceedings of American Marketing Association Educators' Conference*, American Marketing Association, Chicago, 1981, pp. 166–169.

[45] C. Merle Crawford, "When Consumers Complain," *Sales Management*, November 15, 1970, pp. 29–31.

[46] E. Patrick McGuire, *The Consumer Affairs Department: Organization and Functions*, The Conference Board, Inc., New York, 1973, p. 5; and Ann Harvey, "Complaint Handling," *Public Relations Journal*, 35:47, December 1979.

[47] Richard T. Hise, Peter L. Gillett, and J. Patrick Kelly, "The Corporate Consumer Affairs Effort," *MSU Business Topics*, 26:17–26, Summer 1978.

[48] James U. McNeal, "Consumer Education as a Competitive Strategy," *Business Horizons*, 21:50–56, February 1978.

CASES
FOR PART SIX

CASE 6-1
IMPULSE SHOPPERS*

"The sweater was following me," the 38-year-old man said. "I had gone on to a different part of the store, but it pulled me back to the men's department, where I finally bought it."

That might be an extreme example, but similar feelings are common among people who engage in impulse buying, says Dennis Rook, an assistant professor of marketing at the University of Southern California.

Nine out of ten people have succumbed to the urge to make an unplanned purchase, and most regret it later, says Rook, who recently surveyed more than 300 people to find out how they feel when that happens and how they resist the urge.

Many said the sudden urge to buy is exciting, thrilling, stimulating—almost like falling in love. "The impulse can be so strong that it even produces physical symptoms such as goose bumps, hot flashes, and tingling sensations," Rook said.

"But at the same time, the impulse also triggers feelings of guilt, distress, helplessness, and even panic," he added. "This ambivalence emphasizes the psychological complexity," he said. "Much marketing research has treated it simply as 'unplanned' purchasing, but it's not just that. Essentially, impulse buying is an irrational process in which the urge to gratify an impulse triumphs over the rational parts of the mind." And it can be a powerful force.

"Some said they feel hypnotized or mesmerized during an impulse buying episode," he said. "They said they would find themselves moving toward a cashier as if in a dream. Others animated the objects of their desires. . . . They talked about candy bars calling out to them, about shoes staring at them. This way of thinking allowed them to transfer some of their guilt onto the product itself."

Resistance often is not easy, and people use a wide variety of strategies to maintain, or regain, self-control, the survey showed. More than 70 percent of the respondents said they try to conduct an emergency cost-benefit analysis on the spot, asking themselves questions such as these: Do I really want it? Can I afford it? Would I get my money's worth or would I use the product once and forget it?

Other techniques were reported by the respondents: (1) distancing themselves in time or space by trying to wait for the urge to go away or by leaving the store or the department; (2) substituting a small purchase for a larger, more costly or fattening one; (3) imposing rationing devices such as leaving credit cards at home and carrying a limited amount of cash; and (4) inviting others to shop with them, knowing they are more likely to succumb to the impulse-buying urge when they are alone.

But Rook says the survey shows that such strategies frequently fail. "At their strongest, impulses to consume are impossible to resist," he said. "And recent marketing innovations such as twenty-four-hour retailing, instant credit, and telemarketing make the urge to buy even easier to gratify, without even setting foot in a shopping center."

And more than 80 percent of the respondents said they had suffered negative consequences in the wake of impulse buying episodes, he added. These included financial difficulties, disappointment in the product, and the disapproval of other people.

"Some people suffer a tremendous amount of guilt just for having the impulse, whether they give in to it or not," he said. "On the other hand," he added, "some people said that impulse buying elevates their mood and boosts their energy. For them, giving in to the urge is a highly satisfying experience—a way to fill the emptiness of their lives, either literally or figuratively."

Question
What consumerism issues exist for impulse shopping?

CASE 6-2
RHODE ISLAND CONSUMERS' COUNCIL*

Mr. Edwin Palumbo, executive director of the Rhode Island Consumers' Council, was reflecting on the activities and accomplishments of the council. He decided to initiate a survey in order to obtain a better understanding of the needs of its "market" and to gain a "sense of direction" for the future strategy the organization might adopt.

The Rhode Island Consumers' Council was created by legislative enactment to promote the health, prosperity, and welfare of the people of Rhode Island by providing a comprehensive system for consumer protection in the marketplace. The council was composed of seven private citizens and an executive director with responsibility for the general supervision of all council operational activities. There were six full-time employees at the council's only office, located

*From Vic Pollard, "'Impulse Shoppers' Say Shoes, Candy Call Out to Them," *News Star World*, April 27, 1986, p. 2D. Reprinted by permission of Gannett News Service.

*The original version of this case was prepared by David L. Loudon and Albert J. Della Bitta.

approximately 1 mile from the central downtown district of Providence, the state's capital.

Rhode Island is the smallest of the fifty states, measuring 48 miles long and 37 miles wide. It had a population of approximately 1 million and is the second most densely populated state, with an average of 905 persons per square mile. However, this population density varies substantially over the state. For example, Providence and its seven surrounding cities and towns comprised only 13 percent of the land area but accounted for approximately 56 percent of the population of the state.

Most states had some form of specifically designated consumer offices. The responsibilities and powers of these offices varied widely among the several states, from advisory capacities to actual promotion, support, and enforcement of consumer protection laws. In Rhode Island, the Consumers' Council was an independent agency of state government. It represented the public in matters affecting consumer interest, and its legislative charge ranged from conducting studies for the recommendation of legislative programs to furthering consumer education and mediating and resolving individual consumer complaints. To carry out its purpose, the council had recourse to any remedy provided by law. It participated before administrative hearing bodies as the consumers' advocate, and it reported violations of law or regulations affecting consumers to the attorney general for prosecution.

The Consumers' Council was organized into two divisions, the Division of Consumer Affairs and the Division of Credit Counseling.

DIVISION OF CONSUMER AFFAIRS

The Division of Consumer Affairs was responsible for all council activities designed to assure effective protection against commercial injustice. It was concerned with mediation, education, legislation, and regulatory hearing representation.

Mediation

The Division of Consumer Affairs made every effort to resolve consumer-business disputes, and mediation was used when appropriate. For example, when a buyer filed an oral or written complaint about a product or service with the council, the seller involved was notified of the complaint (usually by letter), in order to afford an opportunity to present his or her account of the transaction. Such an approach created an atmosphere in which the division could concentrate its efforts toward bringing accord between the disputing parties. Where circumstances warranted, referrals were made to other governmental departments for enforcement and, where necessary, for prosecution. Even when the resolution of a complaint occurred, the council might still require that the business practice in question be reviewed for possible

prosecution by a state or federal agency. Sometimes resolution itself required that a court test case be initiated by the council.

The number and monetary value of consumer complaints processed by the division rose steadily each year, with the vast majority of the complaints satisfactorily resolved. It was projected that the council would have responded to approximately 3000 complaints and inquiries this year, compared to 268 complaints processed during the council's first year of operation six years ago.

To the extent that contract cancellations and cash refunds amounted to many thousands of dollars since the inception of the council, the division felt that its complaint settlement procedure was fair and effective.

Education

The Division of Consumer Affairs believed that an effective program of consumer protection had to be anchored in an imaginative consumer education effort. Consequently, the division sponsored a comprehensive consumer education program to assist consumers in making sound buying decisions, acquiring skill in personal money management, and recognizing and avoiding consumer frauds and deceptions.

The program was tailored to the needs and interests of several separate groups. These included junior and senior high school and college students, as well as young and middle-age families, the elderly, and the poor.

The report of the National Advisory Commission on Civil Disorders indicated that residents of poor neighborhoods believed that they suffered from constant abuses by local merchants. Thus, the division directed much of its consumer education activity to poor people, among whom consumer grievances were significant. To respond to the overall consumer need for more readily available and easy-to-understand facts about goods and services, the division aimed a consumer-information program at the entire community, publishing and distributing pamphlets on tips to help consumers become more alert buyers and distributing consumer interest publications of federal departments and agencies.

Legislation

Recognizing a pressing need to make the law do more for consumers, the division was particularly active in promoting legislation prohibiting unfair and deceptive selling practices. The council initiated and supported consumer laws at the state and federal level. Through its executive director and staff, the council testified before state and federal government bodies. Listed below are some of the legislative proposals encouraged by the council and implemented by the state:

To allow consumers three days to cancel a contract signed in their homes

To allow consumers to use small claims court in civil actions with a top value of $300

To allow consumers to treat as a gift any unordered merchandise mailed to them

To allow class-action suits

To prohibit unfair and deceptive selling practices including misleading advertising

To prohibit referral selling schemes

To prohibit the shut-off of any publicly regulated utility service on a weekend or holiday preceding the weekend

To prohibit tampering with an automobile mileage recorder with intent to defraud

To require all credit and finance charges in writing and in agreement with the provisions of the Federal Truth-in-Lending Law

To require that all blank spaces in a contract be filled before it is legal

To require retailers to display the unit prices of all items for sale

To regulate games of chance used as a business promotion

To regulate the sale of out-of-state land and developments

To establish a wages receivership program for financially troubled individuals and families

Regulatory Affairs

To provide the public with competent representation in public utility matters, the legislation creating the Rhode Island Consumers' Council decreed that the council "shall appear for and in behalf of the people of the State" in all regulatory matters affecting rates and service. A goal of the council was to provide consumers with a responsible alternative voice in regulatory matters and to provide the regulatory agencies with the freedom to exercise their quasijudicial function without appearing to act as both advocate and judge.

To fulfill this responsibility, the council administered a vigorous program to protect the people's interests in matters ranging from utility requests for rate increases or service curtailments to requests for changes in Blue Cross/Blue Shield rates and proposals for higher auto insurance rates. The council pursued its regulatory responsibilities not only within the state but also at the federal level. Its representatives

appeared before federal regulatory bodies and commissions as well as in courts of law, including the Supreme Court of the United States. The council's efforts helped control numerous increases sought by various regulated industries and brought about many significant reforms.

This aspect of the Consumers' Council's activities attracted much public attention. Prior to the council's intervention, the public could not be certain of representation unless the matter was sufficiently large enough to affect nearly all the people of the state. In all other cases "public representation" was meager and disorganized, even when the public was represented by highly competent special counsel. The fact that attorneys and their expert witnesses were not able to carry on a continuing observation of regulated companies hampered their long range effectiveness. By exercising a continuing surveillance, the Consumers' Council helped to provide consumers with the type of active interest and review necessary to achieving public utility consumer protection.

DIVISION OF CREDIT COUNSELING

A legislative amendment set up the Division of Credit Counseling within the council to accomplish the following goals:

To aid individuals and families already overburdened with debt by offering advice on money management or developing a debt-liquidation plan

To prevent debt problems from arising in the first place through an educational program on the intelligent use of credit

This service was unique in that it was completely sponsored by a state agency. Its success had prompted other states to ask the division for advice on how to establish similar programs. In the four years since the creation of the credit counseling service, the division had assisted 471 families. Its activities included counseling, development of individual family financial budgets, and the implementation of a debt management program.

CURRENT CONCERNS

As Mr. Palumbo reflected on the council's many accomplishments over its seven-year existence, his thoughts turned to several areas of concern. It seemed to him that the council had been fairly successful in establishing its identity as a consumer agency in Rhode Island. However, he recognized that there was an ever-present need to remind consumers about the council and its services and to reach those who were not aware of the council or its services. There was undoubtedly a large segment of Rhode Islanders who had heard or read about the council but did not understand how it could serve their needs.

In order to increase the council's visibility in Rhode Island, a greater emphasis had to be given to public service spot announcements over the Providence radio and television stations that reached the entire state. Some of the spots that were run are presented in Table 1. Mr. Palumbo was unsure of the actual effectiveness of such spot announcements. He felt, initially, that they would acquaint people with the council and, over a period of time, would surely attract more consumers to use the services of the council.

Another facet of his concern was the ability of the Consumers' Council to handle a potentially large influx of consumers desiring the group's free services. The staff of six would be rather hard-pressed to serve a sharply expanded clientele. Thus, Mr. Palumbo wondered whether the council should be promoting itself as vigorously as it had been. He thought that perhaps there were two groups to whom he needed to promote: consumers on whom he expended resources, and legislators and other groups from whom he attracted resources. He was particularly concerned as to whether or not the council would be able to obtain adequate funding to fulfill the requests made on the Consumers' Council by the people of Rhode Island. He wondered how he might generate such support.

These issues then focused Mr. Palumbo's thoughts on the basic direction taken by the Rhode Island Consumers' Council. He noted that a neighboring state's consumer-protection organization had shifted its emphasis more to research about consumer problems and the development of position papers. This move to a more passive role contrasted sharply with the Rhode Island Council's approach to consumer protection. Thus, Mr. Palumbo wondered whether the Rhode Island group should not also pursue such an approach. He did not want to see a reduction in the services provided directly to the people. And he liked the prospect of enlarging the council's research role. Thus, he wondered to what extent the Rhode Island group could pursue such an approach.

With these thoughts in mind, Mr. Palumbo formulated a questionnaire (Table 2, page 716) to be used in surveying part of the council's market. The questionnaire was expected to provide information on respondent awareness and use of the council's services and on respondent interest in learning more about consumer topics. He wondered to what extent the responses obtained would provide the council with a better sense of direction as to its future strategy.

Question

How would you advise Mr. Palumbo?

TABLE 1

Spot Announcements

Announcer: This is "Buyer Be Alert." The subject is Small Claims Court.
             (Or) Unit Prices.
             (Or) Referral Selling Schemes.
             (Or) Wages Receivership Program.

The Rhode Island Consumers' Council is the official voice of the consumer at the state level. The Rhode Island Consumer Law allows you to use small claims court in civil actions with a top value of $300.
    (Or) The Rhode Island Consumer Law requires retailers to display the unit prices of items.
    (Or) The Rhode Island Consumer Law prohibits referral selling schemes.
    (Or) The Rhode Island Consumer Law established a Wages Receivership Program for financially troubled individuals and families.

If you feel your Rhode Island Consumers' Council can be of service, contact us at telephone number 277-2764.

1   Do you know about the Rhode Island Consumer's Council and its activities?
Yes_____ No_____

2   How did you learn about the council?_____

3   Have you ever used its services?
Yes_____ No_____

4   What was the nature of your complaint or problem?_____

5   Was your complaint or problem satisfactorily resolved?
Yes_____ No_____
Remarks:_____

6   Are you dissatisfied with any product or service recently purchased?
Yes_____ No_____

7   What is the nature of your complaint?_____

8   Did you register your complaint with a public or private consumer protective agency?
Yes_____ No_____
Explain:_____

9   Do you wish to register your complaint with the Rhode Island Consumers' Council?
Yes_____ No_____

10 Would you be interested in knowing more about the Consumers' Council and consumer topics such as:
a Laws passed to protect you as a consumer_____
b The different types and costs of credit_____
c Money management_____
d Printed materials distributed by the council_____
e Other_____

11 Would you like to see a film or films on these subjects in a group with your neighbors?
Yes_____ No_____

12 Would you be interested in attending some consumer discussion meetings in a group with your neighbors?
Yes_____ No_____

Interviewer's remarks:_____

Interviewed by:_____

INDEX